Modern Poems

Second Edition

W.W. NORTON & COMPANY, INC.
also publishes

THE NORTON ANTHOLOGY OF AMERICAN LITERATURE
edited by Nina Baym et al.

THE NORTON ANTHOLOGY OF ENGLISH LITERATURE
edited by M. H. Abrams et al.

THE NORTON ANTHOLOGY OF MODERN POETRY
edited by Richard Ellmann and Robert O'Clair

THE NORTON ANTHOLOGY OF LITERATURE BY WOMEN
edited by Sandra M. Gilbert and Susan Gubar

THE NORTON ANTHOLOGY OF POETRY
edited by Alexander W. Allison et al.

THE NORTON ANTHOLOGY OF SHORT FICTION
edited by R. V. Cassill

THE NORTON ANTHOLOGY OF
CONTEMPORARY SHORT FICTION
edited by R. V. Cassill

THE NORTON ANTHOLOGY OF WORLD MASTERPIECES
edited by Maynard Mack et al.

THE NORTON FACSIMILE OF
THE FIRST FOLIO OF SHAKESPEARE
prepared by Charlton Hinman

THE NORTON INTRODUCTION TO LITERATURE
edited by Carl E. Bain, Jerome Beaty, and J. Paul Hunter

THE NORTON INTRODUCTION TO THE SHORT NOVEL
edited by Jerome Beaty

THE NORTON READER
edited by Arthur M. Eastman et al.

THE NORTON SAMPLER
edited by Thomas Cooley

and
THE NORTON CRITICAL EDITIONS

Modern Poems

A Norton Introduction

Second Edition

EDITED BY

RICHARD ELLMANN
Late Goldsmiths' Professor Emeritus, Oxford University

AND

ROBERT O'CLAIR
Late Professor Emeritus, Manhattanville College

W · W · NORTON & COMPANY
New York · London

Copyright © 1989, 1976, 1973 by W. W. Norton & Company, Inc.
All rights reserved.

Printed in the United States of America.
The text of this book is composed in Caledonia, with
display type set in Deepdene. Composition by Vail-Ballou
Manufacturing by R. R. Donnelley

Second Edition

Library of Congress Cataloging-in-Publication Data

Modern poems : a Norton introduction / edited by Richard Ellmann and
    Robert O'Clair.—2nd ed.
        p.   cm.
    Bibliography: p.
    Includes indexes.
    ISBN 0-393-95907-4
        1. American poetry—20th century.   2. English poetry—20th century.
3. American poetry—19th century.   4. English poetry—19th century.
I. Ellmann, Richard, 1918–1987.   II. O'Clair, Robert.
PS613.M58   1989
821'.008—dc20   89-3345

ISBN 0-393-95907-4

W. W. Norton & Company, Inc., 500 Fifth Avenue, New York, N.Y. 10110

W. W. Norton & Company, Ltd., 10 Coptic Street, London WC1A 1PU

    3 4 5 6 7 8 9 0

Contents

x   *Contents*

xx   *Contents*

Preface to the First Edition

Modern Poems: An Introduction to Poetry has come into being because of what we have learned as teachers of American college students and as editors of *The Norton Anthology of Modern Poetry*. Students, when they can choose, often prefer to plunge at once into the poetry of their own century. It responds, after all, to the social and historical conditions in which they find themselves, and its ways of thinking and feeling are those in which they feel most at home. And, of course, much of it is written in contemporary English, the idiom we speak today. In gathering the selections for our longer survey of modern poetry, we came to see that many of these poems would be especially pertinent and moving to students beginning the study of poetry in college, and that their teachers might well share our feeling that such an introduction can be particularly suitable.

Because *Modern Poems* is an *introduction*, we begin the book by presenting, in a section called "Reading Poems," the necessary terms and definitions for the discussion of poetry. Most examples given in these pages are taken from the poems in this book. Teachers may want to use this section as general background, or they may prefer to select one of the topics here and use particular poems from the body of the anthology to illustrate it. The essay has been prepared under the supervision of our editor, John Francis; in trying to make it as useful as possible, we have sought the advice of Albert and Barbara Gelpi (Stanford University), Ronald Sharp (Kenyon College), Robert Phelps, and Scott Elledge (Cornell University), whose sensitive and practical suggestions we acknowledge with thanks.

In selecting the poems themselves, our aim has been to offer a range of work, from the easily accessible to the more difficult, which represents the major modes and aspects of all poetry, regardless of period. We have also sought to represent the principal directions in modern poetry: the most prominent writers and literary groupings appear in sufficient depth so that their interconnections may be studied, and the essay "Modern Poetry in English: A Brief History" offers the setting in which the poems can be regarded.

So that students will be able to read the poems included here without consulting reference books, each poem has been annotated, and each author is briefly introduced in biographical terms. Finally, a bibliography is provided of all the books of poetry and the principal works of prose by each poet.

A note about texts: as a rule, the version here of each poem is the last over which the author may be presumed to have exercised editorial control. Certain exceptions have been made as necessary, and occasionally lines from alternative versions are also given; these textual questions are presented in the footnotes. The poems of each author are arranged chronologically, by the date of first publication in book form. (This date is given immediately following each poem.) Poems without titles are identified by their first lines. Except for a few very long poems, all selections are printed in their entirety; the few exceptions are represented by self-contained excerpts, their omitted portions being indicated by asterisks. Individualities of spelling, punctuation, and typography have been preserved.

This book has profited greatly from the assistance of friends. We wish to thank Professor M. H. Abrams for his timely and valuable counsel. John Francis performed prodigies of editing, and John Benedict, also of W. W. Norton & Company, helped us at crucial junctures; their colleagues Lee Miller and Calvin Towle carried out others of the necessary preparations for this undertaking. We hope that the complete book warrants their manifold exertions.

R. E.
R. O'C.

Publisher's Preface
to the Second Edition

The first edition of *Modern Poems* was that rare thing, a pedagogical experiment which succeeded: never before had editors compiled an anthology consisting entirely of modern poems for introductory poetry courses. Teachers who used the book for such a course agreed that Richard Ellmann and Robert O'Clair had been correct in their judgment that students, if allowed the choice, prefer to begin the study of poetry with poems of their own time. It has turned out that other teachers have also found the anthology an excellent text for short courses in modern poetry.

In preparing this revised edition, the editors have sought to deepen and to broaden the selection of poets and poems. They have not, however, altered the simplicity of the way the first edition was organized, which made the book helpful and easy to use.

As before, the text begins with a section entitled "Reading Poems," which sets forth the terms and definitions most useful for analyzing and discussing poetry. In accordance with advice from some teachers, this essay has been streamlined, some of its sections have been rearranged, and its tone has, we believe, been made more inviting. All but two of the examples in this section are from poems included in this anthology.

In selecting the poems to be included in the volume, the editors—as in their *Norton Anthology of Modern Poetry*—were guided by two main principles. The first was to choose poems that are teachable to introductory students; the other was to represent the main directions and types of modern and contemporary poetry. The editors also tried to maintain a balance between including a considerable number of poems by each major figure and representing notable works written by less celebrated poets. In compliance with teachers' wishes, hardly any poets in this edition of *Modern Poems* are represented by merely a single poem.

The editors have taken pains to bring this volume up to date by adding some of the best and most representative work by poets who have continued writing since the first edition came out in 1976, as well as by reviewing their representation of works by earlier poets. As a consequence, of the 119 poets in the new edition, the selections for 76 have been changed or supplemented. Among the poets whose work has been updated by recent poems are Robert Penn Warren, Elizabeth Bishop, Gwendolyn Brooks, Philip Larkin, Adrienne Rich, and Derek Walcott.

Thirty-eight new poets are included in this edition. Some of these have been added because the editors, in hindsight, judge them to have been unwarrantedly omitted from the first edition: these include Lewis Carroll, Rudyard Kipling, Isaac Rosenberg, Louise Bogan, and Judith Wright. Others are younger poets who have only recently achieved prominence, such as Tony Harrison, Margaret Atwood, Robert Pinsky, Marilyn Hacker, Norman Dubie, Craig Raine, and Leslie Marmon Silko.

Many of the best modern poets are women. This edition includes twenty-six women, of whom half are new to the book. They range from Emily Dickinson, included in the first edition as a prime precursor in modern verse, through Amy Clampitt and Denise Levertov to Cathy Song, the youngest poet in the anthology.

The new *Modern Poems* also reflects the growing and justified concern for what have come to be called "other American" literary traditions. To the poets in the earlier edition representing the Harlem Renaissance and, more generally, the Black experience are added such younger writers as Audre Lorde, Michael Harper, and Rita Dove. Also represented are literary traditions which, although they extend back for generations, have only recently become additions to the recognized literary heritage in America. The anthology includes two younger Native Americans, Leslie Marmon Silko and Louise Erdrich, and two Mexican-Americans, Gary Soto and Alberto Ríos.

The present edition also casts its geographical net more widely than the earlier edition. It includes more poets whose roots are in the American West, such as William Stafford, Richard Hugo, and Galway Kinnell. It brings the representation of Irish poetry up to date, by a larger and more diversified selection of Seamus Heaney's poems and the inclusion of Paul Muldoon, one of the best of the younger Ulster poets. In accordance with the advice of teachers and critics in Canada, the selections by writers in that country have been radically revamped: there are now seven Canadian poets, ranging from Earl Birney to Margaret Atwood.

In making new selections of all poets and poems, the editors were guided by the responses of teachers who have used the earlier edition, as well as by Robert O'Clair's sense of how well a poem works in the classroom. The difficult decisions to omit some of the poets and poems in the first edition were based on a canvass of teachers, which showed that these materials were seldom if ever taught.

The editors have also taken into account the fact that these days, an increasing number of poets are writing long poems. Despite the limited confines of this introductory text, they have, accordingly, increased the representation of self-contained and teachable excerpts from long poems written throughout the course of modern poetry, from Walt Whitman's *Song of Myself* and H. D.'s *Tribute to the Angels* through James Merrill's *The Changing Light at Sandover* to Seamus Heaney's *Station Island*. They include also a number of long poems in their entirety; among these are Earl Birney's "The Gray Woods Exploding," James Dickey's "Falling," Adrienne Rich's "Yom Kippur 1984," and Michael Harper's "Debridement."

Users of the first edition of *Modern Poems* will find that the introductions to the individual authors are more substantial, and include critical appraisal designed to invite students into the poems. The editors have done this in accordance with the suggestions of teachers who felt that bare summations of biographical facts failed to attract students' interest. The editors have also amplified many explanatory footnotes, and have revised and updated the essay, "Modern Poetry in English: A Brief History," which concludes the volume. Other editorial procedures remain as described in the Preface to the first edition.

In this work of revision, the editors have incurred debts to many friends for many things. They are listed in a separate Acknowledgments section that follows.

Richard Ellmann—seconded by Robert O'Clair—insisted on one other small editorial change. Rather than giving a living poet's dates as, say,

"1923–   ," they preferred "b. 1923." The difference, they argued, is that the former suggests that we are morbidly waiting to fill in the death date; the latter suggests a life being lived.

Since both Ellmann and O'Clair lived such full lives, it is intolerable to us that their own death dates have both been filled in: Ellmann's on May 13, 1987, O'Clair's on May 15, 1989. Ellmann had finished his work on *The Norton Anthology of Modern Poetry* but did not live to see the new edition published; O'Clair, ironically, had just finished his work on the alternate edition, *Modern Poems,* but did not live to see it published. The publisher hopes that both volumes may reflect in some measure their learning, their wit, their concern for good teaching, and their devotion to the art of poetry.

Acknowledgments

We are indebted to five teacher-scholars who provided invaluable critiques of the first edition of *Modern Poems:* Michael Blumenthal (Harvard University), Earl W. Booth (University of Maine), Russell Brown (University of Toronto), James Dollar (Anne Arundel Community College), and Thomas C. Foster (University of Michigan at Flint). M. H. Abrams (Cornell University) and Jon Stallworthy (Oxford University) read and improved drafts of "Reading Poems" and made many other invaluable suggestions.

Since *The Norton Anthology of Modern Poetry* is the "parent" of *Modern Poems,* it seems only proper to render thanks once again for help with that book. In addition to the help provided by Abrams and Stallworthy, further advice throughout the work was provided by William Alfred (Harvard University) and Julian Moynahan (Rutgers University).

For the hard work of researching the new Bibliography, we are indebted to William B. Millard (Rutgers University).

Of especial help in making some selections of both poets and poems were Larry Evers (University of Arizona), Perry Nodelman (University of Winnipeg), Raymond A. Paredes (University of California at Los Angeles), and Craig Raine. For aid in Kipling matters, we are grateful to Elliot Gilbert (University of California at Davis), and for alerting us to needed corrections in Frost's texts we are indebted to Lloyd Schwartz (University of Massachusetts, Boston, Harbor Campus). For help in obtaining books and texts, we thank Harry Ford (Atheneum Publishers), Alice Quinn (Alfred A. Knopf, Inc.), and Maureen Shea-Zell.

Robert O'Clair would like to thank his friends Katherine Kane, Carlotta Marshall, Rosemary Middleton, and Alan Pattillo, and the libraries of Simon's Rock Early College and Williams College.

The following people gave us detailed and thought-provoking critiques of the first edition of *The Norton Anthology of Modern Poetry* Daniel Albright (University of Virginia), Bruce Berline (Colgate University), Steven Blume (Marietta College), Russell Brown (Scarborough College), Albert Gelpi (Stanford University), William Harmon (University of North Carolina), David Johnson (Columbus College), Ronald McFarland (University of Idaho), R. G. N. Marken (University of Saskatchewan), Diane Middlebrook (Stanford University), Ralph Mills (University of Illinois), David Perkins (Harvard University), Robert Phillips, Merrill Skaggs (Drew University), Susan van Dyne (Smith College), Helen Vendler (Harvard University), and Linda Wagner (Michigan State University). John H. Timmerman (Calvin College) shared his students' opinions with us.

For help with knotty footnotes we are grateful to Martin Bemis, Barry Brook (The Graduate School and University Center of the City University of New York), Claire Brook (W. W. Norton & Company), Patrick Cunnane, Richard Dutton, M.D., Steven Forman (Norton), Michael Fysh, George Gibian (Cornell University), Nason Hamlin, M.D., Bernard Klein (Random House), Barbara Lewalski (Harvard University), Ruth Mandel (Norton), and Stanley Wolpert (University of California at Los Angeles). Norman Dubie, William Everson, and Adrienne Rich graciously allowed us to reprint, in our footnotes, extracts from private letters or talks that help to explicate passages in their poems.

Robert O'Clair and the publisher's editor would like to salute the editor's former colleague-assistant Carol Stiles Bemis and present colleague-assistant Elizabeth Parish for their intelligent, efficient, and supportive help throughout. They are also indebted to Jacques Chazaud for help with the new edition's design, and to several colleagues at W. W. Norton: Donald S. Lamm, who cut Gordian knots; Ruth Dworkin, who read proof with an eagle's eye; Diane O'Connor, who made the book into a physical fact; and Candace Watt, who transformed copy editing into a creative contribution to the anthology.

Reading Poems

Words and Word Order

Words

But when the Man-Moth
pays his rare, although occasional, visits to the surface,
the moon looks rather different to him . . .
                    (Elizabeth Bishop, "The Man-Moth")

What exactly is a "man-moth"? Bishop spends several haunting stanzas describing this science-fiction–like beast, who crawls up buildings, must "be carried through artificial tunnels," and will give us "one tear, his only possession," if we watch him. Did the poet say to herself, "Now I will create a strange being?" Not according to her footnote, which tells us that *man-moth* was a newspaper's misprint for *mammoth*. Bishop didn't start with an idea; she started with a word.

Words are, in fact, the building blocks of poems. We use words whenever we speak, and writers use them in fiction, nonfiction (autobiography, biography, essays, etc.), and drama. But in those kinds of writings, and in conversation, our primary interest is usually in the narrative, plot, or argument. Poets, however, generally try to exploit all the expressive resources of words: not only their "plain" meanings, but their emotional associations, and even their sounds. As W. H. Auden once said of young poets, "As a rule, the sign that a beginner has a genuine original talent is that he is more interested in playing with words than in saying something original."

This is not to say that a poem has no ideas. It may of course have an intellectual content that can be paraphrased in prose, but in a poem that "prose meaning" is inseparable from the emotional content that only certain words in a certain order can express. The manner of saying something affects what is being said.

To begin with "plain meanings." Most English words have more than one plain meaning, or **denotation.** Even in an abridged dictionary, the word *dig* has a number of denotations: "to break up earth with an implement," "to unearth," "to excavate," "to thrust," "to prod," "to understand," "to admire," "to work hard," "to advance"; it can also mean "a cutting remark" and "an archeological site." But *dig* doesn't carry all these meanings with it every time it is used, since the context usually eliminates most of them. In the sentence "I will dig a hole," *dig* most likely means that I will break up earth with an implement; it is unlikely that I will "prod" or "admire" a hole.

Sometimes a word in one context can still be taken to mean more than one thing. If you say, "Be sure to take the right road," do you mean the *correct* road, or the one *branching to the right?* The right road could be the wrong road, and the left road the right road. Here, the word *right* is ambiguous. When the aim is to provide clear exposition or directions, ambiguity can be a problem. But writers, and especially poets, may enjoy exploiting a word's multiple denotations. In the poem "Spelling," Margaret Atwood says that her little daughter is

> learning how to spell,
> spelling,
> how to make spells.

In the first line of the example, *spell* means "name the letters of the alphabet," while in the third line *spells* means "magical incantations." In the middle line, *spelling* can mean both.

In this example there is a special kind of ambiguity:

> The violence of beast on beast is *read*
> As natural law, but *upright* man
> Seeks his divinity by inflicting pain.
>
> (Derek Walcott, "A Far Cry from Africa")

Walcott means *read* here as "interpreted," but the sound is the same as *red,* the color of blood; the first meaning is made ominous by the second meaning, which would be missed by a reader who was not listening to the poem. (Walcott may also be recalling, consciously or unconsciously, Alfred, Lord Tennyson's line in *In Memoriam:* "Nature, red in tooth and claw.") When the possible meanings of a word contrast sharply, as they do here, the result is a **pun.** (Puns are often funny, but they needn't be.) *Upright,* too, is ambiguous because man is upright because he stands on two legs rather than four, but the word also means "morally correct," a view of humanity which Walcott questions in the following line.

Poets are concerned with much more about a word than its denotations, numerous and suggestive as these may be. They are also sensitive to what might be called a word's atmosphere or "feel," which it acquires from hundreds of years of use in many different contexts.

Take the noun *dust.* Any dictionary will give us its denotation: powdered earth (or other matter), large enough to feel but small enough to be blown about. But poets like the word for its other associations, too. It builds up on furniture; it gets in your eyes; it's useful in phrases like "dust bowl." And for hundreds of years it has symbolized disintegration, things wearing away or being ground down to almost nothing. It has also come to stand for human disintegration, or death:

> For dust thou art, and unto dust shalt thou return.
>
> (Genesis 3:19)

> I will show you fear in a handful of dust.
>
> (T. S. Eliot, *The Waste Land*)

These associations are the word's **connotations.**

Another example: the word *dirt.* In some expressions, dust is merely dry dirt: "to shake the dust off one's feet." But substitute one word for the other, and dirt has very different connotations:

> For dirt thou art, and unto dirt shalt thou return.

> I will show you fear in a handful of dirt.

Dirt's meaning in Old English was "excrement"—some people still use it in this sense—and it carries a connotation of intense disapproval or disgust, as in such expressions as "dirty tricks," "dirty work," "dirty movies." Slanderous or derogatory information about someone is "dirt." (Dirt also has positive connotations: plants grow in dirt, you can "hit pay dirt." In this sense it means the opposite of dry, sterile dust.)

Though poems as words on the page are visual objects, they are also intended to be spoken aloud, and the full poetic experience involves words' sound-qualities as well as their meanings. The sounds of most words have nothing to do with their meanings: we may say *yes*, but an Italian or Spaniard will say *si*, a Frenchman *oui*, a German *ja*, a Russian *da*, and a Japanese *hai*, and all mean exactly the same thing to their compatriots. Some do sound like their meanings (*buzz, hiss, clickety-clack*); this matching of sound and sense is called **onomatopoeia.** But even onomatopoeic words vary from language to language. English roosters say *Cock-a-doodle-doo*, but French roosters say *Co-co-ri-co*. So, rather than depending on onomatopoeia, poets are likely to interweave the sounds and senses of their words in lines and sentences. This management of sound is illustrated below under RHYME and SOUND EFFECTS WITHIN THE LINE.

Word Order

Word order signifies simply the sequence of words that compose a sentence.

She did all the work.   (*A matter-of-fact statement*)

It was she who did all the work. (*Not he or they or I*)

All the work was done by her.   (*Emphasizing how much work*)

In all the simple sentences above, the basic information is the same. In each one, however, the structure is changed to focus attention on different words and so to communicate a subtly different meaning. The structure of a sentence is called its **syntax.**

Here is another way of changing the word order in the sentence above:

All the work did she.

This word order, which you would probably never hear in ordinary conversation, is called **inversion,** because it inverts or reverses the usual sequence of syntactic units in English—subject, verb, object—without changing the role each word plays in the sentence. The basic meaning remains unchanged because of a grammatical rule: the word *she* cannot be the object of a verb (though *her* can). Otherwise, the inversion would not be possible: "Susan saw Tom" is not the same as "Tom saw Susan." "All the work did she" has about the same placement of emphasis as "All the work was done by her," but its effect is quite different. The inversion substitutes for the passive voice (which is a way of speaking we routinely use) an unusual word order that calls attention to itself.

These effects, emphasizing particular words and attracting attention to the way it is being done, are constructive uses of inversion. But poets past and present have often used inversion merely to make their rhythms more even or to get rhyming words at the ends of lines. The technique has consequently acquired a bad reputation in modern poetry. As a young man, W. B. Yeats used inversion in this less rigorous way—"And a small cabin build there," for example, from "The Lake Isle of Innisfree"—and he later regretted the word order as undesirably stilted for the poem, though the rhythm of the line prevented him from revising to eliminate it. But Yeats and other modern poets have also used inversion to powerful expressive effect:

> . . . Hold them cheap
> May who ne'er hung there. Nor does long our small
> Durance deal with that steep or deep.
> (Gerard Manley Hopkins, "No Worst, There Is None")

With the words rearranged in more ordinary order, these sentences could read:

> Who ne'er hung there may hold them cheap.
> Nor does our small durance deal [for] long with that steep or deep.

But Hopkins's inversion in the first sentence keeps us in suspense, waiting to find out who could possibly hold "them" (i.e., "the mind's mountains") cheaply, and emphasizing the "who." The second inversion forces us to contrast "long" and "small."

Inversion is not the only way in which the word order a poet has chosen guides us in our response:

> We romped until the pans
> Slid from the kitchen shelf;
> My mother's countenance
> Could not unfrown itself.
> (Theodore Roethke, "My Papa's Waltz")

In the first two lines, the poet does not say that the boisterous romp made the pans fall down, although that is probably the prose sense of what happened; rather, the word "until" implies that the romping somehow isn't complete until the pans fell. In the next two lines, again, the prose sense is probably that his mother refused to smile. But "could not unfrown itself" suggests that her face is controlled not by her feelings but by some outside force—the romp.

Levels of Diction

Poets strive not only to ensure that the words they choose have the denotations and connotations they want, but also to ensure that the words be appropriate to the subject and the situation.

> And obscure as that heaven of the Jews,
> Thy guerdon . . . Accolade thou dost bestow
> Of anonymity time cannot raise:
> Vibrant reprieve and pardon thou dost show.
> (Hart Crane, "Proem: to Brooklyn Bridge")

> At times, indifferent to his inconsolable
> eye, the women drifted
> through the soft gray fathered light,
> maintaining stillness, the moments in between.
> (Cathy Song, "Beauty and Sadness")

> So how is life with your new bloke?
> Simpler, I bet. Just one stroke
> of his quivering oar and the skin
> of the Thames goes into a spin . . .
> (Craig Raine, "An Attempt at Jealousy")

Alexis saying, "Shit.
He could be Jesus. Died to save you,
didn't he?"
DeLiza nod she head.
God do not seem entirely to be dead.
(June Jordan, "DeLiza Spend the Day in the City")

Each of these examples is a different **level of diction.** Crane's is formal or
elevated; by it we know he wants to present a grand subject in appropriate
language. Song writes in what we might call standard or middle diction—
the style in which much modern poetry (and, for that matter, prose) is
written. Raine's lines, slightly slangy, seek to show an ordinary (British)
person talking. Jordan delights in a very appropriate Black street-talking
idiom. In each case, the poet has captured a level of diction—and, especially in the last two selections, the mode of speech of a particular social
class—suitable to his or her subject.

Speaker and Tone

The Speaker

I am afraid, this morning, of my face.
It looks at me
From the rear-view mirror, with the eyes I hate,
The smile I hate. Its plain, lined look
Of gray discovery
Repeats to me: "You're old." That's all, I'm old.
(Randall Jarrell, "Next Day")

Reading this passage all by itself, we might think that the author is
recounting a sudden fit of self-loathing and the sense that the best of life
has passed. Reading other poems by the same poet, we'd recognize the
same feelings being expressed. And the feelings certainly sound authentic
enough: surely they express what the poet himself feels. But let's go back
to an earlier passage:

When I was young and miserable and pretty
And poor, I'd wish
What all girls wish: to have a husband,
A house and children.

That's odd. The person speaking in the poem is a woman, whereas Randall
Jarrell was a man.

All poems are, of course, personal in that they are the expressions of a
living human voice. But often a poet creates a **speaker,** a person who "talks"
the poem and who is different from its author. Indeed, even the most per-
sonal-sounding poems may be spoken by a character at some remove from
the author. As Diane Wakoski puts it, "The Diane who's in my poems is
not a real person. She's a person I would like to be, that I can imagine
myself being; even though I put all my faults in my poems, it doesn't mean
[Diane's] not a fantasy or imagined person."

I said thanks but reminded him he still hadn't told me why
Why? O—the bloody cliff!

        Cant you guess? The past caught up again
        &—well we've all got lots to grizzle about
                (Earl Birney, "The Gray Woods Exploding")

Sometimes, as here, a poem may have two speakers: another character (here, "he") in addition to the speaker of the poem. In this case, Birney has added a footnote that not only warns us that the whole poem is a fiction but that "even the 'i' is only half al(i)ve."

Sometimes the speaker of a poem is called a **persona**. *Persona* is the Greek word for *mask*, as worn by actors performing classical Greek drama. The term expresses the fact that the voice we hear in a poem may be that of a dramatic character who is, in whole or in part, invented by the poet.

In "Gray Woods," the speaker is telling a story as well as participating in the poem. In other poems that tell a story, the speaker is simply the story-teller, never speaking of himself or herself as "I." Examples of such story, or **narrative**, poems, are Lewis Carroll's "The Walrus and the Carpenter" (p. 33) and Robert Frost's "The Bearer of Evil Tidings" (p. 136).

We may, of course, speak of "the poet," "Jarrell," "Birney," "Carroll," or "Frost" in referring to the source of a poetic utterance. When, however, in analyzing a poem, we want to stress an important distinction, it is well to refer to the poetic voice as that of a speaker or persona, rather than that of the poet.

The Listener

    Since speech is a means of communication, we can assume that if there is a speaker, there is often a listener as well:

        Let us go, through certain half-deserted streets,
        The muttering retreats
        Of restless nights in one-night cheap hotels
        And sawdust restaurants with oyster-shells:
        Streets that follow like a tedious argument
        Of insidious intent
        To lead you to an overwhelming question . . .
        Oh, do not ask, 'What is it?'
        Let us go and make our visit.
           (T. S. Eliot, "The Love Song of J. Alfred Prufrock")

Prufrock is obviously speaking to someone: he uses the word *us* and *you;* he invites somebody to accompany him on a journey and even forestalls a question. But is he speaking directly to us, the readers? Are we invited to "get inside" the poem with him and join him on his visit? There must in this instance be a fictional listener in the poem itself, whose presence influences strongly what Prufrock says and how he says it. And similarly in other poems: just as the poet and the speaker or persona may never be precisely the same as the poet, so the listener may not be the same as the reader.

Eliot's "Prufrock" is a **dramatic monologue**, in which a single speaker utters the entire poem in a specific situation, interacts with one or more people (who do not themselves speak), and in doing so reveals his or her temperament or character. Many other kinds of lyric poems include particular listeners within them:

        Speak earth and bless me with what is richest
        make sky flow honey out of my hips
        rigid as mountains

and hoots and trills,
location-notes and love calls,
whistles and grunts. . . .
(Stanley Kunitz, "The Wellfleet Whale")

It stinks, though; like a hospital,
of antiseptics and sickness,
and, on some days, blood
which smells the same anywhere,
here or at the butcher's.
(Margaret Atwood,
"Footnote to the Amnesty Report on Torture")

I can feel the tug
of the halter at the nape
of her neck, the wind
on her naked front.

(Seamus Heaney, "Punishment")

These are not, of course, the sum total of the sensations we might feel if we were in the situation described by the poet; they are details chosen to evoke the essence of a sensuous perception.

But poets don't limit themselves to the direct presentation of concrete detail in their efforts to transform a perception into words. They may also compare that perception to something else, often quite different. In making such a comparison, they are using **figurative language.**

Figurative language is not some secret formula available only to poets, however; we all use it all the time in order to enliven, or to achieve nuances of significance in, our daily conversation. We may speak, for example, of "to deep six": the phrase, which comes from measuring water depths at sea, means to get rid of something so it can't be recovered. Or a special day can be a "red-letter day." We also use comparisons to strengthen our points: "He's as happy as a pig in clover"; "She's as spry as a chipmunk."

In ordinary conversation, the images that quickly come to mind have often had their effectiveness worn away by overuse. Take the phrase "dog and pony show." In circus talk, this evokes rather vividly a small, unimportant circus: one with no acrobats or lions, just dogs and ponies. It has now entered the business world, where it is used to describe almost any presentation of material to other people and has lost its circus connotation entirely. Such terms, whose real meaning has worn out, are called **clichés.** It should be noted that poets can enjoy violating expected clichés in order to revitalize them:

And once *below a time* I lordly had the trees and leaves
(Dylan Thomas, "Fern Hill")

Simile

. . . *playing* catch or tag
or touch-last *like a terrier*
turning the same thing over and over
(Amy Clampitt, "Beach Glass")

I have a *life* that did not become,
That turned aside and stopped,

spread over a valley
carved out by the mouth of rain.
(Audre Lorde, "Love Poem")

Old horse,
what will it be like
when the next young filly
comes along? . . .
(Michael Blumenthal, "Back from the Word-Processing Course I Say to
My Old Typewriter")

Thirtyfive years
I lived with my husband.
The plumtree is white today
with masses of flowers.
(William Carlos Williams,
"The Widow's Lament in Springtime")

"A Love Poem" is just that. It may or may not have been an actual communication from the poet to her beloved; we are strangers to both speaker and listener, who are inside the poem. The speaker in "Back from the Word-Processing Course . . ." is addressing a typewriter, as if it could understand him. This rhetorical device of speaking to an absent or dead person, or to a nonhuman object or abstraction, is called **apostrophe.** In Williams's poem, on the other hand, the widow does not seem to be speaking to anyone in the poem or to readers. She is speaking to herself, in a **soliloquy.** The poem as a poem is addressed by the poet to the reader, but within the poem a speaker who is not the poet muses aloud; it is as though what she says to herself gets overheard by the audience of readers.

Tone

Poets enjoy the appropriateness of words to subject. This is not only a matter of the right level of diction, as noted above, but also of **tone** of voice.

My father, who had flown in World War I,
Might have continued to invest his life
In cloud banks well above Wall Street and wife.
But the race was run below, and the point was to win.

Too late now, I make out in his blue gaze
(Through the smoked glass of being thirty-six)
The soul eclipsed by twin black pupils, sex
And business; time was money in those days.
(James Merrill, "The Broken Home")

Sundays too my father got up early
And put his clothes on in the blueblack cold,
then with cracked hands that ached
from labor in the weekday weather made
banked fires blaze. No one ever thanked him.
(Robert Hayden, "Those Winter Sundays")

There's a stake in your fat black heart
And the villagers never liked you.

They are dancing and stamping on you.
They always *knew* it was you.
Daddy, daddy, you bastard, I'm through.
(Sylvia Plath, "Daddy")

These poems are all written at about the middle level of diction, and they are all about the speakers' fathers. Yet the tone of each is very different. Merrill's speaker's tone seems to be cynically rueful. He tries to make light of his father's total commitment to a businessman's life by creating puns ("invest" in "cloud *banks*") and echoing the clichés by which his father lived: "the race was run," "the point was to win," "time was money." The tone of Hayden's poem is distanced, an effect enforced by the word "labor" (instead of "work") and the slightly elevated "weekday weather," but only to be altered in the sudden realization of what lay behind the labor the speaker in his youth had taken for granted. The title of Plath's poem, "Daddy," accords with the speaker's deliberately simple vocabulary; *fat* and *black* contrast brutally with this normally affectionate word. In these poems and many others, it is tone that tells us the speaker's attitude to the person who is addressed or the subject that is described.

Irony

. . . They winter
In Palm Beach; cross the Water in June; attend,
When suitable, the nice Art Institute;
Buy the right books in the best bindings; saunter
On Michigan,* Easter mornings, in sun or wind.
(Gwendolyn Brooks, "The Lovers of the Poor")

There is nothing intrinsically wrong with an art institute being "nice," or with "the right books" being well bound. The poem is, however, setting up a contrast between the rich female "lovers of the poor" and the poor themselves. The speaker is using *nice* and *right* scornfully, echoing words that the ladies might themselves use, but in a way that gives these words a very different significance, and makes them express a very different attitude.

This sharp distinction between the apparent meaning and the actual meaning is a good example of **irony.** The word derives, as the critic M. H. Abrams tells us, from a character in Greek comedy known as the *eiron,* a "dissembler" who "characteristically spoke in understatement and deliberately pretended to be less intelligent than he was. In most of the critical uses of the term "irony," Abrams goes on, "There remains the root sense of dissembling or hiding what is actually the case; not, however, in order to deceive, but to achieve special rhetorical or artistic effects." Irony should not, therefore, be taken merely as saying one thing and meaning its opposite; it is also any way of being oblique rather than straightforward, and of seeming to say one thing while actually saying another. The effect of irony, in the reader's recognition of the discrepancy between what seems to be said and what is actually meant, is usually humorous; often (as in Brooks's poem), the humor is used to ridicule a person or group.

Smart lad, to slip betimes away
From fields where glory does not stay . . .

*Michigan Avenue in Chicago.

Now you will not swell the rout
Of lads that wore their honours out,
Runners whom renown outran
And the name died before the man.
(A. E. Housman, "To an Athlete Dying Young")

The speaker's tone is congratulatory: "smart lad." But the athlete has not retired, he has died, and the occasion for this poem is his funeral: the speaker's words belie the emotions which, as pallbearer and eulogist, he may be presumed to feel, and which are perceptible in the rest of the poem below its ironic surface.

Situations and events may be no less ironic than words. The death of an athlete, as in Housman's poem, is ironic because it involves a contradiction between appearances and reality. Athletes in their prime symbolize health, physical vigor, youthfulness—all the qualities that we associate with irrepressible life and the denial of death—yet death will not, finally, be denied, and even youth and beauty may fall victim to accident, murder, suicide. Another poem that presents an ironic view of the universe is Thomas Hardy's poem about the sinking of the *Titanic,* "The Convergence of the Twain":

And as the smart ship grew
In stature, grace, and hue,
In shadowy silent distance grew the Iceberg too.

Alien they seemed to be:
No mortal eye could see
The intimate welding of their later history.

The speaker points up the irony of the situation: while the English were building and fitting out the worlds' most luxurious and "unsinkable" ocean liner, nature (guided, Hardy believed, by a supernatural force he calls the Immanent Will) was rearing the iceberg to smash the ship on her first voyage.

Figurative Language

Image and Figurative Language

What usually sticks in our minds after we finish reading a poem? Probably not so much its argument or its ideas, as the vivid **images** (the verbal pictures and the representations of sensation the poet has created). The images may describe an object seen or heard, a smell, a taste, a touch, or the feeling of one's own body moving. All these are nonverbal sensations; here are some ways poets have put them into words.

. . . Remember this bureau—

battered wood, the fake drawer and split mirror?
And even the glass marks, ring within ring
Of spilled drinks . . .
(Louise Erdrich, "Francine's Room")

You have your language too,
an eerie medley of clicks

astonished:
I hold it in me *like a pregnancy or
as on my lap a child*
(A. R. Ammons, "Easter Morning")

What could have made her peaceful as with a *mind*
'That nobleness made *simple as a fire,*
With beauty like a tightened bow. . . .
(W. B. Yeats, "No Second Troy")

Notice that all the comparisons above declare themselves by using words such as *like, as,* or *as if.* These are called **similes.**

Metaphor

Mary is
a *rose in a whiskey glass.*
(Gwendolyn Brooks, "The Blackstone Rangers")

The *moon* is a *sow*
and grunts in my throat . . .
(Denise Levertov, "Song for Ishtar")

The provinces of his body revolted,
The squares of his mind were empty,
Silence invaded the suburbs.
(W. H. Auden, "In Memory of W. B. Yeats")

My lizard, my lovely writher
(Theodore Roethke, "Wish for a Young Wife")

These examples do without *like* or *as.* The comparisons here suggest that the thing compared and the thing it's compared to are not merely similiar but, for the purposes of the poem, somehow identical. This kind of comparison is called **metaphor.** The first two examples make it easy for us, since they demonstrate the equivalence between the two terms by the word *is.* The Auden lines don't use *is,* but simply make the poet's body equivalent to a country; Roethke's line makes the *you* to whom the poem is addressed equivalent to a lizard.

Sometimes a poet will carry a metaphor beyond the first flash of correspondence and explore the comparison in detail:

The yellow fog that rubs its back upon the window-panes,
The yellow smoke that rubs its muzzle on the window-
    panes.
Licked its tongue into the corners of the evening,
Lingered upon the pools that stand in drains,
Let fall upon its back the soot that falls from chimneys,
Slipped by the terrace, made a sudden leap,
And seeing that it was a soft October night,
Curled once about the house, and fell asleep.
(T. S. Eliot, "The Love Song of J. Alfred Prufrock")

This is an example of **extended metaphor.** Eliot never says that the fog is *like* a cat; he never uses the word *cat* at all. But he makes the fog behave in so catlike a way that we know with certainty what is being compared to what. This nightmarish image—imagine a cat large enough to curl about a house—helps to characterize the speaker, J. Alfred Prufrock.

A metaphor can be a whole poem:

OREAD

Whirl up, sea—
whirl your pointed pines,
splash your great pines
on our rocks,
hurl your green over us,
cover us with your pools of fir.

(H.D.)

Other Kinds of Figurative Language

Now the opulent
Treacherous woman called Life
Forsakes her claim . . .

(William Everson, "The Poet is Dead")

The figure which gives human attributes to a nonhuman object, or else to an abstract concept ("Life", above) is called **personification.**

The hand that signed the paper felled a city;
Five sovereign fingers taxed the breath,
Doubled the globe of dead and halved a country;

(Dylan Thomas, "The Hand That Signed the Paper")

In this figure of speech, a part of a thing or an action is used to stand for the whole: the "hand" signing the declaration of war stands for an entire country and its military actions. This figure of speech is called **synecdoche.**

All we want is a bank balance and a bit of skirt in a taxi.

(Louis MacNeice, "Bagpipe Music")

Here, a person (or thing or action) is replaced by one of its attributes, or by something closely associated with it: "skirt" stands for "girl." It is a nice example of **metonymy.**

Symbol

Symbols, like the figures of speech we have been looking at, can extend the range of a poem's significance or associations. But a symbol is not merely another kind of figurative language; put most simply, a **symbol** is an object or event which in turn signifies something, or has a range of reference, beyond itself.

A nation's flag is, for example, a symbol. Of itself, it is only a rectangular piece of colored cloth. But to the people living in that nation, it signifies the nation's past, present, and future—all that the nation has meant or will mean. It draws forth powerful emotions of love or hate, both to the nation's citizens and to those affected by it. Another, more universal, symbol is a cross. A simple geometric form, it nevertheless stands, for billions of Christians, as a symbol of Christ's Crucifixion—itself a symbolic event which represents the attitude of the Christian God toward humanity and, conversely, Christians' attitudes toward God, the cosmos, and themselves.

A flag and the cross are conventional symbols—also called "signs"—in that while people and nations may fight over the validity of the concepts they symbolize, most or all know, in general, what the symbols mean. Many other symbols have come to be nearly as well known through their repeated use in writing. The color green, for example, often stands for the time of fresh leaves and grass, the spring, and therefore indirectly for youth and love; it may also have political overtones, as in Yeats's line, "Wherever green is worn" ("Easter 1916"). Or the ascent of a mountain can stand for effort, progress, or courage, while the descent might stand for surrender or failure.

In the past it may have been easier for poets to use a symbol like the cross, green, or a mountain with some confidence that their readers would understand its implications. Nowadays, however, poets may be more likely to trust their own private symbols (from whatever depths in the poet they may come) as more directly expressing their meaning. This can sometimes make for a problem in reading, as the poet's private symbols may be hard for readers to identify. The only initial clue to a poem's symbolic level of meaning may be that something in it doesn't act quite naturally, or that the speaker seems interested in it in some odd way.

Still, with some study, the meaning can very likely be teased out. Take, as an example, Adrienne Rich's "Diving into the Wreck" (p. 704). Most of the poem seems to be an account of a scuba dive after sunken treasure. But the very first line is surprising: what does a "book of myths" have to do with "diving into the wreck"? Why is the ladder hanging over the side of the schooner "innocently"? And what does the speaker mean by saying, "We know what it is for, / we who have used it"? Toward the end, the speaker makes an identification:

> we are the half-destroyed instruments
> that once held to a course
> the water-eaten log
> the fouled compass
>
> we are, I am, you are
> by cowardice or courage
> the one who find our way
> back to this scene
> carrying a knife, a camera
> a book of myths
> in which
> our names do not appear.

The metaphorical connection between the *we* here and the nautical instruments that measure speed, distance, and direction suggests that the sunken ship is much more than merely a sunken ship. Likewise, the observation that it requires "cowardice or courage," not merely curiosity, to "find our way back to this scene," suggests that in "diving into the wreck" the speaker feels some emotional risk. The sunken ship, the schooner on the surface, and the ladder and water between them seem to symbolize a particular kind of human experience, that of exploring one's memories, sunk deep in the past. The surface coherence of the narrative about the literal act of diving is so strong that we might easily overlook this symbolic meaning altogether—but to do so would be to read a different and less complex poem than the one the poet wrote.

Some poets have invented private symbologies, or systems of symbols and their associations, that are almost a philosophy or religion. Robert Graves's book *The White Goddess* sets forth a complex interrelationship of supernatural and natural personages, events, and symbols which, he maintains, are inevitably the inspiration of "all true poetry"; "To Juan at the Winter Solstice" (p. 331) is among other things an abstract of Graves's system. William Butler Yeats adopted and adapted several symbologies, each of which often makes unexpected use of familiar symbols, and adds new ones as well:

> Red Rose, proud Rose, sad Rose of all my days!
> Come near me, while I sing the ancient ways . . .
>
> . . . thine own sadness, whereof stars, grown old
> In dancing silver sandalled on the sea,
> Sing in their high and lonely melody.
> Come near, that no more blinded by man's fate,
> I find under the boughs of love and hate,
> In all poor foolish things that live a day,
> Eternal beauty wandering on her way.
>   (W. B. Yeats, "To the Rose upon the Rood of Time")

For Yeats the rose was a symbol of love and fulfillment, as it has been for many writers. Here, however, he infuses this traditional symbol with new meaning by imagining it as flowering from the intersecting arms of the Rood (Christ's cross)—itself a symbol of time and suffering, which the rose transfigures into beauty. The rose isn't allowed to behave as roses ordinarily do, nor do any of its attributes except its beauty apply in any literal way to the things Yeats uses it to stand for.

Myth and Archetype

A **myth** is like a symbol, but involves an extended plot: it is a *story* which stands for, or symbolizes, something else. In traditional societies myths are thought to explain the origins and qualities of natural forces, recurring situations in human life and history, and social customs and observances, through the lives and actions of—usually—superhuman beings. Such beings are often imagined as having human passions and ambitions, but may well be exempt from mortal conditions and possess energies and skills superior to our own. Some of these beings personify natural forces (fertility, the sea); others personify abstract human qualities (love, wisdom). In some mythologies—for example the Native American—the idea-beings are associated with animals such as the eagle or coyote, or are believed to be embodied in the actual animals.

A **mythology** (a collection of myths) embodies the beliefs of a particular culture at a particular time; moreover, most myths were apparently connected with the performance of religious rituals. Some of us, if we no longer believe them, may view myths as quaint old stories. But for many poets writing over the centuries and today, myths have had an undeniable force, because they remain powerful symbols for certain kinds of feeling and experience.

Among the mythologies most commonly used by poets in the past have been the Greek, the Roman, and the Germanic. Poets have also used the stories of supernatural events in the Old and New Testaments as though they were myths. More recently, writers in various American traditions such as the Indian have drawn on, and made alive, the myths of their own heritage or tribe. One example in this anthology is Louise Erdrich's "Windigo" (p. 876), about a mythic demon; another is Leslie Marmon Silko's "Toe'osh: A Laguna Coyote Story" (p. 842). In this latter poem, the situation clearly informs us that the poet didn't merely look the myth up in a book, but drew it out of her own oral heritage. Similarly, Audre Lorde revives African myth in "The Women of Dan" (p. 751).

Scholars have compared the mythologies of widely different societies at different times and places and have found that each possesses some stories, themes, and personages in common with the others. Naturally enough, few mythologies are without a creation myth, giving the physical universe a supernatural origin; many others also have in common a story about murder and resurrection, such as that of Osiris in Egyptian religion, or of Christ. Still another motif (common theme or dominant idea) is the quest, a long and dangerous journey to achieve a desired goal. Among famous quest stories are Ishtar's descent into the Underworld to bring back her lover Tammuz, or the quest of King Arthur's knights for the Holy Grail. A basic book of comparative mythology, Sir James Frazer's *The Golden Bough*, provided T. S. Eliot with some of the raw material for *The Waste Land* (p. 282), including the mythical motifs of the quest.

Some literary critics call these common mythical elements archetypes, from a Greek word meaning "ancient patterns." The term is used to describe such patterns as they occur not only in myths and works of literature, but also in ordinary people's dreams and fantasies. Such critics find archetypes in themes, characters, and images, and even in literary form and kinds. Perhaps because these "ancient patterns" appear to be so pervasive in religion, literature, and our own minds, they enable us to share deep common human experiences.

Because of their power, then, myths and archetypes appear in many poems. Rarely, however, will a poet merely retell one of the stories; more often than not myth may be used allusively, or the archetypal situation may be buried deeply, expressed mainly through seemingly ordinary surface narratives. Louise Bogan's "Medusa" (p. 334) sets a Greek myth in the foreground, as does Yeats's "Leda and the Swan" (p. 85). Rich's "Yom Kippur 1984" (p. 708) takes root in the Old Testament, while D. H. Lawrence's "Ship of Death" (p. 210) uses Etruscan archetypal elements as part of its underpinning.

Allusion

> And then to awake, and the farm, like a wanderer white
> With the dew, come back, the cock on his shoulder: it was all
>   Shining, it was Adam and maiden,
>   The sky gathered again
>   And the sun grew round that very day.
> So it must have been after the birth of the simple light
> In the first, spinning place . . .

(Dylan Thomas, "Fern Hill")

In this poem, Thomas is describing the farm where he spent summers as a boy. Why, then, does he speak of Adam and a "maiden"? If we know the story in Genesis, we can assume the maiden is Eve, and so infer that the speaker is comparing the farm to the Garden of Eden. This inference is strengthened by "the birth of the simple light / In the first spinning place," which must be a reference to the biblical account of the creation: "And God said, Let there be light: and there was light." Thomas gives the reader just enough to make the metaphorical comparison, and then moves swiftly on.

This kind of reference, whether explicit or implicit, to a well-known literary work, or a person, place, or event, is called an **allusion.** Here are some more:

> she is not Justice with eyes
> blindfolded like Love's;
>
> I grant you the dove's symbolic purity,
> I grant you her face was innocent
>
> and immaculate and her veils
> like the Lamb's Bride,
>   (H. D., "Tribute to the Angels")
>
> Where the beggars raffle the banknotes
> And the Giant is enchanting to Jack,
> And the Lily-white Boy is a Roarer,
> And Jill goes down on her back.
>   (W. H. Auden, "As I Walked Out One Evening")
>
> Will I find O solitude
> your plumes, your breasts, your hair
> against my face, as in childhood, your voice like the
> mockingbird's
>   (Adrienne Rich, "Yom Kippur 1984")

These allusions are to a variety of sources. H. D. alludes to figures and symbols of myth and religion: the representations of Justice and Cupid as both blindfolded; the dove, an important Christian symbol of the Holy Ghost; and the tradition of the Lamb as Christ and his Bride the Church. Auden alludes to nursery rhymes: the giant of "Jack and the Bean Stalk" becomes a sweet-talking hustler; the "lily-white" (presumably pure) boy is a boisterous reveler; Jill, of "Jack and Jill," is seduced. Finally, Rich's mockingbird alludes to Whitman's line in "Out of the Cradle Endlessly Rocking," "Out of the mocking-bird's throat, the musical shuttle."

In discussing her poem, Rich said that "there was a real mockingbird singing in the tree outside my window where I was working day after day." This is a piece of her own private experience that most readers wouldn't know. In other words, whereas many allusions—especially in older poems—are to materials that are more or less common knowledge, others may not be:

> the hand, then those breasts coming toward me
> like the quarter-arms of the amputee Joaquín
> who came back from the war to sit
> in the park, reaching always for children
> until one day he had to be held back.
>   (Albert Ríos, "Madre Sofía")

Only Ríos knows whether his speaker is here alluding to a real Joaquín. Such allusions must make their points by themselves, without support from their sources, as part of the poem. This image, whatever the allusion, certainly does.

In "A Martian Sends a Postcard Home," Craig Raine invented what might be called a reverse allusion:

> Caxtons are mechanical birds with many wings
> and some are treasured for their markings—
>
> they cause the eyes to melt
> or the body to shriek without pain.

Caxtons, here, are books, which William Caxton (c. 1422–1491) was the first to print in English, while the second couplet is the Martian's descripton of crying and laughing. The allusions in this case are to very ordinary things and activities, which we must puzzle out through the Martian speaker's perceptions.

Sound and Form

Jon Stallworthy has called a poem "a composition written for performance by the human voice." That is to say, a group of lines is like a musical score, waiting to be spoken; as readers, we hear in imagination the words' sounds as we read them. Most poets, indeed, would agree that how a poem sounds is as important as what it says. "It don't mean a thing," the famous jazz musician Duke Ellington said in a song lyric, "if it ain't got that swing." In fact, many poets say that sound is more important than sense. Richard Hugo once remarked that "knowing" about something in writing a poem "can be a limiting thing. If the population of a town is nineteen, but the poem needs the sound seventeen, seventeen is easier to say if you don't know the population."

Rhythm

One of the most important things we hear, when we listen to others speaking, is a variation in the degree of emphasis:

> In **fact, m**any **po**ets say that **sound** is **more** imp**or**tant than **sense.**

Every English word of more than one syllable emphasizes, or **stresses,** one syllable more than another: we say *syll*able, not syl*lable.* The same is true of groups of words: some one-syllable words are emphasized, others are not, according to their importance in the sentence.

In the written form of language, we can **scan** the verbal rhythm; that is, we can use marks to indicate the pattern of stresses:

> ´ strong
> ˘ weak

Thus:

> In fáct, mány póets sáy thăt sóund ĭs móre impórtănt thăn sénse.

Although there are many degrees of stress between the strongest and weakest syllables, it is usual in scanning verse to differentiate only between a strong and a weak stress.

When a substantial pause occurs naturally, marking the end of a phrase, it is called a **caesura** (from Latin, "to cut"). In scansion, a caesura is indicated by a pair of parallel lines: ‖

In **fact,** ‖ many **poets** say ‖ that **sound** is **more** important than **sense.**

It should be noted that the pattern of stress in a given sentence can vary according to the elements in the sentence we want to emphasize. If someone, for example, were to argue against the proposition in our sample sentence, we might respond by putting a greater emphasis on *is*, as follows:

In **fact,** many **poets** say that **sound** **is** more important than **sense.**

Meter

If the lines of a poem are structured into recurrent, similar rhythmical units, we say that the poem is written in **meter;** without such a regular, recurrent pattern, it is called **free verse.** Meter goes back to poetry's origins as song or chanting, and metrical poetry can therefore be "heard" against an imagined background of regular metrical units; divergences from this ideal, or perfectly regular, meter are local effects, for emphasis and variety. Free verse, on the other hand, is based on what the poet perceives as the actual rhythms of human speech, wherein the stresses and accents of the words fall much less regularly and predictably. We will treat free verse later in this section.

Here is the scansion of a passage of poetry:

> The tumult and the shouting dies;
>   The Captains and the Kings depart:
> Still stands Thine ancient sacrifice,
>   An humble and a contrite heart.

(Rudyard Kipling, "Recessional")

These lines are in relatively regular meter: with only three exceptions, weak and strong stresses alternate one after the other throughout. In scansion, the smallest repeated unit of the pattern (here, ˘ ´) is called a **foot,** and the entire line can be marked off into sequence of feet:

> Still stands | thine an|cient sac|rifice

The foot is the basic unit of meter. In the imagined, ideally regular meter that we can sense behind the actual rhythm of a poem, each foot always includes one strong stress and one or more weak stresses, and all the feet within a line are the same.

Because they are often discussed, these meters, and the feet of which they are composed, have names:

˘ ´ the **iamb;** iambic (examples: propose, delete)

´ ˘ the **trochee;** trochaic (examples: single; enter)

˘ ˘ ´ the **anapest;** anapestic (examples: afternoon, in a hole)

´ ˘ ˘ the **dactyl;** dactylic (examples: emphasis, juniper)

´ ´ the **spondee;** spondaic (examples: hard times, foul ball)

˘ ˘ the **pyrrhic foot** (examples: in a, of the)

The other metrical attribute of a line is its length, which is stated in terms of the number of its feet. A line of two feet is in **dimeter;** three, **trimeter;** four, **tetrameter;** five, **pentameter;** six, **hexameter;** and seven (the longest line normally found in English poetry), **heptameter.** If we want to describe the line of a poem, we use the adjectival form of the name of the foot: thus the Kipling lines are in *iambic tetrameter*.

To write every line to exactly the same rhythm would make a poet sound like a metronome and make listeners or readers annoyed or amused. Every able poet using a meter knows how to play skillful variations on the prevailing meter. Thus Kipling varies the opening lines of "Recessional":

> God of | our fath|ers, known | of old,
> Lord of | our far-|flung bat|tle-line,

Only in the third line does he use without variation the iambic meter which is the norm of the poem.

> Beneath | whose aw|ful hand | we hold
> Domin|ion ov|er palm and pine—

We can notice something else about these lines. In the group of lines quoted first, each clause ends when the line does; when this happens, we say that a line is **end-stopped.** In the next quoted group, in the third line, "Beneath whose awful hand we hold," the transitive verb *hold* requires an object, *dominion*, which does not occur until the next line. When a syntactic unit thus requires a closure that runs over the end of the verse line, the result is called **enjambment,** from the French "striding over."

The best way to understand how a poet can vary rhythms is to scan a complete poem, such as this by Robert Frost:

RANGE FINDING

> The bat|tle rent | a cob|web dia|mond strung
> And cut | a flower | beside | a ground | bird's nest
> Before | it stained | a sing|le hum | an breast.
> The stri|cken flower | bent dou|ble and | so hung.
> And still | the bird | revis|ited | her young.   5
> A but|terfly | its fall | had dis|possessed,
> A mom|ent sought | in air | his flower | of rest,
> Then light|ly stooped | to it | and flut|tering clung.
> On the | bare up|land pas|ture there | had spread
> O'ernight | 'twixt mul|lein stalks | a wheel | of thread   10
> And strain|ing cab|les wet | with sil|ver dew.
> A sud|den pas|sing bul|let shook | it dry.
> The indwel|ling spi|der ran | to greet | the fly,
> But find|ing no|thing, sul|lenly | withdrew.

We need to say, first of all, that there is no fixed way to read, and therefore to scan, any extended poetic passage. Different readers, equally skilled, will read this poem with somewhat different patterns of stress—although, in these divergent readings, the iambic meter established in the earlier lines will come across as the prevailing one. In lines 2, 4, and 7, for example, *flower* could be read by some as a two-syllable word; by others (including Frost?), as a one-syllable word. Or, in line 9, might *On* be stressed or not?

In any case, we can perceive that Frost varies the meter as the poem proceeds. The first seven lines are all but regular, especially if *flower* is pronounced as *flour*. Line 8 seems to speed up with the additional stress in the final foot (*tering clung*), while lines 9 and 10 are slowed down by the spondees in the second feet (*bare up* and *twixt mul*). The meter has been briefly disturbed, as the battle disturbs nature. But nature goes on, as does the regular iambic pentameter of the last four lines.

Other Rhythmic Forms

Gerard Manley Hopkins noticed that the ear counts metrical feet, not by the number of syllables (strong or weak), but by the number of strong stresses in the line. In what he called **sprung rhythm,** he kept the number of strong stresses constant but varied the number of weak stresses. Here is how he scanned the first three lines of "The Windhover":

I caught this morning morning's minion, king-

dom of daylight's dauphin, dapple-dawn-drawn Falcon, in his riding

Of the rolling level underneath him steady air, and striding . . .

(The curved lines mark what Hopkins called "outriders"—syllables added to a foot to create an "extra-metrical effect," with stronger stress on the preceding strong syllable and a short pause after the outrider.)

Another departure from metrical verse is called **syllabic meter.** Marianne Moore, the virtuoso in this meter, established a set number of syllables in a line, but did not regularize the number or placement of strong stresses:

THE FISH

	(syllables:)
wade	1
through black jade.	3
Of the crow-blue mussel shells, one keeps	9
adjusting the ash heaps;	6
opening and shutting itself like	9
an	1
injured fan.	3
The barnacles which encrust the side	9
of the wave, cannot hide	6
there for the submerged shafts of the	8
sun,	1
split like spun	3
glass, move themselves . . .	etc.

The rhythm of the poem is casual in its effect, like speech. Even the one-syllable line that begins each stanza is sometimes stressed heavily (*wade*), sometimes lightly (*an*); and the longer lines of the first two stanzas scan so irregularly that we can draw no conclusions about the meter:

Of the crow-blue mussel shells, one keeps

The barnacles which encrust the side

But Moore certainly means her lines to be experienced as lines; she even rhymes them. And lest this kind of versification become too mathematical, she occasionally adds (or subtracts) a syllable, as in the last line of each of the quoted stanzas. This is playful verse: the poem incorporates the title as part of its first sentence, and each stanza takes an interesting shape on the page. Despite the rhyming, and the counting of syllables, we are a long way from metrical rhythm, and moving toward free verse.

Free Verse

Though "free verse" is not constrained by the need for metrical regularity, it does not therefore renounce form; as T. S. Eliot remarked, no verse is free for the poet who want to do a good job. What we classify as free verse includes a wide variety of identifiable rhythmic procedures:

> And no rock
> If there were rock
> And also water
> And water
> A spring
> A pool amond the rock
> If there were the sound of water only
> Not the cicada*
> And dry grass singing
> But sound of water over a rock
> Where the hermit-thrush sings in the pine trees
> Drip drop drip drop drop drop drop
> But there is no water
> > (T. S. Eliot, *The Waste Land*)

> Zeus lies in Ceres' bosom
> Taishan is attended of loves
> > under Cythera, before sunrise
> and he said: "Hay aquí mucho catolicismo—(sounded
> > catoli*th*ismo)
> > y muy proco reliHión"
> and he said: "Yo creo que los reyes desaparecen"
> (Kings will, I think, disappear)
> That was Padre José Elizondo
> > in 1906 and 1917
> or about 1917
> > (Ezra Pound, "Canto 81")

> So my bare feet
> and my thin green silks
> my bells and finger cymbals
> offend them—frighten their old-young bodies.
> While the men simper and leer—
> glad for the vicarious experience and exercise.
> They do not realize how I scorn them:
> or how I dance for their frightened,
> unawakened, sweet
> women.
> > (Diane Wakoski, "Belly Dancer")

---

*Grasshopper.

> And when the elk have passed
> behind them
> a crystal train of snowflakes
> strands of mist
> tangled in rocks
> and leaves.
> (Leslie Marmon Silko, "In Cold Storm Light")

The one rhythmic aspect these varied selections have in common is that none falls into a regular, predictable meter. A free-verse poem by a skilled poet is allowed to find its own distinctive form.

Like metrical poetry, free verse is written in lines, and often the breaks between lines have the same purpose in both modes of versification. We may therefore usefully begin the analysis of the diverse forms of free verse by studying the way it uses the line.

Traditional Forms of Free Verse

Modern free verse has ancient ancestors. Here is a passage from the most influential of them:

Behold, thou art fair, my love; behold, thou art fair; thou hast doves' eyes
within thy locks: thy hair is as a flock of goats, that appear from Mount
Gilead.
Thy teeth are like a flock of sheep that are even shorn, which came up from
the washing; whereof every one bear twins, and none is barren among
them.
Thy lips are like a thread of scarlet, and thy speech is comely: thy temples
are like a piece of a pomegranate within thy locks.
Thy neck is like the tower of David builded for an armory, whereon there
hang a thousand bucklers, all shields of mighty men.
Thy two breasts are like two young roes that are twins, which feed among
the lilies.

> (Song of Solomon 4:1–5)

This is, of course, the Bible, in the seventeenth-century translation called the King James Version. These lines roll along in irregular line lengths and indeterminate meters, but their rhythm carries great power.

Walt Whitman, the father of free verse in American poetry, wrote lines which echo such biblical cadences:

Stop this day and night with me and you shall possess the origin of
all poems,
You shall possess the good of the earth and sun, (there are millions of
suns left,)
You shall no longer take things at second or third hand, nor look
through the eyes of the dead, nor feed on the spectres in books.
You shall not look through my eyes either, nor take things from me.
You shall listen to all sides and filter them from your self.

> ("Song of Myself")

Whitman's line is usually a unit such as a sentence or an independent clause, and is usually end-stopped. His rhetoric, which also imitates that of the Old Testament, is primarily one of using parallel syntactic structures to reflect a parallelism in meaning. Whitman's long line has been emulated by later free-verse poets such as Robinson Jeffers, William Everson, and Allen

Ginsberg. Another older form of free verse is Old English alliterative verse. Richard Wilbur imitated it in his "Junk":

> An áxe ángles
> > from my neighbor's áshcan;
> It is héll's hándiwork,
> > the wóod not híckory,
> The flów of thé grain
> > not fáithfully fóllowed.

The "stepped" line is divided by a caesura, before and after which there are usually two strong stresses and a varying number of weak stresses; each line includes at least one sequence of alliterative words (i.e., words that repeat initial speech sounds) that extends across the caesura.

> *Modern Free Verse*
>
> so much depends
> upon
>
> a red wheel
> barrow
>
> glazed with rain
> water
>
> beside the white
> chickens.
>
> > (William Carlos Williams,
> > "The Red Wheelbarrow")

There is probably no poem so famous as "The Red Wheelbarrow" that seems less artful, more prosy, when taken word for word. Why, then, this elaborate division of its fourteen words into eight lines? This suggests that the rhythm of the poem may be important, and it may be useful to mark the stresses:

> só múch depénds
> upŏn
>
> ă réd whéel
> bárrow
>
> glázed with ráin
> wătĕr
>
> bĕsíde thĕ whíte
> chíckĕns.

Is there a pattern here? In each stanza, the first line has two or three strong stresses, one always at the end of the line. On the other hand, the placement of the single strong stress in each of the second lines varies: in the first stanza it is preceded by a weak stress, in others the weak stress follows. Rhythmically, this means that in the first stanza the first line seems to glide into the second. But in the remainder of the poem, the line break within each stanza comes between two strong stresses, making for a slower, more deliberate movement from line to line. There appears, then, to be a rhythmic contrast between the opening statement and the following description.

How do these intricate relationships help to express the poem's meaning? Williams doesn't permit a very definite answer, as he never specifies just what it is that "depends" on the wheelbarrow, or how. But the rhythm suggests that the emphasis in the poem is on the objects *as objects*. This emphasis is enhanced by the fact that each of the three objects, in the last three stanzas, is identified by the same pattern of stress:

wheel barrow   rain water   white chickens

Williams intends for us to take in the effect of every detail: rainwater, chickens which are white, a wheelbarrow which is red and which is also a combination of a wheel and a barrow. Though one might propose a more far-reaching interpretation of the poem, and many critics have, this aspect of it suggests that "so much depends," at least in part, on accuracy of observation and freshness of reponse.

THE EVENT

Ever since they'd left the Tennessee ridge
with nothing to boast of
but good looks and a mandolin,

the two Negroes leaning
on the rail of a riverboat   5
were inseparable: Lem plucked

to Thomas' silver falsetto.
But the night was hot and they were drunk.
They spat where the wheel

churned mud and moonlight,   10
they called to the tarantulas
down among the bananas

to come out and dance.
You're so fine and mighty; let's see
what you can do, said Thomas, pointing   15

to a tree-capped island.
Lem stripped, spoke easy: *Them's chestnuts,*
I believe. Dove

quick as a gasp. Thomas, dry
on deck, saw the green crown shake   20
as the island slipped

under, dissolved
in the thickening stream.
At his feet

a stinking circle of rags,   25
the half-shell mandolin.
Where the wheel turned the water

gently shirred.*

(Rita Dove)

Here, free verse helps to tell a harrowing story in twenty-eight lines. The
rhythm is at first that of ordinary conversation: almost no two lines scan
similarly. Lines 1 and 2 are the closest to regular meter, and the poet perhaps uses their music to draw us into the story. Her skillful use of enjamb-
ment keeps us moving from line to line and from stanza to stanza. In lines
18 and 19 Lem takes action, and the rhythm enhances that action:

> Ĭ bĕliéve. | Dóve

> quíck | ăs ă gásp. | Thómăs, | drý

The sudden spondee ("Dóve / quíck"), spanning the stanza break between
lines 18 and 19, emphasizes the suddenness of his dive; the anapest "as a
gasp" underscores its speed. The enjambments at lines 21–22 and 24–25
are the most dramatic: the first gives intensity to the island's movement,
while the second draws us to the finality of what Lem has left behind. The
last line is only three syllables long—

> géntly | shírred

—and the two strong stresses underscore the finality of the death.

Rhyme

The largest English dictionaries list over four hundred thousand words,
but linguists set the number of distinct sounds of which these words are
composed at about thirty-five. The result? English is full or words that rhyme.
Rhyme may be quickly defined as the repetition in sound of the final stressed
syllable, plus any weak-stress syllables that may follow. For centuries rhyme
has been one of the most used formal devices of poetry.

Why? There are many possible answers, none definitive. Children find
rhyming an entrancing game, and many poets and readers feel the same
kind of enjoyment. Light verse almost always rhymes, and sometimes the
rhyming is much of the fun:

Higgledy Piggledy, my white hen;
She lays eggs for gentlemen.
You cannot persuade her with gun or lariat
To come across for the proletariat.

(Dorothy Parker)

Most popular songs have rhymed lyrics: poetry and song have long been
related, and the recurrences of rhyme are often equivalent to the recurrences of melody. And some poets use the requirements of rhyme to make
poems harder to write but more engaging to them and their readers, because
of the effect that rhyme gives of a difficulty that has been aptly overcome.

*Drew together.

More importantly, if poetry is, as W. H. Auden said, "memorable speech," then rhyme helps to keep that speech in our memories.

One of the most obvious uses of rhyme is to draw more attention to the end of the poetic line, and to the break between one line and the next. Because of this, poets often put key words into rhyming positions:

> The chestnut casts his flambeaux,* and the flowers
> Stream from the hawthorn on the wind away,
> The doors clap to, the pane is blind with showers.
> Pass me the can,† lad; there's an end of May.
>   (A. E. Housman, "The Chestnut Casts His Flambeaux")

The inversion which sets "away" at the end of the second line might, in another poem, be merely a convenience of a poet seeking a rhyme for "May." But the theme of these four lines, and of the poem, is that time passes, leaves us, streams *away* like spring flowers; the wait for, and the slight emphasis on, "away," then, underline the poem's meaning. Often words whose sounds rhyme have some relation in meaning as well—they are similar, or opposite, or ask to be compared:

> Miniver Cheevy, born too late,
>   Scratched his head and kept on thinking;
> Miniver coughed, and called it fate,
>   And kept on drinking.
>   (Edwin Arlington Robinson, "Miniver Cheevy")

The rhyme between "born too late" (Miniver Cheevy's situation) and "called it fate" (his response to it) has a kind of unforced conclusiveness about it, while the rhyme between "thinking" and "drinking," emphasized by the short final line, is a witty comment on the quality of Cheevy's thinking and seems to "clinch" the poem.

In the second and fourth lines of the Housman stanza, and the first and third lines of the Robinson stanza, the last stressed syllables are also the last syllables of the line: *away / May; late / fate*. Such single-syllable rhymes have come to be called **masculine rhymes**. The other rhymes are two-syllable rhymes: *flowers / showers; thinking / drinking;* these are called **feminine rhymes**.

Rhymes are often used to unify a poem: to draw us along with rising expectations of an inevitable rhyme, and to fulfill those expectations at a crucial point in the poem. The poems by Housman and Robinson share the same pattern of rhymes, or **rhyme scheme**. Lines one and two begin a though in such a way that we can't predict the conclusions or the rhymes, the third line completes the thought and provides one of the rhymes, and the last line is the clincher. Other rhyme schemes work in other ways:

> But I say it's fine. Honest, I do.
> And I'd like to be a bad woman, too.
> And wear the brave stockings of night-black lace
> And strut down the street with paint on my face.
>   (Gwendolyn Brooks, "A Song in the Front Yard")

> I had come to the house, in a cave of trees,
> Facing a sheer sky.

---

*Torches (chestnut flowers are vivid red).   †I.e., mug of ale.

> Everything moved,—a bell hung ready to strike,
> Sun and reflection wheeled by.
>
> > (Louise Bogan, "Medusa")

> One dark night,
> my Tudor Ford climbed the hill's skull;
> I watched for love-cars. Lights turned down,
> they lay together, hull to hull,
> where the graveyard shelves on the town. . . .
> My mind's not right.
>
> > (Robert Lowell, "Skunk Hour")

Brooks's stanza is in **couplets** (pairs of rhymed lines). The rhymes tie together lines closely connected by their meaning and slightly separate them from the other couplets. In couplets the rhymes are very noticeable because they follow upon each other so closely. The couplet is therefore a favorite rhyme scheme when the rhymes themselves are unusual or funny, as in light or comic verse. In Bogan's poem only half the lines rhyme, still exploiting the effect of rhyme but more sparingly than do Housman and Robinson.

Lowell, on the other hand, rhymes his poem more complexly, and to keep track of the rhymes we can outline their pattern. The first rhyme is usually marked *a*, the second *b*, and so on, while unrhymed lines are marked *x*. The rhyme scheme in "Miniver Cheevy" is *abab*; Brooks's is *aabb*; Bogan's *xaxa*. Lowell's is *abcbca*. The middle four lines set up the same pattern of expectation and fulfillment that we saw earlier, but within a much longer arc that takes off from *night* and comes to rest with *right*. Such a long wait for the rhyme may well imply a meaningful connection between the two *a* lines.

Rhymes may also occur within the line, in which case they are called **internal rhymes**:

> "No, baby, *no,* you may not *go,*
> For the dogs are fierce and wild . . ."
>
> > (Dudley Randall, "Ballad of Birmingham")

> The wilderness rose up to it,
> And sprawled *around,* no longer wild.
> The jar was *round* upon the *ground*
> And tall and of a port in air.
>
> > (Wallace Stevens, "Anecdote of the Jar")

Since rhyming words command attention, their appearance in midline usually signals that something important is happening, as when the mother in Randall's poem emphatically tells her daughter not to go downtown. Stevens's poem, otherwise unrhymed, clusters three rhyming words in its middle, perhaps suggesting the control the jar attains over the formless wilderness at this point in the poem.

The examples we have looked at so far have all been cases of so-called **perfect rhyme**—wherein the sounds match exactly. English-speaking poets have followed this convention for centuries, though occasionally permitting themselves what is called **eye-rhyme** (*cough* / *enough,* for example), wherein the words are spelled alike but don't sound alike. Many modern poets, however, consider that a true rhyme is too noticeable, or too well-ordered, to serve their purposes. They have preferred to use one or another kind of **near-rhyme** (also called half-rhyme, or off-rhyme, or slant rhyme):

> I heard a Fly buzz—when I died—
> The Stillness in the *Room*
> Was like the Stillness in the Air
> Between the Heaves of *storm*—
>
> (Emily Dickinson, J. 465)

In "Room" and "storm" Dickinson retains the final consonant but varies the vowel sound.

Vowel-rhymes are less emphatic than consonant rhymes:

> Now as I was young and easy under the apple *boughs*
> About the lilting house and happy as the grass was *green,*
>   The night above the dingle* *starry,*
>   Time let me hail and *climb*
>   Golden in the heydays of his *eyes,*
> And honoured among wagons I was prince of the apple *towns*
> And once below a time I lordly had the trees and *leaves*
>   Trail with daisies and *barley*
>   Down the rivers of the windfall *light.*
>
> (Dylan Thomas, "Fern Hill")

5

Thomas rhymes only the vowels of *boughs* and *towns; green* and *leaves; starry* and *barley, climb, eyes,* and *light.*

In **pararhyme,** the stressed vowel sounds differ but are flanked by identical or similar consonants. The term was coined by Edward Blunden to describe Wilfred Owen's use of such rhymes:

> It seemed that out of battle I e*scaped*
> Down some profound dull tunnel, long since *scooped*
> Through granites which titanic wars had *groined.*
> Yet also there encumbered sleepers *groaned,*
> Too fast in thought or death to be be*stirred*
> Then, as I probed them, one sprang up, and *stared* . . .
>
> ("Strange Meeting")

As Jon Stallworthy has pointed out, "the second rhyme is usually lower in pitch (has a deeper vowel sound) than the first, producing sound effects of dissonance, failure, and unfulfillment that subtly reinforce Owen's themes." Thus, above, *scooped* sounds lower than *scaped,* and *groaned* than *groined.*

Sound Effects Within the Line

The sounds of rhymes stand out in a poem because they echo each other so closely, especially when they come at the ends of lines. But poets take just as much care with the less noticeable sounds of the other words in the poem. "Let's say you have a choice of adjectives," says Denise Levertov, "and one has an onomatopoeic quality which you want, but it also has a couple of s's in it, and the rest of the line, or the line just before it, is already pretty sibilant, but you feel that line is right. You might have to forego the word that you've just found and keep on looking, because you can't have all those s's jammed together." For Levertov, as for many other poets, it's clearly not a matter of merely letting the sounds take care of themselves.

The most frequent sound patterns within a line are **alliteration** (in which the consonant sounds, especially at the beginnings of words, are the same)

---

*Small wooded valley.

and **assonance** (when several words near to each other have identical or very similar vowel sounds). Here are some examples:

> Only the *stutter*ing rifles' rapid *ratt*le
> Can pa*tter* out their hasty orisons.
>> (Wilfred Owen, "Anthem for Doomed Youth")

> the sudden angel *aff*righted me—light *eff*acing
> my *f*eeble beam,
> a *f*orest of torches, *f*eathers of *f*lame, sparks up*f*lying:
>> (Denise Levertov, "Caedmon")

> It *g*athers to a *g*reatness, like the *oo*ze of *o*il
> Crushed. Why do m*e*n then *now* n*o*t r*e*ck his r*o*d?
>> (Gerard Manley Hopkins, "God's Grandeur")

The alliteration in the first two examples and the assonance (together with more alliteration) in the third help to unify these passages, and could, not unfancifully, be said to imitate, or at least to suggest, the actions being described.

Stanza and Verse Paragraph

Many of the examples in the discussion of rhyme are stanzas. **Stanzas** are regular groups of lines within a poem set off from each other by a space:

> Ah, be content!—the scorpion's tail
> Atones for much; without avail
> Under the sizzling solar pan
> Our sleeping servant pulls the fan.
>
> Even in this island richly blest,
> Where Beauty walks with naked breast,
> Earth is too harsh for Heaven to be
> One little hour in jeopardy.
>> (Edna St. Vincent Millay, "To a Calvinist in Bali")

Most stanzas within a poem have the same number of lines and use the same rhyme scheme, as in the example above.

In many poems, stanzas are like verses of a song; each encompasses a complete thought, and each ends at the end of a sentence. But not always:

> Well, I was ten and very much afraid.
> In my kind world the dead were out of range
> And I could not forgive the sad or strange
> In beast or man. My father took the spade
>
> And buried him. Last night I saw the grass
> Slowly divide (it was the same scene
> But now it glowed a fierce and mortal green)
> And saw the dog emerging. I confess
>
> I felt afraid again, but still he came . . .
>> (Richard Wilbur, "The Pardon")

Here Wilbur is playing against the stanza divisions, and carrying enjamb-ment across the stanza break. It is as if his strong emotions forced the speaker to break the formal divisions of the poem.

Stanzas should not be confused with verse paragraphs, even though both are divided by white spaces. A **verse paragraph** is simply a section of a poem, and it can be any length the poet chooses; it is much like a paragraph of prose. In T. S. Eliot's "Little Gidding" (p. 295), sections I, III, and V contain verse paragraphs of varying lengths, whereas the opening of section II and all of section IV are made up of stanzas.

Many types of stanza have been used so often that their characteristic forms have become fixed; and there are types of poems, such as the sonnet, which are also fixed.

Poetic Kinds, Forms, and Stanzas: a Glossary

Though many modern poets prefer to shape their own forms, others have chosen to adopt traditional formal patterns which over the centuries have become fixed. Even a poet who chooses not to use these forms may want to write one of the traditional kinds or genres of poetry, which impose no specific scheme or rhyme or meter but which suggest specific ways in which certain subjects may be treated. This glossary defines the most common traditional forms and kinds of poetry.

Ballad   A short narrative poem, originally a "folk ballad"—that is, an anon-ymous poem that was sung. Modern literary ballads imitate the folk bal-lad's simple diction, its use of **refrain** (one or more lines repeated at the close of each stanza), and the ballad stanza form: four lines, ususally rhyming *xaxa*, of which lines one and three are iambic tetrameter, and lines two and four are iambic trimeter.
(Example: Edwin Muir, "Ballad of Hector in Hades")

Blank verse   Unrhymed iambic pentameter.
(Example: Robert Frost, "Birches")

Canto   A large division of a long poem, usually a narrative poem.
(Example: Ezra Pound, "Canto I")

Couplet   A pair of lines, usually rhymed and in the same meter. Closed couplets are end-stopped at the second line; heroic couplets are in iambic pentameter.
(Examples: Rudyard Kipling, "A Song to Mithras"; Robert Graves, "The Persian Version")

Elegy   Either a poem about a specific death, often of a friend, a relative, or a famous person; or else a general meditation on death. The term implies no particular formal organization.
(Examples: W. H. Auden, "In Memory of W. B. Yeats"; June Jordan, "July 4, 1984: For Buck")

Epigram   A short, usually rhymed poem, distinguished by its terseness and usually concluding with a witty surprise.
(Example: A. R. Ammons, "Small Song")

Epistle   A letter in verse.
(Examples: Jon Stallworthy, "A Letter from Berlin"; Norman Dubie, "The Czar's Last Christmas Letter: A Barn in the Urals")

Epitaph   A poem to be inscribed on a tomb, or an imitation of such.
(Example: Randall Jarrell, "The Death of the Ball Turret Gunner")

Lyric A relatively short poem concerning itself mainly with the speaker's emotional state, or else with the process of the speaker's thought and feelings. The term originally signified a poem to be sung; in recent times, however, the term has been extended to include any poem not primarily narrative, satiric, or instructional in purpose. (Most short poems in this anthology are lyrics.)

Octave A group of eight lines set off in the poem either by a stanza break or by a distinctive rhyme scheme, as for example in the opening of a Petrarchan sonnet.
(Example: Edwin Arlington Robinson, "For a Dead Lady")

Ode A meditative poem of considerable length, whose subject gives rise to philosophical reflection. It is usually formally elaborate, but the term implies no specific type of organization. A Horatian ode repeats a stanza form of the poet's choice; the Pindaric or irregular ode is composed of stanzas or sections of different patterns.
(Examples: Robert Lowell, "For the Union Dead"—Horatian; Allen Tate, "Ode to the Confederate Dead"—irregular)

Ottava rima A stanza form in eight pentameter lines, rhymed *abababcc*.
(Example: William Butler Yeats, "Among School Children")

Quatrain A group of four lines set off in the poem either by a stanza break or by a distinctive rhyme scheme.
(Examples: Emily Dickinson, "Because I Could Not Stop for Death"; Gwendolyn Brooks, "Sadie and Maud")

Sestet A group of six lines set off in the poem either by a stanza break or by a distinctive rhyme scheme, as for example at the conclusion of a Petrarchan sonnet.
(Examples: Thomas Hardy, "Drummer Hodge"; Seamus Heaney, "The Harvest Bow")

Sestina An Old French verse form in six sestets and a tercet, usually unrhymed and in iambic pentameter. The words at the end of each of the lines of the first sestet are repeated as the end words of the other sestets, though each time in a different order; all six end-words are employed in the closing tercet. The scheme by which the order of the end-words was varied is less strictly followed than it once was. Here is the scheme of the strict sestina:

Stanza	Order of end-words:
1	1 2 3 4 5 6
2	6 1 5 2 4 3
3	3 6 4 1 2 5
4	5 3 2 6 1 4
5	4 5 1 3 6 2
6	2 4 6 5 3 1
7	2, 5; 4, 3; 6, 1

(Example: Anthony Hecht, "Sestina d'Inverno")

Sonnet A lyric poem in fourteen lines, normally in iambic pentameter, and rhymed according to one of a number of set patterns. The three most common rhyme patterns are the Petrarchan sonnet (*abba abba cdcd cd* or *cded ce*); the Shakespearean sonnet (*abab cdcd efef gg*); and the Spenserian sonnet (*abab bcbc cdcd cc*). Gerard Manley Hopkins invented a form called the curtal (or shortened) sonnet (*abcabc dbcdc*). Often the evolution of the content of a sonnet mirrors its form; when the rhyme pattern changes (at the closing sestet in the Petrarchan sonnet, or at the closing couplet in the Shakespearean or Spenserian) the poet also turns from making assertions to drawing conclusions.

(Examples: Edwin Arlington Robinson, "The Sheaves"—Petrarchan; Edna St. Vincent Millay, "Hearing Your Words, and Not a Word Among Them"—Shakespearian; Gerard Manley Hopkins, "Pied Beauty"—curtal)

Sonnet variations   Marilyn Hacker and Tony Harrison are among recent poets who have rung their own changes on the sonnet form. Hacker, in the sonnets reprinted in this anthology, slightly varies the Petrarchan rhyme scheme in her octets: (*abba cddc*) and works out her own sestet: in "Runaways," *effgge;* in "Mythology," *eefefe.* Harrison in his *School of Eloquence* enlarges the sonnet length to sixteen lines, which usually rhyme *abab cdcd efef ghgh;* sometimes he varies the third quatrain: *effe.* (George Meredith, in his sonnet sequence *Modern Love* (1862), used a similar sixteen-line form.)

Tercet   A group of three lines set off in the poem either by a stanza break or by a distinctive rhyme scheme.

(Examples: Elizabeth Bishop, "One Art"; Sylvia Plath, "Ariel")

Terza rima   A sequence of tercets whose rhymes link them together in the pattern *aba bcb cdc ded efe* and so on. Best known as the verse form of Dante's *Divine Comedy*, it is not often strictly used in modern English poetry, but a sequence of tercets in blank verse may be made to have a similar effect.

(Examples: Robert Frost, "Acquainted with the Night"; A. R. Ammons, "City Limits"; Seamus Heaney, "Station Island" XII)

Villanelle   An Old French form in six stanzas on two rhymes, usually in iambic pentameter. The first and last lines of the opening tercet serve alternately as the closing line of the following four tercets, and the two together conclude the final quatrain: *AbA' abA abA' abA abA' abAA'.*

(Examples: Theodore Roethke, "The Waking"; Dylan Thomas, "Do Not Go Gentle into That Good Night")

Index of Terms

Modern Poems

Second Edition

WALT WHITMAN
1819–1892

Walt Whitman was one of the great innovative figures in nineteenth-century Anglo-American literature and remains a uniquely important presence in the poetry of the twentieth century. As one reads modern American poets, one doesn't so much trace Whitman's influence as locate individual writers by their attitude towards him. In the history of modern poetry, Whitman has been a rallying cry, a battle ground, an inspiration, and a bad example. He raised most of the important issues that confront modern poets and their readers. His joyful experiments with language, his pretense of telling all while leaving much to be gathered, his reckless assumption that the poet, his language, his subject matter, and his readers are all part of one expanding community, have endowed him with patriarchal importance. Whitman eludes and sometimes exasperates us because, just as he prophesied, he has become part of our environment, the way we look at and thus create our world.

In his poems Whitman appears as the archetypal over-reacher, and nothing human is alien to him (if he can help it) or negligible. He rescues for poetry the unpoetic, the vulgar, the profane, and the obscene. His mainstay was the English language, augmented from time to time with a gaily worn foreign phrase; his liberation was the realization that poems need no longer look like poems—with their smart couplets and quatrains—need, for that matter, no longer sound like poems. They can sound like the Book of Psalms or Fourth-of-July orations; it was all one to Walt Whitman. He launched his long periodic sentences in search of their subject matter, gave names to everything he saw, and became for later poets a great natural resource, like a forest or a uranium mine.

Walt Whitman was born on May 31, 1819, in then-rural Huntington, Long Island. His father was of British, his mother of Dutch ancestry. His indifference to religious orthodoxy, his insistence on the worth of individual experience and on private charity, may owe something to the fact that there were Quakers on both sides of his family. When Whitman was still very young his father, who was both a farmer and a carpenter, moved the family to Brooklyn, then a city of less than 10,000, where he worked at building houses. Whitman's childhood happily alternated between the growing city and the countryside and seacoast. He attended school for only five years, for in 1830, when he was eleven, he went to work as an office boy, first to an attorney, who encouraged him to read Sir Walter Scott, and then to a physician. He soon turned, however, to printing and journalism, and until the early 1850s—with occasional periods of school teaching—he worked as a newspaperman.

More than most poets, Walt Whitman had a carefully developed public personality, and he fostered the impression that he was ill-read and indolent. This was not in fact the case. As a youth he read the Old and New Testaments (to this reading his revolutionary cadences bear witness), Shakespeare, McPherson's Ossian, Homer, Aeschylus and Sophocles, the Nibelungenlied, the "ancient Hindoo poems," and Dante. He was also influenced by such contemporary sages as Goethe, Carlyle, and Emerson. As an occasional book reviewer for his newspapers and an energetic amateur of the theater and opera, he accumulated the rich experience that would find expression in his poems.

Whitman had been experimenting with poetry since 1847. In 1851 he moved in with his parents, supported himself with part-time carpentry, and began work on *Leaves of Grass*. The first edition appeared on July 4, 1855; like all but two of the first seven editions, it was privately printed, and the author himself set the type. It consisted of twelve untitled poems, the first and by far the longest of which would eventually be titled "Song of Myself." It is a foretaste of the poems that were to follow. The incantatory rhythms of the unrhymed lines, the catalogues of North

1

Americans busy with their lives and occupations, the rapid alternations from joy to disaster, disaster sometimes natural, sometimes visited on men and women by their fellow human beings, the moving cinema-like eye which homes in on a detail, then springs back to survey a panorama, the narrator, sexually and socially undefined, never, despite the awesome egocentricity of the poem's title ("Song of Myself" indeed!), to be isolated from his creations—all of this richness is available to the poet from his beginnings. The book did not sell well, but it attracted attention in important quarters. Emerson, to whom Whitman had sent a copy, wrote a famous acknowledgment: "I greet you at the beginning of a great career, which yet must have had a long foreground somewhere, for such a start. I rubbed my eyes a little to see if this sunbeam were no illusion, but the solid sense of the book is a sober certainty. It has the best merits, namely, of fortifying and encouraging."[1]

In the second and third editions of *Leaves of Grass* (1856, 1860) Whitman's particular mode of composition began to display itself. He slowly discovered that he was writing an increasingly long and complexly orchestrated poem, the unity of which was clear to him only as he worked at it. *Leaves of Grass* is Whitman's one book, a book which appeared in many versions and was transformed in response to changes in its author's life and in the history of his nation. It is Whitman's contribution to that peculiarly nineteenth-century form, the subjective epic, like Wordsworth's *Prelude* a work of heroic introspection, which views the experience of one man so that it will include multitudes. "I can hardly tell why," he wrote, "but feel very positively that if anything can justify my revolutionary attempts & utterances, it is such *ensemble*— like a great city to modern civilization & a whole combined clustering paradoxical unity, a man, a woman. . . ."

Whitman from the first added new poems to his initial slim volume—twenty in 1856, 124 in 1860—and in a letter to Emerson he promised that there would be more to come. He began to give titles to individual poems and to divide the poems into groups. The first of these groups is called "Calamus"—the title refers to a plant, a "very large & aromatic grass, or rush, growing about water-ponds in the valleys . . . often called 'sweet flag' "[2]—and it celebrates masculine friendship or, as Whitman calls it, "adhesiveness." In the second group of poems, "Children of Adam," Whitman is bent on celebrating procreation, but the emotional center of the poem is his admiration for the masculine body at work and play.

From the beginning of his career as a writer, Whitman as experimental poet aligned himself with the great social and political experiment of American democracy. His was a "new style . . . necessitated by new theories, new themes . . . , forced upon us for American purposes."[3] "Every really new person," he explained, "(poet or other,) *makes* his style—sometimes a little removed from the previous models—sometimes very far removed."[4] His ambition, Whitman wrote, was "to give something to our literature which will be our own; with neither foreign spirit, nor imagery nor form, but adapted to our case, grown out of our associations, boldly portraying the West, strengthening and intensifying the national soul, and finding the entire fountains of its birth and growth in our own country."[5] Whitman's relationship with his own country was brought to a dramatic resolution—one might almost say consummation—by the Civil War.

In 1862 Whitman went to the front in Virginia to be with his soldier brother George, who had been reported wounded. George's wounds were slight, but Whitman for a few weeks stayed on near the fighting and then went to Washington. He took a part-time job in the Army paymaster's office in aid of his main activity, the ministering to wounded soldiers, Union and Confederate alike. Unsponsored, living meagerly so

1. Emerson's letter to Whitman, July 21, 1855.
2. Letter to Moncure D. Conway, November 1, 1867, *Letters* 1, New York, 1961, p. 347.
3. Letter to the Editors, *Harper's Magazine,*
Letters 1, p. 46.
4. The same.
5. Letter to William D. O'Connor, 1866, *Letters* 1, p. 288.

that he would have a little money for his charities, Whitman made daily visits to the Washington hospitals: he comforted the dying, dressed wounds, wrote letters home for the soldiers, brought them gifts of flowers, fruit, and tobacco, and read aloud to them, though never from his own poems. Though his first reactions to the war had been conventionally pro-Union, his awareness of the sufferings on both sides and his readily aroused sympathy for all the wounded and dying young men give his poems about the war—eventually collected and published as "Drum Taps" and later incorporated in *Leaves of Grass*—a beautifully modulated compassion. Whitman's tenderness for the soldiers presages the series of sentimental friendships with young working-class men in which his emotional life found its main expression. He was unaware that his sentiments might be considered unorthodox, and when the English critic John Addington Symonds, himself a homosexual, questioned Whitman about his sexual preferences, the poet was horrified and as evidence of his heterosexuality adduced six bastard children, hastily invented for the occasion.

Whitman remained in Washington after the war ended. In 1865 he was appointed to a clerkship in the Office of Indian Affairs, but lost his post within six months when it was discovered that he had written an allegedly indecent book—*Leaves of Grass*. He quickly found employment in the Attorney General's Office, where he remained until he suffered a stroke in 1873. During these postwar years in Washington, he brought out two more editions of the *Leaves of Grass* (1867, 1871), which included "Drum Taps" and "Sequel to Drum Taps." Whitman never completely recovered from his stroke. For a time he lived as an invalid at the home of his brother George in Camden, New Jersey. Between 1876 and 1891 Whitman produced the autobiographical prose work *Specimen Days* and three collections of new poems, first published separately and then added to *Leaves of Grass*, which during this period appeared in five further editions. He spent his last eight years in a small house in Camden which he was just prosperous enough to buy for himself. His European and American reputation was already considerable, and he was unembarrassed by disciples who saw him as the founder of a new religion of political and sexual liberation and who treated his poems as sacred texts. Whitman died on March 26, 1892, in his seventy-third year.

From Song of Myself

1

I celebrate myself, and sing myself,
And what I assume you shall assume,
For every atom belonging to me as good belongs to you.

I loafe[1] and invite my soul,
I lean and loafe at my ease observing a spear of summer grass.   5
My tongue, every atom of my blood, form'd from this soil, this air,
Born here of parents born here from parents the same, and their parents
    the same,
I, now thirty-seven years old in perfect health begin,
Hoping to cease not till death.

Creeds and schools in abeyance,   10
Retiring back a while sufficed at what they are, but never forgotten,
I harbor for good or bad, I permit to speak at every hazard,
Nature without check with original energy.

---

1. Whitman's spelling of "loaf": be idle, lounge around.

2

Houses and rooms are full of perfumes, the shelves are crowded with per-
   fumes,
I breathe the fragrance myself and know it and like it,   15
The distillation would intoxicate me also, but I shall not let it.

The atmosphere is not a perfume, it has no taste of the distillation, it is
   odorless,
It is for my mouth forever, I am in love with it,
I will go to the bank by the wood and become undisguised and naked,
I am mad for it to be in contact with me.   20

The smoke of my own breath,
Echoes, ripples, buzz'd whispers, love-root, silk-thread, crotch and vine,
My respiration and inspiration, the beating of my heart, the passing of blood
   and air through my lungs,
The sniff of green leaves and dry leaves, and of the shore and dark-color'd
   sea-rocks, and of hay in the barn,
The sound of the belch'd words of my voice loos'd to the eddies of the wind, 25
A few light kisses, a few embraces, a reaching around of arms,
The play of shine and shade on the trees as the supple boughs wag,
The delight alone or in the rush of the streets, or along the fields and hill-
   sides,
The feeling of health, the full-noon trill, the song of me rising from bed and
   meeting the sun.

Have you reckon'd a thousand acres much? have you reckon'd the earth
   much?   30
Have you practis'd so long to learn to read?
Have you felt so proud to get at the meaning of poems?

Stop this day and night with me and you shall possess the origin of all
   poems,
You shall possess the good of the earth and sun, (there are millions of suns
   left,)
You shall no longer take things at second or third hand, nor look through
   the eyes of the dead, nor feed on the spectres in books,   35
You shall not look through my eyes either, nor take things from me,
You shall listen to all sides and filter them from your self.

3

I have heard what the talkers were talking, the talk of the beginning and
   the end,
But I do not talk of the beginning or the end.

There was never any more inception than there is now,   40
Nor any more youth or age than there is now,
And will never be any more perfection than there is now,
Nor any more heaven or hell than there is now.

Urge and urge and urge,
Always the procreant urge of the world.

Out of the dimness opposite equals advance, always substance and increase,
    always sex,   45
Always a knit of identity, always distinction, always a breed of life.

To elaborate is no avail, learn'd and unlearn'd feel that it is so.

Sure as the most certain sure, plumb in the uprights, well entretied,[2] braced
    in the beams,
Stout as a horse, affectionate, haughty, electrical,   50
I and this mystery here we stand.

Clear and sweet is my soul, and clear and sweet is all that is not my soul.

Lack one lacks both, and the unseen is proved by the seen,
Till that becomes unseen and receives proof in its turn.

Showing the best and dividing it from the worst age vexes age,[3]   55
Knowing the perfect fitness and equanimity of things, while they discuss I
    am silent, and go bathe and admire myself.

Welcome is every organ and attribute of me, and of any man hearty and
    clean,
Not an inch nor a particle of an inch is vile, and none shall be less familiar
    than the rest.

I am satisfied—I see, dance, laugh, sing;
As the hugging and loving bed-fellow sleeps at my side through the night,
    and withdraws at the peep of the day with stealthy tread,   60
Leaving me baskets cover'd with white towels swelling the house with their
    plenty,
Shall I postpone my acceptation and realization and scream at my eyes,
That they turn from gazing after and down the road,
And forthwith cipher[4] and show me to a cent,
Exactly the value of one and exactly the value of two, and which is ahead? 65

4

Trippers[5] and askers surround me,
People I meet, the effect upon me of my early life or the ward and city I
    live in, or the nation,
The latest dates, discoveries, inventions, societies, authors old and new,
My dinner, dress, associates, looks, compliments, dues,
The real or fancied indifference of some man or woman I love,   70
The sickness of one of my folks or of myself, or ill-doing or loss or lack of
    money, or depressions or exaltations,
Battles, the horrors of fratricidal war, the fever of doubtful news, the fitful
    events;
These come to me days and nights and go from me again,
But they are not the Me myself.

Apart from the pulling and hauling stands what I am,   75
Stands amused, complacent, compassionating, idle, unitary,

---

2. Cross-braced (carpenter's term).
3. In the first four editions of *Leaves of Grass*, Whitman had a comma between *worst* and *age*.
4. Calculate.
5. That is, travelers.

Looks down, is erect, or bends an arm on an impalpable certain rest,
Looking with side-curved head curious what will come next,
Both in and out of the game and watching and wondering at it.

Backward I see in my own days where I sweated through fog with linguists
    and contenders,   80
I have no mockings or arguments, I witness and wait.

           5
I believe in you my soul, the other I am must not abase itself to you,
And you must not be abased to the other.

Loafe with me on the grass, loose the stop from your throat,
Not words, not music or rhyme I want, not custom or lecture, not even the
    best,   85
Only the lull I like, the hum of your valvèd voice.

I mind how once we lay such a transparent summer morning,
How you settled your head athwart my hips and gently turn'd over upon
    me,
And parted the shirt from my bosom-bone, and plunged your tongue to my
    bare-stript heart,
And reach'd till you felt my beard, and reach'd till you held my feet.   90

Swiftly arose and spread around me the peace and knowledge that pass all
    the argument of the earth,
And I know that the hand of God is the promise of my own,
And I know that the spirit of God is the brother of my own,
And that all the men ever born are also my brothers, and the women my
    sisters and lovers,
And that a kelson[6] of the creation is love,   95
And limitless are leaves stiff or drooping in the fields,
And brown ants in the little wells beneath them,
And mossy scabs of the worm fence, heap'd stones, elder, mullein and poke-
    weed.[7]

           6
A child said *What is the grass?* fetching it to me with full hands;
How could I answer the child? I do not know what it is any more than he.   100

I guess it must be the flag of my disposition, out of hopeful green stuff
    woven.

Or I guess it is the handkerchief of the Lord,
A scented gift and remembrancer designedly dropt,
Bearing the owner's name someway in the corners, that we may see and
    remark, and say *Whose?*

Or I guess the grass is itself a child, the produced babe of the vegetation. 105

Or I guess it is a uniform hieroglyphic,
And it means, Sprouting alike in broad zones and narrow zones,

---

6. That is, a basic structural unit; a "keelson" or kelson is a reinforcing timber bolted to the keel of a ship.

7. A shrub, an herb, and a weed, respectively.

Growing among black folks as among white,
Kanuck, Tuckahoe, Congressman, Cuff,[8] I give them the same, I receive
  them the same.

And now it seems to me the beautiful uncut hair of graves.   110

Tenderly will I use you curling grass,
It may be you transpire from the breasts of young men,
It may be if I had known them I would have loved them,
It may be you are from old people, or from offspring taken soon out of their
  mothers' laps
And here you are the mothers' laps.   115

This grass is very dark to be from the white heads of old mothers,
Darker than the colorless beards of old men,
Dark to come from under the faint red roofs of mouths,

O I perceive after all so many uttering tongues,
And I perceive they do not come from the roofs of mouths for nothing.   120

I wish I could translate the hints about the dead young men and women,
And the hints about old men and mothers, and the offspring taken soon out
  of their laps.

What do you think has become of the young and old men?
And what do you think has become of the women and children?

They are alive and well somewhere,   125
The smallest sprout shows there is really no death,
And if ever there was it led forward life, and does not wait at the end to
  arrest it,
And ceas'd the moment life appear'd.

All goes onward and outward, nothing collapses,
And to die is different from what any one supposed, and luckier.   130

7
Has any one supposed it lucky to be born?
I hasten to inform him or her it is just as lucky to die, and I know it.

I pass death with the dying and birth with the new-wash'd babe, and am
  not contain'd between my hat and boots,
And peruse manifold objects, no two alike and every one good,
The earth good and the stars good, and their adjuncts all good.   135

I am not an earth nor an adjunct of an earth,
I am the mate and companion of people, all just as immortal and fathomless
  as myself,
(They do not know how immortal, but I know.)

Every kind for itself and its own, for me mine male and female,
For me those that have been boys and that love women,   140

8. French-Canadian; Virginian (who ate an Indian food-plant, tuckahoe); Negro (from an African word,
cuffee).

For me the man that is proud and feels how it stings to be slighted,
For me the sweet-heart and the old maid, for me mothers and the mothers
of mothers,
For me lips that have smiled, eyes that have shed tears,
For me children and the begetters of children.

Undrape! you are not guilty to me, nor stale nor discarded,   145
I see through the broadcloth and gingham whether or no,
And am around, tenacious, acquisitive, tireless, and cannot be shaken away.

8

The little one sleeps in its cradle,
I lift the gauze and look a long time, and silently brush away flies with my
hand.

The youngster and the red-faced girl turn aside up the bushy hill,   150
I peeringly view them from the top.

The suicide sprawls on the bloody floor of the bedroom,
I witness the corpse with its dabbled hair, I note where the pistol has fallen.

The blab of the pave,[9] tires of carts, sluff of boot-soles, talk of the promen-
aders,
The heavy omnibus, the driver with his interrogating thumb, the clank of
the shod horses on the granite floor,   155
The snow-sleighs, clinking, shouted jokes, pelts of snow-balls,
The hurrahs for popular favorites, the fury of rous'd mobs,
The flap of the curtain'd litter, a sick man inside borne to the hospital,
The meeting of enemies, the sudden oath, the blows and fall,
The excited crowd, the policeman with his star quickly working his passage
to the centre of the crowd,   160
The impassive stones that receive and return so many echoes,
What groans of over-fed or half-starv'd who fall sunstruck or in fits,
What exclamations of women taken suddenly who hurry home and give
birth to babes,
What living and buried speech is always vibrating here, what howls res-
train'd by decorum,
Arrests of criminals, slights, adulterous offers made, acceptance, rejections
with convex lips,   165
I mind them or the show or resonance of them—I come and I depart.

9

The big doors of the country barn stand open and ready,
The dried grass of the harvest-time loads the slow-drawn wagon,
The clear light plays on the brown gray and green intertinged,
The armfuls are pack'd to the sagging mow.   170

I am there, I help, I came stretch'd atop of the load,
I felt its soft jolts, one leg reclined on the other,
I jump from the cross-beams and seize the clover and timothy,
And roll head over heels and tangle my hair full of wisps.

9. Idle street ("pave") talk ("blab").

10

Alone far in the wilds and mountains I hunt,   175
Wandering amazed at my own lightness and glee,
In the late afternoon choosing a safe spot to pass the night,
Kindling a fire and broiling the fresh-kill'd game,
Falling asleep on the gather'd leaves with my dog and gun by my side.

The Yankee clipper is under her sky-sails, she cuts the sparkle and scud,[1]   180
My eyes settle the land, I bend at her prow or shout joyously from the
    deck.

The boatmen and clam-diggers arose early and stopt for me,
I tuck'd my trowser-ends in my boots and went and had a good time;
You should have been with us that day round the chowder-kettle.

I saw the marriage of the trapper in the open air in the far west, the bride
    was a red girl,   185
Her father and his friends sat near cross-legged and dumbly smoking, they
    had moccasins to their feet and large thick blankets hanging from their
    shoulders,
On a bank lounged the trapper, he was drest mostly in skins, his luxuriant
    beard and curls protected his neck, he held his bride by the hand,
She had long eyelashes, her head was bare, her coarse straight locks
    descended upon her voluptuous limbs and reach'd to her feet.

The runaway slave came to my house and stopt outside,
I heard his motions crackling the twigs of the woodpile,   190
Through the swung half-door of the kitchen I saw him limpsy[2] and weak,
And went where he sat on a log and led him in and assured him,
And brought water and fill'd a tub for his sweated body and bruis'd feet,
And gave him a room that enter'd from my own, and gave him some coarse
    clean clothes,
And remember perfectly well his revolving eyes and his awkwardness,   195
And remember putting plasters on the galls of his neck and ankles;
He staid with me a week before he was recuperated and pass'd north,
I had him sit next me at table, my fire-lock lean'd in the corner.

11

Twenty-eight young men bathe by the shore,
Twenty-eight young men and all so friendly;   200
Twenty-eight years of womanly life and all so lonesome.

She owns the fine house by the rise of the bank,
She hides handsome and richly drest aft the blinds of the window.

Which of the young men does she like the best?
Ah the homeliest of them is beautiful to her.   205

Where are you off to, lady? for I see you,
You splash in the water there, yet stay stock still in your room.

---

1. Here, spray driven by the wind. "Yankee
clippers" were swift full-rigged merchant ships of
the time; "sky-sail": one of several light sails near
the tops of the mast.
2. Limping or swaying.

Dancing and laughing along the beach came the twenty-ninth bather,
The rest did not see her, but she saw them and loved them.

The beards of the young men glisten'd with wet, it ran from their long hair, 210
Little streams pass'd all over their bodies.

An unseen hand also pass'd over their bodies,
It descended tremblingly from their temples and ribs.

The young men float on their backs, their white bellies bulge to the sun,
    they do not ask who seizes fast to them,
They do not know who puffs and declines with pendant and bending arch, 215
They do not think whom they souse with spray.

12

The butcher-boy puts off his killing-clothes, or sharpens his knife at the
    stall in the market,
I loiter enjoying his repartee and his shuffle and break-down[3]

Blacksmiths with grimed and hairy chests environ the anvil,
Each has his main-sledge, they are all out, there is a great heat in the fire. 220

From the cinder-strew'd threshold I follow their movements,
The lithe sheer of their waists plays even with their massive arms,
Overhand the hammers swing, overhand so slow, overhand so sure,
They do not hasten, each man hits in his place.

13

The negro holds firmly the reins of his four horses, the block swags under-
    neath on its tied-over chain, 225
The negro that drives the long dray of the stone-yard, steady and tall he
    stands pois'd on one leg on the string-piece,[4]
His blue shirt exposes his ample neck and breast and loosens over his hip-
    band,
His glance is calm and commanding, he tosses the slouch of his hat away
    from his forehead,
The sun falls on his crispy hair and mustache, falls on the black of his pol-
    ish'd and perfect limbs.

I behold the picturesque giant and love him, and I do not stop there, 230
I go with the team also.

In me the caresser of life wherever moving, backward as well as forward
    sluing,
To niches aside and junior[5] bending, not a person or object missing,
Absorbing all to myself and for this song.

Oxen that rattle the yoke and chain or halt in the leafy shade, what is that
    you express in your eyes? 235
It seems to me more than all the print I have read in my life.

---

3. Two ministrel-show dances: the first involves sliding the feet across the floor; the second is faster and noisier.

4. Long, heavy timber used to keep a load in place.

5. That is, smaller.

My tread scares the wood-drake and wood-duck on my distant and day-long
  ramble,
They rise together, they slowly circle around.

I believe in those wing'd purposes,
And acknowledge red, yellow, white, playing within me,   240
And consider green and violet and the tufted crown[6] intentional,
And do not call the tortoise unworthy because she is not something else,
And the jay in the woods never studied the gamut,[7] yet trills pretty well to
  me,
And the look of the bay mare shames silliness out of me.

14

The wild gander leads his flock through the cool night,   245
Ya-honk he says, and sounds it down to me like an invitation,
The pert may suppose it meaningless, but I listening close,
Find its purpose and place up there toward the wintry sky.

The sharp-hoof'd moose of the north, the cat on the house-sill, the chicka-
  dee, the prairie-dog,
The litter of the grunting sow as they tug at her teats,   250
The brood of the turkey-hen and she with her half-spread wings,
I see in them and myself the same old law.

The press of my foot to the earth springs a hundred affections,
They scorn the best I can do to relate them.

I am enamour'd of growing out-doors,   255
Of men that live among cattle or taste of the ocean or woods,
Of the builders and steerers of ships and the wielders of axes and mauls,
  and the drivers of horses,
I can eat and sleep with them week in and week out.

What is commonest, cheapest, nearest, easiest, is Me,
Me going in for my chances, spending for vast returns,   260
Adorning myself to bestow myself on the first that will take me,
Not asking the sky to come down to my good will,
Scattering it freely forever.

*   *   *

46

I know I have the best of time and space, and was never measured and
  never will be measured.

I tramp a perpetual journey, (come listen all!)
My signs are a rain-proof coat, good shoes, and a staff cut from the woods,
No friend of mine takes his ease in my chair,
I have no chair, no church, no philosophy,   1205
I lead no man to a dinner-table, library, exchange,[8]
But each man and each woman of you I lead upon a knoll,

---

6. Of the wood drake, a bird.   8. Stock exchange.
7. That is, scale of musical notes.

My left hand hooking you round the waist,
My right hand pointing to landscapes of continents and the public road.

Not I, not any one else can travel that road for you,   1210
You must travel it for yourself.

It is not far, it is within reach,
Perhaps you have been on it since you were born and did not know,
Perhaps it is everywhere on water and on land.

Shoulder your duds⁹ dear son, and I will mine, and let us hasten forth,   1215
Wonderful cities and free nations we shall fetch as we go.

If you tire, give me both burdens, and rest the chuff¹ of your hand on my
    hip,
And in due time you shall repay the same service to me,
For after we start we never lie by again.

This day before dawn I ascended a hill and look'd at the crowded heaven,   1220
And I said to my spirit *When we become the enfolders of those orbs, and
    the pleasure and knowledge of every thing in them, shall we be fill'd
    and satisfied then?*
And my spirit said *No, we but level that lift to pass and continue beyond.*

You are also asking me questions and I hear you,
I answer that I cannot answer, you must find out for yourself.

Sit a while dear son,   1225
Here are biscuits to eat and here is milk to drink,
But as soon as you sleep and renew yourself in sweet clothes, I kiss you
    with a good-by kiss and open the gate for your egress hence.

Long enough have you dream'd contemptible dreams,
Now I wash the gum from your eyes,
You must habit yourself to the dazzle of the light and of every moment of
    your life.   1230

Long have you timidly waded holding a plank by the shore,
Now I will you to be a bold swimmer,
To jump off in the midst of the sea, rise again, nod to me, shout, and laugh-
    ingly dash with your hair.

47

I am the teacher of athletes,
He that by me spreads a wider breast than my own proves the width of my
    own,   1235
He most honors my style who learns under it to destroy the teacher.

The boy I love, the same becomes a man not through derived power, but
    in his own right,
Wicked rather than virtuous out of conformity or fear,
Fond of his sweetheart, relishing well his steak,

9. Clothes and personal belongings.   1. Heel of the hand.

Unrequited love or a slight cutting him worse than sharp steel cuts,   1240
First-rate to ride, to fight, to hit the bull's eye, to sail a skiff, to sing a song
    or play on the banjo,
Preferring scars and the beard and faces pitted with small-pox over all lath-
    erers,
And those well-tann'd to those that keep out of the sun.

I teach straying from me, yet who can stray from me?
I follow you whoever you are from the present hour,   1245
My words itch at your ears till you understand them.

I do not say these things for a dollar or to fill up the time while I wait for a
    boat,
(It is you talking just as much as myself, I act as the tongue of you,
Tied in your mouth, in mine it begins to be loosen'd.)

I swear I will never again mention love or death inside a house,   1250
And I swear I will never translate myself at all, only to him or her who
    privately stays with me in the open air.

If you would understand me go to the heights or water-shore,
The nearest gnat is an explanation, and a drop or motion of waves a key,
The maul,[2] the oar, the hand-saw, second my words.

No shutter'd room or school can commune with me,   1255
But roughs and little children better than they.

The young mechanic is closest to me, he knows me well,
The woodman that takes his axe and jug with him shall take me with him
    all day,
The farm-boy ploughing in the field feels good at the sound of my voice,
In vessels that sail my words sail, I go with fishermen and seamen and love
    them.   1260

The soldier camp'd or upon the march is mine,
On the night ere the pending battle many seek me, and I do not fail them,
On that solemn night (it may be their last) those that know me seek me.

My face rubs to the hunter's face when he lies down alone in his blanket,
The driver thinking of me does not mind the jolt of his wagon,   1265
The young mother and old mother comprehend me,
The girl and the wife rest the needle a moment and forget where they are,
They and all would resume what I have told them.

48

I have said that the soul is not more than the body,
And I have said that the body is not more than the soul,   1270
And nothing, not God, is greater to one than one's self is,
And whoever walks a furlong[3] without sympathy walks to his own funeral
    drest in his shroud,
And I or you pocketless of a dime may purchase the pick of the earth,

2. Heavy mallet.   3. One-eighth of a mile.

And to glance with an eye or show a bean in its pod confounds the learning
 of all times,
And there is no trade or employment but the young man following it may
 become a hero,   1275
And there is no object so soft but it makes a hub for the wheel'd universe,
And I say to any man or woman, Let your soul stand cool and composed
 before a million universes.

And I say to mankind, Be not curious about God,
For I who am curious about each am not curious about God,
(No array of terms can say how much I am at peace about God and about
 death.)   1280

I hear and behold God in every object, yet understand God not in the least,
Nor do I understand who there can be more wonderful than myself.

Why should I wish to see God better than this day?
I see something of God each hour of the twenty-four, and each moment
 then,
In the faces of men and women I see God, and in my own face in the glass, 1285
I find letters from God dropt in the street, and every one is sign'd by God's
 name,
And I leave them where they are, for I know that wheresoe'er I go,
Others will punctually come for ever and ever.

49

And as to you Death, and you bitter hug of mortality, it is idle to try to
 alarm me.

To his work without flinching the accoucheur[4] comes,   1290
I see the elder-hand pressing receiving supporting,
I recline by the sills of the exquisite flexible doors,
And mark the outlet, and mark the relief and escape.

And as to you Corpse I think you are good manure, but that does not offend
 me,
I smell the white roses sweet-scented and growing,   1295
I reach to the leafy lips, I reach to the polish'd breasts of melons.

And as to you Life I reckon you are the leavings of many deaths,
(No doubt I have died myself ten thousand times before.)

I hear you whispering there O stars of heaven,
O suns—O grass of graves—O perpetual transfers and promotions, 1300
If you do not say any thing how can I say any thing?

Of the turbid pool that lies in the autumn forest,
Of the moon that descends the steeps of the soughing[5] twilight,
Toss, sparkles of day and dusk—toss on the black stems that decay in the
 muck,
Toss to the moaning gibberish of the dry limbs.   1305

---

4. Midwife, obstetrician; "elder-hand": the guid- 5. Sighing.
ing hand of the midwife or obstetrician.

I ascend from the moon, I ascend from the night,
I perceive that the ghastly glimmer is noonday sunbeams reflected,
And debouch[6] to the steady and central from the offspring great or small.

50

There is that in me—I do not know what it is—but I know it is in me.

Wrench'd and sweaty—calm and cool then my body becomes,   1310
I sleep—I sleep long.

I do not know it—it is without name—it is a word unsaid,
It is not in any dictionary, utterance, symbol.

Something it swings on more than the earth I swing on,
To it the creation is the friend whose embracing awakes me.   1315

Perhaps I might tell more. Outlines! I plead for my brothers and sisters.

Do you see O my brothers and sisters?
It is not chaos or death—it is form, union, plan—it is eternal life—it is
    Happiness.

51

The past and present wilt—I have fill'd them, emptied them,
And proceed to fill my next fold of the future.   1320

Listener up there! what have you to confide to me?
Look in my face while I snuff the sidle of evening,[7]
(Talk honestly, no one else hears you, and I stay only a minute longer.)

Do I contradict myself?
Very well then I contradict myself,   1325
(I am large, I contain multitudes.)
I concentrate toward them that are nigh, I wait on the door-slab.

Who has done his day's work? who will soonest be through with his supper?
Who wishes to walk with me?

Will you speak before I am gone? will you prove already too late?   1330

52

The spotted hawk swoops by and accuses me, he complains of my gab and
    my loitering.

I too am not a bit tamed, I too am untranslatable,
I sound my barbaric yawp over the roofs of the world.

The last scud of day holds back for me,
It flings my likeness after the rest and true as any on the shadow'd wilds,   1335
It coaxes me to the vapor and the dusk.

---

6. Pour forth.
7. To "snuff" is to put out, as in extinguishing
a candle; here, the light is the last light of day,
idling or moving along edgeways.

I depart as air, I shake my white locks at the runaway sun,
I effuse my flesh in eddies, and drift it in lacy jags.

I bequeath myself to the dirt to grow from the grass I love,
If you want me again look for me under your boot-soles.   1340

You will hardly know who I am or what I mean,
But I shall be good health to you nevertheless,
And filter and fibre your blood.

Failing to fetch me at first keep encouraged,
Missing me one place search another,   1345
I stop somewhere waiting for you.

                                                1855, 1881

When I Heard at the Close of the Day

When I heard at the close of the day how my name had been receiv'd with
    plaudits in the capitol, still it was not a happy night for me that fol-
    low'd,
And else when I carous'd, or when my plans were accomplish'd, still I was
    not happy,
But the day when I rose at dawn from the bed of perfect health, refresh'd,
    singing, inhaling the ripe breath of autumn,
When I saw the full moon in the west grow pale and disappear in the morn-
    ing light,
When I wander'd alone over the beach, and undressing bathed, laughing
    with the cool waters, and saw the sun rise,   5
And when I thought how my dear friend my lover was on his way coming,
    O then I was happy,
O then each breath tasted sweeter, and all that day my food nourish'd me
    more, and the beautiful day pass'd well,
And the next came with equal joy, and with the next at evening came my
    friend,
And that night while all was still I heard the waters roll slowly continually
    up the shores,
I heard the hissing rustle of the liquid and sands as directed to me whisper-
    ing to congratulate me,   10
For the one I love most lay sleeping by me under the same cover in the
    cool night,
In the stillness in the autumn moonbeams his face was inclined toward me,
And his arm lay lightly around my breast—and that night I was happy.

                                                1860, 1867

Cavalry Crossing a Ford

A line in long array where they wind betwixt green islands,
They take a serpentine course, their arms flash in the sun—hark to the
    musical clank,
Behold the silvery river, in it the splashing horses loitering stop to drink,
Behold the brown-faced men, each group, each person a picture, the neg-
    ligent rest on the saddles,

Some emerge on the opposite bank, others are just entering the ford—
while,   5
Scarlet and blue and snowy white,
The guidon flags flutter gayly in the wind.

1865, 1867

A Sight in Camp in the Daybreak Gray and Dim

A sight in camp in the daybreak gray and dim,
As from my tent I emerge so early sleepless,
As slow I walk in the cool fresh air the path near by the hospital tent,
Three forms I see on stretchers lying, brought out there untended lying,
Over each the blanket spread, ample brownish woolen blanket,   5
Gray and heavy blanket, folding, covering all.

Curious I halt and silent stand,
Then with light fingers I from the face of the nearest the first just lift the
blanket;
Who are you elderly man so gaunt and grim, with well-gray'd hair, and
flesh all sunken about the eyes?
Who are you my dear comrade?   10
Then to the second I step—and who are you my child and darling?
Who are you sweet boy with cheeks yet blooming?

Then to the third—a face nor child nor old, very calm, as of beautiful yellow-white ivory;
Young man I think I know you—I think this face is the face of the Christ
himself,
Dead and divine and brother of all, and here again he lies.   15

1865, 1867

Respondez![8]

RESPONDEZ! Respondez!
(The war is completed—the price is paid—the title is settled beyond recall;)
Let every one answer! let those who sleep be waked! let none evade!
Must we still go on with our affectations and sneaking?
Let me bring this to a close—I pronounce openly for a new distribution of
roles;   5
Let that which stood in front go behind! and let that which was behind
advance to the front and speak;
Let murderers, bigots, fools, unclean persons, offer new propositions!
Let the old propositions be postponed!
Let faces and theories be turn'd inside out! let meanings be freely criminal,
as well as results!
Let there be no suggestion above the suggestion of drudgery!   10
Let none be pointed toward his destination! (Say! do you know your desti-
nation?)

8. This poem first appeared in the 1856 edition of *Leaves of Grass* with the title "Poem of the Propositions of Nakedness"; it was included without title in 1860, and, with revisions, as "Respondez" in 1867,
1871, and 1876. Whitman excluded the poem from the 1881 and later editions, but used lines 6–8, 65,
and 66 to make a poem called "Reversals" and lines 46, 44, and 22 for another, "Transpositions."

Let men and women be mock'd with bodies and mock'd with Souls!
Let the love that waits in them, wait! let it die, or pass still-born to other
    spheres!
Let the sympathy that waits in every man, wait! or let it also pass, a dwarf,
    to other spheres!
Let contradictions prevail! let one thing contradict another! and let one line
    of my poems contradict another!   15
Let the people sprawl with yearning, aimless hands! let their tongues be
    broken! let their eyes be discouraged! let none descend into their hearts
    with the fresh lusciousness of love!
(Stifled, O days! O lands! in every public and private corruption!
Smother'd in thievery, impotence, shamelessness, mountain-high;
Brazen effrontery, scheming, rolling like ocean's waves around and upon
    you, O my days! my lands!
For not even those thunderstorms, nor fiercest lightnings of the war, have
    purified the atmosphere;)   20
—Let the theory of America still be management, caste, comparison! (Say!
    what other theory would you?)
Let them that distrust birth and death still lead the rest! (Say! why shall
    they not lead you?)
Let the crust of hell be neared and trod on! let the days be darker than the
    nights! let slumber bring less slumber than waking time brings!
Let the world never appear to him or her for whom it was all made!
Let the heart of the young man still exile itself from the heart of the old
    man! and let the heart of the old man be exiled from that of the young
    man!   25
Let the sun and moon go! let scenery take the applause of the audience! let
    there be apathy under the stars!
Let freedom prove no man's inalienable right! every one who can tyrannize,
    let him tyrannize to his satisfaction!
Let none but infidels be countenanced!
Let the eminence of meanness, treachery, sarcasm, hate, greed, indeceny,
    importance, lust, be taken for granted above all! let writers, judges,
    governments, households, religions, philosophies, take such for granted
    above all!
Let the worst men beget children out of the worst women!   30
Let the priest still play at immortality!
Let death be inaugurated!
Let nothing remain but the ashes of teachers, artists, moralists, lawyers,
    and learn'd and polite persons!
Let him who is without my poems be assassinated!
Let the cow, the horse, the camel, the garden-bee—let the mud-fish, the
    lobster, the mussel, eel, the sting-ray, and the grunting pig-fish—let
    these, and the like of these, be put on a perfect equality with man and
    woman!   35
Let churches accommodate serpents, vermin, and the corpses of those who
    have died of the most filthy of diseases!
Let marriage slip down among fools, and be for none but fools!
Let men among themselves talk and think forever obscenely of women! and
    let women among themselves talk and think obscenely of men!
Let us all, without missing one, be exposed in public, naked, monthly, at
    the peril of our lives! let our bodies be freely handled and examined
    by whoever chooses!
Let nothing but copies at second hand be permitted to exist upon the earth! 40

Let the earth desert God, nor let there ever henceforth be mention'd the
    name of God!
Let there be no God!
Let there be money, business, imports, exports, custom, authority, prece-
    dents, pallor, dyspepsia, smut, ignorance, unbelief!
Let judges and criminals be transposed! let the prison-keepers be put in
    prison! let those that were prisoners take the keys! (Say! why might
    they not just as well be transposed?)
Let the slaves be masters! let the masters become slaves!   45
Let the reformers descend from the stands where they are forever bawling!
    let an idiot or insane person appear on each of the stands!
Let the Asiatic, the African, the European, the American, and the Austra-
    lian, go armed against the murderious stealthiness of each other! let
    them sleep armed! let none believe in good will!
Let there be no unfashionable wisdom! let such be scorn'd and derided off
    from the earth!
Let a floating cloud in the sky—let a wave of the sea—let growing mint,
    spinach, onions, tomatoes—let these be exhibited as shows, at a great
    price for admission!
Let all the men of These States stand aside for a few smouchers! let the few
    seize on what they choose! let the rest gawk, giggle, starve, obey!   50
Let shadows be furnish'd with genitals! let substances be deprived of their
    genitals!
Let there be wealthy and immense cities—but still through any of them,
    not a single poet, savior, knower, lover!
Let the infidels of These States laugh all faith away!
If one man be found who has faith, let the rest set upon him!
Let them affright faith! let them destroy the power of breeding faith!   55
Let the she-harlots and the he-harlots be prudent! let them dance on, while
    seeming lasts! (O seeming! seeming! seeming!)
Let the preachers recite creeds! let them still teach only what they have
    been taught!
Let insanity still have charge of sanity!
Let books take the place of trees, animals, rivers, clouds!
Let the daub'd portraits of heroes supersede heroes!   60
Let the manhood of man never take steps after itself!
Let it take steps after eunuchs, and after consumptive and genteel persons!
Let the white person again tread the black person under his heel! (Say!
    which is trodden under heel, after all?)
Let the reflections of the things of the world be studied in mirrors! let the
    things themselves still continue unstudied!
Let a man seek pleasure everywhere except in himself!   65
Let a woman seek happiness everywhere except in herself!
(What real happiness have you had one single hour through your whole
    life?)
Let the limited years of life do nothing for the limitless years of death!
    (What do you suppose death will do then?)

1867, 1881

To a Locomotive in Winter

Thee for my recitative,
Thee in the driving storm even as now, the snow the winter-day declining,

Thee in thy panoply, thy measur'd dual throbbing and thy beat convulsive,
Thy black cylindric body, golden brass and silvery steel,
Thy ponderous side-bars, parallel and connecting rods, gyrating, shuttling
    at thy sides,   5
Thy metrical, now swelling pant and roar, now tapering in the distance,
Thy great protruding head-light fix'd in front,
Thy long, pale, floating vapor-pennants, tinged with delicate purple,
The dense and murky clouds out-belching from thy smoke-stack,
Thy knitted frame, thy springs and valves, the tremulous twinkle of thy
    wheels,   10
Thy train of cars behind, obedient, merrily following,
Through gale or calm, now swift, now slack, yet steadily careering;
Type of the modern—emblem of motion and power—pulse of the conti-
    nent,
For once come serve the Muse and merge in verse, even as here I see thee,
With storm and buffeting gusts of wind and falling snow,   15
By day thy warning ringing bell to sound its notes,
By night thy silent signal lamps to swing.

Fierce-throated beauty!
Roll through my chant with all thy lawless music, thy swinging lamps at
    night,
Thy madly-whistled laughter, echoing, rumbling like an earthquake, rous-
    ing all,   20
Law of thyself complete, thine own track firmly holding,
(No sweetness debonair of tearful harp or glib piano thine,)
Thy trills of shrieks by rocks and hills return'd,
Launch'd o'er the prairies wide, across the lakes,
To the free skies unpent and glad and strong.   25

                                     1876, 1881

EMILY DICKINSON
1830–1886

Emily Dickinson is bracketed with Walt Whitman because, unknown to each other
and almost simultaneously, they all but invented American poetry. At first glance
they seem at opposite poles, he with his invasions of large experiences, she with her
careful preservations of private ones. She felt no urge to read him; in 1862 her new
friend and future editor Thomas Wentworth Higginson asked if she knew his work,
and she replied, "You speak of Mr. Whitman—I never read his Book—but was told
that he was disgraceful."[1] Yet the poets join in a concern to salvage from the English
language something specifically American. William Carlos Williams, with the same
aim, thought of Emily Dickinson as his "patron saint." "She was an independent
spirit. She did her best to get away from too strict an interpretation. And she didn't
want to be confined to rhyme or reason. . . . And she followed the American idiom.
She didn't know it, but she followed it nonetheless. . . . She was a real good guy."[2]

    Her letters show that she set great store by Valentine's Day, and several of her
earliest poems were valentines, as if the most banal occasion could serve to stir her
strange, explosive ponderings. Her later verse is filled with questions and riddles;

1. *Letters*, 3 vols., ed. Thomas H. Johnson, vol.
2, Cambridge, Mass., 1958, p. 404.

2. *Writers at Work: Third Series*, New York,
1967, pp. 13–14.

even at this stage in her life, her imagination could conceal its wildness under a mask of mischief. She did not write for publication and was easily discouraged from it; only a few of her nearly 1800 poems were published during her lifetime. Her personal reticence was fulfilled by obscurity. It had its roots in an upbringing which has been variously described as Puritan, Calvinist, and simply Protestant, but this was confirmed by some mysterious catastrophe in her youth, probably having to do with unrequited love. After it she sequestered herself, and she spent the rest of her days in memorializing her oblique visions in lines which she punctuated, as she did her recipes, only with dashes. Yet her Puritanism, if it was that which impeded her immersion in social experience, had a more beneficial effect upon her verse. Since William Blake no other poet has found such inspiration in the Protestant hymnology and in the biblical imagery it employs. Nor, whatever her sense of life's copiousness, which almost at times embarrasses her, can she long forget the terrifying approaches of death, a presence that inspires in her something like sexual excitement.

The key moment in Emily Dickinson's verse is often the transformation of poverty into riches. Her poems find in the happenings of a village life all that is required to reveal the cosmos. The speaker is usually in a state of deprivation, but has a vision of the Kingdom which might, by virtue of imaginative energy, be brought into being. "I dwell in Possibility," she says, and describes her occupation as "spreading wide my narrow hands / To gather Paradise." There are sudden intoxications: "Inebriate of Air—am I— / And Debauchee of Dew." She is aware of impediment, agitated by it, but the impediment is sometimes defied or burst through by "the imperial heart." Out of herself, yet with the help of a literary tradition stretching back to the Metaphysical poets, she wrote several dozen of the greatest poems of her century. Her poems are like Donne's and Herbert's in their assumption that difficult states of mind require hard words and troubled syntax. Higginson and Mabel Loomis Todd, her first editors, tidied up some of her roughnesses when they brought out the first posthumous volume in 1890. Over the following decades her scope was gradually revealed, as several additional collections appeared, and only in 1955, when all her poems were published for the first time, was her text reproduced without editorial improvements. In this belated appreciation of her work she is like her contemporary Gerard Manley Hopkins, another recreator of the Metaphysical mode. In the twentieth century she was greeted at last as not only a precursor, but a poet of contemporary feeling.

Emily Dickinson's life is surprisingly documented by her poems, her letters, and the recollections of her friends and neighbors. She was born in Amherst, Massachusetts, on December 10, 1830, the daughter of a respected lawyer, Edward Dickinson. He was an awesome figure—Emily Dickinson observed that even in going to fetch the kindling he "steps like Cromwell"—and on his death in 1874 she wrote, "His heart was pure and terrible, and I think no other like it exists." A residue of her father and his faith may be found in her work, particularly in the divine paternal figure which she variously finds laughable, terrifying, and consoling. She had a sister, Lavinia, who like Emily never married, and a brother, Austin. We can imagine her life as a group of concentric circles: at the center the poet herself, her imagination and her creations; then the life of her family, a family trusted and respected, yet harboring at least one scandalous secret, her brother's longtime love affair with Mabel Loomis Todd, the wife of an Amherst astronomer and Dickinson's future editor; and, beyond *that*, the life of the village itself, in which the poet participated and which she observed.

From childhood on Emily Dickinson's life was circumscribed: she always lived in her father's house, and rarely left Amherst. But her mind was well traveled. In the same letter that disclaimed any knowledge of Whitman, she told Higginson that she had read Keats and the Brownings for poetry, and Ruskin, Sir Thomas Browne, and the biblical Book of Revelation for prose. She might have added, from among her contemporaries, Emerson, who probably stimulated her preference for imperfect rhymes and her eagerness to see nature as an emblem, as well as the Brontë sisters, George Eliot, and many others. Her acquaintance with Higginson himself she owed to having read one of his magazine articles, which led her to write to him enclosing four poems, and asking for critical advice. The variety of her reading and the vigor of her correspondence belie the assumption that she was merely provincial.

When she was seventeen, Emily Dickinson graduated from Amherst Academy, and the next month she entered Mount Holyoke Female Seminary in South Hadley, Massachusetts. It was only a few miles away, but she was gruelingly homesick, and she returned to Amherst joyfully after less than a year. It was not so much a retreat as a violent attachment for the place where she would remain. She found her occupations and amusements. In 1856 she won second prize in the bread division at the local cattle show, and in 1857 she served as one of the judges. There are references in her letters to local merriment. She was given to infatuated friendships, though few of the persons she loved can have known the parts they played in her inner life. With Benjamin F. Newton, one of her father's law apprentices, she seems to have had a relationship which went a little beyond an exchange of flirtatious valentines. Newton had an energetic mind, and he encouraged her to question conventional beliefs, but he was poor and otherwise an unsuitable candidate to be her husband. He left Amherst when she was eighteen, and died soon after. Emily Dickinson was probably thinking of him when years later she wrote to Higginson, "My dying Tutor told me that he would like to live till I had been a poet."[3] Perhaps the man she most admired was Reverend Charles Wadsworth, whom she met in Philadelphia in 1855 on one of her rare trips beyond Amherst. He visited her at home in 1860 shortly before he was called to a church in San Francisco. She took his departure hard, and her greatest poems, written in the early 1860s, are reenactments of this pain and broodings on it. In her second letter to Higginson she was driven to confide in veiled terms, "I had a terror—since September—I could tell to none—and so I sing, as the Boy does by the Burying Ground—because I am afraid."[4]

In his diary Higginson wrote what a visit to Emily Dickinson was like: "a step like a pattering child's in entry . . . a little plain woman with two smooth bands of reddish hair and a face . . . with no good feature. . . . She came to me with two day-lilies, which she put in a sort of childlike way into my hand and said 'These are my introduction,' in a soft, frightened, breathless childlike voice—and added under her breath, 'Forgive me if I am frightened; I never see strangers, and hardly know what I say'—but she talked soon and thenceforth continuously—and deferentially—sometimes stopping to ask me to talk instead of her—but readily recommencing." She became in the 1860s a recluse; she dressed in white, saw fewer and fewer visitors, and finally none. She worked without stint at her poems, frequently including them in letters; the poems often seem inseparable from the letters, the cadences of the verse chiming with those of the prose. As with Whitman, her period of most intense activity coincided with the Civil War, but she managed to see this chiefly as it impinged on the lives of her fellow villagers. The possibility of death, "that bareheaded life under the grass," held her imagination.

Emily Dickinson died on May 15, 1886, and shortly before her death she wrote her beloved cousins, the Norcross sisters, "Little Cousins,—Called back.—Emily." She had once written that "Nature is a Haunted House—but Art—a House that tries to be haunted."[5] The remark has her yearning elusiveness, a marked trait in her, but she had stronger, sterner qualities too: "Every day life feels mightier, and what we have the power to be, more stupendous."[6] In her turn, like her father, she is "pure and terrible."

3. *Letters* 2, p. 408.
4. The same, p. 404.

5. The same, p. 554.
6. The same, p. 436.

49[1]

I never lost as much but twice,
And that was in the sod.
Twice have I stood a beggar
Before the door of God!

Angels—twice descending   5
Reimbursed my store—
Burglar! Banker—Father!
I am poor once more!

1890

249

Wild Nights—Wild Nights!
Were I with thee
Wild Nights should be
Our luxury!

Futile—the Winds—   5
To a Heart in port—
Done with the Compass—
Done with the Chart!

Rowing in Eden—
Ah, the Sea!   10
Might I but moor—Tonight—
In Thee!

1891

258

There's a certain Slant of light,
Winter Afternoons—
That oppresses, like the Heft[2]
Of Cathedral Tunes—

Heavenly Hurt, it gives us—   5
We can find no scar,
But internal difference,
Where the Meanings, are—

None may teach it—Any—
'Tis the Seal Despair—   10
An imperial affliction
Sent us of the Air—

1. The order and numbering of the poems is that established by Thomas H. Johnson in his edition of *The Poems of Emily Dickinson*, Cambridge, Mass., 1955.   2. Weight.

When it comes, the Landscape listens—
Shadows—hold their breath—
When it goes 'tis like the Distance   15
On the look of Death—[3]

1890

341

After great pain, a formal feeling comes—
The Nerves sit ceremonious, like Tombs—
The stiff Heart questions was it He, that bore,
And Yesterday, or Centuries before?

The Feet, mechanical, go round—   5
Of Ground, or Air, or Ought—
A Wooden way
Regardless grown,
A Quartz contentment, like a stone—

This is the Hour of Lead—   10
Remembered, if outlived,
As Freezing persons, recollect the Snow—
First—Chill—then Stupor—then the letting go—

1929

441

This is my letter to the World
That never wrote to Me—
The simple News that Nature told—
With tender Majesty

Her Message is committed   5
To Hands I cannot see—
For love of Her—Sweet—countrymen—
Judge tenderly—of Me

1890

465

I heard a Fly buzz—when I died—
The Stillness in the Room
Was like the Stillness in the Air—
Between the Heaves of storm—

The Eyes around—had wrung them dry—   5
And Breaths were gathering firm

---

3. "I suppose there are depths in every Consciousness, from which we cannot rescue ourselves—to which none can go with us—which represent to us Mortally—the Adventure of Death—" Letter to Mrs. J. G. Holland, June 1878, in *Letters* 2, p. 555.

For that last Onset—when he King
Be witnessed—in the Room—

I will my Keepsakes—Signed away
What portion of me be
Assignable—and then it was
There interposed a Fly—

With Blue—uncertain stumbling Buzz—
Between the light—and me—
And then the Windows failed—and then
I could not see to see—

1896

632

The Brain—is wider than the Sky—
For—put them side by side—
The one the other will contain
With ease—and You—beside—

The Brain is deeper than the sea—
For—hold them—Blue to Blue—
The one the other will absorb—
As Sponges—Buckets—do—

The Brain is just the weight of God—
For—Heft them—Pound for Pound—
And they will differ—if they do—
As Syllable from Sound—

1896

712

Because I could not stop for Death—
He kindly stopped for me—
The Carriage held but just Ourselves—
And Immortality.[4]

We slowly drove—He knew no haste
And I had put away
My labor and my leisure too,
For His Civility—

We passed the School, where Children strove
At Recess—in the Ring—

4. In a letter to T. W. Higginson, June 9, 1866, she writes: "You mention Immortality. That is the Flood subject. I was told that the Bank was the safest place for a Finless Mind. I explore but little since my mute Confederate, yet the 'infinite Beauty'—of which you speak comes too near to seek. To escape enchantment, one must always flee. Paradise is of the option. Whosoever will Own in Eden notwithstanding Adam and Repeal." *Letters* 2, p. 454.

We passed the Fields of Gazing Grain—
We passed the Setting Sun—

Or rather—He passed Us—
The Dews drew quivering and chill—
For only Gossamer, my Gown—   15
My Tippet⁵—only Tulle—

We paused before a House that seemed
A Swelling of the Ground—
The Roof was scarcely visible—
The Cornice—in the Ground—   20

Since then—'tis Centuries—and yet
Feels shorter than the Day
I first surmised the Horses' Heads
Were toward Eternity—

                                               1890

986

A narrow Fellow in the Grass
Occasionally rides—
You may have met Him—did you not
His notice sudden is—

The Grass divides as with a Comb—   5
A spotted shaft is seen—
And then it closes at your feet
And opens further on—

He likes a Boggy Acre
A Floor too cool for Corn—   10
Yet when a Boy, and Barefoot—
I more than once at Noon
Have passed, I thought, a Whip lash
Unbraiding in the Sun
When stooping to secure it   15
It wrinkled, and was gone—

Several of Nature's People
I know, and they know me—
I feel for them a transport
Of cordiality—   20

But never met this Fellow
Attended, or alone
Without a tighter breathing
And Zero at the Bone—

                                               1866

5. Cape.

1670

In Winter in my Room
I came upon a Worm—
Pink, lank and warm—
But as he was a worm
And worms presume   5
Not quite with him at home—
Secured him by a string
To something neighboring
And went along.

A Trifle afterward   10
A thing occurred
I'd not believe it if I heard
But state with creeping blood—
A snake with mottles rare
Surveyed my chamber floor   15
In feature as the worm before
But ringed with power—

The very string with which
I tied him—too
When he was mean and new   20
That string was there—

I shrank—"How fair you are"!
Propitiation's claw—
"Afraid," he hissed
"Of me"?   25
"No cordiality"—
He fathomed me—
Then to a Rhythm *Slim*
Secreted in his Form
As Patterns swim   30
Projected him.

That time I flew
Both eyes his way
Lest he pursue
Nor ever ceased to run   35
Till in a distant Town
Towns on from mine
I set me down
This was a dream.

1914

1732⁶

My life closed twice before its close;
It yet remains to see

6. The poem perhaps alludes to the death of Emily Dickinson's father and to her love for a Philadelphia clergyman, Charles Wadsworth, whom she met in May 1855, and who went to San Francisco about 1861.

If Immortality unveil
A third event to me,

So huge, so hopeless to conceive   5
As these that twice befell.
Parting is all we know of heaven,
And all we need of hell.

1896

LEWIS CARROLL
1832–1898

Charles Lutwidge Dodgson, the future lecturer and fellow in mathematics at Oxford University, was born on January 27, 1832; Lewis Carroll, the nom de plume which Dodgson was to adopt for his children's books—*Alice's Adventures in Wonderland, Through the Looking-Glass,* and *The Hunting of the Snark*—did not completely emerge until 1865, when Dodgson was thirty-three. His adoption of a pseudonym does not seem to have any psychological resonances: in fact, the mathematician-logician and the teller of tales for children seem to have been on uncommonly good terms with each other.

Dodgson was to grow into a type familiar to students of the milder forms of British eccentricity. He was one of eleven children, and his childhood, at least as he recollected it, was a time of bliss. Young Charles was especially close to his sisters; for their amusement he devised family newspapers, wrote and performed puppet plays and amateur theatricals, and exercised his considerable ingenuity in fashioning word and number games.

From home Dodgson was sent to Rugby School, which he survived but did not much enjoy. Then at the age of nineteen he went to Christ Church, Oxford, and there, first as a student, later as a teacher and minor college official, he remained for the rest of his life. Dodgson was an awkward young man: he stammered (a family trait, which may be mimicked in the name of the Dodo in *Alice in Wonderland*), his face was strikingly asymmetrical, and he was deaf in one ear. By profession, Dodgson was a mathematician and logician, and under his own name he published some thirty books and pamphlets, several of which continue to be of interest. His students found his lectures tedious. In his spare time, Dodgson interested himself in the affairs of the college and in the games and theatricals which had amused him as a child. He was an important amateur photographer, in those days messy and even dangerous work. His favorite subjects were pre-adolescent girls, sometimes photographed in costume, sometimes in the nude.

Dodgson found his main happiness in life in the society of these pretty children. He sought them out, often at the seashore, delicately courted them, wrote them charming and elaborate letters, and quietly quit the scene whenever a child or her parents seemed at all concerned that Dodgson might become a nuisance. For him the child was his muse, and his extraordinary tales were told and then written, at least initially, to please his muse as she had assumed the form of one little girl, Alice Liddell (her family name rhymes with *riddle*). She was the daughter of the Master of Christ Church and Alice and her two sisters were special favorites of Dodgson's. He took tea with them, was at pains to make himself amusing, and occasionally Mrs. Liddell, a model of maternal caution, allowed him to arrange a picnic for the three sisters.

On July 4, 1862, the children, another don, and Dodgson went on such a picnic, and he entertained the company with a fanciful tale. When the day was over, young

Alice asked Dodgson to write the story down. In 1864 he presented Alice with a manuscript book, illustrated by himself, called *Alice's Adventures Underground*. This small book, enlarged, revised, and decorated with illustrations by Sir John Tenniel, was published in 1865 as *Alice's Adventures in Wonderland*. It was a success, and in 1872 it was followed by *Through the Looking-Glass and What Alice Found There*. In 1876 Dodgson published his third masterpiece, *The Hunting of the Snark: An Agony, in Eight Fits*, a small epic and a consummate piece of nonsense.

Lewis Carroll—for convenience's sake, we should now so refer to him—as writer flourished in the near-decade 1865–76. The remaining twenty-two years of his life were comfortable if self-constricted. He described college life as "by no means unmixed misery," though he admitted that "married life has no doubt many charms to which I am a stranger." He had what amounted to a duplex set of rooms at Christ Church. The success of the Alice books assured his financial independence. He died in 1898, a fussy old bachelor whose interior life had been more exciting and strange than most of his contemporaries expected.

Lewis Carroll's poems, apart from *The Hunting of the Snark*, are to be found imbedded in his prose narratives. Some of them were written long before the Alice books were contemplated, although most would eventually find their place there. With the narratives the poems share certain characteristics: they are parodies of more solemn verses, they point no moral and the tale they tell is outlandish, and in their uses of language they are nonsensical. Here are two lines from "Jabberwocky" that can demonstrate Carroll's nonsense words:

> 'Twas brillig, and the slithy toves
> Did gyre and gimble in the wabe.

Humpty Dumpty, in *Through the Looking-Glass*, glosses *slithy* as "lithe and slimy. . . . You see it's like a portmanteau [a two-sectioned traveling case]—there are two meanings packed up into one word." *Tove* he explains as "something like badgers— they're something like lizards—and they're something like corkscrews. . . . also they live on cheese." With this word and Carroll's unhelpful gloss we begin an ascent into the world of pure nonsense, a world where we experience the unalloyed bliss of freedom from common sense, where words are not our masters or our slaves, but playmates, fellow-conspirators, participants in a game whose rules are subject to changes without notice.

Much of Lewis Carroll's nonsense subverts the meanings and morals of earlier poems, for most of the poems are parodies, reworkings of the instructive originals to produce a fresher, more liberating world with the aid of nonsense. Here the poet joins forces with the child-reader to issue a declaration of irrelevance; his poems, and his narrative as well, invite us to join him in the creation of experiences which are puzzling, sometimes frightening, but never improving.

Of parodies one always asks the question: Does it matter whether the reader is familiar—or not familiar—with the poem being parodied? Yes, it does matter. Most of Dodgson's models would be long forgotten had not Lewis Carroll used them in the creation of the Alice books, but the contemporary reader needs to be reminded how unremittingly moralistic most of the poems written for Victorian children were. "The White Knight's Song" is a different matter; it is a parody of Wordsworth's great and noble poem "Resolution and Independence," yet in no sense does it make fun of Wordsworth's poem. The one poem does not contrive to put the other out of business; and Lewis Carroll's drink-cadging old geezer lives amicably enough in the same neighborhood with Wordsworth's aged solitary.

[A Long Tale]¹

"Fury said to
a mouse, That
he met in the
house, 'Let
us both go
to law: *I*
will prose-
cute *you.*—
Come, I'll
take no de-
nial: We
must have
the trial;
For really
this morn-
ing I've
nothing
to do.'
Said the
mouse to
the cur,
'Such a
trial, dear
sir, With
no jury
or judge,
would
be wast-
ing our
breath.'
'I'll be
judge,
I'll be
jury,'
said
cun-
ning
old
Fury:
'I'll
try
the
whole
cause,
and
con-
demn
you to
death.'"

1865

Jabberwocky²

There was a book lying near Alice on the table, and while she sat watching the White King (for she was still a little anxious about him, and had the ink all ready to throw over him, in case he fainted again), she turned over the leaves, to find some part that she could read, "—for it's all in some language I don't know," she said to herself.

It was like this.

1. From *Alice's Adventures in Wonderland*, chapter 3.   2. From *Through the Looking-Glass*, chapter 1.

Jabberwocky

'Twas brillig, and the slithy toves
Did gyre and gimble in the wabe:
All mimsy were the borogoves,
And the mome raths outgrabe.

She puzzled over this for some time, but at last a bright thought struck her. "Why, it's a Looking-glass book, of course! And, if I hold it up to a glass, the words will all go the right way again."

This was the poem that Alice read.

Jabberwocky

'Twas brillig, and the slithy toves
    Did gyre and gimble in the wabe:
All mimsy were the borogoves,
    And the mome raths outgrabe.

"Beware the Jabberwock, my son!   5
    The jaws that bite, the claws that catch!
Beware the Jubjub bird, and shun
    The frumious Bandersnatch!"

He took his vorpal sword in hand:
    Long time the manxome foe he sought—   10
So rested he by the Tumtum tree,
    And stood awhile in thought.

And, as in uffish thought he stood,
    The Jabberwock, with eyes of flame,
Came whiffling through the tulgey wood,   15
    And burbled as it came!

One, two! One, two! And through and through
    The vorpal blade went snicker-snack!
He left it dead, and with its head
    He went galumphing back.   20

"And, hast thou slain the Jabberwock?
    Come to my arms, my beamish boy!
O frabjous day! Callooh! Callay!"
    He chortled in his joy.

'Twas brillig, and the slithy toves   25
    Did gyre and gimble in the wabe:
All mimsy were the borogoves,
    And the mome raths outgrabe.

Humpty Dumpty's Explication[3]

"When *I* use a word," Humpty Dumpty said, in rather a scornful tone, "it means just what I choose it to mean—neither more nor less."

---

3. From *Through the Looking-Glass,* chapter 6.

"The question is," said Alice, "whether you *can* make words mean so many different things."

"The question is," said Humpty Dumpty, "which is to be master—that's all."

Alice was too much puzzled to say anything; so after a minute Humpty Dumpty began again. "They've a temper, some of them—particularly verbs: they're the proudest—adjectives you can do anything with, but not verbs—however, *I* can manage the whole lot of them! Impenetrability! That's what *I* say!"

"Would you tell me please," said Alice, "what that means?"

"Now you talk like a reasonable child" said Humpty Dumpty, looking very much pleased. "I meant by 'impenetrability' that we've had enough of that subject, and it would be just as well if you'd mention what you mean to do next, as I suppose you don't mean to stop here all the rest of your life."

"That's a great deal to make one word mean," Alice said in a thoughtful tone.

"When I make a word do a lot of work like that," said Humpty Dumpty, "I always pay it extra."

"Oh!" said Alice. She was too much puzzled to make any other remark.

"Ah, you should see 'em come round me of a Saturday night," Humpty Dumpty went on, wagging his head gravely from side to side, "for to get their wages, you know."

(Alice didn't venture to ask what he paid them with; and so you see I ca'n't tell *you*.)

"You seem very clever at explaining words, Sir," said Alice. "Would you kindly tell me the meaning of the poem called 'Jabberwocky'?"

"Let's hear it," said Humpty Dumpty. "I can explain all the poems that ever were invented—and a good many that haven't been invented just yet."

This sounded very hopeful, so Alice repeated the first verse:—

> " 'Twas brillig, and the slithy toves
> Did gyre and gimble in the wabe:
> All mimsy were the borogoves,
> And the mome raths outgrabe."

"That's enough to begin with," Humpty Dumpty interrupted: "there are plenty of hard words there. '*Brillig*' means four o'clock in the afternoon—the time when you begin *broiling* things for dinner."

"That'll do very well," said Alice: "and '*slithy*'?"

"Well, '*slithy*' means 'lithe and slimy' 'Lithe' is the same as 'active.' You see it's like a pormanteau[4]—there are two meanings packed up into one word."

"I see it now," Alice remarked thoughtfully: "and what are '*toves*'?"[5]

"Well '*toves*' are something like badgers—they're something like lizards—and they're something like corkscrews."

"They must be very curious-looking creatures."

"They are that," said Humpty Dumpty; "also they make their nests under sun-dials—also they live on cheese."

"And what's to '*gyre*' and to '*gimble*'?"

---

4. A portmanteau is a large leather suitcase which opens, like a book, into two separate compartments.
5. Of the pronunciation of "slithy toves," Carroll later wrote, "The 'i' in 'slithy' is long, as in 'writhe'; and 'toves' is pronounced so as to rhyme with 'groves.' Again, the first 'o' in 'borogoves' is pronounced like the 'o' in 'borrow.' I have heard people try to give it the sound of the 'o' in 'worry.' Such is Human Perversity."

"To '*gyre*' is to go round and round like a gyroscope. To '*gimble*' is to make holes like a gimlet."

"And '*the wabe*' is the grass-plot round a sun-dial, I suppose?" said Alice, surprised at her own ingenuity.

"Of course it is. It's called '*wabe*' you know, because it goes a long way before it, and a long way behind it—"

"And a long way beyond it on each side," Alice added.

"Exactly so. Well then, '*mimsy*' is 'flimsy and miserable' (there's another portmanteau for you). And a '*borogove*' is a thin shabby-looking bird with its feathers sticking out all round—something like a live mop."

"And then '*mome raths*'?" said Alice. "I'm afraid I'm giving you a great deal of trouble."

"Well, a '*rath*' is a sort of green pig: but '*mome*' I'm not certain about. I think it's short for 'from home'—meaning that they'd lost their way, you know."

"And what does '*outgrabe*' mean?"

"Well, '*outgribing*' is something between bellowing and whistling, with a kind of sneeze in the middle: however, you'll hear it done, maybe—down in the wood yonder—and, when you've once heard it, you'll be *quite* content. Who's been repeating all that hard stuff to you?"

"I read it in a book," said Alice.

1871

The Walrus and the Carpenter[6]

The sun was shining on the sea,
  Shining with all his might:
He did his very best to make
  The billows smooth and bright—
And this was odd, because it was   5
  The middle of the night.

The moon was shining sulkily,
  Because she thought the sun
Had got no business to be there
  After the day was done—   10
"It's very rude of him," she said,
  "To come and spoil the fun!"

The sea was wet as wet could be,
  The sands were dry as dry.
You could not see a cloud, because   15
  No cloud was in the sky:
No birds were flying overhead—
  There were no birds to fly.

The Walrus and the Carpenter
  Were walking close at hand: 20
They wept like anything to see

6. Recited by Tweedledee in *Through the Looking-Glass*, chapter 4. The poem is written in the meter of Thomas Hood's "The Dream of Eugene Aram" (1832), which tells of a schoolteacher who is found to be a murderer.

Such quantities of sand:
"If this were only cleared away,"
They said, "it would be grand!"

"If seven maids with seven mops   25
    Swept it for half a year,
Do you suppose," the Walrus said,
    "That they could get it clear?"
"I doubt it," said the Carpenter,
    And shed a bitter tear.   30

"O Oysters, come and walk with us!"
    The Walrus did beseech.
"A pleasant walk, a pleasant talk,
    Along the briny beach:
We cannot do with more than four,   35
    To give a hand to each."

The eldest Oyster looked at him,
    But never a word he said:
The eldest Oyster winked his eye,
    And shook his heavy head—   40
Meaning to say he did not choose
    To leave the oyster-bed.

But four young Oysters hurried up,
    All eager for the treat:
Their coats were brushed, their faces washed,   45
    Their shoes were clean and neat—
And this was odd, because, you know,
    They hadn't any feet.

Four other Oysters followed them,
    And yet another four;   50
And thick and fast they came at last,
    And more, and more, and more—
All hopping through the frothy waves,
    And scrambling to the shore.

The Walrus and the Carpenter   55
    Walked on a mile or so,
And then they rested on a rock
    Conveniently low:
And all the little Oysters stood
    And waited in a row.   60

"The time has come," the Walrus said,
    "To talk of many things:
Of shoes—and ships—and sealing wax—
    Of cabbages—and kings—
And why the sea is boiling hot—   65
    And whether pigs have wings."

"But wait a bit," the Oysters cried,
  "Before we have our chat;
For some of us are out of breath,
  And all of us are fat!"   70
"No hurry!" said the Carpenter.
  They thanked him much for that.

"A loaf of bread," the Walrus said,
  "Is what we chiefly need:
Pepper and vinegar besides   75
  Are very good indeed—
Now, if you're ready, Oysters dear,
  We can begin to feed."

"But not on us!" the Oysters cried,
  Turning a little blue.   80
"After such kindness, that would be
  A dismal thing to do!"
"The night is fine," the Walrus said.
  "Do you admire the view?

"It was so kind of you to come!   85
  And you are very nice!"
The Carpenter said nothing but
  "Cut us another slice.
I wish you were not quite so deaf—
  I've had to ask you twice!"   90

"It seems a shame," the Walrus said,
  "To play them such a trick,
After we've brought them out so far,
  And made them trot so quick!"
The Carpenter said nothing but   95
  "The butter's spread too thick!"

"I weep for you," the Walrus said:
  "I deeply sympathize."
With sobs and tears he sorted out
  Those of the largest size,   100
Holding his pocket-handkerchief
  Before his streaming eyes.

"O Oysters," said the Carpenter,
  "You've had a pleasant run!
Shall we be trotting home again?"   105
  But answer came there none—
And this was scarcely odd, because
  They'd eaten every one.

                                      1871

The White Knight's Song[7]

I'll tell thee everything I can:
   There's little to relate.
I saw an aged aged man,
   A-sitting on a gate.
"Who are you, aged man?" I said.   5
   "And how is it you live?"
And his answer trickled through my head,
   Like water through a sieve.

He said "I look for butterflies
   That sleep among the wheat: 10
I make them into mutton-pies,
   And sell them in the street.
I sell them unto men," he said,
   "Who sail on stormy seas;
And that's the way I get my bread—   15
   A trifle, if you please."

But I was thinking of a plan
   To dye one's whiskers green,
And always use so large a fan
   That they could not be seen.   20
So, having no reply to give
   To what the old man said,
I cried "Come, tell me how you live!"
   And thumped him on the head.

His accents mild took up the tale: 25
   He said "I go my ways,
And when I find a mountain-rill,
   I set it in a blaze;
And thence they make a stuff they call
   Rowland's Macassar-Oil—[8]   30
Yet twopence-halfpenny is all
   They give me for my toil."

But I was thinking of a way
   To feed oneself on batter,
And so go on from day to day   35
   Getting a little fatter.
I shook him well from side to side,
   Until his face was blue:
"Come, tell me how you live," I cried,
   "And what it is you do!"   40

He said "I hunt for haddocks' eyes
   Among the heather bright,

---

7. Sung by the White Knight in *Through the Looking-Glass*, chapter 8. The poem burlesques William Wordsworth's famous "Resolution and Independence" (1807), in which the speaker, inexplicably suffering "dim sadness," is heartened by his talk with an old leech-gatherer; the poem ends, " 'God,' said I, 'be my help and stay secure; / I'll think of the Leech-gatherer on the lonely moor!' "

8. A popular hair oil.

And work them into waistcoat-buttons
    In the silent night.
And these I do not sell for gold   45
    Or coin of silvery shine,
But for a copper halfpenny,
    And that will purchase nine.

"I sometimes dig for buttered rolls,
    Or set limed twigs[9] or crabs: 50
I sometimes search for grassy knolls
    For wheels of Hansom-cabs.[1]
And that's the way" (he gave a wink)
    "By which I get my wealth—
And very gladly will I drink   55
    Your Honour's noble health."

I heard him then, for I had just
    Completed my design
To keep the Menai bridge[2] from rust
    By boiling it in wine.   60
I thanked him much for telling me
    The way he got his wealth,
But chiefly for his wish that he
    Might drink my noble health.

And now, if e'er by chance I put   65
    My fingers into glue,
Or madly squeeze a right-hand foot
    Into a left-hand shoe,
Or if I drop upon my toe
    A very heavy weight,   70
I weep, for it reminds me so
Of that old man I used to know—
Whose look was mild, whose speech was slow,
Whose hair was whiter than the snow,
Whose face was very like a crow,   75
With eyes, like cinders, all aglow,
Who seemed distracted with his woe,
Who rocked his body to and fro,
And muttered mumblingly and low,
As if his mouth were full of dough,   80
Who snorted like a buffalo——
That summer evening long ago,
    A-sitting on a gate.

                                         1871

9. Branches covered with lime to catch birds.   hire.
1. Two-wheeled horse-drawn carriages, often for   2. Suspension bridge in Wales.

THOMAS HARDY
1840–1928

Thomas Hardy and Gerard Manley Hopkins stand like two warders at the portals of modern poetry. Hopkins died before the twentieth century began, while Hardy lived to 1928. Hopkins might be heraldically represented with an eye turned upwards, while Hardy, for a characteristic trait, would be posed casting a backward look. His poetry differs from that of most subsequent poets in its quality of retrospection.

Hardy was born at Upper Bockhampton in Dorset, England, and apart from three long absences it was in this region that he chose to live and die. His date of birth, June 2, 1840, four years before Hopkins, isolates him from the great Victorian poets, Tennyson (born 1809), Browning (born 1812), and Arnold (born 1822). From being their junior during the nineteenth century, he became in this century the senior of all the new poets. Proud of his longevity, he prepared in 1928 a book called *Winter Words* for the press, and in the preface declared, "So far as I am aware, I happen to be the only English poet who has brought out a new volume of verse on his ———— birthday . . ." He meant to write in *eighty-ninth*, but did not quite make it: the volume appeared posthumously. The title *Winter Words* would have suited just as well the poems he wrote in youth; Hardy had something of the premature old age of the child called "Father Time" in *Jude the Obscure*. His earlier books, with titles like *Time's Laughingstocks, Satires of Circumstance,* and *Human Shows—Far Phantasies,* have the same bleakness of outlook.

Hardy's father was a master mason, and the son's first ambition was to design buildings. At sixteen he was apprenticed to a local ecclesiastical architect. But while he could see the possibilities of a livelihood in this profession, he was extremely interested in his school studies in Latin and his private studies in Greek, a language he had taught himself. William Barnes, a good dialect poet, was a neighbor, and encouraged Hardy's literary interests. But a career in letters did not then present itself as a practical course, and Hardy took no wild risks. Having finished his apprenticeship, Hardy went to London in 1862 and became assistant to an architect there. But after five years he returned to Dorset, and, while continuing his architectural work, he began to write novels. The first of them was acceptable to a publisher, but the publisher's reader, who was the novelist George Meredith, called Hardy in and, after praising the book, warned him that its publication would arouse hostility and impair his career. Hardy, strangely docile before this prudential advice—he saw the universe as a many-leveled snub—put the book aside and began another. This new one and thirteen other novels were published without difficulty, but he may never have lost his feeling that prose had a meretricious element and was full of compromises. At any rate, when in 1895 *Jude the Obscure* was lampooned as *Jude the Obscene,* Hardy (perhaps gratefully) turned altogether to verse. Besides volumes of lyrics and dramatic monologues, he published, in the first years of the century, his three-part epic-drama entitled *The Dynasts,* about England's wars with Napoleon, in which the events are shown to be controlled by demiurges.

Hardy said in a late poem that "he never expected much" of the world or life, but one period, of courtship, was exempt from the general belittlement. In 1870 he went to Cornwall to restore a church. He there met Emma Lavinia Gifford and in due course (four years) married her. Their marriage did not go well; Mrs. Hardy was more troubled than pleased by her husband's success, especially when this became social as well as literary. She increasingly withheld herself from his friends, preferring to plead illness and stay home alone. Eventually she became mentally deranged. After she died in 1912, however, Hardy wrote his most passionate poems, evocations of her as she was in her "air-blue gown" almost half a century before.

Hardy himself was always modest about his poems; in a preface dated 1901 he called them "unadjusted impressions," which however might, by "humbly recording diverse readings of phenomena as they are forced upon us by chance and change," lead to a philosophy. He told a friend that he wanted to avoid "the jewelled line"; his awkwardness, often an ostentatious laboriousness, was both natural and cultivated. He is the first of the poets, so numerous now, who are suspicious of writing well. He broke away from poetic diction towards a quite unexpected vocabulary. With similar purposes he insisted upon provincialism in art. Against Matthew Arnold's disparagement, Hardy said that "a certain provincialism of feeling is invaluable. It is of the essence of individuality, and is largely made up of that crude enthusiasm without which no great thoughts are thought, no great deeds done."[1] More largely, he said that "Art is a disproportioning . . . of realities, to show more clearly the features that matter in those realities."[2] The awkwardness was intended to give a sense of penetrating through the facade of language and syntax as well as the deceptions of circumstance. Younger poets have found these tenets congenial. W. H. Auden, for instance, spent a year when he was nineteen or twenty reading Hardy, and wrote later, "My first Master was Thomas Hardy, and I think I was very lucky in my choice. He was a good poet, perhaps a great one, but not *too* good. Much as I loved him, even I could see that his diction was often clumsy and forced and that a lot of his poems were plain bad. This gave me hope where a flawless poet might have made me despair."[3] Philip Larkin also testified to Hardy's influence, and Dylan Thomas, though he thought Yeats the greatest of modern poets, considered Hardy his favorite.

In later life Hardy combined with this feeling of settled thwart a conviction that the force that governs the universe cannot comfortably be described as God. When a clergyman wrote to ask how certain horrors of human and animal life might be reconciled with God's goodness, Hardy replied, with formal finality, "Mr. Hardy regrets that he is unable to offer any hypothesis which would reconcile the existence of such evils as Dr. Grosart describes with the idea of omnipotent goodness."[4] With no confidence in a supernatural god, Hardy was nonetheless fond of a pantheon of forces for which he kept devising new names. These are the demiurges who move us pathetically about. They are animated, Hardy usually insists, not by malignity but merely by indifference, as in "The Subalterns." In this poem the poet is relieved to discover that the forces that control us are themselves controlled. To Yeats, as to Kafka, this vision of a will-less universe in which dolls control lesser dolls is monstrous; to Hardy there is a kind of comfort in the amorality that operates so much at loggerheads with human morality. Sometimes Hardy said that he should not be described as a pessimist but as an evolutionary meliorist, and that his poems were questionings as a first step in the soul's betterment.[5]

Although Hardy is bitter about the supernatural, he is fond and affectionate towards the preternatural. His poems are full of ghosts: some ghosts are the shadows of unrealized ideals, some are ghosts of a commoner sort, garden-variety ghosts. His intense feelings are usually expressed by or about ghosts as ways of displacing the human condition, of justifying detachment from it, of expressing afterthoughts rather than thoughts, experiences remasticated rather than devoured, or of keeping a residue, however ephemeral, from what's gone.

The archetypal scene in a Hardy poem is a man meditating on his losses, surrounded by ghosts of what he has loved or hoped for, preserving his identity in a friendless landscape only by the momentary intensity of his feeling. Time is not regained, as in Proust; memory only deepens loss. The poem is a thermometer of present chill and past heat. The tone is almost always low-pitched. Shared emotion, especially compassion, is his proffered anodyne for the bleakness of the universe.

1. Florence Emily Hardy (Hardy's second wife), *The Life of Thomas Hardy 1840–1928*, New York, 1968, p. 147.
2. The same, p. 229.
3. *The Dyer's Hand*, New York, 1962, p. 38.
4. Florence Hardy, p. 205.
5. *Collected Poems*, London, 1932, p. 526.

It may be a flaw in Hardy's poetry, as in Housman's, that it is so dominated by a sense of general blight, as if the universe found its fulfillment in illustrating over and over again his theory about it. There is strength, but also perhaps a certain complacency, in seeing one's view so inveterately borne out, proved to the point of-stereotype. And while Hardy's sympathy goes out to those who are indifferently mistreated by indifferent masters of the world, there may be in him also a secret admiration for indifference, for power without feeling as opposed to human feeling without power— for the transcendence of human imperfection by the perfection of absolute zero. There is perhaps a secret longing to be free of choice and concern, the unshakable aspects of human existence, and to ally himself with the workings of inhuman will. Yet his conscious purpose is always to defend and fortify, insofar as possible, the human.

Hap

If but some vengeful god would call to me
From up the sky, and laugh: "Thou suffering thing,
Know that thy sorrow is my ecstasy,
That thy love's loss is my hate's profiting!"

Then would I bear it, clench myself, and die,   5
Steeled by the sense of ire unmerited;
Half-eased in that a Powerfuller than I
Had willed and meted me the tears I shed.

But not so. How arrives it joy lies slain,
And why unblooms the best hope ever sown?   10
—Crass Casualty obstructs the sun and rain,
And dicing Time for gladness casts a moan . . .
These purblind Doomsters had as readily strown
Blisses about my pilgrimage as pain.

                                                  1898

Neutral Tones

We stood by a pond that winter day,
And the sun was white, as though chidden of God,
And a few leaves lay on the starving sod;
    —They had fallen from an ash, and were gray.

Your eyes on me were as eyes that rove   5
Over tedious riddles of years ago;
And some words played between us to and fro
    On which lost the more by our love.

The smile on your mouth was the deadest thing
Alive enough to have strength to die;   10
And a grin of bitterness swept thereby
    Like an ominous bird a-wing. . . .

Since then, keen lessons that love deceives,
And wrings with wrong, have shaped to me

Your face, and the God-curst sun, and a tree,   15
    And a pond edged with grayish leaves.

          1898

Drummer Hodge

I

They throw in Drummer Hodge, to rest
    Uncoffined—just as found:
His landmark is a kopje-crest[1]
    That breaks the veldt[2] around;
And foreign constellations west[3]   5
    Each night above his mound.

II

Young Hodge the Drummer never knew—
    Fresh from his Wessex home—[4]
The meaning of the broad Karoo,[5]
    The Bush,[6] the dusty loam,
And why uprose to nightly view   10
    Strange stars amid the gloam.

III

Yet portion of that unknown plain
    Will Hodge for ever be;
His homely Northern breast and brain   15
    Grow to some Southern tree,
And strange-eyed constellations reign
    His stars eternally.

          1901

The Subalterns[7]

I

"Poor wanderer," said the leaden sky,
    "I fain would lighten thee,
But there are laws in force on high
    Which say it must not be."

II

—"I would not freeze thee, shorn one," cried   5
    The North, "knew I but how
To warm my breath, to slack my stride;
    But I am ruled as thou."

1. A small hill, in Afrikaans, the language used in South Africa. Drummer Hodge is a soldier killed in the Boer War, 1899–1902, when Great Britain fought the Transvaal Republic and the Orange Free State.
2. Plain.
3. The foreign constellations are those with which Hodge, being from a northern country, is unfamiliar. "West" means to set in the west.
4. An ancient Saxon kingdom centered in Sal-

isbury plain. Hardy revived the name and first used it in his novel, *Far from the Madding Crowd*, to include his native shire of Dorset and all or parts of five adjoining shires.
5. The Karoo is the high plateau in the Cape of Good Hope, South Africa.
6. Tracts of land in South Africa, covered with brushwood and shrubby vegetation.
7. In the British Army, officers below the rank of captain.

III

—"To-morrow I attack thee, wight,"
    Said Sickness. "Yet I swear
I bear thy little ark no spite,   10
    But am bid enter there."

IV

—"Come hither, Son," I heard Death say;
    "I did not will a grave
Should end thy pilgrimage to-day,   15
    But I, too, am a slave!"

V

We smiled upon each other then,
    And life to me had less
Of that fell look it wore ere when
    They owned their passiveness.   20

                        1901

The Darkling Thrush

I leant upon a coppice[8] gate
    When Frost was spectre-gray,
And Winter's dregs made desolate
    The weakening eye of day.
The tangled bine-stems[9] scored the sky   5
    Like strings of broken lyres,
And all mankind that haunted nigh
    Had sought their household fires.

The land's sharp features seemed to be
    The Century's corpse[1] outleant,   10
His crypt the cloudy canopy,
    The wind his death-lament.
The ancient pulse of germ and birth
    Was shrunken hard and dry,
And every spirit upon earth   15
    Seemed fervourless as I.

At once a voice arose among
    The bleak twigs overhead
In a full-hearted evensong
    Of joy illimited;   20
An aged thrush, frail, gaunt, and small,
    In blast-beruffled plume,
Had chosen thus to fling his soul
    Upon the growing gloom.

So little cause for carolings   25
    Of such ecstatic sound

---

8. Thicket.
9. Stems of a climbing, twisting plant.

1. The poem was written on the last day of the nineteenth century.

Was written on terrestrial things
    Afar or nigh around,
That I could think there trembled through
    His happy good-night air   30
Some blessed Hope, whereof he knew
    And I was unaware.

                 1901

Channel Firing

That night your great guns, unawares,
Shook all our coffins as we lay,
And broke the chancel window-squares,
We thought it was the Judgment-day

And sat upright.   While drearisome   5
Arose the howl of wakened hounds:
The mouse let fall the altar-crumb,
The worms drew back into the mounds,

The glebe[2] cow drooled.   Till God called, "No;
It's gunnery practice out at sea   10
Just as before you went below;
The world is as it used to be:

"All nations striving strong to make
Red war yet redder.   Mad as hatters
They do no more for Christés sake   15
Than you who are helpless in such matters.

"That this is not the judgment-hour
For some of them's a blessed thing,
For if it were they'd have to scour
Hell's floor for so much threatening. . . .   20

"Ha, ha.   It will be warmer when
I blow the trumpet (if indeed
I ever do; for you are men,
And rest eternal sorely need)."

So down we lay again.   "I wonder,   25
Will the world ever saner be,"
Said one, "than when He sent us under
In our indifferent century!"

And many a skeleton shook his head.
"Instead of preaching forty year,"   30
My neighbour Parson Thirdly said,
"I wish I had stuck to pipes and beer."

Again the guns disturbed the hour,
Roaring their readiness to avenge,

2. A small field.

As far inland as Stourton Tower,   35
And Camelot, and starlit Stonehenge.[3]

1914

The Convergence of the Twain

Lines on the loss of the "Titanic"[4]

I

In a solitude of the sea
Deep from human vanity,
And the Pride of Life that planned her, stilly couches she.

II

Steel chambers, late the pyres
Of her salamandrine[5] fires,   5
Cold currents thrid,[6] and turn to rhythmic tidal lyres.

III

Over the mirrors meant
To glass the opulent
The sea-worm crawls—grotesque, slimed, dumb, indifferent.

IV

Jewels in joy designed   10
To ravish the sensuous mind
Lie lightless, all their sparkles bleared and black and blind.

V

Dim moon-eyed fishes near
Gaze at the gilded gear
And query: "What does this vaingloriousness down here?" . . .   15

VI

Well: while was fashioning
This creature of cleaving wing,
The Immanent Will that stirs and urges everything

VII

Prepared a sinister mate
For her—so gaily great—   20
A Shape of Ice, for the time far and dissociate.

VIII

And as the smart ship grew
In stature, grace, and hue,
In shadowy silent distance grew the Iceberg too.

3. Stourton Tower, or King Alfred's Tower, is a tower erected in the eighteenth century in Stourhead Park, Wiltshire, near where, in 878, King Alfred collected his scattered followers and prepared his decisive victory at Edington in the same year. Camelot, the legendary site of King Arthur's court, is associated usually with Tintagel in Cornwall. Hardy and others associated Stonehenge with druidic rites.

4. On the night of April 14, 1912, the British White Star liner *Titanic*, the largest ship afloat and on her maiden voyage to New York from Southampton, collided with an iceberg in the North Atlantic and sank in less than three hours; 1500 of 2206 passengers were lost.

5. Bright red. The salamander was supposed to be able to live in fire.

6. Thread.

IX

Alien they seemed to be: 25
No mortal eye could see
The intimate welding of their later history,

X

Or sign that they were bent
By paths coincident
On being anon twin halves of one august event,   30

XI

Till the Spinner of the Years
Said "Now!" And each one hears,
And consummation comes, and jars two hemispheres.

1914

I Found Her Out There[7]

I found her out there
On a slope few see,
That falls westwardly
To the salt-edged air,
Where the ocean breaks   5
On the purple strand,
And the hurricane shakes
The solid land.

I brought her here,
And have laid her to rest   10
In a noiseless nest
No sea beats near.
She will never be stirred
In her loamy cell
By the waves long heard   15
And loved so well.[8]

So she does not sleep
By those haunted heights
The Atlantic smites
And the blind gales sweep,   20
Whence she often would gaze
At Dundagel's famed head,[9]
While the dipping blaze
Dyed her face fire-red;

---

7. In *Some Recollections* Emma Hardy wrote of her first meetings with her future husband in North Cornwall: "Scarcely any author and his wife could have had a much more romantic meeting with its unusual circumstances, in bringing them together from two different though neighbouring counties to this one at this very remote spot, with beautiful sea-coast, and the wild Atlantic ocean rolling in with its magnificent waves and spray, its white gulls and black choughs and grey puffins, its cliffs and rocks and gorgeous sun settings sparkling redness in a track widening from the horizon to the shore. All this should be seen in the winter to be truly appreciated. No summer visitors can have a true idea of its power to awaken heart and soul."

8. Emma Gifford Hardy died November 27, 1912. Circumstances prevented her being buried in St. Juliot, Cornwall, where Hardy and she had met in connection with his architectural work on the church, so she was buried at Stinsford, a mile from Dorchester.

9. Dunderhole Point, southwest of Tintagel on the road to Trebarwith Strand, is near the legendary site of Camelot.

And would sigh at the tale   25
Of sunk Lyonnesse,[1]
As a wind-tugged tress
Flapped her cheek like a flail;
Or listen at whiles
With a thought-bound brow   30
To the murmuring miles
She is far from now.

Yet her shade, maybe,
Will creep underground
Till it catch the sound   35
Of that western sea
As it swells and sobs
Where she once domiciled,
And joy in its throbs
With the heart of a child.   40

                                                      1914

The Voice[2]

Woman much missed, how you call to me, call to me,
Saying that now you are not as you were
When you had changed from the one who was all to me,
But as at first, when our day was fair.

Can it be you that I hear?   Let me view you, then,   5
Standing as when I drew near to the town
Where you would wait for me: yes, as I knew you then,
Even to the original air-blue gown!

Or is it only the breeze, in its listlessness
Travelling across the wet mead to me here,   10
You being ever dissolved to wan wistlessness,
Heard no more again far or near?

        Thus I; faltering forward,
        Leaves around me falling,
Wind oozing thin through the thorn from norward,   15
        And the woman calling.

                                                      1914

Lines

To a Movement in Mozart's E-Flat Symphony[3]

Show me again the time
When in the Junetide's prime

---

1. The legendary scene of several Arthurian stories. Hardy associated the name with the whole of Cornwall.

2. A poem on his first wife's death.
3. Most likely Mozart's K.349, which was popular in Hardy's day.

We flew by meads[4] and mountains northerly!—
Yea, to such freshness, fairness, fulness, fineness, freeness,
   Love lures life on.   5

   Show me again the day
   When from the sandy bay
We looked together upon the pestered sea!—
Yea, to such surging, swaying, sighing, swelling, shrinking,
   Love lures life on.   10

   Show me again the hour
   When by the pinnacled tower
We eyed each other and feared futurity!—
Yea, to such bodings, broodings, beatings, blanchings, blessings,
   Love lures life on.   15

   Show me again just this:
   The moment of that kiss
Away from the prancing folk, by the strawberry-tree!—
Yea, to such rashness, ratheness,[5] rareness, ripeness, richness,
   Love lures life on.   20

1917

The Oxen

   Christmas Eve, and twelve of the clock.
     "Now they are all on their knees,"[6]
   An elder said as we sat in a flock
     By the embers in hearthside ease.

   We pictured the meek mild creatures where   5
     They dwelt in their strawy pen,
   Nor did it occur to one of us there
     To doubt they were kneeling then.

   So fair a fancy few would weave
     In these years!   Yet, I feel,   10
   If someone said on Christmas Eve,
     "Come; see the oxen kneel,

   "In the lonely barton by yonder coomb[7]
     Our childhood used to know,"
   I should go with him in the gloom,   15
     Hoping it might be so.

1917

4. Old word for meadows.
5. From "rathe," an old word for early-blooming or early-bearing.
6. A folk belief that the oxen kneel every Christmas as the ox kneeled in the manger when Christ was born.
7. Valley; "barton": farmyard.

In Time of "The Breaking of Nations"[8]

I

Only a man harrowing clods
  In a slow silent walk
With an old horse that stumbles and nods
  Half asleep as they stalk.

II

Only thin smoke without flame   5
  From the heaps of couch-grass;
Yet this will go onward the same
  Though Dynasties pass.

III

Yonder a maid and her wight
  Come whispering by: 10
War's annals will fade into night
  Ere their story die.

                                 1917

The Harbour Bridge

From here, the quay,[9] one looks above to mark
The bridge across the harbour, hanging dark
Against the day's-end sky, fair-green in glow
Over and under the middle archway's bow:
It draws its skeleton where the sun has set,   5
Yea, clear from cutwater to parapet;[1]
On which mild glow, too, lines of rope and spar
  Trace themselves black as char.[2]

Down here in shade we hear the painters shift
Against the bollards[3] with a drowsy lift,   10
As moved by the incoming stealthy tide.
High up across the bridge the burghers[4] glide
As cut black-paper portraits hastening on
In conversation none knows what upon:
Their sharp-edged lips move quickly word by word   15
  To speech that is not heard.

There trails the dreamful girl, who leans and stops,
There presses the practical woman to the shops,

8. From Jeremiah 51:20: "Thou art my battle axe and weapons of war: for with thee will I break in pieces the nations: and with thee will I destroy kingdoms." Hardy commented on this poem, "I believe it would be said by people who knew me well that I have a faculty (possibly not uncommon) for burying an emotion in my heart or brain for forty years, and exhuming it at the end of that time as fresh as when interred. For instance, the poem entitled 'The Breaking of Nations' contains a feeling that moved me in 1870, during the Franco-Prussian war, when I chanced to be looking at such an agricultural incident [the old horse harrowing the arable field in the valley below] in Cornwall.

But I did not write the verses till during the war with Germany of 1914, and onwards. Query: where was that sentiment hiding itself during more than forty years?" (Florence E. Hardy, *The Life of Thomas Hardy*, New York, 1965, pp. 378–79).
  9. Wharf.
  1. That is, from the base of the bridge at the waterline up to the low wall at the top.
  2. Charcoal; "spar": mast.
  3. Mooring posts on a wharf; "painters": ropes attaching boats to the bollards.
  4. That is, citizens, usually prosperous and middle-class.

There is a sailor, meeting his wife with a start,
And we, drawn nearer, judge they are keeping apart.   20
Both pause. She says: "I've looked for you. I thought
We'd make it up." Then no words can be caught.
At last: "Won't you come home?" She moves still
        nigher:
        " 'Tis comfortable, with a fire."

"No," he says gloomily. "And, anyhow,   25
I can't give up the other woman now:
You should have talked like that in former days,
When I was last home." They go different ways.
And the west dims, and yellow lamplights shine:
And soon above, like lamps more opaline,   30
White stars ghost forth, that care not for men's wives,
        Or any other lives.

                                                    1925

He Never Expected Much

(OR)
a consideration
(A reflection) on my eighty-sixth birthday

Well, World, you have kept faith with me,
        Kept faith with me;
Upon the whole you have proved to be
        Much as you said you were.
Since as a child I used to lie   5
Upon the leaze[5] and watch the sky,
Never, I own, expected I
        That life would all be fair.

'Twas then you said, and since have said,
        Times since have said,   10
In that mysterious voice you shed
        From clouds and hills around:
"Many have loved me desperately,
Many with smooth serenity,
While some have shown contempt of me   15
        Till they dropped underground.

"I do not promise overmuch,
        Child; overmuch;
Just neutral-tinted haps and such,"
        You said to minds like mine.   20
Wise warning for your credit's sake!
Which I for one failed not to take,
And hence could stem such strain and ache
        As each year might assign.

                                                    1928

5. Pasture.

GERARD MANLEY HOPKINS
1844–1889

Gerard Manley Hopkins, who wrote so little and died so young, was one of the most original poets to write in English at any period. He worked out his innovations in private, and during his lifetime only three of his poems were published. His friend from college days, Robert Bridges, the Poet Laureate, collected and edited Hopkins's poetry in 1918, having delayed so long because of his desire to find the propitious moment. The work caught on at once and has been a favorite of the younger poets, from Auden to Lowell.

The life of Hopkins, whatever its inner satisfactions, must seem melancholy in summary. He was the eldest of eight children. His father was a man of some cultivation who wrote not only books about marine insurance but also a volume of poems. His mother was conspicuously pious. Hopkins went to Highgate School in London, where he won a poetry prize. In 1863 Hopkins enrolled at Balliol College, Oxford, to read Greats (classics, ancient history, and philosophy). At that time his ambition was to become a painter, but his plans changed because, with three of his friends, he was drawn to Catholicism. "All our minds you see were ready to go at a touch," he wrote John Henry (later Cardinal) Newman.[1] His parents were strongly opposed, but he was resolved. He was received into the Church by Newman in October 1866, and the experience of conversion determined the rest of his life. After having taken a first class degree in 1867, he taught at the Oratory School, Birmingham, under Newman's eye. One year later he decided to become a Jesuit. It was at this time that he burnt all his early verses as too worldly. "I am a eunuch," he later wrote Robert Bridges, "but it is for the kingdom of God's sake." In 1877 Hopkins was ordained. He served variously as priest and teacher until 1884, when he was appointed professor of classics at University College, Dublin (founded by Newman as the Catholic University in 1853). Here until his death in 1889 he remained, out of place in the Irish scene but at home in a state of exalted misery. His health was poor and in 1889 he came down with typhoid; he died of that disease and its complications at the age of forty-four.

After he entered his Jesuit novitiate Hopkins wrote no poems, though he had not given up the thought of relating his two vocations of priest and poet. In 1875 he told his superior how moved he felt by the wreck of the *Deutschland*, a ship carrying five nuns exiled from Germany by the Falk Laws. His superior kindly expressed the hope that someone would write a poem about it, and, thus encouraged, Hopkins wrote his first important work. The poem brought together his own conversion and the chief nun's transfiguring death, God's wrath and God's love, with the force of an epigram. Against such a view as Hardy's of the indifference of the creator to his creation, Hopkins celebrated the bond between them.

Not that this conclusion was wrung from him without pain: religion was in no sense an escape or refuge for him, as in a way skepticism was a refuge for Hardy in that it confirmed his sense of being neither wanted nor deceived about being wanted. Hopkins's faith was a source of anguish; he said that he never wavered in it, but that he never felt worthy of it. He made his misery clear in many poems, most notably in the "Terrible Sonnets" which he wrote in his last years.

Most of his poems set anguish and rapture against each other, either in the same poem or in parallel poems. "Hurrahing in Harvest," like "Spring and Fall" a poem about the seasons, shows Christ as immanent: the poet, suddenly in electric touch with him, feels as if his earthly self had been hurled, or half-hurled, off under his feet. On the other hand, "Spring and Fall" tenderly admits the mortality of earth,

---

1. *Further Letters of Hopkins*, 2d ed., ed. C. C. Abbott, London, 1956, p. 30.

with no reference to salvation. Hopkins is at his best in poems where the combat is continued to the last moment, as in "Carrion Comfort," where Christ is adversary as well as savior. This poetry needs pain as the principal ingredient in joy, but the pain is the more convincing.

Hopkins was unwilling to accept any of the usual appurtenances of nineteenth-century poetry—its stanza forms, meters, language. He was altogether at odds with the view implicit in Hardy that one had better not write too well for fear of losing something central in an experience. He held that difficulty of composition was a means of achieving poetic value, as difficulty of spiritual exercises was productive of higher qualities. He approved William Barnes's use of dialect words, because thereby Barnes was tied "down to the things that he or another Dorset man has said or might say, which though it narrows his field heightens his effects."[2] Hopkins himself borrowed from dialect such words as *fettle, sillion,* and *burl.* He also invented new words, such as *beechbole* (trunk of a beech tree), *bloomfall* (fall of flowers), *bower of bone* (body), *churlsgrace* (grace of a churl or laborer), *firedint* (spark), *firefolk* (stars), *leafmeal* (a fusion of "leaf" and "piecemeal"), *unleaving* (losing leaves). He advised Bridges to concentrate by dispensing with articles: instead of "The eye marvelled, the ear hearkened," he urged "eye marvelled, ear hearkened," as in his own poem, "Spring and Fall."[3] The effect is to convey the meaning more abruptly. In addition, Hopkins made new and original use of internal rhyme, alliteration, consonance, dissonance.

He felt the need for a new set of terms to explain what he was doing in his poetry. His earlier expression, "vividness of idea," gave way to *inscape.* This word, formed on the analogy of landscape, meant "individually distinctive beauty." W. A. M. Peter explains more fully that inscape for Hopkins is "the unified complex of the sensible qualities of the object of perception that strike us as inseparably belonging to and most typical of it, so that through the knowledge of this unified complex of sense-data we may gain an insight into the individual essence of the object." It is the "whatness" of a thing, suddenly apprehended like an electrical impulse, a divine spark. Hopkins wrote in his *Notebooks,*[4] "All things therefore are charged with love, are charged with God and if we know how to touch them give off sparks and take fire, yield drops and flow, ring and tell of him" (1881).

A second term Hopkins needed arose from a conception of "liveliness," which he made more precise as *instress.* This is the power that holds inscape together, like the force that binds the atom. The sense of all things as not just passively meaningless or meaningful, but as actively asserting their totality of symbolical being, connects Hopkins with other symbolist poets.

In technique, Hopkins's most important new term (he has others as well) is *sprung rhythm:* this is often defined as simply counting stresses instead of syllables, but W. H. Gardner has shown that it is a new method of timing both the stressed and unstressed syllables. Its use is basic to the effect Hopkins so often achieves, of a sudden rush or an equally sudden slowing down of tension and hypertension and momentary tranquillity. Hopkins contended that it was in fact the rhythm "nearest to the rhythm of prose, that is the native and natural rhythm of speech, the least forced, the most rhetorical and emphatic of all possible rhythms."

The density of his verse made for difficulties of comprehension. In a letter to Bridges[5] he defended these: "Epic and drama and ballad and many, most, things should be at once intelligible; but everything need not and cannot be. Plainly if it is possible to express a subtle and recondite subject in a subtle and recondite way and

---

2. Letter of Aug. 14, 1879, in *Letters of Gerard Manley Hopkins to Robert Bridges,* ed. C. C. Abbott, London, 1935, p. 89.

3. Letter of Jan. 26, 1881, in *Letters to Bridges,* p. 122.

4. Ed. Humphry House, London and New York, 1937, p. 342.

5. Letter of Nov. 6, 1887, in *Letters to Bridges,* pp. 265–66.

with great felicity and perfection, in the end, something must be sacrificed, with so trying a task, in the process, and this may be the being at once, nay perhaps even the being without explanation at all, intelligible."

He responded also to another criticism of the oddness of his verse. On Feb. 15, 1879, he wrote Bridges, "No doubt my poetry errs on the side of oddness. I hope in time to have a more balanced and Miltonic style. But as air, melody, is what strikes me most of all in music and design in painting, so design, pattern or what I am in the habit of calling 'inscape' is what I above all aim at in poetry. Now it is the virtue of design, pattern, or inscape to be distinctive and it is the vice of distinctiveness to become queer. This vice I cannot have escaped."[6] These defenses have been echoed by poets following him in defense of their own difficulty or oddity.

6. The same, p. 66.

Heaven-Haven

A nun takes the veil

I have desired to go
　　Where springs not fail,
To fields where flies no sharp and sided hail
　　And a few lilies blow.

And I have asked to be   5
　　Where no storms come,
Where the green swell is in the havens dumb,
　　And out of the swing of the sea.

1918

The Habit of Perfection

Elected Silence,[1] sing to me
And beat upon my whorlèd ear,
Pipe me to pastures still and be
The music that I care to hear.

Shape nothing, lips; be lovely-dumb: 5
It is the shut,[2] the curfew sent
From there where all surrenders come
Which only makes you eloquent.

Be shellèd, eyes, with double dark
And find the uncreated light:[3]   10
This ruck and reel which you remark
Coils,[4] keeps, and teases simple sight.

Palate, the hutch[5] of tasty lust,
Desire not to be rinsed with wine:
The can[6] must be so sweet, the crust   15
So fresh that come in fasts divine!

1. The priest has elected—or freely chosen— the life of renunciation celebrated in the poem.
2. Closing in of evening, shut of day.
3. "*Lux increata* of the Schoolmen, the creative energy of God's mind." (*The Poems of Gerard Manley Hopkins*, 4th ed., ed. W. H. Gardner and N. H. MacKenzie, London, 1967, p. 252)
4. Ensnares.
5. Storage chest.
6. Tankard.

Nostrils, your careless breath that spend
Upon the stir and keep[7] of pride,
What relish shall the censers send
Along the sanctuary side!   20

O feel-of-primrose hands, O feet
That want the yield of plushy sward,
But you shall walk the golden street
And you unhouse and house the Lord.[8]

And, Poverty, be thou the bride   25
And now the marriage feast begun,
And lily-coloured clothes provide
Your spouse not laboured-at nor spun.[9]

1918

God's Grandeur

Sonet – has turns

The world is charged with the grandeur of God.   *14 lines*
    It will flame out, like shining from shook foil;[1]
    It gathers to a greatness, like the ooze of oil
Crushed. Why do men then now not reck his rod?[2]   *Not in touch*
Generations have trod, have trod, have trod;   *w/ Earth or*
    And all is seared with trade; bleared, smeared with toil;   *god*
    And wears man's smudge and shares man's smell: the soil
Is bare now, nor can foot feel, being shod.

And for all this, nature is never spent;
    There lives the dearest freshness deep down things;   10
And though the last lights off the black West went
    Oh, morning, at the brown brink eastward, springs—
Because the Holy Ghost over the bent
    World broods with warm breast and with ah! bright wings.

1918

The Windhover:[3]

To Christ our Lord

I caught this morning morning's minion,[4] King-
    dom of daylight's dauphin, dapple-dawn-drawn Falcon, in his riding
    Of the rolling level underneath him steady air, and striding
High there, how he rung upon the rein[5] of a wimpling[6] wing

7. Upkeep.
8. Remove the Host from the tabernacle and then return it.
9. "And why are you anxious about clothing? Consider the lilies of the field, how they grow; they neither toil nor spin; yet I tell you, even Solomon in all his glory was not arrayed like one of these" (Matthew 6:28–29).
1. "I mean foil in its sense of leaf or tinsel. . . . Shaken goldfoil gives off broad glares like sheet lightning and also, and this is true of nothing else, owing to its zig-zag dints and creasings and network of small many cornered facets, a sort of fork lightning too." (*Letters of Gerard Manley Hopkins to Robert Bridges*, ed. C. C. Abbott, 1955, p. 169)
2. Heed his authority.
3. The kestrel, a European falcon resembling the American sparrow hawk; the bird hovers in the air with its head to the wind.
4. Darling, favorite.
5. To "ring on the rein" is a riding term, "said of a horse that circles at the end of a long rein held by its trainer" (*Poems*, p. 267).
6. Rippling.

In his ecstasy! then off, off forth on swing,   5
     As a skate's heel sweeps smooth on a bow-bend: the hurl and gliding
     Rebuffed the big wind. My heart in hiding
Stirred for a bird,—the achieve of, the mastery of the thing!

Brute beauty and valour and act, oh, air, pride, plume here
     Buckle![7] AND the fire that breaks from thee then, a billion   10
     Times told lovelier, more dangerous, O my chevalier!

     No wonder of it: shéer plód makes plough down sillion[8]
Shine, and blue-bleak embers, ah my dear,
     Fall, gall themselves, and gash gold-vermilion.

                                                                              1918

Pied Beauty

          Glory be to God for dappled things—
               For skies of couple-colour as a brinded cow;
                    For rose-moles all in stipple upon trout that swim;
          Fresh-firecoal chestnut-falls;[9] finches' wings;
               Landscape plotted and pieced—fold, fallow, and plough;   5
               And áll trádes, their gear and tackle and trim.[1]

          All things counter,[2] original, spare, strange;
               Whatever is fickle, freckled (who knows how?)
                    With swift, slow; sweet, sour; adazzle, dim;
          He fathers-forth whose beauty is past change: 10
                    Praise him.

                                                                              1918

Binsey Poplars[3]

felled 1879

          My aspens dear, whose airy cages quelled,
          Quelled or quenched in leaves the leaping sun,
               All felled, felled, are all felled;
               Of a fresh and following folded rank
                    Not spared, not one   5
                    That dandled a sandalled
               Shadow that swam or sank
          On meadow and river and wind-wandering weed-winding bank.

          O if we but knew what we do   10
                    When we delve or hew—
               Hack and rack the growing green!
               Since country is so tender

To touch, her being só slender,
That, like this sleek and seeing ball
But a prick will make no eye at all
Where we, even where we mean
   To mend her we end her,
  When we hew or delve:
After-comers cannot guess the beauty been.
  Ten or twelve, only ten or twelve
  Strokes of havoc únselve
   The sweet especial scene,
  Rural scene, a rural scene,
  Sweet especial rural scene.

15
20
25
1918

Felix Randal

Felix Randal the farrier,[4] O he is dead then? my duty all ended,
Who have watched his mould of man, big-boned and hardy-handsome
Pining, pining, till time when reason rambled in it and some
Fatal four disorders, fleshed there, all contended?

Sickness broke him. Impatient he cursed at first, but mended
Being anointed and all; though a heavenlier heart began some
Months earlier, since I had our sweet reprieve and ransom[5]
Tendered to him. Ah well, God rest him all road ever he offended!

This seeing the sick endears them to us, us too it endears.
My tongue had taught thee comfort, touch had quenched thy tears,
Thy tears that touched my heart, child, Felix, poor Felix Randal;

How far from then forethought of, all thy more boisterous years,
When thou at the random grim forge, powerful amidst peers,
Didst fettle for the great grey drayhorse his bright and battering sandal!

5
10
1918

Spring and Fall:

to a young child

  Márgarét, áre you gríeving
  Over Goldengrove unleaving?
  Leáves, líke the things of man, you
  With your fresh thoughts care for, can you?
  Áh! ás the heart grows older
  It will come to such sights colder
  By and by, nor spare a sigh
  Though worlds of wanwood leafmeal[6] lie;
  And yet you *will* weep and know why.
  Now no matter, child, the name:

5
10

---

4. One who shoes horses.
5. Confession, absolution, and communion.
6. That is, wan forest with scattered leaves.

"Leafmeal" is coined by analogy with "piece-meal."

Sórrow's spríngs áre the same.
Nor mouth had, no nor mind, expressed
What heart heard of, ghost[7] guessed:
It ís the blight man was born for,
It is Margaret you mourn for.

1918

[Carrion Comfort]

Not, I'll not, carrion comfort, Despair, not feast on thee;
Not untwist—slack they may be—these last strands of man
In me ór, most weary, cry *I can no more*. I can;
Can something, hope, wish day come, not choose not to be.
But ah, but O thou terrible, why wouldst thou rude on me   5
Thy wring-world right foot rock? lay a lionlimb against me? scan
With darksome devouring eyes my bruisèd bones? and fan,
O in turns of tempest, me heaped there; me frantic to avoid thee and flee?

  Why? That my chaff might fly; my grain lie, sheer and clear.
Nay in all that toil, that coil, since (seems) I kissed the rod,   10
Hand rather, my heart lo! lapped strength, stole joy, would laugh, chéer.
Cheer whom though? the hero whose heaven-handling flung me, fóot tród
Me? or me that fought him? O which one? is it each one? That night, that year
Of now done darkness I wretch lay wrestling with (my God!) my God.

1918

[No Worst, There Is None. Pitched Past Pitch of Grief]

No worst, there is none. Pitched past pitch of grief,
More pangs will, schooled at forepangs, wilder wring.
Comforter, where, where is your comforting?
Mary, mother of us, where is your relief?
My cries heave, herds-long; huddle in a main, a chief   5
Woe, world-sorrow; on an age-old anvil wince and sing—
Then lull, then leave off. Fury had shrieked 'No ling-
ering! Let me be fell:[8] force[9] I must be brief'.
  O the mind, mind has mountains; cliffs of fall
Frightful, sheer, no-man-fathomed. Hold them cheap   10
May who ne'er hung there. Nor does long our small
Durance deal with that steep or deep. Here! creep,
Wretch, under a comfort serves in a whirlwind: all
Life death does end and each day dies with sleep.

1918

---

7. Spirit.
8. Cruel, terrible.

9. Perforce; of necessity.

[I Wake and Feel the Fell of Dark, Not Day]

I wake and feel the fell of dark, not day.
What hours, O what black hours we have spent
This night! what sights you, heart, saw; ways you went!
And more must, in yet longer light's delay.
With witness I speak this. But where I say   5
Hours I mean years, mean life. And my lament
Is cries countless, cries like dead letters sent
To dearest him that lives alas! away.

I am gall, I am heartburn. God's most deep decree
Bitter would have me taste: my taste was me;   10
Bones built in me, flash filled, blood brimmed the curse.
Selfyeast of spirit a dull dough sours. I see
The lost are like this, and their scourge to be
As I am mine, their sweating selves; but worse.

1918

[Thou Art Indeed Just, Lord, If I Contend]

Justus quidem tu es. Domine, si disputem tecum: verumtamen justa
loquar ad te: Quare via impiorum prosperatur? etc.[1]

Thou art indeed just, Lord, if I contend
With thee; but, sir, so what I plead is just.
Why do sinners' ways prosper? and why must
Disappointment all I endeavour end?

Wert thou my enemy, O thou my friend,   5
How wouldst thou worse, I wonder, than thou dost
Defeat, thwart me? Oh, the sots and thralls[2] of lust
Do in spare hours more thrive than I that spend,

Sir, life upon thy cause. See, banks and brakes
Now, leavèd how thick! lacèd they are again   10
With fretty chervil, look, and fresh wind shakes

Them; birds build—but not I build; no, but strain,
Time's eunuch, and not breed one work that wakes.
Mine, O thou lord of life, send my roots rain.

1918

---

1. "Righteous art thou, O Lord, when I complain to thee; yet I would plead my case before thee. Why does the way of the wicked prosper?" (Jeremiah 12:1). Hopkins quotes this much as his epigraph; the imagery of his poem may owe something to the next verses: "Why do all who are treacherous thrive? Thou plantest them and they take root; they grow and bring forth fruit; thou art near in their mouth and far from their heart."
2. Prisoners.

A. E. HOUSMAN
1859–1936

Housman refused to have his poems included in an anthology of the nineties, saying that it "would be just as technically correct, and just as essentially inappropriate, as to include Lot in a book on Sodomites."[1] But it is not quite so inappropriate as that. Certain poems of Yeats, Lionel Johnson, and Ernest Dowson are quite close to poems by Housman. The interest in a small, predominantly rural area, whether Ireland or Shropshire, the use of ballad meters, the sense of the world's unsatisfactoriness, and the reiterated theme of unrequited love, are aspects that Housman shared with the early Yeats in particular. The two poets also shared an intense admiration for Blake, whom Housman put second only to Shakespeare. But Housman admires Blake for his lyrical intensity and subordination of idea to passion, while Yeats is much more occupied with Blake's system and its interpretation. Housman minimizes and disparages the intellect in poetry, while Yeats, like other poets of larger scope, recognizes the necessity of incorporating it. Housman, when he can, *excludes*, while Yeats *includes*. It was characteristic of Housman to devote much of his life to editing a minor work, the *Astronomicon* of Manilius, as against classical poems of greater enterprise.

Housman appears to have thought of himself as a loser, predestined to see hopes dashed and love unrequited. He could have considered social convention to be the vanquishing evil, but he preferred to represent the adversary as death. Often the method of dying is by execution, society being implicated as executioner. His poems, written mostly after he was thirty-five, deal chiefly with young men between the ages of twenty-one—or, as he would say, one-and twenty—and twenty-five. Youth and life and love end at a stroke. He extracts all possible ironies from this situation. Nature adds to the gloom either by baleful destructiveness or by its phantasmal parade of meaningless fertility and beauty.

Alfred Edward Housman was born March 26, 1859, in Fockbury, which is in Worcestershire and not, as might be supposed from his verse, in Shropshire. His "sentimental" attachment to Shropshire came, he said, from the fact that "its hills were our western horizon," and he confessed indifferently to having some of his topographical details "quite wrong."[2] His father was a solicitor from Lancashire; his mother was Cornish. After her death in 1870, a stepmother entered the home. He was brought up in the High Church party of the Church of England, "which is much the best religion I have ever come across."[3] But at the age of eight—which was also the year he first tried writing poetry—he was converted to paganism by Lemprière's *Classical Dictionary*. Of his later religious career he commented flatly, "I became a deist at 13 and an atheist at 21."[4]

Housman did well at school and won a scholarship to St. John's College, Oxford, where he read Classical Moderations and then Greats, the latter a combination of classics, ancient history, and philosophy. "Oxford had not much effect on me," he said, "except that I there met my greatest friend."[5] This was effect enough. The friend was Moses Jackson, a bright and versatile student. He was receptive to friendship, but Housman wanted a more intimate relationship. In a posthumously published verse, he wrote, "Because I liked you better / Than suits a man to say, / It irked you, and I promised / To throw the thought away."

At first Housman did well academically, but either because of amorous commotion or because of disaffection from some required studies in his course, he did not even

1. Grant Richards, *Housman: 1897–1936*, London, 1941, p. 245.
2. Letter to Maurice Pollet, quoted in John Carter and John Sparrow, *A. E. Housman, An Annotated Hand-List*, London, 1952, p. 46.
3. The same.
4. The same.
5. The same.

answer many of the examination questions, and was failed. The following fall, 1881, he returned ignominiously to complete a marginal, "pass" degree. Meanwhile Jackson had taken a job in the Patent Office and encouraged Housman to pass a civil service examination and join him there. Housman did so, and for a time the two shared rooms in London. But both had ambitions to transcend their circumstances: Jackson was at work on a doctorate in science, and Housman, scorned for his scholarship by Oxford, was determined to prove himself in classics and spent most of his nights at the British Museum.

Living at such close quarters with Jackson was probably too anguishing. At any rate, Housman in 1886 moved into his own place in Highgate (North London) and lived there a life of total and solitary concentration. Jackson was one of the few people allowed to visit. He, however, had decided upon marriage and upon a career in India. Towards the end of 1887 he resigned from the Patent Office and sailed to India, where he became principal of a small college. Two years later he returned to England to marry the woman who had promised to wait for him. Housman wrote sadly in "Epithalamium," "Friend and comrade yield you o'er / To her that hardly loves you more." He was left to mourn as the Jacksons went to India again. Most of his poems were written in the early 1890s. Besides his grief for Moses Jackson's marriage he had another sorrow, the death of young Adalbert Jackson, brother of Moses, from typhoid in 1892. The removal from his life of these two brothers marked a pivotal moment for Housman. He commented afterwards, "I did not begin to write poetry in earnest until the really emotional part of my life was over."[6]

Housman's extraordinary capacity in classical scholarship earned signal recognition in 1892, when he was elected to the chair of Greek and Latin at University College, London. In 1894 his father died, and then occurred a death which afflicted Housman sharply even though he did not know the dead man. It was of a Woolwich cadet, eighteen years old, who committed suicide and left a note reported in a newspaper article that Housman kept for life. It was possible to read the cadet's statement as referring to a hopeless homosexual love, "that one thing I have no hope of obtaining." Suicide is a chronic theme in Housman. In the nineties, homosexuals were in danger of victimization by the law: in 1895 Oscar Wilde was convicted on this charge and sentenced to two years in prison. Housman, in sympathy, sent him a copy of his book of poems. This book, a product of all Housman's misfortunes and anxieties, was put together in 1896. Its original title was *The Poems of Terence Hearsay,* Terence being a character in them, and Hearsay perhaps a disclaimer of personal involvement. But the publisher wisely proposed *A Shropshire Lad* as a better title. When the book was published in 1896, Housman sent the first copy to Jackson. He was later to dedicate to Jackson his five-volume edition of Manilius, which he published sporadically from 1903 to 1930.

When in 1910 a chair of classics fell vacant at Cambridge, Housman was elected to it, and he lived there from 1911 until his death. His later life is even barer of incident. In 1922 he gathered together a second slender volume lugubriously entitled *Last Poems,* and in the prefatory note remarked that "I can no longer expect to be visited by the continuous excitement" which he had experienced in the early 1890s. His friend Jackson died a year later. Housman lived a retired life at Cambridge, though in 1933 he delivered his famous Leslie Stephen lecture, "The Name and Nature of Poetry," which created a profound impression. He died April 30, 1936. His brother Laurence Housman edited *More Poems* later in that year; more recently some additional poems, as well as the manuscripts of all his verse, have been published.

In his lecture Housman attributed to poetry a "superior terseness" over prose, but denied that ideas used in poetry had any special poeticality. They could mostly be

6. George L. Watson, *A. E. Housman,* London, 1957, p. 135.

expressed better in prose, he declared. The function of poetry is "to transfuse emotion—not to transmit thought but to set up in the reader's sense a vibration corresponding to what was felt by the writer. . . ." Blake in particular offered to "entangle the reader in a net of thoughtless delight." Housman insisted that poetry should be "more physical than intellectual," and he gave his famous touchstone of poetry, which was that when a line of genuine poetry entered his head while he was shaving, he could feel his skin bristle, his spine shiver, and the pit of his stomach receive something like a spear.

Loveliest of Trees, the Cherry Now

Loveliest of trees, the cherry now
Is hung with bloom along the bough,
And stands about the woodland ride
Wearing white for Eastertide.

Now, of my threescore years and ten,   5
Twenty will not come again,
And take from seventy springs a score,
It only leaves me fifty more.

And since to look at things in bloom
Fifty springs are little room,   10
About the woodlands I will go
To see the cherry hung with snow.

                                                    1896

To an Athlete Dying Young

The time you won your town the race
We chaired you through the market-place;
Man and boy stood cheering by,
And home we brought you shoulder-high.

To-day, the road all runners come,   5
Shoulder-high we bring you home,
And set you at your threshold down,
Townsman of a stiller town.

Smart lad, to slip betimes away
From fields where glory does not stay   10
And early though the laurel grows
It withers quicker than the rose.

Eyes the shady night has shut
Cannot see the record cut,
And silence sounds no worse than cheers   15
After earth has stopped the ears:

Now you will not swell the rout
Of lads that wore their honours out,

Runners whom renown outran
And the name died before the man.   20

So set, before its echoes fade,
The fleet foot on the sill of shade,
And hold to the low lintel up
The still-defended challenge-cup.

And round that early-laurelled head   25
Will flock to gaze the strengthless dead
And find unwithered on its curls
The garland briefer than a girl's.

1896

Terence, This Is Stupid Stuff

'Terence,[1] this is stupid stuff:
You eat your victuals fast enough;
There can't be much amiss, 'tis clear,
To see the rate you drink your beer.
But oh, good Lord, the verse you make,   5
It gives a chap the belly-ache.
The cow, the old cow, she is dead;
It sleeps well, the horned head:
We poor lads, 'tis our turn now
To hear such tunes as killed the cow.   10
Pretty friendship 'tis to rhyme
Your friends to death before their time
Moping melancholy mad:
Come, pipe a tune to dance to, lad.'

Why, if 'tis dancing you would be,   15
There's brisker pipes than poetry.
Say, for what were hop-yards meant,
Or why was Burton built on Trent?
Oh many a peer of England brews
Livelier liquor than the Muse.[2]   20
And malt does more than Milton can
To justify God's ways to man.[3]
Ale, man, ale's the stuff to drink
For fellows whom it hurts to think:
Look into the pewter pot   25
To see the world as the world's not.
And faith, 'tis pleasant till 'tis past:
The mischief is that 'twill not last.
Oh I have been to Ludlow[4] fair
And left my necktie God knows where,   30
And carried half-way home, or near,

1. The original title of *A Shropshire Lad* was *The Poems of Terence Hearsay*,
2. A comparison of the fountains of Mount Ida, tended by the Muses, with the breweries of Burton-on-Trent, some of whose owners were raised to the peerage, as sources of poetic inspiration.
3. An allusion to Milton's promise in *Paradise Lost* (I, 17–26) to "justify the ways of God to men."
4. A Shropshire town.

Pints and quarts of Ludlow beer:
Then the world seemed none so bad,
And I myself a sterling lad;
And down in lovely muck I've lain,   35
Happy till I woke again,
Then I saw the morning sky:
Heigho, the tale was all a lie;
The world, it was the old world yet,
I was I, my things were wet,   40
And nothing now remained to do
But begin the game anew.

Therefore, since the world has still
Much good, but much less good than ill,
And while the sun and moon endure
Luck's a chance, but trouble's sure,   45
I'd face it as a wise man would,
And train for ill and not for good.
'Tis true, the stuff I bring for sale
Is not so brisk a brew as ale:
Out of a stem that scored the hand   50
I wrung it in a weary land.
But take it: if the smack is sour,
The better for the embittered hour;
It should do good to heart and head   55
When your soul is in my soul's stead;
And I will friend you, if I may,
In the dark and cloudy day.

There was a king reigned in the East:
There, when kings will sit to feast,   60
They get their fill before they think
With poisoned meat and poisoned drink.
He gathered all that springs to birth
From the many-venomed earth;
First a little, thence to more,   65
He sampled all her killing store;
And easy, smiling, seasoned sound,
Sate the king when healths went round.
They put arsenic in his meat
And stared aghast to watch him eat;   70
They poured strychnine in his cup
And shook to see him drink it up:
They shook, they stared as white's their shirt:
Them it was their poison hurt.
—I tell the tale that I heard told.   75
Mithridates, he died old.[5]

1896

<hr>

5. Mithridates VI, a pre-Christian king of Pon-
tus, was said to have made himself immune to
attempts to poison him by taking poison in small
quantities.

The Chestnut Casts His Flambeaux

The chestnut casts his flambeaux,[6] and the flowers
    Stream from the hawthorn on the wind away,
The doors clap to, the pane is blind with showers.
    Pass me the can, lad; there's an end of May.

There's one spoilt spring to scant our mortal lot,   5
    One season ruined of our little store.
May will be fine next year as like as not:
    Oh ay, but then we shall be twenty-four.

We for a certainty are not the first
    Have sat in taverns while the tempest hurled   10
Their hopeful plans to emptiness, and cursed
    Whatever brute and blackguard made the world.

It is in truth iniquity on high
    To cheat our sentenced souls of aught they crave,
And mar the merriment as you and I   15
    Fare on our long fool's-errand to the grave.

Iniquity it is; but pass the can.
    My lad, no pair of kings our mothers bore;
Our only portion is the estate of man:
    We want the moon, but we shall get no more.   20

If here to-day the cloud of thunder lours
    To-morrow it will hie on far behests:
The flesh will grieve on other bones than ours
    Soon, and the soul will mourn in other breasts.

The troubles of our proud and angry dust   25
    Are from eternity, and shall not fail.
Bear them we can, and if we can we must.
    Shoulder the sky, my lad, and drink your ale.

                1922

Eight O'Clock

He stood, and heard the steeple
    Sprinkle the quarters on the morning town.
One, two, three, four, to market-place and people
    It tossed them down.

Strapped, noosed, nighing his hour,   5
    He stood and counted them and cursed his luck;
And then the clock collected in the tower
    Its strength, and struck.

                1922

6. Torches; chestnut blossoms are a vivid red in color.

Hell Gate

Onward led the road again
Through the sad uncoloured plain
Under twilight brooding dim,
And along the utmost rim
Wall and rampart risen to sight   5
Cast a shadow not of night,
And beyond them seemed to glow
Bonfires lighted long ago.
And my dark conductor broke
Silence at my side and spoke,   10
Saying, "You conjecture well:
Yonder is the gate of hell."

Ill as yet the eye could see
The eternal masonry,
But beneath it on the dark   15
To and fro there stirred a spark.
And again the sombre guide
Knew my question, and replied:
"At hell gate the damned in turn
Pace for sentinel and burn."   20

Dully at the leaden sky
Staring, and with idle eye
Measuring the listless plain,
I began to think again.
Many things I thought of then,   25
Battle, and the loves of men,
Cities entered, oceans crossed,
Knowledge gained and virtue lost,
Cureless folly done and said,
And the lovely way that led   30
To the slimepit and the mire
And the everlasting fire.
And against a smoulder dun
And a dawn without a sun
Did the nearing bastion loom,   35
And across the gate of gloom
Still one saw the sentry go,
Trim and burning, to and fro,
One for women to admire
In his finery of fire.   40
Something, as I watched him pace,
Minded me of time and place,
Soldiers of another corps
And a sentry known before.

Ever darker hell on high   45
Reared its strength upon the sky,
And our footfall on the track
Fetched the daunting echo back.
But the soldier pacing still

The insuperable sill,   50
Nursing his tormented pride,
Turned his head to neither side,
Sunk into himself apart
And the hell-fire of his heart.
But against our entering in   55
From the drawbridge Death and Sin
Rose to render key and sword
To their father and their lord.
And the portress foul to see
Lifted up her eyes on me   60
Smiling, and I made reply:
"Met again, my lass," said I.
Then the sentry turned his head,
Looked, and knew me, and was Ned.

Once he looked, and halted straight,   65
Set his back against the gate,
Caught his musket to his chin,
While the hive of hell within
Sent abroad a seething hum
As of towns whose king is come   70
Leading conquest home from far
And the captives of his war,
And the car of triumph waits,
And they open wide the gates.
But across the entry barred   75
Straddled the revolted guard,
Weaponed and accoutred well
From the arsenals of hell;
And beside him, sick and white,
Sin to left and Death to right   80
Turned a countenance of fear
On the flaming mutineer.
Over us the darkness bowed,
And the anger in the cloud
Clenched the lightning for the stroke;   85
But the traitor musket spoke.

And the hollowness of hell
Sounded as its master fell,
And the mourning echo rolled
Ruin through his kingdom old.   90
Tyranny and terror flown
Left a pair of friends alone,
And beneath the nether sky
All that stirred was he and I.

Silent, nothing found to say,   95
We began the backward way;
And the ebbing lustre died
From the soldier at my side,
As in all his spruce attire
Failed the everlasting fire.   100

Midmost of the homeward track
Once we listened and looked back;
But the city, dusk and mute,
Slept, and there was no pursuit.

1922

Epitaph on an Army of Mercenaries

These, in the day when heaven was falling,
    The hour when earth's foundations fled,
Followed their mercenary calling
    And took their wages and are dead.

Their shoulders held the sky suspended;   5
    They stood, and earth's foundations stay;
What God abandoned, these defended,
    And saved the sum of things for pay.

1922

Tell Me Not Here, It Needs Not Saying

Tell me not here, it needs not saying,
    What tune the enchantress plays
In aftermaths of soft September
    Or under blanching mays,
For she and I were long acquainted   5
    And I knew all her ways.

On russet floors, by waters idle,
    The pine lets fall its cone;
The cuckoo shouts all day at nothing
    In leafy dells alone;   10
And traveller's joy beguiles in autumn
    Hearts that have lost their own.

On acres of the seeded grasses
    The changing burnish heaves;
Or marshalled under moons of harvest   15
    Stand still all night the sheaves;
Or beeches strip in storms for winter
    And stain the wind with leaves.

Possess, as I possessed a season,
    The countries I resign,   20
Where over elmy plains the highway
    Would mount the hills and shine,
And full of shade the pillared forest
    Would murmur and be mine.

For nature, heartless, witless nature,   25
    Will neither care nor know
What stranger's feet may find the meadow
    And trespass there and go,

Nor ask amid the dews of morning
If they are mine or no.

1922

WILLIAM BUTLER YEATS
1865–1939

When Swinburne died in 1909, Yeats remarked to one of his sisters that he was now "king of the cats." He had in fact achieved the crown ten years before with the publication of *The Wind among the Reeds*. His reign continued until his death in 1939, and after it his fame continued to swell during the forties and fifties. In the sixties and seventies there was much grumbling because of his politics, dismissed (on slender evidence) as fascistic; because of his occultism, represented by critics as more naive than it was; and because of his theatricality; as if he were not anti-theatrical as well. In spite of these cavils, no other poet holds so central a place.

Though he described himself in his *Autobiography* as a timid man, timidity only enlarged his ambitions. Half-consciously at least, he prepared himself for the role of a major literary figure. Though he had no knack for languages, he informed himself through translations about the Western cultural tradition and then, as no important poet in English had done before him, about the Eastern tradition. Though not learned, he knew instinctively what it would be necessary for him to know. His range of allusion comprehends Homer's "unchristened heart," a prophecy from Virgil's Sixth Eclogue, Dante's "multifoliate rose," a sentence from Hafiz or Tagore or a Noh play. Goethe remarked that a poet must know all philosophy, but keep it out of his work. Yeats disobediently wrote philosophical lyrics in which he invoked theories of "golden-thighed Pythagoras," "ghostly Plato" and "solider Aristotle," Berkeley "who thought all things a dream," and contemporaries like "profound McTaggart." He knew also the *à rebours* philosophical tradition as expounded by Theosophists, Rosicrucians, spiritualists; he doctored the English of Tagore's Bengali mysticism, based upon the immanence of the divine in everyday life, and translated with the aid of a Hindu swami *The Ten Principal Upanishads*.

Yeats did not neglect the tradition of English verse. With E. J. Ellis he edited and interpreted all the writings of William Blake, including some he was the first to transcribe. He had fresh theories about Shakespeare and the early nineteenth-century poets, as well as about William Morris, Shaw, Wilde, and other figures of the nineties. He pursued the Irish tradition to the earliest saga literature and followed it to his own day. He edited the stories of the early nineteenth-century Irish writer William Carleton; he compiled anthologies of Irish tales, fairy and folk, and of poems. Not content to minister to the dead, he drew into creative activity the Irish play-wrights Lady Augusta Gregory and John Synge, and to some extent James Joyce, not to mention many young writers who were obliged, sometimes reluctantly, to recognize his lofty standards and strong purposes. When with Lady Gregory's help he founded and developed the Abbey Theatre, Yeats demonstrated that he had ability in "management of men" as well as in "this sedentary trade" of poetry.

However international his reading and his interests, Yeats clung to Ireland as source of his imagery, center of his local allusions, and arena of most of his activities. His talent burst the national boundaries, but he was pleased to be an Irish senator as well as a Nobel prize-winner. His deliberate Irishism began at the age of twenty, when he accepted the view of John O'Leary—an aging patriot just returned from exile—that a national literature was both necessary and possible. The first book of the new poets was *Poems and Ballads of Young Ireland* (1888), and the next year Yeats published his *The Wanderings of Oisin and Other Poems*, in which for the first time Irish legend found original expression in a modern consciousness.

From this time until the end of the century, Yeats was busy hammering his thoughts into unity (his own phrase for it). The thoughts included literary and political nationalism, research in the dexterities of English verse, and a "spiritual philosophy" to go with provincial themes. A dominant motif was his adherence to symbolism, the implicit kind to be found in poets like Whitman and the explicit kind in mystics and occultists like Madame Blavatsky and Swedenborg. With the help of Arthur Symons he read Mallarmé and other French members of the Symbolist school. Yeats came to feel that most poets had written within schemes of systematic images, and he traced in Blake, and also in Shelley, the recurrent symbols.

That in the nineties he should have worked out his own symbology was a predictable result. Images hit upon perhaps accidentally began to recur with doubled meaning; at first these were common ones, such as rose, lily, or star, but gradually uncommon ones were added, such as the two trees and the Valley of the Black Pig, and all were given an Irish inflection. In *The Wind among the Reeds* Yeats gathered together an array of themes, attitudes, scenes, and images to form a symbolic cluster.

Although Yeats worked out his symbology with subtlety, it did not wholly content him. It became associated in his mind with "the Celtic twilight" (his term for the persistent spirituality he found in the peasantry) just when he began to feel a need for Irish daylight. He determined therefore to enlarge his means and his scenes, to present himself in his poems with robustness rather than slenderness. Mortal conditions did not need to be transcended; they might be accepted with such intensity that they would no longer hamper him. He need not go to the Lake Isle of Innisfree to shun the world of affairs; he might master it in Dublin. Corporeal love need not be filtered and attenuated in what he once called "the autumn of the body"; it might achieve "profane perfection" in a belated spring.

With this resolution Yeats "came into his force." He spoke with new pungency, as when he astounded Lady Gregory by telling her, "We must accept the baptism of the gutter." His Crazy Jane would say later, "Nothing can be sole or whole / That has not been rent." And in his own person Yeats declared, "I must lie down where all the ladders start, / In the foul rag-and-bone shop of the heart." The world of the rose and that of the cross might enter into many relations: they could encroach upon each other instead of fusing, for example. What is sought is not so much the raising of mortal to immortal but an interpenetration. Instead of sanctifying the human, one must laicize the world of spirit, or, more simply, achieve a *lay sanctity*.

Yeats regarded his new energy as based upon incarnation and the old as based upon transfiguration. In the new, spirit became flesh; in the old, flesh became spirit. He developed a new symbology which would express this opposition, among others, more concretely. It took an intermediate form in those of his poems and prose writings which dwelt upon the battle within each individual mind, between what one is and what one would like to be, the real and the image of its opposite. It is as if every man put on a mask which expressed his antiself and struggled to make it fuse wih his face. But after his marriage Yeats greatly expanded this imagery. He now conceived of all consciousness as a conflict of opposites, which he represented by two interpenetrating cones or *gyres*, the apex of one in the base of the other. These were like his earlier use of the cross as an emblem of earthly pain. Beyond the gyres is a sphere which represents a totality which they merely subdivide. It is comparable to the emblematic rose of his early poetry.

This symbology Yeats put into his book *A Vision*, one of the strangest works of the century. It can profitably be read in connection with his poems, but it also has an intrinsic fascination as the most complete symbology since Blake's, written so well that at moments it leans towards philosophy and at other moments towards poetry. After he had composed it Yeats did not stay still; he was working on new ideas and new symbols, and would probably have published still another edition, or perhaps a second vision.

As Yeats grew older his sense of life sharpened, and he dwelt more boldly upon its lust and rage, its mire and fury, but also envisaged more passionately the state of completeness to which incompleteness may attain. Feelings rarefied when he was young became thick with substance later. He was determined to "beat upon the wall / Till truth obeyed his call," as he said Blake had done; and he pushed to the most extreme point his thought and his expression, content to be, as he said, "for the song's sake a fool."

The relation of Yeats's life to his work is close though not simple. His mythmaking imagination was so powerful that it transforms events which in another writer might be commonplace. It may be helpful, however, to bear in mind some unadorned facts. He was born in Dublin on June 13, 1865, the son of John Butler Yeats, later well known as a portrait-painter. His mother came from the Pollexfen family which lived near Sligo, and Yeats spent much of his childhood with them. In 1874 the family went to London so that J. B. Yeats might continue his art studies, but in 1880 they returned to Dublin. Here Yeats attended high school and then art school, the latter from 1884 to 1886. He gave up painting abruptly and threw himself into literary work. From now on his life expanded in many different directions. He founded Irish literary societies in both Dublin and London. In 1889 he met Maud Gonne and "the troubles of my life began." A nationalist, and a beauty, she became his ideal love and his coadjutor in various nationalistic activities. But eventually, in 1903, she married Major John MacBride. Her political extremism completed her separation from Yeats. She remained a figure in his poetry till the end.

The Irish dramatic movement, which Yeats began to organize in 1899, took up more and more of his time, especially after the founding of the Abbey Theatre in 1904. It was necessary to tread perilously between chauvinists on the one side and British authorities on the other, and Yeats frequently ran afoul of both. As a result he felt some "estrangement" from his country, or at least from large groups within it. But the Easter Rebellion in 1916, though put down at once by the British, awoke his old sympathy and his best political poems. The following year, 1917, Yeats married an Englishwoman, Georgie (changed by Yeats to George) Hyde-Lees. The early days of their marriage were troubled by his concern that his marriage was ill-advised. Mrs. Yeats, in an endeavor to distract her husband, attempted automatic writing, and his doubts evaporated. Some of her script proved so relevant to his own concerns that Yeats began to work it into the book which eventually became *A Vision*.

The Yeatses had a son and a daughter, both memorialized in verse, and they lived off and on in a Norman tower called Thoor (Castle) Ballylee near Lady Gregory's house at Coole. This tower in turn became the setting of several of his poems and gave him the title of one of his books; its winding stair provided the title of another.

After the Irish Free State was formed Yeats served six years in the senate, and after his term he continued to devote himself to various schemes for invigorating the country. Some of these were harebrained, but they always came back to his own ideal of a nation of people free to cultivate their imaginative capacities. All governments began to appall him, and the grim prophecy in his poem "The Second Coming" seemed to him more and more apt. He died on January 28, 1939, in southern France, just before the Second World War began. After it was over, his body was exhumed and brought back to Ireland by an Irish destroyer. He was buried, as his poem had directed, near Sligo, "under Ben Bulben."

The Song of the Happy Shepherd[1]

The woods of Arcady are dead,
And over is their antique joy;

---

1. Originally the epilogue to Yeats's early play, *The Island of Statues,* in which the shepherdess Naschina finds Arcady, a terrestrial paradise of shepherds and shepherdesses ruled by Pan.

Of old the world on dreaming fed;
Gray Truth[2] is now her painted toy;
Yet still she turns her restless head: 5
But O, sick children of the world,
Of all the many changing things
In dreary dancing past us whirled,
To the cracked tune that Chronos[3] sings,
Words alone are certain good.   10
Where are now the warring kings,
Word be-mockers?—By the Rood[4]
Where are now the warring kings?
An idle word is now their glory,
By the stammering schoolboy said,   15
Reading some entangled story:
The kings of the old time are dead,
The wandering earth herself may be
Only a sudden flaming word,
In clanging space a moment heard,   20
Troubling the endless reverie.

Then no wise worship dusty deeds,
Nor seek; for this is also sooth;[5]
To hunger fiercely after truth,
Lest all thy toiling only breeds   25
New dreams, new dreams; there is no truth
Saving in thine own heart. Seek, then,
No learning from the starry men,
Who follow with the optic glass
The whirling ways of stars that pass—   30
Seek, then, for this is also sooth,
No word of theirs—the cold star-bane
Has cloven and rent their hearts in twain,
And dead is all their human truth.
Go gather by the humming sea   35
Some twisted, echo-harbouring shell,[6]
And to its lips thy story tell,
And they thy comforters will be,
Rewording in melodious guile,
Thy fretful words a little while,   40
Till they shall singing fade in ruth,[7]
And die a pearly brotherhood;
For words alone are certain good:
Sing, then, for this is also sooth.

I must be gone: there is a grave   45
Where daffodil and lily wave,
And I would please the hapless faun,[8]
Buried under the sleepy ground,
With mirthful songs before the dawn.

---

2. Yeats was dismayed, as he indicates in his
Autobiography, by the rationalistic, anti-imagina-
tive atmosphere of his time.
3. Time (Greek).
4. Old word for the cross.

5. Reality.
6. In the original version, this poem was spoken by "a satyr, carrying a sea-shell."
7. Compassion.
8. A deity of fields and herds.

His shouting days with mirth were crowned;   50
And still I dream he treads the lawn,
Walking ghostly in the dew,
Pierced by my glad singing through,
My songs of old earth's dreamy youth:
But ah! she dreams not now; dream thou!   55
For fair are poppies on the brow:
Dream, dream, for this is also sooth.

1889

Down by the Salley Gardens[1]

Down by the salley gardens my love and I did meet;
She passed the salley gardens with little snow-white feet.
She bid me take love easy, as the leaves grow on the tree;
But I, being young and foolish, with her would not agree.

In a field by the river my love and I did stand,   5
And on my leaning shoulder she laid her snow-white hand.
She bid me take life easy, as the grass grows on the weirs;
But I was young and foolish, and now am full of tears.

1889

To the Rose upon the Rood of Time[2]

Red Rose, proud Rose, sad Rose of all my days!
Come near me, while I sing the ancient ways:
Cuhoollin[3] battling with the bitter tide;
The Druid, gray, wood-nurtured, quiet-eyed,
Who cast round Fergus dreams, and ruin untold:[4]   5
And thine own sadness, whereof stars, grown old
In dancing silver sandalled on the sea,
Sing in their high and lonely melody.
Come near, that no more blinded by man's fate,
I find under the boughs of love and hate,   10
In all poor foolish things that live a day,
Eternal beauty wandering on her way.

Come near, come near, come near—Ah, leave me still
A little space for the rose-breath to fill!
Lest I no more hear common things that crave;   15

1. Originally entitled "An Old Song Resung."
Yeats explained that it was "an extension of three
lines sung to me by an old woman at Ballisodare."
Later scholarship indicates that line 2 of the first
stanza and the whole of the last stanza were Yeats's
own, and that he also modified considerably the
other three lines. "Salley" is a variety of willow
tree.
2. The rose, as an image of transfiguration and
fulfillment, is a frequent symbol in Yeats's poetry
of this period. In a note dated 1925, he remarks of
it "that the quality symbolised as The Rose differs
from the Intellectual Beauty of Shelley and of
Spenser in that I have imagined it as suffering with
man and not as something pursued and seen from

afar." The title indicates, and line 12 confirms, that
the rose is here eternal beauty, which flowers from
the cross of time and sacrifice.
3. Cuchulain, the Irish mythological hero. His
name means "Hound of Culain." Yeats intended
this poem to be prefatory to several poems having
to do with "the ancient ways," one of them being
"Cuchulain's Fight with the Sea."
4. Priest of the ancient druidic religion.
According to Yeats's poem "Fergus and the Druid"
he gave King Fergus, in response to the latter's
entreaties, a bag of dreams. These made the king
know everything but feel that he had grown to be
nothing.

The weak worm hiding down in its small cave,
The field mouse running by me in the grass,
And heavy mortal hopes that toil and pass;
But seek alone to hear the strange things said
By God to the bright hearts of those long dead,   20
And learn to chaunt a tongue men do not know.[5]
Come near; I would, before my time to go,
Sing of old Eire[6] and the ancient ways:
Red Rose, proud Rose, sad Rose of all my days.

1892

The Lake Isle of Innisfree[7]

I will arise and go now,[8] and go to Innisfree,
And a small cabin build there, of clay and wattles made;
Nine bean rows will I have there, a hive for the honey bee,
And live alone in the bee-loud glade.

And I shall have some peace there, for peace comes dropping slow,   5
Dropping from the veils of the morning to where the cricket sings;
There midnight's all a glimmer, and noon a purple glow,
And evening full of the linnet's wings.[9]

I will arise and go now, for always night and day
I hear lake water lapping with low sounds by the shore;   10
While I stand on the roadway, or on the pavements gray,
I hear it in the deep heart's core.

1892

When You Are Old[1]

When you are old and gray and full of sleep,
And nodding by the fire, take down this book,
And slowly read, and dream of the soft look
Your eyes had once, and of their shadows deep;

5. If the poet is too caught up in eternal beauty, he may lose touch with the lesser, but still eternity-penetrated, life around him.
6. Ireland.
7. Innisfree, which means "Heather Island" in Irish, is a small island in Lough Gill near Sligo in the west of Ireland. In his *Autobiography* Yeats writes: "I had still the ambition, formed in Sligo in my teens, of living in imitation of Thoreau on Innisfree . . . and when walking through Fleet Street very homesick I heard a little tinkle of water and saw a fountain in a shop-window which balanced a little ball upon its jet, and began to remember lake water. From the sudden remembrance came my poem *Innisfree*, my first lyric with anything in its rhythm of my own music. I had begun to loosen rhythm as an escape from rhetoric and from that emotion of the crowd rhetoric brings, but I only understood vaguely and occasionally that I must for my special purpose use nothing but the common syntax. A couple of years later I would not have written that first line with its conventional archaism—'Arise and go'—nor the inversion in the last stanza."

8. "I will arise and go to my father" (Luke 15:18).
9. An early draft of the poem read as follows:

I will arise and go now and go to the island of
    Innisfree
And live in a dwelling of wattles, of woven wattles and wood-work made.
Nine bean-rows will I have there, a yellow hive
    for the honey-bee,
And this old care shall fade.

There from the dawn above me peace will come
    down dropping slow,
Dropping from the veils of the morning to where
    the household cricket sings;
And noontide there be all a glimmer, and midnight be a purple glow,
And evening full of the linnet's wings.

1. An adaptation from a poem by Pierre Ronsard (1524–1585), which begins: *Quand vous serez bien vieille, au soir à la chandelle* (When you are quite old, in the evening by candle-light).

How many loved your moments of glad grace,   5
And loved your beauty with love false or true;
But one man loved the pilgrim soul in you,
And loved the sorrows of your changing face.

And bending down beside the glowing bars
Murmur, a little sadly, how love fled   10
And paced upon the mountains overhead
And hid his face amid a crowd of stars.

1892

Who Goes with Fergus?[2]

Who will go drive with Fergus now,
And pierce the deep wood's woven shade,
And dance upon the level shore?[3]
Young man, lift up your russet brow,
And lift your tender eyelids, maid,   5
And brood on hopes and fears no more.

And no more turn aside and brood
Upon Love's bitter mystery;
For Fergus rules the brazen cars,[4]
And rules the shadows of the wood,   10
And the white breast of the dim sea
And all dishevelled wandering stars.[5]

1892

The Man Who Dreamed of Faeryland

He stood among a crowd at Drumahair;[6]
His heart hung all upon a silken dress,
And he had known at last some tenderness,
Before earth made of him her sleepy care;
But when a man poured fish into a pile,   5
It seemed they raised their little silver heads,
And sang how day a Druid twilight sheds
Upon a dim, green, well-beloved isle,
Where people love beside star-laden seas;
How Time may never mar their faery vows   10
Under the woven roofs of quicken boughs:
The singing shook him out of his new ease.

He wandered by the sands of Lisadill;[7]
His mind ran all on money cares and fears,
And he had known at last some prudent years   15

---

2. This poem was originally a lyric in Yeats's play, *The Countess Cathleen* (1892).
3. According to one story, King Fergus of Ulster decided to abdicate his throne and live with a few companions in the woods.
4. Chariots.

5. These four lines evoke the four elements of air, earth, water, and fire.
6. A town in County Leitrim.
7. Near Raghly, County Sligo, the demesne of the Gore-Booth family.

Before they heaped his grave under the hill;
But while he passed before a plashy place
A lug-worm with its gray and muddy mouth
Sang how somewhere to north or west or south
There dwelt a gay, exulting, gentle race;   20
And how beneath those three times blessed skies
A Danaan[8] fruitage makes a shower of moons,
And as it falls awakens leafy tunes:
And at that singing he was no more wise.

He mused beside the well of Scanavin,[9]   25
He mused upon his mockers: without fail
His sudden vengeance were a country tale,
Now that deep earth has drunk his body in;
But one small knot-grass growing by the pool
Told where, ah, little, all-unneeded voice!   30
Old Silence bids a lonely folk rejoice,
And chaplet their calm brows with leafage cool;
And how, when fades the sea-strewn rose of day,
A gentle feeling wraps them like a fleece,
And all their trouble dies into its peace: 35
The tale drove his fine angry mood away.

He slept under the hill of Lugnagall;[1]
And might have known at last unhaunted sleep
Under that cold and vapour-turbaned steep,
Now that old earth had taken man and all: 40
Were not the worms that spired about his bones
A-telling with their low and reedy cry,
Of how God leans His hands out of the sky,
To bless that isle with honey in His tones;
That none may feel the power of squall and wave,   45
And no one any leaf-crowned dancer miss
Until He burn up Nature with a kiss:
The man has found no comfort in the grave.

                                              1892

Michael Robartes Bids His Beloved Be at Peace[2]

I hear the Shadowy Horses, their long manes a-shake,
Their hoofs heavy with tumult, their eyes glimmering white;

8. Refers to the mythical people Tuatha De
Danaan, loosely identified with the fairies.
9. A townland in County Sligo.
1. A hill near Ben Bulben, County Sligo.
2. Yeats's elaborate note on this poem in *The
Wind among the Reeds* gave this explanation:
"November, the old beginning of winter, or of the
victory of the Fomor, or powers of death, and dismay, and cold, and darkness, is associated by the
Irish people with the horse-shaped Púcas, who are
now mischievous spirits, but were once Fomorian
divinities. I think that they may have some connection with the horses of Mannannan, who reigned
over the country of the dead, where the Fomorian
Tethra reigned also; and the horses of Mannannan, though they could cross the land as easily as
the sea, are constantly associated with the waves.
Some neo-platonist, I forget who, describes the
sea as a symbol of the drifting indefinite bitterness
of life, and I believe there is like symbolism
intended in the many Irish voyages to the islands
of enchantment, or that there was, at any rate, in
the mythology out of which these stories have been
shaped. I follow much Irish and other mythology,
and the magic tradition, in associating the North
with night and sleep, and the East, the place of
sunrise, with hope, and the South, the place of
the sun when at its height, with passion and desire,
and the West, the place of sunset, with fading and
dreaming things." A reference to the Four Horsemen of the Apocalypse may also be intended.
Michael Robartes, whose name appears in several
poems by Yeats, was a character in some of his
early stories. In later versions of this poem its title
became, "He Bids His Beloved Be at Peace."

The North unfolds above them clinging, creeping night,
The East her hidden joy before the morning break,
The West weeps in pale dew and sighs passing away,   5
The South is pouring down roses of crimson fire:
O vanity of Sleep, Hope, Dream, endless Desire,
The Horses of Disaster plunge in the heavy clay:
Beloved, let your eyes half close, and your heart beat
Over my heart, and your hair fall over my breast,   10
Drowning love's lonely hour in deep twilight of rest,
And hiding their tossing manes and their tumultuous feet.

1899

The Cap and Bells[3]

The jester walked in the garden:
The garden had fallen still;
He bade his soul rise upward
And stand on her window-sill.

It rose in a straight blue garment,   5
When owls began to call:
It had grown wise-tongued by thinking
Of a quiet and light footfall;

But the young queen would not listen;
She rose in her pale night gown;   10
She drew in the heavy casement
And pushed the latches down.

He bade his heart go to her,
When the owls called out no more;
In a red and quivering garment   15
It sang to her through the door.

It had grown sweet-tongued by dreaming,
Of a flutter of flower-like hair;
But she took up her fan from the table
And waved it off on the air.   20

"I have cap and bells" he pondered,
"I will send them to her and die;"
And when the morning whitened
He left them where she went by.

She laid them upon her bosom,   25
Under a cloud of her hair,
And her red lips sang them a love song:
Till stars grew out of the air.[4]

3. Of this poem, Yeats wrote: "I dreamed this story exactly as I have written it, and dreamed another long dream after it, trying to make out its meaning. . . . The poem has always meant a great deal to me, though, as is the way with symbolic poems, it has not always meant quite the same thing. Blake would have said 'The authors are in eternity' . . ."
4. The jester, after first sending the queen the trappings of common romance, finally offers the cap and bells which are his alone, and she, obdurate before the familiar and grandiloquent gifts of heart and soul, yields when the jester sends what is most essential and individual in him. (Ellmann, *The Identity of Yeats*, New York, 1964, p. 251). Yeats used to quote this poem in lectures as "the way to win a woman."

She opened her door and her window,
And the heart and the soul came through,   30
To her right hand came the red one,
To her left hand came the blue.

They set up a noise like crickets,
A chattering wise and sweet,
And her hair was a folded flower   35
And the quiet of love in her feet.

1894

Adam's Curse[5]

We sat together at one summer's end
That beautiful mild woman your close friend
And you and I,[6] and talked of poetry.
I said, "A line will take us hours maybe,
Yet if it does not seem a moment's thought   5
Our stitching and unstitching has been naught.
Better go down upon your marrow bones
And scrub a kitchen pavement, or break stones
Like an old pauper in all kinds of weather;
For to articulate sweet sounds together   10
Is to work harder than all these and yet
Be thought an idler by the noisy set
Of bankers, schoolmasters, and clergymen
The martyrs call the world."

                    That woman then
Murmured with her young voice, for whose mild sake   15
There's many a one shall find out all heartache
In finding that it's young and mild and low.
"There is one thing that all we women know
Although we never heard of it at school,
That we must labour to be beautiful."[7]   20

I said, "It's certain there is no fine thing
Since Adam's fall but needs much labouring.
There have been lovers who thought love should be
So much compounded of high courtesy
That they would sigh and quote with learned looks   25
Precedents out of beautiful old books;
Yet now it seems an idle trade enough."

We sat grown quiet at the name of love.
We saw the last embers of daylight die
And in the trembling blue-green of the sky   30

---

5. When evicted from the Garden of Eden, Adam was cursed by God with a life of pain and hard work (Genesis 3:17–19).
6. Although Yeats deliberately does not name the two women in this poem, they are modeled on Maud Gonne and her sister Kathleen.
7. Kathleen's remark that it was hard work being beautiful is recorded in Maud Gonne's autobiography, *A Servant of the Queen* (1938), p. 328.

A moon, worn as if it had been a shell
Washed by time's waters as they rose and fell
About the stars and broke in days and years.

I had a thought for no one's but your ears;
That you were beautiful and that I strove   35
To love you in the old high way of love;
That it had all seemed happy, and yet we'd grown
As weary hearted as that hollow moon.

                                                           1903

No Second Troy[8]

Why should I blame her that she filled my days
With misery, or that she would of late
Have taught to ignorant men most violent ways,
Or hurled the little streets upon the great,
Had they but courage equal to desire?[9]   5
What could have made her peaceful with a mind
That nobleness made simple as a fire,
With beauty like a tightened bow, a kind
That is not natural in an age like this,
Being high and solitary and most stern?   10
Why, what could she have done, being what she is?
Was there another Troy for her to burn?

                                                           1910

On Hearing that the Students of Our New University Have Joined the Agitation Against Immoral Literature[1]

Where, where but here have Pride and Truth,
That long to give themselves for wage,
To shake their wicked sides at youth
Restraining reckless middle-age?

                                                           1912

Friends

Now must I these three praise—
Three women[2] that have wrought
What joy is in my days:

8. This poem, based upon the unnamed Maud Gonne, who is compared with Helen of Troy, is one of the several poems reshaping Greek legend for contemporary purposes which Yeats wrote in middle life.
9. The reference is to Maud Gonne's revolutionary activities.
1. The "new university" was founded as the Catholic University, but soon became known as the Royal University. In 1908 it was renamed the National University and made the parent body of colleges in Cork, Dublin, Galway, and Maynooth. Yeats has the Dublin students in mind.
2. The first is Lady Gregory (1852–1932), Irish playwright and Yeats's collaborator in the Abbey Theatre; after their meeting in 1896, they shared an interest in folklore and the drama. The second is Olivia Shakespear, a novelist and a cousin of Lionel Johnson; with her Yeats had his first love affair about 1895. The third is Maud Gonne.

One because no thought,
Nor those unpassing cares,   5
No, not in these fifteen
Many-times-troubled years,
Could ever come between
Mind and delighted mind;
And one because her hand   10
Had strength that could unbind
What none can understand,
What none can have and thrive,
Youth's dreamy load, till she
So changed me that I live   15
Labouring in ecstasy.
And what of her that took
All till my youth was gone
With scarce a pitying look?
How could I praise that one?   20
When day begins to break
I count my good and bad,
Being wakeful for her sake,
Remembering what she had,
What eagle look still shows,   25
While up from my heart's root
So great a sweetness flows
I shake from head to foot.

    1912

September 1913[3]

What need you,[4] being come to sense,
But fumble in a greasy till
And add the halfpence to the pence
And prayer to shivering prayer, until
You have dried the marrow from the bone?   5
For men were born to pray and save:
Romantic Ireland's dead and gone,
It's with O'Leary[5] in the grave.

Yet they were of a different kind,
The names that stilled your childish play,   10
They have gone about the world like wind,
But little time had they to pray
For whom the hangman's rope was spun,
And what, God help us, could they save?
Romantic Ireland's dead and gone,   15
It's with O'Leary in the grave.

---

3. Originally entitled "Romance in Ireland (On Reading Much of the Correspondence against the Art Gallery)" and published in the *Irish Times*, September 8, 1913. Sir Hugh Lane had offered to give his valuable collection of French Impressionist paintings to Dublin if the city would build a proper gallery. There was unexpected opposition and he withdrew the gift, though an unwitnessed codicil to his will renewed his benefaction.
4. The new Catholic middle class.
5. John O'Leary (1830–1907) was a heroic nationalist who, after five years' imprisonment and fifteen years' exile, returned to Dublin in 1885. Yeats, then twenty, was one of the young men and women whom O'Leary rallied to the cause of literary nationalism.

Was it for this the wild geese[6] spread
The grey wing upon every tide;
For this that all that blood was shed,
For this Edward Fitzgerald died,   20
And Robert Emmet and Wolfe Tone,[7]
All that delirium of the brave?
Romantic Ireland's dead and gone,
It's with O'Leary in the grave.

Yet could we turn the years again,   25
And call those exiles as they were
In all their loneliness and pain,
You'd cry, 'Some woman's yellow hair
Has maddened every mother's son':
They weighed so lightly what they gave.   30
But let them be, they're dead and gone,
They're with O'Leary in the grave.

                                                                      1913

The Magi

Now as at all times I can see in the mind's eye,
In their stiff, painted clothes, the pale unsatisfied ones
Appear and disappear in the blue depth of the sky
With all their ancient faces like rain-beaten stones,
And all their helms of silver hovering side by side,   5
And all their eyes still fixed, hoping to find once more,
Being by Calvary's turbulence[8] unsatisfied,
The uncontrollable mystery on the bestial floor.[9]

                                                                      1914

A Coat[1]

I made my song a coat
Covered with embroideries
Out of old mythologies
From heel to throat;
But the fools caught it,   5
Wore it in the world's eyes
As though they'd wrought it.
Song, let them take it,
For there's more enterprise
In walking naked.   10

                                                                      1914

6. A widely used name for the Irishmen who, because of the penal laws against Catholics, were forced to go to the continent from 1691 until Catholic Emancipation.
7. Lord Edward Fitzgerald (1763–1798), the Irish rebel and patriot. He joined the United Irishmen to foment a rising but was taken prisoner and died of wounds received in the struggle over his arrest. Robert Emmet (1778–1803), another Irish patriot, and also a member of the United Irishmen, started an unsuccessful rising in 1802, but was captured, tried, and executed. Wolfe Tone (1763–1798) brought a French force to Ireland but was captured and died in prison, perhaps at his own hand, before execution.
8. The human death of Christ by crucifixion.
9. His miraculous birth in the stable at Bethlehem.
1. Yeats was distressed by the feeble imitations of his verse that were becoming current in Dublin.

The Wild Swans at Coole

The trees are in their autumn beauty,
The woodland paths are dry,
Under the October twilight the water
Mirrors a still sky;
Upon the brimming water among the stones   5
Are nine-and-fifty swans.

The nineteenth autumn has come upon me
Since I first made my count;[2]
I saw, before I had well finished,
All suddenly mount   10
And scatter wheeling in great broken rings
Upon their clamorous wings.

I have looked upon those brilliant creatures,
And now my heart is sore.
All's changed since I, hearing at twilight,   15
The first time on this shore,
The bell-beat of their wings above my head,
Trod with a lighter tread.

Unwearied still, lover by lover,
They paddle in the cold   20
Companionable streams or climb the air;
Their hearts have not grown old;
Passion or conquest, wander where they will,
Attend upon them still.

But now they drift on the still water,   25
Mysterious, beautiful;
Among what rushes will they build,
By what lake's edge or pool
Delight men's eyes when I awake some day
To find they have flown away?[3]   30

                                                            1917

An Irish Airman Foresees His Death[4]

I know that I shall meet my fate
Somewhere among the clouds above;
Those that I fight I do not hate,
Those that I guard I do not love;
My country is Kiltartan Cross,[5]   5
My countrymen Kiltartan's poor,
No likely end could bring them loss
Or leave them happier than before.
Nor law, nor duty bade me fight,

---

2. Yeats had made his first long visit to Coole in 1897.
3. When the poem was first published, this stanza came immediately after the second.
4. Lady Gregory's son, Major Robert Gregory, was killed in action on the Italian front on January 23, 1918. This is one of the poems Yeats wrote in his memory.
5. Near Coole.

Nor public men, nor cheering crowds,   10
A lonely impulse of delight
Drove to this tumult in the clouds;
I balanced all, brought all to mind,
The years to come seemed waste of breath,
A waste of breath the years behind   15
In balance with this life, this death.

                                                          1919

Easter 1916[6]

I have met them at close of day
Coming with vivid faces
From counter or desk among grey
Eighteenth-century houses.
I have passed with a nod of the head   5
Or polite meaningless words,
Or have lingered awhile and said
Polite meaningless words,
And thought before I had done
Of a mocking tale or a gibe   10
To please a companion
Around the fire at the club,
Being certain that they and I
But lived where motley is worn:
All changed, changed utterly: 15
A terrible beauty is born.[7]

That woman's days were spent
In ignorant good-will,
Her nights in argument
Until her voice grew shrill.   20
What voice more sweet than hers
When, young and beautiful,
She rode to harriers?[8]
This man had kept a school
And rode our wingèd horse;[9]   25
This other his helper and friend[1]
Was coming into his force;
He might have won fame in the end,
So sensitive his nature seemed,
So daring and sweet his thought.   30
This other man I had dreamed
A drunken, vainglorious lout.[2]

6. Yeats was moved by the Easter Rebellion on April 24, 1916, when republicans seized buildings and a park in the center of Dublin. They were killed or captured by April 29 and the leaders were executed in May.

7. Yeats plays on Easter as the day of Christ's resurrection as well as the day of the Irish insurrection.

8. Countess Markiewicz, née Constance Gore-Booth, (1868–1927) took a prominent part in the rebellion.

9. Patrick Pearse (1879–1916) had founded St. Enda's School for Boys at Rathfarnham, near Dublin. He was the leader of the insurrection. The winged horse is Pegasus, the poet's mythical charger; Pearse wrote verse in Irish and English.

1. Thomas MacDonagh (1878–1916), a poet and dramatist.

2. Major John MacBride, Maud Gonne's husband. He and his wife had separated long since because of his drinking and other alleged offenses.

He had done most bitter wrong
To some who are near my heart,
Yet I number him in the song;   35
He, too, has resigned his part
In the casual comedy;
He, too, has been changed in his turn,
Transformed utterly:
A terrible beauty is born.   40

Hearts with one purpose alone
Through summer and winter seem
Enchanted to a stone
To trouble the living stream.
The horse that comes from the road,   45
The rider, the birds that range
From cloud to tumbling cloud,
Minute by minute they change;
A shadow of cloud on the stream
Changes minute by minute;   50
A horse-hoof slides on the brim,
And a horse plashes within it;
The long-legged moor-hens dive,
And hens to moor-cocks call;
Minute by minute they live: 55
The stone's in the midst of all.

Too long a sacrifice
Can make a stone of the heart.
O when may it suffice?
That is Heaven's part, our part   60
To murmur name upon name,
As a mother names her child
When sleep at last has come
On limbs that had run wild.
What is it but nightfall?   65
No, no, not night but death;
Was it needless death after all?
For England may keep faith
For all that is done and said.[3]
We know their dream; enough   70
To know they dreamed and are dead;
And what if excess of love
Bewildered[4] them till they died?
I write it out in a verse—
MacDonagh and MacBride   75
And Connolly and Pearse
Now and in time to be,
Wherever green is worn,
Are changed, changed utterly:
A terrible beauty is born.   80

1916

---

3. England had promised Home Rule for Ireland.

4. Both "confused" and "made wild."

The Second Coming[5]

Turning and turning in the widening gyre[6]
The falcon cannot hear the falconer;
Things fall apart; the centre cannot hold;
Mere anarchy is loosed upon the world,
The blood-dimmed tide is loosed, and everywhere   5
The ceremony of innocence is drowned;
The best lack all conviction, while the worst
Are full of passionate intensity.

Surely some revelation is at hand;
Surely the Second Coming is at hand.   10
The Second Coming! Hardly are those words out
When a vast image out of *Spiritus Mundi*[7]
Troubles my sight: somewhere in sands of the desert
A shape with lion body and the head of a man,[8]
A gaze blank and pitiless as the sun,   15
Is moving its slow thighs, while all about it
Reel shadows of the indignant desert birds.
The darkness drops again; but now I know
That twenty centuries[9] of stony sleep
Were vexed to nightmare by a rocking cradle[1]   20
And what rough beast, its hour come round at last,
Slouches toward Bethlehem[2] to be born?

                                                      1921

A Prayer for My Daughter[3]

Once more the storm is howling, and half hid
Under this cradle-hood and coverlid
My child sleeps on. There is no obstacle
But Gregory's wood[4] and one bare hill
Whereby the haystack- and roof-levelling wind,   5
Bred on the Atlantic, can be stayed;
And for an hour I have walked and prayed
Because of the great gloom that is in my mind.

---

5. Written in January 1919, this poem reflects Yeats's attitude toward the Black and Tan War in Ireland, when British auxiliary troops were sent in to put down the republicans. The title fuses Christ's prediction of his second coming in Matthew 24 and John's vision of the coming of the Beast of the Apocalypse, or Antichrist (1 John 2:18). In a letter in 1938 Yeats quoted the poem as evidence that he was not indifferent or callous towards the rise of Fascism: "Every nerve trembles with horror at what is happening in Europe. 'The ceremony of innocence is drowned.'"
6. The motion of the falcon, but Yeats also used two interlocking gyres or cones as symbolic of the conflicting forces in life. In this poem he uses a single gyre which is widening towards its maximum, at which point the age will turn upon itself, there will be violence and a new era. The widening gyre is also expressed by the loss of control or

relation between the falcon, in its circling flight, and the falconer.
7. A Yeats term for a kind of divine inspiration, or a storehouse of images which the poet does not invent but receives.
8. The Egyptian sphinx (unlike the Greek) is male.
9. That is, the twenty centuries of Christianity.
1. Of Christ, as if Christianity prepared its own opposite.
2. Christ's birthplace, here ironically made the birthplace of the Antichrist, whose violent cruelty is to dominate the new era.
3. Yeats's daughter was Anne Butler Yeats, born February 26, 1919.
4. Lady Gregory's wood at Coole, not far from the tower, Thoor Ballylee, where Yeats was then living.

I have walked and prayed for this young child an hour
And heard the sea-wind scream upon the tower,   10
And under the arches of the bridge, and scream
In the elms above the flooded stream;
Imagining in excited reverie
That the future years had come,
Dancing to a frenzied drum.   15
Out of the murderous innocence of the sea.

May she be granted beauty and yet not
Beauty to make a stranger's eye distraught,
Or hers before a looking-glass, for such,
Being made beautiful overmuch,   20
Consider beauty a sufficient end,
Lose natural kindness and maybe
The heart-revealing intimacy
That chooses right, and never find a friend.

Helen being chosen found life flat and dull   25
And later had much trouble from a fool,[5]
While that great Queen,[6] that rose out of the spray,
Being fatherless could have her way
Yet chose a bandy-leggèd smith for man.[7]
It's certain that fine women eat   30
A crazy salad with their meat
Whereby the Horn of Plenty is undone.

In courtesy I'd have her chiefly learned;
Hearts are not had as a gift but hearts are earned
By those that are not entirely beautiful;   35
Yet many, that have played the fool
For beauty's very self, has charm made wise,
And many a poor man that has roved,
Loved and thought himself beloved,
From a glad kindness cannot take his eyes.   40

May she become a flourishing hidden tree
That all her thoughts may like the linnet[8] be,
And have no business but dispensing round
Their magnanimities of sound,
Nor but in merriment begin a chase,   45
Nor but in merriment a quarrel.
O may she live like some green laurel
Rooted in one dear perpetual place.

My mind, because the minds that I have loved,
The sort of beauty that I have approved,   50
Prosper but little, has dried up of late,
Yet knows that to be choked with hate
May well be of all evil chances chief.
If there's no hatred in a mind

5. Menelaus, the husband of Helen, whom she deserted in favor of Paris.
6. Venus, born from the sea.
7. Vulcan, the gods' blacksmith, was her husband.
8. A songbird.

Assault and battery of the wind   55
Can never tear the linnet from the leaf.

An intellectual hatred is the worst,
So let her think opinions are accursed.
Have I not seen the loveliest woman[9] born
Out of the mouth of Plenty's horn,   60
Because of her opinionated mind
Barter that horn and every good
By quiet natures understood
For an old bellows full of angry wind?

Considering that, all hatred driven hence,   65
The soul recovers radical innocence
And learns at last that it is self-delighting,
Self-appeasing, self-affrighting,
And that its own sweet will is Heaven's will;
She can, though every face should scowl   70
And every windy quarter howl
Or every bellows burst, be happy still.

And may her bridegroom bring her to a house
Where all's accustomed, ceremonious;
For arrogance and hatred are the wares   75
Peddled in the thoroughfares.
How but in custom and in ceremony
Are innocence and beauty born?
Ceremony's a name for the rich horn,
And custom for the spreading laurel tree.   80

                                                                   1921

Leda and the Swan[1]

A sudden blow: the great wings beating still
Above the staggering girl, her thighs caressed
By the dark webs, her nape caught in his bill,
He holds her helpless breast upon his breast.[2]

Panting

How can those terrified vague fingers push   5
The feathered glory from her loosening thighs?

9. Maud Gonne, whose political attitudes became increasingly militant (and less and less to Yeats's taste).

1. "I wrote Leda and the Swan because the editor of a political review [George Russell] asked me for a poem. I thought, 'After the individualist, demagogic movement, founded by Hobbes and popularized by the Encyclopaedists and the French Revolution, we have a soil so exhausted that it cannot grow that crop again for centuries.' Then I thought, 'Nothing is now possible but some movement from above preceded by some violent annunciation.' My fancy began to play with Leda and the Swan for metaphor, and I began this poem; but as I wrote, bird and lady took such possession of the scene that all politics went out of it, and my friend tells me that his 'conservative readers would

misunderstand the poem' " (Yeats's note). For Yeats Leda's rape by the Swan is the beginning of a new age, as was the annunciation to Mary by the Dove of Christ's conception. According to legend, Leda bore, as a result of her rape by Zeus, two eggs, containing the twins Castor and Pollux, Helen, and Clytemnestra. Helen deserted her husband, King Menelaus, to go with Paris to Troy, and so caused the Trojan War; Clytemnestra became the wife of the Greek king Agamemnon, and after the latter's return from Troy murdered him.

2. A first draft of the first four lines reads: "Now can the swooping godhead have his will / Yet hovers, though her helpless thighs are pressed / By the webbed toes; and that all-powerful bill / Has suddenly bowed her face upon his breast."

And how can body, laid in that white rush,
But feel the strange heart beating where it lies?

A shudder in the loins engenders there
The broken wall, the burning roof and tower   10
And Agamemnon dead.[3]
                    Being so caught up,
So mastered by the brute blood of the air,
Did she put on his knowledge with his power[4]
Before the indifferent beak could let her drop?

                                        1924

Sailing to Byzantium[5]

I

That[6] is no country for old men. The young
In one another's arms, birds in the trees
—Those dying generations—at their song,
The salmon-falls, the mackerel-crowded seas,
Fish, flesh, or fowl, commend all summer long   5
Whatever is begotten, born, and dies.
Caught in that sensual music all neglect
Monuments of unageing intellect.

II

An aged man is but a paltry thing,
A tattered coat upon a stick, unless   10
Soul clap its hands and sing,[7] and louder sing
For every tatter in its mortal dress,
Nor is there singing school but studying[8]
Monuments of its own magnificence;
And therefore I have sailed the seas and come   15
To the holy city of Byzantium.

III

O sages[9] standing in God's holy fire
As in the gold mosaic of a wall,[1]
Come from the holy fire, perne in a gyre,[2]

---

3. The tragic conclusions of the events caused by Leda's daughters are here foreshadowed by the sexual violence.
4. The union of these two qualities would be an attribute of godhead.
5. Byzantium (Constantinople) was for Yeats a kind of city of the soul, especially of the artist's soul; he admired its stylization and assurance. (See also "Byzantium," p. 90.) As he said in *A Vision* (1937, pp. 279–80), he would, if given a month to spend in antiquity, have chosen to spend it in Byzantium, "a little before Justinian opened St. Sophia and closed the Academy of Plato. I think I could find in some little wine-shop some philosophic worker in mosaic who could answer all my questions, the supernatural descending nearer to him than to Plotinus even. . . . I think that in early Byzantium, maybe never before or since in recorded history, religious, aesthetic and practical life were one, that architect and artificers . . . spoke to the multitude and the few alike. The painter, the mosaic worker, the worker in gold and silver, the illuminator of sacred books, were almost

impersonal, almost perhaps without the consciousness of individual design, absorbed in their subject-matter and that the vision of a whole people. They would copy out of old gospel books those pictures that seemed as sacred as the text, and yet weave all into a vast design, the work of many that seemed the work of one, that made building, picture, pattern, metalwork of rail and lamp, seem but a single image. . . ."
6. Ireland, as suggested by the salmon-falls (line 4).
7. William Blake saw the soul of his dead brother rising to heaven, "clapping his hands for joy."
8. That is, but for studying.
9. A deliberate change from saints, as if to secularize the vision.
1. The fire and mosaic are made so indissolubly one that it is impossible to distinguish the metaphor from the thing described.
2. "Perne" refers to the winding or unwinding of thread on a bobbin. The poet asks the sages to whirl down from their timeless setting to his point in time.

And be the singing-masters of my soul.   20
Consume my heart away; sick with desire
And fastened to a dying animal
It knows not what it is; and gather me
Into the artifice of eternity.[3]

IV

Once out of nature I shall never take   25
My bodily form from any natural thing,
But such a form as Grecian goldsmiths make
Of hammered gold and gold enamelling
To keep a drowsy Emperor awake;[4]
Or set upon a golden bough to sing   30
To lords and ladies of Byzantium
Of what is past, or passing, or to come.

1927

Among School Children[5]

I

I walk through the long schoolroom questioning;[6]
A kind old nun in a white hood replies;
The children learn to cipher and to sing,
To study reading-books and history,
To cut and sew, be neat in everything   5
In the best modern way—the children's eyes
In momentary wonder stare upon
A sixty-year-old smiling public man.

II

I dream of a Ledaean body,[7] bent
Above a sinking fire, a tale that she   10
Told of a harsh reproof, or trivial event
That changed some childish day to tragedy—
Told, and it seemed that our two natures blent
Into a sphere from youthful sympathy,
Or else, to alter Plato's parable,[8]   15
Into the yolk and white of the one shell.

III

And thinking of that fit of grief or rage
I look upon one child or t'other there
And wonder if she stood so at that age—
For even daughters of the swan can share   20

3. In a story, "The Tables of the Law," Yeats spoke of "that supreme art which is to win us from life and gather us into eternity like doves into their dove-cots."

4. In a note to this poem, Yeats writes, "I have read somewhere that in the Emperor's palace at Byzantium was a tree made of gold and silver, and artificial birds that sang." Compare also Hans Christian Andersen's story, "The Emperor's Nightingale," about a mechanical bird.

5. Yeats wrote in a notebook, about March 14, 1926: "Topic for poem—School children and the thought that life will waste them perhaps that no possible life can fulfill our dreams or even their teacher's hope. Bring in the old thought that life prepares for what never happens."

6. Yeats, as part of his work in the Irish Senate, visited some schools.

7. A body like Leda's, the lover of Zeus. (See "Leda and the Swan," p. 85.) Yeats has Maud Gonne in mind, though he does not name her.

8. In Plato's *Symposium*, it is suggested that man was originally both male and female, but fell into division, and that the resulting two beings come together and embrace each other to become one again.

Something of every paddler's heritage—
And had that colour upon cheek or hair,
And thereupon my heart is driven wild:
She stands before me as a living child.

IV

Her present image[9] floats into the mind—   25
Did Quattrocento finger[1] fashion it
Hollow of cheek as though it drank the wind
And took a mess of shadows[2] for its meat?
And I though never of Ledaean kind
Had pretty plumage once—enough of that,   30
Better to smile on all that smile, and show
There is a comfortable kind of old scarecrow.

V

What youthful mother, a shape[3] upon her lap
Honey of generation[4] had betrayed,
And that must sleep, shriek, struggle to escape   35
As recollection or the drug decide,
Would think her son, did she but see that shape
With sixty or more winters on its head,
A compensation for the pang of his birth,
Or the uncertainty of his setting forth?   40

VI[5]

Plato thought nature but a spume that plays
Upon a ghostly paradigm[6] of things;
Solider Aristotle played the taws
Upon the bottom of a king of kings;
World-famous golden-thighed Pythagoras[7]   45
Fingered upon a fiddle-stick or strings
What a star sang and careless muses heard:
Old clothes upon old sticks to scare a bird.

VII

Both nuns and mothers worship images,
But those the candles light are not as those   50
That animate a mother's reveries,
But keep a marble or a bronze repose.

---

9. In old age, Maud Gonne was thin and almost skeletal.

1. That is, the skill of a fifteenth-century Italian painter.

2. "Esau selleth his birthright for a mess of pottage" (chapter heading to Genesis 25 in the Geneva Bible).

3. A baby, though the word "shape" is intentionally vague.

4. The pleasure of sexual intercourse. Yeats's note says, "I have taken the 'honey of generation' from Porphyry's essay on 'The Cave of the Nymphs,' but find no warrant in Porphyry for considering it the 'drug' that destroys the 'recollection' of prenatal freedom. He blamed a cup of oblivion given in the zodiacal sign of Cancer." Porphyry (233–c.304), a Neoplatonist philosopher, tried to explain the soul's passage from the blissful state of eternity into the prison of time.

5. On September 24, 1926, Yeats wrote Mrs. Olivia Shakespear, "Here is a fragment of my last curse upon old age. It means that even the greatest men are owls, scarecrows, by the time their fame has come. Aristotle, remember, was Alexander's tutor, hence the taws (form of birch). [Yeats then quotes a slightly earlier version of stanza VI.] Pythagoras made some measurement of the intervals between notes on a stretched string. It is a poem of seven or eight similar verses" (*Letters*, p. 719). Plato thought nature merely an image, an imitation of a world that exists elsewhere; Aristotle was "solider" because he regarded this world as the authentic one.

6. Pattern.

7. Iamblichus, in his life of his teacher Pythagoras, said that the philosopher had once shown a friend that he had a golden thigh.

And yet they too break hearts—O Presences
That passion, piety or affection knows,
And that all heavenly glory symbolise—   55
O self-born mockers of man's enterprise;

VIII

Labour is blossoming or dancing where
The body is not bruised to pleasure soul,
Nor beauty born out of its own despair,[8]
Nor blear-eyed wisdom out of midnight oil.   60
O chestnut-tree, great-rooted blossomer,
Are you the leaf, the blossom or the bole?
O body swayed to music, O brightening glance,
How can we know the dancer from the dance?

                                                                 1927

Coole Park and Ballylee, 1931[9]

Under my window-ledge the waters race,
Otters below and moor-hens on the top,
Run for a mile undimmed in Heaven's face
Then darkening through "dark" Raftery's "cellar" drop,
Run underground, rise in a rocky place   5
In Coole demesne, and there to finish up
Spread to a lake and drop into a hole.[1]
What's water but the generated soul?[2]

Upon the border of that lake's a wood
Now all dry sticks under a wintry sun,   10
And in a copse of beeches there I stood,
For Nature's pulled her tragic buskin[3] on
And all the rant's a mirror of my mood:
At sudden thunder of the mounting swan[4]
I turned about and looked where branches break   15
The glittering reaches of the flooded lake.

Another emblem there! That stormy white
But seems a concentration of the sky;
And, like the soul, it sails into the sight
And in the morning's gone, no man knows why;   20
And is so lovely that it sets to right
What knowledge or its lack had set awry,

8. That is, out of despair at its own lack.
9. Coole Park was Lady Gregory's property, and Thoor Ballylee, nearby, was Yeats's. Both are in County Galway, Ireland.
1. In *The Celtic Twilight* Yeats wrote of "dark" (blind) Anthony Raftery: "I talked . . . about a poem in Irish, Raftery, a famous poet, made about her [Mary Lavelle], and how it said, 'there is a strong cellar in Ballylee.' He said the strong cellar was the great hole where the river sank underground, and he brought me to a deep pool, where an otter hurried away under a grey boulder, and told me that many fish came up out of the dark water at early morning 'to taste the fresh water coming down from the hills.' "
2. In *The Celtic Twilight*, Yeats wrote, "Did not the wise Porphyry [the Neoplatonic philosopher] think that all souls come to be born because of water. . . ?"
3. Half-boot worn by actors in Greek tragedies.
4. Yeats wrote his wife on February 3, 1932, "I am turning the introductory verses to Lady Gregory's 'Coole' [a book published by the Cuala Press] into a poem of some length—various sections with more or less symbolic matter. Yesterday I wrote an account of the sudden ascent of a swan—a symbol of inspiration I think."

So arrogantly pure, a child might think
It can be murdered with a spot of ink.

Sound of a stick upon the floor, a sound   25
From somebody that toils from chair to chair;[5]
Beloved books that famous hands have bound,
Old marble heads, old pictures everywhere;
Great rooms where travelled men and children found
Content or joy; a last inheritor[6]   30
Where none has reigned that lacked a name and fame
Or out of folly into folly came.

A spot whereon the founders lived and died
Seemed once more dear than life; ancestral trees,
Or gardens rich in memory glorified   35
Marriages, alliances and families,
And every bride's ambition satisfied.
Where fashion or mere fantasy decrees
We shift about—all that great glory spent—
Like some poor Arab tribesman and his tent.   40

We were the last romantics—chose for theme
Traditional sanctity and loveliness;
Whatever's written in what poets name
The book of the people; whatever most can bless
The mind of man or elevate a rhyme;   45
But all is changed, that high horse[7] riderless,
Though mounted in that saddle Homer rode
Where the swan drifts upon a darkening flood.

                                                                           1932

Byzantium[8]

The unpurged images of day[9] recede;
The Emperor's drunken soldiery are abed;
Night resonance recedes, night-walkers' song
After great cathedral gong;
A starlit or a moonlit dome[1] disdains   5
All that man is,
All mere complexities,
The fury and the mire of human veins.[2]

---

5. Lady Gregory, then in old age.
6. Lady Gregory's son was killed in the First World War, but left a son.
7. Pegasus, symbol of poetry.
8. In Yeats's 1930 Diary he noted, as "subject for a poem," "Describe Byzantium as it is in the system towards the end of the first Christian millennium. A walking mummy. Flames at the street corners where the soul is purified, birds of hammered gold singing in the golden trees, in the harbour [dolphins] offering their backs to the wailing dead that they may carry them to Paradise." In this poem Byzantium is both the city of art and the valley of the blest. (Also see "Sailing to Byzantium," p. 86.)

9. As distinguished from the imaginative images of midnight which are purged.
1. Of the great church of St. Sophia.
2. The first stanza of the poem read in its first draft:

When the emperor's brawling soldiers are abed
The last benighted victims dead or fled—
When silence falls on the cathedral gong
And the drunken harlot's song
A cloudy silence, or a silence lit
Whether by star or moon
I tread the emperor's tower
All my intricacies grown clear and sweet.

Before me floats an image, man or shade,[3]
Shade more than man, more image than a shade;   10
For Hades' bobbin bound in mummy-cloth[4]
May unwind the winding path;[5]
A mouth that has no moisture and no breath
Breathless mouths[6] may summon;
I hail the superhuman;   15
I call it death-in-life and life-in-death.[7]

Miracle, bird or golden handiwork,
More miracle than bird or handiwork,
Planted on the star-lit golden bough,
Can like the cocks of Hades crow,[8]   20
Or, by the moon embittered, scorn aloud
In glory of changeless metal
Common bird or petal
And all complexities of mire or blood.[9]

At midnight on the Emperor's pavement flit   25
Flames that no faggot feeds, nor steel has lit,
Nor storm disturbs, flames begotten of flame,
Where blood-begotten spirits come
And all complexities of fury leave,
Dying into a dance,   30
An agony of trance,
An agony of flame that cannot singe a sleeve.[10]

Astraddle on the dolphin's mire and blood,
Spirit after spirit. The smithies break the flood,
The golden smithies of the Emperor!   35
Marbles of the dancing floor
Break bitter furies of complexity,
Those images that yet
Fresh images beget,
That dolphin-torn, that gong-tormented sea.   40

                                                              1932

Crazy Jane Talks with the Bishop[1]

I met the Bishop on the road
And much said he and I.

---

3. An image would be twice removed from a living man, the shade being intermediate.
4. "Hades' bobbin" is the soul, which winds up the mummy-cloth of experience during life.
5. That is, even in life the soul can communicate with the timeless world.
6. The mouths of the living, enraptured by vision.
7. Such images are dead from the point of view of our life, but under the aspect of eternity it is they that are alive and we who are dead.
8. On Roman tombstones the cock is a herald of rebirth, thus of the continuing cycle of human life.
9. The golden birds are another form of art, which contemns earthly life ("mire or blood").
10. In notes for *A Vision*, Yeats spoke of how the dead are at first subject to destiny, but at a later stage, "the point in the Zodiac where the whirl becomes a sphere once reached, we may escape from the constraint of our nature and that of external things, entering upon a state where all fuel becomes flame, where there is nothing but the state itself, nothing to constrain it or end it. We attain it always in the creation or enjoyment of a work of art. . . . Philosophy has always explained its moment of moments in much the same way; nothing can be added to it, nothing taken away; that all progressions are full of illusion, that everything is born there like a ship in full sail" (quoted in Ellmann, *The Identity of Yeats*, p. 221).
1. Crazy Jane was modeled to some extent upon an old woman named Cracked Mary who lived near Lady Gregory. Yeats used her as a spokeswoman in a group of poems.

"Those breasts are flat and fallen now,
Those veins must soon be dry;
Live in a heavenly mansion,   5
Not in some foul sty."

"Fair and foul are near of kin,
And fair needs foul," I cried.
"My friends are gone, but that's a truth
Nor grave nor bed denied,[2]   10
Learned in bodily lowliness
And in the heart's pride.

"A woman can be proud and stiff
When on love intent;
But Love has pitched his mansion in   15
The place of excrement;[3]
For nothing can be sole or whole
That has not been rent."

1933

Lapis Lazuli[4]

(For Harry Clifton)

I have heard that hysterical[5] women say
They are sick of the palette and fiddle-bow,
Of poets that are always gay,
For everybody knows or else should know
That if nothing drastic is done   5
Aeroplane and Zeppelin[6] will come out,
Pitch like King Billy bomb-balls in[7]
Until the town lie beaten flat.

All perform their tragic play,
There struts Hamlet, there is Lear,   10
That's Ophelia, that Cordelia;
Yet they, should the last scene be there,
The great stage curtain about to drop,
If worthy their prominent part in the play,
Do not break up their lines to weep.   15
They know that Hamlet and Lear are gay;
Gaiety transfiguring all that dread.[8]
All men have aimed at, found and lost;[9]

2. That friends depart is a truth that may be learned from death and also from detumescence.
3. Compare Blake, *Jerusalem:* "For I will make their places of love and joy excrementious."
4. Yeats had received a piece of lapis lazuli "carved by some Chinese sculptor into the semblance of a mountain with temple, trees, paths, and an ascetic and pupil about to climb the mountain." He wrote of it to Dorothy Wellesley: "Ascetic, pupil, hard stone, eternal theme of the sensual east. The heroic cry in the midst of despair. But no, I am wrong, the east has its solutions always and therefore knows nothing of tragedy. It is we, not the east, that must raise the heroic cry" (*Let-* *ters*, pp. 8–9).
5. Because Europe was (in 1936) close to war.
6. The German Zeppelins (dirigibles) seemed at this time to be formidable weapons.
7. King William III, who routed the forces of James II at the Battle of the Boyne in Ireland in 1690. A popular ballad says, "King William he threw his bomb-balls in, / And set them on fire."
8. "The arts are all the bridal chambers of joy" (Yeats, *On the Boiler*, Dublin, 1939, p. 27).
9. Though they die, they complete their images of themselves in death, thus achieving a kind of timeless state. Hamlet, having played his part of Hamlet to the end, is forever Hamlet.

Black out; Heaven blazing into the head:
Tragedy wrought to its uttermost.   20
Though Hamlet rambles and Lear rages,
And all the drop-scenes drop at once
Upon a hundred thousand stages,
It cannot grow by an inch or an ounce.

On their own feet they came, or on shipboard,   25
Camel-back, horse-back, ass-back, mule-back,[1]
Old civilisations put to the sword.
Then they and their wisdom went to rack:
No handiwork of Callimachus,[2]
Who handled marble as if it were bronze,   30
Made draperies that seemed to rise
When sea-wind swept the corner, stands;
His long lamp-chimney shaped like the stem
Of a slender palm, stood but a day;
All things fall and are built again,   35
And those that build them again are gay.

Two Chinamen, behind them a third,
Are carved in lapis lazuli,
Over them flies a long-legged bird,
A symbol of longevity;   40
The third, doubtless a serving-man,
Carries a musical instrument.

Every discoloration of the stone,
Every accidental crack or dent,
Seems a water-course or an avalanche.   45
Or lofty slope where it still snows
Though doubtless plum or cherry-branch
Sweetens the little half-way house
Those Chinamen climb towards, and I
Delight to imagine them seated there;   50
There, on the mountain and the sky,
On all the tragic scene they stare.
One asks for mournful melodies;
Accomplished fingers begin to play.
Their eyes mid many wrinkles, their eyes,   55
Their ancient, glittering eyes, are gay.

                                                               1938

Long-Legged Fly

That civilisation may not sink,
Its great battle lost,
Quiet the dog, tether the pony
To a distant post;
Our master Caesar is in the tent   5

---

1. Egyptians, Arabians, Christians, Moham-
medans.
2. An Athenian sculptor (fifth century B.C.),
believed the first to employ the running borer for
drilling marble.

Where the maps are spread,
His eyes fixed upon nothing,
A hand under his head.
Like a long-legged fly upon the stream
His mind moves upon silence.[3]   10

That the topless towers be burnt
And men recall that face,[4]
Move most gently if move you must
In this lonely place.
She thinks, part woman, three parts a child,   15
That nobody looks; her feet
Practise a tinker shuffle
Picked up on a street.
Like a long-legged fly upon the stream
Her mind moves upon silence.   20

That girls at puberty may find
The first Adam in their thought,
Shut the door of the Pope's chapel,
Keep those children out.
There on that scaffolding reclines   25
Michael Angelo.[5]
With no more sound than the mice make
His hand moves to and fro.
Like a long-legged fly upon the stream
His mind moves upon silence.   30

1939

The Circus Animals' Desertion

I

I sought a theme and sought for it in vain,
I sought it daily for six weeks or so.
Maybe at last, being but a broken man,
I must be satisfied with my heart, although
Winter and summer till old age began   5
My circus animals were all on show,
Those stilted boys, that burnished chariot,
Lion and woman and the Lord knows what.[6]

II

What can I but enumerate old themes?
First that sea-rider Oisin led by the nose   10
Through three enchanted islands,[7] allegorical dreams,

3. Individual actions of men of genius must seem silent, slow, and commonplace, like a fly's movements upon a stream.
4. Of Helen of Troy. Yeats alludes to Marlowe's *Dr. Faustus:* "Was this the face that launched a thousand ships / And burnt the topless towers of Ilium?"
5. Yeats refers to the painting of "The Creation of Man" on the Sistine Chapel ceiling in the Vatican.

6. Yeats alludes to the ancient Irish heroes of his early work ("Those stilted boys") and to the making of an elaborate carriage in his play, *The Unicorn from the Stars.* The lion appears in several poems of Yeats, including "The Second Coming" (p. 83).
7. In "The Wanderings of Oisin," the fairy Niamh leads Oisin to the Islands of Delight, of Many Fears, and of Forgetfulness.

Vain gaiety, vain battle, vain repose,
Themes of the embittered heart, or so it seems,
That might adorn old songs or courtly shows;
But what cared I that set him on to ride,   15
I, starved for the bosom of his faery bride?[8]

And then a counter-truth filled out its play,
The Countess Cathleen[9] was the name I gave it;
She, pity-crazed, had given her soul away,
But masterful Heaven had intervened to save it.   20
I thought my dear must her own soul destroy,
So did fanaticism and hate enslave it,
And this brought forth a dream and soon enough
This dream itself had all my thought and love.

And when the Fool and Blind Man stole the bread   25
Cuchulain fought the ungovernable sea;[1]
Heart-mysteries there, and yet when all is said
It was the dream itself enchanted me:
Character isolated by a deed
To engross the present and dominate memory.   30
Players and painted stage took all my love,
And not those things that they were emblems of.

III

Those masterful images because complete
Grew in pure mind, but out of what began?
A mound of refuse or the sweepings of a street,   35
Old kettles, old bottles, and a broken can,
Old iron, old bones, old rags, that raving slut
Who keeps the till. Now that my ladder's gone,
I must lie down where all the ladders start,
In the foul rag-and-bone shop of the heart.[2]   40

1939

Under Ben Bulben[3]

I

Swear by what the sages spoke
Round the Mareotic Lake
That the Witch of Atlas knew,[4]
Spoke and set the cocks a-crow.

---

8. Niamh. Yeats suggests that it was his own unsatisfied longing for a beloved that led him to write about Oisin.

9. A play, first published in 1892, in which the Countess (modeled on an idealized version of Maud Gonne) sells her immortal soul to save the people of Ireland.

1. An allusion to his play, *On Baile's Strand*, in which Cuchulain, crazed by his discovery that he has killed his son, goes out to do battle with the sea. Yeats implies that the play reflected his own anguish, presumably at losing Maud Gonne.

2. Yeats perhaps intends this line to express a revulsion that is highly qualified, since all his works—as he has said—derive from this source in actuality.

3. Ben Bulben is a mountain near Sligo. Yeats is in fact buried within sight of it, in Drumcliff Churchyard.

4. "The Witch of Atlas" is a poem by Shelley. Yeats, in an essay on Shelley, writes: "When the Witch has passed in her boat from the caverned river, that is doubtless her own destiny, she passes along the Nile 'by Moeris and the Mareotic lakes,' and sees all human life shadowed upon its waters . . . and because she can see the reality of things she is described as journeying 'in the calm depths' of 'the wide lake' we journey over unpiloted." Lake Mareotis, an ancient center of Neoplatonist philosophy, was near Alexandria, Egypt.

Swear by those horsemen,[5] by those women   5
Complexion and form prove superhuman,
That pale, long-visaged company
That air in immortality
Completeness of their passions won;
Now they ride the wintry dawn   10
Where Ben Bulben sets the scene.

Here's the gist of what they mean.

II
Many times man lives and dies
Between his two eternities,
That of race and that of soul,[6]   15
And ancient Ireland knew it all.
Whether man die in his bed
Or the rifle knocks him dead,
A brief parting from those dear
Is the worst man has to fear.   20
Though grave-diggers' toil is long,
Sharp their spades, their muscles strong,
They but thrust their buried men
Back in the human mind again.

III
You that Mitchel's prayer have heard,   25
'Send war in our time, O Lord!'[7]
Know that when all words are said
And a man is fighting mad,
Something drops from eyes long blind,
He completes his partial mind,   30
For an instant stands at ease,
Laughs aloud, his heart at peace.
Even the wisest man grows tense
With some sort of violence
Before he can accomplish fate,   35
Know his work or choose his mate.

IV
Poet and sculptor, do the work,
Nor let the modish painter shirk
What his great forefathers did,
Bring the soul of man to God,   40
Make him fill the cradles right.

Measurement began our might:
Forms a stark Egyptian thought,
Forms that gentler Phidias wrought.
Michael Angelo left a proof   45

---

5. Superhuman beings, like the Sidhe.

6. Yeats wrote Dorothy Wellesley on June 22, 1938, "This is the proposition on which I write: There is now overwhelming evidence that man stands between two eternities, that of his family and that of his soul" (*Letters*, p. 911).

7. John Mitchel (1815–1875), an Irish nationalist. After having been transported to Australia, he escaped to the United States, but returned to Ireland in 1874. Yeats is quoting from Mitchel's *Jail Journal.*

On the Sistine Chapel roof,
Where but half-awakened Adam
Can disturb globe-trotting Madam[8]
Till her bowels are in heat,
Proof that there's a purpose set   50
Before the secret working mind:
Profane perfection of mankind.

Quattrocento[9] put in paint
On backgrounds for a God or Saint
Gardens where a soul's at ease;   55
Where everything that meets the eye,
Flowers and grass and cloudless sky,
Resemble forms that are or seem
When sleepers wake and yet still dream,[1]
And when it's vanished still declare,   60
With only bed and bedstead there,
That heavens had opened.
                    Gyres run on;
When that greater dream had gone
Calvert and Wilson, Blake and Claude,[2]
Prepared a rest for the people of God,   65
Palmer's phrase,[3] but after that
Confusion fell upon our thought.

V

Irish poets, learn your trade,
Sing whatever is well made,
Scorn the sort now growing up   70
All out of shape from toe to top,
Their unremembering hearts and heads
Base-born products of base beds.
Sing the peasantry, and then
Hard-riding country gentlemen,   75
The holiness of monks, and after
Porter-drinkers' randy laughter;
Sing the lords and ladies gay
That were beaten into the clay
Through seven heroic centuries;[4]   80
Cast your mind on other days
That we in coming days may be
Still the indomitable Irishry.

VI

Under bare Ben Bulben's head
In Drumcliff churchyard Yeats is laid.   85

---

8. Compare "Long-Legged Fly," p. 93.
9. Fifteenth-century Italian art.
1. Yeats implies that art, by shaping our images of ourselves and of our loves, affects our children.
2. Edward Calvert (1799–1883) was an English painter and a follower of William Blake. Richard Wilson (1714–1782), an English painter, was a disciple of Claude Lorraine (1600–1682), the French landscape painter.

3. Samuel Palmer (1805–1881), an English landscape painter, said of Blake's illustrations to Virgil, "They are like all this wonderful artist's work, the drawing aside of the fleshly curtain, and the glimpse which all the most holy, studious saints and sages have enjoyed, of the rest which remains to the people of God."
4. Since the conquest of Ireland by the Normans in the twelfth-century reign of Henry II.

An ancestor was rector there
Long years ago,[5] a church stands near,
By the road an ancient cross.
No marble, no conventional phrase;
On limestone quarried near the spot   90
By his command these words are cut:
> *Cast a cold eye*
> *On life, on death.*
> *Horseman,[6] pass by!*

1939

5. Rev. John Yeats (1774–1846), Rector of   evoked at the beginning of the poem, who were
Drumcliff, Sligo.   believed to ride near Ben Bulben.
6. Presumably one of the legendary horsemen

RUDYARD KIPLING
1865–1936

From fairly early in his career as poet and writer of fiction, his readers—both those who enjoyed him and those who did not—have found the works of Kipling difficult to deal with. A survey of Kipling criticism suggests that readers found it hard to decide whether he was a poet to be reckoned with—as we reckon with his near-contemporaries Hardy and Yeats—or whether he was an entertainer and a rabble-rouser, a jingoist, a racist, a reactionary, always ready to write verses calculated to send young men off to be killed. There is a measure of truth in these charges, and yet even his detractors have been distracted by the possibility that in Kipling there is something more and something else, that while many of his poems have the sound of military music, there are others which sound quieter, less overstated, more tender and poignant.

Readers new to Kipling must be reminded that he was a man of his age and culture. Born in India of British parents, he was a child of Empire, and of Empire at a time when it seemed invulnerable. He believed that, on the whole, the citizens of Western Europe had a responsibility to journey east, and teach—by force, if necessary—backward peoples, as they were then called, how they might better their lives. Much evil and some good came from this. Although many of the West who had gone to India and to Africa had gone quite openly for plunder, there were others whose motives were disinterested, even benign, and who, at great personal cost, had tried to make a civilization there, a civilization which combined creatively two vastly different civilizations.

Kipling is a true conservative. He believed in civilization, the ideal of a human community whose model is the city, where there is room for love, truth, and justice, and where the many sorts of mankind go about their tasks. Thus Kipling celebrates the workman at his work, the expert who knows what he is about, be he engineer, mariner, soldier, any one of the precious members of society who devise the machinery of society and keep it going. Kipling is a poet of great imagination—he wrote ghost stories, science fiction, animal fables—and he has as well a sharp, canny eye, an inquisitiveness about people and their inventions, expressed in both his poetry and his prose. The dark side of Kipling's view of civilization comes from his realization that the city is perpetually in danger—besieged from without by hostile tribes, within menaced by betrayers, mendacious and greedy. Constantly Kipling reminds his readers that the social fabric we are inclined to take for granted is fragile and that we must be forever watchful.

Kipling's father Lockwood was married on March 18, 1865, and he and his bride left immediately for India, where he had a post as a resident artist and museum curator; the poet was born in Bombay on December 30 of the same year. For the first years of his life Kipling enjoyed privileges and luxuries as the spoiled child of two cultures. When Kipling was six, his parents decided, following the practice of Anglo-Indians, to send the child and his younger sister back to England, where the climate was thought to be salubrious and where they might be taught that they were in fact English. The two children spent their first English years with a couple who made life a hell on earth. Kipling's eyes were always bad, he was clumsy and defenseless, and he was constantly bullied. This ghastly situation was put to rights when Mrs. Kipling visited her children and noted that when she was about to kiss her son goodnight, he flinched as if to ward off a blow. Rescued by his parents from what he was to call the House of Desolation, Kipling was eventually sent to a distinctly minor public school which turned out to be just the place for him.

When he was seventeen, Kipling returned to India, where he wrote for several newspapers and, on his own, wrote his first poems and short stories. He found himself at the center of a great web of gossip and information about the English in India, and the scandals, comic and tragic, gave Kipling the material he would shape into his poems and stories. Inevitably he often wrote of soldiers—not of generals and viceroys, but of the common soldiers, who, in Housman's words, "saved the sum of things for pay." And he wrote of them using their own vernacular, their own jargon and slang.

In 1889 Kipling returned to England, his works already well known. He quickly made the acquaintance of influential literary people and by age twenty-five, his literary reputation was consolidated. In 1892 he married an American woman, the sister of a dear friend of Kipling's who had recently died. For a time it seemed that Kipling would translate himself permanently to the United States: he and his wife bought property in her hometown, Brattleboro, Vermont, and built a house there. But their neighbors found the Kiplings' way of life a little genteel for Brattleboro tastes, and Kipling had an embarrassing encounter with a drunken lout who happened to be his brother-in-law. Kipling took legal action, reporters descended, and the writer and his wife left the country. Back in England, they bought a country house—a curiously grim and menacing building—and here Kipling spent the rest of his days, though scarcely as a prisoner. He and his family traveled constantly, to Africa, the Orient, and to Canada, but not back to India. He had three children: two girls, one of whom died of an ailment that nearly felled her father, and a son, who died in World War I.

During the Boer War (1900–1902) Kipling was strong in the cause of the English against the Afrikaners, though many of his fellow men of letters were pro-Boer. Kipling had long been suspicious of the Germans, styling them among the "lesser breeds without the law," and so when World War I came, he was at least psychologically prepared. He raised money, in his poems exhorted young men to join the services, believed and retailed every tale of German enormities that he heard. The war brought out a strain of cruelty in Kipling, which is revolting but must also be seen as a source of his power as a writer.

Kipling lived for sixteen years after the Armistice, long enough to see his work go out of fashion, to be treated almost with contempt. He continued to find pleasure in careful work, be it the construction of a water wheel or of a story or poem, and in entertaining small children. He died in 1936, well towards the end of the long afternoon that presaged the Second World War. Kipling and King George V died within days of each other; and it was said, "The King has gone and taken his trumpeter with him."

Danny Deever

"What are the bugles blowin' for?" said Files-on-Parade.[1]
"To turn you out, to turn you out," the Colour-Sergeant said.
"What makes you look so white, so white?" said Files-on-Parade.
"I'm dreadin' what I've got to watch," the Colour-Sergeant said.
  For they're hangin' Danny Deever, you can hear the Dead March play,   5
  The Regiment's in 'ollow square[2]—they're hangin' him to-day;
  They've taken of his buttons off an' cut his stripes[3] away,
  An' they're hangin' Danny Deever in the mornin'.

"What makes the rear-rank breathe so 'ard?" said Files-on-Parade.
"It's bitter cold, it's bitter cold," the Colour-Sergeant said.   10
"What makes that front-rank man fall down?" said Files-on-Parade.
"A touch o' sun, a touch o' sun," the Colour-Sergeant said.
  They are hangin' Danny Deever, they are marchin' of 'im round,
  They 'ave 'alted Danny Deever by 'is coffin on the ground;
  An' 'e'll swing in 'arf a minute for a sneakin' shootin' hound—   15
  O they're hangin' Danny Deever in the mornin'!

" 'Is cot was right-'and cot to mine," said Files-on-Parade.
" 'E's sleepin' out an' far to night," the Colour-Sergeant said.
"I've drunk 'is beer a score o' times, said Files-on-Parade.
" 'E's drinkin' bitter beer[4] alone," the Colour-Sergeant said.   20
  They are hangin' Danny Deever, you must mark 'im to 'is place,
  For 'e shot a comrade sleepin'—you must look 'im in the face;
  Nine 'undred of 'is county[5] an' the Regiment's disgrace,
  While they're hangin' Danny Deever in the mornin'.

"What's that so black agin the sun?" said Files-on-Parade.   25
"It's Danny fightin' 'ard for life," the Colour-Sergeant said.
"What's that that whimpers over'ead?" said Files-on-Parade.
"It's Danny's soul that's passin' now," the Colour-Sergeant said.
  For they're done with Danny Deever, you can 'ear the quickstep play,
  The Regiment's in column, an' they're marchin' us away.   30
  Ho! the young recruits are shakin', and' they'll want their beer to-day,
  After hangin' Danny Deever in the mornin'!

    1892

The Widow at Windsor

  'Ave you 'eard o' the Widow at Windsor
    With a hairy gold crown on 'er 'ead?
  She 'as ships on the foam—she 'as millions at 'ome,
    An' she pays us poor beggars in red.
      (Ow, poor beggars in red!)   5

---

1. Army private. A "Colour-Sergeant" was a high-ranking non-commissioned officer.
2. In this ceremonial formation, the troops line four sides of a parade square and face inwards.
3. Chevrons denoting rank.

4. Or simply "bitter," a favorite variety of beer in British pubs; the grim pun is intentional.
5. English regiments often bear the name of the county from which most of the soldiers have been recruited.

There's 'er nick on the cavalry 'orses,[6]
  There's 'er mark on the medical stores—
An' 'er troopers[7] you'll find with a fair wind be'ind
  That takes us to various wars.
    (Poor beggars!—barbarious wars!)   10
      Then 'ere's to the Widow at Windsor,
        An' 'ere's to the stores an' the guns,
      The men an' the 'orses what makes up the forces
        O' Missis Victorier's sons.
        (Poor beggars! Victorier's sons!)   15

Walk wide o' the Widow at Windsor,
  For 'alf o' Creation she owns:
We 'ave bought 'er the same with the sword an' the flame,
  An' we've salted it down with our bones.
    (Poor beggars!—it's blue with our bones!)   20
Hands off o' the sons o' the Widow,
  Hands off o' the goods in 'er shop,
For the Kings must come down an' the Emperors frown
  When the Widow at Windsor says "Stop!"
    (Poor beggars!—we're sent to say "Stop!")   25
      Then 'ere's to the Lodge o' the Widow,[8]
        From the Pole to the Tropics it runs—
      To the Lodge that we tile with the rank an' the file,
        An' open in form with the guns.
        (Poor beggars!—it's always they guns!)   30

We 'ave 'eard o' the Widow at Windsor,
  It's safest to leave 'er alone:
For 'er sentries we stand by the sea an' the land
  Wherever the bugles are blown.
    (Poor beggars!—an' don't we get blown!)   35
Take 'old o' the Wings o' the Mornin',
  An' flop round the earth till you're dead;
But you won't get away from the tune that they play
  To the bloomin' old rag over'ead.
    (Poor beggars!—it's 'ot over'ead!)   40
      Then 'ere's to the Sons o' the Widow,
        Wherever, 'owever they roam.
      'Ere's all they desire, an' if they require
        A speedy return to their 'ome.
        (Poor beggars!—they'll never see 'ome!)   45
                                                                     1892

Shillin' a Day

My name is O'Kelly, I've heard the Revelly[9]
From Birr to Bareilly, from Leeds to Lahore,

---

6. A "nick" on one of its hooves indicated that a horse belonged to the army and therefore to the queen. Her "mark" was "V.R.I." (*Victoria Regina et Imperatrix*," Victoria, Queen and Empress).
7. Troopships.

8. The queen and her family used lodges in the forest surrounding Windsor castle as country retreats; by extension, here, the British Empire.
9. That is, reveille, trumpet signal to arise in the morning.

Hong-Kong and Peshawur,
Lucknow and Etawah,
And fifty-five more all endin' in "pore."[1]   5
Black Death and his quickness, the depth and the thickness
Of sorrow and sickness I've known on my way,
But I'm old and I'm nervis,
I'm cast from the Service,
And all I deserve is a shillin' a day.[2]   10

> (*Chorus*)   Shillin' a day,
>   Bloomin' good pay—
>   Lucky to touch it, a shillin' a day!

Oh, it drives me half crazy to think of the days I
Went slap for the Ghazi,[3] my sword at my side,   15
When we rode Hell-for-leather
Both squadrons together,
That didn't care whether we lived or we died.
But it's no use despairin', my wife must go charin'[4]
An' me commissairin', the pay-bills to better,   20
So if me you be'old
In the wet and the cold,
By the Grand Metropold,[5] won't you give me a letter?

> (*Full chorus*)   Give 'im a letter—
>   'Can't do no better,   25
>   Late Troop-Sergeant-Major an'—runs with a letter!
>   Think what 'e's been,
>   Think what 'e's seen.
>   Think of his pension an'——
>   GAWD SAVE THE QUEEN!   30

                                                         1892

The Derelict

"And reports the derelict *Margaret Pollock* still at sea."
                                        —Shipping News

I was the staunchest of our fleet
Till the sea rose beneath my feet
Unheralded, in hatred past all measure.
Into his pits he stamped my crew,
Buffeted, blinded, bound and threw,   5
Bidding me eyeless wait upon his pleasure.

1. With the exception of Leeds (in England) and Hong Kong, all the places (including those "ending in 'pore' ") are in India, where the speaker served his army career.
2. That is, his pension; a shilling was then worth about a dollar.
3. Term used by the British for tribal fanatics along the Indian frontier, who committed acts of violence against British officials in the belief that these acts would win them a place in paradise.
4. Or "charring": house-cleaning; "commissairin' " or "commissionairing"; the commissionaires were an organization of pensioned ex-soldiers employed as porters or messengers.
5. Grand Metropole, a swanky London hotel.

Man made me, and my will
Is to my maker still,
Whom now the currents con,[6] the rollers steer—
  Lifting forlorn to spy
  Trailed smoke along the sky,   10
Falling afraid lest any keel come near!

  Wrenched as the lips of thirst,
  Wried, dried, and split and burst,
Bone-bleached my decks, wind-scoured to the graining;   15
  And, jarred at every roll,
  The gear that was my soul
Answers the anguish of my beams' complaining.

  For life that crammed me full,
  Gangs of the prying gull   20
That shriek and scrabble on the riven hatches.
  For roar that dumbed the gale,
  My hawse-pipes[7] guttering wail,
Sobbing my heart out through the uncounted watches.

  Blind in the hot blue ring   25
  Through all my points[8] I swing—
Swing and return to shift the sun anew.
  Blind in my well-known sky
  I hear the stars go by,
Mocking the prow that cannot hold one true.   30

  White on my wasted path
  Wave after wave in wrath
Frets 'gainst his fellow, warring where to send me.
  Flung forward, heaved aside,
  Witless and dazed I bide   35
The mercy of the comber[9] that shall end me.

  North where the bergs careen,
  The spray of seas unseen
Smokes round my head and freezes in the falling.
  South where the corals breed,   40
  The footless, floating weed
Folds me and fouls me, strake on strake[1] upcrawling.

  I that was clean to run
  My race against the sun—
Strength on the deep—am bawd to all disaster;   45
  Whipped forth by night to meet
  My sister's careless feet,
And with a kiss betray her to my master.[2]

6. Steer.
7. Metal cylinders through which a ship's cables run.
8. Of the compass; that is, in all directions.
9. Ocean wave.
1. Plank.
2. Judas betrayed Christ with a kiss.

Man made me, and my will
  Is to my maker still—
To him and his, our peoples at their pier: 50
  Lifting in hope to spy
  Trailed smoke along the sky,
Falling afraid lest any keel come near!

1896

Recessional[3]

God of our fathers, known of old,
  Lord of our far-flung battle-line,
Beneath whose awful Hand we hold
  Dominion over palm and pine—
Lord God of Hosts, be with us yet,   5
Lest we forget—lest we forget!

The tumult and the shouting dies;
  The Captains and the Kings depart:
Still stands Thine ancient sacrifice,
  An humble and a contrite heart.[4]   10
Lord God of Hosts, be with us yet,
Lest we forget—lest we forget!

Far-called, our navies melt away;
  On dune and headland sinks the fire:[5]
Lo, all our pomp of yesterday   15
  Is one with Nineveh and Tyre![6]
Judge of the Nations, spare us yet,
Lest we forget—lest we forget!

If, drunk with sight of power, we loose
  Wild tongues that have not Thee in awe   20
Such boastings as the Gentiles use,
  Or lesser breeds without the Law[7]—
Lord God of Hosts, be with us yet,
Lest we forget—lest we forget!

For heathen heart that puts her trust   25
  In reeking tube and iron shard,
All valiant dust that builds on dust,
  And guarding, calls not Thee to guard,
For frantic boast and foolish word—
Thy mercy on Thy People, Lord!   30

1899, 1903

---

3. Hymn sung as clergy and choir leave the church at the end of the service. Kipling wrote this on the occasion of the Jubilee celebrations in honor of Victoria's sixtieth year as queen, events which had prompted much chauvinistic boasting.
4. "The sacrifices of God are a broken spirit: a broken and a contrite heart, O God, thou wilt not despise" (Psalm 51:17).

5. On Jubilee night, bonfires were lighted all over England.
6. Once capitals of great empires, in Assyria and Phoenicia respectively.
7. "For when the Gentiles, which have not the law, do by nature the things contained in the law, these, having not the law, are a law unto themselves" (Romans 2:14).

The Prodigal Son[8]

WESTERN VERSION

(*Enlarged from* Kim)[9]

Here come I to my own again,
Fed, forgiven and known again,
Claimed by bone of my bone again
And cheered by flesh of my flesh.
The fatted calf is dressed for me,   5
But the husks have greater zest for me.
I think my pigs will be best for me,
So I'm off to the Yards[1] afresh.

I never was very refined, you see,
(And it weighs on my brother's mind, you see)   10
But there's no reproach among swine, d'you see,
For being a bit of a swine.
So I'm off with wallet[2] and staff to eat
The bread that is three parts chaff to wheat,
But glory be!—there's a laugh to it,   15
Which isn't the case when we dine.

My father glooms and advises me,
My brother sulks and despises me,
And Mother catechises me
Till I want to go out and swear.   20
And, in spite of the butler's gravity,
I know that the servants have it I
Am a monster of moral depravity,
And I'm damned if I think it's fair!

I wasted my substance, I know I did,   25
On riotous living,[3] so I did,
But there's nothing on record to show I did
More than my betters have done.
They talk of the money I spent out there—
They hint at the pace that I went out there—   30
But they all forget I was sent out there
Alone as a rich man's son.

So I was a mark for plunder at once,
And lost my cash (can you wonder?) at once,
But I didn't give up and knock under at once.   35
I worked in the Yards, for a spell,
Where I spent my nights and my days with hogs,
And shared their milk and maize[4] with hogs,
Till, I guess, I have learned what pays with hogs
And—I have that knowledge to sell!   40

---

8. Luke 15:11–32 tells the parable of the prodigal son, who left his father's house, spent all he had, and was reduced to eating husks fed to pigs. He finally repented and returned home; his father killed the fatted calf (see line 5) in celebration.
9. Famous novel (1901) by Kipling. Presumably Kipling called his poem a "Western Version" to distinguish it from the biblical—or (near) eastern—version.
1. Stockyards.
2. Traveler's bag or pouch.
3. In Luke 15:13, the "younger son" "wasted his substance with riotous living."
4. That is, corn.

So back I go to my job again,
Not so easy to rob again,
Or quite so ready to sob again
On any neck that's around.
I'm leaving, Pater.   Good-bye to you!   45
God bless you, Mater!⁵   I'll write to you. . . .
I wouldn't be impolite to you,
But, Brother, you *are* a hound!

1901, 1913

A Song to Mithras⁶

HYMN OF THE XXX LEGION: CIRCA A.D. 350

("On the Great Wall"—*Puck of Pook's Hill*)

Mithras, God of the Morning, our trumpets waken the Wall!
"Rome is above the Nations, but Thou art over all!"
Now as the names are answered, and the guards are marched away,
Mithras, also a soldier, give us strength for the day!

Mithras, God of the Noontide, the heather swims in the heat.   5
Our helmets scorch our foreheads, our sandals burn our feet.
Now in the ungirt hour—now lest we blink and drowse,
Mithras, also a soldier, keep us true to our vows!

Mithras, God of the Sunset, low on the Western main—
Thou descending immortal, immortal to rise again!   10
Now when the watch is ended, now when the wine is drawn,
Mithras, also a soldier, keep us pure till the dawn!

Mithras, God of the Midnight, here where the great Bull dies,⁷
Look on Thy children in darkness.   Oh, take our sacrifice!
Many roads Thou hast fashioned—all of them lead to the
      Light!   15
Mithras, also a soldier, teach us to die aright!

1906

The Runes on Weland's Sword⁸

("Old Men at Pevensey"—*Puck of Pook's Hill*)

A Smith makes me
To betray my Man
In my first fight.

5. These Latin words were often used by upper-class English youths for "father" and "mother."

6. Or Mithra, Persian sun god, whose cults spread over most of Europe in the first centuries A.D.; he was especially popular among the legions of the Roman Empire, as the ideal divine companion and warrior. Kipling wrote this song and several others in our selection for his story *Puck of Pook's Hill* (1905), wherein the legendary sprite of the English countryside, Puck, takes two children back to meet figures in early British history. Before the present song, the children have visited a Roman guard of the 300th Legion on the "Great Wall"—or Hadrian's Wall—which had been built across the narrow part of the island in the second century A.D.

7. In Mithraic mythology, Mithras captured and sacrificed a sacred bull, from whose body came all good earthly things.

8. "Old Men at Pevensey" is another chapter in *Puck of Pook's Hill*. Earlier, Puck has told the children about Weland, an old Norse god "who came down in the world" and worked as a blacksmith, or metal worker. "Runes," the ancient Norse alphabet, were supposed to have magical powers. The language and the meter of the poem imitate those of Norse and Old English riddles.

To gather Gold
At the world's end
I am sent.   5

The Gold I gather
Comes into England
Out of deep Water.

Like a shining Fish   10
Then it descends
Into deep Water.

It is not given
For goods or gear,
But for The Thing.   15

The Gold I gather
A king covets
For an ill use.

The Gold I gather
Is drawn up   20
Out of deep Water.

Like a shining Fish
Then it descends
Into deep Water.

It is not given   25
For goods or gear,
But for The Thing.

                                        1906

The Way through the Woods

("Marklake Witches"—*Rewards and Fairies*)[9]

They shut the road through the woods
Seventy years ago.
Weather and rain have undone it again,
And now you would never know
There was once a road through the woods   5
Before they planted the trees.
It is underneath the coppice and heath
And the thin anemones.[1]
Only the keeper sees
That, where the ring-dove broods,   10
And the badgers roll at ease,
There was once a road through the woods,

Yet, if you enter the woods
Of a summer evening late,

---

9. A sequel (1910) to *Puck of Pook's Hill.*
1. Herbal flowers; "coppice": grove of small   trees; "heath": level, uncultivated land.

When the night-air cools on the trout-ringed pools   15
Where the otter whistles his mate,
(They fear not men in the woods,
Because they see so few.)
You will hear the beat of a horse's feet,
And the swish of a skirt in the dew,   20
Steadily cantering through
The misty solitudes,
As though they perfectly knew
The old lost road through the woods. . . .
But there is no road through the woods.   25

1910

The Nurses

("The Bold 'Prentice")[2]

When, with a pain he desires to explain to his servitors, Baby
Howls himself back in the face, toothlessly striving to curse;
And the six-months-old Mother begins to inquire of the Gods if it may be
Tummy, or Temper, or Pins—what does the adequate Nurse?

See!   At a glance and a touch his trouble is guessed; and, thereafter,   5
She juggles (unscared by his throes) with drops of hot water and spoons,
Till the hiccoughs are broken by smiles, and the smiles pucker up into
        laughter,
And he lies o'er her shoulder and crows, and she, as she nurses him,
        croons! . . .

When, at the head of the grade, tumultuous out of the cutting
Pours the belated Express, roars at the night, and draws clear,   10
Redly obscured or displayed by her fire-door's opening and shutting—
Symbol of strength under stress—what does her small engineer?

Clamour and darkness encircle his way.   Do they deafen or blind him?
No!—nor the pace he must keep.   He, being used to these things,
Placidly follows his work, which is laying his mileage behind him,   15
While his passengers placidly sleep, and he, as he nurses her, sings! . . .

When, with the gale at her heel, the ship lies down and recovers—
Rolling through forty degrees, combing the stars with her tops,
What says the man at the wheel, holding her straight as she hovers
On the summits of wind-screening seas; steadying her as she drops?   20

Behind him the blasts without check from the Pole to the Tropic, pursue
        him,
Heaving up, heaping high, slamming home, the surges he must not regard:
Beneath him the crazy wet deck, and all Ocean on end to undo him:
Above him one desperate sail, thrice-reefed but still buckling the yard![3]

2. A story by Kipling; the story and poem were printed next to each other in *Land and Sea Tales*. In collecting his shorter works into books, Kipling often placed a poem or poems next to a short story so that the poem(s) would provide associative commentary. In his introduction to his *Choice of Kipling's Verse*, T. S. Eliot credited Kipling with having invented this kind of juxtaposition.
3. Spar to which sail is tied ("reefed").

Under his hand fleet the spokes[4] and return, to be held or set free again;   25
And she bows and makes shift to obey their behest, till the master-wave
   comes
And her gunnel[5] goes under in thunder and smokes, and she chokes in the
   trough of the sea again—
Ere she can lift and make way to its crest; and he, as he nurses her, hums! . . .

These have so utterly mastered their work that they work without thinking;
Holding three-fifths of their brain in reserve for whatever betide.   30
So, when catastrophe threatens, of colic, collision, or sinking,
They shunt the full gear into train, and take that small thing in their stride.

1919

The Storm Cone[6]

This is the midnight—let no star
Delude us—dawn is very far.
This is the tempest long foretold—
Slow to make head but sure to hold.

Stand by!   The lull 'twixt blast and blast   5
Signals the storm is near, not past;
And worse than present jeopardy
May our forlorn to-morrow be.

If we have cleared the expectant reef,
Let no man look for his relief.   10
Only the darkness hides the shape
Of further peril to escape.

It is decreed that we abide
The weight of gale against the tide
And those huge waves the outer main   15
Sends in to set us back again.

They fall and whelm.   We strain to hear
The pulses of her labouring gear,
Till the deep throb beneath us proves,
After each shudder and check, she moves!   20

She moves, with all save purpose lost,
To make her offing from the coast;
But, till she fetches open sea,
Let no man deem that he is free!

1932

4. That is, of the ship's steering wheel.   6. That is, center of the storm.
5. Or "gunwale," a ship's uppermost planking.

EDGAR LEE MASTERS
1868–1950

The characterization of a small town attracted poets early in this century as a new theme and binding agent for lyrical verse. Edwin Arlington Robinson wrote about his native Gardiner, Maine, under the name of Tilbury Town, and A. E. Housman situated his Shropshire lad in the actual town of Ludlow. Edgar Lee Masters combined an interest in the small town as the place where he had spent his childhood with a novelist's search for individual peculiarities. The technique which proved most important for him was to portray a dead town rather than a live one. After death lives are clarified, delusions are gone and pretensions with them; and if one could write true epitaphs, instead of conventional ones, a whole community might appear as it actually was rather than as it seemed to be. These ideas animated Masters's *Spoon River Anthology*, his one memorable book in a lifetime of writing. It shares that painful realism which was achieved by several writers in the Chicago school of poets and also in the prose of Dreiser and later of Hemingway.

Masters was born on August 23, 1868, in Garnett, Kansas. His family soon moved to Illinois, and he grew up in Lewistown, near Springfield. His childhood was rendered difficult by his father's unsuccess as a lawyer. Masters managed to attend Knox College in Galesburg for a year, but was then obliged by his father to withdraw and study law privately. In 1892 he went to Chicago, and as he struggled for a foothold took a job collecting bills for the Edison Company there, but gradually he built up a successful law practice. For eight years he was a partner of the greatest criminal lawyer and defender of lost causes of the day, Clarence Darrow. Masters shared Darrow's liberal, agnostic, humanitarian outlook.

An early interest in the English Romantic poets, and in Edgar Allen Poe, had not left him, and in the first years of this century he published three books. But more important than what he published was a book he never wrote, a novel he projected in 1906 about people and their interrelationships in a small Illinois town. The idea was revived in 1913 as the result of a fortunate chance. Masters had been submitting conventional poems to William Marion Reedy, the editor of *Reedy's Mirror* in St. Louis. Reedy sent them back, but kept up the acquaintance. Perhaps to wean Masters from Romantic verse, Reedy gave him a copy of J. W. Mackail's *Selected Epigrams from the Greek Anthology*, which had been revised and reissued in 1907. Masters felt the challenge to see what he could do with adapting the mode to modern circumstances. Always an admirer of Whitman, whose biography he was to write, he determined on free verse. His first efforts were perhaps intended as parodic updatings of classical epitaphs, but Reedy received them so enthusiastically that Masters went forward in a burst of creative force. The universality of classical poetry might be blended with the localism of the American Middle West.

Spoon River in the title is the name of an actual river in Illinois, but the town is a combination of Lewistown and Petersburg, where Masters's grandparents lived, and the river itself includes the Saugamon River as well. By virtue of being far removed, in his Chicago office, from the small towns of his childhood, Masters was in a position to scrutinize them with affection and detachment. As the poems came to be written and sometimes published, they were discovered by Harriet Monroe, the editor of *Poetry*. She published some of them and helped Masters to issue them in book form in 1915. *Spoon River Anthology* had an instant and undreamed-of success. Perhaps no book of verse has gone so quickly through so many editions. In part it was because Masters appeared to be laying bare the dark side of small-town life, its suicides, murders, illicit loves. Many of its vignettes have grim stories to tell. But Masters himself emphasized later that the book was organized in terms of hell, purgatory, and heaven (on earth), and began with ne'er-do-wells, moved on to mixed, purgatorial types, and concluded with those who had achieved some illumination.

Masters's later life proved to be anticlimactic. He published thirty-nine books (none destined to last) during the thirty-five years he lived after the *Spoon River Anthology*. There were novels, plays, and even a biography of Lincoln. In 1923 Masters left Chicago and settled, for most of his remaining years, in New York. He died on March 5, 1950, in a convalescent home in Philadelphia.

From *SPOON RIVER ANTHOLOGY*[1]

Elsa Wertman

I was a peasant girl from Germany,
Blue-eyed, rosy, happy and strong.
And the first place I worked was at Thomas Greene's.
On a summer's day when she was away
He stole into the kitchen and took me   5
Right in his arms and kissed me on my throat,
I turning my head.   Then neither of us
Seemed to know what happened.
And I cried for what would become of me.
And cried and cried as my secret began to show.   10
One day Mrs. Greene said she understood,
And would make no trouble for me,
And, being childless, would adopt it.
(He had given her a farm to be still.)
So she hid in the house and sent out rumors,   15
As if it were going to happen to her.
And all went well and the child was born—They were so kind to me.
Later I married Gus Wertman, and years passed.
But—at political rallies when sitters-by thought I was crying
At the eloquence of Hamilton Greene—   20
That was not it.
No!   I wanted to say:
That's my son!   That's my son!

1915

Hamilton Greene

I was the only child of Frances Harris of Virginia
And Thomas Greene of Kentucky,

---

1. The title derives from the *Greek Anthology*, a collection of poems—many of them epitaphs—written by authors from the seventh century B.C. to the tenth century A.D. An epigram on love from a 1906 translation of the anthology reads: "Within my heart Love himself has moulded Heliodora with her lovely voice, the soul of my soul." A sailor's epitaph: "Not dust nor the light weight of a stone, but all this sea that you behold is the tomb of Erasippus; for he perished with his ship, and in some unknown place his bones moulder, and the seagulls alone know them to tell." Another epitaph: "I Dionysius of Tarsus lie here at sixty, having never married; and I would that my father had not."

In an essay in the *American Mercury*, January 1933, Masters wrote: "There are two hundred and forty-four characters in the book, not counting those who figure in the Spooniad and the Epilogue. There are nineteen stories developed by interrelated portraits. Practically every ordinary human occupation is covered except those of the barber, the miller, the cobbler, the tailor and the garage man . . . and all those were depicted later in the *New Spoon River*. What critics overlook when they call the Anthology Zolaesque, and by doing so mean to degrade it, is the fact that when the book was put together in its definitive order . . . the fools, the drunkards, and the failures came first, the people of one-birth minds got second place, and the heroes and the enlightened spirits came last, a sort of Divine Comedy, which some critics were acute enough to point out at once."

Of valiant and honorable blood both.
To them I owe all that I became,
Judge, member of Congress, leader in the State.   5
From my mother I inherited
Vivacity, fancy, language;
From my father will, judgment, logic.
All honor to them
For what service I was to the people!   10

1915

Anne Rutledge[2]

Out of me unworthy and unknown
The vibrations of deathless music;
"With malice toward none, with charity for all."[3]
Out of me the forgiveness of millions toward millions,
And the beneficent face of a nation   5
Shining with justice and truth.
I am Anne Rutledge who sleep beneath these weeds,
Beloved in life of Abraham Lincoln,
Wedded to him, not through union,
But through separation.   10
Bloom forever, O Republic,
From the dust of my bosom!

1915

Lucinda Matlock[4]

I went to the dances at Chandlerville,
And played snap-out at Winchester.
One time we changed partners.
Driving home in the moonlight of middle June,
And then I found Davis.   5
We were married and lived together for seventy years,
Enjoying, working, raising the twelve children,
Eight of whom we lost
Ere I had reached the age of sixty.
I spun, I wove, I kept the house, I nursed the sick,   10
I made the garden, and for holiday
Rambled over the fields where sang the larks,
And by Spoon River gathering many a shell,
And many a flower and medicinal weed—
Shouting to the wooded hills, singing to the green valleys. 15
At ninety-six I had lived enough, that is all,
And passed to a sweet repose.
What is this I hear of sorrow and weariness,
Anger, discontent and drooping hopes?

---

2. Ann Rutledge was a girl Abraham Lincoln knew in New Salem, Illinois. She died at the age of nineteen, and one of Lincoln's biographers insisted that she was the only true love of his life.

3. From Lincoln's Second Inaugural Address, March 4, 1865.
4. Lucinda Matlock was the maiden name of Masters's grandmother.

Degenerate sons and daughters,   20
Life is too strong for you—
It takes life to love Life.

1915

EDWIN ARLINGTON ROBINSON
1869–1935

Edwin Arlington Robinson was born in the same decade as Yeats and, like him, had to change centuries in mid-career. Yeats managed to be at home in both centuries, Robinson in neither; his verse is somewhere between the two. As he said himself, his style had been pretty well formed by the time of his first book, *The Torrent and the Night Before* (1896). He traced himself to Victorian and Romantic predecessors: "When I was younger, I was very much under the influence of Wordsworth and Kipling, but never at all, so far as I am aware, under that of Browning, as many seem to believe."[1] Robinson's language is in fact smoother than Browning's, but a more basic resemblance (in spite of his disclaimer) is their use of dramatic monologues. Robinson invites comparison also with Frost, his junior by a few years; but while Frost presents the same New England landscape, he imposes a more original diction, based upon even greater colloquialism. Frost treated Robinson as a venerable figure, but did not venerate him. To a later writer like T. S. Eliot, for whom a poet's language was the touchstone, Robinson was not important. It does seem that the course of literature was not altered by him, either in diction or otherwise; a humorous gentlemanliness seems to keep him from the final urgencies which great poets successfully achieve. Yet he is very good at what he does, and is altogether a winning figure.

Robinson objected to John Donne for his "rather uninteresting religious enthusiasm" and for his "half-mystical sexual uneasiness." Almost any ideological fervor seems to him unwarranted. Yet, especially in his longer poems, Robinson is addicted to an imagery which reflects an ideology: some gloomy impasse is suddenly (but regularly) broken by the intromission of a saving illumination. This is stored up till the end, there to burst out like Calvinistic grace but unsanctified by Christian thought. Up to this final stage his characters live in a rational world with which they cannot cope; when it is reached, the terms of reference are inexplicably changed, and they are bathed with unearned radiance.

Robinson was born, "with his skin inside out" (as he said), in Head Tide, Maine, on December 22, 1869. At the age of one he was taken by his parents to another small, bleak Maine town, Gardiner. It was here that he spent his childhood, and it was in Gardiner, which he renamed Tilbury Town, that he situated much of his poetry. Robinson had a difficult childhood. He wrote Amy Lowell that at the age of six, as he remembered, he sat in a rocking chair and wondered why he had been born. His life seems to have been singularly lacking in happiness, a matter instead of family ties and low-pitched affections for men and women friends.

In 1890 he formed the ambition to be a writer, as he recounted afterwards with his usual humorous self-deprecation: "I realized finally . . . that I was doomed, or elected, or sentenced for life, to the writing of poetry. . . . I kept the grisly secret to myself. . . . My father died—two years later—without suspecting it. . . ."[2] Or, as he wrote in 1896 to a woman friend, Edith Brower, "My father died four years ago with a quite natural impression that I was a failure, and four months ago my mother

---

1. *Selected Letters of Edwin Arlington Robinson*, New York, 1940, p. 102.

2. Quoted in Chard Powers Smith, *Where the Light Falls*, New York, 1965, p. 105.

followed him—though with a little better opinion of me. . . . What strength I have is the result of tedious and almost intolerable isolation."[3]

Robinson attended Harvard as a special student (rather than a degree candidate) from 1891 to 1893. "Two years at Harvard opened my eyes in many ways," he wrote Miss Brower. "I went there to save myself from going to pieces, and I did it."[4] He committed himself increasingly to literature. He published in 1896, at his own expense ($52), *The Torrent and the Night Before,* and dedicated it with modesty to "any man, woman or critic who will cut the pages." The people to whom he sent copies replied encouragingly. In 1897 he published *The Children of the Night.* Unsuccessful in earning his living in New York by his writing, he took a job as a time-checker in the New York subway system. His next book, *Captain Craig* (1902), exhibited more talent. It came to the notice of President Theodore Roosevelt, who resolved to be of help. He wrote a magazine article in praise of Robinson and found him a sinecure in the New York Custom House. Robinson wrote a friend, "The strenuous man has given me some of the most powerful loafing that has ever come my way."[5] He stayed in the Custom House five years, from 1905 to 1910. The "job" seems to have encouraged him in his drinking, which was a regular habit, though he never started until six o'clock in the evening.

Between 1910 and 1920 Robinson published the three books which established his reputation. During the twenties (and until his death on April 6, 1935) he began to publish a series of long poems, some on Arthurian subjects, some on modern (though scarcely contemporaneous) ones. Whether he wrote of Tristram or of Cavender, his characters were tormented by up-to-date anxieties. These poems continue to have their admirers, but they tend to suffer from the last-minute mysticism already mentioned and from a tendency, hard to understand except in terms of Robinson's stubbornness and isolation, to make every sentence repeat its key words and worry their meaning.

Because these mannerisms are chiefly confined to his longer works, most readers prefer his short lyrics, where in melodious yet intellectual language he offers a deeply felt account of the indignities of living and of its occasional mysterious rewards.

3. *Edwin Arlington Robinson's Letters to Edith Brower,* ed. Richard Cary, Cambridge, Mass., 1968, p. 34.

4. The same, p. 35.
5. *Selected Letters,* p. 62.

Luke Havergal

Go to the western gate, Luke Havergal,
There where the vines cling crimson on the wall,
And in the twilight wait for what will come.
The leaves will whisper there of her, and some,
Like flying words will strike you as they fall;   5
But go, and if you listen she will call.
Go the western gate, Luke Havergal—
Luke Havergal.

No, there is not a dawn in eastern skies
To rift the fiery night that's in your eyes;   10
But there, where western glooms are gathering,
The dark will end the dark, if anything:
God slays Himself with every leaf that flies,
And hell is more than half of paradise.
No, there is not a dawn in eastern skies—   15
In eastern skies.

Out of a grave I come to tell you this,
Out of a grave I come to quench the kiss
That flames upon your forehead with a glow
That blinds you to the way that you must go.   20
Yes, there is yet one way to where she is,
Bitter, but one that faith may never miss.
Out of a grave I come to tell you this—
To tell you this.

There is the western gate, Luke Havergal,   25
There are the crimson leaves upon the wall.
Go, for the winds are tearing them away,—
Nor think to riddle the dead words they say,
Nor any more to feel them as they fall;
But go, and if you trust her she will call.   30
There is the western gate, Luke Havergal—
Luke Havergal.

1896

Supremacy

There is a dear and lonely tract of hell
From all the common gloom removed afar:
A flat, sad land it is, where shadows are,
Whose lorn estate my verse may never tell,
I walked among them and I knew them well: 5
Men I had slandered on life's little star
For churls and sluggards; and I knew the scar
Upon their brows of woe ineffable.

But as I went majestic on my way,
Into the dark they vanished, one by one,   10
Till, with a shaft of God's eternal day,
The dream of all my glory was undone,—
And, with a fool's importunate dismay,
I heard the dead men singing in the sun.

1896

Miniver Cheevy

Miniver Cheevy, child of scorn,
    Grew lean while he assailed the seasons;
He wept that he was ever born,
    And he had reasons.

Miniver loved the days of old   5
    When swords were bright and steeds were prancing;
The vision of a warrior bold
    Would set him dancing.

Miniver sighed for what was not,
    And dreamed, and rested from his labors;   10

He dreamed of Thebes and Camelot,
   And Priam's neighbors.[1]

Miniver mourned the ripe renown
   That made so many a name so fragrant;
He mourned Romance, now on the town,   15
   And Art, a vagrant.

Miniver loved the Medici,[2]
   Albeit he had never seen one;
He would have sinned incessantly
   Could he have been one.   20

Miniver cursed the commonplace
   And eyed a khaki suit with loathing;
He missed the mediæval grace
   Of iron clothing.

Miniver scorned the gold he sought,   25
   But sore annoyed was he without it;
Miniver thought, and thought, and thought,
   And thought about it.

Miniver Cheevy, born too late,
   Scratched his head and kept on thinking;
Miniver coughed, and called it fate,   30
   And kept on drinking.

                                               1910

For a Dead Lady

No more with overflowing light
Shall fill the eyes that now are faded,
Nor shall another's fringe with night
Their woman-hidden world as they did.
No more shall quiver down the days   5
The flowing wonder of her ways,
Whereof no language may requite
The shifting and the many-shaded.

The grace, divine, definitive,
Clings only as a faint forestalling;   10
The laugh that love could not forgive
Is hushed, and answers to no calling;
The forehead and the little ears
Have gone where Saturn keeps the years;[3]
The breast where roses could not live   15
Has done with rising and with falling.

1. Thebes was the setting of many Greek legends, including that of King Oedipus; Camelot was the location of King Arthur's court; Priam was the last king of Troy, and his neighbors included Helen, Aeneas, and Hector.
2. Florentine merchant-princes of the Renaissance who were famous both as powerful rulers and as patrons of the arts.
3. Saturn, or Cronos, the deposed ruler of the gods, was often erroneously associated with time ("Chronos").

The beauty, shattered by the laws
That have creation in their keeping,
No longer trembles at applause,
Or over children that are sleeping;   20
And we who delve in beauty's lore
Know all that we have known before
Of what inexorable cause
Makes Time so vicious in his reaping.

1910

Eros Turannos[4]

She fears him, and will always ask
    What fated her to choose him;
She meets him in his engaging mask
    All reasons to refuse him;
But what she meets and what she fears   5
Are less than are the downward years,
Drawn slowly to the foamless weirs
    Of age, were she to lose him.

Between a blurred sagacity
    That once had power to sound him,   10
And Love, that will not let him be
    The Judas that she found him,
Her pride assuages her almost,
As if it were alone the cost.—
He sees that he will not be lost,   15
    And waits and looks around him.

A sense of ocean and old trees
    Envelops and allures him;
Tradition, touching all he sees,
    Beguiles and reassures him;   20
And all her doubts of what he says
Are dimmed with what she knows of days—
Till even prejudice delays
    And fades, and she secures him.

The falling leaf inaugurates   25
    The reign of her confusion;
The pounding wave reverberates
    The dirge of her illusion;
And home, where passion lived and died,
Becomes a place where she can hide,   30
While all the town and harbor side
    Vibrate with her seclusion.

We tell you, tapping on our brows,
    The story as it should be,—
As if the story of a house   35

4. Love, the tyrant (Greek).

Were told, or ever could be;
We'll have no kindly veil between
Her visions and those we have seen,—
As if we guessed what hers have been,
    Or what they are or would be.   40

Meanwhile we do no harm; for they
    That with a god have striven,
Not hearing much of what we say,
    Take what the god has given;
Though like waves breaking it may be   45
Or like a changed familiar tree,
Or like a stairway to the sea
    Where down the blind are driven.

                                                1916

The Dark Hills

Dark hills at evening in the west,
Where sunset hovers like a sound
Of golden horns that sang to rest
Old bones of warriors under ground,
Far now from all the bannered ways   5
Where flash the legions of the sun,
You fade—as if the last of days
Were fading, and all wars were done

                                                1920

Mr. Flood's Party

Old Eben Flood, climbing alone one night
Over the hill between the town below
And the forsaken upland hermitage
That held as much as he should ever know
On earth again of home, paused warily.   5
The road was his with not a native near;
And Eben, having leisure, said aloud,
For no man else in Tilbury Town to hear:

"Well, Mr. Flood, we have the harvest moon
Again, and we may not have many more;   10
The bird is on the wing, the poet says,
And you and I have said it here before.
Drink to the bird."   He raised up to the light
The jug that he had gone so far to fill,
And answered huskily: "Well, Mr. Flood,   15
Since you propose it, I believe I will."

Alone, as if enduring to the end
A valiant armor of scarred hopes outworn,
He stood there in the middle of the road

Like Roland's ghost winding a silent horn.[5]   20
Below him, in the town among the trees,
Where friends of other days had honored him,
A phantom salutation of the dead
Rang thinly till old Eben's eyes were dim.

Then, as a mother lays her sleeping child   25
Down tenderly, fearing it may awake,
He set the jug down slowly at his feet
With trembling care, knowing that most things break;
And only when assured that on firm earth
It stood, as the uncertain lives of men   30
Assuredly did not, he paced away,
And with his hand extended paused again:

"Well, Mr. Flood, we have not met like this
In a long time; and many a change has come
To both of us, I fear, since last it was   35
We had a drop together.   Welcome home!"
Convivially returning with himself,
Again he raised the jug up to the light;
And with an acquiescent quaver said:
"Well, Mr. Flood, if you insist, I might.   40

"Only a very little, Mr. Flood—
For auld lang syne.   No more, sir; that will do."
So, for the time, apparently it did,
And Eben evidently thought so too;
For soon amid the silver loneliness   45
Of night he lifted up his voice and sang,
Secure, with only two moons listening,
Until the whole harmonious landscape rang—

"For auld lang syne."   The weary throat gave out,
The last word wavered, and the song was done.   50
He raised again the jug regretfully
And shook his head, and was again alone.
There was not much that was ahead of him,
And there was nothing in the town below—
Where strangers would have shut the many doors   55
That many friends had opened long ago.

                                                                      1920

The Sheaves

Where long the shadows of the wind had rolled,
Green wheat was yielding to the change assigned;
And as by some vast magic undivined
The world was turning slowly into gold.
Like nothing that was ever bought or sold   5

5. In the *Chanson de Roland,* a medieval French poem, Roland and the soldiers under his command
were trapped and killed in a battle at the mountain pass of Roncevaux. He refused to blow his horn, the
signal for help from Charlemagne's army, until the moment of his death.

It waited there, the body and the mind;
And with a mighty meaning of a kind
That tells the more the more it is not told.

So in a land where all days are not fair,
Fair days went on till on another day   10
A thousand golden sheaves were lying there,
Shining and still, but not for long to stay—
As if a thousand girls with golden hair
Might rise from where they slept and go away.

                                                           1925

ROBERT FROST
1874–1963

Robert Frost wished to be identified with rural New England, especially New Hampshire and Vermont, so that it comes as a surprise to learn that he was born and lived to the age of eleven in San Francisco, and that he spent his high school years in a Massachusetts mill town, not a farm center. He presented himself in many of his poems—which are almost always in the first person—as building soil, chopping wood, cleaning out the spring, patching fences, picking apples; he was familiar enough with these activities, but happily was spared the necessity of relying entirely upon them for his livelihood.

In his poems Frost, even as a young man, seemed wise, as if he were expressing the sempiternal processes of nature. In his life he displayed, like most men and women, the pettiness which his verse abjured or overlooked. "I always hold that we get forward as much by hating as by loving," he remarked.[1] This startling statement underlies a poem like "Fire and Ice," and it also suggests Frost's own preference to place himself at the center of extreme situations where he has to struggle midway, to find existence possible amidst challenge.

To Frost composition was a process of letting the poem take over from him; he said in an essay, "The Figure a Poem Makes," that "like a piece of ice on a hot stove the poem must ride on its own melting." But while he often composed poems as extremely compact units, they can hardly be said to escape into impersonality. He planned to call one of his books "Melanism"—meaning dark pigmentation—and since his death critics have discovered darkness to be more prominent a counter-theme to the cheeriness often ascribed to him. It could be said that Frost wished to play the game both ways, evincing despair and then dispelling it by household philosophy or offhandedness. He was convinced that he could always grab the reins just before the horse left the road, yet it is possible to glimpse madness in his sanity. One indication was his conservatism in age after a radical youth; the maintenance of social and political order became equivalent to the retention of control over his own mind. Liberalism became for him a form of insanity, and towards the really insane, such as his sister, Frost was notably hardhearted. Even simple humanitarianism offended him; he could say that he was *enjoying* the First World War, and he discouraged concern for the poor, saying, "I need them in my business."[2] Yet Frost's mainstay is always irony, the art of sustaining the self between extremes, and his balances are precarious.

The image of his father, William Prescott Frost, Jr., kept its hold on him in spite of his father's early death. W. P. Frost was born in New Hampshire, the state to which Robert Frost made his devious way back. William Frost transmitted to his son

---

1. Quoted in Lawrance Thompson, *Robert Frost,* vol. 2, New York, 1970, p. 120.   2. Thompson, vol. 2, p. 102.

an appetite for fighting. In the father's case, this had to be satisfied in political battles, though in adolescence he had dreamed of military glory and had applied for admission to West Point. Turned down, he enrolled instead at Harvard. Following his degree with honors, William Frost determined to go west, but to earn money for a year first as headmaster at a small private school in Pennsylvania. The school had only one other teacher, Isabelle Moodie, a woman six years older than himself, whom he courted and married.

Isabelle Moodie had been brought over, at the age of nine, from her native Scotland to live in the house of a rich uncle in Columbus, Ohio. She was an ardent Swedenborgian, and her religion affected her son, though it is hard to say how much. Robert Frost found it possible to include God in his poetic scheme, but Swedenborgianism was a more benign creed than his own, which he once referred to as a grafting of Schopenhauer upon Christianity.

A sensitive, mild woman, Isabelle Frost seems to have been bullied a good deal by her husband. She and William Frost threw up their teaching jobs at the end of the school year and went out to San Francisco. He found work on the *San Francisco Bulletin* and spent the rest of his life in journalism, serving on various papers in important posts. It soon became clear that he was a difficult husband; his propensity to drink led to sporadic brutality. He died in 1885.

His instructions were that he be buried in Lawrence, Massachusetts, and his widow discharged this wish and then remained in the East. She found a teaching job in Salem, New Hampshire, but had to give it up after a year because she could not keep discipline. She returned to Lawrence, and her son attended high school there from 1888 to 1892. Robert Frost was an excellent student of classics, and he also began to be known as a poet. In the school another student of equal excellence was Elinor White. The two were co-valedictorians. Frost resolved to marry her, and it was characteristic of his tenacity that he succeeded in doing so in spite of her delays and doubts. He won a scholarship to Dartmouth, and she went to St. Lawrence College. Before a semester was over, Frost had dropped out. It may have been now that he, like the speaker of "The Lockless Door," decided "to hide in the world." He had hoped to persuade Elinor White to marry him at once, but she insisted upon waiting until she had finished college. The ceremony did not occur until 1895.

Frost continued to write poetry while making a living in miscellaneous ways. In 1897 he decided he must have his Harvard education after all, and persuaded the authorities to admit him as a special student (rather than a degree candidate). He was to say in later life that this was a turning-point for him. At Harvard he could try himself against the cultural powers of his time, and he could listen to philosophers like Santayana and James. But again, in March 1899, he withdrew of his own accord. On medical advice he thought he would live in the country, and his grandfather bought him a farm in Derry, New Hampshire. These years, when money was short and family life was especially difficult—the Frosts had five children by 1905 (the first, Elliott, had died in 1900)—were gloomy ones for Frost. He more than once meditated suicide. A lift came when in 1906 he took a teaching job at Pinkerton Academy. During the next five years he reformed its English syllabus, directed plays, and wrote most of the poems later included in his first book.

In 1911 he sold his farm, and the next year marked a second turning-point in his life, when in September 1912 he took ship with his family to Glasgow and then went on to London. The move was perhaps a caprice, but it was a fortunate one. There was little reason to hope that publication of his verse would be any easier in England than in the United States, but a month after his arrival he submitted his poems to the English publisher Alfred Nutt, and they were accepted. A *Boy's Will* was published in 1913 and a second book, *North of Boston*, in 1914.

In England Frost came to know the poets of the time. Ezra Pound introduced him to Yeats, whom he had long admired, and Frost also met imagists like F. S. Flint and Amy Lowell and became friendly with the Georgian poets. Among these last his closest friend was Edward Thomas, in whom he recognized something like an *alter ego*. This pleasant idyll in England was broken into by the war, which forced him to return in 1915 to the United States. There his luck held: the publisher Henry Holt was easily persuaded to publish both his earlier books as well as subsequent ones. Although Frost could not live on his poems, his poetry made him much sought after by colleges and universities. In 1917 he began to teach at Amherst, and he kept up for many years a loose association with this college, intermixed with periods as professor or poet in residence elsewhere.

Frost's personal life was never easy. He demanded great loyalty and was quick to suspect friends of treachery. In 1938 his wife died, and in 1940 a son committed suicide. He was thwarted by never receiving the Nobel Prize, which Yeats and Eliot had both won; the reason may have been his determined provincialism. Nonetheless, he was showered with honors. Perhaps the most conspicuous was, at John F. Kennedy's invitation, to read a poem at the presidential inauguration ceremony in 1961. From being the most unrecognized poet in America during the days of his youth, he had become by far the most recognized. He lived about as long as Thomas Hardy, dying at the age of eighty-eight on January 29, 1963.

The poetry of Frost has some kinship with that of Robinson in its choice of a New England setting and in its attempt to be true to the peculiarities of the region. But Frost's idiom is much less literary, and here he seems to have learned a little from Hardy and from Yeats's peasant plays. But even his earliest poems show a successful striving for utter colloquialism. This did not entail any surrender of form; he prided himself, for all his country accents, on being close to his favorite Latin poet Horace in the way his poems were chiseled out. Free verse was like playing tennis without a net, he said. To secure his effect Frost emptied his verse of any hint of the grand manner; John Crowe Ransom has remarked that he was startled during his own boyhood to discover that Frost's poetry had no kings or queens in it. He prided himself, too, on staying close to earth, and objected to what he called "Platonism" in poetry, an insistence on essence without matter.

Yet his flatness is not so open as it at first appears. He works with *paysages moralisés*, moralized landscapes. "Poetry," he said, "provides the one permissible way of saying one thing and meaning another. People say, 'Why don't you say what you mean?' We never do that, do we, being all of us too much poets. We like to talk in parables and in hints and in indirections—whether from diffidence or some other instinct."[3] At the same time, he is different from other poets who practice obliquity. He is countrified where Wallace Stevens is not; he is conclusive where Williams is not. Unlike Yeats and Eliot, he has almost nothing to say in prose, whether from guardedness or economy, except for some gnomic and highly quotable statements. Aside from long meditative poems, highly charged dramatic monologues, and two masques, he wrote only lyrics. Frost presents, in comparison with other eminent writers of his time, an example of reserve or holding back in genre, diction, theme, and even philosophy, which is impressive but also, as seen after his death by a generation bent on extravagance, cautious. This from time to time bitter and mischief-making man left his readers poems which they quite simply love; and to love a poem by Frost is to begin, at each rereading of a poem, to hear a voice which does not set aside its task to perform before that task has been performed.

3. "Education by Poetry," in Frost, *Selected Prose*, ed. H. Coxe and E. C. Latham, New York, 1956, pp. 36–37.

Mending Wall

Something there is that doesn't love a wall,
That sends the frozen-ground-swell under it,

And spills the upper boulders in the sun;
And makes gaps even two can pass abreast.
The work of hunters is another thing: 5
I have come after them and made repair
Where they have left not one stone on a stone,
But they would have the rabbit out of hiding,
To please the yelping dogs. The gaps I mean,
No one has seen them made or heard them made,   10
But at spring mending-time we find them there.
I let my neighbor know beyond the hill;
And on a day we meet to walk the line
And set the wall between us once again.
We keep the wall between us as we go.   15
To each the boulders that have fallen to each.
And some are loaves and some so nearly balls
We have to use a spell to make them balance:
'Stay where you are until our backs are turned!'
We wear our fingers rough with handling them.   20
Oh, just another kind of outdoor game,
One on a side. It comes to little more:
There where it is we do not need the wall:
He is all pine and I am apple orchard.
My apple trees will never get across   25
And eat the cones under his pines, I tell him.
He only says, 'Good fences make good neighbors.'
Spring is the mischief in me, and I wonder
If I could put a notion in his head:
'Why do they make good neighbors? Isn't it   30
Where there are cows? But here there are no cows.
Before I built a wall I'd ask to know
What I was walling in or walling out,
And to whom I was like to give offense.
Something there is that doesn't love a wall,   35
That wants it down.' I could say 'Elves' to him,
But it's not elves exactly, and I'd rather
He said it for himself. I see him there
Bringing a stone grasped firmly by the top
In each hand, like an old-stone savage armed.   40
He moves in darkness as it seems to me,
Not of woods only and the shade of trees.
He will not go behind his father's saying,
And he likes having thought of it so well
He says again, 'Good fences make good neighbors.'   45

1914

After Apple-Picking[1]

My long two-pointed ladder's sticking through a tree
Toward heaven still,
And there's a barrel that I didn't fill

---

1. "One thing to notice is that but one poem in the book [*North of Boston*] will intone and that is 'After Apple-Picking.' The rest talk." Frost, *Letters*, New York, 1964, pp. 129–30.

Beside it, and there may be two or three
Apples I didn't pick upon some bough.   5
But I am done with apple-picking now.
Essence of winter sleep is on the night,
The scent of apples: I am drowsing off.
I cannot rub the strangeness from my sight
I got from looking through a pane of glass   10
I skimmed this morning from the drinking trough
And held against the world of hoary grass.
It melted, and I let it fall and break.
But I was well
Upon my way to sleep before it fell,   15
And I could tell
What form my dreaming was about to take.
Magnified apples appear and disappear,
Stem end and blossom end,
And every fleck of russet showing clear.   20
My instep arch not only keeps the ache,
It keeps the pressure of a ladder-round.
I feel the ladder sway as the boughs bend.
And I keep hearing from the cellar bin
The rumbling sound   25
Of load on load of apples coming in.
For I have had too much
Of apple-picking: I am overtired
Of the great harvest I myself desired.
There were ten thousand thousand fruit to touch,   30
Cherish in hand, lift down, and not let fall.
For all
That struck the earth,
No matter if not bruised or spiked with stubble,
Went surely to the cider-apple heap   35
As of no worth.
One can see what will trouble
This sleep of mine, whatever sleep it is.
Were he not gone,
The woodchuck could say whether it's like his   40
Long sleep, as I describe its coming on,
Or just some human sleep.

1914

The Road Not Taken[2]

Two roads diverged in a yellow wood,
And sorry I could not travel both

2. According to Lawrance Thompson, this poem was a slightly mocking parody of the behavior of Frost's friend, Edward Thomas (p. 145), who used to choose a direction for their country walks, then, before they had finished, berate himself for not having chosen a different, more interesting way. Frost, says Thompson, did not approve of romantic "sighing over what might have been."
  On the other hand, E. S. Sergeant, in *Robert Frost: The Trial by Existence* (New York, 1960, pp. 87–88), quotes a letter from Frost, written February 10, 1912, in which he describes how, going down a lonely cross-road on a recent evening, he saw someone who "looked for all the world like myself coming down the other, his approach to the point where our paths must intersect being so timed that unless one of us pulled up we must inevitably collide. I felt as if I was going to meet my own image in a slanting mirror. . . . I stood still in wonderment and let him pass by."

And be one traveler, long I stood
And looked down one as far as I could
To where it bent in the undergrowth;   5

Then took the other, as just as fair,
And having perhaps the better claim,
Because it was grassy and wanted wear;
Though as for that the passing there
Had worn them really about the same,   10

And both that morning equally lay
In leaves no step had trodden black.
Oh, I kept the first for another day!
Yet knowing how way leads on to way,
I doubted if I should ever come back.   15

I shall be telling this with a sigh
Somewhere ages and ages hence:
Two roads diverged in a wood, and I—
I took the one less traveled by,
And that has made all the difference.   20

1916

An Old Man's Winter Night

All out-of-doors looked darkly in at him
Through the thin frost, almost in separate stars,
That gathers on the pane in empty rooms.
What kept his eyes from giving back the gaze
Was the lamp tilted near them in his hand.   5
What kept him from remembering what it was
That brought him to that creaking room was age.
He stood with barrels round him—at a loss.
And having scared the cellar under him
In clomping here, he scared it once again   10
In clomping off;—and scared the outer night,
Which has its sounds, familiar, like the roar
Of trees and crack of branches, common things,
But nothing so like beating on a box.
A light he was to no one but himself   15
Where now he sat, concerned with he knew what,
A quiet light, and then not even that.
He consigned to the moon, such as she was,
So late-arising, to the broken moon
As better than the sun in any case   20
For such a charge, his snow upon the roof,
His icicles along the wall to keep;
And slept. The log that shifted with a jolt
Once in the stove, disturbed him and he shifted,
And eased his heavy breathing, but still slept.   25
One aged man—one man—can't keep a house,
A farm, a countryside, or if he can,
It's thus he does it of a winter night.

1916

The Oven Bird

There is a singer everyone has heard,
Loud, a mid-summer and a mid-wood bird,
Who makes the solid tree trunks sound again.
He says that leaves are old and that for flowers
Mid-summer is to spring as one to ten.   5
He says the early petal-fall is past
When pear and cherry bloom went down in showers
On sunny days a moment overcast;
And comes that other fall we name the fall.
He says the highway dust is over all.   10
The bird would cease and be as other birds
But that he knows in singing not to sing.
The question that he frames in all but words
Is what to make of a diminished thing.

1916

Birches

When I see birches bend to left and right
Across the lines of straighter darker trees,
I like to think some boy's been swinging them.
But swinging doesn't bend them down to stay
As ice-storms do. Often you must have seen them   5
Loaded with ice a sunny winter morning
After a rain. They click upon themselves
As the breeze rises, and turn many-colored
As the stir cracks and crazes their enamel.
Soon the sun's warmth makes them shed crystal shells   10
Shattering and avalanching on the snow-crust—
Such heaps of broken glass to sweep away
You'd think the inner dome of heaven had fallen.
They are dragged to the withered bracken by the load,
And they seem not to break; though once they are bowed   15
So low for long, they never right themselves:
You may see their trunks arching in the woods
Years afterwards, trailing their leaves on the ground
Like girls on hands and knees that throw their hair
Before them over their heads to dry in the sun.   20
But I was going to say when Truth broke in
With all her matter-of-fact about the ice-storm
I should prefer to have some boy bend them
As he went out and in to fetch the cows—
Some boy too far from town to learn baseball,   25
Whose only play was what he found himself,
Summer or winter, and could play alone.
One by one he subdued his father's trees
By riding them down over and over again
Until he took the stiffness out of them,   30
And not one but hung limp, not one was left
For him to conquer. He learned all there was
To learn about not launching out too soon

And so not carrying the tree away
Clear to the ground. He always kept his poise 35
To the top branches, climbing carefully
With the same pains you use to fill a cup
Up to the brim, and even above the brim.
Then he flung outward, feet first, with a swish,
Kicking his way down through the air to the ground. 40
So was I once myself a swinger of birches.
And so I dream of going back to be.
It's when I'm weary of considerations,
And life is too much like a pathless wood
Where your face burns and tickles with the cobwebs 45
Broken across it, and one eye is weeping
From a twig's having lashed across it open.
I'd like to get away from earth awhile
And then come back to it and begin over.
May no fate willfully misunderstand me 50
And half grant what I wish and snatch me away
Not to return. Earth's the right place for love:
I don't know where it's likely to go better.
I'd like to go by climbing a birch tree,
And climb black branches up a snow-white trunk 55
Toward heaven, till the tree could bear no more,
But dipped its top and set me down again.
That would be good both going and coming back.
One could do worse than be a swinger of birches.

1916

Range-Finding[3]

The battle rent a cobweb diamond-strung
And cut a flower beside a ground bird's nest
Before it stained a single human breast.
The stricken flower bent double and so hung.
And still the bird revisited her young. 5
A butterfly its fall had dispossessed
A moment sought in air his flower of rest,
Then lightly stooped to it and fluttering clung.
On the bare upland pasture there had spread
O'ernight 'twixt mullein stalks a wheel of thread 10
And straining cables wet with silver dew.
A sudden passing bullet shook it dry.
The indwelling spider ran to greet the fly,
But finding nothing, sullenly withdrew.

1916

---

3. Frost wrote to Amy Lowell, "Would it amuse you to learn that Range Finding belongs to a set of war poems I wrote in time of profound peace (circa 1902)? Most of them have gone the way of waste paper. Range Finding was only saved from going the same way by Edward Thomas who liked it . . . he thought it so good a description of No Man's Land" (*Letters*, p. 220).

The Witch of Coös[4]

I stayed the night for shelter at a farm
Behind the mountain, with a mother and son,
Two old-believers. They did all the talking.

MOTHER. Folks think a witch who has familiar spirits
She could call up to pass a winter evening,   5
But won't, should be burned at the stake or something.
Summoning spirits isn't 'Button, button,
Who's got the button,' I would have them know.

SON. Mother can make a common table rear
And kick with two legs like an army mule.   10

MOTHER. And when I've done it, what good have I done?
Rather than tip a table for you, let me
Tell you what Ralle the Sioux Control[5] once told me.
He said the dead had souls, but when I asked him
How could that be—I thought the dead were souls—   15
He broke my trance. Don't that make you suspicious
That there's something the dead are keeping back?
Yes, there's something the dead are keeping back.

SON. You wouldn't want to tell him what we have
Up attic, mother?   20

MOTHER. Bones—a skeleton.

SON. But the headboard of mother's bed is pushed
Against the attic door: the door is nailed.
It's harmless. Mother hears it in the night
Halting perplexed behind the barrier   25
Of door and headboard. Where it wants to get
Is back into the cellar where it came from.

MOTHER. We'll never let them, will we, son! We'll never!

SON. It left the cellar forty years ago
And carried itself like a pile of dishes   30
Up one flight from the cellar to the kitchen,
Another from the kitchen to the bedroom,
Another from the bedroom to the attic,
Right past both father and mother, and neither stopped it.
Father had gone upstairs; mother was downstairs.   35
I was a baby: I don't know where I was.

MOTHER. The only fault my husband found with me—
I went to sleep before I went to bed,
Especially in winter when the bed

---

4. A county in New Hampshire.
5. A "control" is a ghostly intermediary who, in   spiritualist séances, facilitates the communication
between the medium and the spirits of the dead.

Might just as well be ice and the clothes snow.   40
The night the bones came up the cellar stairs
Toffile had gone to bed alone and left me,
But left an open door to cool the room off
So as to sort of turn me out of it.
I was just coming to myself enough   45
To wonder where the cold was coming from,
When I heard Toffile upstairs in the bedroom
And thought I heard him downstairs in the cellar.
The board we had laid down to walk dry-shod on
When there was water in the cellar in spring   50
Struck the hard cellar bottom. And then someone
Began the stairs, two footsteps for each step,
The way a man with one leg and a crutch,
Or a little child, comes up. It wasn't Toffile:
It wasn't anyone who could be there.   55
The bulkhead double-doors were double-locked
And swollen tight and buried under snow.
The cellar windows were banked up with sawdust
And swollen tight and buried under snow.
It was the bones. I knew them—and good reason.   60
My first impulse was to get to the knob
And hold the door. But the bones didn't try
The door; they halted helpless on the landing,
Waiting for things to happen in their favor.
The faintest restless rustling ran all through them.   65
I never could have done the thing I did
If the wish hadn't been too strong in me
To see how they were mounted for this walk.
I had a vision of them put together
Not like a man, but like a chandelier.   70
So suddenly I flung the door wide on him.
A moment he stood balancing with emotion,
And all but lost himself. (A tongue of fire
Flashed out and licked along his upper teeth.
Smoke rolled inside the sockets of his eyes.)   75
Then he came at me with one hand outstretched,
The way he did in life once; but this time
I struck the hand off brittle on the floor,
And fell back from him on the floor myself.
The finger-pieces slid in all directions.   80
(Where did I see one of those pieces lately?
Hand me my button-box—it must be there.)
I sat up on the floor and shouted, 'Toffile,
It's coming up to you.' It had its choice
Of the door to the cellar or the hall.   85
It took the hall door for the novelty,
And set off briskly for so slow a thing,
Still going every which way in the joints, though,
So that it looked like lightning or a scribble,
From the slap I had just now given its hand.   90
I listened till it almost climbed the stairs
From the hall to the only finished bedroom,
Before I got up to do anything;

Then ran and shouted, 'Shut the bedroom door,
Toffile, for my sake!' 'Company?' he said,   95
'Don't make me get up; I'm too warm in bed.'
So lying forward weakly on the handrail
I pushed myself upstairs, and in the light
(The kitchen had been dark) I had to own
I could see nothing. 'Toffile, I don't see it.   100
It's with us in the room though. It's the bones.'
'What bones?' 'The cellar bones—out of the grave.'
That made him throw his bare legs out of bed
And sit up by me and take hold of me.
I wanted to put out the light and see   105
If I could see it, or else mow the room,
With our arms at the level of our knees,
And bring the chalk-pile down. 'I'll tell you what—
It's looking for another door to try.
The uncommonly deep snow has made him think   110
Of his old song, *The Wild Colonial Boy*,
He always used to sing along the tote road.
He's after an open door to get outdoors.
Let's trap him with an open door up attic.'
Toffile agreed to that, and sure enough,   115
Almost the moment he was given an opening,
The steps began to climb the attic stairs.
I heard them. Toffile didn't seem to hear them.
'Quick!' I slammed to the door and held the knob.
'Toffile, get nails.' I made him nail the door shut   120
And push the headboard of the bed against it.
Then we asked was there anything
Up attic that we'd ever want again.
The attic was less to us than the cellar.
If the bones liked the attic, let them have it.   125
Let them stay in the attic. When they sometimes
Come down the stairs at night and stand perplexed
Behind the door and headboard of the bed,
Brushing their chalky skull with chalky fingers,
With sounds like the dry rattling of a shutter,   130
That's what I sit up in the dark to say—
To no one any more since Toffile died.
Let them stay in the attic since they went there.
I promised Toffile to be cruel to them
For helping them be cruel once to him.   135

SON. We think they had a grave down in the cellar.

MOTHER. We know they had a grave down in the cellar.

SON. We never could find out whose bones they were.

MOTHER. Yes, we could too, son. Tell the truth for once.
They were a man's his father killed for me.   140
I mean a man he killed instead of me.
The least I could do was to help dig their grave.
We were about it one night in the cellar.

Son knows the story: but 'twas not for him
To tell the truth, suppose the time had come.   145
Son looks surprised to see me end a lie
We'd kept all these years between ourselves
So as to have it ready for outsiders.
But tonight I don't care enough to lie—
I don't remember why I ever cared.   150
Toffile, if he were here, I don't believe
Could tell you why he ever cared himself. . . .
She hadn't found the finger-bone she wanted
Among the buttons poured out in her lap.
I verified the name next morning: Toffile.   155
The rural letter box said Toffile Lajway.

                                                                 1923

Fire and Ice

Some say the world will end in fire,
Some say in ice.
From what I've tasted of desire
I hold with those who favor fire.
But if it had to perish twice,   5
I think I know enough of hate
To say that for destruction ice
Is also great
And would suffice.

                                                                 1923

Stopping by Woods on a Snowy Evening

Whose woods these are I think I know.
His house is in the village though;
He will not see me stopping here
To watch his woods fill up with snow.

My little horse must think it queer   5
To stop without a farmhouse near
Between the woods and frozen lake
The darkest evening of the year.

He gives his harness bells a shake
To ask if there is some mistake.   10
The only other sound's the sweep
Of easy wind and downy flake.

The woods are lovely, dark and deep,
But I have promises to keep,
And miles to go before I sleep,   15
And miles to go before I sleep.[6]

                                                                 1923

6. Frost always insisted that the repetition of the line in the last stanza was not supposed to invoke
death but only to imply a somnolent dreaminess in the speaker.

To Earthward

Love at the lips was touch
As sweet as I could bear;
And once that seemed too much;
I lived on air

That crossed me from sweet things   5
The flow of—was it musk
From hidden grapevine springs
Downhill at dusk?

I had the swirl and ache
From sprays of honeysuckle   10
That when they're gathered shake
Dew on the knuckle.

I craved strong sweets, but those
Seemed strong when I was young;
The petal of the rose   15
It was that stung.

Now no joy but lacks salt
That is not dashed with pain
And weariness and fault;
I crave the stain   20

Of tears, the aftermark
Of almost too much love,
The sweet of bitter bark
And burning clove.

When stiff and sore and scarred   25
I take away my hand
From leaning on it hard
In grass and sand,

The hurt is not enough:
I long for weight and strength   30
To feel the earth as rough
To all my length.

                                        1923

Acquainted with the Night

I have been one acquainted with the night.
I have walked out in rain—and back in rain.
I have outwalked the furthest city light.

I have looked down the saddest city lane.
I have passed by the watchman on his beat   5
And dropped my eyes, unwilling to explain.

I have stood still and stopped the sound of feet
When far away an interrupted cry
Came over houses from another street,

But not to call me back or say good-by;   10
And further still at an unearthly height,
One luminary clock against the sky

Proclaimed the time was neither wrong nor right.
I have been one acquainted with the night.

                                                                1928

Two Tramps in Mud Time

Out of the mud two strangers came
And caught me splitting wood in the yard.
And one of them put me off my aim
By hailing cheerily 'Hit them hard!'
I knew pretty well why he dropped behind   5
And let the other go on a way.
I knew pretty well what he had in mind:
He wanted to take my job for pay.

Good blocks of oak it was I split,
As large around as the chopping block;   10
And every piece I squarely hit
Fell splinterless as a cloven rock.
The blows that a life of self-control
Spares to strike for the common good
That day, giving a loose to my soul,   15
I spent on the unimportant wood.

The sun was warm but the wind was chill.
You know how it is with an April day
When the sun is out and the wind is still,
You're one month on in the middle of May.   20
But if you so much as dare to speak,
A cloud comes over the sunlit arch,
A wind comes off a frozen peak,
And you're two months back in the middle of March.

A bluebird comes tenderly up to alight   25
And turns to the wind to unruffle a plume
His song so pitched as not to excite
A single flower as yet to bloom.
It is snowing a flake: and he half knew
Winter was only playing possum.   30
Except in color he isn't blue,
But he wouldn't advise a thing to blossom.

The water for which we may have to look
In summertime with a witching-wand,
In every wheelrut's now a brook,   35

In every print of a hoof a pond.
Be glad of water, but don't forget
The lurking frost in the earth beneath
That will steal forth after the sun is set
And show on the water its crystal teeth.   40

The time when most I loved my task
These two must make me love it more
By coming with what they came to ask.
You'd think I never had felt before
The weight of an ax-head poised aloft,   45
The grip on earth of outspread feet.
The life of muscles rocking soft
And smooth and moist in vernal heat.

Out of the woods two hulking tramps
(From sleeping God knows where last night,   50
But not long since in the lumber camps).
They thought all chopping was theirs of right.
Men of the woods and lumberjacks,
They judged me by their appropriate tool.
Except as a fellow handled an ax,   55
They had no way of knowing a fool.

Nothing on either side was said.
They knew they had but to stay their stay
And all their logic would fill my head:
As that I had no right to play   60
With what was another man's work for gain.
My right might be love but theirs was need.
And where the two exist in twain
Theirs was the better right—agreed.

But yield who will to their separation,   65
My object in living is to unite
My avocation and my vocation
As my two eyes make one in sight.
Only where love and need are one,
And the work is play for mortal stakes,   70
Is the deed ever really done
For Heaven and the future's sakes.

                                            1936

Desert Places

Snow falling and night falling fast, oh, fast
In a field I looked into going past,
And the ground almost covered smooth in snow,
But a few weeds and stubble showing last.

The woods around it have it—it is theirs.   5
All animals are smothered in their lairs.
I am too absent-spirited to count;
The loneliness includes me unawares.

And lonely as it is that loneliness
Will be more lonely ere it will be less—   10
A blanker whiteness of benighted snow
With no expression, nothing to express.

They cannot scare me with their empty spaces
Between stars—on stars where no human race is.
I have it in me so much nearer home   15
To scare myself with my own desert places.

                                            1936

Neither Out Far nor In Deep

The people along the sand
All turn and look one way.
They turn their back on the land.
They look at the sea all day.

As long as it takes to pass   5
A ship keeps raising its hull;
The wetter ground like glass
Reflects a standing gull.

The land may vary more;
But wherever the truth may be—   10
The water comes ashore,
And the people look at the sea.

They cannot look out far.
They cannot look in deep.
But when was that ever a bar   15
To any watch they keep?

                                            1936

Design[7]

I found a dimpled spider, fat and white,
On a white heal-all, holding up a moth
Like a white piece of rigid satin cloth—
Assorted characters of death and blight
Mixed ready to begin the morning right,   5
Like the ingredients of a witches' broth—
A snow-drop spider, a flower like a froth,
And dead wings carried like a paper kite.

7. The original version, entitled "In White," was written early in 1912 and sent in a letter, as Lawrance Thompson points out. It read as follows:

A dented spider like a snowdrop white
On a white Heal-all, holding up a moth
Like a white peace of lifeless satin cloth—
Saw ever curious eye so strange a sight?
Portent in little, assorted death and blight
Like the ingredients of a witches' broth?

The beady spider, the flower like a froth,
And the moth carried like a paper kite.
What had that flower to do with being white,
The blue Brunella every child's delight?
What brought the kindred spider to that height?
(Make we no thesis of the miller's [miller-moth's] plight.)
What but design of darkness and of night?
Design, design! Do I use the word aright?

What had that flower to do with being white,
The wayside blue and innocent heal-all?
What brought the kindred spider to that height,
Then steered the white moth thither in the night?
What but design of darkness to appall?[8]—
If design govern in a thing so small.

1936

Provide, Provide

The witch that came (the withered hag)
To wash the steps with pail and rag,
Was once the beauty Abishag[9],

The picture pride of Hollywood.
Too many fall from great and good
For you to doubt the likelihood.

Die early and avoid the fate.
Or if predestined to die late,
Make up your mind to die in state.

Make the whole stock exchange your own!
If need be occupy a throne,
Where nobody can call *you* crone.

Some have relied on what they knew;
Others on being simply true.
What worked for them might work for you.

No memory of having starred
Atones for later disregard
Or keeps the end from being hard.

Better to go down dignified
With boughten friendship at your side
Than none at all. Provide, provide!

1936

The Bearer of Evil Tidings

The bearer of evil tidings,
When he was halfway there,
Remembered that evil tidings
Were a dangerous thing to bear.

So when he came to the parting
Where one road led to the throne
And one went off to the mountains
And into the wild unknown,

8. Literally, to make pale.
9. A beautiful young woman who nursed King David in his old age.

He took the one to the mountains.
He ran through the Vale of Cashmere,   10
He ran through the rhododendrons
Till he came to the land of Pamir.

And there in a precipice valley
A girl of his age he met
Took him home to her bower,   15
Or he might be running yet.

She taught him her tribe's religion:
How ages and ages since
A princess en route from China
To marry a Persian prince   20

Had been found with child; and her army
Had come to a troubled halt.
And though a god was the father
And nobody else at fault,

It had seemed discreet to remain there   25
And neither go on nor back.
So they stayed and declared a village
There in the land of the Yak.

And the child that came of the princess
Established a royal line,   30
And his mandates were given heed to
Because he was born divine.

And that was why there were people
On one Himalayan shelf;
And the bearer of evil tidings   35
Decided to stay there himself.

At least he had this in common
With the race he chose to adopt:
They had both of them had their reasons
For stopping where they had stopped.   40

As for his evil tidings,
Belshazzar's overthrow,
Why hurry to tell Belshazzar
What soon enough he would know?[1]

                                                        1936

Never Again Would Birds' Song Be the Same

He would declare and could himself believe
That the birds there in all the garden round

---

1. Though Frost uses the names of a real place (Pamir, bounded by Kashmir, Afghanistan, China, and Russia) and a real person (Belshazzar, the last great king of Babylonia), he invented the rest.

From having heard the daylong voice of Eve
Had added to their own an oversound,
Her tone of meaning but without the words.   5
Admittedly an eloquence so soft
Could only have had an influence on birds
When call or laughter carried it aloft.
Be that as may be, she was in their song.
Moreover her voice upon their voices crossed   10
Had now persisted in the woods so long
That probably it never would be lost.
Never again would birds' song be the same.
And to do that to birds was why she came.

1942

The Subverted Flower[2]

She drew back; he was calm:
'It is this that had the power.'
And he lashed his open palm
With the tender-headed flower.
He smiled for her to smile,   5
But she was either blind
Or willfully unkind.
He eyed her for a while
For a woman and a puzzle.
He flicked and flung the flower,   10
And another sort of smile
Caught up like finger tips
The corners of his lips
And cracked his ragged muzzle.
She was standing to the waist   15
In goldenrod and brake,
Her shining hair displaced.
He stretched her either arm
As if she made it ache
To clasp her—not to harm;   20
As if he could not spare
To touch her neck and hair.
'If this has come to us
And not to me alone—'
So she thought she heard him say;   25
Though with every word he spoke
His lips were sucked and blown
And the effort made him choke
Like a tiger at a bone.
She had to lean away.   30
She dared not stir a foot,
Lest movement should provoke
The demon of pursuit
That slumbers in a brute.

2. Based, according to Lawrance Thompson, on an episode during Frost's courtship of Elinor White, who later became his wife.

It was then her mother's call 35
From inside the garden wall
Made her steal a look of fear
To see if he could hear
And would pounce to end it all
Before her mother came. 40
She looked and saw the shame:
A hand hung like a paw,
An arm worked like a saw
As if to be persuasive,
An ingratiating laugh 45
That cut the snout in half,
An eye became evasive.
A girl could only see
That a flower had marred a man,
But what she could not see 50
Was that the flower might be
Other than base and fetid:
That the flower had done but part,
And what the flower began
Her own too meager heart 55
Had terribly completed.
She looked and saw the worst.
And the dog or what it was,
Obeying bestial laws,
A coward save at night, 60
Turned from the place and ran.
She heard him stumble first
And use his hands in flight.
She heard him bark outright.
And oh, for one so young 65
The bitter words she spit
Like some tenacious bit
That will not leave the tongue.
She plucked her lips for it,
And still the horror clung. 70
Her mother wiped the foam
From her chin, picked up her comb,
And drew her backward home.

1942

The Gift Outright

The land was ours before we were the land's.
She was our land more than a hundred years
Before we were her people. She was ours
In Massachusetts, in Virginia,
But we were England's, still colonials, 5
Possessing what we still were unpossessed by,
Possessed by what we now no more possessed.
Something we were withholding made us weak
Until we found out that it was ourselves
We were withholding from our land of living, 10

And forthwith found salvation in surrender.
Such as we were we gave ourselves outright
(The deed of gift was many deeds of war)
To the land vaguely realizing westward,
But still unstoried, artless, unenhanced,   15
Such as she was, such as she would become.

1942

Directive

Back out of all this now too much for us,
Back in a time made simple by the loss
Of detail, burned, dissolved, and broken off
Like graveyard marble sculpture in the weather,
There is a house that is no more a house   5
Upon a farm that is no more a farm
And in a town that is no more a town.
The road there, if you'll let a guide direct you
Who only has at heart your getting lost,
May seem as if it should have been a quarry—   10
Great monolithic knees the former town
Long since gave up pretense of keeping covered.
And there's a story in a book about it:
Besides the wear of iron wagon wheels
The ledges show lines ruled southeast northwest.   15
The chisel work of an enormous Glacier
That braced his feet against the Arctic Pole.
You must not mind a certain coolness from him
Still said to haunt this side of Panther Mountain.
Nor need you mind the serial ordeal   20
Of being watched from forty cellar holes
As if by eye pairs out of forty firkins.
As for the woods' excitement over you
That sends light rustle rushes to their leaves,
Charge that to upstart inexperience.   25
Where were they all not twenty years ago?
They think too much of having shaded out
A few old pecker-fretted apple trees.
Make yourself up a cheering song of how
Someone's road home from work this once was,   30
Who may be just ahead of you on foot
Or creaking with a buggy load of grain.
The height of the adventure is the height
Of country where two village cultures faded
Into each other. Both of them are lost.   35
And if you're lost enough to find yourself
By now, pull in your ladder road behind you
And put a sign up CLOSED to all but me.
Then make yourself at home. The only field
Now left's no bigger than a harness gall.   40
First there's the children's house of make believe,
Some shattered dishes underneath a pine,
The playthings in the playhouse of the children.

Weep for what little things could make them glad.
Then for the house that is no more a house,   45
But only a belilaced cellar hole,
Now slowly closing like a dent in dough.
This was no playhouse but a house in earnest.
Your destination and your destiny's
A brook that was the water of the house,   50
Cold as a spring as yet so near its source,
Too lofty and original to rage.
(We know the valley streams that when aroused
Will leave their tatters hung on barb and thorn.)
I have kept hidden in the instep arch   55
Of an old cedar at the waterside
A broken drinking goblet like the Grail
Under a spell so the wrong ones can't find it,
So can't get saved, as Saint Mark says they mustn't.[3]
(I stole the goblet from the children's playhouse.)   60
Here are your waters and your watering place.
Drink and be whole again beyond confusion.

                                                                    1947

---

3. Frost's allusion is to Mark 4:11–12, in which Jesus says to his disciples: "To you has been given the secret of the kingdom of God, but for those outside everything is in parables; so that they may indeed see but not perceive, and may indeed hear but not understand; lest they should turn again, and be forgiven."

CARL SANDBURG
1878–1967

Carl Sandburg, like Edgar Lee Masters, belonged to a group of writers centered in Chicago who sought to liberate verse from gentility. After Whitman American poetry lost intensity, and at the end of the nineteenth century, except for Robinson (who was just beginning to publish), there were no models capable of satisfying the young. T. S. Eliot, coming a little later, had to go to France for his examples of live poetry. Sandburg took Whitman as his example and America for his subject matter. In part perhaps because he was the child of immigrant parents, he saw with gusto and exaltation what poets of established families took for granted or disparaged.

There can be no doubt that Sandburg helped to blow a new wind into American verse, in part by his very lack of subtlety. He was a sharp observer and an engaged one: he wrote a poem attacking Billy Sunday the evangelist and another defending Sacco and Vanzetti the anarchists. It was a poetry more immediately political and sociological than Whitman's, with a journalistic delight in timeliness, yet honest and unaffected. Sandburg regarded himself as the defender of the people, and expressed their basic drives in two modes, one rough-and-ready, the other tender.

This change necessitated changes in techniques. "It is a time of confusions," he wrote. "Particularly in America is it a period of chaos, in the economic America that hurls forms and images of new designs so rapidly and changefully that artists who honestly relate their own epoch to older epochs understand how art today, if it is to get results, must pierce exteriors and surfaces by ways different from artists of older times."[1] He was in revolt against what he considered "Arrow Collar" literature.[2] Free

1. *The Letters of Carl Sandburg,* ed. Herbert Mitgang, New York, 1968, p. 209.

2. The same, p. 221.

verse and prose were natural media for him as he embraced his countrymen with loose formulations and noble generalities.

Carl Sandburg was born in Galesburg, Illinois, on January 6, 1878. His father and mother had come from Sweden. At first he exhibited little of the tenacity that marked his father's work as a machinist's blacksmith: he left school after the eighth grade and took on all kinds of jobs. When he was twenty the Spanish-American War gave him an opportunity to enlist as a volunteer. He served as a private in Puerto Rico and sent back letters about his army experiences for a Galesburg newspaper. The war ended, he applied to West Point, and would have been appointed if he had not abjectly failed the examinations in grammar and mathematics.

Sandburg now entered Lombard College in Illinois and supported himself by working in the town fire department. At college he distinguished himself by his writing, but he left in 1902 without a degree. The next ten years took him to many places and many jobs. At first he traveled about the country selling stereoscopic photographs. But he also rode the rails, enjoying the company of hobos; on one occasion he was arrested and made to serve ten days in a Pittsburgh jail. His sympathy for underdogs was fixed by such experiences. In 1904 he returned to work for a Galesburg newspaper, and in this year published his first poems under the romantic title *In Reckless Ecstasy*. They were not yet in his mature manner.

Two years later, in 1906, Sandburg saw, at the fortieth anniversary of the Lincoln-Douglas debate in Galesburg, Lincoln's son, Robert Todd Lincoln. This encounter cemented his lifelong interest in the president, which he appeased by writing a four-volume biography. He also wrote a biography of Lincoln's wife. But in the meantime he took other jobs: in 1907 he became assistant editor of *Tomorrow Magazine* in Chicago, and began to do itinerant lecturing on such subjects as Whitman and Bernard Shaw. In 1907–1908 he worked as an organizer for the Social Democratic party and campaigned with Eugene Victor Debs, the presidential candidate. He returned to Chicago and took on a variety of journalistic jobs for the next dozen years until he was able to support himself entirely as a writer.

In 1914 Harriet Monroe, the editor of *Poetry*, published there some of Sandburg's work under the title of "Chicago Poems," and her assistant editor persuaded Henry Holt to publish a book with the same title two years later. Sandburg quickly became a popular figure. He toured the country giving ballad concerts, he wrote articles, books for children, an autobiography, his biographies of the Lincolns, and a series of books of verse. His fellow poets were not all as impressed as the public: Robert Frost, scarcely ingenuous himself, used to call Sandburg a fraud. But Sandburg was not pretentious, and if anything took satisfaction in modesty. William Carlos Williams, a kindlier man than Frost, regretted that Sandburg "deliberately invited" failure by inattention to the demands of craft. Sandburg was not artless, but his principal interest was in subject, and he is often makeshift in form. The reading public felt his genuineness and was not put off by his clumsiness. Like Frost, he enjoyed in old age extraordinary acclaim. The governor of Illinois proclaimed his seventy-fifth birthday as "Carl Sandburg Day," the King of Sweden decorated him, the United States Congress invited him to address a joint session in 1959 on Lincoln Day, schools bearing his name were opened in Illinois, and in 1964 he received from President Lyndon B. Johnson the Presidential Medal of Freedom. Sandburg died on July 22, 1967.

While his poetry invites comparison with Whitman's, it suffers from that comparison. Sandburg tends to ramble around his subjects as once he rambled around America. His poems do not so much encompass as expand a point of view, Sandburg imitating Whitman's inventories of American life without often transcending a sensitive reportage combined with an old socialist's sympathy. He respected the sturdy and reliable repetitiveness of life and death, like Marinetti and the Futurists he admired dynamism, he hated injustice, and he trusted in his fellow countrymen's ability to handle what might come.

Chicago[1]

Hog Butcher for the World,
Tool Maker, Stacker of Wheat,
Player with Railroads and the Nation's Freight Handler;
Stormy, husky, brawling,
City of the Big Shoulders: 5

They tell me you are wicked and I believe them, for I have seen your
    painted women under the gas lamps luring the farm boys.
And they tell me you are crooked and I answer: Yes, it is true I have seen
    the gunman kill and go free to kill again.
And they tell me you are brutal and my reply is: On the faces of women
    and children I have seen the marks of wanton hunger.
And having answered so I turn once more to those who sneer at this my
    city, and I give them back the sneer and say to them:
Come and show me another city with lifted head singing so proud to be
    alive and coarse and strong and cunning.   10
Flinging magnetic curses amid the toil of piling job on job, here is a tall
    bold slugger set vivid against the little soft cities;
Fierce as a dog with tongue lapping for action, cunning as a savage pitted
    against the wilderness,
        Bareheaded,
        Shoveling,
        Wrecking,   15
        Planning,
        Building, breaking, rebuilding,
Under the smoke, dust all over his mouth, laughing with white teeth,
Under the terrible burden of destiny laughing as a young man laughs,
Laughing even as an ignorant fighter laughs who has never lost a battle,   20
Bragging and laughing that under his wrist is the pulse, and under his ribs
    the heart of the people,
        Laughing!
Laughing the stormy, husky, brawling laughter of Youth, half-naked,
    sweating, proud to be Hog Butcher, Tool Maker, Stacker of Wheat,
    Player with Railroads and Freight Handler to the Nation.

                                                                            1916

Grass

Pile the bodies high at Austerlitz and Waterloo.[2]
Shovel them under and let me work—
        I am the grass; I cover all.

1. Sandburg wrote of Chicago to a friend on July
30, 1913, "You might say at first shot that this is
the hell of a place for a poet but the truth is it is a
good place for a poet to get his head knocked when
he needs it. In fact, it is so good a place for a healthy
man who wants to watch the biggest, most intense,
brutal and complicated game in the world—the
game by which the world gets fed and clothed—
the method of control—the economics and waste—
so good a place is it from this viewpoint that I think
you will like it" (*The Letters of Carl Sandburg,*
ed. Herbert Mitgang, New York, 1968, pp. 99–
100).
    2. Austerlitz (Slavkov, Czechoslovakia) was in
1805 the scene of one of Napoleon's great victories, while Waterloo, in Belgium, was where he
met his final defeat in 1815.

And pile them high at Gettysburg[3]
And pile them high at Ypres and Verdun.[4]   5
Shovel them under and let me work.
Two years, ten years, and passengers ask the conductor:
What place is this?
Where are we now?

I am the grass.   10
Let me work.

1918

Cool Tombs

When Abraham Lincoln was shoveled into the tombs, he forgot the
copperheads[5] and the assassin . . . in the dust, in the cool tombs.

And Ulysses Grant lost all thought of con men and Wall Street, cash and
collateral turned ashes . . . in the dust, in the cool tombs.

Pocahontas'[6] body, lovely as a poplar, sweet as a red haw in November or a
pawpaw in May, did she wonder? does she remember? . . . in the
dust, in the cool tombs?

Take any streetful of people buying clothes and groceries, cheering a hero
or throwing confetti and blowing tin horns . . . tell me if the lovers are
losers . . . tell me if any get more than the lovers . . . in the dust . . .
in the cool tombs.

1918

Gargoyle

I saw a mouth jeering. A smile of melted red iron ran over it. Its laugh was
full of nails rattling. It was a child's dream of a mouth.
A fist hit the mouth: knuckles of gun-metal driven by an electric wrist and
shoulder. It was a child's dream of an arm.
The fist hit the mouth over and over, again and again. The mouth bled
melted iron, and laughed its laughter of nails rattling.
And I saw the more the fist pounded the more the mouth laughed. The fist
is pounding and pounding, and the mouth answering.

1918

---

3. The city in Pennsylvania near which the
Confederate army suffered a major defeat in 1863.
4. Ypres, Belgium, and Verdun, in France, were
the centers of some of the fiercest fighting in the
First World War.
5. A derogatory nickname during the Civil War
for a northerner with sympathy for Southern
secession.
6. Pocahontas (1595?–1617), daughter of the
Indian chief Powhatan, intervened to save the life
of Captain John Smith. The "red haw" is a type of
American hawthorn tree; "pawpaw" is colloquial
for the fruit of the papaya tree.

EDWARD THOMAS
1878–1917

Although Edward Thomas has some superficial affinities with the Georgian poets—like them he is a city-born nature lover and he began writing during the First World War—he is unusual for the intensity of his vision and the durability of his reputation. In 1932 F. R. Leavis praised Thomas as a "very original poet who devoted great technical subtlety to the expression of a distinctively modern sensibility,"[1] and since then his genuine distinction has been recognized.

Edward Thomas was born in Lambeth, a section of London, on March 3, 1878, and he spent most of his early life in the city. Both of his parents were Welsh; his father, a dour man, discouraged Thomas's early interest in poetry and urged the wisdom of a career in the civil service. Thomas was educated at St. Paul's School and Lincoln College, Oxford. At sixteen he fell in love with a girl two years his senior, and he married her while still in his third year at Oxford. Thomas was poor, he soon had a family to support, and he was given to periods of terrible self-doubt and melancholy. His marriage was often miserable because he did not feel that he could equal his wife's love for him. He wrote at one point that he found himself in an "unfathomable, deep forest where all must lose their way."[2] Thomas supported himself as a reviewer and hack writer, and when he died at thirty-eight he had written thirty books of prose and edited many others. He came to poetry late, and he lived to see only six of his poems in print.

A transforming moment in Thomas's life was his reading of the poetry of Robert Frost and his meeting soon thereafter with the poet himself, who had come to England. Frost's poems seem to have suggested to Thomas a way that he might himself write poetry. Frost, who knew from his own experience how much self-distrust and violence may be contained in a marriage, eased Thomas's domestic situation and convinced him that he had long neglected his true vocation, which was poetry. And Thomas was proud to say of a poem that it "sounded" like Frost. Once he had begun to write poems, Thomas wrote happily and with ease, but, as a well-known reviewer of other men's poems, he was shy about publishing his own work.

In 1915 Thomas, whose poems constantly find consolation in the particularities of his native countryside, enlisted as a private soldier to fight for England. He went to France, where the experience of war both alleviated his chronic depression and encouraged his writing. Easter Sunday, 1917, found him in Arras; he wrote his wife, "You would have laughed to see us dodging shells to-day."[3] The next day, April 9, 1917, he was killed.

Frost used to tease his friend Thomas for his indecisiveness, and later said that his poem "The Road Not Taken" was inspired by Thomas's frequent dreaming over what might have been. Many of Thomas's poems are told from the point of view of a questioning, sometimes benighted traveler. In "The Owl" the voice of the owl, coming out of the darkness from which the traveler has just escaped, salts and sobers his repose—that is, reminds him of human misery and seasons his relief in present safety.

The Owl

Downhill I came, hungry, and yet not starved;
Cold, yet had heat within me that was proof

1. F. R. Leavis, *New Bearings in English Poetry: A Study of the Contemporary Situation*, London, 1954, p. 69.
2. Quoted in Lawrance Thompson, *Robert Frost*, vol. 2, New York, 1966, p. 463.
3. Quoted in G. F. Whicher, "Edward Thomas," *Yale Review* 9, 558.

Against the North wind; tired, yet so that rest
Had seemed the sweetest thing under a roof.

Then at the inn I had food, fire, and rest,   5
Knowing how hungry, cold, and tired was I.
All of the night was quite barred out except
An owl's cry, a most melancholy cry

Shaken out long and clear upon the hill,
No merry note, nor cause of merriment,   10
But one telling me plain what I escaped
And others could not, that night, as in I went.

And salted was my food, and my repose,
Salted and sobered, too, by the bird's voice
Speaking for all who lay under the stars,   15
Soldiers and poor, unable to rejoice.

                                                            1917

October

The green elm with the one great bough of gold
Lets leaves into the grass slip, one by one,—
The short hill grass, the mushrooms small, milk-white,
Harebell and scabious and tormentil,[1]
That blackberry and gorse, in dew and sun,   5
Bow down to; and the wind travels too light
To shake the fallen birch leaves from the fern;
The gossamers wander at their own will.
At heavier steps than birds' the squirrels scold.
The rich scene has grown fresh again and new   10
As Spring and to the touch is not more cool
Than it is warm to the gaze; and now I might
As happy be as earth is beautiful,
Were I some other or with earth could turn
In alternation of violet and rose,   15
Harebell and snowdrop, at their season due,
And gorse that has no time not to be gay.
But if this be not happiness,—who knows?
Some day I shall think this a happy day,
And this mood by the name of melancholy   20
Shall no more blackened and obscurèd be.

                                                            1917

The Green Roads

The green roads that end in the forest
Are strewn with white goose feathers this June,

Like marks left behind by someone gone to the forest
To show his track. But he has never come back.

---

1. Varieties of British herbs.

Down each green road a cottage looks at the forest.   5
Round one the nettle towers; two are bathed in flowers.

An old man along the green road to the forest
Strays from one, from another a child alone.

In the thicket bordering the forest,
All day long a thrush twiddles his song.   10

It is old, but the trees are young in the forest,
All but one like a castle keep, in the middle deep.

That oak saw the ages pass in the forest:
They were a host, but their memories are lost,

For the tree is dead: all things forget the forest   15
Excepting perhaps me, when now I see

The old man, the child, the goose feathers at the edge of the forest,
And hear all day long the thrush repeat his song.

                                                                    1917

The Gallows

    There was a weasel lived in the sun
    With all his family,
    Till a keeper shot him with his gun
    And hung him up on a tree,
    Where he swings in the wind and rain,   5
    In the sun and in the snow,
    Without pleasure, without pain,
    On the dead oak tree bough.

    There was a crow who was no sleeper,
    But a thief and a murderer   10
    Till a very late hour; and this keeper
    Made him one of the things that were,
    To hang and flap in rain and wind,
    In the sun and in the snow.
    There are no more sins to be sinned   15
    On the dead oak tree bough.

    There was a magpie, too,
    Had a long tongue and a long tail;
    He could both talk and do—
    But what did that avail?   20
    He, too, slaps in the wind and rain
    Alongside weasel and crow,
    Without pleasure, without pain,
    On the dead oak tree bough.

    And many other beasts   25
    And birds, skin, bone, and feather,

Have been taken from their feasts
And hung up there together,
To swing and have endless leisure
In the sun and in the snow,   30
Without pain, without pleasure,
On the dead oak tree bough.

1917

February Afternoon

Men heard this roar of parleying starlings, saw,
   A thousand years ago even as now,
   Black rooks with white gulls following the plough
So that the first are last until a caw
Commands that last are first again,—a law   5
   Which was of old when one, like me, dreamed how
   A thousand years might dust lie on his brow
Yet thus would birds do between hedge and shaw.
Time swims before me, making as a day
   A thousand years, while the broad ploughland oak   10
   Roars mill-like and men strike and bear the stroke
Of war as ever, audacious or resigned,
And God still sits aloft in the array
   That we have wrought him, stone-deaf and stone-blind.

1918

The Gypsy

A fortnight before Christmas Gypsies were everywhere:
Vans were drawn up on wastes, women trailed to the fair.
"My gentleman," said one, "you've got a lucky face."
"And you've a luckier," I thought, "if such a grace
And impudence in rags are lucky. "Give a penny   5
For the poor baby's sake." "Indeed I have not any
Unless you can give change for a sovereign,[2] my dear."
"Then just half a pipeful of tobacco can you spare?"
I gave it. With that much victory she laughed content.
I should have given more, but off and away she went   10
With her baby and her pink sham flowers to rejoin
The rest before I could translate to its proper coin
Gratitude for her grace. And I paid nothing then,
As I pay nothing now with the dipping of my pen
For her brother's music when he drummed the tambourine   15
And stamped his feet, which made the workmen passing grin,
While his mouth-organ changed to a rascally Bacchanal dance
"Over the hills and far away."[3] This and his glance
Outlasted all the fair, farmer, and auctioneer,
Cheap-jack,[4] balloon-man, drover with crooked stick, and steer,   20
Pig, turkey, goose, and duck, Christmas corpses to be.

2. An English gold piece bearing the king's   4. A peddler, often of inferior or worthless
portrait and worth about $5.00.   goods.
3. An old English folksong.

Not even the kneeling ox had eyes like the Romany.[5]
That night he peopled for me the hollow wooded land,
More dark and wild than stormiest heavens, that I searched and scanned
Like a ghost new-arrived. The gradations of the dark   25
Were like an underworld of death, but for the spark
In the Gypsy boy's black eyes as he played and stamped his tune,
"Over the hills and far away," and a crescent moon.

1918

5. Gypsy.

WALLACE STEVENS
1879–1955

Since the deaths of Yeats and Eliot, it has become clear that a third great imaginative force in the first part of this century was Wallace Stevens. Compared to these other poets, he was extraordinarily self-effacing. He spent his daytime life as an executive of the Hartford Accident and Indemnity Company and never presented himself as a literary figure to his business associates. He had little to do with other writers, and his correspondence reveals that he was on a first-name basis with almost no one. Yet his verse is prodigiously exciting and unexpectable. Stevens, a near-contemporary of Frost, brings into modern poetry a Keatsian color in contrast with Frost's Words-worthian plainness. Frost called him a bric-a-brac poet, in private, while Stevens, professing virtual ignorance of Frost's verse, remarked, "His work is full (or said to be full) of humanity."

Stevens seems to have formed quite early the idea expressed later in "Sunday Morning," that the poet must rediscover the earth. He commented in "Imagination as Value," an essay written in later life, that "the great poems of heaven and hell have been written and the great poem of the earth remains to be written."[1] Just what the world is, is not always so plain. Stevens boasts to his wife, "I believe that with a bucket of sand and a wishing lamp I could create a world in half a second that would make this one look like a hunk of mud."[2] Yet he is quick to insist that "the imagination creates nothing. We are able to romanticize and to give blue jays fifteen toes, but if there was no such thing as a bird we could not create it. . . . Dreams are hash."[3] Precisely what is the domain of the imagination, and what that of the world, is a question that Stevens prefers to keep asking and answering. In this quality he is comparable to Mallarmé and to Yeats, for whom the changing relation of image to fact is also to be explored rather than arrested.

Stevens held that in a time when religion no longer could satisfy, poetry must replace it. He pondered a good deal what satisfactions poetry might offer, and evolved a theory of necessary fictions. Among them poetry is "the supreme fiction." What it provides is "a freshening of life."[4] "What makes the poet the potent figure that he is, or was, or ought to be, is that he creates the world to which we turn incessantly and without knowing it and that he gives to life the supreme fictions without which we are unable to conceive of it."[5]

His thoughts return to this problem, which underlies his early work but is there expressed more obliquely. "If one no longer believes in God (as truth)," he writes, "it is not possible merely to disbelieve; it becomes necessary to believe in something else. Logically, I ought to believe in essential imagination, but that has its difficulties.

1. *The Necessary Angel*, New York, 1965, p. 142.
2. *Letters of Wallace Stevens*, ed. Holly Stevens, New York, 1966, p. 80.
3. The same, p. 465.
4. The same, p. 293.
5. *The Necessary Angel*, p. 31.

It is easier to believe in a thing created by the imagination. A good deal of my poetry recently has concerned an identity for that thing."[6] Yet he objected to what he called the romantic view of the imagination because it excluded the abstract in favor of minor wish-fulfillments, presumably word-pictures of no lasting value in the great task of replacing religion. "The imagination is the liberty of the mind. . . . It is intrepid and eager and the extreme of its achievement lies in abstraction."[7] The abstraction must be blooded, he writes in "Notes for a Supreme Fiction." It must not leave the world behind, but must "express an agreement with reality."[8]

Stevens was born on October 2, 1879, in Reading, Pennsylvania. He attended high school in Reading and then entered Harvard as a special student, like Robert Frost. He remained for three years, 1897 to 1900, during which he studied French and German and, following his philosophical bent, became friendly with the philosopher-poet George Santayana. He was later to write "To an Old Philosopher in Rome" in Santayana's honor. Stevens became president of the *Harvard Advocate* and, like Eliot, published his early poems in it.

Apart from his interest in writing, he was not sure how to make a livelihood. His first job was on the *New York Herald Tribune*, and he did not like it. At his father's suggestion he resigned and entered the New York Law School in the fall of 1901. In 1904 he was admitted to the New York Bar and began, unsuccessfully, to practice law. A partnership failed, and then he worked in several other law firms. In January 1908 he entered the legal staff of an insurance firm and at last felt secure enough to marry, in 1909, Elsie Moll, a young woman whom he had met in Reading five years before. In 1916 he joined the New York office of the Hartford Accident and Indemnity Company and a few months later moved to Hartford. In 1934 he became vice-president. His routine labors at first seemed stultifying: "I certainly do not exist from nine to six, when I am at the office," he wrote Elsie Moll before their marriage.[9] But he told a reporter five years before his death, "It gives a man character as a poet to have this daily contact with a job."[10]

Stevens began to publish his mature poems in 1914, chiefly in *Poetry*. But he held off from publishing a volume until 1923, when *Harmonium* appeared. The following year his only child, Holly, was born. He led a "quiet, normal," but full life. He worked hard at his business; he read; he wrote his poems; and he regularly corresponded with a variety of men and women who shared his interest in all the arts. He collected his share of honorary degrees, and he seems to have been pleased with the attention he received from younger poets and readers. His life, although it may seem short on events, was a feast of the imagination, a feast he shared with all who knew his poems. He continued to work until his death on August 2, 1955.

The source of our Stevens texts is *The Palm at the End of the Mind*, edited by Holly Stevens (New York, 1967). We reprint our selections in the chronological order of composition followed in that book.

6. *Letters*, p. 370.
7. *The Necessary Angel*, pp. 138–39.
8. *Letters*, p. 463.

9. The same, p. 121.
10. *New York Times* obituary, August 3, 1955, p. 23.

Sunday Morning[1]

I

Complacencies of the peignoir,[2] and late
Coffee and oranges in a sunny chair,
And the green freedom of a cockatoo

1. "This is not essentially a woman's meditation on religion and the meaning of life. It is anybody's meditation. . . . The poem is simply an expression of paganism, although, of course, I did not think that I was expressing paganism when I wrote it" (*Letters of Wallace Stevens*, ed. Holly Stevens, New York, 1966, p. 250).
2. Loose negligée.

Upon a rug mingle to dissipate
The holy hush of ancient sacrifice.   5
She dreams a little, and she feels the dark
Encroachment of that old catastrophe,
As a calm darkens among water-lights.
The pungent oranges and bright, green wings
Seem things in some procession of the dead,   10
Winding across wide water, without sound.
The day is like wide water, without sound,
Stilled for the passing of her dreaming feet
Over the seas, to silent Palestine,
Dominion of the blood and sepulchre.[3]   15

II
Why should she give her bounty to the dead?
What is divinity if it can come
Only in silent shadows and in dreams?
Shall she not find in comforts of the sun,
In pungent fruit and bright, green wings, or else   20
In any balm or beauty of the earth,
Things to be cherished like the thought of heaven?
Divinity must live within herself:
Passions of rain, or moods in falling snow;
Grievings in loneliness, or unsubdued   25
Elations when the forest blooms; gusty
Emotions on wet roads on autumn nights;
All pleasures and all pains, remembering
The bough of summer and the winter branch.
These are the measures destined for her soul.   30

III
Jove in the clouds had his inhuman birth.[4]
No mother suckled him, no sweet land gave
Large-mannered motions to his mythy mind.
He moved among us, as a muttering king,
Magnificent, would move among his hinds,[5]   35
Until our blood, commingling, virginal,
With heaven, brought such requital to desire
The very hinds discerned it, in a star.
Shall our blood fail? Or shall it come to be
The blood of paradise? And shall the earth   40
Seem all of paradise that we shall know?
The sky will be much friendlier then than now,
A part of labor and a part of pain,
And next in glory to enduring love,
Not this dividing and indifferent blue.   45

IV
She says, "I am content when wakened birds,
Before they fly, test the reality

---

3. The sepulchre of Christ is located in Palestine; the "blood" may allude either to the many
wars fought in that area, or to Christ's reference
to the wine of his last Passover as his "blood of the
new testament" (Matthew 25:28).

4. According to legend, Jove, or Zeus, was
actually born in Crete, the son of a Titan, Rhea.
During his childhood he was hidden in a cave and
suckled by the goat Amalthea.
5. Shepherds.

Of misty fields, by their sweet questionings;
But when the birds are gone, and their warm fields
Return no more, where, then, is paradise?"   50
There is not any haunt of prophecy,
Nor any old chimera[6] of the grave,
Neither the golden underground, nor isle
Melodious, where spirits gat them home,
Nor visionary south, nor cloudy palm   55
Remote on heaven's hill, that has endured
As April's green endures; or will endure
Like her remembrance of awakened birds,
Or her desire for June and evening, tipped
By the consummation of the swallow's wings.   60

                              V
She says, "but in contentment I still feel
The need of some imperishable bliss."
Death is the mother of beauty; hence from her,
Alone, shall come fulfilment to our dreams
And our desires. Although she strews the leaves   65
Of sure obliteration on our paths,
The path sick sorrow took, the many paths
Where triumph rang its brassy phrase, or love
Whispered a little out of tenderness,
She makes the willow shiver in the sun   70
For maidens who were wont to sit and gaze
Upon the grass, relinquished to their feet.
She causes boys to pile new plums and pears
On disregarded plate.[7] The maidens taste
And stray impassioned in the littering leaves.   75

                             VI
Is there no change of death in paradise?
Does ripe fruit never fall? Or do the boughs
Hang always heavy in that perfect sky,
Unchanging, yet so like our perishing earth,
With rivers like our own that seek for seas   80
They never find, the same receding shores
That never touch with inarticulate pang?
Why set the pear upon those river-banks
Or spice the shores with odors of the plum?
Alas, that they should wear our colors there,   85
The silken weavings of our afternoons,
And pick the strings of our insipid lutes!
Death is the mother of beauty, mystical,
Within whose burning bosom we devise
Our earthly mothers waiting, sleeplessly.   90

                             VII
Supple and turbulent, a ring of men
Shall chant in orgy on a summer morn

6. Imaginary monster.
7. "Plate is used in the sense of so-called family
plate [that is, household silver]. Disregarded refers
to the disuse into which things fall that have been
possessed for a long time. I mean, therefore, that
death releases and renews. What the old have come
to disregard, the young inherit and make use of"
(*Letters,* p. 183).

Their boisterous devotion to the sun,
Not as a god, but as a god might be,
Naked among them, like a savage source. 95
Their chant shall be a chant of paradise,
Out of their blood, returning to the sky;
And in their chant shall enter, voice by voice,
The windy lake wherein their lord delights,
The trees, like serafin,[8] and echoing hills, 100
That choir among themselves long afterward.
They shall know well the heavenly fellowship
Of men that perish and of summer morn.
And whence they came and whither they shall go
The dew upon their feet shall manifest. 105

VIII

She hears, upon that water without sound,
A voice that cries, "The tomb in Palestine
Is not the porch of spirits lingering.
It is the grave of Jesus, where he lay."
We live in an old chaos of the sun, 110
Or old dependency of day and night,
Or island solitude, unsponsored, free,
Of that wide water, inescapable.
Deer walk upon our mountains, and the quail
Whistle about us their spontaneous cries; 115
Sweet berries ripen in the wilderness;
And, in the isolation of the sky,
At evening, casual flocks of pigeons make
Ambiguous undulations as they sink,
Downward to darkness, on extended wings. 120

1915   1923, 1931

Peter Quince at the Clavier[9]

I

Just as my fingers on these keys
Make music, so the selfsame sounds
On my spirit make a music, too.

Music is feeling, then, not sound;
And thus it is that what I feel, 5
Here in this room, desiring you,

Thinking of your blue-shadowed silk,
Is music. It is like the strain
Waked in the elders by Susanna.[1]

---

8. Or seraphim, angels who guard the throne of the Lord.

9. A keyboard instrument, an early form of the piano. Peter Quince is one of the "rude mechanicals" or comic rustics who perform an unintentionally funny tragedy in Shakespeare's *Midsummer Night's Dream;* Shakespeare implies that Quince wrote it.

1. Two elders, or Hebrew tribal councilors, attempted to seduce Susanna, who repulsed them; they then brought against her false accusations of an illicit relationship with a young man; Daniel, however, saved her from punishment. The story is told in Daniel 13, a chapter in the Apocrypha.

Of a green evening, clear and warm,   10
She bathed in her still garden, while
The red-eyed elders watching, felt

The basses of their beings throb
In witching chords, and their thin blood
Pulse pizzicati of Hosanna.[2]   15

II

In the green water, clear and warm,
Susanna lay.
She searched
The touch of springs,
And found   20
Concealed imaginings.
She sighed,
For so much melody.

Upon the bank, she stood
In the cool   25
Of spent emotions.
She felt, among the leaves,
The dew
Of old devotions.

She walked upon the grass,   30
Still quavering.
The winds were like her maids,
On timid feet,
Fetching her woven scarves,
Yet wavering.   35

A breath upon her hand
Muted the night.
She turned—
A cymbal crashed,
And roaring horns.   40

III

Soon, with a noise like tambourines,
Came her attendant Byzantines.[3]

They wondered why Susanna cried
Against the elders by her side;

And as they whispered, the refrain   45
Was like a willow swept by rain.

---

2. Expression of great praise; "pizzicati": notes or passages played by plucking strings.
3. That is, people of the Byzantine Empire, which flourished from roughly the fourth through the fifteenth centuries A.D. "Somebody once called my attention to the fact that there were no Byzantines in Susanna's time. I hope that that bit of precious pedantry will seem as unimportant to you as it does to me" (*Letters*, p. 250).

Anon, their lamps' uplifted flame
Revealed Susanna and her shame.

And then, the simpering Byzantines
Fled, with a noise like tambourines.   50

IV

Beauty is momentary in the mind—
The fitful tracing of a portal;[4]
But in the flesh it is immortal.

The body dies; the body's beauty lives.
So evenings die, in their green going,   55
A wave, interminably flowing.
So gardens die, their meek breath scenting
The cowl[5] of winter, done repenting.
So maidens die, to the auroral
Celebration of a maiden's choral.   60

Susanna's music touched the bawdy strings
Of those white elders; but, escaping,
Left only Death's ironic scraping.
Now, in its immortality, it plays
On the clear viol of her memory,   65
And makes a constant sacrament of praise.

1915   1923, 1931

Thirteen Ways of Looking at a Blackbird[6]

I
Among twenty snowy mountains,
The only moving thing
Was the eye of the blackbird.

II
I was of three minds,
Like a tree   5
In which there are three blackbirds.

III
The blackbird whirled in the autumn winds.
It was a small part of the pantomime.

IV
A man and a woman
Are one.   10
A man and a woman and a blackbird
Are one.

4. A reference, perhaps, to the gates of dreams of classical mythology: one was of ivory, the other of horn, and through them came false and true dreams, respectively.

5. Hood on a monk's or nun's habit.
6. "This group of poems is not meant to be a collection of epigrams or of ideas, but of sensations" (*Letters*, p. 251).

V

I do not know which to prefer,
The beauty of inflections
Or the beauty of innuendoes,   15
The blackbird whistling
Or just after.

VI

Icicles filled the long window
With barbaric glass.
The shadow of the blackbird   20
Crossed it, to and fro.
The mood
Traced in the shadow
An indecipherable cause.

VII

O thin men of Haddam,[7]   25
Why do you imagine golden birds?
Do you not see how the blackbird
Walks around the feet
Of the women about you?

VIII

I know noble accents   30
And lucid, inescapable rhythms;
But I know, too,
That the blackbird is involved
In what I know.

IX

When the blackbird flew out of sight,   35
It marked the edge
Of one of many circles.

X

At the sight of blackbirds
Flying in a green light,
Even the bawds of euphony[8]   40
Would cry out sharply.

XI

He rode over Connecticut
In a glass coach.
Once, a fear pierced him,
In that he mistook   45
The shadow of his equipage[9]
For blackbirds.

---

7. A town in Connecticut. "The thin men of
Haddam are entirely fictitious although some years
ago one of the citizens of that place wrote to me to
ask what I had in mind. I just like the name. It is
an old whaling town, I believe. In any case, it has
a completely Yankee sound" (*Letters*, p. 786).

8. "What was intended by X was that the bawds
of euphony would suddenly cease to be academic
and express themselves sharply: naturally, with
pleasure, etc." (*Letters*, p. 340).

9. That is, coach.

XII

The river is moving.
The blackbird must be flying.

XIII

It was evening all afternoon.   50
It was snowing
And it was going to snow.
The blackbird sat
In the cedar-limbs.

1917   1923, 1931

Anecdote of the Jar

I placed a jar in Tennessee,
And round it was, upon a hill.
It made the slovenly wilderness
Surround that hill.

The wilderness rose up to it,   5
And sprawled around, no longer wild.
The jar was round upon the ground
And tall and of a port in air.

It took dominion everywhere.
The jar was gray and bare.   10
It did not give of bird or bush,
Like nothing else in Tennessee.

1919   1923, 1931

The Snow Man[1]

One must have a mind of winter
To regard the frost and the boughs
Of the pine-trees crusted with snow;

And have been cold a long time
To behold the junipers shagged with ice,   5
The spruces rough in the distant glitter

Of the January sun; and not to think
Of any misery in the sound of the wind,
In the sound of a few leaves,

Which is the sound of the land   10
Full of the same wind
That is blowing in the same bare place

---

1. "I shall explain The Snow Man as an example of the necessity of identifying oneself with reality in order to understand it and enjoy it" (*Letters*, p. 464).

For the listener, who listens in the snow,
And, nothing himself, beholds
Nothing that is not there and the nothing that is.   15

1921   1923, 1931

Bantams in Pine-Woods

Chieftain Iffucan of Azcan in caftan
Of tan with henna hackles,[2] halt!

Damned universal cock, as if the sun
Was blackamoor to bear your blazing tail.

Fat! Fat! Fat! Fat! I am the personal.   5
Your world is you. I am my world.

You ten-foot poet among inchlings. Fat!
Begone! An inchling bristles in these pines,

Bristles, and points their Appalachian tangs,
And fears not portly Azcan nor his hoos.[3]   10

1922   1923, 1931

The Emperor of Ice-Cream[4]

Call the roller of big cigars,
The muscular one, and bid him whip
In kitchen cups concupiscent curds.[5]
Let the wenches dawdle in such dress
As they are used to wear, and let the boys   5
Bring flowers in last month's newspapers.
Let be be finale of seem.[6]
The only emperor is the emperor of ice-cream.

Take from the dresser of deal,[7]
Lacking the three glass knobs, that sheet   10

2. "Iffucan" and "Azcan" are Stevens's coin-
ages, perhaps intended to be suggestive of the
Aztecs or Mayans; a "caftan" is an ankle-length
robe, commonly worn in the Near East. The rooster being addressed (the "bantams" of the title are
small fowl) has "hackles" or neck-feathers of a red-
dish-brown color. In this poem, these facts are very
likely less important than the sounds of the words.
3. Interjections of surprise; again, however,
Stevens probably chose the word for its sound, as
also "Appalachian" (a range of mountains in the
eastern United States).
4. In 1933 Stevens wrote to William Rose Benét:
"I think I should select from my poems as my
favorite the Emperor of Ice Cream. This wears a
deliberately commonplace costume, and yet seems
to me to contain something of the essential gau-
diness of poetry; that is the reason why I like it."
In a later letter to Benét, he continued: "I do not
remember the circumstances under which this
poem was written, unless this means the state of
mind from which it came. I dislike niggling, and
like letting myself go. This poem is an instance of

letting myself go. . . . This represented what was
in my mind at the moment, with the least possible
manipulation" (*Letters*, pp. 263–64).
5. Literally, lustful milk solids. Stevens wrote,
however, that "the words 'concupiscent curds' have
no genealogy; they are merely expressive: at least,
I hope they are expressive. They express the con-
cupiscence of life, but, by contrast with the things
in relation in the poem, they express or accen-
tuate life's destitution, and it is this that gives them
something more than a cheap lustre" (*Letters*, p.
500).
6. ". . . the true sense of Let be be the finale
of seem is let being become the conclusion or
denouement of appearing to be: in short, ice cream
is an absolute good. The poem is obviously not
about ice cream, but about being as distinguished
from seeming to be" (*Letters*, p. 341). "Finale":
the concluding section of a musical composition,
often loud and full of flourishes. Also, the final end,
catastrophe.
7. Plain, unfinished wood.

On which she embroidered fantails[8] once
And spread it so as to cover her face.
If her horny feet protrude, they come
To show how cold she is, and dumb.
Let the lamp affix its beam.   15
The only emperor is the emperor of ice-cream.

1922   1923, 1931

The Idea of Order at Key West[9]

She sang beyond the genius[1] of the sea.
The water never formed to mind or voice,
Like a body wholly body, fluttering
Its empty sleeves; and yet its mimic motion
Made constant cry, caused constantly a cry,   5
That was not ours although we understood,
Inhuman, of the veritable ocean.

The sea was not a mask. No more was she.
The song and water were not medleyed sound
Even if what she sang was what she heard,   10
Since what she sang was uttered word by word.
It may be that in all her phrases stirred
The grinding water and the gasping wind;
But it was she and not the sea we heard.

For she was the maker of the song she sang.   15
The ever-hooded, tragic-gestured sea
Was merely a place by which she walked to sing.
Whose spirit is this? we said, because we knew
It was the spirit that we sought and knew
That we should ask this often as she sang.   20

If it was only the dark voice of the sea
That rose, or even colored by many waves;
If it was only the outer voice of sky
And cloud, of the sunken coral water-walled,
However clear, it would have been deep air,   25
The heaving speech of air, a summer sound
Repeated in a summer without end
And sound alone. But it was more than that,
More even than her voice, and ours, among
The meaningless plungings of water and the wind,   30
Theatrical distances, bronze shadows heaped
On high horizons, mountainous atmospheres
Of sky and sea.

8. ". . . the word fantails does not mean fans, but fantail pigeons . . ." (*Letters*, p. 500).
9. "In 'The Idea of Order at Key West' life has ceased to be a matter of chance. It may be that every man introduces his own order into the life about him and that the idea of order in general is simply what Bishop Berkeley [the eighteenth-century English philosopher] might have called a fortuitous concourse of personal orders. But still there is order. . . . I never thought that it was a fixed philosophic proposition that life was a mass of irrelevancies any more than I now think that it is a fixed philosophic propostion that every man introduces his own order as part of a general order. These are tentative ideas for the purposes of poetry" (*Letters*, p. 293). Key West is the southernmost of several small coral islands off the coast of Florida.
1. Attendant spirit or deity.

                    It was her voice that made
The sky acutest at its vanishing.   35
She measured to the hour its solitude.
She was the single artificer of the world
In which she sang. And when she sang, the sea,
Whatever self it had, became the self
That was her song, for she was the maker.[2] Then we,   40
As we beheld her striding there alone,
Knew that there never was a world for her
Except the one she sang and, singing, made.

Ramon Fernandez,[3] tell me, if you know,
Why, when the singing ended and we turned   45
Toward the town, tell why the glassy lights,
The lights in the fishing boats at anchor there,
As the night descended, tilting in the air,
Mastered the night and portioned out the sea,
Fixing emblazoned zones and fiery poles,   50
Arranging, deepening, enchanting night.

Oh! Blessed rage for order, pale Ramon,
The maker's rage to order words of the sea,
Words of the fragrant portals, dimly-starred,
And of ourselves and of our origins,   55
In ghostlier demarcations, keener sounds.

1934   1936

Farewell to Florida

I

Go on, high ship, since now, upon the shore,
The snake has left its skin upon the floor.
Key West sank downward under massive clouds
And silvers and greens spread over the sea. The moon
Is at the mast-head and the past is dead.   5
Her mind will never speak to me again.
I am free. High above the mast the moon
Rides clear of her mind and the waves make a refrain
Of this: that the snake has shed its skin upon
The floor. Go on through the darkness. The waves fly back.   10

II

Her mind had bound me round. The palms were hot
As if I lived in ashen ground, as if
The leaves in which the wind kept up its sound
From my North of cold whistled in a sepulchral South
Her South of pine and coral and coraline sea,   15
Her home, not mine, in the ever-freshened Keys,

---

2. The Greek *poietes*, or poet, also means "maker."
3. Stevens pointed out to a correspondent that in choosing this name he had simply combined two common Spanish names at random, without conscious reference to Ramon Fernandez the French critic: "Ramon Fernandez was not intended to be anyone at all" (*Letters*, p. 798).

Her days, her oceanic nights, calling
For music, for whisperings from the reefs.
How content I shall be in the North to which I sail
And to feel sure and to forget the bleaching sand . . .   20

III

I hated the weathery yawl[4] from which the pools
Disclosed the sea floor and the wilderness
Of waving weeds. I hated the vivid blooms
Curled over the shadowless hut, the rust and bones,
The trees likes bones and the leaves half sand, half sun.   25
To stand here on the deck in the dark and say
Farewell and to know that that land is forever gone
And that she will not follow in any word
Or look, nor ever again in thought, except
That I loved her once . . . Farewell. Go on, high ship.   30

IV

My North is leafless and lies in a wintry slime
Both of men and clouds, a slime of men in crowds.
The men are moving as the water moves,
This darkened water cloven by sullen swells
Against your sides, then shoving and slithering,   35
The darkness shattered, turbulent with foam.
To be free again, to return to the violent mind
That is their mind, these men, and that will bind
Me round, carry me, misty deck, carry me
To the cold, go on, high ship, go on, plunge on.   40

1936   1936

From The Man with the Blue Guitar[5]

I

The man bent over his guitar,
A shearsman of sorts.[6] The day was green.

They said, "You have a blue guitar,
You do not play things as they are."

---

4. A light fishing boat with sails.
5. "[The sections of 'The Man with the Blue Guitar'] deal with the relation or balance between imagined things and real things which, as you know, is a constant source of trouble to me. . . . Actually, they are not abstractions, even though what I have just said about them suggests that. Perhaps it would be better to say that what they really deal with is the painter's problem of realization: I have been trying to see the world about me both as I see it and as it is" (*Letters*, p. 316). During his last years, Stevens amplified these remarks: "The general intention of the Blue Guitar was to say a few things that I felt impelled to

say 1. about reality; 2. about the imagination; 3. their interrelations; and 4. principally, my attitude toward each of these things. This is the general scope of the poem, which is confined to the area of poetry and makes no pretense of going beyond that area" (*Letters*, p. 788). Though the title describes a painting from Picasso's "blue period," *Blind Guitar-Player* (1903), Stevens asserted in 1953, "I had no particular painting of Picasso's in mind" (*Letters*, p. 786).
6. "This refers to the posture of the speaker, squatting like a tailor (a shearsman) as he works on his cloth" (*Letters*, p. 783).

The man replied, "Things as they are   5
Are changed upon the blue guitar."

And they said then, "But play, you must,
A tune beyond us, yet ourselves,

A tune upon the blue guitar
Of things exactly as they are."   10

1937   1937

A Rabbit as King of the Ghosts

The difficulty to think at the end of day,
When the shapeless shadow covers the sun
And nothing is left except light on your fur—

There was the cat slopping its milk all day,
Fat, cat, red tongue, green mind, white milk   5
And August the most peaceful month.

To be, in the grass, in the peacefullest time,
Without that monument of cat,
The cat forgotten in the moon;

And to feel that the light is a rabbit-light,   10
In which everything is meant for you
And nothing need be explained;

Then there is nothing to think of. It comes of itself;
And east rushes west and west rushes down,
No matter. The grass is full   15

And full of yourself. The trees around are for you,
The whole of the wideness of night is for you,
A self that touches all edges,

You become a self that fills the four corners of night.
The red cat hides away in the fur-light   20
And there you are humped high, humped up,

You are humped higher and higher, black as stone—
You sit with your head like a carving in space
And the little green cat is a bug in the grass.

1937   1942

The Man on the Dump

Day creeps down. The moon is creeping up.
The sun is a corbeil of flowers the moon Blanche[7]

7. Presumably "Blanche" is the name of the moon (subject of "places"); "corbeil": basket of flowers or
fruit, or sculptural representation thereof.

Places there, a bouquet. Ho-ho . . . The dump is full
Of images. Days pass like papers from a press.
The bouquets come here in the papers. So the sun,   5
And so the moon, both come, and the janitor's poems
Of every day, the wrapper on the can of pears,
The cat in the paper-bag, the corset, the box
From Esthonia:[8] the tiger chest, for tea.

The freshness of night has been fresh a long time.   10
The freshness of morning, the blowing of day, one says
That it puffs as Cornelius Nepos[9] reads, it puffs
More than, less than or it puffs like this or that.
The green smacks in the eye, the dew in the green
Smacks like fresh water in a can, like the sea   15
On a cocoanut—how many men have copied dew
For buttons, how many women have covered themselves
With dew, dew dresses, stones and chains of dew, heads
Of the floweriest flowers dewed with the dewiest dew.
One grows to hate these things except on the dump.   20

Now in the time of spring (azaleas, trilliums,
Myrtle, viburnums, daffodils, blue phlox),
Between that disgust and this, between the things
That are on the dump (azaleas and so on)
And those that will be (azaleas and so on),   25
One feels the purifying change. One rejects
The trash.

          That's the moment when the moon creeps up
To the bubbling of bassoons. That's the time
One looks at the elephant-colorings of tires.   30
Everything is shed; and the moon comes up as the moon
(All its images are in the dump) and you see
As a man (not like an image of a man),
You see the moon rise in the empty sky.

One sits and beats an old tin can, lard pail.   35
One beats and beats for that which one believes.
That's what one wants to get near. Could it after all
Be merely oneself, as superior as the ear
To a crow's voice? Did the nightingale torture the ear,
Pack the heart and scratch the mind? And does the ear   40
Solace itself in peevish birds? Is it peace,
Is it a philosopher's honeymoon, one finds
On the dump? Is it to sit among mattresses of the dead,
Bottles, pots, shoes and grass and murmur *aptest eve:*
Is it to hear the blatter of grackles and say   45
Invisible priest; is it to eject, to pull
The day to pieces and cry *stanza my stone?*
Where was it one first heard of the truth? The the.

1938   1942

8. On the Baltic Sea; formerly a country in northeastern Europe (now a republic of the USSR). 9. Roman historian (c.100 B.C.–c.25 B.C.). As elsewhere, his name may well have been chosen for its sound.

The Sense of the Sleight-of-Hand Man

One's grand flights, one's Sunday baths,
One's tootings at the weddings of the soul
Occur as they occur. So bluish clouds
Occurred above the empty house and the leaves
Of the rhododendrons rattled their gold,   5
As if someone lived there. Such floods of white
Came bursting from the clouds. So the wind
Threw its contorted strength around the sky.

Could you have said the bluejay suddenly
Would swoop to earth? It is a wheel, the rays   10
Around the sun. The wheel survives the myths.
The fire eye in the clouds survives the gods.
To think of a dove with an eye of grenadine
And pines that are cornets,[1] so it occurs,
And a little island full of geese and stars: 15
It may be that the ignorant man, alone,
Has any chance to mate his life with life
That is the sensual, pearly spouse, the life
That is fluent in even the wintriest bronze.

1939   1942

Of Modern Poetry

The poem of the mind in the act of finding
What will suffice. It has not always had
To find: the scene was set; it repeated what
Was in the script.
                    Then the theatre was changed   5
To something else. Its past was a souvenir.

It has to be living, to learn the speech of the place.
It has to face the men of the time and to meet
The women of the time. It has to think about war
And it has to find what will suffice. It has   10
To construct a new stage. It has to be on that stage
And, like an insatiable actor, slowly and
With meditation, speak words that in the ear,
In the delicatest ear of the mind, repeat,
Exactly, that which it wants to hear, at the sound   15
Of which, an invisible audience listens,
Not to the play, but to itself, expressed
In an emotion as of two people, as of two
Emotions becoming one. The actor is
A metaphysician in the dark, twanging   20
An instrument, twanging a wiry string that gives
Sounds passing through sudden rightnesses, wholly
Containing the mind, below which it cannot descend,
Beyond which it has no will to rise.

---

1. Cones; "grenadine": orange-red in color.

                 It must   25
Be the finding of a satisfaction, and may
Be of a man skating, a woman dancing, a woman
Combing. The poem of the act of the mind.

1940   1942

A Quiet Normal Life

His place, as he sat and as he thought, was not
In anything that he constructed, so frail,
So barely lit, so shadowed over and naught,

As, for example, a world in which, like snow,
He became an inhabitant, obedient   5
To gallant notions on the part of cold.

It was here. This was the setting and the time
Of year. Here in his house and in his room,
In his chair, the most tranquil thought grew peaked

And the oldest and the warmest heart was cut   10
By gallant notions on the part of night—
Both late and alone, above the crickets' chords,

Babbling, each one, the uniqueness of its sound.
There was no fury in transcendent forms.
But his actual candle blazed with artifice.   15

1952   1954

To an Old Philosopher in Rome[2]

On the threshold of heaven, the figures in the street
Become the figures of heaven, the majestic movement
Of men growing small in the distances of space,
Singing, with smaller and still smaller sound,
Unintelligible absolution and an end—   5

The threshold, Rome, and that more merciful Rome
Beyond, the two alike in the make of the mind.
It is as if in a human dignity
Two parallels become one, a perspective, of which
Men are part both in the inch and in the mile.   10

2. The poem is addressed to the Spanish-born American philosopher, George Santayana (1863–1952), also a poet, who retired from teaching at Harvard in 1912 and went to Italy to live. Stevens met Santayana while an undergraduate at Harvard. "While I did not take any of his courses and never heard him lecture, he invited me to come to see him a number of times and, in that way, I came to know him a little. I read several poems to him and he expressed his own view of the subject of them in a sonnet ['Cathedrals by the Sea: Reply to a sonnet beginning "Cathedrals are not built along the sea" '] which he sent me, and which is in one of his books. This was forty years ago [in 1905], when I was a boy and when he was not yet in mid-life. . . . It would be easy to speak of his interest and sympathy. . . . I always came away from my visits to him feeling that he made up in the most genuine way for many things that I needed. He was then still definitely a poet" (*Letters*, pp. 481–82). This poem was written less than a year before Santayana's death in the nursing home of a Roman Catholic order in Rome: "He seems to have gone to live at the convent, in which he died, in his sixties, probably gave them all he had and asked them to keep him, body and soul" (*Letters*, pp. 761–72).

How easily the blown banners change to wings . . .
Things dark on the horizons of perception
Become accompaniments of fortune, but
Of the fortune of the spirit, beyond the eye,
Not of its sphere, and yet not far beyond,   15

The human end in the spirit's greatest reach,
The extreme of the known in the presence of the extreme
Of the unknown. The newsboys' muttering
Becomes another murmuring; the smell
Of medicine, a fragrantness not to be spoiled . . .   20

The bed, the books, the chair, the moving nuns,
The candle as it evades the sight, these are
The sources of happiness in the shape of Rome,
A shape within the ancient circles of shapes,
And these beneath the shadow of a shape   25

In a confusion on bed and books, a portent
On the chair, a moving transparence on the nuns,
A light on the candle tearing against the wick
To join a hovering excellence, to escape
From fire and be part only of that of which   30

Fire is the symbol: the celestial possible.
Speak to your pillow as if it was yourself.
Be orator but with an accurate tongue
And without eloquence, O, half-asleep,
Of the pity that is the memorial of this room,   35

So that we feel, in this illumined large,
The veritable small, so that each of us
Beholds himself in you, and hears his voice
In yours, master and commiserable man,
Intent on your particles of nether-do,   40

Your dozing in the depths of wakefulness,
In the warmth of your bed, at the edge of your chair, alive
Yet living in two worlds, impenitent
As to one, and, as to one, most penitent,
Impatient for the grandeur that you need   45

In so much misery; and yet finding it
Only in misery, the afflatus[3] of ruin,
Profound poetry of the poor and of the dead,
As in the last drop of the deepest blood,
As it falls from the heart and lies there to be seen,   50

Even as the blood of an empire, it might be,
For a citizen of heaven though still of Rome.
It is poverty's speech that seeks us out the most.

3. Inspiration.

It is older than the oldest speech of Rome.
This is the tragic accent of the scene.   55

And you—it is you that speak it, without speech,
The loftiest syllables among loftiest things,
The one invulnerable man among
Crude captains, the naked majesty, if you like,
Of bird-nest arches and of rain-stained vaults.   60

The sounds drift in. The buildings are remembered.
The life of the city never lets go, nor do you
Ever want it to. It is part of the life in your room.
Its domes are the architecture of your bed.
The bells keep on repeating solemn names   65

In choruses and choirs of choruses,
Unwilling that mercy should be a mystery
Of silence, that any solitude of sense
Should give you more than their peculiar chords.
And reverberations clinging to whisper still.   70

It is a kind of total grandeur at the end,
With every visible thing enlarged and yet
No more than a bed, a chair and moving nuns,
The immensest theatre, the pillared porch,
The book and candle in your ambered room,   75

Total grandeur of a total edifice,
Chosen by an inquisitor of structures
For himself. He stops upon this threshold,
As if the design of all his words takes form
And frame from thinking and is realized.   80

1952   1954

The Plain Sense of Things[4]

After the leaves have fallen, we return
To a plain sense of things. It is as if
We had come to an end of the imagination,
Inanimate to an inert savoir.[5]

It is difficult even to choose the adjective   5
For this blank cold, this sadness without cause.
The great structure has become a minor house.
No turban walks across the lessened floors.

The greenhouse never so badly needed paint.
The chimney is fifty years old and slants to one side.   10
A fantastic effort has failed, a repetition
In a repetitiousness of men and flies.

---

4. "Now that these poems [a group of poems which included "The Plain Sense of Things"] have been completed they seem to have nothing to do with anything in particular, except poetry" (*Letters*, p. 884).
5. Knowledge (French, "to know").

Yet the absence of the imagination had
Itself to be imagined. The great pond,
The plain sense of it, without reflections, leaves,   15
Mud, water like dirty glass, expressing silence

Of a sort, silence of a rat come out to see,
The great pond and its waste of the lilies, all this
Had to be imagined as an inevitable knowledge,
Required, as a necessity requires.   20

1952   1954

WILLIAM CARLOS WILLIAMS
1883–1963

William Carlos Williams has attracted more followers in the last forty years than has Yeats or Eliot. He is the center of much postwar poetry, especially in the United States. The young men and women who trace their branches to his roots regard many other important poets of the century as merely makers of what Verlaine dismissed as "literature." If at one time these older poets were considered liberators, Williams had to liberate poetry from them.

In this conception Williams joins his disciples; he sees most writing as having taken a wrong turn and regards his own efforts, even if stumbling, as at least in the right direction. This mixture of humility and assertiveness can be found in his poems as well, for example, in "Danse Russe," where the naked dance of the writer before his mirror characterizes him first as a ludicrous figure, then as "the happy genius of my household."

In the same way, many of Williams's dicta about poetry make points that were made also by Eliot and Pound. "The language is worn out," Williams declares in *Paterson*; Pound had said the same in the *Cantos* and Eliot in *Four Quartets*. He was on their side, though he thought himself opposed to them, when he wrote Harriet Monroe, editor of *Poetry*, in 1913, "Most current verse is dead from the point of view of art. . . . Now life is above all things else at any moment subversive of life as it was the moment before—always new, irregular. Verse to be alive must have infused into it something of the same order, some tincture of disestablishment, something in the nature of an impalpable revolution, an ethereal reversal, let me say. I am speaking of modern verse." Pound was to insist in the same way on "making it new," though he annoyed Williams by his belief that a great deal of the remote past was capable of modernization.

Williams was by profession a general practitioner of medicine—the most important literary doctor since Chekhov. Notwithstanding his insistent Americanism, his background and education were cosmopolitan. He was born September 17, 1883, in Rutherford, New Jersey, and died in the same city on March 4, 1963. His father had emigrated from Birmingham, England, and his mother (whose mother was Basque and whose father was of Dutch-Spanish-Jewish descent) from Puerto Rico. Williams attended schools in Rutherford until 1897, when he was sent for two years to a school near Geneva and to the Lycée Condorcet in Paris. On his return he attended the Horace Mann High School in New York City. After having passed a special examination, he was admitted in 1902 to the medical school of the University of Pennsylvania. There he met two poets, Hilda Doolittle and Ezra Pound. The latter friendship had a permanent effect; Williams said he could divide his life into *Before Pound* and *After Pound*.

Williams did his internship in New York City from 1906 to 1909, writing verse in between patients. He published a first book, *Poems*, in 1909. Then he went to Leipzig in 1909 to study pediatrics, and after that returned to Rutherford to practice medicine there for the rest of his life. In 1913 Pound secured a London publisher for Williams's second book, *The Tempers*. But his first distinctly original book was *Al Que Quiere!* (To Him Who Wants It), published in Boston in 1917. In the following years he wrote not only poems but short stories, novels, essays, and an autobiography. In 1946 he began the fulfillment of a long-standing intention, to write an epic, with the publication of *Paterson*, Book I. The four following books appeared in 1948, 1949, 1951, and 1958; at the time of his death he was working on a sixth book.

Williams set himself to write poetry which would have its basis in the language as spoken in the United States. He disapproved of Pound's expatriation, and Eliot's, and said that the publication of *The Waste Land* in 1922 was "the great catastrophe" which, by its genius, interrupted the "rediscovery of a primary impetus, the elementary principles of all art, in the local conditions."[1] He refused to present himself as an artist, insisting instead that he was like other men, using slang to avoid pretentiousness and allowing himself to be thought a fool in preference to being considered a subtle artificer. His object was to communicate with the world directly: "There is a constant barrier between the reader and his consciousness of immediate contact with the world," he wrote in *Spring and All* (1923).[2] In explaining an aphorism in *Paterson*, "No ideas but in things," Williams said, "The poet does not . . . permit himself to go beyond the thought to be discovered in the context of that with which he is dealing. . . . The poet thinks with his poem."

Wallace Stevens, in a famous review of Williams, called his work "anti-poetic," and the adjective has its pertinence if poetry is regarded as bookish and allusive. Williams always emphasizes that the poem must have its own idiom, that it must deal with "those things which lie under the direct scrutiny of the senses, close to the nose."[3] In a poem like "The Red Wheelbarrow" he flouts the great subject and makes clear how any object, rightly regarded, can display its special signature. "The particular thing offers a finality that sends us spinning through space. . . ."[4] Each line is suspended to make it demand another line to complete it, and the whole poem shows the dependence of everything (in the poem, but also, since a microcosm is implied, in the world) upon the red wheelbarrow. "To refine, to clarify, to intensify that eternal moment in which we alone live there is but a single force—the imagination,"[5] says Williams, with something of William Blake's radiant energy. "The only realism in art is of the imagination."[6]

To secure this contact, this immediacy and momentary finality, new forms have to be invented. Williams commends Whitman for his daring, and praises Poe for clearing the ground. In "The Poem as a Field of Action," he writes, "I propose sweeping changes from top to bottom of the poetic structure. . . . I say we are *through* with the iambic pentameter as presently conceived, at least for dramatic verse; through with the measured quatrain, the staid concatenations of sounds in the usual stanza, the sonnet."[7]

In freeing himself from the mediation of other writers, Williams seeks "radiant gists," as he calls them in *Paterson*. These are not so unlike Pound's topflight or magic moments as Williams believes. To attain them there must be a totality of experiencing rather than partial or copycat experiencing.

Although he is ostentatiously in the American grain, Williams is no flagwaver. "I believe all art begins in the local and must begin there since only then will the senses find their material," he said. "Our own language is the beginning of that which makes

1. *The Autobiography of William Carlos Williams*, New York, 1951, p. 146
2. *The William Carlos Williams Reader*, ed. M. L. Rosenthal, New York, 1966, p. 321.
3. *Reader*, p. xix.
4. The same, p. 109.
5. The same, p. 322.
6. The same, p. 327.
7. *Selected Essays*, New York, 1954, p. 281.

and will continue to make an American poetry distinctive. . . ."[8] In "A Poem for Norman MacLeod," he says, "The revolution / is accomplished / noble has been / changed to no bull." This purging of staidness and search for new forms and vital, local language led Williams to conceive his poem, *Paterson,* in which the city is at once a giant in the landscape, like Finnegan in Joyce's *Finnegans Wake,* and a city, and a person. "I took the city as my 'case' to work up. . . . It called for a poetry such as I did not know, it was my duty to discover or make such a context on the 'thought.' To *make* a poem, fulfilling the requirements of the art, and yet new, in the sense that in the very lay of the syllables Paterson as Paterson would be discovered . . . it would be as itself, locally, and so like every other place in the world. For it is in that, that it be particular to its own idiom, that it lives."[9] The poem is about the difficulties of bringing the particulars into poetry, and in the course of this process it suggests the blockage of feeling and thought in the modern city. But like Hart Crane in *The Bridge,* Williams emerges from the waste land. As he wrote in a news release about the last book of *Paterson,* "I had to think hard as to how I was going to end the poem. It wouldn't do to have a grand and soul satisfying conclusion because I didn't see any in my subject. It didn't belong to the subject. It would have been easy to make a great smash up with a 'beautiful' sonnet at sea, or a flight of pigeons, love's end and the welter of man's fate. Instead, after the little girl gets herself mixed up at last in the pathetic sophistication of the great city, no less defeated and understandable, even lovable than she is herself, we come to the sea at last. Odysseus swims in as man must always do, he doesn't drown, he is too able but, accompanied by his dog, strikes inland again (towards Camden) to begin again."

8. The same, p. 89.   *Williams,* Middleboro, Vt., 1964, p. 98.
9. Linda Wagner, *The Poems of William Carlos*

Tract

I will teach you my townspeople
how to perform a funeral
for you have it over a troop
of artists—
unless one should scour the world—   5
you have the ground sense necessary.

See! the hearse leads.
I begin with a design for a hearse.
For Christ's sake not black—
nor white either—and not polished!   10
Let it be weathered—like a farm wagon—
with gilt wheels (this could be
applied fresh at small expense)
or no wheels at all:
a rough dray to drag over the ground.   15

Knock the glass out!
My God—glass, my townspeople!
For what purpose? Is it for the dead
to look out or for us to see
how well he is housed or to see   20
the flowers or the lack of them—
or what?

To keep the rain and snow from him?
He will have a heavier rain soon:
pebbles and dirt and what not.   25
Let there be no glass—
and no upholstery, phew!
and no little brass rollers
and small easy wheels on the bottom—
my townspeople what are you thinking of?   30

A rough plain hearse then
with gilt wheels and no top at all.
On this the coffin lies
by its own weight.

                  No wreaths please—   35
especially no hot house flowers.
Some common memento is better,
something he prized and is known by:
his old clothes—a few books perhaps—
God knows what! You realize   40
how we are about these things
my townspeople—
something will be found—anything
even flowers if he had come to that.
So much for the hearse.   45

For heaven's sake though see to the driver!
Take off the silk hat! In fact
that's no place at all for him—
up there unceremoniously
dragging our friend out to his own dignity!   50
Bring him down—bring him down!
Low and inconspicuous! I'd not have him ride
on the wagon at all—damn him—
the undertaker's understrapper!
Let him hold the reins   55
and walk at the side
and inconspicuously too!

Then briefly as to yourselves:
Walk behind—as they do in France,
seventh class, or if you ride   60
Hell take curtains! Go with some show
of inconvenience; sit openly—
to the weather as to grief.
Or do you think you can shut grief in?
What—from us? We who have perhaps   65
nothing to lose? Share with us
share with us—it will be money
in your pockets.
               Go now
I think you are ready.   70
                         1917

The Widow's Lament in Springtime[1]

Sorrow is my own yard
where the new grass
flames as it has flamed
often before but not
with the cold fire   5
that closes round me this year.
Thirtyfive years
I lived with my husband.
The plumtree is white today
with masses of flowers.   10
Masses of flowers
loaded the cherry branches
and color some bushes
yellow and some red
but the grief in my heart   15
is stronger than they
for though they were my joy
formerly, today I notice them
and turned away forgetting.
Today my son told me   20
that in the meadows,
at the edge of the heavy woods
in the distance, he saw
trees of white flowers.
I feel that I would like   25
to go there
and fall into those flowers
and sink into the marsh near them.

                                                          1921

The Great Figure

Among the rain
and lights
I saw the figure 5
in gold
on a red   5
firetruck
moving
tense
unheeded
to gong clangs   10
siren howls
and wheels rumbling
through the dark city.

                                                          1921

1. The poem is a tribute to Williams's mother.

Spring and All

By the road to the contagious hospital[2]
under the surge of the blue
mottled clouds driven from the
northeast—a cold wind. Beyond, the
waste of broad, muddy fields   5
brown with dried weeds, standing and fallen

patches of standing water
the scattering of tall trees

All along the road the reddish
purplish, forked, upstanding, twiggy   10
stuff of bushes and small trees
with dead, brown leaves under them
leafless vines—

Lifeless in appearance, sluggish
dazed spring approaches—   15

They enter the new world naked,
cold, uncertain of all
save that they enter. All about them
the cold, familiar wind—

Now the grass, tomorrow   20
the stiff curl of wildcarrot leaf
One by one objects are defined—
It quickens: clarity, outline of leaf

But now the stark dignity of
entrance—Still, the profound change   25
has come upon them: rooted, they
grip down and begin to awaken

                                                              1923

The Red Wheelbarrow[3]

so much depends
upon

a red wheel
barrow

glazed with rain   5
water

beside the white
chickens.

                                                              1923

---

2. That is, hospital for contagious diseases.
3. "The rhythm, though no more than a frag-   ment, denotes a certain unquenchable exaltation"
(Williams, in *Sewanee Review*, Autumn 1944).

Portrait of a Lady

Your thighs are appletrees
whose blossoms touch the sky.
Which sky? The sky
where Watteau hung a lady's
slipper.[4] Your knees   5
are a southern breeze—or
a gust of snow. Agh! what
sort of man was Fragonard?
—as if that answered
anything. Ah, yes—below   10
the knees, since the tune
drops that way, it is
one of those white summer days,
the tall grass of your ankles
flickers upon the shore—   15
Which shore?—
the sand clings to my lips—
Which shore?
Agh, petals maybe. How
should I know?   20
Which shore? Which shore?
I said petals from an appletree.

1934

This Is Just to Say

I have eaten
the plums
that were in
the icebox

and which   5
you were probably
saving
for breakfast

Forgive me
they were delicious   10
so sweet
and so cold

1934

The Yachts

contend in a sea which the land partly encloses
shielding them from the too-heavy blows
of an ungoverned ocean which when it chooses

---

4. Jean Antoine Watteau (1684–1721), a French painter, was famous for his pictures of outdoor gatherings of people. However, Williams evidently has in mind *The Swing*, a famous painting by another French artist, Jean Honoré Fragonard (1732–1806, line 8), in which the girl on the swing has kicked off her slipper, which hangs perpetually in mid-air.

tortures the biggest hulls, the best man knows
to pit against its beatings, and sinks them pitilessly.   5
Mothlike in mists, scintillant in the minute

brilliance of cloudless days, with broad bellying sails
they glide to the wind tossing green water
from their sharp prows while over them the crew crawls

ant-like, solicitously grooming them, releasing,   10
making fast as they turn, lean far over and having
caught the wind again, side by side, head for the mark.

In a well guarded arena of open water surrounded by
lesser and greater craft which, sycophant, lumbering
and flittering follow them, they appear youthful, rare   15

as the light of a happy eye, live with the grace
of all that in the mind is fleckless, free and
naturally to be desired. Now the sea which holds them

is moody, lapping their glossy sides, as if feeling
for some slightest flaw but fails completely.   20
Today no race. Then the wind comes again. The yachts

move, jockeying for a start, the signal is set and they
are off. Now the waves strike at them but they are too
well made, they slip through, though they take in canvas.

Arms with hands grasping seek to clutch at the prows.   25
Bodies thrown recklessly in the way are cut aside.
It is a sea of faces about them in agony, in despair

until the horror of the race dawns staggering the mind,
the whole sea become an entanglement of watery bodies
lost to the world bearing what they cannot hold. Broken,   30

beaten, desolate, reaching from the dead to be taken up
they cry out, failing, failing! their cries rising
in waves still as the skillful yachts pass over.

1935

The Young Housewife

At ten A.M. the young housewife
moves about in negligee behind
the wooden walls of her husband's house.
I pass solitary in my car.

Then again she comes to the curb   5
to call the ice-man, fish-man, and stands
shy, uncorseted, tucking in
stray ends of hair, and I compare her
to a fallen leaf.

The noiseless wheels of my car   10
rush with a cracking sound over
dried leaves as I bow and pass smiling.

1938

Raleigh Was Right[5]

We cannot go to the country
for the country will bring us no peace
What can the small violets tell us
that grow on furry stems in
the long grass among lance shaped leaves?   5

Though you praise us
and call to mind the poets
who sung of our loveliness
it was long ago!
long ago! when country people   10
would plow and sow with
flowering minds and pockets at ease—
if ever this were true.

Not now. Love itself a flower
with roots in a parched ground.   15
Empty pockets make empty heads.
Cure it if you can but
do not believe that we can live
today in the country
for the country will bring us no peace.   20

1941

The Dance

In Breughel's great picture, The Kermess,[6]
the dancers go round, they go round and
around, the squeal and the blare and the
tweedle of bagpipes, a bugle and fiddles
tipping their bellies (round as the thick-   5
sided glasses whose wash they impound)
their hips and their bellies off balance
to turn them. Kicking and rolling about
the Fair Grounds, swinging their butts, those
shanks must be sound to bear up under such   10

---

5. Williams is in agreement with a poem by Sir Walter Raleigh (c. 1552–1618), "The Nymph's Reply to the Shepherd"; this in turn was a rebuttal of Christopher Marlowe's poem, "The Passionate Shepherd to His Love," in which the shepherd urged the woman he loved to come to the country and enjoy with him its simple pleasures. Raleigh pointed out that even such an idyllic life was no escape from decay and death.

6. Pieter Bruegel (sometimes spelled Brueghel, Breugel, or Breughel) the Elder (1521?–1569), the Flemish painter, was most famous for his pictures of peasant life, set in ordinary Dutch farms and villages. A kermess is an outdoor festival or fair held to benefit a church on the town's patron saint's day.

rollicking measures, prance as they dance
in Breughel's great picture, The Kermess.

1944

Burning the Christmas Greens

Their time past, pulled down
cracked and flung to the fire
—go up in a roar

All recognition lost, burnt clean
clean in the flame, the green   5
dispersed, a living red,
flame red, red as blood wakes
on the ash—

and ebbs to a steady burning
the rekindled bed become   10
a landscape of flame

At the winter's midnight
we went to the trees, the coarse
holly, the balsam and
the hemlock for their green   15

At the thick of the dark
the moment of the cold's
deepest plunge we brought branches
cut from the green trees

to fill our need, and over   20
doorways, about paper Christmas
bells covered with tinfoil
and fastened by red ribbons

we stuck the green prongs
in the windows hung   25
woven wreaths and above pictures
the living green. On the

mantle we built a green forest
and among those hemlock
sprays put a herd of small   30
white deer as if they

were walking there. All this!
and it seemed gentle and good
to us. Their time past,
relief! The room bare. We   35

stuffed the dead grate
with them upon the half burnt out

log's smoldering eye, opening
red and closing under them

and we stood there looking down.   40
Green is a solace
a promise of peace, a fort
against the cold (though we

did not say so) a challenge
above the snow's   45
hard shell. Green (we might
have said) that, where

small birds hide and dodge
and lift their plaintive
rallying cries, blocks for them   50
and knocks down

the unseeing bullets of
the storm. Green spruce boughs
pulled down by a weight of
snow—Transformed!   55

Violence leaped and appeared.
Recreant! roared to life
as the flame rose through and
our eyes recoiled from it.

In the jagged flames green   60
to red, instant and alive. Green!
those sure abutments . . . Gone!
lost to mind

and quick in the contracting
tunnel of the grate   65
appeared a world! Black
mountains, black and red—as

yet uncolored—and ash white,
an infant landscape of shimmering
ash and flame and we, in   70
that instant, lost,

breathless to be witnesses,
as if we stood
ourselves refreshed among
the shining fauna of that fire.   75
                                                1944

Paterson

"*Paterson* is a long poem in four parts—that a man in himself is a city, beginning,
seeking, achieving and concluding his life in ways which the various aspects of a city

may embody—if imaginatively conceived—any city, all the details of which may be made to voice his most intimate convictions. Part One introduces the elemental character of the place. The Second Part comprises the modern replicas. [Part] Three will seek a language to make them vocal, and [Part] Four, the river below the falls, will be reminiscent of episodes—all that any one man may achieve in a life-time" (*Paterson*, Book I, Author's Note). The poem as Williams originally planned it was completed in 1951 with the publication of Book IV. In 1958 Williams published an unanticipated fifth book.

In his *Autobiography* Williams describes the genesis and aims of the poem: "The first idea centering upon the poem, *Paterson*, came alive early: to find an image large enough to embody the whole knowable world about me. The longer I lived in my place, among the details of my life, I realised that these isolated observations and experiences needed pulling together to gain 'profundity.' I already had the river. . . . I wanted, if I was to write in a larger way than of the birds and flowers, to write about the people close about me: to know in detail, minutely what I was talking about. . . . That is the poet's business. Not to talk in vague categories but to write particularly, as a physician works, upon a patient, upon the thing before him, in the particular to discover the universal. John Dewey had said . . . 'The local is the only universal, upon that all art builds.' "

Twentieth-century Paterson is an industrial city located on the Passaic River in northeast New Jersey. It is situated mostly on a plain surrounded by hills on the north and northwest; part of it is near the Passaic Falls.

From *PATERSON*

From Book I
The Delineaments of the Giants

From *I*

Paterson lies in the valley under the Passaic Falls
its spent waters forming the outline of his back. He
lies on his right side, head near the thunder
of the waters filling his dreams! Eternally asleep,
his dreams walk about the city where he persists   5
incognito. Butterflies settle on his stone ear.
Immortal he neither moves nor rouses and is seldom
seen, though he breathes and subtleties of his
          machinations
drawing their substance from the noise of the pouring
          river
animate a thousand automatons. Who because they   10
neither know their sources nor the sills of their
disappointments walk outside their bodies aimlessly
          for the most part,
locked and forgot in their desires—unroused.

—Say it, no ideas but in things—
nothing but the blank faces of the houses   15
and cylindrical trees
bent, forked by preconception and accident—

split, furrowed, creased, mottled, stained—
secret—into the body of the light!

From above, higher than the spires, higher   20
  even than the office towers, from oozy fields
    abandoned to grey beds of dead grass,
black sumac, withered weed-stalks,
mud and thickets cluttered with dead leaves—
the river comes pouring in above the city   25
and crashes from the edge of the gorge
in a recoil of spray and rainbow mists—

  (What common language to unravel?
    .   .   combed into straight lines
  from that rafter of a rock's   30
  lip.)

A man like a city and a woman like a flower
—who are in love. Two women. Three women.
Innumerable women, each like a flower.

                                        But   35
    only one man—like a city.

*In regard to the poems I left with you; will you be so kind as to return them
to me at my new address? And without bothering to comment upon them if you
should find that embarrassing—for it was the human situation and not the literary one that motivated my phone call and visit.*

*Besides, I know myself to be more the woman than the poet; and to concern
myself less with the publishers of poetry than with . . . living . . .*

*But they set up an investigation . . . and my doors are bolted forever (I hope
forever) against all public welfare workers, professional do-gooders and the like.*[7]

              Jostled as are the waters approaching
              the brink, his thoughts
              interlace, repel and cut under,
              rise rock-thwarted and turn aside   40
              but forever strain forward—or strike
              an eddy and whirl, marked by a
              leaf or curdy spume, seeming
              to forget   .
              Retake later the advance and   45
              are replaced by succeeding hordes
              pushing forward—they coalesce now
              glass-smooth with their swiftness,
              quiet or seem to quiet as at the close
              they leap to the conclusion and   50
              fall, fall in air! as if
              floating, relieved of their weight,
              split apart, ribbons; dazed, drunk

---

7. Williams interpolates prose materials throughout *Paterson*, and a number of these are from letters
Williams actually received. In part, Williams is making the poem by using different kinds of language;
in part he is representing the grab-bag contents of Mr. (later "Dr.") Paterson's mind.

with the catastrophe of the descent
floating unsupported   55
to hit the rocks: to a thunder,
as if lightning had struck

All lightness lost, weight regained in
the repulse, a fury of
escape driving them to rebound   60
upon those coming after—
keeping nevertheless to the stream, they
retake their course, the air full
of the tumult and of spray
connotative of the equal air, coeval,   65
filling the void

And there, against him, stretches the low mountain.
The Park's her head, carved, above the Falls, by the quiet
river;[8] Colored crystals the secret of those rocks;
farms and ponds, laurel and the temperate wild cactus,   70
yellow flowered   .   .   facing him, his
arms supporting her, by the *Valley of the Rocks*, asleep.
Pearls at her ankles, her monstrous hair
spangled with apple-blossoms is scattered about into
the back country, waking their dreams—where the deer run   75
and the wood-duck nests protecting his gallant plumage.

*In February 1857, David Hower, a poor shoemaker with a large family, out
of work and money, collected a lot of mussels from Notch Brook near the City
of Paterson. He found in eating them many hard substances. At first he threw
them away but at last submitted some of them to a jeweler who gave him twenty-
five to thirty dollars for the lot. Later he found others. One pearl of fine lustre
was sold to Tiffany for $900 and later to the Empress Eugenie[9] for $2,000 to be
known thenceforth as the "Queen Pearl," the finest of its sort in the world today.*

*News of this sale created such excitement that search for the pearls was started
throughout the country. The Unios (mussels) at Notch Brook and elsewhere
were gathered by the millions and destroyed often with little or no result. A
large round pearl, weighing 400 grains which would have been the finest pearl
of modern times, was ruined by boiling open the shell.*

Twice a month Paterson receives
communications from the Pope and Jacques
                    Barzun
(Isocrates).[1] His works
have been done into French   80
and Portuguese. And clerks in the post-
office ungum rare stamps from
his packages and steal them for their
childrens' albums   .

---

8. In *Paterson*'s symbolism, the park (that is, nature) is associated with the female principle, the city with the male.

9. Wife of Napoleon III and Empress of the French from 1853 to 1871; Tiffany's is a famous jewelry store. This passage interpolates another kind of prose—city history.

1. Presumably Isocrates, an orator and rhetorician of ancient Greece, is to be identified with Barzun, a twentieth-century scholar and teacher at Columbia University. Dr. Paterson "hears from" him because Barzun was a sponsor of the Readers' Subscription, a highbrow mail-order book club, to which the doctor subscribed.

Say it! No ideas but in things. Mr.   85
Paterson has gone away
to rest and write. Inside the bus one sees
his thoughts sitting and standing. His
thoughts alight and scatter—

Who are these people (how complex   90
the mathematic) among whom I see myself
in the regularly ordered plateglass
of his thoughts, glimmering before shoes and bicycles?
They walk incommunicado, the
equation is beyond solution, yet   95
its sense is clear—that they may live
his thought is listed in the Telephone
Directory—
        And derivatively, for the Great Falls,
PISS-AGH! the giant lets fly!² good *Muncie*, too   100

        They craved the miraculous!

                        *   *   *

                    They begin!
        The perfections are sharpened
        The flower spreads its colored petals
                wide in the sun
        But the tongue of the bee   110
                misses them
        They sink back into the loam
                crying out
        —you may call it a cry
        that creeps over them, a shiver   115
                as they wilt and disappear:
        Marriage come to have a shuddering
                implication

                Crying out
        or take a lesser satisfaction: 120
                a few go
        to the Coast without gain—
        The language is missing them
                they die also
                incommunicado.   125

        The language, the language
                fails them³
        They do not know the words
                or have not
        the courage to use them   .   130
                —girls from

2. The Great Falls are imagined as the giant   inadequate language is evidence of a cultural trag-
urinating.   edy.
3. Here and elsewhere Williams insists that an

families that have decayed and
taken to the hills: no words.
They may look at the torrent in
     their minds
and it is foreign to them.   .   135

They turn their backs
and grow faint—but recover!
    Life is sweet
they say: the language!   140
        —the language
is divorced from their minds,
the language . . the language!

            *   *   *

         From *III*

         *   *   *

      Thought clambers up,
snail like, upon the wet rocks
hidden from sun and sight—   220
         hedged in by the pouring torrent—
and has its birth and death there
in that moist chamber, shut from
the world—and unknown to the world,
cloaks itself in mystery—   225

        And the myth
that holds up the rock,
that holds up the water thrives there—
in that cavern, that profound cleft,
         a flickering green   230
inspiring terror, watching   . .

And standing, shrouded there, in that din,
Earth, the chatterer, father of all
speech . . . .

                      1946

From Book II
Sunday in the Park[4]

I

Outside
         outside myself
                there is a world,
he rumbled, subject to my incursions
—a world   5

4. This section of the poem follows Dr. Paterson's Sunday walk through the park, reporting on what
he sees and also what he thinks. The park is thus both a physical place and a mental occasion.

(to me) at rest,
                    which I approach
concretely—

        The scene's the Park
        upon the rock,   10
        female to the city

—upon whose body Paterson instructs his thoughts
(concretely)
                    —late spring,
        a Sunday afternoon!   15

—and goes by the footpath to the cliff (counting:
the proof)

                    himself among the others,
—treads there the same stones
on which their feet slip as they climb,   20
paced by their dogs!

laughing, calling to each other—

                    Wait for me!

 .   .   the ugly legs of the young girls,
pistons too powerful for delicacy!   .   25
the men's arms, red, used to heat and cold,
to toss quartered beeves and   .

                    Yah! Yah! Yah! Yah!

—over-riding
                    the risks: 30
                          pouring down!⁵
For the flower of a day!

Arrived breathless, after a hard climb he,
looks back (beautiful but expensive!) to
the pearl-grey towers! Re-turns   35
and starts, possessive, through the trees,

                    — that love,
that is not, is not in those terms
to which I'm still the positive
in spite of all;   40
the ground dry,—passive-possessive

Walking —

        Thickets gather about groups of squat sand-pine,
        all but from bare rock   .

5. The working people of the city, who represent America to Dr. Paterson. He wants to be a poet of the people, but feels estranged from them: sometimes he is contemptuous of them, sometimes admiring. They are more physical and natural than he, so he is sometimes related to them as mind is to body.

—a scattering of man-high cedars (sharp cones),   45
antlered sumac   .

—roots, for the most part, writhing
upon the surface
                    (so close are we to ruin every
day!)   50
searching the punk-dry rot

Walking —

The body is tilted slightly forward from the basic standing
position and the weight thrown on the ball of the foot,
while the other thigh is lifted and the leg and opposite   55
arm are swung forward (fig. 6b). Various muscles, aided   .[6]

Despite my having said that I'd never write to you again, I do so now because
I find, with the passing of time, that the outcome of my failure with you has
been the complete damming up of all my creative capacities in a particularly
disastrous manner such as I have never before experienced.

For a great many weeks now (whenever I've tried to write poetry) every
thought I've had, even every feeling, has been struck off some surface crust of
myself which began gathering when I first sensed that you were ignoring the
real contents of my last letters to you, and which finally congealed into some
impenetrable substance when you asked me to quit corresponding with you
altogether without even an explanation.

That kind of blockage, exiling one's self from one's self—have you ever expe-
rienced it? I dare say you have, at moments; and if so, you can well understand
what a serious psychological injury it amounts to when turned into a perma-
nent day-to-day condition.

How do I love you?[7] These!

(He hears! Voices   .   indeterminate! Sees them
moving, in groups, by twos and fours   —   filtering
off by way of the many bypaths.)   60

I asked him, What do you do?

He smiled patiently, The typical American question.
In Europe they would ask, What are you doing? Or,
What are you doing now?

What do I do? listen, to the water falling. (No   65
sound of it here but with the wind!) This is my entire
occupation.

No fairer day ever dawned anywhere than May 2, 1880, when the German
Singing Societies of Paterson met on Garret Mountain, as they did many years
before on the first Sunday in May.

However the meeting of 1880 proved a fatal day, when William Dalzell, who
owned a piece of property near the scene of the festivities, shot John Joseph

---

6. Another kind of prose material—from a medical textbook.

7. Paraphrase of a line from *Sonnets from the Portuguese* (1850) by Elizabeth Barrett Browning.

Van Houten. Dalzell claimed that the visitors had in previous years walked
over his garden and was determined that this year he would stop them from
crossing any part of his grounds.

Immediately after the shot the quiet group of singers was turned into an
infuriated mob who would take Dalzell into their own hands. The mob then
proceeded to burn the barn into which Dalzell had retreated from the angry
group.

Dalzell fired at the approaching mob from a window in the barn and one of
the bullets struck a little girl in the cheek. . . . Some of the Paterson Police
rushed Dalzell out of the barn [to] the house of John Ferguson some half
furlong away.

The crowd now numbered some ten thousand,

"a great beast!"[8]

for many had come from the city to join the conflict. The
case looked serious, for the Police were greatly outnumbered. The crowd then
tried to burn the Ferguson house and Dalzell went to the house of John
McGuckin. While in this house it was that Sergeant John McBride suggested
that it might be well to send for William McNulty, Dean of Saint Joseph's
Catholic Church.

In a moment the Dean set on a plan. He proceeded to the scene in a hack.
Taking Dalzell by the arm, in full view of the infuriated mob, he led the man
to the hack and seating himself by his side, ordered the driver to proceed.
The crowd hesitated, bewildered between the bravery of the Dean and   .

Signs everywhere of birds nesting, while
in the air, slow, a crow zigzags
with heavy wings before the wasp-thrusts   70
of smaller birds circling about him
that dive from above stabbing for his eyes

Walking —

he leaves the path, finds hard going
across-field, stubble and matted brambles   75
seeming a pasture—but no pasture
—old furrows, to say labor sweated or
had sweated here   .

                    a flame,
spent.   80
           The file-sharp grass   .

When! from before his feet, half tripping,
picking a way, there starts
             a flight of empurpled wings!
—invisibly created (their   85
jackets dust-grey) from the dust kindled
to sudden ardor!

           They fly away, churring! until
their strength spent they plunge
to the coarse cover again and disappear   90

---

8. "The people is a great beast"—a remark attributed to Alexander Hamilton, eighteenth-century
American statesman.

—but leave, livening the mind, a flashing
of wings and a churring song   .

AND a grasshopper of red basalt, boot-long,
tumbles from the core of his mind,
a rubble-bank disintegrating beneath a   95
tropic downpour

Chapultepec![9] grasshopper hill!

—a matt stone solicitously instructed
to bear away some rumor
of the living presence that has preceded   100
it, out-precedented its breath   .

These wings do not unfold for flight—
no need!
the weight (to the hand) finding
a counter-weight or counter buoyancy   105
by the mind's wings   .

He is afraid! What then?

Before his feet, at each step, the flight
is renewed. A burst of wings, a quick
churring sound   :   110

      couriers to the ceremonial of love!

—aflame in flight!
      —aflame only in flight!

      No flesh but the caress!

He is led forward by their announcing wings.   115

If that situation with you (your ignoring those particular letters and then your
final note) had belonged to the inevitable lacrimae rerum[1] *(as did, for instance,*
my experience with Z.) its result could not have been (as it has been) to destroy
the validity for me myself of myself, because in that case nothing to do with
my sense of personal identity would have been maimed—the cause of one's
frustrations in such instances being not in one's self nor in the other person
but merely in the sorry scheme of things. But since your ignoring those letters
was not "natural" in that sense (or rather since to regard it as unnatural I am
forced, psychologically, to feel that what I wrote you about, was sufficiently
trivial and unimportant and absurd to merit your evasion) it could not but
follow that that whole side of life connected with those letters should in con-
sequence take on for my own self that same kind of unreality and inaccessibil-
ity which the inner lives of other people often have for us.

      —his mind a red stone carved to be
      endless flight   .

---

9. Fortress near Mexico City.   1. Tears (shed for) things (Virgil, *Aeneid* 1. 462).

Love that is a stone endlessly in flight,
so long as stone shall last bearing
the chisel's stroke   .   120

.   .   and is lost and covered
with ash, falls from an undermined bank
and — begins churring!
AND DOES, the stone after the life!

The stone lives, the flesh dies   125
—we know nothing of death.

—boot long
window-eyes that front the whole head,
                    Red stone! as if
a light still clung in them   .   130

Love

                    combating sleep
                    ─────────────
                    the sleep
piecemeal

Shortly after midnight, August 20, 1878, special officer Goodridge, when, in front of the Franklin House, heard a strange squealing noise down towards Ellison Street. Running to see what was the matter, he found a cat at bay under the water table at Clark's hardware store on the corner, confronting a strange black animal too small to be a cat and entirely too large for a rat. The officer ran up to the spot and the animal got in under the grating of the cellar window, from which it frequently poked its head with a lightning rapidity. Mr. Goodridge made several strikes at it with his club but was unable to hit it. Then officer Keyes came along and as soon as he saw it, he said it was a mink, which confirmed the theory that Mr. Goodridge had already formed. Both tried for a while to hit it with their clubs but were unable to do so, when finally officer Goodridge drew his pistol and fired a shot at the animal. The shot evidently missed its mark, but the noise and powder so frightened the little joker that it jumped out into the street, and made down into Ellison Street at a wonderful gait, closely followed by the two officers. The mink finally disappeared down a cellar window under the grocery story below Spangermacher's large beer saloon, and that was the last seen of it. The cellar was examined again in the morning, but nothing further could be discovered of the little critter that had caused so much fun.

Without invention nothing is well spaced,   135
unless the mind change, unless
the stars are new measured, according
to their relative positions, the
line[2] will not change, the necessity
will not matriculate: unless there is   140
a new mind there cannot be a new

2. Throughout his writing, Williams was especially interested in the poetic line, which he saw as the poetry's defining feature. He abjured both old-fashioned metrical lines and the long loose line of free verse.

line, the old will go on
repeating itself with recurring
deadlines: without invention
nothing lies under the witch-hazel   145
bush, the alder does not grow from among
the hummocks margining the all
but spent channel of the old swale,[3]
the small foot-prints
of the mice under the overhanging   150
tufts of the bunch-grass will not
appear: without invention the line
will never again take on its ancient
divisions when the word, a supple word,
lived in it, crumbled now to chalk.   155

Under the bush they lie protected
from the offending sun—
11 o'clock
      They seem to talk

—a park, devoted to pleasure : devoted to   .   grasshoppers!   160

3 colored girls, of age! stroll by
—their color flagrant,
      their voices vagrant
their laughter wild, flagellant, dissociated
from the fixed scene   .   165

But the white girl, her head
upon an arm, a butt between her fingers
lies under the bush   .   .

Semi-naked, facing her, a sunshade
over his eyes,   170
he talks with her

—the jalopy[4] half hid
behind them in the trees—
I bought a new bathing suit, just

pants and a brassier   :   175
the breasts and
the pudenda covered—beneath

the sun in frank vulgarity.
Minds beaten thin
by waste—among   180

the working classes SOME sort
of breakdown
has occurred. Semi-roused

---

3. Hollow or depression, usually in wet or mar-   4. Slang for a beat-up old automobile.
shy ground.

they lie upon their blanket
face to face,   185
mottled by the shadows of the leaves

upon them, unannoyed,
at least here unchallenged.
Not undignified.   .   .

talking, flagrant beyond all talk   190
in perfect domesticity—
And having bathed

and having eaten (a few
sandwiches)
their pitiful thoughts do meet   195

in the flesh—surrounded
by churring loves! Gay wings
to bear them (in sleep)

—their thoughts alight,
away   200
    .   .   among the grass

Walking   —

Across the old swale—a dry wave in the ground
tho' marked still by the line of Indian alders

    .   .   they (the Indians) would weave   205
in and out, unseen, among them along the stream

    .   come out whooping between the log
house and men working the field, cut them
off! they having left their arms in the block-
house, and—without defense—carry them away   210
into captivity. One old man   .

        Forget it! God's sake, Cut
        out that stuff   .

Walking   —

he rejoins the path and sees, on a treeless   215
knoll—the red path choking it—
a stone wall, a sort of circular
redoubt against the sky, barren and
unoccupied. Mount. Why not?
                              A chipmunk,   220
with tail erect, scampers among the stones.

(Thus the mind grows, up flinty pinnacles)

       but as he leans, in his stride,
    at sight of a flint arrow-head
              (it is not)   225
                   —there
    in the distance, to the north, appear
    to him the chronic hills

              Well, so they are.

                 He stops short: 230
    Who's here?

         To a stone bench, to which she's leashed, within the
wall a man in tweeds—a pipe hooked in his jaw—is combing out a new-
washed Collie bitch. The deliberate comb-strokes part the long hair—even
her face he combs though her legs tremble slightly—until it lies, as he
designs, like ripples in white sand giving off its clean-dog odor. The floor,
stone slabs, she stands patient before his caresses in that bare "sea chamber"

                to the right   240
    from this vantage, the observation tower
    in the middle distance stands up prominently
    from its pubic grove

Dear B. Please excuse me for not having told you this when I was over to your
house. I had no courage to answer your questions so I'll write it. Your dog is
going to have puppies although I prayed she would be okey. It wasn't that she
was left alone as she never was but I used to let her out at dinner time while I
hung up my clothes. At the time, it was on a Thursday, my mother-in-law had
some sheets and table cloths out on the end of the line. I figured the dogs
wouldn't come as long as I was there and none came thru my yard or near the
apartment. He must have come between your hedge and the house. Every few
seconds I would run to the end of the line or peek under the sheets to see if
Musty was alright. She was until I looked a minute too late. I took sticks and
stones after the dog but he wouldn't beat it. George gave me plenty of hell and
I started praying that I had frightened the other dog so much that nothing had
happened. I know you'll be cursing like a son-of-a-gun and probably won't ever
speak to me again for not having told you. Don't think I haven't been worrying
about Musty. She's occupied my mind every day since that awful event. You
won't think so highly of me now and feel like protecting me. Instead I'll bet you
could kill. . .

        And still the picnickers come on, now
        early afternoon, and scatter through the   245
        trees over the fenced-in acres   •

                  Voices!
    multiple and inarticulate   •   voices
    clattering loudly to the sun, to
    the clouds. Voices!   250
    assaulting the air gaily from all sides.

    —among which the ear strains to catch
    the movement of one voice among the rest

—a reed-like voice
                        of peculiar accent   255

Thus she finds what peace there is, reclines,
before his approach, stroked
by their clambering feet—for pleasure

                        It is all for
pleasure   .   their feet   .   aimlessly   260
            wandering

The "great beast" come to sun himself
                                as he may
        .   their dreams mingling,
aloof   265

Let us be reasonable!

                    Sunday in the park,
limited by the escarpment, eastward; to
the west abutting on the old road: recreation
with a view! the binoculars chained   270
to anchored stanchions along the east wall—
        beyond which, a hawk
                                soars!

—a trumpet sounds fitfully.

Stand at the rampart (use a metronome   275
if your ear is deficient, one made in Hungary
if you prefer)
and look away north by east where the church
spires still spend their wits against
the sky   to the ball-park   280
in the hollow with its minute figures running
—beyond the gap where the river
plunges into the narrow gorge, unseen

—and the imagination soars, as a voice
beckons, a thundrous voice, endless   285
—as sleep: the voice
that has ineluctably called them—
                        that unmoving roar!

churches and factories
                    (at a price)   290
together, summoned them from the pit   .

—his voice, one among many (unheard)
moving under all.

                    The mountain quivers.
Time! Count! Sever and mark time!   295

So during the early afternoon, from place
to place he moves,
his voice mingling with other voices
—the voice in his voice
opening his old throat, blowing out his lips,   300
kindling his mind (more
than his mind will kindle)
                —following the hikers.

At last he comes to the idlers' favorite
haunts, the picturesque summit, where   305
the blue-stone (rust-red where exposed
has been faulted at various levels
                (ferns rife among the stones)
into rough terraces and partly closed in
dens of sweet grass, the ground gently sloping.   310

Loiterers in groups straggle
over the bare rock-table—scratched by their
boot-nails more than the glacier scratched
them—walking indifferent through
each other's privacy   .

                                                                315

                —in any case,
the center of movement, the core of gaiety.

Here a young man, perhaps sixteen,
is sitting with his back to the rock among
some ferns playing a guitar, dead pan   .   320

The rest are eating and drinking.

                        The big guy
in the black hat is too full to move
                        but Mary
is up!   325
        Come on! Wassa ma'? You got
broken leg?

                It is this air!
                the air of the Midi[5]
and the old cultures intoxicates them: 330
present!
        —lifts one arm holding the cymbals
of her thoughts, cocks her old head
and dances![6] raising her skirts:

                La la la la!   335

5. Region of Europe around the Mediterranean
Sea, including the south of France and part of Italy.
6. Dancing—especially the dancing of old
women—is a recurrent figure of the union of the
human and the natural in Williams's work.

What a bunch of bums! Afraid somebody see
you?   .
            Blah!
            Excrementi!
                        —she spits.   340
Look a'me, Grandma! Everybody too damn
lazy.

This is the old, the very old, old upon old,
the undying: even to the minute gestures,
the hand holding the cup, the wine   345
spilling, the arm stained by it:

                              Remember
      the peon in the lost
      Eisenstein film[7] drinking

            from a wine-skin with the abandon   350
            of a horse drinking

            so that it slopped down his chin?
            down his neck, dribbling

            over his shirt-front and down
            onto his pants—laughing, toothless?   355

                        Heavenly man!

—the leg raised, verisimilitude   .
even to the coarse contours of the leg, the
bovine touch! The leer, the cave of it,
the female of it facing the male, the satyr—   360
        (Priapus!)[8]
with that lonely implication, goatherd
and goat, fertility, the attack, drunk,
cleansed   .

                  Rejected. Even the film   365
      suppressed : but   persistent

The picnickers laugh on the rocks celebrating
the varied Sunday of their loves with
its declining light —

Walking —   370
      look down (from a ledge) into this grassy
      den
            (somewhat removed from the traffic)
                        above whose brows
      a moon! where she lies sweating at his side: 375

7. *Que Viva Mexico*, a film about Mexican
peasants, which the great Russian film director
Sergei Eisenstein (1898–1948) shot many scenes
for but never completed. Parts of it have been
edited and released by others.
    8. Ancient god of lust and male procreation,
often symbolized by a phallus.

                    She stirs, distraught,
against him—wounded (drunk), moves
against him (a lump) desiring,
against him, bored

flagrantly bored and sleeping, a   380
beer bottle still grasped spear-like
in his hand

while the small, sleepless boys, who
have climbed the columnar rocks
overhanging the pair (where they lie   385
overt upon the grass, besieged—

careless in their narrow cell under
the crowd's feet) stare down,
                    from history!
at them, puzzled and in the sexless   390
light (of childhood) bored equally,
go charging off   •

                    There where
the movement throbs openly
and you can hear the Evangelist shouting!   395

                    —moving nearer
    she—lean as a goat—leans
    her lean belly to the man's backside
    toying with the clips of his
    suspenders   •   400

—to which he adds his useless voice:
until there moves in his sleep
a music that is whole, unequivocal (in
his sleep, sweating in his sleep—laboring
against sleep, agasp!)   405
                    —and does not waken.

Sees, alive (asleep)
            —the fall's roar entering
his sleep (to be fulfilled)
                    reborn   410
in his sleep—scattered over the mountain
severally   •

        —by which he woos her, severally.

And the amnesic crowd (the scattered),
called about — strains   415
to catch the movement of one voice   •

                            hears,
        Pleasure! Pleasure!

—feels,

half dismayed, the afternoon of complex   420
voices its own—
and is relieved
(relived)

A cop is directing traffic
across the main road up   425
a little wooded slope toward
the conveniences:

oaks, choke-cherry,
dogwoods, white and green, iron-wood   :
humped roots matted into the shallow soil   430
—mostly gone: rock out-croppings
polished by the feet of the picnickers:
sweetbarked sassafras
leaning from the rancid grease:
deformity—   435

—to be deciphered (a horn, a trumpet!)
an elucidation by multiplicity,
a corrosion, a parasitic curd, a clarion
for belief, to be good dogs   :

NO DOGS ALLOWED AT LARGE IN THIS PARK   440
1948

The Ivy Crown[9]

The whole process is a lie,
unless,
crowned by excess,
it break forcefully,
one way or another,
from its confinement—   5
or find a deeper well.
Antony and Cleopatra[1]
were right;
they have shown   10
the way. I love you
or I do not live
at all.

Daffodil time
is past. This is   15
summer, summer!
the heart says,
and not even the full of it.

---

9. Associated traditionally with an award for
victory or honor. Ivy was sacred to Dionysus, the
ancient Greek god of wine, ecstasy, sacrifice,
regeneration, and poetic inspiration.

1. The Roman warrior Marc Antony (c. 83–30
B.C.) and the Egyptian queen (69–30 B.C.). Their
passionate love affair and eventual suicides are the
subject of Shakespeare's *Antony and Cleopatra*.

                              No doubts
are permitted—   20
              though they will come
                          and may
before our time
              overwhelm us.
                      We are only mortal   25
but being mortal
              can defy our fate.
                      We may
by an outside chance
              even win! We do not   30
                          look to see
jonquils and violets
              come again
                          but there are,
still,   35
              the roses!

Romance has no part in it.
              The business of love is
                          cruelty *which,*
by our wills,   40
              we transform
                          to live together.
It has its seasons,
              for or against,
                          whatever the heart   45
fumbles in the dark
              to assert
                          toward the end of May.
Just as the nature of briars
              is to tear flesh,   50
                          I have proceeded
through them.
              Keep
                          the briars out,
they say.   55
              You cannot live
                          and keep free of
briars.

Children pick flowers.
              Let them.
                          Though having them   60
in hand
              they have no further use for them
                          but leave them crumpled
at the curb's edge.   65
At our age the imagination
              across the sorry facts
                          lifts us
to make roses
              stand before thorns.   70

                          Sure
love is cruel
            and selfish
                        and totally obtuse—
at least, blinded by the light,   75
                  young love is.
                        But we are older,
I to love
            and you to be loved,
                        we have,   80
no matter how,
            by our wills survived
                        to keep
the jeweled prize
            always   85
                        at our finger tips.
We will it so
            and so it is
                  past all accident.

                                                            1955

From Pictures from Bruegel[2]

II. Landscape with the Fall of Icarus[3]

            According to Brueghel
            when Icarus fell
            it was spring

            a farmer was ploughing
            his field   5
            the whole pageantry

            of the year was
            awake tingling
            near

            the edge of the sea   10
            concerned
            with itself

            sweating in the sun
            that melted
            the wings' wax   55

            unsignificantly
            off the coast
            there was

2. Peter Bruegel (or Brueghel) (1521?–1569), Flemish painter of peasant life, often lively and boisterous. *Pictures from Bruegel* is a set of ten poems, each having as its subject a Bruegel painting.
3. In Greek mythology, Icarus's father, Daedalus, made wings for both of them so that they could escape from Crete; Icarus, however, flew too close to the sun, which melted the wax on his wings. In Bruegel's painting of this scene, Icarus's fall is depicted only by a tiny leg sticking out of the sea in one corner of the picture, the title of which is *Fall of Icarus*. See also W. H. Auden's "Musée de Beaux Arts."

a splash quite unnoticed
this was   20
Icarus drowning

VI. Haymaking[4]

The living quality of
the man's mind
stands out

and its covert assertions
for art, art, art!   5
painting

that the Renaissance
tried to absorb
but

it remained a wheat field   10
over which the
wind played

men with scythes tumbling
the wheat in
rows   15

the gleaners[5] already busy
it was his own—
magpies

the patient horses no one
could take that   20
from him
                                              1962

4. The picture is entitled *Haymaking* or *July*.
5. Farm laborers who pick up scattered grain left by reapers.

D. H. LAWRENCE
1885–1930

In an early poem by W. H. Auden, Lawrence is ranked along with Blake and an American psychotherapist named Homer Lane as a healer, and Lawrence would not have objected to this epithet or to the company of Blake. Like Blake, he sees man as imprisoned within his body, his "bowels of steel"—a mechanism grown incapable of genuine feeling. He is imprisoned within his egoism as well; Lawrence speaks of it as a "barbed-wire enclosure of Know Thyself." And he is imprisoned within sexual taboos which destroy his ability to feel and think by isolating the processes of feeling and thinking from each other.

No wonder, then, that in Lawrence's writings the relations of mother and son are perverse—ruined by possessiveness, an excess of feeling; and the relations of lovers perverse too—ruined by frigidity, an excess of thinking. Jehovah (called by Blake

"Nobodaddy") has replaced pulpy Pan and brooding Osiris, for the time at least. The spirit has to break through egoism and become, as a line in one poem says, "Not I, but the wind that blows through me!" To shed self-involvement, to diminish mind, is the way for western man, at least, to achieve secular beatitude. To die is to be risen, "the same as before yet unaccountably new." Only then can a man "let his buttocks prance," in Lawrence's image.

It might seem that Lawrence espouses mindlessness, but he does so only to make his polemic more clear, not because he wishes mere physicality. The self has to be released by "phallic consciousness, which, you understand [as Lawrence wrote to Harriet Monroe, the editor of *Poetry*, who could scarcely have understood], is not the cerebral sex-consciousness, but something really deeper, and the root of poetry, lived or sung."[1] Sexual intercourse is for Lawrence less a physical act than a mystical mode, so that his endorsement of it is oddly grim.

As a young man Lawrence, who liked to present himself at moments as a fool in motley, said he had naturally in this capacity "turned his capering wits to the trapeze of verse."[2] But he was opposed to contemporary verse, whether it derived from Verlaine's insistence on music above everything or from Mallarmé's symbolist inexpressiveness. As he said in the same letter, "My verses are tolerable—rather pretty, but not suave; there is some blood in them. Poetry now-a-days seems to be a sort of plaster-cast craze, scraps sweetly moulded in easy Plaster of Paris sentiment. Nobody chips verses earnestly out of the living rock of his own feeling. . . . Before everything I like sincerity, and a quickening spontaneous emotion. I do not worship music or the 'half-said thing.' "

Lawrence's basic conception of the poetic process was one of self-extinction: "From the first, I was a little afraid of my real poems—not my 'compositions,' but the poems that had the ghost in them. They seemed to me to come from somewhere, I didn't quite know where, out of a me whom I didn't know and didn't want to know, and say things I would much rather not have said: for choice. But there they were. I never read them again."[3] In a preface to his *Collected Poems*, Lawrence remarked, "A young man is afraid of his demon, and puts his hand over the demon's mouth and speaks for him. And the things the young man says are very rarely poetry. So I have tried to let the demon say his say, and to remove the passages where the young man intruded."

Some of Lawrence's critics, especially formalists like R. P. Blackmur, have taken him to task for not valuing more highly the discipline of craft. Lawrence was not indifferent to good writing—the fact that he made many verbal as well as ideological modifications is evidence—but he thought that form must arise spontaneously from the material, not be imposed upon it from above.

This attitude is clarified in the preface to the American edition of *New Poems* (1918). He distinguishes there between two kinds of poetry, that which is perfect, complete, final, conveyed in perfect symmetry of form, like the "gem-like lyrics of Shelley and Keats. But there is another kind of poetry: the poetry of that which is at hand: the immediate present. In the immediate present there is no perfection, no consummation, nothing finished. . . . Life, the ever-present, knows no finality, no finished crystallisation. . . . Give me nothing fixed, set, static. Don't give me the infinite or the eternal: nothing of infinity, nothing of eternity. Give me the still, white seething, the incandescence and coldness of the incarnate moment: the moment, the quick of all change and haste and opposition: the moment, the immediate present, the Now."

David Herbert Lawrence was born on September 11, 1885, in Eastwood, Not-

1. *The Collected Letters of D. H. Lawrence*, ed. Harry T. Moore, vol. 2, New York, 1962, p. 1047.
2. Letter of July 17, 1908, in *Letters*, vol. 1, pp. 20–21.

3. Quoted in Harry T. Moore, *The Life and Works of D. H. Lawrence*, New York, 1951, pp. 52–53.

tinghamshire. His mother was a schoolteacher, his father a miner; their personalities clashed and marked their son's, whose Oedipal feelings play a prominent part in his novel *Sons and Lovers*. Lawrence tended to think of his life as in two parts, the first of them dominated by his mother. Like her he became a schoolteacher, after he had attended the University of Nottingham. He published his first poems in a magazine in 1909; later Ezra Pound wished to adopt him into the Imagists, with whom he had affinities, but Lawrence preferred to play his own game. He published his first novel, *The White Peacock*, in 1911. A month before, in December, his mother had died, and Lawrence felt very conscious of this "wound," as he called it. The second part of his life, a process of recovery, began in April 1912, when he met Frieda von Richthofen Weekley, the wife of a professor of philology and daughter of a German baron. Almost at once they determined to elope to the Continent, although Frieda would have to leave her three children behind. Eventually Frieda secured a divorce and Lawrence married her in 1914. Back in England, Lawrence opposed the First World War and was suspected of being a spy. As soon as it was over, he and his wife left for Italy. They were to travel about a great deal during the remaining years of Lawrence's life. One extended sojourn was at Taos, New Mexico, where he was surrounded by women admirers. Lawrence was so insistent on the importance of bodiliness that his death in Vence, France, on March 4, 1930, from tuberculosis, had a bitter irony.

Lawrence's most notable poems or passages are bursts of unified perception, characterized by brutal honesty of observation. He pries open the lid, whatever the box may hold. It is the honesty of a man with a *parti pris*, not of a detached observer. He disturbs whatever he touches, he goads and is goaded. A second and rather surprising aspect of his poetry is its dignity. Beyond honesty and dignity his verse has a more fundamental quality of dynamism, a concentrated apprehension of the inner beings of animals and flowers. No poet has a more uncanny sense of what it is like to be, for example, a copulating tortoise. Lawrence's view of nature is not, What principles of order and harmony can I find here? Rather it is, What is the center of violent feeling here? This he elicits with great distinctiveness.

The Wild Common[1]

The quick sparks on the gorse-bushes are leaping
Little jets of sunlight texture imitating flame;
Above them, exultant, the peewits[2] are sweeping:
They have triumphed again o'er the ages, their screamings proclaim.

Rabbits, handfuls of brown earth, lie   5
Low-rounded on the mournful turf they have bitten down to the quick.
Are they asleep?—are they living?—Now see, when I
Lift my arms, the hill bursts and heaves under their spurting kick!

The common flaunts bravely; but below, from the rushes
Crowds of glittering king-cups[3] surge to challenge the blossoming bushes;   10
There the lazy streamlet pushes
His bent course mildly; here wakes again, leaps, laughs, and gushes

Into a deep pond, an old sheep-dip,[4]
Dark, overgrown with willows, cool, with the brook ebbing through so slow;

---

1. Uncultivated stretch of land. Although he did not publish this poem until 1916, Lawrence traditionally placed it first in his collections.
2. Birds noted for their irregular flapping flight and shrill wailing cries; "gorse-bushes": spiny evergreen shrubs with yellow flowers.
3. Buttercups.
4. That is, pond in which sheep are washed.

Naked on the steep, soft lip   15
Of the surf I stand watching my own white shadow quivering to and fro.

What if the gorse-flowers shrivelled, and I were gone?
What if the waters ceased, where were the marigolds then, and the gud-
    geon?[5]
What is this thing that I look down upon?
White on the water wimples[6] my shadow, strains like a dog on a string, to
    run on.   20

How it looks back, like a white dog to its master!
I on the bank all substance, my shadow all shadow looking up to me, looking
    back!
And the water runs, and runs faster, runs faster,
And the white dog dances and quivers, I am holding his cord quite slack.

But how splendid it is to be substance, here!   25
My shadow is neither here nor there; but I, I am royally here!
I am here! I am here! screams the peewit; the may-blobs[7] burst out in a
    laugh as they hear!
Here! flick the rabbits. Here! pants the gorse. Here! say the insects far and
    near.

Over my skin in the sunshine, the warm, clinging air
Flushed with the songs of seven larks singing at once, goes kissing me glad. 30
You are here! You are here! We have found you! Everywhere
We sought you substantial, you touchstone of caresses, you naked lad!

Oh but the water loves me and folds me,
Plays with me, sways me, lifts me and sinks me, murmurs: Oh marvellous
    stuff!
No longer shadow!—and it holds me   35
Close, and it rolls me, enfolds me, touches me, as if never it could touch
    me enough.

Sun, but in substance, yellow water-blobs!
Wings and feathers on the crying, mysterious ages, peewits wheeling!
All that is right, all that is good, all that is God takes substance! a rabbit
    lobs[8]
In confirmation, I hear sevenfold lark-songs pealing.[9]
                                                                                      40
                                                                                  1916

Love on the Farm[1]

What large, dark hands are those at the window
    Grasping in the golden light
Which weaves its way through the evening wind
    At my heart's delight?

---

5. Small fish.
6. Ripples.
7. Marigolds.
8. Runs slowly.

9. As in a ringing of bells.
1. Titled "Cruelty and Love" when first published in 1913, and retitled for the *Collected Poems*
(1928).

Ah, only the leaves! But in the west   5
I see a redness suddenly come
Into the evening's anxious breast—
    'Tis the wound of love goes home!

The woodbine[2] creeps abroad
Calling low to her lover: 10
    The sun-lit flirt who all the day
    Has poised above her lips in play
    And stolen kisses, shallow and gay
    Of pollen, now has gone away—
        She woos the moth with her sweet, low word: 15
And when above her his moth-wings hover
Then her bright breast she will uncover
And yield her honey-drop to her lover.

Into the yellow, evening glow
Saunters a man from the farm below;   20
Leans, and looks in at the low-built shed
Where the swallow has hung her marriage bed.
    The bird lies warm against the wall.
    She glances quick her startled eyes
    Towards him, then she turns away   25
    Her small head, making warm display
    Of red upon the throat. Her terrors sway
    Her out of the nest's warm, busy ball,
    Whose plaintive cry is heard as she flies
    In one blue stoop from out the sties[3]   30
    Into the twilight's empty hall.
Oh, water-hen, beside the rushes
Hide your quaintly scarlet blushes,
Still your quick tail, lie still as dead,
Till the distance folds over his ominous tread!   35

The rabbit presses back her ears,
Turns back her liquid, anguished eyes
And crouches low; then with wild spring
Spurts from the terror of *his* oncoming;
To be choked back, the wire ring   40
Her frantic effort throttling:
    Piteous brown ball of quivering fears!
Ah, soon in his large, hard hands she dies,
And swings all loose from the swing of his walk!
Yet calm and kindly are his eyes   45
And ready to open in brown surprise
Should I not answer to his talk
Or should he my tears surmise.

I hear his hand on the latch, and rise from my chair
Watching the door open; he flashes bare   50
His strong teeth in a smile, and flashes his eyes
In a smile like triumph upon me; then careless-wise

---

2. Honeysuckle.   3. Pen for animals.

He flings the rabbit soft on the table board
And comes towards me: ah! the uplifted sword
Of his hand against my bosom! and oh, the broad   55
Blade of his glance that asks me to applaud
His coming! With his hand he turns my face to him
And caresses me with his fingers that still smell grim
Of the rabbit's fur! God, I am caught in a snare![4]
I know not what fine wire is round my throat;   60
I only know I let him finger there
My pulse of life, and let him nose like a stoat[5]
Who sniffs with joy before he drinks the blood.

And down his mouth comes to my mouth! and down
His bright dark eyes come over me, like a hood   65
Upon my mind! his lips meet mine, and a flood
Of sweet fire sweeps across me, so I drown
Against him, die, and find death good.

                                                                   1913

The Bride[6]

My love looks like a girl to-night,
          But she is old.
The plaits[7] that lie along her pillow
          Are not gold,
But threaded with filigree silver,   5
          And uncanny cold.

She looks like a young maiden, since her brow
          Is smooth and fair;
Her cheeks are very smooth, her eyes are closed,
          She sleeps a rare,   10
Still, winsome sleep, so still, and so composed.

Nay, but she sleeps like a bride, and dreams her dreams
          Of perfect things.
She lies at last, the darling, in the shape of her dream;
          And her dead mouth sings   15
By its shape, like thrushes in clear evenings.

                                                                   1916

Gloire de Dijon[8]

When she rises in the morning
I linger to watch her;
She spreads the bath-cloth underneath the window
And the sunbeams catch her
Glistening white on the shoulders,   5

---

4. A wire loop for trapping animals.
5. That is, weasel.
6. The poem is about Lawrence's mother, who died on December 5, 1910.

7. Braids of hair.
8. Literally, "Glory of Dijon"; Dijon is a French town.

While down her sides the mellow
Golden shadow glows as
She stoops to the sponge, and her swung breasts
Sway like full-blown yellow
Gloire de Dijon roses.   10

She drips herself with water, and her shoulders
Glisten as silver, they crumple up
Like wet and falling roses, and I listen
For the sluicing of their rain-dishevelled petals.
In the window full of sunlight   15
Concentrates her golden shadow
Fold on fold, until it glows as
Mellow as the glory roses.

                                                           1917

Piano

Softly, in the dusk, a woman is singing to me;
Taking me back down the vista of years, till I see
A child sitting under the piano, in the boom of the tingling strings
And pressing the small, poised feet of a mother who smiles as she sings.

In spite of myself, the insidious mastery of song   5
Betrays me back, till the heart of me weeps to belong
To the old Sunday evenings at home, with winter outside
And hymns in the cosy parlour, the tinkling piano our guide.

So now it is vain for the singer to burst into clamour
With the great black piano appassionato.[9] The glamour   10
Of childish days is upon me, my manhood is cast
Down in the flood of remembrance, I weep like a child for the past.

                                                           1918

Snake

A snake came to my water-trough
On a hot, hot day, and I in pyjamas for the heat,
To drink there.

In the deep, strange-scented shade of the great dark carob-tree[1]
I came down the steps with my pitcher   5
And must wait, must stand and wait, for there he was at the trough before
    me.

He reached down from a fissure in the earth-wall in the gloom
And trailed his yellow-brown slackness soft-bellied down, over the edge of
    the stone trough
And rested his throat upon the stone bottom,
And where the water had dripped from the tap, in a small clearness,   10

---

9. Played with passion.   1. Mediterranean evergreen tree.

He sipped with his straight mouth,
Softly drank through his straight gums, into his slack long body,
Silently.

Someone was before me at my water-trough,   15
And I, like a second comer, waiting.

He lifted his head from his drinking, as cattle do,
And looked at me vaguely, as drinking cattle do,
And flickered his two-forked tongue from his lips, and mused a moment,
And stooped and drank a little more,   20
Being earth-brown, earth-golden from the burning bowels of the earth
On the day of Sicilian July, with Etna[2] smoking.

The voice of my education said to me
He must be killed,
For in Sicily the black, black snakes are innocent, the gold are venomous. 25

And voices in me said, If you were a man
You would take a stick and break him now, and finish him off.

But must I confess how I liked him,
How glad I was he had come like a guest in quiet, to drink at my water-
     trough
And depart peaceful, pacified, and thankless,   30
Into the burning bowels of this earth?

Was it cowardice, that I dared not kill him?
Was it perversity, that I longed to talk to him?
Was it humility, to feel so honoured?
I felt so honoured.   35

And yet those voices:
If you were not afraid, you would kill him!

And truly I was afraid, I was most afraid,
But even so, honoured still more
That he should seek my hospitality   40
From out the dark door of the secret earth.

He drank enough
And lifted his head, dreamily, as one who has drunken,
And flickered his tongue like a forked night on the air, so black;
Seeming to lick his lips,   45
And looked around like a god, unseeing, into the air,
And slowly turned his head,
And slowly, very slowly, as if thrice adream,
Proceeded to draw his slow length curving round
And climb again the broken bank of my wall-face.   50

And as he put his head into that dreadful hole,
And as he slowly drew up, snake-easing his shoulders, and entered farther,

2. The volcano.

A sort of horror, a sort of protest against his withdrawing into that horrid
    black hole,
Deliberately going into the blackness, and slowly drawing himself after,
Overcame me now his back was turned.   55

I looked round, I put down my pitcher,
I picked up a clumsy log
And threw it at the water-trough with a clatter.

I think it did not hit him,
But suddenly that part of him that was left behind convulsed in undignified
    haste,   60
Writhed like lightning, and was gone
Into the black hole, the earth-lipped fissure in the wall-front,
At which, in the intense still noon, I stared with fascination.

And immediately I regretted it.
I thought how paltry, how vulgar, what a mean act!   65
I despised myself and the voices of my accursed human education.

And I thought of the albatross,[3]
And I wished he would come back, my snake.

For he seemed to me again like a king,
Like a king in exile, uncrowned in the underworld,   70
Now due to be crowned again.

And so, I missed my chance with one of the lords
Of life.
And I have something to expiate;
A pettiness.   75
                                  1923

When I Read Shakespeare

When I read Shakespeare I am struck with wonder
that such trivial people should muse and thunder
in such lovely language.

Lear, the old buffer, you wonder his daughters
didn't treat him rougher,   5
the old chough, the old chuffer![4]

And Hamlet, how boring, how boring to live with,
so mean and self-conscious, blowing and snoring
his wonderful speeches, full of other folks' whoring!

And Macbeth and his Lady, who should have been choring,
such suburban ambition, so messily goring
old Duncan with daggers!

3. In Samuel Taylor Coleridge's "Rime of the
Ancient Mariner" (1798), a ship and its crew fall
under a curse when the Mariner wantonly shoots
an albatross.
    4. Imposter; "chough": chatterer, jabberer.

How boring, how small Shakespeare's people are!
Yet the language so lovely! like the dyes from gas-tar.

1929

Middle of the World[5]

This sea will never die, neither will it ever grow old
nor cease to be blue, nor in the dawn
cease to lift up its hills
and let the slim black ship of Dionysos come sailing in
with grape-vines up the mast,[6] and dolphins leaping.   5

What do I care if the smoking ships
of the P. & O. and the Orient Line and all the other stinkers
cross like clock-work the Minoan[7] distance!
They only cross, the distance never changes.

And now that the moon who gives men glistening bodies   10
is in her exaltation, and can look down on the sun
I see descending from the ships at dawn
slim naked men from Cnossos,[8] smiling the archaic smile
of those that will without fail come back again,
and kindling little fires upon the shores   15
and crouching, and speaking the music of lost languages.

And the Minoan Gods, and the Gods of Tiryns[9]
are heard softly laughing and chatting, as ever;
and Dionysos, young and a stranger
leans listening on the gate, in all respect.   20

1932

Red Geranium and Godly Mignonette[1]

Imagine that any mind ever *thought* a red geranium!
As if the redness of a red geranium could be anything but a sensual experience
and as if sensual experience could take place before there were any senses.
We know that even God could not imagine the redness of a red geranium
nor the smell of mignonette   5
when geraniums were not, and mignonette neither.
And even when they were, even God would have to have a nose
to smell at the mignonette.
You can't imagine the Holy Ghost sniffing at cherry-pie heliotrope.
Or the Most High, during the coal age, cudgelling his mighty brains   10
even if he had any brains: straining his mighty mind

---

5. That is, the Mediterranean Sea, which means, literally, "middle of the earth."
6. In the Seventh Homeric Hymn, the god Dionysus, captured by pirates, turns into a panther (his emblematic beast) and causes a grapevine (his emblem as god of wine) to entwine the ship's mast.
7. Of the brilliant early civilization in Crete.

8. Center of the Minoan civilization in Crete.
9. An ancient city in Greece, perhaps settled by Minoans; these gods are thought of as preceding the divinity of Dionysus.
1. An African herb with greenish-white or greenish-yellow flowers. Its name comes from the French *mignon*, "small."

to think, among the moss and mud of lizards and mastodons
to think out, in the abstract, when all was twilit green and muddy:
"Now there shall be tum-tiddly-um, and tum-tiddly-um,
hey-presto!² scarlet geranium!"   15
We know it couldn't be done.
But imagine, among the mud and the mastodons
God sighing and yearning with tremendous creative yearning, in that dark
    green mess
of, for some other beauty, some other beauty
that blossomed at last, red geranium, and mignonette.   20

1932

Whales Weep Not!

They say the sea is cold, but the sea contains
the hottest blood of all, and the wildest, the most urgent.
All the whales in the wider deeps, hot are they, as they urge
on and on, and dive beneath the icebergs.
The right whales, the sperm-whales, the hammer-heads, the killers   5
there they blow, there they blow, hot wild white breath out of the sea!

And they rock, and they rock, through the sensual ageless ages
on the depths of the seven seas,
and through the salt they reel with drunk delight
and in the tropics tremble they with love   10
and roll with massive, strong desire, like gods.
Then the great bull lies up against his bride
in the blue deep bed of the sea,
as mountain pressing on mountain, in the zest of life:
and out of the inward roaring of the inner red ocean of whale-blood 15
the long tip reaches strong, intense, like the maelstrom-tip, and comes to
    rest
in the clasp and the soft, wild clutch of a she-whale's fathomless body.

And over the bridge of the whale's strong phallus, linking the wonder of
    whales
the burning archangels under the sea keep passing, back and forth,
keep passing, archangels of bliss   20
from him to her, from her to him, great Cherubim³
that wait on whales in mid-ocean, suspended in the waves of the sea
great heaven of whales in the waters, old hierarchies.

And enormous mother whales lie dreaming suckling their whale-tender young
and dreaming with strange whale eyes wide open in the waters of the begin-
    ning and the end.   25

And bull-whales gather their women and whale-calves in a ring
when danger threatens, on the surface of the ceaseless flood
and range themselves like great fierce Seraphim⁴ facing the threat
encircling their huddled monsters of love.

2. Catch-word used by British conjurers.   tice.
3. Angels representing divine wisdom or jus-   4. Angels who guard God's throne.

And all this happens in the sea, in the salt   30
where God is also love, but without words:
and Aphrodite[5] is the wife of whales
most happy, happy she!

and Venus among the fishes skips and is a she-dolphin
she is the gay, delighted porpoise sporting with love and the sea   35
she is the female tunny-fish, round and happy among the males
and dense with happy blood, dark rainbow bliss in the sea.

                                                                                      1932

Bavarian Gentians

Not every man has gentians in his house
in soft September, at slow, sad Michaelmas.[6]

Bavarian gentians, big and dark, only dark
darkening the day-time, torch-like with the smoking blueness of Pluto's
    gloom,[7]
ribbed and torch-like, with their blaze of darkness spread blue   5
down flattening into points, flattened under the sweep of white day
torch-flower of the blue-smoking darkness, Pluto's dark-blue daze,
black lamps from the halls of Dis, burning dark blue,
giving off darkness, blue darkness, as Demeter's pale lamps give off light,
lead me then, lead the way.   10

Reach me a gentian, give me a torch!
let me guide myself with the blue, forked torch of this flower
down the darker and darker stairs, where blue is darkened on blueness
even where Persephone goes, just now, from the frosted September
to the sightless realm where darkness is awake upon the dark   15
and Persephone herself is but a voice
or a darkness invisible enfolded in the deeper dark
of the arms Plutonic, and pierced with the passion of dense gloom,
among the splendour of torches of darkness, shedding darkness on the lost
    bride and her groom.

                                                                                      1932

The Ship of Death[8]

I

Now it is autumn and the falling fruit
and the long journey towards oblivion.

5. Greek goddess of love, known in Rome as Venus (below).

6. September 29, the feast celebrating the Archangel Michael.

7. Pluto (or Dis), in Roman mythology, ruled the underworld. He abducted Persephone, daughter of the grain goddess Demeter, and made her his queen; she was allowed to return from the underworld in April and remain with her mother for six months, but in September had to rejoin her husband.

8. This poem was written near the end of 1929; Lawrence died on March 2, 1930. In his travel book, *Etruscan Places* (1927), Lawrence described ancient Italian tombs in which had been buried, near the body of the dead man, "the little bronze ship that should bear him over to the other world, the vases of jewels for his arraying, the vases of small dishes, the little bronze statuettes and tools, the weapons, the armor: all the amazing impedimenta of the important dead."

The apples falling like great drops of dew
to bruise themselves an exit from themselves.

And it is time to go, to bid farewell   5
to one's self, and find an exit
from the fallen self.

II

Have you built your ship of death, O have you?
O build your ship of death, for you will need it.

The grim frost is at hand, when the apples will fall   10
thick, almost thundrous, on the hardened earth.

And death is on the air like a smell of ashes!
Ah! can't you smell it?

And in the bruised body, the frightened soul
finds itself shrinking, wincing from the cold   15
that blows upon it through the orifices.

III

And can a man his own quietus make
with a bare bodkin?[9]

With daggers, bodkins, bullets, man can make
a bruise or break of exit for his life;   20
but is that a quietus, O tell me, is it quietus?

Surely not so! for how could murder, even self-murder
ever a quietus make?

IV

O let us talk of quiet that we know,
that we can know, the deep and lovely quiet   25
of a strong heart at peace!

How can we this, our own quietus, make?

V

Build then the ship of death, for you must take
the longest journey, to oblivion.
And die the death, the long and painful death   30
that lies between the old self and the new.

Already our bodies are fallen, bruised, badly bruised,
already our souls are oozing through the exit
of the cruel bruise.

9. *Hamlet* 3.1.75–76. "Quietus": death; "bodkin": dagger.

Already the dark and endless ocean of the end   35
is washing in through the breaches of our wounds,
already the flood is upon us.

Oh build your ship of death, your little ark
and furnish it with food, with little cakes, and wine
for the dark flight down oblivion.   40

VI

Piecemeal the body dies, and the timid soul
has her footing washed away, as the dark flood rises.

We are dying, we are dying, we are all of us dying
and nothing will stay the death-flood rising within us
and soon it will rise on the world, on the outside world.   45

We are dying, we are dying, piecemeal our bodies are dying
and our strength leaves us,
and our soul cowers naked in the dark rain over the flood,
cowering in the last branches of the tree of our life.

VII

We are dying, we are dying, so all we can do   50
is now to be willing to die, and to build the ship
of death to carry the soul on the longest journey.

A little ship, with oars and food
and little dishes, and all accoutrements
fitting and ready for the departing soul.   55

Now launch the small ship, now as the body dies
and life departs, launch out, the fragile soul
in the fragile ship of courage, the ark of faith
with its store of food and little cooking pans
and change of clothes,   60
upon the flood's black waste
upon the waters of the end
upon the sea of death, where still we sail
darkly, for we cannot steer, and have no port.

There is no port, there is nowhere to go   65
only the deepening black darkening still
blacker upon the soundless, ungurgling flood
darkness at one with darkness, up and down
and sideways utterly dark, so there is no direction any more.
And the little ship is there; yet she is gone.   70
She is not seen, for there is nothing to see her by.
She is gone! gone! and yet
somewhere she is there.
Nowhere!

VIII

And everything is gone, the body is gone   75
completely under, gone, entirely gone.
The upper darkness is heavy on the lower,
between them the little ship
is gone
she is gone.   80

It is the end, it is oblivion.

IX

And yet out of eternity, a thread
separates itself on the blackness,
a horizontal thread
that fumes a little with pallor upon the dark.   85

Is it illusion? or does the pallor fume
A little higher?
Ah wait, wait, for there's the dawn,
the cruel dawn of coming back to life
out of oblivion.   90

Wait, wait, the little ship
drifting, beneath the deathly ashy grey
of a flood-dawn.

Wait, wait! even so, a flush of yellow
and strangely, O chilled wan soul, a flush of rose.   95

A flush of rose, and the whole thing starts again.

X

The flood subsides, and the body, like a worn sea-shell
emerges strange and lovely.
And the little ship wings home, faltering and lapsing
on the pink flood,   100
and the frail soul steps out, into her house again
filling the heart with peace.

Swings the heart renewed with peace
even of oblivion.

Oh build your ship of death, oh build it!   105
for you will need it.
For the voyage of oblivion awaits you.

1932

EZRA POUND
1885–1972

The most extraordinary career in modern poetry has unchallengeably been that of
Ezra Pound. It was he more than anyone who made poets write modern verse, editors publish it, and readers read it. Yeats asked Pound's help when in 1912 he felt
his style had become abstract; Eliot asked Pound's help when in 1921 he had to sift
The Waste Land out of a mass of ill-assorted material. Pound may also be said to have
discovered Joyce, first as a poet and then as a prose writer, and to have made possible
all his later work. These were major benefactions, but there were innumerable minor
ones as well. Until his later misadventures, Pound's life was a history of openhand-
edness, financial—though he had little money—as well as literary.

His life was centered with great energy on the pursuit of what Arnold called the
best that has been thought and said in the world, and on the attempt to "make it
new" (his slogan) for the present day. He showed an American voracity for swallowing up talented utterance in all languages. Pound was born on October 30, 1885, in
Hailey, Idaho; at the age of two he was taken to Pennsylvania and brought up in the
East. He retained a frontiersman's pleasure in thinking about the opening up of the
West, and prided himself on the exploits of a grandfather who built a railway; he
kept up a rough-and-ready manner, an American bluntness in effete Europe. He
tried to marry continental and Oriental suavities with western directness and even
vulgarity. More profoundly, he sought to bring incandescent moments ("magic
moments," he sometimes called them) out of seeming welter, precision out of seeming improvisation, the most telling English out of conversational or prosy details.
The result of this effort remains controversial. Yeats found Pound's verse to be too
experimental; Eliot, though personally devoted to him, thought it verged on the
"quaint and archaic." Pound himself had misgivings about his literary as well as political directions. But if his poetry is imperfect, it suits the present time, when many
poets feel, without misgivings, that the effect of formal perfection is to betray the
original vision. Pound has had a great effect on verse written in the second half of
the century, notably that of Charles Olson, no less than on verse written in the first
half.

At the age of sixteen Pound enrolled as a special student (rather than as a degree
candidate) at the University of Pennsylvania, to study (as he said) what he thought
important. Then in 1903 he matriculated more conventionally at Hamilton College,
and took a Ph.B. in 1905. His interests were in Romance languages and literatures;
he returned as a fellow in these to the University of Pennsylvania in 1905. He took a
master of arts degree that year, but much more consequential was his meeting with
two poets also just getting started, William Carlos Williams and Hilda Doolittle. She
later became a member of Pound's Imagist group, and Williams and Pound criticized
and befriended each other all their lives.

The next year Pound won a fellowship to go to Provence, Italy, and especially
Spain, in preparation for a dissertation on Lope de Vega. This was never to be written. On his return he became an instructor in Romance languages at Wabash College
in Crawfordsville, Indiana. His generosity in offering his bed to a girl stranded from
a burlesque show was construed by his landladies, and then by the college authorities, as immoral behavior; he was discharged, but was given the rest of his year's
salary, and with this he went to Gibraltar and Venice. In the latter city (which was
to be the scene of his declining years as well) Pound published his first book, *A Lume
Spento* ("With Tapers Extinguished")—he would describe these poems later as "stale
creampuffs," but with all their echoes of Yeats and more exotic poets they are full of
possibility. Pound makes, for example, the first important use in modern verse of
ellipses to indicate the speaker's panicky repressions. From Venice Pound went to

London, where for twelve years he remained a continuing sensation. At that time (1908) Pound was convinced that all English poets except Yeats were on the wrong track, and that Yeats was the greatest poet writing in English. The friendship of these two, which began shortly after Pound's arrival, was important for both. It was the period when Victorianism was giving way to a new idiom: Virginia Woolf said that in 1910 human personality changed, and at any rate it appeared to do so as modern art, music, and architecture began to coalesce with modern literature. In literature Pound was perhaps excessively fond of the troubadours, but he also evinced great respect for a writer like Henry James, the full range of whose modernity was not yet clear to most readers. He profited from the friendship of Ford Madox Ford, a novelist and poet much occupied with bringing the language up to date. Finally, Pound moved in the same circle as T. E. Hulme, who offered the modern movement one of its principal esthetic programs. Hulme, trained in philosophy, was fed up with Romanticism, humanism, and individualism: he thought it important for man to recognize himself as finite and limited, burdened down with original sin. Against the vague outlines and damp emotions which he found in Romantic art, he espoused the formalized lines of Byzantine sculpture and painting and the geometrical qualities of Egyptian art. He said that Romanticism was a well and classicism a bucket, and that the bucket was preferable.

In 1912, Pound founded, with Hilda Doolittle, Richard Aldington, and F. S. Flint, the Imagist group. Their purpose was to sanction experimentation in verse form and to aim at new modes of perception. Pound published in *Poetry* (March 1913) "A Few Don'ts for an Imagist," which set forth three principles:

(1) Direct treatment of the "thing," whether subjective or objective.

(2) To use absolutely no word that does not contribute to the presentation.

(3) As regarding rhythm: to compose in the sequence of the musical phrase, not in the sequence of the metronome.

Pound's most congruent literary relationship in England was with T. S. Eliot, whom he met in September 1914. He was astonished to discover that Eliot had "modernized himself on his own," and he quickly obliged Harriet Monroe to publish "Prufrock" and persuaded the editor of the *Egoist*, Harriet Weaver, to publish Eliot's first book, *Prufrock and Other Observations*. But then both men decided on a change of technique. As Pound wrote, "at a particular date in a particular room, two authors, neither engaged in picking the other's pocket, decided that the dilutation of *vers libre*, Amygism, Lee Masterism, general floppiness had gone too far and that some countercurrent must be set going. Parallel situation centuries ago in China. Remedy prescribed 'Émaux et Camées' [*Enamels and Cameos*, by Théophile Gautier] (or the Bay State Hymn Book). Rhyme and regular strophes. Results: Poems in Mr. Eliot's *second* volume, not contained in his first, . . . also 'H. S. Mauberley'. Divergence later."[1]

Hugh Selwyn Mauberley: Life and Contacts was first published in 1920, though its first section was completed at least a year earlier. It anticipates many of the devices of *The Waste Land* (1922), such as sudden shifts of perspective, unacknowledged quotations in different languages, and the presentation of an individual consciousness against a panorama of the age. It is much more loosely knit, however. Pound was eager to disavow that the poem was autobiographical: "Of course, I'm no more Mauberley than Eliot is Prufrock."[2]

In the meantime Pound had begun his principal work, the *Cantos*, long meditated and destined to occupy him during the rest of his life. He eventually published 117 Cantos, the last ones being incomplete. At various times Pound offered indications of his plan in the *Cantos*, but these varied from each other.

---

1. *Polite Essays*, New York, 1940, p. 14.   D. Paige, New York, 1950, p. 180.
2. *The Letters of Ezra Pound*, 1907–41, ed. D.

The *Cantos*, in the aggregate, display Pound's preference for what is active, bountiful, abundant, passionate, and concrete, over what is passive, usurious, niggardly, ratiocinative, and abstract. They pose a "green world" against a waste land, and instead of the fragments adding up to degradation, as in Eliot, they compose for Pound possibilities and brief realizations. The *Cantos* stand like a monolith in modern literature, not to be avoided or ignored.

In 1920 Pound left England for Paris, where he lived until 1924. Then he moved to Italy, where by 1928 he had settled in Rapallo. In 1925 he published *A Draft of XVI Cantos* as if these versions were to be thought of as tentative. He was later to drop the word "draft" without altering the poems. In 1926 his opera, *The Testament of François Villon*, was performed in Paris. Pound continued to publish the *Cantos* along with books of prose. In 1939 he visited the United States for the first time since 1910. The next year he began to give talks on the Rome radio, denouncing President Roosevelt and supporting various activities of Mussolini as conducive to a new society no longer based on money grubbing. After the United States entered the war he continued to give these talks, and so was indicted in 1943 for treason. The following year the U.S. Army arrested him, and he suffered confinement in a stockade in Pisa. This experience was reflected in some of his best poems, the *Pisan Cantos*. In 1945 he was flown to Washington to stand trial, but was remanded to St. Elizabeth's Hospital for the criminally insane. When in 1949 he was awarded the Bollingen Prize for poetry, a great furore was raised, and Pound's adherents and detractors argued the merits of his case, for a long time afterwards. In 1958, because of the intercession of various poets, including Frost and MacLeish, and of other sympathizers, the indictment for treason was dismissed. Pound went to Italy and resided for a time with his daughter at Schloss Brunnenburg, near Merano, and then with his longtime companion, Olga Rudge, in Venice. He died there on November 1, 1972.

Portrait d'une Femme[1]

Your mind and you are our Sargasso Sea,[2]
London has swept about you this score years
And bright ships left you this or that in fee:
Ideas, old gossip, oddments of all things,
Strange spars of knowledge and dimmed wares of price.   5
Great minds have sought you—lacking someone else.
You have been second always. Tragical?
No. You preferred it to the usual thing:
One dull man, dulling and uxorious,
One average mind—with one thought less, each year.   10
Oh, you are patient, I have seen you sit
Hours, where something might have floated up.
And now you pay one. Yes, you richly pay.
You are a person of some interest, one comes to you
And takes strange gain away.   15
Trophies fished up; some curious suggestion:
Fact that leads nowhere; and a tale or two,
Pregnant with mandrakes, or with something else
That might prove useful and yet never proves,
That never fits a corner or shows use,   20

1. Portrait of a Woman (French).
2. A sea in the north Atlantic which is choked with seaweed; it was widely believed, though eventually disproved, that many ships had been inextricably tangled in the weeds.

Or finds its hour upon the loom of days:
The tarnished, gaudy, wonderful old work;
Idols and ambergris and rare inlays,
These are your riches, your great store; and yet
For all this sea-hoard of deciduous things,   25
Strange woods half sodden, and new brighter stuff:
In the slow float of differing light and deep,
No! there is nothing! In the whole and all,
Nothing that's quite your own.
        Yet this is you.   30
                         1912

The Return[3]

See, they return; ah, see the tentative
    Movements, and the slow feet,
    The trouble in the pace and the uncertain
    Wavering!

See, they[4] return, one, and by one,   5
    With fear, as half-awakened;
    As if the snow should hesitate
    And murmur in the wind,
            and half turn back;
    These were the "Wing'd-with-Awe,"   10
        Inviolable.

Gods of the wingèd shoe![5]
    With them the silver hounds,
        sniffing the trace of air!

Haie! Haie!   15
    These were the swift to harry;
These the keen-scented;
These were the souls of blood.

Slow on the leash,
    pallid the leash-men!   20
                         1912

The River-Merchant's Wife: A Letter[6]

While my hair was still cut straight across my forehead
I played about the front gate, pulling flowers.

3. Pound says of this poem that it "is an objective reality and has a complicated sort of significance," which he compares to that of a modern sculpture (*Gaudier-Brzeska: A Memoir* (1916), p. 98). Compare, in "Hugh Selwyn Mauberley," "Phallic and ambrosial / Made way for macerations" (p. 220, lines 38–39).
4. A deliberately indistinct reference to the pagan gods.
5. A homeric epithet, coined by Pound, to identify the gods; Hermes, their messenger, wore winged shoes.

6. Pound's versions of Chinese poems are based on notes made by the American sinologist Ernest Fenollosa, for whom the Chinese originals were interpreted by various Japanese scholars; neither Fenollosa nor Pound could then read Chinese. Throughout, Pound uses Japanese spellings of Chinese place-names, and even of the name of the poet, Li Po (701–762), who in Japanese is called "Rihaku." This poem is a translation of the first of Li Po's "Two Letters from Chang-Kan" (a suburb of Nanking, called "Chokan" in line 5).

You came by on bamboo stilts, playing horse,
You walked about my seat, playing with blue plums.
And we went on living in the village of Chokan: 5
Two small people, without dislike or suspicion.

At fourteen I married My Lord you.
I never laughed, being bashful.
Lowering my head, I looked at the wall.
Called to, a thousand times, I never looked back.   10

At fifteen I stopped scowling,
I desired my dust to be mingled with yours
Forever and forever and forever.
Why should I climb the look out?

At sixteen you departed,   15
You went into far Ku-tō-en,[7] by the river of swirling eddies,
And you have been gone five months.
The monkeys make sorrowful noise overhead.

You dragged your feet when you went out.
By the gate now, the moss is grown, the different mosses,   20
Too deep to clear them away!
The leaves fall early this autumn, in wind.
The paired butterflies are already yellow with August
Over the grass in the West garden;
They hurt me. I grow older.   25
If you are coming down through the narrows of the river Kiang,
Please let me know beforehand,
And I will come out to meet you
            As far as Chō-fū-Sa.[8]

                                                              1915

A Pact

I make a pact with you, Walt Whitman—
I have detested you long enough.
I come to you as a grown child
Who has had a pig-headed father;
I am old enough now to make friends.   5
It was you that broke the new wood,
Now is a time for carving.
We have one sap and one root—
Let there be commerce between us.

                                                              1916

In a Station of the Metro[9]

The apparition of these faces in the crowd;
Petals on a wet, black bough.

                                                              1916

---

7. An island in the river Ch'ü-t'ang (or Kiang,
in Japanese, as in line 26).
8. A beach several hundred miles upstream of
Nanking.

9. Of this poem Pound writes in *Gaudier-
Brzeska:* "Three years ago in Paris I got out of a
'metro' train at La Concorde, and saw suddenly a
beautiful face, and then another and another, and

Hugh Selwyn Mauberley

LIFE AND CONTACTS[1]

"Vocat æstus in umbram"[2]
Nemesianus Ec. IV.

E. P. *Ode pour L'Election de Son Sepulchre*[3]

I

For three years, out of key with his time,
He strove to resuscitate the dead art
Of poetry; to maintain "the sublime"
In the old sense. Wrong from the start—

No, hardly, but seeing he had been born   5
In a half savage country,[4] out of date;
Bent resolutely on wringing lilies from the acorn;
Capaneus;[5] trout for factitious bait;

"Ἴδμεν γάρ τοι πάνθ', ὅσ' ἐνὶ Τροίη[6]
Caught in the unstopped ear;   10
Giving the rocks small lee-way
The chopped seas held him, therefore, that year.

His true Penelope was Flaubert,[7]
He fished by obstinate isles;
Observed the elegance of Circe's[8] hair   15
Rather than the mottoes on sun-dials.

Unaffected by "The march of events,"
He passed from men's memory in *l'an trentuniesme*

---

then a beautiful child's face, and then another beautiful woman, and I tried all that day to find words for what this had meant to me, and I could not find any words that seemed to me worthy, or as lovely as that sudden emotion. And that evening . . . I was still trying and I found, suddenly, the expression. I do not mean that I found words, but there came an equation . . . not in speech, but in little splotches of colour. . . . The 'one-image poem' is a form of super-position, that is to say, it is one idea getting out of the impasse in which I had been left by my metro emotion. I wrote a thirty-line poem, and destroyed it. . . . Six months later I made a poem half that length; a year later I made the following *hokku*-like sentence."

1. Pound's footnote to this poem describes it as "a farewell to London," and in a letter to Felix E. Schelling on July 9, 1922, he called it "Again a study in form, an attempt to condense the James novel." The use of quatrains he attributed to a feeling shared with Eliot that they must set in motion "some countercurrent" to the excesses of free verse. They both studied the chiseled quatrains of Theophile Gautier (1811–1872) in his *Emaux et Camées* (1852), and in the letter to Schelling Pound said, "The metre in *Mauberley* is Gautier and Bion's *Adonis;* or at least these are the two grafts I was trying to flavour it with. Syncopation from the Greek; and a general distaste for the slushiness and swishiness of the post-Swinburnian British line." Bion, a Greek poet who died

c. 100 B.C., was famous for his "Lament for Adonis."
2. The epigraph is from the Fourth Eclogue of Nemesianus, a third-century Latin poet, and means, "Summer heat calls us into the shade"; it suggests Mauberley's alienation from the contemporary scene.
3. Ode on the Choice of His Tomb. The title is adapted from that of a poem by Pierre de Ronsard (1524–1585), "De l'Election de Son Sepulchre."
4. The United States.
5. One of the seven warriors who attacked Thebes. Having defied Zeus, he was struck down by a thunderbolt.
6. *Idmen gár toi pánth hos eni Troíe* (Greek): "For we know all the things that in Troy . . ." Part of the Sirens' song in *Odyssey* 12. Odysseus filled the ears of his shipmates with wax so that they would be untempted by the song, but he left his own ears open and had himself lashed to the mast so that he might experience the temptation. "Troíe," pronounced "Trohee-ay," rhymes with "leeway;" bilingual rhymes are a recurring device of the poem.
7. Gustave Flaubert (1821–1880), the French novelist, is here a symbol of artistic perfectionism. Penelope, Odysseus's wife, was famous for her long faithfulness to her husband.
8. Circe was the sorceress with whom Odysseus spent a year, delaying his return home from the Trojan War.

De son eage;[9] the case presents
No adjunct to the Muses' diadem.   20

II

The age demanded an image
Of its accelerated grimace,
Something for the modern stage,
Not, at any rate, an Attic grace;

Not, not certainly, the obscure reveries   25
Of the inward gaze;
Better mendacities
Than the classics in paraphrase!

The "age demanded" chiefly a mould in plaster,
Made with no loss of time,   30
A prose kinema,[1] not, not assuredly, alabaster
Or the "sculpture" of rhyme.

III

The tea-rose tea-gown, etc.
Supplants the mousseline of Cos,[2]
The pianola "replaces"   35
Sappho's barbitos.[3]

Christ follows Dionysus,
Phallic and ambrosial
Made way for macerations;[4]
Caliban casts out Ariel.[5]   40

All things are a flowing,
Sage Heracleitus says;[6]
But a tawdry cheapness
Shall outlast our days.

Even the Christian beauty   45
Defects—after Samothrace;[7]
We see τὸ καλόν[8]
Decreed in the market place.

Faun's flesh is not to us,
Nor the saint's vision.   50

9. In the thirty-first year of his life (Old French); Pound adapts the first line of the *Grand Testament* by François Villon (1431–c.1485), Pound was thirty-one when his book of early poems, *Lustra*, was published.
1. Movement (Greek).
2. Cos, a Greek island, was famous in Roman times for its muslin.
3. Lyre (Greek). Sappho (sixth century B.C.), the Greek poet, is Pound's type of the classical poet; most of her surviving works are fragmentary, parts having been lost.
4. That is, the ecstatic, sensual celebrations of Dionysus, the Greek god of wine, have been suc-

ceeded by the "macerations"—excessive fasting—of Christianity.
5. Caliban, a monstrous creature, and Ariel, a spirit of the air, are characters in Shakespeare's *The Tempest*.
6. Heraclitus (c. 535–475 B.C.), the Greek philosopher, held that everything is in eternal flux and therefore cannot ultimately escape dissolution.
7. A Greek island which was visited by St. Paul on his way to convert the Macedonian Jews to Christianity; perhaps Pound objects to the ethic formulated by Paul from Christ's teachings.
8. *Tò kalón* (Greek): "The Beautiful."

We have the press for wafer;
Franchise for circumcision.

All men, in law, are equals.
Free of Pisistratus,[9]
We choose a knave or an eunuch   55
To rule over us.

O bright Apollo,
τίν' ἄνδρα, τίν' ἥρωα, τίνα θεόν,[1]
What god, man, or hero
Shall I place a tin wreath upon!   60

IV

These fought in any case,
and some believing,
                    pro domo,[2] in any case . . .

Some quick to arm,
some for adventure,   65
some from fear of weakness,
some from fear of censure,
some for love of slaughter, in imagination,
learning later . . .
some in fear, learning love of slaughter;   70

Died some, pro patria,
                    non "dulce" non "et decor". . .
walked eye-deep in hell
believing in old men's lies, then unbelieving
came home, home to a lie,   75
home to many deceits,
home to old lies and new infamy;
usury age-old and age-thick
and liars in public places.

Daring as never before, wastage as never before.   80
Young blood and high blood,
fair cheeks, and fine bodies;

fortitude as never before

frankness as never before,
disillusions as never told in the old days,   85
hysterias, trench confessions,
laughter out of dead bellies.

9. Pisistratus (d. 527 B.C.), an Athenian tyrant.
  1. *Tín ándra, tín héroa, tína theón* (Greek): "What man, what hero, what god," a phrase from the Second Olympian Ode by Pindar (c.522–c.402 B.C.), the Greek lyric poet; the original reads, "What god, what hero, what man." Pindar's tone is one of genuine eulogy; Pound puns on "tin," which is the sound of the Greek word for "what."
  2. For [one's] home (Latin), a substitution in the phrase from Horace (65–68 B.C.), *Odes* 3.2.13: "*Dulce et decorum est pro patria mori*"—"It is sweet and fitting to die for one's country." Pound attacks this sentiment in lines 71–72, inserting the negative "non."

V

There died a myriad,
And of the best, among them,
For an old bitch gone in the teeth,   90
For a botched civilization,

Charm, smiling at the good mouth,
Quick eyes gone under earth's lid,

For two gross of broken statues,
For a few thousand battered books.   95

Yeux Glauques[3]

Gladstone[4] was still respected,
When John Ruskin produced
"Kings' Treasuries";[5] Swinburne
And Rossetti still abused.

Fœtid Buchanan lifted up his voice[6]   100
When that faun's head of hers
Became a pastime for
Painters and adulterers.

The Burne-Jones cartons[7]
Have preserved her eyes;   105
Still, at the Tate, they teach
Cophetua to rhapsodize;

Thin like brook-water,
With a vacant gaze.
The English Rubaiyat was still-born[8]   110
In those days.

The thin, clear gaze, the same
Still darts out faun-like from the half-ruin'd face,
Questing and passive. . . .
"Ah, poor Jenny's case' . . .[9]   115

Bewildered that a world
Shows no surprise

3. Sea-green eyes (French), a favorite image in nineteenth-century poetry; the eyes are of Elizabeth Siddal, the model for several paintings by Dante Gabriel Rossetti (1828–1882), the Pre-Raphaelite poet and artist, who married her two years before her death in 1862.
4. William Ewart Gladstone (1809–1898), British prime minister for ten years, and a type of the most rigid Victorian respectability.
5. The first lecture in John Ruskin's *Sesame and Lilies* (1865); it contains a scathing indictment of the English, whom Ruskin found to despise literature, science, art, natural beauty, and human compassion. Pound shared some of Ruskin's views on art and society, and may here be seconding this indictment.
6. Robert Buchanan (1841–1901), the author of the "Fleshly School of Poetry" (1871) which attacked the Pre-Raphaelite poets, among whom Rossetti and Algernon Charles Swinburne (1837–1909) were prominent.
7. Sir Edward Burne-Jones (1833–1898), a Pre-Raphaelite painter. "Cartons," in French, means "cartoons," in the sense of preparatory designs for a painting or tapestry. His painting, *King Cophetua and the Beggar Maid*, at the Tate Gallery in London, used Elizabeth Siddal as a model for the beggar maid.
8. Edward Fitzgerald's *The Rubáiyát of Omar Khayyám*, which Pound thought highly of, was published in 1859 but went unnoticed until Rossetti discovered it the following year.
9. Rossetti's poem, "Jenny," is about a prostitute; Buchanan, a Scotsman with a Calvinistic streak, made much of it in his attack on the Pre-Raphaelites.

At her last maquero's[10]
Adulteries.

"Siena Mi Fe'; Disfecemi Maremma"[1]

Among the pickled fœtuses and bottled bones,   120
Engaged in perfecting the catalogue,
I found the last scion of the
Senatorial families of Strasbourg, Monsieur Verog.[2]

For two hours he talked of Galliffet;[3]
Of Dowson; of the Rhymers' Club;[4]   125
Told me how Johnson (Lionel) died
By falling from a high stool in a pub . . .

But showed no trace of alcohol
At the autopsy, privately performed—
Tissue preserved—the pure mind   130
Arose toward Newman[5] as the whiskey warmed.

Dowson found harlots cheaper than hotels;
Headlam for uplift; Image impartially imbued
With raptures for Bacchus, Terpsichore and the Church.[6]
So spoke the author of "The Dorian Mood,"   135

M. Verog, out of step with the decade,
Detached from his contemporaries,
Neglected by the young,
Because of these reveries.

Brennbaum[7]

The sky-like limpid eyes,   140
The circular infant's face,
The stiffness from spats to collar
Never relaxing into grace;

The heavy memories of Horeb, Sinai and the forty years,[8]
Showed only when the daylight fell   145

10. Or *maquereau* (French), pimp.

1. "Siena made me; Maremma unmade me." (Italian); from Dante's *Purgatorio* 5.133, where it is spoken by Pia de' Tolomei of her birth in Siena and her death in Maremma at her husband's hands. In the *Divine Comedy*, Pia is representative of souls who have found salvation at the last moment.

2. Modeled on Victor Plarr (1863–1929), who was librarian to the Royal College of Surgeons in London; he prepared a catalogue of its manuscripts.

3. The Marquis de Galliffet (1830–1909), a French general and later the French minister of war, led his cavalry brigade courageously in the crucial battle of Sedan during the Franco-Prussian War, which France lost. Pound reproduces part of this conversation in Canto 16:

     wall . . . Strasbourg
     Galliffet led that triple charge . . . Prussians
and he said
         it was for the honour of the army.
And they called him a swashbuckler.

4. Plarr was a member of the Rhymers' Club, an informal association of poets who from 1891 met at the Cheshire Cheese, a London eating-house; other members were Yeats, Ernest Dowson (1867–1900)—whose biography Plarr wrote—and Lionel Johnson (1867–1907), who in fact died from a fall in the street, not in a pub. Plarr's own poems were published in a book called *In the Dorian Mood* (1896).

5. John Henry Cardinal Newman (1801–1890), who like Johnson was a convert to Catholicism.

6. Rev. Stewart D. Headlam (1847–1924), a friend of several writers of the nineties, and Selwyn Image (1849–1930), who edited a literary magazine called *Hobby Horse*, joined to found the Church and Stage Guild. According to K. K. Ruthven, it was Headlam and not Image who was an enthusiast of the dance (Terpsichore).

7. Probably modeled on Max Beerbohm (1872–1956), who was known as "the Incomparable Max." Pound mistakenly thought he was Jewish.

8. Horeb, or Sinai, was the mountain where Moses received the Tables of the Law; after the

Level across the face
Of Brennbaum "The Impeccable."

Mr. Nixon[9]

In the cream gilded cabin of his steam yacht
Mr. Nixon advised me kindly, to advance with fewer
Dangers of delay. "Consider   150
    "Carefully the reviewer.

"I was as poor as you are;
"When I began I got, of course,
"Advance on royalties, fifty at first," said Mr. Nixon,
"Follow me, and take a column,   155
"Even if you have to work free.

"Butter reviewers. From fifty to three hundred
"I rose in eighteen months;
"The hardest nut I had to crack
"Was Dr. Dundas.   160

"I never mentioned a man but with the view
"Of selling my own works.
"The tip's a good one, as for literature
"It gives no man a sinecure.

"And no one knows, at sight, a masterpiece.   165
"And give up verse, my boy,
"There's nothing in it."

·   ·   ·   ·   ·   ·   ·

Likewise a friend of Blougram's[10] once advised me:
Don't kick against the pricks,
Accept opinion. The "Nineties" tried your game   170
And died, there's nothing in it.

X

Beneath the sagging roof
The stylist[1] has taken shelter,
Unpaid, uncelebrated,
At last from the world's welter   175

Nature receives him;
With a placid and uneducated mistress
He exercises his talents
And the soil meets his distress.

Exodus from Egypt, the Israelites spent forty years in the wilderness.
9. Said to be modeled on Arnold Bennett (1867–1931), the highly successful English novelist.
10. Robert Browning's poem, "Bishop Blougram's Apology" (1855), is a priest's casuistic defense of his position.

1. Ford Madox Ford (1873–1939), the English poet, editor, and novelist, is probably the model; Pound always credited Ford with having pointed him towards naturalness and freshness of language, and said that Ford was the only person who was ever able to help him with revision.

The haven from sophistications and contentions   180
Leaks through its thatch;
He offers succulent cooking;
The door has a creaking latch.

XI

"Conservatrix of Milesien"[2]
Habits of mind and feeling,   185
Possibly. But in Ealing[3]
With the most bank-clerkly of Englishmen?

No, "Milésian" is an exaggeration.
No instinct has survived in her
Older than those her grandmother   190
Told her would fit her station.

XII

"Daphne with her thighs in bark
Stretches toward me her leafy hands,"—[4]
Subjectively. In the stuffed-satin drawing-room
I await The Lady Valentine's commands,   195

Knowing my coat has never been
Of precisely the fashion
To stimulate, in her,
A durable passion;

Doubtful, somewhat, of the value   200
Of well-gowned approbation
Of literary effort,
But never of The Lady Valentine's vocation:

Poetry, her border of ideas,
The edge, uncertain but a means of blending   205
With other strata
Where the lower and higher have ending;

A hook to catch the Lady Jane's attention,
A modulation toward the theatre,
Also, in the case of revolution,   210
A possible friend and comforter.

  .   .   .   .

Conduct,[5] on the other hand, the soul
"Which the highest cultures have nourished"

---

2. Pound is quoting a phrase from *Magic Stories, Stratagems* (1894) by Rémy de Gourmont (1858–1915): "Women, conservers of Milesian traditions." The *Milesian Tales* by Aristides of Miletus (second century B.C.) were considered licentious. The word "conservatrix" as applied to this tradition is sardonic.

3. A western part of London, associated with dull respectability.
4. Translated from Gautier, "The Castle of Memory." Daphne, pursued by Apollo, was transformed into a laurel tree to escape him; the sylvan scene is compared with the drawing-room.
5. Here, a verb.

To Fleet St. where
Dr. Johnson flourished;[6]

215

Beside this thoroughfare
The sale of half-hose has
Long since superseded the cultivation
Of Pierian roses.[7]

Envoi (1919)[8]

Go, dumb-born book,
Tell her that sang me once that song of Lawes:[9]
Hadst thou but song
As thou hast subjects known,
Then were there cause in thee that should condone
Even my faults that heavy upon me lie,
And build her glories their longevity.

220

225

Tell her that sheds
Such treasure in the air,
Recking naught else but that her graces give
Life to the moment,
I would bid them live
As roses might, in magic amber laid,
Red overwrought with orange and all made
One substance and one colour
Braving time.

230

235

Tell her that goes
With song upon her lips
But sings not out the song, nor knows
The maker of it, some other mouth,
May be as fair as hers,
Might, in new ages, gain her worshippers,
When our two dusts with Waller's shall be laid,
Siftings on siftings in oblivion,
Till change hath broken down
All things save Beauty alone.

240

245

1920

6. Samuel Johnson (1709–1784), English poet, essayist, and editor, is here a type of the eighteenth-century author; Fleet Street was, and still is, a center of London journalism.
7. In Greek mythology, Pieria, a district on the northern slopes of Mount Olympus, is where the Muses, inspirers of the arts, were born.
8. This poem, presumably written by Mauber-

ley, is an adaptation of "Go, Lovely Rose," a poem by Edmund Waller (1606–1687).
9. Henry Lawes (1598–1662), an English composer, set Waller's poem to music; poet and musician are mentioned, with other Elizabethan composers, in the "libretto" (lines 95–111) of Canto LXXXI, p. 233.

The Cantos

Ezra Pound began to publish the *Cantos* in 1917, when early versions of the first three appeared. In the end, there were 109 complete Cantos and "drafts and fragments" of eight more. From the beginning he was vague about the final dimensions of the work; his decision in 1969 to publish incomplete versions of the latest additions may have meant that he thought he could do no more.

Attempts to establish the *Cantos'* structural plan have so far been unconvincing, and Pound himself offered only partial explanations. He said that the poem constitutes a "commedia agnostica" as against Dante's *Divina Commedia*. In a letter to his father, he suggested an analogy to musical structure: "[The *Cantos* are] rather like, or unlike subject and response and counter subject in fugue," the principal three elements being: "Live man goes down into the world of Dead. The 'repeat in history.' The 'magic moment' or moment of metamorphosis, bust through from quotidien into 'divine or permanent world.' Gods, etc." He also hoped that "Out of the three main classes of themes, permanent, recurrent, and casual (or haphazard), a hierarchy of values should emerge." Though he often intimated that he could provide an "Aquinas-map" of the *Cantos* if he chose, such guidance was not forthcoming.

Pound's intention was to develop a modern epic, a "poem including history," that encompasses not only the world's literature but its art and architecture, myths, economics, the lives of historical figures—in effect "the tale of the tribe"—in a profuse assemblage of particular details that may, or may not, make connections with each other. Underlying this concept are didactic purposes: to present materials which he thinks a civilized reader ought to absorb, and to point, by means of documents and achievements of the past and present, towards a good civilization ruled by right-thinking men of action. The famous obscurity of the *Cantos* results partly from Pound's disjunctive arrangement of his materials, but partly also from the obscurity of the materials themselves; Pound, formidably traveled and read, usually assumes that his readers are as familiar with sixteenth-century Italian architecture, Provençal lyrics, Confucian philosophy, and medieval economic history as he is, as well as with the nearly dozen languages from which he draws, or into which he translates, many of his allusions. In some ways it is easier, armed with patience and the *Annotated Index to the Cantos of Ezra Pound,* to read right through the poem rather than to read excerpts from it, as Pound's hermetic allusions are often tags which are expanded elsewhere.

Cantos 1–7 indicate the poem's procedures and some of its themes. Cantos 8–11 present Sigismundo Malatesta (d. 1468), the Venetian soldier and art patron, as a type of the man of action. Cantos 12–13 contrast modern economic exploitation with the tranquil order of Confucian moral philosophy. Cantos 14–16 describe a passage through hell (in the guise of modern London), ending with a vision of medieval Venice as paradise in Canto 17. American presidents whose policies and personal styles Pound admires are presented in Cantos 31–33 (Jefferson), 34 (John Quincy Adams), 37 (Van Buren), and 62–71 (John Adams); Canto 41 introduces Mussolini, whom Pound, sympathizing with the Fascist economic program and seeming patronage of art, thought the best contemporary leader. As Pound identifies humane civilization and government with Confucian ethics, he sketches a history of ancient China (Cantos 52–61) to show that Chinese prosperity and peace only attended rule by Confucian moral principles—a conclusion that modern historians find dubious. In counterpoint to these "historical" Cantos Pound sets those of the *Fifth Decad of Cantos,* which inveigh against usurious monetary systems (those, according to Pound, based on paper values rather than real ones) and exalt those principles, from the Eleusinian mysteries of ancient Greece to the "social credit" theories of Pound's contemporary C. H. Douglas, which encourage the growth of natural fertility and wealth. During the Second World War Pound wrote two Cantos in Italian which have not been published; at the war's end he was imprisoned near Pisa by the U.S. Army on charges of treason arising from his wartime broadcasts on the Italian radio.

The *Pisan Cantos,* written in the prison camp under great physical and psychological duress while Pound was waiting to be returned to the United States for trial and quite possibly execution, record a "dark night of the soul" through which the poet passes toward a vision of Aphrodite, the goddess of love, and the acceptance of his own death. Available to him were the scenes and events of the detention camp, the Bible, an edition of Confucius, a poetry anthology, and the resources of his extraordinary memory. Under extreme pressure these elements combine, in a "magic moment" recorded in Canto 81. The *Pisan Cantos* are both impressive and difficult, and when they won the Bollingen Prize in 1949 (given by the Library of Congress; the distinguished jury included T. S. Eliot), a controversy was set off involving not only the charge of treason which was still pending against Pound, and the undeniably Fascist and anti-Semitic passages in parts of the poems, but also a reaction against the esthetic of post-symbolist "modernism" as exemplified in all the works of Pound and Eliot.

The later Cantos—*Section: Rock Drill* (1955) and *Thrones* (1959)—consolidate the insights of the earlier Cantos and are yet more cryptic. The *Drafts and Fragments of Cantos CX-CXVII* (1969) hint at an apologia: "But the beauty is not the madness / Tho' my errors and wrecks lie about me. / And I am not a demigod, / I cannot make it cohere" (from Canto 116). In a 1968 conversation with Daniel Cory, Pound said that he had "botched" the work. But despite its unevenness and obscurity, the *Cantos* remains for readers and for other poets one of the great literary challenges and inspirations of the century.

From *THE CANTOS*

I[1]

And then went down to the ship,
Set keel to breakers, forth on the godly sea, and
We[2] set up mast and sail on that swart ship,
Bore sheep aboard her, and our bodies also
Heavy with weeping, and winds from sternward   5
Bore us out onward with bellying canvas,
Circe's this craft, the trim-coifed goddess.[3]
Then sat we amidships, wind jamming the tiller,
Thus with stretched sail, we went over sea till day's end.
Sun to his slumber, shadows o'er all the ocean,   10
Came we then to the bounds of deepest water,
To the Kimmerian lands,[4] and peopled cities
Covered with close-webbed mist, unpierced ever
With glitter of sun rays
Nor with stars stretched, nor looking back from heaven   15
Swartest night stretched over wretched men there.
The ocean flowing backward, came we then to the place
Aforesaid by Circe.
Here did they rites, Perimedes and Eurylochus,[5]
And drawing sword from my hip   20

1. This Canto is, until line 68, a free translation of the opening of *Odyssey* 11, which describes Odysseus's voyage to the end of the earth, where he summons up spirits from the underworld. For Pound, Odysseus is the type of the enterprising, imaginative man, and this voyage is in some sense a symbol or analogy of the poet's own voyage into the darker aspects of his civilization or the buried places of the mind. The verse is alliterative, resembling that of Old English poetry, perhaps to suggest the archaic and archetypal character of this Odyssean experience. Pound believed on internal evidence that Book 11 is the oldest part of the *Odyssey*, and this may also have influenced his choice of the oldest style of English poetry.
2. Odysseus and his shipmates.
3. Odysseus has just left the island where he lived for a year with the goddess Circe. Following her instructions, he is to go to the mouth of the underworld and there consult the prophet Tiresias about his return to his native Ithaca.
4. The Cimmerii were a mythical people living on the edge of the world.
5. Two of Odysseus's men.

I dug the ell-square pitkin;[6]
Poured we libations unto each the dead,
First mead and then sweet wine, water mixed with white flour.
Then prayed I many a prayer to the sickly death's-heads;
As set in Ithaca, sterile bulls of the best   25
For sacrifice, heaping the pyre with goods,
A sheep to Tiresias only, black and a bell-sheep.[7]
Dark blood flowed in the fosse,[8]
Souls out of Erebus,[9] cadaverous dead, of brides
Of youths and of the old who had borne much;   30
Souls stained with recent tears, girls tender,
Men many, mauled with bronze lance heads,
Battle spoil, bearing yet dreory[1] arms,
These many crowded about me; with shouting,
Pallor upon me, cried to my men for more beasts;   35
Slaughtered the herds, sheep slain of bronze;
Poured ointment, cried to the gods,
To Pluto the strong, and praised Proserpine;[2]
Unsheathed the narrow sword,
I sat to keep off the impetuous impotent dead,   40
Till I should hear Tiresias.
But first Elpenor[3] came, our friend Elpenor,
Unburied, cast on the wide earth,
Limbs that we left in the house of Circe,
Unwept, unwrapped in sepulchre, since toils urged other.   45
Pitiful spirit. And I cried in hurried speech:
"Elpenor, how art thou come to this dark coast?
Cam'st thou afoot, outstripping seamen?"
            And he in heavy speech:
"Ill fate and abundant wine. I slept in Circe's ingle.   50
Going down the long ladder unguarded,
I fell against the buttress,
Shattered the nape-nerve, the soul sought Avernus.[4]
But thou, O King, I bid remember me, unwept, unburied,
Heap up mine arms, be tomb by sea-bord, and inscribed: 55
A man of no fortune, and with a name to come.
And set my oar up, that I swung mid fellows."

And Anticlea[5] came, whom I beat off, and then Tiresias Theban,
Holding his golden wand, knew me, and spoke first:
"A second time?[6] why? man of ill star,   60
Facing the sunless dead and this joyless region?
Stand from the fosse, leave me my bloody bever[7]

---

6. A pitkin is Pound's coinage for a small pit; an ell is a measure of length, varying from two to four feet.
7. A bell-sheep is the one which leads the herd. Tiresias, a Theban, was granted the gift of prophecy by the gods. Compare *The Waste Land*, 3 (p. 288).
8. Ditch (Latin).
9. Primeval darkness, Hades.
1. Bloody. (The Old English word is *dreorig*.)
2. Pluto was the Roman god of the underworld; Proserpina was his wife.
3. One of Odysseus's companions. He broke his neck in an accidental fall from the roof of Circe's house; because his companions did not discover his death they failed to perform the burial rites.
. 4. A lake near Cumae and Naples, beside which was the cave through which the Trojan hero Aeneas descended to Hades to learn the future. It is also a name given to the underworld itself.
5. The mother of Odysseus. In the *Odyssey*, Odysseus weeps at the sight of his mother (a detail omitted by Pound), but at Circe's instruction will not allow her to drink the blood, and so to speak with him, until Tiresias has done so.
6. They have met before, in the upper world.
7. Potation (Middle English).

For soothsay."
    And I stepped back,
And he strong with the blood, said then: "Odysseus   65
Shalt return through spiteful Neptune,[8] over dark seas,
Lose all companions." And then Anticlea came.
Lie quiet Divus. I mean, that is Andreas Divus,
In officina Wecheli, 1538, out of Homer.[9]
And he sailed, by Sirens and thence outward and away   70
And unto Circe.[1]
    Venerandam,[2]
In the Cretan's phrase, with the golden crown, Aphrodite,
Cypri munimenta sortita est,[3] mirthful, orichalchi,[4] with golden
Girdles and breast bands, thou with dark eyelids   75
Bearing the golden bough of Argicida.[5] So that:

                           1917, 1925

LXXXI

Zeus lies in Ceres' bosom[6]
Taishan[7] is attended of loves
         under Cythera,[8] before sunrise
and he said: "Hay aquí mucho catolicismo—(sounded catoli*th*ismo)
      y muy poco reliHión"[9]   5
and he said: "Yo creo que los reyes desaparecen"[1]
(Kings will, I think, disappear)
That was Padre José Elizondo[2]
               in 1906 and 1917
or about 1917   10
        and Dolores said "Come pan, niño," (eat bread, me lad)
Sargent[3] had painted her

---

8. An allusion to the shipwreck Odysseus was to undergo. Neptune was the Roman sea-god.

9. Pound here acknowledges that he has been following not the original Greek but a medieval Latin translation of Homer by Andreas Divus, published by the workshop of Wechel in Paris in 1538. Hence also Pound's use of the Roman names for the gods. With these words he abruptly turns from the *Odyssey*.

1. Actually, Odysseus first returned to Circe and then went on to the Sirens. Pound varies the order, perhaps with some idea of a sensual progress from the Sirens (temptation) to Circe (a love affair) and then to Aphrodite, the goddess of love.

2. Commanding reverence (Latin). This is the epithet given to Aphrodite in what is known as the sixth Homeric Hymn. (These Greek hymns were not in fact written by Homer.) Pound is again working from a Latin translation, this one by Georgius Dartona Cretensis ("the Cretan"); it was included in Pound's copy of Divus's Latin *Odyssey*.

3. The citadels of Cyprus were her appointed realm (Latin).

4. Of copper (Latin). The hymn recounts how a votive gift of copper and gold was made, by the attendant Hours, to Aphrodite.

5. Argicida, an epithet usually given to Hermes, the gods' messenger, means "Slayer of Argus" (a mythical herdsman with eyes all over his body, whose watchfulness the goddess Hera had counted on to prevent her husband Zeus from an affair with the mortal woman Io). But Pound is perhaps con-

ferring the epithet upon Aphrodite as slayer of the Argi (Greeks) during the Trojan War. The golden bough was Aeneas's offering to Proserpina before his descent to Hades, and is usually associated with Diana and the sacred wood of Nemi rather than Aphrodite. The Canto's abrupt ending may be taken to suggest that it is not complete in itself, but part of a larger work—the *Cantos*.

6. Zeus, the ruler of the Greek gods, is sometimes said to have married his sister Ceres, goddess of agriculture and natural fertility.

7. A sacred mountain in China, which Pound identified with a cone-shaped mountain visible from his cage in the Disciplinary Training Center near Pisa.

8. Aphrodite, goddess of love; Cythera was an island sacred to her.

9. "There is much Catholicism here and very little religion" (Spanish). The parenthetical instruction is a direction for reading the Canto aloud, and is not itself to be spoken.

1. Translated in the next line.

2. A Spanish priest who had helped Pound to obtain a photostat of manuscripts by Guido Cavalcanti from the Escorial, the palace of the Spanish kings.

3. John Singer Sargent (1856–1925) was much influenced by Velasquez's paintings even before 1880, when he traveled to Spain and copied *The Maids of Honor* and other paintings in the Prado. Dolores is presumably the subject of one of Sargent's Spanish paintings; later he specialized in portraits.

before he descended
(i.e., if he descended)
    but in those days he did thumb sketches,   15
impressions of the Velásquez in the Museo del Prado
and books cost a peseta,
        brass candlesticks in proportion,
hot wind came from the marshes
    and death-chill from the mountains.   20
And later Bowers[4] wrote: "but such hatred,
    I had never conceived such"
and the London reds wouldn't show up his friends
            (i.e., friends of Franco
working in London) and in Alcázar[5]   25
forty years gone, they said: "Go back to the station to eat,
you can sleep here for a peseta"
        goat bells tinkled all night
        and the hostess grinned: "Eso es luto, *haw!*
mi marido es muerto"[6]   30
        (it is mourning, my husband is dead)
when she gave me paper of the locanda[7] to write on
with a black border half an inch or more deep, say 5/8ths,
"We call *all* foreigners frenchies"
    and the egg broke in Cabranez' pocket,
        thus making history.[8] Basil says   35
they beat drums for three days
till all the drumheads were busted
        (simple village fiesta)
and as for his life in the Canaries . . .[9]   40
Possum[1] observed that the local portagoose folk dance
was danced by the same dancers in divers localities
        in political welcome . . .
the technique of demonstration
        Cole studied that (not G.D.H., Horace)[2]   45
"You will find" said old André Spire,[3]
"that every man on that board (Crédit Agricole)[4]
has a brother-in-law."
            "You the one, I the few"
            said John Adams   50
speaking of fears in the abstract
    to his volatile friend Mr. Jefferson,
(To break the pentameter, that was the first heave)
or as Jo Bard[5] says: "They never speak to each other,
if it is baker and concierge visibly   55

4. Claude Gernade Bowers (1878–1958) was the American ambassador to Spain during the Spanish Civil War, 1936–39, won by the right-wing faction led by Francisco Franco.
5. Probably Alcazar de San Juan, a town in central Spain.
6. Translated in the following line.
7. Inn or boarding house (Italian).
8. Perhaps a joke involving one of Pound's Spanish friends; the meaning of this allusion has not been traced.
9. Basil Bunting, the English poet and friend of Pound, lived in the Canary Islands (a Spanish possession off the northwest coast of Africa) from 1933 to 1936 because it was inexpensive, but found the food bad and the Spanish inhabitants cruel.
1. T. S. Eliot (author of *Old Possum's Book of Practical Cats*).
2. Horace Cole was a writer for magazines and a contributor to *20th Century Business Practice*; G. D. H. Cole (1880–1959) was an English economist and novelist.
3. André Spire (1868–1966), a French writer and advocate of Zionism.
4. The French agricultural bank.
5. Joseph Bard, an English essayist.

it is La Rochefoucauld and de Maintenon audibly."[6]
"Te caverò le budella"
          "La corata a te"[7]
In less than a geological epoch
          said Henry Mencken[8]   60
"Some cook, some do not cook,
   some things cannot be altered"
Ἰυγξ . . . ᾿εμὸν ποτί δῶμα τὸν ἄνδρα[9]
What counts is the cultural level,
   thank Benin for this table ex packing box[1]
   "doan yu tell no one I made it"   65
          from a mask fine as any in Frankfurt
"It'll get you offn th' groun"
          Light as the branch of Kuanon[2]
And at first disappointed with shoddy
the bare ramshackle quais, but then saw the   70
high buggy wheels
          and was reconciled,
George Santayana[3] arriving in the port of Boston
and kept to the end of his life that faint *thethear*[4]
of the Spaniard   75
          as a grace quasi imperceptible,
as did Muss the *v* for *u* of Romagna,[5]
and said the grief was a full act
   repeated for each new condoleress
working up to a climax.
And George Horace[6] said he wd/ "get Beveridge" (Senator)   80
Beveridge wouldn't talk and he wouldn't write for the papers
but George got him by campin' in his hotel
and assailin' him at lunch breakfast an' dinner
          three articles
and my my ole man went on hoein' corn   85
   while George was a-tellin' him,
come across a vacant lot
          where you'd occasionally see a wild rabbit
or mebbe only a loose one
          AOI!   90

---

6. The Duc de la Rochefoucauld (1747–1827) and Madame de Maintenon (1635–1719) here not presented as historical figures but as exemplars of elegant prose style, which, Pound indicates, is inherent in the French language.
7. "I'll cut your guts out!" "And I'll tear the liver out of you!" (Italian) In Canto 10 this passage is part of an exchange between Sigismondo Malatesta (1417–1468) and his sworn enemy Federigo d'Urbino (1422–1482).
8. ". . . I believe that all schemes of monetary reform collide inevitably with the nature of man in the mass. He can't be convinced in anything less than a geological epoch." (Quoted as part of a letter from Mencken to Pound in *Guide to Kulchur*, p. 182.) Pound observed, "Above statement does not invalidate geological process."
9. *Iünx, emòn poti doma ton ándra* (Greek): Little wheel, [bring back] that man to my house. From the second Idyll of Theocritus, a dramatic monologue in which a girl uses a magic wheel to

cast a spell on her unfaithful lover.
1. A district in Nigeria, famous for its bronze masks; a collection of them was made by the German anthropologist Leo Frobenius (1873–1938) at the Institute for Cultural Morphology in Frankfurt. The incident Pound tells of occurred in the DTC, where a Black prisoner named Edwards made him a table.
2. The Chinese goddess of mercy.
3. (1863–1952), the Spanish-born American philosopher; lines 70–80 are based on his *Autobiography*.
4. *Cecear* (Spanish) means the Castilian pronunciation of the soft *c*, with a lisp.
5. Mussolini's dialect, in which the sound *w* was pronounced as *v*.
6. George Horace Lorimer (1868–1937) was editor of the *Saturday Evening Post* for over 35 years. He was trying to interview Albert Jeremiah Beveridge (1862–1927), the American senator and historian.

a leaf in the current
           at my grates no Althea[7]

libretto[8]

Yet
Ere the season died a-cold   95
Borne upon a zephyr's shoulder
I rose through the aureate sky
           Lawes and Jenkins guard thy rest
           Dolmetsch ever be thy guest,[9]
Has he tempered the viol's wood   100
To enforce both   the grave   and the acute?
Has he curved us the bowl of the lute?
           Lawes and Jenkins guard thy rest
           Dolmetsch ever be thy guest,
Hast 'ou fashioned so airy a mood   105
           To draw up leaf from the root?
Hast 'ou found   a cloud   so light
           As seemed neither mist nor shade?

           Then resolve me, tell me aright
           If Waller sang or Dowland played.[1]   110

           Your eyen two wol sleye me sodenly
           I may the beauté of hem nat susteyne[2]

And for 180 years almost nothing.

Ed ascoltando il leggier mormorio[3]
           there came new subtlety of eyes into my tent,   115
whether of spirit or hypostasis,[4]
           but what the blindfold hides
or at carneval
                     nor any pair showed anger
           Saw but the eyes and stance between the eyes,   120
colour, diastasis,[5]
           careless or unaware it had not the
           whole tent's room
nor was place for the full Εἰδὼς[6]
interpass, penetrate   125
           casting but shade beyond the other lights

7. From the poem by Richard Lovelace (1618–1657), "To Althea, from Prison": "When Love with unconfined wings / Hovers within my Gates; / And my divine Althea brings / To whisper at the grates . . ."
8. A text to be sung to music.
9. Henry Lawes (1596–1662) and John Jenkins (1592–1678) were English composers; Lawes made a setting of Waller's poem, "Go, Lovely Rose," which is the source of "Envoi" in Pound's "Hugh Selwyn Mauberley." Arnold Dolmetsch (1858–1940), the musicologist and builder of modern reconstructions of old instruments, advocated a revival of interest in pre-Baroque music.

1. Edmund Waller (1606–1687), the English poet, and John Dowland (1563–1626), the composer and lutenist.
2. From Chaucer's "Merciles Beauté": "Your two eyes will slay me quickly; I may not withstand their beauty."
3. And listening to the light murmur (Italian). Pound has remarked that this is "Not a quotation, merely the author using handy language."
4. The substance of the godhead; here, possibly Aphrodite.
5. Separation.
6. *Eidos* (Greek): knowing.

sky's clear
night's sea
green of the mountain pool
shone from the unmasked eyes in half-mask's space.   130
What thou lovest well remains,
                    the rest is dross
What thou lov'st well shall not be reft from thee
What thou lov'st well is thy true heritage
Whose world, or mine or theirs   135
                    or is it of none?
First came the seen, then thus the palpable
    Elysium, though it were in the halls of hell,
What thou lovest well is thy true heritage
What thou lov'st well shall not be reft from thee   140

The ant's a centaur in his dragon world.
Pull down thy vanity,[7] it is not man
Made courage, or made order, or made grace,
    Pull down thy vanity, I say pull down.
Learn of the green world what can be thy place   145
In scaled invention or true artistry,
Pull down thy vanity,
                    Paquin pull down!
The green casque has outdone your elegance.[8]

"Master thyself, then others shall thee beare"[9]   150
    Pull down thy vanity
Thou art a beaten dog beneath the hail,
A swollen magpie in a fitful sun,
Half black half white
Nor knowst'ou wing from tail   155
Pull down thy vanity
                    How mean thy hates
Fostered in falsity,
                    Pull down thy vanity,
Rathe[1] to destroy, niggard in charity,   160
Pull down thy vanity,
                    I say pull down.

But to have done instead of not doing
                    this is not vanity
To have, with decency, knocked   165
That a Blunt[2] should open
            To have gathered from the air a live tradition
or from a fine old eye the unconquered flame
This is not vanity.

7. The tone and language of the following passage are reminiscent of Ecclesiastes 1: "Saith the
preacher, vanity of vanities, all is vanity."
8. The shell of a green insect. Pound had ended
the previous Canto with the words, "sunset grand
couturier"; Paquin is a Parisian dress designer.
9. A variation on Chaucer's "Ballade of Good
Counsel": "Subdue thyself, and others thee shall
hear."
1. Quick (Middle English).
2. Wilfred Scawen Blunt (1840–1922), English
poet and political writer; in 1914 Pound and Yeats
organized a testimonial dinner for him at his house,
and Pound's address on the occasion reads in part:
"We who are little given to respect, / Respect you."

Here error is all in the not done,   170
all in the diffidence that faltered . . .

                                                                      1948

H. D. (Hilda Doolittle)
1886–1961

The American poet and critic R. P. Blackmur paid H. D. a high tribute. He wrote that her "special form of the mode of Imagism—cold, 'Greek,' fast, and enclosed—has become one of the ordinary resources of the poetic language."[1] H. D.'s poems, often modeled on fragments of classical verse and exploiting that very quality of fragmentariness, are reminders that less can be more and that implication is an all-important source of energy in poetry.

Hilda Doolittle was born in Bethlehem, Pennsylvania, on September 10, 1886. Her father was a professor of mathematics and of astronomy at Lehigh University and later at the University of Pennsylvania. She was educated at private schools in Philadelphia and she studied at Bryn Mawr for a time, but because of ill health she left the college in her sophomore year. William Carlos Williams remembered her in those early years:

> There was about her that which is found in wild animals at times, a breath-less impatience, almost a silly unwillingness to come to the point. She had a young girl's giggle and shrug which somehow in one so tall and angular seemed a little absurd. She fascinated me, not for her beauty which was unquestioned if bizarre to my sense, but for a provocative indifference to rule and order which I liked. She dressed indifferently, almost sloppily and looked to a young man, not inviting—she had nothing of that—but irritating, with a smile.[2]

In 1911 H. D. went to Europe for what she thought would be a brief summer's stay. In England she renewed her friendship with Ezra Pound, who several years before had been momentarily in love with her, and he encouraged her to write. "I had never heard of *vers libre*," H. D. recalled, "till I was 'discovered' . . . by Ezra Pound. . . . he was beautiful about my first authentic verses, . . . and sent my poems in for me to Miss Monroe [the editor of *Poetry* magazine]. He signed them for me 'H. D., Imagiste.' The name seems to have stuck somehow."[3] At about the same time H. D. met the English poet Richard Aldington, whom she married; they collaborated on some translations from the Greek, and after he had gone off to war, she was an assistant editor of the magazine called the *Egoist*.

In July 1918, after her break-up with Aldington, H. D., bereft, the mother of an infant child whose paternity was uncertain, was saved from poverty and loneliness by a meeting with the woman whose pen-name and later legal name was Bryher. She was the daughter of the shipping magnate Sir John Ellerman, a man of great wealth. Bryher fell in love with H. D., and she was lovingly devoted to her for the rest of the poet's life. Bryher wrote novels, most of them historical: and she was as well a woman of considerable practical intelligence—Thornton Wilder said she resembled Napoleon—and she made it possible for H. D. to live comfortably, to travel in style, and to have both the society and the solitude she required.

In May 1933 H. D. had yet another momentous encounter. Freud took her on as a "pupil" (H. D.'s word). She went to see Freud because, in her own words, she

---

1. *Language as Gesture*, New York, 1952, p. 352.   3. Quoted in Glenn Hughes, *Imagism and the*
2. *Autobiography*, New York, 1951, pp. 67–68.   *Imagists*, New York, 1960, pp. 110–11.

"wanted to dig down and dig out, root out my personal needs, strengthen my purposes, reaffirm my beliefs, canalize my energies."[4] With Freud she shared an interest in the religions of the past, and her later poems are in their allusions increasingly eclectic. With Bryher she returned to London in 1939 and they spent the war years there. Inspired by her experience of the Blitz, H. D. composed three long meditative poems: here she uses the mythologies of Greece and Egypt, psychoanalysis, astrology, and numerology to come to terms with twentieth-century disaster. These poems were *The Walls Do Not Fall* (1944), *Tribute to the Angels* (1945), and *The Flowering of the Rod* (1946)—brought together in one volume as *Trilogy* (1973). She died in Zurich on September 29, 1961.

H. D.'s poems are exclamations in the face of, and in praise of, actuality, what is seen, what is immediately there. The poet often appears in the role of a priestess who has come to worship and celebrate a natural event. She prays that the event—the heat of the day, the sea, any item of real or imagined life—will overwhelm her, take her by storm. Her early poems are often confident magical spells. The later *The Walls Do Not Fall* is a kind of dejection ode. At first the poet distrusts her ability to identify with, and thus to recreate, what surrounds her; she eventually finds some consolation in the realization that the secret of the gods is "stored / in man's very speech" and that the poet "takes precedence of the priest, / stands second only to the Pharoah."

4. Quoted in Barbara Guest, *Herself Defined: The Poet H. D. and Her World*, New York, 1984.

Sea Rose

Rose, harsh rose,
marred and with stint of petals,
meagre flower, thin,
sparse of leaf,

more precious   5
than a wet rose
single on a stem—
you are caught in the drift.

Stunted, with small leaf,
you are flung on the sand,   10
you are lifted
in the crisp sand
that drives in the wind.

Can the spice-rose
drip such acrid fragrance   15
hardened in a leaf?

1916

Oread[1]

Whirl up, sea—
whirl your pointed pines,
splash your great pines

1. A nymph of the mountains.

on our rocks,
hurl your green over us,   5
cover us with your pools of fir.

1924

Helen[2]

All Greece hates
the still eyes in the white face,
the lustre as of olives
where she stands,
and the white hands.   5

All Greece reviles
the wan face when she smiles,
hating it deeper still
when it grows wan and white,
remembering past enchantments   10
and past ills.

Greece sees unmoved,
God's daughter, born of love,[3]
the beauty of cool feet
and slenderest knees,   15
could love indeed the maid,
only if she were laid,
white ash amid funereal cypresses.

1924

Fragment Sixty-eight

. . . even in the house of Hades.
—Sappho[4]

1

I envy you your chance of death,
how I envy you this.
I am more covetous of him
even than of your glance,
I wish more from his presence   5
though he torture me in a grasp,
terrible, intense.

Though he clasp me in an embrace
that is set against my will
and rack me with his measure,   10
effortless yet full of strength,

2. In Greek legend, wife of the king Menelaus;
her abduction by Paris was the cause of the Trojan
War.
3. Helen was the daughter of Zeus, who, in the
guise of a swan, visited the mortal woman Leda.
4. Greek woman poet (seventh century B.C.)
who gathered a group of like-minded women
around her on the island of Lesbos. Her poems
have come down to us almost entirely in fragments. Hades was the grim and terrible god of the
underworld after death in Greek mythology; the
name was also given to the underworld itself.

and slay me
in that most horrible contest,
still, how I envy you your chance.

Through he pierce me—imperious—   15
iron—fever—dust—
though beauty is slain
when I perish,
I envy you death.

What is beauty to me?   20
has she not slain me enough,
have I not cried in agony of love,
birth, hate,
in pride crushed?

What is left after this?   25
what can death loose in me
after your embrace?
your touch,
your limbs are more terrible
to do me hurt.   30

What can death mar in me
that you have not?

                 2

What can death send me
that you have not?
you gathered violets,   35
you spoke:
"your hair is not less black,
nor less fragrant.
nor in your eyes is less light,
your hair is not less sweet   40
with purple in the lift of lock;"
why were those slight words
and the violets you gathered
of such worth?

How I envy you death;   45
what could death bring,
more black, more set with sparks
to slay, to affright,
than the memory of those first violets,
the chance lift of your voice,   50
the chance blinding frenzy
as you bent?

                 3

So the goddess⁵ has slain me
for your chance smile

5. Probably Aphrodite, goddess of love.

and my scarf unfolding   55
as you stooped to it;
so she trapped me
with the upward sweep of your arm
as you lifted the veil,
and the swift smile and selfless.   60

Could I have known?
nay, spare pity,
though I break,
crushed under the goddess' hate,
though I fall beaten at last,   65
so high have I thrust my glance
up into her presence.

Do not pity me, spare that,
but how I envy you
your chance of death.   70
                                                           1924

From Tribute to the Angels[6]

*   *   *

36

Ah (you say), this is Holy Wisdom,   525
Santa Sophia, the SS of the *Sanctus Spiritus,*[7]

so by facile reasoning, logically
the incarnate symbol of the Holy Ghost;

your Holy Ghost was an apple-tree
smouldering—or rather now bourgeoning   535

with flowers; the fruit of the Tree?[8]
this is the new Eve who comes

clearly to return, to retrieve
what she lost the race,

given over to sin, to death;   285
she brings the Book of Life, obviously.

37

This is a symbol of beauty (you continue),
she is Our Lady universally,

---

6. In this, the second book of *Trilogy,* H.D. revises the biblical book of Revelation—the last book of the New Testament, full of symbols and visions about the end of the world and God's ultimate victory over evil. The speaker has invoked a series of symbolic angels; in the midst of the invocation, she has had a vision of a "a Lady."
7. "Holy Ghost" or "Holy Spirit." *Saint Sophia* means "holy wisdom"; it is also the name of a church in Constantinople (modern Istanbul) which has been, since 360 A.D., central to the city's religious life.
8. The Tree of Knowledge of Good and Evil, which God forbade Adam and Eve to eat the fruit of, in Genesis 2.

I see her as you project her,
not out of place   540

flanked by Corinthian capitals,
or in a Coptic nave,[9]

or frozen above the centre door
of a Gothic cathedral;

you have done very well by her   545
(to repeat your own phrase),

you have carved her tall and unmistakable,
a hieratic[10] figure, the veiled Goddess,

whether of the seven[1] delights,
whether of the seven spear-points.   550

38

O yes—you understand, I say,
this is all most satisfactory,

but she wasn't hieratic, she wasn't frozen,
she wasn't very tall;

she is the Vestal   555
from the days of Numa,[2]

she carries over the cult
of the *Bona Dea*,[3]

she carries a book but it is not
the tome of the ancient wisdom,   560

the pages, I imagine, are the blank pages
of the unwritten volume of the new;

all you say, is implicit,
all that and much more;

but she is not shut up in a cave   565
like a Sibyl;[4] she is not

imprisoned in leaden bars
in a coloured window;

9. That is, central hall in an Egyptian Christian church; "Corinthian capitals" refers to the upper ends of Greek pillars, carved in the lightest and most ornate "Corinthian" style.
10. That is, performing priestly functions.
1. A mystic number.
2. Or Numa Pompilius, legendary king of Rome, who founded most of the city's sacred institutions, such as the temple of Vesta, goddess of the hearth, whose fire was tended by the Vestal Virgins, or Vestals.
3. "Good goddess," in the Roman religion. Of unknown name, she was probably an earth-spirit who protected women, and only women were allowed to attend her rites.
4. Female prophet inspired by a deity, usually Apollo.

she is Psyche,[5] the butterfly,
out of the cocoon.   570

39

But nearer than Guardian Angel
or good Daemon,[6]

she is the counter-coin-side
of primitive terror;

she is not-fear, she is not-war,   575
but she is no symbolic figure

of peace, charity, chastity, goodness,
faith, hope, reward;

she is not Justice with eyes
blindfolded like Love's;[7]   580

I grant you the dove's symbolic purity,[8]
I grant you her face was innocent

and immaculate and her veils
like the Lamb's Bride,[9]

but the Lamb was not with her,   585
either as Bridegroom or Child;

her attention is undivided,
we are her bridegroom and lamb;

her book is our book; written
or unwritten, its pages will reveal   590

a tale of a Fisherman,
a tale of a jar or jars,[1]

the same—different—the same attributes,
different yet the same as before.

40

This is no rune[2] nor symbol,   595
what I mean is—it is so simple

5. Human lover of the Greek god Cupid or Eros, who went to heaven to join him after being set a number of impossible tasks by Aphrodite, including a descent into Hades. Her name means "soul," in Greek, and her symbol is the butterfly.
6. In Greek thought, the indwelling fate or spirit that guides life; humans were occasionally thought to have good and bad daemons.
7. Both Justice and Cupid, god of love, are traditionally represented as being blindfolded.
8. The dove is an important Christian symbol; in Matthew 3:16, for example, the spirit of God descends like a dove at Christ's baptism by John the Baptist.
9. Traditionally, the Lamb is Christ, his bride the Church.
1. These lines anticipate the last book of *Trilogy*, *The Flowering of the Rod*, which retells the Gospel story of the Wise Men's gift of a jar of myrrh (an aromatic gum used for perfuming tabernacle oil and preparing the dead for burial).
2. The letters of the old Norse alphabet, reputed to have magical incantatory powers.

yet no trick of the pen or brush
could capture that impression;

what I wanted to indicate was
a new phase, a new distinction of colour;   600

I wanted to say, I did say
there was no sheen, no reflection,

no shadow; when I said white,
I did not mean sculptor's or painter's white,

nor porcelain; dim-white could   605
not suggest it, for when

is fresh-fallen snow (or snow
in the act of falling) dim?

yet even now, we stumble, we are lost—
what can we say?   610

she was not impalpable like a ghost,
she was not awe-inspiring like a Spirit,

she was not even over-whelming
like an Angel.

41

She carried a book, either to imply   615
she was one of us, with us,

or to suggest she was satisfied
with our purpose, a tribute to the Angels;

yet though the campanili³ spoke,
Gabriel, Azrael,   620

though the campanili answered,
Raphael, Uriel,

thought a distant note over-water
chimed *Annael,* and *Michael*⁴

was implicit from the beginning,   625
another, deep, un-named, resurging bell

answered, sounding through them all:
remember, where there was

3. Bell-tower.
4. All angels invoked elsewhere in the poem, as well.

> no need of the moon to shine . . .
> I saw no temple.

630

*   *   *

1945

SIEGFRIED SASSOON
1886–1967

Siegfried Sassoon was born into a world of leisured ease and country pleasures, a privileged world which in retrospect he transformed into a timeless Eden. "Time went as slowly," he wrote, "as the carrier's van that brought the parcels from the station, and international affairs were comfortably epitomised in the weekly cartoons of *Punch*. France was a lady in a short skirt, Russia a bear, and the performances of the county cricket team more important than either of them."[1] This quiet world exploded in 1914, and Sassoon served in the British Army for four and a half years. During this period he wrote the short satirical poems for which he is best remembered.

He was born in London on September 8, 1886, into a prosperous family of Sephardic Jews. His parents separated when Sassoon was a child; his father died soon thereafter, and he was raised by his mother. He was educated at Marlborough Grammar School and at Clare College, Cambridge, and then spent a few years in London; Sassoon was an attractive young man, well connected and comfortably situated, and his main interests were hunting and poetry. Sassoon was taken up by Sir Edward Marsh, a patron of the arts, and for a time figured in the collections of Georgian poetry he began to publish in 1912.

When war broke out in 1914, Sassoon immediately enlisted and went to France as a second lieutenant. His first war poems were written under the enchantment of a chivalric ideal. His fellow officer Robert Graves showed him his own poems about the war, and Sassoon objected that they were too "realistic," though he would soon change his mind about the war and the proper way to write about it. He set himself the task of observing the war and his reactions to it. Two collections of Sassoon's poems appeared during the war: *The Old Huntsman* (1917) and *Counter Attack* (1918). In 1917 Sassoon was wounded and he was sent home; disgusted with the war and with the civilians who were profiting from it financially and emotionally, he threw his Military Cross into the sea and did his best to get court-martialed so that he could make his views public. Instead he was judged to be "temporarily insane" and thus denied a hearing; he eventually returned to France where he was wounded for a second time.

When the war was over, Sassoon, a declared pacifist, toured the United States, reading his poems and speaking against war. Although he continued to write poetry, his best later work was a three-volume fictionalized autobiography—*Memoirs of a Fox-Hunting Man* (1928), *Memoirs of an Infantry Officer* (1930), and *Sherston's Progress* (1936)—and several volumes of undisguised autobiography. Sassoon became a Roman Catholic in 1957; he died on September 1, 1967.

Sassoon began as a social and poetic radical; in the trenches he used to dream that one day he and Graves would "scandalize the jolly old Gosses and Stracheys,"[2] the established literary figures of their day. Once this wartime exuberance had spent

---

1. Quoted in Michael Thorpe, *Siegfried Sassoon, a Critical Study*, London, 1967, pp. 70–71.

2. Quoted in Robert Graves, *Goodbye to All That*, Harmondsworth, Essex, 1969, p. 210.

itself, Sassoon's views of poetry turned out to be rather old-fashioned. In 1939 he observed that "for the last decade and a half the writing of straightforward and whole-hearted verse has been increasingly out of fashion, and indirect utterance has been indulged in to an unprecedented degree."[3] Clearly Sassoon's sympathies are all on the side of direct utterance, and in his remarks on poetry he shows little interest in exploring the very complex feelings from which simple poetic statements often derive their power. Almost certainly it was the emotion engendered in Sassoon by the war, an emotion for which "urgency" is far too mild a word, that inspired what Graves calls the "extraordinary five years of Siegfried Sassoon's efflorescence (1917–1921)."[4]

3. Quoted in Thorpe, p. 189.   4. The same, p. ix.

"Blighters"

The House is crammed: tier beyond tier they grin
And cackle at the Show, while prancing ranks
Of harlots shrill the chorus, drunk with din;
"We're sure the Kaiser loves the dear old Tanks!"

I'd like to see a Tank come down the stalls,[1]   5
Lurching to ragtime tunes, or "Home, sweet Home,"—
And there'd be no more jokes in Music-halls
To mock the riddled corpses round Bapaume.[2]

                                                              1917

The General

"Good-morning; good-morning!" the General said
When we met him last week on our way to the line.
Now the soldiers he smiled at are most of 'em dead,
And we're cursing his staff for incompetent swine.
"He's a cheery old card," grunted Harry to Jack   5
As they slogged up to Arras[3] with rifle and pack.

              .   .   .

But he did for them both by his plan of attack.

                                                              1918

Everyone Sang

Everyone suddenly burst out singing;
And I was filled with such delight
As prisoned birds must find in freedom,
Winging wildly across the white
Orchards and dark-green fields; on—on—and out of sight.   5

Everyone's voice was suddenly lifted;
And beauty came like the setting sun:

1. Orchestra seats in a theater or music-hall.
2. A town in northern France, one of the main objectives in the costly but successful Allied offen-sive against the Hindenburg Line in 1918. "Music-halls" provided popular variety shows.

3. A city in northern France, in the front line during most of World War I. The British assault against the Germans of the Western Front, on April 9, 1917, was known as the Battle of Arras. The dead "soldiers he smiled at" amounted to 84,000.

My heart was shaken with tears; and horror
Drifted away . . . O, but Everyone
Was a bird; and the song was wordless; the singing will never be done.   10

1919

On Passing the New Menin Gate[4]

Who will remember, passing through this Gate,
The unheroic Dead who fed the guns?
Who shall absolve the foulness of their fate,—
Those doomed, conscripted, unvictorious ones?
Crudely renewed, the Salient[5] holds its own.   5
Paid are its dim defenders by this pomp;
Paid, with a pile of peace-complacent stone,
The armies who endured that sullen swamp.

Here was the world's worst wound. And here
   with pride
"Their name liveth for ever," the Gateway claims.   10
Was ever an immolation so belied
As these intolerably nameless names?
Well might the Dead who struggled in the slime
Rise and deride this sepulchre of crime.

1928

4. The names of 54,889 men are engraved on this World War I memorial.
5. Line of defensive trenches (the long excavations in the earth from which both sides fought in World War I). Since salients jutted out into enemy territory, they were especially vulnerable, exposing the troops in them to fire from the front and both sides.

ROBINSON JEFFERS
1887–1962

Strength is the quality that Robinson Jeffers admires and that he seeks in his own poetry, whether that poetry is full-throated or modulated. He admires "dead men's thoughts" that have "shed weakness" ("Wise Men in Their Bad Hours"). In his prefaces he indicates that his initial conviction was that the poetry of Mallarmé and those who followed him in France, England, and America was "thoroughly defeatist, as if poetry were in terror of prose, and desperately trying to save its soul from the victor by giving up its body. It was becoming slight and fantastic, abstract, unreal, eccentric . . ." Accordingly, his own verse must do something else. "It must reclaim substance and sense, and physical and psychological reality."[1]

The strength he endorses is of two kinds. The first is sudden, swift, flashing, like the hawk's: "I have cut the meshes / And fly like a freed falcon," cries Orestes in *The Tower Beyond Tragedy*. The second kind is enduring, permanent, like the rock's. In "To the Stone Cutters," he says, "The poet as well / Builds his monument mockingly; / For man will be blotted out, the blithe earth die, the brave sun / Die blind and blacken to the heart: / Yet stones have stood for a thousand years, and pained thoughts found / The honey of peace in old poems." Hawk and rock appear in various guises in Jeffers's writings, as principles of dynamism and revered inertness.

1. Foreword to *Selected Poetry*, New York, 1959, p. xiv.

Jeffers's excitement about excitement and admiration for rocks and hawks do not entail an indiscriminate regard for strength. Because incest was his frequent theme, it was supposed at first that he endorsed it. Jeffers was at pains to make clear that he never had a sister; more seriously, he said that the incest theme "breaks taboo more violently than the other irregularities and so *may* be of a more tragic nature; and more important, it seems to symbolize human turned-inwardness."[2] He regarded introversion as the malady from which "all past cultures have died . . . at last, and so will this one . . ."[3] Yet the most violent introversion produces the greatest reaction from it: in *The Tower Beyond Tragedy,* Electra's incestuous love leads her only to futility, but drives her brother Orestes another way, so that in the end, as Jeffers says explicitly, he "had climbed the tower beyond time, consciously." In another long poem, *Roan Stallion* (1925), as in D. H. Lawrence's novel *St Mawr,* a woman loves a horse, prefers it to any human creature. Jeffers says approvingly, "Humanity is the start of the race; I say / Humanity is the mould to break away from, the crust to break through, the coal to break into fire, / The atom to be split. Tragedy that breaks man's face and white fire flies out of it; vision that fools him / Out of his limits, unnatural crime, inhuman science, / Slit eyes in the mask; wild loves that leap over the walls of nature . . ."

With these views, Jeffers saw his work as a kind of liberation. He said in a letter that his theme in *The Women at Point Sur* (1927) was "to uncenter the human mind from itself."[4] In a late book, *The Double Axe* (1948), Jeffers announced with an old man's boldness that he would "present a certain philosophical attitude which might be called inhumanism, a shifting of emphasis and significance from man to not-man."

Jeffers was born January 10, 1887, in Pittsburgh; his father was a professor at the Western Theological Seminary there. Although Jeffers, in "To His Father," contrasted his own unbelief with his father's Scotch-Irish Calvinism, his sense of the primal force in nature bears some resemblance to the God of Calvinism. A more apparent influence came from his father's having been a professor of Greek and Latin; from him Jeffers learned Greek and perhaps also a taste for Greek tragedy. He would later write of Medea as well as of Orestes.

As a boy Jeffers was sent to boarding schools on the Continent in Geneva, Lausanne, Zurich, and Leipzig. When he was fifteen, besides reading Nietzsche, he read Dante Gabriel Rossetti enthusiastically, and later Yeats, Shelley, Tennyson, Milton, and Marlowe. Out of these, and his nature, he composed his own powerful rhetoric. He was brought back from school in 1903, and the next year his family moved from Pittsburgh to California. Jeffers entered Occidental College and was graduated at the age of eighteen. He began graduate work at the University of Southern California, and there, in his nineteenth year, his future was determined: he met, in a German class, Mrs. Una Call Kuster. Apparently she was from now on his lodestar, but her husband stood in Jeffers's way. The next years passed in a series of false starts: he went off to the University of Zurich in 1906, but came quickly back in 1907 to resume studies at Southern California, though in a different course, medicine. His medical interest flagged, and in 1910 he decided to try forestry at the University of Washington. But in 1911 he was back in California. In 1912 he received a modest legacy and published a book entitled *Flagons and Apples.* Una Kuster's husband began to fade from the scene, and on November 17, as Jeffers said in a letter, Una transformed his world. Her own was transformed a few months later by divorce, and quickly thereafter, on August 2, 1913, the two were married. Jeffers spoke with serious rapture of her importance to him, as muse and wife.

They had planned to go to England, but war broke out. In September 1914, they came to the village of Carmel on the California coast, and decided it was there they

2. *Selected Letters, 1897–1962,* ed. Ann N. Ridgeway, Baltimore, 1968, p. 35.

3. The same, p. 116.
4. The same, p. 116.

must live. Jeffers immediately began to have a house built; he was later to build Hawk Tower beside it with his own hands. The rocky coast, the seabirds, the comparative isolation, all suited him. It was still some time before he achieved his mature manner. "Great men have done their work before they were thirty," he said in a letter, "but I wasn't born yet."[5]

Jeffers lived intensely but with few outward incidents. Perhaps his greatest fame came when he translated Euripedes' *Medea* into his own manner, and Judith Anderson played the leading role on Broadway. He risked opprobrium by opposing American participation in the Second World War. Since his death he has become identified with the spectacular Pacific coastline and with basic, violent emotions.

5. The same, p. 108.

Shine, Perishing Republic

While this America settles in the mould of its vulgarity, heavily thickening
    to empire,
And protest, only a bubble in the molten mass, pops and sighs out, and the
    mass hardens,

I sadly smiling remember that the flower fades to make fruit, the fruit rots
    to make earth.
Out of the mother; and through the spring exultances, ripeness and deca-
    dence; and home to the mother.

You making haste haste on decay: not blameworthy; life is good, be it stub-
    bornly long or suddenly   5
A mortal splendor: meteors are not needed less than mountains: shine,
    perishing republic.

But for my children, I would have them keep their distance from the thick-
    ening center; corruption
Never has been compulsory, when the cities lie at the monster's feet there
    are left the mountains.

And boys, be in nothing so moderate as in love of man, a clever servant,
    insufferable master.
There is the trap that catches noblest spirits, that caught—they say—
    God, when he walked on earth.   10

1925

Fawn's Foster-Mother

The old woman sits on a bench before the door and quarrels
With her meager pale demoralized daughter.
Once when I passed I found her alone, laughing in the sun
And saying that when she was first married
She lived in the old farmhouse up Garapatas Canyon.   5
(It is empty now, the roof has fallen
But the log walls hang on the stone foundation; the redwoods
Have all been cut down, the oaks are standing;
The place is now more solitary than ever before.)

"When I was nursing my second baby   10
My husband found a day-old fawn hid in a fern-brake
And brought it; I put its mouth to the breast
Rather than let it starve, I had milk enough for three babies.
Hey, how it sucked, the little nuzzler,
Digging its little hoofs like quills into my stomach.   15
I had more joy from that than from the others."
Her face is deformed with age, furrowed like a bad road
With market-wagons, mean cares and decay.
She is thrown up to the surface of things, a cell of dry skin
Soon to be shed from the earth's old eyebrows,   20
I see that once in her spring she lived in the streaming arteries,
The stir of the world, the music of the mountain.

                                                                    1928

Hurt Hawks

I

The broken pillar of the wing jags from the clotted shoulder,
The wing trails like a banner in defeat,
No more to use the sky forever but live with famine
And pain a few days: cat nor coyote
Will shorten the week of waiting for death, there is game without talons.   5
He stands under the oak-bush and waits
The lame feet of salvation; a night he remembers freedom
And flies in a dream, the dawns ruin it.
He is strong and pain is worse to the strong, incapacity is worse.
The curs of the day come and torment him   10
At distance, no one but death the redeemer will humble that head,
The intrepid readiness, the terrible eyes.
The wild God of the world is sometimes merciful to those
That ask mercy, not often to the arrogant.
You do not know him, you communal people, or you have forgotten him;   15
Intemperate and savage, the hawk remembers him;
Beautiful and wild, the hawks, and men that are dying, remember him.

II

I'd sooner, except the penalties, kill a man than a hawk; but the great redtail
Had nothing left but unable misery
From the bone too shattered for mending, the wing that trailed under his
      talons when he moved.   20
We had fed him six weeks, I gave him freedom,
He wandered over the foreland hill and returned in the evening, asking for
      death,
Not like a beggar, still eyed with the old
Implacable arrogance. I gave him the lead gift in the twilight.
      What fell was relaxed,
Owl-downy, soft feminine feathers; but what   25
Soared: the fierce rush: the night-herons by the flooded river cried fear at
      its rising
Before it was quite unsheathed from reality.

                                                                    1928

New Mexican Mountain

I watch the Indians dancing to help the young corn at Taos[1] pueblo. The
    old men squat in a ring
And make the song, the young women with fat bare arms, and a few shame-
    faced young men, shuffle the dance.

The lean-muscled young men are naked to the narrow loins, their breasts
    and backs daubed with white clay,
Two eagle-feathers plume the black heads. They dance with reluctance,
    they are growing civilized; the old men persuade them.

Only the drum is confident, it thinks the world has not changed; the beating
    heart, the simplest of rhythms,
It thinks the world has not changed at all; it is only a dreamer, a brainless   5
    heart, the drum has no eyes.

These tourists have eyes, the hundred watching the dance, white Ameri-
    cans, hungrily too, with reverence, not laughter;
Pilgrims from civilization, anxiously seeking beauty, religion, poetry; pil-
    grims from the vacuum.

People from cities, anxious to be human again. Poor show how they suck
    you empty! The Indians are emptied,
And certainly there was never religion enough, nor beauty nor poetry here
    . . . to fill Americans.   10

Only the drum is confident, it thinks the world has not changed. Apparently
    only myself and the strong
Tribal drum, and the rockhead of Taos mountain, remember that civiliza-
    tion is a transient sickness.[2]

                                                      1932

Ave Caesar[3]

No bitterness: our ancestors did it.
They were only ignorant and hopeful, they wanted freedom but wealth too.
Their children will learn to hope for a Caesar.
Or rather—for we are not aquiline Romans but soft mixed colonists—
Some kindly Sicilian tyrant who'll keep   5
Poverty and Carthage off until the Romans arrive,[4]

---

1. D. H. Lawrence, a writer whom Jeffers admired, lived in Taos, New Mexico, for a time, and after his death in 1930 the Lawrence cult there was somewhat combined with a Jeffers cult.

2. In a letter to James Rorty, Jeffers wrote, "I don't think industrial civilization is worth the distortion of human nature, and the meanness and loss of contact with the earth, that it entails. I think your Marxist industrialized communism—if it were ever brought into existence—would be only a further step in a bad direction. It would entail less meanness but equal distortion, and would rot people with more complete security. . . . Civilization will have to go on building up for centuries yet, and its collapse will be gradual and tragic and sor-

did, and I have no remedy to propose, except for the individual to keep himself out of it as much as he can conveniently, as you are doing, and as I am doing, and exercise his instincts and self-restraints and powers as completely as possible in spite of it. . . . As to civilization, I am consoled by the knowledge that there was a long time before it and will be a time after it, and by the suspicion that it is not skin-deep, but, say, clothing-deep."

3. Hail, Caesar!

4. For over 200 years the towns of Sicily were ruled by tyrants; this was ended by the First Punic War (264–241 B.C.), in which Rome defeated Carthage and annexed Sicily.

We are easy to manage, a gregarious people,
Full of sentiment, clever at mechanics, and we love our luxuries.

1935

The Purse-Seine[5]

Our sardine fishermen work at night in the dark of the moon; daylight or
    moonlight
They could not tell where to spread the net, unable to see the phospho-
    rescence of the shoals of fish.
They work northward from Monterey, coasting Santa Cruz; off New Year's
    Point or off Pigeon Point
The look-out man will see some lakes of milk-color light on the sea's night-
    purple; he points, and the helmsman
Turns the dark prow, the motorboat circles the gleaming shoal and drifts
    out her seine-net. They close the circle   5
And purse the bottom of the net, then with great labor haul it in.

                                      I cannot tell you
How beautiful the scene is, and a little terrible, then, when the crowded
    fish
Know they are caught, and wildly beat from one wall to the other of their
    closing destiny the phosphorescent
Water to a pool of flame, each beautiful slender body sheeted with flame,
    like a live rocket   10
A comet's tail wake of clear yellow flame; while outside the narrowing
Floats and cordage of the net great sea-lions come up to watch, sighing in
    the dark; the vast walls of night
Stand erect to the stars.

                        Lately I was looking from a night mountain-top
On a wide city, the colored splendor, galaxies of light: how could I help but
    recall the seine-net   15
Gathering the luminous fish? I cannot tell you how beautiful the city appeared,
    and a little terrible.
I thought, We have geared the machines and locked all together into inter-
    dependence; we have built the great cities; now
There is no escape. We have gathered vast populations incapable of free
    survival, insulated
From the strong earth, each person in himself helpless, on all dependent.
    The circle is closed, and the net
Is being hauled in. They hardly feel the cords drawing, yet they shine already.
    The inevitable mass-disasters   20
Will not come in our time nor in our children's, but we and our children
Must watch the net draw narrower, government take all powers—or revo-
    lution, and the new government
Take more than all, add to kept bodies kept souls—or anarchy, the mass-
    disasters.

                    These things are Progress;
Do you marvel our verse is troubled or frowning, while it keeps its reason?
    Or it lets go, lets the mood flow   25

---

5. A fishing net shaped like a bag.

In the manner of the recent young men into mere hysteria, splintered gleams,
    crackled laughter. But they are quite wrong.
There is no reason for amazement: surely one always knew that cultures
    decay, and life's end is death.

1937

Shiva[6]

There is a hawk that is picking the birds out of our sky,
She killed the pigeons of peace and security,
She has taken honesty and confidence from nations and men,
She is hunting the lonely heron of liberty.
She loads the arts with nonsense, she is very cunning,   5
Science with dreams and the state with powers to catch them at last.
Nothing will escape her at last, flying nor running.
This is the hawk that picks out the stars' eyes.
This is the only hunter that will ever catch the wild swan;
The prey she will take last is the wild white swan of the beauty of things.   10
Then she will be alone, pure destruction, achieved and supreme,
Empty darkness under the death-tent wings.
She will build a nest of the swan's bones and hatch a new brood,
Hang new heavens with new birds, all be renewed.

1937

The Deer Lay Down Their Bones

I followed the narrow cliffside trail half way up the mountain
Above the deep river-canyon. There was a little cataract[7] crossed the path,
    flinging itself
Over tree roots and rocks, shaking the jeweled fern-fronds, bright bubbling
    water
Pure from the mountain, but a bad smell came up. Wondering at it I clam-
    bered down the steep stream
Some forty feet, and found in the midst of bush-oak and laurel,   5
Hung like a bird's nest on the precipice brink a small hidden clearing,
Grass and a shallow pool. But all about there were bones lying in the grass,
    clean bones and stinking bones,
Antlers and bones: I understood that the place was a refuge for wounded
    deer; there are so many
Hurt ones escape the hunters and limp away to lie hidden; here they have
    water for the awful thirst
And peace to die in; dense green laurel and grim cliff   10
Make sanctuary, and a sweet wind blows upward from the deep gorge.—I
    wish my bones were with theirs.
But that's a foolish thing to confess, and a little cowardly. We know that life
Is on the whole quite equally good and bad, mostly gray neutral, and can
    be endured
To the dim end, no matter what magic of grass, water and precipice, and
    pain of wounds,
Makes death look dear. We have been given life and have used it—not a
    great gift perhaps—but in honesty   15

6. Shiva (or Siva) is a Hindu god representing
the principle of destruction, and of creation following it.
7. Waterfall.

Should use it all. Mine's empty since my love[8] died—Empty? The flame-
haired grandchild with great blue eyes
That look like hers?—What can I do for the child? I gaze at her and wonder
what sort of man
In the fall of the world . . . I am growing old, that is the trouble. My chil-
dren and little grandchildren
Will find their way, and why should I wait ten years yet, having lived sixty-
seven, ten years more or less,
Before I crawl out on a ledge of rock and die snapping, like a wolf   20
Who has lost his mate?—I am bound by my own thirty-year-old decision:
who drinks the wine
Should take the dregs; even in the bitter lees and sediment
New discovery may lie. The deer in that beautiful place lay down their
bones: I must wear mine.

1954

Vulture

I had walked since dawn and lay down to rest on a bare hillside
Above the ocean. I saw through half-shut eyelids a vulture wheeling high
up in heaven,
And presently it passed again, but lower and nearer, its orbit narrowing, I
understood then
That I was under inspection. I lay death-still and heard the flight-feathers
Whistle above me and make their circle and come nearer.   5
I could see the naked red head between the great wings
Bear downward staring. I said, "My dear bird, we are wasting time here.
These old bones will still work; they are not for you." But how beautiful he
looked, gliding down
On those great sails; how beautiful he looked, veering away in the sea-light
over the precipice. I tell you solemnly
That I was sorry to have disappointed him. To be eaten by that beak and
become part of him, to share those wings and those eyes—   10
What a sublime end of one's body, what an enskyment; what a life after
death.

1963

8. Jeffers's wife Una.

EDWIN MUIR
1887–1959

Edwin Muir wrote in his autobiography, "I was born before the Industrial Revolution, and am now about two hundred years old. But I have skipped a hundred and
fifty years of them. . . . No wonder I am obsessed with Time."[1] He was in fact born
on May 15th, 1887, in Deerness in the Orkney Islands off the coast of Scotland. He
was the son of a small tenant farmer and spent his boyhood, as he later came to
recognize, in a society which had changed little since the Middle Ages. Muir's recollections of this primitive agricultural life, its daily and seasonal rituals, its folk beliefs

1. *The Story and the Fable*, London, 1940, p. 263.

and superstitions, are the material for much of his poetry. His family and their neighbors "had a culture made up of legend, folk-song, and the poetry and prose of the Bible; they had customs which sanctioned their instinctive feelings for the earth; their life was an order, and a good order."[2] His parents seemed to him "fixed allegorical figures in a timeless landscape."

When he was thirteen Muir's family had to give up their farm and move to the industrial city of Glasgow, then famous for its prosperity and for its terrible slums, which were thought to be the worst in the British Isles. His parents found life in the city unbearable and by the time Muir was eighteen both were dead. Muir moved from one shabby job to another. He had left school at fourteen and was forced to continue his education on his own. In June 1919 Muir married Willa Anderson, and he was frequently to say that his marriage was the most important single event of his life. She gave him the courage to devote himself to writing, encouraging him to leave Glasgow and move to London, and some years later collaborated with him on their translations of twentieth-century German writers. Accounts of this extraordinarily happy marriage may be found in Muir's autobiography and in *Belonging*, a book which Mrs. Muir wrote after her husband's death.

He and his wife spent some time in Prague both before and after the Second World War, where he lectured on English literature, and for five years he was the Warden of Newbattle, a residential adult education college in Scotland. In 1955–56 he was Charles Eliot Norton professor at Harvard. He died on January 3, 1959.

Muir is a difficult writer to place, because in his poetry and his criticism he attempts to go his own way and to steer clear of schools and influences. He wrote Stephen Spender, "I think we are all too much moved by a spirit of emulation, and when something 'new' appears feel almost in conscience bound to produce something new, whereas if we wrote from the solidest base within ourselves we should produce something which is new. I know that in my own experience I have generally to burst through to that solid foundation (at least it always feels like that) and only rarely touch it: for me it is the most difficult thing in the world to reach. I am very rarely on it, most of my life is elsewhere."[3]

For Muir the "solidest basis" within himself was the vanished Eden of his childhood. His last book takes its title from the poem "One Foot in Eden," and his tombstone bears lines from his poem "Milton":

> his unblinded eyes
> Saw far and near the fields of Paradise.

Muir's poem "The Horses," which T. S. Eliot described as "that great, that terrifying poem of the 'atomic age',"[4] celebrates the reconstruction of the human and the natural world after the destruction of our mechanized and inhuman "civilization." Because of the enduring simplicities of his recollected childhood, Muir's bent is towards allegory. In 1937 he and his wife translated Kafka's *The Trial*, and his words on that great allegorist are also a summary of Muir's own endeavor and achievement: "He has provided imaginative writers not merely with a way of looking at life, but with a way of dealing with life. In an age obsessed by the time sense, or, as it is called, the historical sense, he has resurrected and made available for contemporary use the timeless story, the archetypal story, in which is the source of all stories."[5]

---

2. *Autobiography*, London, 1954, p. 63.
3. P. H. Butter, *Edwin Muir*, New York, 1967, p. 143.
4. Preface to *Collected Poems*, London, 1952,
p. 5.
5. *Essays on Literature and Society*, London, 1965, p. 124.

Ballad of Hector in Hades[1]

Yes, this is where I stood that day,
Besides this sunny mound.
The walls of Troy are far away,
And outward comes no sound.

I wait. On all the empty plain   5
A burnished stillness lies,
Save for the chariot's tinkling hum,
And a few distant cries.

His helmet glitters near. The world
Slowly turns around,   10
With some new sleight compels my feet
From the fighting ground.

I run. If I turned back again
The earth must turn with me,
The mountains planted on the plain,   15
The sky clamped to the sea.

The grasses puff a little dust
Where my footsteps fall.
I cast a shadow as I pass
The little wayside wall.   20

The strip of grass on either hand
Sparkles in the light;
I only see that little space
To the left and to the right,

And in that space our shadows run,   25
His shadow there and mine,
The little flowers, the tiny mounds,
The grasses frail and fine.

But narrower still and narrower!
My course is shrunk and small,   30
Yet vast as in a deadly dream,
And faint the Trojan wall.
The sun up in the towering sky
Turns like a spinning ball.

The sky with all its clustered eyes   35
Grows still with watching me,

1. Hector, leader of the Trojan army, was killed in battle by the Greek hero Achilles, who dragged the dead body behind his chariot around the walls of Troy. Muir, in his *Autobiography* (1954, pp. 42–43), tells of an incident in his own childhood which inspired this poem. Another boy had chased him home from school: "What I was afraid of I did not know; it was not Freddie, but something else. . . . I was seven at the time, and in the middle of my guilty fears. On that summer afternoon they took the shape of Freddie Sinclair, and turned him into a terrifying figure of vengeance. . . . I got rid of that terror almost thirty years later in a poem describing Achilles chasing Hector round Troy, in which I pictured Hector returning after his death to run the deadly race over again. In the poem I imagined Hector as noticing with intense, dreamlike precision certain little things, not the huge simplified things which my conscious memory tells me I noticed in my own flight. . . . I wrote the poem down, almost complete, at one sitting."

The flowers, the mounds, the flaunting weeds
Wheel slowly round to see.

Two shadows racing on the grass,
Silent and so near,   40
Until his shadow falls on mine.
And I am rid of fear.

The race is ended. Far away
I hang and do not care,
While round bright Troy Achilles whirls   45
A corpse with streaming hair.

                                                     1925

One Foot in Eden

One foot in Eden still, I stand
And look across the other land.
The world's great day is growing late,
Yet strange these fields that we have planted
So long with crops of love and hate.   5
Time's handiworks by time are haunted,
And nothing now can separate
The corn and tares compactly grown.
The armorial weed in stillness bound
About the stalk; these are our own.   10
Evil and good stand thick around
In the fields of charity and sin
Where we shall lead our harvest in.
Yet still from Eden springs the root
As clean as on the starting day.   15
Time takes the foliage and the fruit
And burns the archetypal leaf
To shapes of terror and of grief
Scattered along the winter way.
But famished field and blackened tree   20
Bear flowers in Eden never known.
Blossoms of grief and charity
Bloom in these darkened fields alone.
What had Eden ever to say
Of hope and faith and pity and love   25
Until was buried all its day
And memory found its treasure trove?
Strange blessings never in Paradise
Fall from these beclouded skies.

                                                     1956

The Horses

Barely a twelvemonth after
The seven days war that put the world to sleep,
Late in the evening the strange horses came.

By then we had made our covenant with silence,
But in the first few days it was so still   5
We listened to our breathing and were afraid.
On the second day
The radios failed; we turned the knobs; no answer.
On the third day a warship passed us, heading north,
Dead bodies piled on the deck. On the sixth day   10
A plane plunged over us into the sea. Thereafter
Nothing. The radios dumb;
And still they stand in corners of our kitchens,
And stand, perhaps, turned on, in a million rooms
All over the world. But now if they should speak,   15
If on a sudden they should speak again,
If on the stroke of noon a voice should speak,
We would not listen, we would not let it bring
That old bad world that swallowed its children quick
At one great gulp. We would not have it again.   20
Sometimes we think of the nations lying asleep,
Curled blindly in impenetrable sorrow,
And then the thought confounds us with its strangeness.
The tractors lie about our fields; at evening
They look like dank sea-monsters couched and waiting. 25
We leave them where they are and let them rust:
'They'll moulder away and be like other loam'.
We make our oxen drag our rusty ploughs,
Long laid aside. We have gone back
Far past our fathers' land.   30
                              And then, that evening
Late in the summer the strange horses came.
We heard a distant tapping on the road,
A deepening drumming; it stopped, went on again
And at the corner changed to hollow thunder.[2]   35
We saw the heads
Like a wild wave charging and were afraid.
We had sold our horses in our fathers' time
To buy new tractors. Now they were strange to us
As fabulous steeds set on an ancient shield   40
Or illustrations in a book of knights.
We did not dare go near them. Yet they waited,
Stubborn and shy, as if they had been sent
By an old command to find our whereabouts
And that long-lost archaic companionship.   45
In the first moment we had never a thought
That they were creatures to be owned and used.
Among them were some half-a-dozen colts
Dropped in some wilderness of the broken world,

---

2. In 1958 Muir wrote to a student who had sent him an essay on this poem: "I think you have gone wrong in thinking of the horses as wild horses, or as stampeding. It is less than a year since the seven days' war happened. So the horses are good plough-horses and still have a memory of the world before the war. . . . As for the 'tapping': have you ever listened, on a still evening, to horses trotting in the distance? The sound is really a pretty tapping. The drumming sound indicated that they were drawing nearer: the hollow thunder when they turned the corner meant that they saw the village or farmstead and found their home. . . . The horses are seeking the long lost archaic companionship, accepted in former times by men as an obvious right, so that it never occurred to them that there was anything surprising in using and owning horses. It is the surprise of the return that makes them realize the beauty of that free servitude" (quoted in P. H. Butter, *Edwin Muir*, p. 260).

Yet new as if they had come from their own Eden.   50
Since then they have pulled our ploughs and borne our loads,
But that free servitude still can pierce our hearts.
Our life is changed; their coming our beginning.

1956

MARIANNE MOORE
1887–1972

Marianne Moore is one of the most original poets of her time, original in her mode
of perception, in her kind of poetry, even in the way her stanzas appear on the page.
She proceeds by acute observation, more often centered on animals than on people;
she marvels at peculiarities and generalizes about them, often by ironic comparisons
of lower with higher animals, though one cannot know in advance which group she
will prefer. Her poems are made up of long sentences chopped jaggedly (as it first
seems) into short lines, the latter not usually prefixed with a capital letter, as if she
were eager to speak plainly and, with slight interruptions at line ends, prosily. Yet
the lines do break up the statement and add emphasis, often humorous emphasis, to
what is being said. They also usually rhyme, although finding the rhyme may take
some effort, as if she had determined that this aspect is too purely poetic to be
permitted obtrusiveness or easy detectability. The fact that her verse is patently
verse, yet embraces many characteristics of prose, is almost revolutionary; it reconstitutes the relationship of these two media, and attracted to her many poets equally
concerned to be matter-of-fact and anti-rhetorical. Yet she will not lead them like a
schoolmistress, and is quite capable of suddenly, as in "What Are Years?", bursting
into rhetoric for her own purposes.

Moore was born on November 15, 1887, in St. Louis, ten months before T. S.
Eliot was born in the same city. She too belonged to the generation of Pound and
Williams. While these poets have admired her, perhaps a closer tie is with Wallace
Stevens, because her verse concentrates like his on a highly varied physical scene
and disports with that scene in unaccustomed ways. She shares Stevens's distaste for
what he calls "fops of fancy." Moore is rigorous in adopting a seeming triviality of
detail and in being almost invariably quiet and unpretentious in manner. Her interest in animals, birds, and plants is also more specialized than Stevens's, as if the
variety of the physical universe might be described in its own right, apart from esthetic
and metaphysical problems. Her humility is vast, and she takes the stance neither of
critic nor of connoisseur, both roles being too peacock-tailed and dominating for her
taste.

It might seem that her poems about animals could have been related to D. H.
Lawrence's animal poems, but she is not especially interested in what occupies him—
the deep erotic urges of beasts as contrasted with the flightiness of humans. Moore
is devoted rather to animals' quirkiness, to their stubbornness or flexibility, their
dignity or lack of it. Unlike Lawrence, she offers no depth psychology of the jerboa
or the fish, and makes no attempt—she would consider it futile, in view of the dis-
tinctness of each creature—to share its fundamental drives.

Moore spent a lot of time in the Bronx Zoo, as might be expected, but also at
Ebbets Field, where for many years she applauded the Brooklyn Dodgers until their
unhappy translation to Los Angeles. In the preface to *A Marianne Moore Reader,*
she explains or half-explains her liking for both spectacles:

"Why an inordinate interest in animals and athletes? They are subjects for art and
exemplars of it, are they not? minding their own business. Pangolins, hornbills, pitchers,

catchers, do not pry or prey—or prolong the conversation; do not make us self-conscious; look their best when caring least."[1]

Moore was educated in the Metzger Institute, then at Bryn Mawr College. After taking a degree in 1909, she thought of becoming a painter, a profession for which her extraordinary visual sense might seem to have equipped her. But, perhaps as a stopgap, she went to the Carlisle Commercial College and then taught stenography at the government Indian school in Carlisle, Pennsylvania, from 1911 to 1915. In 1918 she moved to New York and worked as a private tutor, as a secretary, and then, from 1921 to 1925, as an assistant in a branch of the New York Public Library. Her first book of poems was published by the Egoist Press in England, at the instigation of friends and without her knowledge, in 1921. From 1926 to 1929, when it ceased publication, she was editor of the *Dial*, a leading review of the time.

In later life she did a good deal of public reading of her poems, which she continued to write, impervious to changing modes. Moore was also, in spite of her disavowals, a shrewd critic, and published two volumes of brief but pointed essays. She also lived to become a minor but genuine literary celebrity. Her elegant appearance, inevitably set off by a tricorn hat; her passionate interest in baseball; her quiet devotion to Christianity; her generosity; and her intolerance for the second-rate inspired devotion from writers and readers. She once appeared at a convocation of poets wearing an orchid. She explained that it was her "first orchid," and she added, "I admire it." And she herself was admired as well. She died in New York on February 5, 1972.

Her verse is so unassuming that it is almost surprising to see how many poets—Robert Lowell, Ted Hughes, Elizabeth Bishop, and others—acknowledge her as the source for some of their own effects. Her "predilection"—a favorite word with her and more likely to appear than "passion"—is for grace and neatness. Poetry is for her the result of a "heightened consciousness." Her own success must consist also in the quality that Eliot, in a preface to her *Selected Poems*,[2] finds in her, that she is "one of those few who have done the language some service in my lifetime."

1. New York, 1961, p. xvi.   2. New York, 1935, p. viii.

The Fish

wade
through black jade.
    Of the crow-blue mussel shells, one keeps
    adjusting the ash heaps;
        opening and shutting itself like   5

an
injured fan.
    The barnacles which encrust the side
    of the wave, cannot hide
        there for the submerged shafts of the   10

sun,
split like spun
    glass, move themselves with spotlight swiftness
    into the crevices—
        in and out, illuminating   15

    the
turquoise sea
    of bodies. The water drives a wedge
    of iron through the iron edge
        of the cliff; whereupon the stars,[1]   20

    pink
rice-grains, ink-
        bespattered jellyfish, crabs like green
        lilies, and submarine
            toadstools, slide each on the other.   25

    All
external
        marks of abuse are present on this
        defiant edifice—
            all the physical features of   30

    ac-
cident—lack
        of cornice, dynamite grooves, burns, and
        hatchet strokes, these things stand
            out on it; the chasm side is   35

    dead.
Repeated
        evidence has proved that it can live
        on what can not revive
            its youth. The sea grows old in it.   40

                                          1921

Poetry

I, too, dislike it: there are things that are important beyond all this fiddle.
  Reading it, however, with a perfect contempt for it, one discovers in
  it after all, a place for the genuine.[2]
    Hands that can grasp, eyes
      that can dilate, hair that can rise   5
        if it must, these things are important not because a

high-sounding interpretation can be put upon them but because they are
  useful. When they become so derivative as to become unintelligible,
  the same thing may be said for all of us, that we
    do not admire what   10
      we cannot understand: the bat
        holding on upside down or in quest of something to

eat, elephants pushing, a wild horse taking a roll, a tireless wolf under
  a tree, the immovable critic twitching his skin like a horse that feels a
  flea, the base-

---

1. Starfish.   Moore omitted all the poem following this phrase.
2. In the last edition of her *Collected Poems,*

ball fan, the statistician—   15
  nor is it valid
      to discriminate against 'business documents and

school-books';[3] all these phenomena are important. One must make a dis-
    tinction
  however: when dragged into prominence by half poets, the result is not
    poetry,
  nor till the poets among us can be   20
    'literalists of
      the imagination'[4]—above
        insolence and triviality and can present

for inspection, 'imaginary gardens with real toads in them', shall we have
  it. In the meantime, if you demand on the one hand,   25
    the raw material of poetry in
      all its rawness and
        that which is on the other hand
          genuine, you are interested in poetry.

                                                                        1921

A Grave

Man looking into the sea,
taking the view from those who have as much right to it as you have to
    yourself,
it is human nature to stand in the middle of a thing,
but you cannot stand in the middle of this;
the sea has nothing to give but a well excavated grave.   5
The firs stand in a procession, each with an emerald turkey-foot at the top,
reserved as their contours, saying nothing;
repression, however, is not the most obvious characteristic of the sea;
the sea is a collector, quick to return a rapacious look.
There are others besides you who have worn that look—   10
whose expression is no longer a protest; the fish no longer investigate them
for their bones have not lasted:
men lower nets, unconscious of the fact that they are desecrating a grave,
and row quickly away—the blades of the oars
moving together like the feet of water-spiders as if there were no such thing
    as death.   15
The wrinkles progress among themselves in a phalanx[5]—beautiful under
    networks of foam,
and fade breathlessly while the sea rustles in and out of the seaweed;
the birds swim through the air at top speed, emitting catcalls as hereto-
    fore—

---

3. Moore's note quotes the *Diaries of Tolstoy*, New York, 1917, p. 94: "Where the boundary between prose and poetry lies, I shall never be able to understand. The question is raised in manuals of style, yet the answer to it lies beyond me. Poetry is verse: prose is not verse. Or else poetry is everything with the exception of business documents and school books."
4. "The limitation of his [Blake's] view was from the very intensity of his vision; he was a too literal realist of imagination as others are of nature; and because he believed that the figures seen by the mind's eye, when exalted by inspiration, were 'eternal existences,' symbols of divine essences, he hated every grace of style that might obscure their lineaments." W. B. Yeats, "William Blake and His Illustrations," in *Ideas of Good and Evil*, London, 1903, p. 182. (Moore gives this reference.)
5. A body of troops in close array.

the tortoise-shell scourges about the feet of the cliffs, in motion beneath
   them;
and the ocean, under the pulsation of lighthouses and noise of bellbuoys,   20
advances as usual, looking as if it were not that ocean in which dropped
   things are bound to sink—
in which if they turn and twist, it is neither with volition nor consciousness.

1924

The Pangolin[6]

Another armored animal—scale
   lapping scale with spruce-cone regularity until they
form the uninterrupted central
   tail-row! This near artichoke with head and legs and grit-equipped
      gizzard,
the night miniature artist engineer is,   5
   yes, Leonardo da Vinci's replica—
      impressive animal and toiler of whom we seldom hear.
   Armor seems extra. But for him,
      the closing ear-ridge—[7]
         or bare ear lacking even this small   10
         eminence and similarly safe

contracting nose and eye apertures
   impenetrably closable, are not; a true ant-eater,
not cockroach-eater, who endures
   exhausting solitary trips through unfamiliar ground at night,   15
returning before sunrise; stepping in the moonlight,
      on the moonlight peculiarly,[8] that the outside
         edges of his hands may bear the weight and save the claws
   for digging. Serpentined about
      the tree, he draws   20
         away from danger unpugnaciously,
         with no sound but a harmless hiss; keeping

the fragile grace of the Thomas-
   of-Leighton Buzzard Westminster Abbey wrought-iron vine,[9] or
rolls himself into a ball that has   25
   power to defy all effort to unroll it; strongly intailed, neat
head for core, on neck not breaking off, with curled-in feet.
      Nevertheless he has sting-proof scales; and nest
         of rocks closed with earth from inside, which he can thus
            darken.
      Sun and moon and day and night and man and beast   30
         each with a splendor
            which man in all his vileness cannot
            set aside; each with an excellence!

6. The pangolin is an anteater.
(Moore's note).
   7. Moore says she has taken this and certain
other details from Robert T. Henn, "Pangolins,"
Natural History, December 1935.
   8. "See Lyddeker's *Royal Natural History*"
   9. "A fragment of ironwork in Westminister
Abbey" (Moore's note). Leighton Buzzard is an
ancient market town forty miles from London.

"Fearful yet to be feared," the armored
    ant-eater met by the driver-ant does not turn back, but   35
engulfs what he can, the flattened sword-
    edged leafpoints on the tail and artichoke set leg- and body-plates
        quivering violently when it retaliates
            and swarms on him. Compact like the furled fringed frill
                on the hat-brim of Gargallo's[1] hollow iron head of a   40
            matador, he will drop and will
                then walk away
                    unhurt, although if unintruded on,
                    he cautiously works down the tree, helped

by his tail. The giant-pangolin-   45
    tail, graceful tool, as prop or hand or broom or ax, tipped like
an elephant's trunk with special skin,
    is not lost on this ant- and stone-swallowing uninjurable
    artichoke which simpletons thought a living fable
        whom the stones had nourished, whereas ants had done   50
        so. Pangolins are not aggressive animals; between
            dusk and day they have the not unchain-like machine-like
            form and frictionless creep of a thing
                made graceful by adversities, con-

versities. To explain grace requires   55
    a curious hand. If that which is at all were not forever,
why would those who graced the spires
    with animals and gathered there to rest, on cold luxurious
    low stone seats—a monk and monk and monk—between the thus
        ingenious roof supports, have slaved to confuse   60
        grace with a kindly manner, time in which to pay a debt,
        the cure for sins, a graceful use
            of what are yet
                approved stone mullions branching out across
                the perpendiculars? A sailboat   65

was the first machine. Pangolins, made
    for moving quietly also, are models of exactness,
on four legs; on hind feet plantigrade,
    with certain postures of a man. Beneath sun and moon, man slaving
    to make his life more sweet, leaves half the flowers worth having,   70
        needing to choose wisely how to use his strength;
        a paper-maker like the wasp; a tractor of foodstuffs,
        like the ant; spidering a length
            of web from bluffs
                above a stream; in fighting, mechanicked
                like the pangolin; capsizing in   75

disheartenment. Bedizened or stark
    naked, man, the self, the being we call human, writing-
master to this world, griffons a dark
    "Like does not like like that is obnoxious"; and writes error with four   80
    r's. Among animals, *one* has a sense of humor.

---

1. Pablo Gargallo (1881–1934), Spanish sculptor who worked in iron.

Humor saves a few steps, it saves years. Unignorant,
   modest and unemotional, and all emotion,
he has everlasting vigor,
    power to grow,   85
      though there are few creatures who can make one
      breathe faster and make one erecter.

Not afraid of anything is he,
   and then goes cowering forth, tread paced to meet an obstacle
at every step. Consistent with the   90
   formula—warm blood, no gills, two pairs of hands and a few hairs—
     that
is a mammal; there he sits in his own habitat,
    serge-clad, strong-shod. The prey of fear, he, always
      curtailed, extinguished, thwarted by the dusk, work partly
      done,
  says to the alternating blaze,   95
    "Again the sun!
      anew each day; and new and new and new,
      that comes into and steadies my soul."

                                  1936

What Are Years?[2]

    What is our innocence,
  what is our guilt? All are
    naked, none is safe. And whence
  is courage: the unanswered question,
    the resolute doubt—   5
  dumbly calling, deafly listening—that
    in misfortune, even death,
      encourages others
      and in its defeat, stirs

    the soul to be strong? He   10
  sees deep and is glad, who
    accedes to mortality
  and in his imprisonment rises
    upon himself as
  the sea in a chasm, struggling to be   15
  free and unable to be,
      in its surrendering
      finds its continuing.

    So he who strongly feels,
  behaves. The very bird,   20
    grown taller as he sings, steels
    his form straight up. Though he is captive,

2. In a note sent to W. R. Benet and Norman Holmes Pearson, Moore said that the poem was "partly written in 1931 and finished in 1939. The desperation attendant on moral fallibility is mitigated for me by admitting that the most willed and resolute vigilance may lapse, as with the Apostle Peter's denial that he could be capable of denial; but that failure, disgrace, and even death have now and again been redeemed into inviolateness by a sufficiently transfigured courage."

his mighty singing
says, satisfaction is a lowly
thing, how pure a thing is joy.   25
This is mortality,
this is eternity.

1941

JOHN CROWE RANSOM
1888–1974

John Crowe Ransom's poems could never be mistaken for anybody else's. Quirky, even at times eccentric, they are among the most remarkable poems to come out of the southern group to which he belongs with his sometime pupils Allen Tate, Robert Penn Warren, and Donald Davidson. Ransom's wit in such a poem as "The Equilibrists" is metaphysical, but besides the elaborated central image he offers a self-deprecating frivolity in dealing with grave subjects. The implication is that the poem deals both in messages and counter-messages. Yet it is not so much the wit as the diction which leaps first from Ransom's page. Like Spenser in *The Faerie Queene*, he could be said to have "writ no language," since he cultivates archaisms, mock-pedanticisms, unaccustomed usages. It is as if, to express himself in the modern world, he had to don an antique mask. The pull of the past has been powerful, being the past of language, the past of literature, the past of southern society. Archaisms of diction, as he implies in *The World's Body*,[1] go with archaisms of temper. He did not stand still, however, or merely go backwards; both in his verse and his critical writings he passed through phases, each of which was more comprehensive, and more complicated, than its predecessor.

In accepting the Bollingen Prize for verse in 1964, Ransom said, "I know now that when I was writing [my early verse] I had no sound education in poetry, and was in torture trying to escape from the stilted and sentimental verbal habits which conditioned me." He must have decided then that he could be, as the title of one poem suggests, "Agitato ma non Troppo." Perhaps in recollection of his own struggles, he remarked in an essay on "Lycidas" that the poem had been written by Milton smooth and rewritten rough.[2] Not that he seeks roughness exactly, rather it is a game played by the poet on several boards at once, so that logic is mustered on one, "texture" or "particularities" (two of his terms) on another, and formal characteristics on a third. "Suppose we say that the poem is an organism," he writes in "The Concrete Universal: Observations on the Understanding of Poetry."[3] "Then it has a physiology. We will figure its organs, and to me it seems satisfactory if we say they are three: the head, the heart, the feet." The phrase "it seems satisfactory" is one of those elfin glimmers of wit which are never absent from a Ransom sentence. He goes on to explain, "The peculiarity of the joint production is that it still consists of the several products of the organs working individually . . . the head in an intellectual language, the heart in an affective language, the feet in a rhythmical language."

The poem is for Ransom a microcosm of society, and in interchanging poetic and social characteristics Ransom sometimes seemed too attracted to a conservative society. Statements such as "The object of a proper society is to instruct its members how to transform instinctive experience into aesthetic experience"[4] have aroused liberal concern. Ransom did not skirt his own implications, though he outlived many of them: he was a leading member of the Fugitives, a group of southern writers mostly centered at Vanderbilt University who sought to recover and preserve the

---

1. New York, 1938, pp. 70–71.
2. *The World's Body*, p. 12.

3. *Kenyon Review* 16, 1954, p. 560.
4. *The World's Body*, p. 42.

values of the old southern society as against the corruptions of industrialism, which would destroy, like an invading northern army, all delicate gradations. An agrarian culture appeared to be most likely to keep the best in the past together.

Ransom's traditionalism was prominent in his first prose book, *God Without Thunder*.[5] There, adopting the guise of a southern fundamentalist, he urged that religion, or rather religious myth, was necessary because it employed the supernatural "to represent the fullness of the natural." (It was this fullnesss which his theory of organicism in poetry also sought.) This book, with what he later called "home-brew theology," sounded very much like that of a minister's son, which Ransom in fact was. His next book, *The World's Body* (1938), was more urbane and less prescriptive. The fullness of the natural could be represented by poetry rather than by religion. Then in *The New Criticism* (1941), Ransom—after detailed examinations of the leading critics—called for an "ontological critic," one who would be able to demonstrate how in poetry logical structure and variegated detail join in presenting the world's concrete body.

Ransom was born on April 30, 1888, in Pulaski, Tennessee. He received an A.B. degree from Vanderbilt in 1909, and as a Rhodes scholar took a B.A. at Christ Church, Oxford, in 1913. Ransom was a lieutenant in the First World War. Afterwards he returned to Vanderbilt, where he had already done some teaching, and remained there until 1937. In that year, to the surprise of many, he moved north to Kenyon College and became founder and editor of the *Kenyon Review*, which was to be the best-known, and very likely the best, review in the United States, from 1937 until his retirement in 1959. He died in 1974.

5. New York, 1930, pp. 327–28.

Bells for John Whiteside's Daughter

There was such speed in her little body,
And such lightness in her footfall,
It is no wonder her brown study[1]
Astonishes us all.

Her wars were bruited in our high window.   5
We looked among orchard trees and beyond
Where she took arms against her shadow,
Or harried unto the pond

The lazy geese, like a snow cloud
Dripping their snow on the green grass,   10
Tricking and stopping, sleepy and proud,
Who cried in goose, Alas,

For the tireless heart within the little
Lady with rod that made them rise
From their noon apple-dreams and scuttle   15
Goose-fashion under the skies!

But now go the bells, and we are ready,
In one house we are sternly stopped
To say we are vexed at her brown study,
Lying so primly propped.   20

1924

1. Reverie, somber musing.

Here Lies a Lady

Here lies a lady of beauty and high degree,
Of chills and fever she died, of fever and chills,
The delight of her husband, an aunt, an infant of three
And medicos[2] marveling sweetly on her ills.

First she was hot, and her brightest eyes would blaze   5
And the speed of her flying fingers shook their heads.
What was she making? God knows; she sat in those days
With her newest gowns all torn, or snipt into shreds.

But that would pass, and the fire of her cheeks decline
Till she lay dishonored and wan like a rose overblown,   10
And would not open her eyes, to kisses, to wine;
The sixth of which states was final. The cold came down.

Fair ladies, long may you bloom, and sweetly may thole![3]
She was part lucky. With flowers and lace and mourning,
With love and bravado, we bade God rest her soul   15
After six quick turns of quaking, six of burning.

                                                    1924, 1945

Captain Carpenter

Captain Carpenter rose up in his prime
Put on his pistols and went riding out
But had got wellnigh nowhere at that time
Till he fell in with ladies in a rout.

It was a pretty lady and all her train   5
That played with him so sweetly but before
An hour she'd taken a sword with all her main
And twined him of his nose for evermore.

Captain Carpenter mounted up one day
And rode straightway into a stranger rogue   10
That looked unchristian but be that as may
The Captain did not wait upon prologue.

But drew upon him out of his great heart
The other swung against him with a club
And cracked his two legs at the shinny part   15
And let him roll and stick like any tub.

Captain Carpenter rode many a time
From male and female took he sundry harms
He met the wife of Satan crying "I'm
The she-wolf bids you shall bear no more arms."   20

Their strokes and counters whistled in the wind
I wish he had delivered half his blows

---

2. Doctors (slang).   3. Endure.

But where she should have made off like a hind
The bitch bit off his arms at the elbows.

And Captain Carpenter parted with his ears   25
To a black devil that used him in this wise
O Jesus ere his threescore and ten years
Another had plucked out his sweet blue eyes.

Captain Carpenter got up on his roan
And sallied from the gate in hell's despite   30
I heard him asking in the grimmest tone
If an enemy yet there was to fight?

"To any adversary it is fame
If he risk to be wounded by my tongue
Or burnt in two beneath my red heart's flame   35
Such are the perils he is cast among.

"But if he can he has a pretty choice
From an anatomy with little to lose
Whether he cut my tongue and take my voice
Or whether it be my round red heart he choose."   40

It was the neatest knave that ever was seen
Stepping in perfume from his lady's bower
Who at this word put in his merry mien
And fell on Captain Carpenter like a tower.

I would not knock old fellows in the dust   45
But there lay Capatin Carpenter on his back
His weapons were the old heart in his bust
And a blade shook between rotten teeth alack.

The rogue in scarlet and grey soon knew his mind
He wished to get his trophy and depart   50
With gentle apology and touch refined
He pierced him and produced the Captain's heart.

God's mercy rest on Captain Carpenter now
I thought him Sirs an honest gentleman
Citizen husband soldier and scholar enow   55
Let jangling kites⁴ eat of him if they can.

But God's deep curses follow after those
That shore him of his goodly nose and ears
His legs and strong arms at the two elbows
And eyes that had not watered seventy years.   60

The curse of hell upon the sleek upstart
That got the Captain finally on his back
And took the red vitals of his heart
And made the kites to whet their beaks clack clack.

                                                              1924

4. Small carrion-hawks.

Piazza Piece[5]

—I am a gentleman in a dustcoat[6] trying
To make you hear. Your ears are soft and small
And listen to an old man not at all.
They want the young men's whispering and sighing.
But see the roses on your trellis dying   5
And hear the spectral singing of the moon;
For I must have my lovely lady soon,
I am a gentleman in a dustcoat trying.

—I am a lady young in beauty waiting
Until my truelove comes, and then we kiss.   10
But what grey man among the vines is this
Whose words are dry and faint as in a dream?
Back from my trellis, Sir, before I scream!
I am a lady young in beauty waiting.

1927

Dead Boy

The little cousin is dead, by foul subtraction,
A green bough from Virginia's aged tree,
And none of the county kin like the transaction,
Nor some of the world of outer dark, like me.

A boy not beautiful, nor good, nor clever,   5
A black cloud full of storms too hot for keeping,
A sword beneath his mother's heart—yet never
Woman bewept her babe as this is weeping.

A pig with a pasty face, so I had said,
Squealing for cookies, kinned by poor pretense   10
With a noble house. But the little man quite dead,
I see the forbears' antique lineaments.

The elder men have strode by the box of death
To the wide flag porch, and muttering low send round
The bruit[7] of the day. O friendly waste of breath!   15
Their hearts are hurt with a deep dynastic wound.

He was pale and little, the foolish neighbors say;
The first-fruits,[8] saith the Preacher, the Lord hath taken;
But this was the old tree's late branch wrenched away,
Grieving the sapless limbs, the shorn and shaken.   20

1927

---

5. A reenactment of the old folk tale of Death
and the Maiden.
6. Lightweight cloth coat.

7. News.
8. Or first-born, as the Lord killed the Egyptian first-born sons in Exodus.

The Equilibrists[9]

Full of her long white arms and milky skin
He had a thousand times remembered sin.
Alone in the press of people traveled he,
Minding her jacinth, and myrrh, and ivory.

Mouth he remembered: the quaint orifice   5
From which came heat that flamed upon the kiss,
Till cold words came down spiral from the head,
Grey doves from the officious tower illspred.

Body: it was a white field ready for love,
On her body's field, with the gaunt tower above,   10
The lilies grew, beseeching him to take,
If he would pluck and wear them, bruise and break.

Eyes talking: Never mind the cruel words,
Embrace my flowers, but not embrace the swords
But what they said, the doves came straightway flying   15
And unsaid: Honor, Honor, they came crying.

Importunate her doves. Too pure, too wise,
Clambering on his shoulder, saying, Arise,
Leave me now, and never let us meet,
Eternal distance now command thy feet.   20

Predicament indeed, which thus discovers
Honor among thieves, Honor between lovers.
O such a little word is Honor, they feel!
But the grey word is between them cold as steel.

At length I saw these lovers fully were come   25
Into their torture of equilibrium;
Dreadfully had forsworn each other, and yet
They were bound each to each, and they did not forget.

And rigid as two painful stars, and twirled
About the clustered night their prison world,   30
They burned with fierce love always to come near,
But Honor beat them back and kept them clear.

Ah, the strict lovers, they are ruined now!
I cried in anger. But with puddled brow
Devising for those gibbeted and brave   35
Came I descanting: Man, what would you have?

For spin your period out, and draw your breath,
A kinder sæculum[1] begins with Death.
Would you ascend to Heaven and bodiless dwell?
Or take your bodies honorless to Hell?   40

9. People who balance—especially in awkward   1. Age (Latin).
positions, like tightrope walkers or acrobats.

In Heaven you have heard no marriage is,
No white flesh tinder to your lecheries,
Your male and female tissue sweetly shaped
Sublimed away, and furious blood escaped.

Great lovers lie in Hell, the stubborn ones   45
Infatuate of the flesh upon the bones;
Stuprate,[2] they rend each other when they kiss,
The pieces kiss again, no end to this.

But still I watched them spinning, orbited nice.[3]
Their flames were not more radiant than their ice.   50
I dug in the quiet earth and wrought the tomb
And made these lines to memorize their doom:—

EPITAPH

Equilibrists lie here; stranger, tread light;
Close, but untouching in each other's sight;
Mouldered the lips and ashy the tall skull.   55
Let them lie perilous and beautiful.

1927

2. A coinage meaning "infamous."   3. Precisely.

T. S. ELIOT
1888–1965

Thomas Stearns Eliot was born in St. Louis on September 26, 1888, and died in
London on January 4, 1965. He was one of seven children, and the youngest son.
His family had come from Massachusetts and "jealously guarded," as Eliot has written, its New England connections. The poet's father was a successful industrialist,
an executive of the Hydraulic Press Brick Company. He married in 1860 a woman of
literary interests, Charlotte Champe Stearns; she was to write religious verse, including
a dramatic poem about Savonarola. A respect for family tradition and a predisposition
towards intense religious feeling may have come to Eliot through her.

Eliot's geographical movements may reflect his private turbulence. After living for
his first seventeen years in St. Louis, except for annual summer holidays in New
England, he went to Milton Academy in Massachusetts, and then entered Harvard
in 1906. Eliot had the distinction of being the only member of the class to become a
royalist, a label he gave himself, only partly in jest, in 1927—he said he was "classicist
in literature, royalist in politics, and Anglo-Catholic in religion."[1] In St. Louis, he
said, he felt himself to be a New Englander, but in New England he felt himself to
be a southwesterner. He completed his course at Harvard in three years instead of
four.

In 1910 Eliot took a master's degree, and then went to the Sorbonne for a year,
after which he returned to Harvard to write a doctoral dissertation on the philosophy
of F. H. Bradley, the author of *Appearance and Reality*—two concepts which he was
to examine throughout his own poetry. Meanwhile he ranged about in what may
have seemed a haphazard way: he read French poetry, he studied the Sanskrit and
Pali languages, he took a great interest in Indic religion. It was in 1910 also that he

1. Preface to *For Lancelot Andrewes*, London, 1928.

wrote his earliest mature poem, "The Love Song of J. Alfred Prufrock." During the academic year 1913–14 Eliot was an assistant at Harvard. He was then awarded a traveling fellowship, and went to study for the summer at Marburg in Germany. The outbreak of war forced him to Oxford. The year 1914–15 proved to be pivotal, as he then came to three interrelated decisions: to give up the appearance of the philosopher for the reality of the poet, to marry, and to settle in England.

He obtained much encouragement in all three from Ezra Pound, whom he met in September 1914. Pound read the poems which no one had been willing to publish, and pronounced his verdict, that Eliot "has actually trained himself *and* modernized himself *on his own."* Harriet Monroe, the editor of *Poetry*, must publish them, beginning with "Prufrock." It took Pound some time to bring her to the same view, and it was not until June 1915 that Eliot's first publication took place. This was also the month of his first marriage, on June 26. His wife was Vivien Haigh-Wood, and Eliot remained, like Merlin with another Vivian, under her spell, beset and possessed by her intricacies for fifteen years and more. (They separated in 1932; Mrs. Eliot died in 1947.)

He resisted his parents' urging that he return to the United States for a career in teaching philosophy. He would be a poet, and England offered a better atmosphere in which to write. His family did not cut him off, but they offered insufficient help to support the couple. Eliot took a teaching job at the High Wycombe Grammar School, then at Highgate Junior School. He deferred to his parents' wishes so far as to complete his dissertation, and was booked to sail on April 1, 1916, to take his oral examination at Harvard. The crossing was canceled because of wartime complications, and his academic gestures came to an end. In March 1917 he took a job as clerk with Lloyd's Bank in London, and stayed at it for eight years, while he struggled with literary and marital problems too.

The personal life out of which in 1921 came Eliot's poem, *The Waste Land*, began now to be lived in earnest. Vivien Eliot suffered obscurely from nerves, her health was subject to frequent collapses, she complained of neuralgia, of insomnia. Eliot was put under great strain, and the collapse of his marital expectations is probably shadowed in the opening of his poem, "April is the cruellest month." The death of his father in January 1919 was another blow, especially since his father died thinking that Eliot had wasted his ability. Eliot must also have been conscious that he had passed his thirtieth year, and *The Waste Land* was a memorial to his youth as *Mauberley* was a memorial to Pound's.

Much of *The Waste Land* was written by early 1921. Then Eliot had a breakdown, and was advised by a prominent neurologist to take three months away from Lloyd's Bank. When the bank had agreed, he went first to Margate and then to Lausanne, where he had psychiatric treatment. He consulted Pound in Paris, and with Pound's brilliant aid was able to piece *The Waste Land* out of various drafts. The manuscript, edited by his second wife Valerie Eliot, was published in facsimile in 1971.

When the poem itself was published in 1922, it gave Eliot his central position in modern poetry. No one has been able to encompass so much material with so much dexterity, or to express the ennui and the horror of so many aspects of the modern world. Though the poem was made up of fragments, they were like pieces of a jigsaw puzzle which might be joined if certain spiritual conditions were met. After *The Waste Land* he wrote "The Hollow Men," "Ash-Wednesday," and other poems which are stages on his way towards conversion to Christianity and away from secularism. His last important poems, *The Four Quartets*, constitute the achievement of his spiritual quest.

In the year that *The Waste Land* appeared, Eliot founded a new review, the *Criterion*, which became a leading cultural magazine. It began as a quarterly. The sponsor withdrew in 1925, but it resumed publication in 1926, under the sponsorship of the publisher Faber and Gwyer (later Faber & Faber). In 1927 it became a monthly, then proceeded as a quarterly from June 1928 until New Year 1939. Eliot joined the firm of Faber in 1925.

For his part, Eliot was determined to carry his art into other literary forms. After some preliminary attempts, such as "Fragment of an Agon," he began serious play-writing. His first play was *Murder in the Cathedral*, a play about Thomas à Becket with a title which might have suited one of those detective stories of which Eliot was always fond. In subsequent plays Eliot attempted to represent the difficulties of conscience in a conscienceless world, and some of his plays, notably *The Cocktail Party*, achieved a success ordinarily reserved in modern times for plays in prose rather than in verse. Eliot also wrote books on religion, literature, and culture, in which he tried to establish *The Idea of a Christian Society*. In 1948 he was awarded the Nobel Prize for Literature, and it might well seem that with his plays on Broadway, his best lines on every lip, his essays dominating contemporary taste, he was the man of letters *par excellence* of the English-speaking world.

Eliot has said that when he started to write poetry there was no one writing in England or America who could serve him as a model. In December 1908 he happened to come across the newly published second edition of Arthur Symons's *The Symbolist Movement in Literature*, and there for the first time read about Rimbaud, Laforgue, Mallarmé, and others. He remarked that these were the poets from whom he first learned to speak. He drew from them the notion that poetry could carry considerable intellectual as well as emotional content, and that it might be—and, as he thought, in the modern world had to be—exceedingly complex in expression. In his early work Eliot heaped ironies upon each other, yoking—as Dr. Johnson said Metaphysical poets in the seventeenth century did—heterogenous ideas together by violence. His principal models were Laforgue and Corbière. He dealt almost exclusively with decadent, enervated people, yet in all his technical devices revealed a violent, innovative energy. He combined a precise and often formal outward manner with an inner writhing, bound together by wit.

The theme which pervades all his work is, in its various forms, love. Prufrock never sings his love song to a woman; Gerontion (a later hero) finds himself similarly impotent before God; then follows Eliot's laborious and agonized progress, in his own person, towards a higher love. His poetry does not deal much, as Yeats's does, with the love of man and woman, though there are occasional glimpses of erotic exaltation to balance such sordid scenes as that of the typist and the carbuncular clerk in *The Waste Land*. But in one of his late poems, addressed to his wife Valerie, Eliot gives unexpected recognition to the communion of man and woman instead of man and God. Though he upholds the way of the saint as supreme, he allows validity here and in *The Four Quartets* to "the life of significant soil" in which the claims of society, as well as of God, are enforced. With all its strangeness, his poetry conveys a sense of utter painful sincerity, as he sifts and reconstitutes stale into living emotions.

The Love Song of J. Alfred Prufrock[1]

S'io credessi che mia risposta fosse
a persona che mai tornasse al mondo,
questa fiamma staria senza più scosse.
Ma per ciò che giammai di questo fondo
non tornò vivo alcun, s'i'odo il vero,
senza tema d'infamia ti rispondo.[2]

Let us go then, you and I,
When the evening is spread out against the sky

1. Eliot probably finished this poem in 1911, when he was twenty-three, but was not able to have it published until Ezra Pound placed it with *Poetry* in 1915.
2. The epigraph is from Dante's *Inferno*, Canto 27, where the poet asks Guido da Montefeltro, who

Like a patient etherised upon a table;
Let us go, through certain half-deserted streets,
The muttering retreats   5
Of restless nights in one-night cheap hotels
And sawdust restaurants with oyster-shells:
Streets that follow like a tedious argument
Of insidious intent
To lead you to an overwhelming question . . .   10
Oh, do not ask, 'What is it?'
Let us go and make our visit.

In the room³ the women come and go
Talking of Michelangelo.

The yellow fog that rubs its back upon the window-panes,   15
The yellow smoke that rubs its muzzle on the window-panes,
Licked its tongue into the corners of the evening,
Lingered upon the pools that stand in drains,
Let fall upon its back the soot that falls from chimneys,
Slipped by the terrace, made a sudden leap,   20
And seeing that it was a soft October night,
Curled once about the house, and fell asleep.

And indeed there will be time
For the yellow smoke that slides along the street
Rubbing its back upon the window-panes;   25
There will be time, there will be time
To prepare a face to meet the faces that you meet;
There will be time to murder and create,
And time for all the works and days⁴ of hands
That lift and drop a question on your plate;   30
Time for you and time for me,
And time yet for a hundred indecisions,
And for a hundred visions and revisions,
Before the taking of a toast and tea.

In the room the women come and go   35
Talking of Michelangelo.

And indeed there will be time
To wonder, 'Do I dare?' and, 'Do I dare?'
Time to turn back and descend the stair,
With a bald spot in the middle of my hair—   40
(They will say: 'How his hair is growing thin!')
My morning coat, my collar mounting firmly to the chin,
My necktie rich and modest, but asserted by a simple pin—
(They will say: 'But how his arms and legs are thin!')

---

like the other Counsellors of Fraud is wrapped in
a tall flame, to identify himself. Guido, having
sinned with his tongue, has to speak through the
tongue of the flame. He replies, "If I thought that
I was speaking / to someone who would go back to
the world, / this flame would shake no more. / But
since nobody has ever / gone back alive from this
place, if what I hear is true, / I answer you without
fear of infamy." Some readers have understood the
epigraph to mean that Prufrock is speaking not to

another person but to himself as *alter ego*, but Eliot
specifically denied this interpretation. He said that
the "you" of the poem was an unidentified male
companion.
    3. Presumably the room where Prufrock is going
to speak to a woman friend.
    4. The title of a poem by Hesiod (eighth cen-
tury B.C.), the Greek poet, which celebrates farm
work.

Do I dare   45
Disturb the universe?
In a minute there is time
For decisions and revisions which a minute will reverse.

For I have known them all already, known them all—
Have known the evenings, mornings, afternoons,   50
I have measured out my life with coffee spoons;
I know the voices dying with a dying fall
Beneath the music from a farther room.
   So how should I presume?

And I have known the eyes already, known them all—   55
The eyes that fix you in a formulated phrase,
And when I am formulated, sprawling on a pin,
When I am pinned and wriggling on the wall,
Then how should I begin
To spit out all the butt-ends of my days and ways?   60
   And how should I presume?

And I have known the arms already, known them all—
Arms that are braceleted and white and bare
(But in the lamplight, downed with light brown hair!)
Is it perfume from a dress   65
That makes me so digress?
Arms that lie along a table, or wrap about a shawl.
   And should I then presume?
   And how should I begin?

      .   .   .   .   .

Shall I say, I have gone at dusk through narrow streets   70
And watched the smoke that rises from the pipes
Of lonely men in shirt-sleeves, leaning out of windows? . . .

I should have been a pair of ragged claws
Scuttling across the floors of silent seas.

      .   .   .   .   .

And the afternoon, the evening, sleeps so peacefully!   75
Smoothed by long fingers,
Asleep . . . tired . . . or it malingers,
Stretched on the floor, here beside you and me.
Should I, after tea and cakes and ices,
Have the strength to force the moment to its crisis?   80
But though I have wept and fasted, wept and prayed,
Though I have seen my head (grown slightly bald) brought in upon a plat-
      ter,[5]
I am no prophet—and here's no great matter;
I have seen the moment of my greatness flicker,
And I have seen the eternal Footman[6] hold my coat, and snicker,   85
And in short, I was afraid.

---

5. John the Baptist was beheaded by order of   thew 14:3–11).
King Herod, and his head was brought in upon a   6. Probably death or destiny.
silver dish to please the queen, Herodias (Mat-

And would it have been worth it, after all,[7]
After the cups, the marmalade, the tea,
Among the porcelain, among some talk of you and me,
Would it have been worth while,
To have bitten off the matter with a smile,   90
To have squeezed the universe into a ball[8]
To roll it towards some overwhelming question,
To say: "I am Lazarus,[9] come from the dead,
Come back to tell you all, I shall tell you all"—
If one,[1] settling a pillow by her head,   95
    Should say: "That is not what I meant at all.
    That is not it, at all."

And would it have been worth it, after all,   100
Would it have been worth while,
After the sunsets and the dooryards and the sprinkled streets,
After the novels, after the teacups, after the skirts that trail along the floor—
And this, and so much more?—
It is impossible to say just what I mean!
But as if a magic lantern threw the nerves in patterns on a screen: 105
Would it have been worth while
If one, settling a pillow or throwing off a shawl,
And turning toward the window, should say:
    "That is not it at all,
    That is not what I meant, at all."   110

      .   .   .   .   .

No! I am not Prince Hamlet, nor was meant to be;
Am an attendant lord, one that will do
To swell a progress,[2] start a scene or two,
Advise the prince; no doubt, an easy tool,
Deferential, glad to be of use,   115
Politic, cautious, and meticulous;
Full of high sentence, but a bit obtuse;
At times, indeed, almost ridiculous—[3]
Almost, at times, the Fool.

I grow old . . . I grow old . . .   120
I shall wear the bottoms of my trousers rolled.[4]

Shall I part my hair behind? Do I dare to eat a peach?[5]
I shall wear white flannel trousers, and walk upon the beach.
I have heard the mermaids singing, each to each.

I do not think that they will sing to me.   125

---

7. The change of tense indicates that the
moment has passed.
8. In a poem, "To His Coy Mistress," Andrew
Marvell (1621–1678) wrote: "Let us roll all our
strength and all / Our sweetness up into a ball, /
And tear our pleasures with rough strife / Through
the iron gates of life."
9. Raised by Christ from the dead (John 11:1–
44).
1. The woman whom Prufrock has gone to see.

2. A progress was a royal journey, usually made
by most of the court as well as by the sovereign.
3. Prufrock appears to have in mind Polonius,
the king's adviser in *Hamlet.*
4. That is, overfastidiously rolled up so they will
not get wet.
5. That is, shall I comb my hair backwards to
hide a bald spot? Will I get indigestion from eating a peach?

I have seen them riding seaward on the waves
Combing[6] the white hair of the waves blown back
When the wind blows the water white and black.

We have lingered in the chambers of the sea
By sea-girls wreathed with seaweed red and brown   130
Till human voices wake us, and we drown.

                                                                    1917

Whispers of Immortality

Webster[7] was much possessed by death
And saw the skull beneath the skin;
And breastless creatures under ground
Leaned backward with a lipless grin.

Daffodil bulbs instead of balls   5
Stared from the sockets of the eyes!
He knew that thought clings round dead limbs
Tightening its lusts and luxuries.

Donne,[8] I suppose, was such another
Who found no substitute for sense,   10
To seize and clutch and penetrate;
Expert beyond experience,

He knew the anguish of the marrow
The ague of the skeleton;
No contact possible to flesh   15
Allayed the fever of the bone.

                    .   .   .   .   .

Grishkin[9] is nice: her Russian eye
Is underlined for emphasis;
Uncorseted, her friendly bust
Gives promise of pneumatic bliss.   20

The couched Brazilian jaguar
Compels the scampering marmoset
With subtle effluence of cat;
Grishkin has a maisonnette;

The sleek Brazilian jaguar   25
Does not in its arboreal gloom
Distil so rank a feline smell
As Grishkin in a drawing-room.

And even the Abstract Entities
Circumambulate her charm;   30

---

6. (1) As with a hair comb; (2) breaking into foam.
7. John Webster (c. 1580–c. 1625), the English dramatist, whose plays *The Duchess of Malfi* and *The White Devil* are redolent of violent death.
8. The poet and priest John Donne (1572–1631).

9. Though her name is evidently a pseudonym, Grishkin was a real person, according to Ezra Pound, who in Canto 77 mentions finding her photograph—and thinking that Eliot had not done her justice.

But our lot crawls between dry ribs
To keep our metaphysics warm.

1919

Sweeney Among the Nightingales

ὤμοι, πέπληγμαι καιρίαν πληγὴν ἔσω.[1]

Apeneck Sweeney spread his knees
Letting his arms hang down to laugh,
The zebra stripes along his jaw
Swelling to maculate[2] giraffe.

The circles of the stormy moon   5
Slide westward toward the River Plate,[3]
Death and the Raven[4] drift above
And Sweeney guards the hornèd gate.[5]

Gloomy Orion and the Dog[6]
Are veiled; and hushed the shrunken seas;[7]   10
The person in the Spanish cape
Tries to sit on Sweeney's knees

Slips and pulls the table cloth
Overturns a coffee-cup,
Reorganised upon the floor   15
She yawns and draws a stocking up;

The silent man in mocha brown
Sprawls at the window-sill and gapes;
The waiter brings in oranges
Bananas figs and hothouse grapes;   20

The silent vertebrate in brown
Contracts and concentrates, withdraws;
Rachel *née* Rabinovitch
Tears at the grapes with murderous paws;

She and the lady in the cape   25
Are suspect, thought to be in league;
Therefore the man with heavy eyes
Declines the gambit, shows fatigue,

Leaves the room and reappears
Outside the window, leaning in,   30

---

1. Pronounced *ómoi, péplegemai kairían ple-gén éso*. It is from Aeschylus's *Agàmemnon;* when Agamemnon is struck by his wife Clytemnestra, he cries, "Alas, I have been struck a mortal blow." Eliot once remarked that all he consciously set out to create in this poem was a sense of foreboding.
2. Spotted.
3. Or Rio de la Plata, between Uruguay and Argentina in South America.
4. The constellation Corvus.
5. The gate of Hades through which true dreams come.
6. Orion, constellation of the hunter, is close in the sky to Canis Major, the constellation of the dog.
7. The tide is out.

Branches of wistaria
Circumscribe a golden grin;

The host with someone indistinct
Converses at the door apart,
The nightingales are singing near   35
The Convent of the Sacred Heart,[8]

And sang within the bloody wood[9]
When Agamemnon cried aloud
And let their liquid siftings fall
To stain the stiff dishonoured shroud.   40

1919

Gerontion[1]

Thou hast nor youth nor age
But as it were an after dinner sleep
Dreaming of both.[2]

Here I am, an old man in a dry month,
Being read to by a boy, waiting for rain.[3]
I was neither at the hot gates
Nor fought in the warm rain
Nor knee deep in the salt marsh, heaving a cutlass,   5
Bitten by flies, fought.[4]
My house is a decayed house,
And the Jew[5] squats on the window sill, the owner,
Spawned in some estaminet[6] of Antwerp,
Blistered in Brussels, patched and peeled in London.   10
The goat coughs at night in the field overhead;[7]
Rocks, moss, stonecrop, iron, merds.[8]
The woman keeps the kitchen, makes tea,
Sneezes at evening, poking the peevish gutter.[9]
                                        I an old man,   15
A dull head among windy spaces.

Signs are taken for wonders. "We would see a sign!"
The word within a word, unable to speak a word,

8. In the Greek legend of the nightingale, Philomela was raped by her sister Procne's husband, King Tereus. He cut out her tongue to insure her silence, but she depicted his crime on a piece of needlework and sent it to Procne. Procne, to revenge her, killed her son Itys and served up his flesh to her husband. When Tereus attempted to kill the sisters, Philomela was changed into a nightingale and her sister into a swallow. The nightingale appears in Eliot's poem as a symbol of beauty out of betrayal. The Sacred Heart has a comparable significance in Christian thought and persists in isolated convents.
9. Eliot has said he was thinking here of Orpheus, torn apart by the Thracian women for rejecting them. He telescopes this death with that of Agamemnon.
1. Written in 1919, and once proposed by Eliot as a prologue to *The Waste Land*. The title means "little old man" (in Greek).
2. The epigraph comes from Shakespeare's

Measure for Measure, 3.1, where the Duke, to console Claudio who is on the verge of being executed, offers this view of life as unreal and futile.
3. Based on a description of Edward Fitz-Gerald: "Here he sits, in a dry month, old and blind, being read to by a country boy, longing for rain." A. C. Benson, *Edward FitzGerald*, New York and London, 1905, p. 142. Eliot borrows the words, but has more than FitzGerald in mind.
4. Probably references to specific battles: Thermopylae (Greek for "hot gates"), 480 B.C.; Waterloo, 1815; and Cannae, 216 B.C. Compare Prufrock, "No, I am not Prince Hamlet, nor was meant to be."
5. Used unpleasantly by Eliot as a symbol of deracinated man.
6. Tavern.
7. The house is under a "windy knob" (line 33).
8. Excrement (French).
9. British usage for "drain."

Swaddled with darkness.[1] In the juvescence of the year
Came Christ the tiger[2]   20

In depraved May,[3] dogwood and chestnut, flowering judas,[4]
To be eaten, to be divided, to be drunk
Among whispers; by Mr. Silvero
With caressing hands, at Limoges
Who walked all night in the next room;   25

By Hakagawa, bowing among the Titians;
By Madame de Tornquist, in the dark room
Shifting the candles; Fräulein von Kulp
Who turned in the hall, one hand on the door.
                    Vacant shuttles   30
Weave the wind. I have no ghosts,
An old man in a draughty house
Under a windy knob.

After such knowledge,[5] what forgiveness? Think now
History has many cunning passages, contrived corridors   35
And issues, deceives with whispering ambitions,
Guides us by vanities. Think now
She gives when our attention is distracted
And what she gives, gives with such supple confusions
That the giving famishes[6] the craving. Gives too late   40
What's not believed in, or is still believed,
In memory only, reconsidered passion. Gives too soon
Into weak hands, what's thought can be dispensed with
Till the refusal propagates a fear. Think
Neither fear nor courage saves us. Unnatural vices   45
Are fathered by our heroism. Virtues
Are forced upon us by our impudent crimes.
These tears are shaken from the wrath-bearing tree.[7]

The tiger springs in the new year. Us he devours.[8] Think at last
We have not reached conclusion, when I   50

1. Eliot is alluding to several passages in the Gospels, and to Lancelot Andrewes' (1555–1626) commentary on them in *Works* 1.204. Matthew 12:38: "Then some of the scribes and Pharisees said to [Christ], 'Master, we would see a sign from you,' " as a proof of his divinity. John 1:1, 14: "In the beginning was the Word, and the Word was with God, and the Word was God. . . . And the Word became flesh and dwelt among us, full of grace and truth." Luke 2:12, "And this will be a sign for you: you will find a babe [Jesus] wrapped in swaddling cloths and lying in a manger." The passage from Andrewes: "Signs are taken for wonders. 'Master, we would fain see a sign,' that is a miracle. And in this sense it [the Gospel] is a sign to wonder at. Indeed, every word here is a wonder. . . . *Verbum infans* [the infant Word, or the Christ child] the Word without a word; the eternal Word not able to speak a word; the eternal sure. 2. And . . . swaddled; and that a wonder too" (Grover Smith, *T. S. Eliot's Poetry and Plays*, Chicago, 1956, p. 306).
2. Christ's resurrection at Easter reminds Gerontion of power and awesomeness rather than of benevolence and love. "Juvescence" is Eliot's eli-

sion of "juvenescence," or youth.
3. Depraved in these days. Henry Adams, in *The Education of Henry Adams*, Boston and New York, 1918, p. 400, speaks of settling in Washington: "The Potomac and its tributaries squandered beauty. . . . Here and there a Negro log cabin alone disturbed the dogwood and the judas-tree. . . . The tulip and the chestnut tree gave no sense of struggle against a stingy nature. . . . No European spring had shown him [Adams] the same intermixture of delicate grace and passionate depravity that marked the Maryland May. He loved it too much as if it were Greek and half human."
4. A flowering shrub-tree; so-called because of the belief that Judas Iscariot, who betrayed Christ, hanged himself therefrom.
5. The knowledge, however imperfect, of Christ.
6. That is, makes hungry.
7. That is, the flowering judas (line 21); also, perhaps, the Tree of the Knowledge of Good and Evil forbidden to Adam and Eve (Genesis 2 and 3).
8. Instead of the Communion, in which the worshipers "devour" him.

Stiffen in a rented house. Think at last
I have not made this show purposelessly
And it is not by any concitation[9]
Of the backward devils.
I would meet you upon this honestly.   55
I that was near your heart was removed therefrom
To lose beauty in terror, terror in inquisition.
I have lost my passion: why should I need to keep it
Since what is kept must be adulterated?
I have lost my sight, smell, hearing, taste and touch: 60
How should I use them for your closer contact?

These with a thousand small deliberations
Protract the profit of their chilled delirium,
Excite the membrane, when the sense has cooled,
With pungent sauces, multiply variety   65
In a wilderness of mirrors. What will the spider do,
Suspend its operations, will the weevil
Delay? De Bailhache, Fresca, Mrs. Cammel, whirled
Beyond the circuit of the shuddering Bear[1]
In fractured atoms. Gull against the wind, in the windy straits   70
Of Belle Isle, or running on the Horn.
White feathers in the snow, the Gulf claims,
And an old man driven by the Trades
To a sleepy corner.[2]

                              Tenants of the house,
Thoughts of a dry brain in a dry season.

                                                        1920

The Waste Land

In an essay, "*Ulysses*, Order and Myth," Eliot declared that others would follow
Joyce "in manipulating a continuous parallel between contemporaneity and antiquity. . . . It is simply a way of controlling, of ordering, of giving a shape and a significance to the immense panorama of futility and anarchy which is contemporary history.
. . . It is, I seriously believe, a step toward making the modern world possible in
art."

Eliot says of *The Waste Land* itself that "Not only the title, but the plan and a good
deal of the incidental symbolism of the poem were suggested by Miss Jessie L. Weston's book on the Grail legend: *From Ritual to Romance* [1920]. Indeed, so deeply
am I indebted, Miss Weston's book will elucidate the difficulties of the poem much
better than my notes can do; and I recommend it (apart from the great interest of the
book itself) to any who think such elucidation of the poem worth the trouble. To
another work of anthropology I am indebted in general, one which has influenced
our generation profoundly; I mean [Sir James Frazer's] *The Golden Bough* [1890–
1915]; I have used especially the two volumes *Adonis, Attis, Osiris*. Anyone who is
acquainted with these works will immediately recognize in the poem certain references to vegetation ceremonies." Weston contends that the Arthurian romances of

9. Stirring up.
1. The Great Bear, a northern constellation.
2. While the gull attempts the dangerous passage to the extreme north (the Belle Isle straits off
eastern Canada) or south (Cape Horn, at the tip of
South America), he sails with the steady trade-
winds towards the equator.

the quest for the Holy Grail are underlain by pre-Christian fertility myths and rituals such as those described by Frazer. In the Arthurian legend a Fisher King (the fish being an ancient symbol of life) has been maimed or killed, and his country has therefore become a dry Waste Land; he can only be regenerated and his land restored to fertility by a knight (Perceval or Parsifal) who perseveres through various ordeals to the Perilous Chapel and learns the answers to certain ritual questions about the Grail. The Fisher King is seen as analogous to vegetation gods such as Adonis of Greece, Attis of Phrygia, Osiris of Egypt, and perhaps also the Greek deity Hyacinthus, all of whose deaths and rebirths are represented in ancient ritual ceremonies intended to bring about the regeneration of plants after the sterile winter. Weston also connects the symbols of the Arthurian stories with the suits of the tarot deck, today used to tell fortunes but perhaps originally designed by the Egyptians to predict the flooding of the Nile, and the restoration of its valley to fertility.

Eliot wrote most of *The Waste Land* while at Lausanne in 1921, but it had been on his mind since 1919. Indeed, parts of the poem antedate the final version by several years: lines 26–29 were taken from "The Death of Saint Narcissus" (1915), lines 312–21 are adapted from Eliot's French poem "Dans le Restaurant" (1916–17), and Conrad Aiken remarks that lines 377–84 and other passages had "long been familiar" to him "as poems, or part-poems, in themselves" (*A Reviewer's ABC*, 1958).

From the first Eliot gave Ezra Pound much credit for his help in shaping *The Waste Land*, and the manuscript reveals how extensive and crucial this help was. Pound persuaded Eliot to delete 72 lines in rhymed couplets at the beginning of "The Fire Sermon" imitating the style of Pope's "The Rape of the Lock" and the defecation scene in Joyce's *Ulysses* (a book which Eliot had recently read in manuscript and thought "magnificent") and another 82 lines, preceding line 312, based on Dante's description of Ulysses' last voyage and describing the wreck of a New England fishing boat. Pound also disapproved of three short lyrics which Eliot planned as interludes, and dissuaded him from adding "Gerontion" as a preface. Smaller emendations were proposed in order to eliminate patches of conventionally poetic diction and to cut out nonessential verbiage; the effect was often to distort previously regular meter and rhyme. In gratitude for Pound's help Eliot dedicated the poem to him, quoting Dante's tribute to the Provençal poet Arnaut Daniel, "The better craftsman [*il miglior fabbro*] of the mother tongue" (*Purgatorio* 26).

Eliot's 52 footnotes to *The Waste Land*, reproduced here, were prepared for its publication as a book in 1922; they do not accompany the poem in the *Criterion* (London), Eliot's own magazine, or in the *Dial* (New York). He later remarked, "I have sometimes thought of getting rid of these notes; but now they can never be unstuck. They have had almost greater popularity than the poem itself." But Eliot was not unaware of the difficulties his work presented to its readers. In *The Use of Poetry and the Use of Criticism* he emphasized that such difficulties may come from various causes and be of different kinds. "The more seasoned reader . . . does not bother about understanding; not, at least, at first. I know that some of the poetry to which I am most devoted is poetry which I did not understand at first reading; some is poetry which I am not sure I understand yet: for instance, Shakespeare's." He mentions "the difficulty caused by the author's having left out something which the reader is used to finding; so that the reader, bewildered, gropes about for what is absent, and puzzles his head for a kind of 'meaning' which is not there, and is not meant to be there." These remarks, which are somewhat introductory to *The Waste Land*, may be supplemented by Eliot's remark in an interview, "In *The Waste Land* I wasn't even bothering whether I understood what I was saying" (*Writers at Work*, second series, 1963, p. 105). And, though critics immediately began to interpret the poem as Eliot's expression of a generation's spiritual alienation, Eliot himself soon felt the need to disavow any such intention, and is reported to have remarked, "To me it was only the relief of a personal and wholly insignificant grouse against life; it is just a piece of rhythmical grumbling" (T. S. Eliot, *The Waste Land* [Facsimile and Transcript of the Original Drafts . . .], edited by Valerie Eliot, New York, 1971).

The Waste Land

'Nam Sibyllam quidem Cumis ego ipse oculis meis vidi in ampulla pendere, et cum illi pueri dicerent: Σίβυλλα τί θέλεις; respondebat illa: ἀποθανεῖν θέλω.'[3]

For Ezra Pound
il miglior fabbro.

I. The Burial of the Dead[4]

April is the cruellest month, breeding
Lilacs out of the dead land, mixing
Memory and desire, stirring
Dull roots with spring rain.
Winter kept us warm, covering   5
Earth in forgetful snow, feeding
A little life with dried tubers.
Summer surprised us, coming over the Starnbergersee[5]
With a shower of rain; we stopped in the colonnade,
And went on in sunlight, into the Hofgarten,   10
And drank coffee, and talked for an hour.
Bin gar keine Russin, stamm' aus Litauen, echt deutsch.[6]
And when we were children, staying at the arch-duke's,
My cousin's, he took me out on a sled,
And I was frightened. He said, Marie,   15
Marie, hold on tight. And down we went.
In the mountains, there you feel free.
I read, much of the night, and go south in the winter.

What are the roots that clutch, what branches grow
Out of this stony rubbish? Son of man,[7]   20
You cannot say, or guess, for you know only
A heap of broken images, where the sun beats,
And the dead tree gives no shelter, the cricket no relief,[8]
And the dry stone no sound of water. Only
There is shadow under this red rock,[9]   25

3. "For I saw with my own eyes the Sibyl hanging in a jar at Cumae, and when the acolytes said, 'Sibyl, what do you wish?' she replied, 'I wish to die'" (Petronius, *Satyricon*, ch. 48). Apollo had granted the Sibyl eternal life but not eternal youth, and consequently her body shriveled up until she could be put in a bottle.
4. A phrase from the Anglican burial service.
5. A lake near Munich; the Hofgarten is a park in the city. Lines 8–18 resemble some autobiographical reminiscences of Countess Marie Larisch, confidante of Empress Elizabeth of Austria, of the years before Austria's defeat in the First World War lessened the nobility's wealth and influence. According to Valerie Eliot, Eliot based this passage on a conversation he had had with the countess.
6. "I'm not a Russian woman at all; I come from Lithuania, a true German."

7. "Cf. *Ezekiel* II:1" (Eliot's note): "Son of man, stand upon thy feet, and I will speak of thee," says God to Ezekiel. In Ezekiel 37, in the valley of the dry bones, God asks Ezekiel, "Son of man, can these bones live?" and is answered, "O Lord God, thou knowest."
8. "Cf. *Ecclesiastes* 12:5" (Eliot's note), in which the preacher evokes the evil days "when they shall be afraid of that which is high, and fears shall be in the way, and the almond tree shall flourish, and the grasshopper shall be a burden, and desire shall fail . . ."
9. Compare Isaiah 32:2, which tells of a savior who "shall be . . . as rivers of water in a dry place, as the shadow of a great rock in a weary land." Eliot's friend John Hayward suggests that the red rock is the Holy Grail. Eliot perhaps did not intend precise identification.

(Come in under the shadow of this red rock),
And I will show you something different from either
Your shadow at morning striding behind you
Or your shadow at evening rising to meet you;
I will show you fear in a handful of dust.   30

> Frisch weht der Wind
> Der Heimat zu
> Mein Irisch Kind,
> Wo weilest du?[1]

"You gave me hyacinths first a year ago;   35
"They called me the hyacinth girl."
—Yet when we came back, late from the hyacinth garden,
Your arms full, and your hair wet, I could not
Speak, and my eyes failed, I was neither
Living nor dead, and I knew nothing,   40
Looking into the heart of light, the silence.[2]
Oed' und leer das Meer.[3]

Madame Sosostris,[4] famous clairvoyante,
Had a bad cold, nevertheless
Is known to be the wisest woman in Europe,   45
With a wicked pack of cards.[5] Here, said she,
Is your card, the drowned Phoenician Sailor,[6]
(Those are pearls that were his eyes. Look!)[7]
Here is Belladonna,[8] the Lady of the Rocks,
The lady of situations.   50
Here is the man with three staves, and here the Wheel,[9]
And here is the one-eyed merchant,[1] and this card,
Which is blank, is something he carries on his back,
Which I am forbidden to see. I do not find
The Hanged Man. Fear death by water.   55
I see crowds of people, walking round in a ring.
Thank you. If you see dear Mrs. Equitone,

---

1. "V. *Tristan und Isolde*, I, verses 5–8" (Eliot's note). A sailor on the ship which brings Isolde from Ireland to her unloved husband-to-be, King Mark of Cornwall, sings wistfully of a girl he left behind: "Fresh blows the wind / To the homeland; / My Irish darling, / Where do you linger?" "V.": *Vide*, see (Latin).
2. A recollection of a youthful experience, which the speaker cherishes even among the living dead.
3. "Id. III, verse 24" (Eliot's note). Tristan, having been caught in adultery with Isolde and badly wounded, awaits her coming to heal him; but a shepherd, posted as lookout for her ship, says sadly, "Desolate and empty the sea."
4. A fortune-teller who uses the name of the Egyptian pharaoh Sesostris. (Eliot came across it in a comic scene in Aldous Huxley's *Crome Yellow* [1921].)
5. The Tarot deck of cards, with their vestiges of an ancient vegetation myth. Eliot notes: "I am not familiar with the exact constitution of the Tarot pack of cards, from which I have obviously departed to suit my own convenience. The Hanged Man, a member of the traditional pack, fits my purpose in two ways: because he is associated in my mind with the Hanged God of Frazer, and because I associate him with the hooded figure [Christ] in the passage of the disciples to Emmaus in Part V. The Phoenician Sailor and the Merchant appear later;

also the 'crowds of people,' and Death by Water is executed in Part IV. The Man with Three Staves (an authentic member of the Tarot pack) I associate quite arbitrarily, with the Fisher King himself."
6. The Phoenicians were ancient seamen and merchants of the Mediterranean. The sailor reappears as Phlebas in Part IV.
7. From Shakespeare's *The Tempest* 1.2; while the young prince Ferdinand is "Sitting on a bank, / Weeping again the king my father's wrack, / This music crept by me on the waters . . ." The music is a song by the spirit Ariel, who tells Ferdinand (falsely): "Full fathom five thy father lies, / Of his bones are coral made, / Those are pearls that were his eyes. / Nothing of him that doth fade, / But doth suffer a sea-change, / Into something rich and strange."
8. Lovely lady (Italian), but also a poison. Calling her "the Lady of the Rocks" is an ironic allusion to Leonardo de Vinci's "Madonna of the Rocks," a picture of the Virgin Mary.
9. That is, the Wheel of Fortune, and perhaps also the Buddhist "Wheel of Existence" from which the soul endeavors to escape.
1. Mr. Eugenides of Part III. This card, like that of the drowned Phoenician Sailor, is not part of the Tarot deck.

Tell her I bring the horoscope myself:
One must be so careful these days.

Unreal City,[2]   60
Under the brown fog of a winter dawn,
A crowd flowed over London Bridge, so many,
I had not thought death had undone so many.[3]
Sighs, short and infrequent, were exhaled,[4]
And each man fixed his eyes before his feet.   65
Flowed up the hill and down King William Street,
To where Saint Mary Woolnoth kept the hours
With a dead sound on the final stroke of nine.[5]
There I saw one I knew, and stopped him, crying: "Stetson!
"You who were with me in the ships at Mylae![6]   70
"That corpse you planted last year in your garden,
"Has it begun to sprout? Will it bloom this year?
"Or has the sudden frost disturbed its bed?
"O keep the Dog far hence, that's friend to men,
"Or with his nails he'll dig it up again![7]   75
"You! hypocrite lecteur!—mon semblable,—mon frère!"[8]

II. A Game of Chess[9]

The Chair she sat in, like a burnished throne,
Glowed on the marble,[1] where the glass
Held up by standards wrought with fruited vines
From which a golden Cupidon peeped out   80
(Another hid his eyes behind his wing)
Doubled the flames of sevenbranched candelabra
Reflecting light upon the table as
The glitter of her jewels rose to meet it,
From satin cases poured in rich profusion.   85
In vials of ivory and coloured glass

2. "Cf. Baudelaire: '*Fourmillante cité, cité pleine de rêves / Où le spectre en plein jour raccroche le passant*'" (Eliot's note). From Baudelaire's poem, "*Les Sept Vieillards*" (The Seven Old Men). "Swarming city, city full of dreams, / Where the spectre in full daylight accosts the passer-by."
3. "Cf. *Inferno* III, 55–57 . . ." (Eliot's note); Dante describes souls in limbo as "So long a train of people / That I should never have believed / That death had undone so many." They are in limbo because they "lived without praise or blame" or did not know the faith.
4. "Cf. *Inferno* IV, 25–27 . . ." (Eliot's note): "Here, so far as I could tell by listening, / There was no lamentation except sighs, / Which caused the eternal air to tremble." The sighs are uttered by the souls of the virtuous heathen who lived before Christ.
5. "A phenomenon I have often noticed" (Eliot's note). The people cross London Bridge and pass St. Mary Woolnoth (at the corner of King William and Lombard streets) on their way to the financial district of London, known as "the City."
6. A battle in the first Punic War between Rome and Carthage. It merges with the First World War, in which the speaker and Stetson fought; both wars are seen as pointless and futile.
7. "Cf. the Dirge in Webster's *White Devil*" (Eliot's note): "But keep the wolf far thence, that's

foe to man / Or with his nails he'll dig them up again." The dirge is sung by a woman to one of her sons, who has killed the other and is burying him. In fertility rituals, the death of the god heralds his rebirth, but in the Waste Land such rituals are twisted to the point of parody. The god's burial becomes a grim murder, and the dog, perhaps Anubis (the dog-headed Egyptian god of the underworld who helped Isis to reassemble her dismembered brother Osiris), is to be kept away.
8. "V. Baudelaire. Preface to *Fleurs du Mal* [Flowers of Evil]" (Eliot's note). This is the last line of "*Au Lecteur*" ("To the Reader"), which describes ennui as man's worst sin, and well-known to the reader: "Hypocrite reader!—my double—my brother!" With this line Baudelaire and Eliot assault the reader and draw him accusingly into the same plight as themselves.
9. The title comes from Thomas Middleton's (c. 1570–1627) play, *A Game at Chess*, but refers particularly to another play by Middleton, *Women Beware Women*, in which a girl is seduced in one room while her mother-in-law is kept busy at a chess game in the next. The chess moves are an eerie reflection of the erotic maneuvers next door.
1. "Cf. *Antony and Cleopatra*, II.ii.190" (Eliot's note). An ironic adaptation of the famous description of Cleopatra by Enobarbus in Shakespeare's play; here, "she" may be Belladonna (line 49).

Unstoppered, lurked her strange synthetic perfumes,
Unguent, powdered, or liquid—troubled, confused
And drowned the sense in odours; stirred by the air
That freshened from the window, these ascended   90
In fattening the prolonged candle-flames,
Flung their smoke into the laquearia,[2]
Stirring the pattern on the coffered ceiling.
Huge sea-wood fed with copper
Burned green and orange, framed by the coloured stone,   95
In which sad light a carvèd dolphin swam.
Above the antique mantel was displayed
As though a window gave upon the sylvan scene[3]
The change of Philomel,[4] by the barbarous king
So rudely forced;[5] yet there the nightingale   100
Filled all the desert with inviolable voice
And still she cried, and still the world pursues,
"Jug Jug" to dirty ears.[6]
And other withered stumps of time
Were told upon the walls; staring forms   105
Leaned out, leaning, hushing the room enclosed.
Footsteps shuffled on the stair.
Under the firelight, under the brush, her hair
Spread out in fiery points
Glowed into words, then would be savagely still.   110

"My nerves are bad to-night. Yes, bad. Stay with me.
"Speak to me. Why do you never speak. Speak.
   "What are you thinking of? What thinking? What?
"I never know what you are thinking. Think."

I think we are in rats' alley[7]   115
Where the dead men lost their bones.

"What is that noise?"
                    The wind under the door.[8]
"What is that noise now? What is the wind doing?"
                    Nothing again nothing.   120
                                        "Do
"You know nothing? Do you see nothing? Do you remember
"Nothing?"

        I remember
Those are pearls that were his eyes.   125
"Are you alive, or not? Is there nothing in your head?"
                                        But

---

2. "Laquearia. V. *Aeneid*, I, 726 . . ." (Eliot's
note). The word means "panelled ceiling," and Eliot
refers to Virgil's description of the banquet given
by the Carthaginian queen Dido for her lover
Aeneas: "Burning lamps hang from the gold-
panelled ceiling, / And torches dispel the night
with their flames."
3. "Sylvan scene. V. Milton *Paradise Lost*, IV,
140" (Eliot's note). The source is Satan's description of Eden.
4. "V. Ovid. *Metamorphoses*, VI, Philomela"
(Eliot's note). For an account of the myth see

"Sweeney Among the Nightingales," pp. 277–78.
5. "Cf. Part III, line 204" (Eliot's note).
6. Though a familiar representation in Elizabethan literature of the nightingale's song (see note
6, p. 288), it appears here as a further degradation
of Philomela's grief.
7. "Cf. Part III, line 195" (Eliot's note).
8. "Cf. Webster: 'Is the wind in that door still?' "
(Eliot's note). In Webster's *The Devil's Law Case*,
a physician asks this question on finding that the
victim of a murderous attack is still breathing.

O O O O that Shakespeherian Rag—
It's so elegant
So intelligent[9]   130
"What shall I do now? What shall I do?"
"I shall rush out as I am, and walk the street
"With my hair down, so. What shall we do tomorrow?
"What shall we ever do?"
                  The hot water at ten.   135
And if it rains, a closed car at four.
And we shall play a game of chess,[1]
Pressing lidless eyes and waiting for a knock upon the door.

When Lil's husband got demobbed,[2] I said—
I didn't mince my words, I said to her myself,   140
HURRY UP PLEASE ITS TIME[3]
Now Albert's coming back, make yourself a bit smart.
He'll want to know what you done with that money he gave you
To get yourself some teeth. He did, I was there.
You have them all out, Lil, and get a nice set,   145
He said, I swear, I can't bear to look at you.
And no more can't I, I said, and think of poor Albert,
He's been in the army four years, he wants a good time,
And if you don't give it him, there's others will, I said.
Oh is there, she said. Something o' that, I said.   150
Then I'll know who to thank, she said, and give me a straight look.
HURRY UP PLEASE ITS TIME
If you don't like it you can get on with it, I said.
Others can pick and choose if you can't.
But if Albert makes off, it won't be for lack of telling.   155
You ought to be ashamed, I said, to look so antique.
(And her only thirty-one.)
I can't help it, she said, pulling a long face,
It's them pills I took, to bring it off, she said.
(She's had five already, and nearly died of young George.)   160
The chemist[4] said it would be all right, but I've never been the same.
You *are* a proper fool, I said.
Well, if Albert won't leave you alone, there it is, I said,
What you get married for if you don't want children?
HURRY UP PLEASE ITS TIME   165
Well, that Sunday Albert was home, they had a hot gammon,[5]
And they asked me in to dinner, to get the beauty of it hot—
HURRY UP PLEASE ITS TIME
HURRY UP PLEASE ITS TIME
Goonight Bill. Goonight Lou. Goonight May. Goonight.   170
Ta ta. Goonight. Goonight.
Good night, ladies, good night, sweet ladies, good night, good night.[6]

9. Bruce R. McElderry has identified the "Shakespearian Rag" as an actual American ragtime song which was a hit of Ziegfeld's Follies of 1912.

1. "Cf. the game of chess in Middleton's *Women Beware Women*" (Eliot's note), described in note 9, p. 284. Between this and the next line Eliot's manuscript includes another: "The ivory men make company between us." It was cut from the poem at Vivien Eliot's request before publication, but Eliot restored it from memory in a fair copy he wrote out in 1960.

2. Demobilized; discharged from the army after the First World War. (The following passage, according to Eliot, was based on a story told the Eliots by their maid; the manuscript shows that lines 153 and 164 were suggested by Vivien Eliot.)

3. The barkeeper's call at closing time in an English pub.

4. Druggist.

5. Ham.

6. From *Hamlet* 4.5, these words conclude Ophelia's mad speech before her suicide by drowning.

III. The Fire Sermon[7]

The river's tent is broken; the last fingers of leaf
Clutch and sink into the wet bank. The wind
Crosses the brown land, unheard. The nymphs are departed.   175
Sweet Thames, run softly, till I end my song.[8]
The river bears no empty bottles, sandwich papers,
Silk handkerchiefs, cardboard boxes, cigarette ends
Or other testimony of summer nights. The nymphs are departed.
And their friends, the loitering heirs of City directors;   180
Departed, have left no addresses.
By the water of Leman I sat down and wept . . .[9]
Sweet Thames, run softly till I end my song,
Sweet Thames, run softly, for I speak not loud or long.
But at my back in a cold blast I hear[1]   185
The rattle of the bones, and chuckle spread from ear to ear.

A rat crept softly through the vegetation
Dragging its slimy belly on the bank
While I was fishing in the dull canal
On a winter evening round behind the gashouse   190
Musing upon the king my brother's wreck[2]
And on the king my father's death before him.
White bodies naked on the low damp ground
And bones cast in a little low dry garret,
Rattled by the rat's foot only, year to year.   195
But at my back from time to time I hear
The sound of horns and motors, which shall bring
Sweeney to Mrs. Porter in the spring[3]
O the moon shone bright on Mrs. Porter
And on her daughter   200
They wash their feet in soda water[4]
Et O ces voix d'enfants, chantant dans la coupole![5]

---

7. In the *Fire Sermon*, Buddha counsels his followers to conceive an aversion for the burning flames of passion and physical sensation, and thus live a holy life, attain freedom from earthly things, and finally leave the cycle of rebirth for Nirvana. "The complete text of the Buddha's Fire Sermon (which corresponds in importance to the Sermon on the Mount) . . . will be found translated in the late Henry Clarke Warren's *Buddhism in Translation* (Harvard Oriental Series) . . ." (Eliot's note).
8. "V. Spenser, *Prothalamion*" (Eliot's note). This line is the refrain of the Elizabethan poet Edmund Spenser's marriage-song. The nymphs (in the preceding line) are described by Spenser as "lovely Daughters of the Flood", or "Thames-Daughters" as Eliot calls them in his note to line 266.
9. The Psalmist describes the exiled Hebrews mourning for their homeland: "By the rivers of Babylon, there we sat down, yea, we wept, when we remembered Zion" (Psalm 137). Leman is the Swiss name for Lake Geneva, near which, in Lausanne, Eliot was convalescing when he was completing *The Waste Land;* in Elizabethan and earlier English, the common noun meant a lover.
1. "Cf. Marvell, *To His Coy Mistress*" (Eliot's note). Eliot's note, intended for line 196, applies here as well; both are ironic paraphrases of Marvell's lines, "But at my back I always hear / Time's winged chariot hurrying near . . ."
2. "Cf. *The Tempest*, I, ii" (Eliot's note). See line 48.

3. "Cf. Day, *Parliament of Bees:* 'When of the sudden, listening, you shall hear, / A noise of horns and hunting, which shall bring / Actaeon to Diana in the spring, / Where all shall see her naked skin . . .' " (Eliot's note). Diana (the virgin goddess of the woods and hunting, was seen naked by Actaeon the hunter; she then changed him into a stag, to be hunted to death by his own dogs. She was equivalent to the Greek goddess Artemis, whom Frazer discusses as a type of the Hanged God (see note to line 46).
4. "I do not know the origin of the ballad from which these lines are taken: it was reported to me from Sydney, Australia" (Eliot's note). It was sung by Australian troops during the Dardanelles Campaign of World War I; a fuller version reads: "O the moon shone bright on Mrs. Porter / And on the daughter / Of Mrs. Porter. / They wash their feet in soda water / And so they oughter / To keep them clean." As the note for the next line suggests, this may parody the ceremonial washing of feet which is part of the liturgy of Holy Thursday; the act's symbolic meaning is of humility and love, and recapitulates Christ's washing of his disciples' feet as recounted in John 13:1–17.
5. "V. Verlaine, *Parsifal*" (Eliot's note): "And O those children's voices singing in the dome!" Verlaine's poem evokes Wagner's opera about the Grail quest. Parsifal has withstood the enchantress's efforts to seduce him; humbled and purified, she washes his feet to prepare him to enter the Grail Castle, where he heals the Fisher King Amfortas

Twit twit twit
Jug jug jug jug jug jug
So rudely forc'd.
Tereu[6]

205

Unreal City
Under the brown fog of a winter noon
Mr. Eugenides, the Smyrna merchant
Unshaven, with a pocket full of currants
C.i.f. London: documents at sight,[7]

210

Asked me in demotic French
To luncheon at the Cannon Street Hotel[8]
Followed by a weekend at the Metropole.

At the violet hour, when the eyes and back
Turn upward from the desk, when the human engine waits

215

Like a taxi throbbing waiting,
I Tiresias,[9] though blind, throbbing between two lives,
Old man with wrinkled female breasts, can see
At the violet hour, the evening hour that strives
Homeward, and brings the sailor home from sea,[1]

220

The typist home at teatime, clears her breakfast, lights
Her stove, and lays out food in tins.
Out of the window perilously spread
Her drying combinations touched by the sun's last rays,
On the divan are piled (at night her bed)

225

Stockings, slippers, camisoles, and stays.[2]
I Tiresias, old man with wrinkled dugs
Perceived the scene, and foretold the rest—
I too awaited the expected guest.
He, the young man carbuncular,[3] arrives,

230

A small house agent's clerk, with one bold stare,
One of the low on whom assurance sits
As a silk hat on a Bradford millionaire.[4]

---

and becomes king himself. The opera ends with the sound of children's voices singing Christ's praise from the heights of the castle.

6. Another conventional representation of the nightingale's song, alluding to King Tereus and his brutality to Philomel. Compare a song in John Lyle's play, *Campaspe* (1584): "O 'tis the ravished nightingale. / Jug, jug, jug, jug, tereu! she cries. . . ."

7. "The currants were quoted at a price 'carriage and insurance free to London'; and the Bill of Lading etc. were to be handed to the buyer on payment of the sight draft" (Eliot's note).

8. Next to the Cannon Street Station in the City, this hotel was used by businessmen going to or from the Continent by boat-train; it was also a locale for homosexual liaisons. The Metropole is a luxurious hotel in the seaside resort of Brighton.

9. "Tiresias, although a mere spectator and not indeed a 'character,' is yet the most important personage in the poem uniting all the rest. Just as the one-eyed merchant, seller of currants, melts into the Phoenician Sailor, and the latter is not wholly distinct from Ferdinand Prince of Naples [in *The Tempest*], so all the women are one woman, and the two sexes meet in Tiresias. What Tiresias *sees*, in fact, is the substance of the poem . . ."

(Eliot's note). Eliot then quotes a passage in Ovid's *Metamorphoses* (3. 316–38) which tells how Tiresias struck and so separated two snakes that were coupling, and was thereupon turned into a woman; eight years later he saw them again, struck them once more, and was changed back into a man. Jupiter and Juno asked him, since he had been both man and woman, to decide a dispute between them as to whether men or women more enjoyed sexual intercourse. Tiresias infuriated Juno by saying that women did, and was blinded. Jupiter palliated this affliction by granting him the gift of prophecy.

1. "This may not appear as exact as Sappho's lines, but I had in mind the 'long-shore' or 'dory' fisherman, who returns at nightfall" (Eliot's note). Sappho wrote, "Hesperus [the evening star], thou bringest home all things bright morning scattered: thou bringest the sheep, the goat, the child to the mother." Also involved is "Home is the sailor, home from the sea," a line in Robert Louis Stevenson's "Requiem."

2. Corset; "camisoles": fancy underwaists.

3. Pimply.

4. War profiteer. Bradford is an industrial town in the north of England.

The time is now propitious, as he guesses,　　　　　235
The meal is ended, she is bored and tired,
Endeavours to engage her in caresses
Which still are unreproved, if undesired.
Flushed and decided, he assaults at once;
Exploring hands encounter no defence;　　　　　240
His vanity requires no response,
And makes a welcome of indifference.
(And I Tiresias have foresuffered all
Enacted on this same divan or bed;
I who have sat by Thebes below the wall[5]　　　　　245
And walked among the lowest of the dead.)
Bestows one final patronising kiss,
And gropes his way, finding the stairs unlit . . .

She turns and looks a moment in the glass,
Hardly aware of her departed lover;　　　　　250
Her brain allows one half-formed thought to pass:
"Well now that's done: and I'm glad it's over."
When lovely woman stoops to folly and
Paces about her room again, alone,
She smoothes her hair with automatic hand,　　　　　255
And puts a record on the gramophone.[6]

"This music crept by me upon the waters"[7]
And along the Strand, up Queen Victoria Street.
O City city, I can sometimes hear
Beside a public bar in Lower Thames Street,　　　　　260
The pleasant whining of a mandoline
And a clatter and a chatter from within
Where fishmen lounge at noon: where the walls
Of Magnus Martyr[8] hold
Inexplicable splendour of Ionian white and gold.　　　　　265

　　　The river sweats[9]
　　　Oil and tar
　　　The barges drift
　　　With the turning tide
　　　Red sails　　　　　270
　　　Wide
　　　To leeward, swing on the heavy spar.

5. Tiresias, who prophesied in the marketplace by the wall of Thebes, foretold the fall of two Theban kings, Oedipus and Creon. After his death he remained a prophet; Odysseus summoned him from Hades and was given advice to aid his voyage home.
6. "V. Goldsmith, the song in *The Vicar of Wakefield*" (Eliot's note). The seduced Olivia sings, "When lovely woman stoops to folly / And finds too late that men betray, / What charm can soothe her melancholy, / What art can wash her guilt away? / The only art her guilt to cover, / To hide her shame from every eye, / To give repentance to her lover / And wring his bosom—is to die."
7. "V. *The Tempest* as above" (Eliot's note). See note for line 48.
8. "The interior of St. Magnus Martyr is to my mind one of the finest among [Sir Christopher]

Wren's interiors. See *The Proposed Demolition of Nineteen City Churches:* (P. S. King & Son, Ltd.)" (Eliot's note). The church, built in 1676, still stands at the corner of Lower Thames and Fish Streets, between London Bridge and London's fish market. It is here another intimation of a world separated from the Waste Land.
9. "The Song of the (three) Thames-daughters begins here. From line 292 to 306 inclusive they speak in turn. V. *Götterdämmerung*, III, i: the Rhine-daughters" (Eliot's note). In Wagner's opera *The Twilight of the Gods*, the three Rhinemaidens try in vain to seduce and then frighten the hero Siegfried into returning their gold, which brings both power and death to its possessor; since its theft the beauty of their river has gone. Lines 277–78 quote the refrain of their song.

The barges wash
Drifting logs
Down Greenwich reach
Past the Isle of Dogs.[1]   275
          Weialala leia
          Wallala leialala

Elizabeth and Leicester[2]
Beating oars   280
The stern was formed
A gilded shell
Red and gold
The brisk swell
Rippled both shores   285
Southwest wind
Carried down stream
The peal of bells
White towers
          Weialala leia   290
          Wallala leialala

"Trams and dusty trees.
Highbury bore me. Richmond and Kew
Undid me.[3] By Richmond I raised my knees
Supine on the floor of a narrow canoe."   295

"My feet are at Moorgate, and my heart
Under my feet. After the event
He wept. He promised 'a new start.'
I made no comment. What should I resent?"

"On Margate Sands.[4]   300
I can connect

Nothing with nothing.
The broken fingernails of dirty hands.
My people humble people who expect
Nothing."   305
          la la

To Carthage then I came[5]

1. A peninsula in East London formed by a sharp bend in the Thames called Greenwich Reach; Greenwich is a borough on the south bank. It was in Greenwich House that Queen Elizabeth I was born and that she entertained the Earl of Leicester (lines 279–89).
2. "V. [J. A.] Froude, [*The Reign of] Elizabeth*, Vol. I, ch. iv, letter of De Quadra [Spanish bishop and ambassador to England] to [King] Philip of Spain: 'In the afternoon we were in a barge, watching the games on the river. (The queen) was alone with Lord Robert [Earl of Leicester] and myself on the poop, when they began to talk nonsense, and went so far that Lord Robert at last said, as I was on the spot there was no reason why they should not be married if the Queen pleased' " (Eliot's note).
3. "Cf. *Purgatorio*, V, 133 . . ." (Eliot's note). Dante meets the spirit of Pia de' Tolomei of Siena, who tells him that "Siena made me, Maremma unmade me," a reference to her violent death in Maremma at her husband's hands. Ezra Pound used this phrase in "Hugh Selwyn Mauberley" (see p. 233, note 1).
4. Margate, and the other places mentioned above, are in or near London and the Thames.
5. "V. St. Augustine's *Confessions*: 'To Carthage then I came, where a cauldron of unholy loves sang all about mine ear' " (Eliot's note).

Burning burning burning burning[6]
O Lord Thou pluckest me out[7]
O Lord Thou pluckest   310

burning

IV. Death by Water[8]

Phlebas the Phoenician, a fortnight dead,
Forgot the cry of gulls, and the deep sea swell
And the profit and loss.
     A current under sea   315
Picked his bones in whispers. As he rose and fell
He passed the stages of his age and youth
Entering the whirlpool.
     Gentile or Jew
O you who turn the wheel and look to windward,   320
Consider Phlebas, who was once handsome and
tall as you.

V. What the Thunder Said[9]

After the torchlight red on sweaty faces
After the frosty silence in the gardens
After the agony in stony places
The shouting and the crying   325
Prison and palace and reverberation
Of thunder of spring over distant mountains
He who was living is now dead[1]
We who were living are now dying
With a little patience   330

Here is no water but only rock
Rock and no water and the sandy road
The road winding above among the mountains
Which are mountains of rock without water
If there were water we should stop and drink   335
Amongst the rock one cannot stop or think
Sweat is dry and feet are in the sand
If there were only water amongst the rock
Dead mountain mouth of carious[2] teeth that cannot spit
Here one can neither stand nor lie nor sit   340
There is not even silence in the mountains

6. Eliot's note (see note 7, p. 287) to this line alludes to the Buddha's Fire Sermon, but the line is not quoted from it.

7. "From St. Augustine's *Confessions* again. The collocation of these two representatives of eastern and western asceticism, as the culmination of this part of the poem, is not an accident" (Eliot's note). Augustine wrote, "I entangle my steps with these outward beauties, but Thou pluckest me out, O Lord, Thou pluckest me out."

8. The death of Phlebas by drowning was predicted by Madame Sosostris in Part I. Some readers feel that he dies in order to be reborn, as a fertility god; others, that his death is sterile and without hope of resurrection. The likeliest view is

that Phlebas represents the principal speaker's urge to find oblivion, and that his death is not to be taken as a real drowning. This section is a translation, somewhat modified, of the close of Eliot's poem in French, "Dans le Restaurant."

9. "In the first part of Part V three themes are employed: the journey to Emmaus, the approach to the Chapel Perilous (see Miss Weston's book) and the present decay of eastern Europe" (Eliot's note).

1. Christ's agony in the Garden of Gethsemane, his imprisonment, trial, and death on the cross are adumbrated here.

2. That is, rotting.

But dry sterile thunder without rain
There is not even solitude in the mountains
But red sullen faces sneer and snarl
From doors of mudcracked houses
                              If there were water   345
  And no rock
  If there were rock
  And also water
  And water
  A spring   350
  A pool among the rock
  If there were the sound of water only
  Not the cicada[3]
  And dry grass singing
  But sound of water over a rock   355
  Where the hermit-thrush sings in the pine trees
  Drip drop drip drop drop drop drop[4]
  But there is no water

Who is the third who walks always beside you?[5]   360
When I count, there are only you and I together
But when I look ahead up the white road
There is always another one walking beside you
Gliding wrapt in a brown mantle, hooded
I do not know whether a man or a woman   365
—But who is that on the other side of you?

What is that sound high in the air
Murmur of maternal lamentation
Who are those hooded hordes swarming
Over endless plains, stumbling in cracked earth
Ringed by the flat horizon only   370
What is the city over the mountains
Cracks and reforms and bursts in the violet air
Falling towers
Jerusalem Athens Alexandria
Vienna London   375
Unreal[6]

A woman drew her long black hair out tight
And fiddled whisper music on those strings

3. That is, grasshopper. Compare the prophecy of Ecclesiastes, "the grasshopper shall be a burden, and desire shall fail . . ." (and also compare line 23 and its note).

4. "This is *Turdus aonalaschkae pallasii,* the hermit-thrush which I have heard in Quebec Province. Chapman says (*Handbook of Birds of Eastern North America*) 'it is most at home in secluded woodland and thickety retreats. . . . Its notes are not remarkable for variety or volume, but in purity and sweetness of tone and exquisite modulation they are unequalled.' Its 'water-dripping song' is justly celebrated" (Eliot's note).

5. "The following lines were stimulated by the account of one of the Antarctic expeditions (I forget which, but I think one of Shackleton's): it was related that the party of explorers, at the extremity of their strength, had the constant delusion that there was *one more member* than could actually be counted" (Eliot's note). In Luke 24:13–16 two disciples, on their way to Emmaus, discuss Christ's resurrection, and "Jesus himself drew near, and went with them. But their eyes were holden [constrained], that they should not know him."

6. Eliot's note for lines 367–77: "Cf. Hermann Hesse, *Blick ins Chaos* [A Glimpse into Chaos]": "Already half of Europe, and at least half of Eastern Europe, is on the way to Chaos, travels drunk in sacred madness along the brink of the abyss and moreover sings drunken hymns as Dmitri Karamazov sang. The bourgeois, shocked, laughs at these songs: the saint and seer hear them with tears." The "maternal lamentation" is of the women weeping over Christ and perhaps over the deaths of other vegetation gods.

And bats with baby faces in the violet light   380
Whistled, and beat their wings
And crawled head downward down a blackened wall
And upside down in air were towers
Tolling reminiscent bells, that kept the hours
And voices singing out of empty cisterns and exhausted wells   385

In this decayed hole among the mountains
In the faint moonlight, the grass is singing
Over the tumbled graves, above the chapel[7]
There is the empty chapel, only the wind's home.
It has no windows, and the door swings,   390
Dry bones can harm no one.
Only a cock stood on the rooftree
Co co rico co co rico[8]
In a flash of lightning. Then a damp gust
Bringing rain   395

Ganga[9] was sunken, and the limp leaves
Waited for rain, while the black clouds
Gathered far distant, over Himavant.[1]
The jungle crouched, humped in silence.
Then spoke the thunder   400
DA[2]
Datta: what have we given?
My friend, blood shaking my heart
The awful daring of a moment's surrender
Which an age of prudence can never retract   405
By this, and this only, we have existed
Which is not to be found in our obituaries
Or in memories draped by the beneficent spider[3]
Or under seals broken by the lean solicitor[4]
In our empty rooms   410
DA
Dayadhvam: I have heard the key
Turn in the door once and turn once only[5]
We think of the key, each in his prison
Thinking of the key, each confirms a prison   415
Only at nightfall, aethereal rumours

---

7. The Perilous Chapel, which the knight must
enter on his way to the Grail.
8. The cock crows to announce the coming dawn
and the departure of evil spirits, but the efficacy
of his cry is made doubtful by Eliot here.
9. The sacred Indian river Ganges.
1. The Himalayan mountain range.
2. The sound of thunder. " 'Datta, dayadhvam
damyata' (Give, sympathize, control). The fable of
the meaning of the Thunder is found in the Bri-
hadaranyaka-Upanishad, 5, 1 . . ." (Eliot's note).
In the Hindu fable of "The Three Great Disci-
plines," the Creator God instructs the lesser gods
to "control" their unruly natures, men to "give"
alms despite their natural miserliness, and the cruel
demons to "sympathize"; "That very thing is
repeated even today by the heavenly voice, in the
form of thunder as 'Da,' 'Da,' 'Da.' . . . Therefore
one should practice these three things: self-control, giving, and mercy."
3. "Cf. Webster, *The White Devil,* V, vi: ". . .

'they'll remarry / Ere the worm pierce your wind-
ing-sheet, ere the spider / Make a thin curtain for
your epitaphs' " (Eliot's note).
4. Lawyer.
5. "Cf. *Inferno,* XXXIII 46 . . ." (Eliot's note),
which is translated: "And I heard below me the
door of the horrible tower being locked." The traitor Ugolino tells Dante that his enemies imprisoned him and his children in a tower to die of
starvation. Eventually the starving Ugolino ate his
own children. Eliot continues: "Also F. H. Bradley, *Appearance and Reality,* p. 346. 'My external
sensations are no less private to myself than are
my thoughts or my feelings. In either case my
experience falls within my own circle, a circle closed
on the outside; and, with all its elements alike,
every sphere is opaque to the others which surround it. . . . In brief, regarded as an existence
which appears in a soul, the whole world for each
is peculiar and private to that soul.' "

Revive for a moment a broken Coriolanus[6]
DA
Damyata: The boat responded
Gaily, to the hand expert with sail and oar   420
The sea was calm, your heart would have responded
Gaily, when invited, beating obedient
To controlling hands

                            I sat upon the shore
Fishing,[7] with the arid plain behind me   425
Shall I at least set my lands in order?[8]
London Bridge is falling down falling down falling down
Poi s'ascose nel foco che gli affina[9]
Quando fiam uti chelidon—O swallow swallow[1]
Le Prince d'Aquitaine à la tour abolie[2]   430
These fragments I have shored against my ruins
Why then Ile fit you. Hieronymo's mad againe.[3]
Datta. Dayadhvam. Damyata.
            Shantih   shantih   shantih[4]

                                                               1922

Landscapes[5]

I. New Hampshire

Children's voices in the orchard
Between the blossom- and the fruit-time:
Gold head, crimson head,
Between the green tip and the root
Black wing, brown wing, hover over;   5
Twenty years and the spring is over;
To-day grieves, to-morrow grieves,
Cover me over, light-in-leaves;
Golden head, black wing,
Cling, swing,   10
Spring, sing,
Swing up into the apple-tree.

---

6. Roman general, the hero of a play by Shakespeare, who was exiled by the Roman people and then from injured pride led the enemy against Rome.
7. "V. Weston: *From Ritual to Romance;* chapter on the Fisher King" (Eliot's note).
8. Isaiah 38:1: "Thus saith the Lord, Set thine house in order: for thou shalt die, and not live."
9. "V. *Purgatorio,* XXVI, 28 . . ." (Eliot's note). In this passage the soul of the poet Arnaut Daniel speaks to Dante, "Now I pray you, by the goodness that guides you to the top of this staircase [out of Purgatory], be mindful in time of my suffering." Dante continues, "Then he hid himself in the fire which refines them."
1. "V. *Pervigilium Veneris.* Cf. Philomela in Parts II and III" (Eliot's note). In the late Latin poem, "The Vigil of Venus," Philomel asks, "When shall I be like the swallow," continuing, "that I may cease to be silent?" A. C. Swinburne's "Itylus" begins, "Swallow, my sister, O sister swallow, / How can thy heart be full of spring?"
2. "V. Gerard de Nerval, Sonnet *El Desdichado*" (Eliot's note). From Nerval's poem, "The Disinherited," in which the poet compares himself to "The prince of Aquitaine at the ruined tower."
3. "V. Kyd's *Spanish Tragedy*" (Eliot's note). The play's subtitle is "Hieronymo Is Mad Againe"; to avenge his son's murder he feigns madness, and writes a play in which, acting one of the parts, he kills the murderer. "Why then Ile fit you!" (that is, accommodate you) is his answer when requested to write the play.
4. "Repeated as here, a formal ending to an Upanishad. The Peace which passeth understanding' is our equivalent to this word" (Eliot's note). In the 1922 edition of this poem, Eliot phrased his note as "our feeble equivalent to this word."
5. Under this title Eliot grouped five short poems, each dealing with a specific place.

V. Cape Ann[6]

O quick quick quick, quick hear the song-sparrow,
Swamp-sparrow, fox-sparrow, vesper-sparrow
At dawn and dusk. Follow the dance
Of the goldfinch at noon. Leave to chance
The Blackburnian warbler, the shy one. Hail   5
With shrill whistle the note of the quail, the bob-white
Dodging by bay-bush. Follow the feet
Of the walker, the water-thrush. Follow the flight
Of the dancing arrow, the purple martin. Greet
In silence the bullbat. All are delectable. Sweet sweet sweet   10
But resign this land at the end, resign it
To its true owner, the tough one, the sea-gull.
The palaver is finished.

                                                                 1934

Little Gidding[7]

I

Midwinter spring is its own season
Sempiternal though sodden towards sundown,
Suspended in time, between pole and tropic.[8]
When the short day is brightest, with frost and fire,
The brief sun flames the ice, on pond and ditches,   5
In windless cold that is the heart's heat,
Reflecting in a watery mirror
A glare that is blindness in the early afternoon.
And glow more intense than blaze of branch, or brazier,
Stirs the dumb spirit: no wind, but pentecostal fire[9]   10
In the dark time of the year. Between melting and freezing
The soul's sap quivers. There is no earth smell
Or smell of living thing. This is the spring time
But not in time's covenant. Now the hedgerow
Is blanched for an hour with transitory blossom   15
Of snow, a bloom more sudden
Than that of summer, neither budding nor fading,
Not in the scheme of generation.
Where is the summer, the unimaginable
Zero summer?[1]   20

6. On the northern coast of Massachusetts, not far from the New Hampshire border; a wilderness area in the middle of the cape is inhabited by the birds Eliot here describes.
7. This poem, published in 1942, is the last of Eliot's *Four Quartets*, and Eliot considered it the best part of that work, as that work was the best of his poetry. Like the late quartets of Beethoven, they are thematically interwoven with each other. Each of Eliot's *Quartets* is divided into five parts or movements which develop the central theme in quite different ways. Each quartet is based upon one of the four elements, that of *Little Gidding* being fire. Here, as in *The Waste Land* (The Fire Sermon), fire is the torturing element in which we live, but it is also the refining fire which can bring man to salvation. Little Gidding was an Anglican religious community founded in 1625 by Nicholas

Ferrar; it is now a village in Huntingdonshire. Although the community lasted only twenty-two years, the memory of its devotion persisted, and the chapel was rebuilt in the nineteenth century.
8. The sudden fusion of seasons is premonitory, or emblematic, of the intersection of the timeless with time, of the eternal with the present, of God and man. The phrase probably invokes also the sense of the poet's late blossoming.
9. On the feast of Pentecost, the disciples of Christ were assembled, "And suddenly there came a sound from heaven, as of a rushing mighty wind, and it filled all the house where they were sitting. And there appeared unto them cloven tongues, like as of fire. . . . And they were all filled with the Holy Ghost . . ." (Acts 2:2–4).
1. The culmination of what is only presaged by "midwinter spring."

If you came this way,[2]

Taking the route you would be likely to take
From the place you would be likely to come from,
If you came this way in may time, you would find the hedges
White again, in May, with voluptuary sweetness.   25
It would be the same at the end of the journey,
If you came at night like a broken king,[3]
If you came by day not knowing what you came for,
It would be the same, when you leave the rough road
And turn behind the pig-sty to the dull façade   30
And the tombstone. And what you thought you came for
Is only a shell, a husk of meaning
From which the purpose breaks only when it is fulfilled
If at all. Either you had no purpose
Or the purpose is beyond the end you figured   35
And is altered in fulfilment. There are other places
Which also are the world's end, some at the sea jaws,
Or over a dark lake, in a desert or a city—
But this is the nearest, in place and time,
Now and in England.[4]   40

If you came this way,

Taking any route, starting from anywhere,
At any time or at any season,
It would always be the same: you would have to put off
Sense and notion. You are not here to verify,   45
Instruct yourself, or inform curiosity
Or carry report. You are here to kneel
Where prayer has been valid. And prayer is more
Than an order of words, the conscious occupation
Of the praying mind, or the sound of the voice praying.   50
And what the dead had no speech for, when living,
They can tell you, being dead: the communication
Of the dead is tongued with fire beyond the language of the living.
Here, the intersection of the timeless moment
Is England and nowhere. Never and always.   55

II

Ash on an old man's sleeve[5]
Is all the ash the burnt roses leave.
Dust in the air suspended
Marks the place where a story ended.
Dust inbreathed was a house—   60
The wall, the wainscot and the mouse.
The death of hope and despair,
    This is the death of air.

There are flood and drouth
Over the eyes and in the mouth,   65

2. To Little Gidding.
3. King Charles I, who after his final defeat at the battle of Naseby in the English Civil War came to Little Gidding to fortify his spirit.
4. The present time and present place are the point where the spirit exists and has meaning, as opposed to time past and time future, "memory" and "desire" (Part I of *The Waste Land*).
5. The second movement is lyrical, and meditates on the death of the four elements—air, earth, water, and fire—which make up the physical universe.

Dead water and dead sand
Contending for the upper hand.
The parched eviscerate soil
Gapes at the vanity of toil,
Laughs without mirth.   70
    This is the death of earth.

Water and fire succeed
The town, the pasture and the weed.
Water and fire deride
The sacrifice that we denied.   75
Water and fire shall rot
The marred foundations we forgot,
Of sanctuary and choir,[6]
    This is the death of water and fire.

In the uncertain hour before the morning[7]   80
  Near the ending of interminable night
  At the recurrent end of the unending
After the dark dove with the flickering tongue[8]
  Had passed below the horizon of his homing
  While the dead leaves still rattle on like tin   85
Over the asphalt where no other sound was
  Between three districts whence the smoke arose
  I met one walking, loitering and hurried
As if blown towards me like the metal leaves
  Before the urban dawn wind unresisting.   90
  And as I fixed upon the down-turned face
That pointed scrutiny with which we challenge
  The first-met stranger in the waning dusk
  I caught the sudden look of some dead master
Whom I had known, forgotten, half recalled   95
  Both one and many; in the brown baked features
  The eyes of a familiar compound ghost[9]
Both intimate and unidentifiable.
  So I assumed a double part,[1] and cried
  And heard another's voice cry: "What! are *you* here?"   100
Although we were not. I was still the same,
  Knowing myself yet being someone other—
  And he a face still forming; yet the words sufficed
To compel the recognition they preceded.
  And so, compliant in the common wind,   105
  Too strange to each other for misunderstanding,
In concord at this intersection time
  Of meeting nowhere, no before and after,
  We trod the pavement in a dead patrol.
I said: "The wonder that I feel is easy,   110
  Yet ease is cause of wonder. Therefore speak:

6. Parts of a church: the altar is in the "sanctuary," which is connected to the "nave," or main hall, by the "choir."
7. Lines 80--151 are meant to suggest, if not exactly to imitate, the stanzaic pattern of Dante's *Divine Comedy*. Eliot was an air raid warden during the German raids on London in the Second World War, and represents himself here as patrolling the streets after such a raid.
8. The German dive-bomber.
9. Eliot said that he had principally in mind here W. B. Yeats and Jonathan Swift.
1. The dialogue is imagined yet seems real.

I may not comprehend, may not remember."
And he: "I am not eager to rehearse
   My thoughts and theory which you have forgotten.
   These things have served their purpose: let them be.   115
So with your own, and pray they be forgiven
   By others, as I pray you to forgive
   Both bad and good. Last season's fruit is eaten
And the fullfed beast shall kick the empty pail
   For last year's words belong to last year's language   120
   And next year's words await another voice.
But, as the passage now presents no hindrance
   To the spirit unappeased and peregrine[2]
   Between two worlds become much like each other,
So I find words I never thought to speak   125
   In streets I never thought I should revisit
   When I left my body on a distant shore.
Since our concern was speech, and speech impelled us
   To purify the dialect of the tribe[3]
   And urge the mind to aftersight and foresight,   130
Let me disclose the gifts reserved for age
   To set a crown upon your lifetime's effort.
   First, the cold friction of expiring sense
Without enchantment, offering no promise
   But bitter tastelessness of shadow fruit   135
   As body and soul begin to fall asunder.
Second, the conscious impotence of rage[4]
   At human folly, and the laceration
   Of laughter at what ceases to amuse.[5]
And last, the rending pain of re-enactment   140
   Of all that you have done, and been; the shame
   Of motives late revealed, and the awareness
Of things ill done and done to other's harm
   Which once you took for exercise of virtue.
   Then fools' approval stings, and honour stains.   145
From wrong to wrong the exasperated spirit
   Proceeds, unless restored by that refining fire[6]
   Where you must move in measure, like a dancer."[7]
The day was breaking. In the disfigured street
   He left me, with a kind of valediction,   150
   And faded on the blowing of the horn.[8]

III

There are three conditions which often look alike
Yet differ completely, flourish in the same hedgerow:

2. Wandering, foreign.
3. A reference to the line in Stéphane Mallarmé, "Le Tombeau d'Edgar Poe," *Donner un sens plus pur aux mots de la tribu* (To give the words of the tribe a more exact meaning).
4. In Yeats's poem, "The Spur," he spoke of lust and rage as two aspects of old age.
5. Swift's epitaph, written by himself in Latin (and translated by Yeats) says that "Savage indignation now / Cannot lacerate his breast."
6. See note 7, p. 295. But Eliot has also in mind the purgative fires in Yeats's poem, "Byzantium," p. 90.
7. Probably also borrowed from Yeats's "Byzantium" and from his "Among School Children," p. 87.
8. Spirits usually vanish at the crowing of the cock. The horn is the "All Clear" siren after the air raid. Eliot echoes Shakespeare's description of the disappearance of Hamlet's father's ghost: "It faded on the crowing of the cock" (*Hamlet* 1.2.157).

Attachment to self and to things and to persons, detachment
From self and from things and from persons; and, growing between them,
    indifference   155
Which resembles the others as death resembles life,
Being between two lives—unflowering, between
The live and the dead nettle. This is the use of memory:
For liberation—not less of love but expanding
Of love beyond desire, and so liberation   160
From the future as well as the past. Thus, love of a country
Begins as attachment to our own field of action
And comes to find that action of little importance
Though never indifferent. History may be servitude,
History may be freedom. See, now they vanish,   165
The faces and places, with the self which, as it could, loved them,
To become renewed, transfigured, in another pattern.

Sin is Behovely,[9] but
All shall be well, and
All manner of thing shall be well.   170
If I think, again, of this place,
And of people, not wholly commendable,
Of no immediate kin or kindness,
But some of peculiar genius,
All touched by a common genius,   175
United in the strife which divided them;
If I think of a king at nightfall,
Of three men, and more, on the scaffold[1]
And a few who died forgotten
In other places, here and abroad,   180
And of one who died blind and quiet,[2]
Why should we celebrate
These dead men more than the dying?
It is not to ring the bell backward
Nor is it an incantation   185
To summon the spectre of a Rose.[3]
We cannot revive old factions
We cannot restore old policies
Or follow an antique drum.
These men, and those who opposed them   190
And those whom they opposed
Accept the constitution of silence
And are folded in a single party.
Whatever we inherit from the fortunate
We have taken from the defeated   195
What they had to leave us—a symbol:
A symbol perfected in death.
And all shall be well and

9. Necessary to the divine plan. In one of her visions the fourteenth-century English mystic, Dame Julian of Norwich, was told that "sin is behovable but all shall be well . . . and all manner of things shall be well."
1. King Charles I and his two chief aides, Thomas Wentworth, Earl of Strafford, and Archbishop Laud, who were executed by the Puritans in 1649.

2. John Milton, who took Cromwell's side against the King.
3. A pun combining the title of a sentimental ballet, in which a girl dreams of the ghost of a rose she once wore to the ball, and a reference to the Wars of the Roses, Lancaster being the white and York the red, to determine which family would rule England.

All manner of thing shall be well
By the purification of the motive
In the ground of our beseeching.[4]   200

                              IV

The dove descending breaks the air
With flame of incandescent terror
Of which the tongues declare
The one discharge from sin and error.[5]   205
The only hope, or else despair
  Lies in the choice of pyre or pyre—
  To be redeemed from fire by fire.

Who then devised the torment? Love.
Love is the unfamiliar Name   210
Behind the hands that wove
The intolerable shirt of flame
Which human power cannot remove.[6]
  We only live, only suspire[7]
  Consumed by either fire or fire.   215

                              V

What we call the beginning is often the end[8]
And to make an end is to make a beginning.
The end is where we start from. And every phrase
And sentence that is right (where every word is at home,
Taking its place to support the others,
The word neither diffident nor ostentatious,   220
An easy commerce of the old and the new,
The common word exact without vulgarity,
The formal word precise but not pedantic,
The complete consort dancing together)
Every phrase and every sentence is an end and a beginning,   225
Every poem an epitaph. And any action
Is a step to the block, to the fire, down the sea's throat
Or to an illegible stone: and that is where we start.
We die with the dying:
See, they depart, and we go with them.   230
We are born with the dead:
See, they return, and bring us with them.
The moment of the rose and the moment of the yew-tree[9]
Are of equal duration. A people without history
Is not redeemed from time, for history is a pattern   235
Of timeless moments. So, while the light fails

---

4. Dame Julian of Norwich was instructed in a vision that "the ground of our beseeching" is love.

5. The dove is both dive bomber and the symbol of the Holy Ghost with its pentecostal tongues of fire. The two kinds of fire, destructive and refining, form the basis of this lyrical movement.

6. The shirt of Nessus, which Hercules' wife had him put on because she had been falsely informed that it would win back his love for her, clung to his flesh and caused such suffering that he had himself placed on a pyre and burned himself to death.

7. Breathe, sigh.

8. In this section, which begins, like the third, rather flatly, becoming more intense later, Eliot offers an analogy between esthetic and spiritual questing.

9. The rose is a symbol of love and life, as the yew-tree of grief and death.

On a winter's afternoon, in a secluded chapel[1]
History is now and England.

With the drawing of this Love and the voice of this Calling[2]   240

We shall not cease from exploration
And the end of all our exploring
Will be to arrive where we started
And know the place for the first time.
Through the unknown, remembered gate   245
When the last of earth left to discover
Is that which was the beginning;
At the source of the longest river
The voice of the hidden waterfall
And the children in the apple-tree   250
Not known, because not looked for
But heard, half-heard, in the stillness
Between two waves of the sea.[3]
Quick now, here, now, always—
A condition of complete simplicity   255
(Costing not less than everything)
And all shall be well and
All manner of thing shall be well
When the tongues of flame are in-folded
Into the crowned knot[4] of fire   260
And the fire and the rose are one.[5]

1942

1. At Little Gidding.
2. Quoted from *The Cloud of Unknowing,* an anonymous fourteenth-century religious work.
3. The voices of the children and the thrush (the "hidden waterfall"), which occur in the first of the *Four Quartets,* "Burnt Norton," are intimations of the crossing of the time world by the timeless one, of now by always.

4. A nautical term, as George Williamson points out, for a knot finished by interweaving the strands so as to prevent untwisting.
5. The fire suggests the power and intensity of the divine spirit, the rose suggests mercy and love. Whatever meaning is given to the symbols, their union implies the visionary experience within human life.

CLAUDE McKAY
1890–1948

Born in Jamaica, Claude McKay first read the English poets, and his version of the Black experience is expressed in the language and forms of the English Romantics. His revolutionary quality is to be found not in his style but in a new experience—the sufferings, the anger, and the satisfactions of a Black man—discovered for poetry. "The Tropics in New York" commemorates nostalgia in an alien country and climate, a poem in the mode of Wordsworth's "The Reverie of Poor Susan." "America" is an attempt to wrest poetry and manhood out of McKay's conflict with the white man's society. "The Harlem Dancer" is beautiful and idolized, and only the poet guesses her alienation, an alienation as sad as his own.

Claude McKay was born at Sunny Ville, Jamaica, on September 15, 1890. At six he went to live with an older brother, from whom he received all the education he was to have until he emigrated to the United States. Although their parents had been poor farm workers, McKay's brother had become acquainted with major works by T. H. Huxley and Gibbon and had become an agnostic; this was the point from which

McKay was to proceed towards, though eventually away from, a philosophical sympathy with Communist social objectives. Also while a boy McKay began to write poems in the Jamaican dialect, many of which were collected in two books published in 1912; for his work he won a prize which enabled him to come to the United States, where he studied briefly at the Tuskegee Institute and for two years at Kansas State College. In 1914 he moved to Harlem, supporting himself with odd jobs, most often as a restaurant waiter, and during the First World War began to publish some of his most famous poems, including "The Harlem Dancer," under the pseudonym "Eli Edwards." By 1920 his poems were being published regularly in England, and he was living there; the next year McKay returned to the United States as an editor of the radical newspapers *The Liberator* and *The Masses*, and in 1922 his most important book, *Harlem Shadows*, was published.

During the twenties McKay was one of the most prominent members of the Harlem Renaissance; he was the oldest as well as the first to publish. Like many other writers of the time, both black and white, he was attracted to Communism; he traveled to Moscow in 1922 to meet Lenin and Trotsky, and represented the American Workers' Party at the Third Internationale. He remained in Europe, mainly in France and Morocco, and turned to writing fiction; *Home to Harlem* (1928) was a best-selling as well as award-winning novel, and McKay returned to the United States for the rest of his life. In his later years he was a well-known figure in American letters, though he wrote little; his poem "If We Must Die," a response to the Harlem race riots of 1919, was read to the British people by Winston Churchill and into the Congressional Record by American Senator Henry Cabot Lodge, Sr., as a World War II rallying cry. In 1942 he was converted to Catholicism and repudiated his earlier commitment to Communism. He died in Chicago on May 2, 1948.

The Tropics in New York

Bananas ripe and green, and ginger-root,
    Cocoa in pods and alligator pears,
And tangerines and mangoes and grape fruit,
    Fit for the highest prize at parish fairs,

Set in the window, bringing memories   5
    Of fruit-trees laden by low-singing rills,
And dewy dawns, and mystical blue skies
    In benediction over nun-like hills.

My eyes grew dim, and I could no more gaze;
    A wave of longing through my body swept,   10
And, hungry for the old, familiar ways,
    I turned aside and bowed my head and wept.

                          1922

If We Must Die

If we must die, let it not be like hogs
Hunted and penned in an inglorious spot,
While round us bark the mad and hungry dogs,
Making their mock at our accursed lot.
If we must die, O let us nobly die,   5
So that our precious blood may not be shed

In vain; then even the monsters we defy
Shall be constrained to honor us though dead!
O kinsmen! we must meet the common foe!
Though far outnumbered let us show us brave,   10
And for their thousand blows deal one deathblow!
What though before us lies the open grave?
Like men we'll face the murderous, cowardly pack,
Pressed to the wall, dying, but fighting back!

1922

America

Although she feeds me bread of bitterness,
And sinks into my throat her tiger's tooth,
Stealing my breath of life, I will confess
I love this cultured hell that tests my youth!
Her vigor flows like tides into my blood,   5
Giving me strength erect against her hate.
Her bigness sweeps my being like a flood.
Yet as a rebel fronts a king in state,
I stand within her walls with not a shred
Of terror, malice, not a word of jeer.
Darkly I gaze into the days ahead,
And see her might and granite wonders there,
Beneath the touch of Time's unerring hand,
Like priceless treasures sinking in the sand.

1922

The Harlem Dancer

Applauding youths laughed with young prostitutes
And watched her perfect, half-clothed body sway;
Her voice was like the sound of blended flutes
Blown by black players upon a picnic day.
She sang and danced on gracefully and calm,   5
The light gauze hanging loose about her form;
To me she seemed a proudly-swaying palm
Grown lovelier for passing through a storm.
Upon her swarthy neck black shiny curls
Luxuriant fell; and tossing coins in praise,   10
The wine-flushed, bold-eyed boys, and even the girls,
Devoured her shape with eager, passionate gaze;
But looking at her falsely-smiling face,
I knew her self was not in that strange place.

1922

ISAAC ROSENBERG
1890–1918

Isaac Rosenberg was one of those English poets cut off in their youth by the First
World War. As gifted as any of them, he left a small body of excellent work in the

mature style which he achieved only at the end of his short life. He early came under the spell of John Keats, and had Keats's love of splendid phrasing. For Rosenberg the poet was "a part of paradise," though "caught . . . in a cage of earth" ("The Poet I"). Surrounded by the corpses of his fellows, the poet still detects the presence of "fierce imaginings," "sweet laughter," and "joy." Glorifying war is repulsive to him. He succeeds, however, in transforming brute facts by detecting an inner core of exaltation. Many of his poems have what Siegfried Sassoon, another war poet, describes as a biblical or prophetic quality. But he is not without humor either.

Rosenberg was born on November 25, 1890, in Bristol. His Jewish parents had emigrated from Lithuania and Russia. When he was seven the family moved to Whitechapel, London, where their son's abilities as a painter were clearly recognized. At twenty-one, with the help of another Jewish family, he attended the Slade School of Art, from October 1911 to March 1914. He left some fine, fully realized portraits and drawings. Mostly to secure part of his salary for his mother, he enlisted in the army in October 1915. Unlike Rupert Brooke, Wilfred Owen, and Siegfried Sassoon, he was a soldier, not an officer, and writes as one. From August 1916 he was in the trenches in France, except for spells of illness. On April 1, 1918, he was killed at dawn while on night patrol.

The Mirror

It glimmers like a wakeful lake in the dusk narrowing room.
Like drowning vague branches in its depth floats the gloom,
The night shall shudder at its face by gleams of pallid light
Whose hands build the broader day to break the husk of night.

No shade shall waver there when your shadowless soul shall pass,   5
The green shakes not the air when your spirit drinks the grass,
So in its plashless water falls, so dumbly lies therein
A fervid rose whose fragrance sweet lies hidden and shut within.

Only in these bruised words the glass dim-showing my spirit's face,
Only a little colour from a fire I could not trace,   10
To glimmer through eternal days like an enchanted rose,
The potent dreamings of whose scent are wizard-locked beneath its glows.

1937

Break of Day in the Trenches[1]

The darkness crumbles away.
It is the same old druid[2] Time as ever,
Only a live thing leaps my hand,
A queer sardonic rat,
As I pull the parapet's poppy[3]   5
To stick behind my ear.
Droll rat, they would shoot you if they knew
Your cosmopolitan sympathies.

---

1. Much of World War I was fought "in the trenches"—that is, long narrow excavations in the earth which protected the soldiers of the two opposing sides.
2. Member of a Celtic religious order in ancient Gaul, Britain, and Ireland.
3. Poppies were a flower commonly found in Flanders, where much of World War I was fought; "parapet": rampart or breastworks.

Now you have touched this English hand
You will do the same to a German   10
Soon, no doubt, if it be your pleasure
To cross the sleeping green between.
It seems you inwardly grin as you pass
Strong eyes, fine limbs, haughty athletes,
Less chanced than you for life,   15
Bonds to the whims of murder,
Sprawled in the bowels of the earth,
The torn fields of France.
What do you see in our eyes
At the shrieking iron and flame   20
Hurled through still heavens?
What quaver—what heart aghast?
Poppies whose roots are in man's veins
Drop, and are ever dropping;
But mine in my ear is safe—   25
Just a little white with the dust.

June 1916   1922

Louse Hunting

Nudes—stark and glistening,
Yelling in lurid glee. Grinning faces
And raging limbs
Whirl over the floor one fire.
For a shirt verminously busy   5
Yon soldier tore from his throat, with oaths
Godhead might shrink at, but not the lice.
And soon the shirt was aflare
Over the candle he'd lit while we lay.

Then we all sprang up and stript   10
To hunt the verminous brood.
Soon like a demons' pantomime
The place was raging.
See the silhouettes agape,
See the gibbering shadows   15
Mixed with the battled arms on the wall.
See gargantuan hooked fingers
Pluck in supreme flesh
To smutch[4] supreme littleness.
See the merry limbs in hot Highland fling   20
Because some wizard vermin
Charmed from the quiet this revel
When our ears were half lulled
By the dark music
Blown from Sleep's trumpet.   25

1917   1922

---

4. Blacken, besmirch.

Returning, We Hear the Larks

Sombre the night is.
And though we have our lives, we know
What sinister threat lurks there.

Dragging these anguished limbs, we only know
This poison-blasted track opens on our camp—   5
On a little safe sleep.

But hark! joy—joy—strange joy.
Lo! heights of night ringing with unseen larks.
Music showering our upturned list'ning faces.

Death could drop from the dark   10
As easily as song—
But song only dropped,
Like a blind man's dreams on the sand
By dangerous tides,
Like a girl's dark hair for she dreams no ruin lies there,   15
Or her kisses where a serpent hides.

1917   1922

Dead Man's Dump

The plunging limbers[5] over the shattered track
Racketed with their rusty freight,
Stuck out like many crowns of thorns,
And the rusty stakes like sceptres old
To stay the flood of brutish men   5
Upon our brothers dear.

The wheels lurched over sprawled dead
But pained them not, though their bones crunched,
Their shut mouths made no moan,
They lie there huddled, friend and foeman,   10
Man born of man, and born of woman,
And shells go crying over them
From night till night and now.

Earth has waited for them
All the time of their growth   15
Fretting for their decay:
Now she has them at last!
In the strength of their strength
Suspended—stopped and held.

What fierce imaginings their dark souls lit   20
Earth! have they gone into you?
Somewhere they must have gone,
And flung on your hard back

___
5. Two-wheeled vehicles for pulling artillery pieces.

Is their souls' sack,
Emptied of God-ancestralled essences.   25
Who hurled them out? Who hurled?

None saw their spirits' shadow shake the grass,
Or stood aside for the half used life to pass
Out of those doomed nostrils and the doomed mouth,
When the swift iron burning bee   30
Drained the wild honey of their youth.

What of us, who flung on the shrieking pyre,
Walk, our usual thoughts untouched,
Our lucky limbs as on ichor[6] fed,
Immortal seeming ever?   35
Perhaps when the flames beat loud on us,
A fear may choke in our veins
And the startled blood may stop.

The air is loud with death,
The dark air spurts with fire   40
The explosions ceaseless are.
Timelessly now, some minutes past,
These dead strode time with vigorous life,
Till the shrapnel called "an end!"
But not to all. In bleeding pangs   45
Some borne on stretchers dreamed of home,
Dear things, war-blotted from their hearts.

A man's brains splattered on
A stretcher-bearer's face;
His shook shoulders slipped their load,   50
But when they bent to look again
The drowning soul was sunk too deep
For human tenderness.

They left this dead with the older dead,
Stretched at the cross roads.   55
Burnt black by strange decay,
Their sinister faces lie
The lid over each eye,
The grass and coloured clay
More motion have than they,   60
Joined to the great sunk silences.

Here is one not long dead;
His dark hearing caught our far wheels,
And the choked soul stretched weak hands
To reach the living world the far wheels said, 65
The blood-dazed intelligence beating for light,
Crying through the suspense of the far torturing wheels
Swift for the end to break,

6. Ethereal fluid that flowed in the veins of the gods of Greek mythology.

Or the wheels to break,
Cried as the tide of the world broke over his sight.   70

Will they come? Will they ever come?
Even as the mixed hoofs of the mules,
The quivering-bellied mules,
And the rushing wheels all mixed
With his tortured upturned sight,   75
So we crashed round the bend,
We heard his weak scream,
We heard his very last sound,
And our wheels grazed his dead face.

1917   1922

EDNA ST. VINCENT MILLAY
1892–1950

Edna St. Vincent Millay presents a rather unexpected figure in a collection of twentieth-century poetry. Her idiom for the most part avoids local reference, and much
of her verse might have been written at any time. Her diction is not archaic, but the
slightly elevated tone and the movement of the syntax place many of her poems in a
tradition which goes back to the English sixteenth century. Edna Millay made her
reputation (and in the 1920s and 30s it was a very considerable reputation) first with
the long poem "Renascence," and then with a series of lyrics, many of them about
love, in which she created a striking literary personality—dashing, unconventional,
eager for experience, haunted by the brevity of life. In a poem such as "Recuerdo"
the very fact that an experience has passed seems to be one of its chief values, for it
encourages a mood of tender, rueful nostalgia. Edna Millay obviously became dissatisfied with this personality, and in her late poems she found other subjects. That
which seems most to have stirred her imagination is the inevitability of her own
death.

Edna St. Vincent Millay was born on February 22, 1892, in Rockland, Maine. Her
parents were divorced when she was a child, and her mother encouraged her literary
interests. Her first important poem, "Renascence," was published in *The Lyric Year*
in 1912; it is an account of ecstatic self-discovery, full of echoes of Keats and Wordsworth:

> And as I looked a quickening gust
> Of wind blew up to me and thrust
> Into my face a miracle
> Of orchard-breath, and with the smell,—
> I know not how such things can be!—
> I breathed my soul back into me.

She studied for a short time at Barnard, then attended Vassar, where she spent a
good part of her time enjoying the role of the young poet and baiting the college
authorities. When she dared the president to expel her, he explained that he didn't
want a "banished Shelley on my doorstep," and she is supposed to have replied, "On
those terms, I think I can continue to live in this hell hole."[1] In 1917, the year of her
Vassar degree, her first book of poems was published. She moved to Greenwich
Village, then a refuge for young people newly liberated from home and school, and
her poems helped to create the legend of an American Bohemia. She joined the

---

1. Miriam Gurko, *Restless Spirit: The Life of Edna St. Vincent Millay*, New York, 1962, p. 58.

Provincetown Players and published three plays in verse. In 1923 she was awarded the Pulitzer Prize for *The Harp-Weaver;* in the same year she married Eugen Boissevain, a Dutch importer, and moved with her husband to a farm in the Berkshires. Through the twenties and thirties she published regularly. Her work included further collections of poems, the libretto for Deems Taylor's opera *The King's Henchman* (1927), and a translation of Baudelaire's *Flowers of Evil* done in collaboration with George Dillon.

She died in 1950 at the age of fifty-eight, and she lived to see her once-great reputation sadly diminished. In the 1940s she had published two books in which she tried to write poetry adequate to the anguish of the Second World War—*Make Bright the Arrows* (1940) and *The Murder of Lidice* (1942). The poems which retain an interest are those in which she keeps alive the traditions of the English lyric and of the disciplined sonnet.

First Fig

My candle burns at both ends;
It will not last the night;
But ah, my foes, and oh, my friends—
It gives a lovely light!

1920

Recuerdo[1]

We were very tired, we were very merry—
We had gone back and forth all night on the ferry.
It was bare and bright, and smelled like a stable—
But we looked into a fire, we leaned across a table,
We lay on a hill-top underneath the moon;   5
And the whistles kept blowing, and the dawn came soon.

We were very tired, we were very merry—
We had gone back and forth all night on the ferry;
And you ate an apple, and I ate a pear,
From a dozen of each we had bought somewhere;   10
And the sky went wan, and the wind came cold,
And the sun rose dripping, a bucketful of gold.

We were very tired, we were very merry,
We had gone back and forth all night on the ferry.
We hailed, "Good morrow, mother!" to a shawl-covered head, 15
And bought a morning paper, which neither of us read;

And she wept, "God bless you!" for the apples and pears,
And we gave her all our money but our subway fares.

1920

[Love Is Not All: It Is Not Meat nor Drink]

Love is not all: it is not meat nor drink
Nor slumber nor a roof against the rain;

---

1. Memory (Spanish).

Nor yet a floating spar to men that sink
And rise and sink and rise and sink again;
Love can not fill the thickened lung with breath,   5
Nor clean the blood, nor set the fractured bone;
Yet many a man is making friends with death
Even as I speak, for lack of love alone.
It well may be that in a difficult hour,
Pinned down by pain and moaning for release,   10
Or nagged by want past resolution's power,
I might be driven to sell your love for peace,
Or trade the memory of this night for food.
It well may be. I do not think I would.

1931

[Oh, Sleep Forever in the Latmian Cave]

Oh, sleep forever in the Latmian cave,
Mortal Endymion, darling of the Moon![2]
Her silver garments by the senseless wave
Shouldered and dropped and on the shingle strewn,
Her fluttering hand against her forehead pressed,   5
Her scattered looks that trouble all the sky,
Her rapid footsteps running down the west—
Of all her altered state, oblivious lie!
Whom earthen you, by deathless lips adored,
Wild-eyed and stammering to the grasses thrust,   10
And deep into her crystal body poured
The hot and sorrowful sweetness of the dust:
Whereof she wanders mad, being all unfit
For mortal love, that might not die of it.

1931

To a Calvinist in Bali

You that are sprung of northern stock,
And nothing lavish,—born and bred
With tablets at your foot and head,
And CULPA[3] carven in the rock,

Sense with delight but not with ease   5
The fragrance of the quinine trees,
The *kembang-spatu's*[4] lolling flame
With solemn envy kin to shame.

Ah, be content!—the scorpion's tail
Atones for much; without avail   10
Under the sizzling solar pan
Our sleeping servant pulls the fan.

2. Endymion was a beautiful youth who fell
asleep in a cave on Mount Latmos and was visited
by Selene, goddess of the moon. Zeus, the ruler
of the gods, allowed the delighted youth to sleep
there forever.
3. Guilt, fault.
4. A tropical flower.

Even in this island richly blest,
Where Beauty walks with naked breast,
Earth is too harsh for Heaven to be   15
One little hour in jeopardy.

1939

WILFRED OWEN
1893–1918

The subject of war has always been a favorite of poets, but the pity—as distinguished from the heroism—of war is a modern subject. "The Poetry is in the pity," Wilfred Owen wrote in the preface to a book of verse he did not live to see published. Yeats, who regarded pity as an unsatisfactory theme, was not impressed by Owen's verse, which he dismissed as "all blood, dirt & sucked sugar stick." Yet blood, dirt, and sugar are not by nature impossible ingredients. If Owen preserves his youthful romanticism, or at least a shell of it, he uses it to countervail the horrifying scenes he describes, just as he poses his own youth against the age-old spectacle of men dying in pain and futility. In a letter of February 4, 1917, he speaks of "Hideous landscapes, vile noises, foul language . . . everything unnatural, broken, blasted; the distortion of the dead, whose unburiable bodies sit outside the dug-outs all day, all night, the most execrable sights on earth. In poetry we call them the most glorious."[1] In verse, such contrasts are made tense by lines like, "Red lips are not so red / As the stained stones kissed by the English dead." The half-rhymes which Owen discovered for his verse seem to be a reflection, in terms of technique, of the displacement of the old relationships that held together grandeur and patriotic sacrifice.

Owen was born at Oswestry, England, on March 18, 1893. His father had a modest job with the railway, and the family's limited means had their effect on Owen's life. His mother was strict and Calvinistic, but remained closely bound to her son even when, in a letter he wrote her on January 4, 1913, he melodramatically announced, "I have murdered my false creed."[2] She sympathized with his poetic ambition, which began when at the age of about ten she took him for a holiday to Broxton by the Hill. It was there, he wrote her, "I felt my boyhood fill / With uncontainable movements; there was born / My poethood." Owen attended Birkenhead Institute from 1900 to 1907, then Shrewsbury Technical School. He did some work at University College, Reading, in botany, but then matriculated at the University of London. Unfortunately there was no money for fees, so he had to withdraw. He then went to Dunsden, Oxfordshire, as a pupil and lay assistant to the vicar.

At first the notion was that he should take orders, but Owen developed sympathy for the sufferings of the parishioners without a compatible confidence in Christianity's power to relieve them. As a result of his disaffection, he left this post in August 1913 and went to teach at the Berlitz school in Bordeaux. He stayed in the city for two years, the second as tutor for two boys. The coming of war made him restive at "this deflowering of Europe," as he called it.[3] So he returned to England in August or September 1915 in order to enlist. He was trained and then commissioned in the Manchester Regiment, which went to the western front in January 1917. The weather was extremely cold, the fighting was fierce. In June Owen became ill and had to be moved to a hospital and then sent back to England to recuperate. Moved again, to a hospital in Edinburgh, he had the pleasure of meeting Siegfried Sassoon, an army captain and already known as a war poet. "I was always a mad comet; but you have

1. *The Collected Poems of Wilfred Owen*, ed.
C. Day Lewis, London, 1963, p. 22.

2. The same, p. 17.
3. The same, p. 19.

' he wrote to Sassoon in November.[4] Sassoon encouraged him to write
ns, and introduced him to other writers. He also optimistically assured
the time came for Owen to return to the front, that his new experiences
⸳⸳⸳ ᵤₑᵢₚ his poetry. Owen went back to France on August 31, 1918, and was killed
a week before the Armistice, on November 4. His poems were published posthumously by Sassoon in 1920.

Most of Owen's best poems were written during a period of thirteen months, from
August 1917 to September 1918. He felt a burst of energy and confidence during this
time. They are astringent rather than sentimental; they are not patriotic, they are
not self-deceptive, they express community with the intensity of a lover and the
accuracy of an honest man.

The source of our Owen texts is *The Poems of Wilfred Owen*, edited by Jon Stallworthy, New York, 1986.

4. The same, p. 171.

Anthem for Doomed Youth

What passing-bells for these who die as cattle?[1]
　　—Only the monstrous anger of the guns.
　　Only the stuttering rifles' rapid rattle
Can patter out their hasty orisons.[2]
No mockeries now for them; no prayers nor bells;　　　　　　5
　　Nor any voice of mourning save the choirs,—
The shrill, demented choirs of wailing shells;
　　And bugles calling for them from sad shires.[3]

What candles may be held to speed them all?
　　Not in the hands of boys but in their eyes
Shall shine the holy glimmers of goodbyes.
　　The pallor of girls' brows shall be their pall;
Their flowers the tenderness of patient minds,
And each slow dusk a drawing-down of blinds.
September–October 1917　　　　　　　　　　　　　　　　　　1920

Dulce et Decorum Est[4]

Bent double, like old beggars under sacks,
Knock-kneed, coughing like hags, we cursed through sludge,
Till on the haunting flares we turned our backs
And towards our distant rest began to trudge.
Men marched asleep. Many had lost their boots　　　　　　5
But limped on, blood-shod. All went lame; all blind;
Drunk with fatigue; deaf even to the hoots
Of tired, outstripped Five-Nines[5] that dropped behind.

1. Owen may have been responding to the Prefatory Note to *Poems of Today: An Anthology*
(1916): "This book has been compiled in order that
boys and girls, already perhaps familiar with the
great classics of the English speech, may also know
something of the newer poetry of their own day.
Most of the writers are living, and the rest are still
vivid memories among us, while one of the youngest, almost as these words are written, has gone
singing to lay down his life for his country's cause.
. . . there is no arbitrary isolation of one theme
from another; they mingle and interpenetrate
throughout, to the music of Pan's flute, and of

Love's viol, and the bugle-call of Endeavour, and
the passing-bells of Death." (For this and other
footnotes to Wilfred Owen, we are indebted to Jon
Stallworthy, ed., *The Poems of Wilfred Owen*, New
York, 1986.)
2. Prayers.
3. Counties.
4. "The famous Latin tag [from Horace, *Odes*
3.2.13] means, of course, *It is sweet and meet to
die for one's country. Sweet!* and *decorous!*" (letter from Owen to his mother, October 16, 1917).
5. That is, 5.9-inch caliber shells.

Gas! GAS! Quick, boys!—An ecstasy of fumbling,
Fitting the clumsy helmets just in time;   10
But someone still was yelling out and stumbling,
And flound'ring like a man in fire or lime . . .
Dim, through the misty panes[6] and thick green light,
As under a green sea, I saw him drowning.

In all my dreams, before my helpless sight,   15
He plunges at me, guttering, choking, drowning.

If in some smothering dreams you too could pace
Behind the wagon that we flung him in,
And watch the white eyes writhing in his face,
His hanging face, like a devil's sick of sin;   20
If you could hear, at every jolt, the blood
Come gargling from the froth-corrupted lungs,
Obscene as cancer, bitter as the cud
Of vile, incurable sores on innocent tongues,—
My friend,[7] you would not tell with such high zest   25
To children ardent for some desperate glory,
The old Lie: Dulce et decorum est
Pro patria mori.
October 1917   1920

[margin annotation: shift in tense to now]

Strange Meeting

It seemed that out of battle I escaped
Down some profound dull tunnel, long since scooped
Through granites which titanic wars had groined.

Yet also there encumbered sleepers groaned,
Too fast in thought or death to be bestirred.   5
Then, as I probed them, one sprang up, and stared
With piteous recognition in fixed eyes,
Lifting distressful hands, as if to bless.
And by his smile, I knew that sullen hall,—
By his dead smile I knew we stood in Hell.   10

With a thousand pains that vision's face was grained;
Yet no blood reached there from the upper ground,
And no guns thumped, or down the flues made moan.
"Strange friend," I said, "here is no cause to mourn."
"None," said the other, "save the undone years,   15
The hopelessness. Whatever hope is yours,
Was my life also; I went hunting wild
After the wildest beauty in the world,
Which lies not calm in eyes, or braided hair,
But mocks the steady running of the hour,   20
And if it grieves, grieves richlier than here.
For by my glee might many men have laughed,

6. Of the gas mask's celluloid window.
7. Jessie Pope, to whom the poem was originally dedicated, was the author of many prewar
children's books, as well as *Jessie Pope's War Poems*
(1915).

And of my weeping something had been left,
Which must die now. I mean the truth untold,
The pity of war, the pity war distilled.[8]   25
Now men will go content with what we spoiled,
Or, discontent, boil bloody, and be spilled.
They will be swift with swiftness of the tigress.
None will break ranks, though nations trek from progress.
Courage was mine, and I had mystery,   30
Wisdom was mine, and I had mastery:
To miss the march of this retreating world
Into vain citadels that are not walled.
Then, when much blood had clogged their chariot-wheels,
I would go up and wash them from sweet wells,   35
Even with truths that lie too deep for taint.
I would have poured my spirit without stint
But not through wounds; not on the cess[9] of war.
Foreheads of men have bled where no wounds were.

"I am the enemy you killed, my friend.   40
I knew you in this dark: for so you frowned
Yesterday through me as you jabbed and killed.
I parried; but my hands were loath and cold.
Let us sleep now. . . ."
January–March 1918   1920

Greater Love[1]

Red lips are not so red
   As the stained stones kissed by the English dead.
Kindness of wooed and wooer
Seems shame to their love pure.
O Love, your eyes lose lure   5
   When I behold eyes blinded in my stead!

Your slender attitude
   Trembles not exquisite like limbs knife-skewed,[2]
Rolling and rolling there
Where God seems not to care;   10
Till the fierce love they bear
   Cramps them in death's extreme decrepitude.

Your voice sings not so soft,—
   Though even as wind murmuring through raftered loft,—
Your dear voice is not dear,   15
Gentle, and evening clear,

8. Owen, at the time of his death, was preparing a volume of poems. A sketch of the Preface read: "This book is not about heroes. English Poetry is not yet fit to speak of them. Nor is it about deeds, or lands, nor anything about glory, honour, might, majesty, dominion, or power, except War. Above all I am not concerned with Poetry. My subject is War, and the pity of War. The Poetry is in the pity. Yet these elegies are to this generation in no sense consolatory. They may be to the next. All a poet can do to-day is warn. That is why the true Poets must be truthful."
9. As in cesspool.
1. "Greater love hath no man than this, that a man lay down his life for his friends" (John 15:13).
2. That is, distorted by (or like?) a knife.

As theirs whom none now hear,
   Now earth has stopped their piteous mouths that coughed.

Heart, you were never hot
   Nor large, nor full like hearts made great with shot;   20
And though your hand be pale,
Paler are all which trail[3]
Your cross through flame and hail:
   Weep, you may weep, for you may touch them not.[4]
October–November 1917   1920

Disabled

He sat in a wheeled chair, waiting for dark,
And shivered in his ghastly suit of grey,
Legless, sewn short at elbow. Through the park
Voices of boys rang saddening like a hymn,
Voices of play and pleasure after day,   5
Till gathering sleep had mothered them from him.

• • •

About this time Town used to swing so gay
When glow-lamps budded in the light blue trees,
And girls glanced lovelier as the air grew dim,—
In the old times, before he threw away his knees.   10
Now he will never feel again how slim
Girls' waists are, or how warm their subtle hands.
All of them touch him like some queer disease.

• • •

There was an artist silly for his face,
For it was younger than his youth, last year.   15
Now, he is old; his back will never brace;
He's lost his colour very far from here,
Poured it down shell-holes till the veins ran dry,
And half his lifetime lapsed in the hot race
And leap of purple spurted from his thigh.   20

• • •

One time he liked a blood-smear down his leg,
After the matches, carried shoulder-high.[5]
It was after football, when he'd drunk a peg,[6]
He thought he'd better join.—He wonders why.
Someone had said he'd look a god in kilts,   25
That's why; and maybe, too, to please his Meg,
Aye, that was it, to please the giddy jilts[7]
He asked to join. He didn't have to beg;

3. In the military sense of "trail arms": that is, carry a rifle with the butt end near the ground and the muzzle pointing forward.
4. "Jesus said unto [Mary Magdelene], Woman, why weepest thou? . . . Jesus saith unto her, Touch me not; for I am not yet ascended to my Father" (John 21:15–17).

5. Compare A. E. Housman's "To an Athlete Dying Young," lines 1–4: "The time you won your town the race / We chaired you through the market-place; / Man and boy stood cheering by, / And home we brought you shoulder-high."
6. Brandy and soda (slang).
7. Capricious girls.

Smiling they wrote his lie: aged nineteen years.[8]
Germans he scarcely thought of; all their guilt,   30
And Austria's, did not move him. And no fears
Of Fear came yet. He thought of jewelled hilts
For daggers in plaid socks;[9] of smart salutes;
And care of arms; and leave; and pay arrears;
Esprit de corps;[1] and hints for young recruits.   35
And soon, he was drafted out with drums and cheers.

· · ·

Some cheered him home, but not as crowds cheer Goal.
Only a solemn man who brought him fruits
Thanked him; and then enquired about his soul.

· · ·

Now, he will spend a few sick years in institutes,   40
And do what things the rules consider wise,
And take whatever pity they may dole.
Tonight he noticed how the women's eyes
Passed from him to the strong men that were whole.
How cold and late it is! Why don't they come
And put him into bed? why don't they come?[2]
October 1917; July 1918   1920

8. That is, the recruiting officers entered on his enlistment form his lie that he was nineteen years old, the age to enter the army.
9. Kilted Scottish Highlanders used to carry small ornamental daggers *(skene-dhus)* thrust into the top of a stocking.
1. Esteem for the honor and spirit of an organization—here, the army; "pay arrears": back pay.
2. "Dominic Hibberd calls attention to 'a mocking echo of the slogan on a recruiting poster, probably put out in 1914, which shows soldiers in action and in need of reinforcements. The slogan reads, "Will they never come?". . . . The parallel in this poem between playing football and serving in the Army reflects the recruiting drives that had been made at football matches earlier in the war. The Imperial War Museum preserves the following rather amateur poster: "Men and Millwall / Hundreds of Football enthusiasts / are joining the Army daily. / Don't be left behind. / Let the Enemy hear the 'LION'S ROAR'. Join and be in at THE FINAL / and give them a / KICK OFF THE EARTH".' ('Some Contemporary Allusions in Poems by Rosenberg, Owen and Sassoon', N&Q, n.s. xxvi, no. 4 [August 1979], 333)." Quoted in Stallworthy, p. 154.

E. E. CUMMINGS
1894–1962

Cummings is one of the most innovative of modern poets, but it is innovation on a different level from that of Yeats or Stevens. In some ways he is oddly traditional. Though he drops most punctuation and capitalization, and deliberately distorts syntax, he is fond of the sonnet and other regular forms; he likes rhymes and off-rhymes in a way that the innovators of half a century later would find almost reprehensible. Though Cummings alters parts of speech and makes verbs into nouns and nouns into verbs, he does so chiefly to express feelings whose simplicity belies all this complication.

   Edward Estlin Cummings was born in Cambridge, Massachusetts, on October 14, 1894. He was the son of a Unitarian minister who preached in Boston at the South Congregational Church and also taught sociology at Harvard. Cummings took a B.A. degree at Harvard in 1915 and an M.A. in 1916. He then volunteered to go to France as a member of the Norton Harjes Ambulance Corps. A French censor, his suspicions roused by letters written by a fellow volunteer whom Cummings had befriended, caused the poet and his companion to be interned for three months in a concentration camp. Cummings commemorated this experience in the semi-fictional work, *The Enormous Room* (1922), where he celebrates the courageous idiosyncrasies that persisted among the prisoners even in this spirit-destroying situation.

After the war Cummings lived in Paris and took up painting as well as writing. The title of his first book of poems, *Tulips and Chimneys* (1923), suggests the opposition that was to become lifelong in his work, between organic life and what he calls "manunkind" (in the poem, "pity this busy monster,manunkind / not"), or between what he praises in his father—"immeasurable is"—as contrasted with rulebound negation.

Part of Cummings's attack on the establishment was directed against the typographical establishment. He used punctuation only for special effects, and many of his poems exploited odd typographical arrangements, allowing letters of words to trail over from one line to the next in total indifference to syllables. Readers were at first antagonized but eventually gave their assent to this strange panoply. By persisting in his folly, as Blake urged, Cummings won acceptance for it as a kind of wisdom. It became clear that the arrangement of a poem on a page reflected the way it was to be read aloud, roused tensions and effected resolutions, offered an intriguing puzzle, and gave vent to Cummings's iconoclasm. It is in fact the badge which he wears as a self-styled misfit, one still capable of feeling love and lust in an unfeeling, mechanized world. He is in revolt against people in high places, in crowded cities, in ruts, to whom the only pronoun that he considers applicable is "it." One poem begins, "a salesman is an it that stinks Excuse me."

He is set firmly against any form of abstraction. "Knowledge is a polite word for dead but not buried imagination . . . think twice before you think." He is against expressions like "most people," which he runs into one word: "it's no use trying to pretend that mostpeople and ourselves are alike. Mostpeople have less in common with ourselves than the squarerootofminusone. You and I are human beings; mostpeople are snobs. . . . Life,for mostpeople, simply isn't."[1]

Cummings denounces "the cambridge ladies who live in furnished souls" that don't belong to them; the philosophers, scientists, and religious zealots who try to ruin the natural instinctive world by putting unnatural shackles on it; the flagwavers, who keep saying they love America and mean only the "Land of the Cluett Shirt, Boston Garter and Spearmint Girl with the Wrigley eyes." Then there are the artists who write by formula. There are the supposedly wholesome young men ready to die for God, for country, and for Yale, suffering from venereal disease of mind as well as body. There are the warmongers who find the best of reasons for preventing other people from living, and regard freedom as a commodity like a breakfast food. All these live, in short, in negative worlds, full of prohibitions, taboos, manunkindness. It is against them that Cummings shoots his arrows.

Then there are the poor whom he befriends. These range from the man who had fallen among thieves to Olaf the conscientious objector to Buffalo Bill to Cummings's father to every lover. These people have certain things in common: they exist—"is" is their first big word; they love, and love is their second big word; they are spontaneous; they are childlike; and they are themselves.

Cummings's verse did not mature—how could it when maturity was an evil?—but it was sustained at a steadily high level throughout his life as he built up endless variations out of a limited group of ideas. His poems were either lyrical or satirical, and were good in both modes. If his love poems are not the best of his time, they are the most winning, written with a childlike wonder and humor which Cummings has almost to himself in modern poetry, and which he retained into old age. His satirical poems are witty as well as savage. "Only so long as we can laugh at ourselves are we nobody else," he wrote. On the other hand, there is a faint pre-Raphaelite glow about Cummings's unexpected combinations of archaic attitudes in spite of the modern

---

1. Introduction to *Collected Poems 1938*.

diction in which they are couched. He seems in his time to be a triumphant anachronism.

In his last years Cummings was asked to deliver the Charles Eliot Norton lectures at Harvard, and agreed on condition that his lectures should be nonlectures. They appeared under the title *Six Nonlectures* in 1953, and resume that blend of wayward bohemianism and noble intransigence which marks all his work. He died in Conway, New Hampshire, in 1962.

[All in green went my love riding]

All in green went my love riding
on a great horse of gold
into the silver dawn.

four lean hounds crouched low and smiling
the merry deer ran before.   5

Fleeter be they than dappled dreams
the swift sweet deer
the red rare deer.

Four red roebuck at a white water
the cruel bugle sang before.   10

Horn at hip went my love riding
riding the echo down
into the silver dawn.

four lean hounds crouched low and smiling
the level meadows ran before.   15

Softer be they than slippered sleep
the lean lithe deer
the fleet flown deer.

Four fleet does at a gold valley
the famished arrow sang before.   20

Bow at belt went my love riding
riding the mountain down
into the silver dawn.

four lean hounds crouched low and smiling
the sheer peaks ran before.   25

Paler be they than daunting death
the sleek slim deer
the tall tense deer.

Four tall stags at a green mountain
the lucky hunter sang before.   30

All in green went my love riding
on a great horse of gold
into the silver dawn.

four lean hounds crouched low and smiling
my heart fell dead before.   35
                                                              1923

[O sweet spontaneous]

O sweet spontaneous
earth how often have
the
doting

      fingers of   5
prurient philosophers pinched
and
poked

thee
,has the naughty thumb   10
of science prodded
thy

   beauty   .how
often have religions taken
thee upon their scraggy knees   15
squeezing and

buffeting thee that thou mightest conceive
gods
       (but   20
true

to the incomparable
couch of death thy
rhythmic
lover

    thou answerest   25

them only with

    spring)
                                                              1923

[the Cambridge ladies who live in furnished souls]

the Cambridge ladies who live in furnished souls
are unbeautiful and have comfortable minds
(also, with the church's protestant blessings

daughters,unscented shapeless spirited)
they believe in Christ and Longfellow,both dead,   5
are invariably interested in so many things—
at the present writing one still finds
delighted fingers knitting for the is it Poles?
perhaps. While permanent faces coyly bandy
scandal of Mrs. N and Professor D   10
. . . . the Cambridge ladies do not care, above
Cambridge if sometimes in its box of
sky lavender and cornerless,the
moon rattles like a fragment of angry candy

1923

[a man who had fallen among thieves[1]]

a man who had fallen among thieves
lay by the roadside on his back
dressed in fifteenthrate ideas
wearing a round jeer for a hat

fate per a somewhat more than less   5
emancipated evening
had in return for consciousness
endowed him with a changeless grin

whereon a dozen staunch and leal[2]
citizens did graze at pause   10
then fired by hypercivic zeal
sought newer pastures or because

swaddled with a frozen brook
of pinkest vomit out of eyes
which noticed nobody he looked   15
as if he did not care to rise

one hand did nothing on the vest
its wideflung friend clenched weakly dirt
while the mute trouserfly confessed
a button solemnly inert.   20

Brushing from whom the stiffened puke
i put him all into my arms
and staggered banged with terror through
a million billion trillion stars

1926

[i sing of Olaf glad and big]

i sing of Olaf glad and big
whose warmest heart recoiled at war:
a conscientious object-or

---

1. A modern version of Christ's parable of the   2. Loyal.
Good Samaritan (Luke 10:30–37).

his wellbelovéd colonel(trig³
westpointer most succinctly bred)   5
took erring Olaf soon in hand;
but—though an host of overjoyed
noncoms(first knocking on the head
him)do through icy waters roll
that helplessness which others stroke   10
with brushes recently employed
anent this muddy toiletbowl,
while kindred intellects evoke
allegiance per blunt instruments—
Olaf(being to all intents   15
a corpse and wanting any rag
upon what God unto him gave)
responds, without getting annoyed
"I will not kiss your f.ing flag"

straightway the silver bird⁴ looked grave   20
(departing hurriedly to shave)

but—though all kinds of officers
(a yearning nation's blueeyed pride)
their passive prey did kick and curse
until for wear their clarion   25
voices and boots were much the worse,
and egged the firstclassprivates on
his rectum wickedly to tease
by means of skilfully applied
bayonets roasted hot with heat—   30
Olaf(upon what were once knees)
does almost ceaselessly repeat
"there is some s. I will not eat"

our president,being of which
assertions duly notified   35
threw the yellowsonofabitch
into a dungeon, where he died

Christ(of His mercy infinite)
i pray to see; and Olaf,too

preponderatingly because   40
unless statistics lie he was
more brave than me:more blond than you.

1931

[the way to hump a cow is not]

the way to hump a cow is not
to get yourself a stool
but draw a line around the spot
and call it beautifool

---

3. Primly neat.   4. The insignia of an Army colonel.

to multiply because and why   5
dividing thens by nows
and adding and(i understand)
is hows to hump a cows

the way to hump a cow is not
to elevate your tool   10
but drop a penny in the slot
and bellow like a bool

to lay a wreath from ancient greath
on insulated brows
(while tossing boms at uncle toms)   15
is hows to hump a cows

the way to hump a cow is not
to push and then to pull
but practicing the art of swot
to preach the golden rull   20

to vote for me(all decent mem
and wonens will allows
which if they don't to hell with them)
is hows to hump a cows

1940

[my father moved through dooms of love]

my father[5] moved through dooms of love
through sames of am through haves of give,
singing each morning out of each night
my father moved through depths of height

this motionless forgetful where   5
turned at his glance to shining here;
that if(so timid air is firm)
under his eyes would stir and squirm

newly as from unburied which
floats the first who,his april touch   10

5. Rev. Edward Cummings, a Unitarian minister in Boston. His son described him in this way: "He was a New Hampshire man, 6 foot 2, and crack shot & a famous fly-fisherman & a firstrate sailor (his sloop was named The Actress) & a woodsman who could find his way through forests primeval without a compass & a canoist who'd still paddle you up to a deer without ruffling the surface of a pond & an ornithologist & taxidermist & (when he gave up hunting) an expert photographer (the best I've ever seen) & an actor who portrayed Julius Caesar in Sanders Theatre & a painter (both in oils & watercolors) & a better carpenter than any professional & an architect who designed his own houses before building them & (when he liked) a plumber who just for the fun of it installed all his own waterworks & (while at Harvard) a teacher with small use for professors—by whom (Royce, Lanman, Taussig, etc.) we were literally surrounded (but not defeated)—& later (at Doctor Hale's socalled South Congregational really Unitarian church) a preacher who announced, during the last war, that the Gott Mit Uns [God with us] boys were in error since the only thing which mattered was for man to be on God's side (& one beautiful Sunday in Spring remarked from the pulpit that he couldn't understand why anyone had come to hear him on such a day) & horribly shocked his pewholders by crying 'the Kingdom of Heaven is no spiritual roofgarden: it's inside you' " (quoted by Charles Norman, *E. E. Cummings*, New York, 1967, pp. 12–13).

drove sleeping selves to swarm their fates
woke dreamers to their ghostly roots

and should some why completely weep
my father's fingers brought her sleep:
vainly no smallest voice might cry   15
for he could feel the mountains grow.

Lifting the valleys of the sea
my father moved through griefs of joy;
praising a forehead called the moon
singing desire into begin   20

joy was his song and joy so pure
a heart of star by him could steer
and pure so now and now so yes
the wrists of twilight would rejoice

keen as midsummer's keen beyond   25
conceiving mind of sun will stand,
so strictly(over utmost him
so hugely)stood my father's dream

his flesh was flesh his blood was blood:
no hungry man but wished him food;   30
no cripple wouldn't creep one mile
uphill to only see him smile.

Scorning the pomp of must and shall
my father moved through dooms of feel;
his anger was as right as rain   35
his pity was as green as grain

septembering arms of year extend
less humbly wealth to foe and friend
than he to foolish and to wise
offered immeasurable is   40

proudly and(by octobering flame
beckoned)as earth will downward climb,
so naked for immortal work
his shoulders marched against the dark

his sorrow was as true as bread: 45
no liar looked him in the head;
if every friend became his foe
he'd laugh and build a world with snow.

My father moved through theys of we,
singing each new leaf out of each tree   50
(and every child was sure that spring
danced when she heard my father sing)

then let men kill which cannot share,
let blood and flesh be mud and mire,

scheming imagine,passion willed,   55
freedom a drug that's bought and sold

giving to steal and cruel kind,
a heart to fear,to doubt a mind,
to differ a disease of same,
conform the pinnacle of am   60

though dull were all we taste as bright,
bitter all utterly things sweet,
maggoty minus and dumb death
all we inherit,all bequeath

and nothing quite so least as truth   65
—i say though hate were why men breathe—
because my father lived his soul
love is the whole and more than all

                                                                            1940

[plato told]

plato told

him:he couldn't
believe it(jesus

told him;he
wouldn't believe   5
it)lao

tsze[6]
certainly told
him,and general
(yes   10

mam)
sherman;[7]
and even
(believe it
or   15

not)you
told him:i told
him;we told him
(he didn't believe it,no

sir)it took   20
a nipponized bit of
the old sixth

6. Lao Tse, the ancient Chinese philosopher and originator of the doctrine of Taoism.
7. William Tecumseh Sherman (1820–1891), Union general in the Civil War, who is reported to have told a military academy's graduating class that "War is hell."

avenue
el;in the top of his head:to tell

him[8]

25
1944

[maggie and milly and molly and may]

maggie and milly and molly and may
went down to the beach(to play one day)

and maggie discovered a shell that sang
so sweetly she couldn't remember her troubles,and

milly befriended a stranded star   5
whose rays five languid fingers were;

and molly was chased by a horrible thing
which raced sideways while blowing bubbles:and

may came home with a smooth round stone
as small as a world and as large as alone.   10

For whatever we lose(like a you or a me)
it's always ourselves we find in the sea

1958

[now comes the good rain farmers pray for(and]

now comes the good rain farmers pray for(and
no sharp shrill shower bouncing up off
burned earth but a blind blissfully seething
gift wandering deeply through godthanking ground)

bluest whos of this snowy head we call   5
old frank go bluer still as(shifting his life
from which to which)he reaches the barn's immense
doorway and halts propped on a pitchfork(breathing)

lovers like rej and lena smile(while looming
darkly a kindness of fragrance opens around   10
them)and whisper their joy under entirely the coming
quitenotimaginable silenceofsound

(here is that rain awaited by leaves with all
their trees and by forests with all their mountains)

1958

8. A scandal of the late thirties arose over the sale to Japan of scrap metal obtained when the elevated railway over New York's Sixth Avenue was pulled down; it was made into weapons and ammunition which were subsequently used against American forces in the Second World War.

[out of midsummer's blazing most not night]

out of midsummer's blazing most not night
as floats a more than day whose sun is moon,
and our(from inexistence moving)sweet
earth puts on immortality again

—her murdered selves exchanging swiftly for   5
the deathlessness who's beauty:reoccurs
so magically, farthest becomes near
(one silent pasture,all a heartbeat dares;

that mountain,any god)while leaf twig limb
ask every question time can't answer:and   10
such vivid nothing as green meteors swim
signals all some world's millionary[9] mind

never may partly guess—thus,my love,to
merely what dying must call life are you

                                                              1963

9. Having a million (or millions of) dollars.

ROBERT GRAVES
1895–1985

Though Robert Graves claimed that he wrote them only for himself and his muse, his poems do not present the immediate difficulties of much modern poetry; they are not private or eccentric. Graves and his muse demanded a traditionally formed poetry which is intelligible to those who overhear it—craftsmanlike, lucid, orderly, and often companionable in tone. He distinguished between the poetry he wrote for himself and the prose by which he earned his bread and butter; yet the poetry shared with the prose an encouraging civility. Graves chided many of his contemporaries— Yeats, Pound, and Eliot among them—for their slovenliness, their failure to finish the poems they started, and their literary bad manners. Yet his own frequent epigrammatic tidiness did not preclude an allegiance to the irrational and the mythic; like Blake and Yeats, he pieced together his own mythology and proclaimed it the grand original of all true poetry.

Graves's great autobiography *Goodbye to All That* was an account of his life up to 1929. He was born on July 26, 1895, at Wimbledon, near London. His father, Alfred Perceval Graves, was Irish and himself a poet; his mother was German and related to the historian von Ranke. He went to a succession of preparatory schools, where he learned to "keep a straight bat at cricket, and to have a high moral sense."[1] His public school was Charterhouse; Graves found it conventional, hypocritical, and anti-intellectual. He left school a week before the outbreak of the war in 1914 and joined the Royal Welch Fusiliers as an officer, went to France soon after, and saw a good deal of action. Of Graves's school generation one in three died in the war, and on his twenty-first birthday he was himself reported killed in action. Graves's autobiography does not offer a facile contrast between pastoral school days and wartime hell. He finds, of course, a contradiction between the world for which he had been pre-

1. *Goodbye to All That,* Harmondsworth (Sussex), 1971, p. 25.

pared and the horrors of the war. Yet for Graves there are important continuities of experience; the bloody-minded staff officers, for example, were only an exaggeration of schoolmasterly indifference. Though Graves was disgusted with both the officer caste and the civilians, his father among them, who enjoyed the war from a safe distance, he maintained respect for bravery and soldierly values. He became friends with the poet Siegfried Sassoon, and when the latter made a public declaration of his disgust with the pointless fighting, Graves, unknown to Sassoon, connived at his being sent to a mental hospital as an alternative to a probable court-martial and prison sentence.

After the Armistice, Graves studied at Oxford. He was a friend of the psychiatrist W. H. R. Rivers, who had treated Sassoon and Wilfred Owen. Rivers helped his patients through a study of their dream-life, and he led Graves to a psychiatrically based theory of poetry, according to which the poet gives therapeutic expression to unacknowledged internal conflicts. An anthology of poetry is thus a collection of homeopathic medicines; each poet expresses his own neurosis and helps a similarly afflicted reader.

By the late twenties Graves had reached a dead end. He was rescued from his poetic irresolution by his collaboration with the American poet Laura Riding. Graves and Riding left England for Majorca, where apart from wartime absences he continued to live until his death on December 8, 1985. Clearly he found his meeting with Laura Riding a moment of renewal, for his views of poetry changed; poetry, as he now saw it, does not emerge from the poet's subconscious, but the poet discovers a reality beyond himself or herself, a reality which can be opened only by poetry.

Robert Graves had an extraordinarily varied literary career: apart from his poetry, he was a scholar and a mythographer, a literary theorist far more influential than has been realized, a writer of occasional essays and travel books, a translator, a dramatist. Between 1925 and 1957 he wrote fifteen novels, most of them historical. Graves's recreations of the past followed a hint given in his little poem "The Persian Version": here he reminds us that the winners usually write the official version of a battle and that the losers will have different memories. As an historical novelist, he sought to give the "Persian version" of a number of events and figures. For example, the Emperor Claudius has been written off by most historians as a clumsy incompetent, but in *I, Claudius* (1934) and *Claudius the God* (1934) Graves suggested that the historians were duped by a clever man who pretended to be a fool.

It was while doing the research for one of his novels—*Hercules, My Shipmate*—that Graves happened on the trail of evidence which led eventually to a reconstruction of the matriarchal religions of the Neolithic and the Bronze Age. In 1948 he completed his "historical grammar of poetic myth," *The White Goddess*. (He published a revised and enlarged edition in 1952.) In this book Graves gives simultaneously a version of history (he maintains that the Hebrews and Greeks perverted an actual matriarchal society), a view of the personality (the life of an individual man recapitulates the events of the myth), and an account of poetic creation (all true poets worship the same muse). Graves's White Goddess has three aspects: she is the mother who bears man, the beloved woman whom man adores, and the old crone who survives him. The White Goddess frequently recalls the fatal woman of the Romantic poets—the female figure in Blake's "Mental Traveller," the ghastly Death-in-Life of Coleridge's "Rime of the Ancient Mariner," Keats's "La Belle Dame Sans Merci"— but Graves went far beyond these relatively familiar adumbrations of the goddess and tracked her through a whole library of books. In advancing his thesis Graves was almost always urbane, and most readers—apart from specialists, who are quite properly outraged by Graves's speculative foolhardiness—value the book, both for the light it casts on some of Graves's most beautiful poems (especially "To Juan at the Winter Solstice"), and also as a thesaurus of poetic motifs. In later life Graves took note of a Black Goddess behind the White Goddess, and beyond physical passion.

In terms of Graves's poetic theory, *The White Goddess* proclaims his allegiance to objectivity and externality. The early Graves thought of poetry as an expression of unanalyzed interior conflicts; the later Graves saw it as a celebration of a mythic pattern beyond the poet, existing independently of him. Yet as in all such journeys there is probably an ultimate identification between a journey beyond the self and a journey into the depths of the self.

The Cool Web

Children are dumb to say how hot the day is,
How hot the scent is of the summer rose,
How dreadful the black wastes of evening sky,
How dreadful the tall soldiers drumming by.

But we have speech, to chill the angry day,   5
And speech, to dull the rose's cruel scent.
We spell away the overhanging night,
We spell away the soldiers and the fright.

There's a cool web of language winds us in,
Retreat from too much joy or too much fear: 10
We grow sea-green at last and coldly die
In brininess and volubility.

But if we let our tongues lose self-possession,
Throwing off language and its watery clasp
Before our death, instead of when death comes,   15
Facing the wide glare of the children's day,
Facing the rose, the dark sky and the drums,
We shall go mad no doubt and die that way.

                                                          1927

Ogres and Pygmies

Those famous men of old, the Ogres—
They had long beards and stinking arm-pits,
They were wide-mouthed, long-yarded and great-bellied
Yet not of taller stature, Sirs, than you.
They lived on Ogre-Strand, which was no place   5
But the churl's terror of their vast extent,
Where every foot was three-and-thirty inches
And every penny bought a whole hog.
Now of their company none survive, not one,
The times being, thank God, unfavourable   10
To all but nightmare shadows of their fame;
Their images stand howling on the hill
(The winds enforced against those wide mouths),
Whose granite haunches country-folk salute
With May Day kisses, and whose knobbed knees.   15
So many feats they did to admiration:
With their enormous throats they sang louder
Than ten cathedral choirs, with their grand yards

Stormed the most rare and obstinate maidenheads,
With their strong-gutted and capacious bellies   20
Digested stones and glass like ostriches.
They dug great pits and heaped huge mounds,
Deflected rivers, wrestled with the bear
And hammered judgements for posterity—
For the sweet-cupid-lipped and tassel-yarded   25
Delicate-stomached dwellers
In Pygmy Alley, where with brooding on them
A foot is shrunk to seven inches
And twelve-pence will not buy a spare rib.
And who would judge between Ogres and Pygmies—   30
The thundering text, the snivelling commentary—
Reading between such covers he will marvel
How his own members bloat and shrink again.

                                                        1931

Ulysses[1]

To the much-tossed Ulysses, never done
    With woman whether gowned as wife or whore,
Penelope and Circe seemed as one:
She like a whore made his lewd fancies run,
    And wifely she a hero to him bore.   5

Their counter-changings terrified his way:
    They were the clashing rocks, Symplegades,
Scylla and Charybdis too were they;
Now they were storms frosting the sea with spray
    And now the lotus island's drunken ease.   10

They multiplied into the Sirens' throng,
    Forewarned by fear of whom he stood bound fast
Hand and foot helpless to the vessel's mast,
Yet would not stop his ears: daring their song
    He groaned and sweated till that shore was past.[2]   15

One, two and many: flesh had made him blind,
    Flesh had one pleasure only in the act,
Flesh set one purpose only in the mind—
Triumph of flesh and afterwards to find
    Still those same terrors wherewith flesh was racked.   20

His wiles were witty and his fame far known,
Every king's daughter[3] sought him for her own,
    Yet he was nothing to be won or lost.

1. The Greek hero of the Trojan War, whose long journey homeward to Ithaca and his faithful wife Penelope is the subject of Homer's *Odyssey*.
2. Circe, the temptress with whom he stayed a year and who changed his companions into swine; Symplegades, the clashing rocks; Scylla and Charybdis, a man-eating monster and a dangerous whirlpool between which Ulysses' ship had to pass; the land of the drugged lotus-eaters; and the Sirens, fabulous creatures whose singing lured men to sail their ships onto the rocks, were hazards which Ulysses successfully negotiated on his voyage.
3. For example Nausicaa, daughter of King Alcinoos of the Phaeacians, in whose court Ulysses recounted his adventures.

All lands to him were Ithaca: love-tossed
He loathed the fraud, yet would not bed alone.   25

                                                                1933

Down, Wanton, Down!

Down, wanton, down! Have you no shame
That at the whisper of Love's name,
Or Beauty's, presto! up you raise
Your angry head and stand at gaze?

Poor bombard-captain,[4] sworn to reach   5
The ravelin[5] and effect a breach—
Indifferent what you storm or why,
So be that in the breach you die![6]

Love may be blind, but Love at least
Knows what is man and what mere beast;   10
Or Beauty wayward, but requires
More delicacy from her squires.

Tell me, my witless, whose one boast
Could be your staunchness at the post,
When were you made a man of parts   15
To think fine and profess the arts?

Will many-gifted Beauty come
Bowing to your bald rule of thumb,
Or Love swear loyalty to your crown?
Be gone, have done! Down, wanton, down!   20

                                                                1933

The Devil's Advice to Story-Tellers

Lest men suspect your tale to be untrue,
Keep probability—some say—in view.
But my advice to story-tellers is:
Weigh out no gross of probabilities,
Nor yet make diligent transcriptions of   5
Known instances of virtue, crime or love.
To forge a picture that will pass for true,
Do conscientiously what liars do—
Born liars, not the lesser sort that raid
The mouths of others for their stock-in-trade: 10
Assemble, first, all casual bits and scraps
That may shake down into a world perhaps;
People this world, by chance created so,
With random persons whom you do not know—
The teashop sort, or travellers in a train   15

---

4. A "bombard" was a large medieval cannon.
5. Fortified projection from a castle wall.
6. A pun on the verb "to die," in the sense of

"to achieve orgasm" (common from the sixteenth
to the eighteenth centuries).

Seen once, guessed idly at, not seen again;
Let the erratic course they steer surprise
Their own and your own and your readers' eyes;
Sigh then, or frown, but leave (as in despair)
Motive and end and moral in the air;   20
Nice contradiction between fact and fact
Will make the whole read human and exact.

1938

To Juan at the Winter Solstice[7]

There is one story and one story only
That will prove worth your telling,
Whether as learned bard or gifted child;[8]
To it all lines or lesser gauds belong
That startle with their shining   5
Such common stories as they stray into.

Is it of trees you tell, their months and virtues,[9]
Or strange beasts[1] that beset you,
Of birds that croak at you the Triple will?[2]
Or of Zodiac and how slow it turns   10
Below the Boreal Crown,
Prison of all true kings that ever reigned?[3]

Water to water, ark again to ark,
From woman back to woman:
So each new victim treads unfalteringly   15
The never altered circuit of his fate,
Bringing twelve peers as witness
Both to his starry rise and starry fall.[4]

7. This poem epitomizes Graves's "historic grammar of poetic myth," *The White Goddess* (1948), an intuitive study of ancient mythologies (especially Greek and Celtic) which finds the only theme for true poetry in the story of the life-cycle of the Sun-God or -Hero, his marriage with the Goddess and inevitable death at her hands or by her command. Juan is Graves's youngest son; he was born on December 21, 1945, one day before the Winter Solstice, which (as it is the time when the sun gives least heat and light to the North) is in many religions the birthday of the Solar Hero. Some of these heroes are Apollo, Dionysus, Zeus, Hermes, and Hercules of Greek mythology; Horus, the Egyptian sun-god; Merlin and King Arthur; and perhaps Jesus Christ, whose life often parallels that of the Solar Hero, and whose mother Mary shares some characteristics of the Goddess.
8. Graves "decoded" the Celtic riddle-poem, "The Battle of the Trees," by the bard Taliesin, who as a "gifted child" outmatched twenty-four experienced court poets; this insight began the series of researches and intuitions which resulted in *The White Goddess*.
9. Besides "The Battle of the Trees" (see note 8 above) Graves also cites an ancient druidic "tree-calendar" which describes the natural and magic properties of various trees and associates each tree with a month or season of the year.

1. For example, the unicorn, the chimera, and the phoenix, some of the fabulous animals associated with the Goddess.
2. The Goddess sometimes speaks through "prophetic" birds, such as the owl, the crane, and the eagle. She was sometimes called the Triple Goddess or Triple Muse because of her threefold aspect as Goddess of the Underworld, the Earth, and the Sky; further, each of these aspects includes three states of an infinite cycle—as Goddess of the Underworld she symbolizes birth, procreation, and death; as Earth-Goddess she is, in turn, Spring, Summer, and Winter; and, perhaps most important, as Goddess of the Sky she is the Moon-Goddess, proceeding through the cycle of New Moon, Full Moon, and Old Moon.
3. "*Boreal Crown* is Corona Borealis, . . . which in Thracean-Libyan mythology, carried to Bronze Age Britain, was the purgatory where Solar Heroes went after death" (Graves's note). The progression or "turning" of the twelve signs of the Zodiac corresponds to the cycle of months.
4. The King (or Solar Hero), reincarnated, reappears at the Winter Solstice floating in an ark on the water. The "twelve peers" may be, for example, the twelve knights of King Arthur's round table, Christ's apostles, or even the twelve Zodiacal constellations (as suggested by line 18).

Or is it of the Virgin's silver beauty,
All fish below the thighs?   20
She in her left hand bears a leafy quince;
When with her right she crooks a finger, smiling,[5]
How may the King hold back?
Royally then he barters life for love.

Or of the undying snake from chaos hatched,   25
Whose coils contain the ocean,
Into whose chops with naked sword he springs,
Then in black water, tangled by the reeds,
Battles three days and nights,
To be spewed up beside her scalloped shore?[6]   30

Much snow is falling, winds roar hollowly,
The owl hoots from the elder,
Fear in your heart cries to the loving-cup:
Sorrow to sorrow as the sparks fly upward.
The log groans and confesses:[7]   35
There is one story and one story only.

Dwell on her graciousness, dwell on her smiling,
Do not forget what flowers
The great boar trampled down in ivy time.[8]
Her brow was creamy as the crested wave,   40
Her sea-blue eyes were wild[9]
But nothiing promised that is not performed.

1945

The Persian Version

Truth-loving Persians do not dwell upon
The trivial skirmish fought near Marathon.[1]
As for the Greek theatrical tradition

5. Two forms of the Goddess are Aphrodite, Greek goddess of love, whose emblem is the quince (the mythical or Biblical "apple," since the modern apple was not then known), and Rahab, the Hebraic sea-goddess who resembled the modern idea of a mermaid.

6. The snake of Ophion, who was created by the Goddess and mated with her: from their egg the world was hatched by the sun's rays. The Sun-King must kill the serpent to win the Goddess; in turn, in October, the serpent (perhaps reincarnated as the boar of line 39) inevitably kills the King.

7. The owl and the elder tree are occult emblems of death. "The *log* is the Yule log, burned at the year's end" (Graves's note).

8. The boar is another symbol of death; Aphrodite's lover Adonis was killed by a boar. Ivy was eaten as an intoxicant by the priestesses of Dionysus in ancient Greece; if their October revels were interrupted by any man, they tore him to pieces.

9. In another version of this poem, "the crested wave" was replaced by "the long ninth wave"; the ninth wave is said to be the whitest. In the poem to *The White Goddess*, Graves gives a fuller description:

Whose broad high brow was white as any leper's,
Whose eyes were blue, with rowanberry lips,
With hair curled honey-coloured to white hips.

This recalls not only Botticelli's famous painting *The Birth of Venus* but some lines from "The Rime of the Ancient Mariner" by Coleridge:

Her lips were red, her looks were free,
Her locks were yellow as gold,
Her skin was white as leprosy,
The Nightmare Life-in-Death was she,
Who thicks man's blood with cold.

1. The decisive battle of the first war between Persia and Greece, in which an Athenian force routed part of the Persian army. Modern historians consider this war far less significant than the second one, in which the allied Greek city-states defeated an enormous Persian army and navy of 400,000 men. "The Greek theatrical tradition" consists mainly of a play about the wars by Aeschylus; no information has survived about the Persian view of the affair.

Which represents that summer's expedition
Not as a mere reconnaissance in force   5
By three brigades of foot and one of horse
(Their left flank covered by some obsolete
Light craft detached from the main Persian fleet)
But as a grandiose, ill-starred attempt
To conquer Greece—they treat it with contempt;   10
And only incidentally refute
Major Greek claims, by stressing what repute
The Persian monarch and the Persian nation
Won by this salutary demonstration:
Despite a strong defence and adverse weather   15
All arms combined magnificently together.

                                                              1945

The Blue-Fly

Five summer days, five summer nights,
The ignorant, loutish, giddy blue-fly
Hung without motion on the cling peach,
Humming occasionally: "O my love, my fair one!"
    As in the *Canticles*.[2]   5

Magnified one thousand times, the insect
Looks farcically human; laugh if you will!
Bald head, stage-fairy wings, blear eyes,
A caved-in chest, hairy black mandibles,
    Long spindly thighs.   10

The crime was detected on the sixth day.
What then could be said or done? By anyone?
It would have been vindictive, mean and what-not
To swat that fly for being a blue-fly,
    For debauch of a peach.   15

Is it fair, either, to bring a microscope
To bear on the case, even in search of truth?
Nature, doubtless, has some compelling cause
To glut the carriers of her epidemics—
    Nor did the peach complain.   20

                                                              1953

2. That is, the Song of Solomon, chapter 2.

LOUISE BOGAN
1897–1970

Louise Bogan was in life a no-nonsense person. Her mocking temperament made
her suspicious of what she called "ego-airing," and in her relationships with friends
as in her verse she sought directness. She was conscious of not having felt this way

in her childhood: "My great gifts of imagination always took the form of lies, in fact, up to my entrance into puberty, when I became a radical . . ."[1] She considered herself thereafter disabused.

It was like her to notice, and to disclose in an essay, how Victorian woman poets celebrated "the virtues of husbands and connubial bliss," while modern woman poets, often shattered by some recent experience, tended "to vilify and belittle masculine charms."[2] Her own poem, "Women," bitterly pretends to specify the qualities women do not have, but really indicates those they possess.

Louise Bogan was born in Livermore Falls, Maine, on August 11, 1897; it was, she said, "ten years before Auden, Isherwood, and L. MacNeice, and about two thousand years after Sappho."[3] She attended a school in Manchester, New Hampshire, and then the Girls' Latin School in Boston, and finished off her education with a year at Boston University. Her emotional life was tortured: from 1931 on, she had a series of nervous breakdowns. For many years, as poetry editor of *The New Yorker*, she set a standard of fair and unflattering criticism, whether the poets discussed were her friends or not.

In a prose book, *Achievement in American Poetry, 1900–1950* (1951), she celebrated the half century for leaving Victorian deadwood behind and opening up "fresh sources of moral, as well as of aesthetic courage," and for dealing with "subconscious and irrational processes."[4] Her own verse exhibited the same features. She died in 1970.

1. *What the Woman Lived: Selected Letters of Louise Bogan, 1920–1970*, ed. Ruth Limmer, 1973, p. 188.
2. The same, p. 126.
3. The same, p. 189.
4. Louise Bogan, *Achievement in American Poetry, 1900–1950*, Chicago, 1951, pp. 8, 10.

Medusa[1]

I had come to the house, in a cave of trees,
Facing a sheer sky.
Everything moved,—a bell hung ready to strike,
Sun and reflection wheeled by.

When the bare eyes were before me   5
And the hissing hair,
Held up at a window, seen through a door.
The stiff bald eyes, the serpents on the forehead
Formed in the air.

This is a dead scene forever now.   10
Nothing will ever stir.
The end will never brighten it more than this,
Nor the rain blur.

The water will always fall, and will not fall,
And the tipped bell make no sound.   15
The grass will always be growing for hay
Deep on the ground.

And I shall stand here like a shadow
Under the great balanced day,

1. One of the three Gorgons, monstrous sisters with hideous faces, glaring eyes, and snakes for hair; their gaze turned mortals to stone (Greek mythology). Medusa ("Queen") was decapitated by Perseus, but her gaze retained its power even in death.

My eyes on the yellow dust, that was lifting in the wind,   20
And does not drift away.

1923

Women

Women have no wilderness in them,
They are provident instead,
Content in the tight hot cell of their hearts
To eat dusty bread.

They do not see cattle cropping red winter grass,   5
They do not hear
Snow water going down under culverts
Shallow and clear.

They wait, when they should turn to journeys,
They stiffen, when they should bend.   10
They use against themselves that benevolence
To which no man is friend.

They cannot think of so many crops to a field
Or of clean wood cleft by an axe.
Their love is an eager meaninglessness   15
Too tense, or too lax.

They hear in every whisper that speaks to them
A shout and a cry.
As like as not, when they take life over their door-sills
They should let it go by.   20

1923

The Dream

O God, in the dream the terrible horse began
To paw at the air, and make for me with his blows.
Fear kept for thirty-five years poured through his mane,
And retribution equally old, or nearly, breathed through his nose.

Coward complete, I lay and wept on the ground   5
When some strong creature appeared, and leapt for the rein.
Another woman, as I lay half in a swound,
Leapt in the air, and clutched at the leather and chain.

Give him, she said, something of yours as a charm.
Throw him, she said, some poor thing you alone claim.   10
No, no, I cried, he hates me; he's out for harm,
And whether I yield or not, it is all the same.

But, like a lion in a legend, when I flung the glove
Pulled from my sweating, my cold right hand,

The terrible beast, that no one may understand,   15
Came to my side, and put down his head in love.

            1941

The Meeting

For years I thought I knew, at the bottom of the dream,
Who spoke but to say farewell,
Whose smile dissolved, after his first words
Gentle and plausible.

Each time I found him, it was always the same: 5
Recognition and surprise,
And then the silence, after the first words,
And the shifting of the eyes.

Then the moment when he had nothing to say
And only smiled again,   10
But this time toward a place beyond me, where I could not stay—
No world of men.

Now I am not sure. Who are you? Who have you been?
Why do our paths cross?
At the deepest bottom of the dream you are let in,   15
A symbol of loss.

Eye to eye we look, and we greet each other
Like friends from the same land.
Bitter compliance! Like a faithless brother
You take and drop my hand.   20

            1968

HART CRANE
1899–1933

A fairly large group of American poets have sought to embrace America. What attracts them is perhaps the fact that the country is so large, sprawling, and hard to handle. This grandiose sensuality goes back to Whitman, who spoke of how "I embrace multitudes." In this century America's chief lovers have been Masters, Sandburg, and Hart Crane. For all of them America has seemed a center of intense, multifarious feelings. Hart Crane had his own complexities, but he overrode them in his effort to distill an image of America beyond space and time.

This ambition perhaps grew out of the dissatisfactions of his personal life. Crane was born on July 21, 1899, in Garretsville, Ohio, a small town near the Pennsylvania border. He was the son of a candy manufacturer, a stormy, affectionate man who felt insufficiently loved by his wife and stirred up quarrel after quarrel. The two parents separated in 1908, and Mrs. Crane promptly broke down. Then some months later they were reconciled, and lived disharmoniously together until their divorce in 1917. Hart Crane took his mother's part, but his own relations with her were troubled and ended eventually in rupture. After his death, however, she played widow to his memory, seeking to solicit fame for him even while she herself scrubbed floors for a living.

In 1917, following the divorce of his parents, Crane went to live and work in New York instead of finishing high school or attending college. He had little success with jobs, and his personal life was unhappy. His love affairs, which were with men, were short lived, including that with a sailor which became the groundwork of a group of poems called "Voyages." But unsuccess or estrangement did not prevent his finding apocalypse everywhere. He saw all things—bridge, sea, river, ash can—as being on the verge of transformation. By fits and starts of imagination and arduous revision in which he careered his muse more and more violently, he composed the impassioned poetry for which he has become increasingly renowned. His Marlovian rhetoric and preoccupation with ecstasy were congenial to poets like Ginsberg, but these poets did not attempt what is equally distinctive in Crane, his metaphysical compression.

Crane owed in his earlier verse something to Swinburne and Wilde, with their notion of incantatory poetry; but he soon fell under more powerful influences, chiefly T. S. Eliot and the French Symbolist poets. Through them he attempted a poetry close to speech yet many-layered in meaning. As for Eliot, Crane admired his attempt to encompass the present-day scene, but found him, in the early twenties, to be too pessimistic. A letter to Allen Tate, of June 12, 1922, declares: "I have been facing him [Eliot] for *four* years,—and while I haven't discovered a weak spot yet in his armour, I flatter myself a little lately that I have discovered a safe tangent to strike which, if I can possibly explain the position,—goes *through* him toward a *different goal*. . . . Having absorbed him enough we can trust ourselves as never before, in the air or on the sea. I, for instance, would like to leave a few of his 'negations' behind me, risk the realm of the obvious more, in quest of new sensations, *humeurs*."[1] And six months later, on January 5, 1923, he emphasizes his own "more positive, or (if [I] must put it so in a sceptical age) ecstatic goal."[2]

Most of Crane's poems, like his last poem, "The Broken Tower," in fact celebrate crucifixion and resurrection, horror or squalor, out of which suddenly radiate hope and light. In "Chaplinesque" an ash can becomes a grail—a characteristic transformation. In a letter about Charlie Chaplin, he writes, "Chaplin may be a sentimentalist, after all, but he carries the theme with such power and universal portent that sentimentality is made to transcend itself. . . ."[3] The same claim may be made for Crane. His expression of this vision is itself visionary: he takes unusual words, combines them in an unusual way, forms them into unexpected rhythms, as if his technique was intended to expand the boundaries of consciousness in keeping with his subject matter. When he was reproved for the difficulty of his work, Crane explained, in a letter to the editor of *Poetry* in April 1926, that his object was to find a *logic of metaphor* which would not be the *logic of rational thought*. This pursuit of unconscious interconnections of "emotional dynamics" working through abbreviated thoughts is different also from the explained images of the Metaphysical poets; it works by sudden, forced conjunctions which find their justification below rather than above the surface. Crane has as much complexity as any modern poet, but he does not present himself as a difficult poet; rather his powerful speech and rhythms claim the instant response that his intricate images would seem to delay.

Crane's major poem is "The Bridge," published in 1930 and begun early in 1923. "Very roughly," he wrote a friend, "it concerns a mystical synthesis of 'America.' History and fact, location, etc., all have to be transfigured into abstract form that would almost function independently of its subject matter. The bridge suggests something that encompasses and transcends what is below it, as in the "Proem to Brooklyn Bridge," which would subsume all twentieth-century America. Crane accepts the machine, though horrible, as part of this mode of intensity. The poem as a whole is brilliantly written, wonderful in imagery, even if its metaphysic is somewhat unclear and perhaps too dependent on hyperbole. Furious feelings of hope are embodied

1. *Letters of Hart Crane*, ed. Brom Weber, Los Angeles, 1965, p. 90.
2. The same, p. 115.
3. The same, p. 69.
4. The same, p. 124.

rather arbitrarily in the symbol, as if Crane were forcing his material. Instant apocalypse was a danger for him because too tempting.

His life was a series of attempts at renewal. In his last year he made some attempt
to change his sexual direction; he had a love affair in Mexico with a woman, but on
the ship back he suddenly went to her stateroom to bid her goodbye—she thought
he was joking, but he went on deck and jumped into the sea. Accounts differ as to
whether or not he tried to catch the life preserver that was thrown to him. He died
on April 27, 1933.

His poetry is always close to disaster, a form of brinkmanship, but is saved from it
by the power of gathering disaster into a new ecstatic focus. In our time Crane looks
perhaps gaudy, insistent, obscure; we may feel that he strained after intensity. But
there is no doubt that he did establish a polar opposite to Eliot's early poetry; he did
get somewhere the other side of despair (as Eliot himself tried to do later) with his
full-throated, daring, secular but visionary poetry.

The source of our Crane texts is *The Poems of Hart Crane*, ed. Marc Simon, New
York, 1986.

Chaplinesque[1]

We make our meek adjustments,
Contented with such random consolations
As the wind deposits
In slithered and too ample pockets.

For we can still love the world, who find   5
A famished kitten on the step, and know
Recesses for it from the fury of the street,
Or warm torn elbow coverts.

We will sidestep, and to the final smirk
Dally the doom of that inevitable thumb   10
That slowly chafes its puckered index toward us,
Facing the dull squint with what innocence
And what surprise!

And yet these fine collapses are not lies
More than the pirouettes of any pliant cane;   15
Our obsequies are, in a way, no enterprise.
We can evade you, and all else but the heart:
What blame to us if the heart[2] live on.

1. Crane was delighted to see Charlie Chaplin
in *The Kid* in 1921. He considered Chaplin "a dramatic genius that truly approaches the fabulous
sort." In a letter to William Wright of October 17,
1921, he wrote: "As you did not 'get' my idiom in
'Chaplinesque,' I feel rather like doing my best to
explain myself. I am moved to put Chaplin with
the poets (of today); hence the 'we.' In other words,
he, especially in *The Kid*, made me feel myself, as
a poet, as being 'in the same boat' with him. Poetry,
the human feelings, 'the kitten,' is so crowded out
of the humdrum, rushing, mechanical scramble of
today that the man who would preserve them must
duck and camouflage for dear life to keep them or
keep himself from annihilation. I have since learned
that I am by no means alone in seeing these things

in the buffooneries of the tragedian, Chaplin . . .
and in the poem I have tried to express these 'social
sympathies' in words corresponding somewhat to
the antics of the actor" (*Letters*, p. 68). To Gor-
ham Munson, who objected that the film was
sentimental, he replied, "Chaplin may be a sentimentalist, after all, but he carries the theme with
such power and universal portent that sentimentality is made to transcend itself into a new kind of
tragedy, eccentric, homely and yet brilliant. It is
because I feel that I have captured the arrested
climaxes and evasive victories of his gestures in
words, somehow, that I like the poem as much as
anything I have done" (*Letters*, p. 69).
2. According to Crane, a deliberate pun on his
first name.

The game enforces smirks; but we have seen
The moon in lonely alleys make   20
A grail of laughter of an empty ash can,
And through all sound of gaiety and quest
Have heard a kitten in the wilderness.

1926

At Melville's Tomb[3]

Often beneath the wave, wide from this ledge
The dice of drowned men's bones he saw bequeath
An embassy.[4] Their numbers as he watched,
Beat on the dusty shore and were obscured.

And wrecks passed without sound of bells,   5
The calyx of death's bounty giving back
A scattered chapter, livid hieroglyph,
The portent wound in corridors of shells.[5]

Then in the circuit calm of one vast coil,
Its lashings charmed and malice reconciled,   10
Frosted eyes there were that lifted altars;[6]
And silent answers crept across the stars.

Compass, quadrant and sextant contrive
No farther tides[7] . . . High in the azure steeps
Monody shall not wake the mariner.   15
This fabulous shadow only the sea keeps.

1926

Voyages[8]

I

Above the fresh ruffles of the surf
Bright striped urchins flay each other with sand.

3. Herman Melville (1819–1891), the American writer, is buried at Woodlawn Cemetery in New York City.

4. In a letter to Harriet Monroe, editor of *Poetry*, Crane explained: "Dice bequeath an embassy, in the first place, by being ground (in this connection only, of course) in little cubes from the bones of drowned men by the action of the sea, and are finally thrown around the sand, giving 'numbers' but no identification. These being the bones of dead men who never completed their voyage, it seems legitimate to refer to them as the only surviving evidence of certain things, experiences that the dead mariners might have had to deliver. Dice as a symbol of chance and circumstance is also implied." (In Philip Horton, *Hart Crane*, New York, 1937, pp. 333–34.)

5. "This calyx refers in a double ironic sense both to a cornucopia and the vortex made by a sinking vessel. As soon as the water has closed over a ship this whirlpool sends up broken spars, wreckage, etc., which can be alluded to as *livid hieroglyphs*, making a *scattered chapter* so far as any complete record of the recent ship and her crew is concerned. In fact, about as much definite knowledge might come from all this as anyone

might gain from the roar of his own veins, which is easily heard (haven't you ever done it?) by holding a shell close to one's ear."

6. "Refers simply to a conviction that a man, not knowing perhaps a definite god yet being endowed with a reverence for deity—such a man naturally postulates a deity somehow, and the altar of that deity by the very *action* of the eyes *lifted* in searching."

7. "Hasn't it often occurred that instruments originally invented for record and computation have inadvertently so extended the concepts of the entity they were invented to measure (concepts of space etc.) in the mind and imagination that employed them, that they may metaphorically be said to have extended the original boundaries of the entity measured? This little bit of 'relativity' ought not to be discredited in poetry now that scientists are proceeding to measure the universe on principles of pure *ratio*, quite as metaphorical, so far as previous standards of scientific methods extended, as some of the axioms in *Job*."

8. The poem consists of six love poems, the outcome of a passionate affair with Emil Opffer, a merchant seaman.

They have contrived a conquest for shell shucks,
And their fingers crumble fragments of baked weed
Gaily digging and scattering.   5

And in answer to their treble interjections
The sun beats lightning on the waves,
The waves fold thunder on the sand;
And could they hear me I would tell them:

O brilliant kids, frisk with your dog,   10
Fondle your shells and sticks, bleached
By time and the elements; but there is a line
You must not cross nor even trust beyond it
Spry cordage of your bodies to caresses
Too lichen-faithful from too wide a breast.   15
The bottom of the sea is cruel.

II

—And yet this great wink of eternity,
Or rimless floods, unfettered leewardings,
Samite sheeted and processioned where
Her undinal vast belly moonward bends,   20
Laughing the wrapt inflections of our love;

Take this Sea, whose diapason knells
On scrolls of silver snowy sentences,
The sceptred terror of whose sessions rends
As her demeanors motion well or ill,   25
All but the pieties of lovers' hands.

And onward, as bells off San Salvador[9]
Salute the crocus lustres of the stars,
In these poinsettia meadows of her tides,—
Adagios of islands,[10] O my Prodigal,   30
Complete the dark confessions her veins spell.

Mark how her turning shoulders wind the hours,
And hasten while her penniless rich palms
Pass superscription of bent foam and wave,—
Hasten, while they are true,—sleep, death, desire,   35
Close round one instant in one floating flower.

Bind us in time, O Seasons clear, and awe.
O minstrel galleons of Carib fire,
Bequeath us to no earthly shore until
Is answered in the vortex of our grave   40
The seal's wide spindrift gaze toward paradise.

9. Crane alludes to a legend, of which he had heard from Opffer, of a buried city beneath the Pacific Ocean off San Salvador.

10. In an essay, "General Aims and Theories," Crane explained, "When . . . I speak of 'adagios of islands,' the reference is to the motion of a boat through islands clustered thickly, the rhythm of the motion, etc. And it seems a much more direct and creative statement than any more logical employment of words such as 'coasting slowly through the islands,' besides ushering in a whole world of music."

III

Infinite consanguinity it bears—
This tendered theme of you that light
Retrieves from sea plains where the sky
Resigns a breast that every wave enthrones;
While ribboned water lanes I wind   45
Are laved and scattered with no stroke
Wide from your side, where to this hour
The sea lifts, also, reliquary hands.

And so, admitted through black swollen gates   50
That must arrest all distance otherwise,—
Past whirling pillars and lithe pediments,
Light wrestling there incessantly with light,
Star kissing star through wave on wave unto
Your body rocking!   55
       and where death, if shed,
Presumes no carnage, but this single change,—
Upon the steep floor flung from dawn to dawn
The silken skilled transmemberment of song;

Permit me voyage, love, into your hands . . .   60

IV

Whose counted smile of hours and days, suppose
I know as spectrum of the sea and pledge
Vastly now parting gulf on gulf of wings
Whose circles bridge, I know, (from palms to the severe
Chilled albatross's white immutability)   65
No stream of greater love advancing now
Than, singing, this mortality alone
Through clay aflow immortally to you.

All fragrance irrefragably, and claim
Madly meeting logically in this hour   70
And region that is ours to wreathe again,
Portending eyes and lips and making told
The chancel port[11] and portion of our June—

Shall they not stem and close in our own steps
Bright staves of flowers and quills today as I   75
Must first be lost in fatal tides to tell?

In signature of the incarnate word
The harbor shoulders to resign in mingling
Mutual blood, transpiring as foreknown
And widening noon within your breast for gathering 80
All bright insinuations that my years have caught
For islands where must lead inviolably
Blue latitudes and levels of your eyes,—

---

11. The chancel is the part of the church that includes the sanctuary, hence the most sacred or cherished part.

In this expectant, still exclaim receive
The secret oar and petals of all love.   85

                              V

Meticulous, past midnight in clear rime,
Infrangible and lonely, smooth as though cast
Together in one merciless white blade—
The bay estuaries fleck the hard sky limits.

—As if too brittle or too clear to touch!   90
The cables of our sleep so swiftly filed,
Already hang, shred ends from remembered stars.
One frozen trackless smile . . . What words
Can strangle this deaf moonlight? For we

Are overtaken. Now no cry, no sword   95
Can fasten or deflect this tidal wedge,
Slow tyranny of moonlight, moonlight loved
And changed . . . "There's

Nothing like this in the world," you say,
Knowing I cannot touch your hand and look   100
Too, into that godless cleft of sky
Where nothing turns but dead sands flashing.

"—And never to quite understand!" No,
In all the argosy of your bright hair I dreamed   105
Nothing so flagless as this piracy.

                          But now
Draw in your head, alone and too tall here.
Your eyes already in the slant of drifting foam;
Your breath sealed by the ghosts I do not know:
Draw in your head and sleep the long way home.   110

                             VI

Where icy and bright dungeons lift   115
Of swimmers their lost morning eyes,
And ocean rivers, churning, shift
Green borders under stranger skies,

Steadily as a shell secretes
Its beating leagues of monotone,   120
Or as many waters trough the sun's
Red kelson past the cape's wet stone;

O rivers mingling toward the sky
And harbor of the phoenix' breast—
My eyes pressed black against the prow,   125
—Thy derelict and blinded guest

Waiting, afire, what name, unspoke,
I cannot claim: let thy waves rear

More savage than the death of kings,
Some splintered garland for the seer.   130

Beyond siroccos harvesting
The solstice thunders, crept away,
Like a cliff swinging or a sail
Flung into April's inmost day—

Creation's blithe and petalled word   135
To the lounged goddess when she rose
Conceding dialogue with eyes
That smile unsearchable repose—

Still fervid covenant, Belle Isle,
—Unfolded floating dais before   140
Which rainbows twine continual hair—
Belle Isle, white echo of the oar![1]

The imaged Word, it is, that holds
Hushed willows anchored in its glow.
It is the unbetrayable reply   145
Whose accent no farewell can know.

1926

From *THE BRIDGE*

> From going to and fro in the earth,
> and from walking up and down in it.
> —THE BOOK OF JOB

Proem: To Brooklyn Bridge[2]

How many dawns, chill from his rippling rest
The seagull's wings shall dip and pivot him,

1. The meaning appears to be that creation's blithe and petalled word is sounded apart from the siroccos, is like a cliff swinging or a sail flung into the heart of a spring day, as when Venus rose from the sea (that word of creation holds dialogue with her reposeful eyes) or as Belle Isle stands as covenant for love.

2. Crane began writing his epic poem, *The Bridge*, in 1923. On February 18 he continued, "I am too much interested in this *Bridge* thing lately to write letters, ads, or anything. . . . Very roughly, it concerns a mystical synthesis of 'America.' History and fact, location, etc., all have to be transfigured into abstract form that would almost function independently of its subject matter. The initial impulses of 'our people' will have to be gathered up toward the climax of the bridge, symbol of our constructive future, our unique identity, in which is included also our scientific hopes and achievements of the future. The mystic portent of all this is already flocking through my mind . . . but the actual statement of the thing, the marshalling of the forces, will take me months, at best; and I may have to give it up entirely before that; it may be too impossible an ambition. But if I do succeed, such a waving of banners, such ascent of towers, such dancing, etc., will never before have been put down on paper! The form will be symphonic, something like 'F and H' [Faustus and Helen] with its treatment of varied content, and it will probably approximate the same length in lines" (*Letters*, pp. 124–25). In a letter to Waldo Frank of June 20, 1926, he speaks of having what he had thought were authentic materials. "These 'materials' were valid to me to the extent that I presumed them to be (articulate or not) at least organic and active factors in the experience and perceptions of our common race, time and belief. The very idea of a bridge, of course is a form peculiarly dependent on such spiritual convictions. It is an act of faith besides being a communication. The symbols of reality necessary to articulate the span— may not exist where you expected them, however. By which I mean that however great their objective significance to me is concerned—these forms, materials, dynamics are simply nonexistent in the world. I may amuse and delight and flatter myself as much as I please—but I am only evading a recognition and playing Don Quixote in an immorally conscious way. The form of my poem rises out of a past that so overwhelms the present with its worth and vision that I'm at a loss to explain my delusion that there exist any real links between that past and a future destiny worthy of it. . . . The bridge as a symbol today has no significance beyond an economical approach to shorter hours, quicker lunches, behaviorism and toothpicks" (*Letters*, p. 261).

Shedding white rings of tumult, building high
Over the chained bay waters Liberty—

Then, with inviolate curve, forsake our eyes   5
As apparitional as sails that cross
Some page of figures to be filed away;
—Till elevators drop us from our day . . .

I think of cinemas, panoramic sleights
With multitudes bent toward some flashing scene   10
Never disclosed, but hastened to again,
Foretold to other eyes on the same screen;

And Thee, across the harbor, silver-paced
As though the sun took step of thee, yet left
Some motion ever unspent in thy stride,—   15
Implicitly thy freedom staying thee!

Out of some subway scuttle, cell or loft
A bedlamite speeds to thy parapets,
Tilting there momently, shrill shirt ballooning,
A jest falls from the speechless caravan.   20

Down Wall,[3] from girder into street noon leaks,
A rip-tooth of the sky's acetylene;
All afternoon the cloud-flown derricks turn . . .
Thy cables breathe the North Atlantic still.

And obscure as that heaven of the Jews,[4]   25
Thy guerdon[5] . . . Accolade thou dost bestow
Of anonymity time cannot raise:
Vibrant reprieve and pardon thou dost show.

O harp and altar, of the fury fused,
(How could mere toil align thy choiring strings!)   30
Terrific threshold of the prophet's pledge,
Prayer of pariah, and the lover's cry,—

Again the traffic lights that skim thy swift
Unfractioned idiom, immaculate sigh of stars,
Beading thy path—condense eternity: 35
And we have seen night lifted in thine arms.

Under thy shadow by the piers I waited;
Only in darkness is thy shadow clear.
The City's fiery parcels all undone,
Already snow submerges an iron year . . .   40

O Sleepless as the river under thee,
Vaulting the sea, the prairies' dreaming sod,
Unto us lowliest sometime sweep, descend
And of the curveship lend a myth to God.

1930

---

3. Wall Street in Manhattan.
4. Heaven in the Jewish tradition is much vaguer   than in the Christian.
5. Reward.

Royal Palm

For Grace Hart Crane[6]

Green rustlings, more-than-regal charities
Drift coolly from that tower of whispered light.
Amid the noontide's blazed asperities
I watched the sun's most gracious anchorite

Climb up as by communings, year on year   5
Uneaten of the earth or aught earth holds,
And the grey trunk, that's elephantine, rear
Its frondings sighing in aetherial folds.

Forever fruitless, and beyond that yield
Of sweat the jungle presses with hot love   10
And tendril till our deathward breath is sealed—
It grazes the horizons, launched above

Mortality—ascending emerald-bright,
A fountain at salute, a crown in view—
Unshackled, casual of its azured height   15
As though it soared suchwise through heaven too.

1933

The Broken Tower[7]

The bell-rope that gathers God at dawn[8]
Dispatches me as though I dropped down the knell
Of a spent day—to wander the cathedral lawn
From pit to crucifix, feet chill on steps from hell.

Have you not heard, have you not seen that corps   5
Of shadows in the tower, whose shoulders sway
Antiphonal carillons launched before
The stars are caught and hived in the sun's ray?

The bells, I say, the bells break down their tower;
And swing I know not where. Their tongues engrave   10
Membrane through marrow, my long-scattered score
Of broken intervals[9] . . . And I, their sexton slave![1]

---

6. Hart Crane's mother.
7. In his biography of Crane, *Voyager* (New York, 1969, p. 722), John Unterecker quotes Crane's friend, Lesley Simpson, on the beginning of this poem: "I was with Hart Crane in Taxco, Mexico, the morning of January 27, this year [1932], when he first conceived the idea of 'The Broken Tower.' The night before, being troubled with insomnia, he had risen before daybreak and walked down to the village square. . . . Hart met the old Indian bell-ringer who was on his way down to the church. He and Hart were old friends, and he brought Hart up into the tower with him to help ring the bells. As Hart was swinging the clapper of the great bell, half drunk with its mighty music, the swift tropical dawn broke over the mountains. The sublimity of the scene and the thunder of the bells woke in Hart one of those gusts of joy of which only he was capable. He came striding up the hill afterwards in a sort of frenzy, refused his breakfast, and paced up and down the porch impatiently waiting for me to finish my coffee. Then he seized my arm and bore me off to the plaza, where we sat in the shadow of the church, Hart the while pouring out a magnificent cascade of words."
8. The angelus bell commemorates the Incarnation of Christ.
9. Crane's own verse.
1. He is himself the bell ringer, and unable not to be.

Oval encyclicals in canyons heaping
The impasse high with choir. Banked voices slain![2]
Pagodas, campaniles with reveilles outleaping—   15
O terraced echoes prostrate on the plain![3] . . .

And so it was I entered the broken world
To trace the visionary company of love,[4] its voice
An instant in the wind (I know not whither hurled)
But not for long[5] to hold each desperate choice.   20

My word I poured. But was it cognate, scored
Of that tribunal monarch[6] of the air
Whose thigh embronzes earth, strikes crystal Word[7]
In wounds pledged once to hope,—cleft to despair?[8]

The steep encroachments of my blood left me   25
No answer (could blood hold such a lofty tower
As flings the question true?)—or is it she
Whose sweet mortality stirs latent power?—

And through whose pulse I hear, counting the strokes
My veins recall and add, revived and sure   30
The angelus of wars my chest evokes:
What I hold healed, original now, and pure . . .

And builds, within, a tower that is not stone
(Not stone can jacket heaven)—but slip
Of pebbles,—visible wings of silence sown   35
In azure circles, widening as they dip

The matrix of the heart, lift down the eye
That shrines the quiet lake and swells a tower . . .
The commodious, tall decorum of that sky
Unseals her earth, and lifts love in its shower.   40

                                                                  1933

2. Encyclicals are here divinely inspired messages. The impasse is the limit beyond which mortal voices cannot go. At this limit they are slain.
3. These two lines also express the sense of
aspiration and limit.
4. In the attempt of the bells to transfigure life
and to incarnate God, Crane sees an analogue of
his own poetic mission.

5. His inspired moments could not be sustained.
6. Christ as judge and king.
7. Divine revelation, with which the poet hopes
his word is cognate.
8. Christ offers hope of redemption, but himself despaired on the cross. The poet sees in himself a comparable interfusion.

ALLEN TATE
1899–1979

Among the poets who have identified themselves with the southern school, Allen
Tate wrote the most chiseled and complicated verse. He had less directness than
Robert Penn Warren and, though often witty, less humor than John Crowe Ransom.
Warren has managed to extricate himself from the dilemmas of the South, Ransom,
even while sharing them, to acknowledge their partial ludicrousness; Tate seemed
less able to rid himself of the weight of melancholy and regret. Tate's verse was

poised on a problem which, for all his impersonal expression, he felt deeply, of finding and reasserting some affirmable postulates in an atmosphere of disaffection. In "The Meaning of Life," he represented the goal as discovering, amid a world of commentary, the immaculate conception. In this quest Tate became a Fugitive, an agrarian, a Catholic. But he was at once too honest, and too elegant, for the self-denying fervor of these creeds. As a result, he appeared as a rather distant figure, like the speaker in his important "Ode to the Confederate Dead."

Tate's principal literary experience was the shaping effect of one book. He declared this frankly in a prefatory note to *The Swimmers and Other Selected Poems*. To explain the difference between his early and late poems, he said, "By 'early' I mean a poem written before 1922, when I read T. S. Eliot's *Poems* (1920). My early verses now seem to be a conventional and anonymous mixture of Baudelaire (*via* Arthur Symons), Corbière, James Thomson (B.V.), E. A. Robinson, Ernest Dowson, and a little of Ezra Pound, whom I had read before I read Eliot."[1] In the reading of Eliot, and in defending a little later *The Waste Land* against the strictures of John Crowe Ransom (up to then Tate's principal mentor), the young man found his point of separation. His respect for tradition, his unhappiness with the cheapening of values, even his conversion, showed the effect of Eliot, who himself admired Tate's consistency in maintaining "the least popular of political attitudes—that of the sage." Tate also had something of Eliot's precise and sweepingly evaluative manner. In comparison, however, he seems lacking in energy, as if hamstrung by too subtle and exacting a recognition of limits in every view.

John Orley Allen Tate was born in Winchester, Clarke County, Kentucky, on December 19, 1899. His schooling was desultory, with a year at a school in Nashville, three years at one in Louisville, a half year each at two public high schools, a final year at a preparatory school in Washington, D.C. He entered Vanderbilt University in 1918. His readings in philosophy and literature were sufficiently varied to impress John Crowe Ransom, from whom he took two courses and the sense of a way of life. Tate, and later his roommate Robert Penn Warren, were the two undergraduates favored by an invitation to join an adult group who met to discuss poetry and other subjects in Nashville. They called themselves the Fugitives, and published a magazine, *The Fugitive*, to which Tate contributed a number of poems.

Because of a skirmish with tuberculosis, Tate had to take his degree a year late, in 1923. He then did some school teaching in West Virginia, but moved on to New York in the hope of a writing career. To make ends meet he worked on a semi-pornographic magazine called *Telling Tales*. He had meanwhile married Caroline Gordon, also a writer, and they moved to a large house in Patterson, New York, in late 1925 to pursue their writing careers.

The Tates moved back to live in Greenwich Village after a year in Patterson. Allen Tate became through his tales, wit, and perception a well-known and highly respected figure in the literary world. His first book of verse, *Mr. Pope and Other Poems*, was published in New York in 1928. In 1930 he wrote one of the essays in *I'll Take My Stand*, a book in which some eminent southerners took their stand in favor of an agrarian, rather than an industrialized, South. Tate's first book of essays, *Reactionary Essays on Poetry and Ideas* (with its multiple ironies over the meaning of "reactionary"), appeared in 1936. He edited the *Sewanee Review* from 1944 to 1946. In 1950 he became a Roman Catholic. From 1951 until his retirement in 1968 he was a professor of English at the University of Minnesota. He married for the second time in 1967. Besides his verse, he wrote a novel set in the South, *The Fathers*, a biography of Stonewall Jackson and one of Jefferson Davis, and a series of books of elegant criticism. He died in Sewanee, Tennessee, on February 9, 1979.

---

1. *The Swimmers and Other Selected Poems*, London, 1970, p. vii.

Ode to the Confederate Dead[1]

Row after row with strict impunity
The headstones yield their names to the element,
The wind whirrs without recollection;
In the riven troughs the splayed leaves
Pile up, of nature the casual sacrament   5
To the seasonal eternity of death;
Then driven by the fierce scrutiny
Of heaven to their election in the vast breath,
They sough the rumour of mortality.

Autumn is desolation in the plot   10
Of a thousand acres where these memories grow
From the inexhaustible bodies that are not
Dead, but feed the grass row after rich row.
Think of the autumns that have come and gone!—
Ambitious November with the humors of the year,   15
With a particular zeal for every slab,
Staining the uncomfortable angels that rot
On the slabs, a wing chipped here, an arm there:
The brute curiosity of an angel's stare
Turns you, like them, to stone,   20
Transforms the heaving air
Till plunged to a heavier world below
You shift your sea-space blindly
Heaving, turning like the blind crab.[2]

    Dazed by the wind, only the wind   25
    The leaves flying, plunge

You know who have waited by the wall
The twilight certainty of an animal,
Those midnight restitutions of the blood
You know—the immitigable pines, the smoky frieze   30
Of the sky, the sudden call: you know the rage,
The cool pool left by the mounting flood,
Of muted Zeno and Parmenides.[3]
You who have waited for the angry resolution
Of those desires that should be yours tomorrow,   35
You know the unimportant shrift of death

---

1. In an essay, "Narcissus as Narcissus," Tate explains that this poem "is 'about' solipsism, a philosophical doctrine which says that we create the world in the act of perceiving it; or about Narcissism, or any other *ism* that denotes the failure of the human personality to function objectively in nature and society."
2. "The structure of the Ode is simple. Figure to yourself a man stopping at the gate of a Confederate graveyard on a late autumn afternoon. The leaves are falling; his first impressions bring him the 'rumor of mortality'; and the desolation barely allows him, at the beginning of the second stanza, the conventionally heroic surmise that the dead will enrich the earth, 'where these memories grow.' From those quoted words to the end of that passage he pauses for a baroque meditation on the ravages of time, concluding with the figure of the 'blind crab.' This figure has mobility but no direction, energy but, from the human point of view, no purposeful world to use it in: in the entire poem there are only two explicit symbols for the locked-in ego; the crab is the first and less explicit symbol, a mere hint, a planting of the idea that will become overt in its second instance—the jaguar towards the end. The crab is the first intimation of the nature of the moral conflict upon which the drama of the poem develops: the cut-off-ness of the modern 'intellectual man' from the world" (Tate's note).
3. Parmenides and his follower Zeno, both of Elea, were Greek philosophers of the fifth century B.C. They held that the real universe is a single and unchanging whole, while the apparent universe of mutable things is illusory and unknowable.

And praise the vision
And praise the arrogant circumstance
Of those who fall
Rank upon rank, hurried beyond decision—   40
Here by the sagging gate, stopped by the wall.[4]

   Seeing, seeing only the leaves
   Flying, plunge and expire

Turn your eyes to the immoderate past,
Turn to the inscrutable infantry rising   45
Demons out of the earth—they will not last.
Stonewall,[5] Stonewall, and the sunken fields of hemp,[6]
Shiloh, Antietam, Malvern Hill, Bull Run.[7]
Lost in the orient of the thick-and-fast
You will curse the setting sun.   50

   Cursing only the leaves crying
   Like an old man in a storm

You hear the shout, the crazy hemlocks point
With troubled fingers, to the silence which
Smothers you, a mummy, in time.

           The hound bitch   55
Toothless and dying, in a musty cellar
Hears the wind only.

      Now that the salt of their blood
Stiffens the saltier oblivion of the sea,
Seals the malignant purity of the flood,
What shall we who count our days and bow   60
Our heads with a commemorial woe
In the ribboned coats of grim felicity,
What shall we say of the bones, unclean,
Whose verdurous anonymity will grow?[8]

---

4. "The next long passage or 'strophe' . . . states the other term of the conflict. It is the theme of heroism, not merely moral heroism, but heroism in the grand style, elevating even death from mere physical dissolution into a formal ritual: this heroism is a formal ebullience of the human spirit in an entire society, not private, romantic illusion—something better than moral heroism, great as that may be, for moral heroism, being personal and individual, may be achieved by certain men in all ages, even ages of decadence. But the late Hart Crane . . . described the theme as the 'theme of chivalry, a tradition of excess (not literally excess, rather active faith) which cannot be perpetuated in the fragmentary cosmos of today—'those desires which should be yours tomorrow," but which, you know, will not persist nor find any way into action.' The structure then is the objective frame for the tension between the two themes, 'active faith' which has decayed, and the 'fragmentary cosmos' which surrounds us. . . . In contemplating the heroic theme the man at the gate never quite commits himself to the illusion of its availability to him. The most that he can allow himself is the fancy that the blowing leaves are charging soldiers, but he rigorously returns to the refrain: 'Only the wind'—or the 'leaves flying.' . . . More than this, he cautions himself, reminds himself repeatedly, of his subjective prison, his solipsisms, by breaking off the half-illusion and coming back to the refrain of wind and leaves, a refrain that, as Hart Crane said, is necessary to the 'subjective continuity' " (Tate's note).

5. Thomas Jonathan Jackson (1824–1863), Confederate general in the Civil War, earned the nickname Stonewall at the first battle of Bull Run (Virginia), July 21, 1861. He was killed in 1863 at the Battle of Chancellorsville.

6. Sunken because not cultivated during the war.

7. Famous battles of the Civil War, slightly out of chronological order. Shiloh (Tennessee) April 6–7, 1862, ended with the Confederate troops in retreat; Antietam or Sharpsburg (Maryland), September 17, 1862, and Malvern Hill (Virginia), July 2, 1862, also were disadvantageous to the South; the two battles of Bull Run, in 1861 and on August 29–30, 1862, were both victories for the Confederate armies.

8. This line was suggested to Tate by Robert Penn Warren.

The ragged arms, the ragged heads and eyes   65
Lost in these acres of the insane green?
The gray lean spiders come, they come and go;
In a tangle of willows without light
The singular screech-owl's tight
Invisible lyric seeds the mind   70
With the furious murmur of their chivalry.

We shall say only the leaves
Flying, plunge and expire

We shall say only the leaves whispering
In the improbable mist of nightfall   75
That flies on multiple wing;
Night is the beginning and the end
And in between the ends of distraction
Waits mute speculation, the patient curse
That stones the eyes, or like the jaguar leaps   80
For his own image in a jungle pool, his victim.[9]

What shall we say who have knowledge
Carried to the heart?[1] Shall we take the act
To the grave? Shall we, more hopeful, set up the grave
In the house? The ravenous grave?[2]   85

                                        Leave now
The shut gate and the decomposing wall:
The gentle serpent, green in the mulberry bush,
Riots with his tongue through the hush—
Sentinel of the grave who counts us all![3]   90

                                        1928, 1937

9. "This figure of the jaguar is the only explicit rendering of the Narcissus motif in the poem, but instead of a youth gazing into a pool, a predatory beast stares at a jungle stream, and leaps to devour himself" (Tate's note).

1. "This is Pascal's war between heart and head, between *finesse* and *géometrie*." Tate explains that the two themes are gathered here into a final statement.

2. "These two themes struggle for mastery up to [lines 77–78]. . . . It will be observed that the passage begins with a phrase taken from the wind-leaves refrain—the signal that it has won. The refrain has been fused with the main stream of the man's reflections dominating them; and he cannot return even to an ironic vision of the heroes. There is nothing but death, the mere naturalism of death at that—spiritual extinction in the decay of the body. Autumn and the leaves are death; the men who exemplified in a grand style an 'active faith' are dead; there are only the leaves. Shall we then worship death . . . that will take us before our time? The question is not answered, although as a kind of morbid romanticism it might, if answered affirmatively, provide the man with an illusory escape from his solipsism; but he cannot accept it. Nor has he been able to live in his immediate world, the fragmentary cosmos. There is no practical solution, no solution offered for the edification of moralists. . . . The main intention of the poem has been to make dramatically visible the conflict, to concentrate it . . ." (Tate's note).

3. "The closing image, that of the serpent, is the ancient symbol of time, and I tried to give it the credibility of the commonplace by placing it in a mulberry bush—with the faint hope that the silkworm would somehow be implicit. But time is also death. If that is so, then space, or the Becoming, is life; and I believe there is not a single spatial symbol in the poem. 'Sea-space' is allowed the 'blind crab'; but the sea, as appears plainly in the passage beginning, 'Now that the salt of their blood . . .' is life only insofar as it is the source of the lowest forms of life, the source perhaps of all life, but life undifferentiated, halfway between life and death. This passage is a contrasting inversion of the conventional

    . . . inexhaustible bodies that are not
    Dead, but feed the grass . . .

the reduction of the earlier, literary conceit to a more naturalistic figure derived from modern biological speculation. Those 'buried Caesars' will not bloom in the hyacinth but will only make saltier the sea" (Tate's note).

To the Lacedemonians[4]

An old soldier on the night before the veterans' reunion talks
partly to himself, partly to imaginary comrades:[5]

The people—people of my kind, my own
People but strange with a white light
In the face: the streets hard with motion
And the hard eyes that look one way.
Listen! the high whining tone   5
Of the motors, I hear the dull commotion:
I am come, a child in an old play.

I am here with a secret in the night;
Because I am here the dead wear gray.

It is a privilege to be dead; for you   10
Cannot know what absence is nor seize
The odour of pure distance[6] until
From you, slowly dying in the head,
All sights and sounds of the moment, all
The life of sweet intimacy shall fall   15
Like a swift at dusk.

               Sheer time! Stroke of the heart
Towards retirement. . . .

               Gentlemen, my secret is
Damnation: where have they, the citizens, all   20
Come from? They were not born in my father's
House, nor in their fathers': on a street corner
By motion sired, not born; by rest dismayed.
The tempest will unwind—the hurricane
Consider, knowing its end, the headlong pace?   25
I have watched it and endured it, I have delayed
Judgment: it warn't in my time, by God, so
That the mere breed absorbed the generation!

Yet I, hollow head, do see but little;
Old man: no memory: aimless distractions.   30

---

4. Spartans. Sparta, an oligarchic Greek city-state, won the Peloponnesian War (431–404 B.C.) against Athens. It had fought in alliance with other Greek city-states against the Persians at the battle of Thermopylae (480 B.C.). The critic Donald Davidson points out that this poem was first published in the *Richmond* (Virginia) *Times-Dispatch* for June 21, 1932, on the occasion of a reunion of Confederate veterans (most of whom were teen-agers in the war). Davidson also notes that in his *Poems: 1922–1947*, Tate placed this poem and "Ode to the Confederate Dead" as the last two in Part I: "Thus 'To the Lacedemonians' becomes a companion piece and in many ways a counterpart to the 'Ode,'"

5. In the *Times-Dispatch* version, the epigraph reads: "The Old Confederate on the Night Before the Reunion Speaks Partly to Himself. . . ." Tate revised the epigraph to its present reading for *Poems: 1922–1947* (Davidson).

6. Davidson reads these five lines as follows: "I take 'you' to refer to the people of his own kind, now become strange, who lead a life of sensation only and are therefore unable to 'see' the gray-clad [Confederate uniforms were gray] soldiers as anything but 'dead.' To people that are a mere breed 'by motion sired' [line 23], anything belonging to the past is 'dead.' That is the secret upon which he has come in the night—a night both literal and metaphorical . . . the soldier's part is not just to kill, but it is to die, to be willing to die."

I was a boy, I never knew cessation
Of the bright course of blood along the vein;
Moved, an old dog by me, to field and stream
In the speaking ease of the fall rain;
When I was a boy the light on the hills   35
Was there because I could see it, not because
Some special gift of God had put it there.
Men expect too much, do too little,
Put the contraption before the accomplishment,
Lack skill of the interior mind   40
To fashion dignity with shapes of air.
Luxury, yes—but not elegance!
Where have they come from?

                     Go you tell them
That we their servants, well-trained, gray-coated   45
Gray-haired (both foot and horse) or in
The grave, them obey . . . obey them,
What commands?[7]

           My father said
That everything but kin was less than kind.[8]   50
The young men like swine argue for a rind,
A flimsy shell to put their weakness in;
Will-less, ruled by what they cannot see;
Hunched like savages in a rotten tree
They wait for the thunder to speak: Union!   55
That joins their separate fear.

             I fought
But did not care; a leg shot off at Bethel,[9]
Given up for dead; but knew neither shell-shock
Nor any self-indulgence. Well may war be   60
Terrible to those who have nothing to gain
For the illumination of the sense:
When the peace is a trade route, figures
For the budget, reduction of population,
Life grown sullen and immense   65
Lusts after immunity to pain.

There is no civilization without death;
There is now the wind for breath.

Waken, lords and ladies gay, we cried,
And marched to Cedar Run and Malvern Hill,[1]   70
Kinsmen and friends from Texas to the Tide[2]—
Vain chivalry of the personal will!

---

7. In his famous elegy to the Spartans who died defending Greece at Thermopylae, the poet Simonides of Ceos (c.556–c.468 B.C.) wrote: "Stranger, carry the message to the Lacedemonians that we lie here, obeying their commands." "The 'talk' of Tate's old soldier is actually nearer to the idiom of Greek drama" (Davidson).
8. Pun on "kind": (1) kindly, (2) of the same type.

Compare, in Shakespeare's *Hamlet* (1.2.64–65), the usurping King Claudius's address to his stepson as "my cousin Hamlet, and my son," and Hamlet's reply: "A little more than kin, and less than kind."
9. Big Bethel, Virginia, site of a Civil War battle in 1861.
1. Civil War battle in Virginia, 1862.
2. The Tidewater region of eastern Virginia.

Waken, we shouted, lords and ladies gay,
We go to win the precincts of the light,
Unshadowing restriction of our day . . . .
Regard now, in the seventy years of night,[3]   75

Them, the young men who watch us from the curbs:
They hold the glaze of wonder in their stare—
Our crooked backs, hands fetid as old herbs,
The tallow eyes, wax face, the foreign hair!   80

Soldiers, march! we shall not fight again
The Yankees with our guns well-aimed and rammed—
All are born Yankees of the race of men
And this, too, now the country of the damned:

Poor bodies crowding round us! The white face   85
Eyeless with eyesight only, the modern power—
Huddled sublimities of time and space,
They are the echoes of a raging tower

That reared its moment upon a gone land,
Pouring a long cold wrath into the mind—   90
Damned souls, running the way of sand
Into the destination of the wind!

                                                                    1932, 1936

The Swimmers

SCENE: *Montgomery County*
Kentucky, July 1911

Kentucky water, clear springs: a boy fleeing
    To water under the dry Kentucky sun,
    His four little friends in tandem with him, seeing

Long shadows of grapevine wriggle and run
    Over the green swirl; mullein under the ear   5
    Soft as Nausicaä's palm;[4] sullen fun

Savage as childhood's thin harmonious tear:
    O fountain, bosom source undying-dead
    Replenish me the spring of love and fear

And give me back the eye that looked and fled   10
    When a thrush idling in the tulip tree
    Unwound the cold dream of the copperhead.[5]

---

3. Davidson suggests that these, "taken literally, must refer to the seventy years since 1862—
the year of true beginning of the Civil War."
Exactly seventy years before the Confederate soldiers' reunion (see note 1), the Confederate general Robert E. Lee was about to attack the Union
army at Richmond; in this battle, Lee ended "any

possibility of a 'negotiated peace' between the
warring North and South."
    4. The king's daughter who kindly welcomes the
shipwrecked Odysseus in Homer's *Odyssey* (and
see line 15).
    5. Poisonous snake, whose coloring makes it
hard to see among fallen leaves.

—Along the creek the road was winding; we
　Felt the quicksilver sky. I see again
　The shrill companions of that odyssey:　　　　　　　　　　15

Bill Eaton, Charlie Watson, "Nigger" Layne
　The doctor's son, Harry Duèsler who played
　The flute; and Tate, with water on the brain.

Dog-days: the dusty leaves where rain delayed
　Hung low on poison-oak and scuppernong,[6]　　　　　　20
And we were following the active shade

Of water, that bells and bickers all night long.
　"No more'n a mile," Layne said. All five stood still.
　Listening, I heard what seemed at first a song;

Peering, I heard the hooves come down the hill.　　　　25
　The posse passed, twelve horse; the leader's face
　Was worn as limestone on an ancient sill.

Then, as sleepwalkers shift from a hard place
　In bed, and rising to keep a formal pledge
　Descend a ladder into empty space,　　　　　　　　　30

We scuttled down the bank below a ledge
　And marched stiff-legged in our common fright
　Along a hog-track by the riffle's[7] edge:

Into a world where sound shaded the sight
　Dropped the dull hooves again; the horsemen came　　35
　Again, all but the leader: it was night

Momently and I feared: eleven same
　Jesus-Christers unmembered and unmade,
　Whose Corpse had died again in dirty shame.[8]

The bank then levelling in a speckled glade,　　　　　40
　We stopped to breathe above the swimming-hole;
　I gazed at its reticulated[9] shade

Recoiling in blue fear, and felt it roll
　Over my ears and eyes and lift my hair
　Like seaweed tossing on a sunk atoll.　　　　　　　45

I rose again. Borne on the copper air
　A distant voice green as a funeral wreath
　Against a grave: "That dead nigger there."

The melancholy sheriff slouched beneath
　A giant sycamore; shaking his head　　　　　　　　　50
　He plucked a sassafras[1] twig and picked his teeth:

---

6. Fruit common in the South.
7. Of a shallow in the bed of a stream.
8. The oaths—"Jesus Christ!"—uttered by
members of the posse may possibly suggest the
twelve disciples of Christ (their "Corpse").
9. Networked.
1. Aromatic tree.

"We come too late." He spoke to the tired dead
    Whose ragged shirt soaked up the viscous flow
    Of blood in which It lay discomfited.

A butting horse-fly gave one ear a blow   55
    And glanced off, as the sheriff kicked the rope
    Loose from the neck and hooked it with his toe

Away from the blood.—I looked back down the slope:
    The friends were gone that I had hoped to greet.—
    A single horseman came at a slow lope   60

And pulled up at the hanged man's horny feet;
    The sheriff noosed the feet, the other end
    The stranger tied to his pommel in a neat

Slip-knot. I saw the Negro's body bend
    And straighten, as a fish-line cast transverse   65
    Yields to the current that it must subtend.

The sheriff's Goddamn was a murmured curse
    Not for the dead but for the blinding dust
    That boxed the cortège[2] in a cloudy hearse

And dragged it towards our town. I knew I must   70
    Not stay till twilight in that silent road;
    Sliding my bare feet into the warm crust,

I hopped the stonecrop like a panting toad
    Mouth open, following the heaving cloud
    That floated to the court-house square its load   75

Of limber corpse that took the sun for shroud.
    There were three figures in the dying sun
    Whose light were company where three was crowd.[3]

My breath crackled the dead air like a shotgun
    As, sheriff and the stranger disappearing,   80
    The faceless head lay still. I could not run

Or walk, but stood. Alone in the public clearing
    This private thing was owned by all the town,
    Though never claimed by us within my hearing.

                           1953

2. Funerary procession of mourners.   thieves—three in all—on their crosses.
3. Perhaps an echo of Christ and the two

YVOR WINTERS
1900–1968

The poetry of Yvor Winters often celebrates a hard-won victory. In "Sir Gawaine and the Green Knight," for example, the hero is tempted by a lady, who represents natural disorder:

By practice and conviction formed
With ancient stubbornness ingrained,
Although her body clung and swarmed,
My own identity remained.

Winters's formal control, his disregard for twentieth-century poetic fashion, his presence in his poetry and criticism as the lonely, stoic survivor in an alien world—all these are achievements of mind and character over natural and social disorder. Winters often seems to be holding on to the discipline of his verse, and the lucidity it encourages, for dear life. He is not writing to entertain outlandish beliefs for the sake of their poetic effectiveness, a vice for which he censured Yeats. Winters's poems are concerned with discovering and expressing the truth of a particular situation, and thus they are often occasional and epigrammatic. For his models he turned back to the spare, careful poetry of Sir Fulke Greville and Sir Walter Ralegh, Elizabethan courtiers whose work communicates an often bitter wisdom. Though Winters is didactic, he is never bullying, for he knows that the truth is most adequately expressed with delicacy and in a carefully modulated tone.

Yvor Winters was born in Chicago on October 17, 1900. He spent his childhood in California and Oregon, then returned to Chicago, where he went to high school and began studies at the University of Chicago. In his freshman year he was discovered to have tuberculosis, and he was sent to Santa Fe, New Mexico, where he convalesced, taught primary school, and worked as a manual laborer. In 1925 he took an M.A. in Romance languages at the University of Colorado, and in 1928 he began to teach at Stanford University, where he remained until his retirement in 1966. He died in Palo Alto on January 26, 1968. His first book of poems, *The Immobile Wind* (1921), contained experiments in free verse, and early reviewers described Winters as an Imagist. He soon moved to stricter forms, and for the next twenty-five years he wrote the meditative lyrics for which he is best known. Robert Lowell described him as the "kind of conservative who was so original and so radical that his poems were never reprinted in the anthologies for almost twenty years."[1]

John Sutter[1]

I was the patriarch of the shining land,
Of the blond summer and metallic grain;
Men vanished at the motion of my hand,
And when I beckoned they would come again.

The earth grew dense with grain at my desire;   5
The shade was deepened at the springs and streams;
Moving in dust that clung like pillared fire,
The gathering herds grew heavy in my dreams.

Across the mountains, naked from the heights,
Down to the valley broken settlers came,   10
And in my houses feasted through the nights,
Rebuilt their sinews and assumed a name.

1. "Yvor Winters: A Tribute," *Poetry*, April 1961, pp. 40–41.
1. John Sutter (1803–1880), American pioneer, born in Switzerland, was in 1838 granted a huge tract of land on the Sacramento river by the Mexican governor on condition that he develop and fortify it. His settlement, "New Helvetia," became powerful. After California was acquired by the United States, Sutter prepared a new mill; but in the course of digging, gold was found. The news leaked out against his will, the gold rush began, and his property was overrun. When the U.S. Supreme Court found the title to most of his land invalid, he went bankrupt. From 1871 to 1880, when he died, he petitioned Congress annually for redress.

In my clear rivers my own men discerned
The motive for the ruin and the crime—
Gold heavier than earth, a wealth unearned,   15
Loot, for two decades, from the heart of Time.

Metal, intrinsic value, deep and dense,
Preanimate, inimitable, still,
Real, but an evil with no human sense,
Dispersed the mind to concentrate the will.   20

Grained by alchemic change, the human kind
Turned from themselves to rivers and to rocks;
With dynamite broke metal unrefined;
Measured their moods by geologic shocks.

With knives they dug the metal out of stone;   25
Turned rivers back, for gold through ages piled,
Drove knives to hearts, and faced the gold alone;
Valley and river ruined and reviled;

Reviled and ruined me, my servant slew,
Strangled him from the figtree by my door.
When they had done what fury bade them do,   30
I was a cursing beggar, stripped and sore.

What end impersonal, what breathless age,
Incontinent of quiet and of years,
What calm catastrophe will yet assuage   35
This final drouth of penitential tears?

                    1941

Sir Gawaine and the Green Knight[2]

Reptilian green the wrinkled throat,
Green as a bough of yew the beard;
He bent his head, and so I smote;
Then for a thought my vision cleared.

The head dropped clean; he rose and walked;   5
He fixed his fingers in the hair;
The head was unabashed and talked;
I understood what I must dare.

His flesh, cut down, arose and grew.
He bade me wait the season's round,   10
And then, when he had strength anew,
To meet him on his native ground.

The year declined; and in his keep
I passed in joy a thriving yule;

2. Winters's poem is based upon a Middle English poem of the same name. Sir Gawaine cuts off the head of the Green Knight, who tells him to come in a year's time to a castle so as to receive a similar blow. Gawaine arrives, and while his host is out hunting, the lady of the castle woos him. He keeps his virtue, and the Green Knight allows him to depart unscathed.

and whether waking or in sleep,   15
I lived in riot like a fool.

He beat the woods to bring me meat.
His lady, like a forest vine,
Grew in my arms; the growth was sweet;
And yet what thoughtless force was mine!   20

By practice and conviction formed,
With ancient stubbornness ingrained,
Although her body clung and swarmed,
My own identity remained.

Her beauty, lithe, unholy, pure,   25
Took shapes that I had never known;
And had I once been insecure,
Had grafted laurel in my bone.

And then, since I had kept the trust,
Had loved the lady, yet was true,   30
The knight withheld his giant thrust
And let me go with what I knew.

I left the green bark and the shade,
Where growth was rapid, thick, and still;
I found a road that men had made   35
And rested on a drying hill.

                                                    1941

Time and the Garden

The spring has darkened with activity.
The future gathers in vine, bush, and tree:
Persimmon, walnut, loquat, fig, and grape,
Degrees and kinds of color, taste, and shape.
These will advance in their due series, space   5
The season like a tranquil dwelling-place.
And yet excitement swells me, vein by vein:
I long to crowd the little garden, gain
Its sweetness in my hand and crush it small
And taste it in a moment, time and all!   10
These trees, whose slow growth measures off my years,
I would expand to greatness. No one hears,
And I am still retarded in duress!
And this is like that other restlessness
To seize the greatness not yet fairly earned,   15
One which the tougher poets have discerned—
Gascoigne, Ben Jonson, Greville, Raleigh, Donne,[3]
Poets who wrote great poems, one by one,
And spaced by many years, each line an act
Through which few labor, which no men retract.   20

3. These five poets were contemporaries of Shakespeare.

This passion is the scholar's heritage,
The imposition of a busy age,
The passion to condense from book to book
Unbroken wisdom in a single look,
Though we know well that when this fix the head,   25
The mind's immortal, but the man is dead.

1941

LANGSTON HUGHES
1902–1967

Langston Hughes belongs to the same generation of Black poets as Countee Cullen, but does not otherwise resemble him. Cullen was, except for his sense of belonging to a minority, in the English literary tradition; he regarded his work as poetry, not Black poetry. Hughes took a more original direction. He sought to write poems in the spirit of jazz, and found affinities not with Keats, as Cullen did, but with spirituals and blues. Many of his poems were set to music, and he himself wrote operettas. It was not educational difference which separated his poetry from Cullen's—they were both well educated—but choice; Hughes attained a manner of cultivated artlessness.

The color problem was complicated for Hughes by his having a good deal of white and Indian blood. As a result he found discrimination no less poignant, but the more absurd. In his autobiography he tells of being asked in a restaurant in the South whether he was Mexican or Negro; the waiter explained that he might serve a Mexican but not a Negro. Hughes recounts this and many other incidents with amusement rather than indignation. His first thirty years were a series of upheavals, in which color was only one of many agitating factors.

He was born on February 1, 1902, in Joplin, Missouri. His early years were spent in Missouri and Kansas. His parents separated and remarried, but always kept an eye out for him. He lived mostly with his mother in Lawrence, Kansas, until his twelfth year. Hughes went in 1914 to Lincoln, Illinois, to live with his father and stepmother. While there he completed grammar school and was elected class poet, a distinction which compelled him to try writing verse for the first time. He then went to join his mother, also remarried, in Cleveland, and attended high school. He read widely, in Schopenhauer and Nietzsche as well as in Dreiser and Edna Ferber, and he was deeply influenced by Carl Sandburg, Edgar Lee Masters, Vachel Lindsay, and Amy Lowell. Under their influence he wrote free verse; under the influence of the Black poet Paul Lawrence Dunbar, he attempted dialect poetry.

In 1919 a sudden telegram from his father enjoined him to be ready next day to travel to Mexico for the summer. His father had become very clever at business, and found he could do better in Mexico than in the United States. His expectation was that Langston Hughes would become an engineer, and when the boy protested that this was not his interest, his father insisted that he could do well at anything. But eventually Langston was sent, as he had wished, to Columbia University. After one year (1921–22), he dropped out, and shipped out to Africa, and then, on another vessel, to France. The year 1924 was spent in various odd jobs in Paris, the best being that of assistant cook in a fashionable restaurant.

On his return to the United States, Hughes joined his mother, now living in Washington, and took a job as busboy in a hotel. It happened that Vachel Lindsay was dining there, and Hughes, too shy to present himself directly, left some poems beside Lindsay's plate. Lindsay must have seen at once that the poems had that oral, recitative quality which in a different way he aimed at himself. He read some of them to an audience that night, and the busboy poet became locally renowned. On Lindsay's

Langston Hughes

ng, Hughes sent many of his poems to magazines, and one, "The Weary Blues,"
a prize from *Opportunity*, an influential Black magazine. This poem, for which
Hughes was never able to find an ending that satisfied him, became the title poem
in his first volume, published in 1926.

With considerable sense of himself and his future, Hughes accepted a scholarship
to Lincoln University in Pennsylvania. He received a B.A. there in 1929, and in the
same year published his first novel, *Not Without Laughter*. He became a successful
writer, and was also well known for his excellent readings of his poetry. He died May
22, 1967.

The Negro Speaks of Rivers

I've known rivers:
I've known rivers ancient as the world and older than the flow of human
    blood in human veins.

My soul has grown deep like the rivers.

I bathed in the Euphrates when dawns were young.
I built my hut near the Congo and it lulled me to sleep.   5
I looked upon the Nile and raised the pyramids above it.
I heard the singing of the Mississippi when Abe Lincoln went down to New
    Orleans, and I've seen its muddy bosom turn all golden in the sunset.

I've known rivers:
Ancient, dusky rivers.

My soul has grown deep like the rivers.   10

1926

The Weary Blues

Droning a drowsy syncopated tune,
Rocking back and forth to a mellow croon,
    I heard a Negro play.
Down on Lenox Avenue[1] the other night
By the pale dull pallor of an old gas light   5
    He did a lazy sway. . . .
    He did a lazy sway. . . .
To the tune o' those Weary Blues.
With his ebony hands on each ivory key
He made that poor piano moan with melody.   10
    O Blues
Swaying to and fro on his rickety stool
He played that sad raggy tune like a musical fool.
    Sweet Blues!
Coming from a black man's soul.   15
    O Blues!
In a deep song voice with a melancholy tone
    I heard that Negro sing, that old piano moan—

1. A major street in Harlem.

"Ain't got nobody in all this world,
Ain't got nobody but ma self.   20
I's gwine to quit ma frownin'
And put ma troubles on the shelf."
Thump, thump, thump, went his foot on the floor.
He played a few chords when he sang some more—
    "I got the Weary Blues   25
And I can't be satisfied.
Got the Weary Blues
And can't be satisfied—
I ain't happy no mo'
And I wish that I had died."   30
And far into the night he crooned that tune.
    The stars went out and so did the moon.
    The singer stopped playing and went to bed
    While the Weary Blues echoed through his head.
    He slept like a rock or a man that's dead.   35

                                                    1926

Brass Spittoons

Clean the spittoons, boy.
    Detroit,
    Chicago,
    Atlantic City,
    Palm Beach.   5
Clean the spittoons.
The steam in hotel kitchens,
And the smoke in hotel lobbies,
And the slime in hotel spittoons:
Part of my life.   10
    Hey, boy!
    A nickel,
    A dime,
    A dollar,
Two dollars a day.   15
    Hey, boy!
    A nickel,
    A dime,
    A dollar,
    Two dollars   20
Buy shoes for the baby.
House rent to pay.
Gin on Saturday,
Church on Sunday.
    My God!   25
Babies and gin and church
And women and Sunday
All mixed with dimes and
Dollars and clean spittoons
And house rent to pay.   30
    Hey, boy!

A bright bowl of brass is beautiful to the Lord.
Bright polished brass like the cymbals
Of King David's dancers,
Like the wine cups of Solomon.   35
     Hey, boy!
A clean spittoon on the altar of the Lord.
A clean bright spittoon all newly polished—
At least I can offer that.
          Com'mere, boy!   40

                                                              1927

Morning After[2]

I was so sick last night I
Didn't hardly know my mind.
So sick last night I
Didn't know my mind.
I drunk some bad licker that   5
Almost made me blind.

Had a dream last night I
Thought I was in hell.
I drempt last night I
Thought I was in hell.   10
Woke up and looked around me—
Babe, your mouth was open like a well.

I said, Baby! Baby!
Please don't snore so loud.
Baby! Please!   15
Please don't snore so loud.
You jest a little bit o' woman but you
Sound like a great big crowd.

                                                              1942

Madam's Past History

My name is Johnson—
Madam Alberta K.
The Madam stands for business.
I'm smart that way.

I had a   5
HAIR-DRESSING PARLOR
Before
The depression put
The prices lower.

Then I had a   10
BARBECUE STAND

---

2. This poem is in the form of a blues.

Till I got mixed up
With a no-good man.

Cause I had a insurance
The WPA[3]   15
Said, We can't use you
Wealthy that way.

I said,
DON'T WORRY 'BOUT ME!
Just like the song,   20
You WPA folks take care of yourself—
And I'll get along.

I do cooking,
Day's work, too!
Alberta K. Johnson—   25
Madam to you.

                                                          1949

Theme for English B

The instructor said,

*Go home and write
a page tonight.
And let that page come out of you—
Then, it will be true.*   5

I wonder if it's that simple?
I am twenty-two, colored, born in Winston-Salem.
I went to school there, then Durham,[4] then here
to this college[5] on the hill above Harlem.
I am the only colored student in my class.   10
The steps from the hill lead down into Harlem,
through a park, then I cross St. Nicholas,[6]
Eighth Avenue, Seventh, and I come to the Y,
the Harlem Branch Y, where I take the elevator
up to my room, sit down, and write this page: 15

It's not easy to know what is true for you or me
at twenty-two, my age. But I guess I'm what
I feel and see and hear, Harlem, I hear you:
hear you, hear me—we two—you, me, talk on this page.
(I hear New York, too.) Me—who?   20

Well, I like to eat, sleep, drink, and be in love.
I like to work, read, learn, and understand life.
I like a pipe for a Christmas present,

or records—Bessie, bop,[7] or Bach.
I guess being colored doesn't make me *not* like   25
the same things other folks like who are other races.
So will my page be colored that I write?
Being me, it will not be white.
But it will be
a part of you, instructor.   30
You are white—
yet a part of me, as I am a part of you.
That's American.
Sometimes perhaps you don't want to be a part of me.
Nor do I often want to be a part of you.   35
But we are, that's true!
As I learn from you,
I guess you learn from me—
although you're older—and white—
and somewhat more free.   40

This is my page for English B.

1959

7. A kind of jazz; Bessie Smith, the blues singer.

STEVIE SMITH
1902–1971

Stevie Smith's "Was He Married?" is a poetic argument in which one voice questions the depth of Christ's participation in human experience and a second voice expresses the cold comfort of the divine otherness. The first voice is persistent, even nagging— do only human beings "learn too that being comical / Does not ameliorate the desperation?" The second voice replies, "Only human beings feel this, / It is because they are so mixed." Stevie Smith's poems appear at first to be "comical," but a closer look reveals that her adaptations of nursery rhymes, her sometimes *faux-naïf* language, and her references to fairy tales express a perplexed concern over the agonies of our "mixed" lot. Her poems communicate a personality of resolution and stoic toughness. When asked if her attitudes had changed during her life, she replied decisively: "No, they haven't changed at all, I think. One has one's thoughts about things and one takes great pleasure in these thoughts and in working them out. But I should be very surprised, for instance, if one day I said, 'This is absolutely black' and the next day I said, 'This is absolutely white.' "[1] She insists that her poems share with all poems a concern for mortality, but that she doesn't mind much about survival. "I rather like the idea of death," she says strikingly.

Stevie Smith was born Florence Margaret Smith in Hull, Yorkshire, England on September 20, 1902. (Her nickname "Stevie" refers to her smallness; it was borrowed from a famous jockey of the time.) At the age of three she moved to London with her family, and she lived in the same house there until her death. Her first book, published in 1936, was a novel; a year later she published her first collection of poems, illustrated, like all her later collections, with her own drawings, which she described as "something like doodling." Until 1953 she worked in a publisher's office in London; after that she devoted her time to writing and to broadcasts on the BBC.

1. *The Poet Speaks*, ed. Peter Orr, London, 1966, p. 227.

In 1966 she was given the Cholmondely Award, in 1969 the Queen's Gold Medal for Poetry. She died March 8, 1971, and since then her poems have found more and more admiring readers. In 1977 a play based on her life—called simply *Stevie*—was produced, and it has since been made into a film.

Not Waving But Drowning

Nobody heard him, the dead man,
But still he lay moaning:
I was much further out than you thought
And not waving but drowning.

Poor chap, he always loved larking   5
And now he's dead
It must have been too cold for him his heart gave way,
They said.

Oh, no no no, it was too cold always
(Still the dead one lay moaning)   10
I was much too far out all my life
And not waving but drowning.

                                                       1957

Was He Married?

Was he married, did he try
To support as he grew less fond of them
Wife and family?

No,
He never suffered such a blow.   5

Did he feel pointless, feeble and distrait,
Unwanted by everyone and in the way?

From his cradle he was purposeful,
His bent strong and his mind full.

Did he love people very much   10
Yet find them die one day?

He did not love in the human way.

Did he ask how long it would go on,
Wonder if Death could be counted on for an end?

He did not feel like this,   15
He had a future of bliss.

Did he never feel strong
Pain for being wrong?

He was not wrong, he was right,
He suffered from others', not his own, spite.   20

But there *is* no suffering like having made a mistake
Because of being of an inferior make.

He was not inferior,
He was superior.

He knew then that power corrupts but some must govern?   25

His thoughts were different.

Did he lack friends? Worse,
Think it was for his fault, not theirs?

He did not lack friends,
He had disciples he moulded to his ends.   30

Did he feel over-handicapped sometimes, yet must draw even?

How could he feel like this? He was the King of Heaven.

. . . find a sudden brightness one day in everything
Because a mood had been conquered, or a sin?

I tell you, he did not sin.   35

Do only human beings suffer from the irritation
I have mentioned? learn too that being comical
Does not ameliorate the desperation?

Only human beings feel this,
It is because they are so mixed.   40

All human beings should have a medal,
A god cannot carry it, he is not able.

A god is Man's doll, you ass,
He makes him up like this on purpose.

He might have made him up worse.   45

He often has, in the past.

To choose a god of love, as he did and does,
Is a little move then?

Yes, it is.

A larger one will be when men   50
Love love and hate hate but do not deify them?

It will be a larger one.

                                                          1962

Admire Cranmer![1]

Admire the old man, admire him, admire him,
Mocked by the priests of Mary Tudor, given to the flames,
Flinching and overcoming the flinching, Cranmer.

Admire the martyrs of Bloody Mary's reign,
In the shocking arithmetic of cruel average, ninety   5
A year, three-hundred; admire them.

But still I cry: Admire the Archbishop,
The old man, the scholar, admire him.
Not simply, for flinching and overcoming simply,
But for his genius, admire him,   10
His delicate feelings of genius, admire him,

That wrote the Prayer Book
(Admire him!)
And made the flames burn crueller. Admire Cranmer!

   1962

Thoughts about the Person from Porlock[2]

Coleridge received the Person from Porlock
And ever after called him a curse,
Then why did he hurry to let him in?
He could have hid in the house.

It was not right of Coleridge in fact it was wrong   5
(But often we all do wrong)
As the truth is I think he was already stuck
With Kubla Khan.

He was weeping and wailing: I am finished, finished,
I shall never write another word of it,   10
When along comes the Person from Porlock
And takes the blame for it.

It was not right, it was wrong,
But often we all do wrong.

May we inquire the name of the Person from Porlock?   15
Why, Porson, didn't you know?
He lived at the bottom of Porlock Hill
So had a long way to go,

1. Thomas Cranmer, Archbishop of Canterbury during the reign of Henry VIII and a key figure in Henry's break with the Roman Catholic Church and establishment of the Church of England. During the following reign of Queen Mary I (Henry's daughter Mary Tudor, also known as "Bloody Mary") Cranmer was burned at the stake for heresy, as were several hundred others who protested Mary's efforts to reestablish the Roman Catholic Church in England.
2. In the prefatory note to his poem "Kubla Khan" (1816), Samuel Taylor Coleridge wrote that he had dreamed the poem's vision under the effects of opium, and that, on awakening, he immediately started to write the poem. "At this moment," Coleridge says, "he was unfortunately called out by a person on business from Porlock, and detained by him above an hour"; afterwards, trying to finish the poem, Coleridge found, "to his no small surprise and mortification," that the vision had vanished "like the images on the surface of a stream." Compare, below, Amy Clampitt's "A Cure at Porlock" (p. 570).

He wasn't much in the social sense
Though his grandmother was a Warlock,[3]   20
One of the Rutlandshire ones I fancy
And nothing to do with Porlock,

And he lived at the bottom of the hill as I said
And had a cat named Flo,
And had a cat named Flo.   25

I long for the Person from Porlock
To bring my thoughts to an end,
I am becoming impatient to see him
I think of him as a friend,

Often I look out of the window   30
Often I run to the gate
I think, He will come this evening,
I think it is rather late.

I am hungry to be interrupted
For ever and ever amen   35
O Person from Porlock come quickly
And bring my thoughts to an end.

                          •

I felicitate the people who have a Person from Porlock
To break up everything and throw it away
Because then there will be nothing to keep them   40
And they need not stay.

                          •

Why do they grumble so much?
He comes like a benison[4]
They should be glad he has not forgotten them
They might have had to go on.   45

                          •

These thoughts are depressing I know. They are depressing,
I wish I was more cheerful, it is more pleasant,
Also it is a duty, we should smile as well as submitting
To the purpose of One Above who is experimenting
With various mixtures of human character which goes best, 50
All is interesting for him it is exciting, but not for us.
There I go again. Smile, smile, and get some work to do
Then you will be practically unconscious without positively having to go.

                                                          1966

To Carry the Child

To carry the child into adult life
Is good? I say it is not,

---

3. Also the name for a male witch.   4. Blessing.

To carry the child into adult life
Is to be handicapped.

The child in adult life is defenceless   5
And if he is grown-up, knows it,
And the grown-up looks at the childish part
And despises it.

The child, too, despises the clever grown-up,
The man-of-the-world, the frozen,   10
For the child has the tears alive on his cheek
And the man has none of them.

As the child has colours, and the man sees no
Colours or anything,
Being easy only in things of the mind,   15
The child is easy in feeling.

Easy in feeling, easily excessive
And in excess powerful,
For instance, if you do not speak to the child
He will make trouble.   20

You would say a man had the upper hand
Of the child, if a child survive,
But I say the child has fingers of strength
To strangle the man alive.

Oh it is not happy, it is never happy,   25
To carry the child into adulthood,
Let children lie down before full growth
And die in their infanthood
And be guilty of no man's blood.

But oh the poor child, the poor child, what can he do,   30
Trapped in a grown-up carapace,
But peer outside of his prison room
With the eye of an anarchist?

1966

COUNTEE CULLEN
1903–1946

In Countee Cullen Black poetry found one of its gentler voices in the first half of the twentieth century. Cullen was old-fashioned in his admiration for Keats and Millay, in his technical devices, in his mild and wistful protest. To be a poet, and Black, remained for him an unexpected grace. Bitterness was to come later, to others; in Cullen negritude was a subject but not as yet a preemptive cause.

He made his position clear in an anthology of Black poetry which he published in New York in 1927. It had the belletristic title of *Caroling Dusk* (like Yeats's *The Celtic Twilight*), and in the introduction Cullen said, "This country's Negro writers may here and there turn some singular facet toward the literary sun, but in the main, since theirs is also the heritage of the English language, their work will not present any serious aberration from the poetic tendencies of their times."[1] The word "aberration" indicates how contented Cullen was to remain within a literary tradition in which the poet's color was secondary.

As contrasted with Black poets of the second half of the century such as Amiri Baraka, Cullen lived a placid life. He was born in New York City on May 30, 1903. His father was a Methodist minister. While still in high school Cullen began to win prizes for his poems. He went on to New York University, from which he was graduated in 1925. The following year he took an M.A. in English at Harvard. For a time he was assistant editor of *Opportunity: Journal of Negro Life*. Then a Guggenheim Fellowship enabled him to resign and to spend the year 1928 in Paris. During this year he married Yolande Du Bois, daughter of the Black writer W. E. B. Du Bois, but they were divorced a year later. The rest of his life was spent as a teacher in New York schools. He published five respected volumes of verse, a novel, and a translation of Euripides' *Medea*, and he collaborated with Arna Bontemps on a play. His best poetry expresses bewilderment rather than indignation at racial oppression. Cullen died January 9, 1946, just as a new tone began to come into Black literature.

1. Introduction to *Caroling Dusk*, New York, 1927, p. xi.

Yet Do I Marvel

I doubt not God is good, well-meaning, kind,
And did He stoop to quibble could tell why
The little buried mole continues blind,
Why flesh that mirrors Him must some day die,
Make plain the reason tortured Tantalus   5
Is baited by the fickle fruit, declare
If merely brute caprice dooms Sisyphus
To struggle up a never-ending stair.[1]
Inscrutable His ways are, and immune
To catechism by a mind too strewn   10
With petty cares to slightly understand
What awful brain compels His awful hand.
Yet do I marvel at this curious thing:
To make a poet black, and bid him sing!

1925

Incident

(For Eric Walrond)

Once riding in old Baltimore,
    Heart-filled, head-filled with glee,
I saw a Baltimorean
    Keep looking straight at me.

Now I was eight and very small,   5
    And he was no whit bigger,
And so I smiled, but he poked out
    His tongue, and called me, "Nigger."

1. In Hades, the underworld of Greek mythology, Tantalus is forced to starve while food and drink are perpetually just out of his reach; Sisyphus must push to the top of a hill a rock which perpetually rolls back.

I saw the whole of Baltimore
  From May until December;   10
Of all the things that happened there
  That's all that I remember.

                             1925

Heritage

(For Harold Jackman)

What is Africa to me:
Copper sun or scarlet sea,
Jungle star or jungle track,
Strong bronzed men, or regal black
Women from whose loins I sprang   5
When the birds of Eden sang?
One three centuries removed
From the scenes his fathers loved,
Spicy grove, cinnamon tree,
What is Africa to me?   10

So I lie, who all day long
Want no sound except the song
Sung by wild barbaric birds
Goading massive jungle herds,
Juggernauts of flesh that pass   15
Trampling tall defiant grass
Where young forest lovers lie,
Plighting troth beneath the sky.
So I lie, who always hear,
Though I cram against my ear   20
Both my thumbs, and keep them there,
Great drums throbbing through the air.
So I lie, whose fount of pride,
Dear distress, and joy allied,
Is my somber flesh and skin,   25
With the dark blood dammed within
Like great pulsing tides of wine
That, I fear, must burst the fine
Channels of the chafing net
Where they surge and foam and fret.   30

Africa? A book one thumbs
Listlessly, till slumber comes.
Unremembered are her bats
Circling through the night, her cats
Crouching in the river reeds,   35
Stalking gentle flesh that feeds
By the river brink; no more
Does the bugle-throated roar
Cry that monarch claws have leapt
From the scabbards where they slept.   40
Silver snakes that once a year

Doff the lovely coats you wear,
Seek no covert in your fear
Lest a mortal eye should see;
What's your nakedness to me?   45
Here no leprous flowers rear
Fierce corollas in the air;
Here no bodies sleek and wet,
Dripping mingled rain and sweat,
Tread the savage measures of   50
Jungle boys and girls in love.
What is last year's snow to me,[2]
Last year's anything? The tree
Budding yearly must forget
How its past arose or set—   55
Bough and blossom, flower, fruit,
Even what shy bird with mute
Wonder at her travail there,
Meekly labored in its hair.
One three centuries removed   60
From the scenes his fathers loved,
Spicy grove, cinnamon tree,
What is Africa to me?

So I lie, who find no peace
Night or day, no slight release   65
From the unremittent beat
Made by cruel padded feet
Walking through my body's street.
Up and down they go, and back,
Treading out a jungle track.   70
So I lie, who never quite
Safely sleep from rain at night—
I can never rest at all
When the rain begins to fall;
Like a soul gone mad with pain   75
I must match its weird refrain;
Ever must I twist and squirm,
Writhing like a baited worm,
While its primal measures drip
Through my body, crying, "Strip!   80
Doff this new exuberance.
Come and dance the Lover's Dance!"
In an old remembered way
Rain works on me night and day.

Quaint, outlandish heathen gods   85
Black men fashion out of rods,
Clay, and brittle bits of stone,
In a likeness like their own,
My conversion came high-priced;
I belong to Jesus Christ,   90

2. An allusion to Francois Villon's famous epigram on transience, "Where are the snows of yester-year?" from his "Grand Testament."

Preacher of humility;
Heathen gods are naught to me.

Father, Son, and Holy Ghost,
So I make an idle boast;
Jesus of the twice-turned cheek,   95
Lamb of God, although I speak
With my mouth thus, in my heart
Do I play a double part.
Ever at Thy glowing altar
Must my heart grow sick and falter,   100
Wishing He I served were black,
Thinking then it would not lack
Precedent of pain to guide it,
Let who would or might deride it;
Surely then this flesh would know   105
Yours had borne a kindred woe.
Lord, I fashion dark gods, too,
Daring even to give You
Dark despairing features where,
Crowned with dark rebellious hair,   110
Patience wavers just so much as
Mortal grief compels, while touches
Quick and hot, of anger, rise
To smitten cheek and weary eyes.
Lord, forgive me if my need   115
Sometimes shapes a human creed.
All day long and all night through,
One thing only must I do:
Quench my pride and cool my blood,
Lest I perish in the flood.   120
Lest a hidden ember set
Timber that I thought was wet
Burning like the dryest flax,
Melting like the merest wax,
Lest the grave restore its dead.   125
Not yet has my heart or head
In the least way realized
They and I are civilized.

1927

PATRICK KAVANAGH
1904–1967

"My life," wrote Patrick Kavanagh towards its end, "has in many ways been a tragedy
and a failure." He was born in the village of Inniskeen, County Monaghan, Ireland,
on October 21, 1904, and he described the life of the Irish country poor, which he
shared, as "sad, grey, twisted, blind, just awful."[1] Raised a Roman Catholic, Kavanagh continued to be a Christian, though he blamed the Church for causing much
unhappiness, his own included, through its repression of natural feeling. In 1939 he

1. *November Haggard: Uncollected Prose and Poetry,* New York, 1971, p. 16.

went to Dublin. "It was," he wrote, "the worst mistake of my life."[2] The great creative impulse of the Irish Literary Movement was not yet spent, but Kavanagh—in time, at least—scorned it. Though the movement "purported to be frightfully Irish and racy of the Celtic soil," it was, Kavanagh said, a "thorough going English-bred lie."[3] As one who knew the life of the Irish peasant at first hand, he laughed at the writers who claimed "to have their roots in the soil and to be peasants as well."[4] Ferociously independent, forever in a rage with readers who accepted the delusions promoted by successful authors and critics, Kavanagh contrived a meager living as a columnist, movie critic, and, in 1952, publisher of his own magazine, *Kavanagh's Weekly*. His first book of poems to attract much attention, *The Great Hunger* (1942), got him into trouble with the censor because of its alleged obscenity and anti-Catholicism. Kavanagh, who frequently wrote poems which he later disowned, said that there were some "queer and terrible things" in the book, but that it lacked the "nobility and repose of poetry."[5]

Nobility and repose are not qualities one associates with Kavanagh's poetry or prose, and he praised the untroubled acceptance of life with the air of a man who found such acceptance difficult. In 1954 he was gravely ill: he suffered from lung cancer, and one of his lungs had to be surgically removed. During his convalescence, in the summer of 1955, he had the experience described in "Canal Bank Walk," and he was then liberated from his "messianic compulsion." Henceforth his purpose in life, as he described it, "was to have no purpose."[6] He resigned himself to obscurity and failure, finding consolation in the thought that great men "are not concerned with whether or not their work is involved with the ephemeral." The vocation of the true poet, as Kavanagh now saw it, was to "name and name and name the obscure places, people, or events."[7] Kavanagh's efforts to transcend his lifelong anger and pain were made with the help of the comic muse. He came to regard comedy as the "ultimate sophistication," which ordinary people "do not understand and therefore fear."[8] Though he described his own life as tragic, he ultimately believed that in tragedy "there is always something of a lie. . . Comedy is the abundance of life."[9] Kavanagh married for the first time early in 1967 and died later that year, on November 30th, in a Dublin nursing home.

2. *Self-Portrait*, Dublin, 1964, p. 11.
3. The same, p. 9.
4. The same.
5. The same, p. 27.
6. Author's note to *Collected Poems*, New York,
1964, p. xiv.
7. "X," *A Quarterly Review*, 1:2, March 1960, p. 156.
8. *Self-Portrait*, p. 8.
9. "X," *A Quarterly Review*, p. 156.

Tinker's Wife

I saw her amid the dunghill debris
Looking for things
Such as an old pair of shoes or gaiters.
She was a young woman,
A tinker's wife.   5
Her face had streaks of care
Like wires across it,
But she was supple

As a young goat
On a windy hill.   10

She searched on the dunghill debris,
Tripping gingerly
Over tin canisters

And sharp-broken
Dinner plates.   15
                                                                 1936

Inniskeen Road: July Evening[1]

The bicycles go by in twos and threes—
There's a dance in Billy Brennan's barn to-night,
And there's the half-talk code of mysteries
And the wink-and-elbow language of delight.
Half-past eight and there is not a spot   5
Upon a mile of road, no shadow thrown
That might turn out a man or woman, not
A footfall tapping secrecies of stone.

I have what every poet hates in spite
Of all the solemn talk of contemplation.
Oh, Alexander Selkirk[2] knew the plight   10
Of being king and government and nation.
A road, a mile of kingdom, I am king
Of banks and stones and every blooming thing.

                                                                 1936

Canal Bank Walk[3]

Leafy-with-love banks and the green waters of the canal
Pouring redemption for me, that I do
The will of God, wallow in the habitual, the banal,
Grow with nature again as before I grew.
The bright stick trapped, the breeze adding a third   5
Party to the couple kissing on an old seat,
And a bird gathering materials for the nest for the Word
Eloquently new and abandoned to its delirious beat.
O unworn world enrapture me, encapture me in a web
Of fabulous grass and eternal voices by a beech,   10
Feed the gaping need of my senses, give me ad lib
To pray unselfconsciously with overflowing speech
For this soul needs to be honoured with a new dress woven
From green and blue things and arguments that cannot be proven.

                                                                 1960

Come Dance with Kitty Stobling

No, no, no, I know I was not important as I moved
Through the colourful country, I was but a single

---

1. Inniskeen, in the south of County Monaghan, was Kavanagh's native village.
   2. Eighteenth-century seaman whose experiences on an uninhabited island off the coast of Chile
were used by Daniel Defoe for *Robinson Crusoe*.
   3. "It was while recovering from a serious illness in the hot summer of nineteen fifty-five as I
lay on the bank of the Grand Canal [in Dublin]

that I learned the pleasures of being passive"
(*November Haggard*, p. 85). Kavanagh saw this as
a turning point in his poetical career, and claimed
that his "birth as a poet" occurred at that time,
when he was satisfied to "let the water lap idly on
the shores of my mind. My purpose in life was to
have no purpose" (*Collected Poems*, p. xiv).

Item in the picture, the namer not the beloved.
O tedious man with whom no gods commingle.
Beauty, who has described beauty? Once upon a time   5
I had a myth that was a lie but it served:
Trees walking across the crests of hills and my rhyme
Cavorting on mile-high stilts and the unnerved
Crowds looking up with terror in their rational faces.
O dance with Kitty Stobling I outrageously   10
Cried out-of-sense to them, while their timorous paces
Stumbled behind Jove's page boy paging me.
I had a very pleasant journey, thank you sincerely
For giving me my madness back, or nearly.

1960

In Memory of My Mother

I do not think of you lying in the wet clay
Of a Monaghan graveyard; I see
You walking down a lane among the poplars
On your way to the station, or happily

Going to second Mass on a summer Sunday—   5
You meet me and you say:
'Don't forget to see about the cattle—'
Among your earthiest words the angels stray.

And I think of you walking along a headland
Of green oats in June,   10
So full of repose, so rich with life—
And I see us meeting at the end of a town

On a fair day by accident, after
The bargains are all made and we can walk
Together through the shops and stalls and markets   15
Free in the oriental streets of thought.

O you are not lying in the wet clay,
For it is a harvest evening now and we
Are piling up the ricks against the moonlight
And you smile up at us—eternally.   20

1960

EARL BIRNEY
b. 1904

Although Earl Birney counts as a "Canadian poet," he by no means restricts himself
to the landscapes and people of his own country. Birney, a learned wayfarer, a tireless performer of his own poems and those of his compatriots, has given readings
from Vancouver Island to Newfoundland—and at about thirty universities in the
United States. He has also set up his shop, however briefly, in Central and South
America, the Orient, and Africa, and, of course, the British Isles.

Birney's poems are attractive because they are abundant and varied, full of sights and sounds which the poet greets with wonder, and because Birney, with reliable good humor, is willing to try anything new, from the Beats through Projectivist and Concretist poetry, not to speak of Sound poetry, and in the welter of all these influences, some more familiar than others, he remains invigorating and personal. His poems are not so much parts of a great confession as samplings of a mingled stream of observation and imagination.

Not that Earl Birney ever seems fatigued or disenchanted. "The Bear on the Delhi Road" is concerned with the discipline, energy, and pain of creation in the arts. The Himalayan bear would prefer to remain "only an ambling bear / four-footed in berries"; for the Kashmiri hunters who are training him this is hard, dangerous work, necessary to their livelihood.

Earl Birney (there is some disagreement over the spelling of his given name) was born in Calgary, Alberta, on May 13, 1904; he spent his childhood in the Rocky Mountains. He took his B.A. at the University of British Columbia in Vancouver, his M.A. at Toronto, and his Ph.D., which was in Old and Middle English, at the University of California in Berkeley. He was on active duty with the Canadian Army from 1942 to 1945. He has received numerous awards from universities and from the Canadian government.

The Bear on the Delhi Road[1]

Unreal   tall as a myth
by the road the Himalayan bear
is beating the brilliant air
with his crooked arms
About him two men   bare   5
spindly as locusts   leap

One pulls on a ring
in the great soft nose   His mate
flicks   flicks with a stick
up at the rolling eyes   10

They have not led him here
down from the fabulous hills
to this bald alien plain
and the clamorous world   to kill
but simply to teach him to dance   15

They are peaceful both   these spare
men of Kashmir   and the bear
alive is their living   too
If   far on the Delhi way
around him galvanic they dance   20
it is merely to wear   wear
from his shaggy body the tranced
wish forever to stay
only an ambling bear
four-footed in berries   25
It is no more joyous for them

1. In India.

in this hot dust to prance
out of reach of the praying claws
sharpened to paw for ants
in the shadows of deodars[2]   30
It is not easy to free
myth from reality
or rear this fellow up
to lurch   lurch with them
in the tranced dancing of men   35
Srinagar 1958 / Île des Porquerolles 1959   1962, 1972

The Gray Woods Exploding

(For Vin Buckley, who is not in the story,
but helped me straighten my Strine[3])

(1)

Flying from the dry pall of the city
i watch roads wrinkle   dwindle up the dun Range
& disappear in the general pox
of eucalyptus   the skin of a land
hard & vacant as the faces   5
of swagmen[4] in Australian painting

(2)

But suddenly all is tressed
with turbulence
violet smoke rocketing up & away to the Tasman[5]—
Fire is loose   wild in a hundred hills   10
& the gray woods exploding

Somewhere between the red cores
of combustion there must be birds
falling   & screaming horses
in flight from this fearful beauty   15
marsupials   men   ambushed
each creature whirling away
from the palsied will of the trees
to die & immolate all
in a violence of comets over the quiet sea   20

(3)

The plane floats untouched
but i hear again that lone ghost-gum[6] in the Olgas
pricked by a campfire spark
roaring to sacrifice
the air filled in an instant with crimson tongues   25
& the screech & outswoop of parrots

2. East Indian cedars.
3. Australian self-kidding pronounciation of '
"Australian"; that is, Australian accent or talk.
4. Hoboes.
5. The island of Tasmania, south of Australia.
6. Tree common to Australia.

In the time of remembering
i drift beyond sight of perdition
& look down again on mere grayness

Borded & inert as gods we descend   cloudwrapped   30
to the darkening human valleys

(4)

Morning & a Head of English
a bush of hair drab as old tumbleweed
motors me thru such predictable gridirons
of stuccoed cafés & pumps & beer barracks   35
i might be back in Albertan[7] foothills
some town with a fringe collegiate
united by yellowing litter   sex
the profit unsystem   & October's wind
mottling the general flesh   40

But those white splashes are surely not snow
It's spring Down Here & blossoming apples
That *déjà-vu*[8] of an always-too-early fall
was only within me—
or a bleakness breathed by my host   45
this young-old stranger
confronting me now from his business suit
I sit upright in his office cave
hung round with books like stalactites
& stare into pale eyes   a face ungiving   50
obscurely scarred
as he runs down my day's obligings

(5)

Now i'm guesting the inevitable seminar:
Eliot of course   with graduate students
A numismatic exhibition   See!   55
though we live in the Outback
dont our coins ring true as Oxford's ?
& we got them all through reliable dealers . . .
I've faced those lacklustre fronts before
at U.B.C   Berkeley   Toronto: *Academicus anaemicus*   60

Into the usual dismal student caf[9] for sandwiches
The reading follows & some of the faculty come
here   spare me their feelings
But i caught some young eyes softening with laughter
& i'm starting to ease   65

(6)

My chairman-host seems easier too
discards his coat for a rollneck

---

7. That is, in Alberta, Canadian province.
8. Seen before (French).

9. Pronounced "cayf" that is, cafeteria.
"U.B.C.": University of British Columbia.

& takes me into the drywine sunlight
We twist up hills in his landrover
smoking our dust into gumtrees   70
& the ramshackle gates of stations[1]
He's relaxed enough to be quizzing me
in his diffident way   about Canada
The woods thin into mallee scrub[2] & wanness
while we talk large of our countries' identities   75
& cautiously then of our own
He's Australian B.A. with a Master's from London
Set up the local department a few years ago
      And before that?
      Umm—many things   none relevant—   80
      And here's where the road ends

(7)

He means it literally
Leaving the car we tread over leaves like paper
Under a stiff blue sky   & in seconds
stand on a gulf edge—   85
face blotched by vanished cascades
granite sheering to depths unseeable
like an Andean chasm[3]
We sit dangling our feet over silence
The smell of height stirs me   90
& i want to go below surfaces
Is there something tight in this man
he cant untie with words   or wont?
I try to trigger his past with my own:
my early jobs as an axeman   housepainter   95
guide in the Rockies—It works in a fashion:
      Good on you[4] Earle
(at least we've got to first names   i'm no longer Doctor)
      you know what it's like being poor
      & sweating your guts out   100
(a hint of Strine in the London overlay now)
      You too, Jack—you werent always a prof—
But he jumps up so quickly something   a crow?
squawks from a branch in panic
      Too roight!   but it's time we're back   105
      I'll shout you a beer at the motel
      & then we'll feed at my place
      if you'll risk a bachelor's tucker[5]

(8)

I accept quickly & we turn to the rover
Casually he gestures back at the gorge   110
      A mate of mine came here once—
      to jump off   Changed his mind

---

1. Ranches.
2. Low-growing plants.
3. Chasm as deep as in the Peruvian Andes.

4. Australian (or "Strine") for "Good for you!"
5. Food.

Said it queered his pitch[6]
not seeing ahead where he'd land
The flatness of tone belies any joke   115
I search those darting eyes
They are leafgreen now but still unbetraying
    You cant stop there! What's the story?

He climbs to the wheel with a low laugh
    You'd find it boring   & it hasnt an ending   120

(9)

But grudgingly almost he sketches it in
as we bump down through the slaty gums
their trunks radiant now in the slant light
    We can call him Pat
    A fatherless kid from the slums   so he said   125
    on his own early   a slygrogger's runner
    (bootlegger's boy maybe you'd call it
    you'll have to pardon the argot[7]
    but profs' lingo wont do here)
    So then he was copped for theft   130
    & jailed in what they still call a Boys' Home
    School for larrikins rather   for making young thugs

    Well he learned to drive a cat there at least
    broke out   stole new clobber—clothes—duds do you say?   135
    hitched north   took a new nime
    & got a job stripping coral from the Barrier Reef[8]
    It was a Yank oil company
    & the moolah was good
    but he left it & went on the bum

When i asked why   his voice went oddly brusque   140
    How should I know? Just a dopey kid
    Got wet maybe—blew his top—or started to think
    what a bloody thing that was
    to do to the Great Barrier Reef

Jack busied himself with the driving then   145
till i prodded him on
    Ah it's just more of the sime
    He bummed   mainly off sheilas
    popped rabbits   went fossickin   quit
    Got a good set-up then   bulldozing bauxite[9]   150
And he left it in no time—
He shoots me almost a frightened look

    How'd you know?
    Because it was a bloody thing to do to beaches

---

6. That is, disarranged his plans.
7. Local slang. When Jack defines an Austra-lianism (as above, "slygrogger's runner"), we do not gloss it.
8. The Great Barrier Reef, the world's largest coral reef, off the northeastern coast of Australia. "Nime": name.
9. Chemical mixture, source of aluminum; "sheilas": girls; "fossicking": prospecting.

Your Pat was an idealist   155
Was he?
Maybe he just didn't like
spitting out blood with aluminum
He turns his head & his eyes are flecked
He is nettled   I'm being bumptious   160
    No offense Jack   i forgot he was someone close—
    Close? what do you mean by that?
    Look   dont worry   he's not here now
The laugh is friendly   but he pushed the gas
as we bounce in sight of the straggling town   165
    Hell I shouldnt have started this
    It was only because you're a visiting fireman
I wont retail it—but i would like to hear the rest!
    Over the suds then maybe   We'll make for your motel
    I'm perishin thirsty   170

                          (*10*)

We pry a pair of schooners out of the deafening "public"[1]
& set them between us up in my room
I fill him in by request on Canadian liquor control
& persuade him at last back to his story
    Well after the bauxite it seems he went droving   175
    (cattle   that was)   & chucked it
    to be a jackeroo somewhere near Adelyde[2]
    But before that he was up in The Alice I think
    & maybe then he worked as a shearer's rouseabout[3]
    & hunted crocs out from Darwin   180
    Everywhere you can be sure he drank too much
    & got into fights with his flash temper   quit
    He was a barmy bastard for sure
    & crook in the head

I dont believe you really think he was   185
    No?   well he was a bastard   fair dinkum[4]
    & barmy enough to fake still another identity
    & use it to join the bloody rozzers

Who? the police?!   But how could he swing it?
    He'd brines[5] of a sort   read a lot   190
    managed to scrape through the tests
    was posted into a Sinney suburb
    Liked it   he said   & after a bit he was given a rise
    Yeh he was even up for a medal
I *said* he was an idealist!   How did it happen?   195
    Idealist? What does it mean? Is it a dirty word?
    I'm just telling you what a man did   or was done to
He ran through burning bush

---

1. Public bar; "schooners": big glasses of beer.
    2. That is, Adelaide, city in southern Australia;
"jackeroo": new boy on a sheep ranch.
    3. Handyman for a sheepshearer; "The Alice":
Alice Springs, a town on the highway line from
Adelaide to Darwin, a seaport, mentioned in the
next line.
    4. And that's the truth!
    5. That is, brains; "Sinney": Sydney (southeast-
ern Australian city).

& saved a boy cut off in a shack
So he was a one-day hero   then he got sacked   200
or took off   or both really
Sacked! But why?
  Well the blaze had been set
You mean—a pyromaniac?

    No   *entrepreneurs*:   looters   205
  Didnt you know? that's how most bushfires get started
How do they pull it off?
    One cove starts it   & then pisses off
  The rest of them wait for the panic to start
  move in with unmarked lorries   210
  & mike out theyve been sent to help
  They load up the family treasures
  & rev off in the smoke
My God that too was happening below!

But was Pat involved in the looting?   215
    No   but all the other cops were
  Pat was the rookie who didnt know
  & just before he went into the shed for the boy
  he'd recognised a local lout with the truckers
  So he passed the bloke's name to his sergeant   220
  who came to see Pat in the hospital
  The sergeant was in on the fix naturally
  He gave Pat a chance to share in the tike
  But the idiot blew his top & threatened to go to the press
  The sergeant countered he'd reason to think   225
  Pat's papers were phony   It was a stand-off
  Pat just took to the road again.
  & it's time we did too: i'm stahvin'

(11)

We drive through darkening suburbs
to a porchlit cube of stucco   230
& walk through a scraggly hedge
Behind is dead grass with a small waratah[6]
lifting its quiet bonfire of bloom in the dusk

Then the blank house-door opens into a livingroom
so jumping with strangeness & colour   235
i'm mortified again at my own failure
to foresee this professor's complexity
The walls flicker with ochre coils
aboriginal paintings on bark   & Namatjiras
Drysdales   a good Piper (from London days?)   240
Javanese batiks[7]   colour photos of seasnakes & Darwin eagles

---

  6. Australian plant.
  7. These lines set forth Jack's artistic tastes.
"Aboriginal paintings" are by Australian aborigines, or natives. Next cited are painters: Maurice
Namatjira (b. 1939); Sir Russell Drysdale (1912–

1981), a pioneer Australian painter of landscapes
and, later on, of the aborigines; John Piper (b. 1903)
is a prominent English modernist. "Batiks" are
hand-printed textiles made in Indonesia.

Scattered around the floor between ferns
some strangely infolded sculpture

He has a housekeeper after all
an original Australian   ancient creased & gentle   245
We followed her past a piano (with open music)
to savory food & wine as dry & subtle
as the man who drinks it with me
After we've settled over our pipes in his study
(surrounded by Melbourne playbills & photos of Aussie poets)   250
& settled the fate of the Commonwealth
& discussed the sculpture   (his own)
Jack comes back to his tale
It seems Pat found enough forms in police desks
to fake a more useful *curriculum vitae*   255
He hitched & "sundowned" till he'd put a thousand miles
between the past & himself
Then with the last of his money
he enrolled in a university
        A girl in one of his classes fell for him   260
        They were married & she worked to put him through
        He got a degree & a Nuffield[8] to—ah to Cambridge

Jack gets up abruptly & stalks to the brandy tray
        So after a few years he turned up on our staff
        & well—as I said—we got to be cobbers[9]   sort of   265
        And that's how I know his story
        Scarcely an idealist eh? A roughneck I'd call him
        with nothing to skite[1] about
        except his incredible luck—
        And now what about a nightcap   270
        before I take you back to your motel?
I said thanks but reminded him he still hadnt told me why
        Why?   O—the bloody cliff!
        Cant you guess?   The past caught up again
        &—well we've all got lots to grizzle[2] about   275
He is still fiddling with the drinks
        It was our Uni's Registrar plyed the Fury this time—
Jack seems blocked   His voice falters
He comes back silently with the brandies
his face a sallow mask   280
        Then Pat's wife   well he was crazy about her
        And there werent any kids
        She'd just died of cancer   That was the boomer[3]

The professor sits   lifts his glass   gestures a toast
        Well that's it   I warned you   285
His voice swings from dryness to something like anguish
        There's no story   He hadnt the guts to jump
        Anyway there was no need   as it turned out
        The University brass proved frightfully kind & discreet
        kept mum about everything   even found him a job   290

8. That is, a scholarship.   2. Gripe.
9. Pals.   3. Literally, giant kangaroo; that is, the pay-off.
1. Boast.

in one of the new colleges   a long way off
So he's still alive   in a way   somewhere
a good enough teacher   with no ambition
nobody worries him   perhaps he wont drop out this time
ideal eh?   but not idealistic—   295

He gulps the rest of his glass & stands
The laconic tone is back   & the sombre laugh
    Never told that sleeper[4] before   & wont again
    Now how about you? You must be tired
    & your plane goes out damned early   300
    I'll drive you back for some sleep

I get up slow   asking myself what he wanted to say
The silence   the leaden face   are no longer bearable
I hear myself mumbling
    Still alive   somewhere?   I think I *know* where   305
It's the wrong gambit   His face suffuses
till the scars of his burns stand blackly out
    It's nobody's fucking business where!
    Dont imagine I've been telling you *my* life   *Doctor!*—
    Whining & whipping the cat—!   310
We've come face to face   His eyes are flint & sparked with fire
But the next second he's turned
his voice heavy with pale apologies i try bleakly to match

(12)

We step into a chill night without moon
Through a thin cloud-cover the stars are small & dingy   315
I am driven quickly back   He's the calm Head once more
Our talk exchanges routine assurance & wish
The airport bus will pick me up   His goodbye hand is firm

I stand outside the motel till his car disappears
Over a smudge of treetops   in a cloud-rift   320
the heaven reveals strange patterns i've yet to learn
I turn to go in   a meteor flashes
brightens to fireball   in a second burns out
It does not startle   I think i'd looked up[5]
expecting it   out of such skies   325
Australia 1968 / Barclay Street, Vancouver 1973   1975

4. Something that sells slowly.
5. "Warning to all *literalati:* this poem's story is an invention. Pat & Jack are not based on 'actual' people, living or dead. Even the 'i' is only half ali(v)e" (Birney's note). "*Literalati*" is Birney's pseudo-Latin coinage, meaning "people who take things literally."

ROBERT PENN WARREN
b. 1905

Few contemporary American and English men of letters can vie with Robert Penn Warren in scope and aspiration; few have tried their hands at so many different kinds of writing and with such success in all. Warren has written both short lyrics and a narrative poem of book length. He is a novelist who, like his masters Faulkner and Conrad, has endeavored to write fictions that are at once stylistically daunting and yet capable of finding a wide readership. His best-known novel, *All the King's Men* (1946), was in its first form a poetic drama. He is a literary critic, and an influential teacher of literature and creative writing; he founded and edited an influential literary magazine, the *Southern Review*, and he is the co-author, with Cleanth Brooks, of a textbook that sharpened the reading practices of several generations of American college and high school students. Finally, he is a moralist, an observer of the movements of twentieth-century American life, who has spoken for both the values of his ancestors and the present needs of his countrymen.

Despite the impressive range of Warren's lifelong enterprise, there are certain continuities to be found in it, which are evidenced in his poetry as well. As a southerner, he has a deeper and more spontaneously acquired sense of history than most American writers—and readers. He spent the first two decades of his life in the region where he was born, and though much of his later life has been spent far from that home, his feeling of initial rootedness in place and in history is strong. Because he knows where he began, and what was there before him, he thinks of himself as having a special and privileged witness to bear upon the dislocating circumstances of contemporary American life. He describes the modern world as one of "moral confusion," which suffers "from a lack of discipline, of sanction, of community of values, of a sense of mission. . . . It is a world in which the individual has lost his relation to society, the world of the power state in which man is a cipher. It is a world in which man is the victim of abstraction and mechanism, or at least at moments feels himself to be." He concedes the danger of sentimentally harking back to a Golden Age, as his fellow Fugitives and agrarians have been said to do, but reminds us that the past is nonetheless real, and our inevitable resource. "Man's conception of his own role and position has changed from time to time. It is unhistorical to reduce history to some dead level and the mere fact that man in the modern world is worried about his role and position is in itself significant."

Warren's sense of evil leads him to prefer a literature distrustful of the unconditioned and the abstract. In the precepts of his criticism and the exempla of his poems and novels he consistently recommends a view of life that takes account of contradictions and mixed motives. In an important essay called "Pure and Impure Poetry," Warren describes irony as an essential resource for poetry. "The saint," he writes, "proves his vision by stepping cheerfully into the fires. The poet, somewhat less spectacularly, proves his vision by submitting it to the fires of irony . . . in the hope that the fires will refine it. In other words, the poet wishes to indicate that his vision has been earned, that it can survive reference to the contradictions of experience." This ideal of literature might best be called Shakespearean, and to it Warren has been, in the multiplicity of his work, completely dedicated.

He was born in Guthrie, Kentucky, on April 24, 1905. At sixteen he entered Vanderbilt University and studied literature. Among his teachers were John Crowe Ransom and Donald Davidson, who in 1922 founded a literary magazine called *The Fugitive*, and who brought together a number of Vanderbilt teachers and students to read and discuss each other's poetry. As a sophomore, Warren was brought into this circle by his friend Allen Tate, also a student, and he maintained his identification with the Fugitives for years after he graduated in 1925 and went to California, Yale, and Oxford to further his studies. Later he acknowledged, "In a very important way, that group was my education."

While at Oxford on a Rhodes Scholarship, Warren wrote his first book, a biography of John Brown; he also contributed an essay defending racial segregation in the South to the symposium *I'll Take My Stand* (1930), compiled by Ransom to defend southern and agrarian principles in the face of growing northern derision and antagonism, which had recently been provoked by the conviction of John Scopes for teaching the theory of evolution in a Tennessee school. (Later, Warren reversed his position on segregation, and it is characteristic of his sense of honor that he was quick to make public his new attitude.) Returning to the United States, he taught at Vanderbilt, Louisiana State, and Minnesota before joining the Yale faculty in 1950. His style of teaching, as rigorous and detailed as that of his own teacher, John Crowe Ransom, is embodied in *Understanding Poetry* (1938), the textbook he wrote with Cleanth Brooks and which exerted a commanding influence on the study of literature in American colleges. His first book of poems appeared in 1936, and his first novel, *Night Rider*, in 1939; since then he has worked with equal commitment and success in both fiction and verse, and is unique in having won the Pulitzer Prize in both genres, for *All the King's Men* in 1947 and for *Promises* in 1958. His important critical writings have been collected in *Selected Essays* (1958).

Warren retired from Yale in 1973, and since then he has devoted himself principally to his poetry. Many of the poems he has written in the last decade are, not surprisingly, elegiac and retrospective, though they show no diminution of verbal vigor and enterprise. As always, Warren tries to expand the world of a single poem to make it broader and more inclusive; he frequently arranges his poems in clusters. The resilience and strength of Warren's talent—his first book of poems was published more than fifty years ago—have made him a kind of national treasure, a live-and-kicking monument; this eminence was recognized by his appointment as the first Poet Laureate of the United States.

Bearded Oaks

The oaks, how subtle and marine,
Bearded, and all the layered light
Above them swims; and thus the scene,
Recessed, awaits the positive night.

So, waiting, we in the grass now lie   5
Beneath the languorous tread of light:
The grasses, kelp-like, satisfy
The nameless motions of the air.

Upon the floor of light, and time,
Unmurmuring, of polyp made,   10
We rest; we are, as light withdraws,
Twin atolls on a shelf of shade.

Ages to our construction went,
Dim architecture, hour by hour:
And violence, forgot now, lent   15
The present stillness all its power.

The storm of noon above us rolled,
Of light the fury, furious gold,
The long drag troubling us, the depth:
Dark is unrocking, unrippling, still.   20

Passion and slaughter, ruth,[1] decay
Descend, minutely whispering down,

1. Pity.

Silted down swaying streams, to lay
Foundation for our voicelessness.

All our debate is voiceless here,   25
As all our rage, the rage of stone;
If hope is hopeless, then fearless is fear,
And history is thus undone.

Our feet once wrought the hollow street
With echo when the lamps were dead   30
At windows, once our headlight glare
Disturbed the doe that, leaping, fled.

I do not love you less that now
The caged heart makes iron stroke,
Or less that all that light once gave   35
The graduate dark should now revoke.

We live in time so little time
And we learn all so painfully,
That we may spare this hour's term
To practice for eternity.   40
1942

From Mexico Is a Foreign Country:
Four Studies in Naturalism

IV. The Mango on the Mango Tree

The mango on the mango tree—
I look at it, it looks at me,
And thus we share our guilt in decent secrecy

(As once in the crowd I met a face
Whose lineaments were my disgrace   5
And whose own shame my forehead bore from place to place).

The mango is a great gold eye,
Like God's, set in the leafy sky
To harry heart, block blood, freeze feet, if I would fly.

For God has set it there to spy   10
And make report, and here am I,
A cosmic Hawkshaw[2] to track down its villainy.

Gumshoe, *agent provocateur*,
Stool, informer, whisperer
—Each pours his tale into the Great Schismatic's ear.   15

For God well works the Roman plan,
Divide and rule,[3] mango and man,
And on hate's axis the great globe grinds in its span.

2. A detective in a comic strip.
3. The strategy by which Julius Caesar won and controlled the Roman Empire, which at its greatest extent took in nearly all of the known world.

I do not know the mango's crime
In its far place and different time,   20
Nor does it know mine committed in a frostier clime.

But what to God's were ours, who pay,
Drop by slow drop, day after day,
Until His monstrous, primal guilt be washed away,

Who till that time must thus atone   25
In pulp and pit, in flesh and bone,
By our vicarious sacrifice[4] fault not our own?

For, ah, I do not know what word
The mango might hear, or if I've heard
A breath like *pardon, pardon,* when its stiff lips stirred.   30

If there were a word that it could give,
Or if I could only say *forgive,*
Then we might lift the Babel curse[5] by which we live,

And I could leap and laugh and sing
And it could leap, and everything   35
Take hands with us and pace the music in a ring,

And sway like the multitudinous wheat
In a blessedness so long in forfeit—
Blest in that blasphemy of love we cannot now repeat.

                                              1944

Riddle in the Garden

My mind is intact, but the shapes
of the world change, the peach
has released the bough and at last
makes full confession, its *pudeur*[6]
has departed like peach-fuzz wiped off, and   5

We now know how the hot sweetness of flesh and the juice-dark hug
the rough peach-pit, we know its most
suicidal yearnings, it wants
to suffer extremely, it   10

Loves God, and I warn you, do not
touch that plum, it will burn you, a blister
will be on your finger, and you will
put the finger to your lips for relief—oh, do
be careful not to break that soft   15

Gray bulge of fruit-skin of blister, for
exposing that inwardness will

4. For example, the sacrifice of Christ, by which alone humanity is held to have been redeemed from the original sin of Adam and Eve.
5. The inability to communicate, by extension from the biblical legend which attributes the different languages of the earth to God, who thereby confounded the builders of the Tower of Babel.
6. Modesty (French).

increase your pain, for you
are part of the world. You think
I am speaking in riddles. But I am not, for   20

The world means only itself.

1970

Flaubert in Egypt[7]

For Dorothea Tanning

Winterlong, off La Manche,[8] wind leaning. Gray stones of the gray
city sluiced by gray rain. And he dreamed

Of desert and distance, sunlight like murder, lust and new colors whose
names exploded the spectrum like dynamite,
or cancer. So went there,   5

Who did not know what he was, or could be, though hoping he might
find there his fate.[9] Found
what he found: with head shaven,

One lock at the occiput left,[1] red tarboosh wind-flaunted, rode hard at
the Sphinx, at the "Father of Terrors," which,   10
in that perspective and distance, lifted slow from
the desert, like a great ship from hull-down.[2]
At its height,
it swung. His cry burst forth.

In the white-washed room, by the light of wicks in three oil-glasses and to 15
the merciless *screak* of the rebec, with musicians
blind-folded,[3] the dancer, her breasts
cruelly bound to bulge upward and bare, above
pink trousers flesh rippling in bronze, danced
the dance which   20

7. In the fall of 1849, the French novelist Gustave Flaubert made an extended trip to Egypt; he
was then a young man, only twenty-seven, with
his novel *Madame Bovary* still before him. Drawing on Flaubert's travel notes and letters and a
book written thirty years later by Maxime du
Camp, Flaubert's companion, the scholar Francis
Steegmuller compiled the story of this trip in his
Flaubert in Egypt (1972). We extract relevant passages in our notes to show how Warren worked
with his sources.
8. French name for the English Channel, the
strait between England and France.
9. In his introduction to *Flaubert in Egypt*,
Steegmuller writes, "It was no mere idle sightseer
who was about to visit the 'East.' As Jean Bruneau
[a French Flaubert scholar] has put it: 'His love of
the sun, which is the key to his pantheism; his
taste for antiquity, which led to his discovery of
the ancient Orient; his curiosity concerning religions—all this resulted in a deepening of his idea
of the Orient . . . [which was] no mere source of
local color . . . For Flaubert the Orient gradually
became a kind of homeland" (p. 12).
1. "My head is completely shaved, except for
one lock at the occiput [the back of the skull] (by
which Mohammed lifts you up on Judgment Day)

and adorned with a tarboosh [fez-like hat] which
is a screaming red . . ." *(Flaubert in Egypt*, pp.
41–42).
2. "I can contain myself no longer, and dig in
my spurs; my horse bursts into a gallop . . . I begin
to shout in spite of myself . . . *View of the Sphinx.*
Abu-el-Houl (Father of Terror) *(Flaubert in Egypt*,
pp. 50–51). (Steegmuller reminds us in a note that
nowadays "the Sphinx is so familiar from photographs that the actual sight of it is apt to be an
anticlimax . . . But in those pre-photography days
it must have been an amazing sight, enormously
impressive.")
3. Flaubert's notes describe in detail his visits
to courtesans, most especially the famous dancer
Kuchuk Hanem. In this and the following stanzas,
Warren conflates three separate accounts. "We
entered a square whitewashed room . . . [Later]
the room was lighted by three wicks in glasses full
of oil . . . The musicians . . . scrape on the *reba-
bah*, a kind of small violin [which Flaubert elsewhere calls by its European name, "rebec"] . . .
Nothing could be more discordant or disagree-
able." Flaubert goes on to say that the musicians
were blindfolded when Kuchuk performed a strip
dance *(Flaubert in Egypt*, pp. 114–16).

He recalls from the oldest Greek vases—the leap on one foot with
    the free foot crossed over, the fingers
    aquiver, face calm, and
    slow centuries sifting like shadow.[4] Light
    flickers on whitewash. He finds   25
    the *mons veneris* shaven, arse noble.[5]
    That night three *coups,* and once
    performs cunnilingus. Fingers clutching ner necklace,
    he lies. He remembers his boyhood. Her fingers
    and naked thighs twitch in sleep.[6]   30

By day, on the minaret-top, the stork clacked its beak.[7] At the edge of
    the carrion-field, the wild dog,
    snout blue from old blood,
    skulked,[8] and camel bells in the distance.
    On the voyage down-Nile, on the slave boat, old women,   35
    black and slaves too, who had seen all of life, tried
    to persuade the young girls, market-bound,
    to smile.[9] But once,

On the height of Gebel Abusir, looking down on the Cataract, where
    the Nile flung itself to white froth on black granite, he   40
    cried out: "Eureka—the name, it is Emma!"
    And added: "Bovary." Pronouncing the *o,*
    as recorded by his companion, quite short.[1]

So home, and left Egypt, which was: palms black, sky red, and the river
    like molten steel, and the child's hand   45
    plucking his sleeve—"*Baksheesh,*
    and I'll get you my mother to fuck"—and the bath-boy
    he buggared, this in a clinical spirit and as
    a tribute to the host-country. And the chancre, of course,
    bright as a jewel on his member, and borne   50
    home like a trophy.[2]

4. "A woman in pink trousers . . . Kuchuk Hanem is a tall, splendid creature . . . When she bends, her flesh ripples into bronze ridges . . . Kuchuk's dance is brutal. She squeezes her bare breasts together with her jacket . . . She rises first on one foot, then on the other—marvellous movement: when one foot is on the ground, the other moves up and across the front of the shin-bone—the whole thing with a light bound. I have seen this dance on old Greek vases" *(Flaubert in Egypt,* pp. 114–15).

5. Of another courtesan: "These shaved cunts make a strange effect—the flesh is hard as bronze, and my girl had a splendid arse" *(Flaubert in Egypt,* p. 44).

6. "I sucked her [Kuchuk] furiously . . . As for the *coups,* they were good—the third especially . . ." "The lamp, shining feebly, cast a triangular gleam . . . I gave myself over to intense reverie, full of reminiscences . . . I dozed off with my fingers passed through her necklace . . . (As she slept she kept contracting her hands and thighs mechanically, like involuntary shudders.)" *(Flaubert in Egypt,* pp. 129–30, 118–19).

7. "Flaubert . . . a few days before his death in 1880, wrote his niece: 'For the past two weeks I have been gripped by the longing to see a palm-tree standing out against the blue sky, and to hear a stork clacking its beak at the top of a minaret

[tower attached to a mosque from which call to prayers is sounded]" *(Flaubert in Egypt,* p. 222).

8. "Whitish, wolf-like dogs . . . inhabit this malodorous region . . . The muzzles of some of the dogs are purple with clotted blood . . ." *(Flaubert in Egypt,* p. 75).

9. "In the afternoon we board two boats belonging to slave traders . . . the black women are all packed in, in all kinds of positions . . . On all these boats, among the women, there are old negresses who make and remake the trip continually; they are there to console the new slaves and keep up their spirits" *(Flaubert in Egypt,* pp. 131–32).

1. Du Camp wrote that Flaubert's "future novel engrossed him. 'I am obsessed by it,' he would say to me . . . On the borders of Lower Nubia, on the summit of Gebel Abusir, which overlooks the Second Cataract, as we were watching the Nile dash itself against the sharp black granite rocks, he gave a cry: 'I have found it! Eureka! Eureka! I will call her Emma Bovary!' And he repeated it several times; he savored the name Bovary, pronouncing the 'o' very short" *(Flaubert in Egypt,* p. 135).

2. This stanza brings together several widely dispersed notes: " 'If you'll give me five paras [small silver coins] I'll bring you my mother to fuck.' " ("Baksheesh": gift, or money, tip.) "By the way, you ask me if I consummated that business at the

But not to be omitted: on the river at Thebes, having long stared
  at the indigo mountains of sunset, he let
  eyes fix on the motion of three wave-crests that,
  in unison, bowed beneath the wind, and his heart   55
  burst with a solemn thanksgiving to God for
  the fact he could perceive the worth of the
  world with such joy.[3]

Years later, death near, he remembered the palm fronds—
  how black against a bright sky![4]   60

                                                                      1974

There's a Grandfather's Clock in the Hall

There's a grandfather's clock in the hall, watch it closely. The
              minute hand stands still, then it jumps, and
              in between jumps there is no-Time,
And you are a child again watching the reflection of early
              morning sunlight on the ceiling above your bed, 5

Or perhaps you are fifteen feet under water and holding your breath as
              you struggle with a rock-snagged anchor, or holding
              your breath just long enough for one more long,
              slow thrust to make the orgasm really
                        intolerable,   10
Or you are wondering why you do not really give a damn, as they
              trundle you off to the operating room,

Or your mother is standing up to get married and is very pretty and
              excited and is a virgin, and your heart overflows, and
                        you watch her with tears in your eyes, or 15
She is the one in the hospital room and she is really dying.

They have taken out her false teeth, which are now in a
              tumbler on the bedside table, and you know that only
              the undertaker will ever put them back in.
You stand there and wonder if you will ever have to wear false teeth.   20

She is lying on her back, and God, is she ugly, and
With gum-flabby lips and each word a special problem, she is asking
              if it is a new suit that you are wearing.

You say yes and hate her uremic guts, for she has no right to make you
              hurt the way that question hurts. 25

---

baths. Yes—and on a pockmarked young rascal
wearing a white turban." "I must tell you, my dear
sir, that I picked up in Beirut . . . VII chancres
[ulcers on penis, the result of syphilis], which
eventually combined to form two, then one"
(*Flaubert in Egypt*, pp. 38, 203, 215).
  3. On a trip south, on the Nile, Flaubert's boat
stopped briefly at the great ruined city of Thebes:
"Sunset over Medinet Habu. The mountains are
dark indigo [a dark gray-red blue] . . . It was then
. . . just as I was watching three wave-crests

bending under the wind behind us, that I felt a
surge of solemn happiness that reached out towards
what I was seeing, and I thanked God in my heart
for having made me capable of such a joy: I felt
fortunate at the thought, and yet it seemed it me
that I was thinking of nothing: it was a sensuous
pleasure that pervaded my entire being." Later
he spent a longer time in Thebes, which he judged
"the high point of the entire trip."
  4. See note 1 to line 31.

You do not know why that question makes your heart hurt like
                                        a kick in the scrotum,

For you do not yet know that the question, in its murderous triviality, is the
                              last thing she will ever say to you,
Nor know what baptism is occurring in a sod-roofed hut or hole on the now
    night—   30
              swept steppes of Asia, and a million mouths, like ruined
              stars in darkness, make a rejoicing that howls
              like wind, or wolves,

Nor do you know the truth, which is: *Seize the nettle of innocence in*
                    both your hands, for this is the only   35
                              way, and every
Ulcer in love's lazaret may, like a dawn-stung gem, sing—or even
                    burst into whoops of, perhaps, holiness.

But, in any case, watch the clock closely. Hold your breath and wait.
Nothing happens, nothing happens, then suddenly, quick as a wink, and   40
                    slick as a mink's prick, Time
              thrusts through the time
              of no-Time.

                                                                        1974

STANLEY KUNITZ
b. 1905

The seventeenth-century English school of wit is an obvious point of departure for
many of Stanley Kunitz's earlier poems: they are allusive, sometimes recondite, and
usually elaborately patterned. Like Donne, Kunitz sometimes uses the language of
the natural sciences in his unexpected and contrived comparisons. His *Selected Poems,
1938–58* (of which almost a third had been unpublished in book form) and his most
recent books show him working steadily towards a relaxation of form and intimacy of
tone. Some of these poems have affinities with the confessional monologues of Randall Jarrell and the *Life Studies* of Robert Lowell. They are personal in the simplest
sense, fragments of autobiography which mimic the vivid abruptness of notes in a
journal, confrontations between the poet and his loneliness, informed with the
knowledge that all are living and dying at once:

> I stand on the terrible threshold, and I see
> The end and the beginning in each other's arms.

His disciplined tone does not conceal turbulent emotions.

He was born in Worcester, Massachusetts, on July 29, 1905, and studied at Harvard, receiving his B.A. in 1926 and his M.A. the next year. He then joined the staff
of the H.W. Wilson company in New York to edit the *Wilson Library Bulletin*, and
also collaborated with Howard Haycraft to edit four invaluable biographical dictionaries of major English and American authors. His first book of poems, *Intellectual
Things* (1930), attracted little attention. By the time another appeared fourteen years
later, the Second World War was on and Kunitz was serving in the army. After the
war, he joined the faculty of Bennington College, and has taught at various colleges,
since 1963 at Columbia. He had some difficulty in finding a publisher for his *Selected
Poems* (1958), even though he had won several awards, but when it was published it

won him the Pulitzer Prize. He has continued to edit dictionaries of literary biography, most recently *European Authors, 1000–1900* (1967), and from 1969 to 1977 was editor of the Yale Series of Younger Poets.

River Road

That year of the cloud, when my marriage failed,
I slept in a chair, by the flagstone hearth,
fighting my sleep,
and one night saw a Hessian soldier[1]
stand at attention there in full   5
regalia, till his head broke into flames.
My only other callers were the FBI
sent to investigate me as a Russian spy
by patriotic neighbors on the river road;
and flying squirrels parachuting from the elms   10
who squeaked in rodent heat between the walls
and upstairs rumbled at their nutty games.
I never dared open the attic door.
Even my nervous Leghorns[2] joined the act,
indulging their taste for chicken from behind.   15
A glazed look swam into the survivors' eyes;
they caught a sort of dancing-sickness,
a variation of the blind staggers,
that hunched their narrow backs, and struck
a stiffened wing akimbo,   20
as round and round the poultry yard
they flapped and dropped and flapped again.
The county agent shook his head:
not one of them was spared the cyanide.

That year of the cloud, when my marriage failed,   25
I paced up and down the bottom-fields,
tamping the mud-puddled nurslings in
with a sharp blow of the heel
timed to the chop-chop of the hoe:
red pine and white, larch, balsam fir,   30
one stride apart, two hundred to the row,
until I heard from Rossiter's woods
the downward spiral of a veery's[3] song
unwinding on the eve of war.

Lord! Lord! who has lived so long?   35
Count it ten thousand trees ago,
five houses and ten thousand trees,
since the swallows exploded from Bowman Tower
over the place where the hermit sang,
while I held a fantail of squirming roots   40
that kissed the palm of my dirty hand,
as if in reply to a bird.

1. German mercenaries from Hesse fought on   2. A kind of chicken.
the British side in the American Revolution.   3. Tawny thrush's.

The stranger who hammers No Trespass signs
to the staghorn sumac along the road
must think he owns this property.   45
I park my car below the curve
and climbing over the tumbled stones
where the wild foxgrape perseveres,
I walk into the woods I made,
my dark and resinous, blistered land,   50
through the deep litter of the years.

1971

The Wellfleet[4] Whale

A few summers ago, on Cape Cod, a whale foundered on the beach, a sixty-three-foot finback whale. When the tide went out, I approached him. He was lying there, in monstrous desolation, making the most terrifying noises—rumbling—groaning. I put my hands on his flanks and I could feel the life inside him. And while I was standing there, suddenly he opened his eye. It was a big, red, cold eye, and it was staring directly at me. A shudder of recognition passed between us. Then the eye closed forever. I've been thinking about whales ever since.

—Journal entry

1

You have your language too,
    an eerie medley of clicks
        and hoots and trills,
location-notes and love calls,
    whistles and grunts. Occasionally,   5
        it's like furniture being smashed,
or the creaking of a mossy door,
    sounds that all melt into a liquid
        song with endless variations,
as if to compensate   10
    for the vast loneliness of the sea.
        Sometimes a disembodied voice
breaks in, as if from distant reefs,
    and it's as much as one can bear
        to listen to its long mournful cry,   15
a sorrow without a name, both more
    and less human. It drags
        across the ear like a record
running down.

2

No wind. No waves. No clouds.   20
    Only the whisper of the tide,
        as it withdrew, stroking the shore,
a lazy drift of gulls overhead,
    and tiny points of light
        bubbling in the channel.   25
It was the tag-end of summer.
    From the harbor's mouth
        you coasted into sight,
flashing news of your advent,

4. Coastal town on Massachusetts' Cape Cod.

the crescent of your dorsal fin[5]   30
    clipping the diamonded surface.
We cheered at the sign of your greatness
    when the black barrel of your head
        erupted, ramming the water,
and you flowered for us   35
    in the jet of your spouting.

3

All afternoon you swam
    tirelessly round the bay,
        with such an easy motion,
the slightest downbeat of your tail,   40
    an almost imperceptible
        undulation of your flippers,
you seemed like something poured,
    not driven; you seemed
        to marry grace with power.   45
And when you bounded into air,
    slapping your flukes,[6]
        we thrilled to look upon
pure energy incarnate
    as nobility of form.   50
        You seemed to ask of us
not sympathy, or love,
    or understanding,
        but awe and wonder.

That night we watched you   55
    swimming in the moon.
        Your back was molten silver.
We guessed your silent passage
    by the phosphorescence in your wake.
        At dawn we found you stranded on the rocks.   60

4

There came a boy and a man
    and yet other men running, and two
        schoolgirls in yellow halters
and a housewife bedecked
    with curlers, and whole families in beach   65
        buggies with assorted yelping dogs.
The tide was almost out.
    We could walk around you,
        as you heaved deeper into the shoal,
crushed by your own weight,   70
    collapsing into yourself,
        your flippers and your flukes
quivering, your blowhole
    spasmodically bubbling, roaring.
        In the pit of your gaping mouth   75
you bared your fringework of baleen,[7]

---

5. Back fin.   7. A sievelike structure of bone in a whale's
6. That is, tail.   mouth that collects and retains its food.

a thicket of horned bristles.
    When the Curator of Mammals
arrived from Boston
    to take samples of your blood   80
        you were already oozing from below.
Somebody had carved his initials
    in your flank. Hunters of souvenirs
        had peeled off strips of your skin,
a membrane thin as paper.   85
    You were blistered and cracked by the sun.
        The gulls had been pecking at you.
The sound you made was a hoarse and fitful bleating.

What drew us, like a magnet, to your dying?
    You made a bond between us,   90
        the keepers of the nightfall watch,
who gathered in a ring around you,
    boozing in the bonfire light.
        Toward dawn we shared with you
your hour of desolation,   95
    the huge lingering passion
        of your unearthly outcry,
as you swung your blind head
    toward us and laboriously opened
        a bloodshot, glistening eye,   100
in which we swam with terror and recognition.

                        5
Voyager, chief of the pelagic[8] world,
    you brought with you the myth
        of another country, dimly remembered,
where flying reptiles   105
    lumbered over the steaming marshes
        and trumpeting thunder lizards
wallowed in the reeds.
    While empires rose and fell on land,
        your nation breasted the open main,   110
rocked in the consoling rhythm
    of the tides. Which ancestor first plunged
        head-down through zones of colored twilight
to scour the bottom of the dark?
    You ranged the North Atlantic track   115
        from Port-of-Spain to Baffin Bay,[9]
edging between the ice-floes
    through the fat of summer,
        lob-tailing, breaching, sounding,[1]
grazing in the pastures of the sea   120
    on krill-rich orange plankton[2]
        crackling with life.
You prowled down the continental shelf,

---

8. Oceanic.
9. That is, from south to north (literally, from a town in Trinidad to a bay off Greenland).
1. Plummeting to the ocean depths; "lob-tail-ing": beating the water with its flukes; "breach-ing": breaking above the ocean's surface.
2. Minute plants and animals in the water; "krill": minute planktonic shellfish.

    guided by the sun and stars
      and the taste of alluvial silt[3]   125
on your way southward
    to the warm lagoons,
      the tropic of desire,
where the lovers lie belly to belly
    in the rub and nuzzle of their sporting;   130
      and you turned, like a god in exile,
out of your wide primeval element,
delivered to the mercy of time.
    Master of the whale-roads,[4]
let the white wings of the gulls   135
    spread out their cover.
      You have become like us,
disgraced and mortal.

                          1983

---

3. Minute particles of sand and other matter.
4. That is, the ocean; "whale-road" was an Old English "kenning," or conventional poetic expression, for the sea.

JOHN BETJEMAN
1906–1984

A year older than Auden, John (later Sir John) Betjeman also went to Oxford, and he wrote poetry which is just as witty if not so searching. Auden wrote an admiring preface to the American edition of Betjeman's poems in which he praised them as "slick but not streamlined." The two poets invite comparison: Auden always faced the future, however vague that might be, while Betjeman looked over his shoulder at what is gone or going. Hope plays for the one the part that nostalgia plays for the other. Bells—symbols of the old order—appear obsessively in Betjeman's verse. Auden was always eager to move about, and to find new themes far away from home, in Iceland, China, and America. Betjeman in his poetry stayed close, matching contemporary England with old, to the former's disadvantage. His pursuit of the old led him to look closely at then-unfashionable nineteenth-century English architecture. "Architecture," Betjeman observed, "has a wider meaning than that which is commonly given to it. For architecture means not a house, or a single building or a church . . . or the glass at Chartres, but your surroundings, not a town or a street but our whole over-populated island. It is concerned with where we eat, work, sleep, play, congregate, escape. It is our background, alas, often too permanent."[1]

    Betjeman's preference for an older England, more religious, more countrified and less busy, may have arisen from tension between him and his father. His father was involved in factories and "trade," and became increasingly successful and affluent. At first, in childhood, John was encouraged to indulge his appetite for verse, but as his literary interests became more intense, his father tried desperately to shunt him into business, and accused him of snobbery towards "trade." Betjeman held his ground, though not without feelings of guilt; against his father's importunities, and against his classmates' cruelties, he clung to poetry as though it were a religion. This development is described in his excellent autobiographical poem *Summoned by Bells*, a moving and detailed account of difficulties in boyhood and adolescence.

    Betjeman was born on August 28, 1906. At the Highgate School in North London,

---

1. *British Writers* 7, ed. Ian Scott-Kilvert, New York, 1984, p. 359.

he showed his poems to one of the masters, T. S. Eliot by name, who, however, failed to comment on them. Betjeman then attended Marlborough and finally Oxford. On leaving Oxford, desperate to avoid business, he became a schoolteacher. He wrote Shell Guides to Cornwall, Devon, and Shropshire, and books on Oxford and on English landscape. He made a virtue out of anachronism. Perhaps, then, it was only fitting when in 1972 he was named to the anachronistic post of Poet Laureate of Great Britain. He died on May 19, 1984.

The Arrest of Oscar Wilde at the Cadogan Hotel[1]

He sipped at a weak hock and seltzer
    As he gazed at the London Skies
Through the Nottingham lace of the curtains
    Or was it his bees-winged[2] eyes?

To the right and before him Pont Street   5
    Did tower in her new built red,
As hard as the morning gaslight
    That shone on his unmade bed,

"I want some more hock in my seltzer,
    And Robbie,[3] please give me your hand—   10
Is this the end or beginning?
    How can I understand?

"So you've brought me the latest *Yellow Book:*
    And Buchan has got in it now:[4]
Approval of what is approved of   15
    Is as false as a well-kept vow.

"More hock, Robbie—where is the seltzer?
    Dear boy, pull again at the bell!
They are all little better than *cretins,*
    Though this *is* the Cadogan Hotel.   20

"One astrakhan coat is at Willis's—
    Another one's at the Savoy:[5]
Do fetch my morocco portmanteau,
    And bring them on later, dear boy."

A thump, and a murmur of voices—
    ("Oh why must they make such a din?")   25
As the door of the bedroom swung open
    And TWO PLAIN CLOTHES POLICEMEN came in:

1. The poet and playwright Oscar Wilde (1856–1900) was convicted of homosexuality in 1895 and jailed for two years. The circumstances of his arrest were as Betjeman describes them.
2. Beeswing is a gauzy film that forms in old wine.
3. Robert Ross, Wilde's best friend; "hock": wine.
4. The *Yellow Book* (1894–97) was the periodical of the Aesthetic movement of which Wilde was the most famous member, though he had no direct connection with the magazine. John Buchan (1875–1940), later famous for his adventure novels, published two stories in *Yellow Book* in 1896.
5. Wilde had an apartment at the Savoy Hotel, and often took his friends to dinner there and at Willis's Rooms.

"Mr. Woilde, we'ave come for tew take yew
Where felons and criminals dwell: 30
We must ask yew tew leave with us quoietly
For this *is* the Cadogan Hotel."

He rose, and he put down *The Yellow Book.*
He staggered—and, terrible-eyed,
He brushed past the palms on the staircase   35
And was helped to a hansom outside.

                                                                    1937

An Incident in the Early Life of
Ebenezer Jones, Poet, 1828[6]

The lumber of a London-going dray,
The still-new stucco on the London clay,
Hot summer silence over Holloway.[7]

Dissenting chapels,[8] tea-bowers, lovers' lairs,
Neat new-built villas, ample Grecian squares,   5
Remaining orchards ripening Windsor pears.

Hot silence where the older mansions hide
On Highgate Hills' thick elm-encrusted side,
And Pancras, Hornsey, Islington[9] divide.

June's hottest silence where the hard rays strike   10
Yon hill-foot house, window and wall alike,
School of the Reverend Mr. Bickerdike,

For sons of Saints, blest with this world's possessions
(Seceders from the Protestant Secessions),[1]
Good grounding in the more genteel professions.   15

A lurcher dog, which draymen kick and pass,
Tongue lolling, thirsty over shadeless grass,
Leapt up the playground ladder to the class.

---

6. Ebenezer Jones (1820–1860) was a very minor English poet whose one book, *Studies of Sensation and Event* (1943), was so badly received that he published no other poems. Betjeman prefaces this poem with an account of its central incident given by his brother in an 1879 reissue of the book. "We were together at a well-known boarding-school of that day . . . on a hot summer afternoon. . . . Up the ladder-like stairs from the playground a lurcher dog had strayed into the schoolroom, panting with the heat, his tongue lolling out with thirst. The choleric usher who presided, and was detested by us for his tyranny, seeing this, advanced down the room. Enraged at our attention being distracted from our tasks, he dragged the dog to the top of the stairs, and there lifted him bodily up with the evident intention—and we had known him to do similar things—of hurling the poor creature to the bottom. 'YOU SHALL NOT' rang through the room, as little Ebby, so exclaiming at the top of his voice, rushed with kindling face to the spot from among all the boys— some of them twice his age. But even while the

words passed his lips, the heavy fall was heard, and the sound seemed to travel through his listening form and face, as, with a strange look of anguish in one so young, he stood still, threw up his arms, and burst into an uncontrollable passion of tears. With a coarse laugh at this, the usher led him back by his ear to the form; and there he sat long after his sobbing had subsided, like one dazed and stunned."
7. A district of central London.
8. Jones's parents were adherents of Calvinism, an especially strict Protestant sect; like all other Protestants who refused integration into the official Church of England, they were called "dissenters" or "nonconformists," and because of discriminatory laws against them tended to live together in areas such as Holloway.
9. London districts surrounding Holloway.
1. The Church of England seceded from the Roman Catholic Church in the reign of Henry VIII; the Puritans (who were in the habit of calling themselves Saints) considered the Church of England too little reformed and seceded from it.

The godly usher left his godly seat,
His skin was prickly in the ungodly heat,   20
The dog lay panting at his godly feet.

The milkman on the road stood staring in,
The playground nettles nodded 'Now begin"—
And Evil waited, quivering, for sin.

He lifted it and not a word he spoke,   25
His big hand tightened. Could he make it choke?
He trembled, sweated, and his temper broke.

"YOU SHALL NOT!" clear across to Highgate Hill
A boy's voice sounded. Creaking forms were still.
The cat jumped slowly from the window sill.   30

"YOU SHALL NOT!" flat against the summer sun,
Hard as the hard sky frowning over one,
Gloat, little boys! enjoy the coming fun!

"GOD DAMNS A CUR. I AM, I AM HIS WORD!"
He flung it, flung it and it never stirred,   35
'You shall not!—shall not!" ringing on unheard.

Blind desolation! bleeding, burning rod!
Big, bull-necked Minister of Calvin's God!
Exulting milkman, redfaced, shameless clod,

Look on and jeer! Not Satan's thunder-quake   40
Can cause the mighty walls of Heaven to shake
As now they do, to hear a boy's heart break.

1940

A Subaltern's[2] Love-song

Miss J. Hunter Dunn, Miss J. Hunter Dunn,
Furnish'd and burnish'd by Aldershot[3] sun,
What strenuous singles we played after tea,
We in the tournament—you against me!

Love-thirty, love-forty, oh! weakness of joy,   5
The speed of a swallow, the grace of a boy,
With carefullest carelessness, gaily you won,
I am weak from your loveliness, Joan Hunter Dunn.

Miss Joan Hunter Dunn, Miss Joan Hunter Dunn,
How mad I am, sad I am, glad that you won.   10
The warm-handled racket is back in its press,
But my shock-headed[4] victor, she loves me no less.

---

2. "Subaltern": British army term for commissioned officer below the rank of captain.
3. Town in southern England; a large military

camp is located there.
4. That is, with thick, bushy hair.

Her father's euonymus[5] shines as we walk,
And swing past the summer-house, buried in talk,
And cool the verandah that welcomes us in   15
To the six-o'clock news and a lime-juice and gin.

The scent of the conifers,[6] sound of the bath,
The view from my bedroom of moss-dappled path,
As I struggle with double-end evening tie,
For we dance at the Golf Club, my victor and I.   20

On the floor of her bedroom lie blazer and shorts
And the cream-coloured walls are be-trophied with sports,
And westering, questioning settles the sun
On your low-leaded[7] window, Miss Joan Hunter Dunn.

The Hillman[8] is waiting, the light's in the hall,   25
The pictures of Egypt are bright on the wall,
My sweet, I am standing beside the oak stair
And there on the landing's the light on your hair.

By roads "not adopted,"[9] by woodlanded ways,
She drove to the club in the late summer haze,   30
Into nine-o'clock Camberley, heavy with bells
And mushroomy, pine-woody, evergreen smells.

Miss Joan Hunter Dunn, Miss Joan Hunter Dunn,
I can hear from the car-park the dance has begun.
Oh! full Surrey twilight! importunate band!   35
Oh! strongly adorable tennis-girl's hand!

Around us are Rovers and Austins afar,
Above us, the intimate roof of the car,
And here on my right is the girl of my choice,
With the tilt of her nose and the chime of her voice,   40

And the scent of her wrap, and the words never said,
And the ominous, ominous dancing ahead.
We sat in the car park till twenty to one
And now I'm engaged to Miss Joan Hunter Dunn.

1945

The Cottage Hospital[1]

At the end of a long-walled garden
    in a red provincial town,
A brick path led to a mulberry
    scanty grass at its feet.
I lay under blackening branches   5
    where the mulberry leaves hung down

---

5. Small evergreens.
6. Evergreen trees.
7. That is, with a low frame made of lead.
8. Expensive make of automobile.

9. That is, back roads.
1. Small country hospital, without a resident medical staff.

Sheltering ruby fruit globes
  from a Sunday-tea-time heat.
Apple and plum espaliers[2]
  basked upon bricks of brown;
The air was swimming with insects,
  and children played in the street.

Out of this bright intentness
  into the mulberry shade
Musca domestica (housefly)
  swung from the August light
Slap into slithery rigging
  by the waiting spider male
Which spun the lithe elastic
  till the fly was shrouded tight.
Down came the hairy talons
  and horrible poison blade
And none of the garden noticed
  that fizzing, hopeless fight.

Say in what Cottage Hospital
  whose pale green walls resound
With the tap upon polished parquet[3]
  of inflexible nurses' feet
Shall I myself be lying
  when they range the screens around?
And say shall I groan in dying,
  as I twist the sweaty sheet?
Or gasp for breath uncrying,
  as I feel my senses drown'd
While the air is swimming with insects
  and children play in the street?

1954

False Security

I remember the dread with which I at a quarter past four
Let go with a bang behind me our house front door
And, clutching a present for my dear little hostess tight,
Sailed out for the children's party into the night
Or rather the gathering night. For still some boys
In the near municipal acres[4] were making a noise
Shuffling in fallen leaves and shouting and whistling
And running past hedges of hawthorn, spikey and bristling.
And black in the oncoming darkness stood out the trees
And pink shone the ponds in the sunset ready to freeze
And all was still and ominous waiting for dark
And the keeper was ringing his closing bell in the park
And the arc lights[5] started to fizzle and burst into mauve
As I climbed West Hill to the great big house in The Grove,

---

2. Fruit trees trained to grow against a wall.
3. Wooden floor inlaid with patterns.
4. That is, city land.
5. Old-fashioned street lights.

Where the children's party was and the dear little hostess.   15
But halfway up stood the empty house where the ghost is
I crossed to the other side and under the arc
Made a rush for the next kind lamp-post out of the dark
And so to the next and the next till I reached the top
Where the Grove branched off to the left. Then ready to drop   20
I ran to the ironwork gateway of number seven
Secure at last on the lamplit fringe of Heaven.
Oh who can say how subtle and safe one feels
Shod in one's children's sandals from Daniel Neal's.
Clad in one's party clothes made of stuff from Heal's?[6]   25
And who can still one's thrill at the candle shine
On cakes and ices and jelly and blackcurrant wine,
And the warm little feel of my hostess's hand in mine?
Can I forget my delight at the conjuring show?
And wasn't I proud that I was the last to go?   30
Too overexcited and pleased with myself to know
That the words I heard my hostess's mother employ
To a guest departing, would ever diminish my joy,
I WONDER WHERE JULIA FOUND THAT STRANGE, RATHER
    COMMON LITTLE BOY?

1958

6. Upper-class department stores.

WILLIAM EMPSON
1906–1984

In 1963 William Empson gave a talk on the BBC Third Program in which he stated
a need for an alternative to symbolist poetry. By symbolist poetry he meant a poetry
in which the reader is encouraged to infer a mood or dramatic situation by watching
the unreeling of a series of images, a kind of poetry in which the voice and presence
of the poet is suppressed. Empson admitted that the "best poems written in English
during this century are symbolist, and they are very good. But it has gone on long
enough; poets are now finding the rules an obstacle, all the more because literary
theorists commonly talk as if no other kind of poetry is possible but symbolist poetry."[1]
As a promising alternative Empson recommended "argufying in poetry." Poetic
argument, employing tones of voice which are beseeching and quarrelsome, hard-
pressed and passionate, was in fact Empson's poetic procedure, and it explains the
interest taken in his work by the poets of the Movement, who were eager to find an
alternative to the symbolism of Pound and Eliot.

Argument of course assumes conflict. Empson also said that the critical theory
which most influenced his early practice as a poet and critic saw poetry as the expression of an unresolved conflict. He mentioned particularly the early critical writings
of Robert Graves, who used poetry for the therapeutic reenactment of interior conflicts; and Empson was certainly encouraged in this view by his friend and teacher
I. A. Richards, who judged poetry by its success in harmonizing a variety of conflicting impulses. The poet, said Empson, "should write about the things that really
worry him, in fact worry him to the point of madness." Looking back over his poems—

1. *New York Times Book Review*, September 22, 1963, p. 39.

and he published few after 1940—Empson declared that "my few good ones are all on the basis of expressing an unresolved conflict."[2]

For inspiration, Empson turned back to the English Metaphysicals, in particular to Donne and Herbert, whose poems are argumentative in tone and who in their figures of speech bring together discordant terms and images. Using Metaphysical poems as many of his texts, in his first critical work, *Seven Types of Ambiguity* (1930), he taught several generations of readers to look for the moment where a poem hurts, where several, and sometimes contradictory, senses of a word are brought into play at the same time.

Empson's poems are haunted by the figure of Milton's Satan and the accents of his speech. One love poem begins and ends with the resignation of the damned: "It is the pain, it is the pain, endures." In another poem Hell is the reality of life, and our dreams of something better are the necessary illusions: "All those large dreams by which men long live well / Are magic-lanterned on the smoke of hell." Just as Satan is unable to escape his Hell, so modern man is confined by his science: "The world's end is here. / This place's curvature precludes its end." Empson's poem "Ignorance of Death" reviews a number of attitudes towards death and then concludes:

> Otherwise I feel very blank upon this topic,
> And think that though important, and proper for anyone to bring up,
> It is one that most people should be prepared to be blank upon.

In the context of Empson's poetry, "blank" is here not only stupidity and ignorance, though the word includes these meanings; it is the endless nullity of the universe on which man superimposes his poignant visions. But the wry offhand tone of voice of the whole poem suggests that the situation can be lived with.

William Empson was born on September 27, 1906, near Howden, Yorkshire. He was educated at Winchester School and at Magdalene College, Cambridge, where he took degrees first in mathematics, then in English. From 1931 to 1934 he was Professor of English Literature at Tokyo National University. He published his *Poems* in 1935, many of which had been written some years before when he was an undergraduate, and a critical work, *Some Versions of Pastoral*, a reading of a series of literary works with particular attention to their covert social attitudes. Two years later he went to China and taught English at the National University in Peking; his work there was interrupted by the beginning of the Sino-Japanese War. In 1939, when the Second World War was certain, Empson returned to England, where he worked for the BBC and brought out his second collection of poems, *The Gathering Storm* (1940). When the war was over, he returned with his wife and two sons to a teaching post in Peking. He completed a third important critical work, *The Structure of Complex Words*, in 1951, and a year later he returned to live in England. In 1953 he became Professor of English at Sheffield University, and taught there until his retirement in 1971. He died on May 15, 1984.

2. "William Empson in Conversation with Christopher Ricks," *The Modern Poet*, ed. Ian Hamilton, London, 1968, p. 186.

Villanelle[1]

It is the pain, it is the pain, endures.
Your chemic beauty burned my muscles through.
Poise of my hands reminded me of yours.

1. A French poetic form in five tercets (three-line stanzas), followed by a quatrain (four-line stanza). The second lines of all six stanzas keep to the same rhyme, and all other lines of the poem keep to another rhyme. The first and third lines of the first tercet are repeated in alternation as the last line of the succeeding tercets and together as the closing couplet of the quatrain. Empson's "Missing Dates" (p. 407), is another villanelle.

What later purge from this deep toxin cures?
What kindness now could the old salve renew?   5
It is the pain, it is the pain, endures.

The infection slept (custom or change inures)
And when pain's secondary phase was due
Poise of my hands reminded me of yours.

How safe I felt, whom memory assures,   10
Rich that your grace safely by heart I knew.
It is the pain, it is the pain, endures.

My stare drank deep beauty that still allures.
My heart pumps yet the poison draught of you.
Poise of my hands reminded me of yours.   15

You are still kind whom the same shape immures.
Kind and beyond adieu. We miss our cue.
It is the pain, it is the pain, endures.
Poise of my hands reminded me of yours.

                                                               1935

Legal Fiction

Law makes long spokes of the short stakes of men.
Your well fenced out real estate of mind
No high flat of the nomad citizen
Looks over, or train leaves behind.

Your rights extend under and above your claim   5
Without bound; you own land in Heaven and Hell;
Your part of earth's surface and mass the same,
Of all cosmos' volume, and all stars as well.

Your rights reach down where all owners meet, in Hell's
Pointed exclusive conclave, at earth's centre   10
(Your spun farm's root still on that axis dwells);
And up, through galaxies, a growing sector.

You are nomad yet; the lighthouse beam you own
Flashes, like Lucifer, through the firmament.
Earth's axis varies; your dark central cone   15
Wavers, a candle's shadow, at the end.

                                                               1935

Ignorance of Death

Then there is this civilising love of death, by which
Even music and painting tell you what else to love.
Buddhists and Christians contrive to agree about death

Making death their ideal basis for different ideals.
The Communists however disapprove of death   5
Except when practical. The people who dig up

Corpses and rape them are I understand not reported.
The Freudians regard the death-wish as fundamental,
Though "the clamour of life" proceeds from its rival "Eros."

Whether you are to admire a given case for making less clamour   10
Is not their story. Liberal hopefulness
Regards death as a mere border to an improving picture.

Because we have neither hereditary nor direct knowledge of death
It is the trigger of the literary man's biggest gun
And we are happy to equate it to any conceived calm.   15

Heaven me, when a man is ready to die about something
Other than himself, and is it in fact ready because of that,
Not because of himself, that is something clear about himself.

Otherwise I feel very blank upon this topic,
And think that though important, and proper for anyone to bring up,   20
It is one that most people should be prepared to be blank upon.

1940

Missing Dates

Slowly the poison the whole blood stream fills.
It is not the effort nor the failure tires.
The waste remains, the waste remains and kills.

It is not your system or clear sight that mills
Down small to the consequence a life requires;   5
Slowly the poison the whole blood stream fills.

They bled an old dog dry yet the exchange rills
Of young dog blood gave but a month's desires.
The waste remains, the waste remains and kills.

It is the Chinese tombs and the slag hills   10
Usurp the soil,[2] and not the soil retires.
Slowly the poison the whole blood stream fills.

Not to have fire is to be a skin that shrills.
The complete fire is death. From partial fires
The waste remains, the waste remains and kills.   15

It is the poems you have lost, the ills
From missing dates, at which the heart expires.

2. "It is true about the old dog, at least I saw it reported somewhere, but the legend that a fifth or some such part of the soil of China is given up to ancestral tombs is (by the way) not true" (Empson's note).

Slowly the poison the whole blood stream fills.
The waste remains, the waste remains and kills.

1940

W. H. AUDEN
1907–1973

W. H. (Wystan Hugh) Auden stands craggily between the poetry of the first two decades of the century and that of the decade since the Second World War. He wrote abundantly in poetry, prose, drama, and opera libretti. He was less challenged in his position as major poet than any other recent writer in English. Not that he could depend upon steady acclaim: his detractors objected to two tendencies of his later work, towards high-church Christianity and towards low-keyed meditation. But while his later work lacked some of the unexpectedness which made him famous, it remains witty and intelligent to a superlative degree.

From the beginning Auden prided himself on countering the rhetoric and theatricality of others with his own exact understatements. A lover, he insisted on love's transience in the midst of his most passionate lyrics; a poet, he questioned the efficacy of his art even while delighting in it. Though much of his early work was prophetic of social and political change, he repeatedly insisted that poetry could have no value in other spheres.

Auden was born in 1907 in York, England, the third son of a physician. In 1908 his father became Medical Officer and Professor of Public Health at the University of Birmingham. This medical background was absorbed: as a child Auden pored over his father's medical books, and imparted the naughty information there obtained to his schoolmates. In later life he maintained in his verse something of the clinical tradition, its coolness, its diagnostic air, its hatred of the unexplained. Many of his poems dealt with disease, physical or mental, of the individual or of the age, and offered nostrums—revolution (moral rather than physical), love, friendship, "a change of heart."

Auden attended private schools and then Oxford. During his three years at the university, he wrote many poems and collected the best of them in a volume, *Poems* (1928), which his friend Stephen Spender published on a handpress. (These poems, like most of Auden's work, were subjected to severe revision in later collections.) After taking his degree in 1928, Auden traveled to Germany. It was the first of many important journeys which helped him to gather the ingredients of his verse. Most of his poems were related in one way or another to a quest. In Germany he came upon the teachings of Homer Lane, a latter-day American prophet. Lane held, like Rousseau, that civilization distorted instead of ennobled man's natural impulses. But a more important source was Freud, whose help in penetrating psychological arcana Auden movingly acknowledged in his elegy on Freud.

During the thirties Auden became by common consent the principal poet of his generation, and other writers such as Louis MacNeice, Cecil Day Lewis, and Stephen Spender, in spite of their considerable differences from him, were assumed to be writing under his banner. He supported himself at first by teaching, and was to do this sporadically for much of his life. But his urge to travel became conspicuous. In 1937 he and MacNeice published their *Letters from Iceland*, after making a trip to that country at their publisher's expense. The same year Auden went to Spain and wrote a political poem, *Spain*, in support of the Loyalists (another poem which Auden later excluded from his canon). A year later he and Christopher Isherwood went to China, and Auden wrote *Journey to a War*. At that time he was not so prone, as he would later become, to deny the mutual relevance of politics and poetry. In January

1939 Auden and Isherwood left England with the intention of residing permanently in the United States. He became an American citizen in 1946. Most of his time in later life was shared equally between two residences, one in Greenwich Village (New York City) and the other in Kirchstetten, Lower Austria. But in 1972 he was invited to take up lodgings at his old college, Christ Church, Oxford, and consented to do so. He died in Vienna on September 28, 1973.

Auden's early poetry showed a close reading of Hardy and Hopkins, whose effects he emulated. He also admired Eliot for his conversational tone and for his acute inspection of cultural decay, and he liked Yeats's power to treat philosophical matters in lyrics. The early poems of Auden speak, somewhat cryptically, of impending doom, of our general complicity in seemingly individual evil conduct, and of the necessity of reconstituting the affections. Revolution is darkly hinted at, though its exact nature is not specified; the poet seems disposed to urge a conspiracy of men of goodwill. While he concentrated on small, individual gestures, Auden was also fond of invoking large forces—mountains, floods, glaciers, deserts—as symbols of human needs or defects. In this way his witty deflations of grandiloquence joined with large assertions made with great eloquence. The vocabulary was an odd mixture of the homely and the abstract.

Two somewhat divergent tendencies appeared as his work proceeded. On the one hand, Auden regarded poetry as "a game of knowledge," an exploration of possibilities. On the other hand, he insisted upon rigorous honesty, upon a preference for a bit of sense over a good sound. (He often accused Yeats of preferring good lines to good notions.) His art was a stripper of deception, a disenchanter, standing against not only Yeats (whose elegy, notwithstanding, he excellently wrote), but also against the Romantic tradition. Auden was not, however, quite so down-to-earth as he presented himself. His work became increasingly meditative, but it remains what Marianne Moore once called it, "circumspectly audacious."[1] Moreover, its pursuit of the seemingly random but actually significant detail, the extraordinary in the ordinary, gave it reverberations beyond his modest professions for it. Whether he was incorporating bits of Old English poetry, as he did earlier, or bits of popular songs, as later, Auden could not avoid serving as a spokesman for modern sensibility. Throughout his career Auden acknowledged the badness of the times and the nearing of death wittily and without panic, keeping faith with those he loved and with a certain ideal of civilization and civility. He was himself a beacon light in the darkness he sometimes saw spreading, whether its source was dullness, or something worse.

1. *Predilections*, London, 1956, p. 85.

The Letter[1]

From the very first coming down
Into a new valley with a frown
Because of the sun and a lost way,
You certainly remain: to-day
I, crouching behind a sheep-pen, heard   5
Travel across a sudden bird,
Cry out against the storm, and found
The year's arc a completed round
And love's worn circuit re-begun,
Endless with no dissenting turn.   10
Shall see, shall pass, as we have seen
The swallow on the tile, spring's green

1. First published under the title, "The Love Letter."

Preliminary shiver, passed
A solitary truck, the last
Of shunting[2] in the Autumn. But now,   15
To interrupt the homely brow,
Thought warmed to evening through and through,
Your letter comes, speaking as you,
Speaking of much but not to come.

Nor speech is close nor fingers numb,   20
If love not seldom has received
An unjust answer, was deceived.
I, decent with the seasons, move
Different or with a different love,
Nor question overmuch the nod,   25
The stone smile of this country god
That never was more reticent,
Always afraid to say more than it meant.

December 1927   1928

From Five Songs

V

"O where are you going?" said reader to rider,
"That valley is fatal when furnaces burn,
Yonder's the midden[3] whose odours will madden,
That gap is the grave where the tall return."

"O do you imagine," said fearer to farer,   5
"That dusk will delay on your path to the pass,
Your diligent looking discover the lacking,
Your footsteps feel from granite to grass?"

"O what was that bird," said horror to hearer,
"Did you see that shape in the twisted trees?
Behind you swiftly the figure comes softly,   10
The spot on your skin is a shocking disease."

"Out of this house"—said rider to reader,
"Yours never will"—said farer to fearer,
"They're looking for you"—said hearer to horror,   15
As he left them there, as he left them there.

October 1931

The Wanderer[4]

Doom is dark and deeper than any sea-dingle.[5]
Upon what man it fall

2. Traveling back and forth.
3. Dunghill or refuse dump.
4. This poem was first published with the title "Something Is Bound to Happen."
5. Adapted from a Middle English West Mid- land homily, "Sawles Warde," probably written in the thirteenth century, where there is reference to God's judgments as "his dooms that are secret and deeper than any sea dingle." A dingle is an abyss. The rest of the poem owes something to an

In spring, day-wishing flowers appearing,
Avalanche sliding, white snow from rock-face,
That he should leave his house,
No cloud-soft hand can hold him, restraint by women;   5
But ever that man goes
Through place-keepers, through forest trees,
A stranger to strangers over undried sea,
Houses for fishes, suffocating water,
Or lonely on fell as chat,[6]   10
By pot-holed becks[7]
A bird stone-haunting, an unquiet bird.

There head falls forward, fatigued at evening,
And dreams of home,
Waving from window, spread of welcome,   15
Kissing of wife under single sheet;
But waking sees
Bird-flocks nameless to him, through doorway voices
Of new men making another love.   20

Save him from hostile capture,
From sudden tiger's leap at corner;
Protect his house,
His anxious house where days are counted
From thunderbolt protect,   25
From gradual ruin spreading like a stain;
Converting number from vague to certain,
Bring joy, bring day of his returning,
Lucky with day approaching, with leaning dawn.

August 1930   1933

Adolescence[8]

By landscape reminded once of his mother's figure
The mountain heights he remembers get bigger and bigger:
With the finest of mapping pens[9] he fondly traces
All the family names on the familiar places.

In a green pasture straying, he walks by still waters;[1]   5
Surely a swan he seems to earth's unwise daughters,[2]

Old English poem also entitled "The Wanderer," from which Richard Hoggart translates these relevant lines: "Often the solitary man prays for favor, for the mercy of the Lord, though, sad at heart, he must needs stir with his hands for a weary while the icy sea across the watery wastes, must journey the paths of exile; settled in truth is fate! So spoke the wanderer, mindful of hardships. . . . He knows who puts it to the test how cruel a comrade is sorrow for him who has few dear protectors; his is the path of exile, in no wise the twisted gold; a chill body, in no wise the riches of the earth; he thinks of retainers in hall and the receiving of treasure, of how in his youth his gold-friend was kind to him at the feast. The joy has all perished. . . . Then the friendless man wakes again, sees before him the dark waves, the sea-birds bathing, spreading their feathers; frost and snow falling mingles with hail. Then heavier are the wounds in his heart, sore for his beloved; sorrow is renewed."
  6. A kind of bird, a warbler. A "fell" is a moorland ridge.
  7. Stony brooks.
  8. Originally the Prologue to *The Orators: An English Study;* later reprinted by itself under the present title.
  9. Very fine pens.
  1. "He maketh me to lie down in green pastures, He leadeth me beside the still waters" (Psalm 23:2).
  2. As Zeus appeared to Leda in the guise of a swan, in classical myth.

Bending a beautiful head, worshipping not lying,
"Dear" the dear beak in the dear concha[3] crying.

Under the trees the summer bands were playing;
"Dear boy, be brave as these roots," he heard them saying: 10
Carries the good news gladly to a world in danger,
Is ready to argue, he smiles, with any stranger.

And yet this prophet, homing the day is ended,
Receives odd welcome from the country he so defended:
The band roars "Coward, Coward," in his human fever,   15
The giantess[4] shuffles nearer, cries "Deceiver."

March 1931   1932

Our Hunting Fathers[5]

Our hunting fathers told the story
  Of the sadness of the creatures,
Pitied the limits and the lack
  Set in their finished features;
Saw in the lion's intolerant look,   5
  Behind the quarry's dying glare,
Love raging for the personal glory
  That reason's gift would add,
The liberal appetite and power,
  The rightness of a god.   10

Who, nurtured in that fine tradition,
  Predicted the result,
Guessed Love by nature suited to
  The intricate ways of guilt,
That human ligaments could so   15
  His southern gestures modify
And make it his mature ambition
  To think no thought but ours,
To hunger, work illegally,
  And be anonymous?   20

? May 1934   1935

As I Walked Out One Evening[6]

As I walked out one evening,
  Walking down Bristol Street,

---

3. That is, deep in her ear.
4. Presumably the mother.
5. First published under the title "In Father's Footsteps." The poem contrasts two views of love. The first stanza shows how in the eighteenth and nineteenth centuries it was felt to be the driving power which, tempered by reason, provided the individual with his basic motivation . . . The animals are to be pitied because in them the quality is innocent and undirected: only man can consciously put it to a purpose. The second stanza develops the idea that love is, on the contrary, not a noble force at all, but one to be denied because it inevitably leads to the guilt of individualism and self-regard. 'His southern gestures modify' [line 16] means to sublimate love's genital impulses into not a selfish love, but a universal, social love" (John Fuller, A Reader's Guide to W. H. Auden, New York, 1970, p. 101).
6. First published under the title "One Evening."

The crowds upon the pavement
  Were fields of harvest wheat.

And down by the brimming river   5
  I heard a lover sing
Under an arch of the railway:
  "Love has no ending.

"I'll love you, dear, I'll love you
  Till China and Africa meet,   10
And the river jumps over the mountain
  And the salmon sing in the street,

"I'll love you till the ocean
  Is folded and hung up to dry
And the seven stars[7] go squawking   15
  Like geese about the sky.

"The years shall run like rabbits,
  For in my arms I hold
The Flower of the Ages,
  And the first love of the world."   20

But all the clocks in the city
  Began to whirr and chime:
"O let not Time deceive you,
  You cannot conquer Time.

"In the burrows of the Nightmare   25
  Where Justice naked is,
Time watches from the shadow
  And coughs when you would kiss.

"In headaches and in worry
  Vaguely life leaks away.   30
And Time will have his fancy
  To-morrow or to-day.

"Into many a green valley
  Drifts the appalling snow;[8]
Time breaks the threaded dances   35
  And the diver's brilliant bow.

"O plunge your hands in water,
  Plunge them in up to the wrist;
Stare, stare in the basin
  And wonder what you've missed.   40

"The glacier knocks in the cupboard,
  The desert sighs in the bed,

---

7. The constellation the Pleiades, supposed by the ancients to be seven sisters.
8. The phrase "is literal (the snow makes the valleys pale) and yet reinforces a cliché about bad weather" (*Reader's Guide*, p. 108).

And the crack in the tea-cup opens
A lane to the land of the dead.

"Where the beggars raffle the banknotes   45
And the Giant is enchanting to Jack,
And the Lily-white Boy is a Roarer,
And Jill goes down on her back.[9]

"O look, look in the mirror,
O look in your distress;   50
Life remains a blessing
Although you cannot bless.

"O stand, stand at the window
As the tears scald and start;
You shall love your crooked neighbour   55
With your crooked heart."

It was late, late in the evening,
The lovers they were gone;
The clocks had ceased their chiming,
And the deep river ran on.   60

November 1937   1940

Lullaby

Lay your sleeping head, my love,
Human on my faithless arm;
Time and fevers burn away
Individual beauty from
Thoughtful children, and the grave   5
Proves the child ephemeral:
But in my arms till break of day
Let the living creature lie,
Mortal, guilty, but to me
The entirely beautiful.   10

Soul and body have no bounds:
To lovers as they lie upon
Her tolerant enchanted slope
In their ordinary swoon,
Grave the vision Venus[1] sends   15
Of supernatural sympathy,
Universal love and hope;
While an abstract insight wakes
Among the glaciers and the rocks
The hermit's carnal ecstasy.   20

9. The giant of "Jack and the Bean Stalk" becomes a sweet-talking hustler; the "lily-white Boy" (presumably pure) becomes a roisterer, a boisterous reveler; Jill, of "Jack and Jill," is seduced—all perversions of innocent nursery-rhyme morality.
1. Roman goddess of love.

Certainty, fidelity
On the stroke of midnight pass
Like vibrations of a bell
And fashionable madmen raise
Their pedantic boring cry: 25
Every farthing[2] of the cost,
All the dreaded cards foretell,
Shall be paid, but from this night
Not a whisper, not a thought,
Not a kiss nor look be lost.   30

Beauty, midnight, vision dies:
Let the winds of dawn that blow
Softly round your dreaming head
Such a day of welcome show
Eye and knocking heart may bless,   35
Find our mortal world enough;
Noons of dryness find you fed
By the involuntary powers,
Nights of insult let you pass
Watched by every human love.   40

January 1937   1940

Musée des Beaux Arts[3]

About suffering they were never wrong,
The Old Masters: how well they understood
Its human position; how it takes place
While someone else is eating or opening a window or just walking dully
    along;   5
How, when the aged are reverently, passionately waiting
For the miraculous birth, there always must be
Children who did not specially want it to happen, skating
On a pond at the edge of the wood:
They never forgot   10
That even the dreadful martyrdom must run its course
Anyhow in a corner, some untidy spot
Where the dogs go on with their doggy life and the torturer's horse
Scratches its innocent behind on a tree.

In Breughel's *Icarus*,[4] for instance: how everything turns away   15
Quite leisurely from the disaster; the ploughman may
Have heard the splash, the forsaken cry,
But for him it was not an important failure; the sun shone
As it had to on the white legs disappearing into the green
Water; and the expensive delicate ship that must have seen   20

---

2. British coin of very small value (now obsolete).
3. Museum of Fine Arts (French).
4. Pieter Bruegel's painting *The Fall of Icarus* hangs in the Palace of the Royal Museums of Painting and Sculpture in Brussels. Auden borrows the detail of the horse scratching its behind from another Bruegel painting, *The Massacre of the Innocents.* Icarus flew using the wings his father Daedalus had made of feathers and wax, but recklessly went too close to the sun; the wax melted and he fell into the sea. Compare, above, William Carlos Williams's "Landscape with the Fall of Icarus."

Something amazing, a boy falling out of the sky,
Had somewhere to get to and sailed calmly on.

December 1938   1940

In Memory of W. B. Yeats[5]

(d. Jan. 1939)
I

He disappeared in the dead of winter:
The brooks were frozen, the airports almost deserted,
And snow disfigured the public statues;
The mercury sank in the mouth of the dying day.
What instruments we have agree   5
The day of his death was a dark cold day.

Far from his illness
The wolves ran on through the evergreen forests,
The peasant river was untempted by the fashionable quays;
By mourning tongues
The death of the poet was kept from his poems.   10

But for him it was his last afternoon as himself,
An afternoon of nurses and rumours;
The provinces of his body revolted,
The squares of his mind were empty,
Silence invaded the suburbs,   15
The current of his feeling failed; he became his admirers.

Now he is scattered among a hundred cities
And wholly given over to unfamiliar affections;
To find his happiness in another kind of wood[6]
And be punished under a foreign code of conscience.[7]   20
The words of a dead man
Are modified in the guts of the living.

But in the importance and noise of to-morrow
When the brokers are roaring like beasts on the floor of the Bourse,[8]
And the poor have the sufferings to which they are fairly accustomed, 25
And each in the cell of himself is almost convinced of his freedom,
A few thousand will think of this day
As one thinks of a day when one did something slightly unusual.

What instruments we have agree
The day of his death was a dark cold day.   30

---

5. Yeats died on January 29, 1939, in Roque-brune (southern France).
6. An allusion to the beginning of the *Inferno*, where Dante finds himself, in middle life, "in a dark wood." Yeats, by dying, enters a realm of being where poets survive only in their poems.
7. A glance at Yeats's Irish nationalism. The foreign code to which he must now submit is the judgment of the living.
8. Stock exchange (French).

II

You were silly like us;[9] your gift survived it all:
The parish of rich women,[1] physical decay,
Yourself. Mad Ireland hurt you into poetry.
Now Ireland has her madness and her weather still,
For poetry makes nothing happen: it survives   35
In the valley of its making where executives
Would never want to tamper, flows on south
From ranches of isolation and the busy griefs,
Raw towns that we believe and die in; it survives,
A way of happening, a mouth.   40

III

Earth, receive an honoured guest:
William Yeats is laid to rest.
Let the Irish vessel lie
Emptied of its poetry.[2]

In the nightmare of the dark   45
All the dogs of Europe bark,[3]
And the living nations wait,
Each sequestered in its hate;

Intellectual disgrace
Stares from every human face,   50
And the seas of pity lie
Locked and frozen in each eye.

Follow, poet, follow right
To the bottom of the night,
With your unconstraining voice   55
Still persuade us to rejoice;

With the farming of a verse
Make a vineyard of the curse,
Sing of human unsuccess
In a rapture of distress;   60

In the deserts of the heart
Let the healing fountain start,
In the prison of his days
Teach the free man how to praise.[4]

February 1939   1940

---

9. In prose writings, Auden registered various objections to Yeats's thought, especially to his occultism.

1. Yeats as a young man accepted some financial help, later repaid, from Lady Gregory. He was friendly with other wealthy women later.

2. Following this line Auden originally included three stanzas in which Time, which is said to worship language and forgive "everyone by whom [language] lives," is expected to pardon "Kipling and his [imperialistic] views / And will pardon Paul Claudel [a French writer of extreme political conservatism], / Pardons him [Yeats, whose antidemocratic stance was antipathetic to Auden's own] for writing well." Auden deleted these stanzas in the 1966 edition of *Collected Shorter Poems*.

3. The Second World War was to begin in September 1939.

4. The stanza pattern of this section echoes that of Yeats's late poem, 'Under Ben Bulben" (p. 95).

In Memory of Sigmund Freud[5]

(d. Sept. 1939)

When there are so many we shall have to mourn,
when grief has been made so public, and exposed
    to the critique of a whole epoch
    the frailty of our conscience and anguish,

of whom shall we speak? For every day they die   5
among us, those who were doing us some good,
    who knew it was never enough but
    hoped to improve a little by living.

Such was this doctor: still at eighty he wished
to think of our life from whose unruliness   10
    so many plausible young futures
    with threats or flattery ask obedience,

but his wish was denied him: he closed his eyes
upon that last picture, common to us all,
    of problems like relatives gathered   15
    puzzled and jealous about our dying.

For about him till the very end were still
those he had studied, the fauna of the night,
    and shades that still waited to enter
    the bright circle of his recognition   20

turned elsewhere with their disappointment as he
was taken away from his life interest
    to go back to the earth in London,
    an important Jew who died in exile.

Only Hate was happy, hoping to augment   25
his practice now, and his dingy clientele
    who think they can be cured by killing
    and covering the gardens with ashes.

They are still alive, but in a world he changed
simply by looking back with no false regrets;   30
    all he did was to remember
    like the old and be honest like children.

He wasn't clever at all: he merely told
the unhappy Present to recite the Past
    like a poetry lesson till sooner   35
    or later it faltered at the line where

long ago the accusations had begun,
and suddenly knew by whom it had been judged,
    how rich life had been and how silly,
    and was life-forgiven and more humble,   40

5. Austrian neurologist and founder of psychoanalysis (1856–1939). He lived and practiced in Vienna until, forced out by the Nazi regime, he went to London, where he died.

able to approach the Future as a friend
without a wardrobe of excuses, without
    a set mask of rectitude or an
    embarrassing over-familiar gesture.

No wonder the ancient cultures of conceit   45
in his technique of unsettlement foresaw
    the fall of princes, the collapse of
    their lucrative patterns of frustration:

if he succeeded, why the Generalised Life
would become impossible, the monolith   50
    of State be broken and prevented
    the co-operation of avengers.

Of course they called on God, but he went his way
down among the lost people like Dante,[6] down
    to the stinking fosse where the injured   55
    lead the ugly life of the rejected,

and showed us what evil is, not, as we thought,
deeds that must be punished, but our lack of faith,
    our dishonest mood of denial,
    the concupiscence of the oppressor.   60

If some traces of the autocratic pose,
the paternal strictness he distrusted, still
    clung to his utterance and features,
    it was a protective coloration

for one who'd lived among enemies so long;   65
if often he was wrong and, at times, absurd,
    to us he is no more a person
    now but a whole climate of opinion

under whom we conduct our different lives:
Like weather he can only hinder or help,   70
    the proud can still be proud but find it
    a little harder, the tyrant tries to

make do with him but doesn't care for him much:
he quietly surrounds all our habits of growth
    and extends, till the tired in even   75
    the remotest miserable duchy

have felt the change in their bones and are cheered,
till the child, unlucky in his little State,
    some hearth where freedom is excluded,
    a hive whose honey is fear and worry,   80

feels calmer now and somehow assured of escape,
while, as they lie in the grass of our neglect,

---

6. As Dante descended into hell in his *Inferno* (1308–21). "Fosse" (next line): ditch.

so many long-forgotten objects
revealed by his undiscouraged shining

are returned to us and made precious again;   85
games we had thought we must drop as we grew up,
    little noises we dared not laugh at,
    faces we made when no one was looking.

But he wishes us more than this. To be free
is often to be lonely. He would unite   90
    the unequal moieties[7] fractured
    by our own well-meaning sense of justice,

would restore to the larger the wit and will
the smaller possesses but can only use
    for arid disputes, would give back to   95
    the son the mother's richness of feeling:

but he would have us remember most of all
to be enthusiastic over the night,
    not only for the sense of wonder
    it alone has to offer, but also   100

because it needs our love. With large sad eyes
its delectable creatures look up and beg
    us dumbly to ask them to follow:
    they are exiles who long for the future

that lies in our power, they too would rejoice   105
if allowed to serve enlightenment like him,
    even to bear our cry of "Judas,"[8]
    as he did and all must bear who serve it.

One rational voice is dumb. Over his grave
the household of Impulse[9] mourns one dearly loved: 110
    sad is Eros, builder of cities,
    and weeping anarchic Aphrodite.[1]

November 1939   1940

Mundus et Infans[2]

(for Albert and Angelyn Stevens)

Kicking his mother until she let go of his soul
Has given him a healthy appetite: clearly, her rôle
    In the New Order must be
To supply and deliver his raw materials free;
    Should there be any shortage,   5

7. Components, parts.
8. Judas Iscariot was the disciple who betrayed Christ (Matthew 26:14ff.).
9. "The sexual motive that both binds men together socially and creates discord between them personally" (Reader's Guide, p. 176).
1. Goddess of love in ancient mythology, and mother of Eros (which means "love") or Cupid, both members of "the household of Impulse." To build cities requires the creative force of love.
2. The world and the child (Latin). "The title of the poem is borrowed from an early sixteenth-century play" (Reader's Guide, p. 182).

She will be held responsible; she also promises
To show him all such attentions as befit his age.
    Having dictated peace,

With one fist clenched behind his head, heel drawn up to thigh
The cocky little ogre dozes off, ready,   10
    Though, to take the rest
Of the world at the drop of a hat or the mildest
    Nudge of the impossible,
Resolved, cost what it may, to seize supreme power and
Sworn to resist tyranny to the death with all   15
    forces at his command.

A pantheist not a solipsist,[3] he co-operates
With a universe of large and noisy feeling-states
    Without troubling to place
Them anywhere special, for, to his eyes, Funnyface   20
    Or Elephant as yet
Mean nothing. His distinction between Me and Us
Is a matter of taste; his seasons are Dry and Wet;
    He thinks as his mouth does.

Still, his loud iniquity is still what only the   25
Greatest of saints become—someone who does not lie:
    He because he cannot
Stop the vivid present to think, they by having got
    Past reflection into
A passionate obedience in time. We have our Boy-   30
Meets-Girl era of mirrors and muddle to work through,
    Without rest, without joy.

Therefore we love him because his judgments are so
Frankly subjective that his abuse carries no
    Personal sting. We should   35
Never dare offer our helplessness as a good
    Bargain, without at least
Promising to overcome a misfortune we blame
History or Banks or the Weather for: but this beast
    Dares to exist without shame.   40

Let him praise our Creator with the top of his voice,
Then, and the motions of his bowels; let us rejoice
    That he lets us hope, for
He may never become a fashionable or
    Important personage;   45
However bad he may be, he has not yet gone mad;
Whoever we are now, we were no worse at his age;
    So of course we ought to be glad

When he bawls the house down. Has he not a perfect right
To remind us at every moment how we quite   50
    Rightly expect each other

3. One excessively concerned with oneself.

To go upstairs or for a walk, if we must cry over
　　Spilt milk, such as our wish
That, since apparently we shall never be above
Either or both, we had never learned to distinguish   55
　　Between hunger and love?
? August 1942   1945

In Praise of Limestone

If it form the one landscape that we, the inconstant ones,
　　Are consistently homesick for, this is chiefly
Because it dissolves in water. Mark these rounded slopes
　　With their surface fragrance of thyme and, beneath,
A secret system of caves and conduits; hear the springs   5
　　That spurt out everywhere with a chuckle,
Each filling a private pool for its fish and carving
　　Its own little ravine whose cliffs entertain
The butterfly and the lizard; examine this region
　　Of short distances and definite places: 10
What could be more like Mother or a fitter background
　　For her son, the flirtatious male who lounges
Against a rock in the sunlight, never doubting
　　That for all his faults he is loved; whose works are but
Extensions of his power to charm? From weathered outcrop   15
　　To hill-top temple, from appearing waters to
Conspicuous fountains, from a wild to a formal vineyard,
　　Are ingenious but short steps that a child's wish
To receive more attention than his brothers, whether
　　By pleasing or teasing, can easily take.   20

Watch, then, the band of rivals as they climb up and down
　　Their steep stone gennels[4] in twos and threes, at times
Arm in arm, but never, thank God, in step; or engaged
　　On the shady side of a square at midday in
Voluble discourse, knowing each other too well to think   25
　　There are any important secrets, unable
To conceive a god whose temper-tantrums are moral
　　And not to be pacified by a clever line
Or a good lay: for, accustomed to a stone that responds,
　　They have never had to veil their faces in awe   30
Of a crater whose blazing fury could not be fixed;
　　Adjusted to the local needs of valleys
Where everything can be touched or reached by walking,
　　Their eyes have never looked into infinite space
Through the lattice-work of a nomad's comb; born lucky,   35
　　Their legs have never encountered the fungi
And insects of the jungle, the monstrous forms and lives
　　With which we have nothing, we like to hope, in common.
So, when one of them goes to the bad, the way his mind works
　　Remains comprehensible: to become a pimp   40
Or deal in fake jewellery or ruin a fine tenor voice

---

4. A narrow passage between houses or, as here, rocks.

For effects that bring down the house, could happen to all
But the best and the worst of us . . .
                              That is why, I suppose,
    The best and worst never stayed here long but sought   45
Immoderate soils where the beauty was not so external,
    The light less public and the meaning of life
Something more than a mad camp. "Come!" cried the granite wastes,
    "How evasive is your humor, how accidental
Your kindest kiss, how permanent is death." (Saints-to-be   50
    Slipped away sighing.) "Come!" purred the clays and gravels,
"On our plains there is room for armies to drill; rivers
    Wait to be tamed and slaves to construct you a tomb
In the grand manner: soft as the earth is mankind and both
    Need to be altered." (Intendant Caesars rose and   55
Left, slamming the door.)[5] But the really reckless were fetched
    By an older colder voice, the oceanic whisper:
"I am the solitude that asks and promises nothing;
    That is how I shall set you free. There is no love;
There are only the various envies, all of them sad."   60

    They were right, my dear, all those voices were right
And still are; this land is not the sweet home that it looks,
    Nor its peace the historical calm of a site
Where something was settled once and for all: A backward
    And dilapidated province, connected   65
To the big busy world by a tunnel, with a certain
    Seedy appeal, is that all it is now? Not quite:
It has a worldly duty which in spite of itself
    It does not neglect, but calls into question
All the Great Powers assume; it disturbs our rights. The poet,   70
    Admired for his earnest habit of calling
The sun the sun, his mind Puzzle, is made uneasy
    By these marble statues which so obviously doubt
His antimythological myth; and these gamins,
    Pursuing the scientist down the tiled colonnade   75
With such lively offers, rebuke his concern for Nature's
    Remotest aspects: I, too, am reproached, for what
And how much you know. Not to lose time, not to get caught,
    Not to be left behind, not, please! to resemble
The beasts who repeat themselves, or a thing like water   80
    Or stone whose conduct can be predicted, these
Are our Common Prayer,[6] whose greatest comfort is music
    Which can be made anywhere, is invisible,
And does not smell. In so far as we have to look forward
    To death as a fact, no doubt we are right: But if   85
Sins can be forgiven, if bodies rise from the dead,
    These modifications of matter into
Innocent athletes and gesticulating fountains,
    Made solely for pleasure, make a further point:

---

5. John Fuller suggests that this is an allusion
to a remark by Joseph Goebbels, Adolf Hitler's
propaganda minister and, in 1945, his successor:
"If we are defeated, we shall slam the doors of
history behind us" (*Reader's Guide*, p. 213).

6. The Book of Common Prayer is a collection
of prayers in English; assembled during the sixteenth century, it standardizes the devotions of the
Church of England.

The blessed will not care what angle they are regarded from,   90
   Having nothing to hide. Dear, I know nothing of
Either, but when I try to imagine a faultless love
   Or the life to come, what I hear is the murmur
Of underground streams, what I see is a limestone landscape.

May 1948   1951

Their Lonely Betters

As I listened from a beach-chair in the shade
To all the noises that my garden made,
It seemed to me only proper that words
Should be withheld from vegetables and birds.

A robin with no Christian name ran through   5
The Robin-Anthem which was all it knew,
And rustling flowers for some third party waited
To say which pairs, if any, should get mated.

Not one of them was capable of lying,
There was not one which knew that it was dying   10
Or could have with a rhythm or a rhyme
Assumed responsibility for time.

Let them leave language to their lonely betters
Who count some days and long for certain letters:
We, too, make noises when we laugh or weep: 15
Words are for those with promises to keep.

? June 1950   1951

The Shield of Achilles[7]

She looked over his shoulder
   For vines and olive trees,
Marble well-governed cities
   And ships upon untamed seas,
But there on the shining metal   5
   His hands had put instead
An artificial wilderness
   And a sky like lead.

A plain without a feature, bare and brown,
   No blade of grass, no sign of neighborhood,   10

7. Achilles, the chief Greek hero in the war with Troy, loses his armor when his great friend Patroclus, wearing it, is slain by Hector. While Achilles is mourning the death of his friend, his mother, the goddess Thetis, goes to Olympus to entreat Hephaestos to make new armor for him: both she and Hephaestos pity Achilles because he is fated to die soon and because his life has not been happy. The splendid shield, incorporating gold and silver as well as less precious metals, is described at length in Book XVIII of the *Iliad* (lines 478–608), the scenes depicted on it constituting an epitome of the universe and the lives of men. Hephaestos portrays on it the earth, the heavens, the sea, and the planets; a city in peace (with a wedding and a trial-at-law) and a city at war; scenes from country life, including a harvest feast and a grape-gathering; scenes from animal life and the joyful life of young men and maidens. Around all these scenes, closing them in as the outer border, flows the ocean. The shield is usually taken as an emblem of the creative power of the arts in civilization.

Nothing to eat and nowhere to sit down,
   Yet, congregated on its blankness, stood
   An unintelligible multitude,
A million eyes, a million boots in line,
Without expression, waiting for a sign.   15

   Out of the air a voice without a face
      Proved by statistics that some cause was just
   In tones as dry and level as the place:
      No one was cheered and nothing was discussed;
      Column by column in a cloud of dust   20
   They marched away enduring a belief
   Whose logic brought them, somewhere else, to grief.

         She looked over his shoulder
            For ritual pieties,
         White flower-garlanded heifers,   25
            Libation and sacrifice, [8]
         But there on the shining metal
            Where the altar should have been,
         She saw by his flickering forge-light
            Quite another scene.   30

Barbed wire enclosed an arbitrary spot
   Where bored officials lounged (one cracked a joke)
And sentries sweated for the day was hot:
   A crowd of ordinary decent folk
   Watched from without and neither moved nor spoke   35
As three pale figures were led forth and bound
To three posts driven upright in the ground.

The mass and majesty of this world, all
   That carries weight and always weighs the same
Lay in the hands of others; they were small   40
   And could not hope for help and no help came:
   What their foes liked to do was done, their shame
Was all the worst could wish; they lost their pride
And died as men before their bodies died.

         She looked over his shoulder   45
            For athletes at their games,
         Men and women in a dance
            Moving their sweet limbs
            Quick, quick, to music,
            But there on the shining shield   50
         His hands had set no dancing-floor
            But a weed-choked field.

A ragged urchin, aimless and alone,
   Loitered about that vacancy; a bird

---

8. Compare John Keats's "Ode on a Grecian
Urn" (1820): "Who are these coming to the sacrifice? / To what green altar, O mysterious priest, /
Lead'st thou that heifer lowing at the skies, / And
all her silken flanks with garlands dressed?"

Flew up to safety from his well-aimed stone: 55
   That girls are raped, that two boys knife a third,
   Were axioms to him, who'd never heard
Of any world where promises were kept,
Or one could weep because another wept.

   The thin-lipped armorer,   60
     Hephaestos, hobbled away,
   Thetis of the shining breasts
     Cried out in dismay
At what the god had wrought
     To please her son, the strong   65
Iron-hearted man-slaying Achilles
     Who would not live long.

1952   1955

A Lullaby[9]

The din of work is subdued,
another day has westered
and mantling[1] darkness arrived.
Peace! Peace! Devoid your portrait
of its vexations and rest.   5
Your daily round is done with,
you've gotten the garbage out,
answered some tiresome letters
and paid a bill by return,
al *frettolosamente.*[2]   10
Now you have licence to lie,
naked, curled like a shrimplet,
jacent[3] in bed, and enjoy
its cosy micro-climate:
Sing, Big Baby, sing lullay.   15

The old Greeks got it all wrong:
Narcissus[4] is an oldie,
tamed by time, released at last
from lust for other bodies,
rational and reconciled.   20
For many years you envied
the hirsute, the he-man type.
No longer: now you fondle
your almost feminine flesh
with mettled[5] satisfaction,   25
imagining that you are
sinless and all-sufficient,
snug in the den of yourself,
Madonna and *Bambino:*[6]
Sing, Big Baby, sing lullay.   30

9. This poem, sung by the aging poet to himself, is placed last in the *Collected Poems.*
  1. Covering.
  2. Hastily (Italian).
  3. Lying down.
  4. Legendary youth so enamored of his beauty
that he tried to meet his reflection in a stream and
so drowned.
  5. High-spirited.
  6. Literally, "my lady" and "baby" (Italian); used
for the Virgin Mary and the Christ child.

Let your last thinks all be thanks:
praise your parents who gave you
a Super-Ego[7] of strength
that saves you so much bother,
digit friends and dear them all,[8]   35
then pay fair attribution
to your age, to having been
born when you were. In boyhood
you were permitted to meet
beautiful old contraptions,   40
soon to be banished from earth,
saddle-tank locks, beam-engines
and over-shot waterwheels.[9]
Yes, love, you have been lucky:
Sing, Big Baby, sing lullay.   45

Now for oblivion: let
the belly-mind take over
down below the diaphragm,
the domain of the Mothers,
They who guard the Sacred Gates,[1]   50
without whose wordless warnings
soon the verbalising I
becomes a vicious despot,
lewd, incapable of love,
disdainful, status-hungry.   55
Should dreams haunt you, heed them not,
for all, both sweet and horrid,
are jokes in dubious taste,
too jejune[2] to have truck with.
Sleep, Big Baby, sleep your fill.   60

April 1972   1973

7. That part of the psyche that acts as conscience and law-giver (a term from psychoanalysis).
8. Call them all "dear"; "digit": probably in the sense of numbering or counting.
9. Waterwheels with buckets on their rims that turn as the buckets fill with water; "saddle-tanks": water-tanks on the boilers of railway locomotives; "beam-engines": parts of a steam engine.
1. Perhaps the gates of ivory and of horn in classical myth, through which false and true dreams, respectively, issued.
2. Inadequate.

A. D. HOPE
b. 1907

Witty poets have been in short supply during the second half of this century. Witty poets writing of love have been even scarcer. A. D. Hope has, however, established himself as a master of witty, amorous verse, translating into a current idiom the preoccupations of Metaphysical poetry. In his book of essays, *The Cave and the Spring*, Hope regrets the disappearance of "the middle form of poetry: that form in which the uses of poetry approach closest to the uses of prose, and yet remain essentially poetry."[1] It is this middle form which he commands, and he claims poets like Chaucer and Browning as predecessors, poets uninterested in "a profusion of startling images," interested rather in ordinary English.

1. *The Cave and the Spring*, Adelaide, 1965, p. 5.

His occasional pronouncements about poetry have remonstrated against the undigested intensities of his contemporaries. In the preface to a small collection of his poems published in the Australian Poets Series,[2] Hope offers two of his "comfortable prejudices." One is against a "heresy of our times which holds that by excluding those things which poetry has in common with prose, narrative, argument, description, exhortation and exposition, and that by depending entirely on lyric impulse or the evocative power of massed imagery, one can arrive at the pure essence of poetry. 'Pure poetry' seems to me an illusion that has cost us most of the great variety of forms practised in the past and has impoverished those to which we have largely confined ourselves."

His second prejudice is directed against the notion "that poetry can be improved or its range extended by breaking down the traditional structure of English verse or replacing its rhythms by those of prose. The English metre depends upon collocation of metrical and prose rhythms and from this comes its elasticity, its richness of texture and its endless possibilities of variety within a simple pattern. So-called free verse sacrifices all this by trying, and trying in vain, to make the prose rhythms do all the work." He finds both these "heresies" to be derived from Romantic personalism, "the view that poetry is primarily self-expression. On this view the subject becomes a means by which the poet expresses himself, his views, his feelings, his lyric personality. I hold, on the contrary, that poetry is principally concerned to 'express' its subject and is doing so to create an emotion which is the feeling of the poem and not the feeling of the poet. In this I am at one with T. S. Eliot, a poet whose poetry I cannot bring myself to like at all."

Alec Derwent Hope was borne in Coomo, New South Wales, on July 21, 1907, one of the five children of a Presbyterian minister and small-scale farmer, who shortly afterwards moved himself and his family to the island of Tasmania, off the southern coast of Australia. Hope's mother seems to have been chiefly responsible for the children's education. She taught them to read and write, and she and her husband regularly read aloud to the children from the English classics, mostly poetry.

When he was fourteen, Hope was sent to the Australian mainland for his further education. Eventually he took a degree at the University of Sydney, where he bested his contemporaries in both philosophy and English. In 1928 he performed what is for some young Australians a ritual: a return to the Old Country. He enrolled as a student at University College, Oxford, but for Hope the ancient university failed to work its vaunted magic: he was short of funds, probably put off by the English faculty's then indifference to literature written after the Middle Ages, and he took a mediocre third-class degree. Having returned to Australia, it took Hope some years to find a place where he could write his poems and follow his other vocation, teaching. In 1951 he became the first Professor of English at what is now the Australian National University, and in 1955, at the age of forty-eight, he published his first collection of poems, *The Wandering Islands*. Some of its first readers, eager for evidence of an emerging national literature, found the book disappointing, even scandalous. According to his editor, Ruth Morse, he has been "stigmatized as an Augustan, a Romantic, a Nietzschean, a Manichee, and latterly as an elitist and misogynist."[3] All of which means that Hope has exercised every poet's option to explore a variety of ways of looking at the world by impersonating them, by performing them, in his poems.

2. Sydney, 1963, pp. vii–ix.
3. A. D. Hope: *Selected Poems*, ed. Ruth Morse, Manchester, England, 1986, p. 9.

Australia

A Nation of trees, drab green and desolate grey
In the field uniform of modern wars,

Darkens her hills, those endless, outstretched paws
Of Sphinx demolished or stone lion worn away.

They called her a young country, but they lie: 5
She is the last of lands, the emptiest,
A woman beyond her change of life, a breast
Still tender but within the womb is dry.

Without songs, architecture, history:
The emotions and superstitions of younger lands,   10
Her rivers of water drown among inland sands,
The river of her immense stupidity

Floods her monotonous tribes from Cairns to Perth.[1]
In them at last the ultimate men arrive
Whose boast is not: "we live" but "we survive,"   15
A type who will inhabit the dying earth.

And her five cities,[2] like five teeming sores,
Each drains her: a vast parasite robber-state
Where second-hand Europeans pullulate[3]
Timidly on the edge of alien shores.   20

Yet there are some like me turn gladly home
From the lush jungle of modern thought, to find
The Arabian desert of the human mind,
Hoping, if still from the deserts the prophets come,[4]

Such savage and scarlet as no green hills dare   25
Springs in that waste, some spirit which escapes
The learned doubt, the chatter of cultured apes
Which is called civilization over there.

                                                    1939

Observation Car

To be put on the train and kissed and given my ticket,
Then the station slid backward, the shops and the neon lighting,
Reeling off in a drunken blur, with a whole pound note in my pocket
And the holiday packed with Perhaps. It used to be very exciting.

The present and past were enough. I did not mind having my back   5
To the engine. I sat like a spider and spun
Time backward out of my guts—or rather my eyes—and the track
Was a Now dwindling off to oblivion. I thought it was fun:

The telegraph poles slithered up in a sudden crescendo
As we sliced the hill and scattered its grazing sheep;   10
The days were a wheeling delirium that led without end to
Nights when we plunged into roaring tunnels of sleep.

1. Cities on a northeast peninsula and on the southwest coast of Australia, respectively; that is, from one end to the other.
2. Probably Australia's five largest cities—Sydney, Melbourne, Adelaide, Perth, and Hobart.
3. Breed rapidly.
4. In the Old Testament, the prophets—or spokesmen for the Lord—often came out of the desert to speak their prophecies or warnings.

But now I am tired of the train. I have learned that one tree
Is much like another, one hill the dead spit of the next
I have seen tailing off behind all the various types of country   15
Like a clock running down. I am bored and a little perplexed;

And weak with the effort of endless evacuation
Of the long monotonous Now, the repetitive, tidy
Officialdom of each siding, of each little station
Labelled Monday, Tuesday—and goodness! what happened to Friday?   20

And the maddening way the other passengers alter:
The schoolgirl who goes to the Ladies' comes back to her seat
A lollipop blonde who leads you on to assault her,
And you've just got her skirts round her waist and her pants round her feet

When you find yourself fumbling about the nightmare knees   25
Of a pink hippopotamus with a permanent wave
Who sends you for sandwiches and a couple of teas,
But by then she has whiskers, no teeth and one foot in the grave.

I have lost my faith that the ticket tells where we are going.
There are rumours the driver is mad—we are all being trucked   30
To the abattoirs somewhere—the signals are jammed and unknowing
We aim through the night full speed at a wrecked viaduct.

But I do not believe them. The future is rumour and drivel;
Only the past is assured. From the observation car
I stand looking back and watching the landscape shrivel,   35
Wondering where we are going and just where the hell we are,

Remembering how I planned to break the journey, to drive
My own car one day, to have choice in my hands and my foot upon power,
To see through the trumpet throat of vertiginous perspective
My urgent Now explode continually into flower,   40

To be the Eater of Time, a poet and not that sly
Anus of mind the historian. It was so simple and plain
To live by the sole, insatiable influx of the eye.
But something went wrong with the plan: I am still on the train.

1955

The Lingam and the Yoni[5]

The Lingam and the Yoni
Are walking hand in glove,
O are you listening, honey?
I hear my honey-love.

The He and She our movers   5
What is it they discuss?
Is it the talk of Lovers?
And do they speak of us?

5. The Sanskrit names for the phallus and the vulva.

I hear their high palaver—
O tell me what they say!   10
The talk goes on for ever
So deep in love are they;

So deep in thought, debating
The suburb and the street;
Time-payment calculating   15
Upon the bedroom suite.

But ours is long division
By love's arithmetic,
Until they make provision
To buy a box of brick,   20

A box that makes her prisoner,
That he must slave to win
To do the Lingam honour,
To keep the Yoni in.

The mortgage on tomorrow?   25
The haemorrhage of rent?
Against the heart they borrow
At five or six per cent.

The heart has bought fulfilment
Which yet their mouths defer   30
Until the last instalment
Upon the furniture.

No Lingam for her money
Can make up youth's arrears:
His layby on the Yoni   35
Will not be paid in years.

And they, who keep this tally,
They count what they destroy;
While, in its secret valley
Withers the herb of joy.   40
                                                                     1955

Imperial[6] Adam

Imperial Adam, naked in the dew,
Felt his brown flanks and found the rib was gone.
Puzzled he turned and saw where, two and two,
The mighty spoor of Jahweh[7] marked the lawn.

Then he remembered through mysterious sleep   5
The surgeon fingers probing at the bone,

---

6. That is, emperor.   7. Jehovah.

The voice so far away, so rich and deep:
"It is not good for him to live alone."[8]

Turning once more he found Man's counterpart
In tender parody breathing at his side.   10
He knew her at first sight, he knew by heart
Her allegory of sense unsatisfied.

The pawpaw[9] drooped its golden breasts above
Less generous than the honey of her flesh;
The innocent sunlight showed the place of love;   15
The dew on its dark hairs winked crisp and fresh.

This plump gourd severed from his virile root,
She promised on the turf of Paradise
Delicious pulp of the forbidden fruit;
Sly as the snake she loosed her sinuous thighs,   20

And waking, smiled up at him from the grass;
Her breasts rose softly and he heard her sigh—
From all the beasts whose pleasant task it was
In Eden to increase and multiply

Adam had learned the jolly deed of kind:[1]   25
He took her in his arms and there and then,
Like the clean beasts, embracing from behind,
Began in joy to found the breed of men.

Then from the spurt of seed within her broke
Her terrible and triumphant female cry,   30
Split upward by the sexual lightning stroke.
It was the beasts now who stood watching by:

The gravid[2] elephant, the calving hind,
The breeding bitch, the she-ape big with young
Were the first gentle midwives of mankind;   35
The teeming lioness rasped her with her tongue;

The proud vicuña nuzzled her as she slept
Lax on the grass; and Adam watching too
Saw how her dumb breasts at their ripening wept,
The great pod of her belly swelled and grew,   40

And saw its water break, and saw, in fear,
Its quaking muscles in the act of birth,
Between her legs a pigmy face appear,
And the first murderer[3] lay upon the earth.

                                                                 1955

8. "And the Lord said, It is not good that the   1. That is, of nature.
man should be alone" (Genesis 2:18). Eve was cre-   2. Heavy with young.
ated from one of Adam's ribs (compare line 6).   3. Cain, who murdered his brother Abel.
9. Or "papaw," a fruit tree.

Advice to Young Ladies

A.U.C. 334:[4] about this date,
For a sexual misdemeanour which she denied,
The vestal virgin[5] Postumia was tried;
Livy records it among affairs of state.

They let her off: it seems she was perfectly pure;   5
The charge arose because some thought her talk
Too witty for a young girl, her eyes, her walk
Too lively, her clothes too smart to be demure.

The Pontifex Maximus,[6] summing up the case,
Warned her in future to abstain from jokes,   10
To wear less modish and more pious frocks.
She left the court reprieved, but in disgrace.

What then? With her the annalist[7] is less
Concerned than what the men achieved that year:
Plots, quarrels, crimes, with oratory to spare—   15
I see Postumia with her dowdy dress,

Stiff mouth and listless step; I see her strive
To give dull answers. She had to knuckle down.
A vestal virgin who scandalized that town
Had fair trial, then they buried her alive;[8]   20

Alive, bricked up in suffocating dark;
A ration of bread, a pitcher if she was dry,
Preserved the body they did not wish to die
Until her mind was quenched to the last spark.

How many the black maw has swallowed in its time!   25
Spirited girls who would not know their place,
Talented girls who found that the disgrace
Of being a woman made genius a crime.

How many others, who would not kiss the rod,[9]
Domestic bullying broke or public shame?   30
Pagan or Christian, it was much the same:
Husbands, St. Paul declared, rank next to God.

Livy and Paul,[1] it may be, never knew
That Rome was doomed; each spoke of her with pride.
Tacitus,[2] writing after both had died,   35
Showed that whole fabric rotten, through and through.

4. *Ab Urbe Condita*: from the founding of the
city (Latin), that is, Rome, supposedly in 753 B.C.
The historian Livy (58 B.C.–A.D. 17) tells the story
narrated in the first three stanzas in his *History of
Rome from the Foundation*.
   5. One of several young priestesses, from patrician families, who tended the sacred flame of Vesta,
goddess of the earth.
   6. Chief religious officer of ancient Rome, one
of whose special duties was to supervise the Vestals.

7. Historian.
   8. Live burial was the punishment for a Vestal
found guilty of breaking her vow of chastity.
   9. That is, of obedience and punishment.
   1. St. Paul, who said, "Wives, submit yourselves unto your own husbands, as unto the Lord"
(Ephesians 5:22).
   2. The *Histories* of Tacitus (c.77–117) criticize
the degeneracy of the times as exemplified in three
Roman emperors who ruled and were deposed in
68–69.

Historians spend their lives and lavish ink
Explaining how great commonwealths collapse
From great defects of policy — perhaps
The cause is sometimes simpler than they think.   40

It may not seem so grave an act to break
Postumia's spirit as Galileo's, to gag
Hypatia as crush Socrates, or drag
Joan as Giordano Bruno to the stake.[3]

Can we be sure? Have more states perished, then,   45
For having shackled the enquiring mind,
Than those who, in their folly not less blind,
Trusted the servile womb to breed free men?

1965

3. In 1633 the Italian astronomer Galileo was forced by the Church to renounce his own scientific conclusions and was for a time imprisoned. Hypatia, a learned and beautiful lady of Alexandria, was murdered in 415, allegedly at the command of an archbishop, while Socrates was sentenced to die by poison in 399 B.C. on account of his supposedly subversive teachings. Both Joan of Arc and Giordano Bruno were burned at the stake: Joan in 1431 for heresy and sorcery, Bruno in 1600 for theological and scientific heresies.

LOUIS MacNEICE
1907–1963

In 1938 Louis MacNeice published a book called *Modern Poetry: A Personal Essay.* He was then thirty and at the beginning of his career: he had published three books of poems and a translation of the *Agamemnon.* With his friend W. H. Auden he had visited Iceland, and the two young poets had concocted a lively book out of their experiences there. And he was at work on a long poem, *Autumn Journal.* MacNeice describes *Modern Poetry* as a plea for "impure" poetry—that is, for a poetry expressive of the poet's immediate interests and his sense of the natural and the social world. MacNeice is particularly eager to advance the claims of three of his contemporaries, whose work had appeared in the collection *New Signatures:* they were Auden, Spender, and Day Lewis, and theirs, together with MacNeice's own work, is the impure poetry which he defends. These poets are conscious that they have succeeded a race of giants—Yeats and Eliot are particularly threatening figures— and, MacNeice argues, their particular virtue lies in their emotional partisanship. In his conclusion, MacNeice calls for a poetry that is not monastic and consecrated, and which is but one form of human enjoyment among others. "My own prejudice," he writes, ". . . is in favour of poets whose worlds are not too esoteric. I would have a poet able-bodied, fond of talking, a reader of the newspapers, capable of pity and laughter, informed in economics, appreciative of women, involved in personal relationships, actively interested in politics, susceptible to physical impressions."[1]

Louis MacNeice was born in Belfast on September 12, 1907. His father was a clergyman in the Church of Ireland, eventually a bishop. Although he spent most of his adult life in London, where he felt an exile but found life exciting, MacNeice frequently returned in his poems to the landscapes of his childhood, and he took great pride in his Irishness. His mother, troubled by mental illness, died when he was a boy, and he spent the kind of half-neglected childhood which so often seems to be invaluable for a poet. His father was a kindly, literate man, capable of allegiances to unpopular causes, and MacNeice's references to him are affectionate.

1. *Modern Poetry,* Oxford, 1968, p. 198.

MacNeice was educated at Marlborough, a public school, and at Oxford. As an undergraduate MacNeice read philosophy, and his poetry reveals a continuing interest in the classical philosophical problems.

After taking his B.A., MacNeice lectured on classics at Birmingham and then at Bedford College, part of the University of London. Just before the outbreak of the Second World War, he visited the United States and lectured at Cornell University. In 1940 he returned to England and married the singer Hedli Anderson. He gave up teaching to become a writer and producer for the BBC. Like many English poets since the eighteenth century, MacNeice aspired to write poetic drama, and he found an audience through British radio. MacNeice also made translations of the *Agamemnon* and, for radio, of Goethe's *Faust*. In August 1963 MacNeice, on location with a BBC team, insisted on going down into a mine to check personally on sound effects and caught a chill which was not diagnosed as pneumonia until the poet was fatally ill. He died on September 3, just before the publication of his twentieth book of poems, *The Burning Perch.*

MacNeice exercises what he takes to be the modern poet's privilege of irresolution; he dramatizes the mind's tentative advances and questionings, and ultimately he seems to have found the only solution to the problem of belief in the very writing of his poems. In a series of lectures on allegory, MacNeice quotes approvingly Samuel Beckett's statement that he is interested in the "shape of ideas" even if he does not believe in them. MacNeice finds this notion liberating, for "a playwright, like a poet, being a maker . . . is thereby *ipso facto* a shaper (this is true however much he may dispense with plot, metre, etc.), and this very act of shaping may bring him back full circle into something very like belief—rather as if God in the first chapter of Genesis, when he looked at his work and saw that it was good, had found himself forced to believe in himself."[2] MacNeice makes his poetry out of the experience of a fallen world with no wistful glances back at any Eden of undifferentiated sensation or ideological certitude.

2. *Varieties of Parable*, Cambridge, 1965, p. 118.

Snow

The room was suddenly rich and the great bay-window was
Spawning snow and pink roses against it
Soundlessly collateral and incompatible:
World is suddener than we fancy it.

World is crazier and more of it than we think,   5
Incorrigibly plural. I peel and portion
A tangerine and spit the pips and feel
The drunkenness of things being various.

And the fire flames with a bubbling sound for world
Is more spiteful and gay than one supposes—   10
On the tongue on the eyes on the ears on the palms of one's hands—
There is more than glass between the snow and the huge roses.

1935

Bagpipe Music

It's no go the merrygoround, it's no go the rickshaw,
All we want is a limousine and a ticket for the peepshow.

Their knickers are made of crêpe-de-chine, their shoes are made of
    python,
Their halls are lined with tiger rugs and their walls with heads of bison.

John MacDonald found a corpse, put it under the sofa,   5
Waited till it came to life and hit it with a poker,
Sold its eyes for souvenirs, sold its blood for whiskey,
Kept its bones for dumb-bells to use when he was fifty.

It's no go the Yogi-Man, it's no go Blavatsky,[1]
All we want is a bank balance and a bit of skirt in a taxi.   10

Annie MacDougall went to milk, caught her foot in the heather,
Woke to hear a dance record playing of Old Vienna.
It's no go your maidenheads, it's no go your culture,
All we want is a Dunlop tyre and the devil mend the puncture.

The Laird o'Phelps spent Hogmanay[2] declaring he was sober,   15
Counted his feet to prove the fact and found he had one foot over.
Mrs. Carmichael had her fifth, looked at the job with repulsion,
Said to the midwife 'Take it away; I'm through with over production'.

It's no go the gossip column, it's no go the ceilidh,[3]
All we want is a mother's help and a sugar-stick for the baby.   20

Willie Murray cut his thumb, couldn't count the damage,
Took the hide of an Ayrshire cow and used it for a bandage.
His brother caught three hundred cran[4] when the seas were lavish,
Threw the bleeders back in the sea and went upon the parish.

It's no go the Herring Board,[5] it's no go the Bible,   25
All we want is a packet of fags[6] when our hands are idle.

It's no go the picture palace, it's no go the stadium,
It's no go the country cot with a pot of pink geraniums,
It's no go the Government grants, it's no go the elections,
Sit on your arse for fifty years and hang your hat on a pension.   30

It's no go my honey love, it's no go my poppet;
Work your hands from day to day, the winds will blow the profit.
The glass is falling hour by hour, the glass will fall for ever,
But if you break the bloody glass you won't hold up the weather.

          1937

Brother Fire[7]

When our brother Fire was having his dog's day
Jumping the London streets with millions of tin cans

---

1. Madame Helena Petrovna Blavatsky (1831–
1891), a Russian occultist, founded the Theosoph-
ical Society.
2. New Year's Eve (Scots).
3. A sociable evening of singing and story-telling; pronounced "kaley."
4. A measure of fish.

5. A government agency which in the thirties
unsuccessfully tried to save the failing British herring trade.
6. Cigarettes.
7. "Praise to Thee, my Lord, for Brother Fire,
by whom Thou lightest the night; He is lovely and
pleasant, mighty and strong" (St. Francis of Assisi,

Clanking at his tail, we heard some shadow say
"Give the dog a bone"—and so we gave him ours;
Night after night we watched him slaver and crunch away   5
The beams of human life, the tops of topless towers.

Which gluttony of his for us was Lenten fare
Who mother-naked, suckled with sparks, were chill
Though cotted in a grille of sizzling air
Striped like a convict—black, yellow and red;   10
Thus were we weaned to knowledge of the Will
That wills the natural world but wills us dead.

O delicate walker, babbler, dialectician Fire,
O enemy and image of ourselves,
Did we not on those mornings after the All Clear,   15
When you were looting shops in elemental joy
And singing as you swarmed up city block and spire,
Echo your thought in ours? "Destroy! Destroy!"

                                                      1944

The Libertine

In the old days with married women's stockings
Twisted round his bedpost he felt himself a gay
Dog but now his liver has begun to groan,
Now that pick-ups are the order of the day:
O leave me easy, leave me alone.   5

Voluptuary in his 'teens and cynic in his twenties,
He ran through women like a child through growing hay
Looking for a lost toy whose capture might atone
For his own guilt and the cosmic disarray:
O leave me easy, leave me alone.   10

He never found the toy and has forgotten the faces,
Only remembers the props . . . a scent-spray
Beside the bed or a milk-white telephone
Or through the triple ninon[8] the acrid trickle of day:
O leave me easy, leave me alone.   15

Long fingers over the gunwale, hair in a hair-net,
Furs in January, cartwheel hats in May,
And after the event the wish to be alone—
Angels, goddesses, bitches, all have edged away:
O leave me easy, leave me alone.

                                                      20

So now, in middle age, his erotic programme
Torn in two, if after such a delay
An accident should offer him his own
Fulfilment in a woman, still he would say:
O leave me easy, leave me alone.

                                                      1944

"The Song of Brother Sun and of All Creatures").
The occasion for the poem is the German bomb-   ing raids on London during the Second World War.
                                                      8. Light, semi-transparent silk.

Variation on Heraclitus[9]

Even the walls are flowing, even the ceiling,
Nor only in terms of physics; the pictures
Bob on each picture rail like floats on a line
While the books on the shelves keep reeling
Their titles out into space and the carpet   5
Keeps flying away to Arabia nor can this be where I stood—
Where I shot the rapids I mean—when I signed
On a line that rippled away with a pen that melted
Nor can this now be the chair—the chairoplane of a chair—
That I sat in the day that I thought I had made up my mind   10
And as for that standard lamp it too keeps waltzing away
Down an unbridgeable Ganges where nothing is standard
And lights are but lit to be drowned in honour and spite of some dark
And vanishing goddess. No, whatever you say,
Reappearance presumes disappearance, it may not be nice   15
Or proper or easily analysed not to be static
But none of your slide snide rules can catch what is sliding so fast
And, all you advisers on this by the time it is that,
I just do not want your advice
Nor need you be troubled to pin me down in my room   20
Since the room and I will escape for I tell you flat:
One cannot live in the same room twice.

1961

9. Heraclitus (c.540–c.480 B.C.), the Greek philosopher, is known for a number of apothegms on mutability, three of which are relevant to this poem: "All is flux; nothing stands still"; "It is not possible to step twice into the same river"; "Nothing endures but change."

THEODORE ROETHKE
1908–1963

Theodore Roethke was a poet for whom nature took on the aspect of a vast psychic landscape. Some parts of it were projections of his feelings, some were his transcendences of personality. Roethke's authority for making nature a parable came from his love and intensive study of it. He liked to trace this interest to the fact that his grandfather, once Bismarck's chief forester, had emigrated from Prussia in 1870 and then, with his sons, had started some greenhouses in Saginaw, Michigan. The greenhouse, Roethke wrote, "is . . . my symbol for the whole of life, a womb, a heaven-on-earth."[1] He always felt close to elemental processes and inanimate as well as animate objects: "I could say hello to things." He studies the lives on a leaf in "The Minimal," or in "A Field of Light" declares that he could see, suddenly, "the separateness of all things!"

The sense of participation in nature makes for some of his most extreme, and yet most convincing, effects. "I lose and find myself in the long waters," he writes, or, changing elements, "I live in air; the long light is my home," a line from "Her Becoming" which suggests his affinity to Dylan Thomas. Participation is only a short step to transcendence: "I'm wet with another life," or, as he writes in "Snake," "I longed to be that thing, / The pure, sensuous form. / And I may be, some time."

1. *On the Poet and His Craft, Selected Prose of Theodore Roethke*, ed. Ralph J. Mills, Jr., Seattle, 1965, p. 39.

Roethke was six feet two and weighed well over two hundred pounds, but he moves in his verse with great delicacy. Though he was a tormented man, frantic for fame, a prey to breakdowns and a victim of alcoholism, he presented himself in his verse as a naïf. He had, as he insisted, "a driving sincerity,—that prime virtue of any creative worker. I write only what I believe to be the absolute truth,—even if I must ruin the theme in so doing."[2] The sense of a fragile self in a swollen body is pervasive. It reflects a "struggle for personal identity."[3] If only he could "dance with William Blake,"[4] he could possess that purity for which he longs and which nature, in certain aspects, appears to model. Nature can *represent* or, like poetry, *expand* consciousness.

Roethke was born on May 25, 1908, in Saginaw. He went to the University of Michigan and afterwards took some graduate courses at Harvard. Subsequently he taught at several colleges and universities, lending himself generously to his students and even, at one time, coaching tennis. His longest and last post was at the University of Washington, where his sporadic breakdowns were tolerated. When his first book, *Open House*, was published in 1941, Roethke won considerable attention, but he longed for more recognition and was humbly eager to make his verse even better. He wrote little, but with great care. His collected poems, still a slender output, appeared under the title *Words for the Wind* in 1959. By 1963 he was dead.

Sometimes Roethke is boisterous and funny—he was able to write good children's poems—but he is fundamentally serious and intent. He traced his lineage to Emerson, Thoreau, Whitman, Blake, Wordsworth, and Vaughan.[5] In fact, he does belong with them in his visionary intertwining of his spiritual self with leaves, water, light, and lower creatures.

Cuttings

Sticks-in-a-drowse droop over sugary loam,
Their intricate stem-fur dries;
But still the delicate slips keep coaxing up water;
The small cells bulge;

One nub of growth   5
Nudges a sand-crumb loose,
Pokes through a musty sheath
Its pale tendrilous horn.

                                                           1948

Cuttings

(later)

This urge, wrestle, resurrection of dry sticks,
Cut stems struggling to put down feet,
What saint strained so much,
Rose on such lopped limbs to a new life?

I can hear, underground, that sucking and sobbing,   5
In my veins, in my bones I feel it,—
The small waters seeping upward,

2. The same, p. 3.
3. The same, p. 49.
4. Quoted in Ralph J. Mills, Jr., *Theodore Roethke*, Minneapolis, 1963, p. 10.
5. *Selected Letters of Theodore Roethke*, ed. Ralph J. Mills, Jr., Seattle, 1956, p. 230.

The tight grains parting at last.
When sprouts break out,
Slippery as fish,   10
I quail, lean to beginnings, sheath-wet.

                                                                1948

My Papa's Waltz[1]

The whiskey on your breath
Could make a small boy dizzy;
But I hung on like death:
Such waltzing was not easy.

We romped until the pans   5
Slid from the kitchen shelf;
My mother's countenance
Could not unfrown itself.

The hand that held my wrist
Was battered on one knuckle;   10
At every step you missed
My right ear scraped a buckle.

You beat time on my head
With a palm caked hard by dirt,
Then waltzed me off to bed   15
Still clinging to your shirt.

                                                                1948

Dolor[2]

I have known the inexorable sadness of pencils,
Neat in their boxes, dolor of pad and paper-weight,
All the misery of manilla folders and mucilage,
Desolation in immaculate public places,
Lonely reception room, lavatory, switchboard,   5
The unalterable pathos of basin and pitcher,
Ritual of multigraph, paper-clip, comma,
Endless duplication of lives and objects.
And I have seen dust from the walls of institutions,
Finer than flour, alive, more dangerous than silica,   10
Sift, almost invisible, through long afternoons of tedium,
Dropping a fine film on nails and delicate eyebrows,
Glazing the pale hair, the duplicate grey standard faces.

                                                                1948

The Waking

I wake to sleep, and take my waking slow.
I feel my fate in what I cannot fear.
I learn by going where I have to go.

1. Of this poem Roethke said, "I think old Hardy
looks down from heaven on this" (*Selected Let-*   *ters,* p. 158).
                                                    2. Sadness.

We think by feeling. What is there to know?
I hear my being dance from ear to ear.   5
I wake to sleep, and take my waking slow.

Of those so close beside me, which are you?
God bless the Ground! I shall walk softly there,
And learn by going where I have to go.

Light takes the Tree; but who can tell us how?   10
The lowly worm climbs up a winding stair;
I wake to sleep, and take my waking slow.

Great Nature has another thing to do
To you and me; so take the lively air,
And, lovely, learn by going where to go.   15

This shaking keeps me steady. I should know.
What falls away is always. And is near.
I wake to sleep, and take my waking slow.
I learn by going where I have to go.

                                                                              1953

Frau Bauman, Frau Schmidt, and Frau Schwartze[3]

Gone the three ancient ladies
Who creaked on the greenhouse ladders,
Reaching up white strings
To wind, to wind
The sweet-pea tendrils, the smilax,   5
Nasturtiums, the climbing
Roses, to straighten
Carnations, red
Chrysanthemums; the stiff   10
Stems, jointed like corn,
They tied and tucked,—
These nurses of nobody else.
Quicker than birds, they dipped
Up and sifted the dirt;
They sprinkled and shook;   15
They stood astride pipes,
Their skirts billowing out wide into tents,
Their hands twinkling with wet;
Like witches they flew along rows
Keeping creation at ease;   20
With a tendril for needle
They sewed up the air with a stem;
They teased out the seed that the cold kept asleep,—
All the coils, loops, and whorls.
They trellised the sun; they plotted for more than themselves. 25

I remember how they picked me up, a spindly kid,
Pinching and poking my thin ribs

---

3. Roethke's father was a prominent florist in Saginaw, Michigan, and as a boy the poet played around the greenhouses. The employees included the three women of the title.

Till I lay in their laps, laughing,
Weak as a whiffet;[4]
Now, when I'm alone and cold in my bed,   30
They still hover over me,
These ancient leathery crones,
With their bandannas stiffened with sweat,
And their thorn-bitten wrists,
And their snuff-laden breath blowing lightly over me in my first sleep.   35

                                                                         1953

I Knew a Woman

I knew a woman, lovely in her bones,
When small birds sighed, she would sigh back at them;
Ah, when she moved, she moved more ways than one:
The shapes a bright container can contain!
Of her choice virtues only gods should speak,   5
Or English poets who grew up on Greek
(I'd have them sing in chorus, cheek to cheek).

How well her wishes went! She stroked my chin,
She taught me Turn, and Counter-turn, and Stand;
She taught me Touch, that undulant white skin;   10
I nibbled meekly from her proffered hand;
She was the sickle; I, poor I, the rake,
Coming behind her for her pretty sake
(But what prodigious mowing we did make).

Love likes a gander, and adores a goose: 15
Her full lips pursed, the errant note to seize;
She played it quick, she played it light and loose;
My eyes, they dazzled at her flowing knees;
Her several parts could keep a pure repose,
Or one hip quiver with a mobile nose   20
(She moved in circles, and those circles moved).

Let seed be grass, and grass turn into hay:
I'm martyr to a motion not my own;
What's freedom for? To know eternity.
I swear she cast a shadow white as stone.   25
But who would count eternity in days?
These old bones live to learn her wanton ways:
(I measure time by how a body sways).

                                                                         1958

Wish for a Young Wife

My lizard, my lively writher,
May your limbs never wither,
May the eyes in your face

4. Small, young, or unimportant person (probably from "whippet," a small dog).

Survive the green ice
Of envy's mean gaze;   5
May you live out your life
Without hate, without grief,
And your hair ever blaze,
In the sun, in the sun,
When I am undone,   10
When I am no one.

1964

The Far Field[5]

I

I dream of journeys repeatedly:
Of flying like a bat deep into a narrowing tunnel,
Of driving alone, without luggage, out a long peninsula,
The road lined with snow-laden second growth,
A fine dry snow ticking the windshield,   5
Alternate snow and sleet, no on-coming traffic,
And no lights behind, in the blurred side-mirror,
The road changing from glazed tarface to a rubble of stone,
Ending at last in a hopeless sand-rut,
Where the car stalls,   10
Churning in a snowdrift
Until the headlights darken.

II

At the field's end, in the corner missed by the mower,
Where the turf drops off into a grass-hidden culvert,[6]
Haunt of the cat-bird, nesting-place of the field-mouse,   15
Not too far away from the ever-changing flower-dump,
Among the tin cans, tires, rusted pipes, broken machinery,—
One learned of the eternal;
And in the shrunken face of a dead rat, eaten by rain and ground-beetles
(I found it lying among the rubble of an old coal bin)   20
And the tom-cat, caught near the pheasant-run,
Its entrails strewn over the half-grown flowers,
Blasted to death by the night watchman.

I suffered for birds, for young rabbits caught in the mower,
My grief was not excessive.   25
For to come upon warblers in early May
Was to forget time and death:
How they filled the oriole's elm, a twittering restless cloud, all one morn-
     ing,
And I watched and watched till my eyes blurred from the bird shapes,—
Cape May, Blackburnian, Cerulean,—[7]   30
Moving, elusive as fish, fearless,

---

5. The next to last poem in a sequence of six
that comprise "North American Sequence" in
Roethke's last book, *The Far Field* (1964).

6. Drain under a road.
7. Various kinds of warbler.

Hanging, bunched like young fruit, bending the end branches,
Still for a moment,
Then pitching away in half-flight,
Lighter than finches,   35
While the wrens bickered and sang in the half-green hedgerows,
And the flicker drummed from his dead tree in the chicken-yard.

—Or to lie naked in sand,
In the silted shallows of a slow river,
Fingering a shell,   40
Thinking:
Once I was something like this, mindless,
Or perhaps with another mind, less peculiar;
Or to sink down to the hips in a mossy quagmire;
Or, with skinny knees, to sit astride a wet log,   45
Believing:
I'll return again,
As a snake or a raucous bird,
Or, with luck, as a lion.

I learned not to fear infinity,   50
The far field, the windy cliffs of forever,
The dying of time in the white light of tomorrow,
The wheel turning away from itself,
The sprawl of the wave,
The on-coming water.   55

                              III

The river turns on itself,
The tree retreats into its own shadow.
I feel a weightless change, a moving forward
As of water quickening before a narrowing channel
When banks converge, and the wide river whitens;   60
Or when two rivers combine, the blue glacial torrent
And the yellowish-green from the mountainy upland,—
At first a swift rippling between rocks,
Then a long running over flat stones
Before descending to the alluvial plain,[8]   65
To the clay banks, and the wild grapes hanging from the elmtrees,
The slightly trembling water
Dropping a fine yellow silt where the sun stays;
And the crabs bask near the edge,
The weedy edge, alive with small snakes and bloodsuckers,—   70

I have come to a still, but not a deep center,
A point outside the glittering current;
My eyes stare at the bottom of a river,
At the irregular stones, iridescent sandgrains,
My mind moves in more than one place,   75
In a country half-land, half-water.

8. Soil deposited by flowing water, as in river deltas.

I am renewed by death, thought of my death,
The dry scent of a dying garden in September,
The wind fanning the ash of a low fire.
What I love is near at hand,   80
Always, in earth and air.

IV

The lost self changes,
Turning toward the sea,
A sea-shape turning around,—
An old man with his feet before the fire,   85
In robes of green, in garments of adieu.

A man faced with his own immensity
Wakes all the waves, all their loose wandering fire.
The murmur of the absolute, the why
Of being born fails on his naked ears.   90
His spirit moves like monumental wind
That gentles on a sunny blue plateau.
He is the end of things, the final man.

All finite things reveal infinitude:
The mountain with its singular bright shade   95
Like the blue shine on freshly frozen snow,
The after-light upon ice-burdened pines;
Odor of basswood on a mountain-slope,
A scent beloved of bees;
Silence of water above a sunken tree: 100
The pure serene of memory in one man,—
A ripple widening from a single stone
Winding around the waters of the world.

                                                               1964

In a Dark Time[9]

In a dark time, the eye begins to see,
I meet my shadow in the deepening shade;[1]
I hear my echo in the echoing wood—
A lord of nature[2] weeping to a tree.
I live between the heron and the wren,[3]   5
Beasts of the hill and serpents of the den.

What's madness but nobility of soul
At odds with circumstances? The day's on fire!
I know the purity of pure despair,
My shadow pinned against a sweating wall.   10
That place among the rocks—is it a cave,
Or winding path? The edge is what I have.

9. Roethke has said that the title refers to a dark
night of the soul.
  1. "Deepening despair, with a hint of
approaching death" (Roethke's note).

2. "A derisive epithet at this point in the poem"
(Roethke's note).
  3. The heron is solitary, the wren sociable,
among other differences.

A steady storm of correspondences!
A night flowing with birds, a ragged moon,
And in broad day the midnight come again!   15
A man goes far to find out what he is—
Death of the self in a long, tearless night,
All natural shapes blazing unnatural light.

Dark, dark my light, and darker my desire.
My soul, like some heat-maddened summer fly,   20
Keeps buzzing at the sill. Which I is *I*?
A fallen man, I climb out of my fear.
The mind enters itself, and God the mind,
And one is One, free in the tearing wind.[4]

1964

4. The imperfect earth, though Roethke suggests that "tearing" (in contrast to the earlier "tearless")
implies pity on the part of natural forces.

A. M. KLEIN
1909–1972

Among memorable and distinguished Canadian poets of this century, A. M. Klein
has almost classical status. Born in Montreal, he grew up in the Jewish section of that
city and drew strength from the close familial and religious life. His being Jewish
provided him with images and a point of view he embodied in his first book, *Hath
Not a Jew. . . .* It is some lost sense of union between reality and aspiration that gives
him a feeling of "sadness in remembered joy."

The desire to praise is strong in Klein. In his "Portrait of the Poet as Landscape,"
he investigates with humor and sensitivity the writer's behavior. People ignore the
poet, yet it was he "who unrolled our culture from his scroll." He has his moods, of
depression but mostly of joy. Klein elegantly confuses first love of a woman with first
love of language: "Dear limbs adverbial." The poet has also dreams of himself as
Count of Monte Cristo or as convict on parole. He reproves those poets who are too
cerebral, setting "twenty-one jewels into their watches," but unable to tell the time,
and those who are too linguistic or technique-bound. The true poet seeds illusions;
no hero to the world, he "makes of his status as zero a rich garland," and shines "like
phosphorus. At the bottom of the sea."

Klein attended McGill University and the University of Montreal. He began to
practice law in 1933, then became director of education of the Zionist Organization
of Canada. His example of poetry of joyful radiance has not been forgotten.

Portrait of the Poet as Landscape

I

Not an editorial-writer, bereaved with bartlett,
mourns him, the shelved Lycidas.[1]
No actress squeezes a glycerine tear for him.

1. Name of the shepherd poet mourned in John Milton's poem (1638); "bartlett": *Bartlett's Familiar
Quotations*, a collection of memorable sayings.

The radio broadcast lets his passing pass.
And with the police, no record. Nobody, it appears,   5
either under his real name or his alias,
missed him enough to report.

It is possible that he is dead, and not discovered.
It is possible that he can be found some place
in a narrow closet, like the corpse in a detective story,   10
standing, his eyes staring, and ready to fall on his face.
It is also possible that he is alive
and amnesiac, or mad, or in retired disgrace,
or beyond recognition lost in love.

We are sure only that from our real society   15
he has disappeared; he simply does not count,
except in the pullulation[2] of vital statistics—
somebody's vote, perhaps, an anonymous taunt
of the Gallup poll,[3] a dot in a government table—
but not felt, and certainly far from eminent—   20
in a shouting mob, somebody's sigh.

O, he who unrolled our culture from his scroll—
the prince's quote, the rostrum-rounding roar—
who under one name made articulate
heaven, and under another the seven-circled air,   25
is, if he is at all, a number, an x,
a Mr. Smith in a hotel register,—
incognito, lost, lacunal.[4]

II

The truth is he's not dead, but only ignored—
like the mirroring lenses forgotten on a brow   30
that shine with the guilt of their unnoticed world.
The truth is he lives among neighbours, who, though they will allow
him a passable fellow, think him eccentric, not solid,
a type that one can forgive, and for that matter, forgo.

Himself he has his moods, just like a poet.   35
Sometimes, depressed to nadir, he will think all lost,
will see himself as throwback, relict,[5] freak,
his mother's miscarriage, his great-grandfather's ghost,
and he will curse his quintuplet senses, and their tutors.
in whom he put, as he should not have put, his trust.   40

Then he will remember his travels over that body—
the torso verb, the beautiful face of the noun,
and all those shaped and warm auxiliaries!
A first love it was, the recognition of his own.
Dear limbs adverbial, complexion of adjective,   45
dimple and dip of conjugation!

2. That is, rapid increase.
3. George Gallup was the first to take nation-
wide polls.
4. That is, missing.
5. Surviving member of a race or species.

And then remember how this made a change in him
affecting for always the glow and growth of his being;
how suddenly was aware of the air, like shaken tinfoil,
of the patents of nature, the shock of belated seeing,   50
the lonelinesses peering from the eyes of crowds;
the integers of thought; the cube-roots of feeling.

Thus, zoomed to zenith, sometimes he hopes again,
and sees himself as a character, with a rehearsed role:
the Count of Monte Cristo,[6] come for his revenges;   55
the unsuspected heir, with papers; the risen soul;
or the chloroformed prince awaking from his flowers;
or—deflated again—the convict on parole.

III

He is alone; yet not completely alone.
Pins on a map of a colour similar to his,   60
each city has one, sometimes more than one;
here, caretakers of art, in colleges;
in offices, there, with arm-bands, and green-shaded;[7]
and there, pounding their catalogued beats in libraries,—

everywhere menial, a shadow's shadow.   65
And always for their egos—their outmoded art.
Thus, having lost the bevel in the ear,[8]
they know neither up nor down, mistake the part
for the whole, curl themselves in a comma,
talk technics, make a colon their eyes. They distort—   70

such is the pain of their frustration—truth
to something convolute and cerebral.
How they do fear the slap of the flat of the platitude!
Now Pavlov's victims, their mouths water at bell,[9]
the platter empty.   75
                    See they set twenty-one jewels
into their watches; the time they do not tell!

Some, patagonian[1] in their own esteem,
and longing for the multiplying word,
join party and wear pins, now have a message,   80
an ear, and the convention-hall's regard.
Upon the knees of ventriloquists, they own,
of their dandled brightness, only the paint and board.

And some go mystical, and some go mad.
One stares at a mirror all day long, as if   85
to recognize himself; another courts
angels,—for here he does not fear rebuff;

6. In Alexandre Dumas' romance *The Count of Monte Cristo* (1844), the hero, Edmond Dantes, takes revenge on the men who sent him to prison.
7. Office workers used to tuck up their shirt-sleeves with elastic and wear translucent green eyeshades.
8. That is, a workmanlike sense of the language.
9. Ivan Petrovich Pavlov (1849–1936), famous for—among other things—setting up conditioned reflexes in dogs, who salivated at a bell sound.
1. That is, very large.

and a third, alone, and sick with sex, and rapt,
doodles him symbols convex and concave.

O schizoid solitudes! O purities   90
curdling upon themselves! Who live for themselves,
or for each other, but for nobody else;
desire affection, private and public loves;
are friendly, and then quarrel and surmise
the secret perversions of each other's lives.   95

IV

He suspects that something has happened, a law
been passed, a nightmare ordered. Set apart,
he finds himself, with special haircut and dress,
as on a reservation. Introvert.
He does not understand this; sad conjecture   100
muscles and palls thrombotic on his heart.

He thinks an imposter, having studied his personal biography,
his gestures, his moods, now has come forward to pose
in the shivering vacuums his absence leaves.
Wigged with his laurel,[2] that other, and faked with his face,   105
he pats the heads of his children, pecks his wife,
and is at home, and slippered, in his house.

So he guesses at the impertinent silhouette
that talks to his phone-piece and slits open his mail.
Is it the local tycoon who for a hobby   110
plays poet, he so epical in steel?
The orator, making a pause? Or is that man
he who blows his flash of brass in the jittering hall?

Or is he cuckholded by the troubadour
rich and successful out of celluloid?[3]   115
Or by the don who unrhymes atoms? Or
the chemist death built up? Pride, lost impostor'd pride
it is another, another, whoever he is.
who rides where he should ride.

V

Fame, the adrenalin: to be talked about;   120
to be a verb; to be introduced as *The:*
to smile with endorsement from slick paper; make
caprices anecdotal; to nod to the world; to see
one's name like a song upon the marquees played;
to be forgotten with embarrassment; to be—   125
to be.

---

2. The traditional crown of victors was a wreath
of laurel leaves.
3. That is, a singing film star; "cuckholded":
variant spelling of "cuckolded" (dishonored by
adultery). "Don": British university teacher.

It has its attractions, but is not the thing;
nor is it the ape mimesis who speaks from the tree
ancestral; nor the merkin joy . . .[4]
Rather it is stark infelicity
which stirs him from his sleep, undressed, asleep   130
to walk upon roofs and window-sills and defy
the gape of gravity.

VI

Therefore he seeds illusions. Look, he is
the nth Adam taking a green inventory
in world but scarcely uttered,[5] naming, praising,   135
the flowering fiats in the meadow, the
syllabled fur, stars aspirate, the pollen
whose sweet collision sounds eternally.
For to praise
                                                                       140

the world—he, solitary man—is breath
to him. Until it has been praised, that part
has not been. Item by exciting item—
air to his lungs, and pressured blood to his heart.—
they are pulsated, and breathed, until they map,   145
not the world's, but his own body's chart!

And now in imagination he has climbed
another planet, the better to look
with single camera view upon this earth—
its total scope, and each afflated tick,   150
its talk, its trick, its tracklessness—and this,
this he would like to write down in a book!

To find a new function for the *déclassé* craft
archaic like the fletcher's;[6] to make a new thing;
to say the word that will become sixth sense;
perhaps by necessity and indirection bring   155
new forms to life, anonymously, new creeds—
O, somehow pay back the daily larcenies of the lung!

These are not mean ambitions. It is already something
merely to entertain them. Meanwhile, he
makes of his status as zero a rich garland,   160
a halo of his anonymity,
and lives alone, and in his secret shines
like phosphorus.[7] At the bottom of the sea.

1948

4. "Mimesis": imitation; "merkin": obsolete name for a woman's pubic hair (either real or false).
5. That is, in a new Eden; "fiat": command, edict.
6. Maker of arrows; *déclassé*: fallen in status.
7. Chemical element that glows in the dark.

CHARLES OLSON
1910–1970

Charles Olson was the dominant and senior figure in a group that included Robert Creeley, Denise Levertov, Robert Duncan, and other writers centered on Black Mountain College, an experimental school in North Carolina where he was first instructor and later rector, or head. He had a gift for vatic exhortation, the more impressive because it combined the plainest language with bursts of recondite information about Neolithic man and the Pleistocene age, or Hittite poems and Mayan inscriptions, which he would marshal in support of some terse formulation. He worked, as he proudly indicated, in the same direction as Ezra Pound and William Carlos Williams, and was particularly impressed by the *Cantos* and by *Paterson.* But he thought of his own writing as different: Pound's work he found to be "ego-dominated,"[1] hence "no flow," and he urged in a pamphlet entitled *Proprioception,* "Wash the ego out."[2] In Williams he thought the ego was happily eradicated, but objected that *Paterson's* limitation to one city's history was time-bound. Nonetheless, Olson's own epic effort, *The Maximus Poems,* resembles the *Cantos* in its free verse assemblage of heterogeneous incidents, characters, and scenes, and resembles *Paterson* in centering on a specific town, Gloucester, Massachusetts. Olson is bent upon projecting "the complex reality of a real association," a phrase used by a writer he admires, the geographer Carl Sauer.

Instead of calling his type-man Paterson, or, as Joyce does in *Finnegans Wake,* Finnegan, Olson gives him the name of Maximus. "I am not named Maximus / for no cause," he declares.[3] The name is related to his theory of the writer as someone who is totally, maximally here, living in his moment, resuming in his psychological self past and present, and always constituting, as well, a function of his environment.

Olson was born December 27, 1910, in Worcester, Massachusetts. His father was from Sweden, his mother an Irish-American. He speaks of them as his "definers": "the work of each of us is to find out the true lineaments of ourselves by facing up to the primal features of these founders who lie buried in us—that this is us, the Double-Backed Beast."[4] He seeks in effect a juncture of his own past with a mythological past (not to be confused with bloodless history), "the hinges of civilization to be put back on the door."[5] The necessary mythology he discovers as much among the Sumerians and Mayans as among Americans, and so can say, "Just last week / 300,000,000 years ago."[6] Against reason and the art of comparison, Olson offers direct perception and contraries. His pamphlet on *Proprioception* ("one's own perception") speaks forcefully if vaguely of "the data of depth sensibility."[7] In a letter of May 1959, Olson wrote that he would replace "the Classical-representational by the *primitive-abstract.*"[8] Accordingly, he does not so much try to persuade as to confront and overwhelm.

Olson's first book, on Melville (*Call Me Ishmael*), was an attempt to see Melville viscerally rather than critically. It was published in 1947, by which time he was thirty-seven. Up to then his life is somewhat obscured by his own random accounts of it. He was "uneducated" at Wesleyan, Yale, and Harvard: "I have had to learn the simplest things / last," he says.[9] From Wesleyan, anyway, he received a B.A. in 1932 and an M.A. the following year. He taught first at Clark University in Worcester, then, from 1936 to 1939, at Harvard. For the next nine years he had various occupations, which came to a focus in the publication of his Melville book. The following year, 1948, he took the place of his friend, the novelist Edward Dahlberg, at Black

1. *Mayan Letters,* in *Selected Writings,* New York, 1966, pp. 82–83.
2. *Proprioception,* San Francisco, 1964, p. 1.
3. *The Maximus Poems,* New York, 1960, p. 20.
4. *Twentieth-Century Authors,* First Supplement, ed. Stanley Kunitz, p. 741.

5. *Proprioception,* p. 8.
6. *Maximus,* p. 15.
7. *Proprioception,* p. 1.
8. *Selected Writings,* p. 28.
9. *Maximus,* p. 52.

Mountain College. Many of its teachers and students have since been important in painting, music, and the dance as well as in literature. In 1951 Olson became rector (head) of the college, and stayed in this position until 1956. He was to teach later, in his own dynamic, unpredictable fashion, at the State University of New York at Buffalo, and then (briefly) at the University of Connecticut. He died on January 10, 1970.

Olson's poems, though some of them were written earlier, became known and were collected in the sixties. He had been struggling to phrase his esthetic position, and in 1950 succeeded in formulating his essay on "Projective Verse." This became the manifesto for a number of young writers, and William Carlos Williams was so impressed by it that he quoted much of it in his *Autobiography*. In place of inherited line, stanza, formal pattern, all that he calls "closed form" or "verse that print bred," Olson offers "composition by field," open form. "The voice is greater than the eye," he declares.[10] Olson says, "A poem is energy transferred from where the poet got it (he will have some several causations), by way of the poem itself to, all the way over to, the reader. Okay. Then the poem itself must, at all points, be a high energy-construct and, at all points, an energy-discharge."[11] For this poetry, "Form is never more than an extension of content," a quotation from Robert Creeley which Olson incorporates in his poem "A B Cs." The form is somehow to be the product of the breath rather than of the literary tradition. "Who knows what a poem ought to sound like? until it's thar?"[12] This new verse, he insists, "involves a stance toward reality outside a poem as well as a new stance towards the reality of a poem itself."[13]

10. *Human Universe*, ed. Donald Allen, San Francisco, 1965, p. 142.
11. *Selected Writings*, p. 16.
12. *Human Universe*, p. 79.
13. *Selected Writings*, p. 24.

From *THE MAXIMUS POEMS*

I, Maximus of Gloucester,[1] to You

Off-shore, by islands hidden in the blood
jewels & miracles, I, Maximus
a metal hot from boiling water, tell you
what is a lance, who obeys the figures of
the present dance   5

                           1
the thing you're after
may lie around the bend
of the nest (second, time slain, the bird! the bird!
And there! (strong) thrust, the mast! flight
                    (of the bird   10
                    o kylix,[2] o
                    Antony of Padua[3]
                    sweep low, o bless

the roofs, the old ones, the gentle steep ones
on whose ridge-poles the gulls sit, from which they depart,   15

                              And the flake-racks[4]
of my city!

1. Gloucester, Massachusetts, is a fishing town northeast of Boston founded in 1623. Olson, or Maximus, peoples the town with historic figures, invented ones, and with people he knew when he lived there as a boy and young man.
2. A shallow drinking bowl of classical Greece.
3. The Franciscan monk and teacher of the thirteenth century. He preached a famous sermon to the fishes in the Brenta River near Padua.
4. Used for drying fish.

2

love is form, and cannot be without
important substance (the weight
say, 58 carats each one of us, perforce   20
our goldsmith's scale

                feather to feather added
                (and what is mineral, what
                is curling hair, the string
                you carry in your nervous beak, these   25

                make bulk, these, in the end, are
                the sum

                (o my lady of good voyage[5]
                in whose arm, whose left arm rests
no boy[6] but a carefully carved wood, a painted face, a schooner!   30
a delicate mast, as bow-sprit for

                    forwarding

3

the underpart is, though stemmed, uncertain
is, as sex is, as moneys are, facts!
facts, to be dealt with, as the sea is, the demand   35
that they be played by, that they only can be, that they must
be played by, said he, coldly, the
ear!

By ear, he sd.
But that which matters, that which insists, that which will last,   40
that! o my people, where shall you find it, how, where, where shall you
    listen
when all is become billboards, when, all, even silence, is spray-gunned?

when even our bird, my roofs,
cannot be heard

when even you, when sound itself is neoned in?   45

when, on the hill, over the water
where she who used to sing,
when the water glowed,
black, gold, the tide
outward, at evening   50

when bells came like boats
over the oil-slicks, milkweed
hulls

And a man slumped,

5. The Virgin Mary.
6. As in conventional representations of Mary with her child Jesus.

attentionless,   55
against pink shingles

o sea city)

                                   4

one loves only form,
and form only comes
into existence when   60
the thing is born

                 born of yourself, born
                 of hay and cotton struts,
                 of street-pickings, wharves, weeds
                 you carry in, my bird   65

                                of a bone of a fish
                                of a straw, or will
                                of a color, of a bell
                                of yourself, torn

                                   5

love is not easy   70
but how shall you know,
New England, now
that pejorocracy is here, how
that street-cars, o Oregon, twitter
in the afternoon, offend   75
a black-gold loin?

                 how shall you strike,
                 o swordsman, the blue-red black
                 when, last night, your aim
                 was mu-sick, mu-sick, mu-sick   80
                 And not the cribbage game?

                                (o Gloucester-man,
                                weave
                                your birds and fingers
                                new, your roof-tops,   85
                                clean shit upon racks
                                sunned on
                                American
                                braid
                                with others like you, such   90
                                extricable surface
                                as faun and oral,
                                satyr lesbos vase[7]

                                o kill kill kill kill kill
                                those   95
                                who advertise you
                                out)

7. Fauns and satyrs were minor Roman deities of the fields and forests. The island of Lesbos is near Greece.

6

in! in! the bow-sprit, bird, the beak
in, the bend is, in, goes in, the form
that which you make, what holds, which is   100
the law of object, strut after strut, what you are, what you must be, what
the force can throw up, can, right now hereinafter erect,
the mast, the mast, the tender
mast!

> The nest, I say, to you, I Maximus, say   105
> under the hand, as I see it, over the waters
> from this place where I am, where I hear,
> can still hear
>
> from where I carry you a feather
> as though, sharp, I picked up   110
> in the afternoon delivered you
> a jewel,
>   it flashing more than a wing,
> than any old romantic thing,
> than memory, than place,   115
> than anything other than that which you carry
> than that which is,
> call it a nest, around the head of, call it
> the next second
>
> than that which you   120
> can do!

1953

Maximus, to Gloucester

Letter 2

. . . . . tell you? ha! who
can tell another how
to manage the swimming?

he was right: people

don't change. They only stand more   5
revealed. I,
likewise

1

the light, there, at the corner (because of the big elm
and the reflecting houses) winter or summer stays
as it was when they lived there, in the house the street cuts off   10
as though it were a fault,
the side's so sheer

they hid, or tried to hide, the fact the cargo their ships brought back
was black (the Library, too, possibly so founded). The point is

the light does go one way toward the post office,   15
and quite another way down to Main Street. Nor is that all:

coming from the sea, up Middle, it is more white, very white
as it passes the grey of the Unitarian church. But at Pleasant Street,
it is abruptly
black   20

(hidden
city

2

Or now, when such houses are not built,
or such trees planted, it's the doctor knows
what the parents don't know. Or the wife doesn't,   25
of the husband, or the husband, of the other. Sins,

they still call them, and let
pejorocracy thrive. Only the lady

has got it straight. She looks
as the best of my people look   30
in one direction, her direction, they know
it is elements men stand in the midst of,
not these names supported by that false future she,
precisely she,
has her foot upon   35

          (He
made the coast, and though he lost his feet for it,
and the hands he'd purposely allowed to freeze to the oars,
I knew him, drank
with my elders, in his own bar, a toast to him   40

Or my other, the top of whose head a bollard[8] clean took away.
It was four days before they could get him to Chelsea Marine.[9]
This spring I listened to him as good as new, as fresh as it's always been
to hear him talk of the sea. He was puttering in his garden when I came
    up,
looking over his Santa Fe rose. And he took off his hat to show me,   45
how it is all skin where his skull was,
too much of a hole for even the newest metal
to cover

Or the quiet one, who's died since (died as deck-watchman, on his vessel,
    in port).
Years ago I heard from others   50
how he'd pulled two men out of the sea one night
off Eastern Point. They'd not been able to shed their jacks[1]
when the ship went over, and when he caught them
they were going down too. He hauled them into Brace's Cove,
even though the shore wasn't there, it was such a storm and the sea so big 55
it had turned the Lily Pond
into an arm of itself.

8. Post on a wharf to which boats are moored.   1. Jackets.
9. A hospital.

Last, he with muscle as big as his voice, the strength of him
in that blizzard
to have pulled the trawl[2] slack from the very bottom and released   60
his mate from the cod-hook had him out, and almost off,
into the snow. It wasn't that there was so much sea. It was the cold,
and that white, until over the dory went and the two of them,
one still,
were in. The wild thing was, he made the vessel, three miles, and fetched
      her,   65
found that vessel in all that weather, with his fellow dead weight
on him. The sort of eye
which later knew the Peak of Brown's
as though it were his own garden (as Bowditch brought the Eppie Sawyer   70
spot to her wharf a Christmas morning)[3]

                              3
Which is the cream of the milk, of course. And the milk
also of the matter, the most of it, those
who do no more than drink it in a cup of tea alone of such a night, holding
(as she)
a certain schooner   75

What still is, in other words. And the remarkable part of it,
that it still goes on, still is
what counts:

      the lad from the Fort
who recently bought the small white house on Lower Middle   80
(the one diagonally across from the handsome brick with the Bullfinch door)[4]
He stood with me one Sunday
and eyed (with a like eye) a curious ship
we'd both come on, tied to the Gas Company wharf.
She had raked masts, and they were unstepped,   85
fitted loose in her deck, like a neck in a collar.
He was looking idly, as I was, saying nothing.
When suddenly, he turned to a Gloucesterman, a big one,
berthed alongside this queer one, and said:
"I'll own her, one day"   90

                              4
While she stares, out of her painted face,
no matter the deathly mu-sick, the demand
will arouse
some of these men and women

                                                      1953

---

2. Net.
3. Nathaniel Bowditch (1773–1838), a Massachusetts navigator, astronomer, and mathematician, most famous as author of *The New American
Practical Navigator* (1802). In "Maximus, to
Gloucester: Letter 15," Olson writes: "It goes to
show you. It was not the 'Eppie Sawyer.' It was
the ship 'Putnam.' It wasn't Christmas morning, it
was Christmas night, after dark. And the violent
north-easter, with snow, which we were all raised
to believe did show Bowditch such a navigator,
was a gale sprung up from W, hit them outside
the Bay, and had blown itself out by the 23rd. . . .
The whole tale, as we have had it, from his son,
goes by the board."
4. Charles Bulfinch (1763–1844) was an influential Boston architect.

ELIZABETH BISHOP
1911–1979

Elizabeth Bishop's fastidious eye inspects, with a precision like Marianne Moore's, the physical world. What she observes takes form and gathers itself, as if nature were being brought to a boil. She approaches pain or ecstasy more immediately than Marianne Moore. Under her eye, "The Fish" and all around it turn to "rainbow, rainbow, rainbow," while in "The Armadillo" the "dreamlike mimicry" is shattered by the thought of "panic, and a weak mailed fist / clenched ignorant against the sky!" Sometimes the culmination is quieter. She is not so quick as Moore to draw lessons from beast fables or landscapes, although, in her "Invitation to Miss Marianne Moore," she indicates her amused approval of the older poet's penchant: "Manhattan / is all awash with morals this fine morning . . ."

Bishop was born February 8, 1911, in Worcester, Massachusetts. She grew up in New England and Nova Scotia, the latter memorialized in her poem, "First Death in Nova Scotia." She was educated at Vassar, and after that lived for long periods in Key West and, later, Brazil. Travel is a steady theme in her work; in "The Prodigal" she says that even a pigsty, away from home, might attract; and in "Questions of Travel," she asks, "Should we have stayed at home, / wherever that may be?" During her last years she taught at Harvard, and she died in Boston in 1979.

Elizabeth Bishop did not write voluminously. Almost all of the poems begin with an *objet trouvé*, often nondescript ("The Monument" or "Filling Station") yet capable of being contemplated with passion and so rendered aglitter. Her poems offer few elements of her personal life; this may be hinted at in "The Gentleman of Shalott," who is so conscious of inner division. It is hard to be sure. Emotion is usually attributed to rather distant others, as in "Songs for a Colored Singer," which contain the wry promise, "I'm going to go and take the bus / and find someone monogamous." Often she seems determinedly reticent, as if to suggest that her life inheres in the way she observes external phenomena, not in any private events. But in the midst of precise descriptions her verse has frequent spurts of muted feeling, of grief and tenderness, and finds, as in "The Man-Moth," an unfazed sympathy for animal-human plights. Her impeccable work has been greatly admired by other poets such as Lowell and Jarrell as well as by her readers. Her quiet voice is one of the most distinctive of the century.

The Man-Moth[1]

Here, above,
cracks in the buildings are filled with battered moonlight.
The whole shadow of Man is only as big as his hat.
It lies at his feet like a circle for a doll to stand on,
and he makes an inverted pin, the point magnetized to the moon.   5
He does not see the moon; he observes only her vast properties,
feeling the queer light on his hands, neither warm nor cold,
of a temperature impossible to record in thermometers.

But when the Man-Moth
pays his rare, although occasional, visits to the surface,   10
the moon looks rather different to him. He emerges
from an opening under the edge of one of the sidewalks
and nervously begins to scale the faces of the buildings.

---

1. "Newspaper misprint for 'mammoth' " (Bishop's note).

He thinks the moon is a small hole at the top of the sky,
proving the sky quite useless for protection.   15
He trembles, but must investigate as high as he can climb.

        Up the façades,
his shadow dragging like a photographer's cloth behind him,
he climbs fearfully, thinking that this time he will manage
to push his small head through that round clean opening   20
and be forced through, as from a tube, in black scrolls on the light.
(Man, standing below him, has no such illusions.)
But what the Man-Moth fears most he must do, although
he fails, of course, and falls back scared but quite unhurt.

        Then he returns   25
to the pale subways of cement he calls his home. He flits,
he flutters, and cannot get aboard the silent trains
fast enough to suit him. The doors close swiftly.
The Man-Moth always seats himself facing the wrong way
and the train starts at once at its full, terrible speed,   30
without a shift in gears or a gradation of any sort.
He cannot tell the rate at which he travels backwards.

        Each night he must
be carried through artificial tunnels and dream recurrent dreams.
Just as the ties recur beneath his train, these underlie   35
his rushing brain. He does not dare look out the window,
for the third rail, the unbroken draught of poison,
runs there beside him. He regards it as a disease
he has inherited the susceptibility to. He has to keep
his hands in his pockets, as others must wear mufflers.   40

        If you catch him,
hold up a flashlight to his eye. It's all dark pupil,
an entire night itself, whose haired horizon tightens
as he stares back, and closes up the eye. Then from the lids
one tear, his only possession, like the bee's sting, slips.   45
Slyly he palms it, and if you're not paying attention
he'll swallow it. However, if you watch, he'll hand it over,
cool as from underground springs and pure enough to drink.

                                      1946

The Fish

    I caught a tremendous fish
    and held him beside the boat
    half out of water, with my hook
    fast in the corner of his mouth.
    He didn't fight.   5
    He hadn't fought at all.
    He hung a grunting weight,
    battered and venerable
    and homely. Here and there
    his brown skin hung in strips   10

like ancient wallpaper,
and its pattern of darker brown
was like wallpaper:
shapes like full-blown roses
stained and lost through age.
He was speckled with barnacles,   15
fine rosettes of lime,
and infested
with tiny white sea-lice,
and underneath two or three
rags of green weed hung down.   20
While his gills were breathing in
the terrible oxygen
—the frightening gills,
fresh and crisp with blood,
that can cut so badly—   25
I thought of the coarse white flesh
packed in like feathers,
the big bones and the little bones,
the dramatic reds and blacks
of his shiny entrails,   30
and the pink swim-bladder
like a big peony.
I looked into his eyes
which were far larger than mine
but shallower, and yellowed,   35
the irises backed and packed
with tarnished tinfoil
seen through the lenses
of old scratched isinglass.[2]
They shifted a little, but not   40
to return my stare.
—It was more like the tipping
of an object toward the light.
I admired his sullen face,
the mechanism of his jaw,   45
and then I saw
that from his lower lip
—if you could call it a lip—
grim, wet, and weaponlike,
hung five old pieces of fish-line,   50
or four and a wire leader[3]
with the swivel still attached,
with all their five big hooks
grown firmly in his mouth.
A green line, frayed at the end   55
where he broke it, two heavier lines,
and a fine black thread
still crimped from the strain and snap
when it broke and he got away.
Like medals with their ribbons   60

2. A whitish semi-transparent substance used
for windows.

3. Short piece of wire connecting fishhook and
fishline.

frayed and wavering,
a five-haired beard of wisdom
trailing from his aching jaw.
I stared and stared   65
and victory filled up
the little rented boat,
from the pool of bilge
where oil had spread a rainbow
around the rusted engine   70
to the bailer rusted orange,
the sun-cracked thwarts,
the oarlocks on their strings,
the gunnels[4]—until everything
was rainbow, rainbow, rainbow!   75
And I let the fish go.

                                                    1946

Over 2000 Illustrations and a Complete Concordance[5]

Thus should have been our travels:
serious, engravable.
The Seven Wonders of the World are tired
and a touch familiar, but the other scenes,
innumerable, though equally sad and still,   5
are foreign. Often the squatting Arab,
or group of Arabs, plotting, probably,
against our Christian Empire,
while one apart, with outstretched arm and hand
points to the Tomb, the Pit, the Sepulcher.[6]   10
The branches of the date-palms look like files.
The cobbled courtyard, where the Well is dry,
is like a diagram, the brickwork conduits
are vast and obvious, the human figure
far gone in history or theology,   15
gone with its camel or its faithful horse.
Always the silence, the gesture, the specks of birds
suspended on invisible threads above the Site,
or the smoke rising solemnly, pulled by threads.
Granted a page alone or a page made up   20
of several scenes arranged in cattycornered[7] rectangles
or circles set on stippled gray,
granted a grim lunette,[8]
caught in the toils of an initial letter,
when dwelt upon, they all resolve themselves.   25
The eye drops, weighted, through the lines
the burin[9] made, the lines that move apart

---

4. "Bailer": bucket for bailing water out of the
boat; "thwarts": rowers' seats or benches; "oarlocks": metal devices to hold the oars, attached by
a "string" to the boat itself; "gunnels" or "gun-
wales," upper edges of the boat.
5. Part of the title page of an old edition of the
Bible described in the opening lines. It advertises
itself as containing not only the text, but "over 2000
illustrations"—engravings of the Holy Land—and
a concordance (a guide to occurrences of words
and proper names in a book, often found in Bibles).
6. The burial place of Christ, depicted (along
with other places associated with the life of Christ,
such as the Well) among the "2000 illustrations."
7. Placed on a diagonal.
8. The oval, often a segment of an enlarged initial letter, framing an illustration.
9. Engraver's tool.

like ripples above sand,
dispersing storms, God's spreading fingerprint,
and painfully, finally, that ignite   30
in watery prismatic white-and-blue.

Entering the Narrows at St. Johns[1]
the touching bleat of goats reached to the ship.
We glimpsed them, reddish, leaping up the cliffs
among the fog-soaked weeds and butter-and-eggs.   35
And at St. Peter's[2] the wind blew and the sun shone madly.
Rapidly, purposefully, the Collegians[3] marched in lines,
crisscrossing the great square with black, like ants.
In Mexico the dead man lay
in a blue arcade; the dead volcanoes   40
glistened like Easter lilies.
The jukebox went on playing "Ay, Jalisco!"
And at Volubilis[4] there were beautiful poppies
splitting the mosaics; the fat old guide made eyes.
In Dingle[5] harbor a golden length of evening   45
the rotting hulks held up their dripping plush.
The Englishwoman poured tea, informing us
that the Duchess was going to have a baby.
And in the brothels of Marrakesh[6]
the little pockmarked prostitutes   50
balanced their tea-trays on their heads
and did their belly-dances; flung themselves
naked and giggling against our knees,
asking for cigarettes. It was somewhere near there
I saw what frightened me most of all: 55
A holy grave, not looking particularly holy,
one of a group under a keyhole-arched stone baldaquin[7]
open to every wind from the pink desert.
An open, gritty, marble trough, carved solid
with exhortation, yellowed   60
as scattered cattle-teeth;
half-filled with dust, not even the dust
of the poor prophet paynim[8] who once lay there.
In a smart burnoose Khadour looked on amused.

Everything only connected by "and" and "and."   65
Open the book. (The gilt rubs off the edges
of the pages and pollinates the fingertips.)
Open the heavy book. Why couldn't we have seen
this old Nativity[9] while we were at it?
—the dark ajar, the rocks breaking with light,   70
an undisturbed, unbreathing flame,
colorless, sparkless, freely fed on straw,

---

1. City in Newfoundland, on the Atlantic Ocean.
2. The great cathedral in Rome.
3. That is, members of the College of Cardinals in the Vatican, Rome.
4. Ruined Roman city in French Morocco.
5. Town in southwest Ireland.
6. City in French Morocco.
7. Architectual canopy.
8. Archaic literary word for pagan, especially Moslem.
9. Scene of the adoration of the infant Christ.

and, lulled within, a family with pets,
—and looked and looked our infant[1] sight away.

1955

The Armadillo

For Robert Lowell

This is the time of year
when almost every night
the frail, illegal fire balloons appear.
Climbing the mountain height,

rising toward a saint   5
still honored in these parts,
the paper chambers flush and fill with light
that comes and goes, like hearts.

Once up against the sky it's hard
to tell them from the stars—   10
planets, that is—the tinted ones:
Venus going down, or Mars,

or the pale green one. With a wind,
they flare and falter, wobble and toss;
but if it's still they steer between   15
the kite sticks of the Southern Cross,[2]

receding, dwindling, solemnly
and steadily forsaking us,
or, in the downdraft from a peak,
suddenly turning dangerous.   20

Last night another big one fell.
It splattered like an egg of fire
against the cliff behind the house.
The flame ran down. We saw the pair

of owls who nest there flying up   25
and up, their whirling black-and-white
stained bright pink underneath, until
they shrieked up out of sight.

The ancient owls' nest must have burned.
Hastily, all alone,   30
a glistening armadillo left the scene,
rose-flecked, head down, tail down,

and then a baby rabbit jumped out,
short-eared, to our surprise.
So soft!—a handful of intangible ash   35
with fixed, ignited eyes.

---

1. The Latin root of 'infant"—*infans*—means "speechless."

2. A constellation visible only from the southern hemisphere.

Too pretty, dreamlike mimicry!
O falling fire and piercing cry
and panic, and a weak mailed fist
clenched ignorant against the sky!   40

1965

In the Waiting Room

In Worcester, Massachusetts,
I went with Aunt Consuelo
to keep her dentist's appointment
and sat and waited for her
in the dentist's waiting room.   5
It was winter. It got dark
early. The waiting room
was full of grown-up people,
arctics and overcoats,
lamps and magazines.   10
My aunt was inside
what seemed like a long time
and while I waited I read
the *National Geographic*
(I could read) and carefully   15
studied the photographs:
the inside of a volcano,
black, and full of ashes;
then it was spilling over
in rivulets of fire.   20
Osa and Martin Johnson[3]
dressed in riding breeches,
laced boots, and pith helmets.
A dead man slung on a pole
—"Long Pig,"[4] the caption said.   25
Babies with pointed heads
wound round and round with string;
black, naked women with necks
wound round and round with wire
like the necks of light bulbs.   30
Their breasts were horrifying.
I read it right straight through.
I was too shy to stop.
And then I looked at the cover:
the yellow margins, the date.   35

Suddenly, from inside,
came an *oh!* of pain
—Aunt Consuelo's voice—
not very loud or long.
I wasn't at all surprised;   40
even then I knew she was
a foolish, timid woman.

3. Then-popular husband-and-wife team of
explorers and naturalists.

4. Polynesian cannibals' name for the human
carcass.

I might have been embarrassed,
but wasn't. What took me
completely by surprise
was that it was *me:*
my voice, in my mouth.
Without thinking at all
I was my foolish aunt,
I—we—we falling, falling,
our eyes glued to the cover
of the *National Geographic,*
February, 1918.

I said to myself: three days
and you'll be seven years old.
I was saying it to stop
the sensation of falling off
the round, turning world
into cold, blue-black space.
But I felt: you are an *I,*
you are an *Elizabeth,*
you are one of *them.*
Why should you be one, too?
I scarcely dared to look
to see what it was I was.
I gave a sidelong glance
—I couldn't look any higher—
at shadowy gray knees,
trousers and skirts and boots
and different pairs of hands
lying under the lamps.
I knew that nothing stranger
had ever happened, that nothing
stranger could ever happen.
Why should I be my aunt,
or me, or anyone?
What similarities—
boots, hands, the family voice
I felt in my throat, or even
the *National Geographic*
and those awful hanging breasts—
held us all together
or made us all just one?
How—I didn't know any
word for it—how "unlikely" . . .
How had I come to be here,
like them, and overhear
a cry of pain that could have
got loud and worse but hadn't?

The waiting room was bright
and too hot. It was sliding
beneath a big black wave,
another, and another.

Then I was back in it.

The War[5] was on. Outside,   95
in Worcester, Massachusetts,
were night and slush and cold,
and it was still the fifth
of February, 1918.

                                                              1976

Poem

About the size of an old-style dollar bill,
American or Canadian,
mostly the same whites, gray greens, and steel grays
—this little painting (a sketch for a larger one?)
has never earned any money in its life.   5
Useless and free, it has spent seventy years
as a minor family relic
handed along collaterally[6] to owners
who looked at it sometimes, or didn't bother to.

It must be Nova Scotia; only there   10
does one see gabled wooden houses
painted that awful shade of brown.
The other houses, the bits that show, are white.
Elm trees, low hills, a thin church steeple
—that gray-blue wisp—or is it? In the foreground   15
a water meadow with some tiny cows,
two brushstrokes each, but confidently cows;
two minuscule white geese in the blue water,
back-to-back, feeding, and a slanting stick.
Up closer, a wild iris, white and yellow,   20
fresh-squiggled from the tube.
The air is fresh and cold; cold early spring
clear as gray glass; a half inch of blue sky
below the steel-gray storm clouds.
(They were the artist's specialty.)   25
A specklike bird is flying to the left.
Or is it a flyspeck looking like a bird?

Heavens, I recognize the place, I know it!
It's behind—I can almost remember the farmer's name.
His barn backed on that meadow. There it is,   30
titanium white,[7] one dab. The hint of steeple,
filaments of brush-hairs, barely there,
must be the Presbyterian church.
Would that be Miss Gillespie's house?
Those particular geese and cows   35
are naturally before my time.
A sketch done in an hour, "in one breath,"
once taken from a trunk and handed over.
*Would you like this? I'll probably never
have room to hang these things again.*   40
Your Uncle George, no, mine, my Uncle George,
he'd be your great-uncle, left them all with Mother

5. World War I.   7. A very bright white pigment.
6. That is, indirectly.

when he went back to England.
You know, he was quite famous, an R.A.[8] . . .

I never knew him. We both knew this place,   45
apparently, this literal small backwater,
looked at it long enough to memorize it,
our years apart. How strange. And it's still loved,
or its memory is (it must have changed a lot).
Our visions coincided—"visions" is   50
too serious a word—our looks, two looks:
art "copying from life" and life itself,
life and the memory of it so compressed
they've turned into each other. Which is which?
Life and the memory of it cramped,   55
dim, on a piece of Bristol board,[9]
dim, but how live, how touching in detail
—the little that we get for free,
the little of our earthly trust. Not much.
About the size of our abidance   60
along with theirs: the munching cows,
the iris, crisp and shivering, the water
still standing from spring freshets,
the yet-to-be-dismantled elms, the geese.

                                                                    1976

One Art

The art of losing isn't hard to master;
so many things seem filled with the intent
to be lost that their loss is no disaster.

Lose something every day. Accept the fluster
of lost door keys, the hour badly spent.   5
The art of losing isn't hard to master.

Then practice losing farther, losing faster:
places, and names, and where it was you meant
to travel. None of these will bring disaster.

I lost my mother's watch. And look! my last, or   10
next-to-last, of three loved houses went.
The art of losing isn't hard to master.

I lost two cities, lovely ones. And, vaster,
some realms I owned, two rivers, a continent.
I miss them, but it wasn't a disaster.   15

—Even losing you (the joking voice, a gesture
I love) I shan't have lied. It's evident
the art of losing's not too hard to master
though it may look like (*Write* it!) like disaster.

                                                                    1976

8. Member of the Royal Academy of Arts, in   9. Cardboard with a smooth surface.
England.

JOSEPHINE MILES
1911–1985

Josephine Miles was a scholar, and her poems show a scholar's attention to interlocking details. She was also self-deprecating and modest, and some of her best poems amuse and excite by a clash between tone and subject matter. She also had a scholar's preference for indirection. Some of her poems are philosophical puzzles; thus "On Inhabiting an Orange" invites us to consider the paradox that parallel lines drawn on a sphere will always meet. Miles said that she liked the "idea of speech—not images, not ideas, not music, but people talking—as the material from which poetry is made. . . . I like the spare and active interplay of talk."[1] Some of her experiments in the vernacular use tones of voice so confiding and persuasive that one has to think about them a little to realize their quaintness. "All our stones like as much sun as possible" would be an unexceptionable observation to make about flowers, but it is an odd one to make about stones, and the poem which begins "Mother said to call her if the H bomb exploded / and I said I would . . ." presents headline occasions in the mesmerizing tones of an American housewife. She also refused self-pity, even though she suffered a lifelong disabling disease: the "lame old lady" of "Reason" was Miles herself.

Josephine Miles was born on June 11, 1911, in Chicago, Illinois. Her family moved to California five years later, and except for two years in Michigan she lived there from then on. She took her B.A. at UCLA, did graduate work at Berkeley, and remained there as a teacher, first as Professor of English and, from 1973 on, as University Professor. Her scholarly work was devoted to the systematic analysis and comparison of poetic grammars and vocabularies used in different periods of English literary history.

1. *Poet's Choice,* ed. Paul Engle and Joseph Longland, New York, pp. 107–108.

Preliminary to Classroom Lecture

My quiet kin, must I affront you
With a telling tongue?
Will not a mission or request content you
To move as you belong
The fields of doubt among?   5

The voice to burden down a tale upon you
Were indolent with din.
Would better ask and have the answer from you.
And would you then begin
Querying too, querying, my quiet kin?   10

                                                            1941

Belief

Mother said to call her if the H bomb exploded
And I said I would, and it about did
When Louis my brother robbed a service station
And lay cursing on the oily cement in handcuffs.

But by that time it was too late to tell Mother,   5
She was too sick to worry the life out of her
Over *why why.* Causation is sequence
And everything is one thing after another.

Besides, my other brother, Eddie, had got to be President,
And you can't ask too much of one family.   10
The chances were as good for a good future
As bad for a bad one.

Therefore it was surprising that, as we kept the newspapers from Mother,
She died feeling responsible for a disaster unverified,
Murmuring, in her sleep as it seemed, the ancient slogan   15
Noblesse oblige.

                                                                        1955

Reason[1]

Said, Pull her up a bit will you, Mac, I want to unload there.
Said, Pull her up my rear end, first come first serve.
Said, Give her the gun, Bud, he needs a taste of his own bumper.
Then the usher came out and got into the act:

Said, Pull her up, pull her up a bit, we need this space, sir.   5
Said, For God's sake, is this still a free country or what?
You go back and take care of Gary Cooper's horse
And leave me handle my own car.

Saw them unloading the lame old lady,
Ducked out under the wheel and gave her an elbow,   10
Said, All you needed to do was just explain;
Reason, Reason is my middle name.

                                                                        1955

[The Entrepreneur Chicken Shed His Tail Feathers, Surplus]

The entrepreneur chicken shed his tail feathers, surplus
Fat, his comb, wing weight, down to a mere
Shadow, like a Graves bird[2] ready to sing.
For him every morning
Paradise Merchant Mart reopened its doors   5
With regular fire sales, Shoe Parlor
Blackened its aroma, Professional
Building ran its elevators up and down
So fast that pulled teeth turned up in other mouths.

Activity. The tax base broadened in the sunlight   10
As gradually sun spreads wider after coffee.
It was a busy world on that side of the road,
For which the entrepreneur chicken was in his able
Way responsible.
At noon, loans, mortgages, personal interest,   15
At night notarized after-images, as if by sundown
The elevator had turned to moving sidewise
Frames and phrases to be read and reread.

1. " 'Reason' is a favorite one of my poems because I like the idea of speech—not images, not ideas, not music, but people talking—as the material from which poetry is made" (Miles's note).

2. Morris Graves (b. 1910), the American artist, painted a picture (*Guardian*) of a ghostlike, transparent bird.

He was not boss or mayor, but he certainly was
Right on that spinning wheel which spun the public   20
In and out of his stores, and his pleasantries
Began to spin the flesh right off his bones.
That is why the chicken began to sing
High, not loud, and why transparencies
Of pipestems were his legs, his beak aloft,   25
His feathers lean, drawing the busy air,
And why he crossed the road.

1967

Fields of Learning

When we go out into the fields of learning
We go by a rough route
Marked by colossal statues, Frankenstein's
Monsters, AMPAC and the 704,
AARDVARK, and deoxyribonucleic acid.[3]   5
They guard the way.
Headless they nod, wink eyeless,
Thoughtless compute, not heartless,
For they figure us, they figure
Our next turning.   10
They are reading the book to be written.
As we start out
At first daylight into the fields, they are saying,
Starting out.

In every sage leaf is contained a toad   15
Infinitely small.

Carbonized grains of wheat unearthed
From the seventh millennium B.C. town of Jarmo
In the Tigris-Euphrates basin[4]
Match the grains of three kinds of wheat still extant,   20
Two wild, one found only in cultivation.
The separate grains
Were parched and eaten,
Or soaked into gruel, yeasted, fermented.
Took to the idea of bread,   25
Ceres,[5] while you were gone.
Wind whistles in the smokey thatch,
Oven browns its lifted loaf,
And in the spring the nourished seeds,
Hybrid with wild grass,   30
Easily open in a hundred days,
And seeded fruits, compact and dry,
Store well together.
They make the straw for beds,
They ask the caring hand to sow, the resting foot   35
To stay, to court the seasons.

3. Or DNA, the acids that help transmit genetic
information; AMPAC: American Medical Political
Action Committee.

4. In the eastern Mediterrean.
5. Roman goddess of agriculture and the harvest.

Basil: hatred: king over pain.[6]

What did you do on the last day of day camp?
First we did games, running around and playing.
Then we did crafts, making things.   40
Then we did nature, what goes on and on.
Eventually a number
Of boys have got big enough
Through all the hazards of drag-racing, theft, and probation,
To start for junior college, two transfers away,   45
Mysterious as Loch Ness.[7]
While of grandmothers a number
Have stooping arrived to seventy or eighty
And wave the boys on, shaking
With more absentminded merriment than they have mustered   50
In half a century.

King Henry the Eighth consumed many daisies
In an attempt to rid himself of ulcers.

Algebra written across a blackboard hurts
As a tight shoe hurts; it can't be walked in.   55
Music, a song score, hurts,
How far lies one note from another?
Graft hurts, its systems of exploitation
In cold continuance.
Argosies of design, fashions to which the keys   60
Rest restlessly in an Egyptian tomb.

In every sage leaf is contained a toad
Infinitely small.

                                                                          1968

IRVING LAYTON
b. 1912

Irving Layton, born in Romania on March 12, 1912, was brought by his Jewish parents to Canada in the following year. An intense sense of being Jewish has always
characterized his work. He early began to exhibit his restlessness as he worked as a
busboy, waiter, insurance agent, clerk, boxing instructor, and proofreader, and then
took a bachelor of science degree in agriculture. He has been married four times.
From the beginning of his writing career Layton defied what he called the "genteel,
dull, and quite anaemic" verse before him ("Prologue to the King Pea Shooter"). He
opposed "eunuchism," a term he used in the Foreword to his *Collected Poems* (1965).
More seriously, he opposed not only the conservative literary tradition in Canada,
based on English Victorian poetry, but such modern eminences as Eliot. His real
allies, he thought, were Pound and Yeats, before them Nietzsche and Blake, and
after them William Carlos Williams and Robert Creeley. An associate editor of the
Black Mountain Review, and editor of other magazines, he took a prominent role in
the liberation of poetry from standardized modes. Williams saluted him in the intro-

6. Basil is an herb with curative powers; the
word comes from a Greek root meaning "royal."
7. That is, as mysterious as the prehistoric

"monster" reputed to live in Loch Ness, a lake in
Scotland.

duction to Layton's *The Improved Binoculars*,[1] "When I first clapped eyes on the poems of Irving Layton two years ago, I let out a yell of joy."

The purpose of poetry for Layton is transformation. "Whatever else poetry is freedom." The poet has "a prophetic vocation to lead his fellowmen towards sanity and life."[2] Layton has himself been transformed in his long and prolific writing career:

> Almost now I know who I am.
> Almost I have the boldness to be that man.
> ("There Were No Signs")

He has put aside some of the easy asperities of his earlier work, and writes more often now in a subtly imaginative way to which he has won through with difficulty.

1. Highland, N.C., 1956.
2. Foreword to *Collected Poems*, Toronto, 1965, pp. xix, xxi.

The Birth of Tragedy[1]

And me happiest when I compose poems.
    Love, power, the huzza of battle
    are something, are much:
yet a poem includes them like a pool
    water and reflection.   5
In me, nature's divided things—
    tree, mould on tree—
    have their fruition.
I am their core. Let them swap,
bandy, like a flame swerve   10
I am their mouth: as a mouth I serve.

And I observe how the sensual moths
    big with odour and sunshine
    dart into the perilous shrubbery:
or drop their visiting shadows   15
    upon the garden I one year made
of flowering stone to be a footstool
    for the perfect gods:
    who, friends to the ascending orders,
sustain all passionate meditations   20
and call down pardons
    for the insurgent blood.

A quiet madman, never far from tears.
    I lie like a slain thing
    under the green air the trees   25
inhabit, or rest upon a chair
    towards which the inflammable air
tumbles on many robins' wings:
    noting how seasonably
    leaf and blossom uncurl   30
and living things arrange their death,

1. An allusion to *The Birth of Tragedy out of the Spirit of Music* (1872) by the German philosopher Friedrich Nietzsche. In it he posits two responses to the universe: the "Apollonian" or idealistic and orderly, and the "Dionysian," the chaotic underlying the order; he sees Greek tragic playwrights uniting Apollonian form and Dionysian content.

while someone from afar off
blows birthday candles for the world.

1954

A Tall Man Executes a Jig

I

So the man spread his blanket on the field
And watched the shafts of light between the tufts
And felt the sun push the grass toward him;
The noise he heard was that of whizzing flies,
The whistlings of some small imprudent birds,   5
And the ambiguous rumbles of cars
That made him look up at the sky, aware
Of the gnats that tilted[2] against the wind
And in the sunlight turned to jigging motes.
Fruitflies he'd call them except there was no fruit   10
About, spoiling to hatch these glitterings,
These nervous dots for which the mind supplied
The closing sentences from Thucydides,
Or from Euclid[3] having a savage nightmare.

II

Jig jig, jig jig. Like minuscule black links   15
Of a chain played with by some playful
Unapparent hand or the palpitant
Summer haze bored with the hour's stillness.
He felt the sting and tingle afterwards
Of those leaving their orthodox unrest,   20
Leaving their undulant excitation
To drop upon his sleeveless arm. The grass,
Even the wildflowers became black hairs
And himself a maddened speck among them.
Still the assaults of the small flies made him   25
Glad at last, until he saw purest joy
In their frantic jiggings under a hair,
So changed from those in the unrestraining air.

III

He stood up and felt himself enormous.
Felt as might Donatello over stone,   30
Or Plato,[4] or as a man who has held
A loved and lovely woman in his arms
And feels his forehead touch the emptied sky
Where all antinomies[5] flood into light.
Yet jig jig jig, the haloing black jots   35
Meshed with the wheeling fire of the sun:
Motion without meaning, disquietude
Without sense or purpose, ephermerides[6]
That mottled the resting summer air till

---

2. That is, jousted at, charged at.
3. Ancient Greek mathematician and geometrician (fl. 300 B.C.); Thucydides (c.460–400 B.C.): Greek historian.

4. Greek philosopher (c.427–348 B.C.); Donatello: Italian Renaissance sculptor.
5. That is, contradictions.
6. Or "ephemerides," astronomical almanac

Gusts swept them from his sight like wisps of smoke.   40
Yet they returned, bring a bee who, seeing
But a tall man, left him for a marigold.

IV

He doffed his aureole of gnats and moved
Out of the field as the sun sank down,
A dying god upon the blood-red hills.   45
Ambition, pride, the ecstasy of sex,
And all circumstance of delight and grief,
That blood upon the mountain's side, that flood
Washed into a clear incredible pool
Below the ruddied peaks that pierced the sun.   50
He stood still and waited. If ever
The hour of revelation was come
It was now, here on the transfigured steep.
The sky darkened. Some birds chirped. Nothing else.
He thought the dying god had gone to sleep: 55
An Indian fakir on his mat of nails.

V

And on the summit of the asphalt road
Which stretched towards the fiery town, the man
Saw one hill raised like a hairy arm, dark
With pines and cedars against the stricken sun   60
—The arm of Moses or of Joshua.[7]
He dropped his head and let fall the halo
Of mountains, purpling and silent as time,
To see temptation coiled before his feet:
A violated grass snake that lugged   65
Its intestine like a small red valise.
A cold-eyed skinflint it now was, and not
The manifest of that joyful wisdom,
The mirth and arrogant green flame of life;
Or earth's vivid tongue that flicked in praise of earth.   70

VI

And the man wept because pity was useless.
"Your jig's up; the flies come like kites,"[8] he said
And watched the grass snake crawl towards the hedge,
Convulsing and dragging into the dark
The satchel filled with curses for the earth,   75
For the odours of warm sedge, and the sun,
A blood-red organ in the dying sky.
Backwards it fell into a grassy ditch
Exposing its underside, white as milk,
And mocked by wisps of hay between its jaws;   80
And then it stiffened to its final length.
But though it opened its thin mouth to scream
A last silent scream that shook the black sky,
Adamant and fierce, the tall man did not curse.

giving the places of heavenly bodies in the sky.   of Egypt and into the promised land, respectively.
  7. That is, the strong arm of a powerful leader.   8. Small hawks.
These Old Testament figures led the Israelites out

VII

Beside the rigid snake the man stretched out   85
In fellowship of death; he lay silent
And stiff in the heavy grass with eyes shut,
Inhaling the moist odours of the night
Through which his mind tunnelled with flicking tongue
Backwards to caves, mounds, and sunken ledges   90
And desolate cliffs where come only kites,
And where of perished badgers and racoons
The claws alone remain, gripping the earth.
Meanwhile the green snake crept upon the sky,
Huge, his mailed coat glittering with stars that made   95
The night bright, and blowing thin wreaths of cloud
Athwart the moon: and as the weary man
Stood up, coiled above his head, transforming all.

       1963

WILLIAM EVERSON
b. 1912

Like the other members of the Beat Generation, William Everson was eager to find an alternative to the formalism—and, as it seemed to the Beats, the emotional and spiritual aridity—of much postwar American poetry. While Allen Ginsberg and Gary Snyder were finding inspiration for their lives and their poetry in the religions of the East, Everson sought out a tradition closer to home, orthodox Christianity: from 1951 to 1969, he was Brother Antoninus of the Dominican Order of Preachers. For a time strongly indebted to Robinson Jeffers, and probably to D. H. Lawrence as well, Everson's poems then were relentlessly violent, a struggle to achieve a state of spiritual freedom beyond struggle.

He was born in Sacramento, California, on September 10, 1912; brought up by his parents as a Christian Scientist, he became an agnostic during his teens. He attended Fresno State College, but dropped out to write poetry and to marry. Drafted as a conscientious objector in 1943, Everson spent the war years in a succession of work camps in the Pacific Northwest, and in 1944 he published *The Residual Years*, a collection of the verse he had been writing since his college days. After the war Everson went to San Francisco and was one of what he calls "the anarchists and poets around Kenneth Rexroth"; he had divorced and remarried, and his new wife introduced him to Catholicism. In 1949 they separated. After a year on a Guggenheim Fellowship and another doing work in the slums of Oakland, Everson entered the Dominican Order as a lay brother. After six years of self-study and searching he rejoined the literary scene in California, now "identifying openly with the Beat Generation because it proclaimed against a triumphant American pragmatism the necessity for mystical vision"[1] and because of its "dionysian revolt" against the prevailing trends in postwar verse. He published six books of poems as Brother Antoninus and gave readings throughout the country.

He left the order in 1969. He had written his "Tendril in the Mesh" sequence from 1966 to 1968 while "still in vows," but its writing changed him, for it is a poem of deep sexual desire. "By the end of 1969 the karma [that is, fate] of his passion overwhelmed him, and in his final appearance as a monk, on the afternoon of December 7 at the University of California, Davis, he read the ["Tendril"] sequence publicly for the first time . . . concluding his reading, he stripped off his religious habit and

1. *Contemporary Poets of the English Language*, ed. Rosalie Murphy, Chicago, 1970, p. 29.

fled the platform."[2] He married the young woman to whom he had dedicated "Tendril," and, with her young son, they took up residence near San Francisco. He held university posts as poet-in-residence, until in 1982 a grant from the National Endowment for the Arts enabled him to retire from teaching. Since *Man-Fate* (1974), his first published work since leaving the order, he has published twelve books of poetry. He has also had to struggle with the painful onset of Parkinson's disease, "rendering problematical all creativity, but chastening the mind."[3]

In the preface to *Man-Fate*, Everson gives his own perspective on the introductory headnote to his work that appeared in the first edition of this anthology: "A recent anthologist has protested, 'Antoninus' work composes not a spiritual odyssey, but an agony, a bitter quarrel with God.' Actually, his only quarrel is with himself, and his odyssey goes on, no agony can impugn it."[4] Later he has commented, "My preoccupation with the Cross as solution to the mystery of violence . . . has not abated, but in the ecological crisis has shifted to the numen [spirit] subsistent in Nature, as totem, or metaphor, the encounter between man and God . . . In the final phase of my life now opening I look for aboriginal response to the fact of existence on this continent, and in my work will seek to recover the pertinence of Wilderness as purifier to the corrupt civilized dream."[5]

Year's End

The year dies fiercely: out of the north the beating storms,
And wind at the roof's edge, lightning swording the low sky:
This year dying like some traitored Norse stumbling under the deep wounds,
The furious steel, smashing and swinging.

From the northern room I watch in the dusk,   5
And being unsocial regard the coming year coldly,
Suspicious of strangers, distrustful of innovations,
Reluctant to chance one way or another the unknown.
I leave this year as a man leaves wine,
Remembering the summer, bountiful, the good fall, the months mellow
     and full.   10
I sit in the northern room, in the dusk, the death of a year,
And watch it go down in thunder.

                                                          1948

The Poet Is Dead

A Memorial for Robinson Jeffers[1]

To be read with a full stop between the strophes, as in a dirge.[2]

In the evening the dusk
Stipples with lights. The long shore
Gathers darkness in on itself
And goes cold. From the lap of silence
All the tide-crest's pivotal immensity   5
Lifts into the land.

2. William Everson, Preface, *Man-Fate*, New York, 1974, pp. vii–viii.
3. *Contemporary Poets*, New York, 1985, p. 246.
4. Preface, p. ix.
5. *Contemporary Poets*, p. 245.

1. American poet (1887–1962); see above, p. 245.
2. Psalm sung for a departed soul in the Catholic Church; also, any hymn expressing grief. "Strophe": here, stanza.

•

Snow on the headland,
Rare on the coast of California.
Snow on Point Lobos,[3]
Falling all night,
Filling the creeks and the back country,
The strangely beautiful
Setting of death.

•

For the poet is dead.
The pen, splintered on the sheer
Excesses of vision, unfingered, falls.
The heart-crookt hand, cold as a stone,
Lets it go down.

•

The great tongue is dried.
The teeth that bit the bitterness
Are sheathed in truth.

•

If you listen
You can hear the field mice
Kick little rifts in the snow-swirls.
You can hear
Time take back its own.

•

For the poet is dead.
On the bed by the window,
Where dislike and desire
Killed each other in the crystalline interest,
What remains alone lets go of its light. It has found
Finalness. It has touched what it craved: the passionate
Darks of deliverance.

•

At sundown the sea wind,
Burgeoning,
Bled the west empty.

•

Now the opulent
Treacherous woman called Life
Forsakes her claim. Blond and a harlot
She once drank joy from his narrow loins.
She broke his virtue in her knees.

•

In the water-gnawn coves of Point Lobos
The white-faced sea otters

10

15

20

25

30

35

40

3. Promontory south of Carmel, California, where Jeffers lived.

Fold their paws on their velvet breasts
And list waveward.   45

•

But he healed his pain on the wisdom of stone,
He touched roots for his peace.

•

The old ocean boils its wrack,
It steeps its lees.

•

For the poet is dead. The gaunt wolf   50
Crawled out to the edge and died snapping.
He said he would. The wolf
Who lost his mate.[4] He said he would carry the wound,
The blood-wound of life, to the broken edge
And die grinning.   55

•

Over the salt marsh the killdeer,[5]
Unrestrainable,
Cry fear against moon set.

•

And all the hardly suspected
Latencies of disintegration   60
Inch forward. The skin
Flakes loss. On the death-gripped feet
The toenails glint like eyeteeth
From the pinched flesh.
The caged ribs and the bladed shoulders,   65
Ancient slopes of containment,
Imperceptibly define the shelves of structure,
Faced like rock ridges
Boned out of mountains, absently revealed
With the going of the snow.   70

•

In the sleeve of darkness the gopher
Tunnels the sod for short grass
And pockets his fill.

•

And the great phallus shrinks in the groin,
The seed in the scrotum   75
Chills.

•

4. Compare, in Jeffers's poem "The Deer Lay   5. Waterbirds with a shrill cry.
Down Their Bones," lines 20–21 ". . . I crawl out
on a ledge of rock and die snapping, like a wolf /
Who has lost his mate."

When the dawn comes in again,
Thoughtlessly,
The sea birds will mew by the window.

•

For the poet is dead. Beyond the courtyard   80
The ocean at full tide hunches its bulk.
Groping among the out-thrusts of granite
It moans and whimpers. In the phosphorescent
Restlessness it chunks deceptively,
Wagging its torn appendages, dipping and rinsing   85
Its ripped sea rags, its strip-weeded kelp.[6]
The old mother grieves her deathling.
She trundles the dark for her lost child.
She hunts her son.

•

On the top of the tower[7]   90
The hawk will not perch tomorrow.

•

And on surf-swept Point Lobos the cypresses
Stagger in the wind, incestuous
Siblings of the drift. Flexed in transgression
The clenched limbs of lovers press vein to vein,   95
The seethe of their passion
Scrawling a stark calligraphy on the palimpsest of night,
Etched with the swan skein and the leaf,
Impalpably mutable, the gnomic
Marginalia of death.[8]   100

•

But in the gorged rivermouth
Already the steelhead[9] fight for entry.
They feel fresh water
Sting through the sieves of their salt-coarsened gills.
They shudder and thrust.   105

•

So the sea broods. And the aged gull,
Asleep on the water, too stiff to feed,
Spins in a side-rip crossing the surf
And drags down.

•

---

6. Seaweed.
7. Hawk Tower, which Jeffers built from the stone of Carmel Beach, as he did Tor House. Both buildings overlook the sea.
8. Everson has recently (1987) added this strophe to the poem. "*Palimpsests* are written parchments imperfectly erased so that the original words may be made out beneath the later writing. I compare them to the night because Tamar's sin with her brother on Point Lobos in Jeffers' poem named for her reduplicates her father's sin with his sister forty years earlier in the same place. Thus *gnomic* comes through as a kind of cryptic, tangential knowledge, with an implication of deformity about it, wisdom mishapen by the stultification of time" (Everson's note in letter to John Benedict, July 12, 1988).
9. "Marine trout resembling salmon. Unlike the latter they do not die at first spawn, but wrig [sic] back to sea, returning another year. Thus as a libido symbol they mark the turning of the poem" (Everson's note in letter to Benedict, October 3, 1987).

This mouth is shut. I say
The mouth is clamped cold.
I tell you this tongue is dried.   110

•

But the skull, the skull,
The perfect sculpture of bone!—
Around the forehead the fine hair,   115
Composed to the severest
Lineaments of thought,
Is moulded on peace.

•

And the strongly-wrought features,
That keep in the soul's serenest achievement   120
The spirit's virtue,
Set the death mask of all mortality,
The impress of that grace.

•

In the shoal-champed[1] breakers
One wing of the gull   125
Tilts like a fin through the ribbon of spume[2]
And knifes under.

•

And all about there the vastness of night
Affirms its sovereignty. There's not a cliff
Of the coastline, not a reef   130
Of the waterways, from the sword-thrust Aleutians
To the scorpion-tailed stinger Cape Horn[3]—
All that staggering declivity
Grasped in the visionary mind and established—
But is sunken under the dark ordainment,   135
Like a sleeper possessed, like a man
Gone under, like a powerful swimmer
Plunged in a womb-death washed out to sea
And worked back ashore.

•

The gull's eye,   140
Skinned to the wave, retains the ocean's
Imponderable compression,
And burns yellow.

•

The poet is dead. I tell you
The nostrils are narrowed. I say again and again   145
The strong tongue is broken.

•

1. That is, mashed by the shallows.
2. Foam.
3. "That is, the entire Pacific littoral, or shore-
line"—stretching from the Aleutian Islands, off
Alaska, to Cape Horn, at the southernmost tip of
South America (quoted phrase from 1987 letter to
Benedict).

But the owl
Quirks in the cypresses, and you hear
What he says. He is calling for something.
He tucks his head for his mate's   150
Immemorial whisper. In her answering voice
He tastes the grace-note[4] of his reprieve.

•

When fog comes again to the canyons
The redwoods will know what it means.
The giant sisters   155
Gather it into their merciful arms
And stroke silence.

•

You smell pine resin laced in the salt
And know the dawn wind has veered.

•

And on the shelf in the gloom,   160
Blended together, the tall books emerge,
All of a piece. Transparent as membranes
The thin leaves of paper hug their dark thoughts.
They know what he said.

•

The sea, reaching for life,   165
Spits up the gull. He falls spread-eagled,
The streaked wings swept on the sand.
Vague fingers of snow, aimlessly deft, grope for his eyes.
When the blind head snaps
The beak krakes[5] at the sky.   170

•

Now the night closes.
All the dark's negatory[6]
Decentralization
Quivers toward dawn.

•

He has gone into death like a stone thrown in the sea.   175

•

And in far places the morning
Shrills its episodes of triviality and vice
And one man's passing. Could the ears
That hardly listened in life
Care much less now?   180

•

---

4. "Technically an ornamental musical note, but the word 'reprieve' evokes its theological root" (Everson's note in 1987 letter to Benedict).

5. " 'Krakes' is simply an echoic, stemming from 'croaks,' 'creaks,' 'cricks,' 'quacks,' etc., none of which sounded right in the context. 'Krakes' does it" (Everson's note in letter to Carol Stiles, September 19, 1987).

6. Negative.

Snow on the headland,
The strangely beautiful
Oblique concurrence,
The strangely reticent
Setting of death.   185

•

The great tongue
Dries in the mouth. I told you.
The voiceless throat
Cools silence. And the sea-granite eyes.
Washed in the sibilant waters   190
The stretched lips kiss peace.

•

The poet is dead.

•

Nor will ever again hear the sea lions
Grunt in the kelp at Point Lobos.
Nor look to the south when the grunion[7]   195
Run the Pacific, and the plunging
Shearwaters,[8] insatiable,
Stun themselves in the sea.

1964

From Tendril in the Mesh

IV

Daughter of earth and child of the wave be appeased,
Who have granted fulfillment and fed the flesh in the spirit.
A murmur of memory, a feint of infrequent espousals,
And the tug of repose the heart hovers and tilts toward dawn.   230

Somewhere your body relinquishes creeds of defiance.
I have tasted salt salience,[9] and savored its fragrance, have crested repose.
Now appeasement crouches and wends its way through my being.
I sense fulfillment not breached of strings and torches.

Kore! Daughter of dawn! Persephone! Maiden of twilight!   235
Sucked down into Pluto's unsearchable night for your husband.[1]
I see you depart, bearing the pomegranate seed in your groin.
In the node of your flesh you drip my flake of bestowal.

7. Small fish, native to California, which regularly come to the shore to spawn near the time of the full moon.
8. Ocean birds.
9. Emphasis.
1. Persephone (also known as Kore, "the maiden") was carried off by Hades, or Pluto, to be his queen in the underworld. Her mother, Demeter, appealed to Zeus, father of the gods, who was unable to release her completely from the underworld, because she had eaten some pomegranate seeds there (see next line); however, she returns to the earth every spring (thus symbolic of growth and the harvest).

What will you do, back on earth, when you find your mother?
Will the trace of dark lips fade out of your flesh forever? 240
I have knocked your instep with rapture, I have wounded your flank.
Like the little fish in the dredger's boat you bear the teeth of the gaff.[2]

O daughter of God! When the sons of man covet your passion,
Do not forget who placed on your brow his scarab of sovereign possession.
In the service of holy desire bear truth for escutcheon.[3] 245
And when you return to the roost of night wear the mane of the sun!

1974

Runoff[4]

Four wet winters and now the dry.
All the long season a sterile frost
Grips the mountain, the coast like flanged metal
Bent thwart the sea. Above:
Stripped trees, taut-twisted branches 5
Catch stark white light. Below:
Shriveled creekbeds, raw to the air, run naked roots,
Obscenely groined through flaking rock,
The scat[5] of torrents.

        Then early last evening 10
A thin drizzle, gaining toward dusk. Before dark dropped
The low-hanging cloud slit its belly and the rain plunged.
All night long the thirsty slopes drank straight-falling water,
Soaking it up, filling those tilted, deep-shelving seams,
Blue veins of the mountain, zig-zag crevices of fractured shale. 15
When dawn flared and the rain held
The runoff began.

      We rise with the light,
Sally down to the stream to touch fresh water
For a kind of blessing. We find instead a river of ink. 20
All the hoard of tributary creeks, those catchers of leaf-drift—
The strip of alder and the slough of fir,
Acrid shuff of the leathery tan-oak; and laurel,
The redolent, littering leaves of the laurel—
All that autumn-spun opulence 25
Frost drove down and ruthlessly squandered
Four moons back, to rot where it fell,
Now crawls to the sea, a liquid bile.

You look up at last in a wondering way
And exclaim softly, "Why, the mountain is menstruating!" 30
Something in your voice, a tremor there,
Tells of the mutual womanly pulse, the deep sensing,
Its sympathetic pang, its soft vibration.

---

2. Barbed spear.
3. Heraldic emblem; "scarab": talisman in the
shape of an Egyptian beetle.

4. Water from rain or melted snow.
5. Droppings.

Looking, I see indeed it is true:
Leaves like dead cells   35
Long held back in the frigid womb
Begin now to flow—under the rain
A deep cleansing, this rite of renewal.

For me it is runoff but my heart purges.

Touching you and creek-throb in the same impulse   40
I am healed of frost:
Woman and water in the blood-flow.

                                                                    1980

ROBERT HAYDEN
1913–1980

Robert Hayden did not subscribe to any esthetic of Black poetry. Rather he wished
to be read, enjoyed, and judged as a poet writing in English, who happened to
number being an American Black among his endowments. His poems display a strong
interest in narrative and in character. He liked to write about men and women who
are vividly themselves. Hayden presents his characters in direct narrative verse or
in soliloquy by an accumulation of bright detail, sharply apprehended, and rendered
with precision and style.

Hayden's parents were poor and uneducated themselves, but they encouraged
their bookish son, who early showed an interest in writing. After high school Hayden
could not afford to go on immediately to college. Reading on his own, he discovered
the poets of the Harlem Renaissance—he was particularly drawn to Countee Cullen—the more accessible of the twentieth-century Americans (Sandburg, Millay),
and the English classics.

At Detroit City College (now Wayne State University) Hayden majored in foreign
languages, with a special emphasis on Spanish. After college he worked at several
different government-sponsored historical projects, and he was the part-time drama
and music critic for a Detroit Black newspaper. In 1940 he married, published his
first book, and spent a short time in New York City. Hayden then returned to the
Midwest to take an M.A. at the University of Michigan. Among his teachers was
W. H. Auden, whom Hayden came greatly to admire: the older poet was an inven-
tive teacher, incisive in his judgments, and his influence may be seen in the technical
neatness of Hayden's verse.

Once his graduate studies were complete, Hayden did some teaching at the University of Michigan, and for the rest of his life he was to make his living by teaching,
writing his poems as time allowed. Hayden then moved south to Nashville, Tennessee, where he joined the faculty of Fisk University. More than twenty years later, in
1969, he returned to the University of Michigan, where he taught for the rest of his
life. He twice won the Hopwood Award for poetry, and in 1966 he won the Grand
Prize for poetry at the Dakar (Senegal) World Festival of the Arts. Robert Hayden
died in 1980.

The Ballad of Sue Ellen Westerfield

(For Clyde)

She grew up in bedeviled southern wilderness,
but had not been a slave, she said,
because her father wept and set her mother free.
She hardened in perilous rivertowns
and after The Surrender,[1]   5
went as a maid upon the tarnished Floating Palaces.[2]
Rivermen reviled her for the rankling cold
sardonic pride
that gave a knife-edge to her comeliness.

When she was old, her back still straight,   10
her hair still glossy black,
she'd talk sometimes
of dangers lived through on the rivers.
But never told of him,
whose name she'd vowed she would not speak again   15
till after Jordan.[3]

Oh, he was nearer nearer now
than wearisome kith and kin.
His blue eyes followed her
as she moved about her tasks upon the *Memphis Rose*.   20
He smiled and joshed, his voice quickening her.
She cursed the circumstance. . . .

The crazing horrors of that summer night,
the swifting flames, he fought his way to her,
the savaging panic, and helped her swim to shore.   25
The steamer like besieged Atlanta blazing,[4]
the cries, the smoke and bellowing flames,
the flamelit thrashing forms in hellmouth water,
and he swimming out to them,
leaving her dazed and lost.   30
A woman screaming under the raddled trees—
Sue Ellen felt it was herself who screamed.
The moaning of the hurt, the terrified—
she held off shuddering despair
and went to comfort whom she could.   35
Wagons torches bells
and whimpering dusk of morning
and blankness lostness nothingness for her
until his arms had lifted her
into wild and secret dark.   40

---

1. The end of the American Civil War.
2. River steamboats.
3. Until she has passed over the river Jordan
into the Promised Land—that is, until after she
has died.
    4. Atlanta was razed by Union troops during
General Sherman's "march to the sea."

How long how long was it they wandered,
loving fearing loving,
fugitives whose dangerous only hidingplace
was love?
How long was it before she knew   45
she could not forfeit what she was,
even for him—could not, even for him,
forswear her pride?
They kissed and said farewell at last.
He wept as had her father once.   50
They kissed and said farewell.
Until her dying-bed,
she cursed the circumstance.

1962

Mourning Poem for the Queen of Sunday[5]

Lord's lost Him His mockingbird,
His fancy warbler;
Satan sweet-talked her,
four bullets hushed her.
Who would have thought   5
she'd end that way?

Four bullets hushed her. And the world a-clang with evil.
Who's going to make old hardened sinner men tremble now
and the righteous rock?
Oh who and oh who will sing Jesus down   10
to help with struggling and doing without and being colored
all through blue Monday?
Till way next Sunday?

All those angels
in their cretonne[6] clouds and finery   15
the true believer saw
when she rared back her head and sang,
all those angels are surely weeping.
Who would have thought
she'd end that way?   20

Four holes in her heart. The gold works wrecked.
But she looks so natural in her big bronze coffin
among the Broken Hearts and Gates-Ajar,
it's as if any moment she'd lift her head
from its pillow of chill gardenias   25
and turn this quiet into shouting Sunday
and make folks forget what she did on Monday.

Oh, Satan sweet-talked her,
and four bullets hushed her.
Lord's lost Him His diva,[7]   30

---

5. Very probably she was the lead singer in a   6. Cotton or linen fabric.
church choir.   7. Prima donna, singer.

His fancy warbler's gone.
Who would have thought,
who would have thought she'd end that way?

1962

Those Winter Sundays

Sundays too my father got up early
and put his clothes on in the blueblack cold,
then with cracked hands that ached
from labor in the weekday weather made
banked fires blaze. No one ever thanked him.   5

I'd wake and hear the cold splintering, breaking.
When the rooms were warm, he'd call,
and slowly I would rise and dress,
fearing the chronic angers of that house,

Speaking indifferently to him,   10
who had driven out the cold
and polished my good shoes as well.
What did I know, what did I know
of love's austere and lonely offices?

1962

" 'Mystery Boy' Looks for Kin in Nashville"

Puzzle faces in the dying elms
promise him treats if he will stay.
Sometimes they hiss and spit at him
like varmints caught
in a thicket of butterflies.   5

A black doll,
one disremembered time,
came floating down to him
through mimosa's fancy work leaves and blooms
to be his hidden bride.   10

From the road beyond the creepered walls
they call to him now and then,
and he'll take off in spite of the angry trees,
hearing like the loudening of his heart
the name he never can he never can repeat.   15

And when he gets to where the voices were—
Don't cry, his dollbaby wife implores;
I know where they are, don't cry.
We'll go and find them, we'll go
and ask them for your name again.   20

1970

A Plague of Starlings

(Fisk Campus)

Evenings I hear
the workmen fire
into the stiff
magnolia leaves,
routing the starlings   5
gathered noisy and
befouling there.

Their scissoring
terror like glass
coins spilling breaking   10
the birds explode
into mica sky
raggedly fall
to ground rigid
in clench of cold.   15

The spared return,
when the guns are through,
to the spoiled trees
like choiceless poor
to a dangerous   20
dwelling place,
chitter and quarrel
in the piercing dark
about the killed.

Mornings, I pick   25
my way past death's
black droppings:
on campus lawns
and streets
the troublesome   30
starlings
frost-salted lie,
troublesome still.

And if not careful   35
I shall tread
upon carcasses
carcasses when I
go mornings now
to lecture on   40
what Socrates,
the hemlock hour nigh,
told sorrowing
Phaedo and the rest
about the migratory   45
habits of the soul.

1970

A Letter from Phillis Wheatley[8]

London, 1773

Dear Obour[9]
    Our crossing was without
event. I could not help, at times,
reflecting on that first—my Destined—
voyage long ago (I yet   5
have some remembrance of its Horrors)
and marvelling at God's Ways.
    Last evening, her Ladyship presented me
to her illustrious Friends.
I scarce could tell them anything   10
of Africa, though much of Boston
and my hope of Heaven. I read
my latest Elegies to them.
"O Sable Muse!" the Countess[1] cried,
embracing me, when I had done.   15
I held back tears, as is my wont,
and there were tears in Dear
Nathaniel's[2] eyes.
    At supper—I dined apart
like captive Royalty—   20
the Countess and her Guests promised
signatures affirming me
True Poetess, albeit once a slave.
Indeed, they were most kind, and spoke,
moreover, of presenting me   25
at Court (I thought of Pocahontas)—[3]
an Honor, to be sure, but one,
I should, no doubt, as Patriot decline.
    My health is much improved;
I feel I may, if God so Wills,   30
entirely recover here.
Idyllic England! Alas, there is
no Eden without its Serpent. Under
the chiming Complaisance I hear him Hiss;
I see his flickering tongue   35
when foppish would-be Wits
murmur of the Yankee Pedlar
and his Cannibal Mockingbird.
    Sister, forgive th'intrusion of
my Sombreness—Nocturnal Mood   40
I would not share with any save

8. Black slave (c. 1753–1784), who at the age of nineteen published her *Poems on Various Subjects, Religious and Moral,* the first book of poems by a Black woman in America. She had been born in Africa, but was captured and brought to America at an early age, where she was purchased by John and Susannah Wheatley. In 1773 the Wheatleys sent her to London, where her reputation had preceded her. In the poem Hayden echoes her eighteenth-century diction.
9. Obour Tanner, a young free Black who was one of Wheatley's few friends.
1. The Countess of Huntington, one of many Londoners who knew and praised Wheatley's work. "Sable": black (in her poem "On Being Brought from Africa to America," Wheatley refers to her "sable race").
2. The Wheatleys' son, who accompanied her to London.
3. Native-American princess (1595–1617), who reputedly saved the life of Captain John Smith. After being taken prisoner by the English, she married an Englishman and accompanied him to England, where, in 1616, she was presented at the royal court.

your trusted Self. Let me disperse,
in closing, such unseemly Gloom
by mention of an Incident
you may, as I, consider Droll: 45
Today, a little Chimney Sweep,
his face and hands with soot quite Black,
staring hard at me, politely asked:
"Does you, M'lady, sweep chimneys too?"
I was amused, but dear Nathaniel   50
(ever Solicitous) was not.
　　　I pray the Blessings of our Lord
and Saviour Jesus Christ be yours
Abundantly. In his Name,

　　　　　　　　　　Phillis   55
　　　　　　　　　　　　　　　　　　　　　　　1978

Bone-Flower Elegy

In the dream I enter the house
　　wander vast rooms that are
　　　catacombs midnight subway
　　　cavernous ruined movie-palace
　　where presences in vulture masks   5
　　　play scenes of erotic violence
　　　　on a scaffold stage   I want
　　to stay and watch but know somehow
I must not linger and come to the funeral
　　chamber   in its icy nonlight see   10
　　　a naked corpse
　　　　turning with sensual movements
　　　　on its coffin-bed
　　I have wept for you many times
　　I whisper but shrink from the arms   15
　　　that would embrace me
　　　and treading water reach
　　arched portals opening on a desert
groves of enormous nameless flowers
　　　twist up from firegold sand   20
　　skull flowers flowers of sawtooth bone
　　　their leaves and petals interlock
　　　　caging me for you beastangel
　　　　raging toward me
　　angelbeast shining come   25
　　　　to rend me and redeem
　　　　　　　　　　　　　　　　　　　　　　　1978

DUDLEY RANDALL
b. 1914

In 1965 Dudley Randall founded the Broadside Press, an event of crucial importance
in the development of postwar Black American poetry. He started with a capital of

$12.00, which paid the bill for printing the first "broadside"—his poem "Ballad of Birmingham," printed on a single sheet of paper. "I had noticed," Randall said, "how people would carry tattered clippings of their favorite poems in their billfolds, and I thought it would be a good idea to publish them in an attractive form as broadsides."[1] From these beginnings Broadside Press became one of the most influential publishers of contemporary Black poetry. Randall has produced recordings by Black poets reading their own works, and books by Black critics about Black poets.

Although the "Broadside poets" included several who rejected the standard dialect of American English because for them it was the language of the oppressor, Randall is unwilling in his own poems to restrict himself to a jealously guarded Black experience, or to disregard what may be learned from white poets. Randall agrees that a Black writer must write out of his own experience, but he believes that writers who seek to define and work within a "black aesthetic" have a future only as long "as their rejection of 'white standards' reject only what is false."[2] In his own poems he makes creative use of his English literary inheritance; the "Ballad of Birmingham" echoes both Black folk song and Blake's *Songs of Innocence and Experience.* "In any age of poetry," he reasons, "there is a certain ambiance which influences all poets whether they are black or white. The young white poets are using the same freedom as the young black poets."[3]

Born in Washington, D.C., on January 14, 1914, Dudley Randall has spent most of his life in Detroit. During the years when many are in college, he was a foundry worker at the Ford Motor Company, and then became a letter carrier and clerk for the post office. He served with the army in the South Pacific during the Second World War, then resumed his job with the post office and enrolled at Detroit's Wayne State University, where he received a B.A. in 1949. He studied library science at the University of Michigan and, armed with an M.A., worked as a librarian at Lincoln University in Missouri and Morgan State College in Baltimore before returning to Detroit, where he assumed increasingly important positions in the city's public library system. Since 1969 he has been reference librarian and poet-in-residence at the University of Detroit and has taught at the University of Michigan.

1. "Conversation," in *Black World*, December   2. *Negro Digest*, January 1968.
1971, p. 31.   3. "Conversation," p. 31.

Ballad of Birmingham

(On the bombing of a church in Birmingham, Alabama,[1] 1963)

"Mother dear, may I go downtown
Instead of out to play,
And march the streets of Birmingham
In a Freedom March today?"

"No, baby, no, you may not go,   5
For the dogs are fierce and wild,
And clubs and hoses, guns and jails
Aren't good for a little child."

"But, mother, I won't be alone.
Other children will go with me,   10
And march the streets of Birmingham
To make our country free."

1. Site of nonviolent civil-rights demonstrations led by the Black leader Martin Luther King, Jr., which were met with attack dogs, tear gas, cattle prods, and fire hoses.

"No, baby, no, you may not go,
For I fear those guns will fire.
But you may go to church instead   15
And sing in the children's choir."

She has combed and brushed her night-dark hair,
And bathed rose petal sweet,
And drawn white gloves on her small brown hands,
And white shoes on her feet.   20

The mother smiled to know her child
Was in the sacred place,
But that smile was the last smile
To come upon her face.

For when she heard the explosion,   25
Her eyes grew wet and wild.
She raced through the streets of Birmingham
Calling for her child.

She clawed through bits of glass and brick,
Then lifted out a shoe.   30
"O, here's the shoe my baby wore,
But, baby, where are you?"

                                                    1969

Booker T. and W. E. B.

(Booker T. Washington and W. E. B. Du Bois²)

"It seems to me," said Booker T.,
"It shows a mighty lot of cheek
To study chemistry and Greek
When Mister Charlie needs a hand
To hoe the cotton on his land.   5
And when Miss Ann looks for a cook,
Why stick your nose inside a book?"

"I don't agree," said W. E. B.
"If I should have the drive to seek
Knowledge of chemistry or Greek,   10
I'll do it. Charles and Miss can look
Another place for hand or cook.
Some men rejoice in skill of hand,
And some in cultivating land,
But there are others who maintain   15
The right to cultivate the brain."

"It seems to me," said Booker T.,
"That all you folks have missed the boat

---

2. Washington (1856?–1932) and Du Bois (1868–1963) were the two most prominent Black spokesmen of the late nineteenth and early twentieth centuries; Du Bois's opposition to Washington was pretty much on the grounds set forth in the poem.

Who shout about the right to vote,
And spend vain days and sleepless nights   20
In uproar over civil rights.
Just keep your mouths shut, do not grouse,
But work, and save, and buy a house."

"I don't agree," said W. E. B.,
"For what can property avail   25
If dignity and justice fail?
Unless you help to make the laws,
They'll steal your house with trumped-up clause.
A rope's as tight, a fire as hot,
No matter how much cash you've got.   30
Speak soft, and try your little plan,
But as for me, I'll be a man."

"It seems to me," said Booker T.—

"I don't agree,"
Said W. E. B.   35
                                                          1969

A Poet Is Not a Jukebox

A poet is not a jukebox, so don't tell me what to write.
I read a dear friend a poem about love, and she said,
"You're in to that bag now, for whatever it's worth,
But why don't you write about the riot in Miami?"[3]

I didn't write about Miami because I didn't know about Miami.   5
I've been so busy working for the Census, and listening to music all night,
      and making new poems
That I've broken my habit of watching TV and reading newspapers.
So it wasn't absence of Black Pride that caused me not to write about Miami,
But simple ignorance.

Telling a Black poet what he ought to write   10
Is like some Commissar of Culture in Russia telling a poet
He'd better write about the new steel furnaces in the Novobigorsk region,
Or the heroic feats of Soviet labor in digging the trans-Caucausus Canal,
Or the unprecedented achievement of workers in the sugar beet industry
      who exceeded their quota by 400 per cent (it was later discovered to
      be a typist's error).

Maybe the Russian poet is watching his mother die of cancer,   15
Or is bleeding from an unhappy love affair,
Or is bursting with happiness and wants to sing of wine, roses, and night-
      ingales.

I'll bet that in a hundred years the poems the Russian people will read,
      sing, and love

3. In 1980, perhaps one of the severest race riots of the century, in which Blacks took revenge for the
killing of a Black man by four white policemen.

Will be the poems about his mother's death, his unfaithful mistress, or his
    wine, roses, and nightingales,
Not the poems about steel furnaces, the trans-Caucausus Canal, or the sugar
    beet industry.   20
A poet writes about what he feels, what agitates his heart and sets his pen
    in motion.
Not what some apparatchnik[4] dictates, to promote his own career of theo-
    ries.

Yeah, maybe I'll write about Miami, as I wrote about Birmingham,[5]
But it'll be because I want to write about Miami, not because somebody
    says I ought to.

Yeah, I write about love. What's wrong with love?   25
If we had more loving, we'd have more Black babies to become Black broth-
    ers and sisters and build the Black family.

When people love, they bathe with sweet-smelling soap, splash their bod-
    ies with perfume or cologne,
Shave, and comb their hair, and put on gleaming silken garments,
Speak softly and kindly and study their beloved to anticipate and satisfy her
    every desire.
After loving they're relaxed and happy and friends with all the world.   30
What's wrong with love, beauty, joy, or peace?

If Josephine had given Napoleon more loving, he wouldn't have sown the
    meadows of Europe with skulls.
If Hitler had been happy in love, he wouldn't have baked people in ovens.[6]
So don't tell me it's trivial and a cop-out to write about love and not about
    Miami.

A poet is not a jukebox.   35
A poet is not a jukebox.
I repeat, A poet is not a jukebox for someone to shove a quarter in his ear
    and get the tune they want to hear,
Or to pat on the head and call "a good little Revolutionary,"
Or to give a Kuumba Liberation Award.[7]

A poet is not a *jukebox*.   40
A poet is *not* a jukebox.
A *poet* is not a jukebox.

So don't tell *me* what to write.

1981

---

4. Flunky, minor civil servant.
5. See note 1, above.
6. Napoleon, French conqueror of Europe, married Josephine in 1796 and divorced her in 1809; gas ovens were only one feature of Adolf Hitler's extermination camps.
7. Randall received a Kuumba Award in 1973.

WILLIAM STAFFORD
b. 1914

Some poets rebel against the world, against society, against matter, against time, and get their power from such rebelliousness. William Stafford sees no necessity for this. "Your job is to find what the world is trying to be," he is told in "Vocation," and this aptly characterizes his aim. "Even the flaws were good—" he remarks in "At the Fair," and acceptance of life's terms is ingrained in him. He sees the world with the eyes of someone who has lived much in the country as if it were a local habitation, sparsely populated, where its denizens can feel at home. "In scenery I like flat country. / In life I don't like much to happen" ("Passing Remark").

There is no seeking after grandeur; his poetry, he says, is "much like talk, with some enhancement." Nor does he often seek a radiant view of creation in the manner of the seventeenth-century Traherne. He allies himself rather with Thomas Hardy, who he says "is my most congenial landmark" and has the same strong sense of place. (He has little, however, of Hardy's irony.)

William Stafford was born in Hutchinson, Kansas, on January 17, 1914. After taking two degrees at the University of Kansas, he took a doctorate at the University of Iowa. His generally accepting attitude did not prevent his being a conscientious objector during the war. His first book was not published until 1959, when he was forty-five, but he has published a great deal during the ensuing years. His poems mostly have a non-urban locale, and he lives on a lake in Oregon, teaching at Lewis and Clark College in Portland.

Traveling through the Dark

Traveling through the dark I found a deer
dead on the edge of the Wilson River road.
It is usually best to roll them into the canyon:
that road is narrow; to swerve might make more dead.

By glow of the tail-light I stumbled back of the car   5
and stood by the heap, a doe, a recent killing;
she had stiffened already, almost cold.
I dragged her off; she was large in the belly.

My fingers touching her side brought me the reason—
her side was warm; her fawn lay there waiting,   10
alive, still, never to be born.
Beside that mountain road I hesitated.

The car aimed ahead its lowered parking lights;
under the hood purred the steady engine.
I stood in the glare of the warm exhaust turning red;   15
around our group I could hear the wilderness listen.

I thought hard for us all—my only swerving—,
then pushed her over the edge into the river.

1960

At the Bomb Testing Site

At noon in the desert a panting lizard
waited for history, its elbows tense,
watching the curve of a particular road
as if something might happen.

It was looking for something farther off   5
than people could see, an important scene
acted in stone for little selves
at the flute end of consequences.

There was just a continent without much on it
under a sky that never cared less.   10
Ready for a change, the elbows waited.
The hands gripped hard on the desert.

                                                    1966

Monuments for a Friendly Girl at a Tenth Grade Party

The only relics left are those long
spangled seconds our school clock chipped out
when you crossed the social hall
and we found each other alive,
by our glances never to accept our town's   5
ways, torture for advancement,
nor ever again be prisoners by choice.

Now I learn you died
serving among the natives of Garden City,
Kansas, part of a Peace Corps   10
before governments thought of it.

Ruth, over the horizon your friends eat
foreign chaff and have addresses like titles,
but for you the crows and hawks patrol
the old river. May they never   15
forsake you, nor you need monuments
other than this I make, and the one
I hear clocks chip in that world we found.

                                                    1970

Report to Crazy Horse[1]

All the Sioux were defeated. Our clan
got poor, but a few got richer.
They fought two wars. I did not
take part. No one remembers our vision

---

1. Native American chieftain (1849?–1877), who led the Oglala Sioux against General George Custer at the battle of Little Big Horn (1876), the battle in which Custer was killed. Crazy Horse was killed a year later, resisting arrest.

or even your real name. Now
the children go to town and like
loud music. I married a Christian.

Crazy Horse, it is not fair
to hide a new vision from you.
In our schools we are learning
to take aim when we talk, and we have
found out our enemies. They shift when
words do; they even change and hide
in every person. A teacher here says
hurt or scorned people are places
where real enemies hide. He says
we should not hurt or scorn anyone,
but help them. And I will tell you
in a brave way, the way Crazy Horse
talked: that teacher is right.

I will tell you a strange thing:
at the rodeo, close to the grandstand,
I saw a farm lady scared by a blown
piece of paper; and at that place
horses and policemen were no longer
frightening, but suffering faces were,
and the hunched-over backs of the old.

Crazy Horse, tell me if I am right:
these are the things we thought we were
doing something about.

In your life you saw many strange things,
and I will tell you another: now I salute
the white man's flag. But when I salute
I hold my hand alertly on the heartbeat
and remember all of us and how we depend
on a steady pulse together. There are those
who salute because they fear other flags
or mean to use ours to chase them:
I must not allow my part of saluting
to mean this. All of our promises,
our generous sayings to each other, our
honorable intentions—these I affirm
when I salute. At these times it is like
shutting my eyes and joining a religious
colony at prayer in the gray dawn
in the deep aisles of a church.

Now I have told you about new times.
Yes, I know others will report
different things. They have been caught
by weak ways. I tell you straight
the way it is now, and it is our way,
the way we were trying to find.

The chokecherries along our valley
still bear a bright fruit. There is good
pottery clay north of here. I remember   55
our old places. When I pass the Musselshell[2]
I run my hand along those old grooves in the rock.

                                                                    1973

After Arguing against the Contention That Art Must Come from Discontent

Whispering to each handhold, "I'll be back,"
I go up the cliff in the dark. One place
I loosen a rock and listen a long time
till it hits, faint in the gulf, but the rush
of the torrent almost drowns it out, and the wind—   5
I almost forgot the wind: it tears at your side
or it waits and then buffets; you sag outward. . . .

I remember they said it would be hard. I scramble
by luck into a little pocket out of
the wind and begin to beat on the stones   10
with my scratched numb hands, rocking back and forth
in silent laughter there in the dark—
"Made it again!" Oh how I love this climb!
—the whispering to stones, the drag, the weight
as your muscles crack and ease on, working   15
right. They are back there, discontent,
waiting to be driven forth. I pound
on the earth, riding the earth past the stars:
"Made it again! Made it again!"

                                                                    1982

2. In Montana.

RANDALL JARRELL
1914–1965

After Randall Jarrell's death his friend Robert Lowell described him as the most "heartbreaking" poet of his generation, and his friend and teacher John Crowe Ransom spoke of Jarrell's "great flair for the poetry of desperation."[1] Many of Jarrell's early poems were written out of his experience of the Second World War; they are about the losses of war, about young men made childlike by the nearness of death and their obligations as killers. Many of Jarrell's later poems are dramatic monologues which express the painful transformations of life and our desire to be changed into something that we once were or that we ache to become.

Randall Jarrell was born in Nashville, Tennessee, on May 16, 1914. His family soon moved to California, his parents were divorced, and he spent a year or so in Hollywood with grandparents and a great-grandmother. His long poem "The Lost

1. *Randall Jarrell, 1914–1965*, ed. R. Lowell et al., New York, 1967, pp. 103, 160.

World" is a recollection, with echoes of *The Prelude*, in which glimpses of papier-
mâché dinosaurs and pterodactyls and an afternoon spent playing with the Metro-
Goldwyn-Mayer lion are the counterparts to Wordsworth's pastoral. Jarrell returned
to Nashville, where he spent a somewhat drab Depression childhood. His refuge was
books and the local public library. He later wrote two poems about the child as
reader, and other poems refer frequently to books which most people read when
they are very young: *Kim, The Wind in the Willows*, Grimm's *Fairy Tales*. The creatures of fairy tales throng Jarrell's poetry—exiled children, witches, dragons, helpful
animals; they live in a world which is sometimes hostile yet capable of being magically transformed.

Jarrell studied at Vanderbilt University, moving from psychology to English. In
1937–39 he taught at Kenyon College, and his friends there—John Crowe Ransom,
Robert Lowell, and the novelist Peter Taylor—have all written of his gaiety, learning, and bright assurance. In 1942 he published his first book of poems, *Blood from
a Stranger*, and enlisted in the Army Air Corps. He washed out as a pilot, then
served as a control tower operator working with B-29 crews.

The poet Robert Fitzgerald described Jarrell as "practically the only American
poet able to cope with the Second Great War."[2] The war poems are to be found in
two books, *Little Friend, Little Friend* (1945) and *Losses* (1948). The epigraph for the
first is taken from an exchange between a bomber and its fighter escort: ". . . Then I
heard the bomber call me in: 'Little Friend, Little Friend, I got two engines on fire.
Can you see me, Little Friend?' I said, 'I'm crossing right over you. Let's go home.' "
"Losses" is the stock term for military casualties—as in "Our losses were light today"—
and both titles suggest Jarrell's concentration on the murderous mechanisms of war
and the diminished, helpless men who operate them.

After the war in 1946 Jarrell taught at Sarah Lawrence and served as acting literary
editor of the *Nation*. He had, according to Lowell, a "deadly hand for killing what he
despised."[3] His reviews—now collected in *Kipling, Auden, & Co.: Essays and Reviews
1935–1964* (1980)—were hortatory, sometimes cruel, spattered with allusions, full of
memorable epigrams and wisecracks. His contempt for bad poetry—and his pity for
those who were satisfied with it—is explained by a complete devotion to imaginative
literature. He believes that "Human life without some form of poetry is not human
life but animal existence."[4] Poetry may perhaps be our chief defense against that
"want of imagination, that inaccessibility to experience, of which each of us who dies
a natural death will die."[5] His most influential critical essays, those on Whitman and
Frost, are richly documented, passionately argued appeals to readers to pay attention
to poets who were neglected or improperly appreciated because fashionable criticism
didn't know what to do with them.

From 1947 until his death Randall Jarrell taught at the Women's College of the
University of North Carolina at Greensboro; he was occasionally absent on teaching
assignments at other colleges and universities. In addition to his poetry and criticism,
he published a novel, *Pictures from an Institution* (1954), and several books for children. In 1965 he was struck by a car and died on October 14. His last book of poems,
The Lost World, was published in 1966.

In a brief catalogue of some of the perplexities which face us when we trace the
development of modern poetry Jarrell includes the "dramatic monologue, which once
had depended for its effect upon being a departure from the norm," and has now
become "in one form or another the norm."[6] Certainly it becomes the norm for
Jarrell's later poetry. The last poem of Jarrell's last book, "Thinking of the Lost World,"
is a meditation of what mortal man can regain from the past by an act of loving
memory.

2. The same, p. 75.
3. The same, p. 103.
4. *Poetry and the Age*, New York, 1953, p. 22.

5. The same, p. 12.
6. The same.

The Death of the Ball Turret Gunner[1]

From my mother's sleep I fell into the State,
And I hunched in its belly till my wet fur froze.
Six miles from earth, loosed from its dream of life,
I woke to black flak and the nightmare fighters.
When I died they washed me out of the turret with a hose.   5

1945

Eighth Air Force[2]

If, in an odd angle of the hutment,
A puppy laps the water from a can
Of flowers, and the drunk sergeant shaving
Whistles *O Paradiso!*[3]—shall I say that man
Is not as men have said: a wolf to man?   5

The other murderers troop in yawning;
Three of them play Pitch, one sleeps, and one
Lies counting missions, lies there sweating
Till even his heart beats: One; One; One.
O murderers! . . . Still, this is how it's done.   10

This is a war. . . . But since these play, before they die,
Like puppies with their puppy; since, a man,
I did as these have done, but did not die—
I will content the people as I can
And give up these to them: Behold the man![4]   15

I have suffered, in a dream, because of him,
Many things;[5] for this last saviour, man,
I have lied as I lie now. But what is lying?
Men wash their hands, in blood, as best they can:
I find no fault in this just man.   20

1948

A Girl in a Library[6]

An object among dreams, you sit here with your shoes off
And curl your legs up under you; your eyes

1. "A ball turret was a plexiglass sphere set into
the belly of a B-17 or B-24, and inhabited by two
.50 caliber machine-guns and one man, a short
small man. When this gunner tracked with his
machine guns a fighter attacking his bomber from
below, he revolved with the turret; hunched
upside-down in his little sphere, he looked like
the foetus in the womb. The fighters which attacked
him were armed with cannon firing explosive shells.
The hose was a steam hose" (Jarrell's note).
2. " 'Eighth Air Force' is a poem about the air
force which bombed the continent from England.
The man who lies counting missions has one to go
before being sent home. The phrases from the
Gospels compare such criminals and scapegoats as
these with that earlier criminal and scapegoat about
whom the gospels were written" (Jarrell's note).
And, later, Jarrell remarked: " 'Eighth Air Force'

expresses better than any other of the poems I
wrote about the war what I felt about the war."
3. An operatic aria.
4. Pilate offered the Jews their choice whether
Jesus or Barabbas should be released, and the
people chose Barabbas. "Pilate therefore went forth
again, and said to them, Behold, I bring him forth
to you, that you may know that I find no fault in
him. Then came Jesus forth, wearing the crown of
thorns, and the purple robe. And Pilate said unto
them, Behold the man!" (John 19:4–5).
5. Just before calling on the Jews to decide
between Jesus and Barabbas, Pilate received a
message from his wife: "Have nothing to do with
that just man: for I have suffered many things this
day in a dream because of him" (Matthew 27:19).
6. " 'A Girl in a Library' is a poem about the
New World and the Old: about a girl, a student of

Close for a moment, your face moves toward sleep . . .
You are very human.
                         But my mind, gone out in tenderness,
Shrinks from its object with a thoughtful sigh.   5
This is a waist the spirit breaks its arm on.
The gods themselves, against you, struggle in vain.[7]
This broad low strong-boned brow; these heavy eyes;
These calves, grown muscular with certainties;
This nose, three medium-sized pink strawberries   10
—But I exaggerate. In a little you will leave:
I'll hear, half squeal, half shriek, your laugh of greeting—
Then, *decrescendo,* bars of that strange speech
In which each sound sets out to seek each other,
Murders its own father, marries its own mother,   15
And ends as one grand transcendental vowel.[8]

(Yet for all I know, the Egyptian Helen spoke so.)
As I look, the world contracts around you;
I see Brünnhilde had brown braids and glasses
She used for studying; Salome straight brown bangs,   20
A calf's brown eyes, and sturdy light-brown limbs
Dusted with cinnamon, an apple-dumpling's . . .
Many a beast has gnawn a leg off and got free,
Many a dolphin curved up from Necessity—
The trap has closed about you, and you sleep.   25
If someone questioned you, *What doest thou here?*
You'd knit your brows like an orangoutang
(But not so sadly; not so thoughtfully)
And answer with a pure heart, guilelessly:
I'm studying. . . .
                         If only you were not!   30

Assignments,
            recipes,
                    the *Official Rulebook*
Of Basketball—ah, let them go; you needn't mind.
The soul has no assignments, neither cooks
Nor referees: it wastes its time.
                         It wastes its time.
Here in this enclave there are centuries   35
For you to waste: the short and narrow stream
Of Life meanders into a thousand valleys
Of all that was, or might have been, or is to be.
The books, just leafed through, whisper endlessly . . .
Yet it is hard. One sees in your blurred eyes   40
The "uneasy half-soul" Kipling saw in dogs'.[9]

Home Economics and Physical Education, who has
fallen asleep in the library of a Southern college;
about a woman who looks out of one book, Pushkin's *Eugen Onegin,* at this girl asleep among so
many; and about the *I* of the poem, a man somewhere between the two" (Jarrell's note).
     7. From *The Maid of Orleans,* a play by Fried-
rich Schiller (1759–1805): "With stupidity the gods
themselves struggle in vain."
     8. Jarrell's analogy between the girl's way of
talking and an operatic aria is followed by three
comparisons between her and three operatic heroines—the Egyptian Helen, Brünnhilde, and
Salome—whose love led to the deaths of the men
they loved.
     9. Alludes to Rudyard Kipling's poem, "Suppli-
cation of the Black Aberdeen," in which the dog
prays to his master not to leave him, and attributes to him the godlike power of having made "This
dim, distressed half-soul that hurts me so."

One sees it, in the glass, in one's own eyes.
In rooms alone, in galleries, in libraries,
In tears, in searchings of the heart, in staggering joys
We memorize once more our old creation,   45
Humanity: with what yawns the unwilling
Flesh puts on its spirit, O my sister!

So many dreams! And not one troubles
Your sleep of life? no self stares shadowily
From these worn hexahedrons, beckoning   50
With false smiles, tears? . . .
                              Meanwhile Tatyana
Larina[1] (gray eyes nickel with the moonlight
That falls through the willows onto Lensky's tomb;
Now young and shy, now old and cold and sure)
Asks, smiling: "But what is she dreaming of, fat thing?"   55
I answer: She's not fat. She isn't dreaming.
She purrs or laps or runs, all in her sleep;
Believes, awake, that she is beautiful;
She never dreams.
                  Those sunrise-colored clouds
Around man's head[2]—that inconceivable enchantment   60
From which, at sunset, we come back to life
To find our graves dug, families dead, selves dying:
Of all this, Tanya, she is innocent.
For nineteen years she's faced reality:
They look alike already.
                        They say, man wouldn't be   65
The best thing in the world—and isn't he?—
If he were not too good for it.[3] But she
—She's good enough for it.
                          And yet sometimes
Her sturdy form, in its pink strapless formal,
Is as if bathed in moonlight—modulated   70
Into a form of joy, a Lydian mode;[4]
This Wooden Mean's a kind, furred animal
That speaks, in the Wild of things, delighting riddles
To the soul that listens, trusting . . .
                                        Poor senseless Life:
When, in the last light sleep of dawn, the messenger   75
Comes with his message, you will not awake.
He'll give his feathery whistle, shake you hard,
You'll look with wide eyes at the dewy yard
And dream, with calm slow factuality:
"Today's Commencement. My bachelor's degree   80
In Home Ec., my doctorate of philosophy

---

1. The heroine of Pushkin's *Eugen Onegin*,
Tatyana (or Tanya) Larina is a naïve country girl
who is infatuated with the melancholy, cynical
Onegin, but is rejected by him; he kills her friend's
lover, Lensky, in a duel, and then travels abroad.
She marries and becomes a sophisticated beauty,
and on his return Onegin becomes infatuated with
her, but though she still loves him she refuses to
betray her husband.
2. From Wordsworth's *Ode: Intimations of*
Immortality: "But trailing clouds of glory do we
come / From God, who is our home." He believed
that children are endowed with a special awareness of nature that dims and dies after they are
born and grow to adulthood.
3. Jarrell says in his notes that this is a quotation but declines to identify it.
4. A variant of the major scale in music, whose
softer tone has been used by many composers to
express a subdued, religious joy.

In Phys. Ed.
        [Tanya, they won't even *scan*]
Are waiting for me. . . ."
                    Oh, Tatyana,
The Angel comes: better to squawk like a chicken
Than to say with truth, "But I'm a *good* girl,"   85
And Meets his Challenge with a last firm strange
Uncomprehending smile; and—then, then!—see
The blind date that has stood you up: your life.
(For all this, if it isn't, perhaps, life,
Has yet, at least, a language of its own   90
Different from the books'; worse than the books'.)
And yet, the ways we miss our lives are life.
Yet . . . yet . . .
                to have one's life add up to *yet!*

You sigh a shuddering sigh. Tatyana murmurs,
"Don't cry, little peasant"; leaves us with a swift   95
"Good-bye, good-bye . . . Ah, don't think ill of me . . ."
Your eyes open: you sit here thoughtlessly.

I love you—and yet—and yet—I love you.

Don't cry, little peasant. Sit and dream.
One comes, a finger's width beneath your skin,   100
To the braided maidens singing as they spin;
There sound the shepherd's pipe, the watchman's rattle[5]
Across the short dark distance of the years.
I am a thought of yours: and yet, you do not think . . .
The firelight of a long, blind, dreaming story   105
Lingers upon your lips; and I have seen
Firm, fixed forever in your closing eyes,
The Corn King beckoning to his Spring Queen.[6]

                                        1951

Next Day

Moving from Cheer to Joy, from Joy to All,[7]
I take a box
And add it to my wild rice, my Cornish game hens.
The slacked or shorted, basketed, identical
Food-gathering flocks   5
Are selves I overlook. Wisdom, said William James,

Is learning what to overlook.[8] And I am wise
If that is wisdom.
Yet somehow, as I buy All from these shelves
And the boy takes it to my station wagon,   10

5. The "braided maidens," shepherd, and watchman are minor characters in Richard Wagner's operas who have good tunes to sing but are utterly unaware of the significance of the events which transpire around them.
6. "The Corn King and the Spring Queen went by many names; in the beginning they were the man and woman who, after ruling for a time, were torn to pieces and scattered over the fields in order that the grain might grow" (Jarrell's note).
7. Names of detergents.
8. William James (1842–1910) was an American philosopher and psychologist; the quotation, slightly paraphrased, is from *The Principles of Psychology* (1890).

What I've become
Troubles me even if I shut my eyes.

When I was young and miserable and pretty
And poor, I'd wish
What all girls wish: to have a husband,   15
A house and children. Now that I'm old, my wish
Is womanish:
That the boy putting groceries in my car

See me. It bewilders me he doesn't see me.
For so many years   20
I was good enough to eat: the world looked at me
And its mouth watered. How often they have undressed me,
The eyes of strangers!
And, holding their flesh within my flesh, their vile

Imaginings within my imagining,   25
I too have taken
The chance of life. Now the boy pats my dog
And we start home. Now I am good.
The last mistaken,
Ecstatic, accidental bliss, the blind   30

Happiness that, bursting, leaves upon the palm
Some soap and water—
It was so long ago, back in some Gay
Twenties, Nineties, I don't know . . . Today I miss
My lovely daughter   35
Away at school, my sons away at school,

My husband away at work—I wish for them.
The dog, the maid,
And I go through the sure unvarying days
At home in them. As I look at my life,   40
I am afraid
Only that it will change, as I am changing:

I am afraid, this morning, of my face.
It looks at me
From the rear-view mirror, with the eyes I hate,   45
The smile I hate. Its plain, lined look
Of gray discovery
Repeats to me: "You're old." That's all, I'm old.

And yet I'm afraid, as I was at the funeral
I went to yesterday.   50
My friend's cold made-up face, granite among its flowers,
Her undressed, operated-on, dressed body
Were my face and body.
As I think of her I hear her telling me

How young I seem; I *am* exceptional;   55
I think of all I have.
But really no one is exceptional,

No one has anything, I'm anybody,
I stand beside my grave
Confused with my life, that is commonplace and solitary.   60

                                                                          1965

JOHN BERRYMAN
1914–1972

John Berryman's poetry has an air of authority although it is often extremely eccentric and uneven. He succeeded in making the tergiversations of his moody self seem momentous and fascinating, and won a considerable following. Like Robert Lowell, he wrote an intensely personal kind of verse. If it was theatrical, theatricality was an aspect of his personality, and it was only through that aspect that he could express himself.

Berryman was born John Smith on October 25, 1914, in McAlester, Oklahoma. He lived till the age of ten in Anadarko, a nearby town where his father, also named John Smith, was a banker and his mother a schoolteacher. Then the family moved to Tampa, Florida. It was here that his parents' quarrels, furious for years, ended when his father shot himself outside his son's window. In the penultimate poem of *His Toy, His Dream, His Rest,* Berryman described a visit to his father's grave and commented, with unmitigated bitterness, "I spit upon this dreadful banker's grave / who shot his heart out in a Florida dawn." The widow brought John and a younger son to Gloucester, Massachusetts, and then to New York City. Here she married another banker, John Berryman, whose name the children took. The stepfather was soon to divorce his wife, but he remained kind to the children. He sent John to a private school in Connecticut (South Kent School), and then to Columbia College. John Berryman received a B.A. in 1936, and then attended Clare College, Cambridge, on a fellowship. When he returned to the United States he taught for a year at Wayne State, then from 1940 to 1943 at Harvard, and following that, for almost ten years, off and on, at Princeton. From 1955 till his death he taught at the University of Minnesota. A nervous, tense man prone to overdrinking, Berryman lived turbulently. He was married three times. In later life, he was converted back to Roman Catholicism, the faith of his childhood. On January 7, 1972, he threw himself from a bridge in Minneapolis to end his life at the age of fifty-seven.

The influence of Yeats, Auden, Hopkins, Crane, and Pound on him was strong, and Berryman's own voice—by turns nerve-racked and sportive—took some time to be heard. His voice has always been an amalgam, first of other poets but later of Berryman's various selves, formal and informal in unexpected jumps. He shifts from educated language to wild dialect, and almost before he makes a statement begins to question and sometimes to mock it. These characteristics, expressed in contorted syntax, give the poetry an impressive air of painful self-involvement.

Berryman's major work was a series of Dream Songs which appeared in two separate volumes and number 385. They form, like his friend Robert Lowell's *Notebook,* a poetic journal, and represent, half phantasmagorically, the changes in Berryman's mood and attitude. Or as he puts it more grandly in No. 366, they are meant "to terrify and comfort." The tone is often wildly humorous, but turns quickly towards melancholy again. When the first volume, *77 Dream Songs,* was misinterpreted as simply autobiography, Berryman wrote in a prefatory note to the sequel, "The poem then, whatever its cast of characters, is essentially about an imaginary character (not the poet, not me) named Henry, a white American in early middle age sometimes in blackface, who has suffered an irreversible loss and talks about himself sometimes in the first person, sometimes in the third, sometimes even in the second; he has a friend, never named, who addresses himself as Mr. Bones and variants thereof."

("Mr. Bones" is a name from the minstrel show circuit.) When Berryman was asked about the poem's seeming lack of unity, he insisted that it "has a plot. Its plot is the personality of Henry as he moves on in the world," from the age of forty-one to fifty-one. Domestic difficulties, the deaths of friends, personal anxieties, all are fused into verse that thrives on interruptions in syntax, brief asides, and knowing winks. These sustained irregularities are balanced against a surprisingly strict six-line stanza (borrowed, as Berryman said, from Yeats), in which lines 1, 2, 4, and 5 are in pentameter, lines 3 and 6 in trimeter. Each Dream Song is 18 lines long.

Berryman insists that he and his character Henry are not the same; certainly some stylization has occurred, though Berryman's traits are still easily recognizable. The poetry is confessional and neurotic, but is also learned, both in mobilizing traditional literary resources and in savoring all the resources of contemporary diction. Berryman was well versed in English and American literature; he wrote a biography of Stephen Crane (1950) in which he attempted to analyze Crane's psychology as he analyzed his own. What seems likely to survive of his poetry is its pungent and many-leveled portrait of a complex personality which, for all its eccentricity, stayed close to the center of the intellectual and emotional life of the mid-century and after.

A Professor's Song

(. . rabid or dog-dull.) Let me tell you how
The Eighteenth Century couplet ended. Now
Tell me. Troll me the sources of that Song—
Assigned last week—by Blake. Come, come along,
Gentlemen. (Fidget and huddle, do. Squint soon.)   5
I want to end these fellows all by noon.

'That deep romantic chasm'[1]—an early use;
The word is from the French, by your abuse
Fished out a bit. (Red all your eyes. O when?)
'A poet is a man speaking to men':[2]   10
But I am then a poet, am I not?—
Ha ha. The radiator, please. Well, what?

Alive now—no-Blake would have written prose,
But movement following movement crisply flows,
So much the better, better the much so,   15
As burbleth Mozart. Twelve. The class can go.
Until I meet you, then, in Upper Hell
Convulsed, foaming immortal blood: farewell.

1958

From THE DREAM SONGS

14

Life, friends, is boring. We must not say so.
After all, the sky flashes, the great sea yearns,
we ourselves flash and yearn,
and moreover my mother told me as a boy
(repeatedly) 'Ever to confess you're bored   5
means you have no

---

1. Quoted from Coleridge's "Kubla Khan," line 12.   2. Quoted from Wordsworth's preface to the second edition of *Lyrical Ballads*.

Inner Resources.' I conclude now I have no
inner resources, because I am heavy bored.
Peoples bore me,
literature bores me, especially great literature,   10
Henry bores me, with his plights & gripes
as bad as achilles,[3]

who loves people and valiant art, which bores me.
And the tranquil hills, & gin, look like a drag
and somehow a dog   15
has taken itself & its tail considerably away
into mountains or sea or sky, leaving
behind: me, wag.

1964

16

Henry's pelt was put on sundry walls
where it did much resemble Henry and
them persons was delighted.
Especially his long & glowing tail
by all them was admired, and visitors.   5
They whistled: This is *it*!

Golden, whilst your frozen daiquiris
whir at midnight, gleams on you his fur
& silky & black.
Mission accomplished, pal.   10
My molten yellow & moonless bag,
drained, hangs at rest.

Collect in the cold depths barracuda. Ay,
in Sealdah Station some possessionless
children survive to die.
The Chinese communes hum. Two daiquiris
withdrew into a corner of the gorgeous room
and one told the other a lie.

1964

75[4]

Turning it over, considering, like a madman
Henry put forth a book.
No harm resulted from this.
Neither the menstruating   stars (nor man) was moved
at once.   5
Bare dogs drew closer for a second look

and performed their friendly operations there.
Refreshed, the bark rejoiced.
Seasons went and came.
Leaves fell, but only a few.   10

3. Achilles, the Greek warrior whose strength
was needed if the Trojans were to be defeated,
withdrew from fighting over a slight from the
Greeks' general, King Agamemnon.
    4. This Dream Song is dedicated to Berryman's
close friend Saul Bellow, the American novelist.

Something remarkable about this
unshedding bulky bole-proud blue-green moist

thing made by savage & thoughtful
surviving Henry
began to strike the passers from despair   15
so that sore on their shoulders old men hoisted
six-foot sons and polished women called
small girls to dream awhile toward the flashing & bursting tree!

1964

76

Henry's Confession

Nothin very bad happen to me lately.
How you explain that?—I explain that, Mr Bones,
terms o' your bafflin odd sobriety.
Sober as man can get, no girls, no telephones,
what could happen bad to Mr Bones?   5
—If life is a handkerchief sandwich,

in a modesty of death I join my father
who dared so long agone leave me.
A bullet on a concrete stoop
close by a smothering southern sea   10
spreadeagled on an island, by my knee.
—You is from hunger, Mr Bones,

I offers you this handkerchief, now set
your left foot by my right foot,
shoulder to shoulder, all that jazz,   15
arm in arm, by the beautiful sea,[5]
hum a little, Mr Bones.
—I saw nobody coming, so I went instead.

1964

149

This world is gradually becoming a place
where I do not care to be any more. Can Delmore die?[6]
I don't suppose
in all them years a day went ever by
without a loving thought for him. Welladay.   5
In the brightness of his promise,

unstained, I saw him thro' the mist of the actual
blazing with insight, warm with gossip
thro' all our Harvard years
when both of us were just becoming known   10

---

5. A popular song of 1914.
6. Delmore Schwartz was a close friend of Berryman's and in 1940 helped to get him his first
teaching job, at Harvard. *His Toy, His Dream, His*

Rest, the second book of Berryman's *Dream Songs*
(in which this poem appears), is in part dedicated
"to the sacred memory of Delmore Schwartz."

I got him out of a police-station once, in Washington, the world is *tref*[7]
and grief too astray for tears.

I imagine you have heard the terrible news,
that Delmore Schwartz is dead, miserably & alone,   15
in New York: he sang me a song
'I am the Brooklyn poet Delmore Schwartz
Harms & the child I sing,[8] two parents' torts'
when he was young & gift-strong.

          1968

312

I have moved to Dublin to have it out with you,
majestic Shade,[9] You whom I read so well
so many years ago,
did I read your lesson right? did I see through
your phases to the real? your heaven, your hell   5
did I enquire properly into?

For years then I forgot you, I put you down,
ingratitude is the necessary curse
of making things new:[10]
I brought my family to see me through,   10
I brought my homage & my soft remorse,
I brought a book or two

only, including in the end your last
strange poems made under the shadow of death
Your high figures float   15
again across my mind and all your past
fills my walled garden with your honey breath
wherein I move, a mote.

          1968

7. Ritually unclean, according to Jewish law.
8. A parody of the opening words of Virgil's *Aeneid,* "Arms and the man I sing."
9. W. B. Yeats, whom Berryman called his first and last influence. In 1936, while a student at Clare College, Cambridge University, Berryman had tea with Yeats, an event celebrated in Dream Song 215.
10. An adaptation of Ezra Pound's famous slogan, "Make it new."

DYLAN THOMAS
1914–1953

Dylan Thomas used to say in his American readings that his poems had to be read either very soft or very loud, and it is true that he has none of the middle style of Hardy or Auden. He is comparable in some ways to Hart Crane, though he is less interested than Crane in the ineffable ecstasies beyond verbal expression. He liked to speak of his poems as narratives, as in his reply to a questionnaire in 1934: "Poetry is the rhythmic, inevitably narrative, movement from an overclothed blindness to a naked vision that depends in its intensity on the strength of the labour put into the creation of the poetry. My poetry is, or should be, useful to me for one reason: it is the record of my individual struggle from darkness towards some measure of light. . . ."[1]

1. Quoted in Constantine Fitzgibbon, *The Life of Dylan Thomas,* Boston, 1965, p. 142.

At the root of his poetry is a sense of doubleness, of womb and tomb, of the worm as penis and as death, which he embodied in one of his earliest published poems, "The Force That through the Green Fuse Drives the Flower." Out of such paradoxes he builds by crosshatching: as he wrote in a letter, "I make one image—though 'make' is not the word; I let, perhaps, an image be 'made' emotionally in me and then apply to it what intellectual and critical forces I possess—let it breed another, let that image contradict the first, make, of the third image bred out of the other two together, a fourth contradictory image, and let them all, within my imposed formal limits, conflict. Each image holds within it the seed of its own destruction, and my dialectical method, as I understand it, is a constant building up and breaking down of the images that come out of the central seed, which is itself destructive and constructive at the same time . . . Out of the inevitable conflict of images— . . . the womb of war—I try to make that momentary peace which is a poem."[2] He insisted, in a Note to his *Collected Poems* (1952), that "These poems, with all their crudities, doubts, and confusions, are written for the love of Man and in praise of God, and I'd be a damn fool if they weren't."

Thomas was born October 27, 1914, in Swansea, Wales, which he described bitterly as "the smug darkness of a provincial town."[3] Thomas was educated at the Swansea Grammar School, which he left in 1931. His father, a schoolteacher, urged him to go to a university, but Thomas adduced the example of Bernard Shaw to justify his attempting to become a writer at once. His style, in fact, was formed by the time he was seventeen. In 1934 he published, at twenty, his first book, *18 Poems*, and won ecstatic praise from Edith Sitwell and others. He went to live in London in that year. In 1936 he met Caitlin Macnamara, a young Irishwoman whose temperament was as turbulent as his own; they married the following year, and subsequently had three children. Thomas wrote, besides poems, short stories, plays, and film scripts. The most successful was *Under Milk Wood*, a radio script depicting the residents of a small Welsh town by the sea from the middle of one night to middle of the next. He supported himself in his last years in part by long lecture tours in the United States, during which—drunk or sober—he gave magnificent readings of poems (mostly by other writers) on dozens of college campuses. His extravagant drinking gradually usurped most of his time, and chronic alcoholism helped bring about his early death on November 9, 1953, in New York City.

Dylan Thomas appears in modern poetry with the air of a "marvelous boy" (as Wordsworth described Chatterton). He knew no Welsh but he accepted the traditional role of the Welsh bard and was painted by Augustus John as wild and inspired. In fact, his verse played its bravura of language against tight verse forms and was always subjected to stern intellectual ordering. Thomas, a modest man, could berate himself in this way, as a "freak user of words, not a poet,"[4] but he usually felt that his verbal mannerisms were justified: "I am a painstaking, conscientious, involved and devious craftsman in words, however unsuccessful the result so often appears, and to whatever wrong uses I may apply my technical paraphernalia. I use everything and anything to make my poems work and move in the directions I want them to: old tricks, new tricks, puns, portmanteau-words, paradox, allusion, paranomasia, paragram, catachresis, slang, assonantal rhymes, vowel rhymes, sprung rhythm. Every device there is in language is there to be used if you will. Poets have got to enjoy themselves sometimes, and the twistings and convolutions of words, the inventions and contrivances, are all part of the joy that is part of the painful, voluntary work."[5]

The source of our Thomas texts is *The Poems of Dylan Thomas*, edited by Daniel Jones, New York, 1971.

2. Quoted in Henry Treece, *Dylan Thomas*, London, 1936, p. 37.
3. Fitzgibbon, p. 289.
4. The same, p. 120.
5. The same, p. 327.

The Hand That Signed the Paper

The hand that signed the paper felled a city;
Five sovereign fingers taxed the breath,
Doubled the globe of dead and halved a country;
These five kings did a king to death.

The mighty hand leads to a sloping shoulder,   5
The finger joints are cramped with chalk;
A goose's quill has put an end to murder
That put an end to talk.

The hand that signed the treaty bred a fever,
And famine grew, and locusts came;   10
Great is the hand that holds dominion over
Man by a scribbled name.

The five kings count the dead but do not soften
The crusted wound nor stroke the brow;
A hand rules pity as a hand rules heaven;   15
Hands have no tears to flow.

1933   1936

The Force That through the Green Fuse
Drives the Flower

The force that through the green fuse drives the flower
Drives my green age; that blasts the roots of trees
Is my destroyer.
And I am dumb to tell the crooked rose
My youth is bent by the same wintry fever.   5

The force that drives the water through the rocks
Drives my red blood; that dries the mouthing streams
Turns mine to wax.
And I am dumb to mouth unto my veins
How at the mountain spring the same mouth sucks.   10

The hand that whirls the water in the pool
Stirs the quicksand; that ropes the blowing wind
Hauls my shroud sail.
And I am dumb to tell the hanging man
How of my clay is made the hangman's lime.[1]   15

The lips of time leech to[2] the fountain head;
Love drips and gathers, but the fallen blood
Shall calm her sores.
And I am dumb to tell a weather's wind
How time has ticked a heaven round the stars.   20

And I am dumb to tell the lover's tomb
How at my sheet[3] goes the same crooked worm.

1933   1934

1. Quicklime poured in the graves of victims of the public hangman, to quicken decomposition.
2. That is, fasten onto, suck at.
3. Winding sheet (for a corpse).

The Hunchback in the Park[4]

The hunchback in the park
A solitary mister
Propped between trees and water
From the opening of the garden lock
That lets the trees and water enter   5
Until the Sunday sombre bell at dark[5]

Eating bread from a newspaper
Drinking water from the chained cup
That the children filled with gravel
In the fountain basin where I sailed my ship   10
Slept at night in a dog kennel
But nobody chained him up.

Like the park birds he came early
Like the water he sat down
And Mister they called Hey mister   15
The truant boys from the town
Running when he had heard them clearly
On out of sound

Past lake and rockery[6]
Laughing when he shook his paper   20
Hunchbacked in mockery
Through the loud zoo of the willow groves
Dodging the park keeper
With his stick that picked up leaves.

And the old dog sleeper   25
Alone between nurses and swans
While the boys among willows
Made the tigers jump out of their eyes
To roar on the rockery stones
And the groves were blue with sailors   30

Made all day until bell time
A woman figure without fault
Straight as a young elm
Straight and tall from his crooked bones
That she might stand in the night   35
After the locks and chains

All night in the unmade park
After the railings and shrubberies

---

4. "Though the details in this poem . . . could apply to almost any park, this particular park is undoubtedly Cwmdonkin, not far from the Thomas house. There was, indeed, a hunchback who seemed to have nowhere else to go, who stayed from the moment the park opened until it closed. Cwmdonkin Park was a favourite haunt of truants from Swansea Grammar School, because it was bordered on one side by a road that led directly to the school, but sometimes didn't. Thomas and I often met there to read poems to one another or write them, when, perhaps, we should have been learning Geography. But usually our amusements were more boisterous and less 'cultured.' " (*The Poems of Dylan Thomas*, ed. David Jones, New York, 1971, p. 271) Jones was a lifelong friend of Thomas's.
5. The bell that signals the closing of the park at night.
6. Rock garden.

The birds the grass the trees the lake
And the wild boys innocent as strawberries   40
Had followed the hunchback
To his kennel in the dark.

1941   1946

A Refusal to Mourn the Death, by Fire, of a Child in London

Never until the mankind making
Bird beast and flower
Fathering and all humbling darkness
Tells with silence the last light breaking
And the still hour   5
Is come of the sea tumbling in harness

And I must enter again the round
Zion[7] of the water bead
And the synagogue of the ear of corn
Shall I let pray the shadow of a sound   10
Or sow my salt seed
In the least valley of sackcloth to mourn

The majesty and burning of the child's death.
I shall not murder
The mankind of her going with a grave truth   15
Nor blaspheme down the stations of the breath
With any further
Elegy of innocence and youth.

Deep with the first dead lies London's daughter,
Robed in the long friends,   20
The grains beyond age, the dark veins of her mother,
Secret by the unmourning water
Of the riding Thames.[8]
After the first death, there is no other.

1945   1946

Fern Hill[9]

Now as I was young and easy under the apple boughs
About the lilting house and happy as the grass was green,
      The night above the dingle[1] starry,
            Time let me hail and climb
      Golden in the heydays of his eyes,   5
And honoured among wagons I was prince of the apple towns
And once below a time I lordly had the trees and leaves
            Trail with daisies and barley
      Down the rivers of the windfall light.

7. City of God.
8. River that flows through London.
9. A country house where the poet's aunt lived, and where he spent summer holidays as a boy.
1. Small wooded valley.

And as I was green and carefree, famous among the barns   10
About the happy yard and singing as the farm was home,
  In the sun that is young once only,
    Time let me play and be
  Golden in the mercy of his means,
And green and golden I was huntsman and herdsman, the calves   15
Sang to my horn, the foxes on the hills barked clear and cold,
    And the sabbath rang slowly
  In the pebbles of the holy streams.

All the sun long it was running, it was lovely, the hay
Fields high as the house, the tunes from the chimneys, it was air   20
  And playing, lovely and watery
    And fire green as grass.
  And nightly under the simple stars
As I rode to sleep the owls were bearing the farm away,
All the moon long I heard, blessed among stables, the nightjars   25
  Flying with the ricks,[2] and the horses
    Flashing into the dark.

And then to awake, and the farm, like a wanderer white
With the dew, come back, the cock on his shoulder: it was all
  Shining, it was Adam and maiden,   30
    The sky gathered again
  And the sun grew round that very day.
So it must have been after the birth of the simple light
In the first, spinning place, the spellbound horses walking warm
  Out of the whinnying green stable   35
    On to the fields of praise.

And honoured among foxes and pheasants by the gay house
Under the new made clouds and happy as the heart was long,
  In the sun born over and over,
    I ran my heedless ways,   40
  My wishes raced through the house high hay
And nothing I cared, at my sky blue trades, that time allows
In all his tuneful turning so few and such morning songs
    Before the children green and golden
    Follow him out of grace,   45

Nothing I cared, in the lamb white days, that time would take me
Up to the swallow thronged loft by the shadow of my hand,
  In the moon that is always rising,
    Nor that riding to sleep
  I should hear him fly with the high fields   50
And wake to the farm forever fled from the childless land.
Oh as I was young and easy in the mercy of his means,
    Time held me green and dying
    Though I sang in my chains like the sea.
1945   1946

---

2. Stacks of hay; "nightjars": nocturnal birds.

In My Craft or Sullen Art

In my craft or sullen art
Exercised in the still night
When only the moon rages
And the lovers lie abed
With all their griefs in their arms,   5
I labour by singing light
Not for ambition or bread
Or the strut and trade of charms
On the ivory stages
But for the common wages   10
Of their most secret heart.

Not for the proud man apart
From the raging moon I write
On these spindrift[3] pages
Nor for the towering dead   15
With their nightingales and psalms
But for the lovers, their arms
Round the griefs of the ages,
Who pay no praise or wages
Nor heed my craft or art.   20

1945   1946

Do Not Go Gentle into That Good Night[4]

Do not go gentle into that good night,
Old age should burn and rave at close of day;
Rage, rage against the dying of the light.

Though wise men at their end know dark is right,
Because their words had forked no lightning they   5
Do not go gentle into that good night.

Good men, the last wave by, crying how bright
Their frail deeds might have danced in a green bay,
Rage, rage against the dying of the light.

Wild men who caught and sang the sun in flight,   10
And learn, too late, they grieved it on its way,
Do not go gentle into that good night.

Grave men, near death, who see with blinding sight
Blind eyes could blaze like meteors and be gay,
Rage, rage against the dying of the light.   15

---

3. Driven, like sea spray, by the wind.
4. Thomas wrote at the time, "The only person I can't show the little enclosed poem to is, of course, my father, who doesn't know he's dying." Quoted by Jones, who goes on to add that Thomas's father "lingered for more than a year after this, and died on 15th December 1952 . . . It is significant that for this subject and on this occasion, Thomas deliberately chose to discipline himself by the use of a strict form, the villanelle" (*Poems of Dylan Thomas*, p. 275).

And you, my father, there on the sad height,
Curse, bless, me now with your fierce tears, I pray.
Do not go gentle into that good night.
Rage, rage against the dying of the light.

1951   1952

JUDITH WRIGHT
b. 1915

Some of the qualities of Judith Wright's verse derive from her childhood in a rural region of New South Wales in Australia. Living far from the nearest school, she was educated until the age of twelve by a correspondence course organized by the department of education for children of isolated families. She grew up loving the land and the wild animals, and trusting to her feelings for them. Having escaped a conventional education in her earlier years, when she attended the University of Sydney later she chose to take English literature alone rather than the usual variety of courses. Her marriage to the philosopher J. P. McKinney brought her in touch with a philosophy confirming her intimations that the mere intellectual analysis of our world picture has found its limit, and that the time has arrived rather for an intuitive or emotional bond with the world.

Her poems are perhaps the best to come out of Australia. They convey at times a radiant sense of oneness with the country, particularly that part of it in the east known as the New England Plateau. In "The Moving Image" Judith Wright identifies the poet with Tom of Bedlam, the seeming madman whose madness is the ultimate sanity. The sense of the poet as a convergence of outer and inner is explicit in "The Maker":

> . . . into myself I took
> all living things that are,

She laments the death of the wild country, as she regrets the dying out of aboriginal civilization in "Bora Ring," though she suggests that the aboriginal past still haunts the present, and curses it.

Judith Wright was born in Armidale, New South Wales, on May 31, 1915. She has deservedly received many awards for her verse. Her writings include, besides many books of verse, short stories, books for children, and essays, and she has edited several anthologies of Australian poetry.

Bora Ring[1]

The song is gone; the dance
is secret with the dancers in the earth,
the ritual useless, and the tribal story
lost in an alien tale.

Only the grass stands up   5
to mark the dancing-ring: the apple-gums
posture and mime a past corroboree,[2]
murmur a broken chant.

---

1. Site of initiation ceremonies held by Australian aborigines.

2. A nighttime ceremony, held by the aborigines; "apple-gums": Australian timber trees.

The hunter is gone: the spear
is splintered underground; the painted bodies   10
a dream the world breathed sleeping and forgot.
The nomad feet are still.

Only the rider's heart
halts at a sightless shadow, an unsaid word
that fastens in the blood the ancient curse,   15
the fear as old as Cain.[3]

1946

Flood Year

Walking up the driftwood beach at day's end
I saw it, thrust up out of a hillock of sand—
a frail bleached clench of fingers dried by wind—
the dead child's hand.

And they are mourning there still, though I forget,   5
the year of flood, the scoured ruined land,
the herds gone down the current, the farms drowned,
and the child never found.

When I was there the thick hurling waters
had gone back to the river, the farms were almost drained.   10
Banished half-dead cattle searched the dunes; it rained;
river and sea met with a wild sound.

Oh with a wild sound water flung into air
where sea met river; all the country round
no heart was quiet. I walked on the driftwood sand   15
and saw the pale crab crouched, and came to a stand
thinking, A child's hand. The child's hand.

1953

"Dove-Love"

The dove purrs—over and over the dove
purrs its declaration. The wind's tone
changes from tree to tree, the creek on stone
alters its sob and fall, but still the dove
goes insistently on, telling its love   5
        "I could eat you."

And in captivity, they say, doves do.
Gentle, methodical, starting with the feet
(the ham-pink succulent toes
on their thin stems of rose),
baring feather by feather the wincing meat: 10
        "I could eat you."

3. Son of Adam, who, in killing his brother Abel, was our first murderer (Genesis 4:1–16); "the ancient curse" is the curse of the Lord upon Cain.

That neat suburban head, that suit of grey,
watchful conventional eye and manicured claw—
these also rhyme with us. The doves play   15
on one repetitive note that plucks the raw
helpless nerve, their soft "I do. I do.
          I could eat you."

                                                           1962

The Beanstalk, Meditated Later[4]

torture, that we pray it may be mild.
The beans I carried home that careless day
I thought were toys, and I a clever child—
but mother scolded, throwing them away:
"The subtlest traps have just such pretty bait."   5
Well, she was right. The beanstalk reached a sky
where giants cheat us. We must skulk and wait
and steal our fortune back to mock them by.

Who was my father? See where the doubt leads—
the ladder grew so pat out of our garden   10
perhaps my mother recognized its seeds.
Giants have trampled earth and asked no pardon—
Well, nor did I. He took our family's gold.
I stole it back and saw the giant die.
(Four days to bury him.) Now I've grown old,   15
but still the giants trample in the sky.

Yes, still I hear them; and I meditate
(old, rich, respected, maudlin—says my son)
upon our generations and our fate.
Does each repeat the thing the last has done   20
though claiming he rejects it? Once I stood
beside my beanstalk—clever boy—and crowed
I'd killed the giant, Tom Thumb[5] whose luck was good;
but now—what farmer saved the seed I sowed?

For somewhere still that dizzy ladder grows—   25
pathway for tit-for-tat from here to there—
and what's the traffic on it, no man knows.
Sometimes I hug my gold in pure despair
watching my son—my cocky enemy—
big, ugly, boastful. It's the great strain   30
come out in him, I think. I watch, and he
watches me. The gold is in his brain.

I'll post a proclamation—advertise—
find that farmer, buy his whole year's crop,
burn the lot, and see the last seed dies.   35
But one seed—yes—I'll plant. That's for my son.

4. Compare the fairy tale of "Jack and the   5. Name given to Charles Sherwood Stratton,
Beanstalk."   a famous nineteenth-century midget.

I'll send him up it, wait; and when he's crawled
far enough, I'll lay the axe-blows on
and send him sprawling where his grandpa sprawled.

1966

Australia 1970

Die, wild country, like the eaglehawk,
dangerous till the last breath's gone,
clawing and striking. Die
cursing your captor through a raging eye.

Die like the tigersnake   5
that hisses such pure hatred from its pain
as fills the killer's dreams
with fear like suicide's invading stain.

Suffer, wild country, like the ironwood
that gaps the dozer-blade.[6]   10
I see your living soil ebb with the tree
to naked poverty.

Die like the soldier-ant
mindless and faithful to your million years.
Though we corrupt you with our torturing mind.   15
stay obstinate; stay blind.

For we are conquerors and self-poisoners
more than scorpion or snake
and dying of the venoms that we make
even while you die of us.   20

I praise the scoring drought, the flying dust,
the drying creek, the furious animal,
that they oppose us still;
that we are ruined by the thing we kill.

1970

6. Blade of a bulldozer.

P. K. PAGE
b. 1916

Margaret Atwood, another Canadian poet, describes Page as often appearing as a
"tranced observer who verges on mysticism."[1] If the word "mysticism" applies to
Page, it should not suggest a separation of body and spirit, but rather a vision in
which the senses are liberated from immediacies of time and place.

Page's earliest poems were written under the influence of Auden and his circle;

1. Margaret Atwood, Introduction, *The New Oxford Book of Canadian Verse*, ed. Margaret Atwood, Toronto, 1982, p. xxxv.

occasionally they echo the young Auden's social concerns and his rhetoric. One poem is called "Bank Strike"; others, "Offices" and "Typists":

> Crowded together typists touch
> softly as ducks and seem to sense
> each others' anguish with the swift
> sympathy of the deaf and dumb.

"The Stenographers" is a different matter. The women office workers are an emblem of many lives, all of them regimented and emotionally dispossessed to the point of madness.

Page's later poems are less immediately concerned with men, women, and their society. The angels of "Images of Angels" are disturbing because of their remoteness from human beings. They are "never to be loved or petted, never to be friended." And when a child has glimpsed these angels and refuses to tell what he has seen, "his flesh would grow / cold / and snow / would cover the warm and sunny avenue." In "Photos of a Salt Mine" the mine, a world of salt, seems beautiful only at first. The poem concludes with an abrupt change of perspective; now the mine is seen peopled by the damned, one of the circles of Hell.

P(atricia) K(athleen) Page was born in 1916 in Dorset, England; she emigrated to Canada when she was a very young child. She received her formal education at St. Hilda's School in Calgary, Alberta, and at the Art Students League and Pratt Institute in New York City. She has devoted her life to a variety of the arts: she has worked as a radio actress and a script writer, and she is widely known as a painter and printmaker. In addition to her poems, she has written a "romance," short stories, and essays. She now lives in Victoria, British Columbia.

The Stenographers

After the brief bivouac of Sunday,
their eyes, in the forced march of Monday to Saturday,
hoist the white flag,[1] flutter in the snow-storm of paper,
haul it down and crack in the mid-sun of temper.

In the pause between the first draft and the carbon   5
they glimpse the smooth hours when they were children—
the ride in the ice-cart, the ice-man's name,
the end of the route and the long walk home;

remember the sea where floats at high tide
were sea marrows[2] growing on the scatter-green vine   10
or spools of grey toffee, or wasps' nests on water;
remember the sand and the leaves of the country.

Bell rings and they go and the voice draws their pencil[3]
like a sled across snow; when its runners are frozen
rope snaps and the voice then is pulling no burden   15
but runs like a dog on the winter of paper.

Their climates are winter and summer—no wind
for the kites of their hearts—no wind for a flight;

1. Of surrender. "Bivouac": temporary army encampment in the open; "forced march": long march under special difficulties.

2. That is, the "floats" (buoys) looked like sea vegetables.

3. That is, when they take dictation.

a breeze at the most, to tumble them over
and leave them like rubbish—the boy-friends of blood.   20

In the inch of the noon as they move they are stagnant.
The terrible calm of the noon is their anguish;
the lip of the counter, the shapes of the straws
like icicles breaking their tongues, are invaders.

Their beds are their oceans—salt water of weeping   25
the waves that they know—the tide before sleep;
and fighting to drown they assemble their sheep
in columns and watch them leap desks for their fences
and stare at them with their own mirror-worn faces.

In the felt of the morning the calico-minded,   30
sufficiently starched, insert papers, hit keys,
efficient and sure as their adding machines;
yet they weep in the vault, they are taut as new curtains
stretched upon frames. In their eyes I have seen
the pin men[4] of madness in marathon trim   35
race round the track of the stadium pupil.

                                                                     1946

Images of Angels

Imagine them as they were first conceived:
part musical instrument and part daisy
in a white manshape.
Imagine a crowd on the Elysian grass[5]
playing ring-around-a-rosy,   5
mute except for their singing,
their gold smiles
gold sickle moons in the white sky of their faces.
Sex, neither male nor female,
name and race, in each case, simply angel.   10

Who, because they are white and gold, has made them holy
but never to be loved or petted, never to be friended?

Not children, who imagine them more simply,
see them more coloured and a deal more cosy,
yet somehow mixed with the father, fearful and fully   15
realized when the vanishing bed
floats in the darkness,
when the shifting point of focus, that drifting star,
has settled in the head.

More easily perhaps, the little notary[6]   20
who, given one as a pet, could not

---

4. "Stick figures, such as children draw" (Page's
note).
5. On the Elysian Fields, happy home of the
blessed after death in classical mythology.
6. Certifier of deeds and other papers; minor
public official.

walk the sun-dazzled street
with so lamb-white a companion.
For him its loom-large skeleton—
one less articulated than his own—   25
would dog his days with doom
until behind the lethal lock
used for his legal documents
he guiltily shut it up.
His terror then that it escape   30
and smiling call for him at work.
Less dreadful for his public shame
worse for his private guilt
if in the hour that he let it out
he found it limp and boneless as a flower.   35

Perhaps, more certainly perhaps, the financier.
What business man would buy as he buys stock
as many as could cluster on a pin?[7]
Angels are dropping, angels going up.
He could not mouth such phrases and chagrin   40
would sugar round his lips as he said "angel".
For though he mocks their mention he cannot
tie their tinsel image to a tree
without the momentary lowering of his lids
for fear that they exist in worlds which he   45
uneasy, reconstructs from childhood's memory.

The anthropologist with his tidy science
had he stumbled upon one unawares,
found as he finds an arrowhead, an angel—
a what-of-a-thing   50
as primitive as a daisy,
might with his ice cold eye have assessed it coolly.
But how, despite his detailed observations
could he face his learned society and explain?
"Gentlemen, it is thought that they are born   55
with harps and haloes
as the unicorn with its horn.
Study discloses them white and gold as daisies."

Perhaps only a dog could accept them wholly,
be happy to follow at their heels   60
and bark and romp with them in the green fields.
Or, take the nudes of Lawrence[8] and impose
a-sexuality upon them; those
could meet with ease these gilded albinos.

Or a child, not knowing they were angels could   65
wander along an avenue hand in hand
with his new milk-white playmates,
take a step

---

7. The question "How many angels can dance on the head of a pin?" agitated some medieval theologians.

8. D. H. Lawrence (1885–1930), British author, was also a painter of sensuous scenes.

and all the telephone wires would become taut
as the high strings of a harp   70
and space be merely the spaces between strings
and the world mute, except for a thin singing,
as if a sphere—big enough to be in it
and yet small
so that a glance through the lashes   75
would show it whole—
were fashioned very finely out of wire
and turning in a wind.

But say the angelic word
and *this* innocent   80
with his almost-unicorn
would let it go—
(even a child would know
that angels should be flying in the sky!)
and feeling implicated in a lie,   85
his flesh would grow
cold
and snow
would cover the warm and sunny avenue.

                                                                            1967

Photos of a Salt Mine

How innocent their lives look,
how like a child's
dream of caves and winter, both combined;
the steep descent to whiteness
and the stope   5
with its striated walls[9]
their folds all leaning as if pointing to
the great whiteness still,
that great white bank
with its decisive front,   10
that seam upon a slope,
salt's lovely ice.

And wonderful underfoot the snow of salt
the fine
particles a broom could sweep,   15
one thinks
muckers might make angels in its drafts
as children do in snow,
lovers in sheets,
lie down and leave imprinted where they lay   20
a feathered creature holier than they.[1]

And in the outworked stopes
with lamps and ropes

9. With parallel grooves; "stope": steplike excavation in a mine.
1. A common children's pastime is to lie on the snow and move one's arms up and down; the resulting impression looks like an angel with wings.

up miniature matterhorns[2]
the miners climb   25
probe with their lights
the ancient folds of rock—
syncline and anticline[3]—
and scoop from darkness an Aladdin's cave:
rubies and opals glitter from its walls.   30

But hoses douse the brilliance of these jewels,
melt fire to brine.
Salt's bitter water trickles thin and forms,
slow fathoms down,
a lake within a cave,   35
lacquered with jet—
white's opposite.
There grey on black the boating miners float
to mend the stays and struts of that old stope
and deeply underground   40
their words resound,
are multiplied by echo, swell and grow
and make a climate of a miner's voice.

So all the photographs like children's wishes
are filled with caves or winter,   45
innocence
has acted as a filter,
selected only beauty from the mine.
Except in the last picture,
it is shot   50
from an acute high angle. In a pit
figures the size of pins are strangely lit
and might be dancing but you know they're not.
Like Dante's vision of the nether hell[4]
men struggle with the bright cold fires of salt,   55
locked in the black inferno of the rock:
the filter here, not innocence but guilt.

                                                         1967

Kaleidoscope

i

A Little Fantasy

"I send you a very well-constructed Kaleidoscope, a recently invented Toy."
—letter from James Murray to Byron,[5] 1818.

So—Murray to Byron in Italy
when B. was falling in love again. In love.
Teresa this time. Guiciolli.[6]

2. The Matterhorn is a mountain peak in the Alps; it was first scaled in 1865, but not before four of the climbers had fallen to their deaths.
3. A "syncline" is a trough of stratified rock (here, salt) in which the beds of ore (here again, salt) tip toward each other; an "anticline" is the reverse: an arch, with the beds tipping away from each other. "Aladdin's cave" in the next line refers to the cave full of jewels in the Arabian Nights story.
4. The innermost circle of Hell, in Dante's *Inferno*, is made of ice.
5. George Gordon, Lord Byron (1788–1824), British poet; Murray was his publisher.
6. Byron's mistress during his stay in Italy.

What a gift
to view her through that tube!   5
Her palms, sand dollars[7]—
pale, symmetrical—
changed with his breathing
into petalled stars.
Four hearts her mouth, then eight,   10
a single flower
become a bunch
to kiss and kiss and kiss
and kiss a fourth time.
What a field of mouths!   15
Her navel—curling, complex—
shells and pearls
quadrupling for him
and her soft hair—ah,
the flat, sweet plait of it   20
beneath the glass—
a private hair brooch
such as ladies wear
pinned to their *peau de soie*.[8]

Byron is breathing heavily,   25
the tube—a lover's perfect toy—
weighting his palm.
"Quite a celestial kaleidoscope."[9]
But Murray demands more cantos.
(Damn the man!)   30
Oh, multiple Teresa,
Don Juan calls.

ii
A Little Reality

My eye falls headlong
down this slender tube,
its eye-beam glued   35
to shift and flux and flow.
(Mirrors. A trick with mirrors.)
I cannot
budge from this cylinder.
An octagonal rose   40
holds me as though I were its stem.
We move
interdependent
paired in serious play
that is not play.   45
Part of the art
of dance.

Gwendolyn,
your garden of square roots[1]

---

7. Flat sea urchins; their shells bear an outline
in the shape of a five-pointed star.
8. Japanese silk.
9. *"Don Juan*, XCIII" (Page's note). *Don Juan*,
Byron's comic masterpiece, is a long narrative poem
divided into cantos.
    1. "Gwendolyn MacEwen, *The Garden of
Square Roots*" (Page's note). MacEwen (b. 1941)
is a Canadian poet.

grows in this circle: 50
from my pots and pans—
a silver chaparral[2] of leaves & flowers—
the tap's drip dew
upon them—diamonds, stars;
the yellow plastic   55
of my liquid soap—
a quatrefoil[3] of buttercups—
unfolds
in four-leaf clovers on a field of gold.

Nothing is what it seems.   60
Through this glass eye
familiar becomes foreign
fresh and fair
as never seen before.
Each single thing is other   65
all-ways joined
to every other thing,
for this kaleidoscope
this optic tube
sight's magic conduit   70
fashions—look who dares!—
the perfect, all-inclusive metaphor.

                                                              1987

2. Dense impenetrable thicket.
3. Conventionalized representation of a flower with four petals.

ROBERT LOWELL
1917–1977

Robert Lowell presented himself in his poetry as a gnarled, knotty, unwieldy figure—a gargoyle or a personification of a disfavored metaphysical poem. This portrait
is not what might be anticipated from a member of a patrician New England family,
with James Russell Lowell for great-great-uncle and Amy Lowell for distant cousin.
Lowell insisted upon his own version of the family history. In the prose autobiography which forms a large part of his book *Life Studies,* he began that history by insisting that one of his great-great-grandfathers was Mordecai Myers, a Jew. He showed
little indulgence towards later members, such as his parents, and relentlessly recalled
his parents' lifelong dialogue as that of a shrew and a wobbler: " '*Weelawaugh, we-
ee-eeelawaugh, weelawaugh,*' shrilled Mother's high voice. '*But-and, but-and, but
and!*' Father's low mumble would drone in answer."[1] With other ancestors whom he
presented more attractively, with dead writers like Jonathan Edwards, Hawthorne,
T. S. Eliot, Berryman, and Pound, and live ones like Mary McCarthy, Lowell constructed a new family for himself, patricians not of blood but of tortured talent. These
he memorialized in poems and dedications.

  Whether he was discussing the intricacies of the Puritan conscience, or writing as
Catholic or agnostic, Lowell was, like his *Phaedra,* "Always, always agonized."[2] (That
he should translate this play of Racine, with its incestuous heroine, accorded with

1. *Life Studies*, New York, 1967, p. 19.   Lowell, New York, 1961, p. 21.
2. Jean Baptiste Racine, *Phaedra,* tr. Robert

Lowell's Jacobean taste for violent passion.) He beat against what he called awkwardly—and a deliberate awkwardness jackets many of his poems—"blind alleys of our rooms."

He was born March 1, 1917, in "this planned / Babel of Boston where our money talks." He spent his early years there except for several periods in Washington and Philadelphia, where his father, a naval officer, was stationed. In "Commander Lowell" and other poems in *Life Studies*, Lowell offers a chilly, relentless picture of his father, who died in 1950. He attended St. Mark's School, and came to know the poet Richard Eberhart who was teaching there. He also grew interested in art, and began to glimpse in the work of Cézanne and other painters possible parallels with literary work. Now, or soon after, Lowell began to prepare himself with uncanny deliberateness for the life of a poet. He enrolled at Harvard, and immersed himself in courses in English literature; but after two years he abruptly transferred to Kenyon College so he could study with John Crowe Ransom. Under Ransom's guidance he studied the classics, logic, and philosophy. After graduation in 1940, Lowell attended Louisiana State University, where he studied with Robert Penn Warren and Cleanth Brooks. At the same time he formed a close friendship with Allen Tate, so that he was immersed in the school of New Criticism and in their predilection for "formal, difficult poems."

In 1940, the year he was graduated from Kenyon College, Lowell married the novelist Jean Stafford. (They were divorced in 1948, and he married his second wife, Elizabeth Hardwick, in 1949.) He also, like Allen Tate, was converted to Catholicism, and found a new intensity, a new vantage point, in the change from his family's Episcopalianism.

Lowell was greatly disturbed by the advent of the Second World War. At first he tried, unsuccessfully, to enlist. Then in 1943, as his apocalyptic view sharpened, he grew horrified, particularly by the bombing of civilians; he declared himself a conscientious objector and was sent to jail. He was released after six months, and afterwards lived for a time in Black Rock, near Bridgeport, Connecticut, where he found imagery for some of his best poems, reflecting the acute distress he then felt, for the world and himself.

Lowell said that he thought Hart Crane the most successful poet of the twenties, in part because Crane sought to be "at the center of things" in his time, and "got out more than anybody else."[3] In his own way Lowell also sought to be at the center. One way he attempted this is stylistic: like many poets of the century, he attempted in middle age to break through his own formality and obscurity, to write at once more intimately of his own experience and more publicly. The change was marked by a looser meter and form, beginning with *Life Studies*. Another alteration was in symbolism: Lowell gave up the Christian symbols of his early work, and said of his later work, "you couldn't possibly say what creed I believed in."[4] On the other hand, he felt that his later poems were even more religious, and depicted "the same sort of struggle, light and darkness, the flux of experience. The morality seems much the same."[5] His manner, however, became less forbidding, and the details were presented less viscously, with more individual sharpness. He also found dramatic vehicles for his moods by adapting for the stage stories by Melville and Hawthorne.

Lowell confronted important events with courage and conviction. He was at the center of things especially during the Vietnam War, both through poems and by public action. In June 1965 he formally refused an invitation to the White House Festival of the Arts from President Lyndon B. Johnson, as a form of protest against the war. During the Democratic primary campaign for the presidency in 1968, Lowell accompanied Senator Eugene McCarthy, whose anti-war platform he supported.

3. "Interview with Robert Lowell," Frederick Seidel, in *Writers at Work*, Second Series, New York, 1963, pp. 383–84.

4. The same, p. 352.

5. The same.

In 1970 he withdrew from the political scene by moving to England and marrying still another writer, Caroline Blackwood. The strain of his episodes of mental illness was more than she could bear, and he was on his way back to his second wife and daughter when, on September 12, 1977, he died in a taxi from Kennedy Airport.

Lowell's later works included *Notebook 1967–68*, which traces in broken sequence his private actions and the public events of that time. As if caught between formality and informality (his early and late styles), he made the book a sonnet sequence, but the sonnets are unrhymed. Not as savage as his earlier work, and with an awareness of other people—wife, daughter, friends—these poems kept what Lowell called his "surrealism," by which he meant the grotesquerie which was always his brand and distinction. He rewrote and greatly expanded this book in *History* (1973), where he insisted ("Last Things, Black Pines at 4 a.m.") that "imperfection is the language of art." His work was imperfect, as his own persistent revisions of it suggested, but touched the nerve of the time.

The confessional aspect of Lowell's poetry, and his impingement upon crucial events in the world, brought him as close to being central in recent verse as the disorganization of the literary scene allowed. Because of his sense of himself, his impressive personality, his wit, intelligence, and talent, he throned it over his rivals from about 1950 to 1970.

The Quaker Graveyard in Nantucket

(For Warren Winslow,[1] Dead at Sea)

Let man have dominion over the fishes of the sea and the fowls of the air and the beasts
and the whole earth, and every creeping creature that moveth upon the earth.[2]

I

A brackish reach of shoal off Madaket,—[3]
The sea was still breaking violently and night
Had steamed into our North Atlantic Fleet,
When the drowned sailor clutched the drag-net. Light
Flashed from his matted head and marble feet,   5
He grappled at the net
With the coiled, hurdling muscles of his thighs:
The corpse was bloodless, a botch of reds and whites,
Its open, staring eyes
Were lustreless dead-lights   10
Or cabin-windows on a stranded hulk
Heavy with sand.[4] We weight the body, close
Its eyes and heave it seaward whence it came,[5]
Where the heel-headed dogfish barks its nose
On Ahab's void and forehead;[6] and the name   15

1. Warren Winslow, a cousin of Lowell, died at sea when his naval vessel went down.
2. The epigraph is slightly paraphrased from Genesis 1:26.
3. A place on the west side of Nantucket Island.
4. The imagery of these lines is largely borrowed from Henry David Thoreau, *Cape Cod* (Boston, 1898, pp. 5–6), as Hugh B. Staples has pointed out:
"The brig *St. John*, from Galway, Ireland, laden with emigrants, was wrecked on Sunday morning; it was now Tuesday morning, and the sea was still breaking violently on the rocks. . . . I saw many marble feet and matted heads as the clothes were raised, and one livid, swollen, and mangled body of a drowned girl . . . ; the coiled-up wreck of a human hulk, gashed by the rocks or fishes, so that the bone and muscle were exposed, but quite bloodless,—merely red and white,—with wide-open and staring eyes, yet lustreless, dead-lights; or like the cabin windows of a stranded vessel, filled with sand . . ."
5. The origin of life.
6. Ahab is the monomaniacal hunter of the white whale in Herman Melville's *Moby-Dick*. This phrase, used for "heart and head," implies the emptiness of Ahab's heart and the strength of his will.

Is blocked in yellow chalk.
Sailors, who pitch this portent at the sea
Where dreadnaughts shall confess
Its hell-bent deity,
When you are powerless   20
To sand-bag this Atlantic bulwark, faced
By the earth-shaker, green, unwearied, chaste
In his steel scales: ask for no Orphean lute
To pluck life back.[7] The guns of the steeled fleet
Recoil and then repeat   25
The hoarse salute.

II
Whenever winds are moving and their breath
Heaves at the roped-in bulwarks of this pier,
The terns and sea-gulls tremble at your death
In these home waters. Sailor, can you hear   30
The Pequod's[8] sea wings, beating landward, fall
Headlong and break on our Atlantic wall
Off 'Sconset,[9] where the yawing S-boats splash
The bellbuoy, with ballooning spinnakers,
As the entangled, screeching mainsheet clears   35
The blocks: off Madaket, where lubbers[1] lash
The heavy surf and throw their long lead squids
For blue-fish? Sea-gulls blink their heavy lids
Seaward. The winds' wings beat upon the stones,
Cousin, and scream for you and the claws rush   40
At the sea's throat and wring it in the slush
Of this old Quaker graveyard where the bones
Cry out in the long night for the hurt beast[2]
Bobbing by Ahab's whaleboats in the East.

III
All you recovered from Poseidon[3] died   45
With you, my cousin, and the harrowed brine
Is fruitless on the blue beard of the god,
Stretching beyond us to the castles in Spain,
Nantucket's[4] westward haven. To Cape Cod
Guns, cradled on the tide,   50
Blast the eelgrass about a waterclock
Of bilge and backwash, roil the salt and sand
Lashing earth's scaffold, rock
Our warships in the hand
Of the great God, where time's contrition blues   55
Whatever it was there Quaker sailors lost
In the mad scramble of their lives. They died
When time was open-eyed,
Wooden and childish; only bones abide

---

7. Orpheus went to Hades and by his music
persuaded Perspehone to let his wife, Eurydice,
return to earth.
8. Ahab's ship, which the whale Moby-Dick
destroyed.
9. Siasconset, on eastern Nantucket. S-boats are
large racing sailboats once popular in New England.

1. Landlubbers.
2. Moby-Dick.
3. Greek god of the sea.
4. From this island, off the coast of Massachusetts, the whalers put to sea. Many of them were
Quakers.

There, in the nowhere, where their boats were tossed   60
Sky-high, where mariners had fabled news
Of IS,[5] the whited monster. What it cost
Them is their secret. In the sperm-whale's slick
I see the Quakers drown and hear their cry:
"If God himself had not been on our side,   65
If God himself had not been on our side,
When the Atlantic rose against us, why,
Then it had swallowed us up quick."

IV

This is the end of the whaleroad[6] and the whale
Who spewed Nantucket bones on the thrashed swell   70
And stirred the troubled waters to whirlpools
To send the Pequod packing off to hell:
This is the end of them, three-quarters fools,
Snatching at straws to sail
Seaward and seaward on the turntail whale,   75
Spouting out blood and water as it rolls,
Sick as a dog to these Atlantic shoals:
Clamavimus,[7] O depths. Let the sea-gulls wail

For water, for the deep where the high tide
Mutters to its hurt self, mutters and ebbs.   80
Waves wallow in their wash, go out and out,
Leave only the death-rattle of the crabs,
The beach increasing, its enormous snout
Sucking the ocean's side.
This is the end of running on the waves;   85
We are poured out like water. Who will dance
The mast-lashed master of Leviathans[8]
Up from this field of Quakers in their unstoned graves?

V

When the whale's viscera go and the roll
Of its corruption overruns this world   90
Beyond tree-swept Nantucket and Wood's Hole[9]
And Martha's Vineyard, Sailor, will your sword
Whistle and fall and sink into the fat?
In the great ash-pit of Jehoshaphat[1]
The bones cry for the blood of the white whale,   95
The fat flukes arch and whack about its ears,
The death-lance churns into the sanctuary, tears
The gun-blue swingle, heaving like a flail,
And hacks the coiling life out: it works and drags

5. Moby-Dick, here identified with God, who told Moses, "I AM THAT I AM" and instructed him to say to the Israelites, "I AM hath sent me to you" (Exodus 3:14). "Whited monster" is adapted from "whited sepulchre" (Matthew 23:27).
6. An Old English kenning (or epithet) for the sea.
7. We have cried (Latin). Compare Psalm 130:1—"Out of the depths have I cried unto thee, O Lord."
8. Leviathan is a great water animal, mentioned in the Old Testament, here identified with the whale.
9. The closest point on the mainland of Massachusetts to Martha's Vineyard, an island near Nantucket.
1. "The valley of judgment. The world, according to some prophets and scientists, will end in fire" (Lowell, writing to Kimon Friar and John Malcolm Brinnin). Compare: "Let the heathen be wakened, and come unto the valley of Jehoshaphat; for there will I sit to judge all the heathen round about" (Joel 3:12).

And rips the sperm-whale's midriff into rags,   100
Gobbets of blubber spill to wind and weather,
Sailor, and gulls go round the stoven timbers
Where the morning stars sing out together
And thunder shakes the white surf and dismembers
The red flag hammered in the mast-head.[2] Hide,   105
Our steel, Jonas Messias,[3] in Thy side.

VI
Our Lady of Walsingham[4]

There once the penitents took off their shoes
And then walked barefoot the remaining mile;
And the small trees, a stream and hedgerows file
Slowly along the munching English lane,   110
Like cows to the old shrine, until you lose
Track of your dragging pain.
The stream flows down under the druid tree,
Shiloah's whirlpools gurgle and make glad
The castle of God. Sailor, you were glad   115
And whistled Sion[5] by that stream. But see:

Our Lady, too small for her canopy,
Sits near the altar. There's no comeliness
At all or charm in that expressionless
Face with its heavy eyelids. As before,   120
This face, for centuries a memory,
Non est species, neque decor,
Expressionless, expresses God: it goes
Past castled Sion. She knows what God knows,
Not Calvary's Cross nor crib at Bethlehem   125
Now, and the world shall come to Walsingham.

VII

The empty winds are creaking and the oak
Splatters and splatters on the cenotaph,
The boughs are trembling and a gaff
Bobs on the untimely stroke   130
Of the greased wash exploding on a shoal-bell[6]

2. At the end of *Moby-Dick*, as the *Pequod* is sinking, the Indian Tashtego's arm rises from the water to nail Ahab's flag to the sinking mast. A sky-hawk is caught between hammer and flag, and Melville says that the "bird of heaven" is dragged down with the satanic ship.

3. Jonah (in the New Testament, Jonas) is identified with the Messiah or Christ because Lowell imagines the whaler's harpoon penetrating the whale, and Jonah within it, just as the centurion's spear pierced the side of Christ, and also because Jonah, like Christ, emerged after a three-day "burial."

4. Adapted, Lowell has said, from E. I. Watkins, *Catholic Art and Culture*, London, 1947, p. 177: "For centuries the shrine of Our Lady of Walsingham has been an historical memory. Now once again pilgrims visit her image erected in a mediaeval chapel, where, it is said, they took off their shoes to walk barefoot the remaining mile to the shrine. . . . The road to the chapel is a quiet country lane shaded with trees, and lined on one side by a hedgerow. On the other, a stream flows beneath the trees, the water symbol of the Holy Spirit, 'the waters of Shiloah that go softly,' the 'flow of the river making glad the city of God.' Within the chapel, an attractive example of Decorated architecture, near an altar of mediaeval fashion, is seated Our Lady's image. It is too small for its canopy, and is not superficially beautiful. 'Non est species neque decor,' there is no comeliness or charm in that expressionless face with heavy eyelids. But let us look carefully. . . . We become aware of an inner beauty more impressive than outward grace. That expressionless countenance expresses what is beyond expression. . . . Mary is beyond joy and sorrow. . . . No longer the Mother of Sorrows nor yet of the human joy of the crib, she understands the secret counsel of God to whose accomplishment Calvary and Bethlehem alike ministered."

5. Or Zion. Compare Isaiah 51:11: "Therefore the redeemed of the Lord shall return, and come with singing unto Zion."

6. A bell buoy marking shallow waters.

In the old mouth of the Atlantic. It's well;
Atlantic, you are fouled with the blue sailors,
Sea-monsters, upward angel, downward fish:
Unmarried and corroding, spare of flash   135
Mart once of supercilious, wing'd clippers,
Atlantic, where your bell-trap guts its spoil
You could cut the brackish winds with a knife
Here in Nantucket, and cast up the time
When the Lord God formed man from the sea's slime   140
And breathed into his face the breath of life,
And blue-lung'd combers lumbered to the kill.
The Lord survives the rainbow of His will.

                                                                  1946

Memories of West Street and Lepke[7]

Only teaching on Tuesdays, book-worming
in pajamas fresh from the washer each morning,
I hog a whole house on Boston's
"hardly passionate Marlborough Street,"[8]
where even the man   5
scavenging filth in the back alley trash cans,
has two children, a beach wagon, a helpmate,
and is a "young Republican."
I have a nine months' daughter,
young enough to be my granddaughter.   10
Like the sun she rises in her flame-flamingo infants' wear.

These are the tranquillized *Fifties*,
and I am forty. Ought I to regret my seedtime?
I was a fire-breathing Catholic C.O.,[9]
and made my manic statement,   15
telling off the state and president, and then
sat waiting sentence in the bull pen
beside a Negro boy with curlicues
of marijuana in his hair.

Given a year,   20
I walked on the roof of the West Street Jail, a short
enclosure like my school soccer court,
and saw the Hudson River once a day
through sooty clothesline entanglements
and bleaching khaki tenements.   25
Strolling, I yammered metaphysics with Abramowitz,
a jaundice-yellow ("it's really tan")
and fly-weight pacifist,
so vegetarian,
he wore rope shoes and preferred fallen fruit.   30

---

7. In 1943 Lowell was sentenced to a year in
New York's West Street jail for his refusal to serve
in the army. Among the other prisoners was Lepke
Buchalter, head of Murder, Inc., an organized
crime syndicate, who had been convicted of murder.
8. William James's phrase for a street in the
elegant Back Bay section of Boston, where Lowell
lived in the 1950s.
9. Conscientious objector (to war).

He tried to convert Bioff and Brown,
the Hollywood pimps, to his diet.
Hairy, muscular, suburban,
wearing chocolate double-breasted suits,
they blew their tops and beat him black and blue.   35

I was so out of things, I'd never heard
of the Jehovah's Witnesses.[1]
"Are you a C.O.?" I asked a fellow jailbird.
"No," he answered, "I'm a J.W."
He taught me the "hospital tuck,"[2]   40
and pointed out the T-shirted back
of *Murder Incorporated's* Czar Lepke,
there piling towels on a rack,
or dawdling off to his little segregated cell full
of things forbidden the common man: 45
a portable radio, a dresser, two toy American
flags tied together with a ribbon of Easter palm.
Flabby, bald, lobotomized,
he drifted in a sheepish calm,
where no agonizing reappraisal   50
jarred his concentration on the electric chair—
hanging like an oasis in his air
of lost connections. . . .

                                                            1959

"To Speak of Woe That Is in Marriage"[3]

It is the future generation that presses into being by means of these exuberant
feelings and supersensible soap bubbles of ours.
                                        —Schopenhauer[4]

"The hot night makes us keep our bedroom windows open.
Our magnolia blossoms. Life begins to happen.
My hopped up husband drops his home disputes,
and hits the streets to cruise for prostitutes,
free-lancing out along the razor's edge.   5
This screwball might kill his wife, then take the pledge.
Oh the monotonous meanness of his lust. . . .
It's the injustice . . . he is so unjust—
whiskey-blind, swaggering home at five.
My only thought is how to keep alive.   10
What makes him tick? Each night now I tie
ten dollars and his car key to my thigh. . . .
Gored by the climacteric of his want,
he stalls above me like an elephant."

                                                            1959

1. Christian revivalist sect opposed to war and
denying the power of the country in matters of
conscience.
2. Standard way of making beds in a hospital.
3. In *The Canterbury Tales* by Geoffrey Chaucer (1340?–1400), the Wife of Bath begins to tell
of her several marriages with this line.
4. Arthur Schopenhauer (1788–1860), pessimistic German philosopher.

Skunk Hour[5]

(*For Elizabeth Bishop*)[6]

Nautilus Island's hermit
heiress still lives through winter in her Spartan cottage;
her sheep still graze above the sea.
Her son's a bishop. Her farmer
is first selectman in our village;   5
she's in her dotage.

Thirsting for
the hierarchic privacy
of Queen Victoria's century,
she buys up all   10
the eyesores facing her shore,
and lets them fall.

The season's ill—
we've lost our summer millionaire,
who seemed to leap from an L. L. Bean[7]   15
catalogue. His nine-knot yawl
was auctioned off to lobstermen.
A red fox stain covers Blue Hill.[8]

And now our fairy
decorator brightens his shop for fall;   20
his fishnet's filled with orange cork,
orange, his cobbler's bench and awl;
there is no money in his work,
he'd rather marry.

One dark night,[9]   25
my Tudor Ford climbed the hill's skull;
I watched for love-cars. Lights turned down,
they lay together, hull to hull,
where the graveyard shelves on the town. . . .
My mind's not right.   30

A car radio bleats,
"Love, O careless Love. . . ."[1] I hear
my ill-spirit sob in each blood cell,
as if my hand were at its throat. . . .

---

5. The scene is Castine, Maine, where Lowell had a summer house. As he has written, "The first four stanzas are meant to give a dawdling more or less amiable picture of a declining Maine sea town. I move from the ocean inland. Sterility howls through the scenery, but I try to give a tone of tolerance, humor, and randomness to the sad prospect" (*The Contemporary Poet as Artist and Critic*, ed. Anthony Ostroff, p. 107).
6. "The dedication is to Elizabeth Bishop, because re-reading her suggested a way of breaking through the shell of my old manner. . . . 'Skunk Hour' is modelled on Miss Bishop's 'The Armadillo' [p. 463]. . . . Both . . . use short line stanzas, start with drifting description and end with a single animal" (Lowell's note).
7. A Maine mail order house that deals in sporting goods, including clothes for the outdoors.
8. "Meant to describe the rusty reddish color of autumn on Blue Hill, a Maine mountain near where we were living" (Lowell's note).
9. A reference, Lowell says, to *The Dark Night of the Soul* of St. John of the Cross.
1. A popular song of the time, entitled "Careless Love," which contains the two lines: "Now you see what careless love will do . . . / Make you kill yourself and your sweetheart too."

I myself am hell;[2]
nobody's here—

35

only skunks, that search
in the moonlight for a bite to eat.
They march on their soles up Main Street:
white stripes, moonstruck eyes' red fire
under the chalk-dry and spar spire
of the Trinitarian Church.

40

I stand on top
of our back steps and breathe the rich air—
a mother skunk with her column of kittens swills the garbage pail.
She jabs her wedge-head in a cup
of sour cream, drops her ostrich tail,
and will not scare.[3]

45

1959

For the Union Dead[4]

"Relinquunt Omnia Servare Rem Publicam."[5]

The old South Boston Aquarium stands
in a Sahara of snow now. Its broken windows are boarded.
The bronze weathervane cod has lost half its scales.
The airy tanks are dry.

Once my nose crawled like a snail on the glass;
my hand tingled
to burst the bubbles
drifting from the noses of the cowed, compliant fish.

5

My hand draws back. I often sigh still
for the dark downward and vegetating kingdom
of the fish and reptile. One morning last March,
I pressed against the new barbed and galvanized

10

fence on the Boston Common. Behind their cage,
yellow dinosaur steamshovels were grunting
as they cropped up tons of mush and grass
to gouge their underworld garage.

15

Parking spaces luxuriate like civic
sandpiles in the heart of Boston.

2. An adaptation of Lucifer's line, "Which way
I fly is Hell; myself am Hell," in *Paradise Lost*
4.75.
3. "The skunks," says Lowell, "are both quix-
otic and barbarously absurd, hence the tone of
amusement and defiance." Their "affirmation" is
therefore "ambiguous."
4. The poem was first published with the title,
"Colonel Shaw and the Massachusetts 54th." The
monument it describes is a bronze relief by

Augustus Saint-Gaudens (1848–1907) depicting
Robert Gould Shaw (1837–1863), commander of
the first Negro regiment organized in a free state,
who was killed in the assault his troops led against
Fort Wagner, South Carolina. The relief, dedicated in 1897, stands on Boston Common opposite
the Massachusetts State House.
5. They give up everything to preserve the
Republic (Latin).

A girdle of orange, Puritan-pumpkin colored girders
braces the tingling Statehouse,   20

shaking over the excavations, as it faces Colonel Shaw
and his bell-cheeked Negro infantry
on St. Gaudens' shaking Civil War relief,
propped by a plank splint against the garage's earthquake.

Two months after marching through Boston,   25
half the regiment was dead;
at the dedication,
William James[6] could almost hear the bronze Negroes breathe.

Their monument sticks like a fishbone
in the city's throat.   30
Its Colonel is as lean
as a compass-needle.

He has an angry wrenlike vigilance,
a greyhound's gentle tautness;
he seems to wince at pleasure,   35
and suffocate for privacy.

He is out of bounds now. He rejoices in man's lovely,
peculiar power to choose life and die—
when he leads his black soldiers to death,
he cannot bend his back.   40

On a thousand small town New England greens,
the old white churches hold their air
of sparse, sincere rebellion; frayed flags
quilt the graveyards of the Grand Army of the Republic.

The stone statues of the abstract Union Soldier   45
grow slimmer and younger each year—
wasp-waisted, they doze over muskets
and muse through their sideburns . . .

Shaw's father wanted no monument
except the ditch,   50
where his son's body was thrown[7]
and lost with his "niggers."

The ditch is nearer.
There are no statues for the last war[8] here;
on Boylston Street,[9] a commercial photograph   55
shows Hiroshima boiling

over a Mosler Safe, the "Rock of Ages"
that survived the blast. Space is nearer.

---

6. (1842–1910), American philosopher and psychologist, who taught at Harvard.
7. By the Confederate soldiers at Fort Wagner.

8. That is, the Second World War.
9. A street in downtown Boston.

When I crouch to my television set,
the drained faces of Negro school-children rise like balloons.   60

Colonel Shaw
is riding on his bubble,
he waits
for the blessèd break.

The Aquarium is gone. Everywhere,   65
giant finned cars nose forward like fish;
a savage servility
slides by on grease.

                                                            1959

Ezra Pound

Horizontal in a deckchair on the bleak ward,[1]
some feeble-minded felon in pajamas, clawing
a Social Credit[2] broadside from your table, you saying,
". . . here with a black suit and black briefcase; in the briefcase,
an abomination, Possum's[3] *hommage* to Milton."   5
Then sprung; Rapallo,[4] and then the decade gone;
then three years, then Eliot dead, you saying,
"And who is left to understand my jokes?
My old Brother in the arts . . . and besides, he was a smash of poet."
He showed us his blotched, bent hands, saying, "Worms.   10
When I talked that nonsense about Jews on the Rome
wireless,[5] she knew it was shit, and still loved me."
And I, "Who else has been in Purgatory?"
And he, "To begin with a swelled head and end with swelled feet."

                                                            1969

Robert Frost

Robert Frost at midnight, the audience gone
to vapor, the great act laid on the shelf in mothballs,
his voice musical, raw and raw—he writes in the flyleaf:
"Robert Lowell from Robert Frost, his friend in the art."
"Sometimes I feel too full of myself," I say.   5
And he, misunderstanding, "When I am low,
I stray away. My son[6] wasn't your kind. The night
we told him Merrill Moore[7] would come to treat him,
he said, 'I'll kill him first.' One of my daughters thought things,
knew every male she met was out to make her;   10
the way she dresses, she couldn't make a whorehouse."
And I, "Sometimes I'm so happy I can't stand myself."

1. Lowell visited Pound when the latter was in St. Elizabeth's Hospital for the criminally insane, in Washington.
2. A dubious economic program which Pound fanatically supported.
3. Eliot, who originally denounced Milton, as Pound did, and then later recanted.
4. Released from the hospital, Pound went back to Rapallo, Italy, to live.
5. Pound talked several times on the Italian radio during the Second World War. "She" is Olga Rudge, Pound's companion.
6. Frost's son committed suicide.
7. A poet and psychoanalyst.

And he, "When I am too full of joy, I think
how little good my health did anyone near me."

1969

After the Convention[8]

Life, hope, they conquer death, generally, always;
and if the steamroller goes over the flower, the flower dies.
Some are more solid earth; they stood in lines,
blouse and helmet, a creamy de luxe sky-blue—
their music, savage and ephemeral. . . .   5
After five nights of Chicago: police and mob,
I am so tired and had, clichés are wisdom,
the clichés of paranoia. On this shore,
the fall of the high tide waves is a straggling, joshing
march of soldiers . . . on the march for me. . . .   10
How slender and graceful, the double line of trees,
how slender, graceful, irregular and underweight,
the young in black folk-fire circles below the trees—
under their bodies, the green grass turns to hay.
September 1, 1968   1969

Dolphin

My Dolphin,[9] you only guide me by surprise,
captive as Racine, the man of craft,
drawn through his maze of iron composition
by the incomparable wandering voice of Phèdre.[1]
When I was troubled in mind, you made for my body   5
caught in its hangman's-knot of sinking lines,
the glassy bowing and scraping of my will. . . .
I have sat and listened to too many
words of the collaborating muse,
and plotted perhaps too freely with my life,   10
not avoiding injury to others,
not avoiding injury to myself—
to ask compassion . . . this book, half fiction,
an eelnet made by man for the eel fighting—

my eyes have seen what my hand did.   15

1973

Epilogue[2]

Those blessèd structures, plot and rhyme—
why are they no help to me now

8. At the Democratic National Convention in Chicago in 1968, counterculture groups staged a "festival of life" in protest against what they called the Democrats' "festival of death"; they were dispersed by police using clubs and tear gas.
9. According to legend, the dolphin saves drowning sailors. Lowell called his third wife, Caroline Blackwood (m. 1972), his "dolphin," saying that she had saved his life.
1. Heroine of tragedy (1677) by Jean Racine, a play which Lowell translated in 1961.
2. The poem is printed as the last piece (excluding a few translations) in Lowell's final book, *Day by Day* (1977).

I want to make
something imagined, not recalled?
I hear the noise of my own voice: 5
The painter's vision is not a lens,
it trembles to caress the light.
But sometimes everything I write
with the threadbare art of my eye
seems a snapshot,   10
lurid, rapid, garish, grouped,
heightened from life,
yet paralyzed by fact.
All's misalliance.
Yet why not say what happened?   15
Pray for the grace of accuracy
Vermeer[3] gave to the sun's illumination
stealing like the tide across a map
to his girl solid with yearning.
We are poor passing facts,   20
warned by that to give
each figure in the photograph
his living name.

                                                                 1978

3. Jan Vermeer (1632–75), Dutch painter noted for his subtle handling of the effects of light.

GWENDOLYN BROOKS
b. 1917

The first poems of Gwendolyn Brooks, those published before the early seventies, led her readers to see her as a member of an earlier generation of Black poets who found in their race special and enviable characteristics, but were more concerned to depict them than to change the conditions which very frequently left them miserable and deprived. The early Brooks knows her people and her themes, and though she writes in irregular lines, she keeps close control on manner and matter alike. Her verse deals with "Bronzeville"—her name for the Black ghetto. Like Edgar Lee Masters (another Illinois poet) in *Spoon River Anthology,* she often presents the "characters" of local people—the preacher, the independent man, the madam of a brothel. She lights up the most ordinary details by a sudden rhythm, passionate observation, or exciting refrain. She seems to agree with the title character of "Big Bessie Throws Her Son into the Street": "Hunt out your own or make your own alone. / Go down the street." She is for gumption, not for compromise.

In 1967 Brooks had an experience which changed the temper of many of her poems and which expanded her interests as a Black woman and poet. This revelation took place at the Second Fisk University Writers' Conference. Here she met some of the younger Black poets, notably Amiri Baraka (then LeRoi Jones), and, thanks to them, Brooks felt that she had awakened "in some inscrutable and uncomfortable wonderland." She was later to write: "Until 1967 I had sturdy ideas about writing and about writers which I announced sturdily. . . . Until 1967 my own blackness did not confront me with a shrill spelling of itself."[1] On her return to Chicago, she began to organize a poetry workshop for young Blacks who wanted to write; she assisted in

1. Quoted in D. H. Melhem, *Gwendolyn Brooks: Poetry and the Heroic Voice,* Lexington, Ky., 1987, p. 174.

community programs, and tirelessly worked to inspire her fellow Blacks and to inform the white community of the awakening of Black writers whose poems, like her own later poems, are expressions of love and rage.

Gwendolyn Brooks was born June 17, 1917, in Topeka, Kansas. But she grew up in Chicago, was educated at the Englewood High School and Wilson Junior College there, and identifies herself with that city. After her graduation in 1936 she worked for a quack "spiritual advisor," her job being to write hundreds of letters to prospective patients. Her office was in the Mecca Building on South State Street, where many poor families and derelicts lived. When she refused to take on the duties of "Assistant Pastor," she was honorably fired from her job. Her book, *In the Mecca* (1968), draws much of its material, as well as its title, from this period.

Brooks then attended art school at the South Side Community Center. Her main interest, however, was poetry, and she began to demonstrate her talent. She won contests sponsored by *Poetry* magazine and various organizations, and was able to publish her first book in 1945. She later won a Pulitzer Prize for her book *Annie Allen*. She has traveled in East Africa and in the Soviet Union. Of the awards made to her perhaps the most agreeable to the poet was, in 1981, the dedication of the Gwendolyn Brooks Junior High School in Harvey, Illinois. She is married to Henry Blakely and they have a son and a daughter.

A Song in the Front Yard

I've stayed in the front yard all my life.
I want to peek at the back
Where it's rough and untended and hungry weed grows.
A girl gets sick of a rose.

I want to go in the back yard now   5
And maybe down the alley,
To where the charity children play.
I want a good time today.

They do some wonderful things.
They have some wonderful fun.   10
My mother sneers, but I say it's fine
How they don't have to go in at quarter to nine.
My mother, she tells me that Johnnie Mae
Will grow up to be a bad woman.
That George'll be taken to Jail soon or late   15
(On account of last winter he sold our back gate).

But I say it's fine. Honest, I do.
And I'd like to be a bad woman, too,
And wear the brave stockings of night-black lace
And strut down the streets with paint on my face.   20

                                                                    1945

Sadie and Maud

Maud went to college.
Sadie stayed at home.
Sadie scraped life
With a fine-tooth comb.

She didn't leave a tangle in.
Her comb found every strand.
Sadie was one of the livingest chits
In all the land.

Sadie bore two babies
Under her maiden name.   10
Maud and Ma and Papa
Nearly died of shame.

When Sadie said her last so-long
Her girls struck out from home.
(Sadie had left as heritage   15
Her fine-tooth comb.)

Maud, who went to college,
Is a thin brown mouse.
She is living all alone
In this old house.   20

                                                              1945

The Lovers of the Poor

        arrive. The Ladies from the Ladies' Betterment
    League
Arrive in the afternoon, the late light slanting
In diluted gold bars across the boulevard brag
Of proud, seamed faces with mercy and murder hinting   5
Here, there, interrupting, all deep and debonair,
The pink paint on the innocence of fear;
Walk in a gingerly manner up the hall.
Cutting with knives served by their softest care,
Served by their love, so barbarously fair.   10
Whose mothers taught: You'd better not be cruel!
You had better not throw stones upon the wrens!
Herein they kiss and coddle and assault
Anew and deadly in the innocence
With which they baffle nature. Who are full,   15
Sleek, tender-clad, fit, fiftyish, a-glow, all
Sweetly abortive, hinting at fat fruit,
Judge it high time that fiftyish fingers felt
Beneath the lovelier planes of enterprise.
To resurrect. To moisten with milky chill.   20
To be a random hitching-post or plush.
To be, for wet eyes, random and handy hem.
            Their guild is giving money to the poor.
The worthy poor. The very very worthy
And beautiful poor. Perhaps just not too swarthy?   25
Perhaps just not too dirty nor too dim
Nor—passionate. In truth, what they could wish
Is—something less than derelict or dull.
Not staunch enough to stab, though, gaze for gaze!
God shield them sharply from the begger-bold!   30
The noxious needy ones whose battle's bald

Nonetheless for being voiceless, hits one down.
              But it's all so bad! and entirely too much for them.
The stench; the urine, cabbage, and dead beans,
Dead porridges of assorted dusty grains,   35
The old smoke, *heavy* diapers, and, they're told,
Something called chitterlings. The darkness. Drawn
Darkness, or dirty light. The soil that stirs.
The soil that looks the soil of centuries.
And for that matter the *general* oldness. Old   40
Wood. Old marble. Old tile. Old old old.
Not homekind Oldness! Not Lake Forest, Glencoe.[1]
Nothing is sturdy, nothing is majestic,
There is no quiet drama, no rubbed glaze, no
Unkillable infirmity of such   45
A tasteful turn as lately they have left,
Glencoe, Lake Forest, and to which their cars
Must presently restore them. When they're done
With dullards and distortions of this fistic
Patience of the poor and put-upon.   50
               They've never seen such a make-do-ness as
Newspaper rugs before! In this, this "flat,"
Their hostess is gathering up the oozed, the rich
Rugs of the morning (tattered! the bespattered. . . .)
Readies to spread clean rugs for afternoon.   55
Here is a scene for you. The Ladies look,
In horror, behind a substantial citizeness
Whose trains clank out across her swollen heart.
Who, arms akimbo, almost fills a door.
All tumbling children, quilts dragged to the floor   60
And tortured thereover, potato peelings, soft-
Eyed kitten, hunched-up, haggard, to-be-hurt.
               Their League is allotting largesse to the Lost.
But to put their clean, their pretty money, to put
Their money collected from delicate rose-fingers   65
Tipped with their hundred flawless rose-nails seems . . .
               They own Spode, Lowestoft,[2] candelabra,
Mantels, and hostess gowns, and sunburst clocks,
Turtle soup, Chippendale,[3] red stain "hangings,"
Aubussons and Hattie Carnegie.[4] They Winter   70
In Palm Beach; cross the Water in June; attend,
When suitable, the nice Art Institute;
Buy the right books in the best bindings; saunter
On Michigan,[5] Easter mornings, in sun or wind.
Oh Squalor! This sick four-story hulk, this fibre   75
With fissures everywhere! Why, what are bringings
Of loathe-love largesse? What shall peril hungers
So old old, what shall flatter the desolate?
Tin can, blocked fire escape and chitterling
And swaggering seeking youth and the puzzled wreckage   80
Of the middle passage, and urine and stale shames

---

1. Prosperous suburbs north of Chicago.
2. English chinaware.
3. Eighteenth-century English furniture.
4. Aubussons are expensive French rugs; Hattie Carnegie was a fashionable American clothing
designer.
    5. Michigan Avenue, known as the "Magnifi-
cent Mile."

And, again, the porridges of the underslung
And children children children. Heavens! That
Was a rat, surely, off there, in the shadows? Long
And long-tailed? Gray? The Ladies from the Ladies'   85
Betterment League agree it will be better
To achieve the outer air that rights and steadies,
To hie to a house that does not holler, to ring
Bells elsetime, better presently to cater
To no more Possibilities, to get   90
Away. Perhaps the money can be posted.
Perhaps they two may choose another Slum!
Some serious sooty half-unhappy home!—
Where loathe-love likelier may be invested.
            Keeping their scented bodies in the center   95
Of the hall as they walk down the hysterical hall,
They allow their lovely skirts to graze no wall,
Are off at what they manage of a canter,
And, resuming all the clues of what they were,
Try to avoid inhaling the laden air.   100
                                     1960

Boy Breaking Glass

To Marc Crawford[6]
From Whom the Commission

Whose broken window is a cry of art
(success, that winks aware
as elegance, as a treasonable faith)
is raw: is sonic: is old-eyed première.
Our beautiful flaw and terrible ornament.   5
Our barbarous and metal little man.

"I shall create! If not a note, a hole.
If not an overture, a desecration."

Full of pepper and light
and Salt and night and cargoes.   10

"Don't go down the plank
if you see there's no extension.
Each to his grief, each to
his loneliness and fidgety revenge.

Nobody knew where I was and now I am no longer there."   15

The only sanity is a cup of tea.
The music is in minors.

Each one other
is having different weather.

6. "A black writer and editor . . . who suggested that Brooks write a poem about ghetto blacks surviving 'inequity and white power' " (*Gwendolyn Brooks*, p. 176).

"It was you, it was you who threw away my name!   20
And this is everything I have for me."

Who has not Congress, lobster, love, luau,
the Regency Room, the Statue of Liberty,
runs. A sloppy amalgamation.
A mistake.   25
A cliff.
A hymn, a snare, and an exceeding sun.

1968

The Blackstone Rangers[7]

I
AS SEEN BY DISCIPLINES[8]

There they are.
Thirty at the corner.
Black, raw, ready.
Sores in the city
that do not want to heal.   5

II
THE LEADERS

Jeff. Gene. Geronimo. And Bop.[9]
They cancel, cure and curry.
Hardly the dupes of the downtown thing
the cold bonbon,
the rhinestone thing. And hardly   10
in a hurry.
Hardly Belafonte, King,
Black Jesus, Stokely, Malcolm X or Rap.
Bungled trophies.
Their country is a Nation on no map.   15

Jeff, Gene, Geronimo and Bop
in the passionate noon,
in bewitching night
are the detailed men, the copious men.
They curry, cure,   20
they cancel, cancelled images whose Concerts
are not divine, vivacious; the different tins
are intense last entries; pagan argument;
translations of the night.

The Blackstone bitter bureaus   25
(bureaucracy is footloose) edit, fuse

---

7. A tough Chicago street gang. Blackstone Street is the eastern boundary of the Chicago's Black ghetto.
8. That is, law enforcers. "Vexed by some who misread this first section as her own condemnation, Brooks insists that, in any reprinting, the entire poem be published as a unit . . ." (*Gwendolyn Brooks*, p. 181).
9. Name of a kind of jazz; Geronimo was also the name of an Apache Indian chief who led raids against the whites in Arizona.

unfashionable damnations and descent;
and exulting, monstrous hand on monstrous hand,
construct, strangely, a monstrous pearl or grace.

III
Gang Girls

A RANGERETTE

Gang Girls are sweet exotics.   30
Mary Ann
uses the nutrients of her orient,
but sometimes sighs for Cities of blue and jewel
beyond her Ranger rim of Cottage Grove.[1]
(Bowery Boys, Disciples, Whip-Birds will   35
dissolve no margins, stop no savory sanctities.)

Mary is
a rose in a whiskey glass.

Mary's
Februaries shudder and are gone. Aprils   40
fret frankly, lilac hurries on.
Summer is a hard irregular ridge.
October looks away.
And that's the Year!
              Save for her bugle-love.   45
Save for the bleat of not-obese devotion.
Save for Somebody Terribly Dying, under
the philanthropy of robins. Save for her Ranger
bringing
an amount of rainbow in a string-drawn bag.   50
"Where did you get the diamond?" Do not ask:
but swallow, straight, the spirals of his flask
and assist him at your zipper; pet his lips
and help him clutch you.

Love's another departure.   55
Will there be any arrivals, confirmations?
Will there be gleaming?

Mary, the Shakedancer's child
from the rooming-flat, pants carefully, peers at
her laboring lover. . . .   60
              Mary! Mary Ann!
Settle for sandwiches! settle for stocking caps!
for sudden blood, aborted carnival,
the props and niceties of non-loneliness—
the rhymes of Leaning.   65

1968

---

1. Street of overcrowded tenements in the Black ghetto.

Young Africans[2]

of the furious

Who take Today and jerk it out of joint
have made new underpinnings and a Head.

Blacktime is time for chimeful
poemhood
but they decree a   5
Jagged chiming now.

If there are flowers flowers
must come out to the road. Rowdy!—
knowing where wheels and people are,
knowing where whips and screams are,   10
knowing where deaths are, where the kind kills are.

As for that other kind of kindness,
if there is milk it must be mindful.
The milkofhumankindness[3] must be mindful
as wily wines.   15
Must be fine fury.
Must be mega,[4] must be main.

Taking Today (to jerk it out of joint)
the hardheroic maim the
leechlike-as-usual who use,   20
adhere to, carp, and harm.

And they await,
across the Changes and the spiraling dead,
our Black revival, our Black vinegar,
our hands, and our hot blood.   25

                                                                   1981

The Boy Died in My Alley[5]

Without my having known.
Policeman said, next morning,
"Apparently died Alone."
"You heard a shot?" Policeman said.
Shots I hear and Shots I hear.   5
I never see the dead.

The Shot that killed him yes I heard
as I heard the Thousand shots before;

---

2. "The title indicates its Pan-African impetus of common struggle against economic and political bondage" (*Gwendolyn Brooks*, p. 205). "The *furious*" are described in the first lines.
   3. Compare Lady Macbeth, on Macbeth's "milk of human kindness" (1.5.17).
   4. Large, great.
   5. This poem "allegorizes a tragic shooting in Brooks's neighborhood . . . the poem originates in separate incidents involving two black youths. One, Kenneth Alexander, a high school honors student . . . was killed running from a policeman. The other, a boy observed [by Brooks] in Ghana, 1974 . . . Both black youths, in their running, become symbols of 'impulse, not achievement, [Brooks said]" (*Gwendolyn Brooks*, p. 222).

careening tinnily down the nights
across my years and arteries.   10

Policeman pounded on my door.
"Who is it?" "POLICE!" Policeman yelled.
"A Boy was dying in your alley.
A Boy is dead, and in your alley.
And have you known this Boy before?"   15

I have known this Boy before.
I have known this Boy before, who
ornaments my alley.
I never saw his face at all.
I never saw his futurefall.   20
But I have known this Boy.

I have always heard him deal with death.
I have always heard the shout, the volley.
I have closed my heart-ears late and early.
And I have killed him ever.   25

I joined the Wild and killed him
with knowledgeable unknowing.
I saw where he was going.
I saw him Crossed. And seeing,
I did not take him down.   30

He cried not only "Father!"
but "Mother!
Sister!
Brother."
The cry climbed up the alley.   35
It went up to the wind.
It hung upon the heaven
for a long
stretch-strain of Moment.

The red floor of my alley   40
is a special speech to me.

                                                                 1981

AL PURDY
b. 1918

Al Purdy suspects that the far north may hold the secret of the Canadian national
character, and in 1965 he spent a summer among the Eskimos of Baffin Island. From
his experiences there he fashioned his book *North of Summer* (1967). In a postscript
he writes, "Queerly enough I didn't have the sense of vast and lonely barren distance
in the Arctic, even tho it certainly is vast and lonely. I looked at things close up,
flowers, rivers, and people: above all, people. Besides you'd have a helluva time

shoving vast lonely distances into poems."[1] Much of Purdy's best poetry comes from looking at things "close up." He did not, however, go to Baffin Island "consciously seeking for new poems, because it would get to sounding as goddam self-conscious as hell . . . I'm interested in going to Baffin Island because I'm interested in going to Baffin Island."[2] Purdy likes to travel, because he believes that new areas of landscape may "awake old areas of one's self,"[3] and the people he meets along the way provide the occasions for his poems. These give the impression of a generous, friendly, observant man, carefully unpretentious, impatient with the requirements of both social and poetic form. His lines have a special clipped quality, as if many useless words had been omitted and the sentiment bared down to the bone. He "listens" for poems: "After you've lived your whole life writing poetry (and I started writing at thirteen), I think you've always got one ear cocked, listening to know if you're good enough to put it into a poem."[4]

Al (fred Wellington) Purdy was born in Wooller, Ontario, on December 30, 1918. He was educated at Albert College, Belleville, and during World War II he served in the Royal Canadian Air Force. Before 1960, when he settled in southeastern Ontario, he worked a number of jobs, "factory and otherwise, too numerous to mention." His first book of poems was published in 1944, and was not followed by another until 1955; since then he has published regularly. With more than twenty books to his credit, he is one of Canada's most prolific poets. During the seventies, he was poet-in-residence at various Canadian universities. Purdy's work has been awarded a number of prizes and awards, including the Governor General's Award for poetry in 1976 and the Jubilee Medal in 1978.

1. *North of Summer*, Toronto, 1967, p. 83. Geddes, Toronto, 1985, p. 634.
2. Interview with Gary Geddes in *Twentieth-*   3. The same, p. 635.
Century Poetry & Poetics, 3d ed., ed. Gary   4. The same.

Winter Walking

Sometimes I see churches
like tons of light,
triangles and hexagons
sideways in air.
Sometimes an old house   5
holds me watching, still,
with no idea of time,
waiting for the grey shape
to reassemble in my mind,
and I carry it away   10
(translated back
to drawing board, concept,
mathematic and symbol);
I puzzle myself
with form and line   15
of an old house
that goes where man goes.
A train's violent anapest[1]
(- - —! - - —!)
cries in my ears,   20
and leaves me a
breathless small boy.

1. A metrical foot in poetry (scanned in the next line).

What entered me trembling
was not the steel's dream.
And walking by,   25
in a pile of old snow
under a high wall
a patch of brilliant
yellow dog piss
glows, and joins   30
things in the mind.
Sometimes I stand still,
like a core at the centre
of my senses, hidden and still—
All the heavy people,   35
clouds and tangible buildings,
enter and pass thru me:
stand like a spell
of the wild gold sunlight,
knowing the ache stones have,   40
how mountains suffer,
and a wet blackbird feels
flying past in the rain.
This is the still centre,
an involvement in silences—   45

1963

The Madwoman on the Train

I've always been going somewhere—Vancouver[2]
or old age or somewhere ever since I can remember:
and this woman leaning over me, this madwoman,
while I was sleeping, whispering, "Do you take drugs?"
And the sight of her yellow-white teeth biting   5
the dark open wide and white eyes like marbles

children play with but no children play with marbles
like those—saying, "Do you take drugs?" And Vancouver
must be somewhere near this midnight I can't remember
where tho only the sister[3] holding the madwoman,   10
fighting her: me saying stupidly, "No, no drugs."
She wanting to talk and sitting there biting

at something I couldn't see what the hell she was biting,
only her white eyes like aching terrible marbles
and mouth crying out, "I don't want to go to Vancouver!   15
Don't let them take me!" She didn't remember
the sad scared children, children of the madwoman
herself, recognized only me the stranger, asking what drugs

I took and wouldn't stop asking that. What such drugs
do besides closing those eyes and keeping those teeth
from biting   20

---

2. City in British Columbia, Canada.   3. Nurse (British).

that tongue into rags and soothing a forehead damp
                                    as marble's
cold stone couldn't be altogether bad eh? All the way
                                    to Vancouver
where I was going and thought I could remember
having lived once I comforted the madwoman

while the sister minded her frightened children: madwoman,   25
courtesan, mother, wife, in that order. Such drugs
as I know of don't cause this snapping and biting
at shadows or eyes like glaring lacustral marbles[4]
and mouth crying, "Don't let them take me to Vancouver!"
And leaning her head on my shoulder's scared calm . . .
                                    I remember   30

now the promise I made and do not wish to remember
going somewhere and falling asleep on the train and
                                    the madwoman
shakes me softly awake again and, "Yes, I do take drugs,"
I say to her and myself: "I get high on hemp and peyote
                                    biting
at scraps of existence I've lost all the smoky limitless
                                    marbles   35
I found in my life once lost before Vancouver—"

I've forgotten that child, his frantic scratching and biting
for something he wanted and lost—but it wasn't marbles.
I remember the Mountie[5] waiting, then the conductor's
                        "Vancouver next! Vancouver!"   40
                                                        1965

Lament for the Dorsets

(*Eskimos extinct in the 14th century* A.D.)

Animal bones and some mossy tent rings
scrapers and spearheads   carved ivory swans
all that remains of the Dorset giants
who drove the Vikings back to their long ships
talked to spirits of earth and water   5
—a picture of terrifying old men
so large they broke the backs of bears
so small they lurk behind bone rafters
in the brain of modern hunters
among good thoughts and warm things   10
and come out at night
to spit on the stars

The big men with clever fingers
who had no dogs and hauled their sleds

---

4. That is, marbles in a lake.
5. Member of the Royal Canadian Mounted Police.

over the frozen northern oceans   15
awkward giants

        killers of seal
they couldn't compete with little men
who came from the west with dogs
Or else in a warm climatic cycle   20
the seals went back to cold waters
and the puzzled Dorsets scratched their heads
with hairy thumbs around 1350 A.D.
—couldn't figure it out
went around saying to each other   25
plaintively
        'What's wrong? What happened?
        Where are the seals gone?'
And died

Twentieth century people   30
apartment dwellers
executives of neon death
warmakers with things that explode
—they have never imagined us in their future
how could we imagine them in the past   35
squatting among the moving glaciers
six hundred years ago
with glowing lamps?
As remote or nearly
as the trilobites[6] and swamps   40
when coal became
or the last great reptile hissed
at a mammal the size of a mouse
that squeaked and fled

Did they ever realize at all   45
what was happening to them?
Some old hunter with one lame leg
a bear had chewed
sitting in a caribou skin tent
—the last Dorset?   50
Let's say his name was Kudluk
carving 2-inch ivory swans
for a dead grand-daughter
taking them out of his mind
the places in his mind   55
where pictures are
He selects a sharp stone tool
to gouge a parallel pattern of lines
on both sides of the swan
holding it with his left hand   60
bearing down and transmitting
his body's weight
from brain to arm and right hand

6. Extinct marine animals—among the earliest fossils known.

and one of his thoughts
turns to ivory   65
The carving is laid aside
in beginning darkness
at the end of hunger
after a while wind
blows down the tent and snow   70
begins to cover him
After 600 years
the ivory thought
is still warm

                                                            1968

Spinning

For Colleen Thibaudeau

'Can't see out of my left eye
nothing much happens on the left anyway'
—you have to spin around right quickly
then just catch a glimpse
of coat tails leaving the room   5
(lace doilies on the settee)
light foot rising and disappearing
the last shot fired at Batoche
or maybe it was Duck Lake
—though I saw someone I knew   10
and turned faster and faster
said wait for me
it was my grandmother I never knew
before I was born she died
—sometimes I turned fast enough   15
and nearly caught up with the sun
it bounded like a big red ball
forward and then went backwards
over the mountains somewhere
—thought I saw someone I knew   20
she was young in an old summer
I tried to remember very carefully
balanced on one foot
and concentrated and concentrated
lightfoot white feet in the long grass   25
running to meet her lover
I couldn't stop turning then
wait for me wait for me

                                                            1981

ROBERT DUNCAN
1919–1988

Among the diverse writers who worked with Charles Olson at Black Mountain College in North Carolina, Robert Creeley and Denise Levertov developed their art in
sudden, short-lived lyrical insights, but Robert Duncan developed a mystical esthetic.

Olson did not meet him until 1947, but at once praised him as "a beautiful poet," with "ancient, permanent wings of Eros—& of Orphism." Much of Olson's reading was in the sciences, but Duncan was primarily interested in metaphysics, or rather, in philosophy and poetry that implied or recognized a "secret doctrine." He was erudite in this literature, in a way that Creeley and Levertov are not, and became an exponent of it in prose as well as in verse.

Duncan was fond of the image of himself as a wanderer, both in geographical terms and in terms of "areas of being."[1] He was born January 7, 1919, in Oakland, California, and at the age of six months was adopted by a family named Symmes; his early poetry was signed with that name. His homoerotic direction was important in his life and in his work: of it he wrote, "Perhaps the sexual irregularity underlay and led to the poetic; neither as homosexual nor as poet could one take over readily the accepted paradigms of the Protestant ethic." His education at the University of California at Berkeley, which began in 1936, was interupted by a love affair; during his sophomore year he dropped out and followed his lover east. Subsequently he spent some time in the army but was granted a psychiatric discharge in 1941. He returned to the university at Berkeley from 1948 to 1950, and edited then the *Berkeley Miscellany* (1948–49). He taught sporadically at universities, notably with Olson at Black Mountain College in 1956.

In his early period Duncan eagerly embraced the influences of a great many poets, the most influential being the most romantic. By the age of eighteen he had recognized his vocation as poetry, and had come to think of that art as an unfolding of his inner nature.[2] Under "demi-surrealists" such as Dylan Thomas, poetry was a mode of rhetoric, as far-reaching as possible. He sought a dithyrambic verse, and learned a good deal not only from the rhetoricians, but also from the discontinuous and unportentous verse of Williams and Pound. He insisted, however, that he regarded himself as an isolated figure until he read Levertov's "The Shifting" in 1952, Creeley's "The Gold Diggers" in 1954, and Olson's *Maximus Poems* in the fifties.

For Duncan poetry was ultimately magical. "Every moment of life is an attempt to come to life," he said.[3] Poetry is a magic linking of life and Life, or of appearance and reality. Yet he preferred not to regard it as a fusion, but as a confusion, a melee of wisdom and intuition, of reading and mother wit, of adulthood and childishness, all "higglety-pigglety."[4] He learned from one of his teachers in school to regard "poetry not as a cultural commodity or an exercise to improve sensibility, but as a vital process of the spirit."[5] The making of a poem is the exercise of his "faculties at large," which some achieve by making war or love. In this making, as he learned from another teacher, "to form is to transform."

In the sixties Duncan was outraged by the Vietnam War, and began to introduce political events into his work. His method was based upon William Blake's Prophetic Books; like Blake writing about the French Revolution, or about battles in the mind, Duncan wrote of President Lyndon Johnson, "Now Johnson would go up to join the great simulacra of men, / Hitler and Stalin, to work his fame / with planes roaring out from Guam over Asia."[6] Johnson becomes, like Urizen, an antipoetic principle of mythical proportions. Duncan carries this difficult maneuver off with considerable address.

During the 1970s, in contrast with his earlier prolific work, Duncan published little. In his most recent book, *Ground Work* (1984), he "retreated" to what he "called, in an unpublished piece, 'speculations and appreciations, rantings if need be, phantasies, lectures, nocturnes and mind and soul and spirit dances and inventions.' "[7] He died on February 3, 1988.

---

1. *The Years as Catches*, rev. ed., Berkeley, 1966, p. ii.
2. The same, p. i.
3. *The New American Poetry*, ed. Donald M. Allen, p. 405.
4. The same, p. 406.
5. The same, p. 432.
6. "Up Rising, Passages 25."
7. Quoted in *Contemporary Poets*, 4th ed., ed. James Vinson, New York, 1985, p. 211.

In the introduction to *Bending the Bow*, he wrote, "Working in words I am an escapist. . . . But I want every part of the actual world involved in my escape. I bring the laws that bound me into an aerial structure in which they are unbound as outlines of a prison unfolding."[8] Out of such paradoxes Duncan worked towards a sense in which there is "no duality but the variety of the one."[9] His work allows a structural looseness to play against its thematic intensities. There is a steady convergence towards images of fire, music, dancing, possession, greenness, light, opening, and speech itself. Ultimately the poems, which often have love as their subject, seek to illumine as with love the entire poetic situation. Duncan moves toward the vividness of the "first day."[10]

8. *Bending the Bow*, New York, 1968, p. v.   10. "Passages 13."
9. *The Years as Catches*, p. x.

Poetry, a Natural Thing

Neither our vices nor our virtues
further the poem. "They came up
    and died
just like they do every year
    on the rocks."   5

    The poem
feeds upon thought, feeling, impulse,
    to breed   itself,
a spiritual urgency at the dark ladders leaping.

This beauty is an inner persistence   10
    toward the source
striving against (within) down-rushet of the river,
    a call we heard and answer
in the lateness of the world
    primordial bellowings   15
from which the youngest world might spring,

salmon not in the well where the
    hazelnut falls
but at the falls battling, inarticulate,
    blindly making it.   20

This is one picture apt for the mind.

A second: a moose painted by Stubbs,[1]
where last year's extravagant antlers
    lie on the ground.
The forlorn moosey-faced poem wears   25
    new antler-buds,
    the same,

"a little heavy, a little contrived",

his only beauty to be
    all moose.   30

1960

1. George Stubbs (1724–1806), English painter of animals.

Passage over Water

We have gone out in boats upon the sea at night,
lost, and the vast waters close traps of fear about us.
The boats are driven apart, and we are alone at last
under the incalculable sky, listless, diseased with stars.

Let the oars be idle, my love, and forget at this time   5
our love like a knife between us
defining the boundaries that we can never cross
nor destroy as we drift into the heart of our dream,
cutting the silence, slyly, the bitter rain in our mouths
and the dark wound closed in behind us.   10

Forget depth-bombs, death and promises we made,
gardens laid waste, and, over the wastelands westward,
the rooms where we had come together bombd.

But even as we leave, your love turns back. I feel
your absence like the ringing of bells silenced. And salt   15
over your eyes and the scales of salt between us. Now,
you pass with ease into the destructive world.
There is a dry crash of cement. The light fails,
falls into the ruins of cities upon the distant shore
and within the indestructible night I am alone.   20

1966

Childhood's Retreat

It's in the perilous boughs of the tree
out of blue sky   the wind
sings loudest surrounding me.

And solitude, a wild solitude
's reveald, fearfully, high I'd climb   5
into the shaking uncertainties,

part out of longing, part   daring my self,
part to see that
widening of the world,   part

to find my own, my secret   10
hiding sense and place, where from afar
all voices and scenes come back

—the barking of a dog,   autumnal burnings,
far calls, close calls—   the boy I was
calls out to me   15
here the man where I am   "Look!

I've been where you

most fear to be."

1984

A Little Language

I know a little language of my cat, though Dante[2] says
that animals have no need of speech and Nature
abhors the superfluous.   My cat is fluent.   He
converses when he wants with me.   To speak

is natural.   And whales and wolves I've heard   5
in choral soundings of the sea and air
know harmony and have an eloquence that stirs
my mind and heart—they touch the soul.   Here

Dante's religion that would set Man apart
damns the effluence of our life from us   10
to build therein its powerhouse.

It's in his animal communication Man is
         true, immediate, and
in immediacy, Man is all animal.

His senses quicken in the thick of the symphony,   15
         old circuits of animal rapture and alarm,
attentions and arousals in which an identity rearrives.
         He hears
particular voices among
         the concert, the slightest   20
rustle in the undertones,
         rehearsing a nervous aptitude
yet to prove *his*. He sees the flick
         of significant red within the rushing mass
of ruddy wilderness and catches the glow   25
         of a green shirt
to delite him in a glowing field of green
         —it *speaks* to him—
and in the arc of the spectrum color
         speaks to color.   30
The rainbow articulates
         a promise he remembers
he but imitates
         in noises that he makes,

this speech in every sense   35
the world surrounding him.

He picks up on the fugitive tang of mace[3]
         amidst the savory mass,
and taste in evolution is an everlasting key.
         There is a pun of scents in what makes sense.   40

         Myrrh[4] it may have been,
the odor of the announcement that filld the house.

---

2. Italian poet (1265–1321), who said this in his
essay, *De Vulgari Eloquentia (Of the Vulgar* [i.e.,
common] *Speech).*

3. A highly aromatic spice.
4. Bitter gum resin found in North Africa and
Arabia.

He wakes from deepest sleep

upon a distant signal and waits

as if crouching, springs 45

to life.

1984

WILLIAM MEREDITH
b. 1919

William Meredith creates in his poems a world in which creatures and objects are seen separated from one another and yet located in a silent, statuesque, composed relationship. In one of his war poems he describes a convoy of battleships as moving with the ceremonious, processional beauty of the stars above them:

> A company of vessels on the sea
> Running in darkness, like a company
> Of stars. . . .

The vision which identifies the works of man with those of nature is a healing one and it induces a momentary serenity. Isolated as we are, we communicate, Meredith suggests, by a fellow feeling that recognizes our common solitude and the rituals we invent to make it tolerable. The poet reminds us that "all go to the grave several ways / and compose themselves elaborately as for an end." The newly awakened bachelor in one of Meredith's poems is "given a vision of the unity / That informs a small apartment." In another poem, surrounded by the animals he has taken in on a winter's night, aware of the ghostly presences of "Parents with whom we would but cannot talk," the poet invites his reader to participate in a kinship of solitude, a relationship based on individual privacy, dignity, and guilt:

> We dream there is no ravening or guile
> And take it kindly of the beasts to come
> And suffer hospitality.

William Meredith was born in New York City on January 9, 1919. He attended the Lenox School in Massachusetts and earned a B.A. magna cum laude from Princeton in 1940. Meredith spent five years in the service, most of it as a naval aviator in the Pacific theater. After his release from active duty in 1946, Meredith became a Woodrow Wilson Fellow at Princeton, then a Resident Fellow in creative writing. From 1955 until 1983 he taught at Connecticut College. He has been the recipient of several poetry awards, and in 1978–80 served as poetry consultant to the Library of Congress. He is Chancellor of the Academy of American Poets.

On Falling Asleep by Firelight

The wolf and the lamb shall feed together, and the lion shall eat straw
like the bullock, and dust shall be the serpent's meat
—Isaiah 65

Around the fireplace, pointing at the fire,
As in the prophet's dream of the last truce,

The animals lie down; they doze or stare,
Their hooves and paws in comical disuse;
A few still run in dreams. None seems aware   5
Of the laws of prey that lie asleep here too,
The dreamer unafraid who keeps the zoo.

Some winter nights impel us to take in
Whatever lopes outside, beastly or kind;
Nothing that gibbers in or out of mind   10
But the hearth bestows a sleepy sense of kin.
Promiscuous hosts, we bid the causeless slime
Come in; its casualness remains a crime
But metaphysics bites less sharp than wind.

Now too a ghostly, gradually erect   15
Company lies down, weary of the walk,
Parents with whom we would but cannot talk;
Beside them on the floor, their artifacts—
Weapons we gave them which they now bring back.
If they see our privilege, they do not object,   20
And we are not ashamed to be their stock.

All we had thought unkind were all the while
Alike, the firelight says and strikes us dumb;
We dream there is no ravening or guile
And take it kindly of the beasts to come   25
And suffer hospitality; the heat
Turns softly on the hearth into that dust
Isaiah said would be the serpent's meat.

                                                       1958

Bachelor

A mystic in the morning, half asleep,
He is given a vision of the unity
That informs a small apartment, barefooted.
He takes the long view of toes in the bath-tub
And shaves a man whose destiny is mild.   5
He perceives hidden resemblances; particularly
He is struck by how breakfast equipment imitates her,
The object of his less than mystic dream.
Sunlight, orange-juice, newsprint, kitchenware:
Is it love's trick of doubling? Everywhere   10
Like those little dogs in Goya,[1] objects show
A gift for mimicry. His coffee is morose.
A clock goes off next-door where probably
Someone has parodied his dream; and here
The solemn little mongrels of the day   15
Stare out at him, trying to look like her.

---

1. Francisco Goya y Lucientes (1746–1828), Spanish painter. In his portrait of the Duchess of Alba, who wears a white dress and a red bow, she is mimicked by a little white dog also wearing a red bow.

They leer and flirt.
                    Let saints and painters deal
With the mystery of likeness. As for him,
It scares him wide awake and dead alone;
A man of action dials the telephone.   20

1958

Crossing Over

It was now early spring, and the river was swollen and turbulent; great cakes of
floating ice were swinging heavily to and fro in the turbid waters. Owing to a peculiar form of the shore, on the Kentucky side, the land bending far out into the
water, the ice had been lodged and detained in great quantities, and the narrow
channel which swept round the bend was full of ice, piled one cake over another,
thus forming a temporary barrier to the descending ice, which lodged, and formed
a great undulating raft. . . . Eliza stood, for a moment, contemplating this unfavorable aspect of things.
                                    —Uncle Tom's Cabin *(Chapter VII, "The Mother's*
                                        Struggle") / Harriet Beecher Stowe[2]

That's what love is like. The whole river
is melting. We skim along in great peril,

having to move faster than ice goes under
and still find foothold in the soft floe.

We are one another's floe. Each displaces the weight   5
of his own need. I am fat as a bloodhound,[3]

hold me up. I won't hurt you. Though I bay,
I would swim with you on my back until the cold

seeped into my heart. We are committed, we
are going across this river willy-nilly.   10

No one, black or white, is free in Kentucky,
old gravity owns everybody. We're weighty.

I contemplate this unfavorable aspect of things.
Where is something solid? Only you and me.

Has anyone ever been to Ohio?   15
Do the people there stand firmly on icebergs?

Here all we have is love, a great undulating
raft, melting steadily. We go out on it

anyhow. I love you, I love this fool's walk.
The thing we have to learn is how to walk light.   20

1980

2. The epigraph is from the well-known scene
in which the slave girl Eliza, with her young son,
struggles to cross the Ohio River; the novel was
published in 1852.
    3. Bloodhounds were often used to track runa-
way slaves.

Dying Away

(Homage to Sigmund Freud)[4]

"Toward the person who has died
we adopt a special attitude:
something like admiration
for someone who has accomplished
a very difficult task," he said,   5

and now hospitals and rest-homes
are filled with heroes and heroines
in smocks, at their out-sized, unwonted tasks,
now the second date on tombstones is a saint's day[5]
and there is no craven in any graveyard,   10

no malingerer there, no trivial person.
It is you and I, still milling around,
who evade our callings, incestuous
in our love for the enduring trees and the snowfall,
for brook-noise and coins, songs, appetites.   15

And with the one we love most,
the mated one we lose track of ourselves in—
who's giving, who's taking that fleshy pleasure?—
we call those calmings-away, those ecstasies
dyings,[6] we see them as diligent rehearsals.   20

The love of living disturbs me,
I am wracked like a puritan by eros[7] and health,
almost undone by brotherhood, rages
of happiness seize me, the world, the fair world,
and I call on the name of the dark healer, Freud.   25

His appetites, songs, orgasms died away,
his young brother, his daughter, his huge father,
until he saw that the *aim* of life was death.
But a man cannot learn heroism from another,
he owes the world some death of his own invention.   30

Then he said, "My dear Schur,[8] you certainly remember
our first talk. You promised me then not to forsake me
when my time came. Now it is nothing but torture
and makes no sense any more."
Schur gave him two centigrams of morphine.   35

At what cost he said it, so diligent of life,
so curious, we can't guess
who are still his conjurings. He told us

---

4. Austrian neurologist and founder of psychoanalysis (1856–1939).
5. Day in the church calendar on which a saint
is commemorated.
6. In the seventeenth century "dying" was a
poetic term for sexual intercourse, on the grounds
that every orgasm shortens one's life a little.
7. Love.
8. Max Schur (1897–1969), Freud's doctor.

it is impossible to imagine our own deaths,
he told us, this may be the secret of heroism.

40

1980

KEITH DOUGLAS
1920–1944

Keith Douglas was killed in his twenties in World War II as his poetic compatriots,
Wilfred Owen and Rupert Brooke, were killed in World War I. Douglas was not
inclined to claim much in the way of heroism: he spoke in "Aristocrats" of "this gentle
/ obsolescent breed of heroes," with "their stupidity and chivalry." Nor is there place
for patriotism, but only sympathy, a sympathy which he expresses even for the enemy
in whom lover and killer were mingled ("Vergissmeinnicht").

His early work was lyrical; he came to disdain lyricism because he related it to
innocence and could no longer feel in that way. His poems all have about them an
unexpectedness, which he associated with "the nature of poetry." As he said, "Poetry
is like a man, whom thinking you know all his movements and appearance you will
presently come upon in such a posture that for a moment you can hardly believe it a
position of the limbs you know."[1] He wanted to sing "of what the others have never
set eyes on" ("Desert Flowers"). His images, often sardonic, are sharp and pictorial,
and appear, though naturally, in odd frames.

Douglas was born at Tunbridge Wells, Kent, on January 24, 1920. He began to
write poems with some expertness while still at school, and at Oxford, where he
spent two years before being called up for active service, he began to publish a good
deal in magazines. He received a commission and went to the Middle East; his experiences there are described in his war journal, *Alamein to Zem Zem*. He insisted on
being in the front line here and then in the Normandy invasion. On June 9, 1944,
during the landings, Douglas was killed after getting information from behind the
enemy lines, for which he was officially commended.

1. *Collected Poems,* ed. J. Waller and G. S. Fraser, London, 1951, p. 148.

Aristocrats[1]

"I think I am becoming a God"

The noble horse with courage in his eye,
clean in the bone, looks up at a shellburst:
away fly the images of the shires[2]
but he puts the pipe back in his mouth.

Peter was unfortunately killed by an 88:[3]   5
it took his leg away, he died in the ambulance.
I saw him crawling on the sand, he said
It's most unfair, they've shot my foot off.

How can I live among this gentle
obsolescent breed of heroes, and not weep?   10

1. Desmond Graham, editor of *The Complete
Poems of Keith Douglas* (1978), prefers and prints
on p. 110 another, perhaps later but inferior, version of this poem, entitled "Sportsmen." The dying
words of the Roman emperor Vespasian (died 79

A.D.) were supposedly: "Alas! I suppose I am turning into a god."
2. Counties.
3. German tank fitted with an 88-millimeter gun.

Unicorns, almost,
for they are falling into two legends
in which their stupidity and chivalry
are celebrated. Each, fool and hero, will be an immortal.

The plains were their cricket pitch[4]   15
and in the mountains the tremendous drop fences[5]
brought down some of the runners. Here then
under the stones and earth they dispose themselves,
I think with their famous unconcern.
It is not gunfire I hear, but a hunting horn.[6]   20

Tunisia, 1943   1946

Vergissmeinnicht[7]

Three weeks gone and the combatants gone
returning over the nightmare ground
we found the place again, and found
the soldier sprawling in the sun.

The frowning barrel of his gun   5
overshadowing. As we came on
that day, he hit my tank with one
like the entry of a demon.

Look. Here in the gunpit spoil
the dishonoured picture of his girl   10
who has put: *Steffi. Vergissmeinnicht*
in a copybook gothic script.

We see him almost with content,
abased, and seeming to have paid
and mocked at by his own equipment   15
that's hard and good when he's decayed.

But she would weep to see today
how on his skin the swart flies move;
the dust upon the paper eye
and the burst stomach like a cave.   20

For here the lover and killer are mingled
who had one body and one heart.
And death who had the soldier singled
has done the lover mortal hurt.

Tunisia, May–June 1943   1946

---

4. Field on which the game of cricket is played.
5. Fences in the course of a steeplechase horse race.
6. "Lt.-Col. J. D. Player, killed in Tunisia, Enfidaville, February, 1943, left £3,000 to the Beaufort Hunt, and directed that the incumbent of the living in his gift [that is, the church whose vicar he was entitled to appoint] should be a 'man who approves of hunting, shooting, and all manly sports, which are the backbone of the nation' " (Douglas's note on one of the manuscripts of "Aristocrats," noted by Jon Stallworthy. Player was in fact killed in April).
7. Forget me not (German).

Soissons

M. l'Epicier[8] in his white hat
in an outhouse by the cathedral, makes
devils from the selfsame stone
men used in the religious century.
The cathedral itself in new masonry   5
of white, stands openly in this sunlit town,
Soissons. Down the long hill snakes
the hard hot road into the town's heart.

In the evening when the late sunlight abandons
buildings still glimmering from shadow on shadow   10
someone leans from the window eavesdropping our
strange voices so late in the cathedral square.
From the barracks of the 19th Regiment you can hear
the equivalent of Lights Out. Now the sweet-sour
wine clambers in our heads. Go in. Tomorrow   15
tiptoes with us along the dark landing.

'A Laon, belle Cathédrale',[9] making
a wave of his white hat, explains
the maker of gargoyles. So we take
a route for Laon and Rheims leaving you   20
Soissons, a simplified medieval view
taken from a Book of Hours.[1] How dark
seems the whole country we enter. Now it rains,
and trees like ominous old men are shaking.

Oxford, 1940   1951

Simplify Me When I'm Dead

Remember me when I am dead
and simplify me when I'm dead.

As the processes of earth
strip off the colour and the skin
take the brown hair and blue eye   5

and leave me simpler than at birth,
when hairless I came howling in
as the moon came in the cold sky.

Of my skeleton perhaps
so stripped, a learned man will say   10
'He was of such a type and intelligence,' no more.

---

8. Literally, "Mr. Grocer." The "devils" he carves are gargoyles, decorations for the cathedral.
9. At Laon, a beautiful cathedral (French). Soissons, Laon, and Rheims are equidistant from each other.
1. Book containing prayers to be said at designated times; medieval ones were often decorated with paintings and illuminations.

Thus when in a year collapse
particular memories, you may
deduce, from the long pain I bore

the opinions I held, who was my foe   15
and what I left, even my appearance
but incidents will be no guide.

Time's wrong-way telescope will show
a minute man ten years hence
and by distance simplified.   20

Through that lens see if I seem
substance or nothing: of the world
deserving mention or charitable oblivion

not by momentary spleen
or love into decision hurled,   25
leisurely arrive at an opinion.

Remember me when I am dead
and simplify me when I'm dead.

1951

HOWARD NEMEROV
b. 1920

One of Howard Nemerov's favorite words for describing his own poetry and poetry
in general is "subversive." He likes to approach his subjects obliquely, to take his
readers a little by surprise, and to upset our conventional ways of seeing things. His
poems combat fixities; Nemerov deplores any kind of idolatry, any institution or
cliché that blinds our appreciation of the free and lively movements of life. The
literary atmosphere in which he grew up—dominated by Eliot, Yeats, and Auden,
the poets whom he began by imitating—encouraged the view of "irony, paradox and
wit [as] the primary means of imagination, . . . a view that did not always sharply
divide the funny from the serious, and even the sorrowful."[1] Nemerov has since
come to realize that the poetry of paradox may have "cut poets off from great ranges
of experience that begin and end in places deeper than consciousness can be happy
in."[2] His own poetry has moved steadily from an obligation to ambiguity towards
lucidity and precision; Nemerov now regards "simplicity and the appearance of ease
in the measure as primary values, and the detachment of a single thought from its
ambiguous surroundings as a worthier object than the deliberate cultivation of ambiguity."[3] Despite the changes in his poetry, however, Nemerov retains a commitment
to wit in the old-fashioned sense, the power to see relationships among disparate
phenomena and to create metaphors. For him, poetry is the art of "combination, or
discovering the secret valencies which the most widely differing things have for one
another."[4] Nemerov's new combinations of experience often emerge as jokes, and

1. "Attentiveness and Obedience," from *Poets
on Poetry*, ed. Howard Nemerov, New York, 1966,
p. 240.
  2. The same, p. 243.
  3. The same, p. 240.

4. Quoted by Robert D. Harvey in "A Prophet
Armed: An Introduction to the Poetry of Howard
Nemerov," in *Poets in Progress*, ed. Edward
Hungerford, Chicago, 1967, p. 125.

ɟ of reading his poems is in watching the shifts in his comic sense.
one of the plelly raised by literary critics," he writes, "has been that my poems
"The chargead jokes. I incline to agree, insisting however that they are bad
are jokes, errible jokes, emerging from the nature of things as well as from my
jokes, aɔming at things a touch subversively, and from the blind side, or the
prope ide everyone concerned with 'values' would just as soon forget."[5]
darʰmerov was born in New York City on March 1, 1920, and lived there
ʰen he enrolled at Harvard. He received his B.A. in 1941, then enlisted
ʎian Air Force and became a pilot; he joined the U.S. Army Air Corps
two years of the war. Married in 1944, Nemerov returned to New York
ischarge and lived there for a year, working as an editor of the literary
ɩ *Furioso* and completing his first book of poems, *The Image and the Law*,
as published in 1947. Since then he has been a college teacher at several
ʿs, most recently Washington University. "I like teaching," he remarks, "partly
ɩ is . . . a fairly agreeable way of making a dollar, partly because it makes
a more or less quiet life (if you have sense enough to stop talking after hours),
ɩrtly because teaching has been for me an education (Lord knows what it has
for my students)."[6] A Kenyon Review Fellow in fiction in 1955 (he has written
ɔe novels and a number of short stories) and a Guggenheim Fellow in 1968, Nem-
.ov served as Consultant in Poetry to the Library of Congress in 1963–64. In 1978
ʰe won the Pulitzer Prize for his *Collected Poems*.

5. "Attentiveness and Obedience," p. 246.
6. "An Interview with Howard Nemerov," *Trace*, January 1960.

I Only Am Escaped Alone to Tell Thee[1]

I tell you that I see her still
At the dark entrance of the hall.
One gas lamp burning near her shoulder
Shone also from her other side
Where hung the long inaccurate glass   5
Whose pictures were as troubled water.
An immense shadow had its hand
Between us on the floor, and seemed
To hump the knuckles nervously,
A giant crab readying to walk,   10
Or a blanket moving in its sleep.

You will remember, with a smile
Instructed by movies to reminisce,
How strict her corsets must have been,
How the huge arrangements of her hair   15
Would certainly betray the least
Impassionate displacement there.
It was no rig for dallying,
And maybe only marriage could
Derange that queenly scaffolding—   20
As when a great ship, coming home,
Coasts in the harbor, dropping sail

1. In Job 1:14–19, the words of the messengers who tell Job of the destruction of his family and possessions. Herman Melville in *Moby-Dick* sets these words at the head of the epilogue, which is a report by the only survivor of Captain Ahab's maniacal hunt for the white whale.

And loosing all the tackle that had laced
Her in the long lanes . . .
                    I know
We need not draw this figure out
But all that whalebone[2] came from whales   25
And all the whales lived in the sea,
In calm beneath the troubled glass,
Until the needle drew their blood.

I see her standing in the hall,
Where the mirror's lashed to blood and foam,
And the black flukes of agony
Beat at the air till the light blows out.

Wolves in the Zoo

They look like big dogs badly drawn, drawn wrong.
A legend on their cage tells us there is
No evidence that any of their kind
Has ever attacked man, woman, or child.

Now it turns out there were no babies dropped   5
In sacrifice, delaying tactics, from
Siberian sleds; now it turns out, so late,
That Little Red Ridinghood and her Gran

Were the aggressors with the slavering fangs
And tell-tale tails; now it turns out at last   10
That grey wolf and timber wolf are near extinct,
Done out of being by the tales we tell

Told us by Nanny in the nursery;
Young sparks[3] we were, to set such forest fires
As blazed from story into history   15
And put such bounty on their wolvish heads

As brought the few survivors to our terms,
Surrendered in happy Babylon among
The peacock dusting off the path of dust,
The tiger pacing in the stripéd shade.[4]   20

1975

Reading Pornography in Old Age

Unbridled licentiousness with no holds barred,
Immediate and mutual lust, satisfiable

2. That is, in her corset.
3. Also in the sense of young spark, bright
youngster.
4. The zoo is compared to the ancient city of
Babylon by association with the tower of Babel

(Hebrew version of "Babylon") because the animals' cries sound like the confusion of languages
which was the result of the tower (Genesis 11:1–
9). The bars on his cage casting shadows on its
floor cause the tiger's "striped shade."

In the heat, upon demand, aroused again
And satisfied again, lechery unlimited,

Till space runs out at the bottom of the page   5
And another pair of lovers, forever young,
Prepotent,[5] endlessly receptive, renews
The daylong, nightlong, interminable grind.

How decent it is, and how unlike our lives
Where "fuck you" is a term of vengeful scorn   10
And the murmur of "sorry, partner" as often heard
As ever in mixed doubles or at bridge.

Though I suspect the stuff is written by
Elderly homosexuals manacled to their
Machines, it's mildly touching all the same,   15
A reminiscence of the life that was in Eden

Before the Fall, when we were beautiful
And shameless, and untouched by memory:
Before we were driven out to the laboring world
Of the money and the garbage and the kids   20
In which we read this nonsense and are moved
At all that was always lost for good, in which
We think about sex obsessively except
During the act, when our minds tend to wander.

1984

More Joy in Heaven[6]

This bird that a cat sprang loose in the house,
Still flyably warm and wet from the cat's mouth,
Beat like a heart set fluttering with fear;
The bird's heart first, but ours beat after it.

Some comedy came of this, the saner sort   5
Opening doors, the others batting at cats
With brooms, or flying towels at the bird
To muffle it safe from enemy and self;

Who after getting confused among the drapes
And flopping back from a window, from a wall,   10
Found out the empty daylight of a door
Left open, and left, thinking the good thoughts

It would tell its children in our children's books
About an ultimate kindness to the world
Where once, in a legend of the Golden Age,[7]   15
One ecosystem beat the other, once.

1987

---

5. Having exceptional power, very potent.
6. "I say unto you that likewise joy shall be in
heaven over one sinner that repenteth, more than
over ninety and nine just persons, which need no
repentance" (Luke 15:7).
7. Legendary time of innocent happiness.

AMY CLAMPITT
b. 1920

Amy Clampitt is open about her debts to older poets who have helped her to shape her own verse. They include Gerard Manley Hopkins, from whom she borrowed the epigraph for her first volume of poems *The Kingfisher* ("As kingfishers catch fire, dragonflies draw flame . . ."), and John Keats, to whom she dedicates a sequence of biographical poems. In these two poets Clampitt finds a compacted sensuousness to which she herself aspires. And, like her older contemporary Marianne Moore, she writes lines which are often odd assortments, poems in which the quotidian is pondered and transformed. Such a transformation takes place in "Gooseberry Fool." The title refers to an English dessert, a stewed, rather acid-tasting fruit garnished with heavy cream. The gooseberry comes to stand for a certain human temperament or stage of life—a person shy, withdrawn, prickly, *farouche*. The round green berry which rouses these associations, as the poet with her own modesty and arrogance realizes, is her alternative to the "great globe itself."

The organization of Clampitt's poems is often playful, even when the subject is usually considered more gravely and portentously. "Beach Glass" begins with a brief account of the poet's companion, who is "turning over concepts" in a meditation which she does not share. She then watches the ocean—they are taking a walk along the beach—which she imagines as a sleepy, ageless keeper of the inventory of the worn out and cast away: "For the ocean, nothing / is beneath consideration." The poet herself is a collector; she keeps an eye out for bits of glass (beer and wine bottles, the bright blue fragments of laxative bottles). Finally, the poet realizes that the grand structures of the past, treasured by the well-traveled poet, will be worn away, leaving only fragments to be collected and wondered at. It is the lot of the past to be, often without comprehension, turned over and over, as the ocean shifts and moves its inheritance, and it is our lot to do our share of the turning.

Amy Clampitt, born in 1920, was raised in New Providence, Iowa. She studied at Grinnell College, then worked for the Oxford University Press and as a reference librarian. She then became a free-lance writer and editor. She lives in New York City.

Beach Glass

While you walk the water's edge,
turning over concepts
I can't envision, the honking buoy
serves notice that at any time
the wind may change,   5
the reef-bell clatters
its treble monotone, deaf as Cassandra
to any note but warning.[1] The ocean,
cumbered by no business more urgent
than keeping open old accounts   10
that never balanced,
goes on shuffling its millenniums
of quartz, granite, and basalt.

---

1. The "reef bell" is a bell that warns ships of a reef of rocks or sand beneath the surface of the water. Cassandra is the Trojan prophetess in Homer's *Iliad* who prophesied the fall of Troy; because of Apollo's curse, however, no one believed her. Since doom was all that she prophesied, she is deaf "to any note but warning."

It behaves
toward the permutations of novelty—   15
driftwood and shipwreck, last night's
beer cans, spilt oil, the coughed-up
residue of plastic—with random
impartiality, playing catch or tag
or touch-last[2] like a terrier   20
turning the same thing over and over,
over and over. For the ocean, nothing
is beneath consideration.
                     The houses
of so many mussels and periwinkles[3]   25
have been abandoned here, it's hopeless
to know which to salvage. Instead
I keep a lookout for beach glass—
amber of Budweiser, chrysoprase
of Almadén and Gallo, lapis[4]   30
by way of (no getting around it,
I'm afraid) Phillips'
Milk of Magnesia, with now and then a rare
translucent turquoise or blurred amethyst
of no known origin.   35
                     The process
goes on forever: they came from sand,
they go back to gravel,
along with the treasuries
of Murano, the buttressed
astonishments of Chartres,[5]   40
which even now are readying
for being turned over and over as gravely
and gradually as an intellect
engaged in the hazardous   45
redefinition of structures
no one has yet looked at.

                                       1987

Gooseberry Fool[6]

The gooseberry's no doubt an oddity,
an outlaw or pariah[7] even—thorny
and tart as any
kindergarten martinet, it can harbor
like a fernseed, on its leaves' under-   5
side, bad news for pine trees,
whereas the spruce
resists the blister rust
it's host to. That veiny Chinese
lantern, its stolid jelly   10

---

2. A game like kick-the-can.
3. Varieties of shellfish.
4. Or lapis lazuli, a rich, azure blue color (and the name of a semiprecious stone); "chryso-phrase": apple-green color (also a semiprecious stone).

5. Chartres Cathedral, in France, is noted for the beauty of its stained-glass windows; Murano, in Italy, is famous for its glass work.
6. Dessert made of mashed fruit with custard and cream.
7. Outcast.

of a fruit, not only has
no aroma but is twice as tedious
as the wild strawberry's sunburst
stem-end appendage: each one must
be between-nail-snipped at both extremities.   15

Altogether, gooseberry virtues
take some getting
used to, much as does trepang,
tripe à la mode de Caen,[8]
or having turned thirteen.   20
The acerbity of all things green
and adolescent lingers in
it—the arrogant, shrinking,
prickling-in-every-direction thorn-
iness that loves no company except its,   25
or anyhow that's what it gets:
bristling up through gooseberry ghetto sprawl
are braced thistles' silvery, militantly symmetrical
defense machineries. Likewise inseparably en-
tangled in the disarray of an   30
uncultivated childhood, where gooseberry bushes (since
rooted out) once flourished, is
the squandered volupté of lemon-
yellow-petaled roses' luscious flimflam—
an inkling of the mingling into one experience   35
of suave and sharp, whose supremely im-
probable and far-fetched culinary
embodiment is a gooseberry fool.

Tomorrow, having stumbled into
this trove of chief ingredients   40
(the other being very thickest cream)
I'll demonstrate it for you. Ever since,
four summers ago, I brought you,
a gleeful Ariel,[9] the trophy
of a small sour handful,   45
I've wondered what not quite articulated thing
could render magical
the green globe of an unripe berry.
I think now it was simply
the great globe itself's too much to carry.[1]   50
                                                                1985

A Cure at Porlock[2]

For whatever did it—the cider
at the Ship Inn, where the crowd

---

8. A gourmet dish made out of tripe (from a cow's
stomach); presumably an acquired taste, like "trepang," a cooked sea-worm dish eaten in the Far
East.
9. The airy sprite who does the bidding of the
magician Prospero in Shakespeare's *The Tempest*
(1611).

1. Compare Prospero's speech toward the end
of the *Tempest*: "The great globe itself, / Nay, all
which it inherit, shall dissolve" (4.1.153–54).
2. "'In the summer of the year 1797, the
Author, then in ill health, had retired to a lonely
farm-house between Porlock and Linton, on the
Exmoor confines of Somerset and Devonshire. In

from the bar that night had overflowed
singing into Southey's Corner,[3] or

an early warning of appendicitis—
the remedy the chemist in the High Street   5
purveyed was still a dose of kaopectate[4]
in morphine—the bane and the afflatus

of S.T.C.[5] when Alph, the sacred river,
surfaced briefly in the unlikely   10
vicinity of Baker Farm,[6] and as quickly
sank again, routed forever by the visitor

whose business, intent and disposition—
whether ill or well is just as immaterial—
long ago sunk Lethewards,[7] a particle   15
of the unbottled ultimate solution.[8]

I drank my dose, and after an afternoon
prostrate, between heaves, on the
coldly purgatorial tiles of the W.C.
found it elysium[9] simply to recline,   20

sipping flat ginger beer as though it were
honeydue,[1] in that billowy bed,
under pink chenille, hearing you read
The Mystery of Edwin Drood! For whether

the opium was worth it for John Jasper,[2]   25
from finding being with you, even sick
at Porlock, a rosily addictive picnic,
I left less likely ever to recover.

1985

consequence of a slight indisposition, an anodyne [pain-killing drug] had been prescribed, from the effect of which he fell asleep in his chair. . . . The Author continued for about three hours in a profound sleep, at least of the external senses, during which time he has the most vivid confidence that he could not have composed less than from two to three hundred lines. . . . On waking he appeared to himself to have a distinct recollection of the whole, and taking his pen, ink, and paper, instantly and eagerly wrote down the lines that are here preserved. At this moment he was unfortunately called out by a person on business from Porlock, and detained by him above an hour, and on his return to his room, found . . . that . . . with the exception of some eight or ten scattered lines and images, all the rest had been passed away like the images of the surface of a stream into which a stone had been cast. . . .' This is Samuel Taylor Coleridge's account, written some years later, of the composition of 'Kubla Khan' [1816]. The anodyne he mentions was presumably a form of opium, to which he was addicted for much of his adult life" (Clampitt's note). Compare, above, Stevie Smith's "Thoughts about the Person from Porlock."
3. Named after the poet Robert Southey, a contemporary of Coleridge's.

4. An anti-diarrhetic mixture with a pain-deadening drug; "chemist": U.S. pharmacist; "High Street": U.S. "Main Street."
5. Samuel Taylor Coleridge (his friend Charles Lamb often referred to him as "STC"); "afflatus": divine inspiration.
6. The farm where Coleridge was living (see note 9); "Alph, the sacred river" appears in "Kubla Khan" (line 3).
7. That is, toward the river in Hades (classical underworld) whose waters cause forgetfulness; compare also John Keats's "Ode to a Nightingale" (1819): "and Lethe-wards had sunk" (line 4).
8. (1) Liquid mixture, as of medicine; (2) answer (as in Adolf Hitler's attempt to exterminate the Jews as "the Final Solution").
9. That is, bliss (Elysium was the abode of the blessed dead in classical mythology); "W. C.": water-closet, Britishism for bathroom.
1. Compare "Kubla Khan" once more: "For he on honeydew hath fed, / And drunk the milk of Paradise" (lines 53–54); "ginger beer" is similar to U.S. ginger ale.
2. "The ravages of [opium] addiction, as embodied in the character of John Jasper, form a major theme of Dickens's unfinished last novel, *Edwin Drood* [1870]" (Clampitt's note).

RICHARD WILBUR
b. 1921

In the geography of modern verse, Richard Wilbur situates himself at an opposite pole from Robert Lowell. Possibly with this difference in mind, Lowell distinguished two kinds of modern poetry, the cooked and the raw—a distinction originally made by the French anthropologist Claude Lévi-Strauss. Wilbur's poetry is elaborately cooked, or, to elevate the metaphor, he is Apollonian while Lowell is Dionysian: that is, he centers his work in the achievement of illuminated, controlled moments rather than in sudden immersions in chaos and despair. But, just as Lowell is not merely chaotic, so Wilbur is not merely measured and self-possessed. He is alive to inner challenges, and while his mode of expression is more sedate, and more deft, than Lowell's, it begins in cross-purposes and cross-sympathies even if it culminates in quintessences of a terrestrial paradise.

His serious attempts to write poetry began during the Second World War and arose out of it. As he has said, "It was not until World War II took me to Cassino, Anzio and the Siegfried Line that I began to versify in earnest. One does not use poetry for its major purposes, as a means of organizing oneself and the world, until one's world somehow gets out of hand. A general cataclysm is not required; the disorder must be personal and may be wholly so, but poetry, to be vital, does seem to need a periodic acquaintance with the threat of Chaos."[1] Wilbur endorses organization without wanting it to be easy: so in "The Beacon" he salutes a human artifact ("sighted ship / Assembles all the sea") while in "Caserta Garden" he cautions, in speaking of the "garden of the world," that "Its shapes escape our simpler symmetries."

Wilbur announced in his first book two of his principal poetic interests. In "Cigales," with which *The Beautiful Changes* begins, he praises the song made by crickets because it both puzzles and joys; though not straightly apprehended (or as T. S. Eliot said of poetry, "not perfectly understood"), it has a healing power for others. Paradoxically, it has none for the crickets, since, according to the naturalist Fabre, they cannot hear their own song. This is a bow to pure, gratuitous verse, as opposed to social protest or religious affirmation. The next poem, "Water Walker," compares the poet not to a motiveless critic, but to a caddis fly, which lives in two elements, air and water, as the poet, ironic and ambiguous, subsists at once in two atmospheres, spirit and its ground in fact.

Wilbur was born March 1, 1921, in New York City. His father, Lawrence Wilbur, was an artist; Wilbur's poem about him, "My Father Paints the Summer," praises him for disregarding the actual rain to paint a perfect summer's day, "always an imagined time." Wilbur's mother came from a family prominent in journalism, a direction which he was to follow briefly later. Two years after his birth, the family took a very old house in North Caldwell, New Jersey, and he developed there, he has said, his taste for country things; he has written a poem about the potato and writes brilliantly, as in "Seed Leaves," of plant growth—"the doom of taking shape." He worked on student newspapers at his high school and then at Amherst College. At Amherst, too, he was encouraged by his English courses to develop Horatian poems—that is, poems at once formal and rural. After the war he took an M.A. at Harvard and was elected a member of the Society of Fellows, where for three years he devoted himself to verse. He then taught at Harvard (1950–54), Wellesley (1955–57), and at Wesleyan; in 1987 he left his position as writer-in-residence at Smith to become Poet Laureate of the United States, succeeding Robert Penn Warren. Besides five small volumes of verse Wilbur has made splendid translations of Molière's *The*

---

1. *Twentieth Century Authors*, First Supplement, ed. Stanley Kunitz, 1955, p. 1080.

Misanthrope and *Tartuffe*, and of Racine's *Phèdre*. With Lillian Hellman he wrote lyrics for a comic opera, *Candide*, based on Voltaire's novel. In the wit and form of these French originals his talent finds an obvious kinship.

The Pardon

My dog lay dead five days without a grave
In the thick of summer, hid in a clump of pine
And a jungle of grass and honeysuckle-vine.
I who had loved him while he kept alive

Went only close enough to where he was   5
To sniff the heavy honeysuckle-smell
Twined with another odor heavier still
And hear the flies' intolerable buzz.

Well, I was ten and very much afraid.
In my kind world the dead were out of range   10
And I could not forgive the sad or strange
In beast or man. My father took the spade

And buried him. Last night I saw the grass
Slowly divide (it was the same scene
But now it glowed a fierce and mortal green)   15
And saw the dog emerging. I confess

I felt afraid again, but still he came
In the carnal sun, clothed in a hymn of flies,
And death was breeding in his lively eyes.
I started in to cry and call his name,   20

Asking forgiveness of his tongueless head.
. . . I dreamt the past was never past redeeming:
But whether this was false or honest dreaming
I beg death's pardon now. And mourn the dead.

1950

Grasse:[1] The Olive Trees

For Marcelle and Ferdinand Springer

Here luxury's the common lot. The light
Lies on the rain-pocked rocks like yellow wool
And around the rocks the soil is rusty bright
From too much wealth of water, so that the grass
Mashes under the foot, and all is full   5
Of heat and juice and a heavy jammed excess.

Whatever moves moves with the slow complete
Gestures of statuary. Flower smells

---

1. Grasse is a city in southern France.

Are set in the golden day, and shelled in heat,
Pine and columnar cypress stand. The palm   10
Sinks its combs in the sky. This whole South swells
To a soft rigor, a rich and crowded calm.

Only the olive contradicts. My eye,
Traveling slopes of rust and green, arrests
And rests from plenitude where olives lie   15
Like clouds of doubt against the earth's array.
Their faint disheveled foliage divests
The sunlight of its color and its sway.

Not that the olive spurns the sun; its leaves
Scatter and point to every part of the sky,   20
Like famished fingers waving. Brilliance weaves
And sombers down among them, and among
The anxious silver branches, down to the dry
And twisted trunk, by rooted hunger wrung.

Even when seen from near, the olive shows   25
A hue of far away. Perhaps for this
The dove brought olive back, a tree which grows
Unearthly pale, which ever dims and dries,
And whose great thirst, exceeding all excess,
Teaches the South it is not paradise.

                                                             1950

The Death of a Toad[2]

A toad the power mower caught,
Chewed and clipped of a leg, with a hobbling hop has got
    To the garden verge, and sanctuaried him
    Under the cineraria leaves, in the shade
        Of the ashen heartshaped leaves, in a dim,   5
        Low, and a final glade.

The rare original heartsblood goes,
Spends on the earthen hide, in the folds and wizenings, flows
    In the gutters of the banked and staring eyes. He lies
    As still as if he would return to stone,   10
        And soundlessly attending, dies
        Toward some deep monotone,

Toward misted and ebullient seas
And cooling shores, toward lost Amphibia's emperies.[3]
    Day dwindles, drowning, and at length is gone   15

2. This poem, according to Wilbur, is "the only
instance in which I went straight from something
that happened to me to writing a poem about it,
with very little violation of the actual circumstances, though I put more into it before I was
through than I'd felt at the time."
3. Wilbur, asked about this word, replied: "I
may have found it in John Donne in the first place,
but I think I wanted to use it here as a kind of
confession that I'm doing rather a lot with that toad.
I'm turning him into the primal energies of the
world in the course of this poem. And so I get a
little bombastic as a way of acknowledging that I'm
going rather far." Amphibia is imagined as the
presiding spirit of the toad's (and of all amphib-
ians') universe.

In the wide and antique eyes, which still appear
  To watch, across the castrate lawn,
    The haggard daylight steer.

                              1950

Ceremony

A striped blouse in a clearing by Bazille[4]
Is, you may say, a patroness of boughs
Too queenly kind toward nature to be kin.
But ceremony never did conceal,
Save to the silly eye, which all allows,   5
How much we are the woods we wander in.

Let her be some Sabrina[5] fresh from stream,
Lucent as shallows slowed by wading sun,
Bedded on fern, the flowers' cynosure:
Then nymph and wood must nod and strive to dream   10
That she is airy earth, the trees, undone,
Must ape her languor natural and pure.

Ho-hum. I am for wit and wakefulness,
And love this feigning lady by Bazille.
What's lightly hid is deepest understood,   15
And when with social smile and formal dress
She teaches leaves to curtsey and quadrille,
I think there are most tigers in the wood.

                              1950

Love Calls Us to the Things of This World[6]

    The eyes open to a cry of pulleys,
And spirited from sleep, the astounded soul
Hangs for a moment bodiless and simple
As false dawn.
            Outside the open window
The morning air is all awash with angels.   5

    Some are in bed-sheets, some are in blouses,
Some are in smocks: but truly there they are.
Now they are rising together in calm swells
Of halcyon feeling, filling whatever they wear
With the deep joy of their impersonal breathing;   10

---

4. Frédéric Bazille (1841–1871), French painter associated with the Impressionists. Most of his paintings show figures in close association with a landscape.
5. The nymph of the river Severn, in Milton's *Comus*, but here identified with thoughtless, unceremonious nature, and contrasted with Bazille's lady.
6. The title is quoted from St. Augustine. "You must imagine the poem as occurring at perhaps seven-thirty in the morning; the scene is a bedroom high up in a city apartment building; outside the bedroom window, the first laundry of the day is being yanked across the sky and one has been awakened by the squeaking pulleys of the laundry-line" (Wilbur, in *Poets in Progress*, New York, 1966, p. 169).

Now they are flying in place, conveying
The terrible speed of their omnipresence, moving
And staying like white water; and now of a sudden
They swoon down into so rapt a quiet
That nobody seems to be there.

The soul shrinks   15

From all that it is about to remember,
From the punctual rape of every blessed day,
And cries,
      "Oh, let there be nothing on earth but laundry,
Nothing but rosy hands in the rising steam
And clear dances done in the sight of heaven."

20

Yet, as the sun acknowledges
With a warm look the world's hunks and colors,
The soul descends once more in bitter love[7]
To accept the waking body, saying now
In a changed voice as the man yawns and rises,

25

"Bring them down from their ruddy gallows;
Let there be clean linen for the backs of thieves;
Let lovers go fresh and sweet to be undone,
And the heaviest nuns walk in a pure floating
Of dark habits,
      keeping their difficult balance."

30
1956

Pangloss's Song[8]

I

Dear boy, you will not hear me speak
   With sorrow or with rancor
Of what has paled my rosy cheek
   And blasted it with canker;
'Twas Love, great Love, that did the deed
   Through Nature's gentle laws,
And how should ill effects proceed
   From so divine a cause?

5

Sweet honey comes from bees that sting,
   As you are well aware;
To one adept in reasoning,
Whatever pains disease may bring
Are but the tangy seasoning
   To Love's delicious fare.

10

---

7. "Plato, St. Theresa, and the rest of us in our degree have known that it is painful to return to the cave, to the earth, to the quotidian: Augustine says that it is love that brings us back. That is why the love of line 23 has got to be bitter . . ." (Wilbur, in *The Contemporary Poet as Artist and Critic,* p. 18).

8. A lyric written for the comic operetta based on Voltaire's *Candide,* produced in New York in 1956. Dr. Pangloss is the optimistic philosopher who assures his friend, the ingenuous Candide, that all evils, even syphilis, are for the best, and that this is the best of all possible worlds.

II

Columbus and his men, they say,   15
   Conveyed the virus hither
Whereby my features rot away
   And vital powers wither;
Yet had they not traversed the seas
   And come infected back,   20
Why, think of all the luxuries
   That modern life would lack!

All bitter things conduce to sweet,
   As this example shows;
Without the little spirochet   25
We'd have no chocolate to eat,
Nor would tobacco's fragrance greet
   The European nose.

III

Each nation guards its native land
   With cannon and with sentry,   30
Inspectors look for contraband
   At every port of entry,
Yet nothing can prevent the spread
   Of Love's divine disease:
It rounds the world from bed to bed   35
   As pretty as you please.

Men worship Venus everywhere,
   As plainly may be seen;
The decorations which I bear
Are nobler than the Croix de Guerre,   40
And gained in service of our fair
   And universal Queen.

                                  1961

Playboy

High on his stockroom ladder like a dunce
The stock-boy sits, and studies like a sage
The subject matter of one glossy page,
As lost in curves as Archimedes[9] once.

Sometimes, without a glance, he feeds himself.   5
The left hand, like a mother-bird in flight,
Brings him a sandwich for a sidelong bite,
And then returns it to a dusty shelf.

What so engrosses him? The wild décor
Of this pink-papered alcove into which   10

---

9. (c.287–212 B.C.), Greek mathematician and inventor, known for his invention of a tubular helix, or screw, used to lift water from the hold of a ship.

A naked girl has stumbled, with its rich
Welter of pelts and pillows on the floor,

Amidst which, kneeling in a supple pose,
She lifts a goblet in her farther hand,
As if about to toast a flower-stand   15
Above which hovers an exploding rose

Fired from a long-necked crystal vase that rests
Upon a tasseled and vermilion cloth
One taste of which would shrivel up a moth?
Or is he pondering her perfect breasts?   20

Nothing escapes him of her body's grace
Or of her floodlit skin, so sleek and warm
And yet so strangely like a uniform,
But what now grips his fancy is her face,

And how the cunning picture holds her still   25
At just that smiling instant when her soul,
Grown sweetly faint, and swept beyond control,
Consents to his inexorable will.

                                                        1969

The Writer

In her room at the prow of the house
Where light breaks, and the windows are tossed with linden,
My daughter is writing a story.

I pause in the stairwell, hearing
From her shut door a commotion of typewriter-keys   5
Like a chain hauled over a gunwale.[1]

Young as she is, the stuff
Of her life is a great cargo, and some of it heavy:
I wish her a lucky passage.

But now it is she who pauses,   10
As if to reject my thought and its easy figure.[2]
A stillness greatens, in which

The whole house seems to be thinking,
And then she is at it again with a bunched clamor
Of strokes, and again is silent.   15

I remember the dazed starling
Which was trapped in that very room, two years ago;[3]
How we stole in, lifted a sash

---

1. Upper edge of a boat's rail.
2. Here, poetic image.

3. A bird trapped in a house portends a death,
according to New England superstition.

And retreated, not to affright it;
And how for a helpless hour, through the crack of the door,   20
We watched the sleek, wild, dark

And iridescent creature
Batter against the brilliance, drop like a glove
To the hard floor, or the desk-top,

And wait then, humped and bloody,   25
For the wits to try it again; and how our spirits
Rose when, suddenly sure,

It lifted off from a chair-back,
Beating a smooth course for the right window
And clearing the sill of the world.   30

It is always a matter, my darling,
Of life or death, as I had forgotten. I wish
What I wished you before, but harder.

1976

PHILIP LARKIN
1922–1985

Philip Larkin's first book, *The North Ship* (1945), was strongly influenced by Yeats. His later books caught his own tone, which is that of a man who has lost opportunities, failed to get the girl he wanted and got another instead (that not lasting either), and always found life less than it might have been. As an undergraduate at Oxford, Larkin belonged to the group that came to be known as the Movement, its revolt being against rhetorical excess or cosmic portentousness. The search was instead for a more even-tempered, conversational idiom, more accurate than magniloquent. Among these poets, included in an anthology called *New Lines*, Larkin, Donald Davie, and Thom Gunn have proved the most important.

Larkin was saved from the influence of Yeats by the poetry of Thomas Hardy. He inherited some of Hardy's toughness as well as dourness. Just as Hardy in "The Oxen" half wishes that he might believe a tradition out of Christian folklore, so Larkin in "Church Going" leaves the little country church with the sense that something precious, something in which he can no longer believe, has been lost. He is gentler and funnier than Hardy, however, more amused by ineptitude, more affectionate towards his readers.

In an interview Larkin summarized his discontent with "Modernism":

> What I do feel a bit rebellious about is that poetry seems to have got into the hands of a critical industry which is concerned with culture in the abstract, and this I do rather lay at the door of Eliot and Pound . . . I think a lot of this myth-kitty business has grown out of that, because first of all you have to be terribly educated, you have to read everything to know these things, and secondly you've got somehow to work them in to show that you are working them in. But to me the whole of the ancient world, the whole of classical and biblical mythology

means very little, and I think that using them today not only fills poems full of dead spots but dodges the writer's duty to be original.[1]

We should note that here Larkin is speaking as a poet, and that he is naming some of the poets who have been of use to him. Pound's eclecticism is not for him, and even readers who are poets may sometimes feel that there are parts of the *Cantos* which are rather like a tour of an ethnographic museum led by a sporadically demented guide.

Larkin was born on August 9, 1922, in Coventry, Warwickshire. His miseries as a student at Oxford are depicted in *Jill*, the first of his two novels. After taking his Oxford degree in 1943, he worked as a librarian mostly at the University of Hull. Against his rather sequestered career Larkin's poetry sparkles and asserts itself. He published only a few small books of verse. Because their manner is so quiet, and because their matter is so often melancholy contemplation, Larkin somewhat repelled critics looking for radical novelty in technique and for urgent encroachments upon the present in theme. He seems, however, to have survived this criticism. And in fact he is not without defenses. As the misquotation from Hamlet which is the title of one of his books implies, he is "the less deceived," instead of "the more deceived." Others may proceed from rapture to disenchantment, but his enchantment was never as thoroughgoing as theirs.

Larkin was not the poet to celebrate poetry, but in finding affection even when love fails, creative possibilities in loneliness, humility blossoming from unsuccess, he was more resurgent than recumbent. Two of the sustaining elements in his poems, and in his consciousness, are a sense of what "unfenced existence" might be ("Here"), and a recognition of what brilliance images have before they dissipate or diminish, as when he talks of the "bright incipience" of love in "Love Songs in Age," or notes, with complex feelings, the unrealizable aspirations of "The Whitsun Weddings." The reverse of grandiose or straining, Larkin's poetry is so evidently integral with its author, and so witty and deft, that it speaks with singular authority and aplomb.

When Sir John Betjeman died in 1984, it was widely thought that Larkin might succeed him as Poet Laureate, and it is pleasant to imagine a Royal Birthday Ode from the pen of the man who wrote the striking first lines of "This Be the Verse" and "High Windows," but Larkin's own death intervened. He died on December 2, 1985.

---

1. Philip Larkin and Ian Hamilton, "Four Conversations," *London* magazine, November 1964, pp. 71–72.

Church Going

Once I am sure there's nothing going on
I step inside, letting the door thud shut.
Another church: matting, seats, and stone,
And little books; sprawlings of flowers, cut
For Sunday, brownish now; some brass and stuff   5
Up at the holy end; the small neat organ;
And a tense, musty, unignorable silence,
Brewed God knows how long. Hatless, I take off
My cycle-clips in awkward reverence,[1]

---

1. Men commonly show reverence in a church by taking off their hats; since the speaker is "hatless," he instead takes off his bicycle-clips (usually made of metal, these prevent the trouser legs from getting entangled in the bicycle chain).

Move forward, run my hand around the font.　　　　　10
From where I stand, the roof looks almost new—
Cleaned, or restored? Someone would know: I don't.
Mounting the lectern, I peruse a few
Hectoring large-scale verses,[2] and pronounce
"Here endeth" much more loudly than I'd meant.　　15
The echoes snigger briefly. Back at the door
I sign the book, donate an Irish sixpence.[3]
Reflect the place was not worth stopping for.

Yet stop I did: in fact I often do,
And always end much at a loss like this,　　　　　20
Wondering what to look for; wondering, too,
When churches fall completely out of use
What we shall turn them into, if we shall keep
A few cathedrals chronically on show,
Their parchment, plate and pyx[4] in locked cases,　25
And let the rest rent-free to rain and sheep.
Shall we avoid them as unlucky places?

Or, after dark, will dubious women come
To make their children touch a particular stone;
Pick simples[5] for a cancer; or on some　　　　　30
Advised night see walking a dead one?
Power of some sort or other will go on
In games, in riddles, seemingly at random;
But superstition, like belief, must die,
And what remains when disbelief has gone?　　　35
Grass, weedy pavement, brambles, buttress, sky,

A shape less recognisable each week,
A purpose more obscure. I wonder who
Will be the last, the very last, to seek
This place for what it was, one of the crew　　　40
That tap and jot and know what rood-lofts[6] were?
Some ruin-bibber, randy for antique,
Or Christmas-addict, counting on a whiff
Of gown-and-bands and organ-pipes and myrrh?[7]
Or will he be my representative,　　　　　　　　45

Bored, uninformed, knowing the ghostly silt
Dispersed, yet tending to this cross of ground[8]
Through suburb scrub because it held unspilt
So long and equably what since is found
Only in separation—marriage, and birth,　　　　50
And death, and thoughts of these—for whom was built

---

2. That is, verses from a Bible printed in large type for reading aloud; "lectern": reading desk in a church.
3. Of no value in England.
4. "Parchment": church documents written on expensive paper; "plate": the church's metalware; "pyx": box, often made of gold or silver, in which communion wafers are kept.
5. Medicinal herbs.
6. A loft or gallery above the rood screen, which, in an old church, separates the nave, or main hall, from the chancel, which contains the altar; the rood-loft properly holds a rood, or cross.
7. A bitter aromatic gum used in, among other things, making incense; "gown-and-bands": the dress of an old-fashioned clergyman, consisting of a long black gown or robe and a set of narrow white strips of cloth at the neck.
8. Churches were usually built in the form of a cross.

This special shell? For, though I've no idea
What this accoutred frowsty barn[9] is worth,
It pleases me to stand in silence here;

A serious house on serious earth it is,   55
In whose blent air all our compulsions meet,
Are recognised, and robed as destinies.
And that much never can be obsolete,
Since someone will forever be surprising
A hunger in himself to be more serious,   60
And gravitating with it to this ground,
Which, he once heard, was proper to grow wise in,
If only that so many dead lie round.

                                                          1955

The Whitsun[1] Weddings

That Whitsun, I was late getting away:
            Not till about
One-twenty on the sunlit Saturday
Did my three-quarters-empty train pull out,
All windows down, all cushions hot, all sense   5
Of being in a hurry gone. We ran
Behind the backs of houses, crossed a street
Of blinding windscreens, smelt the fish-dock, thence
The river's level drifting breadth began,
Where sky and Lincolnshire and water meet.   10

All afternoon, through the tall heat that slept
            For miles inland,
A slow and stopping curve southwards we kept.
Wide farms went by, short-shadowed cattle, and
Canals with floatings of industrial froth;   15
A hothouse flashed uniquely: hedges dipped
And rose: and now and then a smell of grass
Displaced the reek of buttoned carriage-cloth
Until the next town, new and nondescript,
Approached with acres of dismantled cars.   20

At first, I didn't notice what a noise
            The weddings made
Each station that we stopped at: sun destroys
The interest of what's happening in the shade,
And down the long cool platforms whoops and skirls   25
I took for porters larking with the mails,
And went on reading. Once we started, though,
We passed them, grinning and pomaded, girls
In parodies of fashion, heels and veils,
All posed irresolutely, watching us go,   30

---

9. Christ was born in a barn or manger (Luke
2:7); "frowsty": stuffy.
1. Or Whitsunday, the seventh Sunday after
Easter, and one of the six British bank-holidays
(legal holidays), or long weekends.

As if out on the end of an event
    Waving goodbye
To something that survived it. Struck, I leant
More promptly out next time, more curiously,
And saw it all again in different terms: 35
The fathers with broad belts under their suits
And seamy foreheads; mothers loud and fat;
An uncle shouting smut; and then the perms,
The nylon gloves and jewelery-substitutes,
The lemons, mauves, and olive-ochres that   40

Marked off the girls unreally from the rest.
    Yes, from cafés
And banquet-halls up yards, and bunting-dressed
Coach-party annexes, the wedding-days
Were coming to an end. All down the line   45
Fresh couples climbed aboard: the rest stood round;
The last confetti and advice were thrown,
And, as we moved, each face seemed to define
Just what it saw departing: children frowned
At something dull; fathers had never known   50

Success so huge and wholly farcical;
    The women shared
The secret like a happy funeral;
While girls, gripping their handbags tighter, stared
At a religious wounding. Free at last,   55
And loaded with the sum of all they saw,
We hurried towards London, shuffling gouts of steam.
Now fields were building-plots, and poplars cast
Long shadows over major roads, and for
Some fifty minutes, that in time would seem   60

Just long enough to settle hats and say
    I nearly died,
A dozen marriages got under way.
They watched the landscape, sitting side by side
    An Odeon[2] went past, a cooling tower,   65
And someone running up to bowl[3]—and none
Thought of the others they would never meet
Or how their lives would all contain this hour.
I thought of London spread out in the sun,
Its postal districts packed like squares of wheat: 70

There we were aimed. And as we raced across
    Bright knots of rail
Past standing Pullmans, walls of blackened moss
Came close, and it was nearly done, this frail
Travelling coincidence; and what it held   75
Stood ready to be loosed with all the power
That being changed can give. We slowed again,

2. One of a chain of English movie houses.   the batsman.
3. In the sport of cricket, to pitch the ball to

And as the tightened brakes took hold, there swelled
A sense of falling, like an arrow-shower
Sent out of sight, somewhere becoming rain.   80

                                                             1964

MCMXIV[4]

Those long uneven lines
Standing as patiently
As if they were stretched outside
The Oval or Villa Park,[5]
The crowns of hats, the sun   5
On moustached archaic faces
Grinning as if it were all
An August Bank Holiday[6] lark;

And the shut shops, the bleached
Established names on the sunblinds,   10
The farthings and sovereigns,[7]
And dark-clothed children at play
Called after kings and queens,
The tin advertisements
For cocoa and twist, and the pubs   15
Wide open all day;[8]

And the countryside not caring:
The place-names all hazed over
With flowering grasses, and fields
Shadowing Domesday lines[9]   20
Under wheat's restless silence;
The differently-dressed servants
With tiny rooms in huge houses,
The dust behind limousines;

Never such innocence,   25
Never before or since,
As changed itself to past
Without a word—the men
Leaving the gardens tidy,[1]
The thousands of marriages   30
Lasting a little while longer:
Never such innocence again.

                                                             1964

---

4. 1914. The poem envisions England at the
outbreak of World War I.
5. That is, outside a cricket ground or a professional soccer field; the men are queuing, or waiting in line, to enlist in the army.
6. National summer holiday.
7. British coins, both now obsolete; a farthing
was worth one-fourth of a penny; a sovereign was
worth a little more than a pound.
8. That is, before a law in 1915 restricted tav-
erns' business hours; "twist": tobacco.
9. Lines demarcating property, as listed in the
Domesday Book, drawn up by William the Conqueror in 1085–86.
1. That is, when they go off to war.

Sunny Prestatyn[2]

Come to Sunny Prestatyn
Laughed the girl on the poster,
Kneeling up on the sand
In tautened white satin.
Behind her, a hunk of coast, a   5
Hotel with palms
Seemed to expand from her thighs and
Spread breast-lifting arms.

She was slapped up one day in March.
A couple of weeks, and her face   10
Was snaggle-toothed and boss-eyed;
Huge tits and a fissured crotch
Were scored well in, and the space
Between her legs held scrawls
That set her fairly astride   15
A tuberous cock and balls

Autographed *Titch Thomas*, while
Someone had used a knife
Or something to stab right through
The moustached lips of her smile.   20
She was too good for this life.
Very soon, a great transverse tear
Left only a hand and some blue.
Now *Fight Cancer* is there.

                                    1964

High Windows

When I see a couple of kids
And guess he's fucking her and she's
Taking pills or wearing a diaphragm,
I know this is paradise

Everyone old has dreamed of all their lives—   5
Bonds and gestures pushed to one side
Like an outdated combine harvester,[3]
And everyone young going down the long slide

To happiness, endlessly. I wonder if
Anyone looked at me, forty years back,   10
And thought, *That'll be the life;*
No God any more, or sweating in the dark

About hell and that, or having to hide
What you think of the priest. He
And his lot will all go down the long slide   15
Like free bloody birds. And immediately

---

2. Prestatyn is a seaside resort in north Wales;   3. Farm machine for harvesting grain.
it is not inevitably sunny.

Rather than words comes the thought of high windows:
The sun-comprehending glass,
And beyond it, the deep blue air, that shows
Nothing, and is nowhere, and is endless.   20

                                                           1974

This Be the Verse

They fuck you up, your mum and dad.
    They may not mean to, but they do.
They fill you with the faults they had
    And add some extra, just for you.

But they were fucked up in their turn   5
    By fools in old-style hats and coats,
Who half the time were soppy-stern
    And half at one another's throats.

Man hands on misery to man.
    It deepens like a coastal shelf.[4]   10
Get out as early as you can.
    And don't have any kids yourself.

                                                           1974

Sad Steps[5]

Groping back to bed after a piss
I part thick curtains, and am startled by
The rapid clouds, the moon's cleanliness.

Four o'clock: wedge-shadowed gardens lie
Under a cavernous, a wind-picked sky.   5
There's something laughable about this,

The way the moon dashes through clouds that blow
Loosely as cannon-smoke to stand apart
(Stone-coloured light sharpening the roofs below)

High and preposterous and separate—   10
Lozenge[6] of love! Medallion of art!
O wolves of memory! Immensements! No,

One shivers slightly, looking up there.
The hardness and the brightness and the plain
Far-reaching singleness of that wide stare   15

Is a reminder of the strength and pain
Of being young; that it can't come again,
But is for others undiminished somewhere.

                                                           1974

---

4. Underwater land off a coast.
5. Compare Sir Philip Sidney's *Astrophil and Stella*, Sonnet 31: "With how sad steps, O moon, thou climb'st the skies" (1591).
6. Diamond-shaped pattern.

The Explosion

On the day of the explosion
Shadows pointed toward the pithead:[7]
In the sun the slagheap slept.

Down the lane came men in pitboots
Coughing oath-edged talk and pipe-smoke,   5
Shouldering off the freshened silence.

One chased after rabbits; lost them;
Came back with a nest of lark's eggs;
Showed them; lodged them in the grasses.

So they passed in beards and moleskins,[8]   10
Fathers, brothers, nicknames, laughter,
Through the tall gates standing open.

At noon, there came a tremor; cows
Stopped chewing for a second; sun,
Scarfed as in a heat-haze, dimmed.   15

The dead go on before us, they
Are sitting in God's house in comfort,
We shall see them face to face—

Plain as lettering in the chapels
It was said, and for a second   20
Wives saw men of the explosion

Larger than in life they managed—
Gold as on a coin, or walking
Somehow from the sun towards them,

One showing the eggs unbroken.   25
                                                           1974

7. Entrance to a coal mine.   8. Clothes made of a heavy industrial fabric.

ANTHONY HECHT
b. 1923

Anthony Hecht's first poems, those published in *A Summoning of Stones* (1954), are extraordinarily accomplished; he develops his themes with a baroque profusion, seemingly finding a place for every improbable detail. Hecht pleases by his erudition, his skill in attaching one bit of information to another, his power to sustain a long, periodic sentence, and to maintain a quality of improvisation while at the same time meeting the requirements of a daunting verse form. One of the pleasures that poetry affords is the pleasure of rhyme—a satisfaction that Valéry crystallized in his observation that while God provides the first line of a couplet, the poet must seek out the second—and for amateurs of rhyming and other technical ingenuities, Hecht is an endlessly rewarding poet. He resembles Andrew Marvell in his deftness, his

civility, and his preference for gardens as against the wilderness or the city.
Hecht's own comments on his first book are dismissive. He describes it as "something like an advanced apprenticework. I was still trying to write in the most careful, craftsmanly way that would please me and give pleasure. The subject matter, in fact, didn't have a pressing, immediate need for me; I'd write about anything that came to hand." In his second book, *The Hard Hours* (1968), which won the Pulitzer Prize, Hecht surrenders to his obsessions, the subjects that will not let him go. The later poems, as he describes them, "are about things that had an enormous emotional importance to me; I was prepared to attack them, whether they came out technically perfect or not." Without surrendering his craft, Hecht now endeavors to confront experience on its own painful terms. He is aware of the "grotesqueness of modern life," of the incongruities between life as it is fabled for his children on the television screen and as it really is—or as it might have been. His mainstay is irony, which, in Hecht's own words, "provides a way of stating very powerful and positive emotions and of taking, as it were, the heaviest possible stance towards some catastrophe."

Anthony Hecht was born in New York City on January 16, 1923. He graduated from Bard College in 1944 and immediately entered the army, with which he served in Europe and Japan; he has said about the significance of those years that "the cumulative sense of these experiences is grotesque beyond anything I could possibly write." After his release from the army he taught briefly at several universities while working for his M.A. at Columbia, and he has continued his activity as a teacher, most recently at the University of Rochester.

"More Light! More Light!"[1]

For Heinrich Blücher and Hannah Arendt[2]

Composed in the Tower before his execution
These moving verses, and being brought at that time
Painfully to the stake, submitted, declaring thus:
"I implore my God to witness that I have made no crime."

Nor was he forsaken of courage, but the death was horrible,   5
The sack of gunpowder failing to ignite.
His legs were blistered sticks on which the black sap
Bubbled and burst as he howled for the Kindly Light.[3]

And that was but one, and by no means one of the worst;
Permitted at least his pitiful dignity;   10
And such as were by made prayers in the name of Christ,
That shall judge all men, for his soul's tranquility.

We move now to outside a German wood[4]
Three men are there commanded to dig a hole
In which the two Jews are ordered to lie down   15
And be buried by the third, who is a Pole.

1. Reputedly the last words of Johann Wolfgang von Goethe (1749–1832), German poet.
2. Husband and wife; she is the author of several books on totalitarianism. They emigrated from Germany to the United States in 1941.
3. "The details are conflated from several executions, including Latimer and Ridley [Anglican bishops who were executed for heresy in 1555] whose deaths at the stake are described by Foxe in *Acts and Monuments*. But neither of them wrote poems just before their deaths, as others did" (Hecht's note).
4. At Buchenwald, the Nazi concentration camp. This incident, which occurred in 1944, is described in Eugen Kogon's *The Theory and Practice of Hell*, New York, 1958, p. 97.

Not light from the shrine at Weimar[5] beyond the hill
Nor light from heaven appeared. But he did refuse.
A Lüger settled back deeply in its glove.
He was ordered to change places with the Jews.   20

Much casual death had drained away their souls.
The thick dirt mounted toward the quivering chin.
When only the head was exposed the order came
To dig him out again and to get back in.

No light, no light in the blue Polish eye.   25
When he finished a riding boot packed down the earth.
The Lüger hovered lightly in its glove.
He was shot in the belly and in three hours bled to death.

No prayers or incense rose up in those hours
Which grew to be years, and every day came mute   30
Ghosts from the ovens, sifting through crisp air,
And settled upon his eyes in a black soot.

                                                          1967

Sestina d'Inverno[6]

Here in this bleak city of Rochester,
Where there are twenty-seven words for "snow,"[7]
Not all of them polite, the wayward mind
Basks in some Yucatan[8] of its own making,
Some coppery, sleek lagoon, or cinnamon island   5
Alive with lemon tints and burnished natives,

And O that we were there.[9] But here the natives
Of this grey, sunless city of Rochester
Have sown whole mines of salt about their land
(Bare ruined Carthage[1] that it is) while snow   10
Comes down as if The Flood[2] were in the making.
Yet on that ocean Marvell called the mind

An ark sets forth which is itself the mind,
Bound for some pungent green,[3] some shore whose natives
Blend coriander, cayenne, mint in making   15
Roasts that would gladden the Earl of Rochester[4]
With sinfulness, and melt a polar snow.
It might be well to remember that an island

5. The city where Goethe lived for many years.
6. Sestina for Winter (Italian). A sestina is a complex medieval verse form in which the same six words must end the six lines of each stanza, according to a predetermined order.
7. An allusion to the Eskimos' having many words for snow. Rochester is a city in upstate New York, site of the university where Hecht has taught.
8. City in southern Mexico.
9. In Heaven (the phrase is from an old Christmas carol).

1. After defeating the Phoenician city of Carthage in 146 B.C., the Romans reputedly sowed the land with salt to make it unfertile; "bare ruined" is a phrase from Shakespeare's sonnet 73, line 4.
2. The flood of Noah (Genesis 7–8).
3. In his poem "The Garden" (1681), Andrew Marvell calls the mind "that ocean," and goes on to say that it annihilates "all that's made / To a green thought in a green shade" (lines 43, 47–48). The "ark" is Noah's.
4. Poet, courtier, and rake (1621–1680).

Was a blessed haven once, more than an island,
The grand, utopian dream of a noble mind.   20
In that kind climate the mere thought of snow
Was but a wedding cake; the youthful natives,
Unable to conceive of Rochester,
Made love, and were acrobatic in the making.

Dream as we may, there is far more to making   25
Do than some wistful reverie of an island,
Especially now when hope lies with the Rochester
Gas and Electric Co., which doesn't mind
Such profitable weather, while the natives
Sink, like Pompeians,[5] under a world of snow.   30

The one thing indisputable here is snow,
The single verity of heaven's making,
Deeply indifferent to the dreams of the natives
And the torn hoarding-posters[6] of some island.
Under our igloo skies the frozen mind   35
Holds to one truth: it is grey, and called Rochester.

No island fantasy survives Rochester,
Where to the natives destiny is snow
That is neither to our mind nor of our making.

1977

The Deodand[7]

What are these women up to? They've gone and strung
Drapes over the windows, cutting out light
And the slightest hope of a breeze here in mid-August.
Can this be simply to avoid being seen
By some prying *femme-de-chambre*[8] across the boulevard   5
Who has stepped out on a balcony to disburse
Her dustmop gleanings on the summer air?
And what of these rugs and pillows, all haphazard,
Here in what might be someone's living room
In the swank, high-toned sixteenth *arrondissement?*[9]   10
What would their fathers, husbands, *fiancés,*
Those pillars of the old *haute-bourgeoisie,*[1]
Think of the strange charade now in the making?
Swathed in exotic finery, in loose silks,
Gauzy organzas[2] with metallic threads,   15
Intricate Arab vests, brass ornaments
At wrist and ankle, those small sexual fetters,
Tight little silver chains, and bangled gold

Suspended like a coarse barbarian treasure
From soft earlobes pierced through symbolically,   20
They are preparing some *tableau vivant*.[3]
One girl, consulting the authority
Of a painting, perhaps by Ingres or Delacroix,[4]
Is reporting over her shoulder on the use
Of kohl[5] to lend its dark, savage allurements.   25
Another, playing the slave-artisan's role,
Almost completely naked, brush in hand,
Attends to these instructions as she prepares
To complete the seductive shadowing of the eyes
Of the blonde girl who appears the harem favorite,   30
And who is now admiring these effects
In a mirror held by a fourth, a well-clad servant.
The scene simmers with Paris and women in heat,
Darkened and airless, perhaps with a faint hum
Of trapped flies, and a strong odor of musk.   35
For whom do they play at this hot indolence
And languorous vassalage?[6] They are alone
With fantasies of jasmine and brass lamps,
Melons and dates and bowls of rose-water,
A courtyard fountain's firework blaze of prisms,   40
Its basin sown with stars and *poissons d'or*,[7]
And a rude stable smell of animal strength,
Of leather thongs, hinting of violations,
Swooning lubricities and lassitudes.
What is all this but crude imperial pride,   45
Feminized, scented and attenuated,
The exploitation of the primitive,
Homages of romantic self-deception,
Mimes of submission glamorized as lust?
Have they no intimation, no recall   50
Of the once queen who liked to play at milkmaid,
And the fierce butcher-reckoning that followed
Her innocent, unthinking masquerade?[8]
Those who will not be taught by history
Have as their curse the office to repeat it,[9]   55
And for this little spiritual debauch
(Reported here with warm, exacting care
By Pierre Renoir in 1872—
Apparently unnoticed by the girls,
An invisible voyeur, like you and me)   60
Exactions shall be made, an expiation,
A forfeiture. Though it take ninety years,
All the retributive iron of Racine[1]
Shall answer from the raging heat of the desert.

3. Literally, "living picture," in which the participants, appropriately costumed, pose to represent a painting.
4. Nineteenth-century French painters, both of whom painted pictures of Near Eastern subjects.
5. Dark eye makeup used in Arabia and Egypt.
6. Slavery.
7. Goldfish.
8. Marie Antoinette, Queen of France, one of whose expensive hobbies was dressing up as a milkmaid, was guillotined in 1793, during the French Revolution.
9. "Those who cannot remember the past are condemned to repeat it" (George Santayana, *Life of Reason*). "Office": duty.
1. Jean Racine, seventeenth-century French playwright, most of whose plays were tragedies of revenge.

In the final months of the Algerian war   65
They captured a very young French Legionnaire.[2]
They shaved his head, decked him in a blonde wig,
Carmined his lips grotesquely, fitted him out
With long, theatrical false eyelashes
And a bright, loose-fitting skirt of calico,   70
And cut off all the fingers of both hands.
He had to eat from a fork held by his captors.
Thus costumed, he was taken from town to town,
Encampment to encampment, on a leash,
And forced to beg for his food with a special verse   75
Sung to a popular show tune of those days:
"*Donnez moi à manger de vos mains*
Car c'est pour vous que je fais ma petite danse;
Car je suis Madeleine, la putain,
Et je m'en vais le lendemain matin,   80
Car je suis La Belle France."[3]

                                                                           1980

An Old Malediction[4]

What well-heeled knuckle-head, straight from the unisex
Hairstylist and bathed in *Russian Leather*,
Dallies with you these late summer days, Pyrrha,
In your expensive sublet? For whom do you
Slip into something simple by, say, Gucci?   5
The more fool he who has mapped out for himself
The saline latitudes of incontinent grief.
Dazzled though he be, poor dope, by the golden looks
Your locks fetched up out of a bottle of *Clairol*,
He will know that the wind changes, the smooth sailing   10
Is done for, when the breakers wallop him broadside,
When he's rudderless, dismasted, thoroughly swamped
In that mindless rip-tide that got the best of me
Once, when I ventured on your deeps, Piranha.

                                         (FREELY FROM HORACE)[5]
                                                                           1980

2. Member of the French Foreign Legion, an army of volunteers originally founded to control the French colony of Algiers (northern Africa); Algiers fought bloodily for its independence from 1954 to 1962, and won.
3. "The concluding lines in French may be rendered:
  'Let me be given nourishment at your hands / Since it's for you I perform my little dance. / For I am the street-walker, Magdalen, / And come the dawn I'll be on my way again, / The beauty queen, Miss France" (Hecht's note).
4. Curse.
5. That is, translated from a poem by the Roman poet Horace (65–8 B.C.); Hecht's note says it is Book 1, Ode 1.

JAMES DICKEY
b. 1923

James Dickey practices surrealism as writers in the nineteenth century practiced realism. Illusions, often terrifying, are what he calls "lies," and he insists, as Oscar Wilde did, that art is the fashioning of falsehoods. Once his imagination takes hold of some strange, often monstrous event, like "Falling"—the fall from a plane of a young airline stewardess—he pursues it relentlessly until it subsides in darkness. "As Longinus points out, there's a razor's edge between sublimity and absurdity. And that's the edge I try to walk. Sometimes *both* sides are ludicrous! . . . But I don't think you can get to sublimity without courting the ridiculous."[1]

Dickey spent six of his mature years in advertising. In between writing advertisements for Coca-Cola he composed some of his best poems, and the same secretary typed both the ads and poems. Dickey has in his verse a purposiveness and insistence, a demand for attention and for recognition, that is perhaps not so much an echo of his days in advertising as an indication of why he was good at it.

As a boy Dickey read Byron, and he recalls that Byron's poems were the first he ever bought. The idea of the poet as a man of action has been with him from the start, and it has suited his powers as an athlete. He has wanted to be an "intensified man" or a "totally responsive man."[2] Dickey was born in a suburb of Atlanta on February 2, 1923. Already tall—six feet three—as a boy, he became a high school football star. His interest in poetry had been awakened by his father, a lawyer, who delighted in oratory and used to read to him famous speeches to the jury. Dickey went on to Clemson College in South Carolina in 1942, but left after a year to enlist in the air force. In between a hundred combat missions in the Pacific, he read Conrad Aiken and an anthology of modern poetry by Louis Untermeyer.

On his return from the war Dickey went to Vanderbilt, where he worked with an older student's zeal to learn about anthropology, astronomy, and philosophy, and to study foreign languages as well as English literature. A friendly professor, Monroe K. Spears, encouraged him to write more poetry, and when he found that Dickey felt he must only describe actual experiences, urged him to write as the poem, rather than the experience, necessitated. "That idea was the bursting of a dam for me," said Dickey.[3] He was determined to write, but thought he might do graduate work as well, first at Vanderbilt, and then at Rice University in Texas. The air force recalled him to active service for the Korean War. On his return he went, after a year in Europe, to the University of Florida; he abruptly resigned in April 1956, and went to New York at the age of thirty-three. McCann-Ericson took him on as a writer of advertising copy. He stayed there for a time, then shifted to Atlanta agencies, and finally gave up this work in 1961 to accept a Guggenheim Fellowship and spend a year in Italy. Since that time he has taught, lectured, written, and been for two years (from 1966 to 1968) Poetry Consultant to the Library of Congress. He published a novel, *Deliverance*, in 1970, and another, *Alnilam*, in 1987.

---

1. *Self-Interviews*, New York, 1970, p. 65.   3. The same, p. 33.
2. The same, p. 34.

The Hospital Window

I have just come down from my father.
Higher and higher he lies
Above me in a blue light
Shed by a tinted window.
I drop through six white floors   5
And then step out onto pavement.

Still feeling my father ascend,
I start to cross the firm street,
My shoulder blades shining with all
The glass the huge building can raise.   10

Now I must turn round and face it,
And know his one pane from the others.

Each window possesses the sun
As though it burned there on a wick.
I wave, like a man catching fire.   15
All the deep-dyed windowpanes flash,
And, behind them, all the white rooms
They turn to the color of Heaven.

Ceremoniously, gravely, and weakly,
Dozens of pale hands are waving   20
Back, from inside their flames.
Yet one pure pane among these
Is the bright, erased blankness of nothing.
I know that my father is there,

In the shape of his death still living.   25
The traffic increases around me
Like a madness called down on my head.
The horns blast at me like shotguns,
And drivers lean out, driven crazy—
But now my propped-up father   30

Lifts his arm out of stillness at last.
The light from the window strikes me
And I turn as blue as a soul,
As the moment when I was born.
I am not afraid for my father—   35
Look! He is grinning; he is not

Afraid for my life, either,
As the wild engines stand at my knees
Shredding their gears and roaring,
And I hold each car in its place   40
For miles, inciting its horn
To blow down the walls of the world

That the dying may float without fear
In the bold blue gaze of my father.
Slowly I move to the sidewalk   45
With my pin-tingling hand half dead
At the end of my bloodless arm.
I carry it off in amazement,

High, still higher, still waving,
My recognized face fully mortal,   50
Yet not; not at all, in the pale,
Drained, otherworldly, stricken,
Created hue of stained glass.
I have just come down from my father.

1962

Buckdancer's Choice[1]

So I would hear out those lungs,
The air split into nine levels,
Some gift of tongues of the whistler

In the invalid's bed: my mother,
Warbling all day to herself   5
The thousand variations of one song;

It is called Buckdancer's Choice.
For years, they have all been dying
Out, the classic buck-and-wing men

Of traveling minstrel shows;   10
With them also an old woman
Was dying of breathless angina,

Yet still found breath enough
To whistle up in my head
A sight like a one-man band,   15

Freed black, with cymbals at heel,
An ex-slave who thrivingly danced
To the ring of his own clashing light

Through the thousand variations of one song
All day to my mother's prone music,   20
The invalid's warbler's note,

While I crept close to the wall
Sock-footed, to hear the sounds alter,
Her tongue like a mockingbird's break

Through stratum after stratum of a tone   25
Proclaiming what choices there are
For the last dancers of their kind,

For ill women and for all slaves
Of death, and children enchanted at walls
With a brass-beating glow underfoot,   30

Not dancing but nearly risen
Through barnlike, theatrelike houses
On the wings of the buck and wing.

1965

---

1. A buckdancer is a man who does the buck-and-wing, a tap dance often performed with wooden shoes.

Falling

"A 29-year-old stewardess fell . . . to her death tonight when she was swept
through an emergency door that suddenly sprang open . . . The body . . . was
found . . . three hours after the accident."

—New York Times

The states when they black out and lie there rolling   when they turn
To something transcontinental   move by   drawing moonlight out of the
     great
One-sided stone hung off the starboard wingtip   some sleeper next to
An engine is groaning for coffee   and there is faintly coming in
Somewhere the vast beast-whistle of space. In the galley with its racks   5
Of trays   she rummages for a blanket   and moves in her slim tailored
Uniform to pin it over the cry at the top of the door. As though she blew

The door down with a silent blast from her lungs   frozen   she is black
Out finding herself   with the plane nowhere and her body taking by the
     throat
The undying cry of the void   falling   living   beginning to be some-
     thing   10
That no one has ever been and lived through   screaming without enough
     air
Still neat   lipsticked   stockinged   girdled by regulation   her hat
Still on   her arms and legs in no world   and yet spaced also strangely
With utter placid rightness on thin air   taking her time   she holds it
In many places   and now, still thousands of feet from her death she seems 15
To slow   she develops interest   she turns in her maneuverable body

To watch it. She is hung high up in the overwhelming middle of things in
     her
Self   in low body-whistling wrapped intensely   in all her dark dance-
     weight
Coming down from a marvellous leap   with the delaying, dumfounding
     ease
Of a dream of being dawn   like endless moonlight to the harvest soil   20
Of a central state of one's country   with a great gradual warmth coming
Over her   floating   finding more and more breath in what she has been
     using
For breath   as the levels become more human   seeing clouds placed
     honestly
Below her left and right   riding slowly toward them   she clasps it all
To her and can hang her hands and feet in it in peculiar ways   and   25
Her eyes opened wide by wind, can open her mouth as wide   wider and
     suck
All the heat from the cornfields   can go down on her back with a feeling
Of stupendous pillows stacked under her   and can turn   turn as to
     someone
In bed   smile, understood in darkness   can go away   slant   slide
Off tumbling   into the emblem of a bird with its wings half-spread   30
Or whirl madly on herself   in endless gymnastics in the growing warmth
Of wheatfields rising toward the harvest moon.   There is time to live
In superhuman health   seeing mortal unreachable lights far down seeing
An ultimate highway with one late priceless car probing it   arriving
In a square town   and off her starboard arm the glitter of water catches 35

The moon by its own shaken side   scaled, roaming silver   My God it is
   good
And evil   lying in one after another of all the positions for love
Making   dancing   sleeping   and now cloud wisps at her no
Raincoat   no matter   all small towns brokenly brighter from inside
Cloud   she walks over them like rain   bursts out to behold a Grey-
   hound
                                                                          40
Bus shooting light through its sides   it is the signal to go straight
Down like a glorious diver   then feet first   her skirt stripped beautifully
Up   her face in fear-scented cloths   her legs deliriously bare   then
Arms out   she slow-rolls over   steadies out   waits for something great
To take control of her   trembles near feathers   planes head-down   45
The quick movements of bird-necks turning her head   gold eyes the insight-
eyesight of owls blazing into the hencoops   a taste for chicken over-
   whelming
Her   the long-range vision of hawks enlarging all human lights of cars
Freight trains   looped bridges   enlarging the moon racing slowly
Through all the curves of a river   all the darks of the midwest blazing   50
From above. A rabbit in a bush turns white   the smothering chickens
Huddle   for over them there is still time for something to live
With the streaming half-idea of a long stoop   a hurtling   a fall
That is controlled   that plummets as it wills   turns gravity
Into a new condition, showing its other side like a moon   shining   55
New Powers   there is still time to live on a breath made of nothing
But the whole night   time for her to remember to arrange her skirt
Like a diagram of a bat   tightly it guides her   she has this flying-skin
Made of garments   and there are also those sky-divers on TV   sailing
In sunlight   smiling under their goggles   swapping batons back and forth   60
And He who jumped without a chute and was handed one by a diving
Buddy. She looks for her grinning companion   white teeth nowhere
She is screaming   singing hymns   her thin human wings spread out
From her neat shoulers   the air beast-crooning to her   warbling
And she can no longer behold the huge partial form of the world   now   65
She is watching her country lose its evoked master shape   watching it lose
And gain   get back its houses and peoples   watching it bring up
Its local lights   single homes   lamps on barn roofs   if she fell
Into water she might live   like a diver   cleaving   perfect   plunge

Into another   heavy silver   unbreathable   slowing   saving   70
Element: there is water   there is time to perfect all the fine
Points of diving   feet together   toes pointed   hands shaped right
To insert her into water like a needle   to come out healthily dripping
And be handed a Coca-Cola   there they are   there are the waters
Of life   the moon packed and coiled in a reservoir   so let me begin   75
To plane across the night air of Kansas   opening my eyes superhumanly
Bright   to the dammed moon   opening the natural wings of my jacket
By Don Loper   moving like a hunting owl toward the glitter of water
One cannot just fall   just tumble screaming all that time   one must use
It   she is now through with all   through all   clouds   damp hair   80
Straightened   the last wisp of fog pulled apart on her face like wool revealing
New darks   new progressions of headlights along dirt roads from chaos

And night   a gradual warming   a new-made, inevitable world of one's
   own

Country   a great stone of light in its waiting waters   hold   hold out
For water: who knows when what correct young woman must take up her
    body   85
And fly   and head for the moon-crazed inner eye of midwest imprisoned
Water   stored up for her for years   the arms of her jacket slipping
Air up her sleeves to go   all over her? What final things can be said
Of one who starts out sheerly in her body in the high middle of night
Air   to track down water like a rabbit where it lies like life itself   90
Off to the right in Kansas? She goes toward   the blazing-bare lake
Her skirts neat   her hands and face warmed more and more by the air
Rising from pastures of beans   and under her   under chenille bed-
    spreads
The farm girls are feeling the goddess in them struggle and rise brooding
On the scratch-shining posts of the bed   dreaming of female signs   95
Of the moon   male blood like iron   of what is really said by the moan
Of airliners passing over them at dead of midwest midnight   passing
Over brush fires   burning out in silence on little hills   and will wake
To see the woman they should be   struggling on the rooftree to become
Stars: for her the ground is closer   water is nearer   she passes   100
It   then banks   turns   her sleeves fluttering differently as she rolls
Out to face the east, where the sun shall come up from wheatfields she
    must
Do something with water   fly to it   fall in it   drink it   rise
From it   but there is none left upon earth   the clouds have drunk it
    back
The plants have sucked it down   there are standing toward her only   105
The common fields of death   she comes back from flying to falling
Returns to a powerful cry   the silent scream with which she blew down
The coupled door of the airliner   nearly   nearly losing hold
Of what she has done   remembers   remembers the shape at the heart
Of cloud   fashionably swirling   remembers she still has time to die   110
Beyond explanation. Let her now take off her hat in summer air the coutour
Of cornfields   and have enough time to kick off her one remaining
Shoe with the toes   of the other foot   to unhook her stockings
With calm fingers, noting how fatally easy it is to undress in midair
Near death   when the body will assume without effort any position   115
Except the one that will sustain it   enable it to rise   live
Not die   nine farms hover close   widen   eight of them separate, leav-
    ing
One in the middle   then the fields of that farm do the same   there is no
Way to back off   from her chosen ground   but she sheds the jacket
With its silver sad impotent wings   sheds the bat's guiding tailpiece   120
Of her skirt   the lightning-charged clinging of her blouse   the intimate
Inner flying-garment of her slip in which she rides like the holy ghost
Of a virgin   sheds the long windsocks of her stockings   absurd
Brassiere   then feels the girdle required by regulations squirming
Off her: no longer monobuttocked   she feels the girdle flutter   shake   125
In her hand   and float   upward   her clothes rising off her ascending
Into cloud   and fights away from her head the last sharp dangerous shoe
Like a dumb bird   and now will drop in   SOON   now will drop

In like this   the greatest thing that ever came to Kansas   down from all
Heights   all levels of American breath   layered in the lungs from the
    frail   130

Chill of space to the loam where extinction slumbers in corn tassels thickly
And breathes like rich farmers counting: will come among them after
Her last superhuman act   the last slow careful passing of her hands
All over her unharmed body   desired by every sleeper in his dream:
Boys finding for the first time their loins filled with heart's blood   135
Widowed farmers whose hands float under light covers to find themselves
Arisen at sunrise   the splendid position of blood unearthly drawn
Toward clouds   all feel something   pass over them as she passes
Her palms over *her* long legs   *her* small breasts   and deeply between
Her thighs   her hair shot loose from all pins   streaming in the wind   140
Of her body   let her come openly   trying at the last second to land
On her back   This is it   THIS
                              All those who find her impressed
In the soft loam   gone down   driven well into the image of her body
The furrows for miles flowing in upon her where she lies very deep   145
In her mortal outline   in the earth as it is in cloud   can tell nothing
But that she is there   inexplicable   unquestionable   and remember
That something broke in them as well   and began to live and die more
When they walked for no reason into their fields to where the whole earth
Caught her   interrupted her maiden flight   told her how to lie she can-
    not   150
Turn   go away   cannot move   cannot slide off it and assume another
Position   no sky-diver with any grin could save her   hold her in his
    arms
Plummet with her   unfold above her his wedding silks   she can no longer
Mark the rain with whirling women that take the place of a dead wife
Or the goddess in Norwegian farm girls   or all the back-breaking whores   155
Of Wichita. All the known air above her is not giving up quite one
Breath   it is all gone   and yet not dead   not anywhere else
Quite   lying still in the field on her back   sensing the smells
Of incessant growth try to lift her   a little sight left in the corner
Of one eye   fading   seeing something wave   lies believing   160
That she could have made it   at the best part of her brief goddess
State   to water   gone in headfirst   come out smiling   invulnerable
Girl in a bathing-suit ad   but she is lying like a sunbather at the last
Of moonlight   half-buried in her impact on the earth   not far
From a railroad trestle   a water tank   she could see if she could   165
Raise her head from her modest hole   with her clothes beginning
To come down all over Kansas   into bushes   on the dewy sixth green
Of a golf course   one shoe   her girdle coming down fantastically
On a clothesline, where it belongs   her blouse on a lightning rod:

Lies in the fields   in *this* field   on her broken back as though on   170
A cloud she cannot drop through   while farmers sleepwalk without
Their women from houses   a walk like falling toward the far waters
Of life   in moonlight   toward the dreamed eternal meaning of their farms
Toward the flowering of the harvest in their hands   that tragic cost
Feels herself go go toward   go outward   breathes at last fully   175
Not   and tries   less   once   tries   tries   AH, GOD—

                                                                1981

DENISE LEVERTOV
b. 1923

Denise Levertov's writing is a poetry of secrets, in which the poet uncovers something hidden, like a physicist plumbing the atom. This something is recognized with such joyful force that it seems to palpitate or shudder at being known. Her work has close connections, as she realizes, with that of Robert Duncan and Robert Creeley, the first more mystical than she, the second less ecstatic. She regards them as "the chief poets among my contemporaries."[1] Levertov likes to burst through the trivial, and in "A Common Ground" (with its characteristic title) she speaks of "poems stirred / into paper coffee-cups, eaten / with petals on rye in the / sun . . . entering / human lives forever, / unobserved. . . ." This entrance is not achieved by "common speech," as she declares in the same poem, but by "the uncommon speech of paradise."

Levertov's work began in regular stanzas, but after her first book she shifted to free verse. In that medium she has a fine sense of pace and climax. Her effects are precisely calculated: "I believe every space and comma is a living part of the poem and has its function, just as every muscle and pore of the body has its function. And the way the lines are broken is a functioning part essential to the poem's life."

Apart from her contemporary poets, Levertov has been proud to claim a connection with mystics of the past. Her father was descended from a Russian rabbi, Schneour Zaimon, who was renowned as a Hasid, that is, as a member of a Jewish mystical movement that began in the eighteenth century and found a glory in everyday occurrences rather than in sensational events. He was reputed, as she tells in *Overland to the Islands*, to know the speech of birds. Her mother was descended from a Welsh tailor and mystic, Angel Jones of Mold (a town in Wales). Although her father was born Jewish, he became, while a student at Königsberg in the nineties, a convert to Christianity, and formed a lifelong hope of uniting the two religions. He went to England and became an Anglican priest; he pursued his dream of unity by writing a life of St. Paul in Hebrew, and by translating into English parts of the Jewish mystical work, the *Zohar*.

Denise Levertov was born at Ilford, Essex, on October 24, 1923. Her parents sent her neither to school nor to college, preferring to educate her at home. "As a child," she writes, "I 'did lessons' at home under the tutelage of my mother and listened to the BBC Schools Programs. For French, piano, and art I was sent to various teachers for private lessons."[2] In 1947 she was married to the author Mitchell Goodman. (They are now divorced.) In the late sixties, when his indignation with the Vietnam War resulted in his being arraigned with other notable persons for "conspiracy," Levertov wrote a number of poems about the war, expressions of her sympathy with the mistreated people. She also wrote a long poem, "During the Eichmann Trial."

In 1959 she had written: "I do not believe that a violent imitation of the horrors of our times is the concern of poetry. . . . Insofar as poetry has a social function it is to awaken sleepers by other means than shock." But by 1965 Levertov was eager to refocus her view of the powers of poetry, powers to modify and ameliorate. "The poem," she declares, "has a social *effect* of some kind whether or not the poet wills that it have. It has kinetic force, it sets in motion . . . elements in the reader that would otherwise be stagnant." And, we may assume, these elements include both compassion and outrage.[3]

---

1. *The New American Poetry: 1945–1960*, ed. Donald Allen, New York, 1960, p. 412.
2. "The Untaught Teacher," in *The Poet in the*
World, New York, 1973, p. 149.
3. "A Testament and a Postscript," in *The Poet in the World*, pp. 3, 6.

The Dog of Art

That dog with daisies for eyes
who flashes forth
flame of his very self at every bark
is the Dog of Art.
Worked in wool, his blind eyes   5
look inward to caverns and jewels
which they see perfectly,
and his voice
measures forth the treasure
in music sharp and loud,   10
sharp and bright,
bright flaming barks,
and growling smoky soft, the Dog
of Art turns to the world
the quietness of his eyes.   15

1959

Matins[1]

i

The authentic! Shadows of it
sweep past in dreams, one could say imprecisely,
evoking the almost-silent
ripping apart of giant
sheets of cellophane. No.   5
It thrusts up close. Exactly in dreams
it has you off-guard, you
recognize it before you have time.
For a second before waking
the alarm bell is a red conical hat, it   10
takes form.

ii

The authentic! I said
rising from the toilet seat.
The radiator in rhythmic knockings
spoke of the rising steam.   15
The authentic, I said
breaking the handle of my hairbrush as I
brushed my hair in
rhythmic strokes: That's it,
that's joy, it's always   20
a recognition, the known
appearing fully itself, and
more itself than one knew.

---

1. Prayers offered at dawn; in the Roman Catholic church, this is the most important office of the day.

iii

The new day rises
as heat rises,   25
knocking in the pipes
with rhythms it seizes for its own
to speak of its invention—
the real, the new-laid
egg whose speckled shell   30
the poet fondles and must break
if he will be nourished.

iv

A shadow painted where
yes, a shadow must fall.
The cow's breath   35
not forgotten in the mist, in the
words. Yes,
verisimilitude draws up
heat in us, zest
to follow through,   40
follow through,
follow
transformations of day
in its turning, in its becoming.

v

Stir the holy grains, set   45
the bowls on the table and
call the child to eat.

While we eat we think,
as we think an undercurrent
of dream runs through us   50
faster than thought
towards recognition.

Call the child to eat,
send him off, his mouth
tasting of toothpaste, to go down   55
into the ground, into a roaring train
and to school.

His cheeks are pink
his black eyes hold his dreams, he has left
forgetting his glasses.   60

Follow down the stairs at a clatter
to give them to him and save
his clear sight.

Cold air
comes in at the street door.   65

vi

The authentic! It rolls
just out of reach, beyond
running feet and
stretching fingers, down
the green slope and into   70
the black waves of the sea.
Speak to me, little horse, beloved,
tell me
how to follow the iron ball,
how to follow through to the country   75
beneath the waves
to the place where I must kill you and you step out
of your bones and flystrewn meat
tall, smiling, renewed,
formed in your own likeness.   80

vii

Marvelous Truth, confront us
at every turn,
in every guise, iron ball,
egg, dark horse, shadow,
cloud   85
of breath on the air,

dwell
in our crowded hearts
our steaming bathrooms, kitchens full of
things to be done, the   90
ordinary streets.

Thrust close your smile
that we know you, terrible joy.

                                        1962

Song for Ishtar[2]

The moon is a sow
and grunts in my throat
Her great shining shines through me
so the mud of my hollow gleams
and breaks in silver bubbles   5

She is a sow
and I a pig and a poet

When she opens her white
lips to devour me I bite back
and laughter rocks the moon   10

---

2. Life-giving mother-goddess of the ancient Babylonians.

In the black of desire
we rock and grunt, grunt and
shine

1964

Goodbye to Tolerance

Genial poets, pink-faced
earnest wits—
you have given the world
some choice morsels,
gobbets of language presented   5
as one presents T-bone steak
and Cherries Jubilee.
Goodbye, goodbye,
                    I don't care
if I never taste your fine food again,   10
neutral fellows, seers of every side.
Tolerance, what crimes
are committed in your name.

And you, good women, bakers of nicest bread,
blood donors. Your crumbs   15
choke me, I would not want
a drop of your blood in me, it is pumped
by weak hearts, perfect pulses that never
falter: irresponsive
to nightmare reality.   20

It is my brothers, my sisters,
whose blood spurts out and stops
forever
because you choose to believe it is not your business.

Goodbye, goodbye,   25
your poems
shut their little mouths,
your loaves grow moldy,
a gulf has split
                    the ground between us,   30
and you won't wave, you're looking
another way.
We shan't meet again—
unless you leap it, leaving
behind you the cherished   35
worms of your dispassion,
your pallid ironies,
your jovial, murderous,
wry-humored balanced judgment,
leap over, un-   40
balanced? . . . then
how our fanatic tears
would flow and mingle
for joy . . .

January 1973   1975

Prisoners

Though the road turn at last
to death's ordinary door,
and we knock there, ready
to enter and it opens
easily for us,   5
        yet
all the long journey
we shall have gone in chains,
fed on knowledge-apples
acrid and riddled with grubs.   10

We taste other food that life,
like a charitable farm-girl,
holds out to us as we pass—
but our mouths are puckered,
a taint of ash on the tongue.   15

It's not joy that we've lost—
wildfire, it flares
in dark or shine as it will.
What's gone
is common happiness,   20
plain bread we could eat
with the old apple of knowledge.

That old one—it griped us sometimes,
but it was firm, tart,
sometimes delectable . . .   25

The ashen apple of these days
grew from poisoned soil. We are prisoners
and must eat
our ration. All the long road
in chains, even if, after all,   30
we come to
death's ordinary door, with time
smiling its ordinary
long-ago smile.

                                      1984

Caedmon[3]

All others talked as if
talk were a dance.
Clodhopper I, with clumsy feet
would break the gliding ring.
Early I learned to   5

---

3. "The story comes, of course, from the Venerable Bede's *History of the English Church and People,* but I first read it as a child in John Richard Green's *History of the English People,* 1855" (Levertov's note). Caedmon (fl. 658–80) was, according to the story, an illiterate cowherd employed by a monastery; one night he received a divine call to sing verses in praise of God. He is the earliest known English Christian poet.

hunch myself
close by the door:
then when the talk began
I'd wipe my
mouth and wend   10
unnoticed back to the barn
to be with the warm beasts,
dumb among body sounds
of the simple ones.
I'd see by a twist   15
of lit rush[4] the motes
of gold moving
from shadow to shadow
slow in the wake
of deep untroubled sighs.   20
The cows
munched or stirred or were still. I
was at home and lonely,
both in good measure. Until
the sudden angel affrighted me—light effacing   25
my feeble beam,
a forest of torches, feathers of flame, sparks upflying:
but the cows as before
were calm, and nothing was burning,
        nothing but I, as that hand of fire   30
touched my lips and scorched my tongue
and pulled my voice
                    into the ring of the dance.

                                                             1987

4. The piths of rush plants were used for candlewicks.

RICHARD HUGO
1923–1982

In 1973, when both poets were in mid-career, James Wright reviewed a book by his friend Richard Hugo: "Hugo, like Thomas Hardy, is a writer whose work is all of a piece. . . . [He is] one of the precious few poets of our age (how he would hate that phrase! But I can't help it) who has, and sustains, an abiding vision." A vision of what?, Wright goes on to ask, and answers, in part, "The special and secret details of places."[1]

Writers about place are often defined as "regionalists," sometimes pejoratively. To that label Hugo responded once: "You can hang 'regionalist' on me if you want. I don't consider it's a bad thing. As a matter of fact, I think it's a very good thing."[2] Hugo's poems take place, for the most part, in the Pacific Northwest, where he lived his entire life. But he developed a complex relationship between his region and his fictions. "The place triggers the mind to create the place," he once wrote, and devel-

1. James Wright, "Hugo: Secrets of the Inner Landscape," *American Poetry Review* 2:3, May/June 1973, p. 13.
2. David Dillon, "Gains Made in Isolation: An Interview with Richard Hugo," in *A Trout in the Milk: A Composite Portrait of Richard Hugo,* ed. Jack Myers, Lewiston, Idaho, 1982, p. 295.

oped the idea further in his essay "The Triggering Town": the poet finds a town that provides "knowns" sitting "outside of the poem": with these as a base, "the imagination can take off from them and if necessary return."[3] What he wrote of the little-known British poet Bernard Spencer was true of himself: "He took firm, tender, and private emotional possession of a region where he was a foreigner, an intruder perhaps, certainly a stranger."[4]

A stranger, or as Hugo also put it, referring again both to himself and to Spencer, a man "who lived on the edge of things"; or, as the poet Dave Smith called him, "the American orphan."[5] Hugo's mother, a teen-ager, was forced to abandon him after his birth (on December 21, 1923) to the care of his maternal grandparents, working-class people of German descent who lived in the tough neighborhood of White Center, south of Seattle, Washington. Starved of affection, he grew up lonely, shy, terrified of relationships with women, admiring the local bullies, seeking macho friendships with other boys.[6] After high school and facing the draft like the rest of his generation, he joined the army air force and flew thirty-five missions as a bombardier in Italy.

Returning to complete his studies at the University of Washington, he took, especially, courses in poetry given by Theodore Roethke, who had recently joined the English department. Hugo later said of his education, "I simply didn't know who had written what. I'd never heard of Auden, Hopkins, Thomas, or even Yeats. Just the exposure to such poets was worth any tuition fee. But to be exposed to them by a man so passionately committed to their rhythms and tonalities was to be born." Moreover, "I learned that you could be literally outrageous, take an outrageous stance, and create something beautiful out of it. That gave me confidence."[7]

Hugo now went to work for Boeing Aircraft, writing poems slowly on the side, and married in 1951. In 1959 he co-founded the journal *Poetry Northwest;* in 1961, at the age of thirty-seven, he published his first book, *A Run of Jacks* (the "jacks" are both playing cards and fish). He went to Italy in 1963 with his wife to visit places he had known during the war; while there, without a job, he was invited to teach at the University of Montana. In 1964 he and his wife separated, and he went to Montana alone.

Although he was publishing more poems and becoming an increasingly effective and powerful teacher, Hugo was still a prey to loneliness, and now to drinking as well, and in 1971 suffered a "minor-league breakdown";[8] recovering, he reached out to his friends with "letter poems" in *31 Letters and 13 Dreams* (1977). In 1974, he married again. His new wife, Ripley Schemm, and his stepchildren helped foster a new mood of acceptance. A Guggenheim grant, later, enabled him, with Ripley and his stepdaughter, to visit the remote island of Skye off the northern coast of Scotland: the result was the poems in *The Right Madness on Skye* (1980). In them, the regional poet, surer now of his inner region, takes a new region as his own. The last poems—collected posthumously in *Making Certain It Goes On: The Collected Poems of Richard Hugo*—were written, after a serious operation for lung cancer, in a painful but hopeful struggle for new ground; in many of them the images of rivers or the sea, always a part of Hugo's natural landscape, take on increasing importance. Hugo died on October 22, 1982, of leukemia.

The poet William Matthews has written of Hugo's concern with "triggering towns" that "to say 'all towns you look at could be your home town' is not only to say that you are homeless but that you are potentially at home anywhere. It is to say along with Whitman that you can, by continuous imaginative appropriation, belong to America, however beautifully and terrifyingly vast it is."[9] Or, as the poet Adrienne

3. Richard Hugo, *The Triggering Town*, New York, 1979, p. 12.
4. Richard Hugo, *The Real West Marginal Way*, New York, 1986, p. 155.
5. The same, p. 158; Dave Smith, "Getting Right: Richard Hugo's Selected Poems," in *Trout*,
p. 287.
6. *The Real West Marginal Way*, p. 5.
7. *The Triggering Town*, p. 28.
8. Dillon, p. 292.
9. William Matthews, "Introduction: Old Haunts," *The Real West Marginal Way*, p. xx.

Rich said in a letter, "I taught [Hugo] with Whitman on Election Day to illustrate what being 'American' may mean."[10] Perhaps "the American poet" that Emerson called for is in fact a regional poet—feeling, creating, transforming his region.

10. Adrienne Rich, letter to John Benedict, n.d.

The Way a Ghost Dissolves

Where she lived the close remained the best.
The nearest music and the static cloud,
sun and dirt were all she understood.
She planted corn and left the rest
to elements, convinced that God   5
with giant faucets regulates the rain
and saves the crops from frost or foreign wind.

Fate assisted her with special cures.
Rub a half potato on your wart
and wrap it in a damp cloth. Close   10
your eyes and whirl three times and throw.
Then bury rag and spud exactly where
they fall. The only warts that I have now
are memories or comic on my nose.

Up at dawn. The earth provided food   15
if worked and watered, planted green
with rye grass every fall. Or driven wild
by snakes that kept the carrots clean,
she butchered snakes and carrots with a hoe.
Her screams were sea birds in the wind,   20
her chopping—nothing like it now.

I will garden on the double run,
my rhythm obvious in ringing rakes,
and trust in fate to keep me poor and kind
and work until my heart is short,   25
then go out slowly with a feeble grin,
my fingers flexing but my eyes gone gray
from cramps and the lack of oxygen.

Forget the tone. Call the neighbor's trumpet
golden as it grates. Exalt the weeds.   30
Say the local animals have class
or help me say that ghost has gone to seed.
And why attempt to see the cloud again—
the screaming face it was before it cracked
in wind from Asia and a wanton rain.   35

1961

The Lady in Kicking Horse Reservoir[1]

Not my hands but green across you now.
Green tons hold you down, and ten bass curve
teasing in your hair. Summer slime
will pile deep on your breast. Four months of ice
will keep you firm. I hope each spring   5
to find you tangled in those pads
pulled not quite loose by the spillway pour,
stars in dead reflection off your teeth.[2]

Lie there lily still. The spillway's closed.
Two feet down most lakes are common gray.   10
This lake is dark from the black blue Mission range
climbing sky like music dying Indians once wailed.
On ocean beaches, mystery fish
are offered to the moon. Your jaws go blue.
Your hands start waving every wind.   15
Wave to the ocean where we crushed a mile of foam.

We still love there in thundering foam
and love. Whales fall in love with gulls
and tide reclaims the Dolly skeletons[3]
gone with a blast of aching horns to China.   20
Landlocked in Montana here
the end is limited by light, the final note
will trail off at the farthest point we see,
already faded, lover, where you bloat.

All girls should be nicer. Arrows rain   25
above us in the Indian wind. My future
should be full of windy gems, my past
will stop this roaring in my dreams.
Sorry. Sorry. Sorry. But the arrows sing:
no way to float her up. The dead sink   30
from dead weight. The Mission range
turns this water black late afternoons.

One boy slapped the other. Hard.
The slapped boy talked until his dignity
dissolved, screamed a single 'stop'   35
and went down sobbing in the company pond.
I swam for him all night. My only suit
got wet and factory hands went home.
No one cared the coward disappeared.
Morning then: cold music I had never heard.   40

---

1. Both Kicking Horse Reservoir and the Mission mountain range (line 11) are on the Flathead Indian reservation in Montana.
2. This image derives from a documentary film made by Annick Smith and her husband David about Hugo, entitled *Kicking the Loose Gravel Home* (completed 1976–77; see "White Center," line 54). In making an earlier version of the film, shots were taken of Hugo and a lover; the Smiths then superimposed images of flowing water over these shots. The lover, meanwhile, had left Hugo to marry another man (Annick Smith, speech at Richard Hugo Symposium, Seattle, Wash., November 13, 1986).
3. Specifically, here skeletons of the Dolly Varden trout (but see also line 54).

Loners like work best on second shift.
No one liked our product and the factory closed.
Off south, the bison multiply so fast
a slaughter's mandatory every spring
and every spring the creeks get fat   45
and Kicking Horse fills up. My hope is vague.
The far blur of your bones in May
may be nourished by the snow.

The spillway's open and you spill out
into weather, lover down the bright canal   50
and mother, irrigating crops
dead Indians forgot to plant.
I'm sailing west with arrows to dissolving foam
where waves strand naked Dollys.
Their eyes are white as oriental mountains   55
and their tongues are teasing oil from whales.

                                                                   1973

Degrees of Gray in Philipsburg[4]

You might come here Sunday on a whim.
Say your life broke down. The last good kiss
you had was years ago. You walk these streets
laid out by the insane, past hotels
that didn't last, bars that did, the tortured try   5
of local drivers to accelerate their lives.
Only churches are kept up. The jail
turned 70 this year. The only prisoner
is always in, not knowing what he's done.

The principal supporting business now   10
is rage. Hatred of the various grays
the mountain sends, hatred of the mill,
The Silver Bill repeal,[5] the best liked girls
who leave each year for Butte. One good
restaurant and bars can't wipe the boredom out.   15
The 1907 boom, eight going silver mines,
a dance floor built on springs—
all memory resolves itself in gaze,
in panoramic green you know the cattle eat
or two stacks high above the town,   20
two dead kilns, the huge mill in collapse
for fifty years that won't fall finally down.

4. Small town in Montana, which in the early
twentieth century was a thriving community supported by a silver-processing mill. In making the
documentary film about Hugo (see note 2 above),
Annick and David Smith, the film-makers, suggested shooting scenes in Philipsburg's abandoned silver-mill, to which Hugo replied that he
was a fisherman, not a mill-hand. After the shooting was completed, Hugo telephoned the Smiths
early the next morning to read them "Degrees of
Gray," which he had just finished writing. Some
of the images in the poem (for example, "the old
man," who has no teeth, line 33) are in the film
(Annick Smith, Richard Hugo Symposium).
5. Law enacted in 1934 empowering the fed-
eral government to buy silver; Butte is a city in
Montana.

Isn't this your life? That ancient kiss
still burning out your eyes? Isn't this defeat
so accurate, the church bell simply seems   25
a pure announcement: ring and no one comes?
Don't empty houses ring? Are magnesium
and scorn sufficient to support a town,
not just Philipsburg, but towns
of towering blondes, good jazz and booze   30
the world will never let you have
until the town you came from dies inside?

Say no to yourself. The old man, twenty
when the jail was built, still laughs,
although his lips collapse. Someday soon,   35
he says, I'll go to sleep and not wake up.
You tell him no. You're talking to yourself.
The car that brought you here still runs.
The money you buy lunch with,
no matter where it's mined, is silver   40
and the girl who serves your food
is slender and her red hair lights the wall.

                                                                             1973

The Freaks at Spurgin Road Field

The dim boy claps because the others clap.
The polite word, handicapped, is muttered in the stands.
Isn't it wrong, the way the mind moves back.

One whole day I sit, contrite, dirt, L.A.
Union Station, '46, sweating through last night.   5
The dim boy claps because the others clap.

Score, 5 to 3. Pitcher fading badly in the heat.
Isn't it wrong to be or not be spastic?
Isn't it wrong, the way the mind moves back.

I'm laughing at a neighbor girl beaten to scream   10
by a savage father and I'm ashamed to look.
The dim boy claps because the others clap.

The score is always close, the rally always short.
I've left more wreckage than a quake.
Isn't it wrong, the way the mind moves back.   15

The afflicted never cheer in unison.
Isn't it wrong, the way the mind moves back
to stammering pastures where the picnic should have worked.
The dim boy claps because the others clap.

                                                                             1975

Salt Water Story

He loved his cabin: there
nothing had happened. Then his friends were dead.
The new neighbors had different ways.
Days came heavy with regret.
He studied sea charts and charted   5
sea lanes out. He calculated times
to ride the tide rip, times to go ashore and rest.
He memorized the names of bays: those
with plenty of driftwood for fire,
those with oysters. He found a forest   10
he could draw back into
when the Coast Guard came looking, news
of him missing by now broadcast state-wide.
He made no move. He turned out lights
and lit candles and watched his face   15
in the window glow red.

He dreamed a raft
and dreamed this sea lane out, past
long dormant cannons and the pale hermit
who begged to go with him. A blue heron   20
trailed him. A second heron trailed the first,
a third the second and so on. Those who looked for him
checked the skies for a long blue line
of laboring wings.
The birds broke formation, and the world   25
of search and rescue lost track of his wake.
His face glowed red on the glass.
If found, he'd declare himself pro-cloud
and pro-wind and anti-flat hot days.

Then he dreamed wrong   30
what we owe Egypt, what we owe
sea lanes out of the slaves to ourselves
we become one morning, nothing
for us in dawn, and nothing for us in tide.
What we owe Egypt fades   35
into what we owe Greece and then Rome.
What we owe Rome keeps repeating
like what we owe time—namely our lives
and whatever laughter we find to pass on.
He knew grief repeats on its own.   40

One night late, the face in the window
glowed back at him pale. He believed that face
some bum peeking in
and waved "hi." The old face told him,
to navigate a lasting way out   45
he must learn how coins gleam
one way through water, how bones of dead fish
gleam another, and he must learn both gleams
and dive deep. He learned both gleams

and learned to dive fast and come up slow   50
as sky every day.

And we might think someday we'll find him
dead over his charts, the water ways out
a failed dream. Nothing like that.
His cabin stands empty and he   55
sails the straits. We often see him
from shore or the deck of a ferry.
We can't tell him by craft. Some days
he passes by on a yacht, some days a tug.
He's young and, captain or deckhand,   60
he is the one who waves.

                                                             1984

MAXINE KUMIN
b. 1925

Maxine Kumin's poems aim to give a sense of skin and bone, of what it is to live in a
body, especially a woman's body. She imparts the experience of being a daughter
and mother and lover, of being Jewish, living on a farm, participating in the cyclical
processes of nature. She has an extraordinary eye for the lives of bears, woodchuck,
or even of stones, and for the deaths of small animals as well as of people. It comes
naturally to her to write "The Excrement Poem" in which she meditates on the
universality of excretion: "It is done by us all." But she can also treat the death of a
friend by suicide, and ponder, as she wears the friend's blue jacket, her nearness to
that anguish.

Maxine Kumin was born in Philadelphia on June 6, 1925. She took B.A. and M.A.
degrees at Radcliffe. The rural aspects of her verse come from living on a farm in
Warner, New Hampshire, where she grows vegetables and breeds horses. In 1973
she won the Pulitzer Prize for *Up-Country.* She was closely associated with Anne
Sexton, who collaborated with her on several children's books, but she has little of
Sexton's rage, and her sensitivity, while equally acute, is more buoyant and even
humorous.

Seeing the Bones

This year again the bruise-colored oak
hangs on eating my heart out
with its slow change, the leaves at last
spiraling end over end like your
letters home that fall Fridays   5
in the box at the foot of the hill
saying the old news, keeping it neutral.
You ask about the dog, fourteen years
your hero, deaf now as a turnip,
thin as kindling.   10

In junior high your biology class
boiled a chicken down into its bones
four days at a simmer in my pot,

then wired joint by joint
the re-created hen   15
in an anatomy project
you stayed home from, sick.

Thus am I afflicted, seeing the bones.
How many seasons walking
on fallen apples like pebbles in   20
the shoes of the Canterbury faithful[1]
have I kept the garden up
with leaven of wood ash, kitchen leavings
and the sure reciprocation of horse dung?

How many seasons have the foals   25
come right or breeched or in good time
turned yearlings, two-year-olds, and at three
clattered off in a ferment to the sales?
Your ponies, those dapple-gray kings
of the orchard, long gone to skeleton,   30
gallop across the landscape of my dreams.
I meet my father there, dead years before
you left us for a European career.
He is looping the loop on a roller coaster
called Mercy, he is calling his children in.   35

I do the same things day by day.
They steady me against the wrong turn,
the closed-ward babel of anomie.[2]
This Friday your letter in thinnest blue
script alarms me. Weekly you grow   40
more British with your *I shalls*
and now you're off to Africa
or Everest, daughter of the file drawer,
citizen of no return. I give
your britches, long outgrown, to the crows,   45
your boots with a summer visit's worth
of mud caked on them to the shrews
for nests if they will have them.

Working backward I reconstruct
you. Send me your baby teeth, some new   50
nail parings and a hank of hair
and let me do the rest. I'll
set the pot to boil.

                                                                    1982

Spree

My father paces the upstairs hall
a large confined animal

---

1. Pilgrims to a shrine such as Canterbury
Cathedral put pebbles in their shoes for self-mor-
tification.

2. That is, confusion of sounds or voices attendant upon personal disorientation.

neither wild nor yet domesticated.
About him hangs the smell of righteous wrath.
My mother is meekly seated   5
at the escritoire.³ Rosy from my bath
age eight-nine-ten by now I understand
his right to roar, hers to defy
the bill from Wanamaker's in his hand
the bill from Strawbridge's held high   10
the bill from Bonwit Teller
and the all plum-colored Blum Store.⁴

His anger smells like dinner parties
like trays of frothy daiquiris.
Against the pre–World-War-Two prime   15
standing ribs his carving knife
flashes a little drunkenly. He charms
all the other Bonwit-bedecked wives
but something overripe malingers.
I wear his wide cigar bands on my fingers.   20

Oh God it is so noisy!
Under my bed a secret stair
a gold and purple escalator
takes me nightly down under the sea.
Such dancings, such carryings on   25
with the prince of this-or-that
with the duke of ne'er-do-well
I the plain one, a size too large to tell
grow tremulous at stickpin and cravat
I in toe shoes and tutu suddenly   30
see shopping is an art form
a kind of costume ball.

Papá, would we so humbly come
to the scene in the upstairs hall
on the first of every month, except   35
you chose the mice for footmen,⁵ clapped
to call up the coach and four?
You sent to Paris for the ermine muff
that says I'm rich. To think twelve poor
little things had their heads chopped off   40
to keep my hands unseemly warm!
When you went fishing down the well
for fox furs, hats with peacock plumes
velvet evening capes, what else befell?

You paid the bills, Papá. You cast the spell.   45
                                                              1985

Video Cuisine

They are weighing the babies again on color television.
They are hanging these small bags of bones up in canvas slings
to determine which ones will receive the dried-milk mush,
the concentrate made out of ground-up trash fish.

For years we have watched them, back-lit by the desert,   5
these miles of dusty hands holding out goatskins or cups,
their animals dead or dying of rinderpest,[6]
and after the credits come up I continue to sit

through Dinner with Julia,[7] where, in a French fish
poacher big enough for a small brown baby, an   10
Alaska salmon simmers in a court bouillon.
For a first course, steak tartare to awaken the palate.

With it Julia suggests a zinfandel.[8] This scene
has a polite, a touristy flavor to it,
and I let it play. But somewhere Oxfam[9] goes on   15
spooning gluey gruel between the parched lips

of potbellied children, the ones who perhaps can be saved
from kwashiorkor—an ancient Ghanaian word—
though with probable lowered IQs, the voiceover explains,
caused by protein deficiencies linked to the drought   20

and the drought has grown worse with the gradual increase in herds
overgrazing the thin forage grasses of the Sahel.[1]
This, says the voice, can be laid to the natural greed
of the nomad deceived by technicians digging new wells

which means (a slow pan of the sand) that the water table has dropped.   25
And now to Julia's table is borne the resplendent fish.
Always the camera is angled so that the guests look up.
Among them I glimpse that sly Dean, Jonathan Swift.[2]

After the credits come up I continue to sit
with those who are starving to death in a distant nation   30
squatting, back-lit by the desert, hands out, in my head
and the Dublin Dean squats there too, observing the population

that waits for too little dried milk, white rice, trash fish.
Always the camera is angled so they look up
while their babies are weighed in slings on color television,   35
look into our living rooms and the shaded rooms we sleep in.

1985

6. Highly infectious cattle disease.
7. Julia Child, hostess of a popular television show about gourmet cooking.
8. "Court bouillon": mixture of wine, seasonings, and vegetables in which fish is cooked; "steak tartare": chopped raw beef; "Zinfandel": red California wine.
9. Oxford Famine Relief.
1. A region of Africa that has suffered drought.
2. English satirist, one of whose works, "A Modest Proposal" (1729), ironically suggests that, as an economic benefit to the poor, they sell their children to be cooked and eaten.

A. R. AMMONS
b. 1926

In A. R. Ammons a group of possibilities formulated earlier in the century achieves a fresh and unified expression. The perception of human ambiguities and abstract possibilities in homely bits of nature may be said to have originated in Frost; the attention to the intricacies of poetry as a "supreme fiction" has ties with Stevens; the sense of "no ideas but in things" unites Ammons with William Carlos Williams, as do some elements of his technique, such as the short, lightly punctuated lines and metrical innovations.

Ammons comes on with disarming casualness; he presents himself directly, unfazed, wry when necessary, quick to see symbolic possibilities in ordinary landscapes. Often his poems are minor journeys which gradually become momentous: an automobile trip deepens into a trip to the past and the passions, a walk releases him from old forms, disjointed maneuvers of the mind move suddenly "towards divine, terrible love." Observed facts, he says in a poem called "The Misfit," tear us into questionings, push towards the edges of order, of being. Although he says "there is no finality of vision," he has seen enough to be glad.

On the relation of the symbol apple to the real apple, Ammons points out that Williams's slogan, "no ideas but in things," is too limited, and must be supplemented by "no things but in ideas," "no ideas but in ideas," and "no things but in things." The possibilities of poems are not to be numbered. What is more central than any one slogan is the blend of "conscious preparation" and "the unconscious event," art and nature complementing each other. So poems, products of mind, are "body images," and, as he says, "if that isn't / so I will be terribly disappointed. . . ." But mind is also "the history of our organism," and perhaps of all the processes that went into its making.

The most ambitious of his poems, so far, is *Sphere: The Form of a Motion* (1974). It is made up out of 155 sections, each of which is in turn made up of four three-line stanzas; moreover, the entire poem is one continuous sentence. Here the image of the relationship between art and nature is more that of growth from the center:

> . . . the
> poetic consciousness beginning at a center works itself out by
> incorporation until through craft, experience, insight, etc., it
>
> brushes in a fulsome way against the fulsomeness of nature so that
> on the periphery it is so deeply spelt out that it can tangle with
> the coincidental: . . .

The passage is, in fact, about an *ecology* of nature and art, and it should not be a surprise that Ammons used this word in poems long before it became fashionable. The nineteenth-century Transcendentalist philosopher and poet Ralph Waldo Emerson wrote that "poetry was all written before time was, and whenever we are so finely organized that we can penetrate into that region where the air is music, we hear those primal warblings, and write them down" ("The Poet"). In this balance of art and nature Ammons is seeking Emerson's "fine organization."

Ammons, who prefers not to disclose his first names, was born in Whiteville, North Carolina, on February 18, 1926. His early interests were scientific, and he took a bachelor of science degree at Wake Forest College in 1949. Afterwards he attended the University of California at Berkeley for two years. Still uncertain of his direction, he became principal of an elementary school in his home state, and later an executive in a glass-making firm. But in 1964, he accepted a teaching position at Cornell, and in seven years had gone from instructor to full professor. In 1973 his *Collected Poems: 1951–1971* won the National Book Award for poetry; in 1975, *Sphere* won the Bollin-

gen Prize; and in 1982 *A Coast of Trees* won the National Book Critics' Circle Award.
Earlier, in 1981, Ammons was one of the first recipients of a MacArthur Fellowship.

Ammons has remained loyal to science as well as to literature. His poetry, in fact,
embodies both. His first book was entitled *Ommateum* (1955), which means the compound eye of an insect. After its obscure publication in Philadelphia, he waited nine
years to publish a second book. The sense of long, meditative preparation for writing
is imparted by all his poems, however unexpected and seemingly impromptu their
phrasing. The same preparation has enabled him to begin explorations into human
relationships, as in "Parting," or "Easter Morning."

Corsons Inlet[1]

I went for a walk over the dunes again this morning
to the sea,
    then turned right along
        the surf
                        rounded a naked headland   5
                        and returned

        along the inlet shore:

    it was muggy sunny, the wind from the sea steady and high,
    crisp in the running sand,
            some breakthroughs of sun   10
        but after a bit

    continuous overcast:

    the walk liberating, I was released from forms,
    from the perpendiculars
            straight lines, blocks, boxes, binds   15
    of thought
    into the hues, shadings, rises, flowing bends and blends
            of sight:

                        I allow myself eddies of meaning:
    yield to a direction of significance   20
    running
    like a stream through the geography of my work:
        you can find
    in my sayings
                        swerves of action   25
                        like the inlet's cutting edge:
            there are dunes of motion,
    organizations of grass, white sandy paths of remembrance
    in the overall wandering of mirroring mind:

    but Overall is beyond me: is the sum of these events   30
    I cannot draw, the ledger I cannot keep, the accounting
    beyond the account:

1. Located in southeast New Jersey.

in nature there are few sharp lines: there are areas of
primrose
     more or less dispersed;   35
disorderly orders of bayberry; between the rows
of dunes,
irregular swamps of reeds,
though not reeds alone, but grass, bayberry, yarrow, all . . .
predominantly reeds: 40

I have reached no conclusions, have erected no boundaries,
shutting out and shutting in, separating inside
    from outside: I have
    drawn no lines:
    as   45

manifold events of sand
change the dune's shape that will not be the same shape
tomorrow.

so I am willing to go along, to accept
the becoming   50
thought, to stake off no beginnings or ends, establish
    no walls:

by transitions the land falls from grassy dunes to creek
to undercreek: but there are no lines, though
    change in that transition is clear   55
    as any sharpness: but "sharpness" spread out,
allowed to occur over a wider range
than mental lines can keep:

the moon was full last night: today, low tide was low:
black shoals of mussels exposed to the risk   60
of air
and, earlier, of sun,
waved in and out with the waterline, waterline inexact,
caught always in the event of change:
    a young mottled gull stood free on the shoals   65
    and ate
to vomiting: another gull, squawking possession, cracked a crab,
picked out the entrails, swallowed the soft-shelled legs, a ruddy
turnstone running in to snatch leftover bits:

risk is full: every living thing in   70
siege: the demand is life, to keep life: the small
white blacklegged egret, how beautiful, quietly stalks and spears
    the shallows, darts to shore
        to stab—what? I couldn't
see against the black mudflats—a frightened   75
    fiddler crab?

        the news to my left over the dunes and
reeds and bayberry clumps was
        fall: thousands of tree swallows

gathering for flight: 80
an order held
in constant change: a congregation
rich with entropy: nevertheless, separable, noticeable
as one event,
        not chaos: preparations for   85
flight from winter,
cheet, cheet, cheet, cheet, wings rifling the green clumps,
beaks
at the bayberries
    a perception full of wind, flight, curve,   90
    sound:
        the possibility of rule as the sum of rulelessness:
the "field" of action
with moving, incalculable center:

in the smaller view, order tight with shape: 95
blue tiny flowers on a leafless weed: carapace of crab:
snail shell:
        pulsations of order
        in the bellies of minnows: orders swallowed,
broken down, transferred through membranes   100
to strengthen larger orders: but in the large view, no
lines or changless shapes: the working in and out, together
        and against, of millions of events: this,
                so that I make
                no form   105
                formlessness:

orders as summaries, as outcomes of actions override
or in some way result, not predictably (seeing me gain
the top of a dune,
the swallows   110
could take flight—some other fields of bayberry
        could enter fall
        berryless) and there is serenity:

        no arranged terror: no forcing of image, plan,
or thought: 115
no propaganda, no humbling of reality to precept:

terror pervades but is not arranged, all possibilities
of escape open: no route shut, except in
    the sudden loss of all routes:

        I see narrow orders, limited tightness, but will   120
not run to that easy victory:
        still around the looser, wider forces work:
        I will try
        to fasten into order enlarging grasps of disorder, widening
scope, but enjoying the freedom that   125
Scope eludes my grasp, that there is no finality of vision,
that I have perceived nothing completely,
        that tomorrow a new walk is a new walk.

                                                                  1965

Small Song

The reeds give
way to the

wind and give
the wind away

1970

The City Limits

When you consider the radiance, that it does not withhold
itself but pours its abundance without selection into every
nook and cranny not overhung or hidden; when you consider

that birds' bones make no awful noise against the light but
lie low in the light as in a high testimony; when you consider   5
the radiance, that it will look into the guiltiest

swerving of the weaving heart and bear itself upon them,
not flinching into disguise or darkening; when you consider
the abundance of such resource as illuminates the glow-blue

bodies and gold-skeined wings of flies swarming the dumped   10
guts of a natural slaughter or the coil of shit and in no
way winces from its storms of generosity; when you consider

that air or vacuum, snow or shale, squid or wolf, rose or lichen,
each is accepted into as much light as it will take, then
the heart moves roomier, the man stands and looks about, the   15

leaf does not increase itself above the grass, and the dark
work of the deepest cells is of a tune with May bushes
and fear lit by the breadth of such calmly turns to praise.

1971

Easter Morning

I have a life that did not become,
that turned aside and stopped,
astonished:
I hold it in me like a pregnancy or
as on my lap a child   5
not to grow or grow old but dwell on

it is this grave I most
frequently return and return
to ask what is wrong, what was
wrong, to see it all by   10
the light of a different necessity
but the grave will not heal
and the child

stirring, must share my grave
with me, an old man having   15
gotten by on what was left

when I go back to my home country in these
fresh far-away days, it's convenient to visit
everybody, aunts and uncles, those who used to say,
look how he's shooting up, and the   20
trinket aunts who always had a little
something in their pocketbooks, cinnamon bark
or a penny or nickel, and uncles who
were the rumored fathers of cousins
who whispered of them as of great, if   25
troubled, presences, and school
teachers, just about everybody older
(and some younger) collected in one place
waiting, particularly, but not for
me, mother and father there, too, and others   30
close, close as burrowing
under skin, all in the graveyard
assembled, done for, the world they
used to wield, have trouble and joy
in, gone   35

the child in me could not become
was not ready for others to go,
to go on into change, blessings and
horrors, but stands there by the road
where the mishap occurred, crying out for   40
help, come and fix this or we
can't get by, but the great ones who
were to return, they could not or did
not hear and went on in a flurry and
now, I say in the graveyard, here   45
lies the flurry, now it can't come
back with help or helpful asides, now
we all buy the bitter
incompletions, pick up the knots of
horror, silently raving, and go on   50
crashing into empty ends not
completions, not rondures the fullness
has come into and spent itself from
I stand on the stump
of a child, whether myself   55
or my little brother who died, and
yell as far as I can, I cannot leave this place, for
for me it is the dearest and the worst,
it is life nearest to life which is
life lost: it is my place where   60
I must stand and fail,
calling attention with tears
to the branches not lofting
boughs into space, to the barren
air that holds the world that was my world   65

though the incompletions
(& completions) burn out
standing in the flash high-burn
momentary structure of ash, still it
is a picture-book, letter-perfect   70
Easter morning: I have been for a
walk: the wind is tranquil: the brook
works without flashing in an abundant
tranquility: the birds are lively with
voice: I saw something I had   75
never seen before: two great birds,
maybe eagles, blackwinged, whitenecked
and -headed, came from the south oaring
the great wings steadily; they went
directly over me, high up, and kept on   80
due north: but then one bird,
the one behind, veered a little to the
left and the other bird kept on seeming
not to notice for a minute: the first
began to circle as if looking for   85
something, coasting, resting its wings
on the down side of some of the circles:
the other bird came back and they both
circled, looking perhaps for a draft;
they turned a few more times, possibly   90
rising—at least, clearly resting—
then flew on falling into distance till
they broke across the local bush and
trees: it was a sight of bountiful
majesty and integrity: the having   95
patterns and routes, breaking
from them to explore other patterns or
better ways to routes, and then the
return: a dance sacred as the sap in
the trees, permanent in its descriptions   100
as the ripples round the brook's
ripplestone: fresh as this particular
flood of burn breaking across us now
from the sun.

                                                                    1981

Singling & Doubling Together

My nature singing in me is your nature singing:
you have means to veer down, filter through,
and, coming in,
harden into vines that break back with leaves,
so that when the wind stirs   5
I know you are there and I hear you in leafspeech,

though of course back into your heightenings I
can never follow: you are there beyond
tracings flesh can take,

and farther away surrounding and informing the systems,   10
you are as if nothing, and
where you are least knowable I celebrate you most

or here most when near dusk the pheasant squawks and
lofts at a sharp angle to the roost cedar,
I catch in the angle of that ascent,   15
in the justness of that event your pheasant nature,
and when dusk settles, the bushes creak and
snap in their natures with your creaking

and snapping nature: I catch the impact and turn
it back: cut the grass and pick up branches   20
under the elm, rise to the several tendernesses
and griefs, and you will fail me only as from the still
of your great high otherness you fail all things,
somewhere to lift things up, if not those things again:

even you risked all the way into the taking on of shape   25
and time fail and fail with me, as me,
and going hence with me know the going hence
and in the cries of that pain it is you crying and
you know of it and it is my pain, my tears, my loss—
what but grace   30

have I to bear in every motion,
embracing or turning away, staggering or standing still,
while your settled kingdom sways in the distillations of light
and plunders down into the darkness with me
and comes nowhere up again but changed into your   35
singing nature when I need sing my nature nevermore.

1983

Motion's Holdings

The filled out gourd rots, the
ridge rises in a wave
height cracks into peaks, the peaks

wear down to low undoings whose undertowing
throws other waves up: the branch   5
of honeysuckle leaves arcs outward

into its becoming motion but,
completion's precision done, gives
over riddling free to other

motions: boulders, their green and white   10
moss-molds, high-held in moist
hill woods, stir hum with

stall and spill, take in and give
off heat, adjust nearby to
geomagnetic fields, tip liquid with   15

change should a trunk or rock loosen
to let rollers roll, or they loll
inwardly with earth's lie

in space, oxidize at their surfaces
exchanges with fungal[2] thread and rain: 20
things are slowed motion that,

slowed too far, falls loose, freeing debris:
but in the ongoing warps, the butterfly
amaryllis crowds its bowl with bulbs.

1987

2. Of fungus.

JAMES MERRILL
b. 1926

The first poems of James Merrill show none of the clumsiness and uncertainty of apprentice work. They are calm and collected, highly finished works of art which are often about other works of art. The subject matter is international, and Merrill's detached connoisseurship often reminds one of Proust and James. Merrill has a talent for metaphysical wit. "About the Phoenix" begins with an exclamation of impatience with rhetoric (". . . in the end one tires of the high-flown"), but in turning away from the timelessness of art, exemplified by the gorgeous, jeweled bird, the poet must necessarily evoke it.

In Merrill's later poems the earlier exquisite meditative style is combined with a new interest in narrative. The poems are longer, more relaxed, and the wit is more humane. "The Broken Home" is about the relationship between the speaker and his wealthy, energetic father (a situation which Merrill also treats in his play *The Immortal Husband* and his novel *The Seraglio*). The poem begins with Merrill's characteristic opulence:

> Crossing the street,
> I saw the parents and the child
> At their window, gleaming like fruit
> With evening's mild gold leaf.

—but the recollection of the father is at once both offhand and moving.

> Each thirteenth year he married. When he died
> There were already several chilled wives
> In sable orbit—rings, cars, permanent waves.
> We'd felt him warming up for a green bride.

With the publication in 1976 of *Divine Comedies*, Merrill's work took a surprising, even outrageous turn. Nothing in his earlier poems had quite prepared his readers for what Merrill would be up to next. With the help of his friend David Jackson, an accommodating Ouija board, friends (most of them dead), fellow poets, scientists, and a galaxy of guardians from the spirit world, Merrill would over a period of more than twenty years assemble an epic poem which from time to time resembles such different works as Yeats's *A Vision* and the epic poems of Dante, Blake, Wordsworth, and Whitman, not to speak of the prose narratives of Marcel Proust and Henry James. The completed poem, eventually called *The Changing Light at Sandover*, has to be read to be believed. It is a witty, gracious, genial poem, comforting in its assurance that our friends are never lost to us, and that, thanks to the transmigration of souls, human beings slip, rather comically, from one existence to another. As the constructor of a universe, Merrill contradicts himself from time to time, but, as he might argue, so too does the Great Artisan, the Prime Mover, the God Biology, or whatever we choose to call the Creator of the ultimate universe.

James Merrill was born March 3, 1926, in New York City. His education was interrupted by army service at the end of the Second World War, after which he published a book of poems in Greece in 1946 and received his B.A. from Amherst in 1947. He has, since his first "official" book in 1951, published over twenty-five volumes of poetry; some of these have won the National Book Award, the Bollingen Prize, and the Pulitzer Prize. Merrill lives in Connecticut.

The Broken Home

Crossing the street,
I saw the parents and the child
At their window, gleaming like fruit
With evening's mild gold leaf.

In a room on the floor below,   5
Sunless, cooler—a brimming
Saucer of wax, marbly and dim—
I have lit what's left of my life.

I have thrown out yesterday's milk
And opened a book of maxims.   10
The flame quickens. The word stirs.

Tell me, tongue of fire,
That you and I are as real
At least as the people upstairs.

•

My father,[1] who had flown in World War I,   15
Might have continued to invest his life
In cloud banks well above Wall Street and wife.
But the race was run below, and the point was to win.

Too late now, I make out in his blue gaze
(Through the smoked glass of being thirty-six)   20
The soul eclipsed by twin black pupils, sex
And business; time was money in those days.

Each thirteenth year he married. When he died
There were already several chilled wives
In sable orbit—rings, cars, permanent waves.   25
We'd felt him warming up for a green bride.

---

1. Charles E. Merrill, who was a founding partner of the investment firm of Merrill Lynch, Pierce, Fenner & Smith.

He could afford it. He was "in his prime"
At three score ten. But money was not time.

.

When my parents were younger this was a popular act:
A veiled woman would leap from an electric, wine-dark car   30
To the steps of no matter what—the Senate or the Ritz Bar—
And bodily, at newsreel speed, attack

No matter whom—Al Smith or José Maria Sert
Or Clemenceau[2]—veins standing out on her throat
As she yelled *War mongerer! Pig! Give us the vote!*,   35
And would have to be hauled away in her hobble skirt.

What had the man done? Oh, made history,
Her business (he had implied) was giving birth,
Tending the house, mending the socks.

Always that same old story—   40
Father Time and Mother Earth,
A marriage on the rocks.

.

One afternoon, red, satyr-thighed
Michael, the Irish setter, head
Passionately lowered, led
The child I was to a shut door. Inside,   45

Blinds beat sun from the bed.
The green-gold room throbbed like a bruise.
Under a sheet, clad in taboos
Lay whom we sought, her hair undone, outspread,   50

And of a blackness found, if ever now, in old
Engravings where the acid bit.
I must have needed to touch it
Or the whiteness—was she dead?
Her eyes flew open, startled strange and cold.   55
The dog slumped to the floor. She reached for me. I fled.

.

Tonight they have stepped out onto the gravel.
The party is over. It's the fall
Of 1931. They love each other still.

She: Charlie, I can't stand the pace,   60
He: Come on, honey—why, you'll bury us all!

A lead soldier guards my windowsill:
Khaki rifle, uniform, and face.
Something in me grows heavy, silvery, pliable.

2. Alfred E. Smith (1873–1944) was Governor of New York and in 1928 a candidate for the presidency;
José María Sert (1876–1945), the Spanish painter of murals, decorated the lobby of New York's Waldorf
Astoria Hotel in 1930; and Georges Clemenceau (1841–1929), Premier of France during the First World
War, visited the United States in 1922.

How intensely people used to feel!   65
Like metal poured at the close of a proletarian novel,
Refined and glowing from the crucible,
I see those two hearts, I'm afraid,
Still. Cool here in the graveyard of good and evil.
They are even so to be honored and obeyed.   70

                    •

. . . Obeyed, at least, inversely. Thus
I rarely buy a newspaper, or vote.
To do so, I have learned, is to invite
The tread of a stone guest³ within my house.

Shooting this rusted bolt, though, against him,   75
I trust I am no less time's child than some
Who on the heath impersonate Poor Tom⁴
Or on the barricades risk life and limb.

Nor do I try to keep a garden, only
An avocado in a glass of water—   80
Roots pallid, gemmed with air. And later,

When the small gilt leaves have grown
Fleshy and green, I let them die, yes, yes,
And start another. I am earth's no less.

                    •

A child, a red dog roam the corridors,   85
Still, of the broken home. No sound. The brilliant
Rag runners halt before wide-open doors.
My old room! Its wallpaper—cream, medallioned
With pink and brown—brings back the first nightmares,
Long summer colds, and Emma, sepia-faced,   90
Perspiring over broth carried upstairs
Aswim with golden fats I could not taste.

The real house became a boarding-school,
Under the ballroom ceiling's allegory
Someone at last may actually be allowed   95
To learn something; or, from my window, cool
With the unstiflement of the entire story,
Watch a red setter stretch and sink in cloud.

                                        1966

The Victor Dog⁵

for Elizabeth Bishop

Bix to Buxtehude to Boulez,
The little white dog on the Victor label

---

3. Such as the stone statue of the commander of Seville which, in Molière's play *The Stone Feast*, visits his murderer Don Juan and drags him off to Hell.

4. In Shakespeare's *King Lear*, Edgar, disowned by his father, wanders over the heath disguised as a madman and calling himself "Poor Tom."

5. The old trademark for RCA Victor Records showed a small dog listening intently to an old-fashioned gramophone, with the title, "His Mas-

Listens long and hard as he is able.
It's all in a day's work, whatever plays.

From judgment, it would seem, he has refrained.   5
He even listens earnestly to Bloch,
Then builds a church upon our acid rock.[6]
He's man's—no—he's the Leiermann's best friend,[7]

Or would be if hearing and listening were the same.
Does he hear? I fancy he rather smells   10
Those lemon-gold arpeggios in Ravel's
"Les jets d'eau du palais de ceux qui s'aiment."[8]

He ponders the Schumann Concerto's tall willow hit
By lightning, and stays put. When he surmises
Through one of Bach's eternal boxwood mazes[9]
The oboe pungent as a bitch in heat,

Or when the calypso decants its raw bay rum
Or the moon in *Wozzeck*[1] reddens ripe for murder,
He doesn't sneeze or howl; just listens harder.
Adamant[2] needles bear down on him from   20

Whirling of outer space, too black too near—
But he was taught as a puppy not to flinch,
Much less to imitate his bête noire Blanche
Who barked, fat foolish creature, at King Lear.[3]

Still others fought in the road's filth over Jezebel,[4]   25
Slavered on hearths of horned and pelted barons.
His forebears lacked, to say the least, forbearance.
Can nature change in him? Nothing's impossible.

The last chord fades. The night is cold and fine.
His master's voice rasps through the grooves' bare groves.   30
Obediently, in silence like the grave's
He sleeps there on the still-warm gramophone.

Only to dream he is at the première of a Handel
Opera long thought lost—*Il Cane Minore*.[5]
Its allegorical subject is his story!   35
A little dog revolving round a spindle

---

ter's Voice." The poem alludes to a number of
musicians and composers: the jazz trumpeter Bix
Beiderbecke; the eighteenth-century composers
Dietrich Buxtehude, Johann Sebastian Bach, and
George Frideric Handel; the nineteenth-century
Robert Schumann; and the modernists Pierre
Boulez, Ernest Bloch, and Maurice Ravel.
  6. In Matthew 16:18, Christ says to Peter,
"Upon this rock I will build my church."
  7. In Franz Schubert's song *Der Leiermann*
("The Organ-Grinder"), an old man cranks his
barrel organ in the winter cold to an audience of
snarling dogs.
  8. "The fountains of the palace of those who are
in love with each other" (French); "arpeggios":
tones of a chord.
  9. Labyrinth made out of living boxwood plants,

found in the gardens of eighteenth-century palaces.
  1. Opera by Alban Berg (1885–1935), in which
the protagonist murders his unfaithful wife under
a rising moon.
  2. Diamond.
  3. In the storm scene, Lear says, "The little dogs
and all, / Tray, Blanche, and Sweetheart; see, they
bark at me." *Bête noire:* something to be feared or
avoided (literally "black beast," whereas "Blanche"
means white).
  4. When she died, her body was thrown into
the street as punishment for her evil deeds. When
it was recovered for burial, dogs had eaten most
of it, as Elijah had earlier prophesied (I Kings 21ff.).
  5. *The Little Dog* (Italian).

Gives rise to harmonies beyond belief,
A cast of stars. . . . Is there in Victor's heart
No honey for the vanquished? Art is art.
The life it asks of us is a dog's life.   40

                                                                       1972

From *THE CHANGING LIGHT AT SANDOVER*[6]
From The Book of Ephraim

Backdrop: The dining room at Stonington.[7]
Walls of ready-mixed matte "flame" (a witty
Shade, now watermelon, now sunburn).
Overhead, a turn of the century dome
Expressing white tin wreaths and fleurs-de-lys   5
In palpable relief to candlelight.
Wallace Stevens, with that dislocated
Perspective of the newly dead,[8] would take it
For an alcove in the Baptist church next door
Whose moonlit tower saw eye to eye with us.   10
The room breathed sheer white curtains out. In blew
Elm- and chimney-blotted shimmerings, so
Slight the tongue of land, so high the point of view.
1955 this would have been,
Second summer of our tenancy.   15
Another year we'd buy the old eyesore
Half of whose top story we now rented;
Build, above that, a glass room off a wooden
Stardeck;[9] put a fireplace in; make friends.
Now, strangers to the village, did we even   20
have a telephone? Who needed one!
We had each other for communication
And all the rest. The stage was set for Ephraim.

Properties: A milk glass tabletop.
A blue-and-white cup from the Five & Ten.   25
Pencil, paper. Heavy cardboard sheet
Over which the letters A to Z
Spread in an arc, our covenant
With whom it would concern; also
The Arabic numerals, and YES and NO.[1]   30
What more could a familiar spirit want?

---

6. "James Merrill's trilogy provides a series of overlapping fictions to explain the poet's sense of participation in 'other worlds.' Three successive 'worlds' are revealed to him through 'dictation' on a Ouija board. . . . In *The Book of Ephraim* they [the poet JM and his friend DJ] feel the presence of now dead friends, figures who have been in one way or another exemplary for the poet. They are imagined as part of a vast system of reincarnation and eventual purification in a series of stages that free them from earthly ties. In *Mirabell's Books of Number* human perspective is augmented, even replaced, by a scientific fiction: the presence of nonhuman, batlike figures who are said to speak from within the atom" (David Kalstone's note). The *Book of Ephraim* is divided into twenty-six sections, each identified by a letter of the alphabet; our selection is "B" (identified by the large initial letter). *Mirabell* is divided into numerical sections from 1 through 9; our selection is from the first two parts of section 8.
7. In Connecticut; Merrill's family home.
8. Stevens (see above, p. 149) had died in 1955.
9. A deck outside the house.
1. The messages are spelled out by the pointer, the handle of a cup on which the poet JM and his friend DJ or D (David Jackson) each rest a hand. Ephraim is the name of the "familiar spirit" (friendly being from the other world); he is a first-century Greek Jew (*The Book of Ephraim*, section "C").

Well, when he knew us better, he'd suggest
We prop a mirror in the facing chair.
Erect and gleaming, silver-hearted guest,
We saw each other in it. He saw us.   35
(Any reflecting surface worked for him.
Noons, D and I might row to a sandbar
Far enough from town for swimming naked
Then pacing the glass treadmill hardly wet
That healed itself perpetually of us—   40
Unobserved, unheard we thought, until
The night he praised our bodies and our wit,
Our blushes in a twinkling overcome.)
Or we could please him by swirling a drop of rum
Inside the cup that, overturned and seeming   45
Slightly to lurch at such times in mid-glide,
Took heart from us, dictation from our guide.

But he had not yet found us. Who was there?
The cup twitched in its sleep. "Is someone there?"
We whispered, fingers light on Willowware,[2]   50
When the thing moved. Our breathing stopped. The cup,
Glazed zombie of itself, was on the prowl
Moving, but dully, incoherently,
Possessed, as we should soon enough be told,
By one or another of the myriads   55
Who hardly understand, through the compulsive
Reliving of their deaths, that they have died
—By fire in this case, when a warehouse burned.
HELLP O SAV ME scrawled the cup
As on the very wall flame rippled up,   60
Hypnotic wave on wave, a lullaby
Of awfulness. I slumped. D: One more try.
Was anybody there? As when a pike
Strikes, and the line singing writes in lakeflesh
Highstrung runes,[3] and reel spins and mind reels   65
YES a new and urgent power YES
Seized the cup. It swerved, clung, hesitated,
Darted off, a devil's darning needle
Gyroscope our fingers rode bareback
(But stopping dead the instant one lost touch)   70
Here, there, swift handle pointing, letter upon
Letter taken down blind by my free hand—
At best so clumsily, those early sessions
Break off into guesswork, paraphrase.
Too much went whizzing past. We were too nice   75
To pause, divide the alphabetical
Gibberish into words and sentences.
Yet even the most fragmentary message—
Twice as entertaining, twice as wise
As either of its mediums—enthralled them.   80

1976, 1982

---

2. That is, the cup.   thought to have sacred meanings.
3. Characters in the old Norse alphabet, often

From Mirabell's Books of Number[4]

8.1

It starts in the small hours. An interlude
Out of Rossini.[5] Strings in sullen mood
Manage by veiled threats, to recruit a low
Pressure drum and lightning piccolo.
Not until daybreak does the wind machine   5
Start working. The whole house quakes, and one green
Blind snaps at its own coils like a hurt dragon.
Outside, the elm falls for a beachwagon
And ill-assorted objects fill the sky:
Shingles, fishnet, garbage, doghouse. "Hi,   10
What's up?" yawns David, as down Water Street
Wild torrents drive. Attempting to reheat
Last night's coffee, toast some raisin bread,
We find our electricity gone dead.
Now each his own conductor,[6] and at more   15
Than concert pitch, rips through his repertoire
On the piano while the other races
For towels and pots—no end of dripping places.
Horrors, the wine cellar! We lug—Dunkirk[7]—
Six bottles at a time to safety. Work   20
Stops time? Look at your watch. It's after one,
And yet . . . this stillness? Organ point. Indrawn
Breath of barometric chloroform.
The unblinking eye—grey iris—of the storm
Meets ours. A stroll? See how the ebbing Sound   25
Has prinked[8] with jetsam even the high ground,
And underfoot—! Out of what fairy tale
Fell this inchdeep, multicolored hail . . .
Chromosomes on holiday? A vast
Decomposed Seurat?[9] Or has at last   30
The inmost matter of the universe
Called it quits, yet left us none the worse?
Firemen overhead explain the joke:
Cartons bursting, where high water broke
Into the plastic factory, brought down   35
This plague of rainbow gravel on the town—
Unbiodegradable toy blight
Bound to enliven *and* muck up the site
Summers from now. The storm's eye narrows. Gusts
Of wind and rain return, halfhearted guests   40
Seeking however roundabout a way
From Nature's darkening bar and wrecked buffet;
While we, long since at home in the mild bloom
Of candlelight, exchange a look, resume.

4. "By contrast with *The Book of Ephraim*, which looks back over 20 years of experience at the Ouija board and is told largely in Merrill's own voice, *Mirabell* occurs in an almost continuous present. . . . [The visitors from the other world speak] in five-foot iambic capitalized lines" (Kalstone's note).
5. Italian composer of the nineteenth century.

6. (1) of electricity; (2) of an orchestra.
7. French seaport city from which, in the early stages of World War II, more than three hundred thousand British and French troops quickly evacuated after the fall of France to the Germans.
8. Dressed up; the Sound is Long Island Sound.
9. Nineteenth-century French painter whose paintings are made up of many tiny dots of color.

From 8.2

7 MORE TO GO. DID THOSE FIRST VISITORS TO THE SICKROOM   45
(WIND & WATER) TIRE OUR PATIENT? GOD ALLOWS NATURE
THIS TOOL OF WEATHER   & IT WAS 1ST A VITAL ONE WHEN
AFTER THE CATASTROPHE OF WORLD 2 THE WATERS ROSE
COOLING THE RADIUM-HEATED BALL, THEN FROZE OR WITHDREW.[1]
POLES WERE ESTABLISHED   LAND AREAS DEFINED   THEN ATMOSPHERE   50
THEN THE TIMID SNIFFING NOSTRILS. THE VARIOUS FORCES
OF WEATHER & EARTHSHIFT ARE ONE IN NATURE'S LAB WITH HER
BALANCING OF THE NUMBERS OF FEEDING LIVING CREATURES.
ANY IMBALANCE IS YET AGAIN MAN'S WORK   NATURE HAS
CERTAIN PHYSICAL RULES OF THUMB (GREEN): MAN COHABITS   MAN   55
PROCREATES   THIS RULE IS UNIFORM   ITS APPLICATION
VARIES WITH MAN'S INTELLIGENCE. WHEREVER NATURE STILL
NEEDS DROUGHT EARTHQUAKE ET AL TO SLOW THE CROWDING (INDIA
CHINA OR YR WEST COAST) OUR CLONING OF THE COMMISSARS
HAS BEEN INCOMPLETE   TODAY'S STORM WAS TIMED TO THIS BRIEF TALK 60
YR RED ROOM LEAVES U CARELESS OF WEATHER   & YET ITS SMALL
COMPELLING DRAMA FLICKERS IN THE GREEN SPOTLIGHT   ?S

You actually pulled out all those stops,
Frightened millions, damaged towns and crops,
Just to give *us* a taste of Nature's power?   65
YOU HAVE NO IDEA HOW MANY STOPS THERE ARE   ?S
If we remember accurately, you
Take over some of Nature's duties, too—
Rhythms and densities from pole to pole
Which you, instructed by the stars, control?   70
WE ARE NATURE'S MESSENGERS TOO   WE ARE THE PALACE SLAVES.

*   *   *

1978, 1982

From Coda: The Higher Keys

The Ballroom at Sandover[2]

Empty perfection, as I take you in
My heart pounds. Not the shock of elegance,
High ceiling where a faun-Pythagoras[3]
Loses his calipers to barefoot, faintly
Goitrous nymphs, nor pier-glasses[4] between   5
Floral panels of the palest green,
Nor chandeliers—indulgent chaperones—
Aclick, their crystal charges one by one
Accenting the donnée[5] sun-beamed through tall

---

1. The other-world speaker is referring to the gradual formation of our earth, which is presumably "World 2" because his own world of the spirit is "World 1"; thus "our patient" is also the earth, while "7 more to go" refers to the other seven planets in our solar system.
2. The *Changing Light* trilogy is concluded by a third book, *Scripts for the Pageant*, and then a

"Coda: The Higher Keys." Our selection is the last section of the "Coda."
3. Pythagoras was a sixth-century Greek mathematician and philosopher.
4. Large high mirrors; "goitrous": with a swelling in the neck.
5. Literally, "the given."

French window, silver leaf and waxing bud;   10
All a felicity—that does not, however,
Fully account for mine. Great room, I know you?
Somewhere on Earth I've met you in disguise,
Scouted your dark English woods and blood-red
Hangings, and glared down the bison head   15
Above a hearth of stony heraldry—
How many years before your "restoration"
Brought to light this foreign, youthful grace.
Ah, but styles. They are the new friend's face
To whom we sacrifice the tried and true,   20
And are betrayed—or not—by. For affection's
Poorest object, set in perfect light
By happenstance, grows irreplaceable,
And whether in time a room or a romance,
Fails us or redeems us will have followed   25
As an extension of our "feel" for call them
Immaterials, the real right angle,
The golden section[6]—grave proportions here,
Here at the heart of structure, and alone
Surviving now to tell me where I am: 30
In the old ballroom of the Broken Home.[7]

The checkerboard parquet[8] creaks at a step.
A girl in white, dark hair upswept, has entered
Wonderingly, and to no music still
Revolves a moment in remembered arms;   35
Falters, runs to the first window—vainly.[9]
Each in turn she tries them at the last
Resting a bloodless check against the pane.
Next, her fellow guests materialize
In twos and threes. There's tiny Pope! There's Goethe   40
Drumming his fingers while Colette and Maya
Size one another up through jet-set eyes.
Mallarmé looks blank.[1] With a stern nod
Dante agrees to change seats, so that Proust
Be far as possible from Agatha's   45
Huge baby's-breath and rose and goldenrod
Arrangement masking the lectern.[2] Rilke breaks
A bud off,[3] takes it to the girl in white

6. The Pythagorean "golden section" is the division of a line or geometric figure such that the proportion of the smaller part to the greater is the same as that of the greater to the whole; thus a geometrical ideal, as a "real right angle."
7. That is, in his parents' house, where he lived when the events described in his poem "The Broken Home" (above, p. 626) took place.
8. Floor inlaid with a design.
9. The "girl in white" is very likely Mimí, a friend of JM and DJ in Athens, who, earlier in the "Coda," had died suddenly: "Vasíli's voice from Rome, expressionless: / 'Instantaneous . . . no pain, no warning . . .' / Dead? Mimí? And dressed in the white dress" that Vasíli had bought for her. JM and DJ immediately made contact with her in the other world, but she was "dazed": "BUT WHERE AM I?"
1. The guests (some of whom have been heard from earlier in the poem) are all from the other world. Alexander Pope, eighteenth-century English poet; Johann Wolfgang von Goethe (1749–1832), German poet; Colette (1873–1954), French writer. "Maya" is a central character in the poem: "Deren, Elanora ('Maya'), / 1917–61, doyenne [established leader] of our / American experimental film. / Mistress moreover of a life style not / For twenty years to seem conventional" (from the list of speakers in The Book of Ephraim's section "D"). Stéphane Mallarmé, nineteenth-century French poet, wrote a poem called "The Blank."
2. Dante, medieval Italian poet; Marcel Proust (1871–1922), French novelist of sensibilities; Agatha, third-century Italian saint.
3. Rainer Maria Rilke (1875–1925) died of blood poisoning, the result of being scratched by a rose-bush thorn.

Who looks down, blushing with confusion. From
My standpoint just inside the mirror-frame   50
I feel . . . forgotten. Friends are letting me
Compose myself in tactful privacy
When what I need—ha! a young man in gray
Three-piece pinstripe suit has veered my way,
Smiling pleasantly: NOT THE MOMENT QUITE   55
TO GOSSIP BUT THERE'S ONE THING YOU SHOULD KNOW
THESE WORKS YOU UNDERSTAND? THAT OTHERS 'WRITE'
(It's Eliot, he's thinking of Rimbaud)
ARE YET ONE'S OWN[4] That's kind of you to say—
NO DOUBT GRATUITOUS. CHICKEN & EGG   60
AS I BELIEVE YOU PUT IT. (CHER POETE!
CA VA, MERCI, ET VOUS? TOUJOURS A SETE?)[5]
IMAGINE, ESPADRILLES . . . WELL WELL, I SEE
MANY A FACE FROM THE ACADEMY
Oh? Which academy? THERES ONLY ONE   65
PLATO FIRST, OR SO WE LIKE TO THINK,
PRESIDED, DREAMILY PRESENT[6] Who's taken over?
JUVENAL   BUT I'LL BE IN THE SOUP
UNLESS I NIP BACK TO MY OWN AGE GROU
AH!—All necks crane. A gust of freshest air   70
Blowing through the room, LOOK THIS WAY, MAM![7]
But She's already quietly in her chair,
Golden head and the shy girl in white's dark one
Bowed together over the programme.
Ephraim has risen. The room dims. His glance   75
Lights the chandeliers. A reverence,
MAJESTY AND FRIENDS—when shatteringly
The doorbell rings. Our doorbell here in Athens.
We start up. David opens to a form
Gaunt, bespectacled, begrimed, in black,   80
But black worn days, nights, journeyed, sweated in—
Vasíli? Ah sweet Heaven, sit him down,
Take his knapsack, offer food and brandy—.
He shakes his head. Mimí, Mimí in Rome
Buried near Shelley.[8] He can't eat, can't sleep,   85
Can't weep. D makes to put away the Board,
Explaining with a grimace of pure shame
—Because, just as this life takes precedence
Over the next one, so does live despair
Over a poem or a parlor game—   90
Explaining what our friend has stumbled in on.
Lightly I try to shrug it off, lest he,

4. Arthur Rimbaud was a French poet (1854–1891); on T. S. Eliot, see above, p. 270. In *Mirabell* 3.8 JM and DJ had learned of "V work"— "WORK GUIDED BY HIGHER COLLABORATION"— that is, writing on our world being directed by an author in the other; later they were given an example: in the other world Rimbaud "WROTE / THE WASTE LAND   WE FED IT INTO THE LIKE-CLONED ELIOT" (*Mirabell* 6.8).

5. Eliot has turned aside to greet another guest: "Dear poet! I'm fine, and you? Are you still at Sète?" Sète is a French seaport on the Mediterranean; the poet is perhaps the nineteenth-cen-tury French poet Paul Valéry, who was born there. "Espadrilles": flat rope-soled sandals, worn at the seaside.

6. The Academy was originally a grove of olive trees near Athens, where Plato (427–348 B.C.) taught; he was an idealist (hence "DREAMILY") Greek philosopher. Juvenal (*fl.* first century A.D.) was a waspish Roman satirist.

7. A queen of Greece, who had been on Ephraim's "Guest List" from the other world for this gathering.

8. In Rome's Protestant Cemetery, where both Shelley and Keats are buried.

Shrewd leftwing susceptible myth-haunted
As only a Greek novelist can be,
Take Mimí's "presence" at our fête amiss,[9]   95
Or worse, lest anguish take its lover's leap
Into the vortex of credulity
—Vasíli, drink your brandy, get some sleep,
Look, we've these great pills . . . No; he asks instead,
Anything, *anything* to keep his head   100
Above the sucking waves, merely to listen
A little while. So in the hopelessness
Of more directly helping we resume.
Out come cup, notebook, the green-glowing room,
And my worst fear—that, written for the dead,   105
This poem leave a living reader cold—
But there's no turning back. The absolute
Discretion of our circle, as of old,
Takes over. Sympathetic glances bent
Upon the newcomer; murmurs of assent   110
As Ephraim, winding up his Introduction,
Hints that Vasíli is himself a V^1
Work cut out—whereupon Her Majesty
Rises. A rapt hush falls (She can't be wearing,
Yet is, the brightest, bluest, commonest   115
Greek school smock.) Drawing Mimí to her breast,
She dries her tears; praising their constancy,
Their CHILDLESS LOVE and MR BASIL'S[2] WIT
bids him ATTEND AND MAKE GOOD SENSE OF IT
(& CHANGE THAT SHIRT!) NOW POET, READ! A splendor   120
Across lawns meets, in Sandover's tall time-
Dappled mirrors, its own eye. Should rhyme
Calling to rhyme awaken the odd snore,
No harm done. I shall study to ignore
Looks that more boldly with each session yearn   125
Toward the buffet where steaming silver urn,
Cucumber sandwiches, rum punch, fudge laced
With hashish[3] cater to whatever taste.
Something Miss Austen whispers makes Hans laugh.[4]
Then a star trembles in the full carafe   130
As the desk light comes on, illuminating
The page I open to. Both rooms are waiting.
DJ brighteyed (but look how wrinkled) lends
His copy of the score to our poor friend's
Somber regard—captive like Gulliver[5]   135
Or like the mortal in an elfin court
Pining for wife and cottage on this shore
Beyond whose depthless dazzle he can't see.
For *their* ears I begin: "Admittedly . . ."[6]

1982

---

9. Because his lover Mimí is dead and he is still alive.

1. That is, that Vasíli may also take part in "V work" (see footnote 4, above).

2. That is, Vasíli's.

3. The recipe for which was in the British, but not the American, edition of *The Alice B. Toklas Cookbook* (Toklas was Gertrude Stein's companion).

4. Jane Austen (1775–1814); Hans Lodeizen, "1924–50, / Dutch poet," another frequent visitor in the poem.

5. Narrator of Jonathan Swift's satirical *Gulliver's Travels* (1726), who in the first Book is tied down by Lilliputians.

6. The very first lines of *The Changing Light at Sandover* are: "Admittedly I err by undertaking / This in its present form."

The Pier: Under Pisces

The shallows, brighter,
Wetter than water,
Tepidly glitter with the fingerprint-
Obliterating feel of kerosene.

Each piling like a totem   5
Rises from rock bottom
Straight through the ceiling
Aswirl with suns, clear ones or pale bluegreen,

And beyond! where bubbles burst,
Sphere of their worst dreams,   10
If dream is what they do,
These floozy fish—

Ceramic-lipped in filmy
Peekaboo blouses,
Fluorescent body   15
Stockings, hot stripes,

Swayed by the hypnotic ebb and flow
Of supermarket Muzak,
Bolero beat the undertow's
Pebble-filled gourds repeat;   20

Jailbait consumers of subliminal
Hints dropped from on high
In gobbets none
Eschews as minced kin;

Who, hooked themselves—bamboo diviner   25
Bent their way
Vigorously nodding
Encouragement—

Are one by one hauled kisswise, oh
Into some blinding hell   30
Policed by leathery ex-
Justices each

Minding his catch, if catch is what he can,
If mind is what one means—
the torn mouth   35
Stifled by newsprint, working still. If . . . if . . .

The little scales
Grow stiff. Dusk plugs her dryer in,
Buffs her nails, riffles through magazines,
While far and wide and deep   40

Rove the great sharkskin-suited criminals
And safe in this lit shrine

A boy sits. He'll be eight.
We've drunk our milk, we've eaten our stringbeans,

But left untasted on the plate   45
The fish. An eye, a broiled pearl, meeting mine,
I lift his fork . . .
The bite. The tug of fate.

                                                                  1985

ROBERT CREELEY
b. 1926

Robert Creeley is a poet whose work is immediately likable. He has no interest in pompous or oracular utterance, but offers an instantaneous intimacy. He belongs to the school of Charles Olson, but if Olson is Maximus then Creeley is Minimus. His poems are usually short—in total length, in the length of each line, even in title—and always unassuming. He reports brief passages of feeling as minutely as he can, surrounding himself with a situation rather than first entering and then leaving it. When he attempts to describe in prose what he is doing, Creeley is often opaque. In one interview he said that for poets of his school "writing is an occasion given to the person writing rather than one demanded by him. In other words, Olson's concept of projective verse is in the sense of the open field wherein a man's attention has to be momentarily focused; cannot move on any assumption of attitude of feeling but has to momentarily qualify all of its evidence and its intentions."[1] The emphasis is on allowing the theme to play upon the poet rather than to accept an imposed shape.

As a young man, Creeley says, he "was very intent on Williams's sense of how you get the thing stated in its own particulars rather than your assumption of those particulars. In other words, how do you state something so that it occurs in its autonomy rather than your assumption of that autonomy? How do you write the occasion of a truck moving through an intersection so that actually all that it has is movement in all the environment that it was moving through." Like Williams and Olson, Creeley is reverent towards immediate sensation. Perhaps his strongest statement of intention is that, in reaction to poetry that was "too dry and too intellectually articulate," he thought to get, instead, "a more resonant echo of the subconscious or inner experience."[2]

In his preface to *For Love: Poems 1950–1960*, Creeley disavows lofty occasions for writing. "Wherever it is one stumbles (to get to wherever) at least some way will exist, as and when a man takes this or that step—for which, god bless him."[3] His poems are such ways, stumbled into. The title of one poem is "For No Clear Reason," and this might stand as a signpost for Creeley's subrational, or super-rational, motivation and subject.

Although Creeley rejects traditional meters and rhymes, he develops his own rhythms, often catchy and distinct. "It is all a rhythm, / from the shutting / door, to the window / opening," he insists in the opening poem of his book *Words*, which he entitles "The Rhythm." Possibly his most famous statement on esthetics is that which Charles Olson continually quoted from him, "Form is never more than an extension of content." As Creeley says in the title poem of *The Finger* (1968), "whatever is said / in the world, or forgotten, / or not said, makes a form." In his later poetry, while it is still characterized by terseness, reticence, and dramatic pauses, the emotions are

---

1. "Robert Creeley: Interview," William Knief,   2. The same.
Cottonwood Review, 1968.   3. *For Love: Poems 1950–1960*, New York, 1962.

often more sharply outlined and conclusive than in his earlier work.
Creeley's life seems to flow from his theories of poetry. He has moved with something like stumbles from one place to another. Creeley was born in Arlington, Massachusetts, on May 21, 1926. His father, a doctor, died when Robert was very young.
After attending Holderness School in Plymouth, New Hampshire, Creeley entered
Harvard, but soon left, in 1944, to join the American Field Service in India and
Burma. To escape from boredom he took drugs, and some of his poems describe
hallucinatory experiences. He came back to Harvard a year later, and while a student
married, in 1946. A year later, just in time to avoid receiving a degree (he had one
term left), Creeley dropped out again. He and his wife lived on Cape Cod, then
spent three years on a farm in New Hampshire; from there they went to Aix-en-
Provence and then to Majorca, where he started the Divers Press. In 1954 Charles
Olson invited him to join the faculty of Black Mountain College, and he founded and
edited the *Black Mountain Review*. In 1955 he suffered another crisis when his marriage collapsed and he left the college. Following a divorce he married again, in 1957,
and, after a second divorce in 1976, married in 1977 for the third time. From 1956
to 1959 he taught in a boys' school in Albuquerque, and received a B.A. from the
University of New Mexico in 1960. Then he went to Guatemala and taught from 1959
to 1961 on a coffee plantation. He has had many visiting posts, but since 1966 has
been a professor at the State University of New York at Buffalo. When not teaching
he lives in Waldoboro, Vermont.

A Wicker Basket

Comes the time when it's later
and onto your table the headwaiter
puts the bill, and very soon after
rings out the sound of lively laughter—

Picking up change, hands like a walrus,   5
and a face like a barndoor's,
and a head without any apparent size,
nothing but two eyes—

So that's you, man,
or me. I make it as I can,   10
I pick up, I go
faster than they know—

Out the door, the street like a night,
any night, and no one in sight,
but then, well, there she is,   15
old friend Liz—

And she opens the door of her cadillac,
I step in back,
and we're gone.
She turns me on—   20

There are very huge stars, man, in the sky,
and from somewhere very far off someone hands me a slice of apple pie,
and a gob of white, white ice cream on top of it,
and I eat it—

Slowly. And while certainly   25
they are laughing at me, and all around me is racket
of these cats not making it, I make it

in my wicker basket.

1959

The Window

Position is where you
put it, where it is,
did you, for example, that

large tank there, silvered,
with the white church along-   5
side, lift

all that, to what
purpose? How
heavy the slow

world is with   10
everything put
in place. Some

man walks by, a
car beside him on
the dropped   15

road, a leaf of
yellow color is
going to

fall. It
all drops into   20
place. My

face is heavy
with the sight. I can
feel my eye breaking.

1967

"I Keep to Myself Such Measures . . ."

I keep to myself such
measures as I care for,
daily the rocks
accumulate position.

There is nothing   5
but what thinking makes

it less tangible. The mind,
fast as it goes, loses

pace, puts in place of it
like rocks simple markers,   10
for a way only to
hopefully come back to

where it cannot. All
forgets. My mind sinks.
I hold in both hands such weight   15
it is my only description.

1969

Self-Portrait

He wants to be
a brutal old man,
an aggressive old man,
as dull, as brutal
as the emptiness around him,   5

He doesn't want compromise,
nor to be ever nice
to anyone. Just mean,
and final in his brutal,
his total, rejection of it all.   10

He tried the sweet,
the gentle, the "oh,
let's hold hands together"
and it was awful,
dull, brutally inconsequential.   15

Now he'll stand on
his own dwindling legs.
His arms, his skin,
shrink daily. And
he loves, but hates equally.   20

1983

The Faces

The faces with anticipated youth
look out from the current
identifications, judge or salesman,
the neighbor, the man who killed,

mattering only as the sliding world   5
they betoken, the time it never
mattered to accumulate, the fact that
nothing mattered but for what one

could make of it, some passing,
oblique pleasure, a pain immense   10
in its intensity, a sly but
insistent yearning to outwit it

all, be different, move far, far
away, avoid forever the girl
next door, whose cracked, wrinkled   15
smile will still persist, still know you.

1983

ALLEN GINSBERG
b. 1926

It has been frequently said by Allen Ginsberg's admirers, and by Ginsberg himself, that he writes in a tradition that honors William Blake and Walt Whitman as its distinguished pioneers. Ginsberg resembles the two earlier poets in his confidence as a prophet-poet, in his disregard for distinctions between poetry and religion, in his eclecticism—though some early readers were taken in by his occasional pose as a know-nothing. Ginsberg is happily and extravagantly allusive—in his distrust of abstractions and the antiseptically cerebral, and in his desire to compose poetry which invites a complete emotional and physical participation by the audience. Like all poetic innovators, Ginsberg seemed to claim for poetry new areas of experience and new cultural situations. *Howl* is a panoramic vision of the dark side of the complacent Eisenhower years; it discovered for literature an anti-community of waifs and strays, dope addicts and homosexual drifters. Ginsberg's poetry suggested an alternative to the tightly organized, well-mannered poetry written under the influence of the New Criticism; it was emotionally explosive, unashamedly self-preoccupied, metrically expansive, and it helped to create an audience for such influential books of the sixties as Robert Lowell's *Life Studies,* Norman Mailer's *Advertisements for Myself,* and Norman O. Brown's *Life Against Death.*

From Paterson, Ginsberg went to Columbia University. In 1945 he was temporarily suspended, and William Burroughs, whose experiments with drugs are recorded in such frankly disorganized novels as *The Naked Lunch,* took over Ginsberg's literary education. He received a B.A. from Columbia in 1948, and in the summer of that year he underwent an extraordinary experience which he always mentions in accounts of his spiritual development. He was alone in New York, feeling cut off from his friends and uncertain as to his vocation, when one day he heard a voice, which he took to be that of the poet himself, reciting William Blake's "Ah! Sun-Flower" and several other lyrics. The auditory hallucination was accompanied by a feeling of participation in a universal harmony. In one account of the experience Ginsberg recalls that "looking out at the window, through the window at the sky, suddenly it seemed that I saw into the depths of the universe, by looking simply into the ancient sky. The sky suddenly seemed very *ancient*. And this was the very ancient place that he [Blake] was talking about, the sweet golden clime. I suddenly realized that *this* existence was *it!*"[1] Although Ginsberg eventually had to free himself from his dependence on this remembered moment, he continues to believe in it as a personal revelation of a quality common to all high poetry.

In 1953, bearing a letter of introduction to Kenneth Rexroth from Williams, Ginsberg went to San Francisco. He already knew Burroughs, Jack Kerouac, and Gregory Corso, all writers who would be identified with the Beat movement. Having settled around the corner from Lawrence Ferlinghetti's City Lights Bookstore, which would become the publisher of *Howl* and other Beat poems, Ginsberg worked for a time as a market researcher; he was dissatisfied and eager to change his life. In talks with a psychiatrist he found the courage to give up his job and to follow his own sexual bent. He met Peter Orlovsky, who has been his companion ever since, and he finished the first part of *Howl*.

Among the liberating influences on his poetry Ginsberg mentions with particular gratitude the prose of Jack Kerouac. From him Ginsberg learned the sanctity of the uncorrected first draft, and he also learned to make his writing an extension of his own personal relationships. Ginsberg insists that live poetry must not make a distinction between "what you tell your friends and what you tell your Muse."[2] His ideal is a living speech and an organic metric which expresses the poet's physiological state at the time of composition. Thus the recurrences in *Howl*, the long lines each of which is to be read aloud without a pause for catching the breath, express the poet's physical state and induce a similar state in the reader.

In retrospect, Ginsberg speaks wonderingly of the prophetic insights he expressed in his early poems: "Like this was the end of the McCarthy scene, and here I was talking about super-Communist pamphlets on Union Square and the national Golgotha and the Fascists and all the things that turned out to be implicit in a sort of social community revolution that was actually going on."[3] The first edition of *Howl* was printed in England and published at the City Lights Bookstore in October 1956. In March 1957, the U.S. Customs intercepted a second printing. There was a long trial, and after hearing expert testimony from writers and critics, Judge Clayton Horn decided that *Howl* was not without "redeeming social importance." The effect of the trial was to make *Howl* an extraordinary popular success—in 1967 there were 146,000 copies in print—and to draw public attention to Ginsberg and his friends.

Ginsberg, who once described himself as a Buddhist Jew with attachments to Krishna, Siva, Allah, Coyote, and the Sacred Heart,[4] is a spiritual adventurer. He spent the early sixties traveling, for the most part in the East, speaking with wise men of all persuasions and endeavoring to find means of exploring the consciousness other than drugs. One of the wise men he consulted was the Jewish philosopher Martin Buber, who advised him to turn to relationships between one human being and another rather than relationships between the human and the nonhuman. According to Ginsberg, Buber said, " 'Mark my word, young man, in two years you will realize that I was right.' He was right—in two years I marked his words."[5] And from Indian holy men Ginsberg learned the same lesson, the importance of "living in and inhabiting the human form."[6] Ginsberg finally renounced drugs as a submission to the nonhuman.

1. "Interview with Allen Ginsberg," Thomas Clark, *Writers at Work: The Paris Review Interviews*, Third Series, New York 1967, p. 303.
2. The same, p. 288.
3. "Profile of Allen Ginsberg," Jane Kramer, *The New Yorker*, August 17, 1968, p. 60.
4. The same, p. 38.
5. *Writers at Work*, p. 314.
6. The same, p. 315.

In 1965 Ginsberg returned from the East. He successfully applied for a Guggenheim Fellowship and with his friend Orlovsky began a tour of American colleges and universities. He became, in Jane Kramer's phrase, a "kind of ultimate faculty adviser."[7] He chanted his poems to students, talked with them endlessly and patiently, gave sound practical advice, and eventually the institutions he visited gratefully supplied him with classrooms and office space. Ginsberg was unbothered by charges that he had been taken over by the establishment. At poetry readings, peace demonstrations, love-ins and be-ins, before Senate committees and in courtrooms, he has expressed his strongly held radical convictions in a good-humored and disarming way.

In the later sixties Ginsberg became a vivid presence in American life: his face was familiar to those who had never read a line of poetry, and increasingly his poems were lost in a large genial public impression. He has sometimes spoken of his poems rather dismissively as by-products of a spiritual quest. As A. R. Ammons, himself a figure in a revival of Romanticism in American poetry, has observed, "The unity in Ginsberg's work is Ginsberg in search of unity, so that the poems are fragments of the search. The greater poem is possible when the poem is the sought unity, the poet providing the fragments to the whole from his fragmentary experience."[8] The fact that Ginsberg advertises his poems as fragments of a great confession encourages us to believe that we know much more about him than we can learn from any one poem; this belief should not be allowed to obscure the individual exuberance and daring of much of his work.

In recent years Ginsberg has maintained his role as the most earthy and lovable of prophets. Now that his volume of *Collected Poems* has been published (1984), his work can be seen to comprise a history of youth movements, political upheavals, oppressions, and aspirations, and technological changes. It has an index of proper names which comes to hundreds of people, from Buddha to Reagan. Most of his poems are written in his rhapsodic lines but some are in short and easily chantable ones. Always Ginsberg searches for a paradisal self in a paradisal world, and the search is what gives purpose to his pilgrimage to all points of the geographical and spiritual compass.

7. Kramer, p. 33.   8. *Poetry,* June 1964, p. 187.

From Howl[1]

For Carl Solomon

I

I saw the best minds of my generation destroyed by madness, starving hysterical naked,

1. This poem is a chronicle, and also one of the most famous artifacts, of the Beat counterculture of the fifties. It alludes to the experiences of the Beats, especially Carl Solomon to whom it is dedicated, and Ginsberg himself; they met as patients at the Columbia Psychiatric Institute in 1949, and Solomon, whom Ginsberg calls an "intuitive Bronx dadaist and prose-poet," was an inmate of various mental hospitals, undergoing insulin and electroshock therapy, during the fifties. Others mentioned but not named are William S. Burroughs, whose first book, *Junkie* (1953), was published through Solomon's efforts; Herbert E. Huncke, a down-and-out intellectual, Times Square con artist, petty thief, and hipster who, like his friend Burroughs, was a drug addict, and who appears in

Junkie; and Neal Cassady (1926–1968), a hipster from Denver, whose travels around the country with Jack Kerouac (1927–1969) were recorded by the latter in *On the Road* (1957), in which the two appear as Dean Moriarty and Sal Paradise. Line 66 and much else in "Howl" evidently derive from Solomon's "apocryphal history of my adventures," which he told to Ginsberg in 1949 and later, but in *More Mishaps* (1968) he describes this account as "compounded partly of truth, but for the most raving self-justification, crypto-bohemian boasting . . . effeminate prancing and esoteric aphorisms." Line 7 doubtless refers to Ginsberg's two suspensions from Columbia, in 1945 for scraping obscene pictures and phrases on the grimy windows of his dormitory room to provoke the cleaning-woman

dragging themselves through the negro streets at dawn looking for an angry
fix,
angelheaded hipsters burning for the ancient heavenly connection to the
starry dynamo in the machinery of night,
who poverty and tatters and hollow-eyed and high sat up smoking in the
supernatural darkness of cold-water flats floating across the tops of cities contemplating jazz,
who bared their brains to Heaven under the El[2] and saw Mohammedan
angels staggering on tenement roofs illuminated,   5
who passed through universities with radiant cool eyes hallucinating Arkansas and Blake-light tragedy[3] among the scholars of war,
who were expelled from the academies for crazy & publishing obscene odes
on the windows of the skull,
who cowered in unshaven rooms in underwear, burning their money in
wastebaskets and listening to the Terror through the wall,
who got busted in their pubic beards returning through Laredo[4] with a belt
of marijuana for New York,
who ate fire in paint hotels or drank turpentine in Paradise Alley,[5] death,
or purgatoried their torsos night after night   10
with dreams, with drugs, with waking nightmares, alcohol and cock and
endless balls,
incomparable blind streets of shuddering cloud and lightning in the mind
leaping toward poles of Canada & Paterson,[6] illuminating all the
motionless world of Time between,
Peyote solidities of halls, backyard green tree cemetery dawns, wine drunkenness over the rooftops, storefront boroughs of teahead joyride neon
blinking traffic light, sun and moon and tree vibrations in the roaring
winter dusks of Brooklyn, ashcan rantings and kind king light of mind,
who chained themselves to subways for the endless ride from Battery to
holy Bronx[7] on benzedrine until the noise of wheels and children brought
them down shuddering mouth-wracked and battered bleak of brain all
drained of brilliance in the drear light of Zoo,[8]
who sank all night in submarine light of Bickford's[9] floated out and sat through
the stale beer afternoon in desolate Fugazzi's,[1] listening to the crack of
doom on the hydrogen jukebox,   15
who talked continuously seventy hours from park to pad to bar to Bellevue[2]
to museum to the Brooklyn Bridge,
a lost battalion of platonic conversationalists jumping down the stoops off
fire escapes off windowsills off Empire State out of the moon,
yacketayakking screaming vomiting whispering facts and memories and
anecdotes and eyeball kicks and shocks of hospitals and jails and wars,
whole intellects disgorged in total recall for seven days and nights with
brilliant eyes, meat for the Synagogue cast on the pavement,

into cleaning them, and in 1948 when, in danger
of conviction as an accessory to Huncke's burglar-
ies, he volunteered for psychiatric treatment; line
45 describes Huncke's arrival, fresh from jail, at
Ginsberg's Lower East Side apartment in 1948. A
number of the incidents recalled in the poem happened to more than one of the Beats.
2. The elevated railway.
3. Perhaps an allusion to Ginsberg's auditory
hallucination in 1948 of the voice of William Blake
reciting "Ah, Sun-Flower" and "The Sick Rose."
4. A city in Texas, on the Mexican border.
5. A slum courtyard in New York's Lower East

Side, the setting of Jack Kerouac's novel, *The
Subterraneans* (1958).
6. In New Jersey, Ginsberg's birthplace.
7. The southern and northern ends of a New
York subway line.
8. The Bronx Zoo.
9. One of a chain of all-night cafeterias, where
Ginsberg mopped floors and washed dishes during his college years.
1. A bar north of New York City's bohemian
district, Greenwich Village.
2. The public hospital in New York City which
is a receiving center for the mentally disturbed.

who vanished into nowhere Zen New Jersey leaving a trail of ambiguous
    picture postcards of Atlantic City Hall,   20
suffering Eastern sweats and Tangerian bone-grindings and migraines of
    China under junk-withdrawal in Newark's bleak furnished room,
who wandered around and around at midnight in the railroad yard wonder-
    ing where to go, and went, leaving no broken hearts,
who lit cigarettes in boxcars boxcars boxcars racketing through snow toward
    lonesome farms in grandfather night,
who studied Plotinus Poe St. John of the Cross[3] telepathy and bop kaballa[4]
    because the cosmos instinctively vibrated at their feet in Kansas,
who loned it through the streets of Idaho seeking visionary indian angels
    who were visionary indian angels,   25
who thought they were only mad when Baltimore gleamed in supernatural
    ecstasy,
who jumped in limousines with the Chinaman of Oklahoma on the impulse
    of winter midnight streetlight smalltown rain,
who lounged hungry and lonesome through Houston seeking jazz or sex or
    soup, and followed the brilliant Spaniard to converse about America
    and Eternity, a hopeless task, and so took ship to Africa,
who disappeared into the volcanoes of Mexico leaving behind nothing but
    the shadow of dungarees and the lava and ash of poetry scattered in
    fireplace Chicago,
who reappeared on the West Coast investigating the F.B.I. in beards and
    shorts with big pacifist eyes sexy in their dark skin passing out incom-
    prehensible leaflets,   30
who burned cigarette holes in their arms protesting the narcotic tobacco
    haze of Capitalism,
who distributed Supercommunist pamphlets in Union Square[5] weeping and
    undressing while the sirens of Los Alamos[6] wailed them down, and
    wailed down Wall,[7] and the Staten Island ferry also wailed,
who broke down crying in white gymnasiums naked and trembling before
    the machinery of other skeletons,
who bit detectives in the neck and shrieked with delight in policecars for
    committing no crime but their own wild cooking pederasty and intox-
    ication,
who howled on their knees in the subway and were dragged off the roof
    waving genitals and manuscripts,   35
who let themselves be fucked in the ass by saintly motorcyclists, and screamed
    with joy,
who blew and were blown by those human seraphim, the sailors, caresses
    of Atlantic and Caribbean love,
who balled in the morning in the evenings in rosegardens and the grass of
    public parks and cemeteries scattering their semen freely to whomever
    come who may,
who hiccupped endlessly trying to giggle but wound up with a sob behind

---

3. Ginsberg had studied these writers while in college, and perhaps treasured them for their visionary insights into the mystical and symbolic significances of the apparent real world. After his vision of Blake, he immediately reread passages from St. John of the Cross and Plotinus to help him interpret the experience.
4. "Bop" is a style of modern jazz especially influential during the forties and fifties; the Kaballa is a Hebraic system of mystical interpretation of the scriptures, which asserts the supremacy of the spirit over bodily desires.
5. In New York City; it was a center for radical speeches and demonstrations during the thirties.
6. In New Mexico, the site of the laboratory at which the development of the atomic bomb was completed.
7. Wall Street, in New York, but perhaps also the Wailing Wall in Jerusalem where Jews lament their losses and seek consolation.

a partition in a Turkish Bath when the blonde & naked angel came to
    pierce them with a sword,
who lost their loveboys to the three old shrews of fate the one eyed shrew
    of the heterosexual dollar the one eyed shrew that winks out of the
    womb and the one eyed shrew that does nothing but sit on her ass and
    snip the intellectual golden threads of the craftsman's loom,   40
who copulated ecstatic and insatiate with a bottle of beer a sweetheart a
    package of cigarettes a candle and fell off the bed, and continued along
    the floor and down the hall and ended fainting on the wall with a vision
    of ultimate cunt and come eluding the last gyzym of consciousness,
who sweetened the snatches of a million girls trembling in the sunset, and
    were red eyed in the morning but prepared to sweeten the snatch of
    the sunrise, flashing buttocks under barns and naked in the lake,
who went out whoring through Colorado in myriad stolen night-cars, N.C.,[8]
    secret hero of these poems, cocksman and Adonis of Denver—joy to
    the memory of his innumerable lays of girls in empty lots & diner
    backyards, moviehouses' rickety rows, on mountaintops in caves or
    with gaunt waitresses in familiar roadside lonely petticoat upliftings &
    especially secret gas-station solipsisms of johns, & hometown alleys
    too,
who faded out in vast sordid movies, were shifted in dreams, woke on a
    sudden Manhattan, and picked themselves up out of basements hung-
    over with heartless Tokay and horrors of Third Avenue iron dreams &
    stumbled to unemployment offices,
who walked all night with their shoes full of blood on the snowbank docks
    waiting for a door in the East River to open to a room full of steamheat
    and opium,   45
who created great suicidal dramas on the apartment cliff-banks of the Hud-
    son under the wartime blue floodlight of the moon & their heads shall
    be crowned with laurel in oblivion,
who ate the lamb stew of the imagination or digested the crab at the muddy
    bottom of the rivers of Bowery,[9]
who wept at the romance of the streets with their pushcarts full of onions
    and bad music,
who sat in boxes breathing in the darkness under the bridge, and rose up
    to build harpsichords in their lofts,
who coughed on the sixth floor of Harlem crowned with flame under the
    tubercular sky surrounded by orange crates of theology,   50
who scribbled all night rocking and rolling over lofty incantations which in
    the yellow morning were stanzas of gibberish,
who cooked rotten animals lung heart feet tail borsht & tortillas dreaming
    of the pure vegetable kingdom,
who plunged themselves under meat trucks looking for an egg,
who threw their watches off the roof to cast their ballot for Eternity outside
    of Time, & alarm clocks fell on their heads every day for the next
    decade,
who cut their wrists three times successively unsuccessfully, gave up and
    were forced to open antique stores where they thought they were
    growing old and cried,   55

8. Neal Cassady.
9. The avenue in New York famous as the haunt   of alcoholics and derelicts.

who were burned alive in their innocent flannel suits on Madison Avenue[1] amid blasts of leaden verse & the tanked-up clatter of the iron regiments of fashion & the nitroglycerine shrieks of the fairies of advertising & the mustard gas of sinister intelligent editors, or were run down by the drunken taxicabs of Absolute Reality,

who jumped off the Brooklyn Bridge this actually happened and walked away unknown and forgotten into the ghostly daze of Chinatown soup alleyways & firetrucks, not even one free beer,

who sang out of their windows in despair, fell out of the subway window, jumped in the filthy Passaic,[2] leaped on negroes, cried all over the street, danced on broken wineglasses barefoot smashed phonograph records of nostalgic European 1930's German jazz finished the whiskey and threw up groaning into the bloody toilet, moans in their ears and the blast of colossal steam-whistles,

who barreled down the highways of the past journeying to each other's hotrod-Golgotha[3] jail-solitude watch or Birmingham jazz incarnation,

who drove crosscountry seventytwo hours to find out if I had a vision or you had a vision or he had a vision to find out Eternity.   60

who journeyed to Denver, who died in Denver, who came back to Denver & waited in vain, who watched over Denver & brooded & loned in Denver and finally went away to find out the Time, & now Denver is lonesome for her heroes,

who fell on their knees in hopeless cathedrals praying for each other's salvation and light and breasts, until the soul illuminated its hair for a second,

who crashed through their minds in jail waiting for impossible criminals with golden heads and the charm of reality in their hearts who sang sweet blues to Alcatraz,

who retired to Mexico to cultivate a habit,[4] or Rocky Mount to tender Buddha[5] or Tangiers[6] to boys or Southern Pacific to the black locomotive[7] or Harvard to Narcissus to Woodlawn[8] to the daisy-chain or grave,

who demanded sanity trials accusing the radio of hypnotism & were left with their insanity & their hands & a hung jury,   65

who threw potato salad at CCNY lecturers on Dadaism[9] and subsequently presented themselves on the granite steps of the madhouse with shaven heads and harlequin speech of suicide, demanding instantaneous lobotomy,

and who were given instead the concrete void of insulin metrasol electricity hydrotherapy psychotherapy occupational therapy pingpong & amnesia,

who in humorless protest overturned only one symbolic pingpong table, resting briefly in catatonia,

returning years later truly bald except for a wig of blood, and tears and fingers, to the visible madman doom of the wards of the madtowns of the East,

---

1. The avenue in New York which is the center of the advertising industry, in which Burroughs had worked for a year as a copy writer during the thirties. The conventional, middle-class New York businessman was satirized by Sloan Wilson in his novel, *The Man in the Grey Flannel Suit* (1955).
2. The river that flows past Paterson, New Jersey.
3. Golgotha, or "the place of skulls," is the hill near Jerusalem where Christ was crucified.
4. Burroughs.

5. Kerouac, who was then living in Rocky Mount, North Carolina.
6. Both Burroughs and Ginsberg lived in Tangiers for a time.
7. Neal Cassady, who worked as a brakeman for the Southern Pacific Railroad.
8. A cemetery in the Bronx.
9. An artistic movement (c. 1916–1920) based on absurdity and accident. CCNY is the City College of New York.

Pilgrim State's Rockland's and Greystone's[1] foetid halls, bickering with the
echoes of the soul, rocking and rolling in the midnight solitude-bench
dolmen-realms of love, dream of life a nightmare, bodies turned to
stone as heavy as the moon,   70
with mother finally ******,[2] and the last fantastic book flung out of the
tenement window, and the last door closed at 4 AM and the last telephone slammed at the wall in reply and the last furnished room emptied down to the last piece of mental furniture, a yellow paper rose
twisted on a wire hanger in the closet, and even that imaginary, nothing but a hopeful little bit of hallucination—
ah, Carl, while you are not safe I am not safe, and now you're really in the
total animal soup of time—
and who therefore ran through the icy streets obsessed with a sudden flash
of the alchemy of the use of the ellipse the catalog the meter & the
vibrating plane,
who dreamt and made incarnate gaps in Time & Space through images
juxtaposed, and trapped the archangel of the soul between 2 visual
images and joined the elemental verbs and set the noun and dash of
consciousness together jumping with sensation of Pater Omnipotens
Aeterna Deus[3]
to recreate the syntax and measure of poor human prose and stand before
you speechless and intelligent and shaking with shame, rejected yet
confessing out the soul to conform to the rhythm of thought in his
naked and endless head,   75
the madman bum and angel beat in Time, unknown, yet putting down here
what might be left to say in time come after death,
and rose reincarnate in the ghostly clothes of jazz in the goldhorn shadow
of the band and blew the suffering of America's naked mind for love
into an eli eli lamma lamma sabacthani[4] saxophone cry that shivered
the cities down to the last radio
with the absolute heart of the poem of life butchered out of their own bodies
good to eat a thousand years.

                                                                        1956

A Supermarket in California

What thoughts I have of you tonight, Walt Whitman,[5] for I walked down
the streets under the trees with a headache self-conscious looking at the full
moon.

1. Three mental hospitals near New York. Carl
Solomon was an inmate at Pilgrim State and Rockland hospitals, while Ginsberg's mother was a
patient at Greystone Hospital.
2. Naomi Ginsberg, who for many years suffered from aggravated paranoia and was hospital-
ized for it several times, was permanently
institutionalized shortly after Ginsberg graduated
from Columbia. She died in 1956, the year after
"Howl" was written, and is memorialized in Ginsberg's long poem, *Kaddish*.
3. All-powerful Father, Eternal God (Latin). The
phrase was used by Paul Cézanne (1839–1906), the
French Impressionist painter, in a letter of 1904
to Emile Bernard, to describe the sensations he
received from observing and registering the
appearance of the natural world. "The last part of
'Howl' was really an homage to art but also in specific terms an homage to Cézanne's method. . . .
Just as Cézanne doesn't use perspective lines to
create space, but it's a juxtaposition of one color

against another color (that's one element of his
space), so, I had the idea, perhaps over-refined,
that by the unexplainable, unexplained nonper-
spective line, that is, juxtaposition of one *word*
against another, . . . there'd be a *gap* between the
two words which the mind would fill in with the
sensation of existence. . . . So, I was trying to do
similar things with juxtapositions like 'hydrogen
jukebox' or 'winter midnight smalltown streetlight
rain'. . . . like: jazz, jukebox, and all that, and we
have the jukebox from that; politics, hydrogen
bomb, and we have the hydrogen of that, you see
'hydrogen jukebox.' [line 15] And that actually
compresses in one instant like a whole series of
things" (*Writers at Work:* Third Series, New York,
1967, pp. 295–96).
4. Christ's words from the Cross (Matthew
26:46, Mark 15:33): "My God, my God, why have
you forsaken me?"
5. American poet (see above, p. 1).

In my hungry fatigue, and shopping for images, I went into the neon fruit supermarket, dreaming of your enumerations!

What peaches and what penumbras?[6] Whole families shopping at night! Aisles full of husbands! Wives in the avocados, babies in the tomatoes!—and you, García Lorca,[7] what were you doing down by the watermelons?

I saw you, Walt Whitman, childless, lonely old grubber, poking among the meats in the refrigerator and eyeing the grocery boys.

I heard you asking questions of each: Who killed the pork chops? What price bananas? Are you my Angel?   5

I wandered in and out of the brilliant stacks of cans following you, and followed in my imagination by the store detective.

We strode down the open corridors together in our solitary fancy tasting artichokes, possessing every frozen delicacy, and never passing the cashier.

Where are we going, Walt Whitman? The doors close in an hour. Which way does your beard point tonight?

(I touch your book and dream of our odyssey in the supermarket and feel absurd.)

Will we walk all night through solitary streets? The trees add shade to shade, lights out in the houses, we'll both be lonely.   10

Will we stroll dreaming of the lost America of love past blue automobiles in driveways, home to our silent cottage?

Ah, dear father, graybeard, lonely old courage-teacher, what America did you have when Charon quit poling his ferry and you got out on a smoking bank and stood watching the boat disappear on the black waters of Lethe?[8]

                                                                                1956

America[9]

America I've given you all and now I'm nothing.
America two dollars and twentyseven cents January 17, 1956.
I can't stand my own mind.
America when will we end the human war?
Go fuck yourself with your atom bomb.   5
I don't feel good don't bother me.
I won't write my poem till I'm in my right mind.
America when will you be angelic?
When will you take off your clothes?

6. Partial shadows.
7. Early twentieth-century Spanish poet and dramatist; like Ginsberg and Whitman, a homosexual.
8. One of the rivers of Hades (it means "forgetfulness"), across which Charon ferried the dead.
9. By 1956, Senator Joseph McCarthy had been discredited, but the memory of his anti-Communist witch hunts stifled political dissent, and Ginsberg's publication of this poem was a courageous act. He alludes to the repressive twenties and the liberal thirties, his view colored by that of his mother, a Russian immigrant and a fervent member of the Communist Party. The Trotskyites (line 11) were militant American Communists; the Wobblies (line 27) were members of the Industrial Workers of the World, a radical labor organization active from 1905 to 1930, many of whose members

were imprisoned during the "Red scare" of 1919–21. Tom Mooney (1882–1942) (line 57), a labor organizer, was condemned to death on perjured evidence that he had exploded a bomb during a San Francisco parade; he escaped the electric chair and was freed after 23 years in prison, but anarchists Nicola Sacco and Bartholomeo Vanzetti (line 59) were executed in 1927 after what amounted to a political trial. During the thirties the American Communist Party was able to take part openly in political campaigns, and organized support for Tom Mooney, the Scottsboro boys (line 60—eight Blacks condemned to death after a sensational and unfair rape trial in Scottsboro, Alabama), and for the Loyalists (line 58) who fought in support of the Socialist government of Republican Spain against the Fascist revolution led by General Francisco Franco.

When will you look at yourself through the grave?   10
When will you be worthy of your million Trotskyites?
America why are your libraries full of tears?
America when will you send your eggs to India?
I'm sick of your insane demands.
When can I go into the supermarket and buy what I need with my good
    looks?   15
America after all it is you and I who are perfect not the next world.
Your machinery is too much for me.
You made me want to be a saint.
There must be some other way to settle this argument.
Burroughs[1] is in Tangiers I don't think he'll come back it's sinister.   20
Are you being sinister or is this some form of practical joke?
I'm trying to come to the point.
I refuse to give up my obsession.
America stop pushing I know what I'm doing.
America the plum blossoms are falling.   25
I haven't read the newspapers for months, everyday somebody goes on trial
    for murder.
America I feel sentimental about the Wobblies.
America I used to be a communist when I was a kid I'm not sorry.
I smoke marijuana every chance I get.
I sit in my house for days on end and stare at the roses in the closet.   30
When I go to Chinatown I get drunk and never get laid.
My mind is made up there's going to be trouble.
You should have seen me reading Marx.
My psychoanalyst thinks I'm perfectly right.
I won't say the Lord's Prayer.   35
I have mystical visions and cosmic vibrations.
America I still haven't told you what you did to Uncle Max after he came
    over from Russia.

I'm addressing you.
Are you going to let your emotional life be run by Time Magazine?
I'm obsessed by Time Magazine.   40
I read it every week.
Its cover stares at me every time I slink past the corner candystore.
I read it in the basement of the Berkeley Public Library.
It's always telling me about responsibility. Businessmen are serious. Movie
    producers are serious. Everybody's serious but me.
It occurs to me that I am America.   45
I am talking to myself again.

Asia is rising against me.
I haven't got a chinaman's chance.
I'd better consider my national resources.
My national resources consist of two joints of marijuana millions of genitals
    an unpublishable private literature that goes 1400 miles an hour and
    twentyfive-thousand mental institutions.   50
I say nothing about my prisons nor the millions of underprivileged who live
    in my flowerpots under the light of five hundred suns.

---

1. William Burroughs (b. 1914), author of *The Naked Lunch* (1959), was a heroin addict for fifteen
years until cured in 1957; in 1950 he left the United States for Mexico, and then for Tangiers, to avoid
prosecution.

I have abolished the whorehouses of France, Tangiers is the next to go.
My ambition is to be President despite the fact that I'm a Catholic.[2]

America how can I write a holy litany in your silly mood?
I will continue like Henry Ford my strophes[3] are as individual as his auto-
    mobiles more so they're all different sexes.   55
America I will sell you strophes $2500 apiece $500 down on your old strophe
America free Tom Mooney
America save the Spanish Loyalists
America Sacco & Vanzetti must not die
America I am the Scottsboro boys.   60
America when I was seven momma took me to Communist Cell meetings
    they sold us garbanzos a handful per ticket a ticket costs a nickel and
    the speeches were free everybody was angelic and sentimental about
    the workers it was all so sincere you have no idea what a good thing
    the party was in 1935 Scott Nearing was a grand old man a real mensch
    Mother Bloor made me cry I once saw Israel Amter plain.[4] Everybody
    must have been a spy.
America you don't really want to go to war.
America it's them bad Russians.
Them Russians them Russians and them Chinamen. And them Russians.
The Russia wants to eat us alive. The Russia's power mad. She wants to
    take our cars from out our garages.   65
Her wants to grab Chicago. Her needs a Red Readers' digest. Her wants
    our auto plants in Siberia. Him big bureaucracy running our filling-
    stations.
That no good. Ugh. Him make Indians learn read. Him need big black
    niggers. Hah. Her make us all work sixteen hours a day. Help.
America this is quite serious.
America this is the impression I get from looking in the television set.
America is this correct?   70
I'd better get right down to the job.
It's true I don't want to join the Army or turn lathes in precision parts
    factories, I'm nearsighted and psychopathic anyway.
America I'm putting my queer shoulder to the wheel.

                                                                        1956

To Aunt Rose

Aunt Rose—now—might I see you
with your thin face and buck tooth smile and pain
            of rheumatism—and a long black heavy shoe
                for your bony left leg
limping down the long hall in Newark on the running carpet   5
            past the black grand piano
                in the day room
                    where the parties were
        and I sang Spanish loyalist[5] songs

in a high squeaky voice   10
(hysterical) the committee listening
while you limped around the room
collected the money—
Aunt Honey, Uncle Sam, a stranger with a cloth arm
in his pocket   15
and huge young bald head
of Abraham Lincoln Brigade[6]

—your long sad face
your tears of sexual frustration
(what smothered sobs and bony hips   20
under the pillows of Osborne Terrace)
—the time I stood on the toilet seat naked
and you powdered my thighs with calamine
against the poison ivy—my tender
and shamed first black curled hairs   25
what were you thinking in secret heart then
knowing me a man already—
and I an ignorant girl of family silence on the thin pedestal
of my legs in the bathroom—Museum of Newark.

Aunt Rose   30
Hitler is dead, Hitler is in Eternity; Hitler is with
Tamburlane and Emily Brontë[7]

Though I see you walking still, a ghost on Osborne Terrace
down the long dark hall to the front door
limping a little with a pinched smile   35
in what must have been a silken
flower dress
welcoming my father, the Poet, on his visit to Newark
—see you arriving in the living room
dancing on your crippled leg   40
and clapping hands his book
had been accepted by Liveright[8]

Hitler is dead and Liveright's gone out of business
The Attic of the Past and *Everlasting Minute* are out of print
Uncle Harry sold his last silk stocking   45
Claire quite interpretive dancing school
Buba sits a wrinkled monument in Old
Ladies Home blinking at new babies

last time I saw you was the hospital
pale skull protruding under ashen skin   50
blue veined unconscious girl
in an oxygen tent
the war in Spain has ended long ago
Aunt Rose

1961

6. A group of American volunteers who fought
with the loyalists in the Spanish Civil War.
7. Nineteenth-century English poet and novelist, author of *Wuthering Heights;* Tamburlaine
was the Mideastern "scourge" and conqueror (hero
of Christopher Marlowe's *Tamburlaine,* 1588).

8. This leading American publisher of the 1920s
and 1930s (now a subsidiary of W. W. Norton &
Company) published *The Everlasting Minute*
(1937), poems by Allen Ginsberg's father Louis,
whose first book was *The Attic of the Past* (Boston,
1920).

Mugging

I

Tonite I walked out of my red apartment door on East tenth street's[9] dusk—
Walked out of my home ten years, walked out in my honking neighborhood
Tonite at seven walked out past garbage cans chained to concrete anchors
Walked under black painted fire escapes, giant castiron plate covering a
    hole in ground
—Crossed the street, traffic lite red, thirteen bus roaring by liquor store,   5
past corner pharmacy iron grated, past Coca Cola & Mylai[1] posters fading
    scraped on brick
Past Chinese Laundry wood door'd, & broken cement stoop steps For Rent
    hall painted green & purple Puerto Rican style
Along E. 10th's glass splattered pavement, kid blacks & Spanish oiled hair
    adolescents' crowded house fronts—
Ah, tonite I walked out on my block NY City under humid summer sky
    Halloween
thinking what happened Timothy Leary joining brain police for a season?   10
thinking what's all this Weathermen,[2] secrecy & selfrighteousness beyond
    reason—F.B.I. plots?
Walked past a taxicab controlling the bottle strewn curb—
past young fellows with their umbrella handles & canes leaning against a
    ravaged Buick
—and as I looked at the crowd of kids on the stoop—a boy stepped up, put
    his arm around my neck
tenderly I thought for a moment, squeezed harder, his umbrella handle
    against my skull,   15
and his friends took my arm, a young brown companion tripped his foot
    'gainst my ankle—
as I went down shouting Om Ah Hūṃ[3] to gangs of lovers on the stoop
    watching
slowly appreciating, why this is a raid, these strangers mean strange busi-
    ness
with what—my pockets, bald head, broken-healed-bone leg, my softshoes,
    my heart—
Have they knives? Om Ah Hūṃ—Have they sharp metal wood to shove in
    eye ear ass? Om Ah Hūṃ   20
& slowly reclined on the pavement, struggling to keep my woolen bag of
    poetry address calendar & Leary-lawyer notes hung from my shoulder
dragged in my neat orlon shirt over the crossbar of a broken metal door
dragged slowly onto the fire-soiled floor an abandoned store, laundry candy
    counter 1929—
now a mess of papers & pillows & plastic car seat covers cracked cockroach-
    corpsed ground—
my wallet back pocket passed over the iron foot step guard   25
and fell out, stole by God Muggers' lost fingers, Strange—
Couldn't tell—snakeskin wallet actually plastic, 70 dollars my bank money
    for a week,
old broken wallet—and dreary plastic contents—Amex card & Manf. Han-
    over Trust Credit too—business card from Mr. Spears British Home

---

9. On New York City's Lower East Side.   the 1960s.
1. Scene of a massacre during the Vietnam War.   3. Buddhist mantra or chant.
2. Radical group of student protesters during

Minister Drug Squad—my draft card—membership ACLU & Naropa
    Institute Instructor's[4] identification
Om Ah Hūṃ I continued chanting Om Ah Hūṃ
Putting my palm on the neck of an 18 year old boy fingering my back pocket
    crying "Where's the money"   30
"Oh Am Hūṃ there isn't any"
My card Chief Boo-Hoo Neo American Chruch New Jersey & Lower East
    Side
Om Ah Hūṃ—what not forgotten crowded wallet—Mobil Credit, Shell?
    old lovers addresses on cardboard pieces, booksellers calling cards—
—"Shut up or we'll murder you"—"Om Ah Hūṃ take it easy"
Lying on the floor shall I shout more loud?—the metal door closed on
    blackness   35
one boy felt my broken healed ankle, looking for hundred dollar bills behind
    my stocking weren't even there—a third boy untied my Seiko Hong
    Kong watch rough from right wrist leaving a clasp-prick skin tiny bruise
"Shut up and we'll get out of here"—and so they left,
as I rose from the cardboard mattress thinking Om Ah Hūṃ didn't stop em
    enough,
the tone of voice too loud—my shoulder bag with 10,000 dollars full of
    poetry left on the broken floor—

November 2, 1974

II

Went out the door dim eyed, bent down & picked up my glasses from step
    edge I placed them while dragged in the store—looked out—   40
Whole street a bombed-out face, building rows' eyes & teeth missing
burned apartments half the long block, gutted cellars, hallways' charred
    beams
hanging over trash plaster mounded entrances, couches & bedsprings rusty
    after sunset
Nobody home, but scattered stoopfuls of scared kids frozen in black hair
chatted giggling at house doors in black shoes, families cooked For Rent
    some six story houses mid the street's wreckage   45
Nextdoor Bodega,[5] a phone, the police? "I just got mugged" I said
to the man's face under fluorescent grocery light tin ceiling—
puffy, eyes blank & watery, sickness of beer kidney and language tongue
thick lips stunned as my own eyes, poor drunken Uncle minding the store!
O hopeless city of idiots empty eyed staring afraid, red beam top'd car at
    street curb arrived—   50
"Hey maybe my wallet's still on the ground got a flashlight?"
Back into the burnt-doored cave, & the policeman's gray flashlight broken
    no eyebeam—
"My partner all he wants is sit in the car never gets out Hey Joe bring your
    flashlight—
A tiny throwaway beam, dim as a match in the criminal dark
"No I can't see anything here" . . . "Fill out this form"   55
Neighborhood street crowd behind a car "We didn't see nothing"
Stoop young girls, kids laughing "Listen man last time I messed with them
    see this—"

4. Ginsberg's school for the study of poetry and   5. Combined wineshop and store (Spanish).
mysticism in Boulder, Colorado.

rolled up his skinny arm shirt, a white knife scar on his brown shoulder
"Besides we help you the cops come don't know anybody we all get arrested
go to jail I never help no more mind my business everytime"   60
"Agh!" upstreet think "Gee I don't know anybody here ten years lived half
    block crost Avenue C[6]
and who knows who?"—passing empty apartments, old lady with frayed
    paper bags
sitting in the tin-boarded doorframe of a dead house.

December 10, 1974   1977

6. Which runs at right angles to East 10th Street.

FRANK O'HARA
1926–1966

Frank O'Hara's strategies as a poet, and as a sponsor of other people's poetry, are
summed up in characteristically offhand fashion in an essay called "Personism: A
Manifesto." He begins by putting poetry in its place as one among many legitimate
human amusements. "Too many poets," he protests, "act like a middle-aged mother
trying to get her kids to eat too much cooked meat, and potatoes with drippings
(tears). I don't give a damn whether they eat or not. Forced feeding leads to excessive
thinness (effete). Nobody should experience anything they don't need to, if they
don't need poetry bully for them. I like the movies too. And after all, only Whitman
and Crane and Williams, of the American poets, are better than the movies."[1] Though
it reads like a parody of Charles Olson's "Projective Verse," a manifesto published in
the same year, O'Hara's essay is an effort at an accurate statement; he bears out his
poetics by his own practice. He objects to "abstraction in poetry," which he obliquely
defines as the absence of the artist's personal voice or style from his work; this is not
to be confused with abstractness in painting, because even in the work of Abstract
Expressionists like Jackson Pollock and Willem de Kooning, one can still feel the
presence of a personal style. O'Hara wants poetry to avoid "philosophy," or abstract
speculation, but he doesn't opt for "personality or intimacy" either. Once when writing a poem, he says, "I was realizing that if I wanted to I could use the telephone
instead of writing the poem."[2] It is this personal, spur-of-the-moment spontaneity
that pervades his poems by which O'Hara guarantees his continuing presence in
them.

He was born in Baltimore on June 27, 1926, and grew up in Worcester, Massachusetts; after serving in the navy during the Second World War, he studied at Harvard,
where he helped to found the Poets' Theatre, and at the University of Michigan's
graduate school. In 1951 he settled in New York, where he worked for *Art News* and
joined the staff of the Museum of Modern Art, eventually becoming associate curator
of exhibitions of painting and sculpture. During the sixties he became a leading figure
in a group of young poets (Ashbery, Koch, and Schuyler among them) who came to
be known as the New York poets. By their own testimony they derived inspiration
from paintings by Pollock, Franz Kline, de Kooning, and others, many of whom were
O'Hara's friends. As James Schuyler puts it, "New York poets, except I suppose the
color blind, are affected most by the floods of paint in whose crashing surf we all
scramble . . . In New York the art world is a painters' world; writers and musicians
are in the boat, but they don't steer."[3]

1. *Collected Poems*, New York, 1971, p. 498.   3. Quoted in *The New American Poetry: 1945–*
2. The same, p. 499.   *1960*, New York, 1960, p. 418.

O'Hara wrote many of his poems in spare moments snatched from an increasingly busy life in the art world; most were left around his apartment or sent in letters to friends, and the six books of poems he published between 1952 and 1965 gave little idea of his abundance. After O'Hara's death on July 25, 1966 (he was run down by a dune buggy on Fire Island), Donald Allen assembled hundreds of manuscripts to make up O'Hara's *Collected Poems* (1971).

Poem

The eager note on my door said "Call me,
call when you get in!" so I quickly threw
a few tangerines into my overnight bag,
straightened my eyelids and shoulders, and

headed straight for the door. It was autumn   5
by the time I got around the corner, oh all
unwilling to be either pertinent or bemused, but
the leaves were brighter than grass on the sidewalk!

Funny, I thought, that the lights are on this late
and the hall door open; still up at this hour, a   10
champion jai-alai player like himself? Oh fie!
For shame! What a host, so zealous! And he was

there in the hall, flat on a sheet of blood that
ran down the stairs. I did appreciate it. There are few
hosts who so thoroughly prepare to greet a guest   15
only casually invited, and that several months ago.

                                                             1952

The Day Lady Died

It is 12:20 in New York a Friday
three days after Bastille day,[1] yes
it is 1959 and I go get a shoeshine
because I will get off the 4:19 in Easthampton[2]
at 7:15 and then go straight to dinner   5
and I don't know the people who will feed me

I walk up the muggy street beginning to sun
and have a hamburger and a malted and buy
an ugly NEW WORLD WRITING to see what the poets
in Ghana are doing these days   10
        I go on to the bank
and Miss Stillwagon (first name Linda I once heard)
doesn't even look up my balance for once in her life
and in the GOLDEN GRIFFIN I get a little Verlaine
for Patsy with drawings by Bonnard[3] although I do   15

---

1. July 14, French Independence Day.
2. A town on eastern Long Island.
3. An edition of the poems of Paul Verlaine

(1844–1896), the French poet, with illustrations by Pierre Bonnard (1867–1947).

think of Hesiod,[4] trans. Richmond Lattimore or
Brendan Behan's new play[5] or *Le Balcon* or *Les Nègres*
of Genet,[6] but I don't, I stick with Verlaine
after practically going to sleep with quandariness

and for Mike I just stroll into the PARK LANE   20
Liquor Store and ask for a bottle of Strega and
then I go back where I came from to 6th Avenue
and the tobacconist in the Ziegfeld Theatre and
casually ask for a carton of Gauloises and a carton
of Picayunes, and a NEW YORK POST with her[7] face on it   25

and I am sweating a lot by now and thinking of
leaning on the john door in the 5 SPOT
while she whispered a song along the keyboard
to Mal Waldron[8] and everyone and I stopped breathing

1964

Why I Am Not a Painter

I am not a painter, I am a poet.
Why? I think I would rather be
a painter, but I am not. Well,

for instance, Mike Goldberg[9]
is starting a painting. I drop in.   5
"Sit down and have a drink" he
says. I drink; we drink. I look
up. "You have SARDINES in it."
"Yes, it needed something there."
"Oh." I go and the days go by   10
and I drop in again. The painting
is going on, and I go, and the days
go by. I drop in. The painting is
finished. "Where's SARDINES?"
All that's left is just   15
letters, "It was too much," Mike says.

But me? One day I am thinking of
a color: orange. I write a line
about orange. Pretty soon it is a
whole page of words, not lines.   20
Then another page. There should be
so much more, not of orange, of
words, of how terrible orange is
and life. Days go by. It is even in
prose, I am a real poet. My poem   25
is finished and I haven't mentioned

4. (Eighth century B.C.), Greek poet, author of
Works and Days.
5. Probably *The Quare Fellow* (1956) or *The
Hostage* (1958).
6. Jean Genet, French writer, author of the plays
The Balcony (1956) and *The Blacks* (1958).

7. Billie Holiday (1915–1959), or "Lady Day,"
the blues singer.
8. (b. 1925), pianist, Billie Holiday's accompa-
nist from 1957 until her death.
9. (b. 1924), a New York artist who provided
silk screen prints for O'Hara's *Odes* (1960).

orange yet It's twelve poems, I call
it ORANGES. And one day in a gallery
I see Mike's painting, called SARDINES.

1971

ROBERT BLY
b. 1926

Robert Bly speaks of the "underground image"; his poetry can be thought of as an
underground, or better, a mystical, imagism. In a matter-of-fact tone, shunning grandeur and emphasis, he describes external landscapes of his beloved and native Minnesota, and landscapes of the mind as well; the objects specified are given a strange,
fantastic presentness. Poems that appear modestly inconclusive are, if read in the
way he intends, arrogantly conclusive, because details which may seem trivially phe-
nomenal are untrivially noumenal.

This surcharged imagism draws upon Neruda and other foreign poets; it has connections also with the late poetry of Stevens. But Bly's favorite source is the German
mystic Jakob Boehme. The epigraph from Boehme at the beginning of Bly's second
book, *The Light around the Body*, declares: "For according to the outward man, we
are in this world, and according to the inward man, we are in the inward world . . .
Since then we are generated out of both worlds, we speak in two languages, and we
must be understood also by two languages." The poet is bilingual, but, as Bly several
times remarks, the political leader is not. "There are lives the executives / Know
nothing of," he attests ("Romans Angry About the Inner World"), and explains, "The
other world is like a thorn / In the ear of a tiny beast!" The poet can perceive what
President Johnson cannot: "We were the ones we intended to bomb!" ("Driving
through Minnesota During the Hanoi Bombings"). Secret changes occur which the
poet can record: "The mountains alter and become the sea" ("Moving Inward at
Last").

Bly's poetry always begins with a homely setting, whether on a farm or on a trip,
into which meaning is infused so that the final effect is surrealistic. Much of his
poetry has had a political aspect, but it is politics as Blake conceived it. Bly made
this clear in an essay, "On Political Poetry":

> The life of the country can be imagined as a psyche larger than the psyche of
> anyone living, a larger sphere, floating above everyone. In order for the poet to
> write a true political poem, he has to be able to have such a grasp of his own
> concerns that he can leave them for a while, and then leap up, like a grasshop-
> per, into this other psyche. In that sphere he finds strange plants and curious
> many-eyed creatures which he brings back with him. This half-visible psychic
> life he entangles in his language.
>
> Some poets try to write political poems impelled upward by hatred or fear.
> But those emotions are stiff-jointed, rock-like, and are seldom able to escape
> from the gravity of the body. What the poet needs to get up that far and bring
> back something are great leaps of the imagination.[1]

Bly was born in Madison, Minnesota, on December 23, 1926. He is of Norwegian
descent, and remembers it in his verse. He served in the navy during the Second
World War, and then entered St. Olaf's College in Minnesota. After a year there he
transferred to Harvard, from which he graduated in 1950. For several years he lived

---

1. "On Political Poetry," *Nation,* April 24, 1967.

in New York, and then spent one year in Norway. Then he returned to Minnesota, first living on a farm and now in the small town of Moose Lake, in the eastern part of the state. During the Vietnam War he was one of the first poet-protesters, founding in 1966 American Writers against the Vietnam War. Earlier, he began to edit a journal called *The Fifties* (it later became *The Sixties* and then *The Seventies*), the purpose of which was to publish new translations. Bly has himself made a great number of translations, most especially of the fifteenth-century Indian mystic Kabir, whose work embodies the "leaps of imagination" Bly has championed.

Johnson's Cabinet[1] Watched by Ants

1

It is a clearing deep in a forest: overhanging boughs
Make a low place. Here the citizens we know during the day,
The ministers, the department heads,
Appear changed: the stockholders of large steel companies
In small wooden shoes: here are the generals dressed as gamboling lambs. 5

2

Tonight they burn the rice-supplies; tomorrow
They lecture on Thoreau;[2] tonight they move around the trees,
Tomorrow they pick the twigs from their clothes;
Tonight they throw the fire-bombs, tomorrow
They read the Declaration of Independence; tomorrow they are in church. 10

3

Ants are gathered around an old tree.
In a choir they sing, in harsh and gravelly voices,
Old Etruscan[3] songs on tyranny.
Toads nearby clap their small hands, and join
The fiery songs, their five long toes trembling in the soaked earth.   15

1967

Evolution from the Fish

This grandson of fishes holds inside him
A hundred thousand small black stones.
This nephew of snails, six feet long, lies naked on a bed
With a smiling woman, his head throws off light
Under marble, he is moving toward his own life   5
Like fur, walking. And when the frost comes, he is
Fur, mammoth fur, growing longer
And silkier, passing the woman's dormitory,
Kissing a stomach, leaning against a pillar,
He moves toward the animal, the animal with furry head!   10

What a joy to smell the flesh of a new child!
Like new grass! And this long man with the student girl,
Coffee cups, her pale waist, the spirit moving around them,
Moves, dragging a great tail into the darkness.

---

1. Very possibly the presidential cabinet of
Lyndon B. Johnson (1908–1973).
2. Nineteenth-century American philosopher
and essayist.
3. An early Italian people who preceded the
Romans.

In the dark we blaze up, drawing pictures   15
Of spiny fish, we throw off the white stones!
Serpents rise from the ocean floor with spiral motions,
A man goes inside a jewel, and sleeps. Do
Not hold my hands down! Let me raise them!
A fire is passing up through the soles of my feet!   20

1967

My Father's Wedding

1924

Today, lonely for my father, I saw
a log, or branch,
long, bent, ragged, bark gone.
I felt lonely for my father when I saw it.
It was the log   5
that lay near my uncle's old milk wagon.

Some men live with an invisible limp,
stagger, or drag
a leg. Their sons are often angry.
Only recently I thought: 10
Doing what you want . . .
Is that like limping? Tracks of it show in sand.

Have you seen those giant bird-
men of Bhutan?[4]
Men in bird masks, with pig noses, dancing,   15
teeth like a dog's, sometimes
dancing on one bad leg!
They do what they want, the dog's teeth say that!

But I grew up without dogs' teeth,
showed a whole body,   20
left only clear tracks in sand.
I learned to walk swiftly, easily,
no trace of a limp.
I even leaped a little. Guess where my defect is!

Then what? If a man, cautious   25
hides his limp,
Somebody has to limp it! Things
do it; the surroundings limp.
House walls get scars,
the car breaks down; matter, in drudgery, takes it up.   30

On my father's wedding day,
no one was there
to hold him. Noble loneliness
held him. Since he never asked for pity
his friends thought he   35
was whole. Walking alone, he could carry it.

4. In India.

He came in limping. It was a simple
wedding, three
or four people. The man in black,
lifting the book, called for order.   40
And the invisible bride
stepped forward, before his own bride.

He married the invisible bride, not his own.
In her left
breast she carried the three drops   45
that wound and kill. He already had
his barklike skin then,
made rough especially to repel the sympathy

he longed for, didn't need, and wouldn't accept.
They stopped. So   50
the words are read. The man in black
speaks the sentence. When the service
is over, I hold him
in my arms for the first time and the last.

After that he was alone   55
and I was alone.
No friends came; he invited none.
His two-story house he turned
into a forest,
where both he and I are the hunters.   60
                                                                  1981

GALWAY KINNELL
b. 1927

Galway Kinnell is one of those recent poets who, like Robert Lowell, began to write
in a traditional way and suddenly felt compelled to find looser ones. His early verse
had already begun to suggest something strange and perhaps terrifying in the relations of man and woman to nature. His later verse treats these relations with awesome power. The Eskimo speaker in "The Bear" baits a bone sharpened at both ends
with blubber, then follows the track of the bear who, having swallowed the bone, is
slowly dying. When he comes upon the carcass, he hacks "a ravine in his thigh,"
and, having eaten and drunk, opens the bear up and climbs inside him. There he
sleeps and dreams that he has himself become the bear. The "rank flavor of blood"
is the "poetry by which I lived" in the sense that the speaker is bear and bear is the
speaker, and that an awareness of this identity is the mainspring of the poetic consciousness.

Kinnell was born in Providence, Rhode Island, on February 1, 1927. He took a
B.A. at Princeton and an M.A. at Rochester, but the process of writing poetry has
been for him largely a process of de-educating himself so as to come closer to a world
whose existence he at first only suspected. He has taught at more than twenty colleges and universities, and remains a pioneer and an iconoclast. He has been honored
for his poetry with various awards, among them the Pulitzer Prize in 1983.

Flower Herding on Mount Monadnock[1]

1

I can support it no longer.
Laughing ruefully at myself
For all I claim to have suffered
I get up. Damned nightmarer!

It is New Hampshire out here,   5
It is nearly the dawn.
The song of the whippoorwill[2] stops
And the dimensions of depth seizes everything.

2

The song of a peabody bird[3] goes overhead
Like a needle pushed five times through the air,   10
It enters the leaves, and comes out little changed.

The air is so still
That as they go off through the trees
The love songs of birds do not get any fainter.

3

The last memory I have   15
Is of a flower which cannot be touched,

Through the bloom of which, all day,
Fly crazed, missing bees.

4

As I climb sweat gets up my nostrils,
For an instant I think I am at the sea,   20

One summer off Cap Ferrat[4] we watched a black seagull
Straining for the dawn, we stood in the surf,

Grasshoppers splash up where I step,
The mountain laurel crashes at my thighs.

5

There is something joyous in the elegies   25
Of birds. They seem
Caught up in a formal delight,
Though the mourning dove whistles of despair.

---

1. Mountain in southwestern New Hampshire.
2. Seldom-seen nocturnal bird of eastern North America, whose cry is heard at night or just before dawn.
3. Sparrow of eastern North America.
4. A cape in southeastern France, on the Mediterranean.

But at last in the thousand elegies
The dead rise in our hearts,   30
On the brink of our happiness we stop
Like someone on a drunk starting to weep.

6

I kneel at a pool,
I look through my face
At the bacteria I think   35
I see crawling through the moss.

My face sees me,
The water stirs, the face,
Looking preoccupied,
Gets knocked from its bones.   40

7

I weighed eleven pounds
At birth, having stayed on
Two extra weeks in the womb.
Tempted by room and fresh air
I came out big as a policeman   45
Blue-faced, with narrow red eyes.
It was eight days before the doctor
Would scare my mother with me.

Turning and craning in the vines
I can make out through the leaves   50
The old, shimmering nothingness, the sky.

3

Green, scaly moosewoods[5] ascend,
Tenants of the shaken paradise,

At every wind last night's rain
Comes splattering from the leaves,   55

It drops in flurries and lies there,
The footsteps of some running start.

9

From a rock
A waterfall,
A single trickle like a strand of wire,   60
Breaks into beads halfway down.

I know
The birds fly off

5. Maple trees with striped bark, eastern North America.

But the hug of the earth wraps
With moss their graves and the giant boulders.   65

10

In the forest I discover a flower.

The invisible life of the thing
Goes up in flames that are invisible
Like cellophane burning in the sunlight.

It burns up. Its drift is to be nothing.   70

In its covertness it has a way
Of uttering itself in place of itself,
Its blossoms claim to float in the Empyrean,[6]

A wrathful presence on the blur of the ground.

The appeal to heaven breaks off.   75
The petals begin to fall, in self-forgiveness.
It is a flower. On this mountainside it is dying.

1964

The Correspondence School Instructor
Says Goodbye to His Poetry Students

Goodbye, lady in Bangor, who sent me
snapshots of yourself, after definitely hinting
you were beautiful; goodbye,
Miami Beach urologist, who enclosed plain
brown envelopes for the return of your *very*   5
"Clinical Sonnets";[7] goodbye, manufacturer
of brassieres on the Coast, whose eclogues[8]
give the fullest treatment in literature yet
to the sagging-breast motif; goodbye, you in San Quentin,[9]
who wrote, "Being German my hero is Hitler,"   10
instead of "Sincerely yours," at the end of long,
neat-scripted letters demolishing
the pre-Raphaelites:[1]

I swear to you, it was just my way
of cheering myself up, as I licked   15
the stamped, self-addressed envelopes,
the game I had
of trying to guess which one of you, this time,
had poisoned his glue. I did care.

6. That is, the heavens.
7. An allusion to the "Clinical Sonnets" of Merrill Moore, a twentieth-century psychiatrist (he
treated, among others, Robert Lowell and Robert
Frost).
8. Strictly, poems in which idealized shepherds converse; idylls.
9. Prison in California.
1. English artists and writers of the later nineteenth-century who espoused ideals of Italian art
before Raphael (1483–1520).

I did read each poem entire.   20
I did say what I thought was the truth
in the mildest words I knew. And now,
in this poem, or chopped prose, not any better,
I realize, than those troubled lines
I kept sending back to you,   25
I have to say I am relieved it is over:
at the end I could feel only pity
for that urge toward more life
your poems kept smothering in words, the smell
of which, days later, would tingle   30
in your nostrils as new, God-given impulses
to write.

Goodbye,
you who are, for me, the postmarks again
of shattered towns—Xenia, Burnt Cabins, Hornell—   35
their loneliness
given away in poems, only their solitude kept.

                                                                        1968

The Seekonk Woods[2]

When first I walked here I hobbled
along ties set too close together
for a boy to step naturally on each.
When I grew older, I thought, my stride
would reach every other and thereafter   5
I would walk in time with the way
toward the meeting place of rails
in that yellow Lobachevskian haze up ahead.[3]
Right about here we put down our pennies, dark
on shined steel, where they trembled, fell still,   10
and waited for the locomotive rattling berserk
wheel-rods into perfect circles out of Attleboro
to brighten them into wafers,[4] the way a fork
mashes into view the inner light of a carrot
in a stew. In this late March sunshine,   15
crossing the trees at the angle the bow makes
when the violinist effleurages out of the chanterelle[5]
the C three octaves above middle C,
the old vertical birthwood remembers
its ascent lines, shrunken by half,[6] exactly   20
back down, each tree's on its fallen last summer.
Back then, dryads lived in these oaks;

2. Near Seekonk River in northeastern Rhode Island.
3. The railroad tracks are, of course, parallel, and the classic Greek geometrician Euclid postulated that a pair of parallel lines can never meet. Presumably the "haze" is "Lobachevskian" (after the nineteenth-century Russian mathematician Lobachevsky, founder of a non-Euclidean geometry) because it prevents the speaker from seeing whether the tracks meet or not.
4. It used to be an American childhood pastime to put pennies on railroad tracks to be flattened by a train's wheels; "Attleboro": town in southeastern Massachusetts.
5. Highest string on, for example, a violin; "effleurages": strokes lightly.
6. That is, each tree remembers how it used to grow straight.

these rocks were altars, which often asked
blood offerings[7]—but this one, once, bone, too,
the time Billy Wallace tripped and broke out
his front teeth. Fitted with gold replicas,
he asked, speaking more brightly, "What good
is a golden mouth when there's only grass
to eat?" Though it was true Nebuchadnezzar
spent seven years down on all fours eating
vetch and alfalfa,[8] ruminating the mouth-feel
of "bloom" and "wither," earth's first catechism,[9]
until he was healed, nevertheless we knew
if you held a grass blade between both thumbs
and blew hard you could blurt all its shrieks
out of it—like those beseechings leaves oaks
didn't drop last winter just now scratched out
on a least breeze, let-me-die-let-me-die.
Maybe Billy, lured by bones' memory,
comes back sometimes, too, to the Seekonk Woods,
to stand in the past and just look at it.
Here he might kneel, studying this clump of grass,
a god inspecting a sneeze. Or he might stray
into the now untrafficked whistling-lanes
of the mourning doves, who used to call and call
into the future, and give a start, as though,
this very minute, by awful coincidence,
they reach it. And at last traipse off
down the tracks, with stumbling, arrhythmic gait,
as wanderers must do once it hits them:
the over-the-unknown route, too, ends up
right where time wants. On this spot
I skinned the muskrat. I buried the rat.
The musk breezed away. Of the fur
I made a hat, which as soon as put on
began to rot off, and even now stinks
so sharply my scalp crawls. In circles,
of course, keeping to the skull. Though
one day this scrap of damp skin
will crawl all the way off, and the whole organism
follow. but which way? To effuse with musk?
Or rot with rat? Oh no, we don't choose,
there's a law: *As one supremes,*
so one croaks—forever muskrat! When,
a quarter-turn after the sun, the half-moon,
too, goes down and we find ourselves
in the night's night, then somewhere
thereabouts in the dark must be death.
Knowledge beforehand of the end is surely among
existence's most spectacular feats—and yet right here,
on this ordinary afternoon, in these humblest woods,

25

30

35

40

45

50

55

60

65

70

7. That is, of human sacrifice; "dryads": legendary tree nymphs.
8. In Daniel 4:31ff. the Lord curses the Babylonian king Nebuchadnezzar, who is driven from his kingdom to live with the beasts and eat grass;

"vetch" and "alfalfa" are both grasses. "Ruminating": (1) thinking, considering; (2) chewing the cud.
9. Set of questions and answers to be learned before admission to membership in a church.

with a name meaning "black goose" in Wampanoag,[1]
or in modern Seekonkese, "slob blowing fat nose,"
this unlikely event happens—a creature
struggling along the tracks foreknows it.   75
Then too long to touch every tie,[2] my stride
is now just too short to reach every other,
and so I am to be still the wanderer,
in velocity if not in direction, the hobble
of too much replaced by the common limp   80
of too little. But I almost got there.
I almost stepped according to the liturgical,
sleeping gods' snores you can hear singing up
from former times inside the ties. I almost
set foot in that border zone where what follows   85
blows back, shimmering everything, making
walking like sleepwalking, railroad tracks
a lane among poplars on a spring morning,
where a man, limping but blissful, dazedly
makes his way homeward, his lips, which kissing   90
taught to bunch up like that, blowing
from a night so overfilled with affection
it still hasn't completely finished passing
these few bent strands of hollowed-out air,
haunted by future, into a tune on the tracks.   95
I think I'm about to be shocked awake.
As I was in childhood, when I battered myself
back to my senses against a closed door,
or woke up hanging out of an upstairs window.
Somnambulism[3] was my attempt to slip   100
under cover of nightmare across no father's land
and put my arms around a phantasm. If only
I had found a way to enter his hard time
served at labor by day, by night in solitary,
and put my arms around him in reality,   105
I might not now be remaking him
in memory still; anti-alchemizing bass kettle's
golden reverberations again and again back down
to hair, flesh, blood, bone, the base metals.[4]
I want to crawl face down in the fields   110
and graze on the wild strawberries, my clothes
stained pink, even for seven years
if I must, if they exist. I want to lie out
on my back under the thousand stars and think
my way up among them, through them,   115
and a little distance past them, and attain
a moment of nearly absolute ignorance,
if I can, if human mentality lets us.
I have always intended to live forever,
but even more, to live now. The moment   120
I have done one or the other, I here swear,

1. Language of eastern Native American tribe.
2. Railroad tie.
3. Sleepwalking.
4. Alchemy was the science of producing gold
from base metals; here the speaker wants to reverse
the process and remake the "golden" memories of
his father back into the flesh-and-blood man. "Bass
kettle": kettledrum.

I will come back from the living and enter
death everlasting: consciousness defeated.
But I will not offer, no, I'll never
burn my words. Wishful phrases! The once-   125
poplars creosoted asleep under the tracks
have stopped snoring. What does that mean!
The bow saws at G. A leaf rattles on its tree.
The rails may never meet, O fellow Euclideans,[5]
for you, for me. So what if we groan?   130
That's our noise. Laughter is our stuttering
in a language we can't speak yet. Behind,
the world made of wishes goes dark. Ahead,
if not tomorrow then never, shines only what is.

1985

5. See footnote 3 to line 8.

JOHN ASHBERY
b. 1927

John Ashbery, once set aside as bizarre, now seems one of the central American poets of the latter half of the century. Though he had many associations with the New York school, especially Kenneth Koch (his classmate at Harvard), and uses equally wild and witty imagery, he has also his own quality, characteristically cryptic and unconfiding, even impenetrable. The mixture of surrealist tomfoolery and elegant reserve in Ashbery is convincing, though one rarely can fathom what one is being convinced of.

His poems are resolutely contrary to fact or tangential to it. "Worsening Situation" ends,

> My wife
> Thinks I'm in Oslo—Oslo, France, that is.

Needless to say, there is no Oslo, France, and his wife is therefore twice deluded. But delusion and imagination go together. In a more accessible poem, "The Instruction Manual," the poet ignores the manual and conjures up a journey to Guadalajara, which he describes like some archetypal traveler although it becomes apparent that he has never been there.

Ashbery presents reality as do some modern painters, organizing details to create nature rather than imitate it. Old bonding techniques between man, his surroundings, and divinity no longer work. "You can't say it that way any more," he declares in "And *Ut Pictura Poesis* Is Her name." Sometimes, like action painters, the process of poeticizing obsesses him; he describes it amusingly yet seriously too:

> The extreme austerity of an almost empty mind
> Colliding with the lush, Rousseau-like foliage of its desire to communicate
> Something between breaths . . .

In "What Is Poetry" he asks whether poetry is beautiful images, or trying "to avoid / Ideas, as in this poem." Or do we

> Go back to them as to a wife, leaving
> The mistress we desire?

The series of questions is never answered. But his poems do have ideas as well as images, though they are given provisional status only, dependent upon a reality that resists summary and analysis. He is endlessly resourceful in propounding this dilemma.

Ashbery was born in 1927 in Rochester, New York, and grew up on a farm near Lake Ontario. After receiving his B.A. at Harvard in 1949, he wrote an M.A. thesis at Columbia on Henry Green, the English novelist. The choice was characteristic, since Green's works are also impersonal—written almost entirely in witty conversation, with no interpretative aids by the author. When Ashbery went to France as a Fulbright Scholar (1955–57) he embarked on a book on Raymond Roussel, a writer more difficult than Green, and even less compromising in his artifice. (Roussel declared that his books had been composed not out of experience but out of verbal games.)

Ashbery returned to France in 1958 and stayed until 1965, writing art criticism for the European edition of the New York *Herald Tribune* and for *Art News*. Returning to New York in 1965, he edited *Art News* until 1972. Since then he has taught at Brooklyn College and has been art critic for *Newsweek*. Among the many books he has published and the many awards he has received, it is notable that *Self-Portrait in a Convex Mirror* won the three major poetry prizes of 1976.

Ashbery finds his literary predecessors in the early Auden and Wallace Stevens, "the writers who most formed my language as a poet."[1] To be tough, incisive, and mellifluous was perhaps the lesson he derived from these two writers. The musical aspect of his verse has always been the most important to him: "What I like about music is its ability of being convincing, of carrying an argument through successfully to the finish, though the terms of this argument remain unknown quantities. What remains is the structure, the architecture of the argument, scene or story. I would like to do this in poetry." Often Ashbery appears to be writing on the basis of some solid structure which is taken for granted. The poem follows from postulates which are firm but never divulged. A dreamlike quality ensues, and Ashbery has said that he would like to "reproduce the power dreams have of persuading you that a certain event has a meaning not logically connected with it, or that there is a hidden relation among disparate objects."[2] The strangeness and authority of his poetry have drawn readers in spite of the hiddenness of many of its relations.

---

1. Quoted in *The Poets of the New York School*, ed. John Bernard Myers, Philadelphia, 1969.   2. Quoted in Richard Howard, *Alone with America*, New York, 1969, pp. 29–30.

The Instruction Manual

As I sit looking out of a window of the building
I wish I did not have to write the instructional manual on the uses of a new
    metal.
I look down into the street and see people, each walking with an inner
    peace,
And envy them—they are so far away from me!
Not one of them has to worry about getting out this manual on schedule   5
And, as my way is, I begin to dream, resting my elbows on the desk and
    leaning out of the window a little,
Of dim Guadalajara! City of rose-colored flowers!
City I wanted most to see, and most did not see, in Mexico!
But I fancy I see, under the press of having to write the instruction manual,
Your public square, city, with its elaborate little bandstand!   10
The band is playing *Scheherazade* by Rimsky-Korsakov.
Around stand the flower girls, handing out rose- and lemon-colored flowers,

Each attractive in her rose-and-blue striped dress (Oh! such shades of rose
    and blue),
And nearby is the little white booth where women in green serve you green
    and yellow fruit.
The couples are parading; everyone is in a holiday mood.   15
First, leading the parade, is a dapper fellow
Clothed in deep blue. On his head sits a white hat
And he wears a mustache, which has been trimmed for the occasion.
His dear one, his wife, is young and pretty; her shawl is rose, pink, and
    white.
Her slippers are patent leather, in the American fashion,   20
And she carries a fan, for she is modest, and does not want the crowd to see
    her face too often.
But everybody is so busy with his wife or loved one
I doubt they would notice the mustachioed man's wife.
Here come the boys! They are skipping and throwing little things on the
    sidewalk
Which is made of gray tile. One of them, a little older, has a toothpick in
    his teeth.   25
He is silenter than the rest, and affects not to notice the pretty young girls
    in white.
But his friends notice them, and shout their jeers at the laughing girls.
Yet soon all this will cease, with the deepening of their years,
And love bring each to the parade grounds for another reason.
But I have lost sight of the young fellow with the toothpick.   30
Wait—there he is—on the other side of the bandstand,
Secluded from his friends, in earnest talk with a young girl
Of fourteen or fifteen. I try to hear what they are saying
But it seems they are just mumbling something—shy words of love, prob-
    ably.
She is slightly taller than he, and looks quietly down into his sincere eyes. 35
She is wearing white. The breeze ruffles her long fine black hair against her
    olive cheek.
Obviously she is in love. The boy, the young boy with the toothpick, he is
    in love too;
His eyes show it. Turning from this couple,
I see there is an intermission in the concert.
The paraders are resting and sipping drinks through straws   40
(The drinks are dispensed from a large glass crock by a lady in dark blue),
And the musicians mingle among them, in their creamy white uniforms,
    and talk
About the weather, perhaps, or how their kids are doing at school.
Let us take this opportunity to tiptoe into one of the side streets.
Here you may see one of those white houses with green trim   45
That are so popular here. Look—I told you!
It is cool and dim inside, but the patio is sunny.
An old woman in gray sits there, fanning herself with a palm leaf fan.
She welcomes us to her patio, and offers us a cooling drink.
"My son is in Mexico City," she says. "He would welcome you too   50
If he were here. but his job is with a bank there.
Look, here is a photograph of him."
And a dark-skinned lad with pearly teeth grins out at us from the worn
    leather frame.
We thank her for her hospitality, for it is getting late

And we must catch a view of the city, before we leave, from a good high
    place.   55
That church tower will do—the faded pink one, there against the fierce blue
    of the sky. Slowly we enter.
The caretaker, an old man dressed in brown and gray, asks us how long we
    have been in the city, and how we like it here.
His daughter is scrubbing the steps—she nods to us as we pass into the
    tower.
Soon we have reached the top, and the whole network of the city extends
    before us.
There is the rich quarter, with its houses of pink and white, and its crum-
    bling, leafy terraces.   60
There is the poorer quarter, its homes a deep blue.
There is the market, where men are selling hats and swatting flies
And there is the public library, painted several shades of pale green and
    beige.
Look! There is the square we just came from, with the promenaders.
There are fewer of them, now that the heat of the day has increased,   65
But the young boy and girl still lurk in the shadows of the bandstand.
And there is the home of the little old lady—
She is still sitting in the patio, fanning herself.
How limited, but how complete withal, has been our experience of Guada-
    lajara!
We have seen young love, married love, and the love of an aged mother for
    her son.   70
We have heard the music, tasted the drinks, and looked at colored houses.
What more is there to do, except stay? And that we cannot do.
And as a last breeze freshens the top of the weathered old tower, I turn my
    gaze
Back to the instruction manual which has made me dream of Guadalajara.

    1956

The Tennis Court Oath[1]

What had you been thinking about
the face studiously bloodied
heaven blotted region
I go on loving you like water but
there is a terrible breath in the way all of this   5
You were not elected president, yet won the race
All the way through fog and drizzle
When you read it was sincere the coasts
stammered with unintentional villages the
horse strains fatigued I guess . . . the calls . . .   10
I worry

the water beetle head
why of course reflecting all
then you redid you were breathing
I thought going down to mail this   15

---

1. During the first days of the French Revolution, on June 20, 1789, the commoners (Third Estate)
were barred from a regular meeting of the Estates General. They retired to a nearby indoor tennis court
and took an oath to stand together until the Constitution was reformed.

of the kettle you jabbered as easily in the yard
you come through but
are incomparable the lovely tent
mystery you don't want surrounded the real
you dance   20
in the spring there was clouds

The mulatress[2] approached in the hall—the
lettering easily visible along the edge of the *Times*
in a moment the bell would ring but there was time
for the carnation laughed here are a couple of "other"   25

to one in yon house

The doctor and Philip had come over the road
Turning in toward the corner of the wall his hat on
reading it carelessly as if to tell you your fears were justified
the blood shifted you know those walls   30
wind off the earth had made him shrink
undeniably an oboe now the young
were there there was candy
to decide the sharp edge of the garment
like a particular cry not intervening called the dog "he's coming! he's
       coming" with an emotion felt it sink into peace   35

there was no turning back but the end was in sight
he chose this moment to ask her in detail about her family and the others
The person. pleaded—"have more of these
not stripes on the tunic—or the porch chairs
will teach you about men—what it means"   40
to be one in a million pink stripe
and now could go away the three approached the doghouse
the reef. Your daughter's
dream of my son understand prejudice
darkness in the hole   45
the patient finished
They could all go home now the hole was dark
lilacs blowing across his face glad he brought you

                                                                     1962

Knocking Around

I really thought that drinking here would
Start a new chain, that the soft storms
Would abate, and the horror stories, the
Noises men make to frighten themselves,
Rest secure on the lip of a canyon as day   5
Died away, and they would still be there the next morning.

Nothing is very simple.
You must remember that certain things die out for awhile

---

2. Female mulatto (one of mixed white and Black ancestry).

So that they can be remembered with affection
Later on and become holy. Look at Art Deco   10
For instance or the "tulip mania" of Holland:[3]
Both things we know about and recall
With a certain finesse as though they were responsible
For part of life. And we congratulate them.

Each day as the sun wends its way   15
Into your small living room and stays
You remember the accident of night as though it were a friend.
All that is forgotten now. There are no
Hard feelings, and it doesn't matter that it will soon
Come again. You know what I mean. We are wrapped in   20
What seems like a positive, conscious choice, like a bird
In air. It doesn't matter that the peonies are tipped in soot
Or that a man will come to station himself each night
Outside your house, and leave shortly before dawn,
That nobody answers when you pick up the phone.   25
You have all lived through lots of these things before
And know that life is like an ocean: sometimes the tide is out
And sometimes it's in, but it's always the same body of water
Even though it looks different, and
It makes the things on the shore look different.   30
They depend on each other like the snow and the snowplow.

It's only after realizing this for a long time
That you can make a chain of events like days
That more and more rapidly come to punch their own number
Out of the calendar, draining it. By that time   35
Space will be a jar with no lid, and you can live
Any way you like out on those vague terraces,
Verandas, walkways—the forms of space combined with time
We are allowed, and we live them passionately,
Fortunately, though we can never be described   40
And would make lousy characters in a novel.

1979

Paradoxes and Oxymorons[4]

This poem is concerned with language on a very plain level.
Look at it talking to you. You look out a window
Or pretend to fidget. You have it but you don't have it.
You miss it, it misses you. You miss each other.

The poem is sad because it wants to be yours, and cannot.   5
What's a plain level? It is that and other things,
Bringing a system of them into play. Play?
Well, actually, yes, but I consider play to be

---

3. Art Deco was a popular decorative style of
the 1920s and 1930s; in the seventeenth century,
the Dutch invested obsessively in tulips.
4. "Paradoxes" are statements that seem self-
contradictory but turn out to have a deeper meaning (as John Donne's "Death, thou shalt die");
"oxymorons" are paradoxical statements yoking
together two contrary terms (as "cruel kindness").

A deeper outside thing, a dreamed role-pattern,
As in the division of grace these long August days   10
Without proof. Open-ended. And before you know
It gets lost in the steam and chatter of typewriters.

It has been played once more. I think you exist only
To tease me into doing it, on your level, and then you aren't there
Or have adopted a different attitude. And the poem   15
Has set me softly down beside you. The poem is you.

                                                                         1981

Hard Times

Trust me. The world is run on a shoestring.
They have no time to return the calls in hell
And pay dearly for those wasted minutes. Somewhere
In the future it will filter down through all the proceedings

But by then it will be too late, the festive ambience   5
Will linger on but it won't matter. More or less
Succinctly they will tell you what we've all known for years:
That the power of this climate is only to conserve itself.

Whatever twists around it is decoration and can never
Be looked at as something isolated, apart. Get it? And   10
He flashed a mouthful of aluminum teeth there in the darkness
To tell however it gets down, that it does, at last.

Once they made the great trip to California
And came out of it flushed. And now every day
Will have to dispel the notion of being like all the others.   15
In time, it gets to stand with the wind, but by then the night is closed off.

                                                                         1981

W. S. MERWIN
b. 1927

> And I moved forward, because you must live
> Forward, which is away from whatever
> It was that you had, though you think when you have it
> That it will stay with you forever.

These lines, taken from his *Green With Beasts* (1956), suggest W. S. Merwin's preoccupation with time, with the time sense which may be peculiar to twentieth-century
man and thus require a new kind of poetry, and with his own development as a poet.
He was twenty-four when his first book, *A Mask for Janus* (1952), was chosen by
W. H. Auden for the Yale Younger Poets series, and Merwin has published regularly
and prolifically since. Those first poems, technically very accomplished, show Merwin not only "trained . . . thoroughly in the mechanics of verse," as Auden observed,[1]

---

1. *A Mask for Janus*, New Haven, Conn., 1952, p. ix.

but interested in playing with conventional forms. The mode is a kind of contemporary neoclassicism; Merwin has always been on good terms with the poet of the past. His earliest subjects are often mythical or legendary, and many of the poems are about animals, which he invests with an emblematic quality. The dominant image is the sea, which he identifies with the irrational, the demonic, the dangerous powers which the poet must control by expressing them. In "Leviathan," an imitation of Anglo-Saxon meters, Merwin celebrates the great sea beast that lives at the bottom of the world:

> He is that curling serpent that in ocean is,
> Sea-fright he is, and the shadow under the earth.

The Drunk in the Furnace (1960) represents a change in direction for Merwin. His subjects here are more local and personal, and while his first poems show clearly the influence of Stevens, Merwin now tries to capture some of Frost's shifting colloquialism and even his oracular quality. The first lines of one poem, "Fable," might almost be mistaken for Frost.

> However the man had got himself there,
> There he clung, kicking in mid-air,
> Hanging from the top branch of a high tree
> With his grip weakening gradually.

The title poem demonstrates how successfully Merwin has absorbed his new influences. The metrical irregularities give a new sense of a speaking voice ("Where he gets his spirits / It's a mystery. But the stuff keeps him musical . . ."); the straight-faced and outrageous puns ("As he collapses onto the rioting / Springs of a litter of car-seats ranged on the grates, / To sleep like an iron pig.") give the poem a companionable air. Merwin has found a new way to praise the irrational and outrageous forces that disconcert society, fascinate the innocent, and make poetry possible. The old drunk in the furnace is Orpheus in a new and wonderful form.

W. S. Merwin was born in New York City on September 30, 1927, and grew up in Union, New Jersey, and Scranton, Pennsylvania; his father was a Presbyterian minister, and Merwin recalls, "I started writing hymns for my father almost as soon as I could write at all."[2] He received his B.A. from Princeton University, where he encountered John Berryman (who taught creative writing) and the poet and critic R. P. Blackmur, to whom *The Moving Target* (1963) was dedicated. After a year of graduate work there, during which he continued the study of foreign languages which was to equip him to prepare excellent translations from Latin, Spanish, and French, he left the United States and has since lived mainly in England and France. In 1950 he tutored Robert Graves's son on Majorca; from 1951 to 1954 he was in London, supporting himself primarily by making translations of French and Spanish literature for broadcast by the BBC, while his first two books of poetry were published in the United States. In 1956 Merwin was playwright-in-residence at the Poets' Theater in Cambridge, Massachusetts, and in the next few years he wrote four plays, one produced in Cambridge and the others in England; during another brief return to the United States, from 1961 to 1963, he was poetry editor of the *Nation*. Since 1968 he has been living in the United States; here he has continued to publish books of poems and of translations. He received the National Book Award for *The Moving Target*, the Pulitzer Prize for *The Carrier of Ladders* (1970), and the Bollingen Prize for *Feathers from the Hills* (1978).

---

2. *Contemporary Authors*, v. 15–16, 1966, p. 299.

Leviathan[1]

This is the black sea-brute bulling through wave-wrack,
Ancient as ocean's shifting hills, who in sea-toils
Travelling, who furrowing the salt acres
Heavily, his wake hoary behind him,[2]
Shoulders spouting, the fist of his forehead   5
Over wastes gray-green crashing, among horses unbroken
From bellowing fields, past bone-wreck of vessels,
Tide-ruin, wash of lost bodies bobbing
No longer sought for, and islands of ice gleaming,
Who ravening the rank flood, wave-marshalling,   10
Overmastering the dark sea-marches, finds home
And harvest. Frightening to foolhardiest
Mariners, his size were difficult to describe:
The hulk of him is like hills heaving,
Dark, yet as crags of drift-ice, crowns cracking in thunder,   15
Like land's self by night black-looming, surf churning and trailing
Along his shores' rushing, shoal-water boding
About the dark of his jaws; and who should moor at his edge
And fare on afoot would find gates of no gardens,
But the hill of dark underfoot diving,   20
Closing overhead, the cold deep, and drowning.[3]
He is called Leviathan, and named for rolling,[4]
First created he was of all creatures,[5]
He has held Jonah three days and nights,
He is that curling serpent that in ocean is,[6]   25
Sea-fright he is, and the shadow under the earth.
Days there are, nonetheless, when he lies
Like an angel, although a lost angel
On the waste's unease, no eye of man moving,
Bird hovering, fish flashing, creature whatever   30
Who after him came to herit earth's emptiness.
Froth at flanks seething soothes to stillness,
Waits; with one eye he watches
Dark of night sinking last, with one eye dayrise
As at first over foaming pastures. He makes no cry   35
Though that light is a breath. The sea curling,
Star-climbed, wind-combed, cumbered with itself still
As at first it was, is the hand not yet contented
Of the Creator. And he waits for the world to begin.

     1956

1. "Leviathan" comes from a Hebrew word meaning "great water animal," and is traditionally associated with the whale.
2. Compare the description of the whale in Job 41:32: "Behind him he leaves a shining wake; one would think the deep to be hoary."
3. This description is adapted from a more elaborate one in the bestiary included in the important Old English compendium, *The Exeter Book.*
4. In the "Etymology" at the beginning of *Moby-Dick,* Melville quotes "Webster's Dictionary": "WHALE. * * * Sw. and Dan. *hval.* This animal is named from roundness or rolling; for in Dan. *hvalt* is arched or vaulted."
5. According to Genesis 1:21.
6. "In that day the Lord, with his sore, and great, and strong sword, shall punish leviathan the piercing serpent, even leviathan the crooked serpent; and he shall slay the dragon that is in the sea" (Isaiah 27:1).

The Drunk in the Furnace

For a good décade
The furnace stood in the naked gully, fireless
And vacant as any hat. Then when it was
No more to them than a hulking black fossil
To erode unnoticed with the rest of the junk-hill   5
By the poisonous creek, and rapidly to be added
        To their ignorance.

        They were afterwards astonished
To confirm, one morning, a twist of smoke like a pale
Resurrection, staggering out of its chewed hole,   10
And to remark then other tokens that someone,
Cosily bolted behind the eye-holed iron
Door of the drafty burner, had there established
        His bad castle.

        Where he gets his spirits[7]   15
It's a mystery. But the stuff keeps him musical:
Hammer-and-anvilling with poker and bottle
To his jugged bellowings, till the last groaning clang
As he collapses onto the rioting
Springs of a litter of car-seats ranged on the grates,   20
        To sleep like an iron pig.[8]

        In their tar-paper church
On a text about stoke-holes[9] that are sated never
Their Reverend lingers. They nod and hate trespassers.
When the furnace wakes, though, all afternoon   25
Their witless offspring flock like piped rats[1] to its siren
Crescendo, and agape on the crumbling ridge
        Stand in a row and learn.

                                        1960

Home for Thanksgiving

I bring myself back from the streets that open like long
Silent laughs, and the others
Spilled into in the way of rivers breaking up, littered with words,
Crossed by cats and that sort of thing,
From the knowing wires and the aimed windows,   5
Well this is nice, on the third floor, in the back of the bill-board
Which says Now Improved and I know what they mean,
I thread my way in and I sew myself in like money.

Well this is nice with my shoes moored by the bed
And the lights around the bill-board ticking on and off like a beacon,   10
I have brought myself back like many another crusty
Unbarbered vessel launched with a bottle,
From the bare regions of pure hope where

7. (1) Good feelings; (2) liquor.
8. "Pig iron" is crude iron.
9. Furnace mouths.

1. The Pied Piper of Hamlin's piping lured rats from the town; when he was not paid, he lured away the children as well.

For a great part of the year it scarcely sets at all,
And from the night skies regularly filled with old movies of my fingers,   15
Weightless as shadows, groping in the sluices,
And from the visions of veins like arteries, and
From the months of plying
Between can[2] and can, vacant as a pint in the morning,
While my sex grew into the only tree, a joyless evergreen,   20
And the winds played hell with it at night, coming as they did
Over at least one thousand miles of emptiness,
Thumping as though there were nothing but doors, insisting
"Come out," and of course I would have frozen.

Sunday, a fine day, with my ears wiped and my collar buttoned   25
I went for a jaunt all the way out and back on
A street car and under my hat with the dent settled
In the right place I was thinking maybe—a thought
Which I have noticed many times like a bold rat—
I should have stayed making some of those good women   30
Happy, for a while at least, Vera with
The eau-de-cologne and the small fat dog named Joy,
Gladys with her earrings, cooking and watery arms, the one
With the limp and the fancy sheets, some of them
Are still there I suppose, oh no,   35

I bring myself back avoiding in silence
Like a ship in a bottle.
I bring my bottle.
Or there was thin Pearl with the invisible hair nets, the wind would not
Have been right for them, they would have had   40
Their times, rugs, troubles,
They would have wanted curtains, cleanings, answers, they would have
Produced families their own and our own, hen friends and
Other considerations, my fingers sifting
The dark would have turned up other   45
Poverties, I bring myself
Back like a mother cat transferring her only kitten,
Telling myself secrets through my moustache,
They would have wanted to drink ship, sea, and all or
To break the bottle, well this is nice,   50
Oh misery, misery, misery,
You fit me from head to foot like a good grade suit of longies
Which I have worn for years and never want to take off.
I did the right thing after all.

1963

Footprints on the Glacier

Where the wind
year round out of the gap
polishes everything
here this day are footprints like my own
the first ever   5

2. Drinking vessel, beer mug.

frozen
pointing up into the cold

and last night someone
marched and marched on the candle flame
hurrying   10
a painful road
and I heard the echo a long time afterwards
gone and some connection of mine

I scan the high slopes for a dark speck
that was lately here   15
I pass my hands
over the melted wax
like a blind man
they are all
moving into their seasons at last   20
my bones face each other trying
to remember a question

nothing moves while I watch
but here the black trees
are the cemetery of a great battle   25
and behind me as I turn
I hear names leaving the bark
in growing numbers and flying north

                                                                        1970

The Burnt Child

Matches among other things that were not allowed
never would be
lying high in a cool blue box
that opened in other hands and there they all were
bodies clean and smooth blue heads white crowns   5
white sandpaper on the sides of the box scoring
fire after fire gone before

I could hear the scratch and flare
when they were over
and catch the smell of the striking   10
I knew what the match would feel like
lighting
when I was very young

a fire engine came and parked
in the shadow of the big poplar tree   15
on Fourth Street one night
keeping its engine running
pumping oxygen to the old woman
in the basement
when she died the red lights went on burning   20

                                                    1983

JAMES WRIGHT
1927–1980

Of the poems in his first two books James Wright said, "I have tried very hard to write in the mode of Edwin Arlington Robinson and Robert Frost," a choice of models rather surprising for a man whose first books were published in the late fifties. What Wright seems to have admired in these older poets—and in Thomas Hardy as well—is their seriousness. Wright, in his own words, "wanted to make the poems say something humanly important instead of just showing off with language." The poems are typically about people, men and women who find themselves outside society—a convict escaped from prison, a lesbian whose love has been discovered by her neighbors, an old countryman whose wife has just died. Wright's tone is grave and powerful.

Men and women "apart" provided Wright with his most characteristic first subjects. And not only "apart," but poor. Like his friend Richard Hugo, Wright came of a poor family, and grew up in a small western town in the depths of the depression. As Hugo later wrote, "Jim had seen his father enslaved to a lousy factory job during the depression and knew what terrible fears bind people to jobs."[1] Wright himself said, "Hundreds of times I must have heard a man returning home after a long day's futile search for work, any kind of work at all, and dispiritedly [saying] in his baffled loneliness, 'I ain't got a pot to piss in or a window to throw it out of.' "[2] Wright once told Hugo that he and his first wife had married "to escape Martins Ferry"—his home town and the gritty, industrial "triggering town" of a number of his poems, such as "Autumn Comes to Martins Ferry, Ohio."

Sometime after the publication of his second collection, Wright set about changing—or renewing—his style, commenting, "I have changed the way I've written, when it seemed appropriate, and continue to do so."[3] He published translations of the South American poets Pablo Neruda and Cesar Vallejo and the Austrian poet Georg Trakl, all of whom practice a suppression of continuities between images, and Wright adapted their surrealism for his own poetry. His later poetry preserved his compassionate interest in social outcasts and an increasing confidence in the transforming beauty of nature—in Wright's later poetry a very specifically American nature. What was new in Wright's later style was a greater personal openness—he was now less concerned to use poetry for the creation of character—and an interest in political subjects or, rather, deeply felt social concerns. "I try and say," Wright wrote in 1970, "how I love my country and how I despise the way it is treated. I try and speak of the beauty and again of the ugliness in the lives of the poor and neglected."[4]

In 1971 he published a *Collected Poems*, which won the Pulitzer Prize. It contained most of his first book, all of his second, his translations, the two books that followed, *The Branch Will Not Break* and *Shall We Gather at the River*. Critical opinion is apparently divided on the volumes of poetry Wright published after the *Collected*—the last, *This Journey* and *The Temple in Nimes*, posthumously. The critic Helen Vendler says that his "elegiac plangency threatened to dissolve into sentimentality. Alcoholism sapped his creative energy and induced poems of self-hatred and disgust, of terror at the uncontrolled disintegration of his life."[5] Norman Friedman, on the other hand, finds them "a new stage."[6] In the early 1970s he married again, and was able to control his alcoholism.

James Wright was born December 13, 1927, at Martins Ferry, Ohio, and attended

1. Richard Hugo, "James Wright," in *The Real West Marginal Way: A Poet's Autobiography*, ed. Ripley Hugo, Lois Welch, and James Welch, New York, 1986, p. 230.
2. James Wright, "Letter from Europe, Two Notes from Venice, Remarks on Two Poems, and Other Occasional Prose" in *American Poets in 1976*, ed. William Heyen, Indianapolis, 1976, p. 446.

3. James Wright, in *Contemporary Poets*, 4th ed., ed. James Vinson and D. L. Kirkpatrick, New York, 1985, p. 987.
4. The same.
5. Helen Vendler in *The Harper American Literature*, vol. 2, New York, 1987, p. 2486.
6. Norman Friedman, *Contemporary Poetry*, p. 987.

Kenyon College, from which he received his B.A. He served with the United States
Army in Japan during the American occupation, then resumed his studies at the
University of Washington under Theodore Roethke. He received an M.S. and Ph.D.,
and won a Fulbright Scholarship for study in Vienna. He taught at a number of
colleges and universities, first in the Midwest and then at Hunter College in New
York City. He died of throat cancer on March 25, 1980.

Hugo wrote of him later, "No one carried his life more vividly inside him, or
simultaneously in plain and in eloquent ways used the pain of his life to better advan-
tage."[7] Since his death, a James Wright Poetry Festival has been held annually in
Martins Ferry.

7. Hugo, p. 233.

Autumn Begins in Martins Ferry, Ohio

In the Shreve High football stadium,
I think of Polacks nursing long beers in Tiltonsville,
And gray faces of Negroes in the blast furnace at Benwood,
And the ruptured night watchman of Wheeling Steel,
Dreaming of heroes.   5

All the proud fathers are ashamed to go home.
Their women cluck like starved pullets,[1]
Dying for love.

Therefore,
Their sons grow suicidally beautiful   10
At the beginning of October,
And gallop terribly against each other's bodies.

1963

The Minneapolis Poem[2]

1
I wonder how many old men last winter
Hungry and frightened by namelessness prowled
The Mississippi shore
Lashed blind by the wind, dreaming
Of suicide in the river.   5
The police remove their cadavers by daybreak
And turn them in somewhere.
Where?
How does the city keep lists of its fathers
Who have no names?   10
By Nicollet Island I gaze down at the dark water
So beautifully slow.
And I wish my brothers good luck
And a warm grave.

1. Chickens.
2. Nicollet Island, the Walker Art Center, and
the Tyrone Guthrie Repertory Theater, mentioned in the poem, are all Minneapolis land-
marks.

2

The Chippewa young men
Stab one another shrieking
Jesus Christ.
Split-lipped homosexuals limp in terror of assault.
High school backfields search under benches
Near the Post Office. Their faces are the rich
Raw bacon without eyes.
The Walker Art Center crowd stare
At the Guthrie Theater.

3

Tall Negro girls from Chicago
Listen to light songs.
They know when the supposed patron
Is a plainclothesman.
A cop's palm
Is a roach dangling down the scorched fangs
Of a light bulb.
The soul of a cop's eyes
Is an eternity of Sunday daybreak in the suburbs
Of Juárez, Mexico.

4

The legless beggars are gone, carried away
By white birds.
The Artificial Limbs Exchange is gutted
And sown with lime.
The whalebone crutches and hand-me-down trusses
Huddle together dreaming in a desolation
Of dry groins.
I think of poor men astonished to waken
Exposed in broad daylight by the blade
Of a strange plough.

5

All over the walls of comb cells
Automobiles perfumed and blindered
Consent with a mutter of high good humor
To take their two naps a day.
Without sound windows glide back
Into dusk.
The sockets of a thousand blind bee graves tier upon tier
Tower not quite toppling.
There are men in this city who labor dawn after dawn
To sell me my death.

6

But I could not bear
To allow my poor brother my body to die
In Minneapolis.
The old man Walt Whitman our countryman
Is now in America our country
Dead.

But he was not buried in Minneapolis   60
At least.
And no more may I be
Please God.

7

I want to be lifted up
By some great white bird unknown to the police,   65
And soar for a thousand miles and be carefully hidden
Modest and golden as one last corn grain,
Stored with the secrets of the wheat and the mysterious lives
Of the unnamed poor.

1968

In Response To a Rumor That the Oldest Whorehouse in Wheeling, West Virginia, Has Been Condemned

I will grieve alone,
As I strolled alone, years ago, down along
The Ohio shore.[3]
I hid in the hobo jungle weeds
Upstream from the sewer main,   5
Pondering, gazing.

I saw, down river,
At Twenty-third and Water Streets
By the vinegar works,
The doors open in early evening.   10
Swinging their purses, the women
Poured down the long street to the river
And into the river.

I do not know how it was
They could drown every evening.   15
What time near dawn did they climb up the other shore,
Drying their wings?

For the river at Wheeling, West Virginia,
Has only two shores:
The one in hell, the other   20
In Bridgeport, Ohio.[4]

And nobody would commit suicide, only
To find beyond death
Bridgeport, Ohio.

1968

---

3. Of the Ohio river; "hobo jungle": camp made   4. Bridgeport is just across the river from
by hoboes or tramps.   Wheeling.

A Secret Gratitude

"Eugen Boissevain died in the autumn of 1949. I had wondered already, at
the time of our visit, what would happen to Edna [Millay] if he should die first."
(Edmund Wilson)[5]

1

She cleaned house, and then lay down long
On the long stair.

On one of those cold white wings
That the strange fowl provide for us like one hillside of the sea,
That cautery[6] of snow that blinds us,   5
Pitiless light,
One winter afternoon
Fair near the place where she sank down with one wing broken,
Three friends and I were caught
Stalk still in the light.   10

Five of the lights. Why should they care for our eyes?
Five deer stood there.
They looked back, a good minute.
They knew us, all right:
Four chemical accidents of horror pausing   15
Between one suicide or another
On the passing wing
Of an angel that cared no more for our biology, our pity, and our pain.
Than we care.

Why should any mere multitude of the angels care   20
To lay one blind white plume down
On this outermost limit of something that is probably no more
Than an aphid,[7]
An aphid which is one of the angels whose wings toss the black pears
Of tears down on the secret shores   25
Of the seas in the corner
Of a poet's closed eye.
Why should five deer
Gaze back at us?
They gazed back at us.   30
Afraid, and yet they stood there,
More alive than we four, in their terror,
In their good time.

We had a dog.
We could have got other dogs.   35
Two or three dogs could have taken turns running and dragging down

---

5. Quoted from "Epilogue 1952: Edna St. Vincent Millay" in *The Shores of Light: A Literary
Chronicle of the Twenties and Thirties*, New York:
1952, pp. 788–89. Wilson, the eminent American
literary critic, was prompted to write this essay on
his old friend Edna St. Vincent Millay (see above,
p. 308) after reading a memoir of her by Vincent
Sheean, *The Indigo Bunting*. Wilson had proposed marriage to her, but she later married Eugen
Boissevain, who devoted himself to her care until
his death. The night after Millay's death in 1960,
Wilson dreamed about her; later he learned that
she had died going up the stairs of her country
house in upper New York State.
6. Something that burns or sears.
7. Small plant-sucking insect.

Those fleet lights, whose tails must look as mysterious as the
Stars in Los Angeles.
We are men.
It doesn't even satisfy us   40
To kill one another.
We are a smear of obscenity
On the lake whose only peace
Is a hole where the moon
Abandoned us, that poor   45
Girl who can't leave us alone.

If I were the moon I would shrink into a sand grain
In the corner of the poet's eye,
While there's still room.

We are men.   50
We are capable of anything.
We could have killed every one of those deer.
The very moon of lovers tore herself with the agony of a wounded tigress
Out of our side.
We can kill anything.   55
We can kill our own bodies.
Those deer on the hillside have no idea what in hell
We are except murderers.
They know that much, and don't think
They don't.   60
Man's heart is the rotten yolk of a blacksnake egg
Corroding, as it is just born, in a pile of dead
Horse dung.
I have no use for the human creature.
He subtly extracts pain awake in his own kind.   65
I am born one, out of an accidental hump of chemistry.
I have no use.

                                    2

But
We didn't set dogs on the deer,
Even though we know,   70
As well as you know,
We could have got away with it,
Because
Who cares?

                                    3

Boissevain, who was he?   75
Was he human? I doubt it,
From what I know
Of men.

Who was he,
Hobbling with his dry eyes   80
Along in the rain?

I think he must have fallen down like the plumes of new snow,
I think he must have fallen into the grass, I think he
Must surely have grown around
Her wings, gathering and being gathered,   85
Leaf, string, anything she could use
To build her still home of songs
Within sound of water.

4

By God, come to that, I would have married her too,
If I'd got the chance, and she'd let me.   90
Think of that. Being alive with a girl
Who could turn into a laurel tree[8]
Whenever she felt like it.
Think of that.

5

Outside my window just now   95
I can hear a small waterfall rippling antiphonally[9] down over
The stones of my poem.

1971

The Journey

Anghiari[1] is medieval, a sleeve sloping down
A steep hill, suddenly sweeping out
To the edge of a cliff, and dwindling.
But far up the mountain, behind the town,
We too were swept out, out by the wind,   5
Alone with the Tuscan grass.

Wind had been blowing across the hills
For days, and everything now was graying gold
With dust, everything we saw, even
Some small children scampering along a road,   10
Twittering Italian to a small caged bird.
We sat beside them to rest in some brushwood,
And I leaned down to rinse the dust from my face.

I found the spider web there, whose hinges
Reeled heavily and crazily with the dust,   15
Whole mounds and cemeteries of it, sagging
And scattering shadows among shells and wings.
And then she stepped into the center of air
Slender and fastidious, the golden hair
Of daylight along her shoulders, she poised there,   20
While ruins crumbled on every side of her.
Free of the dust, as though a moment before
She had stepped inside the earth, too bathe herself.

---

8. Daphne was a nymph pursued by the god
Apollo; at her entreaty, she was turned into a laurel tree.

9. As if sung responsively.
1. A village in Tuscany, province in western
Italy.

I gazed, close to her, till at last she stepped
Away in her own good time.   25

Many men
Have searched all over Tuscany and never found
What I found there, the heart of the light
Itself shelled and leaved, balancing
On filaments themselves falling. The secret   30
Of this journey is to let the wind
Blow its dust all over your body,
To let it go on blowing, to step lightly, lightly
All the way through your ruins, and not to lose
Any sleep over the dead, who surely   35
Will bury their own, don't worry.

                                                                    1982

PHILIP LEVINE
b. 1928

Philip Levine works with elemental themes—father and son, the deaths of relatives, war—and infuses them with a melancholy luster. His poems, he says, "mostly record my discovery of the people, places, and animals I am not, the ones who live at all cost and come back for more, and who if they bore tattoos—a gesture they don't need—would have them say, 'Don't tread on me' or 'Once more with feeling' or 'no pasaran' or 'Not this pig.' "[1] In an America where the "time will never come / nor ripeness be all," Levine keeps his stoicism (and sense of humor) in trim by seeking out examples of the vital antiheroic. His poems celebrate the failed, the peripheral, and the uncooperative—in his own words,

> . . . the ugly
> who had no chance
>
> the beautiful in
> body, the used and the unused,
> those who had courage
> and those who quit.

He is master of an extraordinarily colloquial diction. The result is bizarre and powerful poems that evoke crucial emotions.

He was born on January 10, 1928, in Detroit and remained there to study with John Berryman at Wayne State University. In 1958 he received a Fellowship in Poetry at Stanford University and still lives in California, though he travels much, particularly in Spain; he acknowledges the importance to him of the Spanish-American surrealist poets and of their advocate, Robert Bly, as well as the influence of Rexroth and the San Francisco poets, who "opened me up." Since 1969 he has been a professor of English at California State University, Fresno. Though he has published in magazines since the mid-fifties, his first book did not appear until 1963; it has been followed by fourteen more, including his *Selected Poems* (1984). In 1980 he won both the National Book Critics' Circle Award and the American Book Award.

---

1. *Not This Pig*, Middletown, Conn., 1968.

To a Child Trapped in a Barber Shop

You've gotten in through the transom
    and you can't get out
till Monday morning or, worse,
    till the cops come.

That six-year-old red face   5
    calling for mama
is yours; it won't help you
    because your case

is closed forever, hopeless.
    So don't drink   10
the Lucky Tiger,[1] don't
    fill up on grease

because that makes it a lot worse,
    that makes it a crime
against property and the state   15
    and that costs time.

We've all been here before,
    we took our turn
under the electric storm
    of the vibrator   20

and stiffened our wills to meet
    the close clippers
and heard the true blade mowing
    back and forth

on a strip of dead skin,   25
    and we stopped crying.
You think your life is over?
    It's just begun.

                                                  1968

They Feed They Lion

Out of burlap sacks, out of bearing butter,
Out of black bean and wet slate bread,
Out of the acids of rage, the candor of tar,
Out of creosote, gasoline, drive shafts, wooden dollies,
They Lion grow.   5

            Out of the grey hills
Of industrial barns, out of rain, out of bus ride,
West Virginia to Kiss My Ass, out of buried aunties,
Mothers hardening like pounded stumps, out of stumps,

---

1. Brand of hair lotion.

Out of the bones' need to sharpen and the muscles' to stretch,   10
They Lion grow.

               Earth is eating trees, fence posts,
Gutted cars, earth is calling her little ones,
"Come home, Come home!" From pig balls,
From the ferocity of pig driven to holiness,   15
From the furred ear and the full jowl come
The repose of the hung belly, from the purpose
They Lion grow.

             From the sweet glues of the trotters[2]
Come the sweet kinks of the fist, from the full flower   20
Of the hams the thorax[3] of caves,
From "Bow Down" come "Rise Up,"
Come they Lion from the reeds of shovels,
The grained arm that pulls the hands,
They Lion grow.   25

           From my five arms and all my hands,
From all my white sins forgiven, they feed,
From my car passing under the stars,
They Lion, from my children inherit,
From the oak turned to a wall, they Lion,   30
From they sack and they belly opened
And all that was hidden burning on the oil-stained earth
They feed they Lion and he comes.

                                    1972

The Life Ahead

I wakened, still a child,
and dressed myself slowly
for the life ahead. It
came at two, after lunch,
the class quieted   5
and the teacher's eyes
clouded and closed.
I could smell our coats
on their hooks, I could
smell my own uncut hair,   10
the hair of a dog, and
when I looked down below
to the dark streets awash
with oil, a small boy—
alone and lost—wandered   15
across the playground.
He climbed the fence
and made it across
the avenue, past the closed
candy store, and down   20

---

2. Cooked pigs' feet.   3. That is, chest cavity.

the street that led to hell.
There was a river in Detroit
and if you crossed it you
were in another country,[4]
but something always   25
called me back, a woman
who had no use for me
or a brother who did, or
the pure white aura
of steel before the forge   30
came down with a groan
like the sea's and we stood
back waiting for one more
leaf of a truck spring, thick
arched leaf of earth. Something   35
called me back to this life,
and I came home to wander
the schoolyard again
as a lost boy and find
above or below the world   40
was here and now, drowning
in oil, second by second
borrowed from the clock.

1979

Genius

Two old dancing shoes my grandfather
gave the Christian Ladies,
an unpaid water bill, the rear license
of a dog that messed on your lawn,
a tooth I saved for the good fairy   5
and which is stained with base metals
and plastic filler. With these images
and your black luck and my bad breath
a bright beginner could make a poem
in fourteen rhyming lines about the purity   10
of first love or the rose's many thorns
or the dew that won't wait long enough
to stand my little gray wren a drink.

1981

4. Canada, on the opposite bank of the Detroit River.

ANNE SEXTON
1928–1974

The attempt to utter raw feeling before time, conventional reassurance, or contemplation have alleviated it is the beginning and ending of Anne Sexton's work. Poetry,

she said, "should be a shock to the senses. It should almost hurt."[1] "There is some
very bad writing in some of my best poems," she conceded, "and yet these flaws
seem to me to make them even better." This conception, that ore is better unrefined
than refined, is a peculiarly contemporary one.

Her work is rooted, quite deliberately, in her existence as a woman, and exhibits
her loves, her children, her parents, her breakdowns, her urges to self-abandonment
and death. As she said in the interview cited above, her poetry is "intensely physical."

Like Sylvia Plath, Anne Sexton studied with Robert Lowell, who encouraged her
with his view that "imperfection is the language of art." She is often labeled a member of the "Confessional School," which is said to have begun with Lowell's sudden
shift towards autobiography, *Life Studies.* She insisted, however, that she had not
read him when she began to write in her own way, and it is probably true that her
work, and his too, were part of a common direction poets took in the late fifties and
early sixties, away from objective and on to subjective poetry. Her first book was
entitled *To Bedlam and Part Way Back* (1960), and its themes of collapse and partial
recovery reverberate in a later volume such as *Live or Die,* where the final, desperate
choice is to persist: "So I won't hang around in my hospital shift, / repeating the
Black Mass and all of it. / I say *Live, Live* because of the sun, / the dream, the
excitable gift." But a consciousness of evil (a word she puts in capitals), and a sense
of the mutualities of madness and other forms of victimization, is the principal tenor
of her work.

Anne (Harvey) Sexton was born November 9, 1928, in Newton, Massachusetts.
She was educated at Garland Junior College, then married and had two daughters.
Those who had followed her career were shocked but hardly surprised in 1974 to
hear of her suicide.

1. Patricia Marx, "Interview with Anne Sexton," *Hudson Review* 18, Winter 1965–66, 560–80.

The Truth the Dead Know

For My Mother, Born March 1902, Died March 1959
and My Father, Born February 1900, Died June 1959

Gone, I say and walk from church,
refusing the stiff procession to the grave,
letting the dead ride alone in the hearse.
It is June. I am tired of being brave.

We drive to the Cape. I cultivate   5
myself where the sun gutters from the sky,
where the sea swings in like an iron gate
and we touch. In another country people die.

My darling, the wind falls in like stones
from the whitehearted water and when we touch   10
we enter touch entirely. No one's alone.
Men kill for this, or for as much.

And what of the dead? They lie without shoes
in their stone boats. They are more like stone

than the sea would be if it stopped. They refuse   15
to be blessed, throat, eye and knucklebone.

1962

All My Pretty Ones

> All my pretty ones?
> Did you say all? O hell-kite! All?
> What! all my pretty chickens and their dam
> At one fell swoop? . . .
> I cannot but remember such things were,
> That were most precious to me.
> —MACBETH[1]

Father, this year's jinx rides us apart
where you followed our mother to her cold slumber,
a second shock boiling its stone to your heart,
leaving me here to shuffle and disencumber
you from the residence you could not afford: 5
a gold key, your half of a woollen mill,
twenty suits from Dunne's, an English Ford,
the love and legal verbiage of another will,
boxes of pictures of people I do not know.
I touch their cardboard faces. They must go.   10

But the eyes, as thick as wood in this album,
hold me. I stop here, where a small boy
waits in a ruffled dress for someone to come . . .
for this soldier who holds his bugle like a toy
or for this velvet lady who cannot smile.   15
Is this your father's father, this commodore
in a mailman suit? My father, time meanwhile
has made it unimportant who you are looking for.
I'll never know what these faces are all about.
I lock them into their book and throw them out.   20

This is the yellow scrapbook that you began
the year I was born; as crackling now and wrinkly
as tobacco leaves: clippings where Hoover outran
the Democrats,[2] wiggling his dry finger at me
and Prohibition; news where the *Hindenburg* went   25
down[3] and recent years when you went flush
on war. This year, solvent but sick, you meant
to marry that pretty widow in a one-month rush.
But before you had that second chance, I cried
on your fat shoulder. Three days later you died.   30

These are the snapshots of marriage, stopped in places.
Side by side at the rail toward Nassau[4] now;
here, with the winner's cup at the speedboat races,
here, in tails at the Cotillion, you take a bow,

---

1. Macduff's lament on learning that Macbeth has had his wife and children brutally murdered. (*Macbeth* 4.3.215–18.)
2. In the presidential election of 1928.
3. The German airship *Hindenburg* was destroyed by fire at Lakeville, N.J., in 1936.
4. In the Bahamas.

here, by our kennel of dogs with their pink eyes,   35
running like show-bred pigs in their chain-link pen;
here, at the horseshow where my sister wins a prize;
and here, standing like a duke among groups of men.
Now I fold you down, my drunkard, my navigator,
my first lost keeper, to love or look at later.   40

I hold a five-year diary that my mother kept
for three years, telling all she does not say
of your alcoholic tendency. You overslept,
she writes. My God, father, each Christmas Day
with your blood, will I drink down your glass   45
of wine? The diary of your hurly-burly years
goes to my shelf to wait for my age to pass.
Only in this hoarded span will love persevere.
Whether you are pretty or not, I outlive you.
bend down my strange face to yours and forgive you.   50

1962

The Starry Night

> That does not keep me from having a terrible
> need of—shall I say the word—religion. Then
> I go out at night to paint the stars.
> —Vincent Van Gogh[5]
> in a letter to his brother

The town does not exist
except where one black-haired tree slips
up like a drowned woman into the hot sky.
The town is silent. The night boils with eleven stars
Oh starry starry night! This is how   5
I want to die.

It moves. They are all alive.
Even the moon bulges in its orange irons
to push children, like a god, from its eye.
The old unseen serpent swallows up the stars.   10
Oh starry starry night! This is how
I want to die:

into that rushing beast of the night,
sucked up by that great dragon, to split
from my life with no flag,   15
no belly,
no cry.

1962

5. (1853–1890), Dutch painter; in his thirties he became insane and finally committed suicide. His
brother was his only confidant; this letter was written to him in September 1888 from Arles, France.
Van Gogh was also painting, in September of 1888, *Starry Night on the Rhône*.

ADRIENNE RICH
b. 1929

In surveying the arc of Adrienne Rich's extraordinary career it may be useful to take as touchstones the titles of two of her books. Her first (1951) was called *A Change of World;* her fifth, twenty years later, was *The Will to Change* (from Charles Olson's "The Kingfishers": "What does not change / is the will to change"). The first marks an acceptance of the world's changes; the second enunciates the possibility of changes in that world and in oneself.

Rich was born, "white and middle-class," the elder of two sisters, in Baltimore, Maryland, on May 16, 1929. Her father encouraged her to read and to write, "so that for twenty years I wrote for a particular man, who criticized me and praised me and made me feel 'special,' " she was later to write in her influential essay "When We Dead Awaken: Writing as Re-Vision."[1] As for Rich's mother, "my gentile grandmother and my mother were also frustrated artists and intellectuals, a lost writer and a lost composer between them."[2]

She graduated from Radcliffe College in 1951, and in the same year W. H. Auden chose *A Change of World* for the Yale Younger Poets series. In his preface Auden wrote, approvingly, "The poems a reader will encounter in this book are neatly and modestly dressed, speak quietly but do not mumble, respect their elders but are not cowed by them, and do not tell fibs . . ."[3] Male poets were her model in those days, for it then seemed that the best a woman could do was to write as well as a man, "the men I was reading as an undergraduate—Frost, Dylan Thomas, Donne, Auden, MacNeice, Stevens, Yeats." But, she later said, "Looking back at poems I wrote before I was twenty-one, I'm startled because beneath the conscious craft are glimpses of the split I even then experienced between the girl who wrote poems, who defined herself writing poems, and the girl who was to define herself by her relationships with men. 'Aunt Jennifer's Tigers' (1951), written while I was a student, looks with deliberate detachment at this split."[4]

Rich's first book "seemed to mean that others agreed I was a poet. Because I was also determined to prove that as a woman poet I could also have what was then defined as a 'full' woman's life," she married in her twenties and bore three sons before she was thirty; she also published another collection, *The Diamond Cutters* (1955), which was praised for its "gracefulness." She seemed to have everything a woman was supposed to want in the American fifties, and "if there were doubts . . . these could only mean that I was ungrateful, insatiable, perhaps a monster."[5]

The fifties and early sixties were desperate years for her. She wrote in a notebook at the time that she felt "paralyzed by the sense that there exists a mesh of relationships—e.g. between my anger at the children, my sensual relationships, pacifism, sex (I mean sex in its broadest significance, not merely sexual desire)—an interconnectedness which, if I could see it, make it valid, would give me back to myself, make it possible to function lucidly and passionately. Yet I grope in and out among these dark webs." She said, later, of this observation, "I think I began at this point to feel that politics was not something 'out there' but something 'in here' and of the essence of my condition." Then, in the late fifties, she "was able to write, for the first time, directly about experiencing myself as a woman," in the poem "Snapshots of a Daughter-in-Law." Prosodically, it was "in a longer, looser mode than I'd ever trusted myself with before."[6]

1. "When We Dead Awaken: Writing as Re-Vision," in *On Lies, Secrets, and Silence: Selected Prose, 1966–1978,* New York, 1979, pp. 38–39.
2. "Split at the Root: An Essay on Jewish Identity," in *Blood, Bread, and Poetry: Selected Prose, 1979–1985,* New York, 1986, p. 102.

3. *A Change of World,* New Haven, 1951, p. 11.
4. "When We Dead Awaken," pp. 39–40.
5. The same, p. 42.
6. The same, p. 44.

It had taken eight years to write the poems of *Snapshots of a Daughter-in-Law* (1963), but now the books began to come more quickly. "Orion," in her next volume (*Leaflets*, 1969), was written as "a poem of reconnection with a part of myself I had felt I was losing, the active principle, the energetic imagination." It also poses a choice "between 'love'—womanly, maternal love, altruistic love—a love defined and ruled by the weight of an entire culture—and egoism—a force directed by men into creation, achievement, ambition, often at the expense of others, but justifiably so. . . . I know now [1971] that the alternatives are false ones—that the word 'love' is itself in need of re-vision."[7] In the late sixties, when her husband accepted a teaching post at the City College of New York, they both became involved in radical politics, especially in opposition to the Vietnam War. She also taught inner-city minority young people, and teaching has since become an important vocation. The new concerns enter the poems of *Diving into the Wreck* and *The Will to Change*. The language in these books becomes more urgent and fragmented, the images starker, and the prosody more jagged. Moreover, ever since "Snapshots," Rich has been dating her poems, as if to underline their provisional or journal-entry nature.

"I had been looking for the Women's Liberation Movement since the 1950s. I came into it in 1970 . . . I identified myself as a radical feminist, and soon after—not as a political act but out of powerful and unmistakable feelings—as a lesbian," she wrote in 1986 in the Foreword to her second collection of essays.[8] She has also found the prose speech or essay a valuable tool in exploring feminist issues. A larger prose work was her book *Of Woman Born: Motherhood as Experience and Institution* (1976; reissued in a Tenth Anniversary Edition, 1986). It is made up of "personal testimony mingled with research, and theory which derived from both,"[9] on the private feelings and social experiences of motherhood.

The essay "It Is the Lesbian in Us . . ." (1976) explores another controversial issue. She does not restrict the word "lesbian" to female homosexuals, but expands it to mean "a primary intensity between women, an intensity" which the world at large has "trivialized, caricatured, or invested with evil . . . I believe it is the lesbian in every woman who is compelled by female energy . . . It is the lesbian in us who drives us to feel imaginatively, render in language, grasp, the full connection between woman and woman. It is the lesbian in us who is creative, for the dutiful daughter of the fathers is only a hack."[10]

In her more recent books—*The Dream of a Common Language* (1978), *A Wild Patience Has Taken Me This Far* (1981), and *Your Native Land, Your Life* (1986)—a number of the poems continue to reshape the "poetry of dialogue" begun so much earlier. The extraordinary sequence "Twenty-One Love Poems"—which recalls only to undermine the Elizabethan sonnet-sequences written by men to an impossibly idealized lady-love—is a dialogue with a lover who becomes a former lover, while other poems are addressed to named and unnamed women in the present and in history: Willa Cather, Ellen Glasgow, Ethel Rosenberg, her own grandmothers. The long poem "Sources" contains a complex and moving talk with her father, the Jewish intellectual—"For years all arguments I carried on in my head were with you. / . . . It is only now, under a powerful, / womanly lens, that I can decipher your suffering and deny no part / of my own"—and her husband, "the other Jew. / . . . both like you and unlike you." In its totality it is, however, as Rich has said, "a 'dialogue of self and soul,' an interior conversation with and about memory."[11] Still another complex dialogue is that with Robinson Jeffers, Walt Whitman, and the Hebrew Bible in "Yom Kippur, 1984."

7. The same, pp. 45–47.
8. Foreword to *Blood, Bread, and Poetry*, pp. vii–viii.
9. *Of Woman Born: Motherhood as Experience and Institution*, Tenth Anniversary Edition, New York, 1976, 1986, p. x.
10. "It Is the Lesbian in Us . . .," in *On Lies, Secrets, and Silence*, pp. 200–201.
11. Adrienne Rich, letter to John Benedict, July 1, 1988.

The best of these new poems, as the ones before, articulate "the dream of a common language" for a poet "neither unique nor universal, but a person in history, a woman and not a man, a white and also Jewish inheritor of a particular Western consciousness, from the making of which most women have been excluded."[12] And a poet who will continue to change.

Rich's work has been signally honored in recent years. In 1986 she was the first winner of the newly inaugurated Ruth Lilly Poetry Prize, awarded by the Modern Poetry Association and the American Council for the Arts, while in 1987 she received a Creative Arts Medal from Brandeis University. She lives in California, and teaches at Stanford University.

12. Foreword to *The Fact of a Doorframe: Poems Selected and New, 1950–1984*, New York, 1984, p. xv.

Aunt Jennifer's Tigers

Aunt Jennifer's tigers prance across a screen,
Bright topaz denizens of a world of green.
They do not fear the men beneath the tree;
They pace in sleek chivalric certainty.

Aunt Jennifer's fingers fluttering through her wool   5
Find even the ivory needle hard to pull.
The massive weight of Uncle's wedding band
Sits heavily upon Aunt Jennifer's hand.

When Aunt is dead, her terrified hands will lie
Still ringed with ordeals she was mastered by.   10
The tigers in the panel that she made
Will go on prancing, proud and unafraid.

1951

Snapshots of a Daughter-in-Law

1

You, once a belle in Shreveport,
with henna-colored hair,[1] skin like a peachbud,
still have your dresses copied from that time,
and play a Chopin prelude
called by Cortot: *"Delicious recollections*   5
float like perfume through the memory."[2]

Your mind now, moldering like wedding-cake,
heavy with useless experience, rich
with suspicion, rumor, fantasy,
crumbling to pieces under the knife-edge   10
of mere fact. In the prime of your life.

1. That is, red; henna is a hair dye.
2. Remark made by the French pianist Alfred Cortot in his *Chopin: 24 Preludes* (1930); he is referring specifically to Chopin's Prelude No. 7; Chopin was a nineteenth-century Polish composer and pianist who settled in Paris in 1831.

Nervy, glowering, your daughter
wipes the teaspoons, grows another way.

2

Banging the coffee-pot into the sink   15
she hears the angels chiding, and looks out
past the raked gardens to the sloppy sky.
Only a week since They said: *Have no patience.*

The next time it was: *Be insatiable.*
Then: *Save yourself; others you cannot save.*
Sometimes she's let the tapstream scald her arm,   20
a match burn to her thumbnail,

or held her hand above the kettle's snout
right in the woolly steam. They are probably angels,
since nothing hurts her anymore, except
each morning's grit blowing into her eyes.   25

3

A thinking woman sleeps with monsters.
The beak that grips her, she becomes. And Nature,
that sprung-lidded, still commodious
steamer-trunk of *tempora* and *mores*[3]
gets stuffed with it all: the mildewed orange-flowers,   30
the female pills, the terrible breasts
of Boadicea[4] beneath flat foxes' heads and orchids.

Two handsome women, gripped in argument,
each proud, acute, subtle, I hear scream
across the cut glass and majolica   35
like Furies[5] cornered from their prey:
The argument *ad feminam*,[6] all the old knives
that have rusted in my back, I drive in yours,
ma semblable, ma soeur![7]

4

Knowing themselves too well in one another: 40
their gifts no pure fruition, but a thorn,
the prick filed sharp against a hint of scorn . . .
Reading while waiting
for the iron to heat,

---

3. Literally, "times" and "customs"—alluding perhaps to the Roman orator Cicero's "O tempora! O mores!" ("Alas for the degeneracy of our times and the low standards of our morals!").
4. British queen in the time of the Emperor Nero, who led her people in a strong but ultimately unsuccessful revolt against Roman rule; "female pills": remedies for menstrual pain.
5. Greek goddesses of vengeance; "cut glass and majolica": expensive glassware and earthenware.

6. Female version of the phrase *ad hominem* ("to the man"), referring to an argument directed not to reason but to personal prejudices and emotions.
7. The last line of Charles Baudelaire's poem "*Au Lecteur*" ("To the Reader") addresses "*Hypocrite lecteur!—mon semblable—mon frère!*" ("Hypocrite reader—like me—my brother!"); Rich substitutes *ma soeur* (my sister). See also T. S. Eliot's *The Waste Land*, above, p. 284, line 76.

writing, *My Life had stood—a Loaded Gun*[8]—   45
in that Amherst pantry while the jellies boil and scum,
or, more often,
iron-eyed and beaked and purposed as a bird,
dusting everything on the whatnot every day of life.

5

Dulce ridens, dulce loquens,[9]   50
she shaves her legs until they gleam
like petrified mammoth-tusk.

6

When to her lute Corinna sings[1]
neither words nor music are her own;
only the long hair dipping   55
over her cheek, only the song
of silk against her knees
and these
adjusted in reflections of an eye.

Poised, trembling and unsatisfied, before   60
an unlocked door, that cage of cages,
tell us, you bird, you tragical machine—
is this *fertilisante douleur?*[2] Pinned down
by love, for you the only natural action,
are you edged more keen   65
to prise the secrets of the vault? has Nature shown
her household books to you, daughter-in-law,
that her sons never saw?

7

"To have in this uncertain world some stay
which cannot be undermined, is   70
of the utmost consequence."[3]
                Thus wrote
a woman, partly brave and partly good,
who fought with what she partly understood.
Few men about her would or could do more,   75
hence she was labeled harpy, shrew and whore.

8

"You all die at fifteen," said Diderot,[4]
and turn part legend, part convention.

8. Rich's note to this line refers to T. H. Johnson's *Emily Dickinson, Complete Poems* (1960); this is the poem numbered 764 in that edition. Dickinson (see above, p. 20) lived her entire life in Amherst, Massachusetts.
9. Sweetly laughing, sweetly speaking (Latin), from Horace's *Ode* XXII.
1. First line of a poem by the English poet Thomas Campion (1567–1620); "Corinna" is a generic name for a shepherdess.
2. "Fertilizing" or "life-giving sorrow."

3. "From Mary Wollstonecraft, *Thoughts on the Education of Daughters*, London, 1787" (Rich's note); Wollstonecraft, one of the first feminist thinkers, is best known for her *Vindication of the Rights of Woman* (1792).
4. Denis Diderot, eighteenth-century French philosopher and writer. Rich's note to this line says that it is quoted from the *Lettres à Sophie Volland* in Simone de Beauvoir's influential *Le Deuxième Sexe*, vol. 2, pp. 123–24 (cited in French by Rich).

Still, eyes inaccurately dream
behind closed windows blankening with steam.   80
Deliciously, all that we might have been,
all that we were—fire, tears,
wit, taste, martyred ambition—
stirs like the memory of refused adultery
the drained and flagging bosom of our middle years.   85

9

Not that it is done well, but
that it is done at all?[5] Yes, think
of the odds! or shrug them off forever.
This luxury of the precocious child,
Time's precious chronic invalid,—   90
would we, darlings, resign it if we could?
Our blight has been our sinecure:
mere talent was enough for us—
glitter in fragments and rough drafts.

Sigh no more, ladies.[6]   95
                Time is male
and in his cups drinks to the fair.
Bemused by gallantry, we hear
our mediocrities over-praised,
indolence read as abnegation,   100
slattern[7] thought styled intuition,
every lapse forgiven, our crime
only to cast too bold a shadow
or smash the mold straight off.

For that, solitary confinement,   105
tear gas, attrition shelling.[8]
Few applicants for that honor.

10

                Well,
she's long about her coming, who must be
more merciless to herself than history.   110
Her mind full to the wind, I see her plunge
breasted and glancing through the currents,
taking the light upon her
at least as beautiful as any boy
or helicopter,[9]   115
                poised, still coming,
her fine blades making the air wince

5. "Sir, a woman's preaching is like a dog's
walking on his hinder legs. It is not done well; but
you are surprised to find it done at all": Samuel
Johnson to James Boswell in Boswell's *Life*.
6. "Sigh no more, ladies, sigh no more, / Men
were deceivers ever" in Shakespeare's *Much Ado
About Nothing* (2.3.65–66). "In his cups": while
drinking.
7. Unkempt, disorderly.
8. That is, bombing.

9. "She comes down from the remoteness of
ages, from Thebes, from Crete, from Chichén-Itzá;
and she is also the totem set deep in the African
jungle; she is a helicopter and she is a bird; and
there is this, the greatest wonder of all: under her
tinted hair the forest murmur becomes a thought,
and words issue from her breasts" (Simone de
Beauvoir, *The Second Sex*, tr. H. M. Parshlev [New
York, 1953], p. 729). (A translation of the passage
from *Le Deuxième Sexe*, vol. 2, p. 574).

but her cargo
no promise then:
delivered   120
palpable
ours.

1958–1960   1963

Orion[1]

Far back when I went zig-zagging
through tamarack pastures
you were my genius, you
my cast-iron Viking, my helmed
lion-heart king in prison.[2]   5
Years later now you're young

my fierce half-brother, staring
down from that simplified west
your breast open, your belt dragged down
by an oldfashioned thing, a sword   10
the last bravado you won't give over
though it weighs you down as you stride

and the stars in it are dim
and maybe have stopped burning.
But you burn, and I know it;   15
as I throw back my head to take you in
an old transfusion happens again:
divine astronomy is nothing to it.

Indoors I bruise and blunder,
break faith, leave ill enough   20
alone, a dead child born in the dark.
Night cracks up over the chimney,
pieces of time, frozen geodes
come showering down in the grate.

A man reaches behind my eyes   25
and finds them empty
a woman's head turns away
from my head in the mirror
children are dying my death
and eating crumbs of my life.   30

Pity is not your forte.
Calmly you ache up there
pinned aloft in your crow's nest,
my speechless pirate!
You take it all for granted   35
and when I look you back

---

1. A constellation named for the giant hunter of
Greek mythology, who at his death was placed
among the stars by the gods.

2. Like Richard I of England (1157–1199), called
"the lion-hearted," who on his return from a Crusade was briefly imprisoned in Austria.

it's with a starlike eye
shooting its cold and egotistical spear
where it can do least damage.
Breathe deep! No hurt, no pardon   40
out here in the cold with you
you with your back to the wall.

1965   1969

Diving into the Wreck

First having read the book of myths,
and loaded the camera,
and checked the edge of the knife-blade,
I put on
the body-armor of black rubber   5
the absurd flippers
the grave and awkward mask.
I am having to do this
not like Cousteau[3] with his
assiduous team   10
aboard the sun-flooded schooner
but here alone.

There is a ladder.
The ladder is always there
hanging innocently   15
close to the side of the schooner.
We know what it is for,
we who have used it.
Otherwise
it is a piece of maritime floss   20
some sundry equipment.

I go down.
Rung after rung and still
the oxygen immerses me   25
the blue light
the clear atoms
of our human air.
I go down.
My flippers cripple me,
I crawl like an insect down the ladder   30
and there is no one
to tell me when the ocean
will begin.

First the air is blue and then
it is bluer and then green and then   35
black I am blacking out and yet
my mask is powerful
it pumps my blood with power

3. Jacques-Yves Cousteau (b. 1910), French underwater explorer and author.

the sea is another story
the sea is not a question of power   40
I have to learn alone
to turn my body without force
in the deep element.

And now: it is easy to forget
what I came for   45
among so many who have always
lived here
swaying their crenellated[4] fans
between the reefs
and besides   50
you breathe differently down here.

I came to explore the wreck.
The words are purposes.
The words are maps.
I came to see the damage that was done   55
and the treasures that prevail.
I stroke the beam of my lamp
slowly along the flank
of something more permanent
than fish or weed   60

the thing I came for:
the wreck and not the story of the wreck
the thing itself and not the myth
the drowned face[5] always staring
toward the sun   65
the evidence of damage
worn by salt and sway into this threadbare beauty
the ribs of the disaster
curving their assertion
among the tentative haunters.   70

This is the place.
And I am here, the mermaid whose dark hair
streams black, the merman in his armored body.
We circle silently
about the wreck   75
we dive into the hold.
I am she: I am he

whose drowned face sleeps with open eyes
whose breasts still bear the stress
whose silver, copper, vermeil[6] cargo lies   80
obscurely inside barrels
half-wedged and left to rot
we are the half-destroyed instruments
that once held to a course

---

4. With repeated indentations.   which formed the prow of old sailing ships.
5. That of the ornamental female figurehead   6. Gilded silver, bronze, or copper.

the water-eaten log   85
the fouled compass

We are, I am, you are
by cowardice or courage
the one who find our way
back to this scene   90
carrying a knife, a camera
a book of myths
in which
our names do not appear.

1972   1973

From Twenty-One Love Poems

II

I wake up in your bed. I know I have been dreaming.
Much earlier, the alarm broke us from each other,
you've been at your desk for hours. I know what I dreamed:
our friend the poet comes into my room
where I've been writing for days,   5
drafts, carbons, poems are scattered everywhere,
and I want to show her one poem
which is the poem of my life. But I hesitate,
and wake. You've kissed my hair
to wake me. *I dreamed you were a poem,*   10
I say, *a poem I wanted to show someone* . . .
and I laugh and fall dreaming again
of the desire to show you to everyone I love,
to move openly together
in the pull of gravity, which is not simple   15
which carries the feathered grass a long way down the upbreathing air.

XI

Every peak is a crater. This is the law of volcanoes,
making them eternally and visibly female.
No height without depth, without a burning core,
though our straw soles shred on the hardened lava.
I want to travel with you to every sacred mountain   5
smoking within like the sibyl[7] stooped over her tripod,
I want to reach for your hand as we scale the path,
to feel your arteries glowing in my clasp,
never failing to note the small, jewel-like flower
unfamiliar to us, nameless till we rename her,   10
that clings to the slowly altering rock—
that detail outside ourselves that brings us to ourselves,
was here before us, knew we would come, and sees beyond us.

---

7. In classical antiquity, a seeress; her tripod held burning incense.

(The Floating Poem, Unnumbered)

Whatever happens with us, your body
will haunt mine—tender, delicate
your lovemaking, like the half-curled frond
of the fiddlehead fern in forests
just washed by sun. Your traveled, generous thighs   5
between which my whole face has come and come—
the innocence and wisdom of the place my tongue has found there—
the live, insatiate dance of your nipples in my mouth—
your touch on me, firm, protective, searching
me out, your strong tongue and slender fingers   10
reaching where I had been waiting years for you
in my rose-wet cave—whatever happens, this is.

XX

That conversation we were always on the edge
of having, runs on in my head,
at night the Hudson trembles in New Jersey light[8]
polluted water yet reflecting even
sometimes the moon   5
and I discern a woman
I loved, drowning in secrets, fear wound round her throat
and choking her like hair. And this is she
with whom I tried to speak, whose hurt, expressive head
turning aside from pain, is dragged down deeper   10
where it cannot hear me,
and soon I shall know I was talking to my own soul

XXI

The dark lintels, the blue and foreign stones
of the great round rippled by stone implements
the midsummer night light rising from beneath
the horizon—when I said "a cleft of light"
I meant this. And this is not Stonehenge[9]   5
simply nor any place but the mind
casting back to where her solitude,
shared, could be chosen without loneliness,
not easily nor without pains to stake out
the circle, the heavy shadows, the great light.   10
I choose to be a figure in that light,
half-blotted by darkness, something moving
across that space, the color of stone
greeting the moon, yet more than stone:
a woman. I choose to walk here. And to draw this circle.   15
1974–1976   1978

---

8. New Jersey is across the Hudson River from New York City's West Side.
9. A circle of great standing stones on Salisbury Plain, England, probably dating back to the Bronze Age.

Yom Kippur[1] 1984

I drew solitude over me, on the lone shore.
—Robinson Jeffers, "Prelude"[2]

For whoever does not afflict his soul throughout
this day, shall be cut off from his people.
—Leviticus 23:29

What is a Jew in solitude?
What would it mean not to feel lonely or afraid
far from your own or those you have called your own?
What is a woman in solitude: a queer woman or a man?
In the empty street, on the empty beach, in the desert   5
what in this world as it is can solitude mean?

The glassy, concrete octagon suspended from the cliffs
with its electric gate, its perfected privacy
is not what I mean
the pick-up with a gun parked at a turn-out in Utah or the Golan Heights[3]   10
is not what I mean
the poet's tower facing the western ocean, acres of forest planted to the
        east,[4] the woman reading in the cabin, her attack dog suddenly risen
is not what I mean

Three thousand miles from what I once called home[5]
I open a book searching for some lines I remember   15
about flowers, something to bind me to this coast as lilacs in the dooryard
        once
bound me back there[6]—yes, lupines on a burnt mountainside,
something that bloomed and faded and was written down
in the poet's book, forever:
Opening the poet's book   20
I find the hatred in the poet's heart: . . . *the hateful-eyed*
and human-bodied are all about me: you that love multitude may have them

Robinson Jeffers, multitude
is the blur flung by distinct forms against these landward valleys
and the farms that run down to the sea; the lupines   25
are multitude, and the torched poppies, the grey Pacific unrolling its scrolls
        of surf,
and the separate persons, stooped
over sewing machines in denim dust, bent under the shattering skies of
        harvest

---

1. The Jewish Day of Atonement, one of the
holiest days in the Judaic year and the last of the
Ten Days of Penitence. The Lord decreed it in
the Leviticus passage from which the second epigraph is taken.
2. "The epigraph and quoted lines from Robinson Jeffers come from *The Woman at Point Sur
and Other Poems* (New York, 1977)" (Rich's note).
On Jeffers see above, p. 245.
3. Hilly area in Syria, site of Arab-Israeli conflicts; "turn-out": parking area adjacent to a highway.
4. Jeffers and his wife lived in Carmel, on the

California coast. His house, Tor House (now a
museum), fronts directly on the Pacific Ocean;
nearby he built Hawk Tower, with his own hands;
he also, to preserve his solitude, planted forest
behind the house to the east.
5. Rich had just moved from the East Coast,
where she had lived for over fifty years, to California.
6. Compare the title of Whitman's poem about
the death of Abraham Lincoln, "When Lilacs Last
in the Dooryard Bloom'd." Lilacs are an eastern
U.S. flower; lupines, a purple wildflower, grow in
profusion in California.

who sleep by shifts in never-empty beds have their various dreams
Hands that pick, pack, steam, stitch, strip, stuff, shell, scrape, scour, belong
    to a brain like no other   30
Must I argue the love of multitude in the blur or defend
a solitude of barbed-wire and searchlights, the survivalist's final solution,[7]
    have I a choice?

To wander far from your own or those you have called your own
to hear strangeness calling you from far away
and walk in that direction, long and far, not calculating risk   35
to go to meet the Stranger without fear or weapon, protection nowhere on
    your mind
(the Jew on the icy, rutted road on Christmas Eve prays for another Jew
the woman in the ungainly twisting shadows of the street: *Make those be
a woman's footsteps;* as if she could believe in a woman's god)

Find someone like yourself.   Find others.
Agree you will never desert each other.   40
Understand that any rift among you
means power to those who want to do you in.
Close to the center, safety; toward the edges, danger.
But I have a nightmare to tell: I am trying to say
that to be with my people is my dearest wish   45
but that I also love strangers
that I crave separateness
I hear myself stuttering these words
to my worst friends and my best enemies
who watch for my mistakes in grammar   50
my mistakes in love.
This is the day of atonement; but do my people forgive me?[8]
If a cloud knew loneliness and fear, I would be that cloud.

To love the Stranger, to love solitude—am I writing merely about privilege
about drifting from the center, drawn to edges,   55
a privilege we can't afford in the world that is,
who are hated as being of our kind: faggot kicked into the icy river, woman
    dragged from her stalled car
into the mist-struck mountains, used and hacked to death
young scholar shot at the university gates on a summer evening walk, his
    prizes and studies nothing, nothing availing his Blackness[9]
Jew deluded that she's escaped the tribe, the laws[1] of her exclusion, the
    men too holy to touch her hand;   Jew who has turned her back   60

7. Nazi Germany's name for the plan to exterminate all Jews.
8. Before the Lord passes judgment on all Jews on Yom Kippur, they must seek forgiveness for their offenses against other Jews.
9. Rich gave a talk at her publishers' office about this poem on April 30, 1987; of this passage she said, "During that summer [before she moved to California] I read of the shooting by police of Edmund Perry, a young Black man who was in fact on his way to Stanford University on a scholarship, shot in the neighborhood of Columbia University. One of many police assaults on Black people during that time and since. I arrived in Santa Cruz, California . . . And the first thing that confronted me was a series of murders in the Santa Cruz Mountains of women [who] had been dragged from their cars and raped and multilated. The police were sending out warnings that women should not drive alone through the mountains and should only drive with locked windows and doors and a full tank of gas. And that was going to be my commute to San José State University. And during the time of working on the poem I read also of the waylaying and beating up of a gay man in Maine who was then dumped into an icy river and who could not swim and died."
1. That is, the laws governing the purity of the priesthood, as detailed in Leviticus 22. According to tradition, the Israelites were divided into twelve tribes.

on *midrash* and *mitzvah*[2] (yet wears the *chai* on a thong between her breasts)
  hiking alone
found with a swastika[3] carved in her back at the foot of the cliffs (did she die
  as a queer or as Jew?)

Solitude, O taboo, endangered species[4]
on the mist-struck spur of the mountain, I want a gun to defend you
In the desert, on the deserted street, I want what I can't have: 65
your elder sister, Justice, her great peasant's hand outspread
her eye, half-hooded, sharp and true[5]
And I ask myself, have I thrown courage away?
have I traded off something I don't name?
To what extreme will I go to meet the extremist?   70
What will I do to defend my want or anyone's want to search for her spirit-
  vision
far from the protection of those she has called her own?
Will I find O solitude
your plumes, your breasts, your hair
against my face, as in childhood, your voice like the mockingbird's[6]   75
singing *Yes, you are loved, why else this song?*
in the old places, anywhere?

What is a Jew in solitude?
What is a woman in solitude, a queer woman or man?
When the winter flood-tides wrench the tower from the rock, crumble the
  prophet's headland,[7] and the farms slide into the sea   80
when leviathan is endangered and Jonah becomes revenger[8]
when center and edges are crushed together, the extremities crushed together
  on which the world was founded
when our souls crash together, Arab and Jew, howling our loneliness within
  the tribes
when the refugee child and the exile's child re-open the blasted and forbidden city
when we who refuse to be women and men as women and men are chartered,[9] tell our stories of solitude spent in multitude   85
in that world as it may be, newborn and haunted, what will solitude mean?

1984–1985   1986

2. Respectively, detailed study and analysis of the Scriptures, and meritorious acts; *chai*: medallion with the Hebrew symbol for "life."
3. Symbol in the shape of a cross with its arms bent at right angles, adopted by the Nazis as their symbol.
4. Current term for a species of animal that, because of human depredation, is threatened by extinction.
5. Justice is often depicted as a female, wearing a blindfold.
6. Compare, from Whitman's "Out of the Cradle Endlessly Rocking," the line, "Out of the mocking-bird's throat, the musical shuttle." "There was a real mockingbird singing in the tree outside of the window where I was working day after day, the most wonderful, wonderful series of songs, of poetic compositions. But that mockingbird transplaced into the poem conjures up that America that Whitman imagined and believed in. Because although he depicts slavery, he depicts hard labor, he depicts prostitution (he names those things),

Whitman's America is very different from the America of my poem" (from Rich's talk); earlier she had said, "I had to address Jeffers in this poem—I knew that. I didn't know I was going to be also in dialogue with Whitman."
7. High land jutting out into the sea; the "prophet" is possibly Jonah (see note below) or Jeffers.
8. The "leviathan" or sea beast that swallows Jonah is often identified as a whale, in California an "endangered species." Since Jonah repents and is released, the Book of Jonah is read in the synagogue on the afternoon of Yom Kippur as an example of the Lord's clemency toward those who repent. As Rich sees him, Jonah "has this terribly personal connection with God and he's arguing with God, trying to disobey God as hard as he can, and is still so connected to God . . . [It gives] Jonah a sense of his ultimate identity and existence and reality" (from Rich's talk).
9. That is, supposed to be (literally, given certain rights by a charter, or document).

THOM GUNN
b. 1929

Thom Gunn is one of the English poets who began to publish during the fifties and who constituted themselves as a third force in the development of contemporary English poetry. They rejected what seemed to them the Romantic excesses of the New Apocalypse (whose most prominent exponent was Dylan Thomas), and they were equally dissatisfied with the modernist revolution led by Pound and Eliot, who, Gunn contends, abandoned important traditional resources of poetry by deciding "to strengthen the images while either banishing concepts or, where they couldn't avoid them, treating them to the same free association as images."[1] The Movement, of which Gunn was one of the youngest members, sought greater concreteness and a less high-flown diction for poetry; he argues that poetry is "impoverished unless one can include the whole of one's attempt to understand the world"—the quotidian as well as the extraordinary.

Unlike much Movement poetry, Gunn's is never cautious, nor does it seem especially English. By the time of his inclusion in *New Lines* (1956), the anthology which announced the Movement to the world, he had been living in California for two years, had studied at Stanford University, where he met Yvor Winters and J. V. Cunningham, two American poets whose esthetic he found congenial, and had won a prize from *Poetry* magazine in Chicago. He writes of Cunningham's work that it uses a higher proportion of abstract words than usual in Anglo-American poetry since the Imagist movement. But Gunn also praises his contemporaries Gary Snyder and Ted Hughes, poets as different from each other as they are from Cunningham but whose work shares with Gunn's own latest poems an informed and sometimes ecstatic identification with the natural world.

Gunn's poems are often concerned with action, or at times merely "the sense of movement" (as he has entitled one of his books), as an existential proof that one has not yet submitted to the conclusive inertness of death. In "Elegy on the Dust," he observes that all "who sought distinction hard" are inevitably brought to the ultimate democracy of dust; the dust remains, imitating the motion of life, but is as purposeless as the "purposeless matter" which "hovers in the dark" after a nuclear catastrophe in another poem, "The Annihilation of Nothing." The faceless soldiers in "Innocence" and "The Byrnies," hardened into instruments of death, are at least capable of action, however limited their choices.

Thomson William Gunn was born in Gravesend, Kent, on August 29, 1929. During his first ten years his family moved often, as his father, a journalist, worked for several different newspapers. After serving for two years in the British Army, he went to Paris, where for several months he worked in the offices of the Métro (the Paris subway) while trying to write a novel. He then matriculated at Trinity College, Cambridge University, where he wrote his first published poems. In 1953 he received his B.A., published his first book of verse, and went to Rome for six months before entering Stanford University as a graduate student. Except for a year teaching in San Antonio, Texas, and occasional travels to England, Gunn has lived in San Francisco ever since, and from 1958 until 1966 taught at the University of California at Berkeley. Since 1975 he has been Visiting Lecturer there. Besides his own books of verse, he has collaborated with his brother Ander Gunn on a book of photographs and verse, *Positives* (1966), and has edited selections of poems by Ben Jonson and Fulke Greville.

1. *Yale Review* 53, 447–80.

The Byrnies[1]

The heroes paused upon the plain.
When one of them but swayed, ring mashed on ring:
   Sound of the byrnie's knitted chain,
Vague evocations of the constant Thing.

   They viewed beyond a salty hill   5
Barbaric forest, mesh of branch and root
   —A huge obstruction growing still,
Darkening the land, in quietness absolute.

   That dark was fearful—lack of presence—
Unless some man could chance upon or win   10
   Magical signs to stay the essence
Of the broad light that they adventured in.

   Elusive light of light that went
Flashing on water, edging round a mass,
   Inching across fat stems, or spent   15
Lay thin and shrunk among the bristling grass.

   Creeping from sense to craftier sense,
Acquisitive, and loss their only fear,
   These men had fashioned a defence
Against the nicker's snap, and hostile spear.   20

   Byrnie on byrnie! as they turned
They say light trapped between the man-made joints,
   Central in every link it burned,
Reduced and steadied to a thousand points.

   Thus for each blunt-faced ignorant one   25
The great grey rigid uniform combined
   Safety with virtue of the sun.
Thus concepts linked like chainmail in the mind.

   Reminded, by the grinding sound,
Of what they sought, and partly understood,   30
   They paused upon that open ground,
A little group above the foreign wood.

                        1961

My Sad Captains

One by one they appear in
the darkness: a few friends, and
a few with historical
names. How late they start to shine!
but before they fade they stand   5
perfectly embodied, all

---

1. Coats of mail (Middle English).

the past lapping them like a
cloak of chaos. They were men
who, I thought, lived only to
renew the wasteful force they   10
spent with each hot convulsion.
They remind me, distant now.

True, they are not at rest yet,
but now that they are indeed
apart, winnowed from failures,   15
they withdraw to an orbit
and turn with disinterested
hard energy, like the stars.

                                                 1961

Moly[2]

Nightmare of beasthood, snorting, how to wake.
I woke. What beasthood skin she made me take?

Leathery toad that ruts for days on end,
Or cringing dribbling dog, man's servile friend,

Or cat that prettily pounces on its meat,   5
Tortures it hours, then does not care to eat:

Parrot, moth, shark, wolf, crocodile, ass, flea.
What germs, what jostling mobs there were in me.

These seem like bristles, and the hide is tough.
No claw or web here: each foot ends in hoof.   10

Into what bulk has method disappeared?
Like ham, streaked. I am gross—grey, gross, flap-eared.

The pale-lashed eyes my only human feature.
My teeth tear, tear. I am the snouted creature

That bites through anything, root, wire, or can.   15
If I was not afraid I'd eat a man.

Oh a man's flesh already is in mine.
Hand and foot poised for risk. Buried in swine.

I root and root, you think that it is greed,
It is, but I seek out a plant I need.   20

Direct me gods, whose changes are all holy,
To where it flickers deep in grass, the moly:

2. A magic herb of Greek mythology. The enchantress Circe transformed Odysseus's shipmates into swine; Odysseus, protected by the herb moly, which he had been given by the gods' messenger Hermes, compelled her to restore them to human shape.

Cool flesh of magic in each leaf and shoot,
From milk flower to the black forked root.

From this fat dungeon I could rise to skin   25
And human title, putting pig within.

I push my big grey wet snout through the green,
Dreaming the flower I have never seen.

                                                              1971

Autobiography

The sniff of the real, that's
what I'd want to get
            how it felt
to sit on Parliament
Hill[3] on a May evening   5
studying for exams   skinny
seventeen   dissatisfied
            yet sniffing such
a potent air, smell of
grass in heat from   10
the day's sun

I'd been walking through the damp
rich ways by the ponds
and now lay on the upper
grass with Lamartine's[4] poems   15

life seemed all
loss, and what was more
I'd lost whatever it was
before I'd even had it

a green dry prospect   20
distant babble of children
and beyond, distinct at
the end of the glow
St Paul's like a stone thimble[5]

longing so hard to make   25
inclusions that the longing has
become   in memory
an inclusion

                                                              1976

Donahue's Sister

She comes level with him at
the head of the stairs

with a slight, arrogant smile
and an inward look, muttering
some injunction to her private world.   5
Drunk for four days now.

He's unable to get through.
She's not there to get through to.
When he does get through,
next week, it will all sound   10
exaggerated. She will apologize as if
all too humanly she has caused him
a minute inconvenience.

That sudden tirade last night,
such conviction and logic   15
—had she always hated him or
was it the zombie speaking?

Scotch for breakfast,
beer all morning.
Fuelling her private world, in which   20
she builds her case against the public.
Catching at ends of phrases
in themselves meaningless,
as if to demonstrate how well
she keeps abreast.   25
          A zombie,
inaccessible and sodden replacement.

He glances at her, her
body stands light and meatless,
and estimates how high he would have   30
to lift it to launch it
into a perfect trajectory over
the narrow dark staircase
so that it would land on its head
on the apartment-house mosaic of the hallway   35
and its skull would break in two
—an eggshell full of alcohol—
leaving, at last, his sister
lying like the garbage by the front door
in a pool of Scotch and beer,   40
understandably, this time, inaccessible.

1982

DEREK WALCOTT
b. 1930

Derek Walcott was born in 1930 on the island of St. Lucia, one of the four Windward
Islands. Although he has been a constant and fortunate (his word) traveler, the center
of his affections and allegiances, the landscape of his memory and his imagination,
remains his natal island in the eastern Caribbean. Despite his devotion to his own
culture, Walcott's account of his early years suggests that he was a little the outsider.

Derek Walcott

:ared a Methodist in a society which was largely Roman Catholic; his father,
when Walcott was not yet a year old, was a talented amateur painter; and
......er, a schoolteacher, had a collection of the English classics, which she
encouraged her son to read. Walcott's probable vocation for a time seemed to be
painting. He informally apprenticed himself to a local painter; and from him Walcott
learned the discipline of art. He later related this interest in craft to his religious
upbringing. "There is," he has said in an interview, "a very strong sense of carpentry
in Protestantism, in making things simply and in a utilitarian way. . . . I think of
myself in a way as a carpenter, as one making frames simply and well."[1] But his
religious training encouraged him in a view of poetry where craft serves as an accom-
plice, but surely not the whole justification. "I have never," he said in the same
interview, "separated the writing of poetry from prayer. I have grown up believing
it is a vocation, a religious vocation."[2]

Although in the wittily titled "A Far Cry from Africa" he speaks of the conflict
between his loyalties to Africa and to the "English tongue I love," Walcott as a poet
seems to be on good terms with his English cultural inheritance. His subject is frequently human isolation, an isolation heightened by the blazing inhumanity of the
tropical landscapes, but Walcott shows no evidence of isolation from the traditions of
English poetry. He does not compulsively define and redefine his dilemmas only in
terms of race. In "Codicil," for example, it is the language of journalism by which
the poet earns his living—a "hack's hired prose," as he calls it—that delays the
achievement of poetic speech and personal fulfillment. "To change your language,"
he reminds himself, "you must change your life."

Walcott, particularly in recent years, has taken on new landscapes and new subjects: he has taken a particular delight in transforming paintings into poems, a splendid instance of the cultivation of two talents, but he insists that some of the qualities
of his verse—its copiousness, its splendid opulence—are part of his Caribbean inheritance. In a tribute to his own culture, he says, "I come from a place that likes
grandeur; it likes large gestures; it is not inhibited by flourish; it is a rhetorical society; it is a society of physical performance; it is a society of style. . . . Modesty is not
possible in performance in the Caribbean, and that's wonderful. It is better to be
large and make huge gestures than to be modest and do tiptoeing types of presenta-
tions of oneself."[3]

Walcott was fourteen when one of his poems was published in a newspaper, and
four years later he published a booklet of twenty-five poems. The money for this
project came from his mother, who could little spare it; he hawked the pamphlet
throughout the island and was able to pay the money back. The next year his play
Henry Christophe was produced. In 1950 he left St. Lucia and entered the University of the West Indies in Jamaica, from which he received a B.A. in 1953. His poetry
began to attract international attention when *In a Green Night* (1962) was published
in England, and he has achieved growing success as a dramatist. Recently he has
spent much time in the United States. He holds a MacArthur Fellowship, and teaches
at Boston University.

1. Derek Walcott, "The Art of Poetry," *Paris Review* 47, 206.

2. The same, p. 203.
3. The same, p. 209.

A Far Cry from Africa

A wind is ruffling the tawny pelt
Of Africa. Kikuyu,[1] quick as flies,

1. An African tribe whose members, as Mau Mau fighters, conducted an eight-year campaign of ter-
rorism against British colonial settlers in Kenya.

Batten upon the bloodstreams of the veldt.
Corpses are scattered through a paradise.
Only the worm, colonel of carrion, cries: 5
'Waste no compassion on these separate dead!'
Statistics justify and scholars seize
The salients of colonial policy.
What is that to the white child hacked in bed?
To savages, expendable as Jews?   10

Threshed out by beaters,[2] the long rushes break
In a white dust of ibises whose cries
Have wheeled since civilization's dawn
From the parched river or beast-teeming plain.
The violence of beast on beast is read   15
As natural law, but upright man
Seeks his divinity by inflicting pain.
Delirious as these worried beasts, his wars
Dance to the tightened carcass of a drum,
While he calls courage still that native dread   20
Of the white peace contracted by the dead.

Again brutish necessity wipes its hands
Upon the napkins of a dirty cause, again
A waste of our compassion, as with Spain,[3]
The gorilla wrestles with the superman.   25

I who am poisoned with the blood of both,
Where shall I turn, divided to the vein?
I who have cursed
The drunken officer of British rule, how choose
Between this Africa and the English tongue I love? 30
Betray them both, or give back what they give?
How can I face such slaughter and be cool?
How can I turn from Africa and live?

                                                   1962

Codicil

Schizophrenic, wrenched by two styles,
one a hack's hired prose, I earn
my exile. I trudge this sickle, moonlit beach for miles,

tan, burn
to slough off   5
this love of ocean that's self-love.

To change your language you must change your life.

I cannot right old wrongs.
Waves tire of horizon and return.
Gulls screech with rusty tongues   10

---

2. In African game hunting, natives are hired
to beat the brush, chasing birds and animals from
their hiding places.

3. Perhaps a reference to the massacres inflicted
on both sides during the Spanish Civil War of 1936–
39.

Above the beached, rotting pirogues,
they were a venomous beaked cloud at Charlotteville.[4]

Once I thought love of country was enough,
now, even I chose, there's no room at the trough.

I watch the best minds root like dogs   15
for scraps of favour.
I am nearing middle-

age, burnt skin
peels from my hand like paper, onion-thin,
like Peer Gynt's riddle.[5]   20

At heart there's nothing, not the dread
of death. I know too many dead.
They're all familiar, all in character,

even how they died. On fire,
the flesh no longer fears that furnace mouth   25
of earth,

that kiln or ashpit of the sun,
nor this clouding, unclouding sickle moon
whitening this beach again like a blank page.

All its indifference is a different rage.   30
                                                                        1965

Frederiksted,[6] Dusk

Sunset, the cheapest of all picture-shows,
was all they waited for; old men like empties
set down from morning outside the almshouse,[7]
to let the rising evening brim their eyes,
and, in one row, return the level stare   5
of light that shares its mortal properties
with the least stone in Frederiksted, as if
more than mortality brightened the air,
like a girl tanning on a rock alone
who fills with light. Whatever it is   10
that leaves bright flesh like sand and turns it chill,
not age alone, they were old, but a state
made possible by their collective will,
would shine in them like something between life
and death, our two concrete simplicities,   15
and waited too in, seeming not to wait,
substantial light and insubstantial stone.
                                                                        1976

---

4. A town on the West Indian island of Tobago.
5. In Ibsen's play, Peer Gynt peels an onion, likening each layer to an aspect of his own character, but discovers that there is nothing at its core.

6. City on the west coast of St. Croix, one of the Virgin Islands in the West Indies.
7. Poorhouse; "empties": that is, empty bottles to be picked up by the milk-deliverer.

Port of Spain[8]

Midsummer stretches before me with a cat's yawn.
Trees with dust on their lips, cars melting down
in a furnace. Heat staggers the drifting mongrels.
The capitol has been repainted rose, the rails
round the parks the color of rusting blood;   5
junta and *coup d'état*,[9] the newest Latino mood,
broods on the balcony. Monotonous lurid bushes
brush the damp air with the ideograms[1] of buzzards
over the Chinese groceries. The oven alleys stifle
where mournful tailors peer over old machines   10
stitching June and July together seamlessly,
and one waits for lightning as the armed sentry
hopes in boredom for the crack of a rifle—
but I feed on its dust, its ordinariness,
on the inertia that fills its exiles with horror,   15
on the dust over the hills with their orange lights,
even on the pilot light in the reeking harbor
that turns like a police car's. The terror
is local, at least. Like the magnolia's whorish whiff.
And the dog barks of the revolution crying wolf.   20

The moon shines like a lost button;
the black water stinks under the sodium lights[2] on
the wharf. The night is turned on as firmly
as a switch, dishes clatter behind bright windows,
I walk along the walls with occasional shadows   25
that say nothing. Sometimes, in narrow doors
there are old men playing the same quiet games—
cards, draughts, dominoes. I give them names.
The night is companionable, the day is as fierce as
our human future anywhere. I can understand   30
Borges's blind love of Buenos Aires,[3]
how a man feels the veins of a city swell in his hand.

1981

The Fortunate Traveller[4]

(*For Susan Sontag*)

And I heard a voice in the midst of the four beasts say,
A measure of wheat for a penny,
and three measures of barley for a penny;
and see thou hurt not the oil and the wine.
—REVELATION 6:6[5]

I

It was in winter. Steeples, spires
congealed like holy candles. Rotting snow

---

8. Seaport city in Trinidad, island off the northern coast of South America.
9. *Junta:* group seizing governmental power; *coup d'état:* sudden takeover or change in policy.
1. Composite character in Chinese writing.
2. That is, yellow lights.
3. The writer Jorge Luis Borges (1899–1987) was blind; he lived most of his life in Buenos Aires, city in Argentina.
4. Compare the title of the picaresque tale by

Thomas Nashe, *The Unfortunate Traveller* (1593). Sontag is an American philosopher and writer (b. 1933).
5. The narrator of this apocalyptic biblical book hears this voice after the Lamb of God has broken the fourth of six seals, and after he has seen the third of four horses, "a black horse, and he that sat on him had a pair of balances in his hand" (Revelation 6:5). This horseman is often taken to be symbolic of famine.

flaked from Europe's ceiling. A compact man,
I crossed the canal in a gray overcoat,
on one lapel a crimson buttonhole   5
for the cold ecstasy of the assassin.
In the square coffin manacled to my wrist:
small countries pleaded through the mesh of graphs,
in treble-spaced, Xeroxed forms to the World Bank[6]
on which I had scrawled the one word, MERCY;   10

        I sat on a cold bench
under some skeletal lindens.[7]
Two other gentlemen, black skins gone gray
as their identical, belted overcoats,
crossed the white river.   15
They spoke the stilted French
of their dark river,
whose hooked worm, multiplying its pale sickle,
could thin the harvest of the winter streets.[8]
"Then we can depend on you to get us those tractors?"   20
"I gave my word."
"May my county ask you why you are doing this, sir?"
Silence.
"You know if you betray us, you cannot hide?"
A tug. Smoke trailing its dark cry.   25

At the window in Haiti, I remember
a gekko[9] pressed against the hotel glass,
with white palms, concentrating head.
With a child's hands. Mercy, monsieur. Mercy.
Famine sighs like a scythe   30
across the field of statistics and the desert
is a moving mouth. In the hold of this earth
10,000,000 shoreless souls are drifting.
Somalia:[1] 765,000, their skeletons will go under the tidal sand.
"We'll meet you in Bristol[2] to conclude the agreement?"   35
Steeples like tribal lances, through congealing fog
the cries of wounded churchbells wrapped in cotton,
gray mist enfolding the conspirator
like a sealed envelope next to its heart.

No one will look up now to see the jet   40
fade like a weevil[3] through a cloud of flour.
One flies first-class, one is so fortunate.
Like a telescope reversed, the traveller's eye.
swiftly screws down the individual sorrow
to an oval nest of antic numerals,   45
and the iris, interlocking with this globe,
condenses it to zero, then a cloud.

---

6. An international loan association.
7. Large European trees, used for city and street planting.
8. "Sickle" refers both to the crescent-shaped farming tool used for cutting grain and to the sickle-cell disease (in which the red blood cells take on crescent shape), to which Blacks are especially prone.
9. Small tropical lizard, with feet that look not unlike human palms.
1. East African republic, site of recent famines.
2. Industrial and shipping city in southwestern England.
3. Insect whose larvae eat grain and flour.

Beetle-black taxi from Heathrow to my flat.[4]
We are roaches,
riddling the state cabinets, entering the dark holes   50
of power, carapaced in topcoats,[5]
scuttling around columns, signalling for taxis,
with frantic antennae, to other huddles with roaches;
we infect with optimism, and when
the cabinets crack, we are the first   55
to scuttle, radiating separately
back to Geneva, Bonn, Washington, London.

Under the dripping planes of Hampstead Heath,[6]
I read her letter again, watching the drizzle
disfigure its pleading like mascara. Margo,   60
I cannot bear to watch the nations cry.
Then the phone: "We will pay you in Bristol."
Days in fetid bedclothes swallowing cold tea,
the phone stifled by the pillow. The telly
a blue storm with soundless snow.   65
I'd light the gas and see a tiger's tongue.
I was rehearsing the ecstasies of starvation
for what I had to do. *And have not charity.*[7]

I found my pity, desperately researching
the origins of history, from reed-built communes   70
by sacred lakes, turning with the first sprocketed
water-driven wheels. I smelled imagination
among bestial hides by the gleam of fat,
seeking in all races a common ingenuity.
I envisaged an Africa flooded with such light   75
as alchemized[8] the first fields of emmer wheat and barley,
when we savages dyed our pale dead with ochre,
and bordered our temples
with the ceremonial vulva of the conch
in the gray epoch of the obsidian adze.[9]   80
I sowed the Sahara with rippling cereals,[1]
my charity fertilized these aridities.

What was my field? Late sixteenth century.
My field was a dank acre. A Sussex don,
I taught the Jacobean anxieties: *The White Devil.*[2]   85
Flamineo's torch startles the brooding yews.
The drawn end comes in strides. I loved my Duchess,[3]

---

4. Britishism for apartment; Heathrow is one of the two major English airports.
5. The coats are compared to the hard outer shells of insects.
6. Park in the London suburb of Hampstead; "planes": plane trees, common in cities.
7. "Though I speak with the tongues of men and of angels, and have not charity, I am become as sounding brass, or a tinkling cymbal" (1 Corinthians 13:1).
8. That is, transmuted; "emmer wheat": a hard red wheat.
9. "Ochre": red or yellow clay; "bordered . . . conch": that is, decorated our temples with the innermost parts of conch shells; "obsidian adze": primitive cutting tool made of volcanic glass.
1. That is, planted grain.
2. Dark revenge tragedy by John Webster, written in the early seventeenth century ("Jacobean"), a pessimistic time by contrast with the more optimistic Elizabethan age. "Don": British university teacher; "Yews": evergreen trees; they are often associated with grief, as are "cypresses" below (line 89).
3. Flamineo is the Machiavellian villain in *The White Devil*; "the Duchess" is Vittoria Corombona, its heroine.

the white flame of her soul blown out between
the smoking cypresses. Then I saw children pounce
on green meat with a rat's ferocity.   90

I called them up and took the train to Bristol,
my blood the Severn's dregs and silver.
On Severn's estuary[4] the pieces flash,
Iscariot's salary,[5] patron saint of spies.
I thought, who cares how many million starve?   95
Their rising souls will lighten the world's weight
and level its gull-glittering waterline;
we left at sunset down the estuary.

England recedes. The forked white gull
screeches, circling back.   100
Even the birds are pulled back by their orbit,
even mercy has its magnetic field.
                            Back in the cabin,
I uncap the whisky, the porthole
mists with glaucoma.[6] By the time I'm pissed,   105
England, England will be
that pale serrated indigo[7] on the sea-line.
"You are so fortunate, you get to see the world—"
Indeed, indeed, sirs, I have seen the world.
Spray splashes the portholes and vision blurs.   110

Leaning on the hot rail, watching the hot sea,
I saw them far off, kneeling on hot sand
in the pious genuflections of the locust,
as Ponce's armored knees crush Florida[8]
to the funeral fragrance of white lilies.   115

II

Now I have to come to where the phantoms live,
I have no fear of phantoms, but of the real.
The sabbath benedictions[9] of the islands.
Treble clef of the snail on the scored leaf,
the Tantum Ergo[1] of black choristers   120
soars through the organ pipes of coconuts.
Across the dirty beach surpliced[2] with lace,
they pass a brown lagoon behind the priest,
pale and unshaven in his frayed soutane,
into the concrete church at Canaries;[3]   125
as Albert Schweitzer moves to the harmonium[4]

4. Water passage where a river meets the sea; the Severn is a river that flows past Bristol.
5. That is, the thirty pieces of silver which Judas Iscariot received for betraying Christ (Matthew 26: 14–16).
6. As one's eyes would mist if one had glaucoma.
7. That is, like dark blue saw teeth.
8. Ponce de Leon, Spanish explorer, discovered Florida in 1513 and attempted to conquer the Indians there in 1521.
9. That is, holy-day blessings.
1. "So much therefore" (from a Latin mass).
2. White ecclesiastical overgarment.
3. Mountain on the island of Santa Lucia in the West Indies; "soutane": priest's robe.
4. Schweitzer (1875–1965) was a musician and organist who became a medical missionary in Africa in 1913; in the jungle, his instrument was the "harmonium," a small reed organ.

of morning, and to the pluming chimneys,
the groundswell lifts *Lebensraum, Lebensraum.*[5]

Black faces sprinkled with continual dew—
dew on the speckled croton, dew
on the hard leaf of the knotted plum tree,   130
dew on the elephant ears of the dasheen.[6]
Through Kurtz's teeth, white skull in elephant grass,
the imperial fiction sings. Sunday
wrinkles downriver from the Heart of Darkness.[7]   135
The heart of darkness is not Africa.
The heart of darkness is the core of fire
in the white center of the holocaust.
The heart of darkness is the rubber claw
selecting a scalpel in antiseptic light,   140
the hills of children's shoes outside the chimneys,
the tinkling nickel instruments on the white altar;
Jacob,[8] in his last card, sent me these verses:
"Think of a God who doesn't lose His sleep
if trees burst into tears or glaciers weep.   145
So, aping His indifference, I write now,
not Anno Domini: After Dachau."[9]

III

The night maid brings a lamp and draws the blinds.
I stay out on the veranda with the stars.
Breakfast congealed to supper on its plate.   150

There is no sea as restless as my mind.
The promontories snore. They snore like whales.
Cetus, the whale, was Christ.[1]
The ember dies, the sky smokes like an ash heap.
Reeds wash their hands of guilt and the lagoon   155
is stained. Louder, since it rained,
a gauze of sand flies hisses from the marsh.

Since God is dead, and these are not His stars,
but man-lit, sulphurous, sanctuary lamps,
it's in the heart of darkness of this earth   160
that backward tribes keep vigil of His Body,[2]
in deya, lampion,[3] and this bedside lamp.
Keep the news from their blissful ignorance.
Like lice, like lice, the hungry of this earth
swarm to the tree of life. If those who starve   165

5. Space required for life.
6. Starchy edible plant of the tropics; "croton": castor-oil plant.
7. Title of novella (1902) by the Polish-English novelist Joseph Conrad; Kurtz, the man who is the goal of the narrator's search in the Congo, is finally depicted as having seen into the very heart of corruption.
8. Very likely Jacob Timmerman, Argentinian journalist and editor imprisoned and tortured for anti-government writings.

9. Concentration camp operated by the Nazis, liberated in 1945.
1. The fish, representing Christ, was one of the earliest symbols in Christian art.
2. "Sanctuary lamps" refers to the practice in high Catholic churches of keeping a lamp lit above the altar (i.e., "sanctuary") when a consecrated wafer is present; since in Holy Communion the wafer represents Christ's body, this practice is a "vigil of His Body."
3. Small lamp.

like these rain-flies who shed glazed wings in light
grew from sharp shoulder blades their brittle vans
and soared toward that tree, how it would seethe—
ah, Justice! But fires
drench them like vermin, quotas   170
prevent them, and they remain
compassionate fodder for the travel book,
its paragraphs like windows from a train,
for everywhere that earth shows its rib cage
and the moon goggles with the eyes of children,   175
we turn away to read. Rimbaud learned that.
                                          Rimbaud, at dusk,
idling his wrist in water past temples
the plumed dates still protect in Roman file,[4]
knew that we cared less for one human face   180
than for the scrolls in Alexandria's ashes,[5]
that the bright water could not dye his hand
any more than poetry. The dhow's[6] silhouette
moved through the blinding coinage of the river
that, endlessly, until we pay one debt,   185
shrouds, every night, an ordinary secret.

                                    IV

The drawn sword comes in strides.
It stretches for the length of the empty beach;
the fishermen's huts shut their eyes tight.
A frisson[7] shakes the palm trees,   190
and sweats on the traveller's tree.
They've found out my sanctuary. Philippe, last night:
"It had two gentlemen in the village yesterday, sir,
asking for you while you was in town.
I tell them you was in town. They send to tell you,   195
there is no hurry. They will be coming back."

In loaves of cloud, *and have not charity*,
the weevil will make a sahara of Kansas,
the ant shall eat Russia.
Their soft teeth shall make, *and have not charity*,   200
the harvest's desolation,
and the brown globe crack like a begging bowl,
and though you fire oceans of surplus grain,
and have not charity,

still, through thin stalks,   205
the smoking stubble, stalks
grasshopper: third horseman,
the leather-helmed locust.[8]

                                                                       1981

---

4. Single file. Arthur Rimbaud, nineteenth-
century French poet, spent the last ten years of
his life in North Africa.
   5. Many of the scrolls in the great Alexandrian
Library (in Egypt) were destroyed by fire in 47
B.C.

6. Arab boat.
7. Shiver.
8. Predatory insects, compared to the third
horseman of the Apocalypse, famine. Compare the
epigraph and note 4.

GARY SNYDER
b. 1930

In the summer of 1948, after he had finished his freshman year at college, Gary Snyder shipped out of New York as an ordinary seaman. "Going to sea," he has said, "was part of a long growth and extension of my sympathies and sensibilities outside simply one area and to many classes and kinds of people and many parts of the world so that now I feel at home everywhere."[1] The notion of life as an odyssey through space and time and of his poems as progress reports, entries in the explorer's journal, is essential to Snyder. His goal is a poise of the mind which will allow him to stand serenely in the midst of conflicting perspectives. Snyder has managed to "feel at home everywhere," not only by visiting foreign places, by investigating alien cultures and submitting himself to their initiatory rituals, but also by an imaginative investigation into the recesses of our common human past. "As poet," Snyder writes, "I hold the most archaic values on earth. They go back to the late Paleolithic: the fertility of the soil, the magic of animals, the power-vision in solitude, the terrifying initiation and re-birth, the love and ecstasy of the dance, the common work of the tribe. I try to hold both history and wilderness in mind, that my poems may approach the true measure of things and stand against the unbalance and ignorance of our times."[2] In Zen Buddhism Snyder has found his way of getting back beyond the archaic to the pre-verbal experience which must unite us with humankind. With characteristic evenhandedness he grants that the poet faces in two directions: "one is to the world of people and language and society, and the other is to the nonhuman, nonverbal world, which is nature as nature is itself; and the world of human nature—the inner world—as it is itself, before language, before customs, before culture. There's no words in that world. There aren't any rules that we know and that's the area that Buddhism studies."[3]

Snyder's is not a superficial acquaintance with Oriental religion and culture; from 1965 to 1968 he studied with a Zen master in Japan, and was described by Kenneth Rexroth as a Buddhist monk. From these studies, and perhaps also from Pound and Williams, Snyder finds direction in his search for the wordless "world of human nature," and takes delight in the bright, particular grains of experience of nature "as nature is itself."

Snyder, though he wholeheartedly rejects mid-twentieth-century American society, does not indulge in a sentimental rejection of society as such. He has worked at a variety of trades and occupations, writes his poetry out of these experiences, and relates the rhythm of sequences of poems with the rhythms of particular occupations.

Gary Snyder was born in San Francisco on May 8, 1930, and was brought up in Oregon and Washington. He received his B.A. in anthropology from Reed College in 1951. He worked as a logger and a Forest Service trail crew member in the Pacific Northwest, then returned to California to study Oriental languages at Berkeley from 1953 to 1956, during which time he also joined Allen Ginsberg, Jack Kerouac, and others in what turned into the Beat movement, and wrote the poems later published as *Myths and Texts* (1960). (Kerouac used Snyder as the protagonist of his novel *The Dharma Bums*.) From 1956 until 1964 he lived mainly in Japan, though he visited India for a year and also worked as a hand on an American tanker in the Indian and South Pacific oceans. He returned to the United States in 1964 to teach at the University of California at Berkeley, then returned to Japan to study Buddhism of the Mahayana-Vajrayana school; some of his experiences are told in the prose book *Earth House Hold* (1969), which is written in the Japanese form of the poetic travel journal. His many books of poems include a number of translations from ancient and modern

1. Quoted in David Kherdian, *Six San Francisco Poets*, Fresno, Calif., 1969, p. 22.

2. The same, p. 26.
3. The same, p. 35.

Japanese poetry. In 1975 he was awarded the Pulitzer Prize. Twice divorced, he now
lives in the United States with his Japanese wife and their son Kai, who is described
in "Axe Handles."

Riprap[1]

Lay down these words
Before your mind like rocks.
        placed solid, by hands
In choice of place, set
Before the body of the mind   5
        in space and time:
Solidity of bark, leaf, or wall
        riprap of things:
Cobble of milky way,
        straying planets,   10
These poems, people,
        lost ponies with
Dragging saddles—
        and rocky sure-foot trails.
The worlds like an endless   15
        four-dimensional
Game of Go.[2]
        ants and pebbles
In the thin loam, each rock a word
        a creek-washed stone   20
Granite: ingrained
        with torment of fire and weight
Crystal and sediment linked hot
        all change, in thoughts,
As well as things.   25

1959

Four Poems for Robin

Siwashing It[3] Out Once in Siuslaw Forest

I slept under   rhododendron
All night   blossoms fell
Shivering on   a sheet of cardboard
Feet stuck   in my pack
Hands deep   in my pockets   5
Barely   able   to   sleep.
I remembered   when we were in school
Sleeping together   in a big warm bed
We were   the youngest lovers
When we broke up   we were still nineteen.   10
Now our   friends are married

1. "A cobble of stone laid on steep slick rock to
make a trail for horses in the mountains" (Snyder's
note).
2. Ancient Japanese game played with black and
white stones, placed one after the other on a
checkered board.
3. Camping or traveling with minimal equipment; roughing it. Siuslaw Forest is west of
Eugene, Oregon.

You teach   school back east
I dont mind   living this way
Green hills   the long blue beach
But sometimes   sleeping in the open   15
I think back   when I had you.

A Spring Night in Shokoku-ji[4]

Eight years ago this May
We walked under cherry blossoms
At night in an orchard in Oregon.
All that I wanted then
Is forgotten now, but you.   5
Here is the night
In a garden of the old capital
I feel the trembling ghost of Yugao[5]
I remember your cool body
Naked under a summer cotton dress.   10

An Autumn Morning in Shokoku-ji

Last night watching the Pleiades,[6]
Breath smoking in the moonlight,
Bitter memory like vomit
Choked my throat.
I unrolled a sleeping bag   5
On mats on the porch
Under thick autumn stars.
In dream you appeared
(Three times in nine years)
Wild, cold, and accusing.   10
I woke shamed and angry:
The pointless wars of the heart.
Almost dawn. Venus and Jupiter.
The first time I have
Ever seen them close.   15

December at Yase[7]

You said, that October,
In the tall dry grass by the orchard
When you chose to be free,
"Again someday, maybe ten years."

After college I saw you   5
One time. You were strange.
And I was obsessed with a plan.

Now ten years and more have
Gone by: I've always known

---

4. A Zen monastery built in the fourteenth century in Kyoto, the ancient capital of Japan.
5. The ghost of the lady Yugao appears to a priest in the Japanese Nō play of the same name.

6. A group of seven brilliant stars in the constellation of Taurus (the Bull).
7. A subdistrict adjoining northeast Kyoto.

where you were—   10
I might have gone to you
Hoping to win your love back.
You still are single.

I didn't.
I thought I must make it alone. I   15
Have done that.

Only in dream, like this dawn,
Does the grave, awed intensity
Of our young love
Return to my mind, to my flesh.   20

We had what the others
All crave and seek for;
We left it behind at nineteen.

I feel ancient, as though I had
Lived many lives.   25

And may never now know
If I am a fool
Or have done what my
        karma[8] demands.

                                                        1968

Axe Handles

One afternoon the last week in April
Showing Kai[9] how to throw a hatchet
One-half turn and it sticks in a stump.
He recalls the hatchet-head
Without a handle, in the shop   5
And go gets it, and wants it for his own.
A broken-off axe handle behind the door
Is long enough for a hatchet,
We cut it to length and take it
With the hatchet head   10
And working hatchet, to the wood block.
There I begin to shape the old handle
With the hatchet, and the phrase
First learned from Ezra Pound[1]
Rings in my ears!   15
"When making an axe handle
        the pattern is not far off."
And I say this to Kai
"Look: We'll shape the handle
By checking the handle   20
Of the axe we cut with—"

8. In Buddhism, the force generated by one's   the cycle of rebirth.
actions that determines the nature of one's next   9. Snyder's son.
incarnation, and that prevents one's liberation from   1. American poet; see above, p. 214.

And he sees. And I hear it again:
It's in Lu Ji's *Wên Fu*, fourth century
A.D. "Essay on Literature"—in the
Preface: "In making the handle   25
Of an axe
By cutting wood with an axe
The model is indeed near at hand."
My teacher Shih-hsiang Chen
Translated that and taught it years ago   30
And I see: Pound was an axe,
Chen was an axe, I am an axe
And my son a handle, soon
To be shaping again, model
And tool, craft of culture,   35
How we go on.

                                               1983

Getting in the Wood

The sour smell,
    blue stain,
        water squirts out round the wedge,

Lifting quarters of rounds[2]
    covered with ants,
        "a living glove of ants upon my hand"   5
the poll of the sledge a bit peened over
so the wedge springs off[3] and tumbles
    ringing like high-pitched bells
        into the complex duff[4] of twigs   10
        poison oak, bark, sawdust,
        shards[5] of logs,

And the sweat drips down.
    Smell of crushed ants.
The lean and heave on the peavey   15
that breaks free the last of a bucked
    three-foot round,[6]
        it lies flat on smashed oaklings

Wedge and sledge, peavey and maul,[7]
    little axe, canteen, piggyback can   20
of saw-mix gas and oil for the chain,[8]
knapsack of files and goggles and rags,

All to gather the dead and the down.[9]
    the young men throw splits on the piles

2. Small logs.
3. The speaker is splitting logs by "sledge"-hammering a wedge into them; here, the flat end of the hammer ("poll") has hit the wedge at the wrong angle ("peened") so that the wedge flies out of the log.
4. Decayed organic matter on a forest floor.
5. Fragments.
6. Sawed-up three-foot log; "peavey": logger's

tool with spike and hook for maneuvering logs.
7. Heavy hammer.
8. Chain saw; "saw-mix gas and oil": a small machine like a chain saw cannot be fueled and lubricated separately; hence the gas and oil for it are mixed. "Piggy-back can": can that can be attached to something else.
9. That is, trees that have died or been felled.

bodies hardening, learning the pace   25
and the smell of tools from this delve[1]
in the winter
         death-topple of elderly oak.
Four cords.[2]

                                                      1983

Geese Gone Beyond

In the cedar canoe gliding and paddling
on mirror-smooth lake;
         a carpet of canada geese
afloat on the water
who talk first noisy   then murmur   5

we stop paddling, let drift.
yellow larch on the shores
morning chill, mist off the
cold gentle mountains beyond

I kneel in the bow   10
in *seiza*, like tea-ceremony
         or watching a Nō play[3]
kneeling, legs aching, silent.

One goose breaks and flies up.

         a rumble of dripping water   15
         beating wings
         full honking sky,
A touch across,
         the trigger,

The one who is the first to feel to go.   20
                                               1983

The Grand Entry

The many American flags
Whip around on horseback,
Carried by cowgirls.
         the whirling lights of pleasure rides,
         the slow whine of an ambulance.   5

Two men on horseback roping head and leg of a calf:
Held immobile, from each end,
         a frieze;[4]
         the crowd's applause;
         released, and scamper off.   10

1. Hollow; "splits": thin pieces of logs.
2. A cord is a stack of wood 4' x 4' x 8'.
3. "In *seiza*": literally, sitting up straight. The
Japanese "tea ceremony" is an elaborate ritual, and
the Nō dance drama highly stylized.
4. As a band of sculpture on a building.

Grassland biome technicians.[5]
More spirit than those alluvial delta
High biomass priest-accountants[6]
Who invented writing—

The announcer speaks again of the flag.   15
          the flag's like a steak: cowboys
          are solar energy-
          grass-to-protein
          conversion-magic priests!

Hamburger offerings all over America   20
Red, white,
and Blue.

Year of the bicentennial,[7]   1983
Nevada County Fair rodeo

Old Woman Nature

Old Woman Nature
naturally has a bag of bones
          tucked away somewhere.
          a whole room full of bones!

A scattering of hair and cartilage   5
          bits in the woods.

A fox scat[8] with hair and a tooth in it.
          a shellmound
                    a bone flake in a streambank.

A purring cat, crunching   10
          the mouse head first,
                    eating on down toward the tail—

The sweet old woman
          calmly gathering firewood in the
                    moon . . .   15

Don't be shocked,
She's heating you some soup.

VII, '81, Seeing Ichikawa Ennosuke in   1983
"Kurozuka"—"Demoness"—at the Kabuki-za in Tokyo[9]

---

5. Literally, technicians who work in the major ecological community ("biome") of the grasslands; that is, cowboys, farmers.
6. "Alluvial delta": flat fan-shaped plain with streams where the river meets the sea, with deposits of earth, as in Egypt; "high biomass": a large amount of living matter; hence the "priest-accountants" are both Egyptian and fat.
7. 1976, the two-hundredth birthday of the United States.
8. Animal dropping.
9. The kabuki is a popular, stylized Japanese drama with singing and dancing.

TED HUGHES
b. 1930

Ted Hughes works with a subject-matter of violence, and his talent in this area has evoked uneasy admiration. He can be compared with Robinson Jeffers, also prone to depiction of brutal acts. Like Jeffers, he has turned to classical as well as to modern violence, his adaptation of Seneca's bloody version of *Oedipus* paralleling Jeffers's portrayal of Agamemnon in *The Tower Beyond Tragedy*. If he looks at nature, he finds there predators and victims; if he shows nature looking at man, as in the crow's-eye view, the same assortment is seen. Perhaps because, as he says, he used to collect animals, birds, and fish as a boy, he "thinks of poems as a sort of animal."[1] He particularly likes, he adds, things that "have a vivid life of their own, outside mine." That life as he writes about it is always anarchic and savage. The poet's imagination whirls with increasing wildness, until some readers long for modulations of this baleful glare, this raucous recognition. These qualities, however, are so rare in English poetry—they are less so in American—and Hughes is so effective as their exponent, that he has attracted, or rather gripped, a considerable audience. He could not have done so by subject alone: his compression, his daring vocabulary, his jarring rhythms all have contributed.

It may be that Hughes longs, as in "Lupercalia," for "this frozen one" to be *touched*, but his poems find a sanctuary in negation: "As the incinerator, as the sun, / As the spider, I had a whole world in my hands. / Flowerlike, I loved nothing."[2] But an index to his own aspiration is evident in his introduction to *A Choice of Emily Dickinson's Verse*,[3] where he speaks with great approval of "her frightening vision" or the sense of an "icy chill," and also of "the conflagration within her." Some blend of fire and ice is the ideal admixture sought in his poems.

In Hughes's Manichaean vision, darkness usually overcomes light. But another aspect of his work appears in *Moortown* (1979), a notebook kept on a farm, which displays an extraordinary intimacy with animals and insects. He has also created new fables, such as *Gaudete* (1977), a book-length narrative about a vicar who is taken off by evil spirits. They form a simulacrum of him, and the simulacrum attracts the farmers' wives into a kind of harem. But he hankers for ordinary life, and so loses the goodwill of the spirits and is destroyed by the angry farmers, while his original wanders about singing hymns to a nameless female deity. That Hughes himself does not often represent ordinary feelings in his verse does not mean that he does not have them. But the expenditure of power is his usual ambiguous theme.

Hughes was born in Mytholmroyd, Yorkshire, on August 17, 1930. He took a B.A. at Cambridge, where after first studying English literature he turned to archeology and anthropology. There he met the American poet Sylvia Plath, who was on a Fulbright Scholarship. They were married in 1956, at first living in the United States, then settling in England. They had two children. But their marriage was troubled, and they were separated at the time of Sylvia Plath's suicide in 1963. As poets they both dealt in raw sensation and lacerated nerves, though Sylvia Plath's work centered in the plight of the victim as that of her husband centered in the consciousness of the predator. Both caught a note in experience of relentless cruelty, which they tried to position in their verse.

Hughes has since remarried. In 1984 he was named Poet Laureate (in succession to John Betjeman), a post he accepted because he thought of England as a tribe for whose chiefs he could write tribal songs.

---

1. *Poetry in the Making*, London, 1967, p. 15.   3. London, 1968.
2. "Mayday on Holderness."

The Thought-Fox

I imagine this midnight moment's forest:
Something else is alive
Beside the clock's loneliness
And this blank page where my fingers move.

Through the window I see no star;   5
Something more near
Though deeper within darkness
Is entering the loneliness:

Cold, delicately as the dark snow,
A fox's nose touches twig, leaf;   10
Two eyes serve a movement, that now
And again now, and now, and now

Sets neat prints into the snow
Between trees, and warily a lame
Shadow lags by stump and in hollow   15
Of a body that is bold to come

Across clearings, an eye,
A widening deepening greenness,
Brilliantly, concentratedly,
Coming about its own business   20

Till, with a sudden sharp hot stink of fox
It enters the dark hole of the head.
The window is starless still; the clock ticks,
The page is printed.

1957

An Otter

I

Underwater eyes, an eel's
Oil of water body, neither fish nor beast is the otter;
Four-legged yet water-gifted, to outfish fish;
With webbed feet and long ruddering tail
And a round head like an old tomcat.   5

Brings the legend of himself
From before wars or burials, in spite of hounds and vermin-poles;
Does not take root like the badger. Wanders, cries;
Gallops along land he no longer belongs to;
Re-enters the water by melting.   10

Of neither water nor land. Seeking
Some world lost when first he dived, that he cannot come at since,
Takes his changed body into the holes of lakes;
As if blind, cleaves the stream's push till he licks
The pebbles of the source; from sea   15

To sea crosses in three nights
Like a king in hiding. Crying to the old shape of the starlit land,
    Over sunken farms where the bats go round,
    Without answer. Till light and birdsong come
    Walloping up roads with the milk wagon.   20

II

The hunt's lost him. Pads on mud,
Among sedges, nostrils a surface bead,
The otter remains, hours. The air,
Circling the globe, tainted and necessary,

Mingling tobacco-smoke, hounds and parsley.   25
Comes carefully to the sunk lungs.
So the self under the eye lies,
Attendant and withdrawn. The otter belongs

In double robbery and concealment—
From water that nourishes and drowns, and from land   30
That gave him his length and the mouth of the hound.
He keeps fat in the limpid integument

Reflections live on. The heart beats thick,
Big trout muscle out of the dead cold;
Blood is the belly of logic; he will lick   35
The fishbone bare. And can take stolen hold

On a bitch otter in a field full
Of nervous horses, but linger nowhere.
Yanked above hounds, reverts to nothing at all,
To this long pelt over the back of a chair.   40
                                                                            1960

Wodwo[1]

What am I? Nosing here, turning leaves over
Following a faint stain on the air to the river's edge
I enter water. What am I to split
The glassy grain of water looking upward I see the bed
Of the river above me upside down very clear   5
What am I doing here in mid-air? Why do I find
this frog so interesting as I inspect its most secret
interior and make it my own? Do these weeds
know me and name me to each other have they
seen me before, do I fit in their world? I seem   10
separate from the ground and not rooted but dropped
out of nothing casually I've no threads

---

1. A Middle English word taken from line 721 of the anonymous poem, *Sir Gawain and the Green Knight*, and translated as "wild man of the woods" or "wood demon." The source, which is the epigraph for the book of which this is the title-poem, describes Gawain's difficult journey to the Green Knight's castle: "Now with serpents he wars, now with savage wolves, / Now with wild men of the woods, that watched from the rocks" (translation by Marie Borroff).

fastening me to anything I can go anywhere
I seem to have been given the freedom
of this place what am I then? And picking   15
bits of bark off this rotten stump gives me
no pleasure and it's no use so why do I do it
me and doing that have coincided very queerly
But what shall I be called am I the first
have I an owner what shape am I what   20
shape am I am I huge if I go
to the end on this way past these trees and past these trees
till I get tired that's touching one wall of me
for the moment if I sit still how everything
stops to watch me I suppose I am the exact centre   25
but there's all this what is it roots
roots roots roots and here's the water
again very queer but I'll go on looking

1967

Crow's First Lesson

God tried to teach Crow how to talk.
"Love," said God. "Say, Love."
Crow gaped, and the white shark crashed into the sea
And went rolling downwards, discovering its own depth.

"No, no," said God, "Say Love. Now try it. LOVE."   5
Crow gaped, and a bluefly, a tsetse,[2] a mosquito
Zoomed out and down
To their sundry flesh-pots.

"A final try," said God. "Now, LOVE."
Crow convulsed, gaped, retched and   10
Man's bodiless prodigious head
Bulbed out onto the earth, with swivelling eyes,
Jabbering protest—

And Crow retched again, before God could stop him.
And woman's vulva dropped over man's neck and tightened.   15
The two struggled together on the grass.
God struggled to part them, cursed, wept—

Crow flew guiltily off.

1970

Roe Deer[3]

In the dawn-dirty light, in the biggest snow of the year
Two blue-dark deer stood in the road, alerted.

---

2. African fly that carries the sleeping-sickness disease.

3. Small European and Asiatic deer, known for their nimbleness and grace.

They had happened into my dimension
The moment I was arriving just there.

They planted their two or three years of secret deerhood   5
Clear on my snow-screen vision of the abnormal

And hesitated in the all-way disintegration
And stared at me. And so for some lasting seconds

I could think the deer were waiting for me
To remember the password and sign   10

That the curtain had blown aside for a moment
And there where the trees were no longer trees, nor the road a road

The deer had come for me.

Then they ducked through the hedge, and upright they rode their legs

Away downhill over a snow-lonely field   15

Towards tree-dark—finally
Seeming to eddy and glide and fly away up

Into the boil[4] of big flakes.
The snow took them and soon their nearby hoofprints as well

Revising its dawn inspiration
Back to the ordinary.
                                                                 1979

Orf[5]

Because his nose and face were one festering sore
That no treatment persuaded, month after month,
And his feet four sores, the same,
Which could only stand and no more,

Because his sickness was converting his growth   5
Simply to strengthening sickness
While his breath wheezed through a mask of flies
No stuff could rid him of

I shot the lamb.
I shot him while he was looking the other way.   10
I shot him between the ears.

He lay down.
His machinery adjusted itself
And his blood escaped, without loyalty.

---

4. Agitation.   5. Sore mouth, a contagious disease of sheep.

But the lamb life in my care   15
Left him where he lay, and stood up in front of me

Asking to be banished,
Asking for permission to be extinct,
For permission to wait, at least,

Inside my head   20
In the radioactive space
From which the meteorite had removed his body.

                                                                1979

GEOFFREY HILL
b. 1932

The poetic scene in England has as one of its dominant presences the powerful and
enigmatic Geoffrey Hill. He is by nature reticent, sardonic, and unyielding, though
his verse presents intense feelings that crisscross each other. Everything he writes is
conscious of itself and ultimately intelligible, though the "drama of reason" as he calls
it[1] is compatible with admiration for mystics like Robert Southwell and St. John of
the Cross.

Hill writes short poems of compressed violence on large and painful subjects, as
for example the concentration camps of Nazi Germany or the Wars of the Roses. He
evokes the terror of nightmare and then controls it by changing perspectives and by
sporadic lyrical grace. His poems exhibit a clenched decision to face the worst life
has to offer. Though they fix their eye on misery, they purify it by their indignant
terseness. Many of the poems are on religious subjects, where Christianity sometimes appears, very tentatively, as a healing presence.

Hill is daring, occasionally witty, linguistically exciting. He aspires to evolve what
he calls "those rare moments in which the inertia of language, which is also the
coercive force of language, seems to have been overcome."[2] The sense of agonized
struggle is inseparable from his achievement.

He was born in Bromsgrove, Worcestershire, on June 18, 1932, the only child of
a police constable and his wife. After attending local schools he went to Keble College of Oxford University. In 1952, while still an undergraduate, he published his
first book of poems. Hill was a professor at the University of Leeds before taking up
a post at Cambridge University.

---

1. Hill, "Redeeming the Time," in *The Lords*   2. "Poetry as Menace and Atonement," the
of Limit, London, 1984, p. 93.   same, p. 2.

In Memory of Jane Fraser

When snow like sheep lay in the fold[1]
And winds went begging at each door
And the far hills were blue with cold
And a cold shroud lay on the moor

She kept the siege. And every day   5
We watched her brooding over death

---

1. Shelter for sheep.

Like a strong bird above its prey.
The room filled with the kettle's breath.

Damp curtains glued against the pane
Sealed time away. Her body froze   10
As if to freeze us all and chain
Creation to a stunned repose.

She died before the world could stir.
In March the ice unloosed the brook
And water ruffled the sun's hair.   15
Dead cones upon the altar shook.

                                                     1959

Requiem for the Plantagenet Kings[2]

For whom the possessed sea littered, on both shores,
Ruinous arms; being fired, and for good,
To sound the constitution of just wars,
Men, in their eloquent fashion, understood.

Relieved of soul, the dropping-back of dust,   5
Their usage, pride, admitted within doors;
At home, under caved chantries,[3] set in trust,
With well-dressed alabaster and proved spurs
They lie; they lie; secure in the decay
Of blood, blood-marks, crowns hacked and coveted,   10
Before the scouring fires of trial-day
Alight on men; before sleeked groin, gored head,
Budge through the clay and gravel, and the sea
Across daubed rock evacuates its dead.

                                                     1959

September Song[4]

born 19.6.32—deported 24.9.42

Undesirable you may have been, untouchable
you were not. Not forgotten
or passed over at the proper time.

As estimated, you died. Things marched,
sufficient, to that end.   5
Just so much Zyklon and leather, patented
terror, so many routine cries.

---

2. The line of English kings from Henry II
(crowned in 1154) to Henry VI (deposed in 1461)—
a period of costly and tumultuous foreign and civil
wars.
   3. Chapels endowed for priests to sing masses
for the souls of those who founded them. Many
chantries have cavelike ceilings of vaulted stone,
and contain effigies—sometimes in alabaster—of
their founders.
   4. The poem is about the gassing of Jews in Nazi
concentration camps; Zyklon-B was the name of
the gas.

(I have made
an elegy for myself it
is true)[5]   10

September fattens on vines. Roses
flake from the wall. The smoke
of harmless fires drifts to my eyes.

This is plenty. This is more than enough.

                                                              1968

From Funeral Music[6]

William de la Pole, Duke of Suffolk: beheaded 1450
John Tiptoft, Earl of Worcester: beheaded 1470
Anthony Woodville, Earl Rivers: beheaded 1483[7]

6

My little son, when you could command marvels
Without mercy, outstare the wearisome
Dragon of sleep, I rejoiced above all—
A stranger well-received in your kingdom.
On those pristine fields I saw humankind   5
As it was named by the Father; fabulous
Beasts rearing in stillness to be blessed.
The world's real cries reached there, turbulence
From remote storms, rumour of solitudes,
A composed mystery. And so it ends.   10
Some parch for what they were; others are made
Blind to all but one vision, their necessity
To be reconciled. I believe in my
Abandonment, since it is what I have.

8

Not as we are but as we must appear,
Contractual ghosts of pity; not as we
Desire life but as they would have us live,
Set apart in timeless colloquy:
So it is required; so we bear witness,   5
Despite ourselves, to what is beyond us,
Each distant sphere of harmony forever

---

5. The critics Christopher Ricks and Jon Stallworthy have pointed out that Hill was born on June
18, 1932 (18.6.32, English-style).
6. "In this sequence I was attempting a florid
grim music broken by grunts and shrieks. . . .
Funeral Music could be called a commination
[denunciation] and an alleluia [that is, song of
praise] for the period popularly but inexactly known
as the Wars of the Roses [1455–1485, for the
English throne, between the noble houses of York
and Lancaster]. It is now customary to play down
the violence of the Wars of the Roses and to present them as dynastic skirmishes fatal, perhaps, to
the old aristocracy but generally of small concern
to the common people . . . In the accounts of the
contemporary chroniclers it was a holocaust" (from
Hill's essay on "Funeral Music").

7. "['Funeral Music'] bears an oblique dedication. In the case of Suffolk the word 'beheaded' is
a retrospective aggrandisement; he was in fact
butchered across the gunwale of a skiff. Tiptoft
enjoyed a degree of ritual, commanding that he
should be decapitated in three strokes 'in honour
of the Trinity'. This was a nice compounding of
orthodox humility and unorthodox arrogance. . . .
The Woodville clan invites irritated dismissal:
pushful, time-serving, it was really not its business to produce a man like Earl Rivers, who was
something of a religious mystic. . . . Suffolk and
Rivers were poets, though quite tame. Tiptoft,
patron of humanist scholars, was known as the
Butcher of England because of his pleasure in
varying the accepted postures of judicial death"
(from Hill's essay).

Poised, unanswerable. If it is without
Consequence when we vaunt and suffer, or
If it is not, all echoes are the same   10
In such eternity. Then tell me, love,
How that should comfort us—or anyone
Dragged half-unnerved out of this worldly place,
Crying to the end 'I have not finished'.

                                                    1968

The Imaginative Life

Evasive souls, of whom the wise lose track,
Die in each night, who, with their day-tongues, sift
The waking-taste of manna[8] or of blood:

The raw magi,[9] part-barbarians,
Entranced by demons and desert frost,   5
By the irregular visions of a god,

Suffragans of the true seraphs.[1] Lust
Writhes, is dumb savage and in their way
As a virulence natural to the earth.

Renewed glories batten on the poor bones;   10
Gargantuan mercies whetted by a scent
Of mortal sweat: as though the sleeping flesh

Adored by Furies,[2] stirred, yawned, were driven
In mid-terror to purging and delight.
As though the dead had *Finis*[3] on their brows.   15

                                                    1968

From An Apology for the Revival of Christian Architecture in England

the spiritual, Platonic old England[4] . . .
—STC, *Anima Poetae*

'Your situation', said Coningsby, looking up
the green and silent valley, 'is absolutely poetic.'
'I try sometimes to fancy', said Mr Millbank,
with a rather fierce smile, 'that I am in
the New World.'
—BENJAMIN DISRAELI, *Coningsby*[5]

1. Quaint Mazes

And, after all, it is to them we return.
Their triumph is to rise and be our hosts:

8. The food miraculously supplied to the Israelites in the wilderness (Exodus 16:3–5, 13–17).
9. Members of the priestly caste in ancient Persia. The Persian religion included belief in the advent of a savior, which may explain the journey of three magi to Bethlehem to pay homage to the child Jesus.
1. Angels who guard the Lord's throne; "suffragans": bishops.

2. In Greek mythology, supernatural avengers of crime.
3. The end (Latin).
4. That is, an idealized orderly rural England. "STC": Samuel Taylor Coleridge (1772–1834), English poet and philosopher; "*Anima Poetae*": the soul of poetry.
5. Novel (1844) by the British writer and statesman. The "New World" is an idealized America.

lords of unquiet or of quiet sojourn,
those muddy-hued and midge-tormented ghosts.

On blustery lilac-bush and terrace-urn
bedaubed with bloom Linnaean pentecosts[6]
put their pronged light; the chilly fountains burn.
Religion of the heart, with trysts and quests

and pangs of consolation, its hawk's hood[7]
twitched off for sweet carnality, again
rejoices in old hymns of servitude,

haunting the sacred well, the hidden shrine.
It is the ravage of the heron wood;
it is the rood[8] blazing upon the green.

9. *The Laurel Axe*

Autumn resumes the land, ruffles the woods
with smoky wings, entangles them. Trees shine
out from their leaves, rocks mildew to moss-green;
the avenues are spread with brittle floods.

Platonic England, house of solitudes,
rests in its laurels and its injured stone,
replete with complex fortunes that are gone,
beset by dynasties of moods and clouds.

It stands, as though at ease with its own world,
the mannerly extortions, languid praise,
all that devotion long since bought and sold,

the rooms of cedar and soft-thudding baize,[9]
tremulous boudoirs where the crystals kissed
in cabinets of amethyst and frost.[1]

11. *Idylls of the King*[2]

The pigeon purrs in the wood; the wood has gone;
dark leaves that flick to silver in the gust,
and the marsh-orchids and the heron's nest,
goldgrimy shafts and pillars of the sun.

Weightless magnificence upholds the past.
Cement recesses smell of fur and bone
and berries wrinkle in the badger-run[3]
and wiry heath-fern scatters its fresh rust.

---

6. That is, fiery, firelike flowers. Linnaeus (1707–1778) was the father of modern botany; at Pentecost, the Holy Ghost descended upon Christ's disciples as "cloven tongues like as of fire" (Acts 2:3).
7. Hunting hawks were hooded until ready to be released.
8. Cross.
9. That is, billiard rooms in British "stately homes"; the "soft-thudding baize" is the soft green cloth covering the billiard tables.
1. That is, glassware.
2. Also the title of the long series of interconnected poems (completed 1891) on the story of King Arthur and his knights, by Alfred, Lord Tennyson.
3. Enclosure for badgers.

'O clap your hands' so that the dove takes flight,
bursts through the leaves with an untidy sound,   10
plunges its wings into the green twilight

above this long-sought and forsaken ground,
the half-built ruins of the new estate,
warheads of mushrooms round the filter-pond.[4]

1979

4. Pond with a false bottom covered with gravel, serving as a filter for the estate's water.

SYLVIA PLATH
1932–1963

There is a tradition in our culture that the writing of poetry is a dangerous vocation, that great wits are, in fact, to madness near allied, and that poets sometimes court emotional disaster, discovering within themselves areas of pain, confusion, and heartbreak which they transform into works of art, occasions for their readers for fear, trembling, and compassion. In plain English: sometimes poets near the brink of emotional disaster fashion poems which comfort and heal. In the poetry written in English in the last thirty years, that written by Sylvia Plath is a signal and undisguised example of the agonizing and yet creative relationship between pain and creativity. Sylvia Plath's first years were years of solid bourgeois success: she did all the things and won all the prizes that a young American woman was meant to. Yet ticking within her was the inevitability, as it seems to us now, of her great tragic poems and her self-inflicted death. Sylvia Plath's poetry is a document of extremity. Her sensitivity is inordinate, but so is her ability to express it. The result is a holy scream, a splendid agony—beyond sex, beyond delicacy, beyond all but art.

For Americans, the familiarity of Sylvia Plath's history heightens the irony. Everyone in New England knows the hotdog stands on the edge of the water, and everyone in America knows the inexorable progress from primary school to high school and to college. The sheer banality of Plath's beginnings—in, for example, Lois Ames's account[1]—is stunning—all saddle shoes and report cards. She is proof that talent is independent of environment—how very much she made of very little.

When he was fifteen, Sylvia Plath's father, Otto Plath, came to the United States from Grabow in Poland. As an adult, he taught biology and German at Boston University and wrote a treatise on bees. His daughter, Sylvia, was born on October 27, 1932. Thereafter, the father anticipated the birth of a son as well, whom Mrs. Plath co-operatively produced—almost exactly at the time her husband specified, April 27, 1935, about two years after Sylvia. (This brother is the subject of several poems.) Otto Plath died in 1940, resulting in his daughter's elegy, "Daddy," an unnerving assault on the parent. Nothing on the family surface prepares us for this outburst, "the brute / Brute heart of a brute like you." One feels perhaps a twinge of sympathy for Otto Plath. And his daughter admitted that her father, long dead and scarcely known, was not to be mistaken for "Daddy," cruel, destructive, the masculine principle gone mad. Apart from the father's premature death, the daughter's history is shallow. In biographical accounts, the events are generally innocuous, even hackneyed. At its time, one arrived at Sylvia Plath's suicide without much premonition of its causes. There are report cards, scholarships at Smith College, prizes like a

1. "Notes toward a Biography" in *The Art of Sylvia Plath*, ed. Charles Newman, Bloomington, Ind., 1970, pp. 155–73.

month's editing of a magazine, election to Phi Beta Kappa, a *summa cum laude* gɪ uation. At the end of the junior year, a breakdown is recorded in *The Bell Jar*, ɪ this is succeeded by a triumphant final year at Smith. A Fulbright year at Cambridgᴄ University is won, and extended through a second year. In 1956 Sylvia Plath marries the English poet Ted Hughes. They come to America for more than a year, and she teaches at Smith. But the reading of students' papers consumes all her energy, and, after a short time in Boston, the couple return to England. They have two children: Frieda, born on April 1, 1960, and Nicholas, born on January 17, 1962. By the end of 1962, Sylvia Plath has moved back alone to London from the family home in Devon, and brought the children with her. In the few months before her death, she is still talking about an *au pair* girl or "mother's helper," to relieve her for writing. Next, on February 11, 1963, at the age of thirty, she is dead:

> Dying
> Is an art, like everything else.
> I do it exceptionally well.

There is always, with her, a sense of not knowing her, and consequently an exceptional sense of the poetry as truth. Her appearance was deceptive: it gave pleasure, it suggested crude health. The only tell-tale sign, perhaps, was the blocking of her sinuses. This was indicative, suggesting Sylvia Plath's repeated barricades against observation, conviviality. In all her suicidal attempts, she preferred a crawling out of sight. In her novel, *The Bell Jar*, there is not only the sensation of being caught and confined, but also that of unremitting light. As she says in "The Hanging Man,"

> By the roots of my hair some god got hold of me.
> I sizzled in his blue volts like a desert prophet.
>
> The nights snapped out of sight like a lizard's eyelid:
> A world of bald white days in a shadeless socket.

The blessed privacy and oblivion of sleep were denied her. In her final success, her head is stuck into the gas oven.

At the same period of her life in London, she concentrates with a dreadful honesty on painful facts. "I am inhabited by a cry," she had written in "Elm," and the cry is heard now in all its ferocity. Tulips were sent to her in the hospital—never was a gift so rudely received! "The vivid tulips eat my oxygen," and they are "A dozen red lead sinkers round my neck." Even the children, whom she cared for faithfully, are abandoned in the verse.

"Fever 103" remembers Hiroshima:

> Greasing the bodies of adulterers
> Like Hiroshima ash and eating in.
> The sin. The sin.

Always the expansion is by conviction: the self pains and the world pains too. The interchange of person and world is at once seamless and profound.

Lady Lazarus[1]

> I have done it again.
> One year in every ten
> I manage it—

---

1. Lazarus was raised from the dead by Jesus Christ (John 11:44).

A sort of walking miracle, my skin
Bright as a Nazi lampshade,[2]
My right foot   5

A paperweight,
My face a featureless, fine
Jew linen.

Peel off the napkin
O my enemy.   10
Do I terrify?—

The nose, the eye pits, the full set of teeth?
The sour breath
Will vanish in a day.   15

Soon, soon the flesh
The grave cave ate will be
At home on me

And I a smiling woman.
I am only thirty.   20
And like the cat I have nine times to die.

This is Number Three.
What a trash
To annihilate each decade.

What a million filaments.   25
The peanut-crunching crowd
Shoves in to see

Them unwrap me hand and foot—
The big strip tease.
Gentleman, ladies,   30

These are my hands,
My knees.
I may be skin and bone,

Nevertheless, I am the same, identical woman.
The first time it happened I was ten.   35
It was an accident.

The second time I meant
To last it out and not come back at all.
I rocked shut

As a seashell.   40
They had to call and call
And pick the worms off me like sticky pearls.

2. The skins of some Jewish victims of the Nazis were used to make lampshades.

Dying
Is an art, like everything else.
I do it exceptionally well.   45

I do it so it feels like hell.
I do it so it feels real.
I guess you could say I've a call.

It's easy enough to do it in a cell.
It's easy enough to do it and stay put.   50
It's the theatrical

Comeback in broad day
To the same place, the same face, the same brute
Amused shout:

"A miracle!"   55
That knocks me out.
There is a charge

For the eyeing of my scars, there is a charge
For the hearing of my heart—
It really goes.   60

And there is a charge, a very large charge,
For a word or a touch
Or a bit of blood

Or a piece of my hair or my clothes.
So, so, Herr Doktor.   65
So, Herr Enemy.

I am your opus,
I am your valuable,
The pure gold baby

That melts to a shriek.   70
I turn and burn.
Do not think I underestimate your great concern.

Ash, ash—
You poke and stir.
Flesh, bone, there is nothing there—   75

A cake of soap,
A wedding ring,
A gold filling.

Herr God, Herr Lucifer,
Beware   80
Beware.

Out of the ash
I rise with my red hair
And I eat men like air.

1966

Ariel[3]

Stasis in darkness.
Then the substanceless blue
Pour of tor and distances.

God's lioness,
How one we grow,   5
Pivot of heels and knees!—The furrow

Splits and passes, sister to
The brown arc
Of the neck I cannot catch,

Nigger-eye   10
Berries cast dark
Hooks—

Black sweet blood mouthfuls,
Shadows.
Something else   15

Hauls me through air—
Thighs, hair;
Flakes from my heels.

White
Godiva, I unpeel—   20
Dead hands, dead stringencies.

And now I
Foam to wheat, a glitter of seas.
The child's cry

Melts in the wall.   25
And I
Am the arrow,

The dew that flies
Suicidal, at one with the drive
Into the red   30

Eye, the cauldron of morning.

                                                                        1966

Daddy

You do not do, you do not do
Any more, black shoe
In which I have lived like a foot
For thirty years, poor and white,
Barely daring to breathe or Achoo.   5

---

3. The airy spirit in Shakespeare's *The Tempest;* also, the name of Sylvia Plath's horse.

Daddy, I have had to kill you.
You died before I had time—
Marble-heavy, a bag full of God,
Ghastly statue with one grey toe
Big as a Frisco seal   10

And a head in the freakish Atlantic
Where it pours bean green over blue
In the waters off beautiful Nauset.
I used to pray to recover you.
Ach, du[4]   15

In the German tongue, in the Polish town[5]
Scraped flat by the roller
Of wars, wars, wars.
But the name of the town is common.
My Polack friend   20

Says there are a dozen or two.
So I never could tell where you
Put your foot, your root,
I never could talk to you.
The tongue stuck in my jaw.   25

It stuck in a barb wire snare.
Ich, ich, ich, ich,[6]
I could hardly speak.
I thought every German was you.
And the language obscene   30

An engine, an engine
Chuffing me off like a Jew.
A Jew to Dachau, Auschwitz, Belsen.
I began to talk like a Jew.
I think I may well be a Jew.   35

The snows of the Tyrol, the clear beer of Vienna
Are not very pure or true.
With my gypsy ancestress and my weird luck
And my Taroc pack and my Taroc pack
I may be a bit of a Jew.   40

I have always been scared of *you*,
With your Luftwaffe,[7] your gobbledygoo.
And your neat moustache
And your Aryan eye, bright blue.
Panzer-man, panzer-man, O You—   45

Not God but a swastika
So black no sky could squeak through.
Every woman adores a Fascist,

4. Ah, you (German).
5. Grabów, Otto Plath's birthplace.
6. I, I, I, I (German).
7. Air Force (German).

The boot in the face, the brute
Brute heart of a brute like you.   50

You stand at the blackboard, daddy,
In the picture I have of you,
A cleft in your chin instead of your foot
But no less a devil for that, no not
Any less the black man who   55

Bit my pretty red heart in two.
I was ten when they buried you.
At twenty I tried to die
And get back, back, back to you.
I thought even the bones would do.   60

But they pulled me out of the sack,
And they stuck me together with glue.
And then I knew what to do.
I made a model of you,
A man in black with a Meinkampf[8] look   65

And a love of the rack and the screw.
And I said I do, I do.
So daddy, I'm finally through.
The black telephone's off at the root,
The voices just can't worm through.   70

If I've killed one man, I've killed two—
The vampire who said he was you
And drank my blood for a year,
Seven years, if you want to know.
Daddy, you can lie back now.   75

There's a stake in your fat black heart
And the villagers never liked you.
They are dancing and stamping on you.
They always _knew_ it was you.
Daddy, daddy, you bastard, I'm through.   80

1966

Blackberrying

Nobody in the lane, and nothing, nothing but blackberries,
Blackberries on either side, though on the right mainly,
A blackberry alley, going down in hooks, and a sea
Somewhere at the end of it, heaving. Blackberries
Big as the ball of my thumb, and dumb as eyes   5
Ebon in the hedges, fat
With blue-red juices. These they squander on my fingers.
I had not asked for such a blood sisterhood; they must love me.
They accommodate themselves to my milkbottle, flattening their sides.

---

8. *Mein Kampf* (My Battle) was the title of Adolf Hitler's political autobiography.

Overhead go the choughs in black, cacophonous flocks—   10
Bits of burnt paper wheeling in a blown sky.
Theirs is the only voice, protesting, protesting.
I do not think the sea will appear at all.
The high, green meadows are glowing, as if lit from within.
I come to one bush of berries so ripe it is a bush of flies,   15
Hanging their blue-green bellies and their wing panes in a Chinese screen.
The honey-feast of the berries has stunned them; they believe in heaven.
One more hook, and the berries and bushes end.

The only thing to come now is the sea.
From between two hills a sudden wind funnels at me,   20
Slapping its phantom laundry in my face.
These hills are too green and sweet to have tasted salt.
I follow the sheep path between them. A last hook brings me
To the hills' northern face, and the face is orange rock
That looks out on nothing, nothing but a great space   25
Of white and pewter lights, and a din like silversmiths
Beating and beating at an intractable metal.

1971

AUDRE LORDE
b. 1934

"I was really sickening with fury," Audre Lorde told Adrienne Rich in an interview, describing the circumstances that led to writing her poem "Power." A white police-man, accused of killing a young Black boy, had just been acquitted by a jury of eleven white men and one Black woman. "I was thinking that the killer had been a student at John Jay [College of Criminal Justice, the New York City police college where Lorde was teaching] . . . Do I kill him? . . . That archaic fear of the total reality of a power that is not on your terms. There is the jury, white male power . . . How do you reach down into threatening difference without being killed or killing? . . . All of those things were riding on that poem. But I had no sense, no understanding at the time, of the connections, just that I *was* that woman . . . And that sense of writing at the edge, out of urgency, not because you choose it but because you have to, that sense of survival—that's what the poem is out of, as well as the pain of my son's death over and over."[1] If, as the Black novelist Ralph Ellison asserted, "Writers are forged in injustice as swords are forged,"[2] then Lorde has been reforging herself through more than twenty years of writing.

Put this way, it might appear as if for Lorde the politics of racial or gender injustice came first, but as she tells us in an essay, it was the poetry that came first: "I was very inarticulate as a youngster. . . . I used to speak in poetry. I would read poems, and I would memorize them. People would say, well, what do you think, Audre. What happened to you yesterday? And I would recite a poem and somewhere in that poem there would be a line or a feeling I would be sharing. . . . And when I couldn't find the poems to express the things I was feeling, that's what started me writing poetry, and that was when I was twelve or thirteen."[3] At first she expressed her

1. Audre Lorde and Adrienne Rich, "An Interview with Audre Lorde," *Signs: Journal of Women in Culture and Society* 6, no. 4, Summer 1981, p. 734.

2. Quoted by Jerome Brooks, "In the Name of the Father: The Poetry of Audre Lorde," in *Black Women Writers (1950–1980): A Critical Evaluation*, ed. Mari Evans, New York, 1983, p. 269.

3. Audre Lorde, "My Words Will Be There," in *Black Women Writers (1950–1980)*, p. 261.

blackness in rebellion (compare the title of her second book: *Cables to Rage*); later, in an ability to turn anger to use in her poems.

She has learned to do so not only from her experience but also from many recent African writers, of whom she says, "It's not a turning away from pain, from error, but seeing these things as part of living and learning from them."[4] It is therefore no accident that among her most fully realized poems are those in which she treats West African history and matriarchal myth. In "The Women of Dan Dance with Swords in Their Hands to Mark the Time When They Were Warriors," she identifies with the Dahomeyan Amazons as woman warriors—"I come as a woman / dark and open / some times I fall like night / softly / and terrible"— and as woman lovers—"I come like a woman / . . . / warming whatever I touch / that is living." Here her use of myth joins her use of the erotic, to paraphrase the title of her essay, "The Uses of the Erotic." "Love," she has said, "is very important because it is a source of tremendous power," and yet women "have not been taught to respect the erotic urge, the place that is uniquely female."[5]

"It's easier to deal with a poet, certainly a Black woman poet, when you categorize her, narrow her so she can fulfill your expectations," she has said. "I am not one piece of myself. I cannot be simply a Black person, and not be a woman, too, nor can I be a woman without being a lesbian . . . I write for myself and my children and for as many people as possible who can read me. When I say myself, I mean not only the Audre who inhabits my body but all those *feisty, incorrigible Black women* who insist on standing up and saying *I am*, and you can't wipe me out, no matter how irritating I am."[6]

Lorde was born on February 18, 1934, of West Indian parents who had moved to New York City's Harlem. She received a B.A. from Hunter College in 1961, and a master of library science degree from Columbia. She married in 1962 and divorced in 1970. She then worked as a librarian and taught school, and spent a year as poet-in-residence at Tougaloo College in Mississippi. Since then she has taught at colleges in New York City, including the John Jay College of Criminal Justice; since 1981 she has been professor of English at Hunter College, New York City.

4. "My Words Will Be There," p. 266.   6. The same, pp. 262, 268.
5. The same, p. 265.

Coal

    I
is the total black, being spoken
from the earth's inside.
There are many kinds of open
how a diamond comes into a knot of flame
how sound comes into a word, colored   5
by who pays what for speaking.
Some words are open like a diamond
on glass windows
singing out within the passing crash of sun
Then there are words like stapled wagers   10
in a perforated book—buy and sign and tear apart—
and come whatever wills all chances
the stub remains
and ill-pulled tooth with a ragged edge.
Some words live in my throat

breeding like adders. Others know sun
seeking like gypsies over my tongue
to explode through my lips
like young sparrows bursting from shell.
Some words   20
bedevil me.

Love is a word, another kind of open.
As the diamond comes into a knot of flame
I am Black because I come from the earth's inside
now take my word for jewel in the open light.   25
1968

Love Poem

Speak earth and bless me with what is richest
make sky flow honey out of my hips
rigid as mountains
spread over a valley
carved out by the mouth of rain.   5

And I knew when I entered her I was
high wind in her forests hollow
fingers whispering sound
honey flowed
from the split cup   10
impaled on a lance of tongues
on the tips of her breasts on her navel
and my breath
howling into her entrances
through lungs of pain.   15

Greedy as herring-gulls
or a child
I swing out over the earth
over and over
again.   20
1974

The Women of Dan[1] Dance with Swords in Their Hands to Mark the Time When They Were Warriors

I did not fall from the sky
I
nor descend like a plague of locusts[2]
to drink color and strength from the earth
and I do not come like rain   5
as a tribute or symbol for earth's becoming

1. "An ancient name for the kingdom of Dahomey" (from Lorde's Glossary); Dahomey, in West Africa, is now Benin.

2. Like the all-consuming plague of locusts that the Lord visited upon Egypt in Exodus 10.

I come as a woman
dark and open
some times I fall like night
softly   10
and terrible
only when I must die
in order to rise again.

I do not come like a secret warrior
with an unsheathed sword in my mouth   15
hidden behind my tongue
slicing my throat to ribbons
of service with a smile
while the blood runs
down and out   20
through holes in the two sacred mounds
on my chest.

I come like a woman
who I am
spreading out through nights   25
laughter and promise
and dark heat
warming whatever I touch
that is living
consuming   30
only
what is already dead.

                                                  1978

Power

The difference between poetry and rhetoric
is being
ready to kill
yourself
instead of your children.   5

I am trapped on a desert of raw gunshot wounds
and a dead child dragging his shattered black
face off the edge of my sleep
blood from his punctured cheeks and shoulders
is the only liquid for miles and my stomach   10
churns at the imagined taste while
my mouth splits into dry lips
without loyalty or reason
thirsting for the wetness of his blood
as it sinks into the whiteness   15
of the desert where I am lost
without imagery or magic
trying to make power out of hatred and destruction
trying to heal my dying son with kisses
only the sun will bleach his bones quicker.   20

The policeman who shot down a 10-year-old in Queens
stood over the boy with his cop shoes in childish blood
and a voice said "Die you little motherfucker" and
there are tapes to prove that. At his trial
this policeman said in his own defense   25
"I didn't notice the size or nothing else
only the color." and
there are tapes to prove that, too.[3]

Today that 37-year-old white man with 13 years of police forcing
has been set free   30
by 11 white men who said they were satisfied
justice had been done
and one black woman who said
"They convinced me" meaning
they had dragged her 4′10″ black woman's frame   35
over the hot coals of four centuries of white male approval
until she let go the first real power she ever had
and lined her own womb with cement
to make a graveyard for our children.

I have not been able to touch the destruction within me.   40
But unless I learn to use
the difference between poetry and rhetoric
my power too will run corrupt as poisonous mold
or lie limp and useless as an unconnected wire
and one day I will take my teenaged plug   45
and connect it to the nearest socket
raping an 85-year-old white woman
who is somebody's mother
and as I beat her senseless and set a torch to her bed
a greek chorus will be singing in ¾ time[4]   50
"Poor thing. She never hurt a soul. What beasts they are."

                                                                  1978

Beams

In the afternoon sun
that smelled of contradiction
quick birds announcing spring's intention
and autumn about to begin
I started to tell you   5
what Eudora[5] never told me
how quickly it goes
the other fork   out of mind's eye

---

3. "'Power' . . . is a poem written about Clifford Glover, the ten-year-old Black child shot by a cop who was acquitted by a jury on which a Black woman sat. In fact, the day I heard on the radio that O'Shea had been acquitted, I was going across town on Eighty-eighth Street and I had to pull over. A kind of fury rose up in me; the sky turned red. I felt so sick. I felt as if I would drive this car into a wall, into the next person I saw. So I pulled over. I took out my journal just to air some of my fury, to get it out of my fingertips. Those expressed feelings are that poem" (Audre Lorde, "My Words Will Be There," in *Black Women Writers (1950–1980)*, ed. Mari Evans, New York, 1983, p. 266). Queens is a borough of New York City.
4. Waltz rhythm; the Greek choruses chanted commentary on the action in classical Greek tragedies.
5. A friend with whom Lorde lived in Mexico in the early 1950s.

choice
becoming a stone wall   10
across possible
beams
outlined on the shapes of winter
the sunset colors of Southampton Beach
red-snapper runs at Salina Cruz[6]
and we slept in the fishermen's nets
a pendulum swing
between the rippling fingers
of a belly dancer with brass rings
and a two-year-old's sleep smell   20
the inexorable dwindling
no body's choice
and for a few short summers
I too was delightful.

Whenever spring comes I wish to burn   25
to ride the flood like a zebra goaded
shaken with sun
to braid the hair of a girl long dead
or is it my daughter grown
and desire for what is gone   30
sealed into hunger   like an abandoned mine
nights when fear came down like a jones[7]
and I lay   rigid with denials
the clarity of frost without
the pain of coldness   35
autumn's sharp precisions and yet
for the green to stay.

Dark women clad in flat and functional leather
finger their breastsummers[8]   whispering
sisterly advice   one dreams of fish   40
lays her lips like spring across my chest
where I am scarred and naked
as a strip-mined hill in West Virginia[9]
and hanging on my office wall
a snapshot of the last Dahomean Amazons[1]   45
taken the year that I was born
three old Black women in draped cloths
holding hands.

A knout of revelation   of a corm[2] of song
and love   a net of possible   50
surrounding all acts of life

6. Beaches on Long Island (New York) and in Mexico, respectively; "red snappers": red food fish, found especially in the Gulf of Mexico.
7. "Drug habit or addiction" (Lorde's note).
8. "*Breastsummer*: a breastplate; also a wooden beam across an empty place" (Lorde's note).
9. To stripmine is to work a mine from the earth's surface, with the result that the scars in the earth show; West Virginia has many such strip-mined hills.
1. "Unlike in other African systems of belief, women in Dahomey, as the Creators of Life, were not enjoined from the shedding of blood. The Amazons were highly prized, well-trained, and ferocious women warriors who guarded, and fought under the direction of, the Panther Kings of Dahomey" (from Lorde's Glossary); they are so called by analogy with the women warriors of Greek legend.
2. "Knout": flogging whip; "corm": underground stem-base of certain plants.

one woman harvesting   all I have ever been
lights up my sky like stars
or flecks of paint   storm-flung
the blast and seep of gone   55
remains
only the peace we make with it
shifts into seasons
lengthening past equinox
sun   wind   come round again   60
seizing us in her arms like a warrior lover
or blowing us into shapes
we have avoided for years
as we turn
we forget what is not possible   65
                                                                         1986

IMAMU AMIRI BARAKA (LeRoi Jones)
b. 1934

"Let my poems be a graph of me," LeRoi Jones wrote in "Balboa, the Entertainer,"
and he turns with relief from the "philosophers of need" and their political abstractions to an expression of his own fearfulness and his personal need. His early poems
find joy in the liberty of art, in the fashioning of works which make their own rules.
In 1959 he wrote, "There cannot be anything I must *fit* the poem into. Everything
must be made to fit into the poem. There must not be any preconceived notion or
design for what the poem ought to be."[1] Jones's first poems are personal and questioning; they stake out areas of domestic tenderness and satisfaction, though the poet
frequently returns to thoughts of his own death. Jones was later to identify his intimations of mortality with the "deathurge of this twisted society"; he became aware
of the "superstructure of filth Americans call their way of life,"[2] and he exhorted his
fellow Blacks to abandon the American way of life and to work to destroy it. Jones
had once described art as the "most beautiful resolution of energies that in another
context might be violent for myself or for anyone else,"[3] and for a time he wrote his
poems to make a life for himself within a hostile society. Jones no longer seeks an
alternative to violence, and his social passion and his poetry now are one.

LeRoi Jones was born in Newark, New Jersey, on October 7, 1934. He was a
student at Howard University, then spent two years as a weatherman and gunner in
the U.S. Air Force. "The Howard thing," Jones has said, "let me understand the
Negro sickness. They teach you how to pretend to be white. But the Air Force made
me understand the white sickness. It shocked me into realizing what was happening
to me and others. By oppressing Negroes, the whites have become oppressors, twisted
in that sense of doing bad things to people and justifying them finally, convincing
themselves they are right, as people have always convinced themselves."[4] As a graduate student at Columbia, he knew some of the writers identified with the Beat
movement, writers with whom he was likely to feel some comradeship since they
shared his interest in Americans who lived on the edge of American society. In the
late fifties he was an active figure in the New York literary underground.

In the middle sixties he began to make his reputation as a dramatist. His short play

---

1. "How You Sound??" quoted in *The New
American Poetry,* 1945–60, ed. Donald Allen, New
York, 1960, pp. 424–25.
2. "An Explanation of the Work," *Black Magic,*

Collected Poetry, 1961–67, New York, 1969.
3. Interview with Judy Stone, *San Francisco
Chronicle,* August 23, 1964.
4. The same.

Dutchman, an encounter in a subway between a young Black and a white woman which ends in murder, had a long run off-Broadway. Two later plays, *The Toilet* and *The Slave,* were less successful; Jones has said that the latter was the last of his works addressed to a Black-white audience. Eager to find a focus for a Black community which would use the arts, Jones moved first to Harlem, where he founded the Black Arts Repertory Theater, and then in 1966 to the Newark slums, where he set up a community called Spirit House. During the riots in the summer of 1967 Jones was arrested and charged with carrying a concealed weapon; he was convicted, and to justify the unusually heavy sentence, the judge quoted lines from "Black People":

> We must make our own
> World, man, our own world, and we can not do this unless the white man
> is dead. Let's get together and killhim, my man, let's get to gather the fruit
> of the sun.

Jones was eventually acquitted on a retrial. In 1968 he founded the Black Community Development and Defense Organization, a group then composed of a hundred men and fifty women; they wear traditional African dress, speak Swahili as well as English, and practice the Muslim religion. He is now known by his Muslim name, Imamu Amiri Baraka, and in recent years he has played an increasingly important role in national Black politics and in relations between the American Black community and the nations of Black Africa. He has now come to feel that his literary works—prose, poetry, and drama—exist only to achieve an end, the liberation of Black Americans. He remains an awesome moral presence, an angry, talented man who must be contended with.

Political Poem

(For Basil)

Luxury, then, is a way of
being ignorant, comfortably
An approach to the open market
of least information. Where theories
can thrive, under heavy tarpaulins   5
without being cracked by ideas.

(I have not seen the earth for years
and think now possibly "dirt" is
negative, positive, but clearly
social. I cannot plant a seed, cannot   10
recognize the root with clearer dent
than indifference. Though I eat
and shit as a natural man. (Getting up
from the desk to secure a turkey sandwich
and answer the phone: the poem undone   15
undone by my station, by my station,
and the bad words of Newark.[1]) Raised up
to the breech, we seek to fill for this
crumbling century. The darkness of love,
in whose sweating memory all error is forced.   20

---

1. Baraka's birthplace, and once again his home.

Undone by the logic of any specific death. (Old gentlemen
who still follow fires, tho are quieter
and less punctual. It is a polite truth
we are left with. Who are you? What are you
saying? Something to be dealt with, as easily.   25
The noxious game of reason, saying, "No, No,
you cannot feel," like my dead lecturer
lamenting thru gipsies his fast suicide.

                                                        1964

Legacy

(*For Blues People*)

In the south, sleeping against
the drugstore, growling under
the trucks and stoves, stumbling
through and over the cluttered eyes
of early mysterious night. Frowning   5
drunk waving moving a hand or lash.
Dancing kneeling reaching out, letting
a hand rest in shadows. Squatting
to drink or pee. Stretching to climb
pulling themselves onto horses near   10
where there was sea (the old songs
lead you to believe). Riding out
from this town, to another, where
it is also black. Down a road
where people are asleep. Towards   15
the moon or the shadows of houses.
Towards the songs' pretended sea.

                                                        1969

Babylon Revisited

The gaunt thing
with no organs
creeps along the streets
of Europe, she will
commute, in her feathered bat stomach-gown   5
with no organs
with sores on her insides
even her head
a vast puschamber
of pus(sy) memories   10
with no organs
nothing to make babies
she will be the great witch of euro-american legend
who sucked the life
from some unknown nigger   15
whose name will be known
but whose substance will not ever

not even by him
who is dead in a pile of dopeskin

This bitch killed a friend of mine named Bob Thompson   20
a black painter, a giant, once, she reduced
to a pitiful imitation faggot
full of American holes and a monkey on his back
slapped airplanes
from the empire state building   25

May this bitch and her sisters, all of them,
receive my words
in all their orifices like lye mixed with
cocola and alaga syrup

feel this shit, bitches, feel it, now laugh your   30
hysterectic laughs
while your flesh burns
and your eyes peel to red mud

1969

A New Reality Is Better Than a New Movie!

How will it go, crumbling earthquake, towering inferno, juggernaut,[2] vol-
          cano, smashup.
in reality, other than the feverish nearreal fantasy of the capitalist flunky
          film hacks
tho they sense its reality breathing a quake inferno scar on their throat even
          snorts of
100% pure cocaine cant cancel the cold cut of impending death to this soci-
          ety. On all the
screens of america, the joint blows up every hour and a half for two dollars
          an fifty cents.   5
They have taken the niggers out to lunch, for a minute, made us partners
          (nigger charlie) or
surrogates (boss nigger) for their horror. But just as superafrikan mobutu
          cannot leopardskinhat his
way out of responsibility for lumumba's death,[3] nor even with his incredible
          billions rockefeller
cannot even save his pale ho's[4] titties in the crushing weight of things as
          they really are.
How will it go, does it reach you, getting up, sitting on the side of the bed,
          getting ready   10
to go to work. Hypnotized by the machine, and the cement floor, the jungle
          treachery of trying
to survive with no money in a money world, of making the boss 100,000 for
          every 200 dollars

2. *The Towering Inferno* was the title of a movie
about a skyscraper impressively on fire; "juggernaut": massive force or vehicle that moves forward
irresistibly and crushes anything in its path.
    3. Patrice Lumumba, a leader in the bloody
struggle for power that followed the independence of Zaire (formerly the Belgian Congo) was
murdered in 1961; the strong-arm president Sese
Soko Mobutu was placed in power by the American CIA to restore order.
    4. Whore.

you get, and then having his brother get you for the rent, and if you want
   to buy the car you
helped build, your downpayment paid for it, the rest goes to buy his old
   lady a foam rubber
rhinestone set of boobies for special occasions when kissinger drunkenly
   fumbles with   15
her blouse, forgetting himself.[5]
If you dont like it, what you gonna do about it. That was the question we
   asked each other, &
still right regularly need to ask. You dont like it? Whatcha gonna do, about
   it??
The real terror of nature is humanity enraged, the true technicolor spectacle that hollywood
cant record. They cant even show you how you look when you go to work,
   or when you come back.   20
They cant even show you thinking or demanding the new socialist reality,
   its the ultimate tidal
wave. When all over the planet, men and women, with heat in their hands,
   demand that society
be planned to include the lives and self determination of all the people ever
   to live. That is
the scalding scenario with a cast of just under two billion that they dare not
   even whisper.
Its called, "We Want It All . . . The Whole World!"   25
                                                                                  1976

5. Henry Kissinger (b. 1923), Secretary of State under Richard Nixon, was, as an eligible Washington
bachelor, often photographed with attractive women.

JON STALLWORTHY
b. 1935

In his poem "Letter to a Friend" Jon Stallworthy defends himself against the charge
that his poems are not concerned with immediate social problems and that he does
not write "with the accent of the age." His answer is that

> my poems all
> Are woven out of love's loose ends;
> For myself and for my friends.

A reading of Stallworthy's poems substantiates his own self-description: he is concerned with the private life—his life as son, father, and friend—and he evaluates
private experience in carefully crafted poems. He is distrustful of fashionably easy
solutions, and he reproves poets who safely boom away in a political cause with small
attention to those who actually died for it. In "A Letter from Berlin" many of Stallworthy's interests converge: the poem is a meticulously rendered rewriting of an
experience of the poet's surgeon father, and readers find themselves in a sort of
ghastly fun house, where one experience is reflected and distorted in another, and
private experience is given a tragic historical dimension.

   Jon Stallworthy was born in London on January 18, 1935; he attended Rugby School
and Magdalen College at Oxford University, from which he received a B.A. in 1958.
In that year he also received the Newdigate Prize for Poetry and completed his first
book of poetry; since then he has published nine more, as well as two volumes of

selected poems; the most recent is *The Anzac Sonata: New and Selected Poems* (1987).
One of his most ambitious and well-realized books is *A Familiar Tree* (1978), in
which, in a series of interlocking poems, some of them epistolary, he traces his family's history from eighteenth-century tenant farmers, by way of a missionary on a
cannibal island and a New Zealand lumberjack, down to the present.

   Stallworthy has said that "I set myself to learn how to make poems as a carpenter
makes tables and chairs. I count myself a maker, and such other things as I have
made with words—studies of Yeats 'at work,' translations of Blok and Pasternak—
have been made with one purpose in view: to learn how to make better poems."[1]
Stallworthy is being characteristically modest here about his critical work—at least
about his biography of Wilfred Owen (1975), which won several prizes. He has edited
the definitive edition of Owen's poems (1986) and collections of poems on love and
on war, and is a contributing editor to *The Norton Anthology of English Literature*.

   Until 1977 he combined a successful career at the Oxford University Press with
teaching occasional courses at Oxford, and then left publishing to become Anderson
Professor of English at Cornell University. In 1986 he returned to teach at Oxford,
saying that the professor could live in America, but that the poet needed to return
to his English roots.

   1. Jon Stallworthy in *Contemporary Poets*, 4th ed., ed. James Vinson and D. L. Kirkpatrick, New
York, 1985, p. 826.

A poem about Poems About Vietnam[1]

The spotlights had you covered [*thunder
in the wings*]. In the combat zones
and in the Circle,[2] darkness. Under
the muzzles of the microphones
you opened fire, and a phalanx[3]   5
of loudspeakers shook on the wall;
but all your cartridges were blanks
when you were at the Albert Hall.

Lord George Byron cared for Greece,[4]
Auden and Cornford cared for Spain,[5]   10
confronted bullets and disease
to make their poems' meaning plain;
but you—by what right did you wear
suffering like a service medal,
numbing the nerve that they laid bare,   15
when you were at the Albert Hall?

The poets of another time—
Owen[6] with a rifle-butt
between his paper and the slime,

1. This poem comments on a much-publicized
and -discussed poetry reading in London's enormous Royal Albert Hall in 1965, at which several
poems opposing the war in Vietnam were read.
   2. That is, the Dress Circle, a ring of box seats
in the Hall.
   3. Body of infantry in ancient Greece.
   4. Lord Byron died in 1824 of illness and
exhaustion at Missolonghi, in Greece, where he
was working for the cause of Greek independence.
   5. W. H. Auden (see above, p. 408) and John
Cornford, both English poets, went to Spain in
1937 to aid the leftist revolutionary faction against
the counterrevolution led by Francisco Franco.
Auden drove an ambulance, and Cornford was
killed in the fighting.
   6. Wilfred Owen; see p. 311.

Donne[7] quitting Her pillow to cut   20
a quill—knew that in love and war
dispatches from the front are all.
We believe them, they were there,
when you were at the Albert Hall.

Poet, they whisper in their sleep   25
louder from underground than all
the mikes that hung upon your lips
when you were at the Albert Hall.

                                                       1969

A Letter from Berlin

My dear,
         Today a letter from Berlin
where snow—the first of '38[8]—flew in,
settled and shrivelled on the lamp last night,
broke moth wings mobbing the window. Light   5
woke me early, but the trams were late:
I had to run from the Brandenburg Gate[9]
skidding, groaning like a tram,[1] and sodden
to the knees. Von Neumann operates at 10
and would do if the sky fell in. They lock   10
his theatre[2] doors on the stroke of the clock—
but today I was lucky: found a gap
in the gallery next to a chap
I knew just as the doors were closing. Last,
as expected, on Von Showmann's list   15
the new vaginal hysterectomy
that brought me to Berlin.
                          Delicately
he went to work, making from right to left
a semi-circular incision. Deft
dissection of the fascia.[3] The blood-
blossoming arteries nipped in the bud.   20
Speculum,[4] scissors, clamps—the uterus
cleanly delivered, the pouch of Douglas[5]
stripped to the rectum, and the cavity
closed. Never have I seen such masterly   25
technique. 'And so little bleeding!' I said
half to myself, half to my neighbour.
                          'Dead',
came his whisper. 'Don't be a fool'
I said, for still below us in the pool
of light the marvellous unhurried hands   30

7. John Donne (1572–1631), the English poet, had experience of love and war before entering the priesthood.
8. The year before Germany's invasion of Poland opened hostilities in the Second World War.
9. A grandiose monument in the center of Berlin.
1. Streetcar.

2. Britishism for operating room.
3. A layer of tissue that holds the inner parts of the body together.
4. Instrument inserted into the body for inspection or medication.
5. Deep recess between the uterus and upper vaginal wall.

were stitching, tying the double strands
of catgut, stitching, tying. It was like
a concert, watching those hands unlock
the music from their score. And at the end
one half expected him to turn and bend   35
stiffly towards us. Stiffly he walked out
and his audience shuffled after. But
finishing my notes in the gallery
I saw them uncover the patient: she
was dead.
       I met my neighbour in the street   40
waiting for the same tram, stamping his feet
on the pavement's broken snow, and said:
'I have to apologize. She was dead,
but how did you know?' Back came his voice
like a bullet'—saw it last month, twice.'   45

Returning your letter to an envelope
yellower by years than when you sealed it up,
darkly the omens emerge. A ritual wound
yellow at the lip yawns in my hand;
a turbulent crater; a trench, filled   50
not with snow only, east of Buchenwald.[6]

1969

The Almond Tree[7]

I

All the way to the hospital
the lights were green as peppermints.
Trees of black iron broke into leaf
ahead of me, as if
I were the lucky prince   5
in an enchanted wood
summoning summer with my whistle,
banishing winter with a nod.

Swung by the road from bend to bend,
I was aware that blood was running   10
down through the delta of my wrist
and under arches
of bright bone. Centuries,
continents it had crossed;
from an undisclosed beginning   15
spiralling to an unmapped end.

---

6. A Nazi concentration camp where, a few years later, German doctors performed experimental surgery on prisoners, often killing them.

7. One of a series of poems in *The Familiar Tree* (1978) in which Stallworthy explores his family history.

II

Crossing (at sixty) Magdalen Bridge[8]
Let it be a son, a son, said
the man in the driving mirror,
Let it be a son. The tower   20
held up its hand: the college
bells shook their blessing on his head.

III

I parked in an almond's
shadow blossom, for the tree
was waving, waving me   25
upstairs with a child's hands.

IV

Up
the spinal stair
and at the top
along   30
a bone-white corridor
the blood tide swung
me swung me to a room
whose walls shuddered
with the shuddering womb.   35
Under the sheet
wave after wave, wave
after wave beat
on the bone coast, bringing
ashore—whom?   40
New-
minted, my bright farthing![9]
Coined by our love, stamped with
our images, how you
enrich us! Both   45
you make one. Welcome
to your white sheet,
my best poem!

V

At seven-thirty
the visitors' bell   50
scissored the calm
of the corridors.
The doctor walked with me
to the slicing doors.

8. Bridge over the river Cherwell in Oxford; it
takes its name from one of the Oxford colleges,
Magdalen College, famous for its medieval tower.

9. Formerly the smallest British coin; not minted
after 1971.

His hand upon my arm,
his voice—*I have to tell*
you—set another bell
beating in my head:
your son is a mongol[1]
the doctor said.

55

60

VI

How easily the word went in—
clean as a bullet
leaving no mark on the skin,
stopping the heart within it.

This was my first death.
The 'I' ascending on a slow
last thermal breath
studied the man below

65

as a pilot treading air might
the buckled shell of his plane—
boot, glove, and helmet
feeling no pain

70

from the snapped wires' radiant ends.
Looking down from a thousand feet
I held four walls in the lens
of an eye; wall, window, the street

75

a torrent of windscreens, my own
care under its almond tree,
and the almond waving me down.
I wrestled against gravity,

80

but light was melting and the gulf
cracked open. Unfamiliar
the body of my late self
I carried to the car.

VII

The hospital—its heavy freight
lashed down ship-shape ward over ward—
steamed into night with some on board
soon to be lost if the desperate

85

charts were known. Others would come
altered to land or find the land
altered. At their voyage's end
some would be added to, some

90

diminished. In a numbered cot
my son sailed from me; never to come

1. Person suffering from congenital mental deficiency.

ashore into my kingdom   95
speaking my language. Better not

look that way. The almond tree
was beautiful in labour. Blood-
dark, quickening, bud after bud
split, flower after flower shook free.   100

On the darkening wind a pale
face floated. Out of reach. Only when
the buds, all the buds, were broken
would the tree be in full sail.

In labour the tree was becoming   105
itself. I, too, rooted in earth
and ringed by darkness, from the death
of myself saw myself blossoming,

wrenched from the caul[2] of my thirty
years' growing, fathered by my son,   110
unkindly in a kind season
by love shattered and set free.

                                                 1978

2. Membrane enclosing the skull of the fetus in the womb.

JUNE JORDAN
b. 1936

"Listen to this white man; he is so weird!"[1] exclaims June Jordan, approving Walt Whitman's grand design for a "people's poetry" of the New World, and his objection to the "great poems, Shakespeare included" of Europe and England, which are "poisonous to the idea of the pride and dignity of the common people."[2] "I too am a descendant of Walt Whitman," she states, and goes on to say that she aligns herself also with other New World poets, like the Chilean poets Pablo Neruda and Gabriela Mistral and the Black American poets Langston Hughes and Margaret Walker.[3]

The critic Saundra Towns notes that Jordan "has clearly been influenced by the Black Arts movement, the cultural arm of the Black Power movement of the 1970s, whose tenets require the work of art to address itself to a Black audience, explore the complexities of Black life, and work towards the building of an autonomous, vital Black culture."[4] This influence is clear in "Poem about My Rights." That poem, while relentlessly gunning down racial and sexual oppression, is able to say "My name is my own my own my own" as resolutely as Whitman announced his self-celebration in "Song of Myself."

Jordan is fortunate in her ability to use poetic comedy, and she enjoys trying on voices, as in "Onesided Dialog" and "Notes on the Peanut." Her character DeLiza, who appears in "DeLiza Spend the Day in the City," and who elsewhere is "last

1. "For the Sake of a People's Poetry: Walt Whitman and the Rest of Us," in *Passion: New Poems, 1977–1980*, Boston, 1980, p. xx.
2. Walt Whitman, "Democratic Vistas," quoted in Jordan, the same.

3. Jordan, the same, pp. xxiv–xxv.
4. Saundra Towns, "June Jordan," in *Contemporary Poets*, 4th ed., ed. James Vinson and D. L. Kirkpatrick, New York, 1985, p. 439.

drink to close the bars she / holler kissy lips she let / you walk yourself away," is a delicious, streetwise, comic creation.

June Jordan was born in New York City on July 9, 1936. At school and at Barnard College, "I diligently followed orthodox directions from *The Canterbury Tales* right through *The Waste Land* by that consummate Anglophile whose name I can never remember";[5] like Adrienne Rich, then, she began with "the poetry of the fathers" until she began to carve her own. She has taught at schools and colleges in Connecticut and New York, and is presently professor of English at the State University of New York at Stony Brook. In addition to her volumes of poetry, she has written books for children.

5. Jordan, the same, p. x.

Onesided Dialog

OK. So she got back the baby
but what happened to the record player?

No shit. The authorized appropriation
contradicts my falling out of love?

You're wrong. It's not that I gave away my keys.   5
The problem is nobody wants to steal me or my house.

1977

You Came with Shells

You came with shells. And left them:
shells.
They lay beautiful on the table.
Now they lie on my desk
peculiar   5
extraordinary under 60 watts.

This morning I disturb I destroy the window
(and its light) by moving my feet
in the water. There.
It's gone.   10
Last night the moon ranged from the left
to the right side
of the windshield. Only white lines
on a road strike me as
reasonable but   15
nevertheless and too often
we slow down for the fog.

I was going to say a natural environment
means this or
I was going to say we remain out of our   20
element or
sometimes you can get away completely

but the shells
will tell about the howling
and the loss   25
                                                              1977

Second Poem from Nicaragua Libre: War Zone

On the night road from El Rama the cows
congregate fully in the middle and you
wait
looking at the cowhide colors bleached
by the high stars above their bodies   5
big with ribs

At some point you just have to trust
somebody else the soldier
wearing a white shirt the poet
wearing glasses the woman   10
wearing red shoes
into combat

At dawn the student gave me a caramel
candy and pigs and dogs ran into the streets
as the sky began the gradual   15
wide burn and towards the top
of a new mountain I saw
the teen-age shadows of two sentries
armed with automatics
checking the horizon   20
for slow stars
                                                              1985

July 4, 1984: For Buck

April 7, 1978–June 16, 1984

You would shrink back / jump up
cock ears / shake head
tonight
at this bloody idea of a birthday
represented by smackajack explosions   5
of percussive lunacy and downright
(blowawayavillage) boom boom
ratatat-tat-zap

Otherwise any threat would make you stand
quivering perfect as a story   10
no amount of repetition could hope to ruin
perfect as the kangaroo boogie you concocted
with a towel in your jaws and your tail
tucked under and your paws
speeding around the ecstatic circle   15

of your refutation of the rain
outdoors

And mostly you would lunge electrical
and verge into the night
ears practically on flat alert   20
nostrils on the agitated sniff
(for falling rawhide meteors) and laugh
at compliments galore and then
teach me to love you
by hand   25
teach me to love you
by heart

as I do now

                                                               1985

DeLiza Spend the Day in the City

DeLiza drive the car to fetch Alexis
running from she building past the pickets
make she gap tooth laugh why don't
they think up something new they picket now
for three months soon it be too cold   5
to care

Opposite the Thrift Shop
Alexis ask to stop at the Botanica[1]
St. Jacques Majeur find oil to heal she
sister lying in the hospital from lymphoma[2]   10
and much western drug agenda

DeLiza stop. Alexis running back
with oil and myrrh and frankincense[3] and coal
to burn these odors free the myrrh like rocks
a baby break to pieces fit inside the palm   15
of long or short lifelines

DeLiza driving and Alexis
point out Nyabinghi's African emporium
of gems and cloth and Kwanza cards[4] and clay:
DeLiza look.   20

Alexis opening the envelope to give DeLiza
faint gray copies of she article on refugees
from Haiti and some other thing on one white
male one
David Mayer   25
sixty-six

---

1. Shop selling herbs and magical charms.
2. That is, tumor.
3. Two kinds of aromatic gum resins anciently used in cures; the Magi brought "gold, and fran-kincense, and myrrh" as gifts to the Christ child (Matthew 2:11).
4. *Kwanza* is Swahili for "fist."

a second world war veteran
who want America to stop atomic arms
who want America to live without the nuclear death
who want it bad enough to say he'll blow   30
the Washington
D.C. Monument into the southside of the White House
where the First White Lady counting up she
$209,000. dollar china plates and cups and bowls
but cops blow him away   35
blow him / he David Mayer
man of peace
away
Alexis saying, "Shit.
He could be Jesus. Died to save you,   40
didn't he?"
DeLiza nod she head.
God do not seem entirely to be dead.

1985

TONY HARRISON
b. 1937

Tony Harrison was born in the large industrial city of Leeds in 1937. The city itself is a child of the nineteenth-century Industrial Revolution, which grew prosperous, and ugly, thanks to coal, cotton, and manufacturing of many sorts, but which has been in a state of economic decline since the Great Depression of the thirties. Its citizens are likely to be active in the trade union movement and to vote Labour; they and their fellow Yorkshiremen are famous throughout the British Isles for the softness of their speech, for their native idiom often incomprehensible to an outsider, and for their hospitality and neighborliness.

Harrison's family was working-class; we learn something of them from his poems, which often recollect his mother and father with love and with a certain remorse. They took great, often uncomprehending, pride in their poet son, who by dint of his energy and education followed a path which veered from their own. And in his turn, the poet fears that he has lost his grip on the regional Yorkshire dialect which he learned from his mother.

If one kind of speech is seemingly lost, there are many others to be found. A collector of languages, Harrison, as every poet must, treasures speech, but he also treasures the silence which is the context of speech and which is the eloquence of the inarticulate. He knows that "Silence and poetry have their own reserves," that the "mute inglorious Miltons" sometimes achieve a force and dignity which are the special property of those for whom any words are a hard-won achievement. Harrison cites the Cato Street conspirator—one of those executed for having plotted to murder the British cabinet for anti-reform policies—who wrote: "Sir, I Ham a very Bad Hand at Righting." The conspirator, unconsciously we presume, makes a bitter pun, for he is no better at *writing* than at putting things to *rights*. "Three cheers for mute ingloriousness!" shouts the poet; at the same time he praises James Murray, the lexicographer who assembled the great *Oxford English Dictionary,* for his hospitable invitation to all words, aristocratic and low-born alike, to join his dictionary.

The jarring dialects of human behavior are of concern to Harrison whether he writes from his Yorkshire memories, his travels in the United States, or from his four-year stay in Northern Nigeria. Harrison never loses his taste for the idiosyncratic and the human. His landscapes are peopled landscapes; he prefers objects with a human mark and human associations—a pair of brass knuckles, an old shoe.

Tony Harrison has written many verse plays, among them versions of Molière's *The Misanthrope* (1973) and Racine's *Phaedra Britannica* (1975), as well as Aeschylus's *Oresteia* (1981). Together with the Cottesloe Company at England's National Theatre he rendered into a very effective dialectal modern English the texts of a number of medieval mystery plays, as *The Mysteries* (1985).

From *THE SCHOOL OF ELOQUENCE*[1]

'In 1799 special legislation was introduced "utterly suppressing and prohibiting" by name the London Corresponding Society and the United Englishmen.[2] Even the indefatigable conspirator, John Binns, felt that further national organization was hopeless . . . When arrested he was found in possession of a ticket which was perhaps one of the last "covers"[3] for the old LCS: *Admit for the Season to the School of Eloquence.*'
(E. P. Thompson, *The Making of the English Working Class*)

Nunc mea Pierios cupiam per pectora fontes
Irriguas torquere vias, totumque per ora
Volvere laxatum gemino de vertice rivum;
Ut, tenues oblita sonos, audacibus alis
Surgat in officium venerandi Musa parentis.
Hoc utcunque tibi gratum, pater optime, carmen
Exiguum meditatur opus, nec novimus ipsi
Aptius a nobis quae possint munera donis
Respondere tuis, quamvis nec maxima possint
Respondere tuis, nedum ut par gratia donis
Esse queat, vacuis quae redditur arida verbis . . .

Si modo perpetuos sperare audebitis annos,
Et domini superesse rogo, lucemque tueri,
Nec spisso rapient oblivia nigra sub Orco,
Forsitan has laudes, decantatumque parentis
Nomen, ad exemplum, servo servabitis aevo.
(John Milton, 1637)[4]

Heredity

How you became a poet's a mystery!
Wherever did you get your talent from?
I say: I had two uncles, Joe and Harry—
one was a stammerer, the other dumb.

1981

On Not Being Milton[5]

for Sergio Vieira & Armando Guebuza (Frelimo)

Read and committed to the flames, I call
these sixteen lines that go back to my roots

1. A sequence of sixteen-line "sonnets," from which all the rest of our selections except the last are taken.
2. Eighteenth-century English workingmen's radical societies.
3. That is, masking device.
4. The first eleven and the last five lines of a Latin poem, *"Ad Patrem"*—"To (My) Father"—by the seventeenth-century English poet. In Douglas Bush's translation the lines read: "Now I wish that the Pierian waters [of a spring on Mt. Olympus sacred to the Muses] would wind their refreshing way through my breast, and that the whole stream flowing from the twin peaks [of Mt. Parnassus; one sacred to Apollo, god of song, one sacred to Dionysis, god of wine and inspiration] would pour over my lips, so that my Muse, forgetting trivial strains, might rise on bold wings to pay tribute to my revered father. The poem she is meditating is a small effort, and perhaps not very pleasing to you, my dear father; yet I do not know what I can more fitly offer in return for your gifts to me, though my greatest gifts could never match yours, much less can yours be equalled by the barren gratitude expressed in mere words. . . . if only you [that is, my youthful poems] dare hope to enjoy lasting life and survive your master's pyre and see the light, and dark oblivion does not carry you down to crowded Orcus [the underworld of the dead], perhaps these praises, and the name of the father they celebrate, you will preserve as an example to a distant age" (*The Complete Poetical Works of John Milton,* ed. Douglas Bush, Boston, 1965, pp. 99–101). In the poem Milton first ascribes the traditional high qualities to poetry and song, and then goes on to thank his father for the extensive education he provided for him.
5. See note to the Latin epigraph, above.

my *Cahier d'un retour au pays natal*,[6]
my growing black enough to fit my boots.

The stutter of the scold out of the branks   5
of condescension, class and counter-class
thickens with glottals to a lumpen mass
of Ludding morphemes closing up their ranks.[7]
Each swung cast-iron Enoch of Leeds stress[8]
clangs a forged music on the frames of Art,   10
the looms of owned language smashed apart!

Three cheers for mute ingloriousness![9]

Articulation is the tongue-tied's fighting.
In the silence round all poetry we quote
Tidd the Cato Street conspirator who wrote: 15

Sir, I Ham a very Bad Hand at Righting.[1]

1981

Me Tarzan[2]

Outside the whistled gang-call, *Twelfth Street Rag*,
then a Tarzan yodel[3] for the kid who's bored,
whose hand's on his liana[4] . . . no, back
to Labienus[5] and his flaming sword.

Off laikin', then to t'fish 'oil all the boys,   5
off tartin', off to t'flicks[6] but on, on, on,
the foldaway card table, the green baize,
De Bello Gallico and lexicon.[7]

It's only his jaw muscles that he's tensed
into an enraged *shit* that he can't go;   10
down with polysyllables, he's against
all pale-face Caesars, *for* Geronimo.[8]

He shoves the frosted attic skylight, shouts:

6. Compare the proverb, "He's as black as his boot." The "sixteen lines" may refer to Harrison's own attempted translation, since burned, of the sixteen Latin lines by Milton quoted in the epigraph. The French phrase means: "Notebook of a return to the native country," and is the title of a work by the Congolese writer Aimé Césaire.
7. "Branks": that is, struttings, airs; "glottals": that is, glottal stops, or constrictions in the vocal cords, common to north-of-England speech; "lumpen": lower-class; "Ludding": early nineteenth-century workers' protests were called "Luddite riots," after a mythical King Ludd, avenger of worker's wrongs; "morphemes": smallest meaningful units of language.
8. Strong syllable in a poetic line; Harrison notes that "an 'Enoch' is an iron sledgehammer used by the Luddites to smash the frames [used for weaving] which were made by the same Enoch Taylor of Marsden. The cry was: 'Enoch made them, Enoch shall break them!' "
9. Compare "some mute inglorious Milton" in Thomas Gray's "Elegy Written in a Country

Churchyard" (1751).
1. The "Cato Street conspiracy" (1820) was a radical plot, which failed, to kill members of the king's cabinet.
2. In the most famous Tarzan movies (starring Johnny Weissmuller and Maureen O'Sullivan) a standard line was, "Me Tarzan. You Jane."
3. In the movies, Tarzan's cry to the jungle animals.
4. Strong climbing plant.
5. Roman politician, Caesar's legate to Gaul in 52 B.C.
6. The movies ("*t*' " is north English dialect for "the"). "Laikin' ": having fun (often with girls); "tartin' ": going after prostitutes; "t' fish 'oil" may refer to the standard British snack of fish and chips (or french-fried potatoes).
7. Julius Caesar's *On the Gallic Wars* (usual first-year Latin reading text) and dictionary; "baize": coarse fabric covering the table.
8. American Apache chieftain (1829–1909) who led spectacular campaigns against the whites.

Ah bloody can't ah've gorra Latin prose.[9]

His bodiless head that's poking out 's   15
like patriarchal Cissy-bleeding-ro's.[1]

                                                          1981

Book Ends

I

Baked the day she suddenly dropped dead
we chew it slowly that last apple pie.

Shocked into sleeplessness you're scared of bed.
We never could talk much, and now don't try.

You're like book ends, the pair of you, she'd say,   5
Hog that grate, say nothing, sit, sleep, stare . . .

The 'scholar' me, you, worn out on poor pay,
only our silence made us seem a pair.

Not as good for staring in, blue gas,
too regular each bud, each yellow spike.[2]   10

A night you need my company to pass
and she not here to tell us we're alike!

Your life's all shattered into smithereens.

Back in our silences and sullen looks,
for all the Scotch we drink, what's still between 's   15
not the thirty or so years, but books, books, books.

II

The stone's too full. The wording must be terse.
There's scarcely room to carve the FLORENCE on it—

Come on, it's not as if we're wanting verse.
It's not as if we're wanting a whole sonnet!   20

After tumblers of neat *Johnny Walker*[3]
(I think that both of us we're on our third)
you said you'd always been a clumsy talker
and couldn't find another, shorter word
for 'beloved' or for 'wife' in the inscription,   25
but not too clumsy that you can't still cut:

---

9. That is, prose translation for homework;
"gorra": dialect for "gotta."
1. "Bleeding," or more usually "bloody," is a
common English expletive; "cissy": sissy; the orations of Cicero, first-century Roman statesman and
orator, are also usual texts in studying Latin.

2. Flames from the gas fire, common in lower-
class English homes; it is often manufactured to
resemble a log, but its flames are more "regular"
than those of a real fire.
3. Brand of Scotch whiskey.

You're supposed to be the bright boy at description
and you can't tell them what the fuck to put!

I've got to find the right words on my own.

I've got the envelope that he'd been scrawling,   30
mis-spelt, mawkish, stylistically appalling
but I can't squeeze more love into their stone.

1981

Turns

I thought it made me look more 'working class'
(as if a bit of chequered cloth could bridge that gap!)
I did a turn in it before the glass.
My mother said: *It suits you, your dad's cap.*[4]
(She preferred me to wear suits and part my hair: 5
You're every bit as good as that lot are!)

All the pension queue[5] came out to stare.
Dad was sprawled beside the postbox (still VR),[6]
his cap turned inside up beside his head,
smudged H A H in purple Indian ink   10
and Brylcreem[7] slicks displayed so folk might think
he wanted charity for dropping dead.

He never begged. For nowt![8] Death's reticence
crowns his life's, and *me*, I'm opening my trap
to busk the class that broke him for the pence   15
that splash like brackish tears into our cap.[9]

1981

Marked with D.[1]

When the chilled dough of his flesh went in an oven[2]
not unlike those he fuelled all his life,
I thought of his cataracts[3] ablaze with Heaven
and radiant with the sight of his dead wife,
light streaming from his mouth to shape her name,   5
'not Florence and not Flo but always Florrie'.
I thought how his cold tongue burst into flame
but only literally, which makes me sorry,
sorry for his sake there's no Heaven to reach.

4. Soft cloth cap with a visor, commonly worn by, as the poem says, members of the "working class."
5. Line of retired people waiting for their pension (that is, social security) checks.
6. Sidewalk mailbox dating from the time of Queen Victoria and bearing her name and Latin title: *Victoria Regina.*
7. Hair oil.
8. Nothing (northern dialect).
9. "Busk": perform in the street in front of ("buskers" usually provide entertainment for people waiting in theater lines, collecting money afterwards in a cap).
1. Compare the nursery rhyme: "Pat-a-cake, pat-a-cake, baker's man, / Bake me a cake as fast as you can; / Pat it and prick it and mark it with a D [or whatever the baby's initial is], / And put it in the oven for baby and me."
2. His father is being cremated.
3. Clouding of the eye's lens.

I get it all from Earth my daily bread   10
but he hungered for release from mortal speech
that kept him down, the tongue that weighed like lead.

The baker's man that no one will see rise
and England made to feel like some dull oaf
is smoke,[4] enough to sting one person's eyes   15
and ash (not unlike flour) for one small loaf.

                                                                            1981

Self Justification

Me a poet! My daughter with maimed limb
became a more than tolerable sprinter.
And Uncle Joe. Impediment spurred him,
the worst stammerer I've known, to be a printer.

He handset type much faster than he spoke.   5
Those cruel consonants, *ms*, *ps*, and *bs*
on which his jaws and spirit almost broke
flicked into order with sadistic ease.

It seems right that Uncle Joe, 'b-buckshee
from the works',[5] supplied those scribble pads   10
on which I stammered my first poetry
that made me seem a cissy[6] to the lads.

Their aggro[7] towards me, my need of them 's
what keeps my would-be mobile tongue still tied—

aggression, struggle, loss, blank printer's ems   15
by which all   eloquence   gets justified.[8]

                                                                            1981

Lines to My Grandfathers

I

Ploughed parallel as print the stony earth.
The straight stone walls defy the steep grey slopes.
The place's rightness for my mother's birth
exceeds the pilgrim grandson's wildest hopes—

Wilkinson farmed Thrang Crag, Martindale.[9]   5

---

4. The syntax of these lines is: "The baker's man—that [i.e. whom] no one will see rise [to Heaven] / And [whom] England made to feel like some dull oaf—/ is smoke . . ."
5. That is, free from the factory.
6. Sissy.
7. Initially short for "aggravation," it now means "mindless violence."
8. (1) Proven to be right; (2) printer's term: to justify is to space lines of type so that the right-hand margins are even. In handset type and lino-type a "blank em" is a small square of metal that, since it has no letter on it, leaves a blank space the width of the letter M; here, the spaces before and after "eloquence" are "2-em spaces."
9. Small town in the Lake District, northwestern England.

Horner was the Haworth signalman.[1]

Harrison kept a pub with home-brewed ale:

fell farmer, railwayman, and *publican*,[2]

and he, while granma slaved to tend the vat[3]
graced the rival bars 'to make comparisons',   10
Queen's Arms, the Duke of this, the Duke of that,
while his was known as just 'The Harrisons".

He carried cane and *guineas*,[4] no coin baser!
He dressed the gentleman beyond his place
and paid in gold for beer and whisky chaser   15
but took his knuckleduster,[5] 'just in case'.

II

The one who lived with us was grampa Horner
who, I remember, when a sewer rat
got driven into our dark cellar corner
booted it to pulp and squashed it flat.   20

He cobbled all our boots. I've got his last.[6]
We use it as a doorstop on warm days.
My present is propped open by their past
and looks out over straight and narrow ways:

the way one ploughed his land, one squashed a rat,   25
kept railtracks clear, or, dressed up to the nines,
with waxed moustache, gold chain, his cane, his hat,
drunk as a lord could foot it on straight lines.

Fell farmer, railwayman and publican,
I strive to keep my lines direct and straight,   30
and try to make connections where I can—

the knuckleduster's now my paperweight!

1981

1. That is, he ran a signal box, with levers for signals to tell a train to proceed or stop.
2. Owner of a pub; "fell": in northern England, high field.
3. In which the ale is brewed.
4. English coin, now obsolete, worth one pound, one shilling.
5. That is, brass knuckles, a metal tool fitting over the knuckles, for fighting.
6. Metal or wooden form in the shape of a foot, on which shoes are made or repaired.

DIANE WAKOSKI
b. 1937

Diane Wakoski admits that her poetry has certain affinities with surrealism, with poetry of the "deep image," but surrealism of a native American sort. She describes her poems as coming out of the "William Carlos Williams tradition, then influenced

by surrealism via Ginsberg, not surrealism via French writers."[1] Though her poems
do sometimes juxtapose images in a shocking and adventurous way, they also have a
strong narrative and even didactic interest. Indeed, she has recently written that "I
think of myself as a narrative poet, creating both a personal narrative and a personal
mythology."[2]

Critics were quick to classify her, on the basis of her earlier work, among such
"confessional" poets as Lowell, Plath, Snodgrass, and Sexton, but she has been equally
quick to resist that categorization: "Their work is not confessional in the sense that
none of these poets are ashamed of what they did. . . . They felt they had human
experiences." Her own imagery she considers to be "physiological . . . My emotions
are very strong and athletic . . ."[3] and thus she is able to make out of "Belly Dancer"
a strongly physical dramatic monologue.

Wakoski was born in Whittier, California, on August 3, 1937, and attended the
University of California at Berkeley, where she studied under Thom Gunn, who
"made me realize that there are lots of rules about poetry that have nothing to do
with poetry in the abstract. Poetry is human art."[4] She received her B.A. in 1960
and then moved to New York City, where she worked as a bookstore clerk and taught
English at Junior High School 22. Her first book of poems appeared in 1962; however, it was not until 1966, when she won a Robert Frost Fellowship and published
Discrepancies and Apparitions, that any quantity of her work received wider circulation, and as of this writing she has published more than forty books of poetry. She
has taught at a variety of institutions and has been, since 1976, writer-in-residence
at Michigan State University.

1. "The Poet Places Herself," *Falcon*, Spring
1971, 51.
2. Diane Wakoski in *Contemporary Poets*, 4th
ed., ed. James Vinson and D. L. Kirkpatrick, New
York, 1985, p. 890.

3. Diane Wakoski in *The Poet's Craft: Interviews from "The New York Quarterly,"* ed. William Packard, New York, 1987, pp. 204, 206
4. The same, p. 202.

Belly Dancer

Can these movements which move themselves
be the substance of my attraction?
Where does this thin green silk come from that covers my body?
Surely any woman wearing such fabrics
would move her body just to feel them touching every part of her.   5

Yet most of the women frown, or look away, or laugh stiffly.
They are afraid of these materials and these movements in some way.
The psychologists would say they are afraid of themselves, somehow.
Perhaps awakening too much desire—   10
that their men could never satisfy?

So they keep themselves laced and buttoned and made up
in hopes that the framework will keep them stiff enough not to feel
the whole register.
In hopes that they will not have to experience that unquenchable desire for
    rhythm and contact.   15

If a snake glided across this floor
most of them would faint or shrink away.
Yet that movement could be their own.
That smooth movement frightens them—
awakening ancestors and relatives to the tips of the arms and toes.   20

So my bare feet
and my thin green silks
my bells and finger cymbals
offend them—frighten their old-young bodies.
While the men simper and leer—   25
glad for the vicarious experience and exercise.
They do not realize how I scorn them:
or how I dance for their frightened,
unawakened, sweet
women.   30
                                                                   1966

Thanking My Mother for Piano Lessons

The relief of putting your fingers on the keyboard,
as if you were walking on the beach
and found a diamond
as big as a shoe;

as if   5
you had just built a wooden table
and the smell of sawdust was in the air,
your hands dry and woody;

as if
you had eluded   10
the man in the dark hat who had been following you
all week;

the relief
of putting your fingers on the keyboard,
playing the chords of   15
Beethoven,
Bach,
Chopin
        in an afternoon when I had no one to talk to,
        when the magazine advertisement forms of soft sweaters   20
        and clean shining Republican middle-class hair
        walked into carpeted houses
        and left me alone
        with bare floors and a few books

I want to thank my mother   25
for working every day
in a drab office
in garages and water companies
cutting the cream out of her coffee at 40
to lose weight, her heavy body   30
writing its delicate bookkeeper's ledgers
alone, with no man to look at her face,
her body, her prematurely white hair
in love
        I want to thank   35
my mother for working and always paying for

my piano lessons
before she paid the Bank of America loan
or bought the groceries
or had our old rattling Ford repaired.   40

I was a quiet child,
afraid of walking into a store alone,
afraid of the water,
the sun,
the dirty weeds in back yards,   45
afraid of my mother's bad breath,
and afraid of my father's occasional visits home,
knowing he would leave again;
afraid of not having any money,
afraid of my clumsy body,   50
that I knew
        no one would ever love

But I played my way
on the old upright piano
obtained for $10,   55
played my way through fear,
through ugliness,
through growing up in a world of dime-store purchases,
and a desire to love
a loveless world.   60

I played my way through an ugly face
and lonely afternoons, days, evenings, nights,
mornings even, empty
as a rusty coffee can,
played my way through the rustles of spring   65
and wanted everything around me to shimmer like the narrow tide
on a flat beach at sunset in Southern California,
I played my way through
an empty father's hat in my mother's closet
and a bed she slept on only one side of,   70
never wrinkling an inch of
the other side,
waiting,
waiting,

I played my way through honors in school,   75
the only place I could
talk
        the classroom,
        or at my piano lessons, Mrs. Hillhouse's canary always
        singing the most for my talents,   80
        as if I had thrown some part of my body away upon entering
        her house
        and was now searching every ivory case
        of the keyboard, slipping my fingers over black
        ridges and around smooth rocks,   85
        wondering where I had lost my bloody organs,

or my mouth which sometimes opened
like a California poppy, wide and with contrasts
beautiful in sweeping fields,
entirely closed morning and night,   90

I played my way from age to age,
but they all seemed ageless
or perhaps always
old and lonely,
wanting only one thing, surrounded by the dusty bitter-smelling   95
leaves of orange trees,
wanting only to be touched by a man who loved me,
who would be there every night
to put his large strong hand over my shoulder,
whose hips I would wake up against in the morning,   100
whose mustaches might brush a face asleep,
dreaming of pianos that made the sound of Mozart
and Schubert without demanding
that life suck everything
out of you each day,   105
without demanding the emptiness
of a timid little life.

I want to thank my mother
for letting me wake her up sometimes at 6 in the morning
when I practiced my lessons   110
and for making sure I had a piano
to lay my school books down on, every afternoon.
I haven't touched the piano in 10 years,
perhaps in fear that what little love I've been able to
pick, like lint, out of the corners of pockets,   115
will get lost,
slide away,
into the terribly empty cavern of me
if I ever open it all the way up again.
Love is a man   120
with a mustache
gently holding me every night,
always being there when I need to touch him;
he could not know the painfully loud
music from the past that   125
his loving stops from pounding, banging,
battering through my brain,
which does its best to destroy the precarious gray matter when I
am alone;
he does not hear Mrs. Hillhouse's canary singing for me,   130
like the sound of my lesson this week,
telling me,
confirming what my teacher says,
that I have a gift for the piano
few of her other pupils had.   135

When I touch the man
I love,

I want to thank my mother for giving me
piano lessons
all those years,   140
keeping the memory of Beethoven,
a deaf tortured man,
in mind;
      of the beauty that can come
from even an ugly   145
past.

                                                  1971

A Valentine for Ben Franklin Who Drives a Truck in California

I cut the deck
and found a magician
driving a mack truck
down the California grapevine.
His eyes were glistening Japanese beetles,   5
and his hands were surveyors of the moon.
He pulled a carnation
out of his sleeve,
and offered me a ride.
I took the flower and said I was leaving   10
to be an illusionist. He said
he specialized in cards
and sleight of hand.
I touched his mouth and ears
with my lips,   15
        "Keep on truckin,"[1]
I said.
But he laughed and told me a bedtime story.
His body was an elm.
His mouth was filled with grapes.   20
His hands turned my body into new honey.

Now I am home alone,
reading directions
for sawing a beautiful woman in half.
First you start with a mirror. . . .   25

Before I turn down
the crisp sheets of my bed,
I shuffle the tarot deck.
But the magician is missing.[2]
Is he   30
still driving the freeways of California?
Or is he

---

1. Line made famous in the sixties by the cartoonist R. Crumb; to "truck" is to roll along in an easy, untroubled way.
2. In the tarot deck, used for fortune-telling, the first of the "major arcana" (individualized picture cards with special significances) is the Magician.

only an illusion
in my own
magician's
head?

35

1978

MICHAEL HARPER
b. 1938

Though they were forbidden by his parents, young Michael Harper had two secret pleasures: one was riding on the New York subway when there were few other passengers, and the other was listening to recordings of jazz from his parents' collection of 78s. Eventually the young Harper revealed his musical enthusiasms by humming the tunes around the house. He concludes that "You learn most by getting caught doing the things you love." His devotion to jazz—and the blues—has not flagged. Jazz, like the other arts, is an example of what the novelist Ralph Ellison calls "antagonistic cooperation": while the individual musician, soloist for a time, improvises, the other musicians both follow and guide him, and the individual must never lose touch with his fellow-performers. As for the blues, which introduce words into the alchemy of jazz, they are important for Harper because they are a bridge between poetry and music and because of what they say. "They always say *yes* to life; meet life's terms but never accept them."[1]

In Harper's context "saying yes to life" is not an undiscriminating affirmation, for the blues take the view, as Harper does repeatedly in his poems, that life is at best a melancholy business, replete with losses and painful farewells, and that we must remember this state of affairs while never acquiescing in it. One emblem of our occasional victory over the chaos of life is art—the art which emboldens the jazz musician to find one more variation for his self-determined theme, which urges the poet, by his use of an old and demanding verse form, to share in the skill and finesse of a surgical procedure. Indeed the poet sometimes thinks of himself as a surgeon; his poems are written in aid of a healing—certainly in the divided psyches of individuals, even a repairing of the harrowing divisions between men and women of different races. Harper's "Debridement," a sequence of poems, describes, almost cinematically, the life, times, and eventual death of a young Black soldier and veteran of the Vietnam War. Saved by skillful surgeons, he later dies because the society for which he fought cannot provide him with a way to survive. Harper's poems are often about crowds, people violently brought together by the necessities of war and physical suffering, and his lines are crowded, word pressing against word, so that each is well-nigh forced to exhibit its individual energies, to cooperate with a certain antagonism.

Michael Harper was born in Brooklyn, New York, on March 18, 1938. He went to the West Coast for much of his education, attending the City College of Los Angeles and California State University at Los Angeles, where he earned an M.A. in English. He also holds an M.A. from the University of Iowa. He is a professor of English at Brown University.

---

1. Michael Harper, "Don't They Speak Jazz?" in *The Generation of 2000: Contemporary American Poets,* ed. William Heyen, Princeton, N.J., 1984, p. 91.

American History

for John Callahan

Those four black girls blown up
in that Alabama church[1]
remind me of five hundred
middle passage blacks,[2]
in a net, under water   5
in Charleston harbor
so *redcoats*[3] wouldn't find them.
Can't find what you can't see
can you?

                                                           1970

Debridement

Debridement

Black men are oaks cut down.

Congressional Medal of Honor Society
United States of America chartered by
Congress, August 14, 1958; this certifies
that STAC John Henry Louis is a member   5
of this society.

"Don't ask me anything about the
medal. I don't even know how I won
it."

Debridement: The cutting away of dead   10
or contaminated tissue from a wound
to prevent infection.[4]

America: love it or give it back.[5]

Corktown

Groceries ring
in my intestines: 15
grits aint groceries
eggs aint poultry
Mona Lisa was a man:
waltzing in sawdust
I dream my card[6]   20
has five holes in it,
up to twenty holes;

1. By white racists as reprisal against 1960s civil-rights demonstrations.
2. Captured, and en route from Africa to be sold as slaves.
3. That is, British soldiers.
4. Debridement (pronounced de-*breed*-ment) is also performed to heal or clean up infection.

5. Compare slogan, "America: love it or leave it," used by those who supported U.S. policy in Vietnam against those who did not.
6. Officially a soldier's record of injections, but also used to mark off time still to serve in the twelve-month tour of duty in Vietnam.

five shots out of seven
beneath the counter;
surrounded by detectives   25
pale ribbons of valor
my necklace of bullets
powdering the operating table.

Five impaled men loop their ribbons
'round my neck   30
listening to whispers of valor:
"Honey, what you cryin' 'bout?
You made it back."

Caves

Four M-48 tank platoons ambushed
near Dak To, two destroyed: 35
the Ho Chi Minh Trail[7] boils,
half my platoon rockets
into stars near Cambodia,
foot soldiers dance from highland woods
taxing our burning half: 40

there were no caves for them to hide.

We saw no action,
eleven months twenty-two days
in our old tank
burning sixty feet away: 45
I watch them burn inside out:
hoisting through heavy crossfire,
hoisting over turret hatches,
hoisting my last burning man
alive to the ground,   50
our tank artillery shells explode
killing all inside:
hoisting blown burned squad
in tank's bladder,[8]
plug leaks with cave blood: 55

there were no caves for them to hide—

In the Projects[9]

Slung basketballs at Jeffries
House with some welfare kids
weaving in their figure eight hunger.

Mama asked if I was taking anything?   60
I rolled up my sleeves:
no tracks, mama:

7. The route through Laos and Cambodia used
by the North Vietnamese to get supplies and to
infiltrate all areas of South Vietnam; derisively
named after North Vietnamese leader.
8. Slang for a tank's interior.
9. That is, housing projects.

"black-medal-man ain't street-poisoned,"
militants called:
"he's an electronic[1] nigger!"   65

"Better keep electronic nigger 'way."
Electronic Nigger?
Mama, unplug me, please.

A White Friend Flies In from the Coast

Burned—black by birth,
burned—armed with .45,   70
burned—submachine gun,
burned—STAC hunted VC,[2]
burned—killing 5-20,[3]
burned—nobody know for sure;
burned—out of ammo,   75
burned—killed one with gun-stock,
burned—VC AK-47[4] jammed,
burned—killed faceless VC,
burned—over and over,
burned—STAC subdued by three men,   80
burned—three shots: morphine,
burned—tried killing prisoners,
burned—taken to Pleiku,[5]
burned—held down, straitjacket,
burned—whites owe him, hear?   85
burned—I owe him, here.

Mama's Report

"Don't fight, honey,
don't let 'em catch you."

Tour over, gear packed,
hospital over, no job.   90

"Aw man, nothin' happened,"
explorer, altar boy—

Maybe it's 'cause they killed people
and don't know why they did?

My boy had color slides of dead people,   95
stacks of dead Vietnamese.

MP's[6] asked if he'd been arrested
since discharge, what he'd been doin':

---

1. Military slang for a soldier who works with
electronic equipment, such as radios.
2. Vietcong, the North Vietnamese.
3. That is, five to twenty enemy soldiers;
"nobody know for sure" because body counts during the war were inaccurate.
4. Russian assault rifle used by the Vietcong.
5. Large provincial city.
6. Military Police.

"Lookin' at slides,
looking' at stacks of slides, mostly." 100

Fifteen minutes later a colonel called
from the Defense Department, said he'd won the medal;

could he be in Washington with his family,
maybe he'd get a job now; he qualified.

The Democrats had lost,[7] the president said; 105
there were signs of movement in Paris:

Fixing Certificates: Dog Tags:[8] Letters Home

Our heliteam had mid-air blowout
dropping flares—5 burned alive.[9]

The children carry hand
grenades to and from piss tubes.[1] 110

Staring at tracer bullets[2]
rice is the focal point of war.

On amphibious raid, our heliteam
found dead VC with maps of our compound.[3]

On morning sick call you unzip; 115
before you piss you get a smear.[4]

"VC reamed that *mustang* a new asshole"—
even at movies: "no round-eye[5] pussy no more"—

Tympanic membrane damage: high gone—
20-40 db loss mid-frequencies.[6] 120

Scrub-typhus, malaria, dengue fever, cholera;
rotting buffalo, maggoted dog, decapped children.[7]

Bangkok: amber dust, watches, C-rations,
elephanthide billfolds, cameras, smack.[8]

Sand&tinroof bunkers, 81/120 mm:[9] 125
"Health record terminated this date by reason of death."

7. That is, the election of 1968, when the Republican Richard Nixon became president.
8. Metal identification tags, to be worn by soldiers at all times; the "certificates" are death certificates.
9. That is, the entire crew, since helicopter teams consisted of four to five men.
1. Local lavatories.
2. Ammunition that gives off a trail of smoke or fire.
3. That is, camp; "amphibious raid": surprise attack using an amphibious vehicle.
4. Test for venereal disease; "sick call": scheduled time for visiting medical officer.
5. Slang for Occidental; "mustangs" were American World War II planes which the Viet-

cong used in the war.
6. That is, loss of hearing in the high and mid frequencies caused by "tympanic membrane" (eardrum) or nerve damage; "db": decibel, unit for measuring intensity of sound.
7. "Scrub-typhus" and the others in line 121 are acute tropical diseases; "rotting buffalo" and "maggoted dog" are slang terms for still more tropical diseases; "decapped": decapitated.
8. Bangkok, capital of Thailand, where items mentioned could be bought; "amber dust": cocaine; "C-rations": canned army field food; "smack": heroin.
9. An 81-millimeter mortar shell or a 120-millimeter field-piece shell; "bunker": fortified dugout.

Vaculoated amoeba, bacillary dysentery, hookworm;[1]
thorazine, tetracycline, darvon for diarrhea.

'*Conitus*': I wanna go home to mama;
Brown's mixture, ETH with codeine, cortisone skin-creams.[2]   130

Written on helipad fantail 600 bed *Repose;*[3]
"no purple heart, hit by 'nother marine."

"Vascular[4] repair, dissection, debridement":
sharp bone edges, mushy muscle, shrapnel: stainless bucket.

Bodies in polyethylene bag: transport: 135
'Tan San Nhat Mortuary'

Blood, endotracheal tube, prep
abdomen,[5] mid-chest to scrotum—

"While you're fixin' me doc,
can you fix them ingrown hairs on my face?"   140

"They didn't get my balls, did they?"
50 mg thorazine—"Yes they did, marine!"

Street-Poisoned

Swans loom on the playground
swooning in the basket air,
the nod of their bills   145
in open flight, open formation.
Street-poisoned, a gray mallard
skims into our courtyard with a bag:

And he poisons them—
And he poisons them—   150

Electronic-nigger-recruiter,
my pass is a blade
near the sternum[6]
cutting in:
you can make this a career.   155

Patches itch on my chest and shoulders—
I powder them with phisohex[7]
solution from an aerosol can:
you can make this a career.

Pickets of insulin[8] dab the cloudy   160
hallways in a spray.

1. Worms in the intestine causing dysentery, disease with acute diarrhea.
2. Antibiotics, tranquilizers, and painkillers, as also in line 128 above.
3. That is, on the takeoff pad at the rear of the (aircraft-carrier) *Repose.* The Purple Heart is a medal given for being wounded or killed in action.
4. Of the blood vessels.
5. Preparing the abdomen for surgery by shaving and cleaning; "endotracheal tube": tube inserted into the trachea to enable breathing during surgery.
6. Breastbone.
7. A brand of antiseptic soap.
8. Hormone used in the treatment of diabetes.

Circuits of change
march to an honor guard—
I am prancing:
I am prancing: 165

you can make this a career.

Makin' Jump Shots

He waltzes into the lane
'cross the free-throw line,
fakes a drive, pivots,
floats from the asphalt turf
in an arc of black light,   170
and sinks two into the chains.[9]

One on one he fakes
down the main, passes
into the free lane   175
and hits the chains.

A sniff in the fallen air—
he stuffs it through the chains
riding high:
"traveling" someone calls—   180
and he laughs, stepping
to a silent beat, gliding
as he sinks two into the chains.

Debridement: Operation Harvest Moon: On Repose

The sestina[1] traces a circle in language and body.

Stab incision below nipple,
left side; insert large chest tube;   185
sew to skin, right side;
catch blood from tube
in gallon drain bottle.
Wash abdomen with phisohex;
shave; spray brown iodine prep.   190

Stab incision below sternum
to symphis pubis[2]
catch blood left side;
sever reddish brown spleen
cut in half;[3] tie off blood supply;   195
check retroperitoneal,
kidney, renal artery[4] bleeding.

Dissect lateral wall
abdominal cavity; locate kidney;

9. That is, of the basketball net.
1. Complex poetic form in which the same six words must be used at the end of the lines in each stanza.
2. Or "symphysis"; that is, the pubic bones.

3. That is, remove the spleen (which had been) cut in half.
4. Artery near the kidneys; "retroperitoneal"; behind the peritoneum, the membrane lining the abdomen.

pack colon, small intestine;   200
cut kidney; suture[5] closely;
inch by inch check bladder,
liver, abdominal wall, stomach:
25 units blood, pressure down.

Venous pressure: 8; lumbar   205
musculature, lower spinal column
pulverized; ligate blood vessels,[6]
right forearm; trim meat, bone ends;
tourniquet above fracture, left arm;
urine, negative: 4 hours; pressure   210
unstable; remove shrapnel flecks.

Roll on stomach; 35 units blood;
pressure zero; insert plastic blood
containers, pressure cuffs; pump chest
drainage tube; wash wounds sterile   215
saline;[7] dress six-inch ace wraps;
wrap both legs, toe to groin; left arm
plaster, finger to shoulder: 40 units blood.

Pressure, pulse, respiration up;
remove bloody gowns; scrub; redrape;   220
5 cc vitamin K; thorazine: sixth
laparotomy; check hyperventilation;[8]
stab right side incision below nipple;
insert large chest tube; catch blood drain bottle . . .

The Family of Debridement

Theory: Inconvenienced subject will return to hospital   225
if loaned Thunderbird
Withdrawn. Hope: Subject returns,
Treatment:
Foreclosure for nine months unpaid mortgage;
wife tells subject hospital wants deposit,   230
Diseased cyst[9] removal:
'Ain't you gonna give me a little kiss good-bye'
Subject-wife: To return with robe and curlers—
Subject tells friend he'll pay $15 to F's stepfather
if he'll drive him to pick up money owed him.   235

"This guy lives down the street,
I don't want him to see me coming."

"It looked odd for a car filled with blacks
to be parked in the dark in a white neighborhood,
so we pulled the car out under a streetlight   240
so everybody could see us."

---

5. That is, stitch.
6. "Venous": of the veins; "lumbar": of the lowest part of the spinal column; "ligate": tie with surgical thread.
7. Salt solution.
8. Excessive rate and depth of breathing; "laparotomy": cutting into the abdominal wall.
9. That is, tumor.

Store manager: *"I first hit him with two bullets*
so I pulled the trigger until my gun was empty."

"I'm going to kill you, you white MF," store manager
told police. Police took cardload, F and F's parents for   245
further questioning. Subject died on operating table: 5 hrs:

Subject buried on grass slope, 200 yards
east of Kennedy Memorial,
overlooking Potomac and Pentagon,
to the south,   250
Arlington National Cemetery.

Army honor guard
in dress blues,
carried out assignment
with precision: 255

1973, 1977

SEAMUS HEANEY
b. *1939*

After the heavily accented melodies of Yeats, and that poet's elegiac celebrations of imaginative glories, Seamus Heaney addresses his readers in a quite different key. There are none of Yeats's Olympians about; the figures who appear in Heaney's verse have quite human dimensions. Nature for him does not mean the lakes, woods, and swans visible from the big house. Instead, a farmer's son, Heaney sees nature as "the dark-clumped grass where cows or horses dunged, / the cluck when pith-lined chestnut shells split open" (the latter a line that Hopkins would have welcomed). These and much else are things to remember "when you have grown away and stand at last / at the very centre of the empty city." Nature is equipment such as a harrow pin, sledge-head, or trowel, as if its center were protrusive objects and not recessive vistas.

At moments this sense of objects as being like people dragging their histories with them moves toward allegory, as in "A Kite for Michael and Christopher," where the soaring kite reminds the poet humorously of the soul, and the sudden feeling of the kite's weight makes him feel "the strumming, rooted, long-tailed pull of grief." He reminds his beloved that their bodies are temples of the Holy Ghost in order to compare the feeling of her underbreast to that of a ciborium in the palm, as if Christianity existed to supply him with erotic imagery ("La Toilette"). The solid Heaney world melts a little, though he never really leaves the earth behind, and subjects it to sharp scrutiny relieved by playfulness.

One of Heaney's most adventurous groups of poems is that entitled "Station Island." Station Island, sometimes known as St. Patrick's Purgatory, is an island in Lough Derg, County Donegal, to which for hundreds of years people have made pilgrimages. No longer a believer, Heaney has had the happy thought of making the pilgrimage on All Souls' Night, with frequent use of Dantean *terza rima*. The poet encounters a series of familiar ghosts: a woodcutter he has known, an old master from his Anahorish School, a priest friend who died of fever in a mission compound, an athletic schoolfellow killed by the Irish Republican Army and a second cousin killed by a Protestant in Northern Ireland, an archeologist, his mother, a first girlfriend. They tell their stories to this Irish Dante, and tell them well, and implicate him in their replies. The principal ghost is that of James Joyce, who rejects the poet's pilgrimage: "Your obligation / is not discharged by any common rite." He urges him instead to "keep at a tangent" and find his own "echo-soundings, searches, probes, allurements, / elver gleams in the dark of the whole sea."

Heaney fittingly finds his model not in Yeats, who was constantly trying to break through the facade of what is, but in Joyce, who "found the living world enough" if sufficiently epiphanized. Joyce gives sanction to the picture Heaney elsewhere gives of himself as "an inner emigré," who pursues "a migrant solitude." Heaney's poems have a tough rind, as though the author knew that for his purposes deferred comprehension is better than instant. Obliquity suits him. Heaney's prodigious talent continues to exfoliate and augment.

Seamus Heaney was born in County Derry in the North of Ireland on April 13, 1939. He was educated at St. Columb's College before going on to take a first class honours degree in English at Queen's University in Belfast. He had various teaching jobs before becoming a professor at Harvard, where he has been spending a part of each year since 1982. The rest of the year he lives with his wife and two children in Dublin.

Requiem for the Croppies[1]

The pockets of our great coats full of barley—
No kitchens on the run, no striking camp—
We moved quick and sudden in our own country.
The priest lay behind ditches with the tramp.
A people, hardly marching—on the hike—   5
We found new tactics happening each day:
We'd cut through reins and rider with the pike
And stampeded cattle into infantry,
Then retreat through hedges where cavalry must be thrown.
Until, on Vinegar Hill, the fatal conclave.   10
Terraced thousands died, shaking scythes at cannon.
The hillside blushed, soaked in our broken wave.
They buried us without shroud or coffin
And in August the barley grew up out of the grave.[2]

1969

Bogland[3]

for T. P. Flanagan

We have no prairies
To slice a big sun at evening—

1. Irish rebels of 1798, who wore their hair cut (cropped) very short in sympathy with the French Revolution. A "requiem" is a dirge or solemn chant for the dead.
2. Heaney notes that this poem "was written in 1966 when most poets in Ireland were straining to celebrate the anniversary of the 1916 Rising [for Irish independence against British rule]. That rising was the harvest of seeds sown in 1798, when revolutionary republican ideals and national feeling coalesced in the doctrines of Irish republicanism and in the rebellion of 1798 itself—unsuccessful and savagely put down. The poem was born of and ended with an image of resurrection based on the fact that some time after the rebels were buried in

common graves, these graves began to sprout with young barley, growing up from barley corn which the 'croppies' had carried in their pockets to eat while on the march. The oblique implication was that the seeds of violent resistance sowed in the Year of Liberty had flowered in what Yeats called 'the right rose tree' of 1916." See Yeats's "Easter 1916," above, p. 81. Seamus Heaney, "Feeling into Words," in his *Preoccupations: Selected Prose 1968–1978*, New York, 1980, p. 56. The phrase "the right rose tree" is in Yeats's poem "The Rose Tree."
3. "I had been vaguely wishing to write a poem about bogland, chiefly because it is a landscape that has a strange assuaging effect on me, one with

Everywhere the eye concedes to
Encroaching horizon,

Is wooed into the cyclops' eye   5
Of a tarn.[4] Our unfenced country
Is bog that keeps crusting
Between the sights of the sun.

They've taken the skeleton
Of the Great Irish Elk   10
Out of the peat,[5] set it up
An astounding crate full of air.

Butter sunk under
More than a hundred years
Was recovered salty and white.   15
The ground itself is kind, black butter

Melting and opening underfoot,
Missing its last definition
By millions of years.
They'll never dig coal here,[6]   20

Only the waterlogged trunks
Of great firs, soft as pulp.
Our pioneers keep striking
Inwards and downwards,

Every layer they strip   25
Seems camped on before.
The bogholes might be Atlantic seepage.
The wet centre is bottomless.[7]

1969

Punishment[8]

I can feel the tug
of the halter at the nape

---

associations reaching back into early childhood. We used to hear about bog-butter, butter kept fresh for a great number of years under the peat. Then when I was at school the skeleton of an elk had been taken out of a bog nearby and a few of our neighbours had got their photographs in the paper, peering out across its antlers. So I began to get an idea of bog as the memory of the landscape, or as a landscape that remembered everything that happened in and to it. In fact, if you go round the National Museum in Dublin, you will realize that a great proportion of the most cherished material heritage of Ireland was 'found in a bog' " (Seamus Heaney, "Feeling into Words," p. 54).

4. Mountain lake or pool; the mythical cyclops had only one eye.

5. Carbonized vegetable tissue in the ground.

6. Because the ground is too wet for it to form.

7. Older people "were afraid we might fall into the pools in the old workings [excavations for mining or quarrying] so they put it about (and we believed them) that *there was no bottom* in the bog-holes. Little did they—or I—know that I would filch it for the last line of a book" (Heaney, the same, p. 56).

8. In 1951 the peat-stained body of a young girl, who lived in the late first century A.D., was recovered from a bog in Windeby, Germany. As P. V. Glob describes her in *The Bog People*, she "lay naked in the hole in the peat, a bandage over the eyes and a collar round the neck. The band across the eyes was drawn tight and had cut into the neck and the base of the nose. We may feel sure that it had been used to close her eyes to this world. There was no mark of strangulation on the neck, so that it had not been used for that purpose." Her hair "had been shaved off with a razor on the left side of the head. . . . When the brain was removed the convolutions and folds of the surface could be clearly seen. [Glob reproduces a photograph of her brain]. . . . this girl of only fourteen had had an inadequate winter diet. . . .

of her neck, the wind
on her naked front.

It blows her nipples   5
to amber beads,
it shakes the frail rigging
of her ribs.

I can see her drowned
body in the bog,   10
the weighing stone,
the floating rods and boughs.

Under which at first
she was a barked sapling
that is dug up   15
oak-bone, brain-firkin:[9]

her shaved head
like a stubble of black corn,
her blindfold a soiled bandage,
her noose a ring   20

to store
the memories of love.
Little adulteress,
before they punished you

you were flaxen-haired,   25
undernourished, and your
tar-black face was beautiful.
My poor scapegoat,

I almost love you
but would have cast, I know,   30
the stones of silence.
I am the artful voyeur

of your brain's exposed
and darkened combs,[1]
your muscles' webbing   35
and all your numbered bones:

I who have stood dumb
when your betraying sisters,
cauled in tar,
wept by the railings,[2]   40

To keep the young body under, some birch
branches and a big stone were laid upon her."
According to the Roman historian Tacitus, the
Germanic peoples punished adulterous women by
shaving off their hair and then scourging them out
of the village or killing them.
    9. Small cask.
    1. Valleys.

2. Women in Belfast, Northern Ireland, are
sometimes shaven, stripped, tarred, and handcuffed to railings as punishment by the IRA for
keeping company with British soldiers. "Cauled":
wrapped or enclosed; a caul is the inner fetal
membrane which at birth, when it is unruptured,
sometimes covers the infant's head.

who would connive
in civilized outrage
yet understand the exact
and tribal, intimate revenge.

1975

The Strand at Lough Beg[3]

In Memory of Colum McCartney

All round this little island, on the strand
Far down below there, where the breakers strive,
Grow the tall rushes from the oozy sand.
—Dante, *Purgatorio,*[4] I, 100–103

Leaving the white glow of filling stations
And a few lonely streetlamps among fields
You climbed the hills toward Newtownhamilton
Past the Fews Forest, out beneath the stars—
Along that road, a high, bare pilgrim's track   5
Where Sweeney fled before the bloodied heads,[5]
Goat-beards and dogs' eyes in a demon pack
Blazing out of the ground, snapping and squealing.
What blazed ahead of you? A faked road block?
The red lamp swung, the sudden brakes and stalling   10
Engine, voices, heads hooded and the cold-nosed gun?
Or in your driving mirror, tailing headlights
That pulled out suddenly and flagged you down
Where you weren't known and far from what you knew:
The lowland clays and waters of Lough Beg,   15
Church Island's[6] spire, its soft treeline of yew.

There you used hear guns fired behind the house
Long before rising time, when duck shooters
Haunted the marigolds and bulrushes,
But still were scared to find spent cartridges,   20
Acrid, brassy, genital, ejected,
On your way across the strand to fetch the cows.
For you and yours and yours and mine fought shy,
Spoke an old language of conspirators
And could not crack the whip or seize the day: 25
Big-voiced scullions, herders, feelers round
Haycocks and hindquarters, talkers in byres,[7]
Slow arbitrators of the burial ground.

Across that strand of yours the cattle graze
Up to their bellies in an early mist   30
And now they turn their unbewildered gaze

3. Lake in Northern Ireland; "strand": beach. "Colum McCartney, a relative of the author's, was the victim of a random sectarian [that is, Catholic vs. Protestant] killing in the late summer of 1975" (Heaney's note).
4. *Purgatorio,* the second part of the Italian medieval poet Dante's *Divine Comedy,* is about the mountain of Purgatory and its various groups

of repentant sinners after death.
5. "Sweeney is the hero of a Middle Irish prose and poem sequence, one part of which takes place in the Fews" (Heaney's note).
6. Island in Lough Beg on which is a spire erected in 1788 by the Earl of Bristol.
7. Barns; "scullions": lowest-ranking kitchen help.

To where we work our way through squeaking sedge[8]
Drowning in dew. Like a dull blade with its edge
Honed bright, Lough Beg half shines under the haze.
I turn because the sweeping of your feet   35
Has stopped behind me, to find you on your knees
With blood and roadside muck in your hair and eyes,
Then kneel in front of you in brimming grass
And gather up cold handfuls of the dew
To wash you, cousin. I dab you clean with moss   40
Fine as the drizzle out of a low cloud.
I lift you under the arms and lay you flat.
With rushes that shoot green again, I plait
Green scapulars[9] to wear over your shroud.

                                                           1979

The Otter

When you plunged
The light of Tuscany[1] wavered
And swung through the pool
From top to bottom.

I loved your wet head and smashing crawl,   5
Your fine swimmer's back and shoulders
Surfacing and surfacing again
This year and every year since.

I sat dry-throated on the warm stones.
You were beyond me.   10
The mellowed clarities, the grape-deep air
Thinned and disappointed.

Thank God for the slow loadening,[2]
When I hold you now
We are closed and deep   15
As the atmosphere on water.

My two hands are plumbed water.
You are my palpable, lithe
Otter of memory
In the pool of the moment,   20

Turning to swim on your back,
Each silent, thigh-shaking kick
Re-tilting the light,
Heaving the cool at your neck.

And suddenly you're out,   25
Back again, intent as ever,
Heavy and frisky in your freshened pelt,
Printing the stones.

                                                           1979

---

8. Coarse, grasslike plants.
9. Religious or fraternal bands of cloth worn front and back over the shoulders; "plait": braid.

1. Area in western Italy.
2. Dialectal version of "loading."

The Harvest Bow

As you plaited the harvest bow[3]
You implicated the mellowed silence in you
In wheat that does not rust
But brightens as it tightens twist by twist
Into a knowable corona,   5
A throwaway love-knot[4] of straw.

Hands that aged round ashplants and cane sticks
And lapped the spurs on a lifetime of game cocks[5]
Harked to their gift and worked with fine intent
Until your fingers moved somnambulant:[6]   10
I tell and finger it like braille,
Gleaning[7] the unsaid off the palpable,

And if I spy into its golden loops
I see us walk between the railway slopes
Into an evening of long grass and midges,   15
Blue smoke straight up, old beds and ploughs in hedges,
An auction notice on an outhouse wall—
You with a harvest bow in your lapel,

Me with the fishing rod, already homesick
For the big lift of these evenings, as your stick   20
Whacking the tips off weeds and bushes
Beats out of time, and beats, but flushes
Nothing: that original townland
Still tongue-tied in the straw tied by your hand.

The end of art is peace   25
Could be the motto of this frail device
That I have pinned up on our deal[8] dresser—
Like a drawn snare
Slipped lately by the spirit of the corn
Yet burnished by its passage, and still warm.   30

1979

From Station Island[9]

XII

Like a convalescent, I took the hand
stretched down from the jetty, sensed again
an alien comfort as I stepped on ground

---

3. Ornamental knot made of straw or grain-stalk; "plaited": braided, tied.
4. Knot tied in a special way, supposedly expressive of love; "corona": that is, circle of light.
5. That is, spent a lifetime polishing (lapping) the metal spurs (worn by) game cocks; "ashplants": walking sticks made from ash saplings.
6. As if sleepwalking.
7. Gathering (as of grain at harvest).
8. Pine.
9. "*Station Island* is a sequence of dream encounters with familiar ghosts, set on Station Island on Lough Derg in Co. Donegal. The island is also known as St Patrick's Purgatory because of a tradition that Patrick was the first to establish the penitential vigil of fasting and praying which still constitutes the basis of the three-day pilgrimage. Each unit of the contemporary pilgrim's exercises is called a 'station,' and a large part of each station involves walking barefoot and praying round the 'beds,' stone circles which are said to be the remains of early medieval monastic cells" (Heaney's note).

to find the helping hand still gripping mine,
fish-cold and bony, but whether to guide   5
or to be guided I could not be certain

for the tall man in step at my side
seemed blind, though he walked straight as a rush
upon his ash plant, his eyes fixed straight ahead.[10]

Then I knew him in the flesh   10
out there on the tarmac[1] among the cars,
wintered hard and sharp as a blackthorn bush.

His voice eddying with the vowels of all rivers[2]
came back to me, though he did not speak yet,
a voice like a prosecutor's or a singer's,   15

cunning,[3] narcotic, mimic, definite
as a steel nib's downstroke, quick and clean,
and suddenly he hit a little basket

with his stick, saying 'Your obligation
is not discharged by any common rite.   20
What you must do must be done on your own

so get back in harness. The main thing is to write
for the joy of it. Cultivate a work-lust
that imagines its haven like your hands at night

dreaming the sun in the sunspot of a breast.   25
You are fasted now, light-headed, dangerous.
Take off from here. And don't be so earnest,

let others wear the sackcloth and the ashes.[4]
Let go, let fly, forget.
You've listened long enough. Now strike your note.'   30

It was as if I had stepped free into space
alone with nothing that I had not known
already. Raindrops blew in my face

as I came to. 'Old father, mother's son,
there is a moment in Stephen's diary   35
for April the thirteenth, a revelation

set among my stars—that one entry
has been a sort of password in my ears,
the collect of a new epiphany,[5]

10. In this last section of the poem, the "familiar ghost" is James Joyce, Irish writer, who was almost blind. "Ash plant": walking-stick made of an ash sapling; Stephen Dedalus, one of the two heroes of James Joyce's *Ulysses*, carries one. Compare the stanza form of Eliot's "Little Gidding" (above, p. 295).
1. That is, surfaced parking lot.
2. The "Anna Livia Plurabelle" section of *Fin-*

negans Wake resounds with the names of many rivers.
3. "The only arms I allow myself to use—silence, exile, and cunning" (Joyce's *Portrait of the Artist As a Young Man*).
4. Traditional dress of penitents.
5. Manifestations of a divine being, as of the infant Christ to the Magi (Matthew 2); in the Christian calendar, the Feast of the Epiphany is

the Feast of the Holy Tundish.'[6] 'Who cares,'   40
he jeered, 'any more? The English language
belongs to us. You are raking at dead fires,

a waste of time for somebody your age.
That subject people stuff is a cod's[7] game,
infantile, like your peasant pilgrimage.   45

You lose more of yourself than you redeem
doing the decent thing. Keep at a tangent.
When they make the circle wide, it's time to swim

out on your own and fill the element
with signatures on your own frequency,   50
echo soundings, searches, probes, allurements,

elver-gleams[8] in the dark of the whole sea.'
The shower broke in a cloudburst, the tarmac
fumed and sizzled. As he moved off quickly

the downpour loosed its screens round his straight walk.   55

1985

Alphabets

I

A shadow his father makes with joined hands
And thumbs and fingers nibbles on the wall
Like a rabbit's head. He understands
He will understand more when he goes to school.

There he draws smoke with chalk the whole first week,   5
Then draws the forked stick that they call a Y.
This is writing. A swan's neck and swan's back
Make the 2 he can see now as well as say.

Two rafters and a cross-tie on the slate[9]
Are the letter some call *ah,* some call *ay.*   10
There are charts, there are headlines, there is a right
Way to hold the pen and a wrong way.

First it is 'copying out', and then 'English'
Marked correct with a little leaning hoe.
Smells of inkwells rise in the classroom hush.   15
A globe in the window tilts like a coloured O.

January 6. "Collect": short prayer assigned to a particular day. "Epiphany" was also the term Joyce used for the prose poems he wrote as a young man; it meant, he said, the "sudden revelation of the whatness of things."

6. "See the end of James Joyce's *Portrait of the Artist as a Young Man*" (Heaney's note): "*13 April:* That tundish [funnel] has been on my mind for a long time. I looked it up and find it English and good old blunt English too. Damn the dean of studies and his funnel! What did he come here for to teach us his own language or to learn it from us? Damn him one way or the other!"

7. Fool's.

8. Gleams as of young eels.

9. Small rectangular sheet of rocklike substance, written on with chalk in school.

II

Declensions sang on air like a *hosanna*[1]
As, column after stratified column,
Book One of *Elementa Latina*,
Marbled and minatory,[2] rose up in him.   20

For he was fostered next in a stricter school
Named for the patron saint of the oak wood[3]
Where classes switched to the pealing of a bell
And he left the Latin forum for the shade

Of new calligraphy[4] that felt like home.   25
The letters of this alphabet were trees.
The capitals were orchards in full bloom,
The lines of script like briars coiled in ditches.

Here in her snooded garment and bare feet,
All ringleted in assonance and woodnotes,[5]   30
The poet's dream stole over him like sunlight
And passed into the tenebrous[6] thickets.

He learns this other writing. He is the scribe
Who drove a team of quills on his white field.
Round his cell door the blackbirds dart and dab.   35
Then self-denial, fasting, the pure cold.

By rules that hardened the farther they reached north
He bends to his desk and begins again.
Christ's sickle[7] has been in the undergrowth.
The script grows bare and Merovingian.[8]   40

III

The globe has spun. He stands in a wooden O.
He alludes to Shakespeare. He alludes to Graves.[9]
Time has bulldozed the school and school window.
Balers drop bales like printouts where stooked sheaves[1]

Made lambdas on the stubble once at harvest   45
And the delta face of each potato pit
Was patted straight and moulded against frost.
All gone, with the omega that kept

1. Cry of adoration; "declensions": changes in word forms according to their grammatical cases (in grammar books these are usually printed in columns).
2. Menacing; *Elementa Latina:* Elements of Latin.
3. St. Louis (1214–1270), king of France, administered justice under an oak tree.
4. Elegant handwriting, as in medieval manuscripts; "forum": public meeting place in old Roman city. The critic Neil Corcoran suggests that the "new calligraphy" is "the Irish script" and that the poem moves from English through Latin to Irish (*Times Literary Supplement*, June 26, 1987, p. 681).

5. "Snooded": with a net or cloth bag holding her hair; "assonance": repetition of vowels in poetry; "woodnotes": natural, artless verbal expressions.
6. Murky.
7. In Revelation 14:14, Christ is portrayed as having "in his hand a sharp sickle," to reap "the harvest of the earth."
8. Characteristic of the first Frankish dynasty (500–751) in northern Europe.
9. British poet (see above, p. 326). Shakespeare, in the Chorus's (or prologue's) first speech in *Henry V*, compares the theater building of his time to a "wooden O."
1. That is, gatherings of grain stalks and ears.

Watch above each door, the good luck horse-shoe.[2]
Yet shape-note language, absolute on air   50
As Constantine's sky-lettered IN HOC SIGNO[3]
Can still command him; or the necromancer[4]

Who would hang from the doomed ceiling of his house
A figure of the world with colours in it
So that the figure of the universe   55
And 'not just single things' would meet his sight

When he walked abroad. As from his small window
The astronaut sees all he has sprung from,
The risen, aqueous, singular, lucent O
Like a magnified and buoyant ovum[5]   60

Or like my own wide pre-reflective stare
All agog at the plasterer on his ladder
Skimming our gable[6] and writing our name there
With his trowel point, letter by strange letter.

         1987

2. These images allude to the shapes of capital letters in the Greek alphabet: lambda: Λ; delta: Δ; omega: Ω.
3. Constantine the Great (d. 337), according to legend, saw, before a battle, a vision in the heavens of a cross and the words *In hoc signo vinces* ("in this sign you will conquer"); he won the battle and converted to Christianity.
4. One who conjures the spirits of the dead in order to reveal the future.
5. That is, cell (also Latin for "egg"); "aqueous": watery; "lucent": glowing with light.
6. That is, putting a thin layer of plaster over the triangular end of our house's roof.

MARGARET ATWOOD
b. 1939

Margaret Atwood, born November 18, 1939, published her first book just after taking her B.A. from Victoria College, University of Toronto, in 1961. She then took an M.A. at Harvard, and spent about five years at that university, publishing several volumes of verse in the meantime. She has since written, besides verse, novels, stories, and critical prose, all excellent in their kinds. Her poems are written with great confidence, though they portray a quality she shares with one of her characters, Susanne Moodie, "the inescapable doubleness of her own vision."[1] Her experiences seem always to rouse contradictory responses.

In poems dealing with concerns the atmosphere is again charged both positively and negatively. In *The Journals of Susanne Moodie* she explores not only her character's attitude towards her native Canada, but her own:

> I am a word
> in a foreign language.
>
> there is no city;
> there is the centre of a forest.

She describes also in prose how Moodie, an actual person, feels:

> She claims to be an ardent Canadian patriot while all the time she is standing back from the country and criticizing it as though she were a detached observer,

1. *The Journals of Susanne Moodie*, Toronto, 1970, p. 63.

a stranger. Perhaps this is the way we still live. We are all immigrants to this place even if we were born here: the country is too big for anyone to inhabit completely, and in the parts unknown to us we move in fear, exiles and invaders. (p. 62)

Attitudes equally interwoven occur when Margaret Atwood describes a love affair. Even the title, *Power Politics*, displays her ambiguous point of view, for she wishes attachment even as she detaches herself. She is a feminist, but that is not the source of her humorous metaphors for a complicated involvement. All the stages and phases take on the aspect of power politics, not because there is any brutality but because of the inescapable otherness of the loved person. Margaret Atwood, though her voice is pitched low, commands instant attention.

This Is a Photograph of Me

It was taken some time ago.
At first it seems to be
a smeared
print: blurred lines and grey flecks
blended with the paper;   5

then, as you scan
it, you see in the left-hand corner
a thing that is like a branch: part of a tree
(balsam or spruce) emerging
and, to the right, halfway up   10
what ought to be a gentle
slope, a small frame house.

In the background there is a lake,
and beyond that, some low hills.

(The photograph was taken   15
the day after I drowned.

I am in the lake, in the center
of the picture, just under the surface.

It is difficult to say where
precisely, or to say   20
how large or small I am:
the effect of water
on light is a distortion

but if you look long enough,
eventually   25
you will be able to see me.)

                                                              1966

The Animals in that Country

In that country the animals
have the faces of people:

the ceremonial
cats possessing the streets

the fox run
politely to earth, the huntsmen
standing around him, fixed
in their tapestry of manners

the bull, embroidered
with blood and given
an elegant death, trumpets, his name
stamped on him, heraldic brand[1]
because

(when he rolled
on the sand, sword in his heart, the teeth
in his blue mouth were human)

he is really a man

even the wolves, holding resonant
conversations in their
forests thickened with legend.

    In this country the animals
    have the faces of
    animals.

    Their eyes
    flash once in car headlights
    and are gone.

    Their deaths are not elegant.

    They have the faces of
    no-one.

1966

Daguerreotype[2] Taken in Old Age

    I know I change
    have changed

    but whose is this vapid face
    pitted and vast, rotund
    suspended in empty paper
    as though in a telescope

    the granular moon

---

1. With a heraldic insignia burned onto him with a hot iron.

2. Early photograph, produced on a silver-coated plate.

I rise from my chair
pulling against gravity
I turn away   10
and go out into the garden

I revolve among the vegetables,
my head ponderous
reflecting the sun
in shadows from the pocked ravines   15
cut in my cheeks, my eye-
sockets 2 craters

along the paths
I orbit
the apple trees   20
white white spinning
stars around me

I am being
eaten away by light

1970

Footnote to the Amnesty Report
on Torture

The torture chamber is not like anything
you would have expected.
No opera set or sexy chains and
leather-goods from the glossy
porno magazines, no thirties horror   5
dungeon with gauzy cobwebs; nor is it
the bare cold-lighted
chrome space of the future
we think we fear.
More like one of the seedier   10
British Railways stations, with scratched green
walls and spilled tea,
crumpled papers, and a stooped man
who is always cleaning the floor.

It stinks, though; like a hospital,   15
of antiseptics and sickness,
and, on some days, blood
which smells the same anywhere,
here or at the butcher's.

The man who works here   20
is losing his sense of smell.
He's glad to have this job, because
there are few others.
He isn't a torturer, he only
cleans the floor: 25

every morning the same vomit,
the same shed teeth, the same
piss and liquid shit, the same panic.

Some have courage, others
don't; those who do what he thinks of   30
as the real work, and who are
bored, since minor bureaucrats
are always bored, tell them
it doesn't matter, who
will ever know they were brave, they might   35
as well talk now
and get it over.

Some have nothing to say, which also
doesn't matter. Their
warped bodies too, with the torn   40
fingers and ragged tongues, are thrown
over the spiked iron fence onto
the Consul's lawn, along with
the bodies of children
burned to make their mothers talk.   45

The man who cleans the floors
is glad it isn't him.
It will be if he ever says
what he knows. He works long hours,
submits to the searches, eats   50
a meal he brings from home, which tastes
of old blood and the sawdust
he cleans the floor with. His wife
is pleased he brings her money
for the food, has been told   55
not to ask questions.

As he sweeps, he tries
not to listen; he tries
to make himself into a wall,
a thick wall, a wall   60
soft and without echoes. He thinks
of nothing but the walk back
to his hot shed of a house,
of the door
opening and his children
with their unmarked skin and flawless eyes   65
running to meet him.

He is afraid of
what he might do
if he were told to,
he is afraid of the door,   70

he is afraid, not
of the door but of the door

opening; sometimes, no matter
how hard he tries,
his children are not there.   75

                                                                          1978

Variations on the Word *Love*

This is a word we use to plug
holes with. It's the right size for those warm
blanks in speech, for those red heart-
shaped vacancies on the page that look nothing
like real hearts. Add lace   5
and you can sell
it. We insert it also in the one empty
space on the printed form
that comes with no instructions. There are whole
magazines with not much in them   10
but the word *love*, you can
rub it all over your body and you
can cook with it too. How do we know
it isn't what goes on at the cool
debaucheries of slugs under damp   15
pieces of cardboard? As for the weed-
seedlings nosing their tough snouts up
among the lettuces, they shout it.
Love! Love! sing the soldiers, raising
their glittering knives in salute.   20

Then there's the two
of us. This word
is far too short for us, it has only
four letters, too sparse
to fill those deep bare   25
vacuums between the stars
that press on us with their deafness.
It's not love we don't wish
to fall into, but that fear.
This word is not enough but it will   30
have to do. It's a single
vowel in this metallic
silence, a mouth that says
O again and again in wonder
and pain, a breath, a finger   35
grip on a cliffside. You can
hold on or let go.

                                                                          1981

Spelling

My daughter plays on the floor
with plastic letters,
red, blue & hard yellow,

learning how to spell,
spelling,   5
how to make spells.

                  •

I wonder how many women
denied themselves daughters,
closed themselves in rooms,
drew the curtains   10
so they could mainline words.

                  •

A child is not a poem,
a poem is not a child.
There is no either / or.
However.   15

                  •

I return to the story
of the woman caught in the war
& in labour, her thighs tied
together by the enemy
so she could not give birth.   20

Ancestress: the burning witch,
her mouth covered by leather
to strangle words.

A word after a word
after a word is power.   25

                  •

At the point where language falls away
from the hot bones, at the point
where the rock breaks open and darkness
flows out of it like blood, at
the melting point of granite   30
when the bones know
they are hollow & the word
splits & doubles & speaks
the truth & the body
itself becomes a mouth.   35

This is a metaphor.

                  •

How do you learn to spell?
Blood, sky & the sun,
your own name first,
your first naming, your first name,   40
your first word.

                                                          1981

ROBERT PINSKY
b. 1940

The clarity, wit, and seriousness of Robert Pinsky's poems probably owe something to the example of Yvor Winters, the poet, critic, and teacher to whom Pinsky pays tribute in the "Peroration, Concerning Genius" of his "Essay on Psychiatrists," and whom he calls the "Old Man. Winters maintained that somewhere in the middle of the eighteenth century, the "logical foundations of Western thought" were lost to poets—and presumably to the rest of us—and that the poets were left with no way to examine their emotions and experiences. This realization that they were castaways in a universe not susceptible to logical examination drove poets and other men of genius to madness. As far as Winters was concerned

> Suffering was life's penalty; wisdom armed one
> Against madness; speech was temporary; poetry was truth.

The sanity exemplified by Winters, a stoicism bolstered by reason and learning, is not the sanity which psychiatrists can help their patients to achieve. They "ponder relative truth and the warm / Dusk of amelioration"; they are the "first citizens of contingency." The genius of physicians and some poets seems to lie in their ability to impart something of their own ability to tolerate, without panic, the contingent— the accidental and the unseen.

Pinsky studies his own feeling for other people, the observed and the created. In "Poem about People" the poet feels tenderness for others when they are seen as a group and at a distance. But when the poet comes closer to the individual, love "falters and flags" at the sight of suffering and need.

In several of his most accomplished poems Pinsky entertains a nihilism, the feeling of desperate meaninglessness which the psychiatrist endeavors to dispel. In "The Figured Wheel" the wheel grinds away the human and the natural world. Man in recognition of its power and its inevitability has decorated the wheel with the symbols of his religions. The wheel may be the instrument of Jesus, "oblivious to hurt turning to give words to the unrighteous" or it may be "Gogol's feeding pig that without knowing it eats a baby chick / And goes on feeding." "The Living," which can be read as a companion piece to "The Figured Wheel," examines the "abrupt good fortune" of being alive. The poem does not suggest some way out of nihilism, but rather that man simply cannot long sustain an unqualified nihilism.

Robert Pinsky was born in 1940 in New Jersey and educated at Rutgers, where he took his B.A., and at Stanford, where he took a Ph.D. in English. His dissertation, later published, was a study of the poetry of Walter Savage Landor, who in his poems cultivated a classical coolness and dispassion, which Landor proposed as an alternative to Romantic extremism. Having taught at Wellesley College, he moved to the University of California, Berkeley, where he is now a professor of English. In 1987 he published *Mindwheel*, an "electronic novel" or complex interactive computer game.

Doctor Frolic

Felicity the healer isn't young
And you don't look him up unless you need him.
Clown's eyes, Pope's nose,[1] a mouth for dirty stories,
He made his bundle in the Great Depression

---

1. "Pope's nose" is an irreverent term for the tail of a plucked bird; hence, his nose looks like the tail of a plucked bird.

And now, a jovial immigrant success 5
In baggy pinstripes, he winks and wheezes gossip,
Village stories that could lift your hair
Or lance a boil; the small town dirt, the dope,

The fishy deals and incestuous combinations,
The husband and the wife of his wife's brother, 10
The hospital contract, the certificate . . .
A realist and hardy omnivore,[2]

He strolls the jetties when the month is right
With a knife and lemons in his pocket, after
Live mussels from among the smelly rocks, 15
Preventative of impotence and goitre.[3]

And as though the sight of tissue healing crooked
Pleased him, like the ocean's vaginal taste,
He'll stitch your thumb up so it shows for life.
And where he once was the only quack in town 20

We all have heard his half-lame joke, the one
About the operation that succeeded,
The tangy line that keeps that clever eye
So merry in the punchinello[4] face.

1975

The Figured[5] Wheel

The figured wheel rolls through shopping malls and prisons,
Over farms, small and immense, and the rotten little downtowns.
Covered with symbols, it mills everything alive and grinds
The remains of the dead in the cemeteries, in unmarked graves and oceans.

Sluiced by salt water and fresh, by pure and contaminated rivers, 5
By snow and sand, it separates and recombines all droplets and grains,
Even the infinite sub-atomic particles crushed under the illustrated,
Varying treads of its wide circumferential track.

Spraying flecks of tar and molten rock it rumbles
Through the Antarctic station of American sailors and technicians, 10
And shakes the floors and windows of whorehouses for diggers and smelters
From Bethany, Pennsylvania to a practically nameless, semi-penal New
    Town

In the mineral-rich tundra[6] of the Soviet northernmost settlements.
Artists illuminate it with pictures and incised mottoes
Taken from the Ten-Thousand Stories and the Register of True Dramas. 15
They hang it with colored ribbons and with bells of many pitches.

With paints and chisels and moving lights they record
On its rotating surface the elegant and terrifying doings

2. One who eats everything.
3. Disease of the thyroid gland which causes
swelling in the neck.

4. Hooknosed clown-hero of puppet shows.
5. Inscribed, decorated, or prophesied.
6. Arctic or subarctic treeless plain.

Of the inhabitants of the Hundred Pantheons of major Gods
Disposed in iconographic stations at hub, spoke and concentric bands,   20

And also the grotesque demi-Gods, Hopi gargoyles and Ibo dryads.[7]
They cover it with wind-chimes and electronic instruments
That vibrate as it rolls to make an all-but-unthinkable music,
So that the wheel hums and rings as it turns through the births of stars

And through the dead-world of bomb, fireblast and fallout   25
Where only a few doomed races of insects fumble in the smoking grasses.
It is Jesus oblivious to hurt turning to give words to the unrighteous,
And is also Gogol's feeding pig that without knowing it eats a baby chick

And goes on feeding.[8] It is the empty armor of My Cid, clattering
Into the arrows of the credulous unbelievers, a metal suit   30
Like the lost astronaut revolving with his useless umbilicus[9]
Through the cold streams, neither energy nor matter, that agitate

The cold, cyclical dark, turning and returning.
Even in the scorched and frozen world of the dead after the holocaust
The wheel as it turns goes on accreting ornaments.   35
Scientists and artists festoon it from the grave with brilliant

Toys and messages, jokes and zodiacs, tragedies conceived
From among the dreams of the unemployed and the pampered,
The listless and the tortured. It is hung with devices
By dead masters who have survived by reducing themselves magically   40

To tiny organisms, to wisps of matter, crumbs of soil,
Bits of dry skin, microscopic flakes, which is why they are called "great,"
In their humility that goes on celebrating the turning
Of the wheel as it rolls unrelentingly over

A cow plodding through car-traffic on a street in Iasi[1]   45
And over the haunts of Robert Pinsky's mother and father
And wife and children and his sweet self
Which he hereby unwillingly and inexpertly gives up, because it is

There, figured and pre-figured in the nothing-transfiguring wheel.

1987

The Living

The living, the unfallen lords of life,
Move heavily through the dazzle
Where all things shift, glitter or swim—

---

7. That is, carved grotesques of the plain-dwelling Native American tribe and tree nymphs of the African Ibo tribe.

8. "There was also a sow with her family; as she scraped in a heap of garbage the sow in passing swallowed a chicken and, without even noticing it, continued unconcernedly to gobble up the water-melon rinds"; from Nikolai Gogol's novel *Dead Souls* (1842) (tr. George Reavey), part 1, chapter 3.

9. Navel; the astronaut's now useless "lifeline" is compared to the human umbilical cord, as in a scene in Stanley Kubrick's movie, *2001* (1968). "My Cid" is El Cid, eleventh-century Spanish military leader; after he died, his followers dressed his corpse in his armor and tied it to a horse, so that he could still lead them into battle.

1. City in Romania.

As on a day at the beach, or under
The stark, absolute blue of a snow morning,   5
With concentric peals of brightness

Ringing in the cold air. They seem drugged.
Their abrupt good fortune clings heavily
With the slow sway and pomp of dirty velvet,

Their purple, the unaccustomed garb—   10
Worn slipshod—of the Court
Of Misrule:[2] animal-headed, staring

As if sleepy or drunk, riding a goat
Or perched backwards on a donkey,
Widdershins,[3] hectic. Beggars, bad governors,   15

We thrive awkwardly—some maimed slightly
In the course of war; some torn by fear sometimes;
Yet not paralyzed: we are moved. The strange

Stories of the degradations of the martyrs—
Crucified upside-down, cooked live   20
On a grille—bother us doubly: in themselves,

And because a strange opiate intervenes
As if they were suffering now, at this
Apex of time, and for some reason we

Could not concentrate, lost on the slopes   25
Below. We ape court manners clumsily;
Or shake fists, in awkward parade,

Exalted and confused. Even in affliction—grotesque
Illnesses, poverty, ruined hopes, the world's
Rage and the body's—the most miserable   30

Find in the mere daylight and air
A miraculous daily bread. Fairy bread:[4]
We eat and are changed. Survivors

After a catastrophe, transported, feel
Nearly as if they could find the lost,   35
Luckless ones, somewhere, perhaps not far—

Crowded, maybe, behind some one
Of the innumerable doors of the palace.
Plump Chance beams like an effigy

Of Mardi Gras[5]—the apparent origin   40
And end of so much: disease, fame,
Unemployment, intrigue. The world, random,

2. The allusion is to a medieval holiday in which a Lord of Misrule was appointed, people wore masks, and traditional hierarchies were overturned.

3. Backwards or counterclockwise.
4. That is, enchanted bread.
5. The Tuesday before Ash Wednesday is traditionally a high-spirited holiday.

Is so real, it is as if our own
Good or bad luck were here only
As a kind of filler, holding together   45

Just that much of the adjacent
Splendor and terror. Only,
Sometimes, a sharp, violent burr, discordant,

Sizzles for one instant in jagged
Hachures[6] in the brain—momentary scream   50
Of the powersaw wincing back

From a buried nail. Seizure: with a rising
Whoop, like a child on a steep slide,
A woman fell heavily to the floor

A few feet away from me, her scalp   55
Split a little, blood on my sleeve
As I raised her shoulders, acting the part

Of a stranger helping—asking a clerk
To please get something to cover her,
Please call for an ambulance, maybe   60

She has had a seizure. Epileptic—
The Falling Evil;[7] something about the tongue,
Something for the teeth. But her mouth

Was not rigid, her eyes open—why
Should she look at me so knowingly,   65
Almost with contempt, was she crazy?—

As if I had made her fall: or were no
Stranger at all but a son, lover, lord
And master who had thus humiliated her

And now, tucking the blanket around her,   70
Hypocritical automaton, pretended
To urge—as if without complicity or shame

Or least sense of betrayal—the old embrace
Of this impenetrable haze, this prolonged
But not infinite surfeit of glory.   75
                                                       1984

The Questions

What about the people who came to my father's office
For hearing aids and glasses—chatting with him sometimes

A few extra minutes while I swept up in the back,
Addressed packages, cleaned the machines; if he was busy

---

6. Short line used for shading; crosshatching.   7. The "falling sickness": epilepsy.

I might sell them batteries, or tend to their questions: 5
The tall overloud old man with a tilted, ironic smirk

To cover the gaps in his hearing; a woman who hummed one
Prolonged note constantly, we called her "the hummer"—how

Could her white fat husband (he looked like Rev. Peale)[8]
Bear hearing it day and night? And others: a coquettish old lady   10

In a bandeau,[9] a European. She worked for refugees who ran
Gift shops or booths on the boardwalk in the summer;

She must have lived in winter on Social Security. One man
Always greeted my father in Masonic gestures and codes.[1]

Why do I want them to be treated tenderly by the world, now   15
Long after they must have slipped from it one way or another,

While I was dawdling through school at the moment—or driving,
Reading, talking to Ellen. Why this new superfluous caring?

I want for them not to have died in awful pain, friendless.
Though many of the living are starving, I still pray for these,   20

Dead, mostly anonymous (but Mr. Monk, Mrs. Rose Vogel)
And barely remembered: that they had a little extra, something

For pleasure, a good meal, a book or a decent television set.
Of whom do I pray this rubbery, low-class charity? I saw

An expert today, a nun—wearing a regular skirt and blouse,   25
But the hood or headdress navy and white around her plain

Probably Irish face, older than me by five or ten years.
The Post Office clerk told her he couldn't break a twenty

So she got change next door and came back to send her package.
As I came out she was driving off—with an air, it seemed to me,   30

Of annoying, demure good cheer, as if the reasonableness
Of change, mail, cars, clothes was a pleasure in itself: veiled

And dumb like the girls I thought enjoyed the rules too much
In grade school. She might have been a grade school teacher;

But she reminded me of being there, aside from that—as a name   35
And person there, a Mary or John who learns that the janitor

Is Mr. Woodhouse; the principal is Mr. Ringleven; the secretary
In the office is Mrs. Apostolacos; the bus driver is Ray.

1987

---

8. Norman Vincent Peale, popular twentieth-century preacher.
9. Hairband.

1. Of the Order of Freemasons, a secret society.

MARILYN HACKER
b. 1942

"I do like words," admits Marilyn Hacker, and few contemporary poets are as venturesome and dexterous in their use, for she likes elaborate ways of organizing words. Both "Feeling and Form" (itself a canzone) and the poem called "Canzone" celebrate the pleasures of making poems—and other pleasures as well. In the latter she exploits the tripartite significance of "tongue": part of the bodily apparatus by which we taste, an instrument in erotic play, and a word for language, as in such a phrase as "native tongue."

Hacker's poems are often addressed to specific friends and lovers, and they usually emerge from recent joys and disappointments. With her mother and her daughter she composes a generational triad which forms, breaks apart, and reforms. Hacker's latest collection is a sequence of poems, most of them sonnets, which describes a love affair and its eventual unhappy conclusion. The sonnets commemorate her grief, but they also testify, with humor, to her bravery and spirit.

Marilyn Hacker was born in New York City on November 27, 1942. She was educated at the Bronx High School of Science, New York University, and the Art Students League. She has been an antiquarian bookseller and a teacher; she has done editorial work for books and magazines. In 1975 she won the National Book Award. She has one daughter, and she spends half of each year in France.

Canzone[1]

Consider the three functions of the tongue:
taste, speech, the telegraphy of pleasure,
are not confused in any human tongue;
yet, sinewy and singular, the tongue
accomplishes what, perhaps, no other organe   5
can. Were I to speak of giving tongue,
you'd think two things at least; and a cooked tongue,
sliced, on a plate, with caper sauce, which I give
my guest for lunch, is one more, to which she'd give
the careful concentration of her tongue   10
twice over, to appreciate the taste
and to express—it would be in good taste—

a gastronomic memory the taste
called to mind, and mind brought back to tongue.
There is a paucity of words for taste;   15
sweet, sour, bitter, salty. Any taste,
however multiplicitous its pleasure,
complex its execution (I might taste
that sauce ten times in cooking, change its taste
with herbal subtleties, chromatic organ   20
tones of clove and basil, good with organ
meats[2]) must be described with those few taste-
words, or with metaphors, to give
my version of sensations it would give

---

1. Medieval Italian lyric poem.   is a spice, "basil" an herb.
2. As, for example, liver and kidneys; "clove"

a neophyte, deciding whether to give   25
it a try. She might develop a taste.
(You try things once; I think you have to give
two chances, though, to know your mind, or give
up on novelties.) Your mother tongue
nurtures, has the subtleties which give   30
flavor to words, and words to flavor, give
the by no means subsidiary pleasure
of being able to describe a pleasure
and recreate it. Making words, we give
the private contemplations of each organ   35
to the others, and to others, organ-

ize sensations into thoughts. Sentient organisms, we symbolize feeling, give
the spectrum (that's a symbol) each sense organ
perceives, by analogy, to others. Disorgan-   40
ization of the senses is an acquired taste
we all acquire; as speaking beasts, it's organic to our discourse. The first organ
of acknowledged communion is the tongue
(tripartite diplomat, which after tongu-   45
ing a less voluble expressive organ
to wordless efflorescences of pleasure
offers up words to reaffirm the pleasure).

That's a primary difficulty: pleasure
means something, and something different, for each organ;   50
each person, too. I may take equisite pleasure
in boiled eel, or blancmange—or not. One pleasure
of language is making known what not to give.
And think of a bar of lavender soap, a pleasure
to see and, moistened, rub on your skin, a pleasure   55
especially to smell, but if you taste
it (though smell is most akin to taste)
what you experience will not be pleasure;
you almost retch, grimace, stick out your tongue,
slosh rinses of ice water over your tongue.   60

But I would rather think about your tongue
experiencing and transmitting pleasure
to one or another multi-sensual organ
—like memory. Whoever wants to give
only one meaning to that, has untutored taste.

                                                                    1980

Runaways Café II

For once, I hardly noticed what I ate
(salmon and broccoli and Saint-Véran).[3]

3. A wine.

My elbow twitched like jumping beans; sweat ran
into my shirtsleeves. Could I concentrate
on anything but your leg against mine   5
under the table? It was difficult,
but I impersonated an adult
looking at you, and knocking back the wine.
Now that we both want to know what we want,
now that we both want to know what we know,   10
it still behooves us to know what to do:
be circumspect, be generous, be brave,
be honest, be together, and behave.
At least I didn't get white sauce down my front.

                                                        1986

Mythology

Penelope as a *garçon manqué*
weaves sonnets on a barstool among sailors,
tapping her iambs out on the brass rail.[4] Ours
is not the high-school text. Persephone
a.k.a. Télémaque-who-tagged-along,[5]   5
sleeps off her lunch on an Italian train
headed for Paris, while Ulysse-Maman[6]
plugs into the Shirelles singing her song
("What Does a Girl Do?"). What *does* a girl do
but walk across the world, her kid in tow,   10
stopping at stations on the way, with friends
to tie her to the mast when she gets too
close to the edge? And when the voyage ends,
what does a girl do? Girl, that's up to you.

                                                        1986

From Coda[7]

Did you love well what very soon you left?
Come home and take me in your arms and take
away this stomach ache, headache, heartache.
Never so full, I never was bereft
so utterly. The winter evenings drift   5
dark to the window. Not one word will make
you, where you are, turn in your day, or wake
from your night toward me. The only gift
I got to keep or give is what I've cried,
floodgates let down to mourning for the dead   10

---

4. Penelope, in Homer's *Odyssey*, is the name
of the wife Odysseus left behind; *garçon manqué:*
that is, a boy in a girl's body; literally, a boy just
lacking in "boyness"; "iambs": metrical feet. The
incident may allude to the story of the German
poet Goethe making love while composing a poem
and tapping out the rhythm on his lover's back-
side.
5. Persephone, in classical mythology, was the
daughter of Ceres, the earth-goddess; abducted by

Pluto, king of the underworld, Persephone spent
the spring and summer on earth, the fall and winter in the underworld. "A.k.a.": also known as;
Télémaque is the French form of Telemachus, the
name of the diffident son of Odysseus, who
accompanies his father on the last part of his wanderings.
6. That is, Mama-Odysseus.
7. Conclusion; this is the final poem in the
"Coda" sequence.

chances, for the end of being young,
for everyone I loved who really died.
I drank our one year out in brine instead
of honey from the seasons of your tongue.

1986

DAVE SMITH
b. 1942

Dave Smith insists upon his nickname, and its informality helps prepare the reader
for an unusual poet. He writes powerfully, using rough words as he inexhaustibly
collates jarring bits of the local scene. The world is full of harsh objects waiting for
him to muster them. It is mostly a world of outdoors: he is at home with goshawks,
antelope, oysters, shark, sawmills, boats. There are occasional hints of literary tradition: Chaucer is mentioned, and Hopkins has obviously had some effect upon him,
as has Robert Penn Warren. But he scorns to use familiar devices such as alliteration
or obviously melodic cadences.

Memory plays a large part in his consciousness. His own childhood is a recurring
theme. There are memories of discovering pornographic pictures in an old sea chest
of his father, and his father haunts Smith's poems. At their best the details seem in
place, and pulsate with a kind of vitalism. Smith himself has said that his poems are
"attempts in their structure to conflate the lyric and the narrative." He conveys as
he says a sense of responsibility, in situations of stress. More grandly, "Poetry is the
knight doing psychic combat for us." Smith's poetry has freshness and unexpectedness as well as inner strength.

Dave Smith was born on December 19, 1942, in Portsmouth, Virginia. He graduated from the University of Virginia, served in the air force, and took graduate
degrees at Southern Illinois University and at Ohio University. In addition to his
books of poetry, he has published a novel, *Onliness* (1981); a volume of short stories;
and a collection of essays on contemporary poetry. He has also edited a book of essays
on James Wright.

Hole, Where Once in Passion We Swam

The sun frets, a fat wafer falling like a trap of failed mesh.
I watch the pin-glare of a mockingbird's eye cut sharply, descend
on the blank water, then emerge from himself naked
as a girl who shimmered here, once, for me.

If we come back like penitents to kneel over water, bass swirling,   5
scattering the mayflies that often, in silence, graze

lips, what is the word floating out from the mouth unbearable
as a bird's black grin or a madman's lust?

The word is not we, but *me*. Giving it again and again

brings no one out of the willows and I, willing to believe   10
like a sap in whatever dives or rises hear no voice
but the mist sizzling on stones. I lift my head

for echoes out of trees, for the flashed recoil of flesh hung
cheap and gaudy, wingless, above the stab of water
that crunched her like a beer can. Toads honk   15

the only answer. Among them, a boy, I felt

the grotesque pull of the moon all night, peeled and went slowly
down in terror, rising, falling through the pulpy leaves
until the sun caught me, drained, and I was no one
wanted, so walked away from all knowing,   20

walked into town and drank, calmly, an illegal beer, then slept.

The hooks, in hairy hands, clawed it smooth as a dish, a superhuman search by flood and fire light. What could they find?
Like many, I have been out of town a long time.

I wish the face floating above the chill at my knees opened   25
the door of a drab hotel. I wish it said *Go to hell*
or *Do you know what time it is*, anything

that, if I heard it, I could kneel to and swear to be faithful.

                                                                1976

The Roundhouse[1] Voices

In full flare of sunlight I came here, man-tall but thin
as a pinstripe, and stood outside the rusted fence
with its crown of iron thorns while
the soot cut into our lungs with tiny diamonds.
I walked through houses with my grain-lovely slugger   5
from Louisville[2] that my uncle bought and stood
in the sun that made its glove soft on my hand
until I saw my chance to crawl under and get past
anyone who would demand a badge and a name.

The guard hollered that I could get the hell from there quick   10
when I popped in his face like a thief. All I ever wanted
to steal was life and you can't get that easy
in the grind of a railyard. *You can't catch me
lardass, I can go left or right good as the Mick,*[3]
I hummed to him, holding my slugger by the neck   15
for a bunt laid smooth where the coal cars
jerked and let me pass between tracks
until, in a slide on ash, I fell safe and heard
the wheeze of his words: *Who the hell are you, kid?*

I hear them again tonight Uncle, hard as big brakeshoes,[4]   20
when I lean over your face in the box of silk. The years

---

1. Circular building for housing and repairing railway engines.
2. "Louisville Slugger," popular brand of baseball bat.
3. Mickey Mantle, famous baseball player, whose peak years were the fifties and early sixties.
4. Part of the trains' brakes.

you spent hobbling from room to room alone crawl
up my legs and turn this house to another
house, round and black as defeat, where slugging
comes easy when you whip the gray softball over
the glass diesel globe. Footsteps thump on the stairs
like that fat ball against bricks and when I miss
I hear you warn me to watch the timing, to keep
my eyes on your hand and forget the fence, 25

hearing also that other voice that keeps me out and away
from you on a day worth playing good ball. Hearing
Who the hell . . . I see myself, like a burning speck
of cinder come down the hill and through a tunnel
of porches like stands, running on deep ash,
and I give him the finger, whose face still gleams
clear as a B & O[5] headlight, just to make him get up
and chase me into a dream of scoring at your feet.
At Christmas that guard staggered home sobbing,
the thing in his chest tight as a torque wrench.[6]
In the summer I did not have to run and now 30 35 40

who is the one who dreams of a drink as he leans over
tools you kept bright as a first-girl's promise? I
have no one to run from or to, nobody to give
my finger to as I steal his peace. Uncle, the light
bleeds on your gray face like the high barbed wire
shadows I had to get through and maybe you don't remember
you said to come back, to wait and you'd show me
the right way to take a hard pitch
in the sun that shudders on the ready man. I'm here 45

though this is a day I did not want to see. In the roundhouse
the rasp and heel-click of compressors[7] is still,
soot lies deep in every greasy fingerprint.
I called you from the pits and you did not come up
and I felt the fear when I stood on the tracks
that are like stars which never lead us
into any kind of light and I don't know who'll
tell me now when the guard sticks his blind snoot
between us: take off and beat the bastard out.
Can you hear him over the yard, grabbing his chest,
cry out *Who the goddamn hell are you, kid?* 50 55 60

I gave him every name in the book, Uncle, but he caught us
and what good did all those hours of coaching do?
You lie on your back, eyeless forever, and I think
how once I climbed to the top of a diesel and stared
into that gray roundhouse glass where, in anger,
you threw up the ball and made a star
to swear at greater than the Mick ever dreamed.
It has been years but now I know what followed there 65

5. Baltimore & Ohio, a railway line.
6. Wrench that measures and indicates the amount of twisting or turning force applied in tightening a bolt or nut.
7. Machine that compresses air or gases.

every morning the sun came up, not light
but the puffing bad-bellied light of words.   70

All day I have held your hand, trying to say back that life,
to get under that fence with words I lined
and linked up and steamed into a cold room
where the illusion of hope means skin torn in boxes
of tools. The footsteps come pounding into words   75
and even the finger I give death is words
that won't let us be what we wanted, each one
chasing and being chased by dreams in a dark place.
Words are all we ever were and they did us
no damn good. Do you hear that?   80

Do you hear the words that, in oiled gravel, you gave me
when you set my feet in the right stance to swing?
They are coal-hard and they come in wings
and loops like despair not even the Mick
could knock out of this room, words softer   85
than the centers of hearts in guards or uncles,
words skinned and numbed by too many bricks.
I have had enough of them and bring them back here
where the tick and creak of everything dies
in your tiny starlight and I stand down   90
on my knees to cry, *Who the hell are you, kid?*

                                                                    1979

Snapshot of a Crab-Picker[8] Among Barrels Spilling Over, Apparently at the End of Her Shift

Clacking and gouging when huddled,
these well-armored warriors[9]
sweat in dimmed sun and scuttle
in the small space each has.
Long arms salute liegelords[1] just   5
passed, shadows, the honed meat
hard under those scarred helmets.
Sea-promised they come and wait,
season and season always the same.

Near these the squat houses, lights   10
burled,[2] where a girl will go step
athwart the sharp road of shells
down to a shadow who's dug in
his feathery heels and hovers now
as the liquid night swells, lifts   15
her with first mooncrest to ride
upon him until she will lie

8. One who sorts crabs by size, for eating.
9. That is, the crabs.
1. Lords to whom feudal service is owed.

2. That is, mottled, like the mottled figures of burls in wood.

pale in the frost's breath, spent
flesh the white flaky treasure
these homebound, wordless, breed.   20

What they offer she will offer,
with sea-smell on her hands
that clean and cradle and keep
against the dull day hours
of simple dreams: hunger, flight,   25
the tidal force like despair
that under moons shall idle,
singing for the armorless one
love she smiles at, a taste,
faint, she cannot flee ever,   30
of legions[3] at her lips biting.

                                                                     1983

3. Roman army units.

MICHAEL ONDAATJE
b. 1943

Ceylon (now Sri Lanka) is a large, pear-shaped island just off the southern tip of
India. For centuries it has seemed to travelers an earthly paradise, albeit a paradise
frequently disrupted by internecine quarrels and violence. It is tropically hot, its
landscape is variegated with mountains and jungles, and its vegetation is of a wild
and dreamlike richness. Michael Ondaatje's family has been in Sri Lanka since 1600.
Culturally they are a mixture of the Sinhalese, the indigenous inhabitants; the Tam-
ils, dark-skinned emigrants from India; and the Dutch, who came to Sri Lanka in
search of spices in the seventeenth century. Ondaatje spent the first eleven years of
his life in Sri Lanka (some of his memories of the island and of his family are preserved in his marvelous autobiography *Running in the Family*, 1982). Making his
way there by way of England, he eventually settled in Canada. Perhaps he finds in
the New World writ large something of the cultural diversity of his native land.
   "We own the country we grow up in," Ondaatje writes, "or we are aliens and
invaders." Two of his acts of expropriation—his invasions, as it were—are book-length
narratives which combine poems with highly charged prose: *The Collected Works of
Billy the Kid* (1970, 1974) is a fantasy on the life of the half-mythical gunslinger, and
Coming through Slaughter (1976) is based on the life of Billy Bolden, the fabulous
Black cornettist who was a figure in the jazz world of New Orleans at the turn of the
century and who eventually went mad and died in an institution. Ondaatje's shorter
poems are often surrealistic snapshots of domestic life.
   Michael Ondaatje was born on September 12, 1943. After his departure from Sri
Lanka, a departure prompted by his parents' divorce, he was educated at Dulwich
College, London, Bishop's University, Quebec, the University of Toronto, and Queen's
University, Kingston, Ontario. Since 1971 he has taught at Glendon College, York
University, in Toronto. He has twice received the Governor-General's Award for
Literature—roughly equivalent to the Pulitzer Prize. In addition to his poems and
anthologies, Ondaatje has directed several films.

Elizabeth

Catch, my Uncle Jack said
and oh I caught this huge apple
red as Mrs Kelly's bum.[1]
It's red as Mrs Kelly's bum, I said
and Daddy roared   5
and swung me on his stomach with a heave.
Then I hid the apple in my room
till it shrunk like a face
growing eyes and teeth ribs.

Then Daddy took me to the zoo   10
he knew the man there
they put a snake around my neck
and it crawled down the front of my dress.
I felt its flicking tongue
dripping onto me like a shower.   15
Daddy laughed and said Smart Snake
and Mrs Kelly with us scowled.

In the pond where they kept the goldfish
Philip and I broke the ice with spades
and tried to spear the fishes;   20
we killed one and Philip ate it,
then he kissed me
with raw saltless fish in his mouth.

My sister Mary's got bad teeth
and said I was lucky, then she said   25
I had big teeth, but Philip said I was pretty.
He had big hands that smelled.

I would speak of Tom, soft laughing,
who danced in the mornings round the sundial
teaching me the steps from France, turning   30
with the rhythm of the sun on the warped branches,
who'd hold my breast and watch it move like a snail
leaving his quick urgent love in my palm.
And I kept his love in my palm till it blistered.

When they axed his shoulders and neck   35
the blood moved like a branch into the crowd.
And he staggered with his hanging shoulder
cursing their thrilled cry, wheeling,
waltzing in the French style to his knees
holding his head with the ground,   40
blood settling on his clothes like a blush;
this way
when they aimed the thud into his back.

---

1. Britishism for "bottom."

And I find cool entertainment now
with white young Essex, and my nimble rhymes.[2]   45

1979

Letters & Other Worlds

*"for there was no more darkness for him and, no doubt
like Adam before the fall, he could see in the dark"*

My father's body was a globe of fear
His body was a town we never knew
He hid that he had been where we were going
His letters were a room he seldom lived in
In them the logic of his love could grow   5

My father's body was a town of fear
He was the only witness to its fear dance
He hid where he had been that we might lose him
His letters were a room his body scared

He came to death with his mind drowning.   10
On the last day he enclosed himself
in a room with two bottles of gin, later
fell the length of his body
so that brain blood moved
to new compartments   15
that never knew the wash of fluid
and he died in minutes of a new equilibrium.

His early life was a terrifying comedy
and my mother divorced him again and again.
he would rush into tunnels magnetized   20
by the white eye of trains
and once, gaining instant fame,
managed to stop a Perahara[3] in Ceylon
—the whole procession of elephants dancers
local dignitaries—by falling   25
dead drunk onto the street.

As a semi-official, and semi-white at that,
the act was seen as a crucial
turningpoint in the Home Rule Movement
and led to Ceylon's independence in 1948.   30

(My mother had done her share too—
her driving so bad

2. The Earl of Essex, a favorite of Queen Elizabeth I (1533–1603; crowned 1558); she also wrote poetry. We can now identify "Daddy" as her father, Henry VIII; Philip is no doubt the young Philip II, later king of Spain, while Mary is Elizabeth's half-sister, queen from 1553 to 1558. "Tom" is Thomas Seymour (1508?–1549), a repeated and always rejected suitor of the young princess Elizabeth; his schemes to displace his brother as protector of the young king Edward VI led to his execution in 1549.

3. Or Anuradhapura Perahara, an annual Ceylonese religious festival commemorating the birth of Vishnu, one of the three primary Hindu gods. On its final night the festival culminates in processions, the elephants carrying shrines and relics.

she was stoned by villagers
whenever her car was recognized)

For 14 years of marriage   35
each of them claimed he or she
was the injured party.
Once on the Colombo[4] docks
saying goodbye to a recently married couple
my father, jealous   40
at my mother's articulate emotion,
dove into the waters of the harbour
and swam after the ship waving farewell.
My mother pretending no affiliation
mingled with the crowd back to the hotel.   45

Once again he made the papers
though this time my mother
with a note to the editor
corrected the report—saying he was drunk
rather than broken hearted at the parting of friends.   50
The married couple received both editions
of *The Ceylon Times* when their ship reached Aden.[5]

And then in his last years
he was the silent drinker,
the man who once a week   55
disappeared into his room with bottles
and stayed there until he was drunk
and until he was sober.

There speeches, head dreams, apologies,
the gentle letters, were composed.   60
With the clarity of architects
he would write of the row of blue flowers
his new wife had planted,
the plans for electricity in the house,
how my half-sister fell near a snake   65
and it had awakened and not touched her.
Letters in a clear hand of the most complete empathy
his heart widening and widening and widening
to all manner of change in his children and friends
while he himself edged   70
into the terrible acute hatred
of his own privacy
till he balanced and fell
the length of his body
the blood screaming in   75
the empty reservoir of bones
the blood searching in his head without metaphor

1979

4. Seaport city, capital of Ceylon, or Sri Lanka.   the Arabian peninsula, in South Yemen; then a
5. The Port of Aden, on the southern coast of   British colony.

Burning Hills

for Kris and Fred

So he came to write again
in the burnt hill region
north of Kingston.[6] A cabin
with mildew spreading down walls.
Bullfrogs on either side of him.   5

Hanging his lantern of Shell Vapona Strip[7]
on a hook in the centre of the room
he waited a long time. Opened
the Hilroy writing pad, yellow Bic pen.
Every summer he believed would be his last.   10
This schizophrenic season change, June to September,
when he deviously thought out plots
across the character of his friends.
Sometimes barren as fear going nowhere
or in habit meaningless as tapwater.   15
One year maybe he would come and sit
for 4 months and not write a word down
would sit and investigate colours, the
insects in the room with him.
What he brought: a typewriter   20
tins of ginger ale, cigarettes. A copy of *StrangeLove*,
of *The Intervals*, a postcard of Rousseau's *The Dream*.[8]
His friends' words were strict as lightning
unclothing the bark of a tree, a shaved hook.
The postcard was a test pattern by the window   25
through which he saw growing scenery.
Also a map of a city in 1900.

Eventually the room was a time machine for him.
He closed the rotting door, sat down
thought pieces of history. The first girl   30
who in a park near his school
put a warm hand into his trousers
unbuttoning and finally catching the spill
across her wrist, he in the maze of her skirt.
She later played the piano   35
when he had tea with the parents.
He remembered that surprised—
he had forgotten for so long.
Under raincoats in the park on hot days.

The summers were layers of civilisation in his memory   40
they were old photographs he didn't look at anymore
for girls in them were chubby not as perfect as in his mind
and his ungovernable hair was shaved to the edge of skin.
His friends leaned on bicycles

6. City in southeastern Ontario.
7. Insect-repellent strip.
8. Painting by the French painter Henri Rousseau (1884–1910), depicting a naked woman on a
sofa in a dreamlike jungle. The other two titles are
of books by Canadian authors.

were 16 and tried to look 21   45
the cigarettes too big for their faces.
He could read those characters easily
undisguised as wedding pictures.
He could hardly remember their names
though they had talked all day, exchanged styles   50
and like dogs on a lawn hung around the houses of girls
waiting for night and the devious sex-games with their simple plots.

Sex a game of targets, of throwing firecrackers
at a couple in a field locked in hand-made orgasms,
singing dramatically in someone's ear along with the record   55
'*How do you think I feel / you know our love's not real*
The one you're mad about / Is just a gad-about
How do you think I feel'[9]
He saw all that complex tension the way his child would.

There is one picture that fuses the 5 summers.   60
Eight of them are leaning against a wall
arms around each other
looking into the camera and the sun
trying to smile at the unseen adult photographer
trying against the glare to look 21 and confident.   65
The summer and friendship will last forever.
Except one who was eating an apple. That was him
oblivious to the significance of the moment.
Now he hungers to have that arm around the next shoulder.
The wretched apple is fresh and white.   70

Since he began burning hills
the Shell strip has taken effect.
A wasp is crawling on the floor
tumbling over, its motor fanatic.
He has smoked 5 cigarettes.   75
He has written slowly and carefully
with great love and great coldness.
When he finishes he will go back
hunting for the lies that are obvious.

                                                          1979

(Inner Tube)[1]

On the warm July river
head back

upside down river
for a roof

slowly paddling   5
towards an estuary[2] between trees

---

9. From a song recorded by Elvis Presley in 1974.
1. Airtight tube that was filled with air inside an automobile tire; often used, as in the poem, by children as a float.
2. Water passage where a river meets the sea.

there's a dog
learning to swim near me
friends on shore

my head   10
dips
back to the eyebrow
I'm the prow
on an ancient vessel,
this afternoon   15
I'm going down to Peru
soul between my teeth

a blue heron
with its awkward
broken backed flap   20
upside down

one of us is wrong

he
his blue grey thud
thinking he knows   25
the blue way
out of here

or me

1984

JAMES TATE
b. 1943

James Tate describes himself as writing in the "tradition of the Impurists," and he
mentions in particular the poetry of Whitman, Williams, and Pablo Neruda. Poetry,
for Tate, is a form of protest, as well as celebration,[1] protest of a kind that runs deeper
than politics because it is endlessly concerned with our vexatious efforts to be in
touch with one another and with the natural world that surrounds us. The dazzling
surrealist world of such a poem as "The Wheelchair Butterfly" is both a heaven and
a hell; there is delight here, but it cannot exist without destruction:

> Today a butterfly froze
> in midair; and was plucked like a grape
> by a child who swore he could take care
>
> of it.

Presumably the poet here identifies with the child, for he speaks of his desire to
"order the world for a moment, freeze it, understand it."

Sometimes his poems seem to coast along on their own rhetoric, propelled by the
energies of the language itself, and by the clash of images. Tate effects his transformations with the speed and efficiency of a first-rate magician. Yet beneath the some-

---

1. *Contemporary Authors*, vol. 21–22, 1969, p. 528.

times giddy surfaces of Tate's poems there is enough pain and disappointment to satisfy the heartiest appetite for poetic distress. As Donald Justice said on the publication of *The Lost Pilot*, "Once despair can be taken for granted, gaiety becomes a possibility, almost a necessity" (notice on dust jacket).

Tate often dreams a world where an armistice will be declared in the warfare of contraries. The blue booby of the Galapagos—who contrives to be at once sad, funny, and beautiful—has found a haven beyond conflict; he exemplifies his creator's dictum, "The poem is man's noblest effort because it is utterly useless."[2]

Tate was born in Kansas City, Missouri, on December 8, 1943, and received his B.A. from Kansas State College in 1965 after two years at the University of Missouri. He then went to the University of Iowa, from which he received an M.F.A. and where he taught creative writing for a year. He has since taught at Berkeley and at Columbia and been poetry editor of the *Dickinson Review*. A prolific poet, he has published more than twenty books of poetry. Since 1967 he has been a member of the department of English at the University of Massachusetts at Amherst.

2. *Contemporary Poets of the English Language*, ed. R. Murphy, Chicago, 1971, p. 1025.

The Blue Booby

<pre>
The blue booby lives
on the bare rocks
of Galápagos[1]
and fears nothing.
It is a simple life: 5
they live on fish,
and there are few predators.
Also, the males do not
make fools of themselves
chasing after the young   10
ladies. Rather,
they gather the blue
objects of the world
and construct from them

a nest—an occasional   15
Gaulois[2] package,
a string of beads,
a piece of cloth from
a sailor's suit. This
replaces the need for   20
dazzling plumage;
in fact, in the past
fifty million years
the male has grown
considerably duller,   25
nor can he sing well.
The female, though,
</pre>

1. Pacific islands famous for their unique species of animal and bird life.

2. A French brand of cigarettes, in a distinctive blue package.

asks little of him—
the blue satisfies her
completely, has
a magical effect   30
on her. When she returns
from her day of
gossip and shopping,
she sees he has found her   35
a new shred of blue foil:
for this she rewards him
with her dark body,
the stars turn slowly
in the blue foil beside them   40
like the eyes of a mild savior.

                                                    1969

The Wheelchair Butterfly

O sleepy city of reeling wheelchairs
where a mouse can commit suicide if he can

concentrate long enough
on the history book of rodents
in his underground town   5

of electrical wheelchairs!
The girl who is always pregnant and bruised
like a pear

rides her many-stickered bicycle
backward up the staircase   10
of the abandoned trolleybarn.

Yesterday was warm. Today a butterfly froze
in midair; and was plucked like a grape
by a child who swore he could take care

of it. O confident city where   15
the seeds of poppies pass for carfare,

where the ordinary hornets in a human's heart
may slumber and snore, where bifocals bulge

in an orange garage of daydreams,
we wait in our loose attics for a new season   20

as if for an ice-cream truck.
An Indian pony crosses the plains
whispering Sanskrit prayers to a crater of fleas.
Honeysuckle says: I thought I could swim.

The Mayor is urinating on the wrong side   25
of the street! A dandelion sends off sparks:
beware your hair is locked!

Beware the trumpet wants a glass of water!
Beware a velvet tabernacle!

Beware the Warden of Light has married   30
an old piece of string!

                                                          1969

The Lost Pilot

for my father, 1922–1944

Your face did not rot
like the others—the co-pilot,
for example, I saw him

yesterday. His face is corn-
mush: his wife and daughter,   5
the poor ignorant people, stare

as if he will compose soon.
He was more wronged than Job.[3]
But your face did not rot

like the others—it grew dark,   10
and hard like ebony;
the features progressed in their

distinction. If I could cajole
you to come back for an evening,
down from your compulsive   15

orbiting, I would touch you,
read your face as Dallas,
your hoodlum gunner, now,

with the blistered eyes, reads
his braille editions. I would   20
touch your face as a disinterested

scholar touches an original page.
However frightening, I would
discover you, and I would not

turn you in; I would not make   25
you face your wife, or Dallas,
or the co-pilot, Jim. You

could return to your crazy
orbiting, and I would not try
to fully understand what   30

---

3. Figure in the Old Testament severely afflicted by God in order to test his faith.

it means to you. All I know
is this: when I see you,
as I have seen you at least

once every year of my life,
spin across the wilds of the sky   35
like a tiny, African god,

I feel dead. I feel as if I were
the residue of a stranger's life,
that I should pursue you.

My head cocked toward the sky,   40
I cannot get off the ground,
and, you, passing over again,

fast, perfect, and unwilling
to tell me that you are doing
well, or that it was mistake   45

that placed you in that world,
and me in this; or that misfortune
placed these worlds in us.

1978

Poem to Some of My Recent Poems

My beloved little billiard balls,
my polite mongrels, edible patriotic plums,
you owe your beauty to your mother, who
resembled a cyclindrical corned beef
with all the trimmings, may God rest   5
her forsaken soul, for it is all of us
she forsook; and I shall never forget
her sputtering embers, and then the little mound.
Yes, my little rum runners, she had defective
tear ducts and could weep only iced tea.   10
She had petticoats beneath her eyelids.
And in her last years she found ball bearings
in her beehive puddings, she swore allegiance
to Abyssinia. What should I have done?
I played the piano and scrambled eggs.   15
I had to navigate carefully around her brain's
avalanche lest even a decent finale be forfeited.
And her beauty still evermore. You see,
as she was dying, I led each of you to her side,
one by one she scorched you with her radiance.   20
And she is ever with us in our acetylene leisure.
But you are beautiful, and I, a slave to a heap of cinders.

1983

A Wedding

She was in terrible pain the whole day,
as she had been for months: a slipped disc,
and there is nothing more painful. She

herself was a nurse's aid, also a poet
just beginning to make a name for her   5
nom de plume.[4] As with most things in life,

it happened when she was changing channels
on her television. The lucky man, on the other
hand, was smiling for the first time

in his life, and it was fake. He was   10
an aspiring philosopher of dubious potential,
very serious, but somehow lacking in

essential depth. He could have been
an adequate undertaker. It was not the first
time for either of them. It was a civil   15

service, with no music, few flowers.
Still, there was a slow and erratic tide
of champagne—corks shot clear into the trees.

And flashcubes, instant photos, some blurred
and some too revealing, cake slices that aren't   20
what they were meant to be. The bride slept

through much of it, and never did we figure out
who was on whose team. I think the groom
meant it in the end when he said, "We never

thought anyone would come." We were not the first   25
to arrive, nor the last to leave. Who knows,
it may all turn out for the best. And who

really cares about such special days, they
are not what we live for.

1986

4. Pen name.

CRAIG RAINE
b. 1944

Craig Raine takes his place among the English poets who are attempting a radical
reconsideration of poetic subjects and attitudes. One of his principal models is James
Joyce. At first his verse appears opaque and riddling; it seems to require explanatory
notes but offers none. Gradually as one reads him his method becomes clearer: his
verse presents real life by what the Soviet critic Victor Shklovsky calls "defamiliari-

zation." Raine made this especially clear by the title poem of his second book, "A Martian Sends a Postcard Home." He would come upon this world as if from outer space. The result is a surrealistic surface. A number of other poets flocked to the Martian banner—James Fenton and Christopher Reid, for example—and were promptly labeled "the Martian school." As James Fenton said, Raine "taught us to become strangers in our familiar world, to release the faculty of perception and allow it to graze at liberty in the field of experience."[1]

Though Raine has been criticized for merely heaping up weird data, his work is closely knit rather than random. Even the Martian postcard seems to proceed from external nature—rain, mist, birds—to internal—"everyone's pain has a different smell." In his recent volume *Rich*, Raine writes not as someone from outer space but as father, lover, office worker. Raine's pleasure in unexpected juxtapositions, in a comedy of displacement, in the recognition of everyday absurdity, is contagious. In spite of the difficulty of his verse, it has secured a large audience.

Craig Raine was born in Bishop Auckland, County Durham, England, on December 3, 1944. He was educated at Oxford and for some years lectured there. He also served in an editorial capacity on several magazines. Since 1981 he has occupied a post formerly held by T.S. Eliot, as poetry editor at the publishing house of Faber & Faber Ltd. In 1986 he wrote the libretto for an opera, *The Electrification of the Soviet Union*, based on a story by Boris Pasternak, to whose niece he is married.

---

1. Quoted in Anthony Thwaite, *Poetry Today*, London and New York, 1985, p. 126.

Nature Study

(for Rona, Jeremy, Sam & Grace)

All the lizards are asleep—
perched pagodas with tiny triangular tiles,
each milky lid a steamed-up window.
Inside, the heart repeats itself life a sleepy gong,
summoning nothing to nothing.   5

In winter time, the zoo reverts to metaphor,
God's poetry of boredom:
the cobra knits her Fair-Isle[1] skin,
rattlers titter over the same joke.
All of them endlessly finish spaghetti.   10
The python runs down like a spring,
and time stops on some ancient Sabbath:[2]

Pythagorean bees are shut inside the hive,
which hymns and hums like Sunday chapel[3]—
drowsy thoughts in a wrinkled brain.   15

The fire's gone out—
crocodiles lie like wet beams,
cross-hatched by flames that no one can remember.
Grasshoppers shiver, chafe their limbs
and try to keep warm,   20

---

1. Name of a distinctively designed, heavily ribbed sweater.
2. Day of rest and worship.
3. Nonconformist (that is, Protestant) church;
the bees are imagined as followers of the ancient Greek mathematician Pythagoras because of the geometric shapes of their honeycombs.

crouching on their marks perpetually.
The African cricket is trussed like a cold chicken:
the sneeze of movement returns it to the same position,
in the same body. There is no change.

The rumple-headed lion has nowhere to go   25
and snoozes in his grimy combinations.[4]
A chaise longue with missing castors,
the walrus is stuck forever on his rock.
Sleepily, the seals play crib,[5]
scoring on their upper lips.   30
The chimps kill fleas and time,
sewing nothing to nothing

Five o'clock—perhaps.
Vultures in their shabby Sunday suits
fidget with broken umbrellas,   35
while the ape beats his breast
and yodels out repentance.
Their feet are an awful dream of bunions—

but the buffalo's brazil nut bugle-horns
can never sound reveille.   40
                                                               1978

A Martian Sends a Postcard Home

Caxtons[6] are mechanical birds with many wings
and some are treasured for their markings—

they cause the eyes to melt
or the body to shriek without pain.[7]

I have never seen one fly, but   5
sometimes they perch on the hand.

Mist is when the sky is tired of flight
and rests its soft machine on ground:

then the world is dim and bookish
like engravings under tissue paper.   10

Rain is when the earth is television.
It has the property of making colours darker.

Model T[8] is a room with the lock inside—
a key is turned to free the world

for movement, so quick there is a film   15
to watch for anything missed.

4. One-piece underwear.
5. That is, cribbage, a card game.
6. That is, books, which William Caxton (c.
1422–1491) was the first to print in English.

7. The Martian does not know the words for
"cry" or "laugh."
8. That is, automobile; the "key" is the ignition
key.

But time is tied to the wrist
or kept in a box, ticking with impatience.

In homes, a haunted apparatus sleeps,
that snores when you pick it up.   20

If the ghost cries, they carry it
to their lips and soothe it to sleep

with sounds. And yet, they wake it up
deliberately, by tickling with a finger.

Only the young are allowed to suffer   25
openly. Adults go to a punishment room

with water but nothing to eat.
They lock the door and suffer the noises

alone. No one is exempt
and everyone's pain has a different smell.   30

At night, when all the colours die,
they hide in pairs

and read about themselves—
in colour, with their eyelids shut.

     1979

An Attempt at Jealousy

So how is life with your new bloke?
Simpler, I bet. Just one stroke
of his quivering oar and the skin
of the Thames goes into a spin,

eh? How is life with an oarsman? Better?   5
More in—out? Athletic? Wetter?
When you hear the moan of the rowlocks,
do you urge him on like a cox?

Tell me, is he bright enough to find
that memo-pad you call a mind?   10
Or has he contrived to bring you out—
given you an in-tray and an out?

How did I ever fall for a paper-clip?
How could I ever listen to office gossip
even in bed and find it so intelligent?   15
Was it straight biological bent?

I suppose you go jogging together?
Tackle the Ridgeway in nasty weather?

Face force 55 gales and chat about prep
or how you bested that Birmingham rep?[9]   20

He must be mad with excitement.
So must you. What an incitement
to lust all those press-ups must be.
Or is it just the same? PE?

Tell me, I'm curious. Is it fun   25
being in love with just anyone?
How do you remember his face
if you meet in a public place?

Perhaps you know him by his shoes?
Or do you sometimes choose   30
another pinstriped clone
by accident and drag that home

instead? From what you say,
he's perfect. For a Chekhov play.
Tall and dark and brightly dim,   35
Kulygin's[1] part was made for him.

Imagine your life with a 'beak'.[2]
Week after week after week
like homework or detention;
all that standing to attention   40

whenever his colleagues drop in
for a spot of what's-your-toxin.
Speech Day, matron, tuck-shop,[3] Christ,
you'll find school fees are over-priced

and leave, but not come back to me.   45
You've done your bit for poetry.
Words, or deeds? You'll stick to youth.
I'm a stickler for the truth—

which makes me wonder what it was
I loved you for. Tell me, because   50
now I feel nothing—except regret.
What is it, love, I need to forget?

1984

---

9. (1) Sales representative from Birmingham; (2) Birmingham Repertory, a theater group. "Prep": homework (English "public"—that is, private—school term).
1. The weak schoolteacher in Anton Chekov's *The Three Sisters* (1901).
2. Britishism for "headmaster."
3. "What's-your-toxin": that is, "What'll you have to drink?" (compare U.S. "Name your poison"). The rest are more English public-school terms: "Speech Day" is the equivalent of U.S. commencement, with prizes and speeches; "matron" is the nurse-housekeeper who looks after, especially, the smaller boys; a "tuck-shop" is a candy store.

NORMAN DUBIE
b. 1945

In a period when narrative verse is in disfavor, and specific times and [
be avoided, Norman Dubie persists in evoking scenes of historical anc
concern. Whether he deals with Czar Nicholas II, Madame Blavatsky, or Queen
Elizabeth I, Dubie seeks out a focus and evolves into a dramatic monologue, spoken by
his character, or by some reflective observer, or both. He gathers together an
extraordinary range of subjects, and presents them as if he were personally involved
in them all. Dubie has a keen eye for detail and he is alive to multiple perspectives.
He can describe also what no man has seen, "a limitless glut of peace" where parallel
things meet ("About Infinity").

In spite of his use of historical materials, Dubie's meaning is not simple, and is
rendered obliquely. His poetry is like a series of parables in which the lessons must
be kept implicit and somewhat indistinct.

Dubie was born in Barre, Vermont, on April 10, 1945. He was educated at God-
dard College in Vermont and at the University of Iowa. Since 1975 he has taught at
Arizona State University.

The Czar's Last Christmas Letter:
A Barn in the Urals[1]

You were never told, Mother, how old Illya[2] was drunk
That last holiday, for five days and nights

He stumbled through Petersburg forming
A choir of mutes, he dressed them in pink ascension gowns[3]

And, then, sold Father's Tirietz stallion so to rent   5
A hall for his Christmas recital: the audience

Was rowdy but Illya in his black robes turned on them
And gave them that look of his; the hall fell silent

And violently he threw his hair to the side and up
Went the baton, the recital ended exactly one hour   10

Later when Illya suddenly turned and bowed
And his mutes bowed, and what applause and hollering

Followed.
All of his cronies were there!

Illya told us later that he thought the voices   15
Of mutes combine in a sound

---

1. The Ural mountains in west central Russia, to which Czar Nicholas II (1868–1918) and his family were exiled after the Russian Revolution forced him to abdicate.
2. "Illya" is not an historical person; he "is the fiction that allowed me to take an interest in the familiar story of the Czar's family. I almost never research a poem. I use what I have already learned, and consequently have somehow made it my own" (Norman Dubie, letter to John Benedict, July 28, 1987).
3. Robes in which to celebrate Ascension Day (commemorating Christ's ascension into heaven); St. Petersburg, the pre-Revolutionary name for Leningrad, was the capital of the Russian Empire; "mutes": people who cannot speak.

Like wind passing through big, winter pines.
Mother, if for no other reason I regret the war

With Japan[4] for, you must now be told,
It took the servant, Illya, from us. *It was confirmed.*   20

He would sit on the rocks by the water and with his stiletto
Open clams and pop the raw meats into his mouth

And drool and laugh at us children.
We hear guns often, now, down near the village.

Don't think me a coward, Mother, but it is comfortable   25
Now that I am no longer Czar. I can take pleasure

From just a cup of clear water. I hear Illya's choir often.
I teach the children about decreasing fractions,[5] that is

A lesson best taught by the father.
Alexandra conducts the French and singing lessons.   30

Mother, we are again a physical couple.
I brush out her hair for her at night.

She thinks that we'll be rowing outside Geneva[6]
By the spring. I hope she won't be disappointed.

Yesterday morning while bread was frying   35
In one corner, she in another washed all of her legs

Right in front of the children. I think
We became sad at her beauty. She has a purple bruise

On an ankle.
Like Illya I made her chew on mint.   40

Our Christmas will be in this excellent barn.
The guards flirt with your granddaughters and I see . . .

I see nothing wrong with it. Your little one, who is
Now a woman, made one soldier pose for her, she did

Him in charcoal, but as a bold nude. He was   45
Such an obvious virgin about it; he was wonderful!

Today, that same young man found us an enormous azure
And pearl samovar. Once, he called me Great Father[7]

And got confused.
He refused to let me touch him.   50

4. In 1904–1905, Russia was roundly beaten.
5. That is, fractions of fractions.
6. In Switzerland. The Czar and his wife had
been estranged earlier, in part because of the Cza-
rina's religious fervor.
7. "Great Father" was one of a Czar's titles;
"samovar": urn used in Russia for boiling water for
tea.

I know they keep your letters from us. But, Mother,
The day they finally put them in my hands

I'll know that possessing them I am condemned
And possibly even my wife, and my children.

We will drink mint tea this evening.   55
Will each of us be increased by death?

With fractions as the bottom integer gets bigger, Mother, it
Represents less.[8] That's the feeling I have about

This letter. I am at your request. The Czar.
And I am Nicholas.   60
                                                               1977

Elizabeth's War with the Christmas Bear

The bears are kept by hundreds within fences, are fed cracked
Eggs; the weakest are
Slaughtered and fed to the others after being scented
With the blood of deer brought to the pastures by Elizabeth's
Men—the blood spills from deep pails with bottoms of slate.   5

The balding Queen[9] had bear gardens in London and in the country.
The bear is baited:[1] the nostrils
Are blown full with pepper, the Irish wolf dogs
Are starved, then, emptied, made crazy with fermented barley:

And the bear's hind leg is chained to a stake, the bear   10
Is blinded and whipped, kneeling in his own blood and slaver, he is
Almost instantly worried by the dogs. At the very moment that
Elizabeth took Essex's head,[2] a giant brown bear
Stood in the gardens with dogs hanging from his fur . . .
He took away the sun, took   15
A wolfhound in his mouth, and tossed it into
The white lap of Elizabeth I—arrows and staves[3] rained

On his chest, and standing, he, then, stood even taller, seeing
Into the Queen's private boxes—he grinned
Into her battered eggshell face.   20
Another volley of arrows and poles, and opening his mouth
He showered
Blood all over Elizabeth and her Privy Council.[4]

The next evening, a cool evening, the Queen demanded
13 bears and the justice of 113 dogs: She slept   25

---

8. As, for example, $\frac{1}{5}$ is less than $\frac{1}{2}$; "integer": number.
9. Queen Elizabeth I (1553–1603).
1. Tied to a stake and attacked by dogs, as described below. Bear-baiting was a popular spectator sport in Elizabethan England.

2. In 1601; the Earl of Essex, who had earlier been Elizabeth's favorite, was executed for treason.
3. Narrow strips of wood.
4. That is, her advisory council.

All that Sunday night and much of the next morning
Some said she was guilty of *this* and *that*.
The Protestant Queen gave the defeated bear
A grave in a Catholic cemetery. The marker said:
Peter, a Solstice Bear, a gift of the Tsarevitch[5] to Elizabeth.   30

After a long winter she had the grave opened. The bear's skeleton
Was cleared with lye, she placed it at her bedside,
Put a candle inside behind the sockets of the eyes, and, then
She spoke to it:

You were a Christmas bear—behind your eyes   35
I see the walls of a snow cave where you are a cub still smelling
Of your mother's blood which has dried in your hair; you have
Troubled a Queen who was afraid
When seated in *shade* which, standing,
You had created! A Queen who often wakes with a dream   40
Of you at night—
Now, you'll stand by my bed in your long white bones; alone, you
Will frighten away at night all visions of bear, and all day
You will be in this cold room—your constant grin,
You'll stand in the long, white prodigy of your bones, and you are,   45

Every inch of you, a terrible vision, not bear, but virgin![6]

                                                                                    1979

Elegy for Wright & Hugo[7]

Saint Jerome lived with a community
Of souls[8] in a stone house.
He had a donkey and a young lion.
Winter evenings the brown donkey
Went out for wood, the proud lion   5
Always his faithful companion.

One night passing merchants seized
The donkey. The lion
Returned to the house
And was accused by Jerome   10
Of having eaten his friend!
The punishment was merciful—the lion
Assumed the donkey's burden
And went alone each winter evening
Across the fields   15
For firewood. The lion missed
The donkey, but he never
Felt wronged or misunderstood.

---

5. The Tsar's (or Czar's) son; "solstice": in celebration of the winter solstice, December 22.
6. Elizabeth I was known as "the Virgin Queen."
7. James Wright and Richard Hugo, American
poets, who died in 1980 and 1982, respectively.

See above, pp. 681 and 606.
8. That is, a monastery. St. Jerome (c. 342–420)
translated the Bible from Greek and Hebrew into
Latin; in art, he is represented as accompanied by
a lion.

Years passed. And then
The merchants, with troubled conscience,   20
Detailing their shame, returned the donkey
To Saint Jerome.
The donkey and the lion
Resumed happily their winter schedules.
Everyone was forgiven. This is where   25
The story usually ends.

But months passed
And the lion, who missed his new usefulness,
Changed, became jealous, and snapped—
He ate the donkey under the stars   30
Among the cold alders.
He returned to the stone house
With a load of wood on his back.
Saint Jerome, not to be confused by experience,
Announced to the community   35
That the donkey was again lost,
That the lion had returned
With firewood, that the lion was bloody,
No doubt from combat, no doubt having attacked
The cruel merchants who had once again   40
Stolen his companion. But Jerome knew—
From then on the downcast lion
Was excused from all work, was left
To age by the fire.

Jerome, dressed in sack,[9]   45
Went out each night
Barefoot across the blue snow
And returned with branches
Tied to his back.

He was a saint. It was like that. . . .   50

1983

Lamentations

The scrub woman for the old bank and jailhouse,
Her face reddening

Over supper on a steamy night
Is thinking of the village spillway being

Answered by a dry clucking over mud, *she is*   5
Touching the burrs on the tongue of the azalea . . .

Exhaustion puts knotted rags in the neck
And shoulders:

---

9. Sackcloth, a coarse cloth worn as penitence.

As a girl, in Poland, she watched her husband
Be dragged through the shade of five pines   10

To the execution wall. A year earlier
She had watched him bathe

In the bronze tub the landlord had put
Out in the field as a trough for horses.

She picked him from among the men   15
Smoking pipes after haying, *she rolled*

Over on her stomach
To study the blue cornflower; she shyly
Rained on the wildflowers, a hot urine . . .
They laughed, and never knew her brother   20

Was taken by train to Hamburg,[1] was infected
With tuberculosis, was

In the last days of the war
Stripped along with six other children

And hanged in the boiler room of a post office.   25
What she has understood

Is there are only
Two speeches the naked make well,

One is of welcome, the other farewell.

                                                             1986

1. In Germany.

LESLIE MARMON SILKO
b. 1948

In Leslie Marmon Silko's *Story Teller*, a collection of prose and poetry, there is a
photograph of a young couple and their child. The man has a high brow, fine observant eyes, and an enormous moustache. The woman's gaze is not fixed on any thing,
but rather might well be an inward scrutiny. The child sits on his mother's lap; he is
a fat, jolly baby, and the only one of the three who seems to be actually participating
in the business of being photographed. The young couple were Silko's great-grand-
parents (and the baby was her grandfather), he a white American, and she a Native
American of the Laguna Pueblo, Marie Anaya Marmon, who would live to be the
elderly woman in "[It Was a Long Time Before]" who dies because there is no one
left in her life to talk with.

The Laguna Pueblo, even in the nineteenth century, was hospitable to mixed
marriages and the children of these marriages. Silko's native culture, preliterate,
orally transmitted generally by story-telling older women, is accessible to her, and
she is building a bridge between that culture and readers of poetry in English. Not
that she is indifferent to the mostly losing struggle between the Native American and

the murderous white invaders. One of her poems imagines a world "no white people / and there was nothing European." The downfall is "witchcraft." The witches of many tribes gather for a contest as to the most mischief. The prize is won by a heretofore unknown witch wι people who live far away: "When they look they see only objects. The wε thing for them / the trees and rivers are not alive / the mountains and sto alive. / The deer and the bear are objects / They see no life." The other ν appalled and plead with the strange witch to recall this curse, but that cι ̣ ̣ ̣ be done: the curse has already started.

Leslie Marmon Silko was born in Albuquerque, New Mexico. In addition to her poems, she has written short stories and a novel, *Ceremony* (1977). In 1974 she received an award from the National Endowment for the Arts and in 1981 a Mac-Arthur Prize Fellowship.

[It Was a Long Time Before]

It was a long time before
I learned that my Grandma A'mooh's
real name was Marie Anaya Marmon.
I thought her name really was "A'mooh."
I realize now it had happened when I was a baby   5
and she cared for me while my mother worked.
I had been hearing her say
            "a'moo'ooh"
which is the Laguna[1] expression of endearment
for a young child   10
spoken with great feeling and love.

Her house was next to ours
and as I grew up
I spent a lot of time with her
because she was in her eighties   15
and they worried about her falling.
So I would go check up on her—which was really
an excuse to visit her.
After I had to go to school
I went to carry in the coal bucket   20
which she still insisted on filling.
I slept with her
in case she fell getting up in the night.

She still washed her hair with yucca roots
or "soap weed" as she called it. She said   25
it kept white hair like hers from yellowing.
She kept these yucca roots on her windowsill
and I remember I was afraid of them for a long time
because they looked like hairy twisted claws.

I watched her make red chili on the grinding stone   30
the old way, even though it had gotten difficult for her

1. A pueblo (either the communal dwelling place of a Native American village or the village itself) in west central New Mexico.

to get down on her knees.
She used to tell me and my sisters
about the old days when they didn't have toothpaste
and cleaned their teeth with juniper ash,   35
and how, instead of corn flakes, in the old days they ate
"maaht'zini" crushed up with milk poured over it.

Her last years they took her away to Albuquerque[2]
to live with her daughter, Aunt Bessie.
But there was no fire to start in the morning   40
and nobody dropping by.
She didn't have anyone to talk to all day
because Bessie worked.
She might have lived without watering morning glories
and without kids running through her kitchen   45
but she did not last long
without someone to talk to.

                                                         1981

In Cold Storm Light

In cold storm light
I watch the sandrock
    canyon rim.

    The wind is wet
       with the smell of piñon.[3]   5
    The wind is cold
       with the sound of juniper.
         And then
          out of the thick ice sky
           running swiftly   10
           pounding
           swirling above the treetops
         The snow elk come,
         Moving, moving
           white song   15
           storm wind in the branches.
  And when the elk have passed
    behind them
       a crystal train of snowflakes
       strands of mist   20
         tangled in rocks
         and leaves.

                                                         1981

Toe'osh: A Laguna Coyote Story

for Simon Ortiz,[4] July 1973

In the wintertime
at night

___

2. City in New Mexico.
3. Low-growing pine.

4. Native American poet.

we tell coyote stories
            and drink Spañada by the stove.
How coyote got his
ratty old fur coat
                bits of old fur
                the sparrows stuck on him
                with dabs of pitch.
That was after he lost his proud original one in a poker game.
anyhow, things like that
are always happening to him,
that's what he said, anyway.

And it happened to him at Laguna
and Chinle
and Lukachukai[5] too, because coyote got too smart for his own good.

But the Navajos say he won a contest once.
It was to see who could sleep out in a
snowstorm the longest
and coyote waited until chipmunk badger and skunk were all
curled up under the snow
and then he uncovered himself and slept all night
inside
and before morning he got up and went out again
and waited until the others got up before he came
in to take the prize.

Some white men came to Acoma[6] and Laguna a hundred years ago
and they fought over Acoma land and Laguna women, and even now
some of their descendants are howling in
the hills southeast of Laguna.

Charlie Coyote wanted to be governor
and he said that when he got elected
he would run the other men off
the reservation
and keep all the women for himself.

One year
the politicians got fancy
at Laguna.
They went door to door with hams and turkeys
and they gave them to anyone who promised
to vote for them.
On election day all the people
stayed home and ate turkey
and laughed.

The Trans-Western pipeline vice president came
to discuss right-of-way.
The Lagunas let him wait all day long
because he is a busy and important man.

5. Pueblos (Native American villages).   6. Pueblo in west central New Mexico.

And late in the afternoon they told him
to come back again tomorrow.   50

They were after the picnic food
that the special dancers left
down below the cliff.
And Toe'osh and his cousins hung themselves
down over the cliff   55
holding each other's tail in their mouth making a coyote chain
until someone in the middle farted
and the guy behind him opened his
mouth to say "What stinks?" and they
all went tumbling down, like that.   60

Howling and roaring
Toe'osh scattered white people
out of bars all over Wisconsin.
He bumped into them at the door
until they said   65
                    "Excuse me"
And the way Simon meant it
was for 300 or maybe 400 years.

                                                                   1981

MICHAEL BLUMENTHAL
b. 1949

Michael Blumenthal's poems flash with verbal energy. He likes to assume the role of
poetic ringmaster, crack his whip, and put the language through its paces. In his
poem "Inventors" he praises the likes of Alexander Fleming and Benjamin Franklin,
not for their actual discoveries, but for the delicious new words they brought into
the language: "penicillin," "electricity." Blumenthal's poem about abandoning his
car in a snowstorm is full of puns and other verbal sideswipes (note his use of "clutch,"
"revving," "stalled.") The poem also converts a misfortune into a liberation: the poet
can say farewell not only to his Toyota, but also to Exxon and Detroit, the sometime
cathedral city of the American automobile.

    Not that Blumenthal is "against" machinery, though he particularly treasures
machines which have grown human by long association. His old typewriter, soon to
be replaced by a word processor, is imagined as a beloved but aging mistress; the
conclusion is pleasant in its promise that there is a dance or two in the old girl yet.
Blumenthal's metaphors invariably enliven and enrich.

    Michael Blumenthal was born on March 8, 1949, in Manhattan, where he grew up
in a German-speaking home. He received a B.A. from the State University of New
York in Binghamton, and a J.D. from the Cornell Law School. He has worked as a
teacher, a lawyer, an editor, an administrator for the National Endowment for the
Arts, and a director of documentary and news films. He is presently Briggs-Copeland
Assistant Professor at Harvard University. His third book, *Laps*, won the Juniper
Prize for poetry from the University of Massachusetts Press.

Inventors

Imagine being the first to say: surveillance . . .
—Howard Nemerov[1]

"Imagine being the first to say: *surveillance,*"
the mouth taking in air like a swimmer, the tongue
light as an astronaut, gliding across the roof
of the mouth, the eyes burning like the eyes of Fleming
looking at mold and thinking: *penicillin.*[2]   5

Imagine Franklin holding his key that dark night,
the clouds rolling across the sky's roof
like a poet's tongue, the air heavy with some
unnamed potential, the whole thing suspended
from a string like a vocal cord waiting to say: 10
electricity.

Or imagine digging for shale[3] in some dull Oklahoma,
how the ground is a parched throat waiting for moisture,
and you all derricky and impatient, knowing something
you have yet no name for might rise and surprise you.   15
Imagine being the first to say: *petroleum.*

Some night, dry as an old well and speechless
beneath a brilliant moon, think of Heisenberg
taking his ruler to the world for a measure
and finding, in the measuring, an irrevocable changing.   20
Imagine being the first to say, with confidence:
uncertainty.[4]

It goes on like this always. A poet stops in the woods
to clear his throat, and out comes: *convolvulus.*
A biologist rolls over during the night to hold   25
her husband, thinking: *peristalsis.*[5] A choreographer
watches the sunrise over Harlem, whispering: *tour-jetté,*
ronde-de-jambe.[6]

Just think of it—
your tongue rolling over the first *pharmacopoeia*[7]   30
like a new lover, the shuddering thrill of it,
the way the air parts in front of your mouth, widening
the world in its constant uncertainty. Go on.

---

1. American poet; see above, p. 564.
2. Sir Alexander Fleming (1881–1955), Scottish bacteriologist, discovered penicillin in 1928.
3. Stratified rock.
4. In 1934 Werner Karl Heisenberg, twentieth-century German physicist, formulated his "uncertainty principle"—that it is impossible, according to ordinary geometry, to state precisely the position and velocity of an atomic particle.

5. Involuntary contraction in the intestine; "convolvulus": herb or shrub of the morning-glory family.
6. Terms in classical ballet: high leap and circular movement of the leg; Harlem is the area above New York City's 125th Street.
7. Book on, or stock of, drugs and medical chemicals.

Let your mind wander. Imagine being the first to say:
I love you, oregano, onomatopoeia.[8]   35

Just imagine it.
                                                                    1980

Abandoning Your Car in a Snowstorm: Rosslyn, Virginia

It is better
than leaving your wife or your nagging lover
could ever be.

It is better than anything
you have ever bought, better   5
than the best nights of sex in your life,
even better than quitting your job.

As you open your door to reclaim your feet
from the hungry clutch, you know
you are on to something: You are suddenly   10
a drowning man whose last stride has found
the ocean floor, a vagabond with a roof
over his head for the first time.

Around you, mothers curse red lights,
men in wide ties are reduced to a hilarious impotence.   15
All the revving in the world will not move them,
all their stalled money cannot buy rain.

And there you are,
Toyota-less and dancing to the Cadillac pace
of sure movement, Johnny Travolta Fred Astaire[9]   20
by God the world is beautiful and glass-less
and the Shah of Iran too is stalled in some Siberia
with his billions and his quiet wife, and all the oil
wells in the world will not lead him from his private Rosslyn.

If you go anywhere, dear Shah,   25
you must learn to trust your feet again,
I call to him from my clean and snow-swept escalator
to the nation's capital, and move on—

a ribbon whirling between the stalled cars
on these beautiful bridges,   30
calling *Goodbye Exxon*
Goodbye gas-line anti-freeze

Goodbye you ugly Detroit.

                                                                    1980

8. Naming a thing or action with a word that supposedly sounds like what it describes, as "buzz" or "hiss"; "oregano" is an herb.
9. Agile dancers in movies.

Back from the Word-Processing Course,
I Say to My Old Typewriter

Old friend, you
who were once in the avant-garde,
you of the thick cord
and the battered plug,
the slow and deliberate characters   5
proportionally spaced, shall we
go on together as before?
Shall we remain married
out of the cold dittos[1] of conviction
and habit? Or should we move on   10
to some new technology of ease
and embellishment—Should I run off
with her, so much like you when
you were young, my aged Puella[2]
of the battered keys, so lovely   15
in that bleached light of the first morning?

Old horse,
what will it be like
when the next young filly
comes along? How will I love you,   20
crate of my practiced strokes,
when she cries out: *new new*
and asks me to dance again?
Oh plow for now, old boat,
through these familiar waters,   25
make the tides come in
once more! Concubined[3] love,
take me again into your easy arms,
make this page wild once more
like a lustful sheet! Be wet,   30
sweet toy, with your old ink:
vibrate those aging hips again
beneath these trembling hands.

1985

---

1. That is, repetitions.
2. Girl (Latin).

3. That is, having become a concubine or mistress.

JAMES FENTON
b. 1949

Although James Fenton gave the Martian poets their name, on the basis of a poem by Craig Raine, he strikes a note of his own. His experiences as a journalist in the Far East and in Germany have provided him with a first-hand vista of suffering. He feels particularly for those people, especially children, whom "geography condemns to war" ("Children in Exile"). In "A German Requiem" a series of negatives sparsely recalls widescale destruction. The simplicity of grief is heightened rather than confused by such a sardonic detail as "Professor Sargnagel was buried with four degrees, two associate memberships . . ." Fenton is at his best in confronting horror with humor, not so much to mitigate as to enhance it. His title "Dead Soldiers" means both consumed bottles of Napoleon brandy and actual dead men; in the poem, the wild party at the beginning gives way to the barbarous civil war at the end. The jocularity is only a cover for pity.

Fenton rarely expresses himself directly, yet in a poem like "Wind" his tacit sympathy goes out to the human chaff blown about:

> I saw a thousand years pass in two seconds.
> Land was lost, languages rose and divided.

Suffering appears to be immemorial. No wonder that he can take up a macabre subject such as "The Staffordshire Murderer," or find the Deity, in "God, A Poem," anything but beneficent. Yet if he has no confidence in redemption, he has some trust in human wit and fantasy. In "The Kingfisher's Boxing Gloves" the animal kingdom is mustered for inspection as in a museum, a spacecraft takes off to the moon, and other delightfully unexplained and often ludicrous things contribute to the sense that the universe, if not buoyant, is at least extremely lively.

James Fenton was born in Lincoln, England, on April 25, 1949. He was educated at Oxford and won the Newdigate Prize for Poetry there. In the 1970s he wrote for the *New Statesman* and *Guardian,* working in Germany and the Far East as well as in London. From 1979 to 1984 he was a theater critic for the *Sunday Times,* and has been since that time a principal reviewer of books for the *Times.*

A German Requiem[1]

(To T. J. G.-A.)

For as at a great distance of place, that which wee look at, appears dimme, and
without distinction of the smaller parts; and as Voyces grow weak, and inarticulate:
so also after great distance of time, our imagination of the Past is weak; and wee lose
(for example) of Cities wee have seen, many particular Streets; and of Actions, many
particular Circumstances. This *decaying sense*, when wee would express the thing it
self, (I mean *fancy* it selfe,) wee call *Imagination*, as I said before: But when we
would express the *decay*, and signifie that the Sense is fading, old, and past, it is
called Memory. So that *Imagination* and *Memory* are but one thing . . .
—Hobbes, *Leviathan*[2]

It is not what they built. It is what they knocked down.
It is not the houses. It is the spaces between the houses.
It is not the streets that exist. It is the streets that no longer exist.
It is not your memories which haunt you.
It is not what you have written down.   5
It is what you have forgotten, what you must forget.
What you must go on forgetting all your life.
And with any luck oblivion should discover a ritual.
You will find out that you are not alone in the enterprise.   10
Yesterday the very furniture seemed to reproach you.
Today you take your place in the Widow's Shuttle.[3]

•

The bus is waiting at the southern gate
To take you to the city of your ancestors

1. Mass or chant for the dead.
2. *Leviathan, or the Matter, Form, and Power of a Commonwealth, Ecclesiastical and Civil* (1651), by the English philosopher Thomas Hobbes.
3. Popular name for bus going to cemetery.

Which stands on the hill opposite, with gleaming pediments,[4]
As vivid as this charming square, your home.   15
Are you shy? You should be. It is almost like a wedding,
The way you clasp your flowers and give a little tug at your veil. Oh,
The hideous bridesmaids, it is natural that you should resent them
Just a little, on this first day.
But that will pass, and the cemetery is not far.   20
Here comes the driver, flicking a toothpick into the gutter,
His tongue still searching between his teeth.
See, he has not noticed you. No one has noticed you.
It will pass, young lady, it will pass.

●

How comforting it is, once or twice a year,   25
To get together and forget the old times.
As on those special days, ladies and gentlemen,
When the boiled shirts[5] gather at the graveside
And a leering waistcoat approaches the rostrum.
It is like a solemn pact between the survivors.   30
The mayor has signed it on behalf of the freemasonry.[6]
The priest has sealed it on behalf of all the rest.
Nothing more need be said, and it is better that way—

●

The better for the widow, that she should not live in fear of surprise,
The better for the young man, that he should move at liberty between the
    armchairs,   35
The better that these bent figures who flutter among the graves
Tending the nightlights and replacing the chrysanthemums
Are not ghosts,
That they shall go home.
The bus is waiting, and on the upper terraces   40
The workmen are dismantling the houses of the dead.

●

But when so many had died, so many and at such speed,
There were no cities waiting for the victims.
They unscrewed the name-plates from the shattered doorways
And carried them away with the coffins.   45
So the squares and parks were filled with the eloquence of young
    cemeteries:
The smell of fresh earth, the improvised crosses
And all the impossible directions in brass and enamel.

●

'Doctor Gliedschirm, skin specialist, surgeries 14-16 hours or by
    appointment.'
Professor Sargnagel was buried with four degrees, two associate
    memberships   50
And instructions to tradesmen to use the back entrance.
Your uncle's grave informed you that he lived on the third floor, left.

---

4. Triangular spaces under roofs.   6. Secret society for mutual help, called "Free
5. (Men wearing) dress shirts with starched   and Accepted Order of Masons."
fronts.

You were asked please to ring, and he would come down in the lift[7]
To which one needed a key . . .

•

Would come down, would ever come down   55
With a smile like thin gruel, and never too much to say.
How he shrank through the years.
How you towered over him in the narrow cage.[8]
How he shrinks now . . .

•

But come. Grief must have its term? Guilt too, then.   60
And it seems there is no limit to the resourcefulness of recollection.
So that a man might say and think:
When the world was at its darkest,
When the black wings passed over the rooftops[9]
(And who can divine His purposes?) even then   65
There was always, always a fire in this hearth.
You see this cupboard? A priest-hole![1]
And in that lumber-room whole generations have been housed and fed.
Oh, if I were to begin, if I were to begin to tell you
The half, the quarter, a mere smattering of what we went through!   70

•

His wife nods, and a secret smile,
Like a breeze with enough strength to carry one dry leaf
Over two pavingstones, passes from chair to chair.
Even the enquirer is charmed.
He forgets to pursue the point.   75
It is not what he wants to know.
It is what he wants not to know.
It is not what they say.
It is what they do not say.

                                                                      1981

Dead Soldiers

When His Excellency Prince Norodom Chantaraingsey[2]
Invited me to lunch on the battlefield
I was glad of my white suit for the first time that day.
They lived well, the mad Norodoms, they had style.
The brandy and the soda arrived in crates.   5
Bricks of ice, tied around with raffia,
Dripped from the orderlies'[3] handlebars.

And I remember the dazzling tablecloth
As the APCs[4] fanned out along the road,

---

7. Britishism for "elevator."
8. Of the wire-screened elevator.
9. Compare Exodus 12:27: "It is the sacrifice of the Lord's passover, who passed over the houses of the children of Israel in Egypt, when he smote the Egyptians, and delivered our houses."
1. Originally a secret hiding place for a Roman Catholic priest during periods of persecution.
2. Uncle of Prince Norodom Sihanouk, former ruler of Cambodia (see below). Fenton was a war correspondent in Vietnam and Cambodia.
3. Soldiers assigned to act as servants for higher officers; "raffia": palm fibers.
4. Armored personnel carriers.

The dishes piled high with frogs' legs,
Pregnant turtles, their eggs boiled in the carapace,
Marsh irises in fish sauce
And inflorescence[5] of a banana salad.

On every bottle, Napoleon Bonaparte
Pleaded for the authenticity of the spirit.[6]
They called the empties Dead Soldiers
And rejoiced to see them pile up at our feet.

Each diner was attended by one of the other ranks
Whirling a table-napkin to keep off the flies.
It was like eating between rows of morris dancers[7]—
Only they didn't kick.

On my left sat the prince;
On my right, his drunken aide.
The frogs' thighs leapt into the sad purple face
Like fish to the sound of a Chinese flute.
I wanted to talk to the prince. I wish now
I had collared his aide, who was Saloth Sar's brother.
We treated him as the club bore. He was always
Boasting of his connections, boasting with a head-shake
Or by pronouncing of some doubtful phrase.
And well might he boast. Saloth Sar, for instance,
Was Pol Pot's[8] real name. The APCs
Fired into the sugar palms but met no resistance.

In a diary, I refer to Pol Pot's brother as the Jockey Cap.
A few weeks later, I find him 'in good form
And very skeptical about Chantaraingsey.'
'But one eats well there,' I remark.
'So one should,' says the Jockey Cap:
'The tiger always eats well,
It eats the raw flesh of the deer,
And Chantaraingsey was born in the year of the tiger.
So, did they show you the things they do
With the young refugee girls?'

And he tells me how he will one day give me the gen.[9]
He will tell me how the prince financed the casino
And how the casino brought Lon Nol[1] to power.
He will tell me this.
He will tell me all these things.
All I must do is drink and listen.

In those days, I thought that when the game was up
The prince would be far, far away—

10

15

20

25

30

35

40

45

50

---

5. That is, cluster (of bananas in salad); "carapace": shell; "march iris": that is, water plant.
6. (1) Soul; (2) alcoholic drink.
7. Vigorous English folk dance.
8. Leader of Cambodian Communist Khmer
Rouge, who in 1976 ousted Lon Nol (see below),
proclaimed the new state of Kampuchea, and
instituted a reign of terror.
9. General information (British slang).
1. Corrupt military leader of Cambodia, who in
1970 overthrew the government of Prince Norodom Sihanouk (see below).

In a limestone faubourg, on the promenade at Nice,[2]
Reduced in circumstances but well enough provided for.
In Paris, he would hardly require his private army.
The Jockey Cap might suffice for café warfare,   55
And matchboxes for APCs.

But we were always wrong in these predictions.
It was a family war. Whatever happened,
The principals were obliged to attend its issue.
A few were cajoled into leaving, a few were expelled,   60
And there were villains enough, but none of them
Slipped away with the swag.

For the prince was fighting Sihanouk,[3] his nephew,
And the Jockey Cap was ranged against his brother
Of whom I remember nothing more   65
Than an obscure reputation for virtue.
I have been told that the prince is still fighting
Somewhere in the Cardamoms or the Elephant Mountains.
But I doubt that the Jockey Cap would have survived his good
    connections.
I think the lunches would have done for him—   70
Either the lunches or the dead soldiers.

                                                                 1981

God, A Poem

A nasty surprise in a sandwich,
A drawing-pin caught in your sock,
The limpest of shakes from a hand which
You'd thought would be firm as a rock,

A serious mistake in a nightie,   5
A grave disappointment all round
Is all that you'll get from th'Almighty,
Is all that you'll get underground.

Oh he *said:* 'If you lay off the crumpet
I'll see you alright[4] in the end.   10
Just hang on until the last trumpet.[5]
Have faith in me, chum—I'm your friend.'

But if you remind him, he'll tell you:
'I'm sorry, I must have been pissed[6]—
Though your name rings a sort of a bell. You   15
Should have guessed that I do not exist.

'I didn't exist at Creation,
I didn't exist at the Flood,

---

2. Paved walkway at Nice, a French resort on the Mediterranean; "faubourg": suburb of a French city.
3. Ruler of Cambodia until ousted by Lon Nol's military coup.

4. That is, I'll take care of you (Britishism); "crumpet": here, Britishism for girls.
5. That is, Judgment Day.
6. Drunk.

And I won't be around for Salvation
To sort out the sheep from the cud—   20

'Or whatever the phrase is. The fact is
In soteriological[7] terms
I'm a crude existential malpractice
And you are a diet of worms.[8]

'You're a nasty surprise in a sandwich.   25
You're a drawing-pin caught in my sock.
You're the limpest of shakes from a hand which
I'd have thought would be firm as a rock,

'You're a serious mistake in a nightie,
You're a grave disappointment all round—   30
That's all that you are,' says th'Almighty,
'And that's all that you'll be underground.'

1983

---

7. Having to do with salvation.
8. (1) Food for worms (after death); (2) conference (or "Diet") held at Worms, Germany, in 1521 to dissuade Martin Luther from his agitations for reform. "Existential malpractice": that is, empirical mistake.

PAUL MUDLOON
b. 1951

Paul Muldoon insists that his books, which typically include a number of short poems and one long poem, should be read as we read other books, starting with the first page and proceeding to the last. Having carefully arranged his individual poems in the sequence that he wants, Muldoon invites his readers to see interconnections. He says: "I've become very interested in structures that can be fixed like mirrors at angles to each other . . . so that new images can emerge from the setting up of the poems in relationship to each other."[1] Muldoon's are often good-humored; he takes pleasure in his skills and in the amiable surprises and tricks he arranges for us, though he pays attention to such grim matters as urban warfare—he is, after all, a native of Northern Ireland—our common mortality, and our generally futile attempts to recover the past. The poems often deal with the commerce between love and sex, and they are sometimes delicately obscene. One poem deals with a situation frequently found in folk humor (the couple who cannot be uncoupled) but treats it with tender reverence.

"Alternate worlds"—Auden's phrase for works of art and what they offer us—are what we find in the situations Muldoon invents for his readers. As he says, "One of the ways in which we are most ourselves is that we imagine ourselves to be going somewhere else. It's important to most societies to have the notion of something out there to which we belong, that our home is somewhere else . . . there's another dimension, something around us and beyond us, which is our inheritance."[2]

Paul Muldoon was born in County Armagh in 1951. He was educated at St. Patrick's College, Armagh, and Queen's University, Belfast. He won his first literary award at the age of twenty-one, and he published his first book of poems a year later. For more than ten years he worked as a producer, first in radio and then in television for

1. "A Literary Flowering in Ulster," *Newsweek*, June 2, 1986, p. 74ff.   2. The same.

the British Broadcasting Corporation in Belfast. In 1986 he left to devote himself to writing and to teaching, at Cambridge and the University of East Anglia. In 1987 he taught poetry workshops in the United States.

The Big House[1]

I was the only girl under the stairs
But I was the first to notice something was wrong.
I was always first up and about, of course.
Those hens would never lay two days running
In the same place. I would rise early   5
And try round the haggard[2] for fresh nests.
The mistress let me keep the egg-money.

And that particular night there were guests,
Mrs de Groot from the bridge set
And a young man who wrote stories for children,   10
So I wanted everything to be just right
When they trooped down to breakfast that morning.

I slept at the very top of that rambling house,
A tiny room with only a sky-light window.
I had brushed my hair and straightened my dress   15
And was just stepping into the corridor
When it struck me. That old boarded-up door
Was flung open. A pile of rubble and half-bricks
Was strewn across the landing floor.

I went on down. I was stooping among the hay-stacks   20
When there came a clatter of hooves in the yard.
The squire's sure-footed little piebald[3] mare
Had found her own way home, as always.
He swayed some. Then fell headlong on the cobbles.

There was not so much as the smell of whiskey on him.   25
People still hold he had died of fright,
That the house was haunted by an elder brother
Who was murdered for his birthright.
People will always put two and two together.

What I remember most of that particular morning   30
Was how calmly everyone took the thing.
The mistress insisted that life would go on quietly
As it always had done. Breakfast was served
At nine exactly. I can still hear Mrs de Groot
Telling how she had once bid seven hearts.   35
The young man's stories were for grown-ups, really.

                                                        1977

---

1. Country name for the home of an aristocrat.   and the barn.
2. On a farm, the open area between the house   3. That is, black and white.

The Weepies

Most Saturday afternoons
At the local Hippodrome
Saw the Pathe-News rooster,[4]
Then the recurring dream

Of a lonesome drifter   5
Through uninterrupted range.
Will Hunter, so gifted
He could peel an orange

In a single, fluent gesture,
Was the leader of our gang.   10
The curtain rose this afternoon
On a lion, not a gong.[5]

When the crippled girl
Who wanted to be a dancer
Met the married man   15
Who was dying of cancer,

Our hankies unfurled
Like flags of surrender.
I believe something fell asunder
In even Will Hunter's hands.   20

1980

Making the Move

When Ulysses braved the wine-dark sea
He left his bow with Penelope,

Who would bend for no one but himself.[6]
I edge along the book-shelf,

Past bad Lord Byron, Raymond Chandler,   5
Howard Hughes; The Hidden Years,[7]

Past Blaise Pascal, who, bound in hide,
Divined the void to his left side:[8]

Such books as one may think one owns
Unloose themselves like stones   10

4. Trademark of the Pathé News newsreels, short movies about current events that used to be shown prior to the main feature film.
5. That is, on an American movie from Metro-Goldwyn-Mayer (whose trademark is a roaring lion), not a British one from J. Arthur Rank (whose trademark was a man beating on a huge gong).
6. Ulysses, or Odysseus, left his wife Penelope at home when he went off to the Trojan War; "who" may refer to Penelope, the bow, or both. "Wine-dark" was a common Homeric epithet for the sea.

7. The English poet George Gordon, Lord Byron (1778–1824) was involved in various scandalous liaisons; Chandler (1888–1959) was a writer of tough-guy private-eye thrillers; Hughes was an eccentric American millionaire.
8. Pascal, seventeenth-century French philosopher and mathematician, published *New Experience of the Void* in 1647; there is also a "void" on the shelf to the left of his book, which is bound in leather.

And clatter down into this wider gulf
Between myself and my good wife;

A primus stove,[9] a sleeping bag,
The bow I bought through a catalogue

When I was thirteen or fourteen   15
That would bend, and break, for anyone,

Its boyish length of maple upon maple
Unseasoned and unsupple.

Were I embarking on that wine-dark sea
I would bring my bow along with me.   20
                                                      1980

The Right Arm

I was three-ish
when I plunged my arm into the sweet-jar
for the last bit of clove-rock.[1]

We kept a shop in Eglish[2]
that sold bread, milk, butter, cheese,   5
bacon and eggs,
Andrews Liver Salts,
and, until now, clove-rock.

I would give my right arm to have known then
how Eglish was itself wedged between   10
ecclesia and *église*.[3]

The Eglish sky was its own stained-glass vault
and my right arm was sleeved in glass
that has yet to shatter.
                                                      1983

Brock[4]

Small wonder
he's not been sighted all winter;
this old brock's
been to Normandy and back

through the tunnels and trenches   5
of his subconscious.[5]
His father fell victim
to mustard-gas at the Somme;

---

9. Oil-burning portable stove.
1. Stick candy flavored with cloves.
2. Small town in Ireland.
3. Latin and French words for "church."

4. Old name for badger.
5. That is, has dreamed he traveled through underground tunnels under the English Channel to Normandy (in France).

one of his sons lost a paw
to a gin-trap at Lisbellaw: 10
another drills
on the Antrim hills'

still-molten lava
in a moth-eaten Balaclava.[6]
An elaborate   15
system of foxholes and duckboards

leads to the terminal moraine[7]
of an ex-linen baron's
croquet-lawn
where he's part-time groundsman.[8]   20

I would find it somewhat *infra-dig*
to dismiss him simply as a pig
or heed Gerald of Wales'[9]
tall tales

of badgers keeping badger-slaves.   25
For when he shuffles
across the esker[1]
I glimpse my grandfather's whiskers

stained with tobacco-pollen.
When he piddles against a bullaun[2]   30
I know he carries bovine TB
but what I *see*

is my father in his Sunday suit's
bespoke lime and lignite,[3]
patrolling his now-diminished estate   35
and taking stock of this and that.

                                            1987

6. The Somme River, in France, was the location of one of World War I's great battles, in which poison gas was used; "gin-trap"; snare for animals; Lisbellaw and Antrim are in Northern Ireland; "Balaclava": hoodlike knitted cap covering the head, neck, and part of the shoulders (named after a village in the Crimea, in present-day USSR, where a battle was fought in 1854 during the Crimean War).
7. "Foxholes": pits dug in the ground to protect individual soldiers from enemy fire; "duckboards": path made of wooden slats to cover muddy ground; "terminal moraine": rocks and stones carried by a glacier and deposited at its end, where the ice is widest.
8. "Linen-baron": tycoon who has made his money in textiles; "groundsman": groundskeeper.
9. Welsh churchman and historian (c.1146–c.1223); *infra dig*: beneath one's dignity.
1. Narrow ridge or mound of sand and gravel.
2. A weed.
3. That is, white or gray and dark brown (the colors of lime and of "lignite," a form of coal); "bespoke": specially ordered, custom-made.

GARY SOTO
b. 1952

In 1848, at the end of the Mexican War, Mexico ceded the rest of its territory above the Rio Grande River to the United States; the Mexicans who lived there automatically became American citizens, but were allowed to maintain their language and traditions. Other Mexicans, dreaming of becoming rich Americans, also came to the Southwest, but all—the new immigrants and the native Mexican-Americans—"soon discovered that the dominant English-speaking majority considered them outsiders," segregating them into barrios—essentially Spanish-speaking ghettos—and considering them "second-class citizens."[1] Or perhaps invisible citizens, since the word "Chicano" did not exist until 1954.[2] A hundred years is a long time to go without a name.

There were literary stirrings within the Chicano community during these years, and a growing group consciousness. But it was not until the late sixties that leaders like César Chávez could make la causa "a powerful national movement affecting all Chicanos in all regions of the country."[3] "La causa" produced a protest literature; it also made way for other Chicano writers to become visible. One of them is Gary Soto, who began publishing in 1977.

The critic Raymund A. Paredes notes that Soto's first two books—*The Element of San Joaquin* (1977) and *The Tale of Sunlight* (1978)—comprise a journey from the ugly urban life of Fresno, California, and the dreary toil of farm work in the San Joaquin Valley "to Taxco in central Mexico, the town where, as Soto's narrator puts it, 'we all begin.'"[4] "The Elements of San Joaquin" asks us to experience the misery of the itinerant ill-paid Chicano farm laborer's life in the weather of that lush California valley. It was a life that Soto himself had experienced. Molina, of "The Map" and other poems in *The Tale of Sunlight*, is an "alter ego to the young poet," while Manuel, of "The Manuel Zaragoza Poems," escapes to the imaginative fantasy he has made for himself—like a poet's—out of a "magical" beam of light ("The Tale of Sunlight").[5]

In his most recent book, *Black Hair* (1985), Soto's themes enlarge to include the possibilities of friendship. Another way he makes sense for himself is in poems that try to make sense of the world for his children.

Gary Soto was born in Fresno, California, on April 2, 1952. He earned a B.A. at California State University at Fresno and an M.F.A. at the University of California at Irvine. He has written a book of prose recollections, *Living Up the Street* (1984), and presently teaches both Chicano Studies and English at the University of California at Berkeley.

1. Luis Leal and Pepe Barrón, "Chicano Literature: An Overview," in *Three American Literatures*, ed. Houston Baker, New York, 1982, pp. 9–10.
2. *Webster's Ninth New Collegiate Dictionary*, Springfield, Mass., 1986, p. 232.

3. Leal and Barrón, p. 22.
4. Raymund A. Paredes, "The Evolution of Chicano Literature," in Baker, the same, pp. 68–69.
5. The same, pp. 70, 71.

From The Elements of San Joaquin[1]

Wind [2]

When you got up this morning the sun
Blazed an hour in the sky,

A lizard hid
Under the curled leaves of manzanita[2]
And winked its dark lids.   5

Later, the sky grayed,
And the cold wind you breathed

1. Valley on either side of the San Joaquin (pronounced "San Wah-*keen*") River in central California; site of many farms, usually worked by Chicano labor. Soto himself has done this work.
2. California shrubs.

Was moving under your skin and already far
From the small hives of your lungs.

Rain

When autumn rains flatten sycamore leaves,
The tiny volcanos of dirt
Ants raised around their holes,
I should be out of work.

My silverware and stacks of plates will go unused   5
Like the old, my two good slacks
Will smother under a growth of lint
And smell of the old dust
That rises
When the closet door opens or closes.   10

The skin of my belly will tighten like a belt
And there will be no reason for pockets.

1977

The Map

When the sun's whiteness closes around us
Like a noose,

It is noon, and Molina squats
In the uneven shade of an oleander.[3]

He unfolds a map and, with a pencil,   5
Blackens Panama[4]

Into a bruise;
He dots rain over Bogotá,[5] the city of spiders,

And x's in a mountain range that climbs
Like a thermometer   10

Above the stone fence
The old never thought to look over.

A fog presses over Lima.[6]
Brazil is untangled of its rivers.

Where there is a smudge,   15
Snow has stitched its cold into the field.

Where the river Orinoco[7] cuts east,
A new river rises nameless

---

3. Poisonous evergreen shrub.
4. Central American country that joins North America to South America.
5. City in the Andes mountains, capital of Col-ombia, South America.
6. Capital of Peru.
7. River in Venezuela which, after it turns east, empties into the Atlantic Ocean.

From the open grasses,
And Molina calls it his place of birth.   20

1978

The Tale of Sunlight[8]

Listen, nephew.
When I opened the cantina[9]
At noon
A triangle of sunlight
Was stretched out   5
On the floor
Like a rug
Like a tired cat.
It flared in
From the window   10
Through a small hole
Shaped like a yawn.
Strange I thought
And placed my hand
Before the opening,   15
But the sunlight
Did not vanish.
I pulled back
The shutters
And the room glowed,   20
But this pyramid
Of whiteness
Was simply brighter.
The sunlight around it
Appeared soiled   25
Like the bed sheet
Of a borracho.[1]
Amazed, I locked the door,
Closed the windows.
Workers, in from   30
The fields, knocked
To be let in,
Children peeked
Through the shutters,
But I remained silent.   35
I poured a beer,
At a table
Shuffled a pack
Of old cards,
And watched it   40
Cross the floor,
Hang on the wall
Like a portrait
Like a calendar

8. One of the last of "The Manuel Zaragoza   9. Small bar (which Manuel owns).
Poems."   1. Drunkard.

Without numbers.
When a fly settled 45
In the sunlight
And disappeared
In a wreath of smoke,
I tapped it with the broom, 50
Spat on it.
The broom vanished.
The spit sizzled.
It is the truth, little one.
I stood eye to blank eye 55
And by misfortune
This finger
This pink stump
Entered the sunlight,
Snapped off 60
With a dry sneeze,
And fell to the floor
As a gift
To the ants
Who know me 65
For what I gave.

1978

Making Money: Drought Year in Minkler, California

"It's a '49," Rhinehardt said, and slammed
The screen door, then worked his way around
The dog turds in the yard
To the Buick gutted from fire—the gears
Teething rust, the fenders sloped 5
Like the shoulders of a fired worker
Out of beer. He circled the car
Kicking the tires, eyeing
The grille that still grinned the ribbed wings
Of a sparrow. He looked inside and flies 10
Lifted like patted dust, settling
Into a loose knot on the visor.
"Yeh, you're right as right . . . it's a '50,"
Rhinehardt spat, his tongue rolling
A false tooth into place. "It's got no 15
Running board." He pressed a buck
Into his son's hand and retired to the porch
Where he towel-flicked
His wife from a chair
And as evening came on watched beyond 20
The street, a kennel of trees,
Where—as he had dreamed—a plane would drop
And bloom fire. Two bucks on that one.

1981

Oranges

The first time I walked
With a girl, I was twelve,
Cold, and weighted down
With two oranges in my jacket.
December. Frost cracking   5
Beneath my steps, my breath
Before me, then gone,
As I walked toward
Her house, the one whose
Porch light burned yellow   10
Night and day, in any weather.
A dog barked at me, until
She came out pulling
At her gloves, face bright
With rouge. I smiled,   15
Touched her shoulder, and led
Her down the street, across
A used car lot and a line
Of newly planted trees,
Until we were breathing   20
Before a drugstore. We
Entered, the tiny bell
Bringing a saleslady
Down a narrow aisle of goods.
I turned to the candies   25
Tiered like bleachers,
And asked what she wanted—
Light in her eyes, a smile
Starting at the corners
Of her mouth. I fingered   30
A nickel in my pocket,
And when she lifted a chocolate
That cost a dime,
I didn't say anything.
I took the nickel from   35
My pocket, then an orange,
And set them quietly on
The counter. When I looked up,
The lady's eyes met mine,
And held them, knowing   40
Very well what it was all
About.

        Outside,
A few cars hissing past,
Fog hanging like old   45
Coats between the trees.
I took my girl's hand
In mine for two blocks,
Then released it to let
Her unwrap the chocolate.   50
I peeled my orange

That was so bright against
The gray of December
That, from some distance,
Someone might have thought   55
I was making a fire in my hands.

1985

RITA DOVE
b. 1952

Rita Dove's poems are often mysterious but they are not perplexing: they make so
strong an appeal to our common humanity that they are to be enjoyed and wondered
at rather than to be figured out. Many of Dove's poems are written out of her sense
of history, with all its elaborate injustices; she expresses this sense by inventing some
incidents (see, for example, "The House Slave") and by making poems out of the lives
of men and women who actually lived and whom she, like Odysseus on his visit to
the Underworld, restores to life long enough to speak to us and thus to endure. The
victory of Dove's poems is that she is able to express a variety of emotions roused by
pain and injustice without angrily cutting all the circuits which bind her to her readers. When she writes about situations which could be easily politicized, she spends
her energies not on the cultivation of outrage, but on the recreation of the human
lot.

Thomas and Beulah might count as a long short story, like Flaubert's *A Simple
Heart* encapsulating a lifetime, in fact two lifetimes, told in a series of short poems.
Dove carefully celebrates the lives of her grandparents, and the whole work shines
with gratitude and joy. Dove has admitted that her purpose, celebration apart, was
also to combat what she sees as a fatuous assumption, that the inner lives of the poor
and unlettered are less complex than the lives of those who are on easier terms with
society. Beulah, the Black woman hidden from the white customers of the dress
shop, ironing the sweaty dress of some white woman, and reflecting on the spoiled
darlings of the French courts, has, thanks to her granddaughter, her own complexity
and her own heroism.

Rita Dove was born on August 28, 1952, in Akron, Ohio, and educated at Miami
University in Oxford, Ohio. She has traveled abroad and is active on writers' panels.
Besides her books of poetry, she has written a play and a volume of short stories,
Fifth Sunday. In 1987 she won the Pulitzer Prize for *Thomas and Beulah*. She teaches
writing at Arizona State University, where two of her colleagues are Norman Dubie
and Alberto Ríos.

The House Slave

The first horn lifts its arm over the dew-lit grass
and in the slave quarters there is a rustling—
children are bundled into aprons, cornbread

and water gourds grabbed, a salt pork breakfast taken.
I watch them driven into the vague before-dawn   5
while their mistress sleeps like an ivory toothpick

and Massa dreams of asses, rum and slave-funk.
I cannot fall asleep again. At the second horn,
the whip curls across the backs of the laggards—

sometimes my sister's voice, unmistaken, among them.   10
"Oh! pray," she cries. "Oh! pray!" Those days
I lie on my cot, shivering in the early heat,

and as the fields unfold to whiteness,
and they spill like bees among the fat flowers,
I weep. It is not yet daylight.   15
                                                                      1980

Banneker[1]

What did he do except lie
under a pear tree, wrapped in
a great cloak, and meditate
on the heavenly bodies?
Venerable, the good people of Baltimore   5
whispered, shocked and more than
a little afraid. After all it was said
he took to strong drink.
Why else would he stay out
under the stars all night   10
and why hadn't he married?

But who would want him! Neither
Ethiopian nor English, neither
lucky nor crazy, a capacious bird
humming as he penned in his mind   15
another enflamed letter
to President Jefferson— he imagined
the reply, polite and rhetorical.
Those who had been to Philadelphia
reported the statue   20
of Benjamin Franklin
before the library

his very size and likeness.
A wife? No, thank you.
At dawn he milked   25
the cows, then went inside
and put on a pot to stew
while he slept. The clock
he whittled as a boy
still ran. Neighbors   30
woke him up
with warm bread and quilts.
At nightfall he took out

his rifle— a white-maned
figure stalking the darkened   35
breast of the Union— and

1. "Benjamin Banneker (1731–1806), first black
man to devise an almanac and predict a solar eclipse
accurately, was also appointed to the commission
that surveyed and laid out what is now Washington, D.C." (Dove's note).

shot at the stars, and by chance
one went out. Had he killed?
I assure thee, my dear Sir!
Lowering his eyes to fields   40
sweet with the rot of spring, he could see
a government's domed city
rising from the morass and spreading
in a spiral of lights. . . .

1983

Parsley[2]

1. *The Cane Fields*[3]

There is a parrot imitating spring
in the palace, its feathers parsley green.
Out of the swamp the cane appears

to haunt us, and we cut it down. El General
searches for a word; he is all the world   5
there is. Like a parrot imitating spring,

we lie down screaming as rain punches through
and we come up green. We cannot speak an R—
out of the swamp, the cane appears

and then the mountain we call in whispers *Katalina.*[4]   10
The children gnaw their teeth to arrowheads.
There is a parrot imitating spring.

El General has found his word: *perejil.*
Who says it, lives. He laughs, teeth shining
out of the swamp. The cane appears   15

in our dreams, lashed by wind and streaming.
And we lie down. For every drop of blood
there is a parrot imitating spring.
Out of the swamp the cane appears.

2. *The Palace*

The word the general's chosen is parsley.   20
It is fall, when thoughts turn
to love and death; the general thinks
of his mother, how she died in the fall
and he planted her walking cane at the grave
and it flowered, each spring stolidly forming   25
four-star blossoms. The general

---

2. "On October 2, 1957, Rafael Trujillo (1891–
1961), dictator of the Dominican Republic, ordered
20,000 blacks to be killed because they could not
pronounce the letter "r" in *perejil,* the Spanish
word for parsley" (Dove's note).

3. This first section is in the form of a (non-
rhyming) villanelle. "Cane": sugar cane.
4. That is, Katarina (since "we cannot speak an
R").

pulls on his boots, he stomps to
her room in the palace, the one without
curtains, the one with a parrot
in a brass ring. As he paces he wonders   30
Who can I kill today. And for a moment
the little knot of screams
is still. The parrot, who has traveled

all the way from Australia in an ivory
cage, is, coy as a widow, practising   35
spring. Ever since the morning
his mother collapsed in the kitchen
while baking skull-shaped candies
for the Day of the Dead,[5] the general
has hated sweets. He orders pastries   40
brought up for the bird; they arrive

dusted with sugar on a bed of lace.
The knot in his throat starts to twitch;
he sees his boots the first day in battle
splashed with mud and urine   45
as a soldier falls at his feet amazed—
how stupid he looked!— at the sound
of artillery. *I never thought it would sing*
the soldier said, and died. Now

the general sees the fields of sugar   50
cane, lashed by rain and streaming.
He sees his mother's smile, the teeth
gnawed into arrowheads. He hears
the Haitians sing without R's
as they swing the great machetes: 55
Katalina, they sing, *Katalina*,

mi madle, mi amol en muelte.[6] God knows
his mother was no stupid woman; she
could roll an R like a queen. Even
a parrot can roll an R! In the bare room   60
the bright feathers arch in a parody
of greenery, as the last pale crumbs
disappear under the blackened tongue. Someone

calls out his name in a voice
so like his mother's, a startled tear   65
splashes the tip of his right boot.
My mother, my love in death.
The general remembers the tiny green sprigs
men of his village wore in their capes
to honor the birth of a son. He will   70
order many, this time, to be killed

for a single, beautiful word.

1983

---

5. Or Corpus Christi (Body of Christ), Roman
Catholic festival.

6. That is, *mi madre, mi amor en muerte:* "my
mother, my love in death."

The Event[7]

Ever since they'd left the Tennessee ridge
with nothing to boast of
but good looks and a mandolin,

the two Negroes leaning
on the rail of a riverboat   5
were inseparable: Lem plucked

to Thomas' silver falsetto.
But the night was hot and they were drunk.
They spat where the wheel

churned mud and moonlight,   10
they called to the tarantulas
down among the bananas

to come out and dance.
You're so fine and mighty; let's see
what you can do, said Thomas, pointing   15

to a tree-capped island.
Lem stripped, spoke easy: *Them's chestnuts,*
I believe. Dove

quick as a gasp. Thomas, dry
on deck, saw the green crown shake   20
as the island slipped

under, dissolved
in the thickening stream.
At his feet

a stinking circle of rags,   25
the half-shell mandolin.
Where the wheel turned the water

gently shirred.[8]

1986

Weathering Out

She liked mornings the best— Thomas gone
to look for work, her coffee flushed with milk,

7. This and the next two poems are from Dove's *Thomas and Beulah*, which she introduces with the statement that "These poems tell two sides of a story and are meant to be read in sequence." In an interview on National Public Radio in the summer of 1987, Dove said that these poems were inspired by incidents in the lives of her grandparents in Akron, Ohio, that her grandmother told her about.

8. Drew together. "There is a particular story which started the entire thing. My grandmother told me the story of my grandfather coming north on the riverboats and . . . his best friend had died on a dare from him. They had a little song and dance team and . . . he dared him to jump off the boat and swim to an island to pick some chestnuts and the friend died in the river . . . my grandmother told me the story after my grandfather had died—I couldn't ask him and so I had to in a way write the poem . . . trying to reconcile the man that I knew as my grandfather with the man that I saw in the story that my grandmother told. I had never realized that he had this guilt to carry around" (from the interview).

outside autumn trees blowsy and dripping.
Past the seventh month she couldn't see her feet

so she floated from room to room, houseshoes flapping,   5
navigating corners in wonder. When she leaned

against a door jamb to yawn, she disappeared entirely.

Last week they had taken a bus at dawn
to the new airdock. The hangar slid open in segments

and the zeppelin nosed forward in its silver envelope.   10
The man walked it out gingerly, like a poodle,

then tied it to a mast and went back inside.
Beulah felt just that large and placid, a lake;

she glistened from cocoa butter smoothed in
when Thomas returned every evening nearly   15

in tears. He'd lean an ear on her belly
and say: *Little fellow's really talking,*

though to her it was more the *pok-pok-pok*
of a fingernail tapping a thick cream lampshade.

Sometimes during the night she woke and found him   20
asleep there and the child sleeping, too.

The coffee was good but too little. Outside
everything shivered in tinfoil— only the clover

between the cobblestones hung stubbornly on,
green as an afterthought. . . .   25
                                                                         1986

The Great Palaces of Versailles[9]

Nothing nastier than a white person!
She mutters as she irons alterations
in the backroom of Charlotte's Dress Shoppe.
The steam rising from a cranberry wool
comes alive with perspiration[1]
and stale Evening of Paris.   5
Swamp she born from, swamp
she swallow, swamp she got to sink again.

The iron shoves gently
into a gusset,[2] waits until   10

9. The magnificent complex of palaces built
principally by Louis XIV (1638–1715) of France.
    1. Beulah "can smell the perspiration. In that
poem, it's one of those rare moments where, with
her rage, she even allows it to come to the surface
in terms of response. It's a political situation,
actually, in the dress shop, because white girls can
sell the dresses in the front of the shop and she,
as the black help, gets to iron in the back room"
(from the interview).
    2. Insert in the seam of a garment.

the puckers bloom away. Beyond
the curtain, the white girls are all
wearing shoulder pads to make their faces
delicate. That laugh would be Autumn,
tossing her hair in imitation of Bacall.[3]   15

Beulah had read in the library
how French ladies at court would tuck
their fans in a sleeve
and walk in the gardens for air. Swaying
among lilies, lifting shy layers of silk,   20
they dropped excrement as daintily
as handkerchieves. Against all rules

she had saved the lining from a botched coat
to face last year's gray skirt. She knows
whenever she lifts a knee   25
she flashes crimson. That seems legitimate;
but in the book she had read
how the *cavaliere*[4] amused themselves
wearing powder and perfume and spraying
yellow borders knee-high on the stucco   30
of the *Orangerie*.[5]

A hanger clatters
in the front of the shoppe.
Beulah remembers how
even Autumn could lean into a settee   35
with her ankles crossed, sighing
I need a man who'll protect me
while smoking her cigarette down to the very end.

                                                                   1986

3. Lauren Bacall, American movie actress.   5. Building housing orange trees at Versailles.
4. Lovers, gallants.

ALBERTO RÍOS
b. 1952

"You see, there are in our countries rivers which have no names, trees which nobody
knows, and birds which nobody has described. . . . Our duty, then, as we understand it, is to express what is unheard of." Alberto Ríos uses this remark—made by
the Chilean poet Pablo Neruda—as the epigraph for his first book, *Whispering to
Fool the Wind* (1981), and can be seen to have adopted it as his own program. Whereas
his contemporary and fellow poet Gary Soto is, in his first books, aware of the barrio
and of the present, Ríos in many poems gently quarries his past and his imagination
for "unheard-of" people and places.

What especially characterizes Ríos's art is that he quietly makes his readers accept,
take friendly pleasure in, and understand the grotesquerie of his "unheard-of" people. The "old Russian" in "A Man Then Suddenly Stops Moving" is merely "surprised" when, out of a plum he has thrown to the ground, emerges his "younger
self," which he simply puts "on the shelf / with the pictures." In these and other

Alberto Ríos

ιe embodies the mixture of fantasy and realism—the "magical realism"—of
nerican writers such as Gabriel Gárcia Márquez.

to Ríos was born on September 18, 1952, in Nogales, Arizona, on the border
υɪ ᴍᴇxɪᴄo. "My father, born in southern Mexico, and my mother, born in England,
gave me a language-rich, story-fat upbringing," he has said. He earned two B.A.s—
one in English, one in psychology—at the University of Arizona. After a brief stint
at law school, which he left because it stopped his writing, he earned an M.F.A. at
the University of Arizona. He has also written a volume of short stories, *The Iguana
Killer: Twelve Stories of the Heart* (1984), which won the 1984 Western States Book
Award. He teaches writing at Arizona State University, where two of his colleagues
are Norman Dubie and Rita Dove.

Madre Sofía[1]

My mother took me because she couldn't
wait the second ten years to know.
This was the lady rumored to have been
responsible for the box-wrapped baby
among the presents at that wedding,   5
but we went in, anyway, through the curtains.
Loose jar-top, half turned
and not caught properly in the threads
her head sat mimicking its original intention
like the smile of a child hitting himself.   10
Central in that head grew unfamiliar poppies
from a face mahogany, eyes half yellow
half gray at the same time, goat and fog,
slit eyes of the devil, his tweed suit, red
lips, and she smelled of smoke, cigarettes,   15
but a diamond smoke, somehow; I inhaled
sparkles, but I could feel them, throat, stomach.
She did not speak, and as a child
I could only answer, so that together
we were silent, cold and wet, dry and hard: 20
from behind my mother pushed me forward.
The lady put her hand on the face
of a thin animal wrap, tossing that head
behind her to be pressured incredibly
as she sat back in the huge chair and leaned.   25
And then I saw the breasts as large as her
head, folded together, coming out of her dress
as if it didn't fit, not like my mother's.
I could see them, how she kept them
penned up, leisurely, in maroon feed bags,   30
horse nuzzles of her wide body,
but exquisitely penned up
circled by pearl reins and red scarves.
She lifted her arm, but only with the tips
of her fingers motioned me to sit opposite.   35
She looked at me but spoke to my mother
words dark, smoky like the small room,

1. "Mother Sofía"; "Sofía" derives from the Greek word meaning "wisdom."

words coming like red ants stepping occasionally
from a hole on a summer day in the valley,
red ants from her mouth, her nose, her ears,   40
tears from the corners of her cinched eyes.
And suddenly she put her hand full on my head
pinching tight again with those finger tips
like a television healer, young Oral Roberts
half standing, quickly, half leaning   45
those breasts swinging toward me
so that I reach with both my hands to my lap
protecting instinctively whatever it is
that needs protection when a baseball is thrown
and you're not looking but someone yells,   50
the hand, then those breasts coming toward me
like the quarter-arms of the amputee Joaquín
who came back from the war to sit
in the park, reaching always for children
until one day he had to be held back.   55
I sat there, no breath, and could see only
hair around her left nipple, like a man.
Her clothes were old.
Accented, in a language whose spine had been
snapped, she whispered the words of a city   60
witch, and made me happy, alive like a man:
The future will make you tall.

                                                               1982

A Dream of Husbands

Though we thought it, Doña[2] Carolina did not die.
She was too old for that nonsense, and too set.
That morning she walked off just a little farther
into her favorite dream, favorite but not nice
so much, not nice and not bad, so it was not death.   5
She dreamed the dream of husbands
and over there she found him after all the years.
Cabrón,[3] she called him, *animal,* very loud
so we could hear it, for us it was a loud truck
passing, or thunder, or too many cats, very loud   10
for having left her for so long and so far. Days now
her voice is the squeak of the rocking chair
as she complains, we hear it, it will not go
not with oils or sanding or shouts back at her.
But it becomes too the sound a spoon makes, her old   15
very large wooden spoon as it stirs a pot of soup.
Dinnertimes, we think of her, the good parts, of her
cooking, we like her best then, even the smell of her.
But then, *cabrones* she calls us, *animales,* irritated,
from over there, from the dream, they come, her words   20
they are the worst sounds of the street in the night
so that we will not get so comfortable about her,

---

2. Lady.   3. He-goat.

so comfortable with her having left us
we thinking that her husband and her long dream
are so perfect, because no, they are not, not so much,   25
she is not so happy this way, not in this dream,
this is not heaven, don't think it. She tells us this,
sadness too is hers, a half measure, sadness at having
no time for the old things, for rice, for chairs.

                                                                        1985

A Man Then Suddenly Stops Moving

The old Russian spits up a plum
fruit of the rasping sound
he has stored in his throat
all these lonely years

made in fact lonely by his wife   5
who left him, God knows
without knowing how to cook for himself.

He examines the plum
notes its purplish consistency
almost the color and shape of her buttocks   10
whose circulation was bad

which is why he himself wears a beret:
black, good wool, certainly warm enough
the times he remembers.

He shoots the plum   15
to the ground like a child
whose confidence is a game of marbles

whose flick of a thumb
is a smile inside his mouth
knowing what he knows will happen.   20

But his wife, Marthe
does not spill out
when the plum breaks open.

Instead, it is a younger self
alive and waving   25
just the size he remembers
himself to have been.

The old Russian puts him onto his finger
like a parakeet
and sits him on the shelf   30
with the pictures.

For the rest of his days
he nags himself constantly

into a half-sleep
surprised by this turn of events.   35

                                                                  1985

LOUISE ERDRICH
b. 1954

"My characters choose me and once they do it's like standing in a field and hearing
echoes," Louise Erdrich has said. "All I can do is trace their passage."[1] She was
speaking of the people in her novel *The Beet Queen* (1986), but the remark applies
as well to the personae of the many remarkable dramatic monologues in her book of
poems, *Jacklight*. They range from a mad medieval French king to a hooker who
rides the rodeo circuit, from a seventeenth-century colonial woman captured by Indians
to a monster of Native American myth. Erdrich never judges the speakers in her
poems, but quietly observes the details of their lives in the almost sympathetic ray
of her "jacklight."

And among them are characters drawn from the people with whom she grew up
near the Turtle Mountain Reservation in North Dakota: Debby, who speaks in "Family Reunion" of her beer-drinking uncle Ray, or the nameless inmates of "Indian
Boarding School," who suffer "long insults" and bear the "worn-down welts / Of
ancient punishments." These are the rootless Native Americans—"Indi'ns"—of the
present day. As the critic Kenneth Lincoln has observed of Erdrich's earlier novel
Love Medicine (1984), there are no "Chippewa chants, no ceremonies to the Great
Spirit, no wizened old medicine people. Instead, there are pickups and bars and
nuns and crazed uncles and fierce aunts."[2]

Louise Erdrich was born on June 7, 1954, in Minnesota, and grew up in a small
town in North Dakota near the Turtle Mountain Reservation, where her grandparents lived. Her French-Chippewa mother and her German-born father both worked
for the Bureau of Indian Affairs. She began writing at Dartmouth College, from
which she received her B.A.; she also has an M.A. from the Writing Seminars at
Johns Hopkins University. Married in 1981, she says that she now "collaborates with
her husband in the writing of her books and his"; they live in Cornish, New Hampshire. She won both the National Book Critics' Circle Award and the American Academy of Arts and Letters prize for *Love Medicine*.

1. Barbara Lovenheim, interview with Louise
Erdrich, *New York Times Book Review*, August
31, 1986, p. 2.

2. Kenneth Lincoln, *Native American Renaissance*, Berkeley, Calif., 1983, p. xv.

Indian Boarding School: The Runaways

Home's the place we head for in our sleep.
Boxcars stumbling north in dreams
don't wait for us. We catch them on the run.
The rails, old lacerations that we love,
shoot parallel across the face and break   5
just under Turtle Mountains.[1] Riding scars
you can't get lost. Home is the place they cross.

1. In North Dakota, site of Chippewa Indian reservation.

The lame guard strikes a match and makes the dark
less tolerant. We watch through cracks in boards
as the land starts rolling, rolling till it hurts   10
to be here, cold in regulation clothes.
We know the sheriff's waiting at midrun
to take us back. His car is dumb and warm.
The highway doesn't rock, it only hums
like a wing of long insults. The worn-down welts   15
of ancient punishments lead back and forth.

All runaways wear dresses, long green ones,
the color you would think shame was. We scrub
the sidewalks down because it's shameful work.
Our brushes cut the stone in watered arcs   20
and in the soak frail outlines shiver clear
a moment, things us kids pressed on the dark
face before it hardened, place, remembering
delicate old injuries, the spines of names and leaves.

                                                                                    1984

Francine's Room

This is Tarsus,[2] one place like anyplace else.
And this is my circuit, the rodeo, fair.
The farmboys blow through here in pickups,[3] wild
as horses in their oat sacks.
The women wear spurs.   5
In the trailers the cattle are pounding for air.

My room is the same as last year. They always give me
end of the corridor, left, the top floor.
Privacy. Why not. I've been through here before.
I'm the town's best   10
customer. A minor attraction.
I buy from their stores. Remember this bureau—

battered wood, the fake drawer and split mirror?
And even the glass marks, ring within ring
of spilled drinks. When I sit here   15
the widest warped links have a center.
Strung out they're a year's worth of slack, a tether
that swings around the spine's dark pole

and swings back. Each time I return
something's different,   20
although there's a few I can always expect.
The cracks in the mirror: always more, never less.
The stains in the bedspread have spread.
And the rip in the window shade lets through more light,
strange light, since I come here to be in the dark.   25

---

2. Midwestern town named after the ancient city   3. Light trucks.
of Tarsus, in Turkey.

Should be taped. A few things can be saved anyhow.
But I don't want to get into that.

I set up my pictures. Mother and Father,
stiffer, more blurred every year.
I turn them to the walls when there's customers, that   30
is the least I can do. What mending there is
occurs in small acts,
and after the fact of the damage,
when nothing is ever enough.
There is always the scar to remind me   35
that things were once perfect, at least

they were new. I first came here when I was a girl.
It surprised me, the things that two people could do
left alone in a room. Not long and I learned.
I learned what the selves are a man can disown   40
till he lets them to life in a room.

It's the region's hard winters, snowed in with the snow
half the year. I'd expect them to think up a few.
But nothing surprises me, not anymore.
The plumbing can only get worse with the cold.   45
It's true, even summers the water is foul
and flows slowly, a thin brown trickle by noon.

Heat pours in the west, freak waves of dry lightning
soak the whole town in a feverish light.
Beneath me, the tables of water[4] have dropped   50
to unheard-of levels. It's been a long drought.
I bend my whole arm to the handle, the valve
yawns open but nothing comes out. What else should I
expect. Wrung cloth. The body washing in dust.

                                                              1984

That Pull from the Left

Butch once remarked to me how sinister it was
alone, after hours, in the dark of the shop
to find me there hunched over two weeks' accounts
probably smoked like a bacon from all those Pall-Malls.[5]

Odd comfort when the light goes, the case lights left on   5
and the rings of baloney, the herring, the parsley,
arranged in the strict, familiar ways.

Whatever intactness holds animals up
has been carefully taken, what's left are the parts.
Just look in the cases, all counted and stacked.   10

---

4. Upper limits of the ground totally saturated   5. Brand of cigarettes.
with water.

Step-and-a-Half Waleski used to come to the shop
and ask for the cheap cut, she would thump, sniff, and finger.
This one too old. This one here for my supper.
Two days and you do notice change in the texture.

I have seen them the day before slaughter.   15
Knowing of the outcome from the moment they enter
the chute, the eye rolls, blood is smeared on the lintel.[6]
Mallet or bullet they lunge toward their darkness.

But something queer happens when the heart is delivered.
When a child is born, sometimes the left hand is stronger.   20
You can train it to fail, still the knowledge is there.
That is the knowledge in the hand of a butcher
that adds to its weight. Otto Kröger could fell
a dray horse[7] with one well-placed punch to the jaw,
and yet it is well known how thorough he was.   25

He never saw down without washing his hands,
and he was a maker, his sausage was *echt*[8]
so that even Waleski had little complaint.
Butch once remarked there was no one so deft
as my Otto. So true, there is great tact involved   30
in parting the flesh from the bones.

How we cling to the bones. Each joint is a web
of small tendons and fibers. He knew what I meant
when I told him I felt something pull from the left,
and how often it clouded the day before slaughter.   35

Something queer happens when the heart is delivered.

                                                                      1984

Windigo

For Angela

The Windigo is a flesh-eating, wintry demon with a man buried deep inside
of it. In some Chippewa stories, a young girl vanquishes this monster by
forcing boiling lard down its throat, thereby releasing the human at the core
of ice.

You knew I was coming for you, little one,
when the kettle jumped into the fire.
Towels flapped on the hooks,
and the dog crept off, groaning,
to the deepest part of the woods.   5

In the hackles of dry brush a thin laughter started up.
Mother scolded the food warm and smooth in the pot

6. As the Israelites, exiled in Egypt, smeared
the blood of sacrificed lambs on the lintels (that is,
above the doors) of their houses, as Moses commanded in Exodus 12.
   7. Workhorse that pulls heavy loads.
   8. Genuine.

and called you to eat.
But I spoke in the cold trees:
New one, I have come for you, child hide and lie still.   10

The sumac pushed sour red cones through the air.
Copper burned in the raw wood.
You saw me drag toward you.
Oh touch me, I murmured, and licked the soles of your feet.
You dug your hands into my pale, melting fur.   15

I stole you off, a huge thing in my bristling armor.
Steam rolled from my wintry arms, each leaf shivered
from the bushes we passed
until they stood, naked, spread like the cleaned spines of fish.

Then your warm hands hummed over and shoveled themselves full   20
of the ice and the snow. I would darken and spill
all night running, until at last morning broke the cold earth
and I carried you home,
a river shaking in the sun.

1984

CATHY SONG
b. 1955

In 1982, the poet Richard Hugo, then judge of the Yale Younger Poet series, chose as the winning manuscript Cathy Song's *Picture Bride*. In his foreword to the book he says, "If we accept Cathy Song's background as it comes through the poem 'Leaving' and through bits and pieces of other poems, we may sense the origin of, and even the necessity for, her passive/receptive sensibility. She need not rave or struggle. She has learned the strength of quiet resolve."[1]

Song's grandmother came from Korea, the poet tells us in the title poem. She was, if we are to believe the poem, a "picture bride" (a mail-order bride), sent for as a wife to Hawaii on the strength of her photograph. Inevitably, then, Song, like her forebears, inhabits both the Old World of Asia and the New World of modern Hawaii, and her poems often explore the gains and losses in moving from one to the other. Thus "Leaving" is both a memory of childhood and a growing detachment from that childhood. In "The Youngest Daughter" the speaker cares for her mother and yet is "planning my escape." And in "Lost Sister," where the sister has indeed escaped, she discovers that, as Hugo puts it, "the psychic price of her rebellion was great."[2] Song's "passive/receptive sensibility" does not miss the harsh reality of the traps that family and society set for women.

In many of the poems in her next book, *Frameless Windows, Squares of Light* (1988), Song continues her exploration of the family—an extended exploration, now, because her own children are part of the family heritage:

> Sometimes my brother would hold me
> the way my son holds onto his sister,
> tightly, for practical reasons,
> to keep them both from flying out of the hammock.
> ("Tribal Scenes")

1. Richard Hugo, foreword to Cathy Song, *Picture Bride*, New Haven, 1983, pp. xiii–xiv.   2. The same, p. xii.

Again, in "Heaven," the speaker muses on an ancestor from China, while she watches her children. Of the poems in this book she has written:

> These are poems about the window and the field, the passages of time that are marked there: your brief history, the time-line that spans the length of your room; the window you occupy day after day, looking at the view, the field beyond where snow falls "on both sides of the glass." What frames the view is the mind in the diamond pinpoint light of concentration tunneling into memory, released by the imagination. Out of that depth, squares of light form, like windows you pass at night, like photographs developing in the dark.[3]

After schooling in Hawaii, Song went to Wellesley College, where she received a B.A., and to Boston University, where she earned an M.A. in creative writing. Like many other poets of her generation, she teaches creative writing at various mainland universities; she maintains a permanent address in Hawaii.

3. Cathy Song to John Benedict, July 31, 1987.

Leaving

Wahiawa is still
a red dirt town[1]
where the sticky smell
of pineapples
being lopped off   5
in the low-lying fields
rises to mix
with the minty leaves
of eucalyptus[2]
in the bordering gulch.   10

We lived there
near the edge
where the orchids grew huge
as lanterns overnight
and the passion fruits rotted   15
on the vines
before they could be picked.

We grew there
in the steady rain
that fell like a gray curtain   20
through which my mother peered:
patches of depression.
She kept the children under cover.
We built houses within houses,
stripping our parents' bed   25
of pillows and sheets,
erecting walls out of
The National Geographic

1. "Small town on the island of Oahu, Hawaii"   2. Evergreen trees with rigid leaves.
(from Song's Glossary to *Picture Bride*).

which my father had subscribed to
for years. We feasted   30
on those pictures of the world,
while the mud oozed
past the windows
knocking over the drab green leaves
of palm fronds   35
as we ate our spinach.
The mildew grew in rings
around the sink
where centipedes came
swimming up the pipes   40
on multiple feet
and the mold grew
around our small fingers
making everything slippery
to touch.   45
We were squeamish and pale.

I remember one night
my sister screamed.
All the lights blinked on
in the house.   50
In the sudden brightness,
we rushed to her room
and found her crumpled
in the far corner of the bed,
her nightgown twisted in a strange shape;   55
her eyes were as huge as mine,
staring into the eyes of the bat
that clung to the screen.
Its rodent fingers
finally letting go   60
as my father jabbed its furry body
with the end of a broom.

1983

Beauty and Sadness

for Kitagawa Utamaro[3]

He drew hundreds of women
in studies unfolding
like flowers from a fan.
Teahouse waitresses, actresses,
geishas,[4] courtesans and maids.   5
They arranged themselves
before this quick, nimble man
whose invisible presence
one feels in these prints
is as delicate   10

3. Japanese artist (1753–1806), who specialized in studies of sensuous and beautiful women.

4. Women trained to provide entertaining, lighthearted company for men.

as the skinlike paper
he used to transfer
and retain their fleeting loveliness.

Crouching like cats,
they purred amid the layers of kimono[5]   15
swirling around them
as though they were bathing
in a mountain pool with irises
growing in the silken sunlit water.
Or poised like porcelain vases,   20
slender, erect and tall; their heavy
brocaded hair was piled high
with sandalwood combs and blossom sprigs
poking out like antennae.
They resembled beautiful iridescent insects,   25
creatures from a floating world.[6]

Utamaro absorbed these women of Edo[7]
in their moments of melancholy
as well as of beauty.
He captured the wisp of shadows,   30
the half-draped body
emerging from a bath; whatever
skin was exposed
was powdered white as snow.
A private space disclosed.   35
Portraying another girl
catching a glimpse of her own vulnerable
face in the mirror, he transposed
the trembling plum lips
like a drop of blood   40
soaking up the white expanse of paper.

At times, indifferent to his inconsolable
eye, the women drifted
through the soft gray feathered light,
maintaining stillness, the moments in between.   45
Like the dusty ash-winged moths
that cling to the screens in summer
and that the Japanese venerate
as ancestors reincarnated;
Utamaro graced these women with immortality   50
in the thousand sheaves of prints
fluttering into the reverent hands of keepers:
the dwarfed and bespectacled painter
holding up to a square of sunlight
what he had carried home beneath his coat   55
one afternoon in winter.

1983

5. Traditional Japanese robe with long sleeves.
6. The pictures "were called 'pictures of the
floating world' because of their preoccupation with
the pleasures of the moment" (Song's Glossary).
7. "Present-day Tokyo" (Song's Glossary).

Lost Sister

1

In China,
even the peasants
named their first daughters
Jade—
the stone that in the far fields   5
could moisten the dry season,
could make men move mountains
for the healing green of the inner hills
glistening like slices of winter melon.

And the daughters were grateful: 10
They never left home.
To move freely was a luxury
stolen from them at birth.
Instead, they gathered patience,
learning to walk in shoes   15
the size of teacups,
without breaking—
the arc of their movements
as dormant as the rooted willow,
as redundant as the farmyard hens.   20
But they traveled far
in surviving,
learning to stretch the family rice,
to quiet the demons,
the noisy stomachs.   25

2

There is a sister
across the ocean,
who relinquished her name,
diluting jade green
with the blue of the Pacific.   30
Rising with a tide of locusts,
she swarmed with others
to inundate another shore.
In America,
there are many roads   35
and women can stride along with men.

But in another wilderness,
the possibilities,
the loneliness,
can strangulate like jungle vines.   40
The meager provisions and sentiments
of once belonging—
fermented roots, Mah-Jong⁸ tiles and firecrackers—set but
a flimsy household

8. Oriental game.

in a forest of nightless cities.   45
A giant snake rattles above,
spewing black clouds into your kitchen.
Dough-faced landlords
slip in and out of your keyholes,
making claims you don't understand,   50
tapping into your communication systems
of laundry lines and restaurant chains.

You find you need China:
your one fragile identification,
a jade link   55
handcuffed to your wrist.
You remember your mother
who walked for centuries,
footless—
and like her,   60
you have left no footprints,
but only because
there is an ocean in between,
the unremitting space of your rebellion.

                                                  1983

Heaven

He thinks when we die we'll go to China.
Think of it—a Chinese heaven
where, except for his blond hair,
the part that belongs to his father,
everyone will look like him.   5
China, that blue flower on the map,
bluer than the sea
his hand must span like a bridge
to reach it.
An octave away.   10

I've never seen it.
It's as if I can't sing that far.
But look—
on the map, this black dot.
Here is where we live,   15
on the pancake plains
just east of the Rockies,
on the other side of the clouds.
A mile above the sea,
the air is so thin, you can starve on it.   20
No bamboo trees
but the alpine equivalent,
reedy aspen with light, fluttering leaves.
Did a boy in Guangzhou[9] dream of this
as his last stop?   25

9. Or Canton, seaport city in southeastern China.

I've heard the trains at night
whistling past our yards,
what we've come to own,
the broken fences, the whiny dog, the rattletrap cars.
It's still the wild west,   30
mean and grubby,
the shootouts and fistfights in the back alley.
With my son the dreamer
and my daughter, who is too young to walk,
I've sat in this spot   35
and wondered why here?
Why in this short life,
this town, this creek they call a river?

He had never planned to stay,
the boy who helped to build
the railroads for a dollar a day.[1]   40
He had always meant to go back.
When did he finally know
that each mile of track led him further away,
that he would die in his sleep,
dispossessed,   45
having seen Gold Mountain,
the icy wind tunneling through it,
these landlocked, makeshift ghost towns?

It must be in the blood,   50
this notion of returning.
It skipped two generations, lay fallow,
the garden an unmarked grave.
On a spring sweater day
it's as if we remember him.   55
I call to the children.
We can see the mountains
shimmering blue above the air.
If you look really hard
says my son the dreamer,   60
leaning out from the laundry's rigging,
the work shirts fluttering like sails,
you can see all the way to heaven.

1988

---

1. The Chinese provided much of the cheap labor that laid the tracks of the transcontinental railroads
in the nineteenth century.

Modern Poetry in English: A Brief History

Just when poetry became "modern" is not easy to determine. It is necessary to pursue less a moment than a context—intellectual and social—in which the innovations we call modern have occurred. Such a search leads, paradoxically perhaps, back to the Romantic movement of the early nineteenth century. Romanticism was influential in the arts and in society as well; before it, poetry more often than not had celebrated the ideals of the society to which the poet belonged, but Romanticism offered sanction for a more copious and diversified expression of the self, for more various relations between the individual and society. An element of subversion is probably present in all great poets, but not until individuality came to be seen as positive, rather than eccentric or antisocial, did the conception of the guerilla poet—outcast, victim, misfit, radical—achieve heroic consequence.

To this extent at least we remain within the purview of the Romantic movement, but after almost two centuries the movement has been much altered from its origins. Modern poets are not necessarily proud of their descent from Romanticism. Yeats called himself one of the last Romantics, but repudiated the second half of the nineteenth century; Eliot, more sternly, repudiated both halves. Yet one relation has persisted: Romantic poets offered subsequent writers an all-important idea, the primacy of the imagination, its power to invest the external world with a new light—or even, as many would contend, to transform it altogether, to invent what W. H. Auden calls "alternative worlds." This idea has bred new forms, just as the revolutionary social ideas that went with it in the beginning of the nineteenth century have overthrown old stratifications of society. The assertion of the imaginative, image-making, untrammeled self becomes a form of individualism, although modern writers often present their special world as an attempt to extend the perceptions of all humanity. They explore these possibilities with an intricacy and an allusiveness which have become characteristic of imaginative life in this century.

Precursors

There were modern poets before there was modern poetry. Walt Whitman stands monolithically at the threshold, as poets like William Carlos Williams, Hart Crane, and June Jordan have eagerly attested, and as Ezra Pound more grudgingly conceded. Whitman expressed a new way of looking at the world: in *Leaves of Grass* (1855), he orchestrates the universe by finding and acknowledging the relationships among the most disparate things, and relating them to himself as poet and as archetypal man. This largeness of conception broke the bonds of conventional prosody. Whitman became the first major poet to write in free verse, a crucial innovation which Pound was to institutionalize fifty years later as a prime tenet of "modernism"— "To break the pentameter, that was the first heave." Beside Whitman stands a second poet, Emily Dickinson. Like him she "wrote a letter to the world," but her world is one of minute examination of her surroundings, a microcosm as opposed to Whitman's macrocosm, expressed as confidences that seem to have been preserved almost accidentally. Her recording eye is a shaping imagination, like Marianne Moore's after her. With short lines which seem the antitheses of Whitman's long ones, with her attentive inspection of domestic and natural objects while he is off to the city or the battlefield embracing farflung multitudes, she too draws all things into cohesion, for to her, as to the symbolists, "the brain is wider than the sky" and can encompass and absorb sky, sea, and all. Her poetry seconds what Yeats and William Blake both asserted, that infinity may be represented by things infinitely small as well as infinitely large.

Gerard Manley Hopkins, a third precursor of the modern movement, was a devout student of Whitman, and remarked in a letter, "I may as well say . . . that I always knew in my heart Walt Whitman's mind to be more like my own than any other man's living. As he is a very great scoundrel this is not a very pleasant confession." Hopkins doubtless thought Whitman a scoundrel because of the latter's unchristian religion and general bravado, but their poetic kinship is unmistakable. The sense of unity overcoming diversity is shared by the two poets, though where Whitman found the multitudinous world's coherence in his own sensibility, Hopkins found it in God. Like Whitman, Hopkins felt the need to transform the apparatus of poetry in the process of re-symbolizing the world. He did not desert rhyme or meter, but he pulled, twisted, and stretched them until they looked like nothing seen before in English verse. One of his affinities with Whitman is the way he confronts and even affronts the reader with new shapes, rhythms, and sounds. Something of this attitude is apparent also in Thomas Hardy, who offers verse based upon tormented syntax and inelegant vocabulary, as if they, rather than suavities, might best contain the uncouth universe. That these poets were out of phase with their time is indicated by the fact that they were little understood while alive; neither Dickinson nor Hopkins was even known. In different ways, each of these four wrote as if the world had a soul, and as if that soul might be apprehended by poetic vision.

Symbolism

A term frequently used to describe post-Romantic verse is "symbolism." This movement was related to idealist conceptions which find truth to inhere in mental operations rather than in the outside world. Against materialism or naturalism—movements adversary to it—practitioners of symbolism in varying ways and degrees proclaimed the supremacy of idea over fact. They rejected the conception of objects uninfluenced by perceiving subjects, and found in seemingly disconnected things secret and unexpected links. Their poetry is an attempt to render organic what appears fragmentary.

The symbolist movement is often said to have begun with Charles Baudelaire, who in *The Flowers of Evil* (1857), published two years after Whitman's first version of *Leaves of Grass*, describes nature as a temple filled with symbols which all secretly echo each other in a complexity of correspondence, the seen echoing the unseen and being echoed back. But the movement is international in origin, and Baudelaire himself traced his inspiration to Edgar Allan Poe, whose works he translated. In a general form, the metaphysical view that underlies symbolism is a very old one, dating back to the Neoplatonists of the third to fifth centuries A.D., and to many Renaissance and Romantic writers after them; they held that all beauty, goodness, and truth in the sensible world are an emanation or radiation from the One, or the Absolute, hence that objects in this world both echo the One and interrelate among each other.

Poe's critical writings encouraged Baudelaire in his assumption that the poet's task is to decipher what nature presents in encoded form. Much of Baudelaire's verse acknowledges the visible corruption of the body in life and death, and in revulsion invents a symbolic world of "wholeness, harmony, and radiance." In the words of a later French poet, Stéphane Mallarmé, this symbolic world is identified as "the mind's native land," no artificial concoction but what we would know at once if we were not taken in by an overlay of false culture. Mallarmé pursued the symbolist position as far as anyone; he spoke of his goal as "the flower absent from all bouquets," by which he meant both an essence and the flower which should be supremely real. He wished, he said, to recover the "orphic language of the earth," as if underlying all phenomena there was a secret code or language which bound them all together, as the double helix pervades and binds DNA.

The term "symbolism" became popular in France about 1886, and after about ten years crossed the English Channel. Arthur Symons had begun writing about the new French poets as "The Decadent Movement in Literature," but eventually called his book, instead, *The Symbolist Movement in Literature*. His change of heart was largely caused by his friend Yeats, with whom he shared rooms for a time in the mid-nineties. Yeats published an essay entitled "The Autumn of the Body" in which he said that the era of externality was over and that a new movement which should renew imaginative control over the environment (the body's world) was now afoot. Yeats reinforced his position with essays on the symbolism in William Blake's paintings and poems, and later with one on Shelley's symbolism. Most important, he published in 1899 *The Wind among the Reeds*, a book of poems which was the culmination of the early symbolist manner in which Symons and other poets of the nineties, as well as Yeats himself, had been writing.

This book was made out of many disparate elements, including Irish nationalism and occult lore, but all were given a new unity in a kind of counter-universe of Yeats's own invention. He created a hierarchy of symbols and of moods attendant upon them. Yeats's book was a discovery of counter-nature, or of a second, human-centered nature, in which all outward things were internalized. The four elements, which he found in stars, sea, winds, and woods, became aspects of feeling; bird and beast alike were bent upon expressing human passion rather than retaining their own identity. The human figures too became archetypes: the lover was Christ suffering sacrificially for his love, his Passion a confirmation of spiritual reality, and the beloved, often symbolized as a pale rose, was an ideal figure, dim and almost spectral. The book appeared in the same year as Freud's *The Interpretation of Dreams*, a discussion of the symbols of the unconscious. Arthur Symons's *The Symbolist Movement in Literature*, dedicated to Yeats, was also published that year. It was this book which introduced to T. S. Eliot the French symbolist poets who provided the models for his early verse.

Yeats in *The Winds among the Reeds* may be said to have achieved his aims only too well. His task now was to make symbolism less lugubrious and less disembodied, to unlock the secrets of nature for a larger and different audience. He began work on a second system, or symbology, which should allow for the whole person thinking and feeling, rather than for a pilgrim amorist ecstatically languishing. Verse must be "athletic," with leaps instead of dying falls. He began to attempt to assemble in verse material eschewed earlier as imperfect and "unpoetic."

In this development, Yeats found unexpected company in an American, Ezra Pound. Pound arrived in London in 1908, at the age of twenty-three, convinced that Yeats was the best poet then writing in English and determined to learn from him. He did so, but Yeats also discovered how much this young man could tell him of new ideas and techniques. Pound's openness to modernism—his exhortation to "make it new"—and his generosity and gregariousness made his apartment in Kensington for a time the headquarters of innovative verse for both England and America. He was helped to chart this new course by the novelist Ford Madox Ford and the philosopher T. E. Hulme, both of whom encouraged him to renounce his earlier Browningesque rhetoric in favor of a more epigrammatic and ironic mode, which became Imagism. Hulme believed that the Romantic view of the individual as a bottomless well of possibilities, which were to be released by the destruction and reconstruction of society, was wrong, and that a new Classicism, taking exactly the opposite view, must check it. In 1912 Pound, with H. D. and others, founded the Imagist movement, demanding "direct treatment of the thing," whether the thing was inside or outside the mind. They warned against slackness and sentimentality and counseled that poetic rhythm, whether free verse or not, should not be determined by the metronome. These were useful rules, but rather bare, and Pound soon shifted from Imagism to Vorticism. In his manifesto for the latter he emphasized not the do's and don'ts of style but the dynamism of content. The vortex, which Pound conceived of as the central image, must energize and double the force of the life it encompassed. Vorticism lasted only for a short time, and after it Pound left off founding movements, but he began to demonstrate in his verse what innovations were possible. He remarked that Henry James had done things in the novel which had not yet been attempted in verse, and in *Hugh Selwyn Mauberley: Life and Contacts* he undertook to try such things and others of his own devising.

His closest confederate was T. S. Eliot, whom Pound may be said to have discovered. The two men met in 1914, when Eliot came to England to study philosophy at Oxford; Pound was astonished by the poems which Eliot showed him, among them "The Love Song of J. Alfred Prufrock," observing that Eliot had modernized himself on his own as, Pound felt, no one else had done. At first it seemed that they were moving in much the same direction. They both wrote about the modern world as a group of fragments, Pound in the first Cantos which he published in *Poetry* (the magazine which, through his efforts and those of its founder Harriet Monroe, became the American clearinghouse for modern verse) and Eliot in *The Waste Land,* which Pound had helped Eliot to complete. Only gradually did it become clear that these very poems embodied divergent views: for Eliot the disjunctiveness of the world was intolerable, and he was determined to mend it (as his eventual conversion to Anglican Christianity helped him to do), but Pound preferred to accept and exploit this disjunctiveness. In the canceled first version of *Canto II*, Pound compared himself with Browning, who had "one whole man," whereas he himself had only "many fragments." But he went on to ask defiantly, "Less worth? Less worth?" He saw how he might accept the fragments and make them material for a modern epic, the *Cantos*, which would achieve its paradise, as well as its hell and purgatory, intermittently.

As a result *The Waste Land,* with the poems by Eliot that became its sequels, and the *Cantos*, which Pound continued to write until his death, may be seen as rival eminences of earlier modern verse. The fragments which Eliot wished to re-combine Pound was willing to keep unchanged. Although Pound wrote Eliot that he envied him his sense of form, he did not emulate it. Eliot's sifting and fusion ended in a surprisingly orthodox religious view which Pound regarded as based upon too limited a number of particulars. Pound preferred his own "ideogrammic method," as he called it, by which he meant the heaping up of the components of thought so that they would eventually cohere almost without artistic intervention. His image was one of iron filings which, drawn towards a piece of glass by a magnet, assume the pattern of a rose. "Hast 'ou seen the rose in the steel dust?" he asks. He realized that such a rose might serve him as the rose of beauty had served Yeats, the Christian rose had served Eliot. The *Cantos* collate slices of time and space, fable and fact, examples from aboriginal tribes and effete cultures. There is no purification or evident exclusion; the poet achieves his effect by collocating diffuse materials. Eliot consolidated his innovations, while Pound restlessly extended his.

The *Waste Land* was published in 1922, and the first collection of Cantos in volume form appeared in 1925. The reaction to Eliot's poem was violently mixed. His friend Conrad Aiken was quick to praise *The Waste Land*, but most poets, while admiring its technical inventiveness and finish, found it hard to like. Yeats felt it was dour and despairing. Robert Graves clung to traditional forms, disparaging their disintegration by Eliot. John Crowe Ransom wrote an adverse review of the poem to which his sometime pupil Allen Tate published a refutation. Hart Crane was moved by *The Waste Land* but thought that Eliot's despair was exaggerated and that his own mission, with the help of Walt Whitman, must be to effect a redemption of Eliot's disintegrated or corrupted world.

William Carlos Williams found it necessary to campaign against the poem; its sinister merit was so powerful that it might well block the movement towards an indigenous American verse. For him it was "the great catastrophe" which by its genius (a quality he admitted) interrupted the "rediscovery of a primal impulse, the elementary principle of all art, in the local [as opposed to cosmopolitan] conditions." Williams considered that Eliot had imposed a shape upon material which should have been allowed to take its own shape. His own conception of poetry he expressed by the poem beginning "So much depends upon / a red wheelbarrow," as if objects in the world should be allowed to retain their nature without being conceptualized into abstract schemas. "No ideas but in things" was the credo Williams espoused in his epic, *Paterson*, which is like Pound's *Cantos* in extending the principles of Imagism, and also rebukes those symbolists who invest "things" with foreign significance. Williams agreed with the poets Verlaine and Rimbaud in opposing "literature" as a phenomenon created by the "establishment"; he regarded language as the vital instrument which must be invigorated by keeping it local rather than cosmopolitan. His own poems, unlike Pound's or Eliot's, are all but devoid of "literary" English, and their unmistakable distinctiveness comes, as he insisted, from contact with native materials. He founded a magazine with *Contact* as its defiant title.

Stevens led a different revolt against the religious presuppositions of *The Waste Land*. In *Harmonium* (1923) and later books, he presented the death of the old gods as a liberation of the imagination. In contradistinction to Eliot's return to Christianity, Stevens asked for a new religion which should be closer to physical life and willing to encompass death, as well as life, in its conception of being. Its paradise must be within the world. The poet's task is to replace the satisfactions of belief once provided by religion with those of verse: "What makes the poet the potent figure that he is, or was, or ought to be, is that he creates the world to which we turn incessantly and without knowing it and that he gives to life the supreme fictions without which we are unable to conceive of it." The creation of these fictions, which he changed even as he affirmed, occupied Stevens steadily.

Apart from Yeats, British poets were less attracted to the problems raised by the symbolists than Americans, and those few who followed the lead of Eliot and Pound made relatively little impact on their readers. In England as in America, the influence of strongly programmatic poetry was balanced by much more traditional modes of verse. These alternatives must next be considered.

Elegant and Inelegant Variations

Yeats was able to proceed from a static symbolism to a more dynamic kind, much as Pound proceeded from Imagism to Vorticism and the ideogrammic method. Others followed the tradition of Kipling, with his boisterous renderings of dialect and his swinging measures, his celebrations of the guardians and workers who keep civilization going. The more introspective and solitary poets, however, looked further back to the Romantics, and infused nature with nationalist feeling. Soon after George V acceded to the throne in 1910, they began to appear in an annual anthology called *Georgian Poetry*, edited by Sir Edward Marsh. Among the poets participating were Robert Graves, Siegfried Sassoon, and for a time even D. H. Lawrence. Curiously, Edward Thomas was omitted from the anthology, though he best epitomized Georgian ideals. At first these poets, with their celebration of the English countryside and its people, seemed to open a window into a more wholesome outdoors, and the movement was received enthusiastically by those who wished to preserve rural England in traditional prosody. Traces of Georgian tendencies can be found in the work of Thomas's friend Robert Frost, who lived in England from 1912 to 1915. Almost from the beginning the Georgians were under critical attack, and the movement succumbed to the First World War, during which Brooke and Thomas died. Innocent greenery was too much at odds with trench warfare and mass slaughter. Robert Graves proved tougher than the movement to which he had belonged. Sassoon, who survived the war, and Owen, who was killed in its last week, became, with Isaac Rosenberg (who was also killed in action), the most famous of the war poets. Their experiences in the trenches withered away their conventional patriotism and stirred them to devise a bitter new rhetoric to express their disillusion and anger at martial inhumanity.

D. H. Lawrence was little more in place as a Georgian than as an Imagist, although both groups had sought to claim him. His praise for the Georgians was more for their potential than their actual accomplishments. He conceded that *Georgian Poetry* had not much concern with love—an understatement—but prophesied that the group were "just ripening to be love poets." He quickly read into their efforts his own doctrine: "If I take my whole, passionate, spiritual and physical love to the woman who in return loves me, that is how I serve God. . . . All of which I read in the anthology of *Georgian Poetry*." As a statement of his own purpose this was accurate. Lawrence sought to break through the tinsel with his burning honesty and directness, and centered his own verse in the passions of tortoises and elephants as well as of men and women. Robinson Jeffers in America, and Ted Hughes in England, were to pursue the same qualities, though in them it often seems that more reality attaches to hate than to love. Unlike the Georgians, Lawrence worked mostly in free verse, but did not share Pound's interest in the minutiae of that technique. He thought that an interest in form usually accompanied an interest in imitation, and preferred to let his subjects command their own shape. He remained an isolated figure, almost an outcast, beset during his short life by the public's unfounded notion that his writings were pornographic. They were in fact the opposite.

In America, during the first two decades of the new century, poets explored their environment with little regard for the symbolist patterns being woven by their compatriots Pound, Eliot, and H. D. in England. Edwin Arlington Robinson exposed the life of his Tilbury Town, and Edgar Lee Masters of his Spoon River, so as to impart public lessons from private scandals. Robert Frost returned from England in 1915, bought a farm in New Hampshire, and consolidated his reputation as America's greatest pastoral poet. For many he was its greatest poet of the twentieth century. Frost brought a toughness to pastoralism; on the one hand he tapped the seasoned country wisdom of New England, on the other he converted his self-disgust and loneliness into verses of Horatian dignity phrased in the accents of New Hampshire and Vermont. His dramatic monologues are often spoken by tormented and lonely men and women whose pain cannot be assuaged by any amount of homely folk wisdom. The more brazen Carl Sandburg wrote of the brawling city of Chicago and its workers. Sandburg's ebullient rhetoric constituted the most "modern" literature to gain much public acceptance in the United States. Many poets who wished a more radical break with tradition left the country to find it, while the early poems of others, such as William Carlos Williams, were printed either privately or abroad. In 1923 the Pulitzer Prize for poetry went not to *The Waste Land* but to three books by Edna St. Vincent Millay.

Some poets of less prominence were to outlast some others who at first achieved greater reputations. In New York two poets, Marianne Moore in Brooklyn and E. E. Cummings in Greenwich Village, were proceeding with subtlety in ways more decisively modern. Marianne Moore, like her friend William Carlos Williams, was a sharp observer, and upholder, of the physical world, but hers was a world which few others knew, made up of rare birds and animals, insects, baseball players and steeplejacks, steamrollers and other creatures. Pretending that her lines were prose, she employed light rhymes and odd stanzaic patterns as if to conceal the finish of her work. Poetry, she alleged, was all "fiddle," and yet, she confided, it had in it "a place for the genuine." Cummings was a more flamboyant poet: he invented an astonishing number of typographical oddities, partly to tantalize and disconcert, partly to amuse, but mostly to indicate to his devotees how the poems might be best read aloud. For all his up-to-date pyrotechnics, however, he kept to the ancient themes of lyric poetry.

The Black poets of the Harlem Renaissance, on the other hand, sought revitalization by content rather than form. They adopted the devices of nineteenth-century verse in expressing their new theme of Black racial consciousness and culture. They rejected the "Uncle Remus" dialect and the exoticism of Paul Laurence Dunbar and other earlier Black poets in order to develop a new intransigence. Claude McKay, politically the most militant if prosodically among the more conservative of the new Black writers, was first with *Harlem Shadows* (1922); then followed Countee Cullen, whose elegiac verse was first published in *Color* (1925). The most prominent and talented member of the group was Langston Hughes, the only one whose work continued to be published regularly in later decades.

The year 1922 saw many important tendencies in modern verse put into motion. It was the year of *The Waste Land* and of Joyce's *Ulysses* (published in Paris), and of several bursts of concerted activity such as the Harlem Renaissance in New York. It was also the year when a group of teachers and students at Vanderbilt University brought out a literary magazine called *The Fugitive*, in which they published their own and others' poems and urged an alternative to the cosmopolitan modernism centered in London. Of the Fugitives, the central figure was John Crowe Ransom, and the younger members of the group included Allen Tate and Robert Penn Warren. The original Fugitives cultivated an astringent wit as an antidote to southern nostalgia; politically, through the Agrarian movement, they hoped to keep for the South some of its traditional values. They came to view their provinciality, their remoteness from metropolitan culture, and their sense of rootedness in time and place as sources of strength for their writing. The magazine ceased publication in 1925; Tate had already moved to New York, Warren (after graduate study at Berkeley, Yale, and Oxford) went to Louisiana State University, and Ransom joined the faculty of Kenyon College and founded the *Kenyon Review*. As writers, teachers, and critics, these, and other poets speaking from the university such as Yvor Winters, continued to compose in a style that younger poets liked for its aloofness and its complexity of motives and materials.

The influence of this style began to take shape during the later twenties and the thirties, when a number of important critical works were published whose general tendency was applauded by John Crowe Ransom in a book, *The New Criticism* (1941), whose title became a byword for the entire movement. In *A Survey of Modernist Poetry* (1927), by Laura Riding and Robert Graves, Riding had been perhaps the first to try the experiment of reading a poem apart from any historical or linguistic context; her intense appreciation of the semantic complexities of a Shakespeare sonnet encouraged the young William Empson to discover the value of exploring every nuance of meaning, with the aid of psychology and sociology. The result was his famous study, *Seven Types of Ambiguity* (1930), which sought to characterize the semantic strategies of multiple meanings which distinguish imaginative writing from straightforward exposition. Another force behind the New Criticism was Empson's teacher, I. A. Richards, who urged that poems be read with active and exclusive attention to what they said, without distortion by the reader's subjective preferences and presuppositions. Eliot, important for his criticism as well as for his verse, agreed that what was needed in reading poetry was "a very highly developed sense of fact." These prescriptions for readers, and by extension for writers, were codified by Robert Penn Warren and Cleanth Brooks in their textbook *Understanding Poetry* (1938), which had a vast influence on the teaching of verse at American colleges in the forties, fifties, and early sixties; the influence was even greater on the many imitative textbooks it spawned. Taken to extremes, the New Criticism implied that the essence of poetry was not to convey ideas or feelings as such but to create intricate structures of language which would manifest the density of psychophysical experience. Some of Empson's own poems are perhaps the most thoroughgoing exemplifications of this principle; few other poets went so far, but they understood his goal. During and immediately after the Second World War, most poets living in the United States came to write in a way that poets of the twenties and critics of the thirties had prepared for them.

In England during the late twenties and early thirties, two important young poets were W. H. Auden and Louis MacNeice, members of a group which prided itself on "understatement" and "social concern." They were eager to express radical political attitudes, and preferred to do so through older verse techniques. Except for their preference for rhyme and meter, they were strenuously ahead of their time, not least in their use of the specialized vocabularies of politics, psychiatry, and the social sciences. They proclaimed their support for a socialist revolution. To some extent, the Second World War obliged them to try to preserve rather than to change. Auden, who went to the United States, wrote sharply and sympathetically about the new problems of community in a divided world. In his later years he became rather religious in his beliefs, and more tender and friendly in his verse. Instead of predicting that something dreadful was about to happen, he preferred to celebrate with great wit what was happening now.

Poetry from 1945 to 1975

The many poets who have published mainly since 1945 may, in general, be said to conduct in their work, or in their thinking about their work, a restless dialogue. Behind these younger poets has loomed a powerful literature which early in the century registered great innovations and consolidations. As they have looked back on this earlier period, they have been apt to see as fixed what was earlier experimental. They have liked to invade areas of awareness, both commonplace and exotic, which were largely neglected by their predecessors. The Second World War may not have markedly divided the poetry written before it from that written after, but many poets who were young during the war have written with greater skepticism of accepted personal and social values than those older poets—Stevens, Cummings, Williams, Frost, Eliot, Pound, Moore—who survived it.

During the war itself a number of British poets emerged whose response to the "age of anxiety," as Auden called it, was vehement and extreme. These were the poets of the New Apocalypse, among whom the major figure was Dylan Thomas. Perhaps in opposition to the understatement of the Auden school, Thomas, with the most spectacular display of language since Hart Crane, reintroduced openly expressed emotion and rhetoric into English verse. In ordinary situations he heard extraordinary reverberations, and like Wordsworth and Coleridge he tried to restore a radiance lost to English nature poetry since the seventeenth century. In reaction to this apocalyptic mode there arose during the fifties a loose association of university poets who called themselves, baldly, the "Movement": the chief of them proved to be Philip Larkin. The Movement had affinities with developments in the other arts, as in the novels of Kingsley Amis and John Wain (themselves poets as well), in the "kitchen-sink" school of painting, in plays by "angry young men" such as John Osborne, and in the concern with ordinary uses of language by philosophers like A. J. Ayer. While objecting to what they saw as the Romantic excesses of the New Apocalypse, the poets of the Movement also rejected the symbolist tradition of Yeats, Pound, and Eliot, and favored wit over prophecy and extravagance, urban and suburban realities over the urbane. They committed themselves to very little. They defined themselves more narrowly in relationship to Graves, Empson, and Edwin Muir, and they aimed to consolidate the achievements of the Auden school, to write a poetry which in its subjects and in its diction would express rather than overthrow the restrictions of ordinary life.

A similar situation obtained in the United States, where a generation of younger poets had emerged during the forties, many of whom were to die—some by suicide—before the sixties were out. A few poets—of whom Randall Jarrell is a prime figure—wrote poems out of their wartime experiences; they were essentially meditative rather than dramatic. Others, such as Theodore Roethke, Robert Lowell, and John Berryman, began to write in an atmosphere of reticence and restraint. For some years after the war, the esthetic of the New Criticism—itself a condensation of the practice of certain poets—helped to shape most new American verse, even that by writers like Lowell and Berryman who fifteen years later would write in quite different ways. The qualities it enshrined, such as metaphysical wit (exemplified by John Donne and Gerard Manley Hopkins), an irony too complex to permit strong commitments, and a technique which often calls attention to its own dexterity, are characteristic elements of what its detractors called an academic style. Whatever it may have lacked in gusto, it is not dull, and it served handsomely as a difficult school for some of the best recent poets. If some poets of the New Criticism gravitated to careers as critics and college teachers, it must be recognized that both criticism and college teaching have become more demanding and exciting pursuits when so many esthetic battles are being waged.

The wry, cultivated quality of much poetry of the fifties is visible in the work of some university poets. The verse of poets like Elizabeth Bishop, Richard Wilbur, Howard Nemerov, Josephine Miles, and Anthony Hecht gives pleasure by the fertility and deftness of their images and phrases; their work is unsentimental and yet alive to senses and sympathies, well made and careful not to repeat itself or become predictable. These are real values and lead to verse that is often more durable, if less sensational, than what has come from more driven talents. These poets are also, it should be noted, capable of abrupt departures from their habitual styles.

In contrast to the influence of the New Critics, that of William Carlos Williams and Ezra Pound was more subversive and therefore less easily accommodated by the academy. Williams continued to live the life of a physician in Rutherford, New Jersey, and was the goal of pilgrimages by young poets, including A. R. Ammons and Allen Ginsberg. Pound, under indictment for treason because of his wartime radio broadcasts from Rome, was returned to the United States in 1945, bringing with him the manuscript of the *Pisan Cantos*. Found mentally incompetent to stand trial, he was immured in a Washington sanatorium, and until his release twelve years later (as incurably insane but harmless) he was a magnet for younger American poets who sought in his work an immersion in experience which they found to be lacking in the poetry of Eliot and Ransom and their followers. Finding strength in their association with the old impresario of *vers libre* and the even older M.D. in Rutherford, they preferred open to closed poetic forms, agreeing with Robert Creeley that "Form is never more than an extension of content."

Creeley was one of the poets who gathered around Charles Olson at Black Mountain College, an experimental and unaccredited school in North Carolina which was to become one of the centers of new American verse. Olson developed the theoretical manifesto of the Black Mountain poets and others of similar aims in his essay on "projective verse," which attempts a dynamism like that of Pound's Vorticism, and offers a conception of "open-field" form. Here, and in his *Maximus Poems* of the sixties, he constituted himself the heir of Pound and Williams. Like Williams he emphasized the breath, rather than the iamb, as the basis of rhythm. Like Pound, Olson in his verse mixed colloquialism and farflung learning. Against subjective verse Olson offered what he called "objectism," a form of verse in which the ego is washed away and the poet "fronts to the whole of reality." He opposed the isolation of literature from the rest of experience; the poet must take a stance towards the world. In his *Maximus Poems* he presented his archetypal hero in terms of a specific area (Gloucester, Massachusetts) which in turn takes its character from history, geology, archaeology, anthropology. The Pleistocene Age was for Olson still an active force in the present of

Gloucester. As a result he called himself an "archaeologist of morning" and maintained that poets can summon up regions of experience which till now have been inaccessible.

The faculty of Black Mountain College included Creeley, who also edited the *Black Mountain Review*; during its short run of seven issues it was a major outlet for the anti-academic verse which was to explode into prominence in the late fifties. Robert Duncan came from San Francisco to join the college staff; Denise Levertov was published in the *Review*. A. R. Ammons, from North Carolina if not from Black Mountain, has much in common with these poets; even Imamu Amiri Baraka, who then called himself LeRoi Jones, acknowledged the fundamental influence of Charles Olson on his poetry.

The Beat poets too aligned themselves with the "open" prosody of Pound and especially of Williams, who wrote an introduction for Allen Ginsberg's *Howl*. They were featured in the last issue of the *Black Mountain Review*, of which Ginsberg was a contributing editor. The Beats, however, tended to dismiss the Black Mountain poets as too much at ease with authority figures; their own consistent opposition to authority made their poetic achievement the most conspicuous and notorious of the fifties. They set themselves against the stuffy majority culture, the anticommunist inquisitions, and the formalistic poetry of the times, and decided to drop out and create among themselves a counterculture based upon inspired improvisation, whether through jazz, drugs, or transcendence by way of Oriental mysticism. Ginsberg and other exiles from New York found a congenial milieu in San Francisco, where a poetic renaissance had already been fomented within "the alternative society," as Kenneth Rexroth called it. Robert Duncan returned to the San Francisco scene after Black Mountain College collapsed in 1956; Gary Snyder returned to his birthplace after years in the lumber camps of Oregon and more years studying Zen Buddhism in a Japanese monastery. Following the example of Walt Whitman, Beat writers like Ginsberg shaped their public utterances out of the private experiences which their first readers found shameful and appalling: they presented, often as visionary experiences, confidences of a kind which were once uttered only to priest or doctor. This kind of poetry came to be known as "confessional," and through the sixties many younger poets vied with each other in unabashed self-revelation.

Frank O'Hara was a member of what was for a time called the "New York school" of poets, as was John Ashbery. They met at Harvard, where they were associated with the Poets' Theater, an experimental drama group of the early fifties. Inspired by the paintings of such contemporary artists as Jackson Pollock and Willem de Kooning, they went to New York and immersed themselves in modern art—Ashbery and O'Hara wrote for *Art News* and O'Hara worked for the Museum of Modern Art. Although some of the painters they have admired were abstractionists, their verse was not abstract; they have practiced a calculated effrontery and discontinuity of perception, as if all the rest were pomposity. The world can only be seen properly by an eye which is never overawed. In their highspirited way they celebrate New York and record its landscape, as when O'Hara, characteristically looking from the window of an art gallery, writes that "the warm traffic going by is my natural scenery." The rootedness of these poets in their locale is as intense as that of the Georgians or the poets of the American South. Ashbery has become the most prominent of these poets, manipulating reality and fantasy and forcing the reader to assume different selves in the process. His distinctive style blends humor with intricate perceptions.

Surrealism, a mode which exploits as material the distortion imposed upon reality by the unconscious, had until the sixties been more common to the visual arts, and to European writing, than to American or English poetry. Now, however, some of these achievements suggested ways for American poets to exploit new perceptions and arrangements of phenomena. Under the sponsorship of Robert Bly's magazine, *The Fifties* (later *Sixties* and *Seventies*), new translations of the South Americans Pablo Neruda and Cesar Vallejo, as well as other surrealist poets, were made available, and a "new surrealism" can be found in some of Bly's own poems and in those of James Wright and W. S. Merwin. Others, like Diane Wakoski, were also periodically attracted to the dislocation of sense and image that is a feature of surrealism.

In Robert Lowell's work the New Critical tradition of elaborate structure and the Whitmanesque tradition of radical contact with subject approached startling fusion during the late fifties. As a young man, Lowell had left Harvard to study at Kenyon College with John Crowe Ransom; he and his older friend Allen Tate became Roman Catholics at the same time; his second book, *Lord Weary's Castle*, showed a technical mastery of rhyme and meter and gave him an established place among young poets. Then followed a long silence, during which Lowell, teaching at the University of Iowa, was struck by some aspects of Beat poetry. In 1959 he published his first book of "confessional" poetry, *Life Studies*, working for the first time in what appeared to be a looser form. It seemed at first that Lowell might himself be becoming a Beat, but in fact his verse is more controlled than it appears. If, as he says in *History*, "Imperfection is the language of art," his constant revisions bore witness to a lingering allegiance to the well-made poem. If he wrote sonnets without rhyme, they were still in fourteen lines. Other poets who wrote in this intensely autobiographical vein, such as Snodgrass, Theodore Roethke, and John Berryman (who invented an "anti-sonnet" of three six-line stanzas for his *Dream Songs*), Sylvia Plath, Anne Sexton, and Adrienne Rich, either played against conventional form or wrote free verse in a peculiarly unrelaxed way. These poets are generally melancholy; they have sought in their lives the key moments of pain much more often than of pleasure, and see such moments as epitomes of the general condition of men and women in their time. Three of them—Sylvia Plath, John Berryman, and Anne Sexton—committed suicide.

Black poets after the war also sought a special rapport with their readers, but on social rather than personal grounds. They regarded agonies as imposed from without rather than from within and against oppression wrote the most political verse of the time. Gwendolyn Brooks began to use authentic Black street language in poems such as "We Real Cool." LeRoi Jones, now Imamu Amiri Baraka, left the white avant-garde during the sixties to move towards a distinctively Black esthetic, which insisted on the importance to Black writers of commitment to the needs of the Black community and the discovery of their artistic resources in it. The sense of racial injustice he expressed turns up, although in different forms, in some of the poets contemporary with him, such as Audre Lorde.

Poetry Since 1975

In the United States, the time since 1975 was, first of all, marked by what the critic David Kalstone called "personal absences." By this he meant the deaths of Elizabeth Bishop and Robert Lowell, two of the most distinctive voices in the older generation of contemporaries; the deaths, as well, of James Wright and Richard Hugo in their fifties; and the comparative silence of others, such as Allen Ginsberg. Only four of the more prominent post-1945 writers have continued to develop and change. John Ashbery, as noted earlier, has become the strongest of the "New York school," while A. R. Ammons has recently blended his descriptive and meditative modes with more personal introspections. James Merrill, in *The Changing Light at Sandover*, has produced a cosmological epic unlike anything by an American poet before him, and Adrienne Rich continues to forge afresh her "dream of a common language" for women.

For the poets who have first begun publishing in the seventies or eighties, the work of these older contemporaries is an accepted part of the poetic landscape, while the major poetic innovations and consolidations earlier in the century are now simply history. It is worth noting that the time span between a poem published in 1989 and a landmark modernist poem such as *The Waste Land* is almost as great as the span between *The Waste Land* and a quintessential Victorian poem such as Tennyson's *In Memoriam*. The poetic past is, for these younger poets, embodied, accepted, or perhaps ignored, but not challenged.

Conducive to this acceptance of the past is what one might call the "academicization" of American poetry. With few exceptions the younger poets have received some training in university-based creative-writing programs. And, by and large, the younger poets then go on to teach in creative-writing programs themselves. The poetry reading—which in the sixties had been a psychedelic or revolutionary event—is now a commonplace campus social activity.

America is a vast country, made up of regions, each with its own history and traditions. Writers in these regions tend to affiliate with each other, as did the southern Fugitives in the 1920s. Even though most of the major publishing houses and some of the more prestigious academies are still located in the Northeast, this region is no longer thought of as the only center of American poetic activity.

In the best of the younger poets—and there are many of them—"regionalism" is not, however, a vague, pastel local-colorism or a tacking-on of local props, but a vigorous use of vivid experiences in a particular place: what Richard Hugo called a "triggering town" that sets a poetic process going. Gary Soto places himself and us strongly in the San Joaquin valley in California, as does Rita Dove in Akron, Ohio, or Cathy Song in small Hawaii towns. These are places where, in earlier poetic generations, poems didn't happen.

One such regional group is that of poets who have lived or worked in the Pacific Northwest, and who were students of Roethke, like James Wright and Richard Hugo, who took creative-writing courses with him at the University of Washington. Hugo later founded, with Carolyn Kizer and other poets of the region, the journal *Poetry Northwest*. All these poets have practiced a kind of disciplined Romanticism, finding their subjects in the American West, as has William Stafford.

There are rich regions other than the strictly geographic, even though they may depend in part on geography. Chicano and Chicana literature, by definition, is located in the American Southwest, but it also expresses a region of ethnic experience, as dictated by generations of ghettoizing of the ethnic minority by the "Anglo" majority. The same may be said of Native-American poets. These are poets of the American West, but they are also poets whose forebears were members of specific regional tribes, each with its own rich set of tales, traditions, and ways of seeing the world. Finally, a younger Black poet such as Rita Dove says that she intended her *Thomas and Beulah* sequence in part to combat the notion that the inner lives of the poor are less complex than those of other classes. She does not, however, express this directly and militantly so much as obliquely, by mining her grandparents' region of experience. There are more women writing poetry today than perhaps ever before. Unlike many of their older sisters, perhaps as a result of the success of earlier struggles, younger poets do not always seem impelled to take gender as their central subject.

With all this diversity it would be hard, if not impossible, to point to poetic trends, or types of poems, common to all these younger poets. The personal—at first as seen in relation to one's parents or immediate ancestors, then with one's own children—is a prominent subject, but this is a concern as old as the Romantic period itself. A significant poetic mode is that of the dramatic monologue. This is not so much at variance with the earlier autobiographical mode as it might seem, for, in the dramatic monologues by poets as seemingly diverse as Norman Dubie and Louise Erdrich, the invented protagonist serves mainly for a metaphor for the personal, within an imagined other self.

The dramatic monologue and the autobiographical self-exploration are not always containable within the brief lyric, and it is significant that many recent poets are writing longer poems or poetic sequences. Among the longer poems are such meditations as Stanley Kunitz's "The Wellfleet Whale," William Everson's "The Poet Is Dead," James Dickey's "Falling," and A. R. Ammons's *Sphere*. Among the sequences are, for example, Adrienne Rich's *Twenty-One Love Poems*, Tony Harrison's *School of Eloquence*, Michael Harper's "Debridement," and Seamus Heaney's "Station Island."

In her introduction to *The New Oxford Book of Canadian Verse in English* (1982), Margaret Atwood observes that in Canada "the modern movement took some time to build a following . . . [because] puritanism and the colonial worship of imports still restricted taste . . . the position of the poet in Canada in the forties was not far removed from that of the lonely obsessive figure—the voice with no hearer—portrayed in A. M. Klein's brilliant poem 'Portrait of the Poet as Landscape.' " Nevertheless, first Earle Birney in the thirties, then Klein himself, Irving Layton, and P. K. Page in the forties found their individual voices. The counterculture in America of the 1960s had its counterpart in Canada, and Al Purdy became one of its foremost spokesmen, followed by Atwood herself.

The revolt against a too polished poetry in America has been paralleled by similar efforts in England. Already in the sixties Ted Hughes had begun to write poems in which he was seeing the world as violent and himself as having a savage role to fill, and finding emblems of violence in the outer world of animals, weather, and physical work he was experiencing as a sheep and cattle farmer. Geoffrey Hill's verse is at once distinctively modern and reminiscent of the Metaphysical exploitation of Christian liturgy by John Donne and other seventeenth-century poets.

In their introduction to *The Penguin Book of Contemporary British Poetry* (1982), Blake Morrison and Andrew Motion identify a new attitude among younger British poets: "as a way of making the familiar strange again, they have exchanged the idea of the poet as the-person-next-door, or knowing insider, for the attitude of the anthropologist or alien invader or remembering exile. . . . The new poetry is often open-ended, reluctant to point to the moral of, or conclude too neatly, what it chooses to transcribe." This attitude is manifest in Craig Raine's "The Martian Sends a Postcard Home," in which an alien invader describes humanity; the poem's title was adopted by fellow poets who call themselves the "Martian school." Similarly in "Dead Soldiers" James Fenton explores the Cambodian wars in terms of a battle-field dinner party. Tony Harrison often writes as a "remembering exile" from his working-class origins; as he says in "Turns," for example, his poet persona is that of a street-entertainer for "the class that broke" his working-class father.

In the early sixties a group of young people, all of them born and brought up in Ulster, and all of them with literary ambitions, began to meet in the apartment of Philip Hobsbaum, then a Lecturer at Queen's University in Belfast. Some of the aspiring writers were Catholics, others Protestants; all were agreed that the endless guerilla warfare between religious *cum* polit-ical factions in Ulster should not divert them from their writing or become, in a bullying way, their sole subject. If the troubles in Ulster were to be treated in poems, they agreed, it must be by indirection. The Ulster poets are traditionalists, though they are far from tame. Seamus Heaney has said that the Irish poet cannot hate the English, because without them he would not have their language, his chief resource as a poet. And they have not so much used the Western literary tradition as ransacked it, from Dante to Dashiell Hammett. Seamus Heaney is the oldest among these poets; Paul Muldoon is one of the youngest. The Ulster poets, all of them still on the young side, have written poems of great freshness and formal elegance; and as with all of the younger poets in this anthology, one looks forward to reading their as yet unwritten books.

Bibliography

This bibliography lists works by each poet in the anthology. Each entry begins with all a poet's books of poetry, except for those poets who are no longer living and whose poems are collected in definitive editions: in those cases, only the definitive editions are cited and, if available, convenient volumes of "selected poems." Also listed for each poet are very selective lists of other books: fiction (f), drama (d), autobiography (a), criticism (c), and other nonfictional prose (p).

A. R. AMMONS

Ommateum, with Doxology (1955); *Expressions of Sea Level* (1964); *Corsons Inlet* (1965); *Tape for the Turn of the Year* (1965); *Northfield Poems* (1966); *Selected Poems* (1968); *Uplands* (1970); *Briefings: Poems Small and Easy* (1971); *Collected Poems, 1951–1971* (1972); *Sphere: The Form of a Motion* (1974); *Diversifications* (1975); *The Snow Poems* (1977); *The Selected Poems 1951–1977* (1977); *Highgate Road* (1977); *For Doyle Fosco* (1977); *Poem* (1977); *Six-Piece Suite* (1979); *Selected Longer Poems* (1980); *A Coast of Trees* (1981); *Worldly Hopes* (1982); *Lake Effect Country* (1983); *The Selected Poems: Expanded Edition* (1986); *Sumerian Vistas* (1987).

JOHN ASHBERY

Turandot and Other Poems (1953); *Some Trees* (1956); *The Poems* (1960); *The Tennis Court Oath* (1962); *Rivers and Mountains* (1966, 1977); *Selected Poems* (1967); *Three Madrigals* (1968); *Sunrise in Suburbia* (1968); *Fragment* (1969); *Evening in the Country* (1970); *The Double Dream of Spring* (1970); *The New Spirit* (1970); *Three Poems* (1972); *The Vermont Notebook* (1975); *The Serious Doll* (1975); *Self-Portrait in a Convex Mirror* (1975); *Houseboat Days* (1977); *As We Know* (1979); *Shadow Train* (1981); *A Wave* (1984); *Selected Poems* (1985).

MARGARET ATWOOD

Double Persephone (1961); *Talismans for Children* (1965); *Kaleidoscopes: Baroque* (1965); *Speeches for Doctor Frankenstein* (1966); *The Circle Game* (1966); *Expeditions* (1966); *Who Was In the Garden* (1969); *The Animals in That County* (1969); *The Journals of Susanna Moodie* (1970); *Procedures for Underground* (1970); *Power Politics* (1971); *You Are Happy* (1974); *Selected Poems* (1976); *Marsh, Hawk* (1977); *Two-Headed Poems* (1978); *Lobsticks* (with others) (n.d.); *True Stories* (1981); *Notes Towards a Poem That Can Never Be Written* (1981); *Snake Poems* (1983); *Interlunar* (1984).
Other:
The Edible Woman (1969) (f); *Surfacing* (1972) (f); *Survival: A Thematic Guide to Canadian Literature* (1972) (c); *Lady Oracle* (1976) (f); *Dancing Girls and Other Stories* (1977) (f); *Days of the Rebels 1815–1840* (1977) (p); *Life Before Man* (1979) (f); *Bodily Harm* (1981) (f); *Second Words: Selected Critical Prose* (1982) (c); *Murder in the Dark: Short Fictions and Prose Poems* (1983) (f); *Unearthing Suite* (1983) (p); *Bluebeard's Egg* (1984) (f); *The Handmaid's Tale* (1986) (f).

W. H. AUDEN

Collected Poems (ed. Edward Mendelson, 1976); *The English Auden: Poems, Essays and Dramatic Writings 1927–1939* (ed. Edward Mendelson, 1977); *Selected Poems* (ed. Edward Mendelson, 1979).
Other:
With C. Isherwood, *The Dog Beneath the Skin* (1935) (d); with Isherwood, *The Ascent of F–6* (1936) (d); with L. MacNeice, *Letters from Iceland* (1937) (p); with Isherwood, *On the Frontier* (1938) (d); with Isherwood, *Journey to a War* (1939) (p); with C. Kallman, *The Rake's Progress* (1951) (d [libretto]); with Kallman,

Elegy for Young Lovers (1961) (d [libretto]); *The Dyer's Hand* (1962) (c); *Selected Essays* (1964) (c); with Kallman, *The Bassarids* (1966) (d [libretto]); *The Dyer's Hand and Other Essays* (1968) (c); ed., *A Certain World: A Commonplace Book* (1970) (p); with Kallman, *Love's Labour's Lost* (1972) (d [libretto]); *Forewords and Afterwords* (1973) (c); *Paul Bunyan* (1976) (d [libretto]).

IMAMU AMIRI BARAKA (LeRoi Jones)
Spring and Soforth (1960); *Preface to a Twenty Volume Suicide Note* (1962); *The Dead Lecturer* (1965); *Black Art* (1966); *A Poem for Black Hearts* (1967); *Black Magic: Poetry 1961–1967* (1969); *It's Nation Time* (1970); *In Our Terribleness: Some Elements and Meaning in Black Style* (with Fundi [Billy Abernathy]) (1970); *Spirit Reach* (1972); *Afrikan Revolution* (1973); *Hard Facts* (1976); *Selected Poetry* (1979); *AM/TRAK* (1979); *Reggae or Not!* (1982).
Other:
The Toilet (1962) (d); *Blues People: Negro Music in White America* (1963) (c); *Four Black Revolutionary Plays, All Praises to the Black Man* (1969) (d); *Selected Plays and Prose* (1979) (d,p); *Daggers and Javelins: Essays 1974–1979* (1984) (p); *The Autobiography of LJ / AB* (1984) (a).

JOHN BERRYMAN
Poems (1942); *The Dispossessed* (1948); *Homage to Mistress Bradstreet* (1956); *His Thought Made Pockets & the Plane Buckt* (1958); *Berryman's Sonnets* (1967); *Short Poems* (1967); *I Have Moved to Dublin...* (1967); *The Dream Songs* (1969); *Love and Fame* (1970); *Delusions, Etc.* (1972); *Selected Poems 1938–1968* (1972); *A Dream Song* (1976); *Henry's Fate and Other Poems 1967–1972* (ed. John Haffenden, 1977).
Other:
Stephen Crane (1950) (p).

JOHN BETJEMAN
Collected Poems (1958, 2d ed. 1962, 3d ed. 1970); *A Nip in the Air* (1972); *Metroland: Verses* (1977); *The Best of B* (ed. John Guest, 1978); *Church Poems* (1981); *Uncollected Poems* (1982).

EARL BIRNEY
David and Other Poems (1942); *Now Is Time* (1945); *The Strait of Anian: Selected Poems* (1948); *Trial of a City and Other Verse* (1952); *Ice Cod Bell or Stone* (1962); *Near False Creek Mouth* (1964); *Selected Poems 1940–1966* (1966); *Memory No Servant* (1968); *The Poems of EB* (1969); *Pnomes, Jukollages and Other Stunzas* (ed. B. P. Nichol, 1969); *Rag and Bone Shop* (1971); *Four Parts Sand: Concrete Poems* (with others) (1972); *The Bear on the Delhi Road: Selected Poems* (1973); *What's So Big about Green?* (1973); *The Collected Poems* (ed. John Newlove, 1975); *The Rugging and the Moving Times: Poems New and Uncollected 1976* (1976); *Alphabeings and Other Seasyours* (1976); *Ghost in the Wheels: Selected Poems 1920–1976* (1977); *Fall by Fury and Other Makings* (1978); *The Mammoth Corridors* (1980); *Copernican Fix* (1986).

ELIZABETH BISHOP
The Complete Poems 1927–1979 (1984).
Other:
The Collected Prose (ed. Robert Giroux, 1984).

MICHAEL BLUMENTHAL
Sympathetic Magic (1980); *Laps: A Poem* (1984); *Days We Would Rather Know: Poems* (1984).

ROBERT BLY
Silence in the Snowy Fields (1962, rev. 1967); *The Light Around the Body* (1967); *Chrysanthemums* (1967); *Ducks* (1968, 1972); *The Morning Glory: Another Thing That Will Never Be My Friend: Twelve Prose Poems* (1969); *The Shadow-Mothers* (1970); *The Teeth-Mother Naked at Last* (1970); *Poems for Tennessee* (with William Stafford and William Matthews) (1971); *Water under the Earth* (1972); *Christmas Eve Service at Midnight at St. Michael's* (1972); *Jumping out of Bed* (1972); *Sleepers Joining Hands* (1973); *The Dead Seal near McClure's Beach* (1973); *The Hockey Poem* (1974); *Point Reyes Poems* (1974); *Old Man Rubbing His Eyes* (1975); *The Morning Glory: Prose Poems* (1975); *Leaping Poetry: An Idea with Poems and Translations* (1975); *The Loon* (1977); *This Body Is Made of Camphor and Gopher–*

wood: Prose Poems (1977); *This Tree Will Be Here for a Thousand Years* (1979); *Visiting Emily Dickinson's Grave and Other Poems* (1979); *The Man in the Black Coat Turns* (1981); *Finding an Old Ant Mansion* (1981); *The Eight Stages of Translation* (1983); *Four Ramages* (1983); *Out of the Rolling Ocean* (1984); *Loving a Woman in Two Worlds* (1985); *Selected Poems* (1986).

LOUISE BOGAN
The Blue Estuaries: Poems, 1923–1968 (1977).
Other:
   Selected Criticism: Prose, Poetry (1955) (c); *What the Woman Lived: Selected Letters of Louise Bogan, 1920–1970* (ed. Ruth Limmer, 1973) (p); *Journey Around My Room: The Autobiography of Louise Bogan: A Mosaic* (ed. Ruth Limmer, 1980) (p).

GWENDOLYN BROOKS
A Street in Bronzeville (1945); *Annie Allen* (1949); *Selected Poems* (1963); *In the Time of Detachment, In the Time of Cold* (1965); *In the Mecca* (1968); *For Illinois 1968: A Sesquicentennial Poem* (1968); *Riot* (1969); *The Wall* (n.d.); *Family Pictures* (1970); *The World of GB* (1971) (v,f); *Aloneness* (1972); *Aurora* (1972); *Beckonings* (1975); *To Disembark* (1981).
Other:
   Maud Martha (1953) (f); *Report from Part One: An Autobiography* (1972) (a).

LEWIS CARROLL (Charles Lutwidge Dodgson)
The Complete Writings of Lewis Carroll (1939); *Alice in Wonderland: A Norton Critical Edition* (containing *Alice in Wonderland, Through the Looking Glass,* and *The Hunting of the Snark*) (ed. Donald J. Gray, 1971); *Lewis Carroll Observed: A Collection of Unpublished Photographs, Drawings, Poetry and New Essays* (ed. Edward Guiliano, 1976) (v,p); *The Wasp in a Wig: A "Suppressed" Episode of Through the Looking-Glass and What Alice Found There* (ed. Edward Guiliano, 1977).

AMY CLAMPITT
Multitudes, Multitudes (1974); *The Isthmus* (1982); *The Kingfisher* (1983); *The Summer Solstice* (1983); *A Homage to John Keats* (1984); *What the Light Was Like* (ed. Alice Quinn, 1985); *Archaic Figures* (1987).

HART CRANE
The Poems of HC (ed. Marc Simon, with intro. by John Unterecker, 1986).

ROBERT CREELEY
Le Fou (1952); *The Immoral Proposition* (1953); *The Kind of Act of* (1953); *A Snarling Garland of Xmas Verses* (1954); *All That Is Lovely in Men* (1955); *Ferrini and Others* (with others) (1955); *...If You* (1956); *The Whip* (1957); *A Form of Women* (1959); *For Love: Poems 1950–1960* (1962); *Distance* (1964); *Two Poems* (1964); *Hi There!* (1965); *Words* (1965); *About Women* (1966); *Poems 1950–1965* (1966); *For Joel* (1966); *A Sight* (1966); *Words: Poems* (1967); *RC Reads* (1967); *The Charm: Early and Uncollected Poems* (1967); *The Finger* (1968, rev. 1970); *5 Numbers* (1968); *The Boy* (1968); *Numbers* (1968); *Divisions and Other Early Poems* (1968); *Pieces* (1968); *Hero* (1969); *A Wall* (1969); *Mazatlan: Sea* (1969); *Mary's Fancy* (1970); *In London* (1970); *For Betsy and Tom* (1970); *For Benny and Sabina* (1970); *As Now It Would Be Snow* (1970); *America* (1970); *Christmas: May 10, 1970* (1970); *A Day Book* (1970) (v,p); *St. Martin's* (1971); *Sea* (1971); *1.2.3.4.5.6.7.8.9.0.* (1971); *For the Graduation* (1971); *Change* (1972); *One Day after Another* (1972); *A Day Book* (1972); *For My Mother* (1973); *Kitchen* (1973); *His Idea* (1973); *Sitting Here* (1974); *Thirty Things* (1974); *Backwards* (1975); *Away* (1976); *Hello* (1976); *Selected Poems* (1976); *Myself* (1977); *Thanks* (1977); *The Children* (1978); *Hello: A Journal, February 29–May 3, 1976* (1978); *Later* (1978); *Desultory Days* (1978); *Later: New Poems* (1979); *Corn Close* (1980); *The Collected Poems of RC 1945–1975* (1982); *Echoes* (1982); *A Calendar: Twelve Poems* (1983); *Mirrors* (1983); *Memories* (1984); *Memory Gardens* (1986).
Other:
   The Collected Prose of RC (1984).

COUNTEE CULLEN
Color (1925); *Copper Sun* (1927); *The Ballad of the Brown Girl* (1928); *The Black Christ* (1929); *The Medea and Some Poems* (1935); *On These I Stand* (1947).

Other:
   One Way to Heaven (1932) (f); *St. Louis Woman* (with others) (1946) (d).
E. E. CUMMINGS
   Complete Poems, 1913–1962 (ed. George James Firmage, 1973); *Etcetera: The Unpublished Poems* (ed. George James Firmage and Richard S. Kennedy, 1982). Translations:
      Louis Aragon, *The Red Front* (1933); Jean Cocteau, *Oedipus Rex* (libretto; opera by Stravinsky) (1955).
   Other:
      The Enormous Room (1922) (f); *him* (1927) (d); *EIMI* (1933) (f); *Tom* (1935) (d); *Santa Claus* (1946) (d); *1: Six Nonlectures* (1953) (p); *EEC: A Miscellany Revised* (ed. George J. Firmage, 1965) (p); *America, I Love You* (1965) (d [libretto: music by David Ahlstrom]); *Three Plays and a Ballet* (ed. George J. Firmage, 1967) (d).
JAMES DICKEY
   Into the Stone (1957); *Drowning with Others* (1962); *Helmets* (1964); *Two Poems of the Air* (1964); *Buckdancer's Choice* (1965); *Poems 1957–1967* (1967); *The Achievement of JD: A Comprehensive Selection of His Poems, with a Critical Introduction* (ed. Lawrence Lieberman, 1968); *The Eye-Beaters, Blood, Victory, Madness, Buckhead and Mercy* (1970); *Exchanges: Being in the Form of a Dialogue with Joseph Trumbull Stickney* (1971); *The Zodiac* (1976); *The Strength of Fields* (1977, rev. 1979); *Veteran Birth: The Gadfly Poems 1947–1949* (1978); *Head-Deep in Strange Sounds: Free-Flight Improvisations from the UnEnglish* (1979); *Falling, May Day Sermon, and Other Poems* (1981); *The Early Motion* (1981); *Puella* (1982); *The Central Motion: Poems 1968–1979* (1983); *False Youth: Four Seasons* (1983); *Night Hurdling: Poems, Essays, Conversations, Commencements, and Afterwords* (1983) (v,p); *Intervisions: Poems and Photographs* (with Sharon Anglin Kuhne) (1983).
   Other:
      Deliverance (1972; also *Deliverance: A Screenplay*, ed. Matthew J. Bruccoli, 1981) (d); *Alnilam* (1987) (f).
EMILY DICKINSON
   The Poems of ED (ed. Thomas A. Johnson, 3 vols., 1955); *Complete Poems* (ed. Thomas A. Johnson, 1960).
H.D. (Hilda Doolittle)
   By Avon River (1949); *Helen in Egypt* (1961, 1974); *Two Poems* (1971); *Hermetic Definition* (1972); *Collected Poems 1912–1944* (ed. Louis L. Martz, 1983). Other:
      Tribute to Freud (1956) (a); *The Gift* (1984) (a); *Her* (1984; U.S. ed. *HERmione*) (f).
KEITH DOUGLAS
   Complete Poems (ed. Desmond Graham, 1977).
   Other:
      Alamein to Zem Zem (1966; rev. 1979) (p); *A Prose Miscellany* (1985) (p).
RITA DOVE
   The Yellow House on the Corner (1980); *Museum* (1983); *Thomas and Beulah* (1986). Other:
      Fifth Sunday (ed. Charles H. Rowell, 1985) (f).
NORMAN DUBIE
   The Horsehair Sofa (1969); *Alehouse Sonnets* (1971); *Indian Summer* (1974); *The Prayers of the North American Martyrs* (1975); *Popham of the New Song and Other Poems* (1975); *In the Dead of Night* (1975); *The Illustrations* (1977); *A Thousand Little Things and Other Poems* (1978); *Odalisque in White* (1978); *The City of the Olesha Fruit* (1979); *The Everlastings* (1980); *The Window in the Field* (1981); *Selected and New Poems* (1983); *The Springhouse* (1986).
ROBERT DUNCAN
   Heavenly City, Earthly City (1947); *Poems 1948–1949* (1949); *Medieval Scenes* (1950); *Song of the Borderguard* (1952); *Caesar's Gate* (1955, 1972); *Letters: Poems 1953–1956* (1958); *Selected Poems 1942–1950* (1959); *The Opening of the Field* (1960); *Roots and Branches* (1964); *Writing, Writing: A Composition Book of Madison*

1953, Stein Imitations (1964); *Wine* (1964); *Uprising* (1965); *A Book of Resemblances: Poems 1950–1953* (1966); *Fragments of a Disordered Devotion* (1966); *Of the War: Passages 22–27* (1966); *The Years as Catches: First Poems 1939–41* (1966); *Boob* (1966); *Epilogos* (1967); *The Cat and the Blackbird* (1967); *Christmas Present, Christmas Presence!* (1967); *Bending the Bow* (1968); *My Mother Would Be a Falconess* (1968); *Names of People* (1968); *The First Decade: Selected Poems 1940–1950*, Vol. 1 (1968); *Derivations: Selected Poems, 1950–1956* (1968); *Play Time, Pseudo Stein* (1969); *Achilles' Song* (1969); *Poetic Disturbances* (1970); *Bring It Up from the Dark* (1970); *Tribunals: Passages 31–35* (1970); *In Memoriam Wallace Stevens* (1972); *Poems from the Margins of Thom Gunn's Moly* (1972); *A Seventeenth Century Suite* (1973); *An Ode and Arcadia* (with Jack Spicer) (1974); *Dante* (1974); *The Venice Poem* (1975); *Veil, Turbine, Cord, and Bird* (1979); *The Five Songs* (1981); *Ground Work: Before the War* (1984).

T. S. ELIOT
The Complete Poems and Plays (1952, 1969); *Collected Poems 1909–1962* (1963); *The Waste Land: A Facsimile and Transcript of the Original Drafts including the Annotations of Ezra Pound* (ed. Valerie Eliot, 1971).
Translation:
St.-John Perse, *Anabasis* (1930).
Other:
The Sacred Wood (1920) (c); *For Lancelot Andrewes: Essays on Style and Order* (1928) (c); *Sweeney Agonistes* (1932) (d); *After Strange Gods, A Primer of Modern Heresy* (1934) (p); *Murder in the Cathedral* (1935) (d); *The Family Reunion* (1939) (d); *Notes toward the Definition of Culture* (1948) (p); *The Cocktail Party* (1950, 1974) (d); *The Three Voices of Poetry* (1953) (c); *The Confidential Clerk* (1954) (d); *The Elder Statesman* (1959) (d); *Collected Plays* (1962) (d); *Selected Essays* (1964, 1972) (c,p); *Selected Prose of TSE* (ed. Frank Kermode, 1975) (c,p).

WILLIAM EMPSON
Collected Poems (1955).
Other:
Seven Types of Ambiguity (1930, rev. 1947) (c); *Some Versions of Pastoral* (1935) (c); *The Structure of Complex Words* (1951) (c).

LOUISE ERDRICH
Jacklight (1984).
Other:
Love Medicine (1984) (f); *The Beet Queen* (1986) (f).

WILLIAM EVERSON
These Are the Ravens (1935); *San Joaquin* (1939); *The Masculine Dead* (1942); *X War Elegies* (1943); *The Waldport Poems* (1943); *War Elegies* (1944); *The Residual Years: Poems 1940–1941* (1944; rev. eds. *Poems: 1934–1946*, 1948, and *Poems: 1934–1948*, 1968); *Poems MCMXLII* (1945); *A Privacy of Speech* (1949); *Triptych for the Living* (1951); *At the Edge* (1952, as Brother Antoninus); *A Fragment for the Birth of God* (1958, as BA); *An Age Insurgent* (1959, as BA); *The Crooked Lines of God: Poems 1949–1954* (1959, as BA); *There Will Be Harvest* (1960); *The Year's Declension* (1961); *The Hazards of Holiness* (1962, as BA); *The Poet Is Dead: A Memorial for Robinson Jeffers* (1964, as BA); *The Rose of Solitude* (1964, as BA); *The Blowing of the Seed* (1966); *The Vision of Felicity* (1966, as BA); *Single Source* (1966); *In the Fictive Wish* (1967); *The Rose of Solitude* [collection] (1967, as BA); *The Achievement of BA: A Comprehensive Selection of His Poems with a Critical Introduction* (ed. William Stafford, 1967); *A Canticle to the Waterbirds* (1968, as BA); *The Springing of the Blade* (1968); *The City Does Not Die* (1969, as BA); *The Last Crusade* (1969, as BA); *Who Is She That Looketh Forth as the Morning* (1972, as BA); *Gale at Dawn* (1972); *Tendril in the Mesh* (1973); *Black Hills* (1973); *Man-Fate: The Swan Song of Brother Antoninus* (1974); *River-Root: A Syzygy for the Bicentennial of These States* (1976); *Missa Defunctorum* (1976); *The Mate-Flight of Eagles: Two Poems on the Love-Death of the Cross* (1977); *Blackbird Sundown* (1978); *Rattlesnake August* (1978); *The Veritable Years: Poems 1949–1966* (1978); *Cutting the Firebreak* (1978); *Blame It on the Jet Stream!* (1978); *The Masks of Drought: Poems, 1972–1979* (1980); *Eastward the Armies: Selected Poems 1935–*

1942 That Present the Poet's Pacifist Poisition Through the Second World War (ed. Les Ferriss, 1980); *Cougar* (1982); *Renegade Christmas* (1984); *In Medias Res* (1984).

JAMES FENTON

Our Western Furniture (1968); *Put Thou Thy Tears into My Bottle* (1969); *Terminal Moraine* (1972); *A Vacant Possession* (1978); *Dead Soldiers* (1981); *A German Requiem* (1981); *The Memory of War: Poems 1968–1982* (1982); *Children in Exile* (1983); *The Memory of War and Children in Exile: Poems 1968–83* (1983); U.S. ed. *Children in Exile*, 1984).

ROBERT FROST

Complete Poems (1949); *The Poetry of RF* (1969); *RF: Poetry and Prose* (ed. Edward C. Lathem and Lawrance R. Thompson, 1972).

Other:

Selected Prose of RF (ed. Hyde Cox and Edward C. Lathem, 1966) (p).

ALLEN GINSBERG

Howl and Other Poems (1956); *Siesta in Xbalba and Return to the States* (1956); *Empty Mirror: Early Poems* (1961); *Kaddish and Other Poems, 1958–1960* (1961); *A Strange New Cottage in Berkeley* (1963); *Reality Sandwiches* (1963); *The Change* (1963); *Kral Majales* (1965); *Prose Contribution to Cuban Revolution* (1966); *Wichita Vortex Sutra* (1966); T.V. *Baby Poems* (1967); *Who Be Kind To* (1967); *Wales— A Visitation, July 29, 1967* (1968); *Scrap Leaves, Hasty Scribbles* (1968); *Message 11* (1968); *Ankor-Wat* (1968); *Planet News: 1961–1967* (1968); *Airplane Dreams* (1968); *The Moments Return* (1970); *Notes after an Evening with William Carlos Williams* (1970); *Iron Horse* (1972); *The Gates of Wrath: Rhymed Poems 1948– 1952* (1972); *Open Head* (with *Open Eye* by Lawrence Ferlinghetti) (1972); *New Year Blues* (1972); *Bixby Canyon Ocean Path Word Breeze* (1972); *The Fall of America: Poems of These States, 1965–1971* (1973); (with others) *8 from Naropa* (1974); *Sad Dust Glories* (1975); *First Blues: Rags, Ballads, and Harmonium Songs 1971–1974* (1975); *Mind Breaths: Poems 1972–1977* (1977); *Poems All Over the Place: Mostly 'Seventies* (1978); *Mostly Sitting Haiku* (1978); *Careless Love: Two Rhymes* (1978); *Straight Hearts' Delight: Love Poems and Selected Letters 1947– 1980* (with Peter Orlovsky) (ed. Winston Leyland, 1980); *Plutonian Ode: Poems 1977–1980* (1981); *Collected Poems 1947–1980* (1984); *White Shroud: Poems, 1980– 1985* (1986).

ROBERT GRAVES

Collected Poems 1975 (2 vols., 1975); *New Collected Poems* (1977).

Other:

On English Poetry (1922) (c); *A Survey of Modernist Poetry* (with Laura Riding) (1927) (c); *Goodbye to All That* (1929, rev. 1957, 1981) (a); *I, Claudius . . .* (1934) (f); *Claudius the God and His Wife Messalina . . .* (1934) (f); *The Long Weekend: A Social History of Great Britain, 1918–1939* (with A. Hodge) (1940) (p); *The Golden Fleece* (1944; U.S. ed. *Hercules, My Shipmate*, 1945) (f); *King Jesus* (1946) (f); *The White Goddess* (1947, rev. 1966) (p); *Homer's Daughter* (1955) (f); *They Hanged My Saintly Billy* (1957) (f); *On Poetry: Collected Talks and Essays* (1969) (c).

THOM GUNN

Fighting Terms (1954, rev. 1962); *The Sense of Movement* (1957); *My Sad Captains and Other Poems* (1961); *Selected Poems* (with Ted Hughes) (1962); *A Geography* (1966); *Positives* (with Ander Gunn) (1966); *Touch* (1967); *The Garden of the Gods* (1968); *The Explorers* (1969); *The Fair in the Woods* (1969); *Poems, 1950–1966: A Selection* (1969); *Sunlight* (1969); *Last Days at Teddington* (1971); *Moly* (1971); *Poem after Chaucer* (1971); *Moly, and My Sad Captains* (1971); *Mandrakes* (1973); *Songbook* (1973); *To the Air* (1974); *Jack Straw's Castle* (1975); *Jack Straw's Castle* [collection] (1976); *The Missed Beat* (1976); *Games of Chance* (1979); *Selected Poems 1950–1975* (1979); *Bally Power Play* (1979); *Talbot Road* (1981); *The Menace* (1982); *The Passages of Joy* (1982).

MARILYN HACKER

The Terrible Children (1967); *Highway Sandwiches* (with Thomas M. Disch and Charles Platt) (1970); *Presentation Piece* (1974); *Separations* (1976); *Taking Notice* (1980); *Assumptions* (ed. Nancy Nicholas, 1985); *Love, Death and the Changing of the Seasons* (1986).

THOMAS HARDY

The Complete Poems (ed. James Gibson, 1976); *The Variorum Edition of the Complete Poems* (ed. James Gibson, 1979); *The Complete Poetical Works* (ed. Samuel Hynes, 3 vols., 1982–1985).
Other:
Far from the Madding Crowd (1874) (f); *The Return of the Native* (1878) (f); *The Mayor of Casterbridge* (1886) (f); *Tess of the D'Urbervilles* (1891) (f); *Jude the Obscure* (1896) (f); *The Works of TH in Prose* (18 vols., 1984) (p).

MICHAEL HARPER

Dear John, Dear Coltrane (1970); *History Is Your Own Heartbeat* (1971); *Photographs: Negatives: History as Apple Tree* (1972); *Song: I Want a Witness* (1972); *Debridement* (1973); *Nightmare Begins Responsibility* (1974); *Images of Kin: New and Selected Poems* (1977); *Rhode Island: Eight Poems* (1981); *Spiritual Warfare* (1984); *Healing Song for the Inner Ear* (1984).

TONY HARRISON

Earthworks (1964); *Newcastle Is Peru* (1969); *The Loiners* (1970); *Ten Poems from the School of Eloquence* (1976); *The School of Eloquence and Other Poems* (1978); *Looking Up* (with Philip Sharpe) (1979); *Continuous: 50 Sonnets from the School of Eloquence* (1981); *A Kumquat for John Keats* (1981); *U.S. Martial* (1981); *Selected Poems* (1984); *The Fire-Gap* (1985).
Other:
Theatre Works 1973–1985 (1985) (d [includes *The Misanthrope, The Bartered Bride, Phaedra Britannica, Bow Down,* and *The Big H*]); *The Mysteries* (1986) (d).

ROBERT HAYDEN

Collected Poems (ed. Frederick Glaysher, 1985).
Other:
Collected Prose (ed. Frederich Glaysher, 1984) (c,p).

SEAMUS HEANEY

Eleven Poems (1965); *Death of a Naturalist* (1966); *A Lough Neagh Sequence* (1969); *Door into the Dark* (1969); *Night Drive* (1970); *A Boy Driving His Father to Confession* (1970); *Land* (1971); *Wintering Out* (1973); *North* (1975); *Bog Poems* (1975); *Stations* (1975); *After Summer* (1978); *Hedge School (Sonnets from Glanmore)* (1979); *Field Work* (1979); *Ugolino* (1979); *Selected Poems 1965–1975* (1980); *Poems 1965–1975* (1980); *Poems and a Memoir* (1982); *An Open Letter* (1983); *Sweeney Astray: A Version from the Irish* (1983) (v,p); *Station Island* (1984); *Hailstones* (1984); *The Haw Lantern* (1987).
Other:
Preoccupations: Selected Prose 1968–1978 (1980) (p).

ANTHONY HECHT

A Summoning of Stones (1954); *The Seven Deadly Sins* (1958); *Struwwelpeter* (1958); *A Bestiary* (1962); *Jiggery-Hokery: A Compendium of Double Dactyls* (with John Hollander and others) (1967); *The Hard Hours* (1967); *Aesopic: Twenty-Four Couplets* . . . (1967); *Millions of Strange Shadows* (1977); *The Venetian Vespers* (1979).

GEOFFREY HILL

For the Unfallen: Poems 1952–1958 (1959); *Preghiere* (1964); *King Log* (1968); *Mercian Hymns* (1971); *Somewhere Is Such a Kingdom: Poems 1952–1971* (1975); *Tenebrae* (1978); *The Mystery of the Charity of Charles Peguy* (1983).

A.D. HOPE

The Wandering Islands (1955); *Poems* (1960); *(Poems)* (ed. Douglas Stewart, 1963); *Collected Poems 1930–1965* (1966); *New Poems, 1965–1969* (1970); *Dunciad Minor: An Heroick Poem* (1970); *Collected Poems 1930–1970* (1972); *Selected Poems* (1973); *The Damnation of Byron* (1973); *A Late Picking: Poems 1965–1974* (1975); *A Book of Answers* (1978); *The Drifting Continent and Other Poems* (1979); *Antechinus: Poems 1975–1980* (1981); *The Age of Reason* (1984); *Selected Poems* (ed. Ruth Morse, 1986).

GERARD MANLEY HOPKINS

Poems (ed. Robert Bridges, 1918; 4th rev. ed., ed. W. H. Gardner and Norman H. Mackenzie, 1967); *Poems and Prose* (ed. W. H. Garnder, 1953) (v,p).

Other:
   Note-books and Papers (ed. Humphry House, 1937; 2 vols, 1959); *Sermons and Devotional Writings* (ed. Christopher Devlin, 1959) (p); *Journals and Papers* (ed. Humphry House and Graham Storey, 1959) (p); *Selected Prose* (ed. Gerald Roberts, 1980) (p).
A. E. HOUSMAN
   Collected Poems (1939, rev. 1953); *Complete Poems* (ed. Basil Davenport, 1959, rev. 1971).
Other:
   Selected Prose (ed. John Carter, 1961) (c); *The Classical Papers of AEH* (ed. J. Diggle and F. R. D. Goodyear, 1972) (c,p).
LANGSTON HUGHES
   The Weary Blues (1926); *Fine Clothes to the Jew* (1927); *Dear Lovely Death* (1931); *The Negro Mother and Other Dramatic Recitations* (1931); *The Dream Keeper and Other Poems* (1932); *Scottsboro Limited* (1932) (v,d); *A New Song* (1938); *Shakespeare in Harlem* (1942); *Jim Crow's Last Stand* (1943); *Lament for Dark Peoples and Other Poems* (1944); *Fields of Wonder* (1947); *One-Way Ticket* (1949); *Montage of a Dream Deferred* (1951); *The LH Reader* (1958, 1966) (v,f,d,p); *Selected Poems* (1959, rev. 1965); *Ask Your Mama: 12 Moods for Jazz* (1961); *The Panther and the Lash: Poems of Our Times* (1967); *Don't You Turn Back* (ed. Lee Bennett Hopkins, 1969).
TED HUGHES
   The Hawk in the Rain (1957); *Pike* (1959); *Lupercal* (1960); *Selected Poems* (with Thom Gunn) (1962); *The Burning of the Brothel* (1966); *Wodwo* (1967); *Recklings* (1967); *Scapegoats and Rabies* (1967); *Animal Poems* (1967); *Gravestones* (1967; as *Poems*, 1968); *I Said Goodbye to Earth* (1969); *A Crow Hymn* (1970); *The Martyrdom of Bishop Farrar* (1970); *A Few Crows* (1970); *Four Crow Poems* (1970); *Crow: From the Life and Songs of the Crow* (1970); *Fighting for Jerusalem* (1970); *Amulet* (1970); *Crow Wakes* (1971); *Poems* (with others) (1971); *In the Little Girl's Angel Gaze* (1972); *Selected Poems 1957–1967* (1972); *Prometheus on His Crag: 21 Poems* (1973); *The Interrogator: A Titled Vultures* (1975); *Cave Birds* (1975; rev. ed. *Cave Birds: An Alchemical Cave Drama*, 1978); *The New World* (1975); *Eclipse* (1976); *Gaudete* (1977); *Chiasmadon* (1977); *Sunstruck* (1977); *A Solstice* (1978); *Orts* (1978); *Moortown Elegies* (1978); *Adam and the Sacred Nine* (1979); *Remains of Elmet: A Pennine Sequence* (1979); *Night-Arrival of Sea Trout, The Iron Wolf, Puma, Brooktrout, Pan, Woodpecker, Wolverine, Eagle, Mosquito, Tapir's Saga* [broadsides] (1979–80); *Four Tales Told by an Idiot* (1979); *Moortown* (1979); *Selected Poems 1957–1981* (1982; U.S. ed. *New Selected Poems*, 1982); *River* (1983); *Flowers and Insects: Some Birds and a Pair of Spiders* (1986).
RICHARD HUGO
   Selected Poems (1979); *Making Certain It Goes On: The Collected Poems of RH* (1984).
Other:
   The Triggering Town: Lectures and Essays on Poetry and Writing (1979) (c); *Death and the Good Life* (1981) (f); *The Real West Marginal Way: A Poet's Autobiography* (ed. Ripley S. Hugo, Lois M. Welch, and James Welch, 1986) (a).
RANDALL JARRELL
   Complete Poems (1969).
Other:
   Poetry and the Age (1953) (c); *Pictures from an Institution* (1954) (f); *Poets, Critics, and Readers* (1959) (c); *A Sad Heart at the Supermarket* (1962) (c); *The Third Book of Criticism* (1969) (c); *Kipling, Auden & Co.: Essays and Reviews 1935–1964* (1980) (c).
ROBINSON JEFFERS
   Flagons and Apples (1912); *Californians* (1916, 1971); *Tamar and Other Poems* (1924); *Roan Stallion* (1925); *The Women at Point Sur* (1927, 1977); *Poems* (1928); *Cawdor and Other Poems* (1928); *Dear Judas and Other Poems* (1929, 1977); *Descent to the Dead: Poems Written in Ireland and Great Britain* (1931); *Thurso's Landing* (1932); *Give Your Heart to the Hawks and Other Poems* (1933); *Solstice and Other*

Poems (1935); *Such Counsels You Gave to Me and Other Poems* (1937); *Poems Known and Unknown* (1938); *Selected Poetry* (1938); *Be Angry at the Sun* (1941); *The Double Axe and Other Poems* (1948; rev. with subtitle *Including Eleven Suppressed Poems,* 1977); *Hungerfield and Other Poems* (1954); *The Beginning and the End* (1963); *Selected Poems* (1965); *J Country: The Seed Plots of RJ's Poetry* (1971); *Tragedy Has Obligations* (1973); *The Alpine Christ and Other Poems* (ed. William Everson, 1973); *Brides of the South Wind: Poems 1917–1922* (ed. William Everson, 1974); *Granite and Cypress: Rubbings from the Rock . . .* (1975); *The Desert* (1976); *"What Odd Expedients" and Other Poems* (ed. Robert Ian Scott, 1980).
Translation:
 Euripides, *Medea* (1946) (d).

JUNE JORDAN
 Some Changes (1971); *Poem: On Moral Leadership as a Political Dilemma (Watergate, 1973)* (1973); *New Days: Poems of Exile and Return* (1974); *Things I Do in the Dark: Selected Poetry* (1977, rev. 1981); *Passion: New Poems 1977–80* (1980); *Living Room: New Poems* (1985).

PATRICK KAVANAGH
 Complete Poems (1972).

GALWAY KINNELL
 What a Kingdom It Was (1960); *Flower Herding on Mount Monadnock* (1964); *Poems of Night* (1968); *Body Rags* (1968); *Far Behind Me on the Trail* (1969); *The Hen Flower* (1970); *First Poems 1946–1954* (1970); *The Book of Nightmares* (1971); *The Shoes of Wandering* (1971); *The Avenue Bearing the Initial of Christ into the New World: Poems 1946–1964* (1974); *Three Poems* (1976); *Brother of My Heart* (1977); *Fergus Falling* (1979); *There Are Things I Tell No One* (1979); *Two Poems* (1979); *Mortal Acts, Mortal Words* (1980); *The Last Hiding Places of Snow* (1980); *Angling, A Day, and Other Poems* (1980); *Selected Poems* (1982); *The Fundamental Project of Technology* (1983); *The Past* (1985).

RUDYARD KIPLING
 RK's Verse: Definitive Edition (1940); *Early Verse by RK, 1879–1889: Unpublished, Uncollected, and Rarely Collected Poems* (ed. Andrew Rutherford, 1986).
Other:
 Soldiers Three, and Other Stories (1880) (f); *Plain Tales from the Hills* (1888) (f); *The Phantom Rickshaw* (1889) (f); *Wee Willie Winkie, and Other Stories* (1889) (f); *The Light That Failed* (1890) (f); *Life's Handicap, Being Stories of Mine Own People* (1891) (f); *Many Inventions* (1893) (f); *The Jungle Book* (1894) (f); *The Second Jungle Book* (1895) (f); *The Seven Seas* (1896) (f); *Captains Courageous* (1897) (f); *The Day's Work* (1898) (f); *Kim* (1901) (f); *The Five Nations* (1903) (f); *Traffics and Discoveries* (1904) (f); *Actions and Reactions* (1909) (f); *Rewards and Fairies* (1909) (f); *A Diversity of Creatures* (1917) (f); *Something of Myself* (1937) (a).

A. M. KLEIN
 Collected Poems (ed. Miriam Waddington, 1974).
Other:
 The Second Scroll (1951) (f); *Beyond Sambation: Selected Essays and Editorials, 1928–1955* (ed. M. W. Steinberg and Usher Caplan, 1982) (p); *Short Stories* (ed. M. W. Steinberg, 1983) (f).

MAXINE KUMIN
 Halfway (1961); *The Privilege* (1965); *The Nightmare Factory* (1970); *Up Country: Poems of New England, New and Selected* (1972); *House, Bridge, Fountain, Gate* (1975); *The Retrieval System* (1978); *Our Ground Time Here Will Be Grief* (1982); *Closing the Ring* (ed. John Wheatcroft, 1984); *The Long Approach* (1985).

STANLEY KUNITZ
 Intellectual Things (1930); *Passport to the War* (1944); *Selected Poems 1928–1958* (1958); *The Testing-Tree* (1971); *The Terrible Threshold: Selected Poems 1940–1970* (1974); *The Coat Without a Seam: Sixty Poems 1930–1972* (1974); *The Lincoln Relics* (1978); *The Poems of SK 1928–1978* (1979); *The Wellfleet Whale and Companion Poems* (1983).

Translations:
Andrei Voznesensky, *Antiworlds* (with others) (1967); *Poems of Anna Akhmatova* (with Max Hayward) (1970); Yevgeny Yevtushenko, *Stolen Apples* (with others) (1972); Anna Akhmatova, *Poems* (with Max Hayward) (1973); Andrei Voznesensky, *Story under Full Sail* (with others) (1974); Ivan Drach, *Orchard Lamps* (with others) (1978).

PHILIP LARKIN
The North Ship (1945, rev. 1966); *XX poems* (1951); *Poems* (1954); *The Less Deceived* (1955); *The Whitsun Weddings* (1964); *The Explosion* (1970); *High Windows* (1974); *Femmes Damnées* (1978); *Aubade* (1980).
Other:
All That Jazz: A Record Diary 1961–68 (1970) (c); *Required Writing: Miscellaneous Pieces 1955–1982* (1983) (p,c).

D. H. LAWRENCE
Complete Poems (3 vols., 1957; rev. ed. by Vivian de Sola Pinto and F. Warren Roberts, 1972).
Other:
Sons and Lovers (1931) (f); *The Prussian Officer* (1914) (f); *The Rainbow* (1915) (f); *Women in Love* (1920) (f); *Aaron's Rod* (1922) (f); *Kangaroo* (1923) (f); *Studies in Classic American Literature* (1923) (c); *The Plumed Serpent* (1926) (f); *Lady Chatterley's Lover* (1928; rev. ed. *John Thomas and Lady Jane: The Hitherto Unpublished Second Version of Lady Chatterley's Lover*, (1972) (f); *The Woman Who Rode Away* (1928) (f); *The Virgin and the Gypsy* (1930) (f); *Selected Literary Criticism* (1955) (c); *Complete Short Stories* (3 vols., 1955) (f); *The Short Novels* (2 vols., 1956) (f); *Complete Plays* (1966) (d).

IRVING LAYTON
Here and Now (1945); *Now Is the Place: Poems and Stories* (1948); *The Black Huntsman* (1951); *Cerberus* (with others) (1952); *Love the Conqueror Worm* (1953); *The Long Pea-Shooter* (1954); *In the Midst of My Fever* (1954); *The Cold Green Element* (1955); *The Blue Propeller* (1955); *The Bull Calf and Other Poems* (1956); *Music on a Kazoo* (1956); *The Improved Binoculars: Selected Poems* (1956, rev. 1957); *A Laughter in the Mind* (1958, rev. 1959); *A Red Carpet for the Sun: Collected Poems* (1959); *The Swinging Flesh* (1961); *Balls for a One-Armed Juggler* (1963); *The Laughing Rooster* (1964); *Collected Poems* (1965); *Periods of the Moon* (1967); *The Shattered Plinths* (1968); *The Whole Bloody Bird (obs, aphs, and pomes)* (1969); *Collected Poems* (1971); *Nail Polish* (1971); *Lovers and Lesser Men* (1973); *The Pole-Vaulter* (1974); *Seventy-five Greek Poems 1951–1974* (1974); *Selected Poems: The Darkening Fire 1945–1968, The Unwavering Eye 1969–1975* (2 vols., 1975); *New Holes in the Wall* (1975); *For My Brother Jesus* (1976); *Uncollected Poems 1936–59* (ed. W. David John, 1976); *The Covenant* (1977); *The Tightrope Dancer* (1978); *Droppings from Heaven* (1979); *There Were No Signs* (1979); *The Love Poems* (1979); *For My Neighbors in Hell* (1980); *Europe and Other Bad News* (1981); *A Wild Peculiar Joy: Selected Poems, 1945–82* (1982); *The Gucci Bag* (1983); *The Reverence and Delight: The Love Poems* (1984); *A Spider Danced a Cozy Jig* (1984).

DENISE LEVERTOV
The Double Image (1946); *Here and Now* (1956); *5 Poems* (1958); *Overland to the Islands* (1958); *With Eyes at the Back of Our Heads* (1960); *The Jacob's Ladder* (1961); *O Taste and See* (1964); *City Psalm* (1964); *Psalm Concerning the Castle* (1964); *The Sorrow Dance* (1967); *A Tree Telling of Orpheus* (1968); *A Marigold from North Viet Nam* (1968); *Three Poems* (1968); *The Cold Spring and Other Poems* (1968); *Embroideries* (1969); *Summer Poems 1969* (1970); *Relearning the Alphabet* (1970); *A New Year's Garland for My Students, MIT 1969–1970* (1970); *To Stay Alive* (1971); *Footprints* (1972); *The Freeing of the Dust* (1975); *Chekhov on the West Heath* (1977); *Modulations for Solo Voice* (1977); *Life in the Forest* (1978); *Collected Earlier Poems 1940–1960* (1979); *Pig Dreams: Scenes from the Life of Sylvia* (1981); *Wanderer's Daysong* (1981); *A Mass for the Day of St. Thomas Didymus* (1982); *Candles in Babylon* (1982); *Poems 1960–1967* (1983); *Oblique Prayers* (1984); *El Salvador—Requiem and Invocation* (1984); *The Menaced World* (1984); *Breathing the Water* (1987).

PHILIP LEVINE

On the Edge (1963); *Silent in America: Vivas for Those Who Failed* (1965); *Not This Pig* (1968); *5 Detroits* (1970); *Thistles* (1970); *Pili's Wall* (1971); *Red Dust* (1971); *They Feed They Lion* (1972); *1933* (1974); *New Season* (1975); *On the Edge and Over: Poems Old, Lost, and New* (1976); *The Names of the Lost* (1976); *7 Years from Somewhere* (1979); *Ashes: Poems New and Old* (1979); *One for the Rose* (1981); *Selected Poems* (1984); *Sweet Will* (1985); *A Walk with Tom Jefferson: Poems* (1988). Other:
> *Don't Ask* (1981) (c).

AUDRE LORDE

The First Cities (1968); *Cables to Rage* (1970); *From a Land Where Other People Live* (1973); *New York Head Shop and Museum* (1975); *Between Our Selves* (1976); *Coal* (1976); *The Black Unicorn* (1978); *Chosen Poems, Old and New* (1982); *Our Dead Behind Us* (1986). Other:
> *Uses of the Erotic: The Erotic as Power* (1978) (p); *The Cancer Journals* (1980) (p); *Zami: A New Spelling of My Name* (1982) (p); *Sister Outsider: Essays and Speeches* (1984) (p).

ROBERT LOWELL

Land of Unlikeness (1944); *Lord Weary's Castle* (1946, rev. 1947); *Poems, 1938–1949* (1950); *The Mills of the Kavanaughs* (1951); *Life Studies* (1959); *Imitations* (1961, 1984); *For the Union Dead* (1964); *Selected Poems* (1965); *The Achievement of RL: A Comprehensive Selection of His Poems with a Critical Introduction* (ed. William J. Martz, 1966); *Near the Ocean* (1967); *Notebook 1967–68* (1969; 3d rev. ed. *Notebook*, 1970); *4 by RL* (1969); *The Dolphin* (1973); *For Lizzie and Harriet* (1973); *History* (1973); *Poems: A Selection* (ed. Jonathan Raban, 1974); *Selected Poems* (1976); *Day by Day* (1977). Translations and Imitations:
> Eugenio Montale, *Poésie* (1960); Jean Racine, *Phaedra* (1961); *The Voyage and Other Versions of Poems by Baudelaire* (1968); Aeschylus, *Prometheus Bound* (1969); Aeschylus, *The Oresteia* (1978). Other:
> *The Old Glory* (1965) (d); *Collected Prose* (ed. Robert Giroux, 1987) (p,c).

CLAUDE MC KAY

The Passion of CM: Selected Poetry and Prose, 1912–1948 (ed. Wayne F. Cooper, 1973) (v,p).

LOUIS MAC NEICE

Collected Poems (1966). Translations:
> Aeschylus, *Agamemnon* (1936) (d); Goethe, *Faust* (with E. L. Stahl) (1951) (d).

EDGAR LEE MASTERS

A Book of Verses (1898); *The Blood of the Prophets* (1905); *Songs and Sonnets* (1910); *Spoon River Anthology* (1915); *Songs and Satires* (1916); *The Great Valley* (1916); *Toward the Gulf* (1918); *Starved Rock* (1919); *Domesday Book* (1920); *The New Spoon River* (1924); *Selected Poems* (1925); *Lee* (1926); *Jack Kelso* (1928); *The Fate of the Jury: An Epilogue to "Domesday Book"* (1929); *Lichee Nuts* (1930); *Godbey* (1931); *The Serpent in the Wilderness* (1933); *Invisible Landscapes* (1935); *The Golden Fleece of California* (1936); *Poems of People* (1936); *The New World* (1937); *More People* (1939); *Illinois Poems* (1941); *The Sangamon* (1942).

WILLIAM MEREDITH

Love Letter from an Impossible Land (1944); *Ships and Other Figures* (1948); *The Open Sea and Other Poems* (1958); *The Wreck of the Thresher and Other Poems* (1964); *Winter Verse* (1964); *Earth Walk: New and Selected Poems* (1970); *Hazard, the Painter* (1975); *The Cheer* (1980).

W. S. MERWIN

A Mask for Janus (1952); *The Dancing Bears* (1954); *Green with Beasts* (1956); *The Drunk in the Furnace* (1960); *The Moving Target* (1963); *The Lice* (1967); *Three Poems* (1968); *Animae* (1969); *The Carrier of Ladders* (1970); *Signs: A Poem* (1971); *Writings to an Unfinished Accompaniment* (1974); *The First Four Books of Poems* (1975); *Three Poems* (1975); *The Compass Flower* (1977); *Feathers from the Hill*

(1978); *Finding the Islands* (1982); *Opening the Hand* (1983); *The Rain in the Trees: Poems* (1988).
Translations:
Lope de Rueda, *Eufemia* (1958); *The Poem of the Cid* (1959); *The Satires of Persius* (1961); *The Life of Lazarillo de Tormes: His Fortunes and Adversities* (1962); *The Song of Roland* (1963); Federico Garcia Lorca, *Yerma* (1966); *Selected Translations, 1948–1968* (1968); Pablo Neruda, *Twenty Love Poems and a Song of Despair* (1969); Pablo Neruda, *Selected Poems: A Bilingual Edition* (ed. Nathaniel Tarn, 1969); *Chinese Figures: Second Series* (1971); *Japanese Figures* (1971); *Asian Figures* (1973); *Selected Poems of Osip Mandelstam* (with Clarence Brown) (1974); *Sanskrit Love Poetry* (with J. Moussaieff Masson) (1977; as *The Peacock's Egg: Love Poems from Ancient India*, 1981); Euripides, *Iphigenia at Aulis* (with George E. Dimock, Jr., 1978); *Selected Translations 1968–1978* (1979); *From the Spanish Morning* (1984); *Four French Plays* (1985).

JOSEPHINE MILES
Lines at Intersections (1939); *Poems on Several Occasions* (1941); *Local Measures* (1946); *After This Sea* (1947); *Prefabrications* (1957); *Poems 1930–1960* (1960); *Civil Poems* (1966); *Bent* (1967); *Kinds of Affection* (1967); *Fields of Learning* (1968); *Saving the Bay* (1969); *American Poems* (1970); *To All Appearances: Poems New and Selected* (1974); *Coming to Terms* (1979); *Collected Poems 1930–1983* (1983).

EDNA ST. VINCENT MILLAY
Collected Poems (ed. Norma Millay, 1956).

MARIANNE MOORE
Poems (1921); *Marriage* (1923); *Observations* (1924); *Selected Poems* (1935); *The Pangolin* (1936); *What Are Years?* (1941); *Nevertheless* (1944); *A Face* (1949); *Collected Poems* (1951); *Like a Bulwark* (1956); *O To Be a Dragon* (1959); *A MM Reader* (1961) (v,p); *The Arctic Ox* (1964); *Tell Me, Tell Me: Granite, Steel, and Other Topics* (1966); *Complete Poems* (1967, 1982).
Translations:
Jean de La Fontaine, *Fables* (1954); Adalbert Stifter, *Rock Crystal: A Christmas Tale* (1954); various, *Selected Fables* (1955).
Other:
Collected Prose (ed. Patricia C. Willis, 1986) (p,c).

EDWIN MUIR
Collected Poems (1960, rev. 1965); *Selected Poems* (1965).
Translations:
Franz Kafka, *The Castle* (with Willa Muir) (1930); *Selected Short Stories of Franz Kafka* (with WM) (1936); Kafka, *The Trial* (with WM) (1937).

PAUL MULDOON
Knowing My Place (1971); *New Weather* (1973); *Spirit of Dawn* (1975); *Mules* (1977); *Names and Addresses* (1978); *Why Brownlee Left* (1980); *Immram* (1980); *Quoof* (1983); *The Wishbone* (1984); *Mules and Earlier Poems* (1986).

HOWARD NEMEROV
The Image and the Law (1947); *Guide to the Ruins* (1950); *The Salt Garden* (1955); *Mirrors and Windows* (1958); *New and Selected Poems* (1960); *The Next Room of the Dream: Poems and Two Plays* (1962); *Departure of the Ships* (1966); *Dangers of Reasoning by Analogy* (1966); *The Blue Swallows* (1967); *A Sequence of Seven* (1967); *The Winter Lightning: Selected Poems* (1968); *The Painter Dreaming in the Scholar's House* (1968); *Gnomes and Occasions* (1972); *The Western Approaches: Poems 1973–1975* (1975); *The Collected Poems of HN* (1977); *By Al Lebowitz's Pool* (1979); *Sentences* (1980); *Inside the Onion* (1984); *War Stories* (1987).

FRANK O'HARA
Collected Poems (ed. Donald Allen, 1971); *Early Poems 1946–1951* (ed. Donald Allen, 1976); *Poems Retrieved 1951–1966* (ed. Donald Allen, 1977).

CHARLES OLSON
Selected Writings (ed. Robert Creeley, 1966) (v,p); *Archaeologist of Morning: The Collected Poems Outside the Maximus Series* (1971); *The Maximus Poems* (ed. George F. Butterick, 1983).

MICHAEL ONDAATJE
The Dainty Monsters (1967); *The Man with Seven Toes* (1969); *The Collected Works of Billy the Kid: Left Handed Poems* (1970); *Rat Jelly* (1973); *Elimination Dance* (1978, rev. 1980); *There's a Trick with a Knife I'm Learning to Do: Poems 1963–1978* (1979); as *Rat Jelly and Other Poems 1963–1978* (1980); *Secular Love* (1984). Other:
> *The Collected Works of Billy the Kid* (1973) (d); *Coming through Slaughter* (1976) (f); *Running in the Family* (1982) (a); *Tin Roof* (1982) (p); *In the Skin of a Lion* (1987) (f).

WILFRED OWEN
The Complete Poems and Fragments of WO (ed. Jon Stallworthy, 2 vols., 1983); *The Poems of WO* (ed. JS, 1985).

P. K. PAGE
Unit of Five (with others, ed. Ronald Hambleton) (1944); *As Ten as Twenty* (1946); *The Metal and the Flower* (1954); *Cry Ararat! Poems New and Selected* (1967); *Poems, Selected and New* (1974); *Five Poems* (1980); *Evening Dance of the Grey Flies* (1981); *The Glass Air: Selected Poems* (1985). Other:
> *The Sun and the Moon, and Other Fictions* (1973) (f).

ROBERT PINSKY
Sadness and Happiness (1975); *An Explanation of America* (1979); *History of My Heart* (1984). Other:
> *The Situation of Poetry: Contemporary Poetry and Its Traditions* (1976) (c); *Mindwheel* (1987) (computer novel).

SYLVIA PLATH
The Collected Poems (ed. Ted Hughes, 1981); *Selected Poems* (ed. Ted Hughes, 1985). Other:
> *The Bell Jar* (as Victoria Lucas, 1963; as SP, 1966) (f); *Johnny Panic and the Bible of Dreams, and Other Prose Writings* (ed. Ted Hughes, 1977) (p).

EZRA POUND
Personae: Collected Poems (1926, rev. 1949); *Collected Shorter Poems* (1968); *The Cantos of EP* (1971); *Collected Early Poems* (ed. Michael John King, 1976). Translations:
> *Sonnets and Ballate of Guido Cavalcanti* (1912); *Cathay: Translations* (1915); *Certain Noble Plays of Japan* (with Ernest Fenellosa) (1916); Confucius, *The Unwobbling Pivot and The Great Digest* (1947); *The Confucian Analects* (1951); *Translations* (1953); *Shih-Ching: The Classic Anthology Defined by Confucius* (1954); Sophocles, *Women of Trachis* (1956) (d); *Rimbaud* (1957); *Love Poems of Ancient Egypt* (with Noel Stock) (1962); *EP's Cavalcanti Poems* (1966); *The Translations of EP* (ed. Hugh Kenner, 1970); Peire Bremon, *From Syria: The Worksheets, Proofs, and Text* (ed. Robin Skelton, 1981); *P's Cavalcanti: An Edition of the Translations, Notes, and Essays* (ed. David Anderson, 1983).

AL PURDY
The Enchanted Echo (1944); *Pressed on Sand* (1955); *Emu, Remember!* (1956); *The Crafte So Longe to Lerne* (1959); *Poems for All the Annettes* (1962, 1968); *The Old Woman and the Mayflowers* (1962); *The Blur in Between* (1963); *The Cariboo Horses* (1965); *North of Summer: Poems from Baffin Island* (1967); *Wild Grape Wine* (1968); *Spring Song* (1968); *The Winemaker's Beat-étude* (1968); *Interruption* (n.d.); *Love in a Burning Building* (1970); *The Quest for Ouzo* (1970); *Poems for Voices* (with others, 1970); *Selected Poems* (1972); *Hiroshima Poems* (1972); *On the Bearpaw Sea* (1972); *Sex and Death* (1973); *Scott Hutcheson's Boat* (1973); *In Search of Owen Roblin* (1974); *Sundance at Dusk* (1976); *The Poems of AP* (1976); *At Marsport Drugstore* (1977); *A Handful of Earth* (1977); *No Second Spring* (1977); *Moths in the Iron Curtain* (1977); *Being Alive: Poems 1958–78* (1978); *The Stone Bird* (1981); *Birdwatching at the Equator: The Galapagos Islands Poems* (1982); *Bursting into Song* (1982); *Piling Blood* (1984); *Collected Poems* (ed. Russell Brown, 1986).

CRAIG RAINE
The Union, Memory (1978); A Martian Sends a Postcard Home (1979); A Journey to Greece (1979); A Free Translation (1981); Rich (1984).

DUDLEY RANDALL
Ballad of Birmingham (1965); Dressed All in Pink (1965); Booker T. and W.E.B. (1966); Poem, Counterpoem (with Margaret Danner) (1966); Cities Burning (1966); On Getting a Natural (1969); Love You (1971); More to Remember: Poems of Four Decades (1971); Green Apples. (1972); After the Killing (1973); A Litany of Friends: Poems Selected and New (1981, rev. 1983).
Other:
   Broadside Memories: Poets I Have Known (1975) (p).

JOHN CROWE RANSOM
Chills and Fever (1914); Poems About God (1919); Grace After Meat (1924); Two Gentlemen in Bonds (1927); Selected Poems (1945, rev. 1963, 1969); Poems and Essays (1955).
Other:
   The New Criticism (1941) (c); Beating the Bushes: Selected Essays 1941–1970 (1972) (c).

ADRIENNE RICH
A Change of World (1951); The Diamond Cutters (1955); Snapshots of a Daughter-in-Law (1963, rev. 1967); Necessities of Life (1966); Selected Poems (1967); Leaflets (1969); The Will to Change (1971); Diving into the Wreck (1973); Poems Selected and New 1950–1974 (1975); Twenty-One Love Poems (1976); The Dream of a Common Language: Poems 1974–1977 (1978); A Wild Patience Has Taken Me This Far: Poems 1978–1981 (1981); Sources (1983); The Fact of a Doorframe: Poems Selected and New 1950–1984 (1984); Your Native Land, Your Life (1986).
Other:
   Of Woman Born: Motherhood as Experience and Institution (1976, Tenth Anniversary Edition 1986); (p); On Lies, Secrets, and Silence: Selected Prose 1966–1978 (1979) (p); Blood, Bread, and Poetry: Selected Prose 1979–1985 (1986) (p).

ALBERTO RÍOS
Whispering to Fool the Wind (1982); Five Indiscretions (1985).
Other:
   The Iguana Killer: Twelve Stories of the Heart (1984) (f).

EDWIN ARLINGTON ROBINSON
Collected Poems (1937); Uncollected Poetry and Prose (ed. Richard Cary, 1975) (v,p).

THEODORE ROETHKE
Collected Poems (1966); Selected Poems (ed. Beatrice Roethke, 1969).
Other:
   On the Poet and His Craft: Selected Prose (1966) (c); Straw for the Fire: From the Notebooks of TR, 1943–1963 (ed. David Wagoner, 1972).

ISAAC ROSENBERG
Collected Works (ed. Ian Parsons, 1979).

CARL SANDBURG
Complete Poems (1950, rev. 1970).
Other:
   Abraham Lincoln, the Prairie Years (2 vols., 1926) (p); Abraham Lincoln, the War Years (4 vols., 1939) (p); Remembrance Rock (1950) (f); Always the Young Strangers (1953) (a); Abraham Lincoln (1 vol. abridged ed., 1954) (p); Ever the Winds of Chance (ed. Margaret Sandburg and George Hendrick) (1983) (a).

SIEGFRIED SASSOON
Collected Poems 1908–1956 (1961); The War Poems of SS (ed. Rupert Hart-Davis, 1983).
Other:
   Memoirs of a Fox-Hunting Man (1928) (f); Memoirs of an Infantry Officer (1930) (f).

ANNE SEXTON
The Complete Poems (1981).

LESLIE MARMON SILKO
Laguna Woman (1974).
Other:
   Ceremony (1977) (f); *Storyteller* (1981) (f).

DAVE SMITH
   Bull Island (1970); *Mean Rufus Throw Down* (1973); *The Fisherman's Whore* (1974); *Drunks* (1974); *Cumberland Station* (1976); *In Dark, Sudden with Light* (1977); *Goshawk, Antelope* (1979); *Dream Flights* (1981); *Blue Spruce* (1981); *Homage to Edgar Allen Poe* (1981); *In the House of the Judge* (1983); *Gray Soldiers* (1983); *The Roundhouse Voices: Selected and New Poems* (1985).

STEVIE SMITH
   Collected Poems (1976); *Me Again: The Uncollected Writings* (ed. Jack Barbera and William McBrien, 1981).
Other:
   Novel on Yellow Paper (1936) (f); *Over the Frontier* (1938) (f); *The Holiday* (1949) (f).

GARY SNYDER
   Riprap (1959); *Myths and Texts* (1960, 1978); *Hop, Skip, and Jump* (1964); *Nanao Knows* (1964); *The Firing* (1964); *Across Lamarack Col* (1964); *Riprap, and Cold Mountain Poems* (1965); *Six Sections of Mountains and Rivers Without End* (1965; rev. as *Six Sections of Mountains and Rivers without End plus One*, 1970); *Dear Mr. President* (1965); *Three Worlds, Three Realms, Six Roads* (1966); *A Range of Poems* (1966); *The Back Country* (1968); *The Blue Sky* (1969); *Sours of the Hills* (1969); *Regarding Wave* (1969, rev. 1970); *Anasazi* (1971); *Manzanita* (1971); *Clear Cut* (n.d.); *Manzanita* [collection] (1972); *The Fudo Trilogy: Spell Against Demons, Smokey the Bear Sutra, The California Water Plan* (1973); *Turtle Island* (1974); *All in the Family* (1975); *True Night* (1980); *Axe Handles* (1983).

CATHY SONG
   Picture Bride (1983); *Frameless Windows, Squares of Light* (1988).

GARY SOTO
   Entrance: Four Chicano Poets (with others, ed. by GS) (1976); *The Elements of San Joaquin* (1977); *The Tale of Sunlight* (1978); *Father Is a Pillow Tied to a Broom* (1980); *Como Arbustos de Niebla* [English and Spanish] (1980); *Where Sparrows Work Hard* (1981); *Black Hair* (1985); *Small Faces* (1986).
Other:
   Living Up the Street, Narrative Recollections (1985) (a).

WILLIAM STAFFORD
   Poems (1959?); *West of Your City* (1960); *Traveling through the Dark* (1962); *The Rescued Year* (1966); *Eleven Untitled Poems* (1968); *Weather* (1969); *Allegiances* (1970); *Temporary Facts* (1970); *Poems for Tennessee* (with others) (1971); *Someday, Maybe* (1973); *That Other Alone* (1973); *In the Clock of Reason* (1973); *Going Places* (1974); *Late, Passing Prairie Farm* (1976); *Braided Apart* (with Kim Robert Stafford) (1976); *Stories That Could Be True: New and Collected Poems* (1977); *The Design on the Oriole* (1977); *Two about Music* (1978); *All about Light* (1978); *Passing a Crèche* (1978); *Tuft by Puff* (1978); *Around You, Your House: and a Catechism* (1979); *The Quiet of the Land* (1979); *Absolution* (1980); *Things That Happen When There Aren't Any People* (1980); *Wyoming Circuit* (1980); *Sometimes Like a Legend* (1981); *A Glass Face in the Rain: New Poems* (1982); *Roving across Fields: A Conversation and Uncollected Poems 1942–1982* (ed. Thom Tammaro, 1983); *Smoke's Way: Poems from Limited Editions (1968–1981)* (1983); *Seques: A Correspondence in Poetry* (with Marvin Bell) (1983); *Listening Deep* (1984); *Stories, Storms, and Strangers* (1984); *Wyoming* (1985).

JON STALLWORTHY
   The Earthly Paradise (1958); *The Astronomy of Love* (1961); *Out of Bounds* (1963); *The Almond Tree* (1967); *A Day in the City* (1967); *Root and Branch* (1969); *Positives* (1969); *A Dinner of Herbs* (1970); *Hand in Hand* (1974); *The Apple Barrel: Selected Poems 1956–1963* (1974); *A Familiar Tree* (1978); *The Anzac Sonata: New and Selected Poems* (1987).
Translations:
   Five Centuries of Polish Poetry (with Jerzy Peterkiewicz) (rev. 1970); Alexander

Blok, *The Twelve and Other Poems* (with Peter France) (1970; as *Selected Poems*, 1974); Boris Pasternak, *Selected Poems* (with Peter France) (1983).
Other:
  Between the Lines: W. B. Yeats's Poetry in the Making (1963) (c); *Vision and Revision in Yeats's "Last Poems"* (1969) (c); *Wilfred Owen* (1974) (p,c); *Poems of the First World War* (1974) (c).

WALLACE STEVENS
Collected Poems (1954); *Opus Posthumous* (ed. Samuel French Morse, 1957) (v,p,d); *The Palm at the End of the Mind* (ed. Holly Stevens, 1971).
Other:
  The Necessary Angel: Essays on Reality and the Imagination (1951) (c).

ALLEN TATE
Mr. Pope and Other Poems (1928); *Poems, 1928–1931* (1932); *The Mediterranean and Other Poems* (1936); *Selected Poems* (1937); *The Winter Sea* (1944); *Poems, 1920–1945* (1947); *Poems, 1922–1947* (1948); *Two Conceits for the Eye to Sing, If Possible* (1950); *Poems* (1960); *Poems* (1961); *The Swimmers and Other Selected Poems* (1970).
Translation:
  Pervigilium Veneris (The Vigil of Venus) (1943).
Other:
  Collected Essays (1959) (c,p); *Essays of Four Decades* (1969) (c); *Memoirs and Opinions: 1926–1974* (1975) (p,c).

JAMES TATE
Cages (1967); *The Destination* (1967); *The Lost Pilot* (1967); *The Torches* (1968, rev. 1971); *Notes of Woe* (1968); *Mystics in Chicago* (1968); *Camping in the Valley* (1968); *Row with Your Hair* (1969); *Is There Anything* (1969); *Shepherds of the Mist* (1969); *The Oblivion Ha-Ha* (1970, 1984); *Amnesia People* (1970); *Deaf Girl Playing* (1970); *Are You Ready Mary Baker Eddy?* (with Bill Knott) (1970); *The Immortals* (1970); *Wrong Songs* (1970); *Hints to Pilgrims* (1971, rev. 1982); *Nobody Goes to Visit the Insane Anymore* (1971); *Absences* (1972); *Apology for Eating Geoffrey Movius' Hyacinth* (1972); *Viper Jazz* (1976); *Riven Doggeries* (1979); *The Land of Little Sticks* (1982); *Constant Defender* (1983); *Reckoner* (1986).

DYLAN THOMAS
The Poems (ed. Daniel Jones, 1971; rev. 1974); *Selected Poems* (ed. Walford Davies, 1974); *The Green Fuse* (1982).
Other:
  Under Milk Wood (1954) (d); *A Child's Christmas in Wales* (1955) (f); *The Doctor and the Devils and Other Scripts* (1966) (d); *Collected Prose* (1969) (p); *Collected Stories* (1983).

EDWARD THOMAS
Collected Poems (ed. Walter de la Mare, 1974); *Collected Poems* (ed. R. George Thomas, 1978).

DIANE WAKOSKI
Coins and Coffins (1961); *Dream Sheet* (1965); *Discrepancies and Apparitions* (1966); *The George Washington Poems* (1967); *Greed: Parts One and Two* (1968); *The Diamond Merchant* (1968); *Inside the Blood Factory* (1968); *A Play and Two Poems* (with Robert Kelly and Ron Loewinsohn) (1968); *Thanking My Mother for Piano Lessons* (1969); *Some Poems for the Buddha's Birthday* (1969); *Greed: Parts 3 and 4* (1969); *The Moon Has a Complicated Geography* (1969); *The Magellanic Clouds* (1970); *The Lament of the Lady Bank Dick* (1970); *Black Dream Ditty for Billy "The Kid" Seen in Dr. Generosity's Bar Recruiting for Hell's Angels and Black Mafia* (1970); *Greed, Parts 5–7* (1971); *Exorcism* (1971); *This Water Baby: For Tony* (1971); *On Barbara's Shore* (1971); *The Motorcycle Betrayal Poems* (1971); *The Pumpkin Pie, or Reassurances Are Always False, Tho We Love Them. Only Physics Counts* (1972); *The Purple Finch Song* (1972); *Sometimes a Poet Will Hijack the Moon* (1972); *Smudging* (1973); *The Owl and the Snake: A Fable* (1973); *Greed, Parts 8, 9, 11* (1973); *Dancing on the Grave of a Son of a Bitch* (1973); *Winter Sequences* (1973); *Trilogy: Coins and Coffins, Discrepancies and Apparitions, The George Washington Poems* (1974); *Looking for the King of Spain* (1974); *The Wandering Tatler* (1974); *Abalone* (1974); *Virtuoso Literature for Two and Four Hands*

(1975); *The Fable of the Lion and the Scorpion* (1975); *Waiting for the King of Spain* (1976); *The Laguna Contract of DW* (1976); *George Washington's Camp Cups* (1976); *The Last Poem* (with *Tough Company* by Charles Bukowski) (1976); *The Ring* (1977); *Overnight Projects with Wood* (1977); *Spending Christmas with the Man from Receiving at Sears* (1977); *The Man Who Shook Hands* (1978); *Pachelbel's Canon* (1978); *Cap of Darkness, Including Looking for the King of Spain and Pachelbel's Canon* (1978); *Trophies* (1979); *Making a Sacher Torte* (1981); *Saturn's Rings* (1982); *The Lady Who Drove Me to the Airport* (1982); *Divers* (1982); *The Magician's Feastletters* (1982); *Looking for Beethoven in Las Vegas* (1983); *The Collected Greed: Parts 1–13* (1984); *Why My Mother Likes Liberace: A Musical Salute* (1985); *The Rings of Saturn* (1986).

DEREK WALCOTT
Twenty-Five Poems (1948); *Epitaph for the Young: XII Cantos* (1949); *Poems* (1951); *In a Green Night: Poems 1948–1960* (1962); *Selected Poems* (1964); *The Castaway* (1965); *The Gulf* (1969); *The Gulf and The Castaway* (1969); *Another Life* (1972); *Sea Grapes* (1976); *Selected Poems* (ed. O. R. Dathorne, 1977); *The Star-Apple Kingdom* (1979); *Selected Poetry* (ed. Wayne Brown, 1980); *The Fortunate Traveller* (1981); *Midsummer* (1983); *The Caribbean Poetry of DW and the Art of Romare Bearden* (1983); *Collected Poems 1948–1984* (1986); *The Arkansas Testament* (1987).
Other:
Dream on Monkey Mountain and Other Plays (1971) (d,p); *Three Plays* (1985) (d).

ROBERT PENN WARREN
Thirty-Six Poems (1936); *Eleven Poems on the Same Theme* (1942); *Selected Poems, 1923–1943* (1944); *Brother to Dragons: A Tale in Verse and Voices* (1953); *To a Little Girl, One Year Old, in a Ruined Fortress* (1956); *Promises: Poems, 1954–1956* (1957); *You, Emperors and Others: Poems 1957–1960* (1960); *Selected Poems: New and Old, 1923–66* (1966); *Incarnations: Poems 1966–1968* (1968); *Audubon: A Vision* (1969); *Or Else: Poem / Poems 1968–1974* (1974); *Selected Poems, 1923–1975* (1976); *Now and Then: Poems 1976–1978* (1978); *Two Poems* (1979); *Being Here: Poetry 1977–1980* (1980); *Rumor Verified: Poems 1979–1980* (1981); *Chief Joseph of the Nez Perce* (1983); *New and Selected Poems 1925–1985* (1985).
Other:
Understanding Poetry (with Cleanth Brooks) (1938) (c); *At Heaven's Gate* (1943) (f); *Understanding Fiction* (with Brooks) (1943) (c); *All the King's Men* (1946) (f); *The Circus in the Attic and Other Stories* (1948) (f); *World Enough and Time: A Romantic Novel* (1950) (f).

WALT WHITMAN
Leaves of Grass (1855, rev. 1856, 1860, 1867, 1871, 1872, 1876, 1881, 1889, 1891; variorum, ed. Emory Holloway and O. L. Triggs, 1924, 1954; *Comprehensive Reader's Edition*, ed. Harold Blodgett and Sculley Bradley, 1965).
Other:
Democratic Vistas (1871) (p); *Specimen Days* (1882) (a).

RICHARD WILBUR
The Beautiful Changes (1947); *Ceremony* (1950); *Things of This World* (1956); *Poems, 1943–56* (1957); *Advice to a Prophet* (1961); *Poems* (1963); *The Pelican from a Bestiary of 1120* (1963); *Prince Souvanna Phouma: An Exchange between RW and William Jay Smith* (1963); *Complaint* (1968); *Walking to Sleep: New Poems and Translations* (1969); *Digging for China* (1970); *Seed-Leaves: Homage to R. F.* (1974); *The Mind-Reader* (1977); *Verses on the Times* (with William Jay Smith) (1978); *Opposites: Poems and Drawings* (1979); *Seven Poems* (1981).
Translations:
Molière, *The Misanthrope* (1955); Voltaire, *Candide* (1956); Molière, *Tartuffe* (1963); Molière, *School for Wives* (1971); Joseph Brodsky, *The Funeral of Bobo* (1974); Molière, *The Learned Ladies* (1977); Racine, *Andromache* (1982); various, *The Whale and Other Uncollected Translations* (1982).

WILLIAM CARLOS WILLIAMS
The Collected Later Poems (1950, rev. 1963); *The Collected Earlier Poems* (1951); *Pictures from Brueghel: Collected Poems 1950–1962* (1967); *Paterson* (1963); *Selected*

Poems (ed. Charles Tomlinson, 1985); *Collected Poems, 1909–1939* (ed. A. Walton Litz and Christopher MacGowan, 1986).
Other:
   In the American Grain (1925) (p); *The Knife of the Times* (1932) (f); the Stecher trilogy—*White Mule* (1937), *In the Money* (1940), *The Build-Up* (1952) (f); *Life Along the Passaic River* (1938) (f); *Make Light of It* (1950) (f); *Autobiography* (1951, 1967) (a); *Selected Essays* (1954, 1969) (c); *In the American Grain* (1956) (c,p); *I Wanted to Write a Poem* (1958) (a); *Many Loves and Other Plays* (1961) (d); *The Farmer's Daughters: Collected Short Stories* (1961) (f); *The Doctor Stories* (ed. Robert Coles, 1984) (f).

YVOR WINTERS
   Collected Poems (1978, rev. 1980).
   Other:
   Primitivism and Decadence: A Study of American Experimental Poetry (1937) (c); *In Defense of Reason* (1947) (c); *On Modern Poets* (1959) (c).

JAMES WRIGHT
   Collected Poems (1971); *Two Citizens* (1973, rev. 1987); *Old Booksellers and Other Poems* (1976); *Moments of the Italian Summer* (1976); *To a Blossoming Pear Tree* (1977); *Two Mallee Days Poems* (1977); *Leave It to the Sunlight* (1981); *The Journey* (1981; as *This Journey*, 1982); *The Temple in Nimes* (1982); *The Shape of Light: Prose Poems* (1986).
   Translations:
   Twenty Poems of Georg Trakl (with Robert Bly) (1963); *Twenty Poems of Cesar Vallejo* (1964); Theodor Storm, *The Rider on the White Horse* (1964); *Twenty Poems of Pablo Neruda* (with Robert Bly) (1968); Hermann Hesse, *Poems* (1970).
   Other:
   Collected Prose (ed. Anne W, 1982) (c).

JUDITH WRIGHT
   The Moving Image (1946); *Woman to Man* (1949); *The Gateway* (1953); *The Two Fires* (1955); *Australian Bird Poems* (1961); *Birds: Poems* (1962); *Poems* (1963); *Five Senses: Selected Poems* (1963); *City Sunrise* (1964); *The Other Half* (1966); *Collected Poems 1942–1970* (1971); *Alive: Poems 1971–72* (1973); *Fourth Quarter and Other Poems* (1976); *The Coral Battleground* (1977); *The Double Tree: Selected Poems 1942–1976* (1978); *Phantom Dwelling* (1985).

WILLIAM BUTLER YEATS
   Collected Poems (1950, rev. 1956); *Variorum Edition of the Poems* (ed. Peter Allt and Russell K. Alspach, 1957, rev. 1966); *Selected Poems and Two Plays* (ed. M. L. Rosenthal, rev. 1966); *The Poems of WBY: A New Edition* (ed. Richard J. Finneran, 1983); *Poems, 1919–1935* (ed. Elizabeth Cullingford, 1984).
   Other:
   A Vision (1925, rev. 1937) (p); *Autobiographies* (1926, rev. 1938, 1955) (a); *Collected Plays* (1953) (d); *Memoirs* (ed. Denis Donoghue, 1973) (a); *Variorum Edition of the Plays* (ed. Russell K. Alspach, 1966) (d).

916

Index